DOING STATISTICS FOR BUSINESS with Excel

Data, Inference, and Decision Making

2nd Edition

Marilyn K. Pelosi, Ph.D.
Western New England College
Springfield, MA

Theresa M. Sandifer, Ph.D.
Southern Connecticut State University
New Haven, CT

JOHN WILEY & SONS, INC.

New York • Chichester • Weinheim • Brisbane • Singapore • Toronto

DEVELOPMENT EDITOR	Caroline Ryan
SUPPLEMENTS EDITOR	Mary Beth Bohman
MARKETING MANAGER	Julie Lindstrom
PRODUCTION SERVICES MANAGER	Jeanine Furino
SENIOR DESIGNER	Karin Gerdes Kincheloe
ILLUSTRATION EDITOR	Anna Melhorn
PHOTO EDITOR	Lisa Gee
PRODUCTION MANAGEMENT SERVICES	Susan L. Reiland
COVER INSET PHOTO	Ken Reid/FPG International
COVER BACKGROUND PHOTO	Dave Cannon/Stone

This book was set in New Baskerville by Progressive Information Technologies, and printed and bound by Courier Companies. The cover was printed by Lehigh Press.

This book is printed on acid-free paper. 

Library of Congress Cataloging in Publication Data:

Pelosi, Marilyn K.
Doing statistics for business with Excel : data, inference, and decision making/Marilyn K. Pelosi, Theresa M. Sandifer.– 2nd ed.
p. cm.
Includes bibliographical references and index.
ISBN 0-471-40829-8 (cloth : alk. paper)
1. Commercial statistics. 2. Statistics. 3. Industial management–Statistical methods.
I. Sandifer, Theresa M. II. Title.

HF1017 .P367 2001
519.5′0285′5369–dc21 2001017837

Printed in the United States of America

10 9 8 7 6 5 4 3 2

PREFACE

OUR GOALS

Our primary goal in writing this text is to teach students how to *do* statistics and how to *use* statistics as a tool for making intelligent, informed decisions in the business world. Statistics is the means to an end, not the end itself. We want students to learn how to analyze data and turn it into useful, inference-based information. At the same time, we want students to develop an intuitive understanding of variability, sampling, probability and inference, and models. While it would be nice if students remembered some of the formulas like the standard deviation or the correlation coefficient, it is not essential. It is much more important that students remember *what* these statistics measure and *why* one might want to use them.

Thus, the pedagogical focus of *Doing Statistics for Business* is data driven, emphasizing statistical reasoning, interpretation and decision making. We want to teach the "practice" of statistics; therefore, the emphasis is on comparison and interpretation rather than rote calculation. To support this approach we include discussions of practice as opposed to theory. For example, we discuss when it is OK to be in violation of an assumption and what to watch out for in applying techniques. In order to focus on decision making, the use of the computer is emphasized to keep students from getting bogged down in the details of the calculations.

All the cases found in *Doing Statistics for Business* are based on real business situations and data that are relevant to student life. Most chapters begin with a "Business Dilemma" based on real-world data. This example is then threaded throughout the chapter and to a lesser extent throughout the book. The data used in many of the examples and exercises are based on our consulting experiences. In order to protect the confidentiality of the companies involved, the data may be rescaled or altered, which does not hinder the usefulness of the data from a pedagogical perspective.

We have adopted a conversational tone so that students may learn the material using vocabulary that is familiar to them. The explanations have an *informal* flavor in order to allow the student to see that the techniques make logical sense. When necessary, we deviate from "pure" mathematics in the interest of understanding, being sure to note when this occurs. The student should see *why* and *how* the technique works. With this kind of understanding, students will know *what* technique to use and *when* to use it.

This book is intended for use in a one or two semester introductory business statistics course. The first 10 chapters cover topics that are usually found in a one-semester course. The remaining chapters are designed to be added or skipped at the instructor's discretion.

KEY FEATURES OF OUR ACTIVITY-BASED LEARNING APPROACH

In writing this book, we reflected on our many years of teaching experience and examined how people learn new things. The pedagogical features which follow represent the activity-based model we have developed over the years in our own classrooms. We have found that students . . .

- **Learn by Trying**

Try It Now! Exercises are checkpoints embedded in the text, with spaces provided for students to do them, making sure that they understand the basics before moving on. Answers are right there (upside down) so that students will have immediate feedback.

Try It Now!

The Glue Company ***Selecting a Simple Random Sample***

Select a sample of five tubes of glue for the glue company. You can assume that each tube of glue has a five-digit ID number, which the company uses to track its inventory.

- **Learn by Practicing**

Learning It! Exercises allow students to practice the basics of computation and include all the techniques covered in the chapter.

2.5.5 Exercises—Learning It!

2.14 The President of the United States wishes to see how popular he/she is after 2 years in office. A sample of 1000 voters is taken from the state of California.

(a) Why might this be a biased sample?

(b) How could you get a simple random sample?

Thinking About It! Exercises emphasize critical thought and ask students to interpret the results of statistical techniques and make decisions based on their analysis.

Thinking About It!

1.1 We have said that quality and statistics go hand in hand. What product or service have you used recently that did not have the quality you thought it should have?

(a) Describe the product or service and the area in which it was lacking in quality.

(b) What corrective action would you recommend?

1.2 Describe a situation in which you had a paradigm shift or change.

Doing It! Exercises use large real-world data sets and ask students to perform the statistical analyses and interpret them to solve a real problem. As students progress in their statistical thinking, these exercises will help them to make judgments about "what to do next." The data sets for these exercises are provided on the Resource CD-ROM.

Doing It!

4.46 The company investigating the golf balls is not satisfied with the limited analysis that it has done. The managers have collected a good deal of data, but they are not sure how to look at them and interpret the output. They decide to hire you to help them understand what the golf balls are doing and how they compare to each other. In addition to measures of the balls' performance, such as the variable *Carry*, the managers know that other factors, both internal (ball-related) and external (environment-related), could affect performance. They tested 36 of each type of ball at three different times using a machine to launch the balls. Data were recorded on 14 different variables. A portion of the data is shown here:

Ball	Model	S1	S2	S3	Wgt	Dw	Dd	Head	Temp	Carry	TotDist	Date	Time
1	M1	81	81	82	45.3	0.145	0.0110	686	77	257	270	8/20	8:15
2	M1	83	83	84	45.2	0.151	0.0111	688	77	255	267	8/20	8:15
3	M1	81	82	84	45.2	0.145	0.0105	687	77	256	267	8/20	8:15
4	M1	81	81	83	45.3	0.144	0.0117	688	77	255	271	8/20	8:15
5	M1	83	81	82	45.5	0.146	0.0108	687	77	255	268	8/20	8:15

- **Learn by Communicating Results**

An item called **Executive Summary** concludes each chapter. This feature highlights an important goal in the business statistics course: how to take statistical results and communicate them to your colleagues in a meaningful way. A memo is depicted, summarizing the analysis of the chapter opening problem. This brings the problem to some closure and models the communication of data analysis for students.

4.6 Executive Summary

THE GOLF BALL COMPANY

TO: Marketing Department
FROM: Data Analyst
RE: Comparison of Two Golf Ball Models

We were asked to compare two different models of golf balls in preparation for an advertising campaign. The study was conducted as a blind study, that is, we did not know the golf ball type while the data were being collected and analyzed. We did this to ensure that our results are as unbiased as possible.

Using a mechanical hitting device, we hit 72 different golf balls, 36 of each type. The balls were hit in batches of 12, alternating brands. To measure distance traveled we used carry, which is the distance from point of impact with the club to the place where the ball first hit the ground, and total distance, which is the distance from point of impact to the final position of the ball. This report focuses on the carry of the two ball types.

• Learn by Using the Computer

Microsoft Excel is used throughout the chapters, with screen shots featured in many of the text's figures and examples. We have chosen Microsoft Excel because it is the leading analytical software used in the business world. There is a greater chance that students will practice statistical thinking if we show them how to do statistics in a software package that is most likely to be on their desktop at home or at work.

4.7.1 Calculating Summary Statistics in Excel

Suppose that we want to calculate a set of summary statistics for the golf ball data. Figure 4.9 shows a portion of that data in an Excel worksheet.

The Data Analysis ToolPak has a function that creates a set of summary statistics for a set of data. To access this function, select **Data Analysis** from the **Tools** menu and choose **Descriptive Statistics** from the list of Analysis tools. The dialog box is shown in Figure 4.10. You will see that it is similar to the one you used to create a histogram.

	A	B	I	J	K	L	M	N
1	Ball#	Model #	Head	Temp	Carry	Tot Dist	Date	Time
2	1	M1	686	77	257	270	8/20	8:15
3	2	M1	688	77	255	267	8/20	8:15
4	3	M1	687	77	256	267	8/20	8:15
5	4	M1	688	77	255	271	8/20	8:15
6	5	M1	687	77	255	268	8/20	8:15
7	6	M1	687	77	256	267	8/20	8:15
8	7	M1	687	77	255	264	8/20	8:15
9	8	M1	690	78	258	269	8/20	8:15
10	9	M1	686	78	252	257	8/20	8:15
11	10	M1	687	78	256	268	8/20	8:15
12	11	M1	687	78	253	263	8/20	8:15

FIGURE 4.9 The golf ball data

The final section of each chapter in the text describes how to implement the techniques taught in the chapter in Excel. In some instances Excel has built-in features to do the necessary statistical calculations. The sections at the end of each chapter walk students through each step in using these features. While Excel does not perform all of the statistical functions found in the text, KADDSTAT 3.0 will do these calculations. KADDSTAT is included on the accompanying Resource CD and the text explains how to use it.

If students are not familiar with using Excel, we have included a short introduction to the basics in Appendix C.

• Learn by Discovery

In the process of trying things, we often discover ideas that eventually lead to understanding. Within most of the chapters students will find *Discovery Exercises.* These exercises are written to achieve a high level of student understanding by directing their line of thinking, leading to an "aha" discovery of a key concept. They are designed to help students see that statistical thinking is logical and that the formulas make sense when students discover where they came from and see why they work.

Several of the *Discovery Exercises* are designed to help students apply the techniques and interpret the results in terms of making a business decision. Most of these exercises require them to *write* a memo or short business report to explain their decisions and recommendations.

Discovery Exercise 2.2
INTRODUCTION TO SAMPLING

Suppose the data shown here represent an entire population. They show the number of people in 50 families living in a small college town in New England. (If you did Discovery Exercise 2.1 then you will recognize this as the same data set.) Now a two-digit ID number has also been included.

New England families: large amount of variability
Average number of people in 50 families: 4.50

ID: 01	1	ID: 02	4	ID: 03	5	ID: 04	7	ID: 05	8
ID: 06	3	ID: 07	9	ID: 08	8	ID: 09	8	ID: 10	8
ID: 11	4	ID: 12	9	ID: 13	9	ID: 14	1	ID: 15	6
ID: 16	4	ID: 17	1	ID: 18	3	ID: 19	9	ID: 20	7
ID: 21	8	ID: 22	2	ID: 23	3	ID: 24	1	ID: 25	9
ID: 26	1	ID: 27	7	ID: 28	5	ID: 29	1	ID: 30	1
ID: 31	1	ID: 32	6	ID: 33	8	ID: 34	2	ID: 35	9
ID: 36	4	ID: 37	1	ID: 38	1	ID: 39	1	ID: 40	3
ID: 41	4	ID: 42	2	ID: 43	4	ID: 44	9	ID: 45	4
ID: 46	1	ID: 47	3	ID: 48	8	ID: 49	1	ID: 50	1

Step 1: Select a sample of five numbers from this population. Use the table of random numbers to do this. Record your sample in the following table.

• Learn by Making Your Case

Many times we learn new material by mastering small chunks at a time, but we don't really "get it" until we step back and put all the small pieces together into a complete whole.

In addition to the exercises and structured cases found in each chapter, this text contains cases that require the use of a variety of the statistical tools introduced in several chapters. Making Your Case takes an overall look at the techniques learned throughout the course, and how the tools can be used in a systematic way to solve real business problems. After all, in the "real world," this is exactly the way it works. For ease of location, these cases are all found in the final chapter. However, these cases can be used *before* the end of the book is reached. Each case references the chapter that introduced the tools appropriate for the case. For example, the first case, "Advising the President," requires the use of many of the tools of descriptive statistics introduced in Chapters 3, 4 and 5.

MAKING YOUR CASE!
Who Spends Money? What Do They Buy?: Inferential Statistics

A large marketing research firm has an international client that has business interests in many consumer industries such as food, apparel, alcohol, and automobile fuel. As a person with some statistical experience, you have been hired by this marketing research company. Before spending any of the client's money on surveying consumers, the client has asked you to report on general trends in consumer spending. Specifically, you are asked which business areas have experienced increases, and what are the characteristics of people who are spending money in these areas. Your report will guide future survey design and eventually new product development and advertising expenditures.

Using your Internet-surfing skills, you find the Web site for the U.S. Census Bureau and find the results of the Consumer Expenditure Survey conducted periodically by the Census Bureau. The most recent survey available on-line is from 1993 and so you decide to use it.

- **Learn by Checking Your Knowledge**

Each chapter ends with summary tables of key terms and formulas. These features are useful when reviewing the material for quizzes and/or exams. Page references are provided so it is easy to return to the more detailed discussion in the chapter.

Key Terms

Term	Definition	Page reference
Biased sample	A **biased sample** is a sample that does not fairly represent the population.	27
Census	A **census** is a study of the entire population.	16
Continuous data	**Continuous data** are data that can take on any one of an infinite number of possible values over an interval on the number line.	34
Descriptive statistics	**Tools of descriptive statistics** allow you to summarize the data.	36
Discrete data	**Discrete data** are data that can take on only certain values. These values are often integers or whole numbers.	34
Inference	An **inference** is a deduction or a conclusion.	37
Inferential statistics	The **techniques of inferential statistics** allow us to draw inferences or conclusions about the population from the sample.	37

SUPPLEMENTS

For the Student:

Resource CD-ROM

An exciting addition to this edition of *Doing Statistics for Business with Excel* is the **Resource CD-ROM,** which accompanies every textbook. The Resource CD contains all of the following elements to help teachers teach and students learn statistics:

The **Student Solutions Manual** contains full solutions to selected problems from the text.
The **PowerPoint Slides** illustrate key concepts from the text.
The **Data Sets,** provided in Microsoft® Excel format, are linked to the *Doing It!* and other exercises from the text.
Excel Interactive: Tutorials for Statistics, developed by Barbara Miller of Indiana University, provides hands-on training in the basic functions of Microsoft® Excel.
KADDSTAT is a menu-driven, statistical analysis program for Excel created by Brian Kilmer, in collaboration with Donald L. Harnett. The programmed statistical routines provide "point and click" computational capability to perform graphic analysis, descriptive statistics, and inferential model analysis activities.

Business Extra

The **Business Extra** program is a partnership between Wiley and the Dow Jones Company that offers an exciting new way to extend your textbook beyond the walls of the classroom. The program gives you a special password for the Business Extra Web site, through which your students get instant access to a wealth of current articles from the *Wall Street Journal,* as well as a special offer for the *Wall Street Journal* Interactive Edition. Business Extra can be packaged with the text by using the set ISBN 0-471-15155-6.

For the Instructor:

The **Instructor's Manual** contains full solutions to the problems from the text as well as additional teaching materials.

EGrade is an on-line assessment system that contains a large bank of skill-building problems and solutions. Instructors can now automate the process of assigning, delivering, grading, and routing all kinds of homework, quizzes, and tests while providing students with immediate scoring and feedback on their work. Wiley *eGrade* "does the math" . . . and much more. For more information, visit www.wiley.com/college/egrade.

PowerPoint Slides are available on the Resource CD that accompanies the text.

Supplements for the instructor can be obtained by sending a request on your institutional letterhead to Mathematics Marketing Manager, John Wiley & Sons Inc., 605 Third Avenue, New York, NY 10158-0012, or by contacting your local Wiley representative.

ACKNOWLEDGMENTS

No work of this magnitude can happen without a lot of help. We would like to take this opportunity to thank those people who have made the book a reality. First and most importantly, we want to thank Brad Wiley II, our editor, who believed in us, and what we wanted to accomplish. We could not have done this without the help of Mary O'Sullivan, who kept us sane during a very difficult process, and Susan Reiland, who carried us through the production process without losing her sense of humor. There are many other people at Wiley who deserve our thanks, in particular, Debbie Berridge, Mary Beth Bohman, Caroline Ryan, Jeanine Furino, Martin Batey, and Peter Janzow.

Part of what makes this book unique is the amount of student input in the development process. We thank all of our students who read and used the book in draft form, finding our errors and making suggestions. In particular, we would like to thank Chris Michaelson and Barbara Dedman. We would also like to thank the following reviewers, who offered helpful suggestions and advice: William Kasperski, Georgia Southern University; Mark Eakin, University of Texas, Arlington; William Seaver, University of Tennessee, Knoxville; Randy Anderson, California State University, Fresno; Kent D. Smith, California Polytechnic State University; Max A. Linn, Florida State University; Alan Humphrey, University of Rhode Island; Anthony Seraphin, University of Delaware; Sung K. Ahn, Washington State University; Jan Case, Mississippi State University; Marla Bell, Kennesaw State University; Frederick W. Derrick, Loyola College; Rene Leo E. Ordonez, Southern Oregon University; Ben Lev, University of Michigan, Dearborn; Joyce McQuade, Westchester Community College; and Lynn Smith, Gloucester County College.

TO THE STUDENT: SUMMARY OF FEATURES IN EVERY CHAPTER

Each element of every chapter in this text is designed to help you change your paradigm so that you may see the world through statistical thinking. More specifically, each chapter

- Begins with a business problem based on an actual situation. The *Business Dilemma* will motivate the material and will be carried throughout the chapter as you learn the techniques needed to solve the problem.

Business Dilemma...

- Lists the *objectives* of the chapter in the first section.
- Provides you with *worked examples* for each statistical concept, tool, or other important idea. For every example in the text, the problem-solving steps will be noted in the margin.

- Provides you with *Try It Now!* exercises to give you some practice. These exercises are like checkpoints. Do not skip them. Space is provided for you to work the problems out, and the answers are given upside down so you may check your work immediately.

- Provides you with *Discovery Exercises.* These are optional, and if they are skipped you will not miss any information. They are designed to help you discover a concept or idea. They will help you see that statistical thinking is logical and that the formulas make sense when you discover where they came from and why. Your instructor will probably use some but not all of these exercises.

- Includes *icons* in the margins to highlight the major themes of **quality** and the **communication** of results.
- Includes many *side margin notes,* which contain keywords, hints, and tips. These help you to review the material and locate key formulas, definitions, and concepts.
- Includes *Definitions* in shaded boxes for easy locating. Any term that is in a definition box will be listed in the end-of-chapter summary.
- Identifies *Formulas* with a label in the margin. All such formulas will appear in the end-of-chapter summary.
- Provides you with more practice problems at the end of most sections. (Chapter 1 does not have any of these.) These are labeled *"Exercises—Learning It"* and by doing them you will master the basics.

- Ends with an *Executive Summary,* which is a business analysis of the dilemma presented at the start of the chapter. This is in the form of a memo or report, and gives you a model for how analysis could be communicated to senior management in the real world.

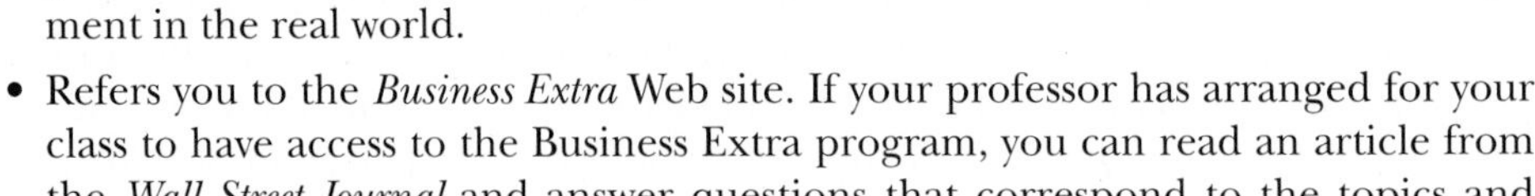

- Refers you to the *Business Extra* Web site. If your professor has arranged for your class to have access to the Business Extra program, you can read an article from the *Wall Street Journal* and answer questions that correspond to the topics and techniques in the chapter.
- Provides you with detailed instruction on how to use Microsoft Excel to perform most of the statistical analyses described in the chapter. These instructions are found in the last section of each chapter. In many cases, if Excel does not provide a convenient or correct way to do the analysis, KADDSTAT 3.0 will perform the function. KADDSTAT is found on the Resource CD-ROM.
- Provides a *Chapter Summary* including tables of key terms and formulas introduced in the chapter.
- Provides you with *End-of-Chapter Exercises. Learning It!* exercises are similar to the end-of-section exercises. *Thinking About It!* exercises ask you to go beyond the basics. You are asked to think about the business implications of the computational result and your thinking may be directed beyond the immediate details of the problem. *Doing It!* exercises are linked to the large data sets that are provided on the Resource CD-ROM. These data sets are designed to let you use the techniques of the chapter in a more realistic setting, one in which you have lots of data to analyze and not a great deal of structure.

HOW DO YOU LEARN BEST?

Now that you've looked over the features in each chapter, take time to find out how you learn best. This quiz was designed to help you find out something about your preferred learning method. Research suggests that each person has preferred ways to receive and communicate information. After you take the quiz, we will help you pinpoint the study aids in this text that will help you learn the material based on your learning style.

Circle the letter of the answer that best explains your preference. Circle more than one if a single answer does not match your perception. Leave blank any question that does not apply.

1. You are about to give directions to a person who is standing with you. She is staying in a hotel in town and wants to visit your house later. She has a rental car. Would you
a. draw a map on paper?
b. tell her the directions?
c. write down the directions (without a map)?
d. pick her up at the hotel in your car?

2. You are not sure whether a word should be spelled "dependent" or "dependant." Do you
c. look it up in the dictionary?
a. see the word in your mind and choose by the way it looks?
b. sound it out in your mind?
d. write both versions down on paper and choose one?

3. You have just received a copy of your itinerary for a world trip. This is of interest to a friend. Would you
b. call her immediately and tell her about it?
c. send her a copy of the printed itinerary?
a. show her on a map of the world?
d. share what you plan to do at each place you visit?

4. You are going to cook something as a special treat for your family. Do you
d. cook something familiar without the need for instructions?
a. thumb through the cookbook looking for ideas from the pictures?
c. refer to a specific cookbook where there is a good recipe?

5. A group of tourists has been assigned to you to find out about wildlife reserves or parks. Would you
d. drive them to a wildlife reserve or park?
a. show them slides and photographs?
c. give them pamphlets or a book on wildlife reserves or parks?
b. give them a talk on wildlife reserves or parks?

6. You are about to purchase a new CD player. Other than price, what would most influence your decision?
b. The salesperson telling you what you want to know.
c. Reading the details about it.
d. Playing with the controls and listening to it.
a. Its fashionable and upscale appearance.

7. Recall a time in your life when you learned how to do something like playing a new board game. Try to avoid choosing a very physical skill, e.g., riding a bike. How did you learn best? By
a. visual clues—pictures, diagrams, charts?
c. written instructions?
b. listening to somebody explaining it?
d. doing it or trying it?

8. You have an eye problem. Would you prefer that the doctor
b. tell you what is wrong?
a. show you a diagram of what is wrong?
d. use a model to show what is wrong?

9. You are about to learn to use a new program on a computer. Would you
d. sit down at the keyboard and begin to experiment with the program's features?
c. read the manual that comes with the program?
b. call a friend and ask questions about it?

10. You are staying in a hotel and have a rental car. You would like to visit friends whose address/location you do not know. Would you like them to
a. draw you a map on paper?
b. tell you the directions?
c. write down the directions (without a map)?
d. pick you up at the hotel in their car?

11. Apart from price, what would most influence your decision to buy a particular book?
d. You have used a copy before.
b. A friend talking about it.
c. Quickly reading parts of it.
a. The appealing way it looks.

12. A new movie has arrived in town. What would most influence your decision to go (or not go)?
b. You heard a radio review about it.
c. You read a review about it.
a. You saw a preview of it.

13. Do you prefer a lecturer or teacher who likes to use
c. a textbook, handouts, readings?
a. flow diagrams, charts, graphs?
d. field trips, labs, practical sessions?
b. discussion, guest speakers?

Count your choices

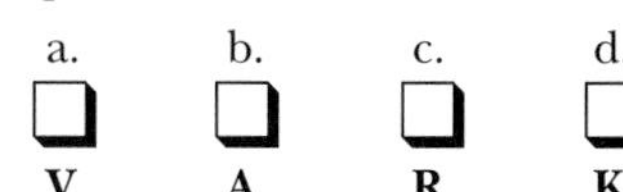

Now match the letter or letters you have recorded most to the same letter or letters in the Learning Styles Chart. You may have more than one learning style preference—many people do. Next to each letter in the Chart are suggestions that will refer you to different learning aids throughout this text.

LEARNING STYLES CHART

V VISUAL

This preference includes the depiction of information in charts, graphs, flow charts, and all the symbolic arrows, circles, hierarchies, and other devices that instructors use to represent what could have been presented in words. *Note:* This definition does not include the use of television, videos, and films. These media are primarily Aural (A) and Kinesthetic (K) because of their presentation of sound and reality (usually). They rarely use graphics.

WHAT TO DO IN CLASS	WHAT TO DO WHEN STUDYING	TEXT FEATURES THAT MAY HELP YOU THE MOST	WHAT TO DO PRIOR TO AND DURING EXAMS
• Pay close attention to charts, drawings, and handouts your instructor uses. • Underline. • Use different colors. • Use symbols, flow charts, graphs, different arrangements on the page, white space.	Convert your lecture notes into "page pictures." To do this: • Use the "In Class" strategies. • Reconstruct images in different ways. • Redraw pages from memory. • Replace words with symbols and initials. • Look at your pages.	**Chapter Objectives** **Worked Examples** **Icons of Quality and Communication** **Definition boxes** **Formulas labeled in margin** **Microsoft Excel instructions** **Chapter Summary**	• Recall your "page pictures." • Draw diagrams where appropriate. • Practice turning your visuals back into words.

AURAL

This perceptual mode describes a preference for information that is "spoken or heard." Students with this modality report that they learn best from lectures, tutorials, and talking to other students.

WHAT TO DO IN CLASS	WHAT TO DO WHEN STUDYING	TEXT FEATURES THAT MAY HELP YOU THE MOST	WHAT TO DO PRIOR TO AND DURING EXAMS
• Attend lectures and tutorials. • Discuss topics with students and instructors. • Explain new ideas to other people. • Use a tape recorder. • Leave spaces in your lecture notes for later recall. • Describe overheads, pictures, and visuals to somebody who was not in class.	You may take poor notes because you prefer to listen. Therefore: • Expand your notes by talking with others and with information from your textbook. • Tape record summarized notes and listen. • Read summarized notes out loud. • Explain your notes to another "aural" person.	***Try It Now!* Exercises** **Discovery Exercises** **Executive Summary** **Business Extra Web site** **Chapter Summary**	• Make these text features aural by explaining/talking about them to classmates and your teacher. • Talk with the instructor. • Spend time in quiet places recalling the ideas out loud. • Practice writing answers to old exam questions.

R READING/WRITING

This preference is for information displayed as words.

WHAT TO DO IN CLASS	WHAT TO DO WHEN STUDYING	TEXT FEATURES THAT MAY HELP YOU THE MOST	WHAT TO DO PRIOR TO AND DURING EXAMS
• Use lists and headings. • Use dictionaries, glossaries, and definitions, • Read handouts, textbooks, and supplementary library readings. • Use lecture notes.	• Write out words again and again. • Reread notes silently. • Rewrite ideas and principles into other words. • Turn charts, diagrams, and other illustrations into statements.	**Chapter Objectives** **Worked Examples** **Side margin notes** **Definition boxes** **Formulas** **Business Extra Web site** **Microsoft Excel instructions** **Chapter Summary** **End-of-Chapter Exercises**	• Write exam answers. • Practice with multiple-choice questions. • Write paragraphs, beginnings and endings. • Write your lists in outline form. • Arrange your words into hierarchies and points.

K KINESTHETIC

This is a preference for the use of experience and practice (simulated or real). Although such an experience may invoke other modalities, the key is that the individual is connected to reality, either through experience, example, practice, or simulation.

WHAT TO DO IN CLASS	WHAT TO DO WHEN STUDYING	TEXT FEATURES THAT MAY HELP YOU THE MOST	WHAT TO DO PRIOR TO AND DURING EXAMS
• Use all your senses. • Go to labs, take field trips. • Listen to real-life examples. • Pay attention to applications. • Use hands-on approaches. • Use trial-and-error methods.	You may take poor notes because topics do not seem concrete or relevant. Therefore: • Put examples in your summaries. • Use case studies and applications to help with principles and abstract concepts. • Talk about your notes with another "kinesthetic" person. • Use pictures and photographs that illustrate an idea.	**Business Dilemma** ***Try It Now!* Exercises** **Discovery Exercises** **End-of-Section Practice Exercises** **Executive Summary** **Microsoft Excel instructions** **Chapter Summary** **End-of-Chapter Exercises**	• Write practice answers. • Role-play the exam situation.

Source: Adapted from VARK pack. There is a VARK Web site at www.active-learning-site.com.

CONTENTS

GETTING STARTED

CHAPTER 13

ADDITIONAL TOPICS

CHAPTER 14

CHAPTER 15

CHAPTER 16

CHAPTER 17

APPENDIX *A*

APPENDIX *B*

APPENDIX *C*

CHAPTER 1

INTRODUCTION: THE ROLE OF STATISTICAL THINKING IN MANAGEMENT

Business Dilemma...

QUALITY PRODUCTS

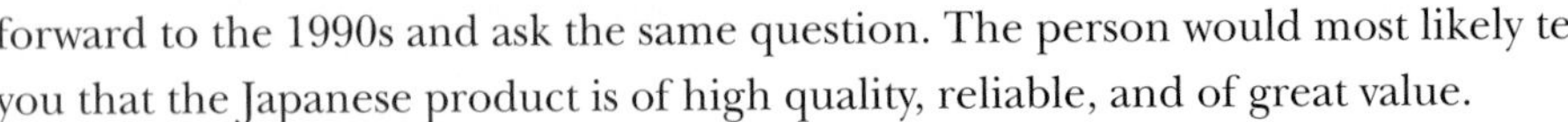

If you asked someone to describe the quality of a product made in Japan in the 1950s, what do you think the response would be? Most likely the person would tell you that the Japanese product made in the 1950s was of low quality, not reliable, and probably junk. Now let's roll forward to the 1990s and ask the same question. The person would most likely tell you that the Japanese product is of high quality, reliable, and of great value.

What happened between 1950 and 1990? During this time period Japanese industries started paying increasingly more attention to the quality of their products. At the same time American companies were enjoying the postwar boom and paying little, if any, attention to quality. Interestingly enough, it was an American statistician named W. Edwards Deming who helped the Japanese focus on quality. Deming tried to get American manufacturers to listen to him but they were not interested at the time. Today, American companies, both service industries and manufacturing concerns, are paying close attention to quality to compete internationally.

1.1 Chapter Objectives

You may be wondering why a story about product quality is used as an introduction to a book on statistics. Students often feel that taking a course in statistics causes unnecessary pain and that they will never again use the statistical techniques they learn. The objective of this book is to refute both of these points: The course need not be painful, and you will certainly be asked to collect and analyze data and use the information to make informed business decisions.

The objective of this chapter is to start you down this path. Specifically, this chapter covers the following topics:

- Dispelling the Myths About Statistics
- What Managers Should Know About Statistics
- Statistical Thinking—A New Paradigm for Management
- Management Themes and Problem-Solving Steps
- Some Situations That Call for Statistical Thinking
- Key Components of Statistical Thinking
- Use of Excel and Other Statistical Software

1.2 Dispelling the Myths About Statistics

We should first dispel some of the common myths about statistics. Listed here are three myths we have run across regularly:

Myth 1: *"If I had one hour left to live, I would choose to live it in statistics class because it would seem to last forever!"*

A student's lament

Myth 2: *"There are three kinds of lies—lies, damned lies, and statistics."*

Benjamin Disraeli

Myth 3: *"If it moves, it's biology; if it changes color, it's chemistry; if it breaks, it's physics; if it puts you to sleep, it's statistics."*

Bob Hogg, University of Iowa

If you are like most people you can relate to one of these myths about the "S-word," *statistics*, or *sadistics* as some people refer to it. Statistics is boring and not useful! This book will lead you to another view of the dreaded S-word—one that sees statistics not as a sleeping pill but as a way in which to view all sorts of exciting, amazing, and valuable things.

Myths and Fears

Identifying Some of Your Own

Be honest. Write down your myths and fears about this subject right now. Get them out in the open so you can deal with them directly and put them behind you. To get you started, a common student fear follows.

- *I am worried about all of the math in this course.*

You have taken the first step. It is easier to combat the myths about statistics when we acknowledge them. Good work. Next we need to see why it is important to learn about the tools of statistics.

1.3 WHAT MANAGERS SHOULD KNOW ABOUT STATISTICS

The use of statistical techniques has long played an important role in quality control and quality improvement in business and industry. Unfortunately, for too long quality has been relegated to the "quality department" and not integrated into the whole organization. The purchasing department would purchase the raw materials needed at the cheapest price without regard to quality and then would throw the material "over the wall" to the engineers. The engineers would make the product, not worrying about the process, since they knew that the quality department would inspect the product before it went out the door. Businesses in the United States have learned that this way of approaching quality does not work and does not allow them to compete internationally. Quality is everyone's job!

Quality and statistics go hand in hand.

One of the reasons that people prefer to have the quality department handle quality issues is that thinking about quality leads to thinking about data analysis. Data analysis requires the use of statistical techniques, which are often viewed as difficult. But statistical thinking is not difficult to comprehend. Everything we do can be thought of as a series of steps that are connected. Each time we repeat a step it will not be precisely the same. Reducing how much the step changes from time to time is one way to improve things. Suppose your company manufactures copy machines. You would like to know that the raw materials you use to make the copy machine are always the same, and the customer would like to know that the copy machine will perform the same from day to day. Statistical thinking is logical, uses data, recognizes the interdependence of activities, and looks at how things vary.

Four issues must be addressed if statistics is to become an integral part of management:

- Managers must understand *why* they need to possess statistical knowledge.
- Current and future managers (that's you) must *have* this knowledge.
- Steps must be taken to ensure that the knowledge is *used*.
- The *payoff* from the knowledge and its application must be measured.

To achieve this integration of statistics into business and industry we are going to have to change the way we see the world. We need a new pair of glasses.

1.4 STATISTICAL THINKING—A NEW PARADIGM FOR MANAGEMENT

Look at Figure 1.1. What do you see? Ask the person next to you what he or she sees. Some of you will see two faces and some of you will see a vase. You probably can see both of these things, but which one did you see first? There is no right or wrong answer here. What you see first depends on your viewpoint, your lens, your glasses. This is your **paradigm**; this is how you *see* things. Each of us has a paradigm or view of the world that has been developed based on our individual experiences. The hard part is changing our lens. There will be many times when you must change your paradigm to see the same picture in a new way. This book is designed to help you shift your paradigm so that you can see the world through the lens of statistical thinking.

A ***paradigm*** is commonly used today to mean a model, theory, perception, assumption, or frame of reference. It was originally a scientific term.

Did you ever take a class on the great artists of the Italian Renaissance? Even if you did not you might have heard of Michelangelo, Leonardo da Vinci, Raphael, and Donatello. If you study Michelangelo, you would probably study his statue of David, and if you study Leonardo, you would certainly learn about his painting of the Mona Lisa. Then you would begin to see David and Mona used in all sorts of advertisements and logos as far away from art as software and tomato sauce! Look at the ones shown in Figure 1.2.

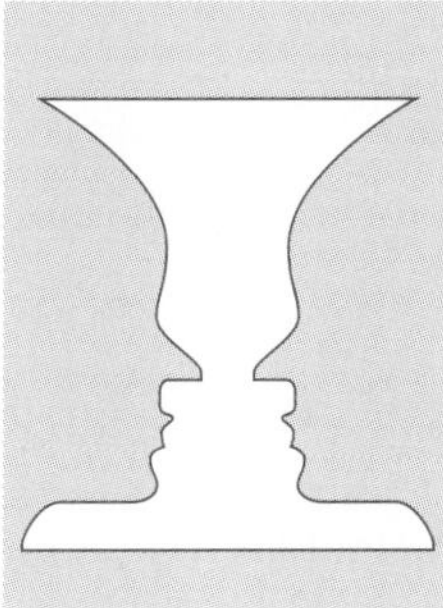

FIGURE 1.1 Two faces or a vase?

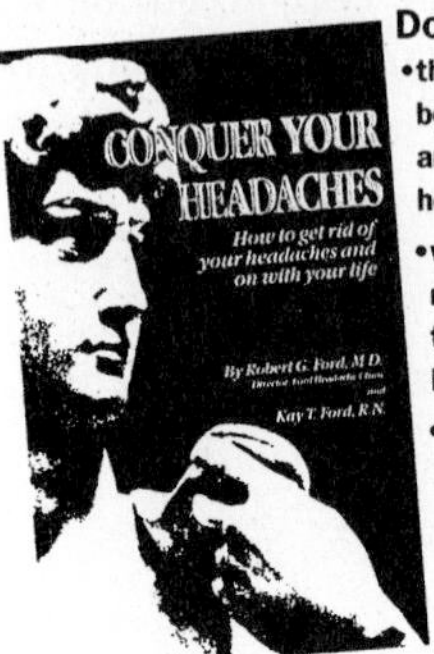

FIGURE 1.2 Advertisements using the status of David and the Mona Lisa

Are these ads new? No, you are just more aware of their existence after having studied about them. This is similar to what happened when you looked at the two faces/vase illustration in Figure 1.1. Once you become aware of the second way of looking at the picture you see both things each time you look at the picture. Similarly, once you study Michelangelo and Leonardo your view is different because you are now aware of their works and begin to see them everywhere. You have a new paradigm or view of the world. Your paradigm has *shifted.*

This book is about changing your paradigm to one that allows you to *see* things using statistical thinking. Statistical thinking is public property. Everyone owns it and everyone must use it—not just statisticians. Over the short term, it can improve the quality of decisions; over the long term, it can help turn people into leaders.

You will learn to see data everywhere you turn and to see the information hidden in the data as well. This information will help you make informed investment, marketing, and management decisions and will help you develop quality processes and product designs. How is this possible? By learning and understanding the tools of statistics you will be able to see the world differently. The tools of statistics are actually quite logical and simple to use, yet many people do not use them because of lack of exposure to statistics or dislike of math. Hence, these people often do not make well-informed decisions. You will be different because you will learn the tools of statistics as decision-making tools and not as mathematical manipulation. Think about this book as a management text, not a math text. You will soon see what we mean.

1.5 MANAGEMENT THEMES AND PROBLEM-SOLVING STEPS

As you learn how to analyze data to make well-informed business decisions you will see the following recurring themes:

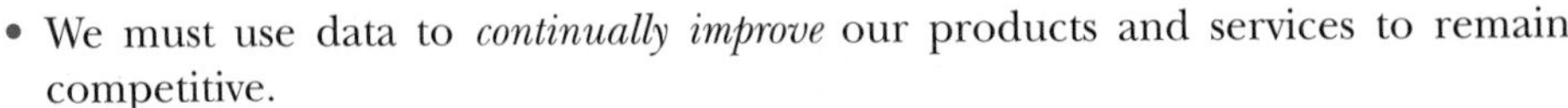

- We must use data to *continually improve* our products and services to remain competitive.

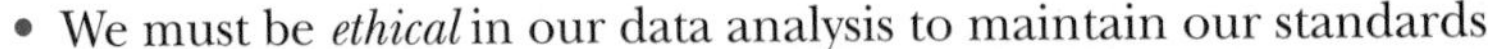

- We must be *ethical* in our data analysis to maintain our standards.

- We must be able to effectively *communicate* our analysis to management and our customers to make our case.

These themes are woven throughout this book. They provide a context for our data analysis. It is not possible to isolate these topics in a single chapter because they pervade virtually every situation that calls for statistical thinking in business.

In the next section you will see three examples. In each situation the data were collected and must be analyzed to *improve* a product or the work environment. You will also see that there are often ways to "*lie* with statistics," as Disraeli warned us in myth 2. Discussions of what not to do and things to watch out for are presented. Finally, you will see that you can be the best data analyst in the world, but if you cannot effectively *communicate* the results of your analysis, then it is as though you never did the analysis. So, you will learn how to synthesize and summarize your analysis so it can be used.

Typically, communicating the results of your analysis is the last step. Sometimes this last step becomes the first step of another analysis, but clearly some systematic steps are generally followed in any type of problem solving. There are many different models to follow in problem solving, but we will use a simple, four-step model in this book:

1. Understand the problem.
2. Collect and analyze the data.
3. Draw conclusions and make recommendations.
4. Communicate the results.

The focus of this book is to teach you the tools to do the second step. Most of your work in this text will be analyzing the data. however, the second step does not take place without there first being a problem to solve or a situation to improve, and the analysis is worthless if it does not lead to conclusions and recommendations that are properly communicated.

The organization of every chapter herein will help you see these steps and get used to recognizing them in several different ways. First, every chapter will open with a problem or opportunity for improvement. This is step 1. The worked examples in the chapter carry out some of the analysis for this opening problem and draw some conclusions based on the analysis. Most of these illustrate steps 2 and 3. Every chapter concludes with an executive summary of the analysis of the opening problem that summarizes the results of the worked examples. This is one part of step 4. Some chapters also include a PowerPoint presentation as another way of communicating the results. To reinforce the communication theme, you will get practice writing memos and executive summaries as part of the exercises.

In addition to written communication, you are often asked to orally communicate your analysis. This might take the form of a PowerPoint presentation. Section 2.9 in the next chapter guides you in preparing such a presentation by addressing questions about what type of visuals to use and how much detail to provide. For some of the case assignments in this book you will be asked to prepare a short presentation of your analysis.

1.6 SITUATIONS THAT CALL FOR STATISTICAL THINKING

After finishing this course and graduating from college, you may find yourself facing decisions similar to any one of the following scenarios. In each case you must make decisions based on what you see in the data. A short discussion of possible approaches you might use to investigate each situation is provided. This should help convince you that the tools of statistics make logical sense.

EXAMPLE 1.1 Tissue Manufacturer

Understand the Problem

Complaints Become Opportunities

Most large companies that manufacture consumer goods receive feedback from their customers. A large manufacturer of paper goods keeps track of consumer complaints for its facial tissue product line. The company receives these complaints through a toll-free number that appears on the product. Next time you pick up a box of tissues see if you can find the toll-free number for making complaints.

The data taken consist of a transcription of the actual complaint and a classification of the complaint into a specific category. The complaint categories are dispensing, foreign material, odor, miscounts, and packaging. There are three subcategories of packaging complaints: damaged, misleading, and defective. The 25 packaging complaints for January 1998 are

Damaged	Misleading	Defective	Damaged	Misleading
Defective	Defective	Damaged	Damaged	Defective
Damaged	Misleading	Misleading	Damaged	Damaged
Misleading	Defective	Damaged	Damaged	Damaged
Defective	Damaged	Misleading	Defective	Damaged

You must examine the complaints about packaging and make some recommendations to management. What is your decision?

Possible approaches and things to think about in making a decision:

- Make a table summarizing how many of each type of packaging complaint occurred.
- Make a graph from this table.
- Look to see whether there are more complaints of one type than others and whether this happens during other months. ■

Let's consider another situation.

EXAMPLE 1.2 Golf Ball Design

Understand the Problem

New Product Design

All companies are currently facing increasing competition at the national and international level. In the face of this competition, American manufacturers are focusing on quality. Customer feedback described in the previous scenario is one aspect of this movement. This change is not simple, but rather encompasses all aspects of the business and all the employees of the company. Managers are learning to listen to the creative ideas of their employees, breaking down the hierarchical management layers, and are monitoring their production processes. In doing so, more and more data are being collected on every aspect of the business. All parts of the organization must work together as a team to achieve Total Quality Management (TQM).

A large manufacturer of golf balls is incorporating some of these concepts. The company is studying two golf balls of equal cost to determine which ball design performs better. Data on how far the ball carried when hit are given (in yards) for 12 balls of each design:

Design 1						Design 2					
257	259	255	256	260	258	254	252	256	255	255	257
260	259	259	257	255	260	253	255	254	254	256	255

You must make a recommendation on which design to pursue. What is your decision?

Possible approaches and things to think about in making a decision:

- For each design, find the average distance the balls carried.
- Compare these averages.
- Think about whether the difference between these averages is large.
- Think about whether the differences that you see in the averages could be caused by something other than the ball design. ■

Here is one more example.

EXAMPLE 1.3 **Dress Down Day**

Impact on Employee Morale

Understand the Problem

Many companies have designated one day a week as dress down day. This idea has been implemented even in long-time conservative companies such as IBM. What reason(s) would management have for adopting such a policy? In April 1992, Levi Strauss and Co. conducted the first national survey on business casual dress issues. This phone survey gathered data and opinions from managers from a wide range of industries.

At the company you work for, your boss has conducted a survey of employees. Thirty employees were asked whether they strongly agree (SA), agree (A), disagree (D), or strongly disagree (SD) with each of the following two statements:

Statement 1: Casual dress improves morale.

A SA A A A D SD SA A A D D A A SA
A A D D A A SA SD A D A A D A SA

Statement 2: I do my best work when dressed casually.

D SD A A A A SA A A A D D A A SA
A A A D A D SD D A D A A D A SA

Your boss would like your recommendation regarding the likely increase in productivity if a dress down day is adopted by your company. What is your decision?

Possible approaches and things to think about in making a decision:

- Summarize the results.
- Examine what percentage of people strongly agreed, agreed, disagreed, or strongly disagreed with the various statements presented to them.
- Consider how productivity was defined in this survey.
- Look to see whether the responses are different in different industries. ■

Discovery Exercise 1.1
STARTING TO THINK STATISTICALLY

This exercise allows you to begin to think statistically. Although you have not yet learned any statistical techniques, you will be surprised to discover that many of the ideas you suggest are the basis for some of the techniques you will learn about later in this book. Do not try to solve the problem, but rather focus on what you might do with the data to analyze the situation and what additional information you would like to know about the data or the situation. Remember that statistical thinking is logical, uses data, recognizes the interdependence of activities, and looks at how things vary.

(continued)

Part I. Reduction in Sick Days Used

It has been a widely held belief that a switch to "participative management" would increase employees' "buy-in" to the company. One of the benefits that should be realized is a reduction in the number of sick days that employees use when they feel that they are an important part of the team. A company that has made the switch in some departments wonders whether this has been true. The company decides to sample 25 employees from each of two manufacturing departments. The first department has been using a participative management style for almost 2 years, and the second is still using a traditional management style. The data on the number of sick days used by each employee in the past 12 months follow:

Participative					Traditional				
1	3	5	5	6	0	5	6	7	9
1	4	5	6	7	3	5	7	7	9
2	4	5	6	8	4	6	7	7	10
2	4	5	6	8	4	6	7	8	11
3	4	5	6	8	5	6	7	8	11

Has the participative management style reduced the number of sick days?

1. What else would you like to know about these data sets before comparing them?

2. How could you compare the two data sets using graphs?

3. What numerical calculations would you perform to compare the two data sets?

Part II. Are We There Yet?

The amount of time it takes to travel is clearly dependent on how far you travel and the type of vehicle you are driving. The data shown here give information about how long it took to travel the distance (in miles) when the vehicle was either a car or a truck. The travel times (in minutes) are listed as the Y values. The distances traveled are listed as the $X2$ values. The vehicles used are listed as $X1$ values with the following coding scheme: $X1 = 0$ if a truck was driven and $X1 = 1$ if a car was driven.

Type of vehicle (car = 1, truck = 0)	Distance (miles)	Travel time (min)
$X1$	$X2$	Y
0	55	35
0	102	56
1	33	23
0	20	12
1	55	65
0	48	34
0	53	23

(continued)

Type of vehicle (car = 1, truck = 0)	Distance (miles)	Travel time (min)
0	22	12
1	45	35
1	44	46
1	12	14
0	45	34

Think about how you would analyze the impact that distance and type of vehicle have on travel time.

1. What else would you like to know about the data?

2. How could you display the relationship between the travel time and distance in a graph?

3. How would you predict the time it would take to travel a distance of 90 miles driving a car?

A picture is worth a thousand words. Did you ever hear that saying? Why is this true? Perhaps it is because your eye can process and understand the millions of tiny dots of paint when they are all put together in a meaningful fashion. In this way you see a beautiful picture. Well, that is exactly what the tools of statistics do for you. They put together millions of bits of data in a meaningful fashion. In this way you can make the best decision based on what you see in the data.

1.7 KEY COMPONENTS OF STATISTICAL THINKING

It is important to understand the components of this new paradigm that we have called statistical thinking. There are three key components:

- We must use data whenever possible to guide us.
- We must look for connections and relationships.
- We must understand why data values differ from each other.

Now it is time to introduce an official definition of statistics.

Statistics is a branch of mathematics dealing with the analysis and interpretation of masses of data.

With statistical thinking as the new paradigm, your way of thinking about numbers has begun to change. You must begin to discipline yourself to think systematically and to collect data systematically. Then you must learn how to see the information contained in the data you have collected. Finally, you must use the information to make informed business decisions. The rest of this book is designed to increase your inventory of specific statistical skills to help you see the information contained in the data and strengthen your decision-making skills. In highly successful organizations, the statistical-thinking paradigm will be linked to other important paradigms, such as providing leadership, promoting teamwork, working toward continuous improvement, creating innovative channels of communication, and delighting customers.

1.8 USE OF EXCEL AND OTHER STATISTICAL SOFTWARE

Many statistical techniques require long and involved calculations. Often you want to look at the data in a variety of different ways to get a clear picture of what the data are telling you. Clearly, you want to use software to assist you. Many different statistical packages are available, including Minitab, SPSS, SAS, Statgraphics, and others. You may have noticed that Excel is not in this list. This is not a mistake. Excel is a spreadsheet tool that also has the ability to perform many statistical functions, but it is not first and foremost a statistics package. Excel is widely used in the business world, and this is precisely why we have chosen to use Excel whenever possible. We do not want you to think of Excel as a statistical package. But if you learn how to do data analysis using Excel, which you will most likely have on your desktop at work, then you will be able to easily apply the statistical tools you learn in this book.

To assist you in using Excel to do data analysis, the last section of each chapter shows how to perform the statistical techniques in Excel. This section can be skipped if you are not using Excel.

You will see Excel output throughout this book. However, if you choose not to use Excel, this will not be a problem because the output is there to show the results of the "number crunching." If you do not use Excel, you will use some other tool that will give you the same results.

In addition to Excel output, you will see output from Minitab and SPSS. These are two commonly used statistical packages. Sometimes we show their output just so you can see a slightly different presentation of the results. However, sometimes output from these other packages is used because Excel does not have the capability to do what needs to be done.

You will first need KADDSTAT in Chapter 4 to do boxplots.

Perhaps the most important point to make about using software to support your data analysis is that you should, whenever possible, choose the tool that does the job easily and correctly. Many of the statistical features of Excel are found in the **Tools** menu under an option called **Data Analysis**. If this option does not appear on your **Tools** pull-down menu, you will be shown how to add it when you first need this feature in Chapter 3. There are some statistical techniques that Excel does not perform. Some of these can be easily added to Excel via an add-in feature called KADDSTAT found on the accompanying CD. The first time you need KADDSTAT you will be instructed on how to add it to Excel. More detailed instruction is also available in Appendix C. However, in some cases even with the add-ins, Excel is not adequate. In these cases you will see output from Minitab and SPSS. Remember that in all cases the software is only there to save you the drudgery of the calculations in step 2 of the problem-solving process. You must interpret the data, draw the conclusions, and communicate the results!

BUSINESS EXTRA

The *Wall Street Journal* is a major source of current business news and information for the business community. If your professor has arranged for your class to have access to the Business Extra feature, you can go to it now and see the techniques of this chapter in action today. Go to the Wiley Web site at http://www.wiley.com/college/pelosi, and click on Business Extra!

CHAPTER 1 SUMMARY

In this chapter you learned how important it is for today's business professional to know how to use the tools of statistics. The business environment is changing rapidly, and one of the key issues facing most businesses is the issue of quality. This is true regardless of whether the business is a manufacturer, a restaurant, a hospital, or an entertainment industry. To remain competitive, businesses must pay attention to the quality of the product or service they provide. At the foundation of the quality movement lies the field of statistics.

Key Terms

Term	Definition	Page reference
Paradigm	A **paradigm** is commonly used today to mean a model, theory, perception, assumption, or frame of reference.	4
Statistics	**Statistics** is a branch of mathematics dealing with the analysis and interpretation of masses of data.	9

CHAPTER 1 EXERCISES

Thinking About It!

1.1 We have said that quality and statistics go hand in hand. What product or service have you used recently that did not have the quality you thought it should have?

(a) Describe the product or service and the area in which it was lacking in quality.

(b) What corrective action would you recommend?

1.2 Describe a situation in which you had a paradigm shift or change.

1.3 There has been an increased use of electronic mail in most organizations. This way of communicating with people changes the dynamics of the exchange of information and how people do business. In fact, you might speculate that e-mail would change the way the organization behaves. It is possible that e-mail is used more by middle management than senior management. It is also possible that e-mail is not used to communicate certain types of decisions. A human resource manager asks 10 senior managers and 10 middle managers how many messages they send each day. The data are

Senior managers: 10, 15, 2, 21, 14, 35, 19, 12, 18, 19

Middle managers: 25, 27, 22, 24, 23, 21, 25, 26, 29, 19

(a) What might you do with these data to investigate whether there is a difference in e-mail usage by level of management?

(b) What factors, other than level of management, might influence e-mail usage?

1.4 You have just been hired to be the manager of the service department for a car dealership in your town. You begin by examining the service time for all the cars worked on last Friday. The service time is the number of minutes between the time the car arrived at the dealership and the time the service was completed. The data for last Friday are

15 125 45 65 35 50 20

(a) What additional data would you like to examine to get a more complete picture of the current level of service?

(b) How would you collect the data identified in part (a)?

CHAPTER 2

THE LANGUAGE OF STATISTICS

THE GLUE COMPANY

Business Dilemma...

All companies are currently facing increasing competition at the national and international level. In the face of this competition, American manufacturers are focusing on quality. Customer feedback is one aspect of this movement. In fact, companies are now building relationships with their vendors to ensure higher quality.

The U.S. automobile industry was hit very hard by international competition. The industry appears to have recovered by paying attention to quality at all levels, right down to the glue that is used in assembling some of the components. One of the large U.S. automobile manufacturers has been building a relationship with the manufacturer of an adhesive product. In doing so, the car company has required a lot of data to support the claims about the performance of the glue. The car company visits the adhesive manufacturer from time to time to further the relationship and discuss product quality problems and solutions.

This type of interaction between the supplier and the customer is much different from the "old days" when the purchasing department bought from the least expensive supplier, which could easily be several different suppliers over a short period of time. There was no long-term commitment on either end of the deal. This short-term mentality led to shortcomings in quality.

2.1 CHAPTER OBJECTIVES

In the first chapter you learned that quality and statistics go hand in hand. You also saw that to truly integrate quality into the organization we must view our environment with a statistical thinking paradigm. Recall that a statistical thinking paradigm is a systematic way of thinking about and applying statistical techniques to data and business problems. The first step in changing your view of the world to a statistical thinking paradigm is to develop a language that can be used to describe this new view. This chapter develops the basic language that you need. The following material is covered:

- The Difference Between the Population and a Sample of the Population
- The Difference Between a Parameter and a Statistic
- Factors That Influence Sample Size: Some Sampling and Sample Size Considerations
- Selecting the Sample
- Types of Data
- The Difference Between Descriptive Statistics and Inferential Statistics
- Ethical Issues in Data Analysis
- Communicating the Results
- Basic Summation Notation

2.2 THE DIFFERENCE BETWEEN THE POPULATION AND A SAMPLE OF THE POPULATION

2.2.1 The Population of Interest

In Section 1.6, we saw several situations that called for statistical thinking. If we step back from the details of these situations we see that regardless of the decision that must be made, there is always a group of people or things that must be studied and understood to make the necessary decision. For the tissue manufacturer it was all the boxes of tissues that the company makes, for the company considering dress down day it was all the employees of the company, and for the golf ball company it was the performance of all the balls made according to each of the two designs. These are examples of what is called the **population** in the statistical thinking paradigm. Thus, *all the boxes of tissues* is the population of interest to the tissue manufacturer, *all the employ-*

ees is the population of interest to the company considering dress down day, and *all the golf balls* is the population of interest to the golf ball manufacturer. In each case, to make a recommendation the decision maker must learn something about how the population of interest behaves.

> The ***population*** is everything you wish to study.

EXAMPLE 2.1 The Glue Company

Understand the Problem

Identifying the Population

For the glue company to be a supplier for the car company it must study and understand the performance of all the tubes of glue made for the car company. Call the type of glue used by the car company type C. Thus, the population of interest is all the tubes of type C glue manufactured by the glue company. ■

Often, when we study a population, we are really interested in knowing about different characteristics of each member of the population. These characteristics are known as **variables**. For each member of the population we may be interested in knowing about one, two, or even more different variables.

> A ***variable*** is used to represent a characteristic of each member of the population.

EXAMPLE 2.2 The Glue Company

Understand the Problem

Possible Variables of Interest

In the case of the glue company, we may wish to know how long the glue will stick but we may also wish to know how the glue smells. In this case we wish to study two variables or characteristics of the members of the population of all the tubes of type C glue manufactured by the glue company. ■

TRY IT NOW!

The In-line Skate Company ***Identifying Possible Variables to Study***

There have been a number of failures on the braking device of a new model of roller blades that your company manufactures. What is the population of interest?

Name two variables or characteristics that you might wish to study.

ANS. ALL BLADES OF THIS MODEL: NUMBER OF HOURS OF USE UNTIL THE BRAKE FAILS, TYPE OF FAILURE THAT OCCURS.

2.2.2 The Sample

Now that you understand what a population is, we need to formally define a sample. The statistical definition of the word *sample* is much like the normal use of the word. If someone tells you to sample the apple pies made by a bakery, then you take a small piece of one and eat it, or you might eat one whole pie out of the many pies made by the bakery. It is the same in statistics. If you take a sample, you take a small piece of the population and look at it or test it. Thus, we have our next definition.

A ***sample*** is a piece of the population.

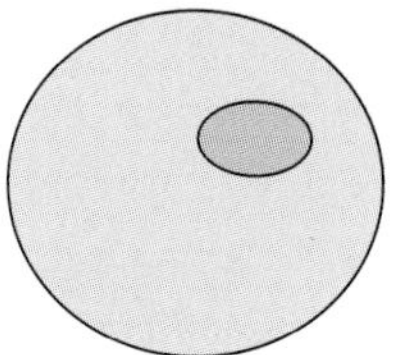

FIGURE 2.1
The population and a sample

If we think about the population as the big oval (all the pies) shown in Figure 2.1, then a sample from this population might be the small oval shown in the figure. This is clearly not the only sample that could be taken from this population; many different samples may be picked. Some of the samples may overlap and some may be bigger or smaller than the one shown.

2.2.3 Why Pick a Sample at All?

Reasons why we can't study the entire population

We have said that the population is everything we wish to study and that the sample is only a piece of the population. A natural question to ask is, Why should we bother to examine a sample when what we really want to know about is the population? Most of the time we cannot study the entire population and must use a sample as a guide. The main reasons are fairly clear when you think about it for a minute:

- It would take too much time to study the entire population.
- It would take too much money to study the entire population.
- It might not be possible to identify all the members of the population.
- If we test the entire population, we might not have anything left to sell.

Let's consider a couple of populations that we have already talked about and see these reasons in action.

EXAMPLE 2.3 **The Glue Company**

Reason Why the Population Cannot Be Studied

Understand the Problem

The glue company must study the performance of all tubes of type C glue that it sells to the car company. It would clearly take a great deal of time and money to test each and every tube of type C glue that the company manufactures. In addition, each tube that is tested is opened and then cannot be sold. So, if every tube were tested there would be no glue to sell to the car company. ■

Here's another example based on one of the situations we looked at in Chapter 1.

EXAMPLE 2.4 **Dress Down Day**

Reason Why the Population Cannot Be Studied

Understand the Problem

A company must study the productivity of the employees before and after a dress down day is adopted. If there are 5000 employees in this company all doing different jobs, it would be virtually impossible to measure productivity for all of them. ■

2.2.4 The Difference Between the Population and the Sample: An Introduction to Sampling Error

It is not necessary to study the entire population

At this point it might look like we should throw up our hands and go home, as we will never have the time, money, or ability to study an entire population. The good news is we don't need to study the entire population. By studying the behavior of a sample we can get a good idea of the behavior of the population. It will not be a perfect picture of the population, but it will be good enough to guide us in our decision making. It is just like eating a piece of the apple pie. You don't know precisely how all the pie tastes but you have a pretty good idea that it is delicious!

Remember, it is really the population that we wish to understand and study. The sample is a means to this end. By understanding and studying a sample, we gain insight and knowledge about the behavior of the population. The amount of information in the sample is not perfect but adequate.

Imagine that you took a picture of the population but let it develop for only a few seconds. You would be able to get an overall sense of what the population looked like but you would not have all of the details. This is like taking a sample and using the sample to determine how the population behaves. If you let this picture develop a few seconds longer, you would get a little clearer view of the population. This is equivalent to taking a bigger sample. Finally, if you let the picture develop completely, then you would have complete information. This is equivalent to studying the entire population. If you study the entire population, then you have taken what is called a **census**.

> A ***census*** is a study of the entire population.

Since the sample is an imperfect snapshot of the population, you know that there will be differences between the sample and the population. This is a bit disconcerting at first. Unless we study the entire population, which we usually cannot do, we will always have incomplete information about the population. That is, unless we study the entire population, we cannot eliminate what is known as **sampling error**.

In addition to sampling error there are other errors that are nonsampling errors. These include the respondent's lying, measurement error, and error due to people not responding.

> ***Sampling error*** is the difference between a characteristic of the entire population and a sample of that population.

The size of the sampling error is determined by two factors. The first of these factors is the *size of the sample*. Clearly, the larger the sample you take, the more similar the sample will be to the population, thus decreasing the sampling error. The second factor that influences the size of the sampling error is the amount of *variation* that exists in the population. Variation in statistics has the same general meaning that it does in typical language usage.

The size of the sample influences the size of the sampling error.

> The amount of ***variation*** refers to how different the members of the population are from each other with regard to the variable being studied.

The amount of variability in the population influences the size of the sampling error.

For example, suppose your population of interest is all attendees at a concert. The variable of interest is the age of these people. If they were exactly the same age then you would say that there was no variation in the age of the members of the population. In this extreme case you would need to take a sample of only one student to have perfect information about the age of the concertgoers.

However, you will almost never be studying a characteristic that has no variability. Suppose that the ages of the concertgoers have a small amount of variability. Let's say the ages range from 18 to 22 years old. Clearly, you have to take a sample of more than one student to understand how the ages vary in this population. Now suppose the ages of the concertgoers range from 17 to 60 years. You have to take a much larger sample to understand how the ages vary in this population. As the amount of variability in the population increases, the sampling error also increases.

2.2.5 Exercises—Learning It!

2.1 The President of the United States wishes to see how popular he/she is after 2 years in office.

(a) What is the population of interest?

(b) Identify which of the reasons for taking a sample (listed on page 15) apply in this case. (There are more than one.)

(c) Identify two variables or characteristics of the members of this population that you may wish to study.

2.2 Tasty Ice Cream Corporation wishes to be sure that all of the half-gallon ice cream cartons do contain one-half gallon of ice cream.

(a) What is the population of interest?

(b) Identify which of the reasons for taking a sample (listed on page 15) apply in this case. (There are more than one.)

(c) Identify two variables or characteristics of the members of this population that you may wish to study.

2.3 A university wishes to know how students view the new athletic center on campus.

(a) What is the population of interest?

(b) What are some reasons why there would be varying views?

(c) Why might the Director of Admissions be interested in these data?

2.4 The U.S. government wishes to know how many people are unemployed.

(a) What is the population of interest?

(b) Suppose you had enough resources to do a census. Why might it be difficult to do a census?

2.5 The accompanying illustration ranks the top 10 international airports in passenger satisfaction.

Source: International Air Transport Association

(a) What is the population of interest?

(b) What is the variable being studied?

(c) Speculate on how the data were obtained.

2.6 The government's goal is to have 90% seat-belt use by the year 2005. As of June 2000, 68% of drivers in the United States used seat belts. That figure is up from about 50% in 1990, 21% in 1985, and 14% in 1983.

(a) What is the population of interest?

(b) What is the variable being studied?

(c) Do you think a census was taken to arrive at these figures? Explain why or why not.

2.7 Before selecting a major, a student decides to study the salaries of individuals working as accountants. The student is thinking that the choice of a major is related to salary. What other factors might cause variation in the salaries of accountants?

Discovery Exercise 2.1

INTRODUCTION TO SAMPLING AND VARIABILITY

Suppose that each set of data in this exercise represents an entire population. Since we don't yet have a way to quantify the amount of variability in a population, the data sets are labeled as having a small amount of variability or a large amount of variability. The first data set shows the number of people in 50 families living in a small college town in New England. The second set of data shows the number of people in 50 families living in a large city in the South.

New England families: large amount of variability
Average number of people in 50 families: 4.50

1	4	5	7	8
3	9	8	8	8
4	9	9	1	6
4	1	3	9	7
8	2	3	1	9
1	7	5	1	1
1	6	8	2	9
4	1	1	1	3
4	2	4	9	4
1	3	8	1	1

Southern families: small amount of variability
Average number of people in 50 families: 4.36

1	3	4	3	5
3	4	6	6	3
6	4	3	4	6
7	5	4	5	5
4	4	5	5	6
3	4	4	7	4
6	3	5	5	5
5	4	4	4	5
4	5	4	3	4
5	4	2	4	4

Step 1. Select a sample of five numbers from each population.

	Sample from NE families	**Sample from Southern families**
Selection 1		
Selection 2		
Selection 3		
Selection 4		
Selection 5		
Average		

Step 2. Calculate the sample average of the five numbers by adding them together and dividing by 5.

Step 3. Calculate how far away the sample average is from the true population average by subtracting the sample average from the population average that is provided for you.

Step 4. Which data set had the greater error—the one with a small amount of variability or the one with a large amount of variability?

Repeat steps 1–4 with a sample of ten numbers.

Step 1. Select a sample of ten numbers from each population.

	Sample from NE families	**Sample from Southern families**
Selection 1		
Selection 2		
Selection 3		
Selection 4		
Selection 5		
Selection 6		
Selection 7		
Selection 8		
Selection 9		
Selection 10		
Average		

Step 2. Calculate the sample average of the ten numbers by adding them together and dividing by 10.

Step 3. Calculate how far away the sample average is from the true population average by subtracting the sample average from the population average that is provided for you.

(continued)

Step 4. Which data set had the greater error—the one with a small amount of variability or the one with a large amount of variability?

Step 5. Record the errors in the following table:

	Sample of size 5	**Sample of size 10**
NE families (large variability)		
Southern families (small variability)		

What happened to the error when you increased the sample size?

2.3 THE DIFFERENCE BETWEEN A PARAMETER AND A STATISTIC

In the last section we saw that by understanding and studying the sample, we can gain insight and knowledge about the behavior of the population. Next we must think about how to describe the behavior of the population to someone else. Suppose you were asked to describe your instructor's behavior in the classroom. You might say that he/she is informative, humorous, organized, and helpful (hopefully)! These are verbal descriptors of your instructor's behavior. If you were asked to provide a visual description of your instructor you might say that she is about 5 feet 2 inches tall, weighs approximately 110 pounds, and is probably about 40 years old. These are numerical descriptors of the person. To paint a picture of a population and a sample, we use descriptors that are both verbal and numerical, just like the ones that we used to describe your instructor.

2.3.1 Parameters: Numerical Descriptors of the Population

There are many different ways to describe the behavior of a population. One of them is to use numerical values to paint a picture of the population. For instance, if you are told that all the values in the population fall between 0 and 10, you form a mental image of the population that is quite different from the picture that is conjured up if you learn that all the values in the population fall between 0 and 1000. This is just one example of a numerical way to describe the population. Chapter 4 shows you the traditional numerical measures that are used to describe the population. They are all examples of what are known as **parameters**.

A ***parameter*** is a number that describes a characteristic of the population.

The following example gives three different parameters that might be of interest to the glue company.

Understand the Problem

EXAMPLE 2.5 The Glue Company

Parameters of Interest

The glue company may wish to know the average number of days that the glue will stick. In this case the parameter of interest is an average value. The company may also wish to know the longest time the glue will stick. In this case the parameter of interest is the maximum stick time. Likewise, the company might wish to know the earliest time that the glue will fail (come unglued). So the shortest stick time is also a parameter of interest. ■

The next example shows that the parameter of interest might be a percentage.

EXAMPLE 2.6 **Dress Down Day**

Parameter of Interest

Understand the Problem

The company thinking of adopting the dress down day would like to know the percentage of employees who had increased productivity as a result of this policy change. The parameter of interest here is a percentage or a proportion. ■

Remember that generally we do not know much about the population. If we did we would not need to take a sample and would not need the tools of statistics (and we could all go home now!). We are usually trying to discover information about these parameters. In particular, we are often trying to *estimate the value of these parameters.* This is the job of statistics.

2.3.2 Statistics: Numerical Descriptors of the Sample

Since we most likely will not know the value of the parameters needed to describe the population, we must resort to using the information contained in the sample. It seems logical that a numerical descriptor for the sample might somehow be used to estimate the corresponding measure for the population. This is the right idea.

So we need numbers to describe the behavior of the sample for two reasons: (1) to paint a picture of the sample and (2) to help us estimate the corresponding population parameter. There is nothing difficult here—in fact, it is quite simple. A statistic is nothing more than a number that describes a characteristic of the sample. Let's put that into a definition box.

A ***statistic*** is a number that describes a characteristic of a sample.

According to this definition we could dream up any formula that we want to describe the sample and it would count as a statistic. Surprisingly enough, this is exactly right. There are, however, a few measures that are typically used because they convey some fairly standard type of information. These are the subject of Chapter 4.

Let's look at two examples: the glue company and the company considering the dress down day policy. In each case we will see what statistics might be calculated.

EXAMPLE 2.7 **The Glue Company and Dress Down Day**

Statistics That Could Be Calculated

Understand the Problem

The glue company might calculate the average stick time from the sample data. This would be one statistic. The company might also record the shortest and the longest stick times in the sample. These are two more statistics.

Let's assume that the company thinking of adopting the dress down day policy has adopted the policy for one department in the company. The company has taken a sample of employees in this department and measured the productivity of each employee in the sample before and after this policy was adopted. Should the policy be adopted companywide? The statistic to calculate is the percentage of employees in the sample who increased their productivity after the dress down policy was adopted. ■

Notice that the statistics that might be calculated from the sample data are closely related to the parameters of interest. This is often the case. Remember that when you calculate the average stick time for the sample it is exactly that: a description of the sample. Is the average stick time for the population of all tubes of type C glue the same as the average you found in the sample? Probably not. Is it close? That depends on how well your sample reflects the population. This is the subject of the next two sections.

2.3.3 Telling the Difference Between Parameters and Statistics

Sometimes it is difficult to tell whether the numbers being reported in the newspaper or on television are parameter values based on a census or statistics based on a sample. To answer this question for yourself, you must ask whether the data are based on complete population information. Sometimes this is the case, but often data are not based on complete information even though they are presented as such. Sometimes you cannot tell from the information provided, and sometimes the writer doesn't want you to think that much about it. This is actually an ethical issue.

For example, the newspapers are always giving lists of "top 10's" such as the top 10 vacation spots, the top 10 car features desired by car owners, the top 10 busiest airports, on the top 10 movies. In the case of the top 10 vacation spots it is possible that a survey was conducted and respondents were asked about their favorite vacation spots. This would make the data reported sample statistics. It is also possible that a count of the number of people staying at hotels in a number of different vacation spots was taken. If hotel registration data were used, this could be census data for the hotels.

Consider the following list of the dollar value of box-office revenues for the top 10 movies for the weekend ending June 16, 2000:

1. Shaft
2. Gone in 60 Seconds
3. Big Momma's House
4. Mission: Impossible 2
5. Titan A.E.
6. Boys and Girls
7. Dinosaur
8. Gladiator
9. Shanghai Noon
10. Road Trip

Are these based on parameter values or statistics? You need to know how they got the data. Most likely they took a sample of movie theaters across the nation, thus the data are statistics.

Now consider the average of the top 10 fastest times for completing the Boston Marathon. This is based on the actual top 10 fastest times and therefore is a parameter for the population of 10 fastest race times. Many sports statistics are based on complete historical information. As such they are parameters. There is no sampling error because the number were calculated based on census data.

Draw Conclusions and Make Recommendations

EXAMPLE 2.8 Affordable Housing Shortage

Look at the accompanying data about the number of families in crisis. Are these population parameters or sample statistics?

Metro area	Number of families in crisis	Portion of all working families
San Jose, Calif.	45,278	**27%**
San Francisco	49,609	**26%**
Oakland	63,952	**22%**
Tampa	56,206	**21%**
Boston	88,573	**20%**
Providence	20,008	**17%**
Washington	90,280	**16%**
Norfolk, Va.	31,965	**15%**
Rochester, N.Y.	17,919	**13%**
Baltimore	44,628	**13%**
Salt Lake City	20,600	**12%**
New York	513,649	**12%**
Houston	55,870	**10%**
Minneapolis-St. Paul	46,496	**10%**
Cincinnati	19,972	**10%**
Los Angeles	401,402	**9%**
Birmingham, Ala.	7,974	**7%**
USA	**3,046,000**	**10%**

SOURCE: The Center for Housing Policy

These data were gathered by the Center for Housing Policy and are most likely census data for the cities listed. But what about the values of the USA shown at the bottom of the table? Are these the totals of the values in the table? Check for yourself—but they are not, although the layout of the table suggests that these figures are totals. So the USA figure is a sample statistic. ■

2.3.4 Exercises—Learning It!

2.8 Consider the illustration shown here.

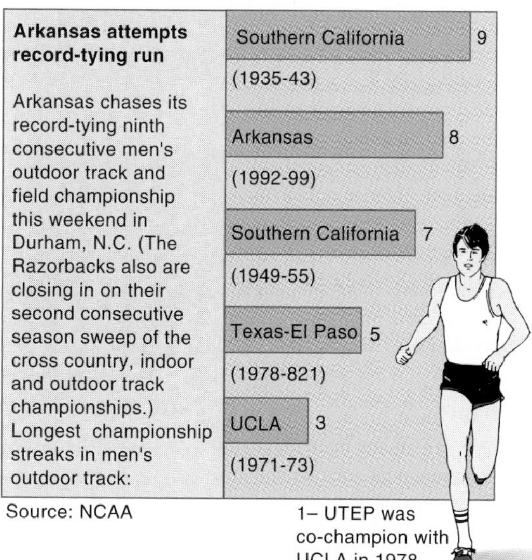

Are the numbers cited parameter values or statistics? Explain your reasoning.

2.9 Tasty Ice Cream Corporation wishes to be sure that all of the half-gallon ice cream cartons do contain one-half gallon of ice cream.

(a) What parameter is of interest?

(b) What statistic might you calculate from the sample?

2.10 The road, it has been said in the concert industry, goes on forever. But in the summer 2000, it mainly circles around New Jersey. If you are mapping out the top markets for the Dave Matthews Band, what is your parameter of interest?

2.11 The university wishes to know how students view the new athletic center on campus.

(a) What parameter is of interest?

(b) What statistic might you calculate from the sample?

2.12 The U.S. government wishes to know how many people are unemployed. The unemployment rate for the United States for 1998 was 4.5%. Is this a statistic or a parameter value? Explain your answer.

2.13 Before selecting a major, a student decides to study the salaries of individuals working as accountants.

(a) What parameter is of interest?

(b) What statistic might you calculate from the sample?

2.4 FACTORS THAT INFLUENCE SAMPLE SIZE: SOME SAMPLING AND SAMPLE SIZE CONSIDERATIONS

The next question is, How big must the sample be? Do we need to eat half of one pie to know how all the pies in a batch taste? What factors will influence our decision in this matter? We touched on this question when we observed the impact of the sample size and the amount of variability on the size of the sampling error. This section reinforces the connection between the sample size and the two factors we have already studied: the amount of variability in the population and the sampling error. In addition, two other factors are introduced.

2.4.1 Size of the Population

The first factor is the **size of the population**. How many tubes of glue are manufactured each day? How many employees are there in the company? How many golf balls are manufactured each hour? How many boxes of tissues are produced in a day? These numbers are the size of the population. Intuitively it should seem that it would take a different sample size to learn about a population of 1000 compared to a population of 100,000. The population size is a factor, but it turns out not to be as important as some of the other factors we have identified.

> The ***size of the population*** is the number of members of the population. It will be referred to as *N*.

2.4.2 Extent of Resources Available

The amount of resources available affects sample size.

The next factor is the amount of time, money, and other resources that you have available. If you need a decision in 6 months rather than next week, the amount of data you could possibly collect and analyze is different. Also, remember that it is expensive to collect and process data, so cost must be a factor. However, we still have not identified the two most important factors.

2.4.3 Amount of Error That Can Be Tolerated

Remember! *A sampling error does not imply that you did anything wrong. It results simply because you have an incomplete picture of the population.*

In Section 2.2.4 we learned that whenever you use a sample to draw conclusions about the population you will have some sampling error. And the bigger the sample we pick, the less error we will have in our conclusions. Returning to the ovals in Figure 2.1, you can see that if you take a bigger sample, then you have captured more of the population. Therefore, the conclusions you draw about the population based on

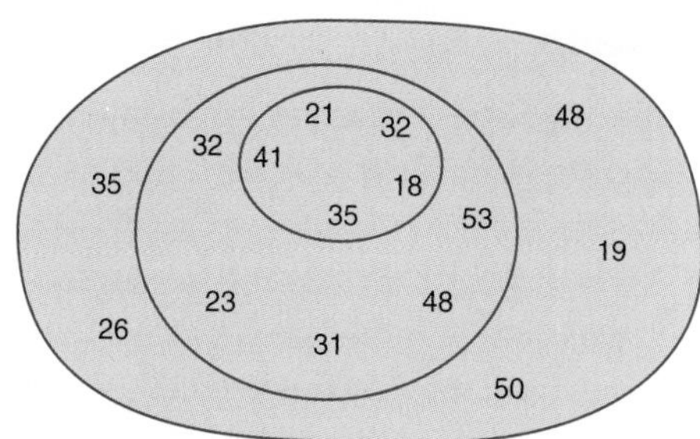

FIGURE 2.2 Bigger and bigger samples

the sample will be more accurate. This is shown by the increasing sample sizes in Figure 2.2. The numbers shown in the large oval are the ages of members of the population being studied. You can see that the smallest oval represents a sample size of 5, since there are five members of the population in it. The next larger oval represents a sample of size 10. In addition to the five members contained in the small oval, it contains five more members of the population.

If we continue taking increasingly bigger sample sizes, eventually we will end up taking a census, or studying the entire population. This is represented by the largest oval. When this happens, the sample size is as big as the population size, *N*, and there is no sampling error.

The amount of error that we can afford is an important factor in determining sample size.

It seems, then, that if we can live with a little more error, then we can get by with a smaller sample size. The more costly the error, the larger our sample size must be. Thus, the *amount of sampling error* (dictated by the cost of the error) we can live with is a factor in determining sample size. We return to this matter in greater detail in Chapters 7–9.

2.4.4 Amount of Variation in the Population

The amount of variation in the population is a key factor in determining sample size.

Even if we can tolerate only a small amount of error we still may not need a really large sample size. One other factor is very important: the *amount of variability* that exists in the population. Suppose for a moment that I wish to study all the students in your college. I wish to be very accurate in my conclusions, but all of the students feel exactly the same about the issue I am studying. How many students do I need to talk to in order to get very precise information about the population? The correct answer is that only one student is needed. A sample size of 1 is adequate despite the need to be very accurate and despite the large size of the population. This is because there is no variation in the population; that is, everyone feels the same way about the issue. Granted, this is not likely to happen, but you can see the impact that this factor has on the sample size needed. The more similar the members of the population are to each other, the less variation there is within the population. So the sample size can be smaller. If the population is highly diversified then you will need to talk to more people to get a sense of how the population feels about the issue.

How will we know the amount of variability in the population?

A natural question to ask is, How will we know the amount of variability of the population to use in determining the sample size? Considering that we are taking a sample to estimate such parameters as variability in the population, it seems a bit of a problem if we need to know the variability to determine the sample size. We are locked in a loop at this point, a classic "catch 22" situation. We could estimate the amount of variability using information about the amount of variability in a population similar to the one we are studying; we could use previous studies of the same population to give us an idea of the amount of variability; or we could do a pilot study. These are some of the ideas for dealing with this dilemma, and they are addressed more completely in Chapter 7.

2.4.5 Summary of Factors Influencing Sample Size

We have identified the following factors that are important in determining the size of the sample needed:

- The amount of variation in the population
- The amount of error that can be tolerated
- The amount of resources available for the project
- The size of the population, N

You will see that the first two factors show up in the formula for determining the size of the sample. These are developed in Chapter 7. For now it is sufficient for you to have a general understanding of the impact that each of these factors has on the sample size determination.

As a final note in this section, we should agree on a label for the sample size. No matter what statistics book you pick up you will always see the **sample size** referred to as n. Remember that the size of the population is labeled N.

> The ***size of the sample*** will be referred to as n.

2.5 SELECTING THE SAMPLE

Now that you have a general idea of which factors influence the size of the sample to be selected, we are ready to think about how we could select a sample. Let's decide what qualities we would like our sample to have.

2.5.1 Selecting an Unbiased Sample

Ideally, we would like the sample to be a miniversion of the population. Remember that we will be using the sample to understand the population. The sample should thus contain all the key features found in the population. It is easiest to understand what this means by looking at some examples of samples that may *not* be a miniversion of the population.

EXAMPLE 2.9 **The Glue Company**

Collect and Analyze the Data

Selecting a Sample

Suppose the glue company decided to use the first 50 tubes of glue made on a Monday morning as the sample.

Why is this not a good idea? It is possible that the manufacturing process varies as the machine runs for a long period of time. It is also possible that different people operate the machine at different times of the day and on different days of the week. And it is possible that a different batch of raw material might lead to differences in the glue performance. If our sample consists of the first 50 tubes made on Monday morning, we may not see the impact of any of these factors on the glue performance. ■

EXAMPLE 2.10 **Dress Down Day**

Collect and Analyze the Data

Selecting a Sample

Suppose the company considering a dress down day decides to use the recently hired female employees as their sample.

Again the problem is that this sample may not truly represent the population of employees of the company. Why not? First of all, the people in this sample are all women. Maybe women in this company are consistently more or less productive than men. Second, they are all new hires and are likely to be putting their best effort into the job. At the same time, they are in training and may make more than the average number of errors. For all of these reasons and probably others this group is not a miniversion of the employees of this company. ■

In both of these situations the proposed sample may not let us see all of the variation that exists in the population. Another way to express this is to say that these samples might be **biased**. The word *bias* in statistics has the same meaning that it has in ordinary usage. It means that the sample is somehow not a fair reflection of the reality we would see in the population. A biased sample would give us an unfair or prejudiced view of the population. This is precisely what we wish to avoid. Let's capture this in a definition.

> A ***biased sample*** is a sample that does not fairly represent the population.

TRY IT NOW!

Stress Relief ***Identifying Possible Biases in a Sample***

You are studying the methods that students at your school use to relieve stress. You decide to use your statistics class as your sample. Why might this be a biased sample?

2.5.2 Selecting a Simple Random Sample

In selecting any sample, we wish to pick an unbiased or fair sample. We also wish to pick a sample that contains as much information as possible. There are many ways to pick a sample but for the purposes of an introductory course we are going to use what is known as a **simple random sample (srs)**. This means that each member of the population has an equal chance of being selected as a member of the sample. In addition, every sample of size n has the same chance of becoming our sample. This is equivalent to placing the names of all the members of the population in a hat and reaching in and picking out members to be in the sample.

> A ***simple random sample*** is a sample that has been selected in such a way that all members of the population have an equal chance of being picked. In addition, every sample of size n has the same chance of becoming our sample.

ANS. THE STUDENTS IN THIS CLASS MAY BE MOSTLY SOPHOMORE BUSINESS STUDENTS.

Simple random sampling is the most obvious way to select a sample. In fact, you might wonder how else you could do it. Suppose you wished to learn about prices charged for advertising in newspapers. Your population would be all companies located in the United States that publish newspapers. If you picked a simple random sample of newspaper companies you might end up with all small companies purely by chance. You might not get any of the "biggies" such as the *New York Times*, the *Boston Globe*, the *Chicago Tribune*, or the *Los Angeles Sun* in the sample. Is this bad? Well, that depends on what variable you are studying. We are interested in prices for advertising in these papers and the larger companies might set the pace for the smaller companies with regard to pricing. In this case you might choose to use something other than simple random sampling to guarantee that you had some "biggies" in your sample.

As you learn more about statistics you will see that simple random sampling does not always provide you with the most information for your money. All of the concepts that you will learn in this book carry over to the other kinds of selection methods, but the formulas might have to change a bit if you use a procedure other than simple random sampling. In Chapter 14 you will learn how to select a sample by designing an experiment.

2.5.3 The Sampling Frame

Now that we have decided that we want to select a simple random sample, we must look at what is needed to pick the sample. Returning to the example of the newspapers from the previous section, we can see that we need a list of all the newspaper publishing companies in the United States. Such a list is known as the **sampling frame**.

A ***sampling frame*** is a list of all members of the population.

There are government agencies and private companies, such as Dun & Bradstreet, whose function is to collect data for sampling frames. However, creating a sampling frame may take a fair amount of time, energy, and money. Thus, the list from which you pick your sample may not be accurate or complete. The difficulty in creating these lists is not the focus of this course or this book. However, you should know what a sampling frame is and know enough to watch out for potential problems.

2.5.4 Using a Table of Random Numbers to Select the Sample

Once you have the sampling frame and you have determined your sample size (using the formula developed in Chapter 7), you are ready to select your sample. Although it is easy to understand the idea of placing the name of each member of the population in a hat and selecting the sample by picking names from the hat, this is not a practical way to select the sample. To imitate this process you can use a **table of random numbers**.

A ***table of random numbers*** is a table that consists of a list of numbers randomly generated and listed in the order in which they were generated.

Such a table is provided in Table 1 in Appendix A. A portion of this table is shown in Figure 2.3.

A random number table should contain roughly as many zeros as ones as twos and so forth. There is a way to check to see that such a table does in fact contain random numbers, but for our purposes we will assume that the random number table has been correctly generated.

	Column						
Row	**1**	**2**	**3**	**4**	**5**	**6**	**7**
1	094632795	711501513	537971597	562758635	410398128	182794408	773761503
2	033413186	653475420	289063704	485441982	460744361	328703833	289612212
3	297556368	658953044	738968017	414437050	296126017	075254187	702140315
4	472960570	785645638	574817322	817883255	976076280	843373358	118284363
5	256883707	716249997	378236162	467694224	193707682	380141891	605807481
6	179451522	878902420	602450872	987686989	686677180	242196303	517640224
7	894964682	704841116	241902107	750429362	794778197	693242123	316755091
8	738120861	744470405	873393138	758824215	394004646	496696605	006936567
9	803156944	653387115	716335974	835667154	066959782	908783760	165946696
10	187636922	321421098	638210137	055734541	493193305	566923120	435549770

FIGURE 2.3 Portion of a table of random numbers

To use this table to identify which members of our population will be selected to be in the sample, we must first assign each member of the population an identification (ID) number. Suppose that you are studying the students at your college or university. Each student probably has a student ID number. Since many schools use the student's social security number as the ID number, let's suppose that the ID number is a 9-digit number. To use a table of random numbers to select a sample of 30 students from this population, you would first select where in the random number table you should start reading. One way to do this is to close your eyes and point to a spot in the table. Suppose that you did this and you selected row 10, column 2 as your starting point. Then you would read the next nine digits from Figure 2.3 as 321421098. This is the ID number of the first member of your sample. The next nine-digit number from the table is 638210137 and this is the ID number of the second member of your sample. You would continue this process until you have selected 30 ID numbers.

The sample obtained in this manner is a simple random sample. However, you would certainly need to read more than 30 ID numbers from the table to get 30 usable ID numbers. Most of the ID numbers you read from the table of random numbers will not correspond to anyone at your school. This would certainly happen, especially if the school is using the student's social security number as the ID number. Although you will eventually find 30 usable ID numbers, you will waste an incredible amount of time.

This method works a little better when you can assign the ID codes to the members of your population in such a way that they are sequential, so that you will not select any nonusable ID numbers. Let's see how this works in the following example.

EXAMPLE 2.11 Student Views

Selecting a Sample Using a Table of Random Numbers

Collect and Analyze the Data

Each student at your college has a mailbox on campus. The mailboxes are numbered from 0000 to 9000. To select a simple random sample of 10 students we can select 10 mailbox numbers at random using the random number table. Suppose we choose to start at row 7, column 3 of the table shown in Figure 2.3. The first student selected has mailbox number 2419, which is a valid number. Continuing to read off 4-digit numbers from this table, the second number selected has mailbox number 0210. The list of all 10 mailbox numbers selected is:

2419 0210 7750 4293 6279 4778 1976 2123 3167 5509

Since the numbers are organized in nine-digit blocks and we need only four-digit mailbox numbers, we just kept reading the numbers sequentially, wrapping

Step 4: If you did Discovery Exercise 2.1, compare the sample you selected using the random number table to the sample you selected without the use of the table. Which one had a sample average closer to the population average?

2.5.5 Exercises—Learning It!

2.14 The President of the United States wishes to see how popular he/she is after 2 years in office. A sample of 1000 voters is taken from the state of California.

(a) Why might this be a biased sample?

(b) How could you get a simple random sample?

2.15 Tasty Ice Cream Corporation wishes to be sure that all of the half-gallon ice cream cartons do contain one-half gallon of ice cream. A sample of 30 cartons are measured. All of the cartons in the sample were filled on Friday.

(a) Why might this be a biased sample?

(b) How could you get a simple random sample?

2.16 A company that manufactures electronic switches wishes to provide the customer with defect-free switches. A sample of five switches is selected every hour throughout the day. Explain why this is most likely an unbiased sample.

2.17 The university wishes to know how students view the new athletic center on campus. A questionnaire is distributed to people as they enter the building.

(a) Why might this be a biased sample?

(b) How could you get a simple random sample?

2.18 The U.S. government wishes to know how many people are unemployed. A sample of 1000 individuals over age 18 is selected from a national listing. Explain why this is probably an unbiased sample.

2.19 The manufacturer of disposable diapers wishes to know how much fluid the diapers can hold before they leak. The diapers are put on children who are playing and fluid is injected every 15 minutes until the diaper leaks. Explain why this is probably an unbiased sample.

2.20 The Coca-Cola Company wishes to know the proportion of people who prefer Coke over Pepsi. A sample of 100 people at a county fair is taken.

(a) Why might this be a biased sample?

(b) How could you get a simple random sample?

2.21 Before selecting a major, a student decides to study the salaries of individuals working as accountants. A sample of accountants is selected from the list of alumni of the school that the student is attending.

(a) Why might this be a biased sample?

(b) How could you get a simple random sample?

2.6 TYPES OF DATA

NOTE: The words ***data*** *and* ***variable*** *are being used interchangeably.*

Although we will not study the whole area of data collection, we do need to think about the different kinds of data or variables that we might encounter. The kind of statistical analysis that we do depends on the type of data we have. There are two major types of variables, **qualitative** and **quantitative**. In this section we concentrate on being able to identify the different types of data. Since different statistical techniques are used with different types of data, it is important to identify the type of data you have before you analyze them so that you don't use the wrong technique.

2.6.1 Qualitative Data

Qualitative data, also known as **nominal** or **categorical** data, are the simplest form of data. Examples of qualitative data are variables such as gender (male or female) or the expected grade in a course (A, B, C, D, or F). Each item in the sample falls into one of a finite number of possible categories.

> ***Qualitative data*** describe a particular characteristic of a sample item. They are most often nonnumerical in nature.

Suppose you are interested in learning about the length of time that a certain glue, type C, adheres. You collect the data from a sample of glue tubes and after analyzing them you find that there appear to be two groups in the data. Each group has sticking times that cluster around a different value. Why would this occur? When you ask some questions about how the data were collected you learn that some of the tubes came from machine A and some came from machine B. When you return to the sticking times you find that all of the machine A values are clustered at the lower number, whereas those of machine B are clustered at the higher number. The variable *machine* is an example of qualitative data. Knowing which machine produced the tube helps to explain the differences in the glue sticking times that you saw in the data.

Dress Down Day ***Possible Qualitative Variables***

The company considering the dress down day tries this policy out with a sample of employees. After the policy has been in effect for some time, the company decides to measure the change in productivity for the employees. It appears that for some employees productivity has increased, whereas for others it has decreased. What qualitative data might have been collected to help the company understand the differences observed?

The statistical techniques that are used to analyze qualitative data are limited, but are often critical to our understanding of the results of statistical analyses. When you are collecting data it is important to think of qualitative data that may be relevant to the problem to be solved. Qualitative data are easily collected at the time, but almost impossible to reconstruct after the fact. When in doubt, qualitative data should always be collected.

Sometimes numbers are used to classify qualitative data. For example, in surveys that ask for gender we often find that a 0 is used to denote "male" and a 1 is used to denote "female." When this is the case the data are referred to as **nominal** data. The numbers are used simply to represent different categories and have no real meaning as numbers.

ANS. GENDER, DEPARTMENT, LEVEL WITHIN THE ORGANIZATION

Data that are created by assigning numbers to different categories when the numbers have no real meaning are called ***nominal data***.

Nominal data are treated the same way as ordinary qualitative data.

The order in which numbers are assigned to qualitative data may have some meaning. When numbers are used to name ordered categories the data are called **ordinal**. In the case of gender, the numbers 0 and 1 could very easily be reversed and so they have no intrinsic meaning. But suppose you asked a group of people to rank five different versions of a new soft drink. The resulting data might look like this:

Version	3	2	5	1	4
Ranking	1	2	3	4	5

In this case the numbers are not entirely meaningless since they indicate a relative position for each version of the product on a scale. However, you cannot tell from this scale whether the person doing the ranking liked version 3 a lot and really hated the other four or whether versions 3 and 2 were similar and much superior to the remaining three versions. The distances between the assigned numbers are not necessarily equal.

Another example of ordinal data would be when a characteristic of a sample item, such as income, is classified as 1 = low, 2 = medium, and 3 = high. Here, the numbers have a relative ordering, but there is no way to compare 1 to 2 to 3 numerically.

Data that are created by assigning numbers to categories where the order of assignment has meaning are called ***ordinal data***.

Most often, ordinal data are analyzed using the same graphical techniques that apply to other qualitative data. There are some limited statistical techniques that can be used to further analyze ordinal data. These techniques are called nonparametric analyses.

2.6.2 Quantitative Data

Data that are inherently numerical in form are called **quantitative** data. This type of data falls into two different categories: **discrete** and **continuous**.

Discrete data usually result when the data being collected involve *counting* or *enumerating*. The only possible values are positive integers or whole numbers. Examples of discrete data are the number of prior convictions for a person who has been arrested or the number of defective items in a sample.

Discrete data are data that can take on only certain values. These values are often integers or whole numbers.

Discrete data that result from counting the number of times that something occurs are important. They are the type of data used in analyzing many public opinion polls and other surveys. You will encounter this kind of data many times in the text.

Continuous data are data that can take on any one of an infinite number of possible values over an interval on the number line. These values are most often the result of measurement.

Numerical data that are not discrete are called **continuous**. Continuous data occur most often as the result of measuring and are sometimes referred to as *measurement data.* Continuous data usually consist of real numbers, which, as far as we are concerned, will be in decimal form.

EXAMPLE 2.12 Study Time

An Example of Continuous Data

Collect and Analyze the Data

Suppose you are interested in learning about the length of time that a typical student spends studying statistics on any given night. Initially, there are an infinite number of possibilities for values, ranging from 0 minutes up. These data are continuous. Once you decide on a measuring device the number of possibilities is limited, but the limitation is caused by the measuring device and not the variable itself. For example, if you measure the time spent studying to the nearest hour, the possible values are 0, 1, 2, ... If, however, you decide to measure to the nearest one-tenth of an hour (6 minutes), the possible values are 0.0, 0.1, 0.2, . . . , 3.0, 3.1, ... The more precise your measuring device, the more possible values your data can assume. ■

2.6.3 Exercises—Learning It!

2.22 The President of the United States wishes to see how popular he/she is after 2 years in office. A sample of voting age adults are asked if they would reelect him or her today.

(a) Is the variable qualitative or quantitative?

(b) If the variable is qualitative, is it nominal or ordinal data? If it is quantitative, is it discrete or continuous?

2.23 Tasty Ice Cream Corporation wishes to be sure that all of the half-gallon ice cream cartons do contain one-half gallon of ice cream.

(a) What is one variable of interest?

(b) Are the data qualitative or quantitative?

(c) If the data are qualitative, are they nominal or ordinal? If they are quantitative, are they discrete or continuous?

2.24 The university wishes to know how students view the new athletic center on campus. Students are asked to rank the new center against four other schools' athletic centers.

(a) Are the data qualitative or quantitative?

(b) If the data are qualitative, are they nominal or ordinal? If they are quantitative, are they discrete or continuous?

2.25 The U.S. government wishes to know how many people are unemployed. A sample of people are asked whether they are employed full time.

(a) Are the data qualitative or quantitative?

(b) If the data are qualitative, are they nominal or ordinal? If they are quantitative, are they discrete or continuous?

2.26 Before selecting a major, a student decides to study the salaries of individuals working as accountants. A sample of accountants are asked their salary.

(a) Are the data qualitative or quantitative?

(b) If the data are qualitative, are they nominal or ordinal? If they are quantitative, are they discrete or continuous?

2.27 Here are a few questions from a survey about the "I Love You" computer virus. For each question, identify what type of data will be collected.

(a) Was your computer infected by the "I Love You" virus?

- Yes, one or more of my computers was infected by it.
- No, none of my computers was infected by it.
- I'm really not sure whether it was.

(b) Do you know anyone else whose computers were infected by the "I Love You" virus?

- Yes
- No

(c) How often do you carefully examine the subject and body of your e-mail messages before opening their attachments?

- Always
- Often
- Occasionally
- Seldom or never

(d) Rewrite the question in part(c) so that it yields quantitative data. Why might this be better?

(e) Please rate this survey on a scale of 1 to 5.

2.7 THE DIFFERENCE BETWEEN DESCRIPTIVE STATISTICS AND INFERENTIAL STATISTICS

So far, we have looked at the concept of population and recognized the usefulness of the sample in gleaning information about the population. We have discussed factors that influence how large the sample needs to be and how we go about picking the sample. And we have looked at the types of data that might be collected from the sample. Now we need an answer to the question, What do I do with the data? The right answer is, It depends. It depends on what type of data you have and on what questions you want answered about the behavior of the population. The rest of this book is devoted to providing tools to answer the question, What do I do with the data? These tools fall into two main categories: the tools of descriptive statistics and the tools of inferential statistics. Although these tools support each other, the jobs they do are quite different.

2.7.1 Descriptive Statistics

The tools of descriptive statistics are usually the first ones encountered in any data analysis. They allow you to *describe* the sample. However, that is all they do. This is generally the first step in any data analysis, once the data have been collected, of course. If you were given the results of a survey on customer satisfaction from 100 customers, the first thing you would want to do is to get a handle on the data by summarizing them. This is precisely what the tools of descriptive statistics do for you: summarize the data.

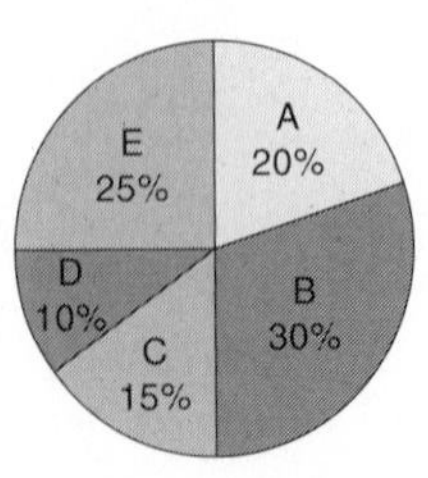

Bar chart

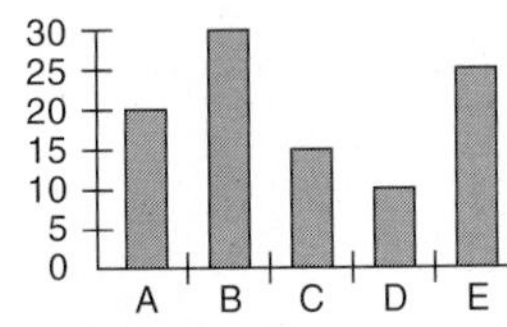

FIGURE 2.4 Pie chart and bar chart

> ***Tools of descriptive statistics*** allow you to summarize the data.

There are *graphical* or *visual descriptive tools*, which generally include bar charts, pie charts, and histograms. These tools are discussed in Chapter 3. Graphical tools help you to see how the data behave and to summarize the data visually. These tools are used all the time. You frequently will see them in newspapers and in reports. Some examples are shown in Figure 2.4.

There are also *numerical descriptive tools*, which allow you to summarize the data numerically. Typically, a numerical summary would provide you with such *statistics* as the average, the median, the mode, and the largest and smallest data values. We used the word statistics in the last sentence because that is precisely what these values are. Remember that a statistic is simply a number that describes the behavior of the sample. These numbers are covered in more detail in Chapter 4.

Descriptive tools would be adequate if all we wanted to do was describe the sample. But remember that the sample is a means to an end. At the end of the day it is not the sample that we care about but the population. Somehow we must make the leap from the information contained in the sample to the population behavior. To do this we need the tools of inferential statistics.

2.7.2 Inferential Statistics

Let's start by defining the word **inference**. If your friend told you not to infer that all business students are brilliant, then your friend is telling you not to reach that *conclusion!*

> An ***inference*** is a deduction or a conclusion.

In our case we wish to draw conclusions about the behavior of the population based on the information in the sample. We have already seen that the sample is only a piece of the population, so we will not have complete information. We have also seen that if the sample is properly selected, then the information contained in the sample will give us reliable information about the population.

How are we going to make this leap from describing the sample data to drawing an inference or conclusion about the behavior of the population? The answer is found in the study of probability. Indeed, without the tools of probability, we could not do anything more than describe the sample data. We could do no inferential statistics.

Think about the population and the sample as the circles shown in Figure 2.5. The larger circle represents the population and the smaller circle represents the sample. This figure is being used to help you see how probability is necessary to draw inferences about the population from the sample. In reality, the sample circle should sit inside the population circle, because it is a piece of it. But for now let us continue with this picture. The line that moves from the sample to the population is labeled "Inferential statistics." The tools of inferential statistics are used to move from sample information to population information. Let's save that thought as a definition.

> The ***techniques of inferential statistics*** allow us to draw inferences or conclusions about the population from the sample.

To understand the line that moves from the population to the sample, consider the following situation. You and I have decided to play poker and I have dealt us each five cards. You see that you have a full house and are wildly excited. However, your excitement is quickly contained as I reveal to you that I have not one, not two, not three, not four, but *five* aces! Immediately you accuse me of cheating (imagine that!). You quickly conclude that I have not used a standard deck.

Let's take a closer look at how you reached that conclusion. First of all, the deck of cards is our population. You had a sample of five cards selected from that population and I had a sample of five cards from that population. On the basis of the information in my sample you calculated the probability of observing five aces if I was using a standard deck and found it to be zero. There is no chance of getting five aces if the population has the behavior of a standard deck. So you quickly rejected the

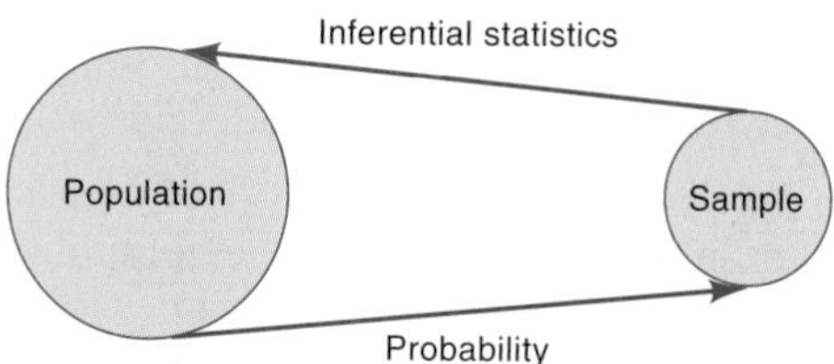

FIGURE 2.5 Relationship between probability and inferential statistics

Reaching a conclusion based on a sample. Did I cheat?

notion that I was using a standard deck. This is precisely what we need to do in general. We need to draw conclusions about a population based on the observed sample and the theory of probability. The conclusions will not always be so obvious as this example. So we have a definition for the line in Figure 2.5 labeled "Probability," which leads from the population to the sample.

> We will use ***probability*** theory to calculate the likelihood of observing or selecting a particular sample from a population.

Although the branch of mathematics known as probability theory is interesting in its own right, we present only those particular parts of probability that will help us in our ultimate goal: to make inferences about the population from the sample.

Let's summarize Figure 2.5. If we make the trip across the bottom line we would be making some assumptions about the population behavior and determining the likelihood of various samples that might come from this population. If we make the trip across the top line we would be taking the information in the sample and drawing conclusions about the population from which it came. The tools of probability ultimately allow us to accomplish what we want, which is to do inferential statistics.

2.7.3 Upcoming Chapters

Based on our discussions in this section, it is clear that the first thing we should do is learn the tools of descriptive statistics. These are covered in Chapters 3, 4, and 5. Chapter 6 presents the necessary probability theory that helps us move beyond simply describing the sample data. Chapters 7–16 present various techniques of inferential statistics. The last chapter (Chapter 17) provides a synthesis of the book and a set of cases.

2.8 ETHICAL ISSUES IN DATA ANALYSIS

In this text we will caution you numerous times to present the data fairly and accurately. You can distort the message of the data by altering the scale of the graphs, by changing the level of α at which you perform the hypothesis test, by withholding data, and by other means.

The American Statistical Association (ASA) is one of the professional associations that statisticians belong to. The ASA is concerned about the misuse of data and has published the following "Ethical Guidelines for Statistical Practice":

1. Statisticians have a public duty to maintain integrity in their professional work, particularly in the application of statistical skills to problems where private interests may inappropriately affect the development or application of statistical knowledge. For these reasons, statisticians should:
   - present their findings and interpretations honestly and objectively
   - avoid untrue, deceptive, or undocumented statements
   - disclose any financial or other interests that may affect, or appear to affect, their professional statements
2. Recognizing that collecting data for a statistical inquiry may impose a burden on respondents, that it may be viewed by some as an invasion of privacy, and that it often involves legitimate confidentiality considerations, statisticians should:
   - collect only the data needed for the purpose of their inquiry
   - inform each potential respondent about the general nature and sponsorship of the inquiry and the intended uses of the data
   - establish their intentions, where pertinent, to protect the confidentiality of information collected from respondents and strive to ensure that these inten-

tions realistically reflect their pledges of confidentiality and their limitations to the respondents

- ensure that the means are adequate to protect confidentiality to the extent pledged or intended, that processing and use of data conform with the pledges made, that appropriate care is taken with directly identifying information, that appropriate techniques are applied to control statistical disclosure
- ensure that, whenever data are transferred to other persons or organizations, this transfer conforms with the established confidentiality pledges, and require written assurance from the recipients of the data that the measures employed to protect confidentiality will be at least equal to those originally pledged

3. Recognizing that statistical work must be visible and open to assessment with respect to quality and appropriateness to advance knowledge and that such assessment may involve an explanation of the assumptions, methodology, and data processing used, statisticians should:
    - delineate the boundaries of the inquiry as well as the boundaries of the statistical inferences that can be derived from it
    - emphasize that statistical analysis may be an essential component of an inquiry and should be acknowledged in the same manner as other essential components
    - be prepared to document data sources used in an inquiry, known inaccuracies in the data, and steps taken to correct or refine the data, statistical procedures applied to the data, and the assumptions required for their application
    - make the data available for analysis by other responsible parties with appropriate safeguards for privacy concerns
    - recognize that the selection of a statistical procedure may to some extent be a matter of judgment and that other statisticians may select alternative procedures
    - direct any criticism of a statistical inquiry to the inquiry itself and not to the individuals conducting it
4. Recognizing that a client or employer may be unfamiliar with statistical practice and be dependent upon the statistician for expert advice, statisticians should:
    - make clear their qualifications to undertake the statistical inquiry at hand
    - inform a client or employer of all factors that may affect or conflict with their impartiality
    - accept no contingency fee arrangements
    - fulfill all commitments in any inquiry undertaken
    - apply statistical procedures without concern for a favorable outcome
    - state clearly, accurately, and completely to a client the characteristics of alternate statistical procedures along with the recommended methodology and the usefulness and implications of all possible approaches
    - disclose no private information about or belonging to any present or former client without the client's approval

2.9 COMMUNICATING THE RESULTS

Before concluding this chapter on the language of statistics, we should talk about the language you should use to communicate your results. Remember that the last step of the problem-solving process is to communicate your results. In a sense you need to make your case, based on your analysis. How should you do this? Should you show all of your analysis or should you show only a summary of your findings? The best data analysis in the world is not worth much if it cannot be presented and explained clearly so that the person who must make decisions based on the data understands it. This section will provide you with some general guidelines for clear communication.

First, you must understand your audience. Consider the technical background of the people you are talking to and make your decisions about level of detail and degree of technical language accordingly. You want to use language that is understandable.

Second, provide your audience with a written summary of your analysis. This is called an executive summary, and the first such example is presented in Section 2.10. Each chapter of this book concludes with an executive summary. Use these as models. They should be at most one page in length.

Third, use an electronic slide show tool, such as PowerPoint, to present the results. Be sure you use only the graphs and results necessary to make your case. Be sure all your graphs have titles and all the axes are properly labeled. Do not show every graph you created but only those that led you to your conclusions and recommendations. Likewise, show only relevant calculations. Begin your slide show with a slide that gives your name, the date, and the project title. Follow this with a slide that outlines your presentation. The results of your analysis should follow next, with summary slides after each point is made. Complete your presentation with a slide that show your conclusions and recommendations.

2.10 Executive Summary:

THE GLUE COMPANY

Business Analysis...

TO: Operations Manager
FROM: Erica Q. Analyst
RE: Data for automotive customers

This company is committed to providing quality adhesive products. It is also committed to building long-term relationships with our customers. Data will be collected on a regular basis and shared with the automotive customers, should they wish to see them. Representatives from the automotive customers are welcome to observe our manufacturing process and to speak to us about our continuous improvement efforts.

The company will study and understand the performance of the adhesive products made for the car company. In particular, data on the maximum stick time will be collected under differing weather conditions. Data on earliest time to failure (it comes unglued) will also be collected under differing weather conditions. These data will be collected on a regular basis.

We will work with the customer to establish their needs and use this information together with information about the variability to stick time to determine a sample size and frequency of sampling. Samples will be selected to ensure that they fairly represent the population.

It is recommended that we collect the following data:

Qualitative variables:	day of the week data are taken
	name of person recording the data
	time of day data are taken
	machine data are taken from
Quantitative variables:	maximum stick time
	minimum stick time

Graphs and numerical summaries will be provided to management on a weekly basis.

The *Wall Street Journal* is a major source of current business news and information for the business community. If your professor has arranged for your class to have access to the Business Extra feature, you can go to it now and see the techniques of this chapter in action today. Go to the Wiley Web site at http://www.wiley.com/college/pelosi, and click on Business Extra!

2.11 BASIC SUMMATION NOTATION

In all of the material that follows this chapter, you will need to be familiar with basic summation notation. If you are familiar with this notation, you may skip this section. But you may wish to use it as a quick review and refer to it as you proceed through the rest of the book. A shorthand notation useful for writing statistical formulas is called **sigma notation.**

> ***Sigma notation*** is shorthand notation used to write formulas. It is so named because it uses the Greek capital letter sigma, written as Σ.

2.11.1 Summing the Data

If we have a sample of size n, we can refer to the individual data values as $x_1, x_2, x_3, \ldots, x_n$, where x_1 represents the first data value, x_2 the second data value, and so on. Many of the formulas you encounter will require that you sum the data values. We could write the sum as $x_1 + x_2 + x_3 + \cdots + x_n$ but this will get cumbersome and be awkward to use.

Remember that we agreed to use the letter n to represent the size of the sample.

Using the sigma notation, we can write the sum $x_1 + x_2 + x_3 + \cdots + x_n$ as

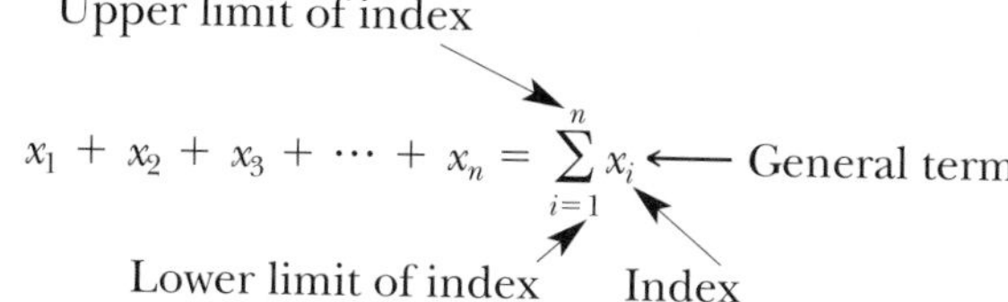

$$x_1 + x_2 + x_3 + \cdots + x_n = \sum_{i=1}^{n} x_i$$

The sigma notation on the right of the equation is read as "the sum of x_i as i goes from 1 to n." The letter under the Σ is called the index and it really doesn't matter what letter you use since you use the same letter in describing the general term. The value of the index indicated on the bottom of the Σ is the starting value for the index and is usually 1, meaning that we are going to start with x_1. The value on the top of the Σ is the ending value for the index and is usually n, the sample size. When the index goes from $i = 1$ to n, all of the data values in the sample are being used.

Let's try some examples.

EXAMPLE 2.13 **The Glue Company**

Using Summation Notation

Collect and Analyze the Data

The glue company studies the performance (i.e., the stickiness) of 10 tubes of type C glue. The data are recorded in terms of number of days until the glue failed. This is what the company found: 233, 167, 289, 221, 254, 198, 210, 225, 240, 203. Thus, x_1 is 233, the first member of the sample. In a similar fashion we can label the rest of the data values: $x_2 = 167$, $x_3 = 289$, $x_4 = 221$, $x_5 = 254$, $x_6 = 198$, $x_7 = 210$, $x_8 = 225$, $x_9 = 240$, and $x_{10} = 203$. The value of n is 10, the size of the sample.

To find $x_1 + x_2 + x_3 + \cdots + x_{10}$ we will first write it as $\sum_{i=1}^{10} x_i$. This means that we start the value of i at 1 and start with x_1, which we know is 233. Check to see whether the value for i is at the upper limit for i, which in this case is 10. Since i is only 1 we continue. Next put a plus sign and change i to be 2 and add in x_2, which we know to be 167. So far we have 233 + 167. Again we check to see whether the value for i is bigger than the upper limit of 10. It is not, so we continue by putting a plus sign and changing i to 3 and adding x_3, which we know is 289. Now we have 233 + 167 + 289. This process continues until the value of i is 10 and we have written down 233 + 167 + 289 + 221 + 254 + 198 + 210 + 225 + 240 + 203 and obtained 2240. ■

The Mail-Order Company *Using Sigma Notation*

A mail-order company wants some information on the daily demand for a product that has been heavily advertised. The company looks at the orders for an 8-day period and obtains the following data:

Demand	31	28	29	32	30	31	29	30

Use sigma notation to write down the expression that means to add up all the data values.

2.11.2 Summing Differences

When we analyze data we often need to look at how *far away* data values are from some number. Clearly, we could state how far away any one of the data values was from a number by simply subtracting the two numbers. For the glue company data shown in Example 2.13 we could say that x_1 is 9 days away from a number, for instance, 224. Remember that x_1 is 233. In addition to being interested in how far away x_1 is from 224, we often have to state how far away the whole data set is from 224. To do this we have to subtract 224 from each value in the data set, each x_i, and then add up all these differences.

ANS. $\sum_{i=1}^{8} x_i$

EXAMPLE 2.14 The Glue Company

Use of Sigma Notation to Calculate Differences

Suppose we wish to quantify how far away the whole data set is from 224 for the glue company. The calculation we want is

$$\begin{aligned}&(233-224)+(167-224)+(289-224)+(221-224)+(254-224)+(198-224)\\&\quad+(210-224)+(225-224)+(240-224)+(203-224)\\&=(9)+(-57)+(65)+(-3)+(30)+(-26)+(-14)+(1)+(16)+(-21)\\&=0\end{aligned}$$

Using the notation x_1 to represent the first data value and x_2 to represent the second data value, we can write this expression more generally as

$$\begin{aligned}&(x_1-224)+(x_2-224)+(x_3-224)+(x_4-224)+(x_5-224)\\&\quad+(x_6-224)+(x_7-224)+(x_8-224)+(x_9-224)+(x_{10}-224)\end{aligned}$$

Taking this one step further, we can use sigma notation to make this expression less cumbersome:

Collect and Analyze the Data

$$\sum_{i=1}^{10}(x_i-224)$$ ■

This shorthand way of writing the long summation will help us when we get to Chapter 4. Now you try one of these.

TRY IT NOW!

The Mail-Order Company ***Using Sigma Notation to Sum Differences***

A mail-order company wants some information on the daily demand for a product that has been heavily advertised. The company looks at the orders for an 8-day period and obtains the following data:

Demand	31	28	29	32	30	31	29	30

Use the sigma notation to write down the expression that means to add up all differences between the data values and the number 30.

2.11.3 Exercises—Learning It!

2.28 Tasty Ice Cream Corporation wishes to be sure that all of the half-gallon ice cream cartons do contain one-half gallon of ice cream. A sample of 30 cartons are inspected. All of the cartons in the sample were filled on Friday. The data (in gallons) are

0.51	0.50	0.49	0.48	0.51	0.50	0.49	0.50	0.50	0.48	0.53	0.50	0.49	0.49	0.51
0.50	0.50	0.51	0.52	0.50	0.48	0.49	0.50	0.47	0.49	0.51	0.50	0.50	0.50	0.49

(a) Write the sigma notation to represent the sum of the 30 data values.

ANS. $\sum_{i=1}^{8}(x_i-30)$

(b) Tasty would like to know how far away from 0.5 (one-half gallon) the data are on the whole. Write the sigma expression to find the sum of the difference between each data value and 0.5.

(c) Evaluate the expression you constructed in part (b).

2.29 The manufacturer of disposable diapers wishes to know how much fluid the diapers can hold before they leak. The diapers are put on 10 children who are playing and fluid is injected every 15 minutes until the diaper leaks. The weight of the diaper (in grams) when it fails is recorded. The data are

503 513 489 499 520 511 525 494 498 501

Write the sigma notation to represent the sum of these data values.

2.30 Before selecting a major, a student decides to study the salaries of individuals working as accountants. A sample of 15 accountants is selected from the list of alumni of the school that the student is attending. The data are

\$25,100	\$33,000	\$27,500	\$29,000	\$35,000	\$26,400	\$29,100	
\$31,050	\$32,100	\$29,100	\$40,000	\$21,000	\$25,000	\$26,500	\$33,000

(a) Write the sigma notation to represent the sum of all the salaries in the sample.

(b) Write the sigma notation to represent the sum of the first five salaries in the sample.

(c) Write the sigma notation to represent the sum of the last five salaries in the sample.

2.12 SELECTING A SAMPLE IN EXCEL

	A	B
1	ID Codes	
2	1	
3	2	
4	3	
5	4	
6	5	
7	6	
8	7	
9	8	
10	9	
11	10	
12	11	
13	12	
14	13	
15	14	
16	15	
17	16	
18	17	
19	18	

FIGURE 2.6 Population of 50 ID codes

There are two ways to use Excel to select a simple random sample from a population. We will look at the method that assumes you have the population values already in a worksheet. Suppose that you have a population with 50 two-digit ID numbers, a portion of which is shown in Figure 2.6.

2.12.1 Selecting a Random Sample from a Population

You can use the **Data Analysis** tools in Excel to select a random sample. From the **Tools** menu, select **Data Analysis**; the dialog box shown in Figure 2.7 opens.

These steps will allow you to select a random sample from the population:

1. Scroll down the **Analysis Tools** list and select **Sampling**. The dialog box shown in Figure 2.8 opens. You must tell Excel three things to obtain the sample: (1) the location of the population, (2) the type of sampling method and the number of samples, and (3) where you want the sample placed.

Note: Make sure the **Tools** *menu contains the* **Data Analysis** *option. If not, you may have to run the* **MS Office Setup** *program to include the* **Analysis ToolPak** *and then execute the* **Tools Add-Ins** *command.*

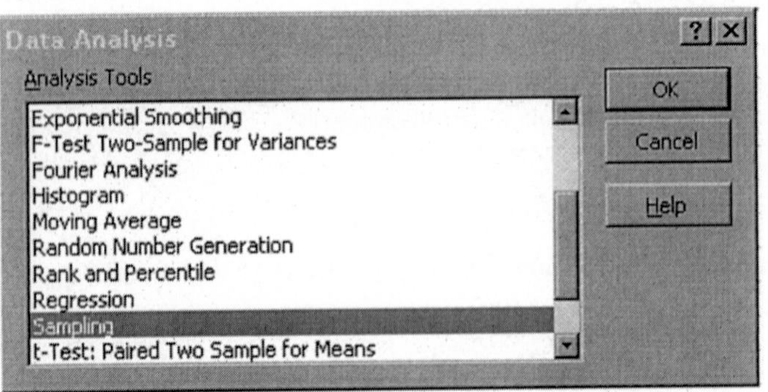

FIGURE 2.7 Data Analysis dialog box

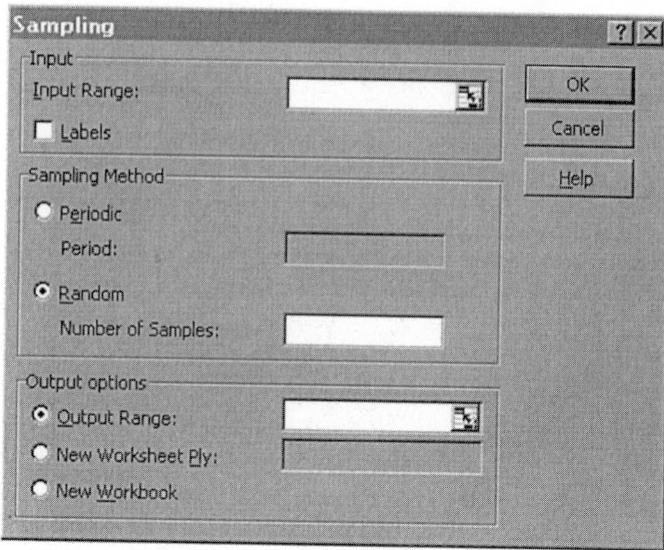

FIGURE 2.8 Sampling dialog box

2. Position the cursor in the box labeled **Input Range** and then highlight the range in the worksheet that contains the data, in this case A1:A51. Since the first row of the population is a title, ID Codes, check the box marked **Labels**.
3. In the section labeled **Sampling Method**, click the radio button for the **Random** sampling method and type "5" in the text box for **Number of Samples:.**
4. In the section labeled **Output Options**, you can specify that the sample be located in a section of the current worksheet, a new worksheet in the same workbook, or a new workbook. In this example, click the radio button for **Output Range:** and position the cursor in the textbox. Then highlight the cell in the worksheet where you want the output to start. The finished dialog box should look like the one in Figure 2.9.
5. Click **OK**; the random sample of five ID codes will appear in the location you specified, in this case cells C1:C5, as shown in Figure 2.10 (page 46). This tells you to sample the items with ID codes 42, 11, 10, 40, and 46.

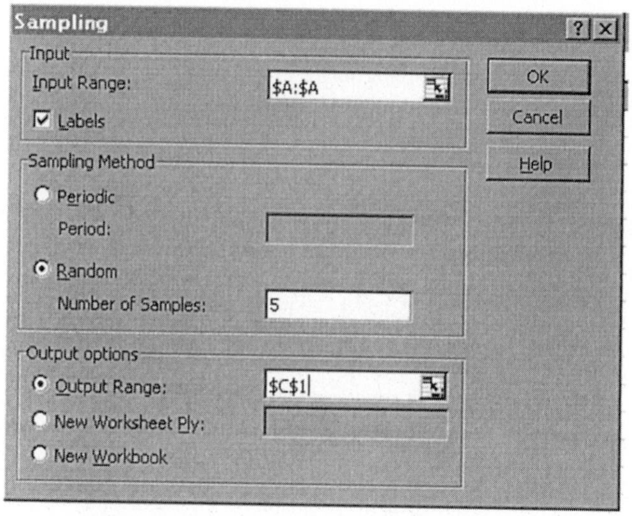

FIGURE 2.9 Completed sampling dialog box

	A	B	C
1	ID Codes		42
2	1		11
3	2		10
4	3		40
5	4		46
6	5		
7	6		
8	7		

FIGURE 2.10 Random sample of five ID codes

CHAPTER 2 SUMMARY

In this chapter you learned the basic language of statistics. You learned that the complete group that you wish to study is called the population. Typically there are several characteristics of each member of the population that you wish to know about. These are called variables. There are two types of variables: quantitative and qualitative. Ideally you would like to study the entire population, or take what is known as a census, but most of the time a census is too expensive and too time-consuming. For these reasons and others you select a sample from a list of the members of the population. In doing so you end up with sampling error, because you are not studying every member of the population. The only way to eliminate sampling error is to study the entire population.

We always want our sample to be a fair representation of the population. This is known as an unbiased sample. There are many ways to select the sample but we will use simple random samples in this book. You learned how to select a simple random sample using a table of random numbers or a software tool such as Excel. You were also introduced to some shorthand notation, known as sigma notation, which is used to write equations throughout the remainder of this book.

Key Terms

Term	Definition	Page reference
Biased sample	A **biased sample** is a sample that does not fairly represent the population.	27
Census	A **census** is a study of the entire population.	16
Continuous data	**Continuous data** are data that can take on any one of an infinite number of possible values over an interval on the number line.	34
Descriptive statistics	**Tools of descriptive statistics** allow you to summarize the data.	36
Discrete data	**Discrete data** are data that can take on only certain values. These values are often integers or whole numbers.	34
Inference	An **inference** is a deduction or a conclusion.	37
Inferential statistics	The **techniques of inferential statistics** allow us to draw inferences or conclusions about the population from the sample.	37
Nominal data	Data that are created by assigning numbers to different categories when the numbers have no real meaning are called **nominal data.**	34
Ordinal data	Data that are created by assigning numbers to categories where the order of assignment has meaning are called **ordinal data**.	34
Parameter	A **parameter** is a number that describes a characteristic of the population.	20

(continued)

Key Terms *(Continued)*

Term	Definition	Page reference
Population	The **population** is everything you wish to study.	14
Population size	The **size of the population** is the number of members of the population. It will be referred to as N.	24
Probability	We use **probability** theory to calculate the likelihood of observing or selecting a particular sample from a population.	38
Qualitative data	**Qualitative data** describe a particular characteristic of a sample item. They are most often nonnumerical in nature.	33
Quantitative data	Data that are inherently numerical in form are called **quantitative** data.	34
Sample	A **sample** is a piece of the population.	15
Sample size	The **size of the sample** will be referred to as n.	26
Sampling error	**Sampling error** is the difference between a characteristic of the entire population and a sample of that population.	16
Sampling frame	A **sampling frame** is a list of all members of the population.	28
Sigma notation	**Sigma notation** is shorthand notation used to write formulas. It is so named because it uses the Greek capital letter sigma, written as Σ.	41
Simple random sample	A **simple random sample** is a sample that has been selected in such a way that all members of the population have an equal chance of being picked. In addition, every sample of size n has the same chance of becoming our sample.	27
Statistic	A **statistic** is a number that describes a characteristic of a sample.	21
Table of random numbers	A **table of random numbers** is a table that consists of a list of numbers randomly generated and listed in the order they were generated.	28
Variable	A **variable** is a characteristic of each member of the population.	14
Variation	The amount of **variation** refers to how different the members of the population are from each other with regard to the variable being studied.	16

CHAPTER 2 EXERCISES

Learning It!

2.31 A golf ball manufacturer wishes to know how far its newly designed super fly ball will go.

(a) What is the population of interest?

(b) Identify which of the reasons for taking a sample (listed on page 15) apply in this case. (There are more than one.)

(c) What type of data would you collect?

2.32 A mall vendor wishes to know how people like his new chocolate chip cookies.

(a) What is the population of interest?

(b) Identify which of the reasons for taking a sample (listed on page 15) apply in this case.

(c) What type of data would you collect?

2.33 A golf ball manufacturer wishes to know how far its newly designed super fly ball will go. A sample of 50 golf balls is hit and the distance is measured.

(a) Why might this be a biased sample?

(b) How could you get a simple random sample?

2.34 A mall vendor wishes to know how people like his new chocolate chip cookies. Fifty shoppers are stopped and given free samples of the new cookies. Do you think this sample is representative of the population of mall shoppers? Explain why or why not.

2.35 A golf ball manufacturer wishes to know how far its newly designed super fly ball will go. A sample of 50 golf balls is hit and the distance is measured in yards. The data are

301	299	307	310	291
300	297	286	297	302
296	290	291	306	302
301	296	287	311	309
309	290	292	287	276
299	302	304	300	309
290	281	308	306	307
317	277	301	298	285
289	288	306	311	293
297	291	285	302	300

(a) Write the sigma notation to represent the sum of the data values.

(b) The golf ball manufacturer wishes to know how different the values are from 300. Write the sigma notation to subtract 300 from each data value and sum the differences.

2.36 You are trying to decide whether your company should advertise during the Olympics. You propose collecting some data before making a decision. You propose the following survey:

- How many (summer) Olympic Games have you lived through?
- Rank the following events in terms of your interest from 1 to 8, with 1 being your favorite.

  Opening Ceremony
  Rowing
  Closing Ceremony
  Cycling
  Gymnastics
  Track and field
  Swimming
  Team sports (soccer, hockey, etc.)

For each question, what kind of data will be collected?

Thinking About It!

2.37 Would your information be accurate if you studied every member of the population? Why or why not?

2.38 In trying to understand the population, what is the only way to eliminate the possibility of reaching the wrong conclusion?

2.39 Is it likely that the value of the statistic calculated from the sample is exactly the same as the value of the population parameter?

2.40 Remembering that the percentage of voters who support the President of the United States is an unknown number, what might you suggest using as a best guess for this percentage?

2.41 This classic story illustrates how the wrong inferences can be reached if the sample is biased. Just before the presidential election between Truman and Dewey the *Chicago Tribune* selected a national sample of voters from the telephone book. These voters overwhelmingly supported Dewey in the presidential race and so the newspaper confidently printed the headline "Dewey Wins" before the results were finally tallied. As we know, the headline was wrong: Truman became the 33rd President in 1945. What mistake did the *Chicago Tribune* make?

2.42 Recall that you want your sample to be a miniversion of the population. Candidates for president think they have found a sample that is a miniversion of the population. Republican and Democratic leaders believe that whoever wins Michigan, a state whose demographic makeup closely mirrors the nation, will be the next president. Examine the following evidence.

1998 data	Michigan	USA
Per-capita income	$14,154	$18,685
Unemployment	3.9%	4.5%
Median age	34.6	34.6
Population over 65	12.5%	12.8%
Minority populations		
Blacks	13.9%	12.1%
Hispanics	2%	9%
Asians	1.1%	2.9%
American Indians	0.6%	0.8%
Portion of workforce in unions	21.6%	13.9%[1]
Median house value	$60,600	$84,209
Married-couple households	55.1%	55.9%

Sources: *The Almanac of American Politics; USA Today* research 1–1999 data

(a) What do you think about this claim?

(b) What other information would you like to know to evaluate this claim?

Doing It!

2.43 The data in this problem are the weekly average closing prices (in $) of Microsoft on the New York Stock Exchange (NYSE) from January 1995 to May 2000.

(a) Consider all the weeks of data to be the population and find the population average.

(b) Select 50 simple random samples of 30 weeks and find the sample average for each of the samples. Which sample average is closest to the population average? Which sample average is the farthest from the population average?

Data file: *MSFT. XXX*

(c) Select 50 random samples of 40 weeks and find the sample average for each of the samples. Which sample average is closest to the population average? Which sample average is the farthest from the population average?

(d) Select 50 random samples of 50 weeks and find the sample average for each of the samples. Which sample average is closest to the population average? Which sample average is the farthest from the population average?

(e) Summarize your findings in a memo. Be sure to explain what happens to the accuracy of the sample average as you increased your sample size from 30 to 40 to 50.

CHAPTER 3

GRAPHICAL DISPLAYS OF DATA

ALUACHA BALACLAVA COLLEGE

Business Dilemma...

Aluacha Balaclava College (ABC) is having trouble with faculty compensation. The faculty claim that they have not received pay raises for several years and that new faculty are being hired at much higher salaries than existing faculty members are getting. The former Provost has just resigned under pressure and the President has hired a new Provost to design a new compensation package that is fair and reasonable. The new Provost knows that, prior to designing anything new, she must first understand the current system and some of the history of the system. She decides that her first step must be to collect some data on faculty salaries.

After some thought, she decides that faculty salaries depend on other factors, so she has the Management Information Systems (MIS) department gather data for each faculty member on current rank (Professor, Associate Professor, Assistant Professor, and Instructor), number of years of service to the college, and current salary. The data, which they provide to her in the form of a list, are not very enlightening. A portion of the data is given here:

Rank	Years of service	1996–97 salary
ASST	22	53316
PROF	11	64375
ASSO	7	63501
ASSO	6	59426

Rank	Years of service	1996–97 salary
ASSO	20	49058
PROF	4	94969
ASST	21	54762
ASSO	9	55516

To gain any information from the data she will need to summarize them, probably with some graphical displays.

3.1 CHAPTER OBJECTIVES

In Chapter 2 you learned about the different types of data and about how data can and should be collected. You learned that people collect data to provide information about something they are interested in understanding, such as why brakes on rollerblades fail or why customers complain about tissues. Usually there is some problem that needs to be solved, like a new brake design, when this understanding is gained.

In this chapter we look at ways to display different types of data. The chapter covers the following material:

- Graphical methods for qualitative data: frequency tables, bar charts, and pie charts
- Graphical methods for quantitative data: frequency tables and histograms
- Other graphical methods: dotplots and Pareto diagrams

3.2 ORGANIZING DATA

If one objective of statistics is to obtain information about a set of data, then we need to organize the data in some way. When data are collected the initial result is usually a *list* of the observations for each variable. This is referred to as the *raw data.* Raw data, such as those given to the Provost at the college, provide almost no information. Statistics provides some tools or techniques for turning raw data into information.

3.2.1 The Frequency Distribution

One way to organize data is to consolidate them by determining how many times each value in the data occurs and making a table that summarizes this information. This is called a **frequency table** or **frequency distribution.** A frequency distribution divides the data into categories or classes. These terms are used interchangeably, although categories usually refer to qualitative data and classes to quantitative data.

> A ***frequency table*** or ***frequency distribution*** is a table containing each category, value, or class of values that a variable might have and the number of times that each one occurs in the data. The frequency of the ith class is denoted f_i.

Frequency Tables for Qualitative Data

Category	Frequency
Category 1	f_1
Category 2	f_2
Total	n

FIGURE 3.1
A frequency table

Creating a frequency table for qualitative data is not difficult. A basic frequency table has two columns. In the first column of the table each row lists one of the values for the variable of interest. The second column lists the corresponding number of times that the value occurred in the set of data. Later on we will add some additional columns to the table, but right now we will work with only two. Figure 3.1 shows the setup for a typical frequency table:

EXAMPLE 3.1 ABC Faculty Salaries

Creating a Frequency Table

The Provost at ABC knows that salary will differ for each faculty member, depending on several factors. One such factor is the current rank of the faculty member. She decides to look at the faculty by rank to see how the faculty is made up as a whole. She puts the data in the form of a frequency table as shown here:

Collect and Analyze the Data

Rank	Frequency
Professor	55
Associate Professor	67
Assistant Professor	77
Instructor	8
Total	**207**

From the frequency table she sees that, although Assistant Professor has the highest frequency, the three highest ranks are not all that different. There are obviously not many faculty at the rank of Instructor. ■

The order for the categories in the frequency table is not important. If there is a logical order, or if you know what the classifications will be before you fill out the table, then you might use a particular order. If you are creating the categories as you make the table, you might list them in the order in which they first appear in the raw data.

EXAMPLE 3.2 Student Distribution

Creating a Frequency Table

Understand the Problem

The faculty in the School of Business at a university are concerned that many students are delaying taking the Introductory Statistics course required by all majors. The course can be taken as early as the freshman year, but traditionally is taken by sophomores. To determine whether the concerns are justified, a section of Introductory Statistics is selected at random and each student is classified as a freshman (F), sophomore (S), junior (J) or senior (Sr) according to the number of credits completed to date. The raw data for the 28 students are shown here:

Sr	Sr	S	S	S	Sr	Sr
S	S	S	S	S	F	F
Sr	S	Sr	Sr	Sr	F	F
J	S	J	S	S	Sr	Sr

Collect and Analyze the Data

To use the data to answer their questions, the faculty organize the data in the form of a frequency table:

Classification	Frequency
Freshman	4
Sophomore	12
Junior	2
Senior	10
Total	**28**

From the table they see that very few students taking the course are freshmen or juniors, and that the rest are about evenly divided between sophomores and seniors. ■

Draw Conclusions

Although the information obtained from the frequency table is certainly better than that from the raw data, it is still not quite as informative as it might be. The values in the frequency table are influenced by the sample size. For large samples the individual frequencies will be much larger numbers than for small samples. This makes comparisons of different samples difficult. To solve this problem we must find a way to express the frequency so that the sample size does not matter. One way to do this is to use the **relative frequency.**

The ***relative frequency*** of a classification is the number of times an observation falls into that classification represented as a portion of the total number of observations. It can be expressed as a *fraction, decimal,* or *percentage.*

Thus, to find the relative frequency for the *i*th classification, rf_i, we use

$$\text{rf}_i = \frac{\text{Frequency of } i\text{th classification}}{\text{Sample size}} = \frac{f_i}{n}$$

EXAMPLE 3.3 ABC Faculty Salaries

Finding Relative Frequency

To get a better idea of how the faculty were distributed among the ranks, the provost decided to calculate the relative frequency for each rank. The calculations and results are shown in the table:

Analyze the Data

Rank	Frequency	Relative frequency	Relative frequency (%)
Professor	55	55/207	26.6
Associate Professor	67	67/207	32.4
Assistant Professor	77	77/207	37.2
Instructor	8	8/207	3.9
Total	**207**	**207/207**	**100.0**

Note: *If you add the percentages for relative frequency, you will not get 100% here, because the percentages have been rounded off.*

Draw Conclusions

Note: Use the actual variable name for the classification to provide the most information.

It appears from the relative frequencies that the three largest classes are not quite as different as she had thought, but no single class constitutes a majority. ■

It does not matter whether you use fraction, decimal, or percentage to calculate the relative frequency. Percentage is easiest for most people to understand. When using percentage you need to be careful about rounding. When you report relative frequency to the nearest percent or even one decimal place, the values may not sum to exactly 100%. This is not a problem.

EXAMPLE 3.4 **Student Distribution**

Calculating the Relative Frequency

Analyze the Data

To get a better picture of the students in the Introductory Statistics course, the person studying the data decides to look at the relative frequency for each classification.

If these calculations are not easy for you, then you should get out a calculator and practice them until they are!

Freshmen:

$$rf_1 = \tfrac{4}{28} = 0.143 \qquad \text{or, as a percentage} = 0.143 \times 100 = 14.3\%$$

Sophomores:

$$rf_2 = \tfrac{12}{28} = 0.429 \qquad \text{or, as a percentage} = 0.429 \times 100 = 42.9\%$$

Juniors:

$$rf_3 = \tfrac{2}{28} = 0.071 \qquad \text{or, as a percentage} = 0.071 \times 100 = 7.1\%$$

Seniors:

$$rf_4 = \tfrac{10}{28} = 0.357 \qquad \text{or, as a percentage} = 0.357 \times 100 = 35.7\%$$

Adding a column to the frequency table gives

Year in school	Frequency	Relative frequency (%)
Freshman	4	14.3
Sophomore	12	42.9
Junior	2	7.1
Senior	10	35.7
Total	**28**	**100.0**

From this table the School of Business can see that 35.7% of the students in the class are seniors, and 35.7% + 7.1% = 42.8% of the students delayed the course beyond the sophomore year. ■

TRY IT NOW!

Student Grades ***Creating a Frequency Table***

A professor in an Introductory Statistics course knows that, although students dread taking the course, they also have unusually high expectations for their performance. She surveys (anonymously, of course) her students and asks them what grade they expect to get in the course. The raw data are listed here:

A C B A A B B
B A B A A C B
B A F C B D C
B B D B A B A

Make a frequency table for the data. Include both frequencies and relative frequencies.

Frequency Tables for Integer Data

Remember from Chapter 2 that one type of quantitative data you might collect results from *counting* the number of times that something occurs in a set of data or from *ranking* or *rating* objects. This type of data takes on integer values.

Creating a frequency table for this type of data is exactly the same as creating one for qualitative data. Each value of the variable represents one category or classification in the table. The only real difference is that since the numbers for these data have some meaning, the categories must be in numerical order. For qualitative data the order in which you list the categories is not rigid.

EXAMPLE 3.5 Student Attitudes

Frequency Table for Integer Data

Understand the Problem

The statistics professor who has been trying to learn about her class is also interested in her students' attitudes toward the study of statistics. She is aware that most of the people are enrolled in the course because it is required, and she wonders if this is reflected in their attitude toward the subject. As part of the last anonymous survey on grades, she asks the class to rank "the importance of statistics in my life" on a scale of 0 to 10, where 0 = of no importance whatsoever and 10 = the most important thing I will ever study. The raw data from the study are

0 10 8 0 0 8 6
5 1 6 1 4 10 8
7 0 10 9 4 10 10
7 6 10 9 1 5 1

ANS. A, 9, 32.1%; B, 12, 42.9%; C, 4, 14.3%; D, 2, 7.1%; F, 1, 3.6%

Collect and Analyze the Data

Since this is not very informative she decides to create a frequency table for the data:

Rating	Frequency	Relative frequency (%)
0	4	4/28 = 14.3
1	4	4/28 = 14.3
2	0	0/28 = 0.0
3	0	0/28 = 0.0
4	2	2/28 = 7.1
5	2	2/28 = 7.1
6	3	3/28 = 10.7
7	2	2/28 = 7.1
8	3	3/28 = 10.7
9	2	2/28 = 7.1
10	6	6/28 = 21.4
Total	**28**	**28/28 = 100**

Draw Conclusions

From the frequency table she sees that most people seemed to have attitudes on either end of the scale, with fewer in the center, neutral, zone. ■

Most data that are truly integer in nature occur from counting, rankings, or ratings. Sometimes data that are really measurements are recorded as integers. In this case it is important to think about where the data came from and the number of possible values before you pick the classes for your frequency table. Since the data are numbers, you cannot leave out a class (value) if there are no observations in it. If the number of possible values is much larger than 15 or 20 you probably do not want to treat the data as integer data. Instead you should use the methods for continuous data shown later in this section.

EXAMPLE 3.6 ABC Faculty Salaries

Looking at Integer Data

The Provost looking at faculty salaries also knows that salary depends on the length of time that the faculty member has been at the College. She decides to summarize these data using a frequency table, and notices that the data are integer data.

She also notices that the shortest length of time involved is 0 years and the longest is 41 years. She realizes that time is a measurement and that it is integer data because it was recorded to the nearest whole year. She sees that treating these data as integer data will not be appropriate. ■

Since quantitative data are *ordered* by nature, it is also interesting to ask questions like, What percentage of the class rates statistics on the bottom half of the scale? Neutral? The top half? You can answer the questions by summing the relative frequencies, or by using the **cumulative relative frequency.**

The ***cumulative relative frequency*** of a class is the sum of the relative frequencies of all classes at or below that class represented as a portion of the total number of observations. It can be expressed as a fraction, decimal, or percentage.

EXAMPLE 3.7 Student Attitudes

Cumulative Frequencies

For the data from the Student Attitudes example, the professor calculated the cumulative frequency for each class in the table:

Analyze the Data

Rating	Frequency	Cumulative relative frequency (%)
0	4	4/28 = 14.3
1	4	8/28 = 28.6
2	0	8/28 = 28.6
3	0	8/28 = 28.6
4	2	10/28 = 35.7
5	2	12/28 = 42.9
6	3	15/28 = 53.6
7	2	17/28 = 60.7
8	3	20/28 = 71.4
9	2	22/28 = 78.6
10	6	28/28 = 100.00
Total	**28**	

Draw Conclusions

From the table, the professor can easily see that 35.7% of the students had negative attitudes toward statistics. To find the percentage of students that have neutral attitudes, she must do some arithmetic first. From the table she can see that 42.9% of the students were in the classes from 5 down. Since she knows that 35.7% were in the classes from 4 down, it seems that 42.9% − 35.7% = 7.2% have a neutral attitude toward statistics. This agrees with the relative frequency from Example 3.5.

To find the percentage with positive attitudes, again a little arithmetic is needed. Since she knows that 42.9% are in the classes from 5 down, the remainder must be in the classes from 6 up. She finds that 100% − 42.9% = 57.1% have positive attitudes toward statistics. Teaching this class may be an uphill battle! ■

At this point you must be thinking that it would be simpler to use the relative frequencies and just add up the ones you are interested in, like you did for the qualitative data. Sometimes this is true, but when there are a lot of classes the procedure becomes very tedious. There are two other reasons for learning how to deal with cumulative relative frequencies: (1) When you are using statistics or spreadsheet software to analyze data, the cumulative frequencies are part of the output, which makes it a much easier job; and (2) certain statistical tables such as probability tables are cumulative and there is just no other way to use them.

TRY IT NOW!

New Product Survey *Cumulative Relative Frequencies*

A marketing research firm conducted a survey of consumers who invariably use a particular brand of bath soap. The consumers were given a competitor's version of the same product with nonallergenic enhancements and asked whether they would consider buying the new product. Their answers were given on a scale of 1 to 5 where 1 = would not ever buy this product and 5 = will buy this product immediately. The raw data from the survey are given at the top of page 58.

(continued)

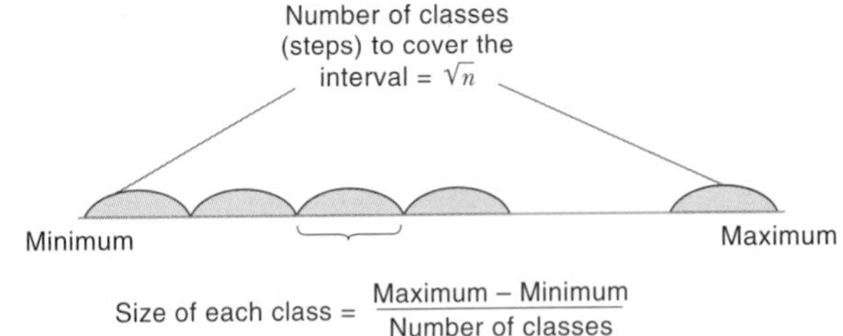

FIGURE 3.2 Number of classes and class interval for continuous data

EXAMPLE 3.9 On-Time Rates

Creating Class Intervals for Continuous Data

Understand the Problem

A major commuter railroad has been looking at the on-time rates for service to a particular city. The railroad collects data for 30 randomly selected days and finds the percent of trains on time each day:

60.4	92.9	67.0	91.6	93.7
71.9	66.4	48.0	66.6	94.6
83.2	68.0	74.3	78.6	40.9
76.4	62.9	67.1	68.5	29.5
69.2	45.8	49.1	34.7	65.1
72.1	40.6	35.0	60.8	54.3

Collect and Analyze the Data

To make some sense of the data the railroad decides to create a frequency table. The first task is to decide how many classes the table should have. The railroad first calculates

$$\sqrt{30} = 5.48$$

and so decides to use five classes.

Next the railroad must decide how large each class should be. The data show that the maximum value is 94.6% and the minimum value is 29.5%. The total distance that needs to be covered by the classes is

$$94.6 - 29.5 = 65.1$$

and the size of each class must be

$$\frac{65.1}{5} = 13.02$$

■

To determine the starting and ending points (boundaries) for each class we must remember that the classes cannot overlap and that there cannot be any gaps in the interval. There are several ways to accomplish this, but we will define a class as containing all observations *more than* the lower boundary, *up to and including* the upper boundary:

$$\text{Lower boundary} < x \leq \text{Upper boundary}$$

where x represents the value of the variable being studied.

Different texts will use different methods for defining intervals, but they will all yield similar results. The interval definition used here is consistent with the major spreadsheet software such as Excel and Lotus 1-2-3. Most statistical packages, such as Minitab and Data Desk, define the classes to *include* the lower boundary and to go up to but *not include* the upper boundary.

$$\text{Lower boundary} \le x < \text{Upper boundary}$$

As we will see later in the chapter, this causes some differences in the final output, but it is not usually a problem.

Remember that the intervals have been defined so that they contain the values *above* the lower boundary. To make sure that the classes you define include the minimum, you need to start just *below* the minimum value in the data set and add the class width. The lower boundary for the next class is the upper boundary for the previous class.

EXAMPLE 3.10 ABC Faculty Salaries

Creating the Class Intervals

The Provost decides that for the data on the number of years of service she will use a computer software package. She will let the software create the frequency distribution for her and see what it comes up with:

Note: When the data contain values of 0, the Excel convention forces the first class to start with negative numbers. This is awkward, so the other method might be better.

Class	Frequency
$-2.928571 < x \le 0.000000$	15
$0.000000 < x \le 2.928571$	19
$2.928571 < x \le 5.857143$	19
$5.857143 < x \le 8.785714$	34
$8.785714 < x \le 11.714286$	16
$11.714286 < x \le 14.642857$	14
$14.642857 < x \le 17.571429$	13
$17.571429 < x \le 20.500000$	17
$20.500000 < x \le 23.428571$	33
$23.428571 < x \le 26.357143$	20
$26.357143 < x \le 29.285714$	4
$29.285714 < x \le 32.214286$	2
$32.214286 < x \le 35.142857$	0
$35.142857 < x \le 38.071429$	0
$38.071429 < x \le 41.000000$	1

Analyze the Data

The results are not quite what she expected, but she sees that there are 15 classes and that the width of each class is 2.92857 years. ■

In Example 3.10 we saw that the frequency table generated by a software package used intervals that had six decimal places! Although this is not bad, it might be more appealing to use intervals that look more like the original data, with the same precision.

EXAMPLE 3.11 On-Time Rates

Creating Class Intervals for Continuous Data

In Example 3.9 we found that the width of each class should be 13.02. The data are measured only to the nearest tenth, so we will use increments of 13.0. Since the smallest value in the data is 29.5, we will start just below that value, at 29.4, and add 13.0. That is, the first class interval contains all values, x, of the variable such that

$$29.4 < x \le 42.4$$

The next class is formed by starting at 42.4 and again adding 13.0:

Analyze the Data

$$42.4 < x \le 55.4$$

It is okay to wind up with one more class than you planned on. Remember the rules are only guidelines.

The remainder of the classes are

$$55.4 < x \leq 68.4$$
$$68.4 < x \leq 81.4$$
$$81.4 < x \leq 94.4$$
$$94.4 < x \leq 107.4$$

We need this last class for the maximum observation, 94.6%.

To create the frequency table for the data we count the number of data values that fall in each interval and complete the table.

On-time rates	Frequency	Relative frequency (%)	Cumulative relative frequency (%)
$29.4 < x \leq 42.4$	5	16.7	16.7
$42.4 < x \leq 55.4$	4	13.3	30.0
$55.4 < x \leq 68.4$	9	30.0	60.0
$68.4 < x \leq 81.4$	7	23.3	83.3
$81.4 < x \leq 94.4$	4	13.3	96.6
$94.4 < x \leq 107.4$	1	3.3	100.0

Draw Conclusions

From the frequency table the railroad management can obtain information such as, "On 83.3% of the days the on-time rate was no greater than 81.4%" or "The on-time rate was greater than 94.4% on only 3.3% of the days." This allows the railroad to judge its performance and take appropriate action. ■

You may be wondering why you need to know how to do this, when you can use a computer to generate the frequency distribution for you. There are two reasons that this knowledge is necessary. First, some software packages require input from the user about how the frequency table is set up. Knowledge of some basic rules will help to answer those questions. The second reason is that even if there is a default setup for the frequency table, the result may not be acceptable. Remember the frequency table for the faculty salaries!

What are we looking for in a frequency table? How can we tell whether the one we have created is good? We already know that we need the classes to be the same size and that they must cover all of the data values. What else is important?

Many times you may want the intervals to be defined in nice, round numbers that are integer data or that end in 0.5 or some other convention. Certainly, it is more appealing to look at classes with numbers like 25, 35, 45, . . . , but software packages follow rules very similar to the ones outlined here and the results are very often not what you want.

Figure 3.3 shows the frequency table produced by Microsoft Excel for the On-Time Rate data.

It is possible to vary both the starting point of the first class and the interval width, within reason. Remember that the decisions for the number of classes and interval widths are guidelines based on the sample size and the range of the data. As long as your final results do not vary too much from the guidelines you can adjust them.

Bin	Frequency	Cumulative %
29.50	1	3.33
42.52	4	16.67
55.54	4	30.00
68.56	10	63.33
81.58	6	83.33
More	5	100.00

In Excel, the number in the Bin column is the highest number that is included in the interval, so the first bin is all numbers less than and including 29.50, and the last bin is all numbers greater than 81.58.

FIGURE 3.3 Microsoft Excel frequency table

EXAMPLE 3.12 ABC Faculty Salaries

Adjusting Class Boundaries

After looking at the results given by the statistical software, the Provost feels that the class intervals do not use numbers with which people will identify. There is no reason to use so many decimal places when the data are measured to the nearest year. Perhaps she should adjust the class intervals a little bit so that they use nice, round numbers. After looking at the data she decides to start just below 0, at -1 rather than at the -3 suggested by the software. She is less sure about the width of each class. Using a class width of 3 years would not be too different from the 2.93 calculated value, but she feels that a width of 5 years might be more appealing. She decides to try both ways and obtains the following frequency tables.

Analyze the Data

Class	Frequency
$-1 < x \leq 2$	34
$2 < x \leq 5$	19
$5 < x \leq 8$	34
$8 < x \leq 11$	16
$11 < x \leq 14$	14
$14 < x \leq 17$	13
$17 < x \leq 20$	17
$20 < x \leq 23$	33
$23 < x \leq 26$	20
$26 < x \leq 29$	4
$29 < x \leq 32$	2
$32 < x \leq 35$	0
$35 < x \leq 38$	0
$38 < x \leq 41$	1

Class	Frequency
$-5 < x \leq 0$	15
$0 < x \leq 5$	38
$5 < x \leq 10$	42
$10 < x \leq 15$	23
$15 < x \leq 20$	29
$20 < x \leq 25$	51
$25 < x \leq 30$	8
$30 < x \leq 35$	0
$35 < x \leq 40$	0
$40 < x \leq 45$	1

The first set of changes does not alter the frequency distribution very much. There are 14 classes instead of 15, and the end classes are fairly empty. The second set of changes reduces the number of classes to 10 and there are fewer empty or nearly empty classes. She is not sure whether this matters, but she will keep it in mind. ■

EXAMPLE 3.13 On-Time Rates

Adjusting Class Boundaries

After examining the frequency table for the on-time rates problem, the railroad managers decide that they would prefer to see the data classified with rounder, more understandable numbers. They look at the data and decide to start the first interval at just above 25.0% and use a width of 10%. The new frequency table would look like this:

Analyze the Data

On-time rates	Frequency	Relative frequency (%)	Cumulative relative frequency (%)
$25.0 < x \leq 35.0$	3	10.0	10.0
$35.0 < x \leq 45.0$	2	6.7	16.7
$45.0 < x \leq 55.0$	4	13.3	30.0
$55.0 < x \leq 65.0$	3	10.0	40.0
$65.0 < x \leq 75.0$	11	36.7	76.7
$75.0 < x \leq 85.0$	3	10.0	86.7
$85.0 < x \leq 95.0$	4	13.3	100.0
Total	**30**	**100.0**	**100.0**

The changes result in seven classes rather than six because the first interval starts at a lower number and the interval widths are not as large.

Another possibility for class intervals would have been to start at just above 25% and use an interval width of 15%. The frequency table for that arrangement would be

On-time rates	Frequency	Relative frequency (%)	Cumulative relative frequency (%)
$25.0 < x \leq 40.0$	3	10.0	10.0
$40.0 < x \leq 55.0$	6	20.0	30.0
$55.0 < x \leq 70.0$	11	36.7	66.7
$70.0 < x \leq 85.0$	6	20.0	86.7
$85.0 < x \leq 100.0$	4	13.3	100.0
Total	**30**	**100.0**	**100.0**

This time the frequency table has only five classes because we used an interval width of more than 13.0%. ■

Assignment Times *Creating a Frequency Table for Continuous Data*

The instructor for an introductory statistics class wonders about the complaints that she is hearing about the time it takes to complete a computer assignment. The assignments are designed to be done in about 25 minutes. She asks the members of the class to time how long it takes to do the next assignment and to hand the data in with the assignment. The data, in minutes, are

22.8	27.0	27.9	30.4	33.4
24.8	27.2	27.9	31.1	33.9
24.8	27.4	28.2	31.4	35.3
26.0	27.4	29.4	32.4	35.7
26.0	27.4	29.6	33.1	36.3
26.1	27.6	29.8	33.2	40.4

Approximately how many classes should the frequency table have?

What should the class width be?

Create a frequency table for the data.

ANS. 6; 3.52; $22.70 < x \leq 26.22$; $26.22 < x \leq 29.74$; $29.74 < x \leq 33.26$; $33.26 < x \leq 36.78$; $36.78 < x \leq 40.30$; $40.30 < x \leq 43.82$; FREQUENCIES 6, 11, 7, 5, 0, 1

3.2.2 Exercises—Learning It!

3.1 The administrators of a local university are trying to determine whether the amount of parking that they have is adequate. They take a random sample of 25 entering freshmen and ask them what mode of transportation they will use to travel to classes. The responses are

Car	Car	Car	Car	Car
Car	Walk	Car	Car	Car
Public	Car	Walk	Car	Car
Other	Car	Bicycle	Car	Car
Public	Car	Car	Public	Walk

(a) Create a frequency table for the responses.

(b) What mode of transportation was the most popular? the least popular?

(c) Does any class in the frequency table constitute a majority? If so, which one?

3.2 To assess the dominance of Microsoft in the operating systems market, a local computer society randomly sampled 30 of its members and asked which operating system they were currently running on their PCs. The data follow:

Mac OS	W 98	W 98	W NT	W 2000
W NT	W NT	W 95	W NT	W 2000
W 2000	W 2000	W NT	W 98	W NT
W NT	W 98	W 98	W NT	W 98
W 2000	W 98	W 98	W 2000	W 98
W 98	W NT	W NT	W 2000	W 2000

(a) Create a frequency table for the data on operating system.

(b) What percentage of the people surveyed used W 98?

(c) What percentage of the people surveyed did not use a Microsoft product?

(d) Was any operating system used by a majority of those surveyed?

3.3 A manufacturing company has been receiving complaints from its warehouse operators about the condition of the product cases that are being stored. The complaints indicate that most of the cases are defective in some way and that it is creating logistics problems for the warehouse employees. The managers of the company decide to take a random sample of the cases produced and examine them for various defects. The data they obtain are

Dented	No defect	No defect	Dented	No defect
No defect	Torn	Crushed	No defect	No defect
Unsealed	No defect	No defect	No defect	No defect
No defect	No defect	No defect	No defect	No defect
No defect	No defect	No defect	Dented	No defect
No defect	Unsealed	No defect	No defect	No defect

(a) Create a frequency table for the defect data.

(b) Based on the data, does the warehouse claim appear justified? Why or why not?

3.4 A survey in a computer newsletter for employees at a large corporation asked readers how many times per week they logged onto the Internet using any one of the available services at the company. The responses from 50 employees are shown here:

1	7	3	4	1
0	7	0	1	8
3	3	4	2	4
3	0	3	3	5
3	3	7	4	1
7	5	3	3	4
4	3	3	3	7

(continued)

6	8	0	7	2
7	0	3	9	3
4	4	4	4	3

(a) Create a frequency table for the data.

(b) What percentage of those surveyed logged onto the Internet exactly five times per week? More than five times per week?

(c) What percentage of those surveyed logged on four, five, or six times per week? Less than twice per week?

3.5 As part of a cost/benefit analysis on service contracts for photocopiers, a large company surveyed all departments with copy machines and asked how many times per week their machines needed to be serviced. The data obtained are

3	2	3	0	3
0	2	2	2	1
3	2	2	1	0
2	3	2	1	2
3	4	2	7	1
2	2	1	3	1
0	3	1	1	2

(a) Create a frequency table for the data. Include relative frequency and cumulative relative frequency.

(b) What percentage of the copiers need repairs more than twice per week?

(c) What percentage need repairs at least four times per week?

(d) Do a majority of the copiers require repairs more than three times per week?

3.6 To determine whether it was reasonable to request that students use computers to write reports, a school surveyed a typical fifth-grade class and asked the students how many computers they had at home. The responses are

1	0	1	1	2
2	2	0	1	0
0	0	3	3	0
0	1	1	2	1
1	2	1	1	0

(a) Create a frequency table for the data. Include relative frequency and cumulative relative frequency.

(b) What percentage of the students did not have access to computers at home?

(c) What percentage of the students had easy access (two or more) to computers at home?

(d) Based on the data collected, do you think that asking students to use computers for reports is reasonable? Why or why not?

3.7 As part of a study to decide whether to renew the contract of a food service company at a local university, the administration surveyed a group of students who used the service on a regular basis. The students were asked to rate the food quality on a scale of 1 to 5, where 1 was extremely bad and 5 was extremely good. The results are

2	4	3	4	1
3	2	3	1	3
1	1	4	1	4
1	3	3	4	1
4	2	3	4	3
3	3	3	1	3

(a) Create a frequency table for the data.

(b) What rating had the highest frequency? The lowest?

(c) Based on the data, do you think that the students like the food provided by the company? Why or why not?

3.8 A local computer group surveyed high school students to find out how many hours per week the students spent logged on to various on-line services. The data are

0.2	4.1	11.9	15.5	17.8
0.8	4.2	13.0	15.5	17.9
1.0	6.9	13.4	15.5	18.4
1.4	8.0	13.5	15.5	18.7
2.5	8.2	14.9	16.7	19.5
2.9	8.6	15.1	16.8	19.7

Create a frequency table for the amount of time spent on-line by students. Include relative frequency and cumulative relative frequency.

3.9 A large corporation that relies on a secretarial service group to do much of its work is trying to decide whether it needs more workers in the group. One of the criteria that will be used to make the decision is the turnaround time experienced by users of the service. The corporation surveys a number of employees who use the service on a regular basis and asks them for the turnaround time (in hours) for the last job they submitted. The following data are obtained:

14	19	21	25	26	29
15	19	22	25	26	29
16	20	22	25	26	30
16	20	23	25	26	31
18	20	23	25	27	31
18	20	23	25	28	35
18	21	24	26	29	40

(a) Create a frequency table for the data. Include relative frequency and cumulative relative frequency.

(b) What percentage of the people who use the service wait more than one day (24 hours) for their jobs to be done?

(c) Modify the class intervals for your frequency table to allow you to easily answer the questions, What percentage of those surveyed wait 20 hours or less? More than 30 hours?

(d) *Approximately* what percentage waited between 20 and 30 hours?

3.10 The Bureau of Weights and Measures conducts random checks of products in various supermarkets. The Bureau decides to check half-gallon containers of a particular brand of orange juice. The contents of each of the containers tested (measured to the nearest 0.1 oz) are

64.8	65.2	65.6	65.7	65.9
64.8	65.3	65.7	65.7	66.0
64.9	65.3	65.7	65.7	66.1
65.1	65.4	65.7	65.8	66.1
65.2	65.4	65.7	65.8	66.3

(a) Create a frequency table for the data.

(b) If the containers are subject to bursting when filled with more than 66 oz of fluid, what percentage of the containers are in danger of bursting?

3.11 The local refuse company in charge of recycling in a town is receiving complaints from the people at the end of the pickup route. The complaints indicate that their recycling is not being picked up at the end of the route because the drivers say that the trucks are too full. In an effort to determine how much capacity is really needed for the route, the refuse company randomly samples the newspaper recycling that is put out and measures each pile to the nearest 0.1 inch. The data obtained are

8.3	9.1	9.9	10.2	11.0
8.5	9.7	9.9	10.4	11.2
8.8	9.8	10.1	11.0	11.4

(continued)

12.0	12.3	13.1	13.6	14.3
12.0	12.3	13.3	13.6	14.4
12.2	12.5	13.3	13.8	14.4
12.2	12.7	13.4	13.9	14.4
12.3	12.8	13.4	14.1	14.8
12.3	12.9	13.4	14.3	15.2

(a) Create a frequency table for the data. Include relative frequency and cumulative relative frequency.

(b) Modify the frequency table you created in part (a) so that you can easily use it to answer the questions in parts (c)–(e).

(c) What percentage of the newspaper recycling piles are more than 1 foot in height?

(d) What percentage of the recycling piles are 10 inches or less?

(e) *Approximately* what percentage of the recycling piles are between 10 and 14 inches?

3.3 GRAPHICAL DISPLAYS OF DATA

Although the frequency distribution does a good job of organizing and summarizing a set of data, it does not have much of a visual impact. To create a more immediate impression from a data set we need to create a pictorial (graphical) representation of the information in the frequency distribution. Most of the work is already done in creating the frequency table. The displays have the same basic structures with some changes to accommodate the type of data being displayed.

3.3.1 Graphical Displays for Qualitative Data

There are two methods that you can use to display qualitative data, a **bar chart** and a **pie chart.**

A ***bar chart*** represents the frequency or relative frequency from the table in the form of a rectangle or bar.

Creating a Bar Chart for Qualitative Data

In a bar chart, one of the axes is used to represent the categories from the frequency table and the other axis is used to represent the frequency or relative frequency for the categories. For qualitative data, assignment of the axes is a matter of preference. We will use the x axis for the categories and the y axis for the frequencies and relative frequencies to be consistent with the graphs for the other types of data.

Steps for creating a bar chart

Step 1: Draw a pair of axes, x and y.

Step 2: At evenly spaced intervals on the x axis put tick marks and label them with the categories from the frequency table.

Step 3: Scale the y axis so that the category with the highest frequency or relative frequency can be graphed. Choose the scale so that you can distinguish different frequencies or relative frequencies from each other.

Step 4: At each category on the x axis, draw a rectangle (bar) whose height is equal to the frequency or relative frequency for the category. The bases of the rectangles must be the same width and the bars should not touch each other.

Step 5: Label the axes and give the graph an appropriate title.

Often there is no predetermined order for the categories for qualitative data, but you might want to think about the order in which you place them, since the order may affect the impact of the graph. Some common choices are by descending or ascending frequency or alphabetical order.

EXAMPLE 3.14 ABC Faculty Salaries

Creating a Bar Chart

The Provost at the college decides to create a bar chart for the data she has collected on faculty rank. The frequency table for the data was

Rank	Frequency	Relative frequency (%)
Professor	55	26.6
Associate Professor	67	32.4
Assistant Professor	77	37.2
Instructor	8	3.9
Total	**207**	**100.0**

She decides to use increasing rank order for the bars on the chart and the resulting bar chart looks like this:

Analyze the Data

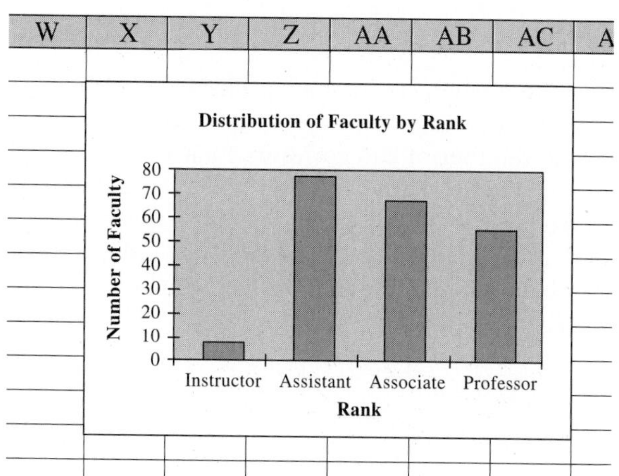

■

You may wonder why you would want to know how to create bar charts by hand when it is very likely that you will use a computer to make the charts. Most computer software requires the user to make decisions about how the chart should be set up. Knowing the basics of how the charts are made helps you to make these decisions.

EXAMPLE 3.15 Student Distribution

Creating a Bar Chart

The School of Business would like to create a bar chart of the data that it collected on the class year of students who are taking the Introductory Statistics course. The frequency table for the data is shown at the top of page 70.

Year in school	Frequency	Relative frequency (%)
Freshman	4	14.3
Sophomore	12	42.9
Junior	2	7.1
Senior	10	35.7
Total	**28**	**100.0**

Analyze the Data

Since in this case there is a natural order for the categories we will use it when labeling the *x* axis. The *y* axis must accommodate a frequency as high as 12, so the scale for that axis will go from 0 to 12 by twos. The completed bar chart is shown in the figure.

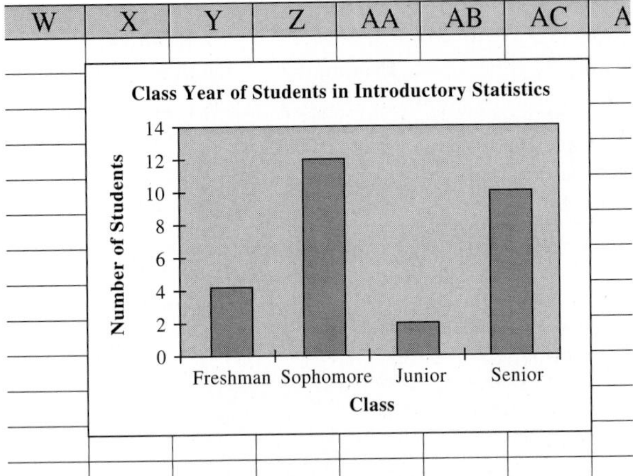

■

One thing to remember when creating a bar chart is that there are no absolute rules. The idea is to create a chart that conveys information to the viewer. In general, it is desirable to keep the number of categories in a bar chart to no more than ten. When there are too many categories, the axis becomes crowded and difficult to read and the viewer is distracted. To accomplish this, categories with very low frequencies are often consolidated into a single category labeled "Other." Even though the "Other" category might have a higher frequency than some of the categories, it must appear last in the bar chart.

Student Grades ***Creating a Bar Chart***

The instructor who surveyed her students about expected grades wants to create a bar chart from the data. The frequency table for the data is

Grade	Frequency	Relative frequency (%)
A	9	32.1
B	12	42.9
C	4	14.3
D	2	7.1
F	1	3.6
Total	**28**	**100.0**

Create a bar chart for the data using relative frequency on the y axis. Be sure to label the axes and include an appropriate title.

Pareto Analysis

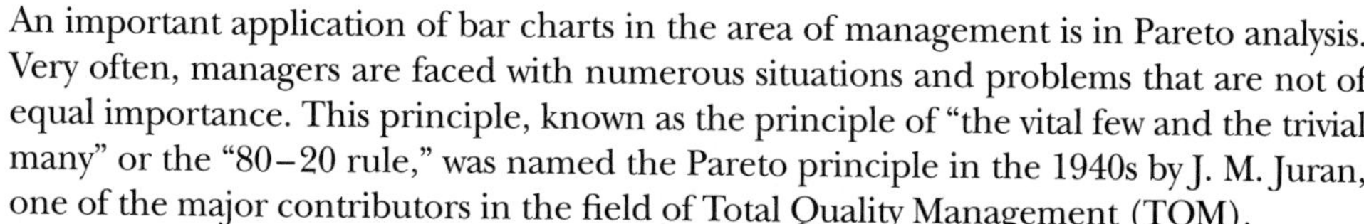

An important application of bar charts in the area of management is in Pareto analysis. Very often, managers are faced with numerous situations and problems that are not of equal importance. This principle, known as the principle of "the vital few and the trivial many" or the "80–20 rule," was named the Pareto principle in the 1940s by J. M. Juran, one of the major contributors in the field of Total Quality Management (TQM).

The idea behind the principle is that, in most cases, 80% of the phenomena being observed fall into only 20% of the categories. For example, in quality control, most customer complaints can be attributed to only a few of the defect categories; in marketing, a small number of customers account for most of the sales; and in human services and employee relations, only a few of the employees account for most of the personnel problems. If managers can identify the key few categories, they can improve quality, increase sales, and improve employer/employee relations.

A tool that helps accomplish this is known as a **Pareto diagram.**

A ***Pareto diagram*** is a bar chart in which the categories are plotted in order of decreasing relative frequency. In addition to the bars, the cumulative relative frequency of the categories is plotted on the same graph.

EXAMPLE 3.16 Tissue Defects

Pareto Diagram

A large consumer products company that manufactures facial tissues has been keeping track of customer complaints and classifying them according to the type of complaint. The company has created a frequency table for the complaints for the previous month. The data, in order of decreasing frequency, are

Understand the Problem

Complaint category	Frequency	Relative frequency (%)	Cumulative relative frequency (%)
Dispensing	127	58.0	58.0
Packaging	44	20.1	78.1
Miscounts	32	14.6	92.7
Softness	12	5.5	98.2
Odor	3	1.4	99.6
Pricing	1	0.5	100.0
Total	**219**	**100.0**	

Collect and Analyze the Data

To create a Pareto diagram for these data, first construct a bar chart using the relative frequency (see figure at the top of page 72).

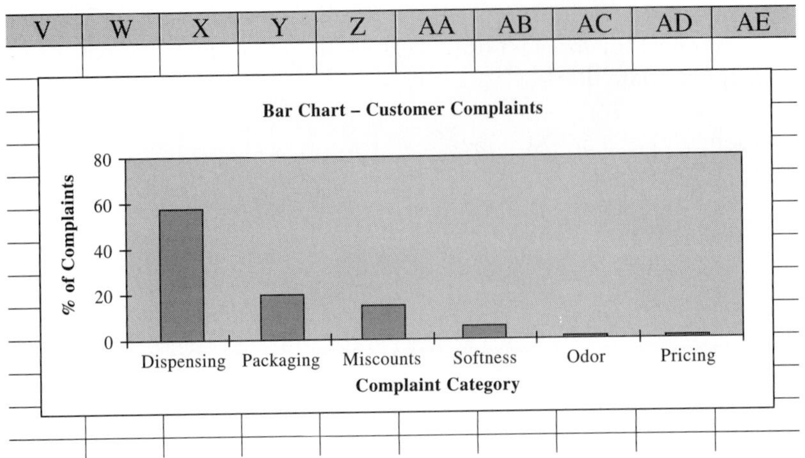

To make the bar chart a Pareto diagram we must add a new, different scale to the right side of the graph. This second scale on the y axis must allow us to graph the cumulative relative frequency, so it must go from 0 to 100%. At the location of each bar, a point is plotted that represents the cumulative relative frequency for that bar. At the end, the points are connected to create a line. The Pareto diagram for the tissue complaint data is shown here:

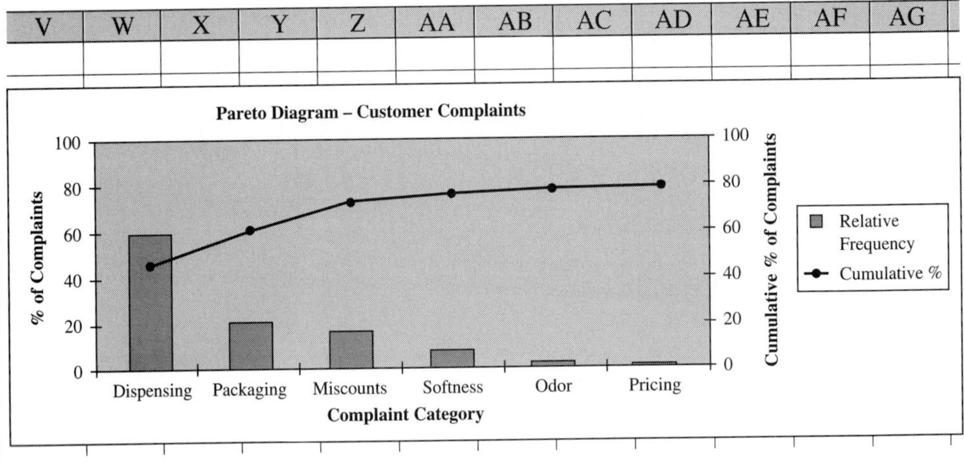

Draw Conclusions

From the Pareto diagram the company can see that almost 80% (78.1%) of the customer complaints that they received in the last month were about dispensing or packaging. If they concentrate on fixing the defects that generate those complaints they can go a long way toward reducing customer complaints. ■

Other Uses for Bar Charts

Bar charts are not limited to situations where the data are frequencies. Very often bar charts are used to display data for different categories where the data are some kind of quantitative measure for each category. For example, a bar chart could be used to display and compare sales revenues for a sample of different software products. In this case, the y axis of the chart would represent the value of the variable being studied.

EXAMPLE 3.17 Food Sales

Bar Charts for Nonfrequency Data

A company did a study of sales for a group of foods that are advertised as having "added nutrients." The company looked at supermarket sales for a 52-week period and found the following:

Product	Manufacturer	Sales ($ million)
Hawaiian Punch	Procter & Gamble	125.7
Yoo Hoo Chocolate Flavored Drink	Austin Nichols	32.9
Life Savers Flavor Pops	Agway	9.4
Wonder Calcium Enriched White Bread	Ralston-Continental Baking	1.0
Vicks Vitamin C Lemon Drops	Procter & Gamble	0.5

Collect and Analyze the Data

The company created a bar chart for the data using the product for the x axis and the sales (in millions of dollars) for the y axis. The chart obtained is shown here:

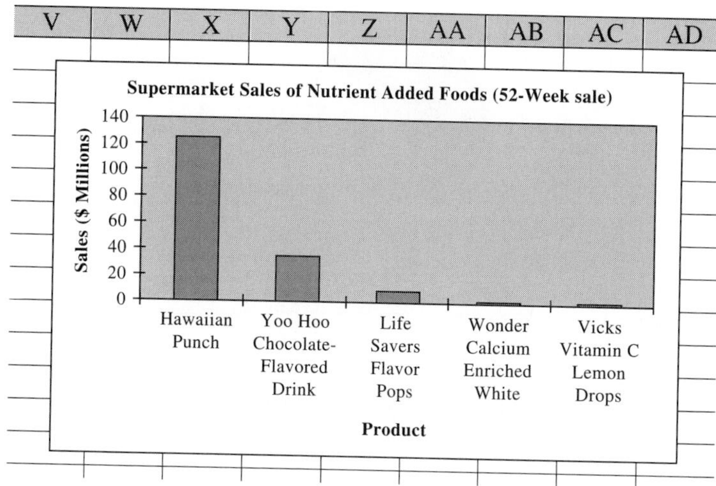

■

Creating a Pie Chart for Qualitative Data

Qualitative data can also be displayed using a **pie chart.** This type of chart is often used when the categories of the data represent some part or portion of a whole.

> A ***pie chart*** represents data in the form of slices or sections of a circle. Each slice represents a category and the size of the slice is proportional to the relative frequency of the category.

Drawing a pie chart by hand requires the use of a protractor to accurately measure the sizes of the slices and is fairly tedious. Since the number of degrees in a circle is 360, you can use the relative frequency to determine how many degrees should be allocated to each slice. Because of this it is usually best to use computer software to create one.

EXAMPLE 3.18 Class Year

Creating a Pie Chart

The School of Business wants to use the data on class year for a presentation to the faculty. They think that a pie chart might have the best impact. From the relative frequency table they determine the following:

Class year	Relative frequency (%)
Freshman	14.3
Sophomore	42.9
Junior	7.1
Senior	35.7
Total	**100.0**

Analyze the Data

They use Microsoft Excel to create a pie chart from the relative frequency table:

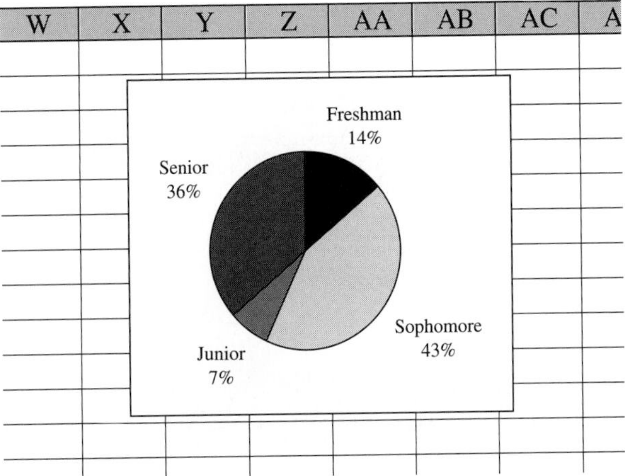

■

3.3.2 Graphical Displays for Quantitative Data

The tool used to display quantitative data is called a **histogram**. A histogram is very similar to a bar chart, but since numbers are naturally ordered, the x axis of the graph must be scaled to reflect this. There are slight differences for dealing with integer and continuous data.

Histograms for Integer Data

As in a bar chart, you use a rectangle to represent each possible data value, with the height of the bar corresponding to the frequency or relative frequency for that value. Remember that integers are numbers and they have a definite ordering. The x axis must accommodate all of the possible values, whether or not there were any observations of the value. The rectangles are centered on the data values as in a bar chart, but the bars are contiguous; that is, they touch each other.

EXAMPLE 3.19 Student Attitudes

Creating a Histogram for Integer Data

The instructor who is interested in student attitudes toward statistics would like to create a graphical display of the data. She feels that this might provide another view of the situation. The frequency table for the data is

Rating	Frequency	Relative frequency (%)
0	4	14.3
1	4	14.3
2	0	0.0
3	0	0.0
4	2	7.1
5	2	7.1
6	3	10.7
7	2	7.1
8	3	10.7
9	2	7.1
10	6	21.4
Total	**28**	**100.0**

Analyze the Data

To create a relative frequency histogram for the data the x axis will be scaled so that the numbers 0 through 10 appear at the center of the bars. The y axis will be scaled to accommodate the relative frequencies, the highest of which is 21.4%. The histogram is shown here:

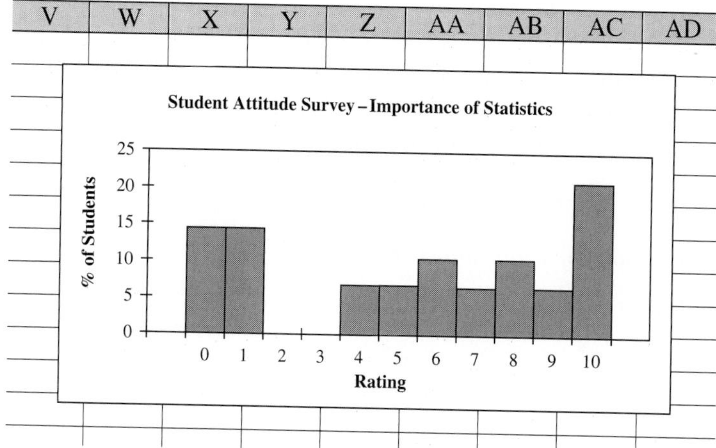

From the histogram the instructor sees that the really negative attitudes are separate from the rest of the group and that the most typical response was a 10. The remainder of the responses were evenly spread out over the 4 through 9 ratings. Although there is no new information in the graph, the visual display does add another dimension to the information. ■

Draw Conclusions

TRY IT NOW!

New Product Survey *Cumulative Relative Frequencies*

The marketing research firm that is conducting a survey about customer attitudes toward a new brand of soap would like to look at its data graphically. The frequency table for the data is shown at the top of page 76.

(continued)

Rating	Frequency	Relative frequency (%)
1	4	13.3
2	5	16.7
3	6	20.0
4	11	36.7
5	4	13.3
Total	**30**	**100.0**

Create a relative frequency histogram for the data.

Histograms for Continuous Data

A histogram for continuous data differs from the one for integer data in that each rectangle represents a class interval, which is a *range of values.* For this reason, the rectangles are not centered on values, but begin and end at each of the class boundaries.

EXAMPLE 3.20 ABC Faculty Salaries

Creating a Histogram for Continuous Data

Analyze the Data

The Provost at ABC wants to make a histogram of the data on number of years of service. She decides to use the frequency distribution that uses intervals of 5 years:

Class	Frequency
$-5 < x \leq 0$	15
$0 < x \leq 5$	38
$5 < x \leq 10$	42
$10 < x \leq 15$	23
$15 < x \leq 20$	29
$20 < x \leq 25$	51
$25 < x \leq 30$	8
$30 < x \leq 35$	0
$35 < x \leq 40$	0
$40 < x \leq 45$	1

The histogram is shown here:

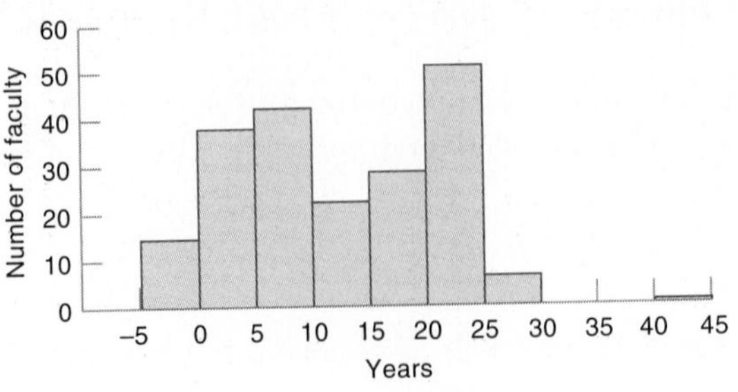

She sees at first glance that the data are certainly heavily concentrated at the bottom half of the class intervals and that the intervals in the upper half are very sparse. ■

Draw Conclusions

Sometimes you will see histograms that do not use the endpoints of the intervals to label the *x* axis. In this case, the bars of the histogram are centered on the axis tick mark and the *midpoint* of the interval is used instead.

EXAMPLE 3.21 On-Time Rates

Creating a Histogram for Continuous Data

The railroad company interested in on-time rates would like to look at a graphical display of the data that have been collected. The frequency table for the data was

On-time rates	Frequency	Relative frequency (%)
$25.0 < x \leq 35.0$	3	10.0
$35.0 < x \leq 45.0$	2	6.7
$45.0 < x \leq 55.0$	4	13.3
$55.0 < x \leq 65.0$	3	10.0
$65.0 < x \leq 75.0$	11	36.7
$75.0 < x \leq 85.0$	3	10.0
$85.0 < x \leq 95.0$	4	13.3
Totals	**30**	**100.0**

The railroad decides to create a relative frequency histogram. To do this the *y* axis must be scaled so that it can accommodate percentages from 0 to 36.7%. So the railroad decides to go from 0 to 40% in increments of 5%. The tick marks on the *x* axis will be the values at the beginning of each of the class intervals. The last tick mark will be at the end of the last interval. The histogram is shown here:

Analyze the Data

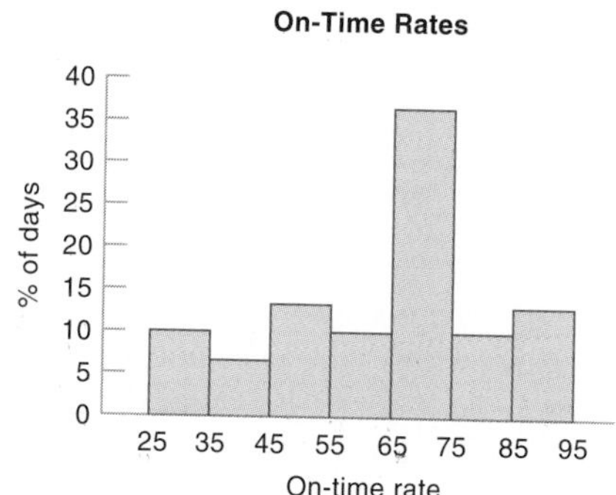

From the histogram the railroad company sees that the most typical on-time rates were in the 65–75% range, and that they were evenly distributed among the other classes. ■

3.3.3 Displaying Small Data Sets

The rules for creating histograms are really not suitable for data sets with less than 25 observations. This is because the number of classes should not be less than five and we determine the number of classes by taking the square root of the sample size. Often when we collect data we do not have more than 25 observations. Is there a way to display these types of data sets graphically? The answer is a graphical method called a **dotplot.**

In a *dotplot*, each observation is plotted as a point on a single, horizontal axis. The axis is scaled so that each of the data points can be located uniquely on the axis. When there is more than one observation with the same value the points are "stacked" on top of each other.

A dotplot can show many of the same features of the data as a histogram.

EXAMPLE 3.22 Bank Customers

Creating a Dotplot for a Data Set

Understand the Problem

A bank is interested in understanding the number of customers that arrive hourly on Fridays preceding holiday weekends. It takes data for 8 hours on each of two different Fridays and obtains the following:

Collect and Analyze the Data

10	14	15	14	19	12	11	14
15	14	20	19	11	12	17	17

After looking at the data the bank decides to use a dotplot to display them because there are not very many observations. An axis is created that is scaled from 10 (the smallest value) to 20 (the largest value) in increments of 1, since the data are integer data:

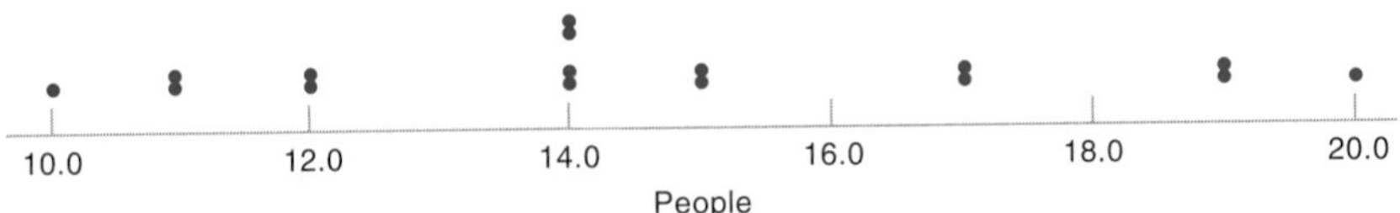

Draw Conclusions and Make Decisions

The dotplot shows that the number of customers per hour varies widely over the interval, although in 25% (4/16) of the hours there were 14 customers, and in 69% (11/16) there were at least 14 (14 or more) customers. The bank decides to use these data to plan the number of tellers that should be working on these Fridays. ■

3.3.4 Using the Computer to Create Graphical Displays

You may be wondering why it is necessary to learn how to create bar charts, pie charts, and histograms by hand, when you will almost certainly be using a computer to create them. The graphs produced by computer software are superior to those produced by hand, but a good deal of critical thought goes into creating a graph that conveys *information* to the viewer. It is not so important that you *create* the charts by hand as it is that you know *how* they are created.

Most computer software packages ask the user for input when creating graphs. Knowing how the charts are created will help you make decisions about how the charts look. In addition, not all software allows the user to make the same decisions. The default graphs produced by computer software offer great starting points for the final graphical display, but they are not usually the end product that you are looking for.

When you create a bar chart by hand you have the freedom to put the bars in any order you want and to combine categories as you wish. Some software will allow you to choose ascending or descending order of frequency for the bars, others will require you to sort the frequency table first, either by frequency or alphabetical order of categories. The same is true about combining categories and using frequency or

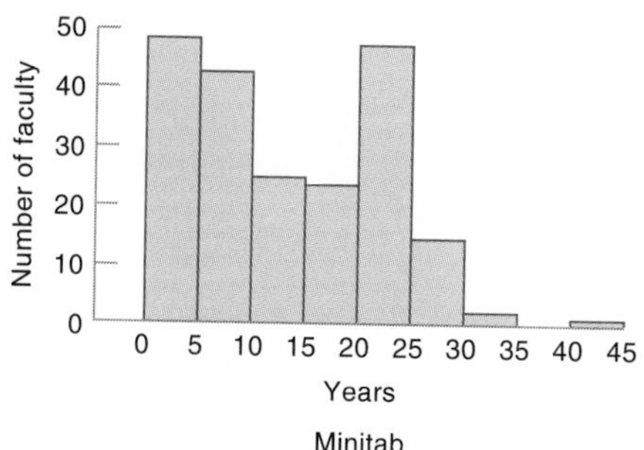

FIGURE 3.4 Histogram from Minitab for ABC years of service

relative frequency. Some computer software packages such as Excel will not create frequency distributions for categorical data and will make bar and pie charts only from already existing frequency tables. If you did not know what the chart should contain you would not know how to process the raw data that you collect.

Creating histograms differs among software packages. There are differences in the way you go about defining and creating the chart. Almost all software packages will create a histogram using a default set of class intervals, but they differ widely in what they will allow the user to specify. You saw in the previous section that when you are trying to make graphical displays to compare different samples, you need to be able to control the *x* axis of the graph. Microsoft Excel will allow you to specify the ending values for each of the classes, but when it creates the histogram from the data, it puts the endpoints in the *center* of the bar. Minitab and SPSS will allow you to specify endpoint values or midpoint values, or the number of classes you want to use, but not both.

There are also differences in the way the final chart looks. Remember that Minitab and SPSS define their intervals to include the lower value and go up to but not include the upper value. The differences in processing cause the histograms from the different software packages to look a little different. Figure 3.4 shows the histogram produced using this method for the data on faculty years of service for Aluacha Balaclava College.

If you compare this histogram to the one shown on page 76, you see that the major difference is in the first class. In the original histogram, this class contains only those people with 0 years of service ($-5 < x \leq 0$), whereas in Figure 3.4 it contains all people with 0, 1, 2, 3, or 4 years of service ($0 \leq x < 5$). This difference does not really change the general appearance of the histograms. Knowing the basics of creating histograms enables you to make smarter, more informed decisions, no matter what software you might use.

3.3.5 Exercises—Learning It!

3.12 The data that the computer society collected on personal computer operating systems are given again here: *Requires Exercise 3.2*

Mac OS	W 98	W 98	W NT	W 2000
W NT	W NT	W 95	W NT	W 2000
W 2000	W 2000	W NT	W 98	W NT
W NT	W 98	W 98	W NT	W 98
W 2000	W 98	W 98	W 2000	W 98
W 98	W NT	W NT	W 2000	W 2000

(a) Suppose you were asked to create a bar chart for the data. What order would you pick for the categories? Why?

(b) Make the bar chart for the data.

3.13 Every month the Department of Transportation (DOT) reports on the number of mishandled baggage reports filed by passengers on U.S. airlines. The data for April 2000 are given here:

Airline	**Reports per 10,000 passengers**
Alaska	277
America West	581
American	502
Continental	397
Delta	381
Northwest	424
Southwest	401
TWA	452
United	587
US Airways	429

(a) Create a bar chart for the number of reported problems per 10,000 passengers.

(b) Comment on any interesting features of the data.

3.14 Columbia University conducted a survey of 637 members of the Authors Guild and the Dramatists Guild, all of whom have published at least one book, one play, or three magazine articles. As part of the survey, the members were asked to classify the amount of money that they made from writing. The accompanying frequency table gives the results of the survey:

Revenue from writing	**Number of members**
More than $50,000	57
More than $20,000 but less than $50,000	127
More than $1000 but less than $20,000	192
More than $0 but less than $1000	102
No money at all	159
Total	**637**

(a) Create a relative frequency bar chart for the data.

(b) From the data would you conclude that a majority of those surveyed can or cannot earn a living solely from writing?

(c) Although the data are numerical, why did you have to make a bar chart rather than a histogram?

(d) What problem do you see with the way that the classes were defined?

Requires Exercise 3.5

3.15 The company that collected data on the number of weekly repairs needed by copy machines decided that it wanted a graphical display of the data to include in a budget report. The data are repeated here:

3	2	3	0	3
0	2	2	2	1
3	2	2	1	0
2	3	2	1	2
3	4	2	7	1
2	2	1	3	1
0	3	1	1	2

Create a histogram for the data.

Requires Exercise 3.3

3.16 After collecting the data on packaging defects, the company decided to ask you how it could make a graph of the data to use in a brainstorming session with the employees in the department. The data are repeated here:

Dented	No defect	No defect	Dented	No defect
No defect	Torn	Crushed	No defect	No defect
Unsealed	No defect	No defect	No defect	No defect

(continued)

No defect	No defect	No defect	No defect	No defect
No defect	No defect	No defect	Dented	No defect
No defect	Unsealed	No defect	No defect	No defect

(a) What type of graph would be appropriate for these data?

(b) Create a graphical display of the data.

(c) What order did you select for the categories? Why?

3.17 A company has recently become concerned about the number of young engineers that seem to be leaving the company and decides to collect some data to try to understand why the engineers are leaving. During the exit interviews with employees the human resources department asks several questions about the reasons the employee has for leaving the company. A table showing the reasons for leaving and the appropriate codes follows.

Dislike engineering	DE
Relocation	L
Raise in pay	P
More responsibilities	R
Relations with manager	M
Colleagues	C
Type of work	B

The human resources department looks at the results from the exit interview process for 40 engineers that have left the company in the last 2 years and finds the following:

DE	P	B	R	R	R	R	DE
P	L	M	DE	M	M	R	P
R	P	L	P	B	P	DE	L
R	R	P	P	P	R	C	C
M	P	R	P	P	M	P	L

(a) Create a Pareto diagram for the data.

(b) What category has the highest relative frequency?

(c) Does it appear that the 80–20 rule is true for these data? Why or why not?

3.18 After a change in the channels provided by the cable television service in a town, subscribers were asked to rate the new service on a scale of 1 = worst service I have ever had to 10 = best service I have ever had. The responses from 40 random subscribers are

1	4	5	7	8
2	4	5	7	9
2	4	5	7	9
3	4	6	7	9
3	4	6	7	9
3	4	6	7	9
3	4	6	8	9
3	5	7	8	10

(a) Create a relative frequency histogram of the ratings.

(b) Are the majority of the ratings favorable, unfavorable, or neither?

3.19 The company that is worried about losing its engineering staff also looked at the length of time, in months, that the engineers in the sample worked for the company:

16.7	26.0	28.0	29.6	30.6	32.6	34.0	35.8
20.9	26.6	28.1	29.7	30.8	32.6	34.6	37.4
25.2	26.6	28.5	30.2	31.1	33.2	34.8	37.8
25.6	27.4	28.8	30.2	31.7	33.5	34.9	38.3
25.8	27.7	28.8	30.3	32.1	33.6	35.2	44.6

Create a relative frequency histogram for the data.

Requires Exercise 3.11

3.20 The refuse company decides to use the data it collected in a presentation to the town. The data are shown again here:

8.3	10.2	12.2	13.1	13.9
8.5	10.4	12.3	13.3	14.1
8.8	11.0	12.3	13.3	14.3
9.1	11.0	12.3	13.4	14.3
9.7	11.2	12.3	13.4	14.4
9.8	11.4	12.5	13.4	14.4
9.9	12.0	12.7	13.6	14.4
9.9	12.0	12.8	13.6	14.8
10.1	12.2	12.9	13.8	15.2

(a) Create a relative frequency histogram for the data.

(b) From the histogram, does it appear that a majority of the newspaper piles put out for recycling exceed 12 inches?

Requires Exercise 3.10

3.21 The Bureau of Weight and Measures that looked at orange juice containers from supermarkets wants to create a graphical display of the following data it obtained:

64.8	65.2	65.6	65.7	65.9
64.8	65.3	65.7	65.7	66.0
64.9	65.3	65.7	65.7	66.1
65.1	65.4	65.7	65.8	66.1
65.2	65.4	65.7	65.8	66.3

Create an appropriate graphical display of the data.

3.4 DESCRIBING AND COMPARING DATA

Since the reason for displaying data is to gain understanding, it is important to know what we can learn from the graph of a data set. For quantitative data we usually want to know what a typical observation might be, and how the actual observations differ from the typical values. We would also like to be able to compare different data sets and make some decisions based on the comparisons.

3.4.1 Describing Quantitative Data

In statistics, the features of interest for a set of numerical data can be classified as **center**, **shape**, and **variability**.

> The ***center*** of a set of data describes where, numerically, the data are centered or concentrated.

> The ***shape*** of a set of data describes how the data are spread out around the center with respect to the symmetry or skewness of the data.

> The ***variability*** of a set of data describes how the data are spread out around the center with respect to the smoothness and magnitude of the variation.

Together these three features describe the distribution of the data. To describe the data it is useful to picture the distribution of the data as being represented by a smooth curve that captures the "shape" of the histogram. One way to achieve this curve is to plot a point at the top of each bar of the histogram and then connect the dots as shown in Figure 3.5.

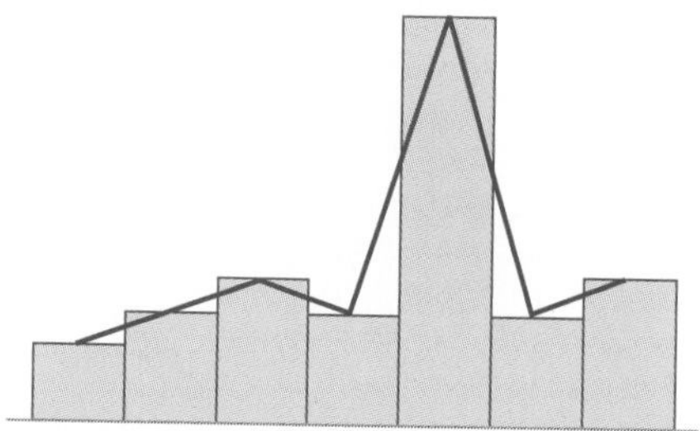

FIGURE 3.5 Histogram with line showing the shape of the distribution

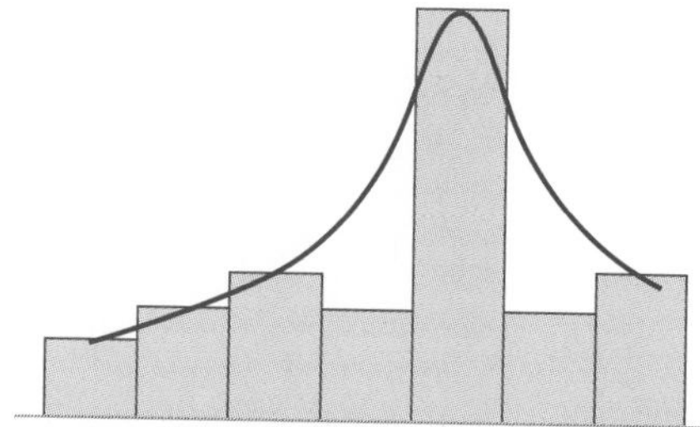

FIGURE 3.6 Histogram with smoothed curve representing the distribution

If you smooth out the plotted line you get a curve that looks like the one shown in Figure 3.6. From the curve you see that the distribution is centered at the bump or high point of the curve. Since the bump in the distribution is the location of the class with the highest frequency, it locates the most typical data points.

The shape of a distribution concerns how the data are spread out on either side of the center, that is, whether they are **symmetric** or **skewed.**

> When data are evenly spread out on both sides of the center, we describe the distribution of the data as ***symmetric.***

A typical symmetric distribution is shown in Figure 3.7.

> When the data are not evenly spread out on either side of the center then we refer to the distribution as being ***skewed.***

Skewness has a direction associated with it, either left (negative) or right (positive). The direction of the skew describes the side on which the distribution of the data covers a larger distance, that is, the direction in which the distribution "tails off" more slowly. Figure 3.8 shows both right and left skewed distributions.

When data are skewed, either left or right, the tailing off of the data is continuous and gradual as shown in Figure 3.9*a* on page 84. When the tailing off involves a gap in the data—a place where classes in the frequency histogram have no observa-

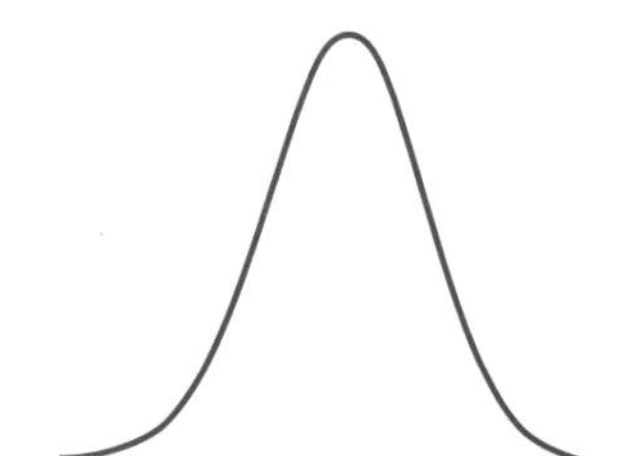

FIGURE 3.7 Typical symmetric distribution

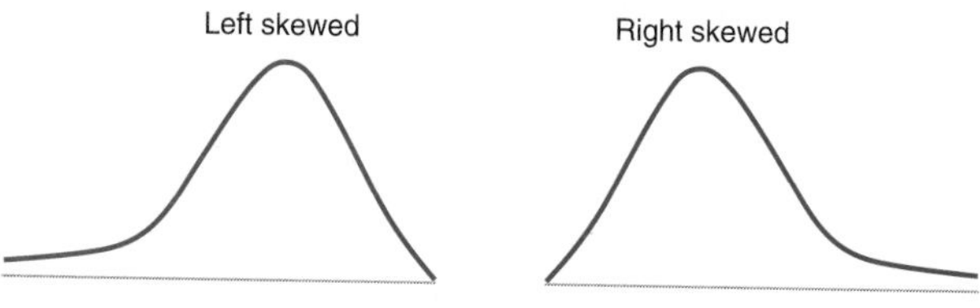

FIGURE 3.8 Typical skewed distributions

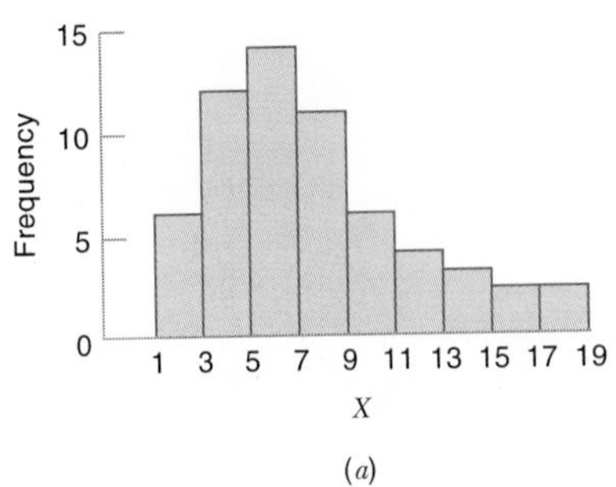

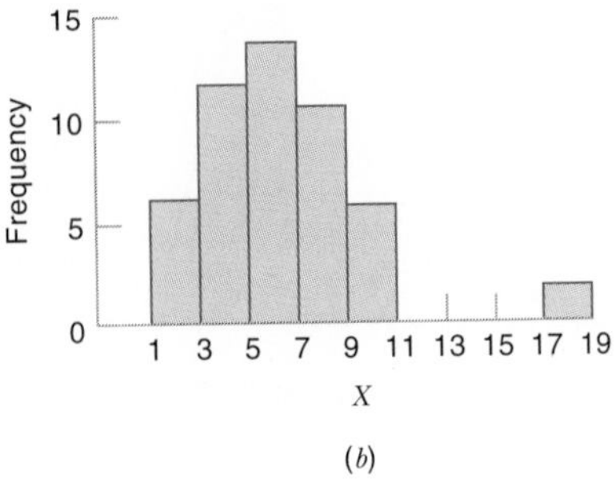

FIGURE 3.9 Histograms with (*a*) skewed data and (*b*) extreme values

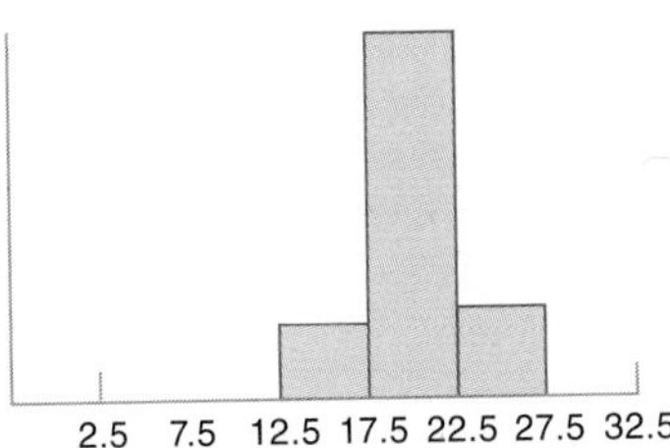

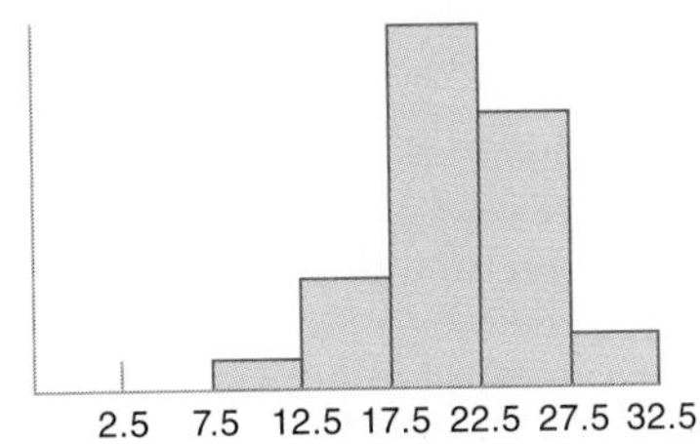

FIGURE 3.10 Histograms with different variability showing spread of data

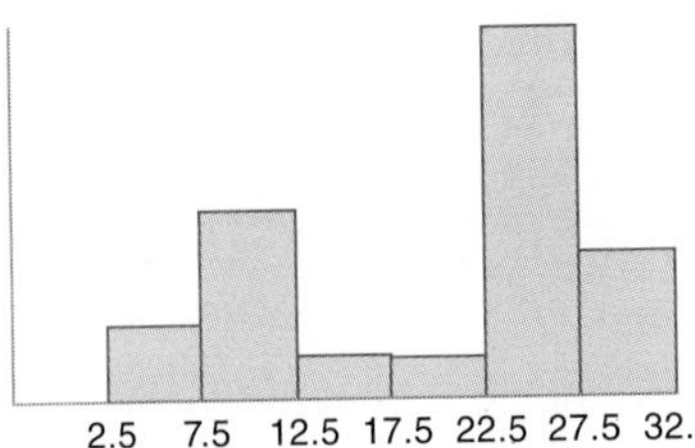

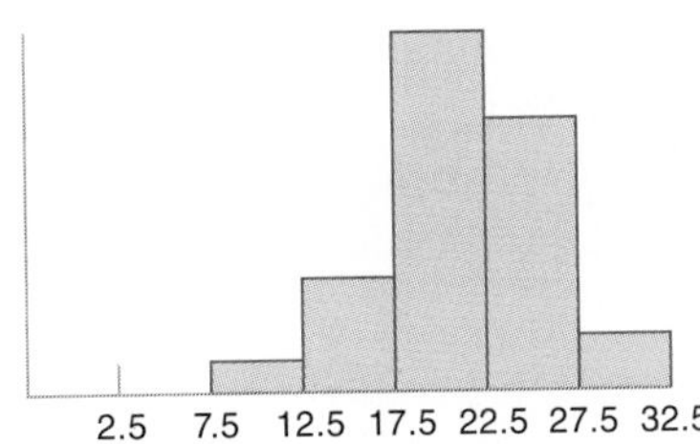

FIGURE 3.11 Histograms with different variability showing smoothness

tions—as shown in Figure 3.9*b*, the data are not really skewed. More likely the data you have contain some extreme or unusual observations. We talk about these extreme values more in Chapter 4 when we discuss outliers.

In addition to center and shape we would like to describe how much the data differ from the center or typical values. This is not easy to do without some way to measure the differences. We examine measures of variability in Chapter 4. At this point we can describe the variability of the distribution in two ways: in terms of (1) the "smoothness" of the curve and (2) the total spread of the data.

When data are not very variable, the frequency of observations decreases steadily as you move away from the center. Sometimes when data are highly variable, the distribution will be jagged. That is, the frequency of data values will not decrease steadily as you move away from the center. Another way to describe variability is to describe the distance from one end of the data to the other. Figures 3.10 and 3.11 show histograms with different degrees of variability.

Dotplots can also be used to describe data distributions, although because they represent small data sets it is often more difficult to describe the data.

EXAMPLE 3.23 ABC Faculty Salaries

Describing Data Distributions

The ABC Provost looked at the distribution of years of faculty service to see whether she could determine how the data are distributed.

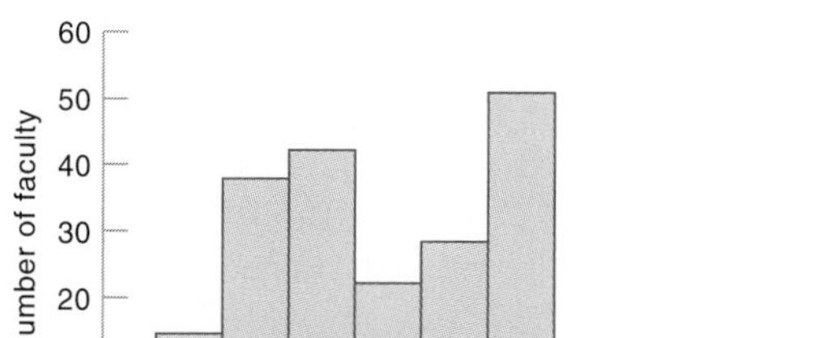

She sees that the data are highly variable and there is no smooth shape to the distribution. In addition, there does not seem to be a unique center or shape. She wonders why this might be. Perhaps another variable is affecting the picture. It might make more sense to look at years of service for each rank separately. ■

Draw Conclusions

Sometimes when you collect data and make a histogram there is no cohesive picture to be seen. This often happens when there are other, underlying variables that have an effect on the variable you are studying. When this happens it is useful to separate the data into groups on the basis of another variable and look at them again.

EXAMPLE 3.24 On-Time Rates

Describing Data Distributions

The railroad company that is looking at on-time rates obtained the following histogram:

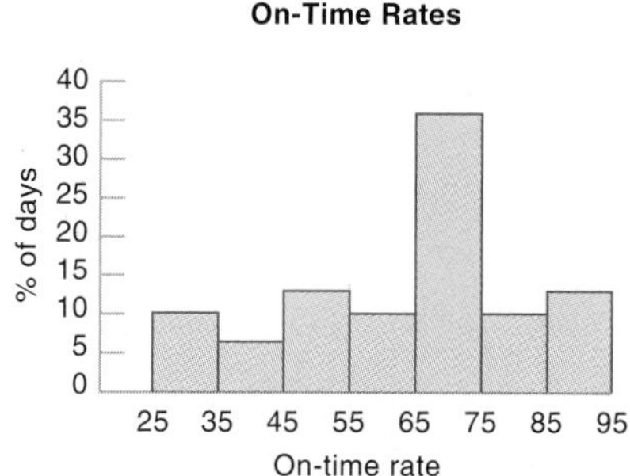

From the histogram we see that the data have a distinct center and that, typically, the on-time rate was between 65% and 75%. The frequency of the data seems to drop off rapidly from the center, and the data are rather uniformly distributed among the other classes. The data seem a little variable. The distribution is skewed to the left, which means that the data are more spread out on the low side (four classes) than on the high side (two classes). ■

Draw Conclusions

The choice of the number of class intervals for a histogram is very important. If your histogram has too many intervals for the number of data values, then the data might appear to have a lot of variability when, in fact, classes are empty or have few observations because of the lack of data. If your histogram has too few intervals, then the distribution will look like a lump and important features of the data might be hidden. It is often important to look at the data in several different ways to make sure that you are getting a true and consistent picture. We see later on that it is possible to distort graphical displays and bias an analysis by playing with the scale.

TRY IT NOW!

Assignment Times *Creating a Frequency Table for Continuous Data*

The instructor for the Introductory Statistics class wants to see, in graphical form, the data she has collected on the amount of time it took the students to do the assignment. The frequency distribution for the data is

Time	Frequency	Relative frequency (%)
$22.70 < x \leq 26.22$	6	20.0
$26.22 < x \leq 29.74$	11	36.7
$29.74 < x \leq 33.26$	7	23.3
$33.26 < x \leq 36.78$	5	16.7
$36.78 < x \leq 40.30$	0	0.0
$40.30 < x \leq 43.82$	1	3.3

Create a relative frequency histogram for the data.

Use the histogram to describe the distribution of the times the students took to complete the assignment.

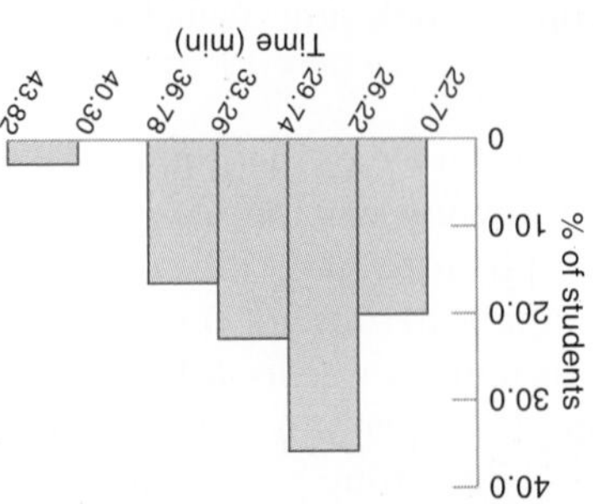

ANS. **Time to Complete Statistics Assignment** TYPICALLY BETWEEN 26.22 AND 29.74 MINUTES, SKEWED RIGHT, NOT VERY VARIABLE.

3.4.2 Comparing Data Distributions

One of the major reasons for doing statistical analyses of data is to obtain facts for making *informed* decisions. As a result, we must often make comparisons between or among samples taken from different populations. When comparing different data sets, we make those comparisons based on the qualities of the data you just learned: center, shape, and variability.

To make valid comparisons it is critical that the data be displayed in the same way. Since the graphical displays have a *visual* impact, it is important that the graphs used are comparable in scale so that the viewers are not misled.

To make visual comparisons about center, shape, and variability, the class intervals for the different graphs should be the same. When this is not the case it is difficult if not impossible to compare these qualities in a meaningful way. The following example shows how using different scales can mask the visual impact of the display.

EXAMPLE 3.25 Loan Application Times

Comparing Data Distributions

A large bank with many branch offices has developed two different procedures for filling out mortgage loan applications. Each procedure is being used in a different branch of the bank in comparable locations. After the procedures are used for several months, some data are collected on the amount of time (in minutes) it took for loan candidates to complete the application. The data for each branch follow:

Understand the Problem

Branch 1					Branch 2				
37.0	39.3	42.1	44.3	47.8	40.4	42.8	43.4	44.3	46.1
37.2	39.9	42.4	44.5	49.3	40.8	42.8	43.5	44.4	46.4
37.6	41.2	42.6	45.3	49.5	41.5	42.8	43.5	44.7	46.5
38.1	41.5	42.7	45.7	50.3	41.5	43.1	43.8	44.7	47.1
38.8	41.6	43.0	46.1	52.1	41.6	43.2	44.0	45.1	47.9
39.2	41.9	43.4	46.2	54.7	42.3	43.3	44.2	45.4	48.6

Collect and Analyze the Data

To better understand the data and to compare the loan application times for the two branches a computer software package is used to create histograms for each of the data sets. The histograms show that the application times for branch 1 are typically between 37.5 and 42.5 minutes and that the data are slightly skewed to the right. The loan application times for branch 2 are typically between 43 and 45 minutes and the data are more symmetric than for branch 1. On first glance it appears that the first bank is using the better method. Or is it?

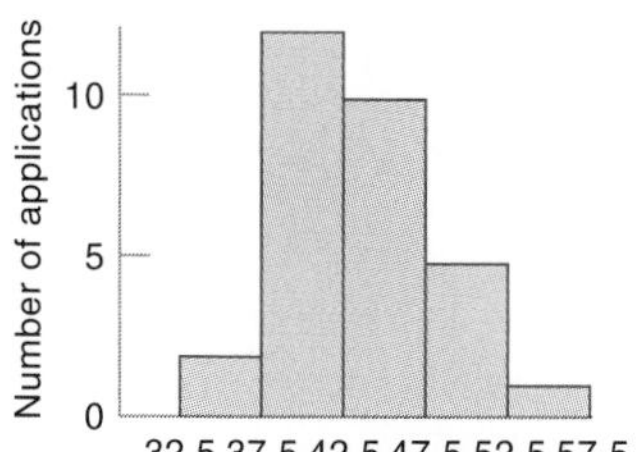

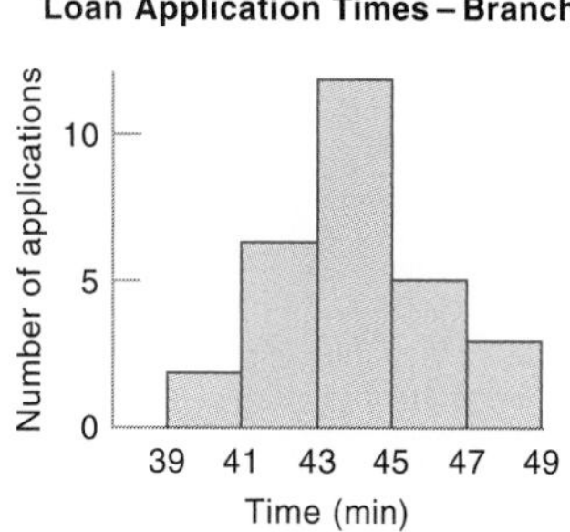

The bank decides to re-create the histograms, this time using a common scale for the x axis. The results are shown in the following histograms.

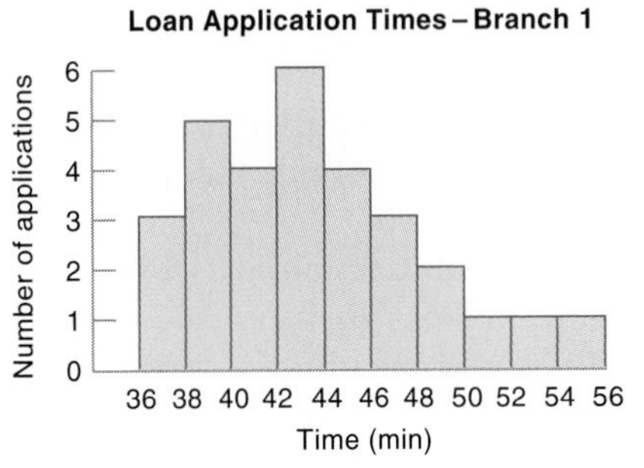

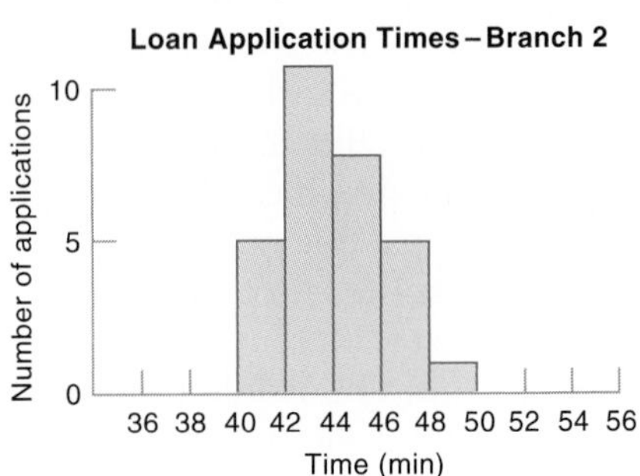

Draw Conclusions

From the second set of histograms it appears that the times for branch 1 are much more variable than those for branch 2. It also seems that the typical times for branch 1 are really not that much different than those for branch 2. They can see from the second set of graphs that the method used for branch 2 is more consistent than that for branch 1 and it has comparable application times. ■

In the previous example it does not really matter that the y axis of the histograms is frequency rather than relative frequency, because the number of observations is the same for each sample. If this is not the case it is necessary to use relative frequency to make valid and meaningful comparisons.

EXAMPLE 3.26 ABC Faculty Salaries

Drawing Conclusions from Graphs

Now that the Provost understands a little more about the characteristics of the faculty at ABC, she decides to look at salaries. It would seem that a faculty member's salary should be related to their years of service. She decides to make a histogram of faculty salaries and compare it to the histogram for years of service. The histogram for faculty salary is shown here:

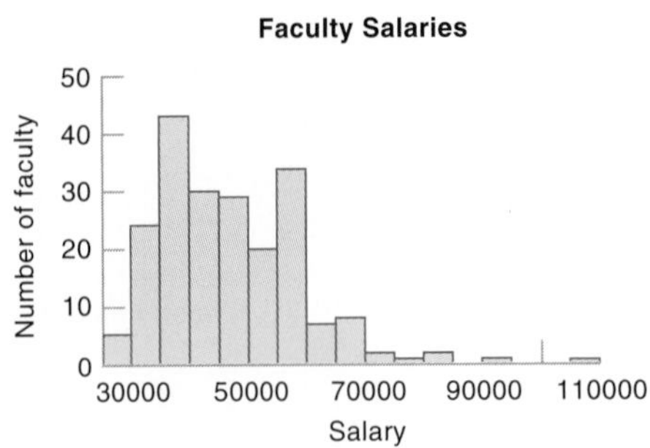

In comparing the two graphs, she sees some similarities. Both graphs appear to be bimodal and highly variable. They both skew to the right, but the salary histogram shows more values that are unusual on the high side. It would appear that there might be other factors to consider in this analysis. ■

Discovery Exercise 3.1
THINKING ABOUT VARIABILITY

A manufacturer of compact discs uses two different suppliers for the jewel boxes used to hold the discs. There have been problems with these boxes in the past. The inside width of the jewel box has critical specifications of 119.0 ± 0.2 mm. If the case is too narrow the disc will not fit in it and if it is too wide, the front label insert slips around. Because it is time to renew the purchasing contracts for the jewel boxes, the CD manufacturer decides to take a look at a sample of the boxes from each supplier. The data (in mm) for each source are

Supplier A				
118.7	118.9	119.0	119.1	119.2
118.8	119.0	119.0	119.1	119.2
118.8	119.0	119.0	119.1	119.2
118.9	119.0	119.1	119.2	119.2
118.9	119.0	119.1	119.2	119.3

Supplier B				
118.8	118.8	118.9	118.9	118.9
118.8	118.8	118.9	118.9	119.0
118.8	118.8	118.9	118.9	119.0
118.8	118.8	118.9	118.9	119.0
118.8	118.9	118.9	118.9	119.1

Make a relative frequency histogram of the data for each supplier.

Describe the distribution of jewel box widths for each supplier and compare them.

Your company has decided to single source its supply of jewel boxes. The purchasing agent in charge of the accounts argues that supplier B should not get a renewed contract since he observes that the jewel boxes from that source are not centered at the target specification of 119.0 mm whereas the jewel boxes from supplier A are right on target. Can you explain to him why, although his observation is true, his decision to use supplier A is not necessarily correct? What factor has he failed to consider?

(continued)

Which supplier would you recommend that your company use? Write a short memo to the manager with your recommendation and your supporting reasons.

3.4.3 Exercises—Learning It!

3.22 A university collected some data on the amount of money ($) that students spend on textbooks in a typical semester:

222	276	303	326	377
225	285	304	331	380
237	289	305	344	395
244	291	306	359	398
247	294	309	361	406
263	297	312	369	409
271	302	316	374	427

(a) Create a histogram of the data.

(b) Where is the center of the distribution located?

(c) Are the data symmetric or skewed? If they are skewed, are they left or right skewed?

(d) Describe the variability of the data.

3.23 The company that is looking at the length of time that engineers stayed at the company wants to summarize its data, shown here:

Requires Exercise 3.19

16.7	26.0	28.0	29.6	30.6	32.6	34.0	35.8
20.9	26.6	28.1	29.7	30.8	32.6	34.6	37.4
25.2	26.6	28.5	30.2	31.1	33.2	34.8	37.8
25.6	27.4	28.8	30.2	31.7	33.5	34.9	38.3
25.8	27.7	28.8	30.3	32.1	33.6	35.2	44.6

(a) Describe the center of the data.

(b) Describe the shape of the data.

(c) Describe the variability of the data.

3.24 The refuse company decides to use the data it collected in a presentation to the town. The data are shown again:

Requires Exercises 3.11, 3.20

8.3	10.2	12.2	13.1	13.9
8.5	10.4	12.3	13.3	14.1
8.8	11.0	12.3	13.3	14.3
9.1	11.0	12.3	13.4	14.3
9.7	11.2	12.3	13.4	14.4
9.8	11.4	12.5	13.4	14.4
9.9	12.0	12.7	13.6	14.4
9.9	12.0	12.8	13.6	14.8
10.1	12.2	12.9	13.8	15.2

Describe the distribution of the data. Remember to include center, shape, and variability.

3.25 The company that is looking at turnaround time from the Office Services department wants to summarize its data:

Requires Exercise 3.9

14	19	21	25	26	29
15	19	22	25	26	29
16	20	22	25	26	30
16	20	23	25	26	31
18	20	23	25	27	31
18	20	23	25	28	35
18	21	24	26	29	40

(a) How long is a typical turnaround time for a job?
(b) What shape is the distribution of turnaround times?
(c) How would you describe the variability in turnaround times?

3.5 *Executive Summary*

ABC COLLEGE

Business Analysis...

TO: President, Aluacha Balaclava College
FROM: Provost, Aluacha Balaclava College
RE: Current Faculty Salaries

Before preparing a new faculty salary scale, it will be helpful to understand the current faculty salary situation. This will give us a frame of reference to use in responding to faculty concerns. To begin with, the MIS group collected data on 207 current faculty members. The variables chosen were rank, years of service, and salary. The results of the analysis are presented in summary form and recommendations follow.

Figure 1 shows the distribution of faculty by rank. No single rank constitutes a majority of the faculty. With the exception of the rank of Instructor, which only makes up 4% of the total faculty, the distribution by rank is fairly uniform. The low percentage in the Instructor rank is not unusual since faculty at this rank do not have a doctorate; therefore, the category consists of special, terminal appointments. It is interesting to note that the percentage of faculty at each of the other ranks (Assistant, 37%; Associate, 32%; Professor, 27%) decreases. This might turn out to be an important phenomenon.

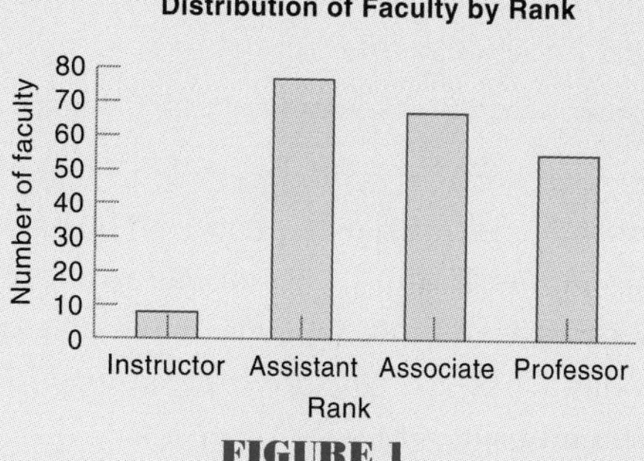

FIGURE 1

The graph showing distribution of years of service (Figure 2) shows that the data are bimodal—that is, they center in two different places. A typical faculty member has between 0 and 10 or between 20 and 25 years of service. The number of faculty with between 10 and 20 years of service is considerably less. This decrease might indicate that faculty at this point in their careers are leaving the college, which is

(continued)

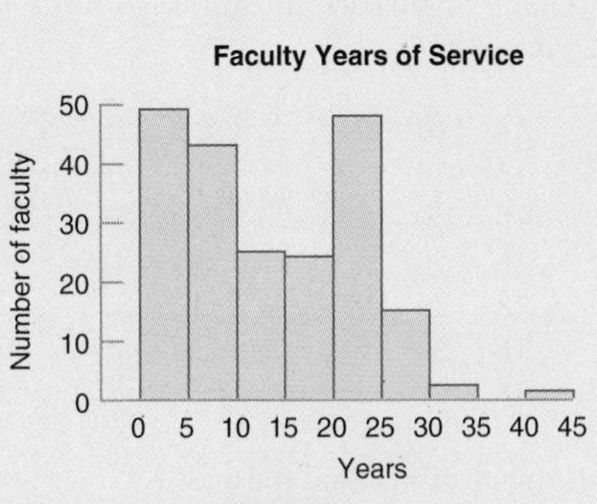

FIGURE 2

cause for some concern. The data are highly variable, indicating that perhaps other factors affect years of service.

The distribution of faculty salaries is shown in Figure 3. It seems reasonable that salary and years of service would be related, so we might expect those distributions to be similar, which they are in several ways. First, the salary histogram is also bimodal, indicating that typical salaries are in the $35,000–$40,000 range and the $55,000–$60,000 range. This is consistent with the data on years of service. The salary data are also highly variable, particularly on the high side. There are several unusually high salaries in the sample. Again, this indicates that other factors should be considered.

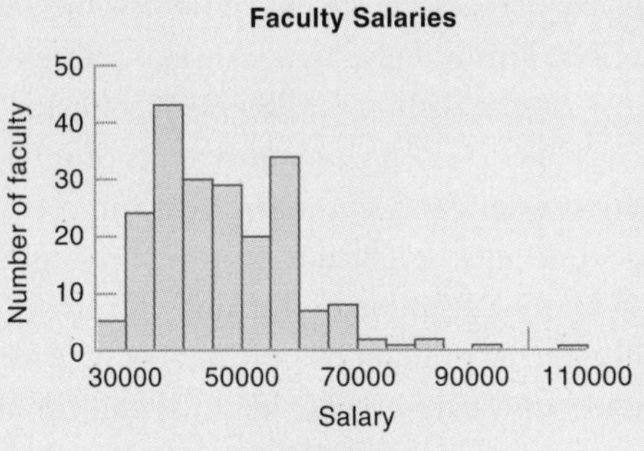

FIGURE 3

I recommend that we continue to study the problem, but include more variables in the study. I am asking the MIS group to generate additional data on gender, tenure, and the School in which the faculty member teaches. I will analyze the data using this additional information and report back within 2 weeks.

The *Wall Street Journal* is a major source of current business news and information for the business community. If your professor has arranged for your class to have access to the Business Extra feature, you can go to it now and see the techniques of this chapter in action today. Go to the Wiley Web site at http://www.wiley.com/college/pelosi, and click on Business Extra!

3.6 CREATING GRAPHICAL DISPLAYS USING EXCEL 97

The graphical displays that you learned about in this chapter can be created easily using Microsoft Excel 97. The power of using a computer package such as Excel to create the graphs is that you can modify them easily. This leads to better graphical displays because it eliminates much of the drudgery. This section will cover the basics of creating a chart using Microsoft Excel, as well as the specific methods for creating bar charts, pie charts, and histograms.

3.6.1 The Basics of Creating a Chart in Excel

Chart Wizard belongs to the Standard Toolbar.

In most cases, graphs and charts in Excel are easily created by using a special assistant called the *Chart Wizard.* The steps for creating a chart or graph using the Chart Wizard are:

1. Highlight the frequency table that you want to graph.
2. Invoke the Chart Wizard by clicking on the icon on the toolbar.
3. Follow the directions and hints from the Chart Wizard.
4. Edit the graph to include any other features or changes that you want.

3.6.2 Creating a Bar Chart in Excel

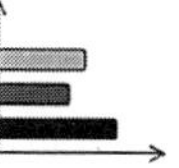

A Bar Chart

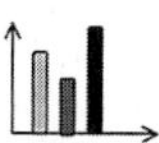

A Column Chart

Excel differentiates between *bar* and *column* charts. The only real difference is the direction (horizontal vs. vertical) of the bars. What we call a bar chart in statistics is called a column chart in Excel. Using the Chart Wizard to create a bar or column chart in Excel assumes that the data have already been tabulated in the form of a frequency table. Once this is done, it is relatively easy to create the chart.

Suppose we want to create a bar chart for the faculty rank data for Aluacha Balaclava College. Figure 3.12 shows the frequency table as part of an Excel worksheet.

	A	B	C
1			
2	Rank	Total	
3	Associate	67	
4	Assistant	77	
5	Instructor	8	
6	Professor	55	
7	Grand Total	207	
8			

FIGURE 3.12 Excel worksheet with frequency table

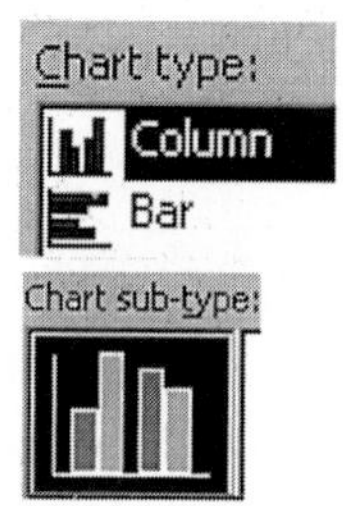

To use the Chart Wizard to create a bar or column chart, select the range that contains the frequency table, in this case **A2:B6,** and click the Chart Wizard icon on the Standard Toolbar.

There are four steps to creating the chart:

1. In the first step you select the *Chart Type.* Select **Column Chart** as the *type* and **Clustered Chart** as the *sub-type,* and then click the **Next>** button.
2. The second step of the process tells Excel where the frequency table is located and how the data are arranged, in columns or in rows. The default setting in this box is usually correct. You can see what your chart will look like. If it does not appear the way you expect, experiment with the settings. Figure 3.13 on page 94 shows what you should see at this point in the process.
3. Once you have indicated where the data are located, you can click on the **Next** button and go to the third step of the process. In this step you will be making decisions about the format of the chart. The dialog box for this step has six tabs: Titles, Axes, Gridlines, Legend, Data Labels, and Data Table. In the **Titles** section, click the **Chart title** box and type **"Aluacha Balaclava College—Faculty Rank".** Next, press TAB and type **"Rank".** Then press TAB and type **"Number**

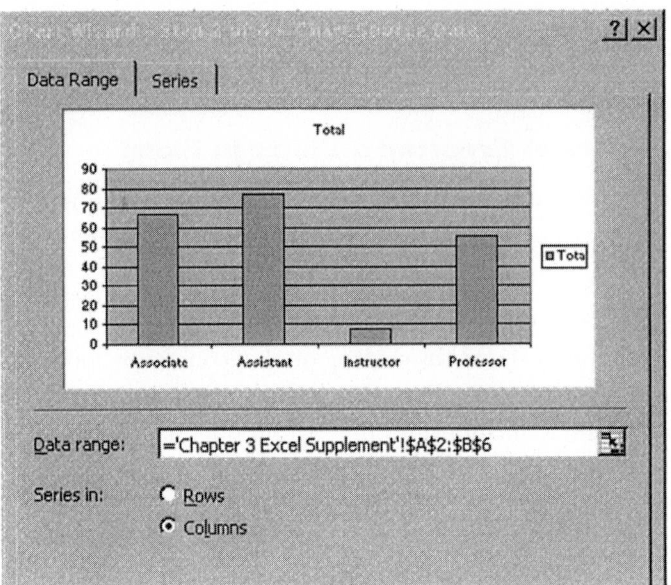

FIGURE 3.13 The Chart Source Data dialog box

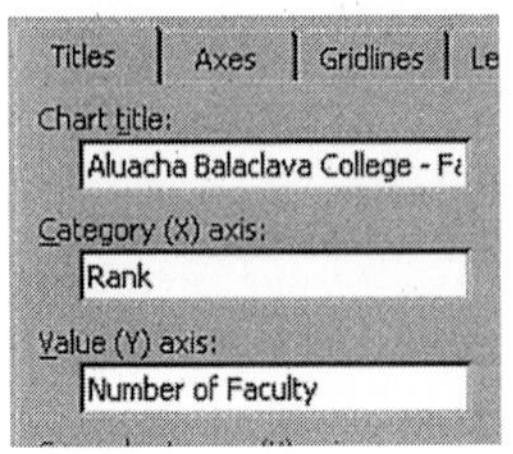

FIGURE 3.14
Adding titles to the chart

of Faculty". Figure 3.14 shows a portion of the dialog box at this point. Click the **Gridlines** tab and clear the **Major gridlines** check box. Then click the **Legend** tab and clear the **Show legend** check box. Finally, click the **Data Labels** tab and click the **Show value** check box. Notice that while you are making these choices, you can see what your chart will look like. When you are finished with this step, click the **Next** button and begin the fourth and last step.

4. The fourth step of the process lets you select where you want the chart to appear. You can either put the chart on a new worksheet or locate the chart on an existing sheet. To have the chart located on the current sheet, check the **As object in** radio button and click **Finish.** Excel will place the chart on the current worksheet. Figure 3.15 shows the chart.

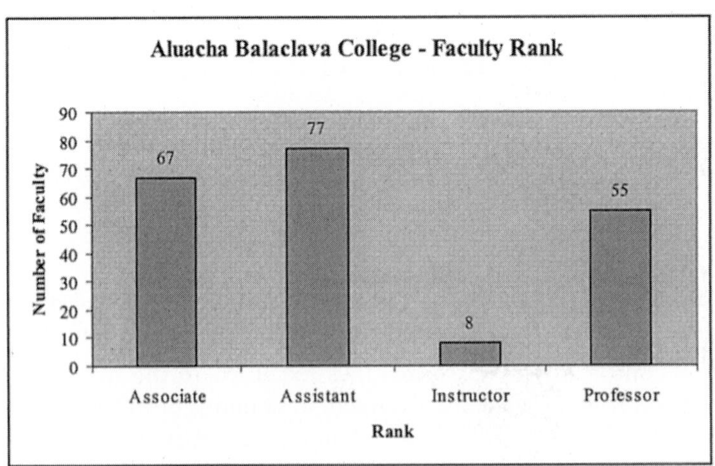

FIGURE 3.15 Finished Excel column chart

3.6.3 Creating a Pie Chart in Excel

Creating a pie chart in Excel uses the same procedure as that for creating a bar chart. The major difference occurs in the first dialog box of the Chart Wizard, where you select a different type of chart: In the first dialog box of the Chart Wizard, select Pie as the type of chart you want. The second step defines the location of the data, just as it did for the bar chart. The real differences are in step 3, where you determine the format of the chart. The dialog box for a pie chart has three tabs: Title, Legend, and Data Labels. The **Title** and **Legend** boxes are the same as those for the bar chart. The **Data Labels** tab allows you to select how the pie slices are labeled. Figure 3.16 shows the dialog box with the selections to label each slice with the category and the percent. The chart to the right updates to show how your selections will look. Note that if you are going to label the slices of the pie, it is not necessary to have a legend as well.

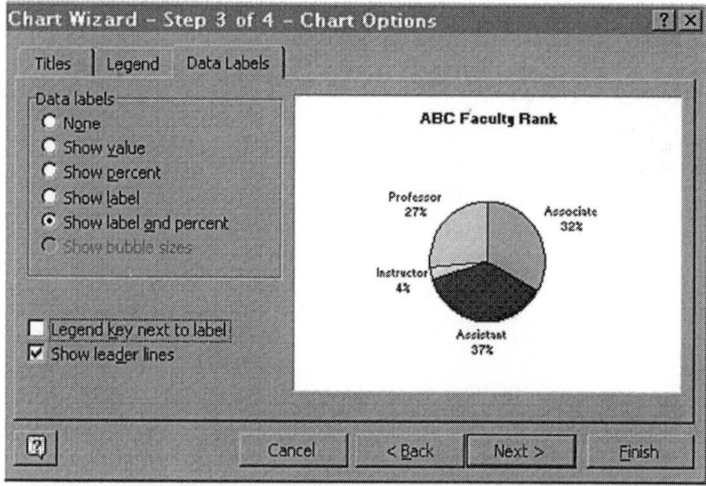

FIGURE 3.16 Formatting the pie chart

3.6.4 Creating a Pareto Diagram in Excel

As you learned in this chapter, a Pareto diagram is a special kind of bar chart used to identify trouble spots in a process. It is really a bar chart with the bars sorted by decreasing frequency. It also has a line that plots the cumulative frequency for the categories.

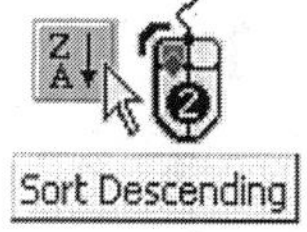

To create a Pareto diagram in Excel, you must first sort your frequency table by using the Sort command. You can do this in two ways. The quick way is to highlight the range that you want to sort—in this case, it is the data in the frequency table for Total—and click on the **Sort Descending** button on the Standard Toolbar. This will sort the range you have selected and will also sort the adjacent data accordingly. You can also highlight the entire table you want to sort and select **Sort** from the **Data** menu. In the dialog box, select the field you want to sort by and indicate whether you want to sort in ascending or descending order.

To create a Pareto diagram, you will also need a column for cumulative relative frequency. You can do this using the SUM function to keep a running total similar to the way you would update a checkbook register. The steps are:

1. Label the cell adjacent to Total in the frequency table Cumulative and copy the frequency of the first category to the adjacent cell.
2. In the cell directly below this, you will enter a formula using the SUM function. You tell Excel that you are entering a formula or function by typing an equal sign "=" and entering the formula or function name. In this case, the function you want to use is SUM, so you type this directly after the equal sign. The SUM function has two parts here, the location of the current subtotal and the location of the data you want to add to that subtotal. For example, looking at the data table in Figure 3.17, you see that the current subtotal is in cell C3 and you want to add the data in cell B4. You can see the formula in cell C4. When you hit Enter, the formula will calculate the value you have indicated.

	A	B	C
1			
2	Rank	Total	Cumulative
3	Associate	67	67
4	Assistant	77	=SUM(C3,B4)
5	Instructor	8	
6	Professor	55	

FIGURE 3.17 Formula for Cumulative Frequency

3. Copy this formula to the rest of the cells in the column labeled Cumulative and you will see the cumulative frequencies calculated.
4. Now you need to calculate the cumulative relative frequencies. Using the next column (you can label it Cumulative Relative Frequency) in the worksheet, you will enter the formula—that is, the cumulative frequency divided by the total. In cell D4 type " = C4/207" and press Enter. The cumulative relative frequency for the first category is calculated. Copy the formula to the remainder of the cells in this column.

Creating the Pareto diagram is easy using one of the custom charts in the Chart Wizard. After starting the Chart Wizard, the steps are as follows:

*Note: If the ranges are not adjacent, hold down the **CTRL** button while you highlight the ranges.*

1. In the first dialog box for chart type, click on the tab labeled **Custom Types** and scroll down until you see a chart called Line–Column on 2 Axes as shown in Figure 3.18. This will plot the first data series in your table as columns and the second as a line. The left axis corresponds to the bars and the right to the line. Click **Next>** to proceed.

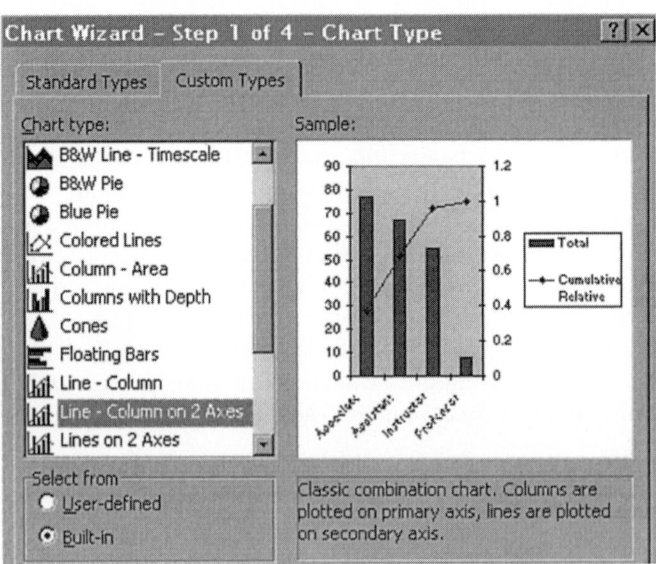

FIGURE 3.18 Custom Chart Type menu

2. The second step lets you specify the location of the data and see that your chart is set up correctly. When this is done, click **Next>** to continue.
3. The third step allows you to format the chart by adding labels. You might want to use the **Legend** tab to relocate the legend to the bottom of the chart

so that it does not interfere with the right axis. When the graph is the way you want it, click **Next>** to continue.

4. In the fourth step you can specify the location of the chart and click **Finish** to see your result. The finished chart is shown in Figure 3.19.

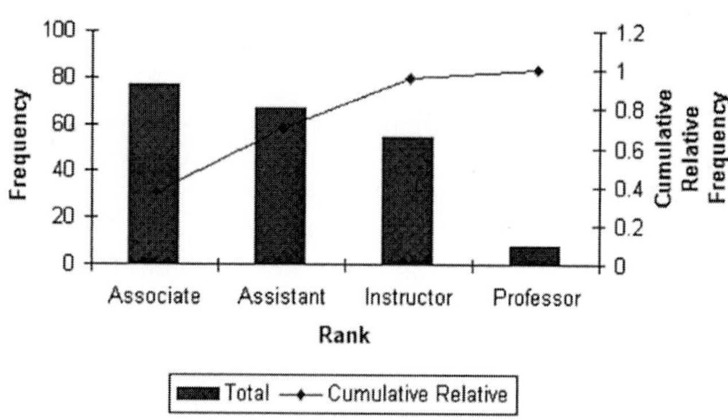

FIGURE 3.19 Pareto diagram

3.6.5 Creating a Frequency Table in Excel

In the previous section, you learned how to use the Chart Wizard to create a bar chart in Excel when you have the frequency table available. If you have the raw data instead of the frequency table, then you need to use **Pivot Table** to create it.

A **Pivot Table** in Excel is a tool that you will use often to manipulate raw data that are qualitative. You can create a pivot table by using the Pivot Table Wizard in Excel. The steps for creating the frequency table are:

1. Highlight the data for which you want to create the frequency table.
2. Invoke the Pivot Table Wizard in Excel by using the **Data > Pivot Table and Pivot Chart Report** menu.
3. Follow the directions that the Pivot Table Wizard gives you.
4. Copy or edit the pivot table to include any changes you want.

Remember that the Provost at Aluacha Balaclava College received the data in raw form; that is, the data had not been summarized. A portion of the data for faculty rank is shown in Figure 3.20.

	A	B	C
1	Rank	Service (Yr)	Salary
2	ASST	22	53316
3	PROF	11	64375
4	ASSO	7	63501
5	ASSO	6	59426
6	ASSO	20	49058
7	PROF	4	94969
8	ASST	21	54762
9	ASSO	9	55516
10	ASSO	18	45932

FIGURE 3.20 Raw data for faculty rank

The frequency table for these data will have a column for each rank that appears and a column for the frequency, or number of times that it appears. You can also add columns for the relative frequency and cumulative relative frequency. Highlight the range that contains the data you want to summarize—in this case, the data are in the range **A1:A208**—and follow these steps:

1. From the **Data** menu select **Pivot Table and Pivot Chart Report.** The Pivot Table Wizard will start by asking what type of data you want to work with. Since you are using data that are already in an Excel worksheet, simply leave the default radio button checked and click on **Next>** to continue.

Note: The data columns must be labeled in the first row.

2. Since you have already highlighted the range that contains your data, you can proceed by clicking **Next>.** If you have not indicated where your data are located, you can do that now by highlighting the range in the worksheet. The next step of the process will define the table you want to create. Click on the box labeled **Layout** and the dialog box shown in Figure 3.21 appears.

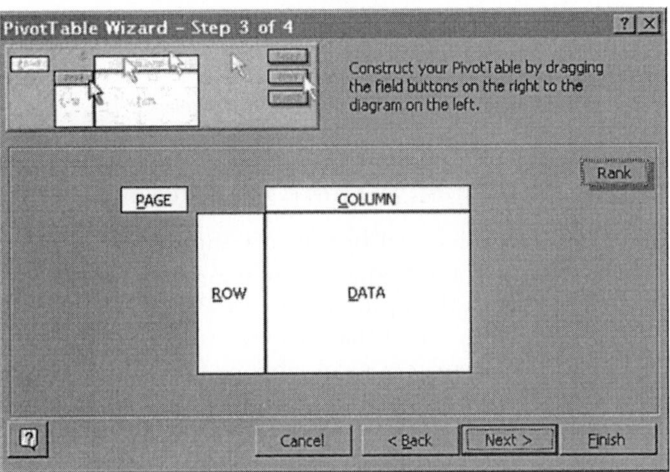

FIGURE 3.21 Creating the table

3. At the right of the dialog box, there are small rectangles called field buttons, which represent all of the variables you have highlighted. In this case, **Rank** is the only one. You create the table by dragging the variable names to the places you want them to appear. Since we want the ranks to appear as rows in the table, click on the **Rank** box and drag it to the area marked **ROW,** as indicated at the top of the dialog box. To get the frequencies, you must tell the

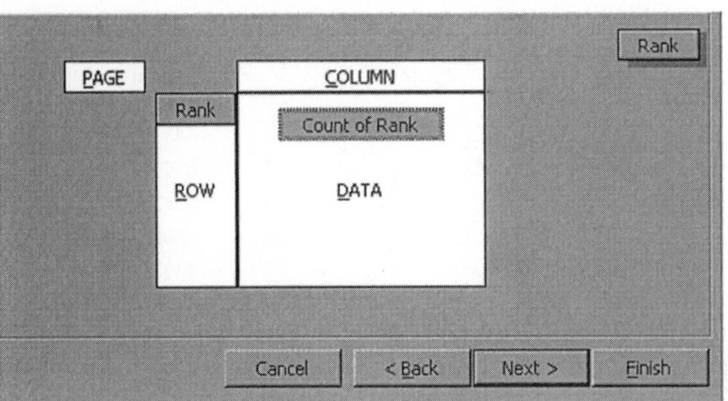

FIGURE 3.22 Defining the table

Pivot Wizard how to process the data. To do this, drag the field button for **Rank** into the area of the dialog box marked **DATA.** The dialog box should now look like the one in Figure 3.22.

The default operation in a Pivot Table is to provide a count (frequency) of each value. If you want to change this, or if you want to provide additional information in the table, you can double click on the field in the DATA area and select a different data operation such as Sum or Average. When you have finished this step, click **Next>** to continue.

4. The last step of the process is to tell Excel where you want the Pivot Table to appear. You can have it appear in the current worksheet or on a new worksheet. To have it appear in the current sheet, select the **Existing worksheet** radio button and then click on the cell in the worksheet where you want the left corner of the table to appear. Click **Next>** and the pivot table shown in Figure 3.23 will appear in the worksheet location you indicated.

    If you want to change the pivot table so that it looks better, you can click on the cell and type in exactly what you want to appear. For example, if you want the ranks to appear as Associate Professor, Assistant Professor, etc., simply edit those cells in the table.

Count of Rank	
Rank	Total
ASSO	67
ASST	77
INST	8
PROF	55
Grand Total	207

FIGURE 3.23
Finished pivot table

Note: Make sure the **Tools** *menu contains the* **Data Analysis** *option. If not, you may have to run the* **MS Office Setup** *program to include the* **Analysis ToolPak** *and then execute the* **Tools| Add-Ins** *command.*

It is possible to change other features of the table by double clicking on the cell in the table with the field label and clicking on the **Advanced** button. This will allow you to change the order of the categories and several other options.

Once you have the frequency table, you can create a bar chart, pie chart, or Pareto diagram as explained previously.

3.6.6 Creating Histograms in Excel

Quantitative data are easier to process using Excel because there are built-in functions for many of the statistical tools. Selecting **Data Analysis** from the **Tools** menu accesses these functions, as shown in Figure 3.24. Macros for other types of analyses are available on the disk that comes with this book.

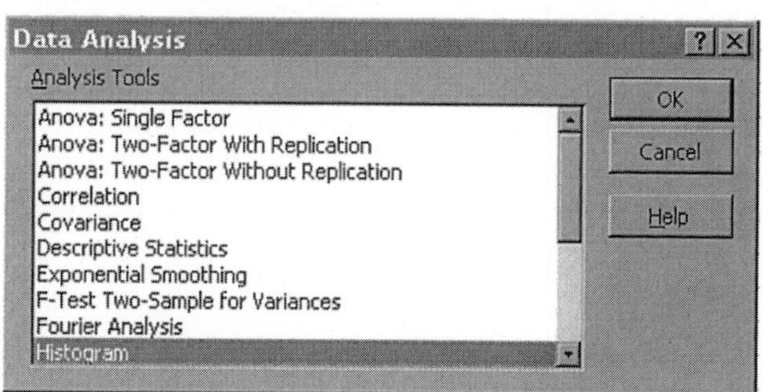

FIGURE 3.24 Data Analysis dialog box

The basics of creating a histogram in Excel are quite simple. Suppose you want to create a histogram for the data on years of service for Aluacha Balaclava College. Figure 3.20 shows the data as part of an Excel file.

To produce a basic histogram, simply follow these steps:

1. From the Data Analysis dialog box, select Histogram and click **OK.** The **Histogram** dialog box will open.
2. Position the cursor in the **Input Range** text box and highlight the range that contains the data, **B1:B208.**

3. Click the check box for **Labels** since the range contains the variable name.
4. Excel calls the class intervals for continuous data Bins. Leave the Bin text box empty this time and let Excel pick the class intervals.
5. Click the radio button for **Output Range,** position the cursor in the text box, and click on the cell where you want the top left corner of the output to appear.
6. Finally, click the check box for **Chart Output.** The completed dialog box is shown in Figure 3.25.
7. Click **OK** and the output will appear as shown in Figure 3.26.

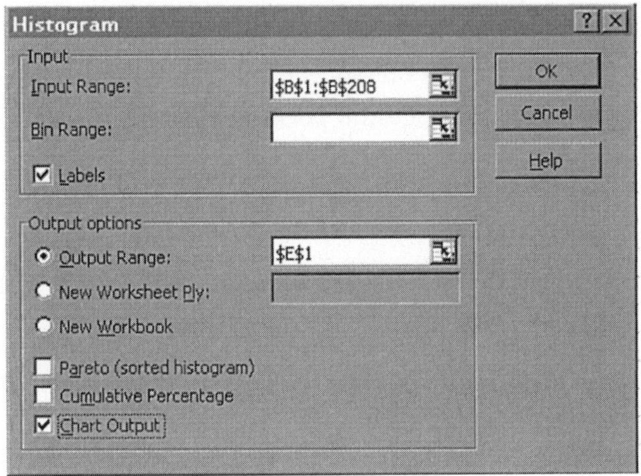

FIGURE 3.25 Completed histogram dialog box

Bin	Frequency
0	15
2.928571	19
5.857143	19
8.785714	34
11.71429	16
14.64286	14
17.57143	13
20.5	17
23.42857	33
26.35714	20
29.28571	4
32.21429	2
35.14286	0
38.07143	0
More	1

FIGURE 3.26 Output from histogram tool

Clearly this is not the output you hoped for, but it is a starting point. There are two basic problems with this output. First, Excel used rules very similar to the ones you learned in this chapter for creating the class intervals or Bins. As a result, the numbers are not particularly friendly. The number that shows in each bin is the *upper* boundary for that class interval. A bin represents all of the data values that are greater than the previous bin number, up to and including the current bin number. That is, the number 2.928571 represents all of the data greater than 0 and less than or equal to 2.928571 ($0 < x \leq 2.928571$). The first class is all data values that are less than or equal to zero, and the last is all data values greater than 38.07143.

The second problem is with the format of the graph. No labels can be seen on the axis, the graph is squashed, and the titles and axis labels are not very useful. This can be fixed by clicking on the parts of the chart that you do not like and editing them. A set of steps for editing the chart in Figure 3.26 follows:

- Click on the chart to select it. Handles appear on the corners and sides.
- Click on the bottom handle and drag it down to increase the height of the chart, as shown in Figure 3.27. You see that the axis labels become visible.

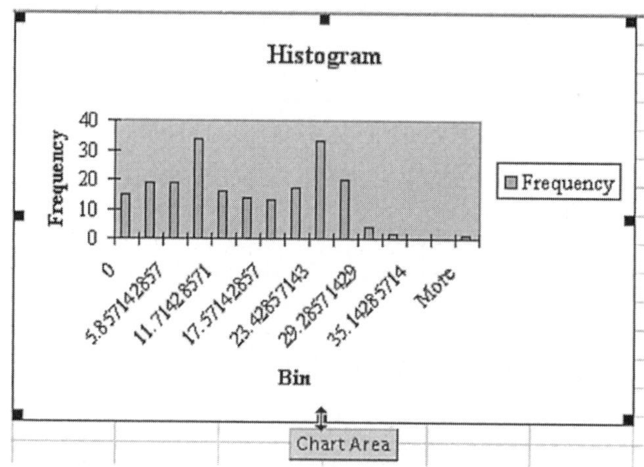

FIGURE 3.27 Changing the size of the chart

To change any portion of the chart, you simply double click on it and the appropriate dialog box opens. There are many changes that can be made to the chart. We will focus on a few that will produce an acceptable finished product.

The major problems with the chart are the way the x axis is labeled, the titles, and the gaps between the bars. We will fix some of these easily by making some changes to the bins in the frequency table. The frequency table and the chart are *linked* so that making changes to the table will update the chart.

- To get a little more room for the chart, click on the **Legend** box and press the Delete key to remove it.
- Since the original data are integers, it really does not make sense to have the classes use six decimal places. Highlight the range in the worksheet that contains the frequency table and select **Cells** from the **Format** menu. The Format Cells dialog box opens. The box has six tabs: Number, Alignment, Font, Border, Patterns, and Protection. Click on the tab for **Number** and select **Number** from the list under **Category.** In the text box for **Decimal places:** type 0, because you want integers. The dialog box is shown in Figure 3.28. Click **OK** to continue. The bins will change to integer values and you will see the changes on the chart.

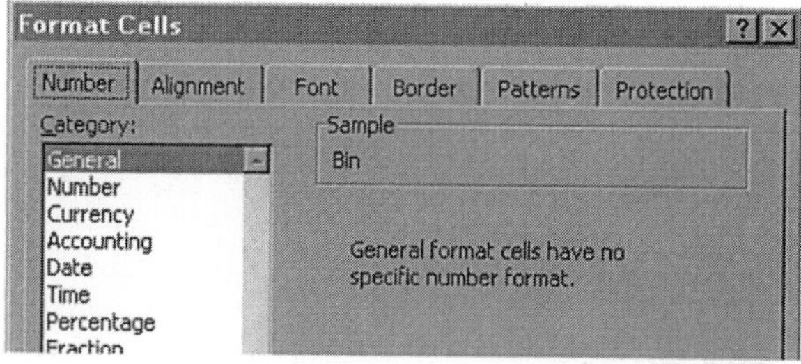

FIGURE 3.28 Format Cells dialog box

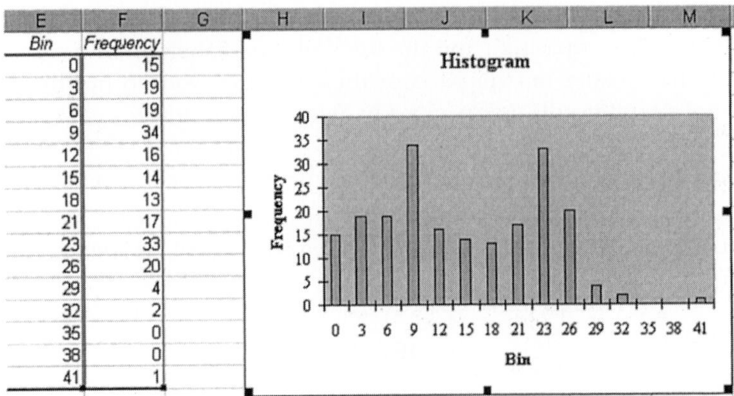

Bin	Frequency
0	15
3	19
6	19
9	34
12	16
15	14
18	13
21	17
23	33
26	20
29	4
32	2
35	0
38	0
41	1

FIGURE 3.29 Edited bins and chart

When you have an extreme outlier in the data, Excel will include it in that last interval regardless of the width of the other intervals.

- Before we proceed, we really need to change the last bin label. Excel automatically labels the bin More, but we know it should be a number. From the updated frequency table, you can see that the class width is 3, so the last number in the bin column should be 38 + 3 = 41. Click on the cell that contains the word "More" and change it to 41. The worksheet should look like the one in Figure 3.29.

  Notice that this changed the orientation of the text on the axis. That happened because the word "More" was too long to fit horizontally. If this change had not occurred, you could have changed the orientation of the text as follows:

- Move the cursor to the chart and click on the *x* axis labels. The **ToolTips** box will say "Category Axis" when your cursor is in the right location. The Format Axis dialog box will open. The box has five tabs: Patterns, Scale, Font, Number, and Alignment. To change the orientation of the text on the axis, click on the **Alignment** tab. Click on the red diamond to orient the text horizontally.

Note: *Clicking and dragging the red diamond will change the orientation of the text to any angle you want.*

We still need to change the title and axis labels and to remove the gaps between the bars.

- To change any title or label, simply click on the title and type the new text.
- To remove the gaps, double click on any of the histogram bars and the **Format Data Series** dialog box will open. This box allows you to change the way the bars in the histogram look. For example, from the Patterns box you can change the color of the bars or from the Data Labels box you can have the frequency for each bar print above the box. To change the spacing between the bars, click on the **Option** tab, and in the text box for **Gap width,** type 0 as shown in Figure 3.30.

Click **OK**, and the chart should look like the one in Figure 3.31.

Even though Excel defines the bin numbers as the endpoints of the class intervals, it prints them in the center of the histogram bars. There is no way to

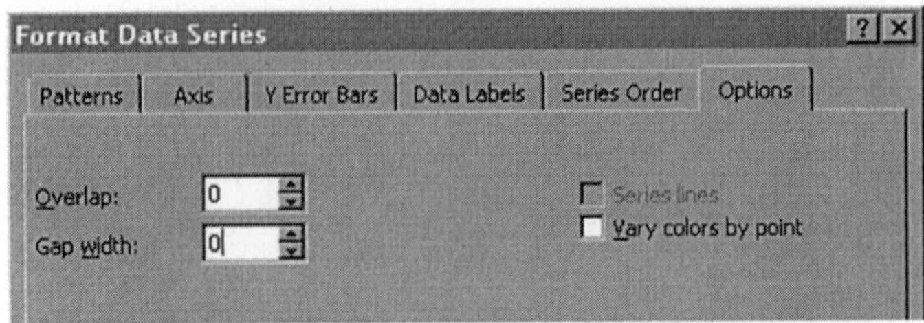

FIGURE 3.30 Changing the gap width

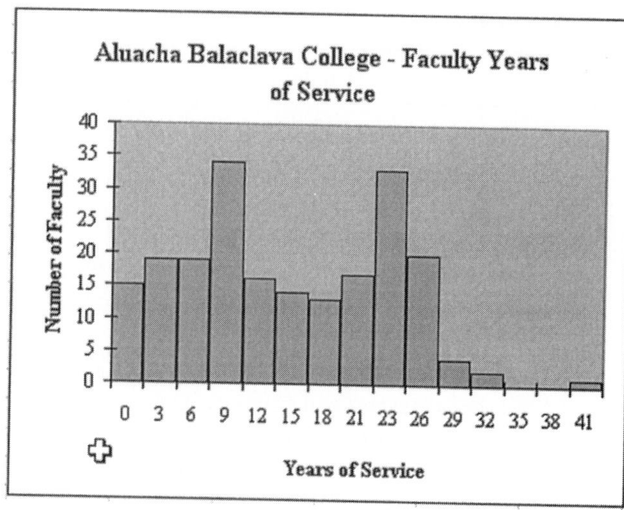

FIGURE 3.31 Completed histogram

change this. It is one of the problems that arise because Excel is not a statistical package.

There are many other changes that you can make to a chart in Excel. Experiment with them and see what improvements you can make to the histogram.

CHAPTER 3 SUMMARY

Raw data are nothing more than a list of words or numbers. The purpose of descriptive statistics is to turn *data* into *information.* One way to do this is by summarizing the data with a frequency distribution and then using a graphical display that is appropriate for the type of data. Qualitative data can be displayed using *bar charts* or *pie charts,* whereas quantitative data are usually displayed using *histograms* or *dotplots.*

Graphical displays of data can be used to describe data in terms of *center, shape,* and *variability.* They can also be used to compare different data sets.

Although it is possible to create graphs by hand, using a computer software package such as Minitab or Excel greatly enhances the quality of the finished product. It is important, however, to know how each graphical technique works so that you can use the software intelligently and make useful (and not just flashy) graphs.

Key Terms

Term	Definition	Page reference
Bar chart	A **bar chart** is a graph that represents the frequency or relative frequency from a frequency table in the form of a rectangle or bar.	68
Center	The **center** of a distribution tells where on the number line the data are centered or concentrated.	82
Cumulative relative frequency	The **cumulative relative frequency** of a class is the sum of the relative frequencies of all classes at or below that class represented as a portion of the total number of observations. It can be expressed as a fraction, decimal, or percentage.	56
Dotplot	A **dotplot** is a graph used for small data sets, in which each observation is plotted as a point on a single, horizontal axis.	78

(continued)

Key Terms (*Continued*)

Term	Definition	Page reference
Frequency table	A **frequency table** or frequency distribution is a table containing each category, value, or class of values that a variable might have and the number of times that each one occurs in the data.	52
Histogram	A **histogram** is very similar to a bar chart, but since numbers are naturally ordered, the x axis of the graph must be scaled to reflect this.	74
Pareto diagram	A **Pareto diagram** is a bar chart in which the categories are plotted in order of decreasing relative frequency. The cumulative relative frequency of the categories is plotted on the same graph.	71
Pie chart	A **pie chart** is a graph in which a circle is used to represent the whole, and each "slice" is used to represent one of the categories. The size of the slice is proportional to the relative frequency of the category.	73
Relative frequency	The **relative frequency** of a classification is the number of times an observation falls into that classification represented as a portion of the total number of observations. It can be expressed as a *fraction, decimal*, or *percentage*.	53
Shape	The **shape** of a distribution describes how the data are spread out around the center with respect to symmetry or skewness.	82
Skewed	When the data are not evenly spread out on either side of the center then we refer to the distribution as being **skewed.**	83
Symmetric	When data are evenly spread out on both sides of the center we describe the distribution of the data as **symmetric.**	83
Variability	The **variability** of a distribution describes how the data are spread out around the center with respect to the magnitude of the variation.	82

CHAPTER 3 EXERCISES

Learning It!

3.26 In a study on housing costs in major international cities, data were collected on the construction cost ($ per square meter) for housing in 23 capital cities. Here are the data:

Jakarta	65	Kingston	157	London	560
Dar Es Salaam	67	Bogota	171	Toronto	608
Karachi	87	Johannesburg	192	Seoul	617
Beijing	90	Rio de Janeiro	214	Hong Kong	641
New Delhi	94	Melbourne	383	Singapore	749
Istanbul	110	Algiers	500	Paris	990
Manila	148	Washington, D.C.	500	Tokyo	2,604
Bangkok	156	Madrid	510		

(a) What kind of graphical display is appropriate for these data? Why?

(b) Create a dotplot of the data.

(c) Use the data to describe housing construction costs for these cities.

(d) Do any of the data values appear to be unusual? If so, which one(s)?

3.27 In an ongoing study of trends in higher education, an article in *Dartmouth Life* (September 15, 1996) reported on the number of students from different classes who enrolled in various majors as freshmen. The data for the class of 1986 are:

Major	1986
Anthropology	10
Art History	28
Asia	11
Biology	31
Chemistry	28
Classics	2
Comparative Literature	5
Drama	13
Earth Science	8
Economics	90
English	156
French	23
Geography	23
Government	147
History	102
Mathematics	35
Music	10
Philosophy	21
Physics	13
Psychology	70
Religion	22
Sociology	17

(a) Create a bar chart for these data.

(b) What percentage of the students majored in the sciences?

(c) What order did you pick for the categories on the *x* axis? Why did you choose this order? Can you think of any other orders that might also be appropriate? If so, what are they?

3.28 The *Chronicle of Higher Education* (June 2000) reported on the distribution of college and university faculty by rank. The data are summarized here:

Academic rank	Relative frequency (%)
Professor	28.9
Associate Professor	22.7
Assistant Professor	23.5
Instructor	12.1
Lecturer	2.3
No Rank	1.0

(a) Create a bar chart for these data.

(b) What do the data tell you about the distribution of faculty over the various ranks?

3.29 A report by the Bureau of Labor Statistics says that in 1998, the last year for which such data are available, 709 homicides occurred while people were on the job. These homicides were classified by the type of job that the victim had, as follows:

Job	People killed on job
Managerial and professional	131
Sales	239
Service industry	145
Drivers/factory workers	129
Other	65

(a) Create a bar chart for these data.

(b) Describe any interesting features of the data.

3.30 The publishing industry has long felt that the field of food magazines is in a recession. They looked at paid circulations for all of the magazines in the field and obtained the following data:

Magazine	Paid circulations
Bon Appetit	1,294,945
Cooking Light	1,119,811
Gourmet	906,299
Food & Wine	734,831
Eating Well	648,697
*Cook's Illustrated**	160,000
*Fine Cooking**	100,000
*Saveur**	100,000

* Publishers' current estimates.

(a) Create a bar chart for the data.

(b) Does one of the magazines account for a majority of the paid circulations in food magazines? If so, which one?

(c) Do you think that *Bon Appetit, Food & Wine,* and *Gourmet* deserve their reputation as the Big Three? Why or why not?

3.31 As part of a survey conducted by the Bureau of Transportation in 1996, drivers were asked questions about the age of the vehicle that they normally drive. The survey recorded the year that the vehicle was manufactured. Data for 50 drivers surveyed are:

1955	1983	1989	1991	1993
1967	1984	1989	1992	1994
1970	1984	1989	1993	1994
1974	1984	1989	1993	1994
1977	1986	1990	1993	1994
1978	1988	1990	1993	1994
1978	1988	1990	1993	1995
1979	1989	1990	1993	1995
1981	1989	1991	1993	1995
1982	1989	1991	1993	1995

(a) Create a histogram for these data.

(b) Use the histogram to describe the distribution of the age of vehicles driven by the people in the sample.

(c) These data are really integer data. Why would a histogram using each year as a separate class not work for these data?

3.32 In addition to information about vehicles, the Personal Transportation Survey conducted by the Bureau of Transportation also asked questions about households, in particular, the number of people who lived in the household. The data for 45 random respondents are:

1	2	2	3	4
1	2	2	3	4
1	2	2	3	4
1	2	2	3	4
1	2	2	3	4
1	2	3	4	4
2	2	3	4	4
2	2	3	4	5
2	2	3	4	5

(a) Create a relative frequency histogram for the data.

(b) What percentage of the households surveyed had three or more people in them?

(c) What percentage of the households had fewer than four people?

3.33 A manufacturer of breakfast cereals packs the cereal in 15-ounce boxes. Periodic quality checks must be made to ensure that the boxes are being filled adequately. A random sample of 35 boxes of the cereal are selected and weighed. The data are

14.91	15.23	15.34	15.40	15.48	15.59	15.62
14.96	15.24	15.34	15.42	15.49	15.60	15.62
15.11	15.28	15.36	15.45	15.50	15.60	15.63
15.21	15.30	15.38	15.46	15.52	15.61	15.64
15.22	15.30	15.39	15.48	15.58	15.61	15.67

(a) Create a relative frequency histogram for the cereal box weights.

(b) Use the histogram to describe the distribution of cereal weights.

3.34 A large company buys computer storage media (diskettes) from one supplier. The company wants to know something about how long the diskettes last before they show signs of wear, so it collects data (in hours) for 20 diskettes from different boxes:

486	494	502	508
490	496	504	510
491	498	505	514
491	498	506	515
494	498	507	517

(a) Create a dotplot for the data.

(b) Use the dotplot to describe the distribution of lifetimes for the 20 diskettes.

3.35 A survey of 40 households asked the head of the household how much was spent on clothing ($) during the previous 3 months. The data are

0.00	0.00	0.00	35.00	210.00
0.00	0.00	0.00	36.75	221.00
0.00	0.00	0.00	60.89	224.00
0.00	0.00	0.00	64.66	303.33
0.00	0.00	10.62	96.00	310.55
0.00	0.00	15.00	114.61	365.95
0.00	0.00	17.21	149.27	365.95
0.00	0.00	21.33	165.37	702.60

(a) Create a frequency table for the data.

(b) Use the frequency table to make a histogram of the data.

(c) Describe the distribution of the amount of money that a household spends on clothing in a 3-month period.

Thinking About It!

3.36 The problem of piracy has long been a concern for the computer software industry. Each year, the amount of revenue lost from piracy is staggering. Since the Internet has become more developed, the problems have become even more severe. In 1994 piracy losses were $15.2 billion. A study showed that the losses were distributed over the world as follows:

Region	% of total
Europe	39
Asia	29
Africa/Middle East	2
Latin America	9
North America	21

SOURCE: *The Economist*, July 27, 1996.

(a) Create a bar chart for these data.

(b) Create a pie chart for these data.

(c) Which chart do you think does a better job of displaying the data and what they mean? Why?

3.37 Consumers are increasingly complaining that it is not worth the effort to clip coupons any more. One of the reasons they cite for this is that the life of the coupons is decreasing and it takes more time to sort and discard expired coupons. In an effort to substantiate these claims a consumer group looked at samples of 500 coupons from both 1995 and 1996. The data are summarized as follows:

	Number of coupons	
Coupon life	**1995**	**1996**
Less than 1 month	28	123
1–4 months	88	140
5–8 months	204	122
9–12 months	141	88
More than 1 year	39	27

(a) Create bar charts for 1995 and 1996.

(b) Compare and describe the data for the two years. Do you think that there has been a change in coupon life? Why or why not?

3.38 The problem of workplace violence is growing. A survey of 600 full-time American workers who were the victims of violence while working reports the following:

Workplace violence survey

Type of violence	% Who reported
Harassment	19
Threat of physical harm	7
Physical attack	3

	Type of violence (%)		
Major effect on worker	**Harassment**	**Threat**	**Physical**
Psychologically	49	53	49
Disrupted work life	34	25	25
Physically injured or sick	13	9	17
No negative effect	4	13	9

Create graphical displays of these data. Use any techniques you feel are appropriate to convey the information in the data.

3.39 The article that looked at majors of students at Dartmouth College also reported data for the classes of 1991 and 1996:

Major	1991	1996
Anthropology	19	17
Art History	20	15
Asia	15	22
Biology	44	108
Chemistry	15	55
Classics	1	8
Comparative Literature	6	6
Drama	8	5
Earth Science	15	7
Economics	66	93
English	143	92
French	15	19
Geography	28	28
Government	172	142
History	125	115

(continued)

Major	1991	1996
Mathematics	23	14
Music	3	11
Philosophy	28	25
Physics	10	16
Psychology	74	87
Religion	31	8
Sociology	26	15

(a) Create bar charts for the 1991 and 1996 data. Design the charts so that you will be able to compare the two classes and also compare them to the data for the class of 1986.

(b) Did the fact that you needed to make comparisons change the way you might have arranged the categories? Why or why not?

(c) Did the fact that you needed to make comparisons affect the way you scaled the *y* axis?

(d) Do you think that there is any basis for the claim that there has been an increase in the number of students who are interested in the sciences? Why or why not?

(e) Make comparative bar charts for only those majors that are sciences. Do you think that these charts make trends in the sciences easier to see? Why or why not?

(f) Compare the distribution of majors in general for each of the classes. Do you see any other changes or trends?

3.40 The company looking at the life of its diskettes, decides to buy some diskettes from a different vendor and do a comparative test. The company selects 45 diskettes from each supplier and distributes them to a random sample of employees. The employees are asked to use the diskettes as they normally would, but to check them regularly for signs of wear using a disk-checking utility. They are to record how long (in hours) their disk lasts before it exhibits signs of wear. The data, for each supplier, are: *Datafile: DISKS.XXX*

Supplier A					Supplier B				
474	492	498	504	511	487	492	495	497	499
486	492	500	505	511	488	492	495	497	499
489	494	501	506	512	489	492	495	497	499
490	494	501	507	513	489	492	495	497	501
490	494	501	508	514	489	493	495	498	502
490	495	502	508	515	491	493	496	498	503
491	496	502	509	517	491	494	496	498	503
491	498	504	509	519	491	494	496	498	505
491	498	504	510	528	492	494	496	499	506

(a) Create histograms for the lifetimes of diskettes from each supplier. Be sure to choose your scales so that you can make meaningful comparisons.

(b) Describe the distribution of diskette lifetimes for each supplier.

(c) Compare the lifetimes for the diskettes from supplier B to those from the company's current supplier, supplier A. Which diskettes would you recommend the company use? Why?

(d) Write a memo to your boss with your recommendations.

3.41 The most recent data from the Department of Justice (June 1995) gives a state by state report on the number of people incarcerated per 100,000 people in the population. The data are shown in the table: *Datafile: PRISON.XXX*

State	# Incarcerated per 100,000	State	# Incarcerated per 100,000
District of Columbia	1151	Arizona	501
Delaware	890	Connecticut	481
Texas	643	Oklahoma	479
South Carolina	512	Alabama	468
Alaska	505	Florida	444

(continued)

State	# Incarcerated per 100,000	State	# Incarcerated per 100,000
Georgia	439	Hawaii	279
Nevada	431	Oregon	275
Maryland	424	Indiana	267
Michigan	424	Tennessee	260
Louisiana	399	Wyoming	239
California	398	Iowa	235
Ohio	390	Idaho	231
New York	382	New Mexico	229
North Carolina	356	Wisconsin	217
Kentucky	354	West Virginia	211
Virginia	354	Washington	197
Missouri	352	Montana	191
Mississippi	346	New Hampshire	183
Kansas	332	Utah	178
Illinois	329	Massachusetts	174
South Dakota	328	Nebraska	173
Arkansas	326	Vermont	173
Pennsylvania	326	Minnesota	139
Rhode Island	310	Maine	117
New Jersey	294	North Dakota	107
Colorado	289		

(a) Create a histogram for the data.

(b) Describe the number of people incarcerated (per 100,000) in the United States.

(c) Do you think that the observation from the District of Columbia has an effect on the way your histogram turned out? If so, what is it?

(d) Recreate the histogram without the data from the District of Columbia.

(e) Use the new histogram to describe the number of people incarcerated (per 100,000) in the United States.

(f) Has your description changed from that of part (b)? If so, what is different?

Requires Exercise 3.18

3.42 The cable company that is looking at its ratings after changing channel selection wonders whether there has been a change in customer feelings about the service. The company looks at the responses from a survey done 6 months prior to the change and finds the following data:

2	3	3	4	5
2	3	3	4	6
2	3	3	4	6
2	3	3	4	6
2	3	4	5	6
2	3	4	5	7
3	3	4	5	8

(a) Create a graphical display for the ratings data before the service changes were made.

(b) Do you think that the company can conclude that the ratings have improved? Why or why not?

3.43 It has been a widely held belief that the switch to participative management would increase employee "buy-in" to the company. One of the benefits that should be realized is a reduction in the number of sick days that employees use. A company that has made the switch in some departments wonders whether this has been true. The company decides to sample 25 employees from each of two manufacturing departments. The first has been using participative management for almost 2 years and the second is still using a traditional management style. The data on the number of sick days used by each employee in the past 12 months are

Participative Management					Traditional				
1	3	5	5	6	0	5	6	7	9
1	4	5	6	7	3	5	7	7	9
2	4	5	6	8	4	6	7	7	10
2	4	5	6	8	4	6	7	8	11
3	4	5	6	8	5	6	7	8	11

(a) Create a graphical display for each of the samples.

(b) Use the graphical display to describe the distribution of sick days for each department.

(c) Based on the data, do you think there is a difference in the number of sick days taken by each group? Why or why not?

(d) Do you think, on the basis of these data, that the company can conclude that participative management reduces the number of sick days taken by employees? Why or why not?

(e) Write a memo to management summarizing your analysis and make recommendations for improving the study.

Doing It!

3.44 A large manufacturer of paper goods keeps track of consumer complaints for its facial tissue product line. The company receives these complaints through a toll-free number that appears on the product. The data taken consist of a transcription of the actual complaint language and a classification of the complaint into a specific category. When a complaint is received, the company generally asks for additional information about the specific package. The information is then used to relate the complaints to manufacturing data so that in the future similar problems can be prevented. The categories and subcategories used for classifying complaints are given here:

Datafile: *COMPLAIN.XXX*

Category	Subcategory
Dispensing	Sheets tear on removal
	Reach in/fallback
Foreign material	Lint/dust
	Other
Odor	
Miscounts	
Packaging	Defective
	Misleading
	Damaged
	Other

For example, if a consumer calls the company and says, "The box of tissues I bought was not full," the customer service representative classifies this as a miscount. Sometimes complaints can be tricky to classify. If a customer calls, for example, after a product change and says, "I eat tissues and I prefer the taste of the old product," into what category should this complaint be placed?

The company is looking at data for 3 different years. It compiles data for five different variables:

Variable name	Description
Month	Month in which complaint occurred
Year	Year of the complaint
Category	Category of complaint
Subcategory	Subcategory of complaint
Number	Number of complaints of the particular category and subcategory in the time period

A portion of the data file is shown here:

Month	Year	Category	Subcategory	Number
JANUARY	1996	DISPENSING	FALLBACK	79
JANUARY	1996	DISPENSING	SHEETS_TEAR	114
JANUARY	1996	FOREIGN MATL.	LINT/DUST	54
JANUARY	1996	FOREIGN MATL.	OTHER	5
JANUARY	1996	MISCOUNTS	MISCOUNTS	41
JANUARY	1996	ODOR	ODOR	10
JANUARY	1996	PACKAGING	ADVERTISING	0

(a) Create a bar chart for customer complaints by subcategory for January 1996. What subcategory has the largest number of complaints? Does any subcategory constitute a majority?

(b) Create similar charts for January 1997 and January 1998. Compare the 3 months. Do you notice any similarities or differences?

(c) Create bar charts for the complaint categories for the same 3 months. Describe and compare the bar charts.

(d) Look at the data for all of 1996. Create a bar chart that displays the total number of complaints by month. Do you notice any trends or interesting features? Does any month or season have considerably more or less complaints than others? Can you offer any explanation for this?

(e) Create similar bar charts of total complaints for 1997 and 1998. Compare these years to 1996 and to each other. Are they similar? Would you expect them to be? Why or why not?

(f) Take the bar chart that you made for January 1996 and modify it so that it is a Pareto chart. Do the same thing for January 1997 and January 1998. As manager of the company, where would you concentrate your resources to eliminate complaints? Why?

(g) Look at the data for July 1996 and make bar charts for both complaint category and complaint subcategory. Compare July 1997 to January 1998. How are they similar? How are they different?

(h) Look at the same data as in part (g), but this time create pie charts. Which chart does a better job at conveying information about customer complaints? Why?

(i) Look at the data by category for each year and make pie charts comparable to the bar charts from parts (d) and (e). Have there been any changes over the 3-year period in the type and number of complaints? If so, what are they?

(j) The management of this company asks for your assessment of the complaint data. In particular, the managers would like to know where their biggest problems are and what the trends seem to be over the past 3 years.

(k) Write a memo to the company management summarizing your analysis. Include your answers to parts (a)–(j) as appendix material.

Datafile: FACULTY.XXX

3.45 The Provost at Aluacha Balaclava College would like to look at the data she has collected in a different way. She has collected data on salary, rank, school, gender, and tenure. A sample of the data is shown here:

Salary ($)	Years of service	Rank	Schools	Gender (M/F)	Tenure (Y/N)
53,316	22	ASST	BUSINESS	F	Y
64,375	11	PROF	BUSINESS	M	Y
63,501	7	ASSO	BUSINESS	M	Y
59,426	6	ASSO	BUSINESS	M	N
49,058	20	ASSO	BUSINESS	M	Y
94,969	4	PROF	BUSINESS	M	N
54,762	21	ASST	BUSINESS	M	Y
55,516	9	ASSO	BUSINESS	M	Y

(a) Create histograms of salary for each rank separately.

(b) Compare the distribution of salaries for the four ranks.

(c) Create histograms of salary for each school separately.

(d) Compare the distributions of salary for the different schools.

(e) Create separate histograms of salary by gender and for tenured/untenured faculty and compare them.

(f) Write a memo to the Provost summarizing your observations. Include your answers to parts (a)–(e) as appendix material to your report.

CHAPTER 4

NUMERICAL DESCRIPTORS OF DATA

THE GOLF BALL COMPANY

A company that manufactures golf balls is preparing for an advertising campaign. The company wants to compare the ball that it manufactures to a competitor's product to see how they differ. In preparation for the study, sample data are collected on a number of different variables for the two types of balls and you are asked to summarize the data and report on what you find. A portion of the data is shown below:

Ball number	Model number	S1	S2	S3	Weight (g)	Dimple width (mm)	Dimple depth (mm)	Head	Temperature (°F)	Carry (yd)	Total distance (yd)	Date	Time
1	M1	81	81	82	45.3	0.1450	0.0110	686	77	257	270	8/20	8:15
2	M1	83	83	84	45.2	0.1510	0.0111	688	77	255	267	8/20	8:15
3	M1	81	82	84	45.2	0.1450	0.0105	687	77	256	267	8/20	8:15
4	M1	81	81	83	45.3	0.1440	0.0117	688	77	255	271	8/20	8:15
5	M1	83	81	82	45.5	0.1460	0.0108	687	77	255	268	8/20	8:15
6	M1	83	83	82	45.3	0.1560	0.0111	687	77	256	267	8/20	8:15
7	M1	81	81	82	45.2	0.1495	0.0111	687	77	255	264	8/20	8:15
8	M1	83	81	82	45.1	0.1505	0.0110	690	78	258	269	8/20	8:15

Business Dilemma...

The company wants to know things like how far most of the balls go when they are hit, how much variation there is in the distance, and what percentage of the balls go beyond a certain distance. You need to figure out which numerical measures will provide the company with the most information.

4.1 CHAPTER OBJECTIVES

Remember that when you looked at different graphical techniques for displaying numerical data you were interested in three characteristics: center, spread or dispersion, and shape. In this chapter we look at different numerical measures that can be used to describe the same features of the data. The chapter covers the following material:

- Numerical measures of center: the mean, the median, and the mode
- Numerical measures of variability: the range and the standard deviation
- Describing a set of data: the empirical rule and boxplots
- Measures of relative standing: percentiles and percentile rank
- Identifying outliers: z-scores and boxplots

4.2 DESCRIBING DATA NUMERICALLY

Although we may say that a picture is worth a thousand words, it is useful to find numerical quantities to describe the data as well. You may wonder why you need to do this, when the graphs let you *see* the data. There are two reasons. First, while you can certainly see the data using histograms and bar charts, it is difficult to *talk* or *write* about pictures. We often need other references to describe the data. A second reason for using numerical descriptors is that we may want to make inferences based on the sample data. To make statistical inferences you need to use *numerical measures.*

When you collect data you may have either a *population* or a *sample* from the population. Numerical measures calculated from the data are known as either **statistics** or **parameters.**

> A ***statistic*** is a numerical descriptor that is calculated from sample data and is used to describe the sample. Statistics are usually represented by Roman letters.

> A ***parameter*** is a numerical descriptor that is used to describe a population. Parameters are usually represented by Greek letters.

Most of the time in statistics you will be working with sample data, but you may sometimes have the entire population available for study. We usually use Greek letters to denote parameters and Roman letters to describe statistics.

When you look at numerical descriptors for a set of data, you want to describe the same properties of the data that you described from the graphical displays. You will find, however, that there are several different statistics that you can use to describe each property and that the choice of the statistic is dependent on the problem you are trying to solve.

4.3 MEASURES OF CENTRAL TENDENCY

The golf ball company would like to know about values that represent a "typical" golf ball. The company would like to measure the *center* of its data. We will look at three different statistics that measure central tendency: the *sample mean*, the *median*, and the *mode*.

4.3.1 The Arithmetic Mean

You are probably already familiar with the most common measure of center, the **sample mean.** The mean, or average, as it is commonly known, is calculated by adding all of the data values in the sample and then dividing by the number of values. The symbol for the sample mean is $\overline{X}$ (this is read as "X bar").

$$\overline{X} = \frac{\text{Sum of all the values in the sample}}{\text{Total number of observations}}$$

> The ***sample mean*** is the center of balance of a set of data, and is found by adding up all of the data values and dividing by the number of observations.

The population parameter that corresponds to the sample mean is the **population mean,** μ (mu).

> The ***population mean*** is represented by the Greek letter μ (mu).

Using the Σ notation that you saw in Chapter 2, we can write the formula for the sample mean as:

SAMPLE MEAN

$$\overline{X} = \frac{\Sigma_{i=1}^{n} x_i}{n} \quad \text{or} \quad \frac{\Sigma x}{n}$$

Most of the time in statistics, it is understood that the sum is over the entire sample and so we can leave out the index on the summation sign.

When we talk about a variable or a statistic in general we use *capital* letters, such as X or $\overline{X}$. When we talk about a *specific value* of a variable we use *lowercase* letters such as x. For example, we write, "The sample mean, $\overline{X}$, is calculated by . . . ," or "The third value in the sample is $x = 27.2$."

EXAMPLE 4.1 **The Mail-Order Company**

Calculating the Sample Mean

Understand the Problem

A mail-order company wants some information about the daily demand for a product that has been heavily advertised. The company wants a measure of what it might typically expect the demand to be. The company looks at the number of orders for a 10-day period and obtains the following data:

Demand	29	28	29	31	30	31	27	29	30	32

Collect and Analyze the Data

Since it is interested in a *typical* value for the demand, the company decides to calculate the sample mean, $\overline{X}$:

$$\overline{X} = \frac{29 + 28 + 29 + 31 + 30 + 31 + 27 + 29 + 30 + 32}{10} = \frac{296}{10} = 29.6 \text{ orders}$$ ■

What Does the Sample Mean Really Measure?

You want to use a dotplot for these data because the sample size is so small.

You can think of the sample mean as the *balance point* of the data. The value of $\overline{X}$ balances the higher values against the lower ones. It is easiest to see this when you look at the mean on a dotplot of the data. In Figure 4.1 you can see that the mean, 29.6, is in the center of the data and that the data are fairly evenly spread out on both sides of the mean.

Suppose that the data on the right (high) side are more spread out than those on the left. What will happen to the value of the sample mean? Remember, we said that the sample mean is the balance point of the data values. When there are a few data points on one side that are far from the bulk of the data (the bump), the sample mean moves toward them to maintain balance with the data on the other side. The next example shows what happens.

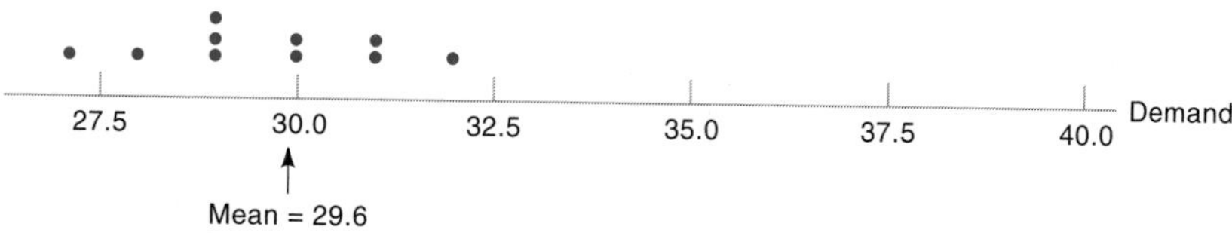

FIGURE 4.1 Dotplot of the data for the mail-order company

EXAMPLE 4.2 The Mail-Order Company

The Sample Mean as a Balance Point

Suppose that when the mail-order company looks at its data it finds the following:

Demand	40	28	29	31	30	31	27	29	39	36

Analyze the Data

Most of the data values are still around 30, but three of them are quite a bit higher. If you calculate the sample mean from the data,

$$\overline{X} = \frac{40 + 28 + 29 + 31 + 30 + 31 + 27 + 29 + 39 + 36}{10} = \frac{320}{10} = 32.0 \text{ items}$$

you see that the sample mean has changed from 29.6 to 32.0. This is not really where the bulk of the data are located. You can see that although the bulk of the data are still located around 30, the value of the sample mean has changed to 32.0 to balance the three data values at the high end.

27.5 30.0 32.5 35.0 37.5 40.0 Demand

Mean = 32.0

■

TRY IT NOW!

Restaurant Table Times *Calculating the Sample Mean*

A restaurant is trying to decide whether it has an adequate number of tables available. The restaurant owner would like some information on the amount of time a table is occupied by a customer. She collects data on the length of time a customer occupies a table for a random sample of ten customers:

Customer	1	2	3	4	5	6	7	8	9	10
Time (min)	59.3	58.6	62.7	65.4	59.0	67.3	62.8	68.1	59.4	63.7

Calculate the sample mean for the length of time a table is occupied.

EXAMPLE 4.3 The Golf Ball Problem

The Sample Mean

Understand the Problem

The company that manufactures golf balls is interested in describing the way the two different golf balls behave so that an advertising campaign can be planned. One way to describe the distance that the balls travel is to use the variable *Carry*, which measures the distance (yd) from the point where the ball was hit to the point where it hit the ground. Since the company is interested in *comparing* the two different designs, it will want to look at the designs separately. Using a computer package, you can calculate a set of descriptive statistics for the two different ball designs. From the output you find the following information:

	Type M1	**Type M2**
Sample size	36	36
Sum of data	9267	9244
Sample mean	257.4	256.8

Analyze the Data

It would appear from these values that there is not much difference in the way a "typical" ball behaves, but at this point that is just conjecture.

To better understand what the numbers really mean you can locate the values obtained for the mean on a histogram of the data. Perhaps the numbers and graphs together will provide more information.

ANS. 62.6 MIN

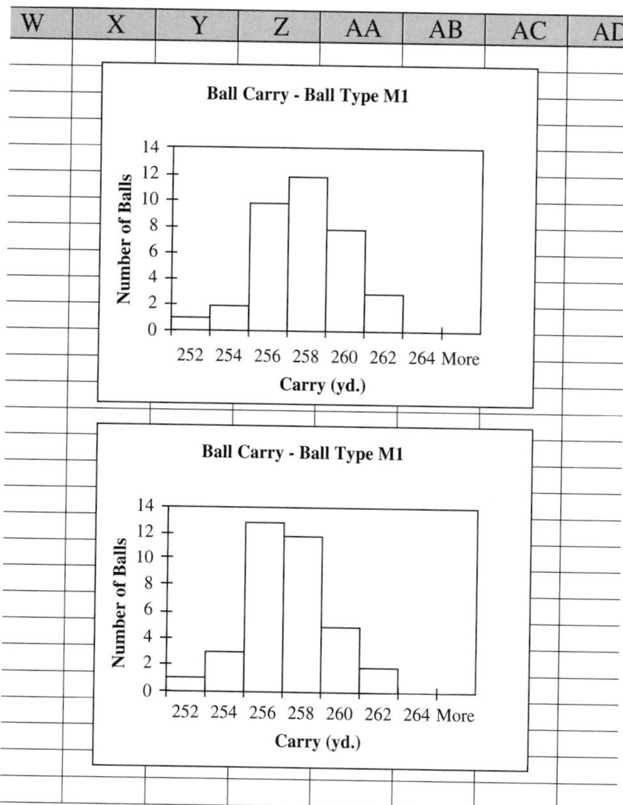

Draw Conclusions

When you locate the mean *Carry* for each ball type on the appropriate histogram you see that the mean appears to be a good measure of the center of the data and that it does not appear to be influenced by extreme values. However, you notice that the sample mean does not provide any information about the number of golf balls that went more than that number of yards or less than that number of yards. This could be useful information, and so it seems that you need another measure of center. ■

4.3.2 The Sample Median

Although the sample mean does measure the center of the data, its value might be influenced by unusually high or low values in the sample and might not present a true picture of the sample data. For this reason we often look at other measures of center in addition to the sample mean so that we will be able to see a better picture of the data.

Another measure of central tendency that is often used is the **sample median.** Although the sample mean is a measure of the center of balance of the data and is sensitive to the actual values, the sample median is a measure of the middle of the data set after it is sorted from lowest to highest.

The ***sample median*** is the value of the middle observation in an ordered set of data.

Finding the sample median requires sorting the data set first. Once this is done, the *sample median* is the value of the observation that is in the middle of the data. The exact location of the middle will depend on whether the number of observations in the sample is even or odd.

Make a dotplot of the data.

From the dotplot, do the data appear symmetric or skewed?

EXAMPLE 4.7 The Golf Ball Problem

Comparing the Mean and the Median

The golf ball company needs another number to describe a "typical" golf ball. Although the mean is a good statistic, you know you can give the company more information if you look at the median, too. You know that the value of the sample median will represent the distance that had half of the golf balls above it and half below it. This will tell the company a little more about how the golf balls behaved.

From the same computer output that gave us the mean, we learn that the median for the M1 balls is 257.5 yd and the median for the M2 balls is 257.0 yd. This information tells the company that 50% of the M1 balls in the sample went farther than 257.5 yards and that 50% of the M2 balls in the sample went farther than 257 yards.

Analyze the Data

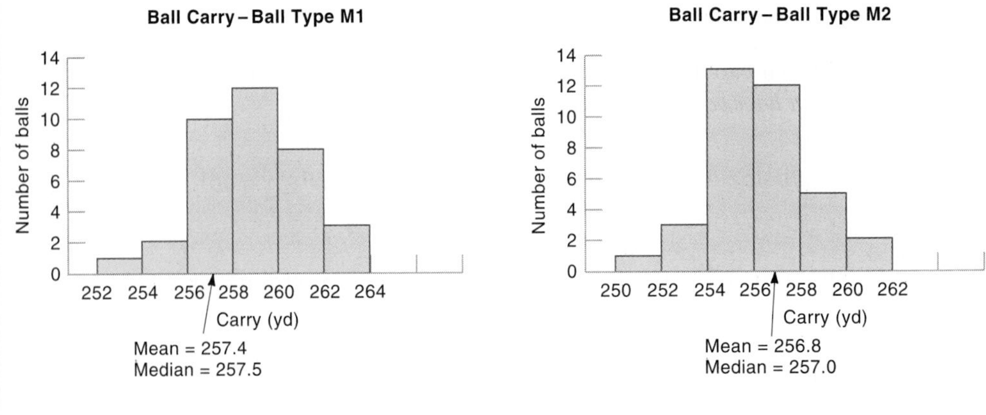

The medians are very close to the sample means. ■

ANS. MEAN = 13.8; MEDIAN = 14; SYMMETRIC

Discovery Exercise 4.1
THE TRIMMED MEAN

Part I. Investigating the Data

In a report to the administration of a large university, the Psychology Department states that the average class size is greater than the 35 students per class allowed by the university charter. The report indicates that the mean class size is 39.4.

No data are appended to the report, but you can obtain the current enrollments easily. The data you find are

3	14	22	26	42
3	15	23	27	45
5	15	24	28	45
9	17	24	28	190
11	21	25	36	193
13	22	26	38	193

(a) Do you think that the mean is a good measure of center for these data? Why or why not?

(b) By simply studying the data, what do you think a typical class size for the Psychology Department is?

(c) What is the median of the data? Is this close to what you thought?

(d) Compare the mean and the median. What does the comparison lead you to believe about the data?

(e) Display the data graphically. Do you still think the same thing?

(continued)

Part II. Solving the Problem

In the first part of this exercise you saw that neither the mean nor the median gives a very good measure of a typical class size. In addition, a comparison of the mean and the median leads you to believe that the data are skewed right! From the histogram you can see that this is not the case.

How can we measure the center of the data when we have extreme values that influence the statistics we usually rely on?

You really can't just discard the extremes without careful investigation of the causes. One way to do this is to use a measure other than the median that removes the effect of the extremes. The ***trimmed mean*** is a statistic that does this. The trimmed mean allows you to drop a specified percentage of the observations in the data set from ***each end***. By doing this you are not simply dropping outliers, but are looking at the center of the data, which may prove to be more reliable. Typically the trimmed mean is used with a percentage of 10%, but the percentage can be varied to suit the specific circumstances.

Computing the Trimmed Mean

To compute a 10% trimmed mean you must first determine how many values will be dropped from each end of the data set.

(a) Find 10% of the sample size.

(b) Do you think that dropping this many values from each end will be effective? Why or why not? If not, how many values do you think would be effective?

(c) Drop the top and bottom three observations from the data and recalculate the mean.

(d) Compare the trimmed mean and the median. What do you think about the data? Do you think this is a more accurate representation?

By using the trimmed mean together with the mean and the median you find that the mean was not influenced by the *skewness* of the data, but by extreme values on the high end.

(e) As an administrator at this university, do you think that the Psychology Department can claim that it exceeds the class size specification of 35 students per section? Use all of the information you have gathered to write a memo explaining your decision.

4.3.4 The Sample Mode

There is another measure of center that is used in statistics to measure the center of the data. This measure is the **mode**. In a bar chart the mode is analogous to the bar with the highest frequency.

The sample ***mode*** is the data value that has the highest frequency of occurrence in the sample.

It would appear that the mode would be a very good measure of a typical value, but there are some obvious reasons why it will not always provide useful information. One is that, depending on the size of the sample and the number of possible data values, there may not be any repeated values in the sample. *That is, for some samples, the mode may not exist.* For continuous data, where there are many different possible values, we do not usually talk about the mode because of the problems just mentioned. In these cases, we often refer to the **modal class** in a frequency distribution or histogram.

The ***modal class*** is the class interval in a frequency distribution or histogram that has the highest frequency.

Another problem with the mode is that there may appear to be more than one mode for a sample. This frequently happens with small samples. When this occurs it is not necessarily a case of two or three values that may occur much more frequently than any others. Rather, it is that most of the values happen to occur more than once.

For these reasons the mode is considered by many people to be an unreliable measure of central tendency. However, sometimes a sample does have more than one distinct mode. This indicates a *bimodal* (two modes) or *multimodal* (many modes) sample and should raise a number of questions in your mind.

1. Is it likely that these data could have two or more distinct centers? What would cause such a phenomenon?
2. Is it possible that the sample represents two or more different populations that were not understood when the data were taken?

(d) In this case the range is a large number, which presumably tells you that there is a large amount of variability in the data. Do you agree? Based on this, do you think that the range is a good measure of variability?

Part III

(a) Hopefully you concluded that the range can, in fact, give a very misleading picture of the amount of variability in the data. The range is quite large for this data set. Why?

(b) What about if we tried measuring how far away each data point is from the middle (i.e., the average) of the data? Let's do this by filling in the following table. Remember that the average is 9.71 days. The first measurement has been done for you.

City	Number of unhealthy days	Distance from middle
Atlanta	18	18 − 9.7 = 8.3
Boston	0	
Chicago	0	
Dallas	5	
Denver	0	
Houston	94	
Kansas City	0	
Los Angeles	1	
New York	13	
Philadelphia	2	
Pittsburgh	3	
San Francisco	0	
Seattle	0	
Washington, D.C.	0	
Average or typical	**9.7**	

(c) This is still not informative because we want a single number that will tell us what the typical deviation from the middle is. What is one way to measure "typical"?

Now, calculate the typical deviation.

(d) Does this value give us a good idea of how much variation there is in the data? Why not?

(e) What caused the typical variation just calculated to be such a small number? How can we fix this?

Part IV

(a) There are two ways to handle this. One way is to convert all the numbers to positive values by squaring them. The other way is to take the absolute value of the numbers. Fill in the following table. Then calculate the typical or average of the values in column 4 and the average of the values in column 5.

City	Number of unhealthy days	Distance from middle	Absolute value of distance from the middle	Distance from the middle squared
Atlanta	18	18 − 9.7 = 8.3	8.3	$(8.3)^2 = 68.89$
Boston	0			
Chicago	0			
Dallas	5			
Denver	0			
Houston	94			
Kansas City	0			
Los Angeles	1			
New York	13			
Philadelphia	2			
Pittsburgh	3			
San Francisco	0			
Seattle	0			
Washington, D.C.	0			
Average	**9.7**			

(b) Why are these two averages not close in magnitude?

(c) The average of the absolute distances (column 4) is called the *mean absolute deviation* (MAD) and the average of the squared distances (column 5) is called the *variance.* What are the units for the MAD and what are the units for the variance?

(continued)

(d) The MAD is actually easier to interpret but is not often used because absolute values do not "behave well." What can we do to the variance to get the magnitude to be about the same as the MAD? Do it.

What you have calculated is called the standard deviation.

4.4 MEASURES OF DISPERSION OR SPREAD

In the previous chapter you saw that simply describing the center of the data or a typical data value does not provide complete information about the data set. In addition to knowing what a typical value for the sample is, it is important to know how diverse the values in the sample can be. That is, we need to know how *spread out* or *dispersed* the data values are relative to the typical values. Understanding the *variation* in a set of data is of critical importance in statistics. When people use statistics to make decisions, it is important to understand not only a typical outcome, but all possibilities as well. We will look at two different measures of dispersion, the *sample range* and the *sample standard deviation.*

4.4.1 The Sample Range

The simplest measure of dispersion, the **sample range,** involves looking at the two extreme values in the sample: the highest (maximum) and the lowest (minimum) values.

The ***sample range, R,*** is the difference between the maximum and minimum observations in the sample.

The sample range is very easy to calculate and understand. It gives information about the distance from one end of an ordered data set to the other. If the sample data are symmetric, then it also gives information about the spread of the data relative to the measures of central tendency.

EXAMPLE 4.9 **The Mail-Order Company**

Calculating the Sample Range

Look at the data on demand from the mail-order company. In Example 4.1 we had the sample data:

Analyze the Data

Position	1	2	3	4	5	6	7	8	9	10
Demand	27	28	29	29	29	30	30	31	31	32

The sample range for this data is

$$R = 32 - 27 = 5$$

This tells the company that the demand for the product has a range or spread of 5 units around its center. In this case the range is a reliable measure of how spread out the demands are.

■

Information on the range *along with a measure of central tendency* gives you a mental image of the data. If the data are symmetric, then the company would expect that a typical demand for the product is 30 units, and that the demand is evenly spread out on either side of the center. The actual demand might be as low as 27.1 (29.6 − 2.5) or as high as 32.1 (29.6 + 2.5). In Example 4.9 these bounds agree very well with the actual data.

It would seem that the range is a good statistic because it gives a clear picture of the spread and is easy to calculate and understand. The next example illustrates why this is not always the case.

EXAMPLE 4.10 Hold Times

Understanding the Sample Range

A company is wondering whether complaints about the amount of time customers spend on hold for technical service are justified or whether the complaints are a result of the "squeaky wheel" phenomenon. The company takes a sample of 15 customer calls to the technical service phone line and records the amount of time each customer spends on hold.

Understand the Problem

Customer	1	2	3	4	5	6	7	8	9	10	11	12	13	14	15
Wait (min)	5.6	10.2	6.6	6.9	9.4	6.7	0.6	9.2	7.6	10.7	9.6	2.9	6.0	8.6	4.6

Collect and Analyze the Data

To find the range, find the minimum and maximum observations and subtract them:

$$R = 10.7 - 0.6 = 10.1 \text{ min}$$

What does the range tell the company?

At first glance, the company would think that the length of time that a customer spends on hold has a spread of 10.1 minutes. If the company considers that the largest value in the sample is 10.7 minutes, it could conclude that the data are quite variable. Or are they?

0.0 2.0 4.0 6.0 8.0 10.0 12.0
Waiting time on hold (min)

A dotplot of the data shows that the value of 0.6 minute is really quite a distance from the next nearest value, whereas there are quite a few observations in the 9- to 10-minute range. The image that the company receives from the data is actually quite distorted. If it calculates the average hold time

$$\overline{X} = \frac{105.2}{15} = 7.0 \text{ min}$$

then the company would think that a typical caller is on hold for 7.0 minutes and that the time a customer spends on hold might be as low as 1.95 (7.0 − 5.05) minutes or as high as 12.05 (7.0 + 5.05) minutes. This is certainly not an accurate picture of the data since the mean is biased downward by the few extremely low values and the range was biased upward by the same values!

■

EXAMPLE 4.12 Hold Times

Calculating the Sample Standard Deviation Using the Definition

The company looking at customer hold times knows that a measure of a typical hold time will not provide enough information about what its customers might encounter. The managers of the company need to know how much the time of a call might vary from the center. They decide to calculate the sample standard deviation for their data on customer hold times:

Customer	1	2	3	4	5	6	7	8	9	10	11	12	13	14	15
Wait (min)	5.6	10.2	6.6	6.9	9.4	6.7	0.6	9.2	7.6	10.7	9.6	2.9	6.0	8.6	4.6

To calculate the sample standard deviation the managers first need to calculate the sample mean, since the standard deviation measures the average of the squared distances from the sample mean. For this set of data we found previously that the mean hold time is 7.0 min.

Analyze the Data

The next part of the calculation for the sample variance finds the distance of each data value, X, from the sample mean, $\overline{X}$, squares each of them, and then adds them. The accompanying table gives the details of each part of the calculation. Each column of the table represents one part of the calculation. The last row of the table is the sum of all of the previous rows.

Customer	**Wait**	$(X - \overline{X})$	$(X - \overline{X})^2$
1	5.6	−1.4	1.96
2	10.2	3.2	10.24
3	6.6	−0.4	0.16
4	6.9	−0.1	0.01
5	9.4	2.4	5.76
6	6.7	−0.3	0.09
7	0.6	−6.4	40.96
8	9.2	2.2	4.84
9	7.6	0.6	0.36
10	10.7	3.7	13.69
11	9.6	2.6	6.76
12	2.9	−4.1	16.81
13	6.0	−1.0	1.00
14	8.6	1.6	2.56
15	4.6	−2.4	5.76
Sum	**105.2**	**0.2**	**110.96**

The last part of the calculation divides the sum of the squared deviations by $n - 1$, in this case, 14. So we have the sample variance

$$s^2 = \frac{110.96}{14} = 7.93 \text{ min}^2$$

and the sample standard deviation

$$s = \sqrt{7.93} = 2.82 \text{ min}$$

This tells the company that although an average call lasts 7.0 minutes, the actual call times will vary from that value. Typically, the variations or differences from the average will be about 2.82 minutes. ■

By now you must be convinced that there has to be a really good reason to use the standard deviation instead of the range! In fact, almost nobody actually *calculates* the sample variance and standard deviation using the definition. There is a shortcut formula that reduces considerably the number of calculations you have to perform:

$$s^2 = \frac{n\Sigma x^2 - (\Sigma x)^2}{n(n-1)}$$

SHORTCUT FORMULA FOR SAMPLE VARIANCE

To calculate the sample variance and sample standard deviation this way you need to sum all of the data values and also to square each value and sum the squares. The next example recalculates both the sample variance and standard deviation from the previous example using the new, shorter method.

EXAMPLE 4.13 Hold Times

Calculating s Using the Shortcut Formula

Using the same data, you would need to sum both the values and the values squared. The table gives the details of the calculations:

Customer	Wait (X)	X^2
1	5.6	31.36
2	10.2	104.04
3	6.6	43.56
4	6.9	47.61
5	9.4	88.36
6	6.7	44.89
7	0.6	0.36
8	9.2	84.64
9	7.6	57.76
10	10.7	114.49
11	9.6	92.16
12	2.9	8.41
13	6.0	36.00
14	8.6	73.96
15	4.6	21.16
Sum	**105.2**	**848.76**

Analyze the Data

Substituting the values in the last row of the table into the formula you get

$$s^2 = \frac{(15)(848.76) - (105.2)^2}{(15)(14)} = \frac{1664.36}{210} = 7.93 \text{ min}^2$$

and

$$s = \sqrt{7.93} = 2.82 \text{ min}$$

which is the same answer we got using the original formula. ■

It is probably hard to convince yourself that this is actually any better than the first set of calculations. Actually it is, but unless you do it several times it is hard to see. In fact, there is really no reason to calculate the sample variance and sample standard deviation by hand more than once or twice in your lifetime. Many calculators available today include statistical calculations like the sample mean and sample standard deviation, and these functions are also built into every spreadsheet package. What is important is understanding what the standard deviation measures and how it can be used to interpret sample data.

CAUTION! Calculators and spreadsheets can calculate more than one type of standard deviation. Be sure that you are finding the ***sample*** *standard deviation.*

TRY IT NOW!

Town Hall Traffic Flow ***Calculating the Sample Variance and Standard Deviation***

The town council looking at the traffic flow problem has seen reports that use the standard deviation, and wants to use it to describe the variability of traffic flow. The data are

Number of Cars	20	27	29	28	37	23	21	28	29	28

What is the sample standard deviation of the traffic flow?

Use whatever method you feel most comfortable with. If you have a statistical calculator learn how to use it NOW!

4.4.3 Interpreting the Standard Deviation—The Empirical Rule

Admittedly, the standard deviation is not as intuitive or appealing as the sample range. From the sample range you get an immediate (although sometimes false) picture of how far the data spread out around the center. The sample standard deviation does not give you the same intuitive response.

One way to understand what information the standard deviation gives is to use the **empirical rule.**

The ***empirical rule*** says that for a mound-shaped, symmetric distribution

- about 68% of all observations are within one standard deviation of the mean
- about 95% of all observations are within two standard deviations of the mean
- almost all (more than 99%) of the observations are within three standard deviations of the mean.

The empirical rule (Figure 4.5) is defined for large data sets and distributions that are symmetric and mound-shaped, often called bell-shaped or normal curves. For distributions that are only slightly skewed the empirical rule is surprisingly accurate as well. It provides sets of bounds for data values from a given population.

In general, if we are talking about sample data we will not know the population mean and standard deviation, so it is necessary to substitute $\overline{X}$ and s for μ and σ. To really understand the empirical rule an example is necessary.

ANS. MEAN = 27 CARS; S = 4.85 CARS

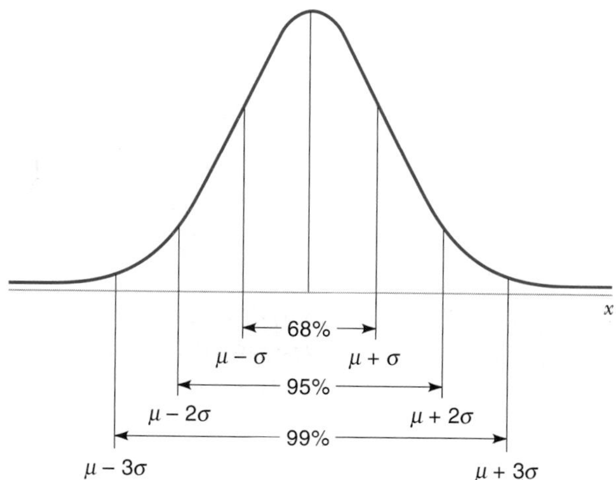

FIGURE 4.5 The empirical rule

EXAMPLE 4.14 Hold Times

The Empirical Rule

Suppose that the company looking at hold times had collected a total of 50 observations on customer hold times. The sorted data are shown here:

0.6	4.6	5.6	6.3	6.8	7.5	7.8	8.3	8.9	9.6
2.9	4.7	6.0	6.3	6.9	7.5	7.9	8.4	9.2	10.1
3.4	5.2	6.0	6.6	6.9	7.6	8.0	8.4	9.2	10.2
3.8	5.5	6.1	6.6	7.0	7.6	8.1	8.6	9.4	10.7
4.5	5.5	6.1	6.7	7.2	7.8	8.2	8.6	9.4	11.1

For a data set this large you should use your calculator or a computer software package to find X and s.

To investigate the empirical rule we need to find the sample mean and sample standard deviation of the data. For this data set $\bar{x} = 7.12$ minutes and $s = 2.08$ minutes. We should also verify that the empirical rule applies—that is, that the data we have follow a normal curve. To do this we can make a histogram of the data:

Analyze the Data

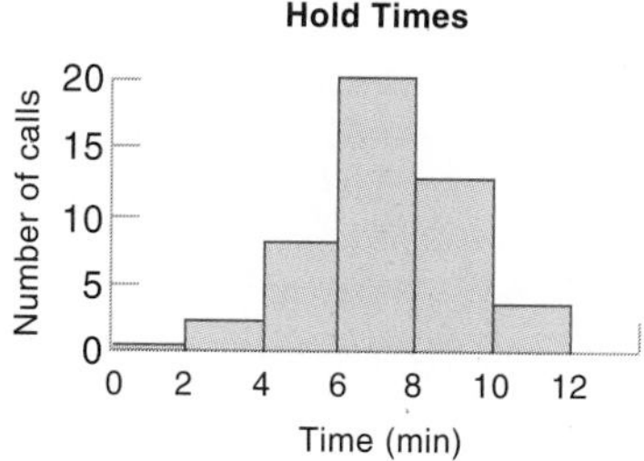

The histogram shows that the data are reasonably symmetric and bell-shaped, so we can use the empirical rule:

$\bar{x} + s = 7.12 + 2.08 = 9.20$ min
$\bar{x} - s = 7.12 - 2.08 = 5.04$ min

About 68% of the data values should be between 5.04 and 9.20 min.

$\bar{x} + 2s = 7.12 + 2(2.08) = 11.28$ min
$\bar{x} - 2s = 7.12 - 2(2.08) = 2.96$ min

About 95% of the data values should be between 2.96 and 11.28 min.

$\bar{x} + 3s = 7.12 + 3(2.08) = 13.36$ min
$\bar{x} - 3s = 7.12 - 3(2.08) = 0.88$ min

Almost all of the data (more than 99%) should be between 0.88 and 13.36 min.

To see how well the data we collected agree with this rule we can calculate the actual percentage of data values that fall within each interval. The following table contains the number of data values and the percentage that fall within each of the three intervals.

Interval	Number of data values	Percentage of data values	Empirical rule (%)
5.04 to 9.20	36	72	68
2.96 to 11.28	48	96	95
0.88 to 13.36	49	98	99

Looking at the table we see that the actual percentages are slightly different from what the empirical rule predicted. Remember that variation in data is to be expected. In statistics it is important to understand when the variation is within the limits of what is expected or typical. When the variation from what is expected is too large, something may be happening to cause it.

In this case actual percentages are fairly close to those predicted by the empirical rule. The largest difference occurs in the first interval. If the percentages are very different from what is expected then the cause is that the data are probably from a distribution that is not symmetric. The more skewed a data set is, the more it will deviate from the empirical rule in the first two intervals. ■

Loan Processing ***The Empirical Rule***

Errors in filling out loan applications can lead to delays in having the loans approved. Bank employees must contact the applicants to correct the errors. This sometimes requires multiple contacts. To understand the extent to which the errors affect the application process a bank collected data on the number of follow-up contacts required before a loan could be processed. The bank looked at 25 different applications and found

0	1	2	3	4
0	2	2	4	4
1	2	3	4	5
1	2	3	4	5
1	2	3	4	7

Make a dotplot of the data.

From the dotplot, do you think that the assumption that the data have a symmetric, bell-shaped distribution is a reasonable one?

Find the mean and standard deviation of the data.

According to the empirical rule, between what two values should 68% of the observations fall?

Between what two values should 95% of the observations fall?

Between what two values should more than 99% of the observations fall?

4.4.4 z-Scores

In the previous section we saw that the standard deviation can be used to measure how likely it is for a data value to occur. Since, for a symmetric, bell-shaped distribution, 68% of the data values fall within one standard deviation of the mean, it is reasonable to assume that data values in that interval will make up about 68% of the sample values. Certainly, most (more than 99%) of the data values in the sample should be within three standard deviations of the mean! We could use this rule as a measure of how "usual" that data value is. This measure is called the ***z*-score.**

> A ***z*-score** measures the number of standard deviations that a data value is from the mean.

To calculate the *z*-score of a data value we first find the *distance* that the data value is from the mean and then divide by the standard deviation:

$$z = \frac{\text{Distance between the data value and the mean}}{\text{Standard deviation}} = \frac{X - \mu}{\sigma}$$

Remember! When we substitute $\overline{X}$ and s for μ and σ we are relying on large sample sizes to ensure that they are good estimates.

As in the empirical rule, for sample data we substitute $\overline{X}$ and s for μ and σ, respectively. A positive *z*-score indicates that the data value is *above* the mean, whereas a negative *z*-score indicates that the data value is *below* the mean.

If you think about the empirical rule together with the *z*-score you can begin to make some inferences on how data values compare to what is expected from a random sample. Table 4.1 on page 144 gives you an idea of how this can be used.

Just because a data value is identified as an outlier does not mean you can discard it from the sample!

It is possible to use the *z*-score of a data value to identify *outliers*. The problem with doing this is that everyone's definition of unusual is not the same and so

ANS. DATA ARE SOMEWHAT SYMMETRIC, BELL-SHAPED. MEAN = 2.8, s = 1.7; 68%, (1.1, 4.5); 95%, (−0.6, 6.2); > 99%, (−2.3, 7.9)

TABLE 4.1 Using the Empirical Rule and z-Scores Together

If the z-score is . . .	The empirical rule says it will occur . . .	You can conclude that . . .
Less than −2 or more than 2	About 5% of the time	It is unusual and possibly an outlier
Less than −3 or more than 3	Less than 1% of the time	It is very unusual and probably an outlier

inconsistencies in data analysis can result. In Chapters 6 and 8, *z*-scores are discussed much more extensively.

EXAMPLE 4.15 The Golf Ball Company

***z*-scores**

From the histograms, the company investigating the two designs of golf balls did not think that any of the data are potential outliers. Still, it is better to be sure, so the company asks you to calculate *z*-scores. Rather than calculate the *z*-score for every data value you know, it will be easier to just look at the maximum and minimum values first. If neither of these have unusual *z*-scores, then you know that none of the other values will either. From the tables of summary statistics you find the information you need and compute the *z*-scores shown in the table. The *z*-scores are indeed in the 2–3 range, but they do not indicate that the extreme sample values are outliers.

Analyze the Data

Ball type	Carry (yd)	Carry (yd)	z-score
M1	Max 262	$\bar{x} =$ 257.4	1.92
	Min 252	$s =$ 2.4	−2.25
M2	Max 262	$\bar{x} =$ 256.8	2.26
	Min 251	$s =$ 2.3	−2.52

■

TRY IT NOW!

Town Hall Traffic ***Calculating z-Scores***

The town that was looking at traffic flow in front of the town hall wonders whether the observation of 37 cars is unusual. Although the town officials know that their sample size of 10 cars is not large enough to ensure accuracy, they want to use *z*-scores to look at the data:

Number of cars	20	27	29	28	37	23	21	28	29	28

What is the *z*-score for the observation of 37 cars?

Comparing the *z*-score to the empirical rule, do you think that the value is unusual?

ANS. z-SCORE = 2.06, POSSIBLE OUTLIER

4.4.5 Exercises—Learning It!

4.9 In addition to knowing the typical time visitors to Disney World wait for a monorail, management wants to know about the variation in waiting times. The data for the waiting times (min) are *Requires Exercise 4.1*

5.5 9.6 5.1 13.6 6.5 8.6 9.3 9.1 9.5 15.0 9.7 14.1

(a) What is the range of the waiting times?

(b) What are the variance and the standard deviation of the waiting times?

4.10 To understand its customer base, a mail-order book club must know something about the frequency with which customers make subsequent purchases. They collect data on the number of purchases that customers make during their initial 3-year membership. From a sample of 15 randomly selected customers they obtain the following data:

12 12 14 15 14 11 13 10 14 14 13 14 14 11 15

(a) Find the range of the number of purchases in a 3-year period.

(b) Find the variance and the standard deviation of the number of purchases.

(c) Do you think that the range or the standard deviation is a better measure of variation for these data? Why?

4.11 A professor in an introductory statistics course is interested in the number of hours that students spend doing homework during the week. A random selection of 12 students yields the following:

4.1 2.8 6.1 4.9 4.2 5.5 3.2 5.9 2.7 5.4 6.9 3.7

(a) Find the range and the standard deviation of the number of hours spent doing homework.

(b) According to the empirical rule, between what two amounts of time will 68% of the students spend on homework? 95%? More than 99%?

(c) How do the actual data compare to the predictions from the empirical rule?

4.12 A manager at XYZ Corporation thinks that the number of travel miles claimed in expense reports of its sales personnel has increased in recent months. To substantiate his idea he collects historical data from expense reports filed in the previous year:

2171 1709 2062 2075 1758 1733 1716 1963 1655 1558 1617 1908

(a) Find the range of the number of miles claimed.

(b) Find the standard deviation of the number of miles claimed.

(c) What is the z-score of the smallest data value? Do you think this value is unusual? Why or why not?

(d) What is the z-score of the largest data value? Do you think this value is unusual? Why or why not?

4.13 The company that sells mail-order computer systems wants to further analyze its typical weekly sales. The data (in thousands of dollars) for the 15 weeks are *Requires Exercise 4.2*

Weekly sales 191 222 222 223 223 225 227 228 229 232 234 234 236 244 253

(a) What are the range and standard deviation of the weekly sales?

(b) According to the empirical rule, between what two values will 68% of the weekly sales fall? 95%? More than 99%?

(c) Do you think that the empirical rule is appropriate for these data? Why or why not?

(d) What is the z-score for the week that had $228,000 in sales? What does this tell you about that observation?

4.14 To make a decision about replacing the cars in its current fleet, a company looks at the amount of money spent on repairs in the past 12 months, for a random sample of ten cars:

472 472 603 459 538 601 449 588 539 521

(a) Find the range, variance, and standard deviation of the amount spent on repairs.

(b) Use the empirical rule to describe the distribution of the amount spent on repairs.

(c) Do you think that the use of the empirical rule was appropriate here? Why or why not?

(d) Find the z-score for each data value. Are any of the values unusual? If so, why?

Requires Exercise 4.3

4.15 Look at the data on percent material loss per day in manufacturing:

Daily loss	10	12	12	13	14	14	18	19	19	20

(a) What is the range of percent material loss for the process?

(b) What is the standard deviation of the percent material loss for the process?

(c) Find the *z*-score for each data value. Do you think that any of the values are unusual? Why or why not?

4.16 A company that buys blank VHS tapes for video recording is concerned about the actual amount of time that the tapes are able to record. The tapes are rated at 120 minutes, but the company knows that there is variation in the actual recording time. The company collects data on 25 randomly selected tapes and finds the actual recording times (min) listed here:

116	118	119	119	120
117	118	119	119	121
117	118	119	120	121
117	119	119	120	121
117	119	119	120	121

(a) What is the range of actual recording times for the tapes? What are the variance and standard deviation of the recording times of the tapes?

(b) Make a dotplot or a histogram of the data.

(c) Use the empirical rule to find the intervals $\bar{X} \pm 1s$, $\bar{X} \pm 2s$, $\bar{X} \pm 3s$, and mark them on the graphical display.

(d) Find the actual number of data points that fall in each interval. Does this agree with the predictions of the empirical rule? Why or why not?

4.17 A large company that sells software has had complaints from customers lately that the disks provided by the company fail to work properly after extended use. The company decides to investigate the complaint and looks at the disks from its current supplier. The disks are rated with a life of 500 hours of use before failure. After testing 20 disks until they fail, the company obtains the following data on disk life (hours):

486	494	502	508
490	496	504	510
491	498	505	514
491	498	506	515
494	498	507	527

(a) Find the range and standard deviation of the time to failure of the disks.

(b) Make a dotplot of the data. Do any of the data values appear unusual?

(c) Do you think that the range or the standard deviation is more reliable for this set of data? Why?

(d) Find the *z*-score of the two largest and the two smallest disk lives. What does this tell you about the observations?

Requires Exercise 4.5

4.18 The company that is looking at cost overruns by a particular department also wants to look at how the overruns vary:

87.3	93.7	96.8	98.4	100.9	107.8
89.9	94.9	97.0	99.6	101.3	109.7
91.5	96.5	97.1	100.3	105.7	111.5
93.6	96.7	97.3	100.4	107.7	114.2

(a) Find the range and standard deviation of the daily overrun by the department.

(b) Use the empirical rule to give the company a picture of how the overruns vary.

(c) Find the z-scores of the maximum and minimum overruns. Is either of these two values unusual? Why or why not?

4.5 MEASURES OF RELATIVE STANDING

Measures of center and dispersion are certainly important, but they are not the only numerical measures that can be used to obtain information about a set of data. Other measures, called measures of relative standing, or *order statistics*, give information about the position of an observation in the sample. We looked at one measure of relative standing, the median, when we looked at measures of center. Now we look at some additional measures.

4.5.1 Percentiles

It is useful in some real situations to know what data value in a sample has a certain percentage of the sample above or below it. This measure is known as the **percentile** of the data.

The *p*th ***percentile*** of a data set is the value that has $p\%$ of the data at or below it.

The methods used for calculating percentiles vary slightly among software packages, and so the values that you get might differ.

Two questions can be asked involving percentiles: What value has $p\%$ of the data at or below it? and What is the percentile rank of a particular data value? The first question involves finding either a particular percentile or set of percentiles, such as the *deciles* (10%, 20%, . . . , 90%). It can be tedious to do by hand, but is easily done using most statistical software packages. It is of particular use when the observations in the data set are to be compared to each other or to some other norm.

EXAMPLE 4.16 **The Golf Ball Company**

Finding Percentiles

The statistics you have provided so far tell the management of the golf ball company a lot about how its golf balls behave when they are hit, but these statistics will not be useful for making statements like "Ninety Percent of Brand X balls go XXX yards when they are hit!" No number that the company has looked at so far seems to provide that information, although the median comes close. The company wonders whether there is a more general statistical measure similar to the median.

Remember! The median gives the data value that has 50% of the values above or below it.

A statistician is consulted who says that the measures the company wants are called percentiles. These percentiles are easily obtained from a statistical software package:

Data vector: GOLFDATA.Carry M1

Percentages		Percentiles
10	=	255
20	=	255
30	=	256
40	=	257
50	=	257.5
60	=	258
70	=	259
80	=	260
90	=	260

Data vector: GOLFDATA.Carry M2

Percentages		Percentiles
10	=	254
20	=	255
30	=	255
40	=	256
50	=	257
60	=	257
70	=	258
80	=	258
90	=	260

Analyze the Data

Draw Conclusions

From this information the golf ball company sees, for example, that 20% of the M1 balls went further than 260 yards, compared to only 10% of the M2 balls. This is really the first difference that the company has seen in the way the two balls behaved, but it might just be part of the natural variation. ■

The second question involves finding the **percentile rank** of a particular value in a data set.

The ***percentile rank*** of a value is the percentage of the data in the sample that are at or below the value of interest.

This measure allows you to determine the *relative standing* of an observation in a set of data. To find the percentile rank of an observation, the data must be put in numerical order. The percentile rank, P, is then found by

PERCENTILE RANK

$$P = \frac{b + \frac{1}{2}e}{n}$$

where

b = the number of data values *below* the value of interest
e = the number of data values *equal* to the value of interest
n = the sample size

EXAMPLE 4.17 **Starting Salaries**

Finding the Percentile Rank

Suppose that in the example where we looked at starting salaries, a person in the group who had a starting salary of $26,200 wanted to know how she ranked relative to her peers. Looking at the data you see that

Analyze the Data

$b = 50$ (there are 50 salaries below $26,200)
$e = 7$ (there are 7 salaries equal to $26,200)
$n = 100$

so

Draw Conclusions

$$P = \frac{50 + \frac{1}{2}(7)}{100} = 0.535 = 53.5\%$$

This tells her that 53.5% of the starting salaries were at or below hers. ■

TRY IT NOW!

Aptitude Test Scores ***Calculating the Percentile Rank***

A group of employees at a manufacturing facility take a test to determine their aptitude for training. The tests are scored on a 400-point scale and are shown here in increasing order:

185	227	241	257	281	299	314	329
195	228	243	261	283	304	318	333
196	234	248	269	283	307	319	335
199	238	250	271	291	309	322	349
223	241	253	272	297	310	328	353

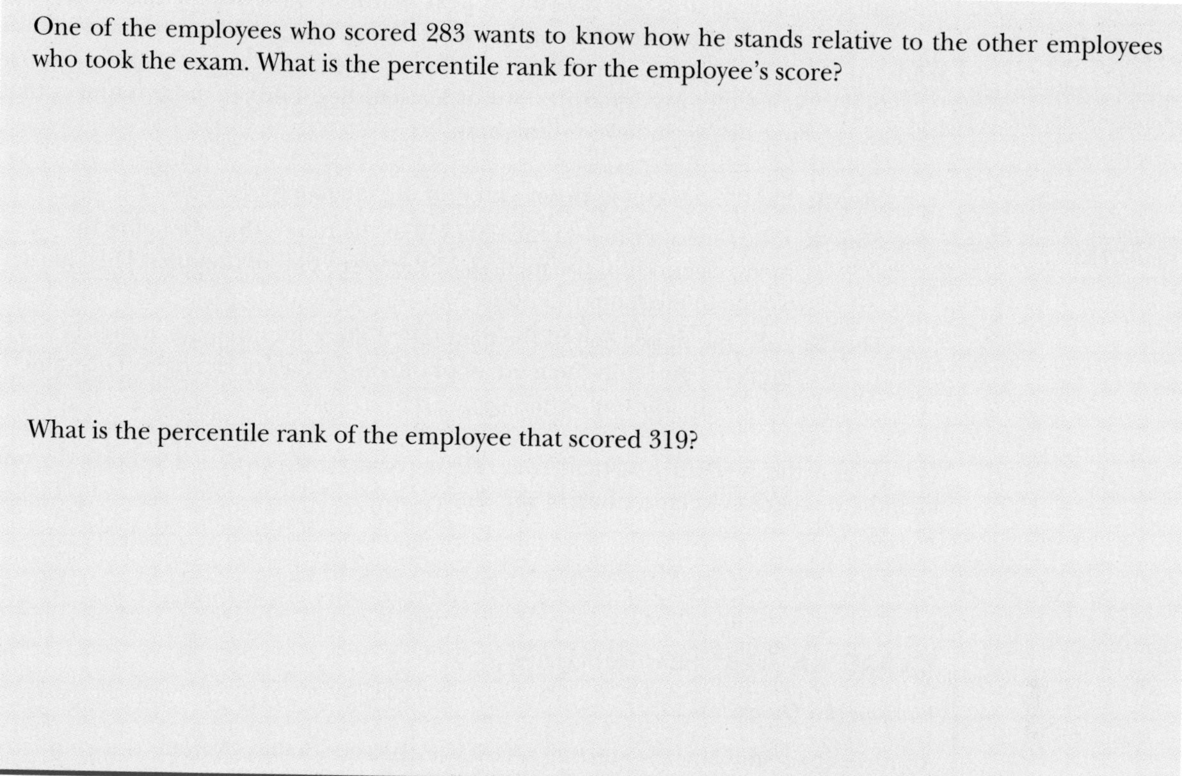

One of the employees who scored 283 wants to know how he stands relative to the other employees who took the exam. What is the percentile rank for the employee's score?

What is the percentile rank of the employee that scored 319?

4.5.2 Quartiles

Although calculating percentiles in general can be tedious, there are certain percentiles that are used frequently. These percentiles are the 25th percentile and the 75th percentile, also known as the **first and third quartiles.**

> The ***first quartile,*** Q_1, is the value in the sample that has 25% of the data at or below it.

> The ***third quartile,*** Q_3, is the value in the sample that has 75% of the data at or below it.

You may be wondering what happened to the second quartile, but we have already seen it! If you think about the definition of the quartile, it is not hard to see that the second quartile, Q_2, must be the median.

Just like finding percentiles, finding the quartiles for a set of data can be tedious, depending on how you choose to do it. Actually, several methods can be used to find the quartiles of a set of data. As with the percentiles, different software packages use different methods and so it is not unusual to get two slightly different answers when using two different packages on the same data set. The method that we use estimates the quartiles and is not really exact. It gives values that are quite close to the more exact methods and it is much simpler.

If you think about the quartiles you see that they divide the data set in fourths. We know that the median divides the data set in half, and that if you take half of

---

ANS. 55%, 81.25%

one-half you get a quarter. So, it would appear that if we find the median of each of the two halves of the data we will have our quartiles! It may sound complicated, but it really isn't.

Since percentiles and quartiles are order statistics, finding them requires that the data set be sorted from lowest to highest.

Steps for FINDING the QUARTILES

Step 1: Put the data set in order and find the median of the data.

Step 2: Take the lower half of the data (all of the values that are below the median) and find the median of the lower half of the data. This value will be the first quartile, Q_1.

Step 3: Take the upper half of the data (all of the values that are above the median) and find the median of the upper half of the data. This value will be the third quartile, Q_3.

When the median is actually one of the data values (when n is odd) do not include the median in either half of the data.

EXAMPLE 4.18 Starting Salaries

Finding the Quartiles

A university is studying the starting salaries of their graduates. Among the graduates sampled, what salary has 25% of the students earning less than that salary and what salary has 25% of the students earning more than that salary? In other words, the university wants to know the quartiles of the data. To make this easier the data set is repeated here:

$25,000	$25,400	$25,600	$25,800	$25,900	$26,200	$26,400	$26,600	$27,000	$28,000
25,100	25,400	25,600	25,800	25,900	26,200	26,400	26,600	27,100	28,200
25,100	25,400	25,600	25,800	26,000	26,200	26,400	26,600	27,100	28,300
25,200	25,500	25,700	25,800	26,000	26,200	26,400	26,600	27,100	28,300
25,200	25,500	25,700	25,800	26,000	26,200	26,400	26,600	27,200	28,400
25,200	25,500	25,700	25,800	26,100	26,200	26,400	26,700	27,300	28,500
25,200	25,500	25,700	25,900	26,100	26,200	26,500	26,700	27,400	28,600
25,300	25,600	25,700	25,900	26,100	26,300	26,500	26,800	27,600	29,400
25,300	25,600	25,700	25,900	26,100	26,300	26,500	26,900	27,700	30,700
25,300	25,600	25,800	25,900	26,100	26,300	26,500	26,900	27,700	30,800

Remember! Since 100 is even you average the two middle values to find the median.

1. Since there are 100 observations in the sample, the median must be the average of the 50th and 51st data values:

$$Q_2 = \frac{26{,}100 + 26{,}200}{2} = \$26{,}150$$

The lower half of the data set, everything *below* the median, consists of the first 50 values, and the upper half of the data, everything above the median, consists of the second 50 values.

Analyze the Data

2. To find the first quartile, find the median of 50 values, which will be the average of the 25th and 26th observations:

$$Q_1 = \frac{25{,}700 + 25{,}700}{2} = \$25{,}700$$

3. To find the median of the 51st through 100th values you will need to average the 75th and 76th observations:

$$Q_3 = \frac{26{,}600 + 26{,}700}{2} = \$26{,}650$$

So, the university finds that 25% of the graduates earn less than $25,700 and 25% of the graduates earn more than $26,650. ■

TRY IT NOW!

Training Aptitude ***Finding the Quartiles***

The company looking at training aptitude wants to give employees who scored in the top 25% on the test the opportunity to attend a seminar on training. The test scores are

185	227	241	257	281	299	314	329
195	228	243	261	283	304	318	333
196	234	248	269	283	307	319	335
199	238	250	271	291	309	322	349
223	241	253	272	297	310	328	353

In the sample, what is the cutoff score for those people who will be able to attend the seminar?

Hint: The value that defines the top 25% is the same as the value that defines the bottom 75%.

Suppose that the company decides that the employees who scored in the bottom 25% need some additional classes on team building. What is the cutoff score for those employees who need the classes on team building?

4.5.3 Displaying the Data Using Boxplots

In Chapter 3 we looked at several different methods for displaying quantitative data. These methods allowed us to look at the data and describe central tendency, shape, variability, and outliers. Both methods, histograms and dotplots, provide displays of the actual data in the data set.

Another method for displaying a set of data uses not the individual data values, but rather a set of summary statistics taken from the data. The plot is called a **boxplot** or a **box and whisker diagram.**

ANS. $Q_3 = 312$, $Q_1 = 241$

A ***boxplot*** or ***box and whisker diagram*** is a graphical display that uses summary statistics to display the distribution of a set of data.

A boxplot summarizes a sample using the quartiles and the median. You know that the median is a measure of center, but how can these statistics be used to show shape and variability? How can they identify outliers?

If you look at the first and third quartiles of a sample, Q_1 and Q_3, you see that 50% of the data in the sample fall between these two values. The distance between these two values is called the **interquartile range (IQR).**

The ***interquartile range*** (**IQR**) is the difference between the third and first quartiles, $Q_3 - Q_1$.

We found that one way of describing the variability of a set of data is to use the empirical rule. Remember, the empirical rule says that approximately 68% of the data in the sample should be within one standard deviation of the mean (in the interval $\mu - 1\sigma$, $\mu + 1\sigma$). The interval from Q_1 to Q_3 is similar to the first interval of the empirical rule.

Note: The parts of a boxplot are defined from the quartiles, not the median.

The main part of the boxplot consists of a rectangle (box) constructed from the median and the quartiles, as shown in Figure 4.6. This provides a partial picture of the data set. To complete the description with the empirical rule we used two additional intervals, $\mu \pm 2\sigma$ and $\mu \pm 3\sigma$. The boxplot uses multiples of the IQR instead of the standard deviation. The second interval in a boxplot is described by the **inner fences.** This is similar to the 2σ interval of the empirical rule. The last interval is described by the **outer fences.**

The ***inner fences*** of a boxplot are located at $\mathbf{Q_1 - 1.5(IQR)}$ and $\mathbf{Q_3 + 1.5(IQR)}$.

The ***outer fences*** of a boxplot are located at $\mathbf{Q_1 - 3(IQR)}$ and $\mathbf{Q_3 + 3(IQR)}$.

The inner and outer fences are not drawn on the boxplot but are used to define the "whisker" portion of the plot. The whiskers are constructed by drawing horizontal lines from the quartiles to the smallest (and largest) observations in the sample that are *within* the inner fences. This is illustrated in Figure 4.7.

Note: In drawing the box the height of the vertical lines is arbitrary. The scale on the x axis should span the values of the data similar to a histogram or dotplot.

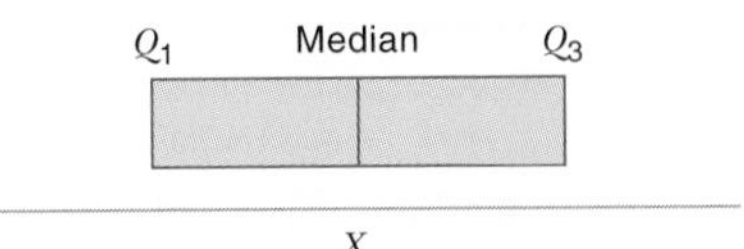

FIGURE 4.6 Box portion of boxplot

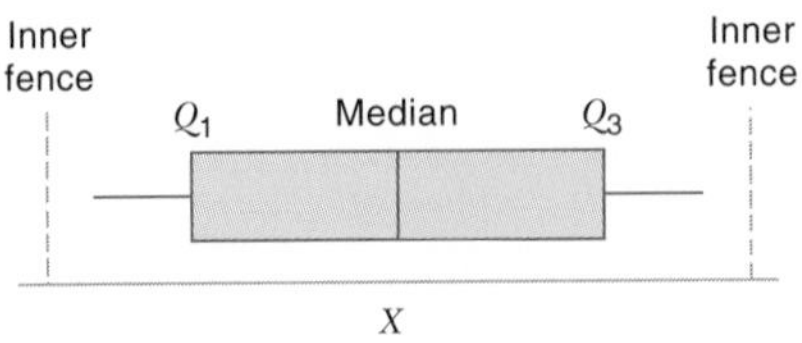

FIGURE 4.7 Boxplot with whiskers

FIGURE 4.8 Boxplots for skewed data

It is easy to see that the median gives us a picture of the center of the data, but you may be wondering how the boxplot shows the shape of the distribution. You know that when data are symmetric the mean and the median are both located at the bump in the distribution and that the distribution tails off at the same rate in both directions. In a boxplot, if the data are symmetric, then you would expect that the median is located halfway between the two quartiles and that the whiskers are the same length.

If data are skewed the median stays located near the bump in the data and one side of the distribution tails at a slower rate than the other. In a boxplot, the median will be closer to one of the quartiles than the other and/or the whisker on the tail side of the distribution will be longer than the other. Figure 4.8 shows boxplots for data that are skewed.

Although all this may seem quite complicated, it really is not. It is actually *easier* to make a boxplot than a histogram because the rules are standard and there is no judgment involved in setting it up. Making a boxplot can be separated into two parts, the calculations and the construction.

CREATING A BOXPLOT

Calculations

Step 1: Find the median and the first and third quartiles for the data.

Step 2: Calculate the interquartile range (IQR) by finding $Q_3 - Q_1$.

Step 3: Find the values for locating the inner and outer fences:

Lower inner fence (LIF):	$Q_1 - 1.5$ (IQR)
Upper inner fence (UIF):	$Q_3 + 1.5$ (IQR)
Lower outer fence (LOF):	$Q_1 - 3$ (IQR)
Upper outer fence (UOF):	$Q_3 + 3$ (IQR)

Construction

Step 1: Draw the *x* axis and select a scale that will allow you to locate the largest and smallest values in the sample.

Step 2: Draw three vertical lines, all of the same height, one at Q_1, one at Q_3, and one at the median.

Step 3: Construct a box using the quartiles as the vertical edges and enclosing the median.

Step 4: Locate the inner fences on the axis. Draw a horizontal line from Q_1 to the smallest value in the sample that is within (larger than) the lower inner fence. Draw a similar horizontal line from Q_3 to the largest sample value that is within (less than) the upper inner fence.

It is probably time for an example!

EXAMPLE 4.19 Starting Salaries

Constructing a Boxplot

Consider the data about starting salaries. We have already summarized the data by constructing a histogram and by looking at sample statistics. What can we learn from a boxplot?

The first step in the calculation portion is done, since in Example 4.18 we found the median and the quartiles for the data to be

Median:	\$26,150
Q_1:	\$25,700
Q_3:	\$26,650

The interquartile range is

Analyze the Data

$$Q_3 - Q_1 = \$26{,}650 - \$25{,}700 = \$950$$

For the inner fences we find that

$$\text{Lower inner fence} = 25{,}700 - 1.5(950) = \$24{,}275$$
$$\text{Upper inner fence} = 26{,}650 + 1.5(950) = \$28{,}075$$

and for the outer fences we find that

$$\text{Lower outer fence} = 25{,}700 - 3(950) = \$22{,}850$$
$$\text{Upper outer fence} = 26{,}650 + 3(950) = \$29{,}500$$

We now have all of the information needed to draw the boxplot.

Select the scale for the x axis so that it will accommodate the smallest and largest values in the sample, in this case \$25,000 and \$30,800. We will let the axis go from \$24,000 to \$31,000 in \$1000 increments.

Locating the box portion of the plot is not difficult. To determine how far to extend the whiskers, compare the minimum and maximum values in the data set to the lower and upper inner fences:

Minimum: \$25,000	Lower inner fence: \$24,275
Maximum: \$30,800	Upper inner fence: \$28,075

You see that the lower whisker can extend all the way to the minimum data value, but the upper whisker cannot go to the maximum because it is beyond the inner fence. Looking back at the data you see that the largest data value that is less than \$28,075 is \$28,000. The boxplot will look like the one shown here:

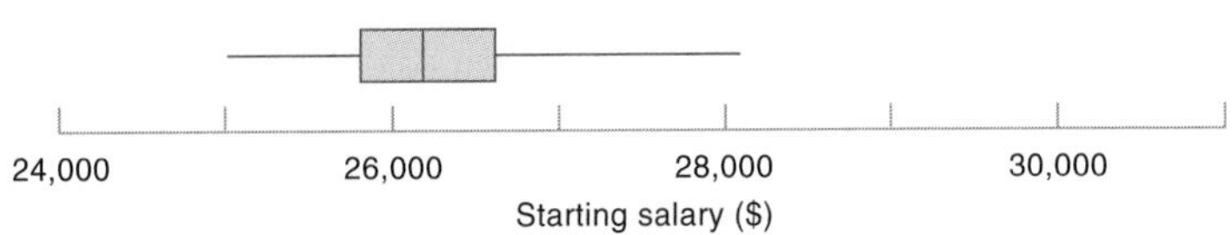

From the boxplot it would appear that the data are only slightly skewed to the right, since the median is located only a little closer to the lower quartile and the right whisker is only slightly longer than the left. ■

4.5.4 Using a Boxplot to Identify Outliers

At this point you may have some questions such as, Why did we find the outer fences if we never use them? What happens to the values from the sample that are beyond the inner fences? Both of these questions are quite reasonable and we are ready to answer them.

When we started talking about boxplots we said that they could be used to identify outliers. The intervals defined by the fences are similar to the 2σ and 3σ intervals from the empirical rule. Sample data that fall between the inner and outer fences are called *possible outliers,* whereas data values that fall beyond the outer fences are called *probable outliers.* If you are having trouble figuring out the difference between *probable* and *possible,* think about the difference in your reaction when your instructor tells you, "It is *possible* that you will pass this course" versus "It is *probable* that you will pass this course."

The observations that fall between the inner and outer fences, the possible outliers, correspond to those that fall between two and three standard deviations from the mean using the empirical rule. Remember that less than 5% of the data should fall in this region, so data values that fall there are fairly unlikely events.

The observations that fall beyond the outer fences, the probable outliers, correspond to those that are more than three standard deviations from the mean in the empirical rule. Less than 1% of the data should fall in this region, so data values that fall there are very unlikely events.

The possible and probable outliers are plotted individually on the boxplot using special symbols, such as an open dot for possible outliers and a closed dot for probable outliers.

EXAMPLE 4.20 **Starting Salaries**

Locating Outliers on a Boxplot

Let's finish up the boxplot for the starting salaries data by identifying the possible and probable outliers. To do this we need to compare the data values that were not included in the whiskers to the inner and outer fences. You remember that nine observations were beyond the inner fence on the upper side of the boxplot. Comparing these values to the values of the inner and outer fences, we find

Analyze the Data

Upper inner fence:	\$28,075
Possible outliers:	\$28,200; 28,300; 28,300; 28,400; 28,500; 28,600; 29,400
Upper outer fence:	\$29,500
Probable outliers:	\$30,700; 30,800

The completed boxplot is shown here:

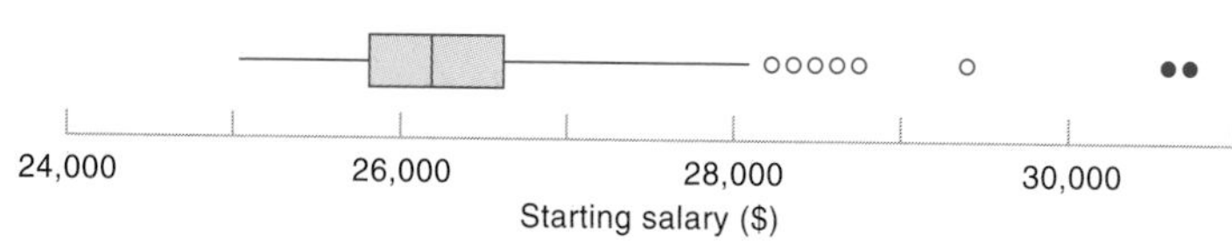

When the outliers are added to the boxplot the extreme skewness shown in the histogram is evident. Further, now we know that it is not just a case of skewed data but that in fact at least two of the data points are very different from the rest of the data. ■

Now that we know that some of the data might be outliers, you might wonder what we will do about it. You remember that when we sample from populations we want our sample to represent the population of interest. An outlier is a data value that has a large variation from the center. The first thing to do when we have identified outliers is to search for the *cause* of the variation. If there is some identifiable, assignable cause that makes the data value *not* representative of the data, then it is reasonable to drop the observation from the sample and redo the analysis. You cannot drop the observation without cause, but you can note in your report or analysis that an observation might have influenced the results.

Why do we need *another* method for displaying sample data and for identifying outliers? One important reason for using the boxplot is that it relies on statistics that are *invariant* (do not change) to the outliers themselves. When we use z-scores to identify outliers we use the mean and the standard deviation, both of which are sensitive to extreme values. If we have cause to actually delete the extreme observations the mean and standard deviation will change and *so will the definition of an outlier!* In a way, using z-scores to identify outliers is like trying to hit a moving target. The median and quartiles, on the other hand, remain relatively stable. Removing outliers does not really affect the locations of the inner and outer fences and so the definition of an outlier stays the same.

Another reason for using boxplots to display data is that they really do give an excellent picture of the distribution and they make it easy to compare samples from the same or different populations. Multiple boxplots lend themselves to being put on the same axis and make comparisons easier than multiple histograms, each of which requires a separate graph.

EXAMPLE 4.21 **The Golf Ball Company**

Comparing Data Using Boxplots

As the statistical consultant, you decide to give the management of the golf ball company a final picture by looking at boxplots for each sample. A statistical software package is used to create the plots and the results are shown here:

Analyze the Data

Draw Conclusions

This is the first time that the two ball types have actually been compared side by side and the boxplots provide new information. From the plots it appears that although the middle 50% of the M1 balls carry between 256 and 259 yards, the middle 50% of the M2 balls only carry between 255 and 258 yards. In addition, based on the size of the plot, it appears that the M2 balls are slightly more variable, but, again, this may be due entirely to the samples selected. ■

Training Aptitude ***Finding the Quartiles***

The company that administered the training aptitude test to its employees would like a better picture of how the employees performed on the test. The data are

185	227	241	257	281	299	314	329
195	228	243	261	283	304	318	333
196	234	248	269	283	307	319	335
199	238	250	271	291	309	322	349
223	241	253	272	297	310	328	353

Previously (page 151), you found the first and third quartiles of the data set. Use these values to complete the calculations needed for a boxplot.

Draw a complete boxplot of the data.

Were there any outliers? If so, which data values were they?

4.5.5 Exercises—Learning It!

4.19 The management of Disney World thinks that between 5 and 10 minutes is about the right amount of time for someone to wait for a monorail. Looking at the sample data, we find

5.1 5.5 6.5 8.6 9.1 9.3 9.5 9.6 9.7 13.6 14.1 15.0

(a) What is the percentile rank of the person who waited 9.7 minutes?

(b) What is the percentile rank of the person who waited 5.1 minutes?

(c) Approximately what percentage of the people in the sample waited between 5 and 10 minutes?

4.20 The transportation department of the small city wants to know what percentage of time there were ten cars backed up at the light. Use the following data: *Requires Exercise 4.7*

4 4 5 6 7 8 9 10 11 12

(a) What is the percentile rank of the observation of ten cars waiting at the light?

(b) What is the percentile rank of the observation of seven cars waiting at the light?

(c) What information does this give the transportation department?

4.21 The mail-order book club wants to know about the percentage of its customers that make subsequent purchases. Use the following sample of 15 randomly selected customers: *Requires Exercise 4.10*

ANS. IQR = 71, LIF = 134.5, UF = 418.5, LOF = 28, UOF = 525; NO OUTLIERS

10 11 11 12 12 13 13 14 14 14 14 14 14 15 15

(a) What is the percentile rank of a person who makes 13 subsequent purchases?

(b) What are the first and third quartiles of the data?

(c) What information do the quartiles give the book club?

Requires Exercise 4.12

4.22 The manager looking at the travel expenses of sales representatives would like to look at the data in terms of percentiles:

1558 1617 1655 1709 1716 1733 1758 1908 1963 2062 2075 2171

(a) Find the first and third quartiles of the data and explain what they mean.

(b) What is the interquartile range? How would you explain what that tells the manager?

(c) Make a boxplot of the data.

(d) Use the boxplot to describe the distribution of travel miles claimed.

(e) Are any of the observations unusual? Why or why not?

Requires Exercise 4.2

4.23 The company that sells mail-order computer systems wants to look at typical weekly sales in terms of quartiles. The data (in thousands of dollars) for the 15 weeks are given here:

191 222 222 223 223 225 227 228 229 232 234 234 236 244 253

(a) Find the first and third quartiles of the data and explain what they mean.

(b) What is the interquartile range? How would you explain what it means?

(c) Make a boxplot of the data.

(d) Use the boxplot to describe the distribution of weekly sales.

(e) Are any of the observations unusual? Why or why not?

4.24 The most recent data available from the Department of Justice (June 1995) give a state-by-state report on the number of people incarcerated per 100,000 people in the population. The data are shown in the table:

State	# Incarcerated per 100,000	State	# Incarcerated per 100,000
District of Columbia	1151	Arkansas	326
Delaware	890	Pennsylvania	326
Texas	643	Rhode Island	310
South Carolina	512	New Jersey	294
Alaska	505	Colorado	289
Arizona	501	Hawaii	279
Connecticut	481	Oregon	275
Oklahoma	479	Indiana	267
Alabama	468	Tennessee	260
Florida	444	Wyoming	239
Georgia	439	Iowa	235
Nevada	431	Idaho	231
Maryland	424	New Mexico	229
Michigan	424	Wisconsin	217
Louisiana	399	West Virginia	211
California	398	Washington	197
Ohio	390	Montana	191
New York	382	New Hampshire	183
North Carolina	356	Utah	178
Kentucky	354	Massachusetts	174
Virginia	354	Nebraska	173
Missouri	352	Vermont	173
Mississippi	346	Minnesota	139
Kansas	332	Maine	117
Illinois	329	North Dakota	107
South Dakota	328		

(a) Make a boxplot of the data.

(b) Use the boxplot to describe the number of people incarcerated in the United States.

(c) Are any of the data values unusual? Why or why not?

4.6 Executive Summary

GOLF BALL COMPANY

Business Analysis...

TO: Marketing Department
FROM: Data Analyst
RE: Comparison of Two Golf Ball Models

We were asked to compare two different models of golf balls in preparation for an advertising campaign. The study was conducted as a blind study, that is, we did not know the golf ball type while the data were being collected and analyzed. We did this to ensure that our results are as unbiased as possible.

Using a mechanical hitting device, we hit 72 different golf balls, 36 of each type. The balls were hit in batches of 12, alternating brands. To measure distance traveled we used carry, which is the distance from point of impact with the club to the place where the ball first hit the ground, and total distance, which is the distance from point of impact to the final position of the ball. This report focuses on the carry of the two ball types.

Table 1 contains summary statistics for the two balls. As you can see, the two models are very similar. The average carry for model 1 is 257.4 yards, and for model 2 it is 256.8 yards. This difference is less than 1 yard and might not be distinguishable to most golfers. The medians for each model are 257.5 and 257.0, respectively. This means that for each model 50% of the balls hit carried farther than this value and 50% carried less. The standard deviation for the carry is 2.4 yards for model 1 and 2.3 yards for model 2. This, along with the ranges, indicates that the variation in carry for the two balls is about the same.

TABLE 1

	Model 1	Model 2
Mean	257.4	256.8
Standard error	0.4	0.4
Median	257.5	257.0
Mode	258.0	255.0
Standard deviation	2.4	2.3
Range	10.0	11.0
Minimum	252.0	251.0
Maximum	262.0	262.0
Count	36.0	36.0

Although these summary statistics indicate that the balls are not very different, we decided to look at some other measures. Table 2 contains some additional measures for the two models. From these statistics you see that for model 1 25% of the balls went farther than 259 yards, whereas for model 2 the top 25% cutoff was 258 yards. In the same way, the bottom 25% for model 1 flew less than 256 yards, whereas for model 2 the value was 255 yards.

(continued)

TABLE 2

	Model 1	Model 2
First quartile	256.0	255.0
Third quartile	259.3	258.0

These results are best illustrated with the boxplots in Figure 1. From the plots you see that the middle 50% of the balls for model 2 (indicated by the box) carry less far than those for model 1. In addition, there is more variation in the carry for model 2.

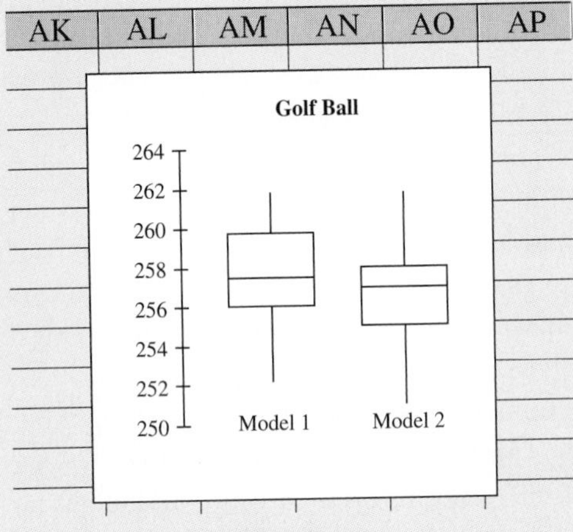

FIGURE 1

At this point, it would be difficult to say that there is any real difference between the two balls. However, we suggest that a similar analysis be done using total distance instead of carry, since this is what matters to most golfers. Also, we recommend that golf balls be hit under a wider variety of conditions to better simulate use by consumers.

The *Wall Street Journal* is a major source of current business news and information for the business community. If your professor has arranged for your class to have access to the Business Extra feature, you can go to it now and see the techniques of this chapter in action today. Go to the Wiley Web site at http://www.wiley.com/college/pelosi, and click on Business Extra!

4.7 NUMERICAL DESCRIPTORS IN EXCEL

This section covers the basics of using Excel to calculate summary statistics and to create boxplots.

4.7.1 Calculating Summary Statistics in Excel

Suppose that we want to calculate a set of summary statistics for the golf ball data. Figure 4.9 shows a portion of that data in an Excel worksheet.

The Data Analysis ToolPak has a function that creates a set of summary statistics for a set of data. To access this function, select **Data Analysis** from the **Tools** menu and choose **Descriptive Statistics** from the list of Analysis tools. The dialog box is shown in Figure 4.10. You will see that it is similar to the one you used to create a histogram.

	A	B	I	J	K	L	M	N
1	Ball#	Model #	Head	Temp	Carry	Tot Dist	Date	Time
2	1	M1	686	77	257	270	8/20	8:15
3	2	M1	688	77	255	267	8/20	8:15
4	3	M1	687	77	256	267	8/20	8:15
5	4	M1	688	77	255	271	8/20	8:15
6	5	M1	687	77	255	268	8/20	8:15
7	6	M1	687	77	256	267	8/20	8:15
8	7	M1	687	77	255	264	8/20	8:15
9	8	M1	690	78	258	269	8/20	8:15
10	9	M1	686	78	252	257	8/20	8:15
11	10	M1	687	78	256	268	8/20	8:15
12	11	M1	687	78	253	263	8/20	8:15

FIGURE 4.9 The golf ball data

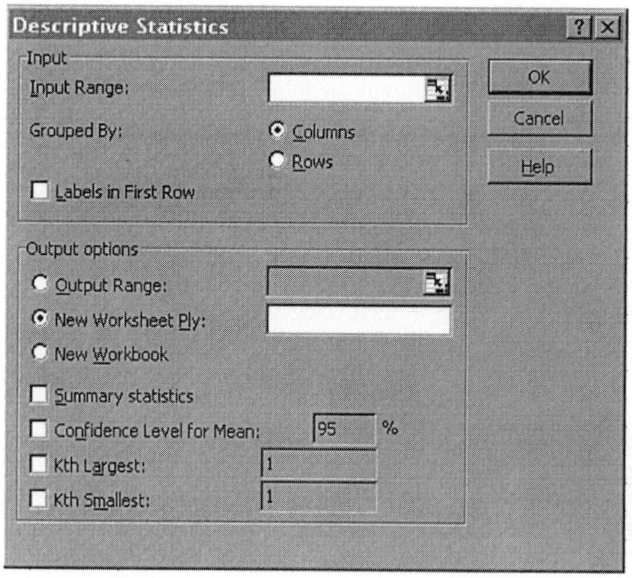

Descriptive Statistics

Input
Input Range:
Grouped By: Columns / Rows
Labels in First Row
OK / Cancel / Help

Output options
Output Range:
New Worksheet Ply:
New Workbook
Summary statistics
Confidence Level for Mean: 95 %
Kth Largest: 1
Kth Smallest: 1

FIGURE 4.10 The Descriptive Statistics dialog box

AE	AF
Carry	
Mean	257.0972
Standard Error	0.274902
Median	257
Mode	258
Standard Deviation	2.332621
Sample Variance	5.441119
Kurtosis	-0.18199
Skewness	-0.04536
Range	11
Minimum	251
Maximum	262
Sum	18511
Count	72

FIGURE 4.11 Output from **Tools> Data Analysis> Descriptive Statistics**

Note: You will have to adjust the column widths to be able to read the first column of the output.

The steps for creating the summary statistics are:

1. Position the cursor in the text box labeled **Input Range** and highlight the range of data for which you want to calculate summary statistics. If your first row contains the variable name, be sure to check the box labeled **Labels in First Row.**
2. You must specify a location for the output, either a section of the current worksheet, or a new worksheet or workbook. Click on the radio button for your choice. If you select **Output Range,** you must specify a location on the worksheet. Position the cursor in the text box for Output Range and click on the cell where you want the upper left corner of the results to appear. If you want to put the results in a new worksheet, you have the option of giving the sheet a name in the text box or just letting Excel create a new, numbered sheet.
3. The last thing you must do is specify what kind of descriptive statistics you want. Click on the box labeled **Summary statistics** and finally click on **OK.** The output will appear in the location you specified and should look like Figure 4.11. The output includes most of the summary statistics that you learned in this chapter, as well as some that you have not yet encountered. The output does not include the quartiles. When a statistic (such as the mode) cannot be computed, the output will read N/A (Not Available).

4.7.2 Making a Boxplot in Excel

Excel does not include boxplots as part of the graphs it can create. However, it is possible to create them if you know how Excel creates graphs. We have provided a macro for creating boxplots on the data disk that comes with this book.

To access the macros, you must use the KADDSTAT add-in located on the CD-ROM that came with this book.

Directions for Installing KADDSTAT

If you do not have the KADDSTAT add-in enabled, you must do this before you can proceed. On the CD-ROM that accompanies this book, find the folder labeled KADDSTAT. KADDSTAT is an add-in for Excel that adds a new item to the main menu bar. You can install KADDSTAT for a single Excel session or as a menu item that will be included every time you use Excel.

To open KADDSTAT for a single session, open the folder and double click on the file labeled **KADD.xla.** Excel will start and you will be warned that you are opening a file that contains macros. Click **Yes** to proceed. When Excel finishes opening, you will see a new menu item labeled **KADD.** If you open KADDSTAT like this, it will *not* appear the next time you open Excel and you will have to repeat the procedure.

To open KADDSTAT as a more permanent menu item, first open Excel and use the same procedure you used to open the **Data Analysis Toolpak.** From the **Tools** menu choose **Add-Ins** and when the dialog box opens, click on **Browse.** Use the **Look in:** drop-down menu to change to the drive and folder that contain the **KADD.xla** file. Double click on the file name and the option **KADDSTAT** will be added to the list of available add-ins. The option will have a check mark in the box. Click **OK** to add KADDSTAT.

Creating a Boxplot with KADDSTAT

1. Click on **KADD** from the menu bar and you will see a list of different statistical analysis tools available as shown in Figure 4.12.

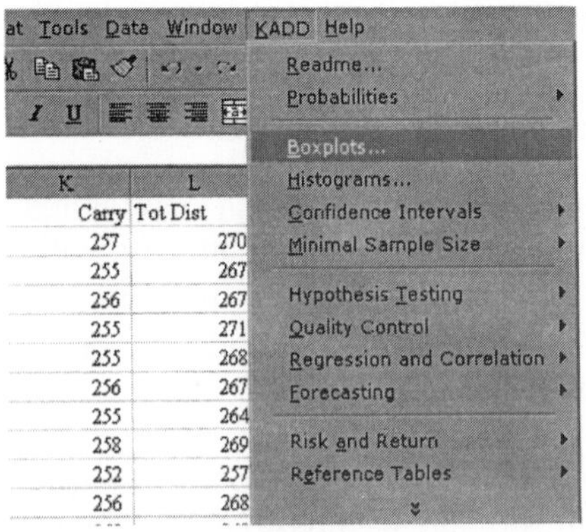

FIGURE 4.12

2. Select **Boxplots . . .** and the dialog box shown in Figure 4.13 opens.
3. Position the cursor in the text box labeled **Input Range** and highlight the cells that contain the data. If the cell range contains a cell that is a label, for example, the name of the variable, then click on the check box labeled **Header Row Included.**

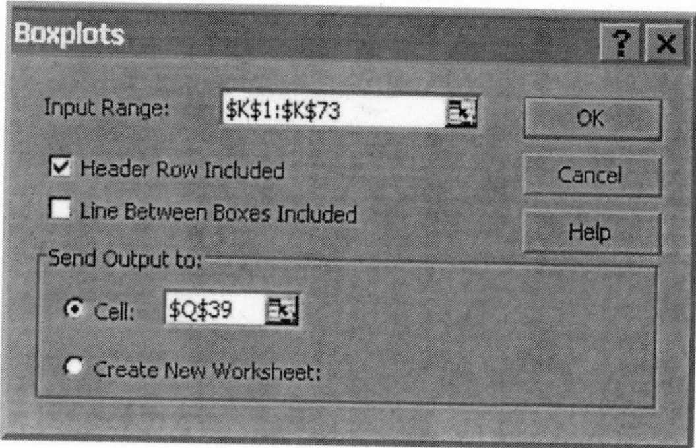

FIGURE 4.13

4. Indicate where you want the boxplot output to appear by either clicking on **Cell** and the cell that will contain the top left corner of the output, or by clicking on **Create New Worksheet.**
5. Click **OK** and output similar to Figure 4.14 should appear in the location you specified.

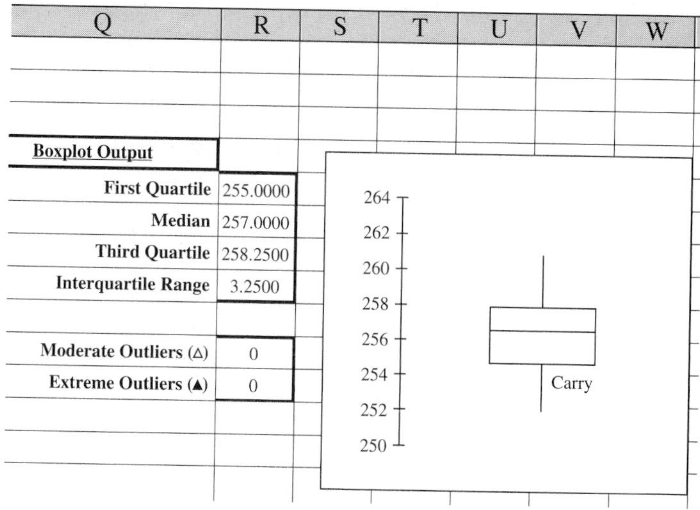

FIGURE 4.14

CHAPTER 4 SUMMARY

There are many ways to describe a set of data using sample statistics. No single number will do the job, nor is there any standard way to proceed. The measures that you choose must reflect the characteristics of the data itself. Most of the time the best descriptions come from the use of multiple measures and the conclusions that can be reached by comparing them.

Rather than summarize a sample with a list of numbers it is often useful to create images of the data using combinations of different statistics. An example of this is the *empirical rule,* which gives a picture of the distribution of the data. Another example of using summary statistics together to get a picture of the distribution is the *boxplot.*

Data analysis is not a static tool. You will need to look at a set of data in every way possible to obtain all of the information that it contains. Sometimes different methods will all lead you to the same conclusions and sometimes one method will yield an insight that is hidden in every other method.

Key Terms

Term	Definition	Page reference
Boxplot	A graphical tool that summarizes a sample using the quartiles and the median.	152
Empirical rule	For a symmetric distribution • about 68% of all observations are within one standard deviation of the mean. • about 95% of all observations are within two standard deviations of the mean. • almost all (more than 99%) of the observations are within three standard deviations of the mean.	140
First quartile, Q_1	The value in the sample that has 25% of the data at or below it.	149
Interquartile range, IQR	The difference between the third and first quartiles, $Q_3 - Q_1$.	152
Median	The value of the middle observation in an ordered set of data.	119
Modal class	The class interval in a frequency distribution or histogram that has the highest frequency.	127
Mode	The data value that has the highest frequency of occurrence in the sample.	127
Parameter	A numerical descriptor that is used to describe a population.	115
***p*th percentile**	The value in the data that has p% of the data at or below it.	147
Population mean	μ (mu)	116
Possible outlier	Observations that fall between the inner and outer fences.	154
Probable outlier	Observations that fall beyond the outer fences.	154
Sample mean	The center of balance of a set of data, found by adding up all of the data values and dividing by the number of observations.	116
Sample range	The difference between the maximum and minimum observations in the sample.	134
Sample standard deviation, s	The positive square root of the sample variance.	137
Sample variance, s^2	The average of the squared deviations of the data values from the sample mean.	137
Statistic	A numerical descriptor that is calculated from sample data and is used to describe the sample.	115
Third quartile, Q_3	The value in the sample that has 75% of the data at or below it.	149
z-score	A **z-score** measures the number of standard deviations that a data value is from the mean.	143

Key Formulas

Term	Formula	Page reference
Inner fences	$Q_1 - 1.5(\text{IQR})$ $Q_3 + 1.5(\text{IQR})$	152
IQR	$Q_3 - Q_1$	152
Outer fences	$Q_1 - 3(\text{IQR})$ $Q_3 + 3(\text{IQR})$	152
Percentile rank	$P = \dfrac{b + \frac{1}{2}e}{n}$	148
Sample mean, $\overline{X}$	$\overline{X} = \dfrac{\sum_{i=1}^{n} x_i}{n}$ or $\dfrac{\sum x}{n}$	116
Sample range, *R*	Max − Min	134
Sample standard deviation, *s*	$s = \sqrt{s^2}$	137
Sample variance, s^2	$s^2 = \dfrac{\sum_{i=1}^{n}(x_i - \overline{x})^2}{n-1}$	137
z-score	$\dfrac{X - \mu}{\sigma}$	143

CHAPTER 4 EXERCISES

Learning It!

4.25 A manufacturer of pain relievers is interested in studying the amount of time it takes a person to be relieved of headache pain after taking the medication. The manufacturer selects a random sample of 12 people and conducts a study. The data (minutes) are

13.0 12.9 13.2 12.7 13.1 13.0 13.1 13.0 12.6 13.1 13.0 13.1

(a) Find the mean, median, and mode of the relief time.

(b) Find the range and standard deviation of the relief time.

(c) What is the percentile rank of the person who took 12.9 minutes to be relieved of their headache pain?

(d) Find the quartiles for the data set and interpret them.

4.26 A group of elderly people in a town filed a grievance with the town council, saying that the length of the walk signals in the town was inadequate for many elderly people to cross safely. In an attempt to investigate the claim, the town collected data on street crossing times for 12 elderly persons. The times, to the nearest tenth of a second, are

21.4 15.1 13.6 16.0 15.0 19.1 21.0 14.2 15.6 20.1 21.1 22.2

(a) Find the mean, median, and mode for the crossing times.

(b) Find the range and standard deviation of the crossing times.

(c) Compare the mean and the median. Do you think the data are skewed?

(d) What is the percentile rank of the person who took 20.1 seconds to cross the street?

(e) Find the quartiles and interpret them.

(f) Make a boxplot of the data.

(g) Describe the distribution of the crossing times.

4.27 A manufacturer of compact discs decides to take a random sample of the discs and measure the diameter. The diameter of the discs is a critical measurement, since if the discs are too large they will not fit in the players and if they are too small then they will not be read properly. The sample of 10 discs yields the following data (in.):

4.74 4.72 4.76 4.72 4.73 4.72 4.76 4.74 4.75 4.75

(a) Find the mean diameter of the compact discs.

(b) Find the median diameter of the compact discs.

(c) Compare the median and the mean. Do you think the distribution of the diameters is symmetric? Why or why not?

(d) Would it make sense to use the mode as a measure of center for this sample? Why or why not?

(e) Find the range of the diameters of the compact discs.

(f) Find the standard deviation of the diameters of the compact discs.

4.28 The vice president of marketing at a large corporation is wondering how many of the company's employees arrive at work before he does. He decides to collect some data by counting the number of cars that are in the parking lot when he arrives at 6:30 A.M.

23 24 24 25 25 25 25 26 26 37

(a) Find the sample mean of the data.

(b) Find the median of the data.

(c) Find the range of the data.

(d) Find the standard deviation of the data.

4.29 A company that sells personal computers via mail order would like to know something about the amount of time that a customer spends on the phone with the Technical Support department during a call. The company collects information on the length of a call in minutes for 20 different customers:

15	23	34	38	41
16	25	37	40	43
19	25	38	40	43
20	28	38	41	44

(a) What is the average length of a call to Technical Support? What is the median length of a call?

(b) What is the range of call length? What is the standard deviation of the call length?

(c) Compare the mean and the median. Do you think the distribution of call times is symmetric or skewed? If it is skewed, which way is it skewed?

(d) Use one of the graphical methods you learned in Chapter 3 to display the data. Does the display agree with your answer to part (c)? If not, why not?

4.30 A manufacturer of breakfast cereals packs the cereal in 15-ounce boxes. Periodic quality checks are made to ensure that the boxes are being filled adequately. A random sample of 35 boxes of the cereal are selected and weighed. The data are

14.91	15.23	15.34	15.40	15.48	15.59	15.62
14.96	15.24	15.34	15.42	15.49	15.60	15.62
15.11	15.28	15.36	15.45	15.50	15.60	15.63
15.21	15.30	15.38	15.46	15.52	15.61	15.64
15.22	15.30	15.39	15.48	15.58	15.61	15.67

(a) Find the mean, median, and mode for the weight of the cereal boxes.

(b) Find the range and the standard deviation of the cereal box weights.

(c) Describe the distribution of the data using the information from parts (a) and (b).

(d) Find the quartiles of the data and interpret them.

(e) Make a boxplot of the data.

4.31 A university collected some data on the amount of money ($) that students spend on textbooks in a typical semester:

222	244	271	289	297
225	247	276	291	302
237	263	285	294	303

(continued)

304	312	344	374	398
305	316	359	377	406
306	326	361	380	409
307	331	369	395	427

(a) Find the mean and the standard deviation of the amount spent on textbooks.

(b) Find the intervals $\overline{X} \pm 1s$, $\overline{X} \pm 2s$, and $\overline{X} \pm 3s$.

(c) Make a histogram of the data and mark the intervals on the histogram.

(d) Calculate the actual percentage of the data that fall within each interval.

(e) Compare the actual percentages with those predicted by the empirical rule.

4.32 To begin a study comparing the monthly salaries of the auditors for a particular company to accountants' salaries in the industry in general, a random sample of 25 auditors was taken and their monthly salaries recorded. The data are

3069	3276	3333	3484	3570
3072	3310	3383	3498	3593
3137	3313	3412	3515	3603
3144	3323	3446	3532	3649
3269	3330	3456	3551	3659

(a) Find the mean and the standard deviation of the monthly salaries.

(b) Find the intervals $\overline{X} \pm 1s$, $\overline{X} \pm 2s$, and $\overline{X} \pm 3s$.

(c) Calculate the actual percentage of the data that fall within each interval.

(d) Compare the actual percentages with those predicted by the empirical rule.

(e) Create a boxplot of the monthly salaries.

(f) Use the boxplot to describe the monthly salaries of auditors in the company.

4.33 It has been a widely held belief that the switch to participative management would increase employees' "buy-in" to the company. One of the benefits that should be realized is a reduction in the number of sick days that employees use. The company decides to sample 25 employees from each of two manufacturing departments. The first department has been participative for almost 2 years and the second is still using a traditional management style. The data on the number of sick days used by each employee in the past 12 months are

Participative Management					**Traditional**				
1	3	5	5	6	0	5	6	7	9
1	4	5	6	7	3	5	7	7	9
2	4	5	6	8	4	6	7	7	10
2	4	5	6	8	4	6	7	8	11
3	4	5	6	8	5	6	7	8	11

(a) Find the mean, median, and mode for the number of sick days used for each group of employees.

(b) Find the range and standard deviation for the two sets of data.

(c) Make a boxplot for each set of data.

Thinking About It!

4.34 Consider the data about the number of cars that are in the parking lot when the vice president arrives: *Requires Exercise 4.28*

23 24 24 25 25 25 25 26 26 37

(a) If the vice president wanted an estimate of the typical number of employees who arrive at work before he does, would the mean or the median be a better statistic to use? Why?

(b) Is the standard deviation or the range more reliable for these data? Why?

(c) Find the *z*-score of the data value of 37 cars. Does it confirm your suspicion that the data value is unusual?

4.35 Grading homework is a real problem. It takes an enormous amount of time and many students do not do a very good job or copy answers from other students or the back of the book. A teacher of Elementary Statistics decided to conduct a study to determine what effect grading homework had on her students' exam scores. She taught three sections of Elementary Statistics and randomly assigned each class one of three conditions: (1) no homework given, (2) homework given but not collected, and (3) homework given, collected, and graded. After the first exam, she collected the data (exam scores) and made histograms of the data and calculated some numerical measures. The histograms and summary data for each group are:

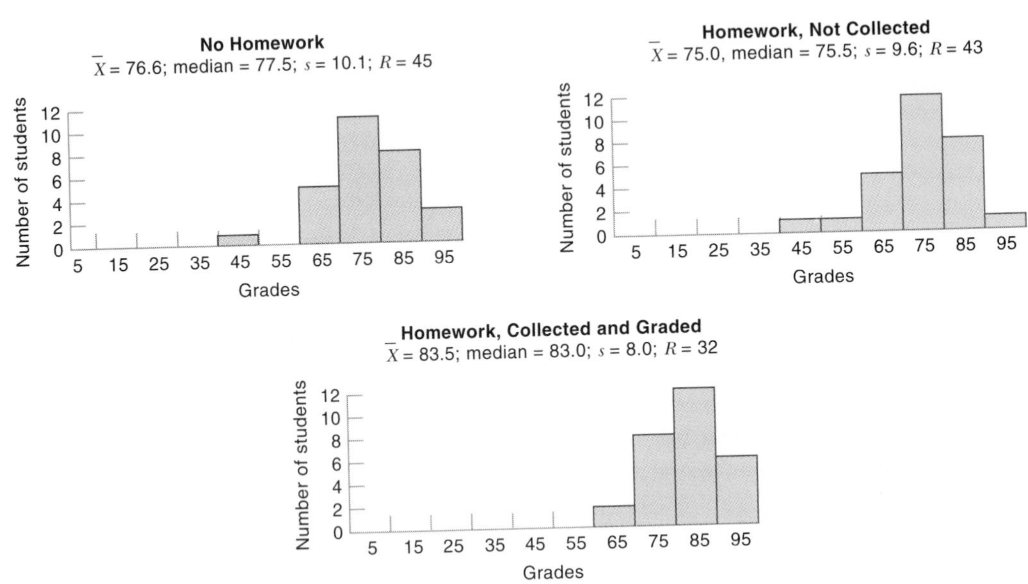

(a) Describe the distribution of the data for each of the groups and use the information to compare the three data sets and come to any conclusions you can about the effects of homework on exam grades.

(b) Do you think that this was a valid way for the instructor to examine the effects of homework on exam scores? Why or why not? What other factors might need to be considered? Based on the data, if you were the instructor, what would you do about assigning homework?

Requires Exercise 4.29

4.36 The mail-order computer firm that collected data on the length of a call to Technical Support is unsure about which sample statistics should be used to summarize the data and what they really mean. The firm calls on you to be its expert. What can you tell the firm about the length of phone calls to its Technical Support lines? Write a memo summarizing your findings.

4.37 A company has been recording data on the number of defective items found in the daily production lots after 100% inspection. The data recorded for the last 5 days had an average of 20 defectives. One of the people on the inspection team thought this seemed strange and realized that on one of the days the number of defectives was really 10 and had been miscopied. When the correct value was written down the average number of defectives changed from 20 to 15. What value had been written down instead of the 10?

Requires Exercises 4.28 and 4.34

4.38 Create a boxplot for the data on the number of cars in the parking lot when the vice president arrives:

23 24 24 25 25 25 25 26 26 37

(a) What does the boxplot indicate about outliers?

(b) Does this agree with the information obtained from the z-score? Why or why not?

(c) Which do you think is a more reliable indicator in this case?

4.39 The software company that is looking at the time to failure of the diskettes it uses decides to look at an alternative supplier of the product. The data for its current supplier and for the new supplier are *Requires Exercise 4.17*

Current Supplier			
486	494	502	508
490	496	504	510
491	498	505	514
491	498	506	515
494	498	507	527

Alternative Supplier			
489	492	495	498
489	492	496	499
491	493	497	502
492	493	497	503
492	494	497	505

(a) Find the mean, median, range, and standard deviation for each supplier.

(b) Make a boxplot of the data for each supplier.

(c) Based on these statistics, describe the diskettes for each supplier and write a recommendation to the company on which supplier to choose. Be sure to support your recommendation with references to the data.

4.40 The university that collected the data on the amount that students spend on textbooks wants to include the information in their catalog on typical semester expenses. The current catalog estimates that students spend $300 on books in a semester. *Requires Exercise 4.31*

(a) Do you think the catalog should be changed?

(b) If you think the catalog should be changed, what amount should be used? Justify your choice. If you think the catalog does not need to be changed, explain why.

(c) Suppose that changing catalog copy is costly considering the number of catalogs that are currently on hand. Does this change your answer to part (b)? If so, why? If not, why not?

4.41 The company that wants to compare its auditors' salaries to the industry in general finds that the average monthly salary of accountants in the industry is $3400 with a standard deviation of $50. The company asks you to interpret the data and to show how its auditors' salaries compare to those of the industry in general. *Requires Exercise 4.32*

4.42 As part of an annual program to calibrate their quality inspectors, each inspector in a company is asked to do a 100% inspection of a lot of 500 items. The data on the number of defectives found by each of the 35 inspectors are

8	10	13	14	15	16	17
9	11	13	15	15	16	18
9	12	13	15	15	17	18
9	12	14	15	15	17	19
10	12	14	15	15	17	20

(a) If you did not know the actual number of defectives in the lot, would you use the sample mean, median, or mode as your estimate of the number of defectives in the lot? Justify your decision.

(b) Suppose that you were the training coordinator for the quality inspectors. How would you interpret the data? What would you do as a result?

4.43 The company that is looking at employee sick days asks you to examine the summary statistics and compare the number of sick days taken by the two groups. *Requires Exercise 4.33*

(a) Based on the data, what would you tell the company?

(b) Are the data sufficient for you to conclude that participative management reduces the number of sick days taken by employees?

(c) If your answer to part (b) is yes, why can you reach this conclusion? If your answer to part (b) is no, why do you think this conclusion is not valid?

(d) As a consultant write a memo to the company. Be sure to include suggestions for additional data collection.

4.44 A study was recently completed by an insurance company concerning a particular surgical procedure. The study looked at the hospital records of 40 patients at two hospitals and compared the length of patient stay. The data were analyzed using Excel. Output showing the descriptive statistics for the data and boxplots of the two samples is shown on page 170.

E	F	G
Boxplot Output	Hospital 1	Hospital 2
First Quartile	6.0000	8.0000
Median	7.5000	10.0000
Third Quartile	9.0000	12.5000
Interquartile Range	3.0000	4.5000
Moderate Outliers (△)	1	0
Extreme Outliers (▲)	0	0

Patient Length of Stay

Hospital 1		*Hospital 2*	
Mean	7.725	Mean	10.35
Standard Error	0.405076	Standard Error	0.52812
Median	7.5	Median	10
Mode	7	Mode	8
Standard Deviation	2.5619254	Standard Deviation	3.340121
Sample Variance	6.5634615	Sample Variance	11.15641
Kurtosis	0.1601082	Kurtosis	-0.47823
Skewness	0.31302	Skewness	0.573241
Range	12	Range	13
Minimum	2	Minimum	5
Maximum	14	Maximum	18
Sum	309	Sum	414
Count	40	Count	40

(a) Using the computer output, describe each of the data sets. Be sure to include information about central tendency, variability, shape, and outliers.

(b) Compare the length of patient stay for the two hospitals.

(c) Proponents of hospital 1 say that this hospital is better than hospital 2 at the surgical procedure because the patients from hospital 1 recover faster than the patients from hospital 2. Can you conclude, on the basis of these data, that hospital 1 is better at the surgical procedure than hospital 2?

(d) If you think that the conclusion described in part (c) is reasonable, justify it. If you think this conclusion is not possible, what can you conclude? What additional information would you, as the insurance company president, find useful?

Requires Exercise 4.26

4.45 The town that is studying crossing times consults you about what the data mean. Currently, the walk signals are set for 15 seconds. Write a report telling the town council what you have found.

Doing It!

Datafile: *GOLFBALL.XXX*

4.46 The company investigating the golf balls is not satisfied with the limited analysis that it has done. The managers have collected a good deal of data, but they are not sure how to look at them and interpret the output. They decide to hire you to help them understand what the golf balls are doing and how they compare to each other. In addition to measures of the balls' performance, such as the variable *Carry*, the managers know that other factors, both internal (ball-related) and external (environment-related), could affect performance. They tested 36 of each type of ball at three different times using a machine to launch the balls. Data were recorded on 14 different variables. A portion of the data is shown here:

Ball	Model	S1	S2	S3	Wgt	Dw	Dd	Head	Temp	Carry	TotDist	Date	Time
1	M1	81	81	82	45.3	0.145	0.0110	686	77	257	270	8/20	8:15
2	M1	83	83	84	45.2	0.151	0.0111	688	77	255	267	8/20	8:15
3	M1	81	82	84	45.2	0.145	0.0105	687	77	256	267	8/20	8:15
4	M1	81	81	83	45.3	0.144	0.0117	688	77	255	271	8/20	8:15
5	M1	83	81	82	45.5	0.146	0.0108	687	77	255	268	8/20	8:15

Variable	Description
Ball	Keeps track of the observation number and goes from 1 to 72
Model	Identifies ball design, M1 and M2
S1, S2, S3	Measurement of circumference at three different points
Wgt	Weight of the ball
Dw, Dd	Dimple width and depth
Head	Head speed of the ball when it is hit
Temp	Environmental temperature in degrees Fahrenheit
Carry	Distance from the point the ball was hit to the point where it first hit the ground, measured in yards
TotDist	Total distance the ball travels from the point where it was hit to its final position
Date	Date of the testing
Time	Time of day that the observation took place. There were three different time periods.

(a) For each model number, calculate the mean, median, mode, range, and standard deviation of the variable *TotDist*.

(b) Describe the distribution of *TotDist* for each ball. How does *TotDist* compare with *Carry*? Which measure do you think is better from a statistical point of view?

(c) What can you tell the company about the effects of temperature during the trials?

(d) What can you say about the variable *Head* over the entire trial? Is it consistent for both ball models? Do you think that head speed needs to be considered as a variable in this trial or is it controlled well enough?

(e) Would you expect there to be much difference in performance from one time period to the next? Examine the effects of *Time* for each model separately and describe what you see. Make sure you look at both *Carry* and *TotDist*.

(f) Look at the variables *S1*, *S2*, and *S3*. The closer these measures are to being equal, the closer to spherical the ball is. Do you think that the balls are spherical? Why or why not?

(g) Look at *Dw* and *Dd*. How do these compare for each ball type?

(h) Think about the problem and analyze the data in any other way that you think might be interesting or important.

(i) Write a summary memo to company management with your analysis. Include the answers to parts (a)–(g) as appendix material.

4.47 Remember the complaint data from the tissue manufacturer that we looked at in the last chapter? Recall that one of the largest categories of customer complaints involved sheets tearing on removal. One of the product variables that can cause tissues to tear is tensile strength. The manufacturer has decided to look at the manufacturing process and to investigate the tensile strength of the tissues. Two hundred samples are taken

Datafile: TISSUES.XXX

from tissues produced on a single-tissue machine. The samples are taken over three different days. A portion of the data file is shown here:

Day	MDStrength	CDStrength
1	1006	422
1	994	440
1	1032	423
1	875	435
1	1043	445

Day keeps track of the day on which the sample was taken and goes from 1 to 3.
MDStrength measures the machine-directional strength and is measured in lb/ream.
CDStrength measures the cross-directional strength and is measured in lb/ream.

(a) Calculate a set of summary statistics for *MDStrength* for the entire 3-day period.

(b) Use the summary statistics to describe the *MDStrength* of the tissues. Be sure to comment on central tendency, variability, shape, and outliers.

(c) Display the data for *MDStrength* for the 3-day period graphically. How does the graph agree with or disagree with your answer to part (b)?

(d) Calculate a set of summary statistics for each day separately. How does the distribution of *MDStrength* for each of the 3 days compare to the overall distribution?

(e) Suppose that the *MDStrength* for the product is supposed to have a mean of 1050 and a standard deviation of 50. Do you think that the manufacturing product is meeting these specifications?

(f) Repeat parts (a)–(e) for the variable *CDStrength.* The specifications for *CDStrength* are a mean of 450 and a standard deviation of 25. In addition to a target mean and standard deviation, each variable has defect limits. For example, *MDStrength* should be between 850 and 1075. If the strength is too low the tissue snaps and causes the machine to shut down. If it is too high the tissues are stiff. The *CDStrength* should be between 390 and 480. If the strength is too low then the tissues will tear when you pull on them to remove them from the box. If it is too high, they will be stiff.

(g) Prepare a report for the management of the tissue company telling them how the actual process compares to the specifications. Include any appropriate graphs or tables of data with the report. Include other analyses as appendix material.

CHAPTER 5

ANALYZING BIVARIATE DATA

ALUACHA BALACLAVA COLLEGE

The Provost at Aluacha Balaclava College decides that there is more to the faculty salary picture than can be seen in the set of data she has currently collected. She decides to look at some additional variables that may help her to understand the problem a little more. She wonders whether the department or school in which the faculty member is employed has an effect on salary, so she decides to look at the data for both variables.

In addition, she decides to collect data on gender and whether the faculty member has tenure at the university. Perhaps these additional variables will give her some insight into how the faculty is paid. A portion of the data is shown here:

Business Dilemma...

Rank	Years of service	Salary	Gender	Tenure?	Schl
ASST	22	53316	F	Y	BUSINESS
PROF	11	64375	M	Y	BUSINESS
ASSO	7	63501	M	Y	BUSINESS
ASSO	6	59426	M	N	BUSINESS
ASSO	20	49058	M	Y	BUSINESS
PROF	4	94969	M	N	BUSINESS
ASST	21	54762	M	Y	BUSINESS

5.1 CHAPTER OBJECTIVES

In Chapters 3 and 4 you learned how to summarize data using both graphical and numerical measures. You learned how to use these techniques to obtain *information* about the data and to use that information to help in making decisions. In this chapter we look at some additional methods for summarizing data and also at how to display and analyze *bivariate* data. The chapter covers the following material:

- Bivariate Qualitative Data: contingency tables, clustered and stacked bar charts
- Identifying Quantitative Relationships: scatter plots and the least-squares line

5.2 QUALITATIVE BIVARIATE DATA

In the previous chapters of this book we have looked at ways to organize, summarize, and describe data that represent a *single* variable or characteristic of the population under study. Most often when data are collected, multiple variables are involved. The reason for doing this is that very often phenomena that occur in one variable are connected to or can be explained by the values of other, related variables. In this section we discuss methods for summarizing and displaying data for two variables, known as *bivariate data.*

5.2.1 Summarizing Two Qualitative Variables

In Chapter 3 you learned that the first step in organizing and summarizing data for a single variable is to create a frequency table. The frequency table contains the number of occurrences of each value of the variable expressed as a count, fraction, decimal, or percentage. When data are collected on two *related* variables, they are organized by using a **cross-classification table** or **contingency table.**

> ***A contingency table*** is a table whose rows represent the possible values of one variable and whose columns represent the possible values for a second variable. The entries in the table are the number of times that each *pair* of values occurs.

Creating a contingency table for a set of bivariate data is similar to creating a frequency table for a single variable. The basic setup of a contingency table is shown in Table 5.1. Each category for one of the variables is represented by a column, whereas each category for the other variable is represented by a row. The numbers in the table, the f_{ij}'s, represent the number of observations in the data set that were in category i of variable 1 *and* category j of variable 2.

TABLE 5.1 Layout of Contingency Table

		Variable 2				
		Category 1	Category 2	. . .	Category n	Total
Variable 1	Category 1	f_{11}	f_{12}	. . .	f_{1n}	
	Category 2	f_{21}	f_{22}	. . .	f_{2n}	
	.	.	.	.	.	
	.	.	.	.	.	
	.	.	.	.	.	
	Category m	f_{m1}	f_{m2}	. . .	f_{mn}	
	Total					

By using a contingency table, we can look at the number, proportion, or percentage of the data that fall into each *pair* of values for variable 1 and variable 2. Adding a second variable to an analysis gives you a different, and sometimes valuable, perspective on the data you have collected.

EXAMPLE 5.1 ABC Faculty Salary

Creating a Contingency Table

Since she is still convinced that rank should be a factor in determining salary, the Provost decides to look at the school in which the faculty member is employed in addition to rank. The college has four schools: Business, Liberal Arts, Professional Studies, and Science. The ranks of the faculty are Professor, Associate Professor, Assistant Professor, and Instructor. She creates a contingency table for the data and finds the following:

Rank	Business	Liberal arts	Professional studies	Science	Total
Professor	6	27	7	15	55
Associate Professor	11	30	9	17	67
Assistant Professor	10	20	15	32	77
Instructor	0	3	3	2	8
Total	27	80	34	66	207

Analyze the Data

Making comparisons with the actual frequencies is difficult, so she decides to use the relative frequencies for each cell. The relative frequency table is shown here:

Rank	Business (%)	Liberal arts (%)	Professional studies (%)	Science (%)	Total (%)
Professor	3	13	3	7	27
Associate Professor	5	14	4	8	32
Assistant Professor	5	10	7	15	37
Instructor	0	1	1	1	4
Total	13	39	16	32	100

The Provost sees that the distribution of faculty over the schools is not as uniform as the distribution over ranks. The Schools of Liberal Arts and Science make up 71% of the faculty, whereas Business and Professional Studies make up only 29%. She wonders whether this has any impact on the distribution of faculty salaries. ■

Draw Conclusions

EXAMPLE 5.2 Student Distribution

Creating a Contingency Table

Understand the Problem

When the faculty of the School of Business looked at the data on students taking the Introductory Statistics course, they wondered whether they could identify a reason why so many seniors were taking the course. They went back to the class and asked again for the information on year, but also asked a few more questions to help them classify the student. One of the questions they asked was whether the student was a transfer student. They guessed that students who transferred into the college might not have had the course previously. The data that they collected looked like this:

Collect the Data

Fr Transfer	So Nontransfer	So Nontransfer	Sr Transfer
Fr Nontransfer	So Nontransfer	So Transfer	Sr Nontransfer
Fr Nontransfer	So Nontransfer	Jr Nontransfer	Sr Transfer
Fr Nontransfer	So Nontransfer	Jr Nontransfer	Sr Transfer
So Nontransfer	So Transfer	Sr Transfer	Sr Transfer
So Nontransfer	So Nontransfer	Sr Transfer	Sr Transfer
So Nontransfer	So Nontransfer	Sr Transfer	Sr Transfer

To make sense of the data they decided to create a contingency table using the students' year as the row variable and the transfer status as the column variable. The table is shown here:

Analyze the Data

	Status		
Year	**Nontransfer**	**Transfer**	**Total**
Fr	3	1	4
So	10	2	12
Jr	2	0	2
Sr	1	9	10
Total	16	12	28

From the table they saw that nine of the seniors who were taking the course were indeed transfer students. To make the table more general, they decided to create the same table expressing each frequency as a percentage of the total:

	Status		
Year	**Nontransfer**	**Transfer**	**Total (%)**
Fr	11	4	14
So	36	7	43
Jr	7	0	7
Sr	4	32	36
Total	57	43	100

Draw Conclusions

From the second table they learned that, in fact, 43% of the students in the class were sophomores, which is supposed to be the norm. They also learned that senior transfer students constituted 32% of the total students enrolled in the course. Since the table also indicated that 43% of the students in the course were transfer students, they decided that establishing a task force to study transfer students was probably a good idea. ■

Creating contingency tables from large data sets can be tedious and time-consuming. Often, when data are collected, many more than two variables are considered and the person doing the analysis wants to look at different pairs of variables. Almost any software package that can be used for statistical analyses can create contingency tables easily. It is the *information* obtained from the tables that is important.

TRY IT NOW!

Quality Problems *Creating a Contingency Table*

A company that manufactures cardboard boxes is trying to understand some of its quality problems. The company has analyzed some data and determined that the major defects are printing, color, and skewness (how square the box is). Further attempts to pinpoint the problems have resulted in many opinions and finger-pointing about responsibility. The company decides to collect some additional data on defect type and the shift during which production occurred. The data (sorted by defect type) are as follows:

Color	1	Color	2	Printing	3
Color	2	Color	1	Printing	1
Color	1	Color	1	Printing	2
Color	3	Color	3	Printing	1
Color	3	Color	1	Printing	2
Color	2	Printing	3	Printing	1
Color	1	Printing	2	Printing	2
Color	1	Printing	1	Printing	1
Color	1	Printing	2	Skewness	2
Color	2	Printing	1	Skewness	2

Create a relative frequency contingency table for the data.

What percentage of the defects were color?

Does there appear to be any credence to the claim that the majority of the defects occur on the third shift?

ANS.

	Shift (%)			
Defect	**1**	**2**	**3**	**Total %**
Color	27	13	10	50
Printing	20	17	7	43
Skewness	0	7	0	7
Total	47	37	17	100

5.2.2 Displaying Contingency Tables

Although there is certainly a great deal of information to be obtained from a contingency table, we learned in Chapter 3 that a visual representation of the data can strengthen our understanding of what is happening. The question then is how can we best represent bivariate data.

If we select one of the variables it would be possible to create bar or pie charts for each of the possible categories of that variable. For the student distribution data in Example 5.2, the corresponding bar charts are shown in Figure 5.1. This accomplishes what we wanted, but it will certainly be cumbersome if the number of possible categories increases! Also, as you learned in Chapter 3, when you are making comparisons on separate charts it is important that the scales of the charts be comparable.

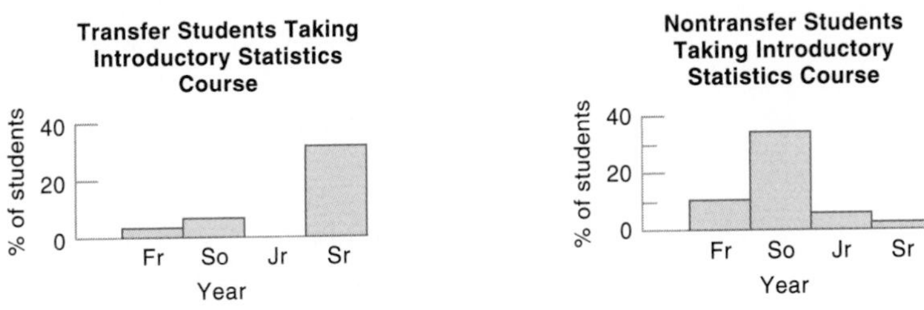

FIGURE 5.1 Two bar charts representing a contingency table

Clustered and Stacked Bar Charts

There is a way to display contingency table data on the same chart, by using what are called *clustered* or *stacked* bar charts. Both of these charts use a different type of bar (color, shading) to represent one of the values of a selected qualitative variable.

Clustered Bar Charts

Clustered bar charts can be used in place of multiple bar charts when you want to compare the data for the values of the selected qualitative variables. An example of a clustered bar chart is shown in Figure 5.2.

> In a ***clustered bar chart,*** the bars for one variable are grouped according to the values of the other qualitative variable.

You can see that a clustered bar chart really *combines* the results of several bar charts into a single chart. A legend is included to identify each of the categories.

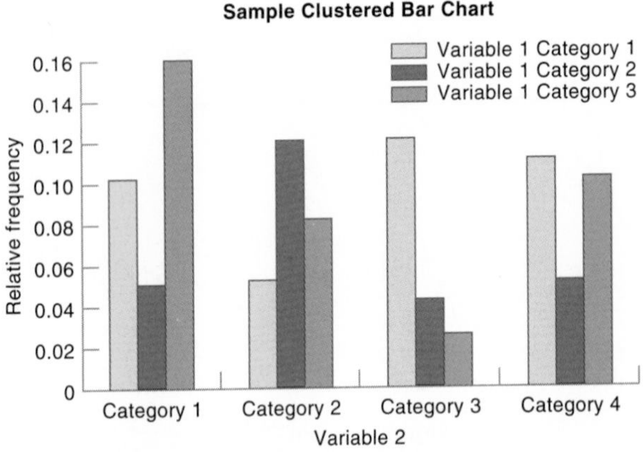

FIGURE 5.2 Example of a clustered bar chart

EXAMPLE 5.3 ABC Faculty Salaries

Creating a Clustered Bar Chart

The Provost is interested in seeing how the faculty of the different schools are distributed over the ranks. She decides to create a clustered bar chart using rank as the category on the x axis and a different bar for each school:

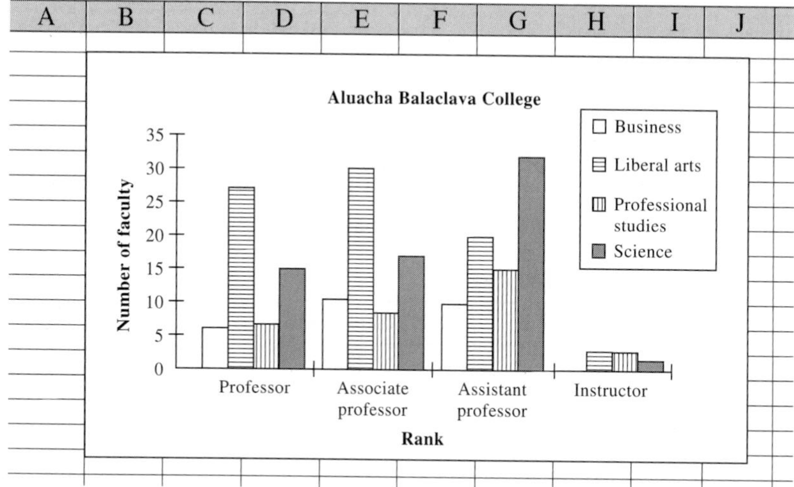

Analyze the Data

Looking at the bar chart, the Provost sees that the faculty in the School of Liberal Arts tends toward the higher ranks, whereas the School of Science has a higher percentage of the faculty in the lower ranks. The School of Business appears to be similar to Liberal Arts, whereas Professional Studies is similar to Science. ■

Draw Conclusions

EXAMPLE 5.4 Student Distribution

Creating a Clustered Bar Chart

In the student distribution example the faculty wanted to compare transfer students to nontransfer students. They decided that to get a good picture of the data they would use a clustered bar chart to display the data they collected. Since the variable that they wanted to compare was student status, they made a bar for each of the two student types for each of the four years. There are really no new calculations to do. The chart that resulted is shown here:

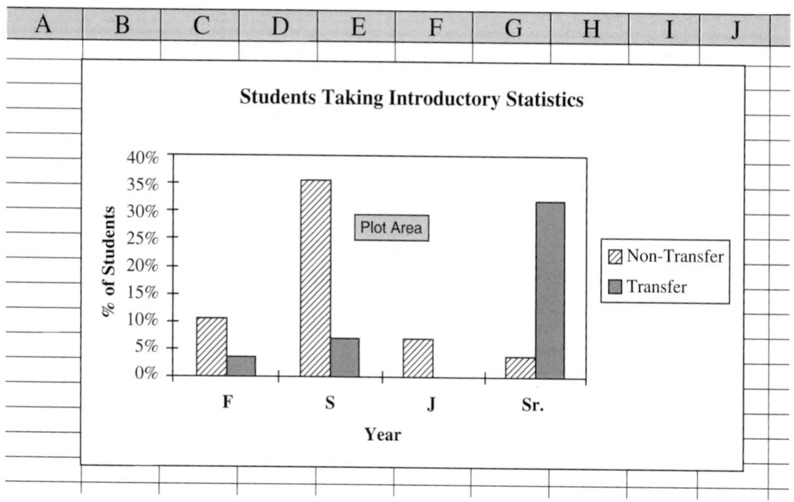

Analyze the Data

The stacked bar chart for this table is shown here:

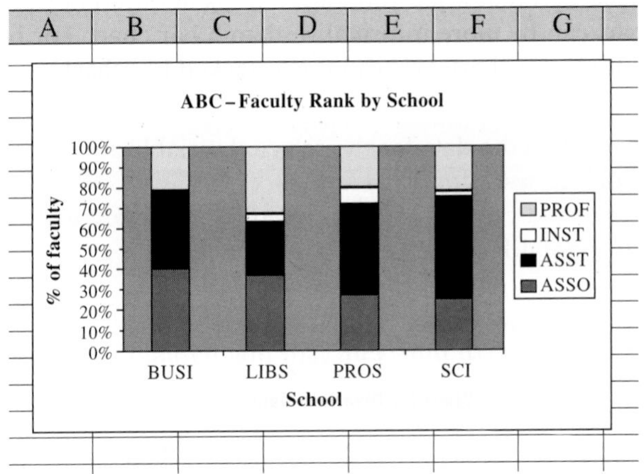

Draw Conclusions

She sees from the graph that the schools of Science and Professional Studies have a higher proportion of Assistant Professors than the other schools and that Liberal Arts has the highest percentage of Professors. ■

EXAMPLE 5.6 Student Distribution

Creating a Stacked Bar Chart

The faculty members of the School of Business decide to look at the data one more time. They want to see whether they can determine the proportion of transfer students enrolled in the course that are freshmen, sophomores, juniors, and seniors. The first task is to figure out the percentages for each column of the contingency table. Since they are trying to express the year as a percentage of the type of student rather than as a percentage of the total, they use the column totals instead of the grand total to calculate them. The original contingency table is shown here:

Analyze the Data

	Status		
Year	**Nontransfer**	**Transfer**	**Total**
Fr	3	1	4
So	10	2	12
Jr	2	0	2
Sr	1	9	10
Total	16	12	28

The number of nontransfer students who are freshmen is 3. To express this as a percentage of the nontransfer students calculate $3/16 = 18.75\%$, or approximately 19%.

In the same way, to find the percentage of transfer students that are freshmen calculate $1/12 = 8.33\%$ or approximately 8%. The completed table follows.

	Status %	
Year	**Nontransfer**	**Transfer**
Fr	19	8
So	63	17
Jr	13	0
Sr	6	75
Total	100	100

The stacked bar chart for the data is

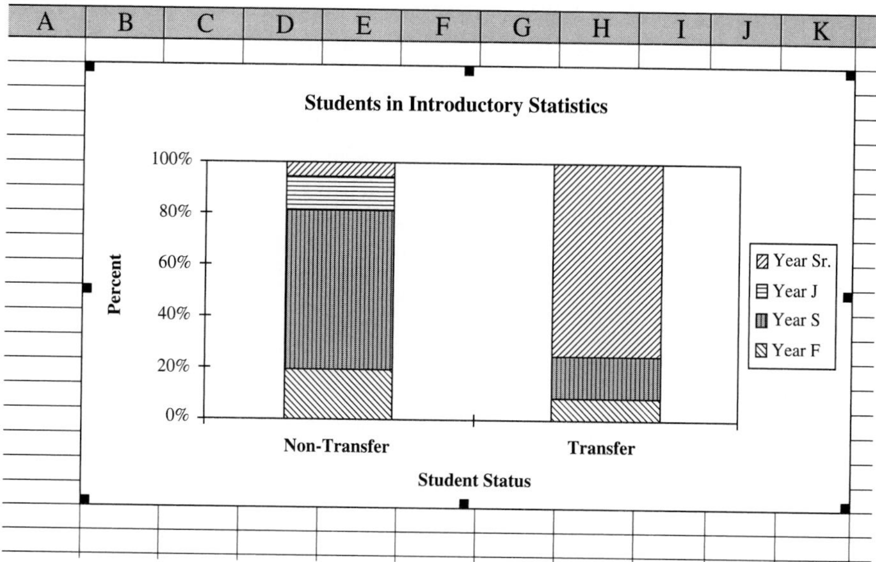

This chart shows that the majority of nontransfer students enrolled in the course are freshmen and sophomores, which is appropriate. The majority of the transfer students are seniors and there are no juniors. This information reinforces the earlier idea that better advising of transfer students might alleviate the problem. ■

Draw Conclusions

TRY IT NOW!

Quality Problems *Creating a Stacked Bar Chart*

The company that manufactures cardboard boxes decides to create a graphical display of the data to show to the employees. What the company wants to do is to display type of defect as a percentage of total defects for each shift. It is hoped that these data will help each shift concentrate on its own priorities. The contingency table for the defect data is shown here:

	Shift			
Defect	**1**	**2**	**3**	**Total**
Color	8	4	3	15
Printing	6	5	2	13
Skewness	0	2	0	2
Total	14	11	5	30

Modify the contingency table to display defect types as a percentage of total defects for each shift.

(continued)

Create a stacked bar chart for the data.

Which defect type should each crew concentrate on? Why?

5.2.3 Exercises—Learning It!

5.1 In an article about Internet access and minorities (*The Truth About the Digital Divide,* April 11, 2000) Forrester Research looked at data obtained from surveying 103,200 households. Data on Internet access for two time periods by race are shown here:

Race/Ethnicity	Percentage On-line (%) January 2000	January 1999
Caucasian-American (C. Am.)	43	34
African-American (Af. Am.)	33	23
Hispanic-American (H. Am.)	47	36
Asian-American (As. Am.)	69	64
All households	43	35

(a) Create a clustered bar chart for the data using the variable *Race/Ethnicity* as the category for the *x* axis.

ANS. CREW 1 COLOR; CREW 2 PRINTING; CREW 3 COLOR

Defect	Shift (%) 1	2	3	Total (%)
Color	57	36	60	50
Printing	43	45	40	43
Skewness	0	18	0	7
Total	100	100	100	100

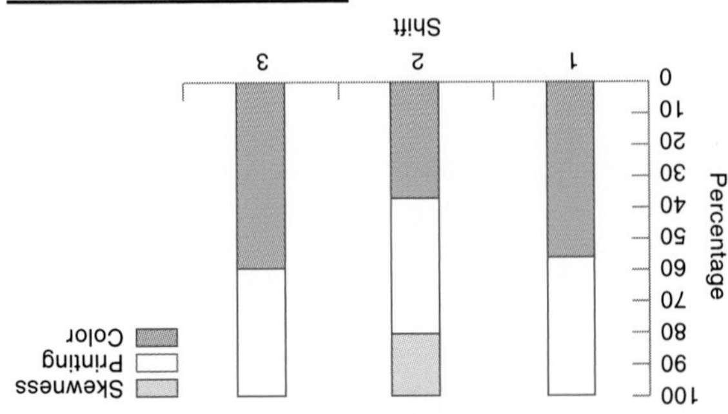

(b) Redo the chart plotting the variable *Time* on the *x* axis.

(c) Which graph do you think was better for presenting this information? Why?

5.2 The Bureau of Labor Statistics (BLS) reports that the second leading cause of on-the-job deaths fell to its lowest level in 7 years in 1998. The accompanying table gives workplace homicides for the retail trade industry, broken down into three subcategories, for 1994 through 1998.

	Year				
Retail Industry	**1994**	**1995**	**1996**	**1997**	**1998**
Grocery stores	196	152	146	141	95
Eating and drinking places	135	121	135	109	69
Gasoline service stations	41	36	23	34	24

(a) Create a clustered bar chart using the year as the *x*-axis category.

(b) Create a clustered bar chart using the type of retail industry as the *x* axis.

(c) Which chart does a better job of illustrating the claim made by the BLS? Why?

(d) Use the data in the table to create a stacked bar chart with the year as the *x*-axis category.

(e) Are homicides more prevalent in any one type of retail industry? What conclusions can you draw about the number of homicides in the different retail industries? Is there any other information you would want to know to better interpret the data?

5.3 The relationship between cities and the economic health of countries is of interest to city planners. The following data show where cities get revenues for eight different developing countries:

	Source of funding (%)		
Country	**Central transfers**	**Local taxes**	**Local fees**
Indonesia	84	7	9
Brazil	65	24	11
Mexico	63	12	25
Turkey	63	10	27
Tunisia	56	34	10
Colombia	42	46	12
India	27	61	12
Kenya	4	38	58

(a) Use a stacked bar chart to display the data. The *x*-axis categories should be the countries.

(b) What interesting features do you see in the data?

5.3 QUANTITATIVE BIVARIATE DATA

In the previous section you learned ways to investigate the relationships among *qualitative* variables. It is also interesting to understand how *quantitative* variables are related.

When we say that two variables are *related* we mean that they vary in some systematic way. For example, as one variable increases, the other might also increase. This would be true for variables such as height and weight, and it might or might not be true for variables such as the amount of time you study and the grade you earn on an exam. Another type of relationship occurs when one variable increases as the other decreases. This might apply to the relationship between the price of a product and sales of that same product.

In statistics, it is often important to investigate the relationships between variables to learn how to predict the value of one variable based on the value of the other, related variable. This is called *regression analysis* and is covered in Chapter 11. But, just as in all statistical studies, before any analytical tool is used it is important to look at the data first to get an understanding of what is happening. Viewing the data with different graphical tools helps a statistician to decide what statistical techniques are appropriate. The most important tool for exploring relationships between quantitative variables is a graphical tool called a **scatter plot.**

5.3.1 Scatter Plots

Each observation of bivariate quantitative data can be thought of as a data pair of the form (x, y), where x represents the values of the first variable and y represents the value of the second variable. The x variable is often called the **independent** variable, and the y variable is often called the **dependent** variable. The type of graph used to display this kind of data is called a **scatter plot.**

> In a ***scatter plot*** an axis is used to represent each of the variables and the data are plotted as points on the graph. Typically, the ***independent variable*** is plotted on the x axis and the ***dependent variable*** is plotted on the y axis.

An example of a scatter plot is shown in Figure 5.4. The plot gives information about whether a relationship exists between two variables and what the form of that relationship might be. From the plot it appears that as the value of X increases, so does the value of Y. Of course, what we know about variation in data tells us that the relationship will not be perfect. If there is a strong enough relationship between the two variables, then it should be apparent even in the presence of normal variation.

Creating a scatter plot is not difficult. Once you have selected which variable is the *independent* variable and which is the *dependent* variable, all you must do is draw a set of axes and scale them so that you can plot all of the data. You might have learned in a mathematics class at some time that when you create a graph on a pair of x–y axes the scales should both start at 0. Although this is often desirable in mathematics, it may not be suitable for a scatter plot in statistics. If your data are very large, then starting both axes at 0 might squash the graph into the top portion and actually hide the relationship. For this reason, we usually pick the starting points on the axes to be some reasonable number that is smaller than the smallest x and y values. When the axes are drawn, the data pairs are plotted as points on the graph.

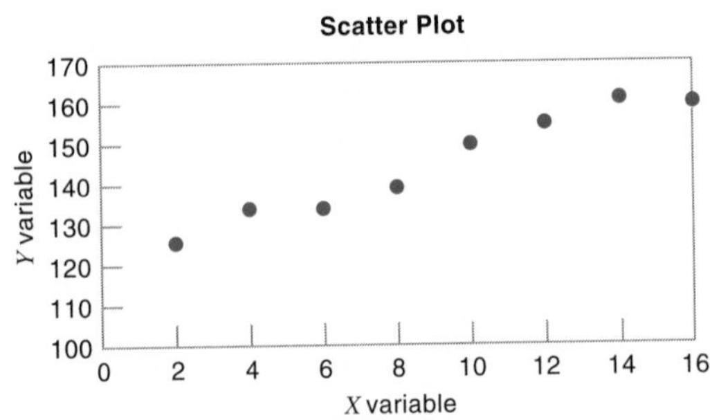

FIGURE 5.4 Scatter plot

EXAMPLE 5.7 ABC Faculty Salaries

Looking for Relationships

The Provost who is looking at faculty salaries is still convinced that there should be a relationship between the number of years of service to the university and faculty salary. She feels that it is time to look at these two variables together. Since both variables are quantitative, she knows that the first step in understanding the relationship will be to make a scatter plot of salary versus the number of years of service. Since she thinks that salary depends on years of service, she picks salary for the y (dependent) variable and years of service for the x (independent) variable. The plot she obtains is shown here:

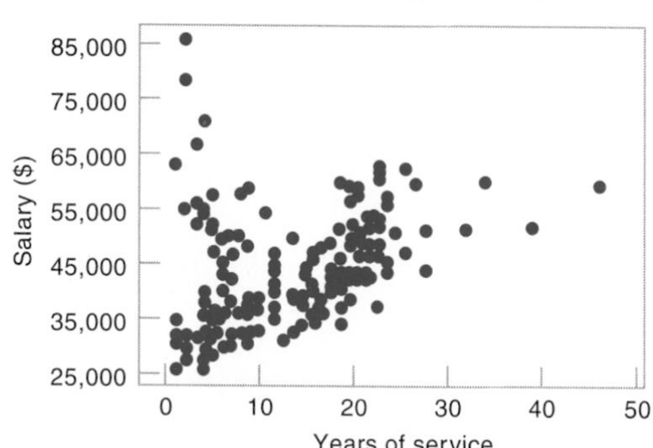

Analyze the Data

She looks at the plot and knows that she is basically correct—that salary and years of service are related and that the relationship is, for the most part, linear. She sees, however, that many data points do not quite fit the picture. She guesses that some of the other qualitative variables that she has been looking at might be of interest. ■

Draw Conclusions

EXAMPLE 5.8 Sales and Advertising

Creating a Scatter Plot

A pharmaceutical company is interested in determining whether there is a relationship between the amount of money spent in advertising and factory sales for a group of over-the-counter products. It seems reasonable to think that spending more on advertising will increase sales, but the company is not sure. The managers collect some data and find the following:

Understand the Problem

Advertising (millions of dollars)	143.8	91.7	43.8	26.7
Factory sales (millions of dollars)	855	360	170	130

Collect the Data

They decide to create a scatter plot to look at the data. Since they are expecting the amount of sales to depend on the amount spent on advertising, they pick sales to be the dependent (y) variable and advertising expenditures to be the independent (x) variable. After looking at the data they choose to scale the x axis from \$0 to \$150 million and the y axis from \$100 to \$900 million. They then plot each of the four data points on the graph.

Analyze the Data

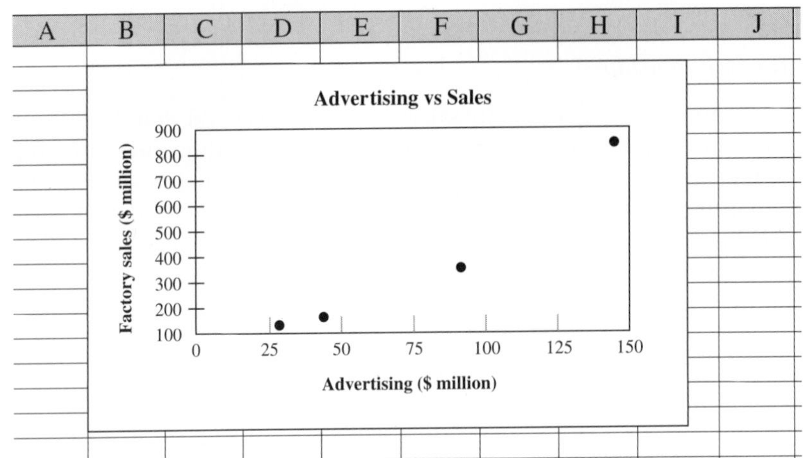

Draw Conclusions

From the graph they see that their idea was correct and that as advertising expenditures increase so do sales. ■

TRY IT NOW!

Airline Fares ***Creating a Scatter Plot***

A travel agency was interested in knowing how airline fares were related to the length of the flight in miles. The agency hypothesized that the longer the flight, the more the airfare. The following data were collected:

Miles	2375	1400	1250	2325	985	2025
Airfare ($)	430	272	252	422	207	373

Which variable is the dependent variable and which is the independent variable?

Make a scatter plot of the data.

From your plot, do you think that the travel agency's hypothesis was correct? Why or why not?

5.3.2 Types of Relationships

Once we determine that two variables are related, we often want to find an equation describing the relationship. This equation shows how the variables are related and can then be used to predict values of the dependent variable for different values of the independent variable. The purpose of a scatter plot is to give a visual clue about whether a relationship exists between two quantitative variables. The scatter plot will also give information about the type of relationship, which can be used to determine the correct method for finding the equation that relates the variables.

When two variables are related, the scatter plot forms some type of pattern that characterizes the form of the relationship. In Figure 5.5 you see some of the different types of relationships that can exist between variables.

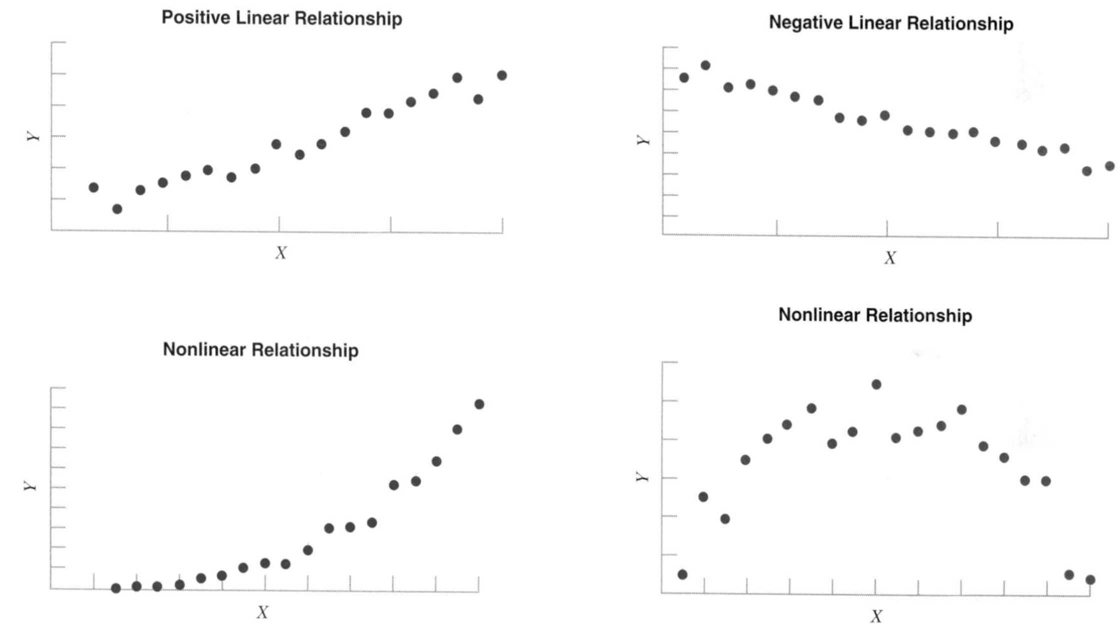

FIGURE 5.5 Various types of relationships between two variables

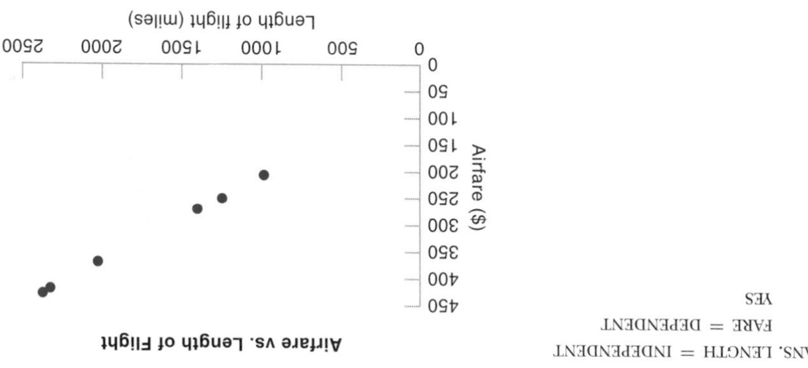

ANS. LENGTH = INDEPENDENT
FARE = DEPENDENT
YES

When two variables are not related, the scatter plot forms no pattern, as is seen in Figure 5.6.

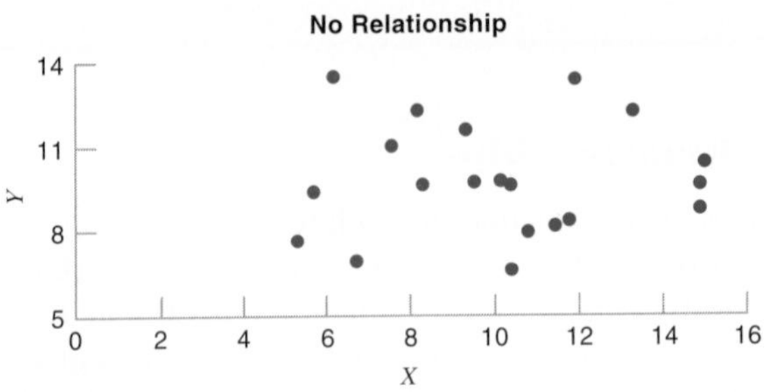

FIGURE 5.6 Scatter plot indicating no relationship between two variables

EXAMPLE 5.9 Training and Performance

Finding the Least-Squares Line

Understand the Problem

A company is interested in determining whether there is a relationship between the number of days that it spends training employees at a particular job and the employees' performance as measured on a standardized test. The managers collect the following data:

Collect the Data

Training days	Score
1.0	41
1.5	60
2.0	72
2.5	91
3.0	99

The first thing they do is display the data on a scatter plot to determine whether the two variables are related. Since they think that the score depends on the number of training days, they plot the score on the y axis and the number of training days on the x axis.

Analyze the Data

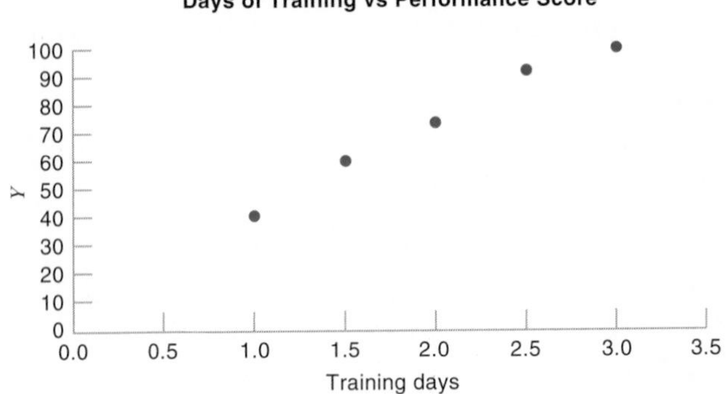

Draw Conclusions

The plot confirms their hypothesis and indicates that a linear relationship is appropriate. ■

Try It Now!

Starting Salaries and Math Courses *Finding the Least-Squares Line*

The Career Planning office of a large university is interested in knowing whether there is a relationship between the starting salary of graduates and the number of mathematics courses the graduates had taken as students. The Career Planning office goes through the records for the last year and finds the following data.

Number of math courses	Starting salary ($)
1	26,284
1	25,470
2	26,777
3	27,269
4	28,553
6	30,054

Which variable is the independent variable? The dependent variable?

Use the grid to create a scatter plot of the data.

(continued)

Do you think that there is a linear relationship between the number of math courses taken and the starting salary? If so, describe the relationship.

Discovery Exercise 5.1
DISCOVERING RELATIONSHIPS

Part I

1. The following data represent data taken on the number of weeks that a student was enrolled in a speed reading program and the speed gain in words per minute that the student has experienced:

Weeks	2	3	4	6	8
Speed gain	49	86	109	164	193

2. Plot the data on the graph paper. Be sure to label your axes and to construct the graph so that it uses most of the paper.

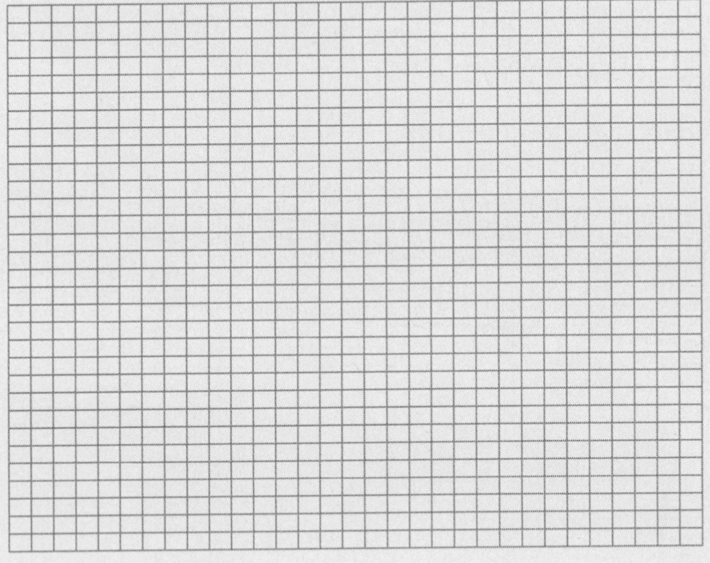

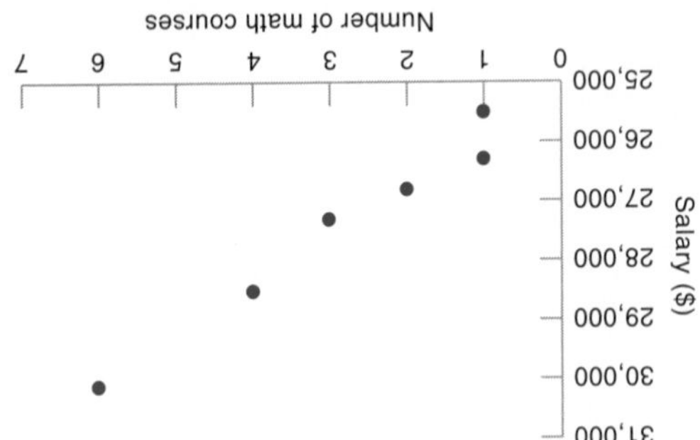

ANS. DEPENDENT—SALARY; INDEPENDENT—NUMBER OF MATH COURSES; YES. AS NUMBER OF MATH COURSES INCREASES, SO DOES SALARY.

3. Draw a straight line through the points that you think best represent the relationship between x and y. What criteria did you use for drawing the line you selected?

Part II

Use your ***line and the graph*** to answer the following questions. Do NOT use the data given:

1. What is the speed gain for a person who has spent 4 weeks in the program as predicted by the line?

2. If you were to select a person at random who had spent 3 weeks in the program, what would your prediction of that person's speed gain be?

3. By how much would you predict speed gain will change for a 1-week increase in time in the program?

4. Draw the line whose equation is $y = 10.1 + 23.9x$ on the graph.
5. Answer the prediction questions you previously answered using the new "best" line.

6. Agree that my line is better than yours (if it is different).

7. What do you think would happen if you used the line to predict the speed gain of a person who had been in the program for 1 week? 0 weeks? Is this reasonable?

8. What problems can you see with what we have done?

5.3.3 Least-Squares Line

If the relationship between the variables looks linear (like a straight line), then a curve-fitting technique called least squares can be used to find the equation of the line that best fits the data. In Chapters 11 and 12 you will use least squares in more depth in a statistical technique called regression analysis. At this point we use least squares to find the equation relating X and Y.

In drawing a line to fit a set of points, we would like to satisfy some criteria. First, we would like the line that is drawn to be unique. It would certainly not be very useful if everyone who saw the same set of data used a technique that produced a *different* line! Second, we would like the line to be as close as possible to all of the points. In Figure 5.7 you see the data points and a line drawn to represent the relationship between the variables. The distances from each point to the line are called the *deviations* or *errors*. We will use **least squares** to find the equation of the line that best represents the relationship between the two variables.

The ***least-squares*** technique finds the equation of the line that minimizes the sum of the squared errors between the actual data points and the line.

The reasons for minimizing the sum of the squared deviations rather than just the deviations or the absolute deviations are mathematical and are discussed in more detail in Chapter 11.

The ***least-squares line*** is defined by

$$\hat{y} = a + bx$$

The value $\hat{y}$ (y-hat) is the **predicted value** of y for a selected value of x. We are also interested in the **deviation** of the data from the least-squares line.

The distance between the predicted value of Y, $\hat{y}$, and the actual value of Y, y, is called the ***deviation*** or ***error***. The ***deviation***, ***e***, is equal to $\hat{y} - y$.

Calculating the Least-Squares Line

The actual method of least squares finds the *slope* and the *y intercept* of the line $\hat{y} = a + bx$. The least squares estimates for the slope, b, and the y intercept, a, are given by

Slope and Intercept of Least-Squares Line

$$b = \frac{n\Sigma XY - \Sigma X \Sigma Y}{n\Sigma X^2 - (\Sigma X)^2} \quad \text{and} \quad a = \frac{\Sigma Y}{n} - b\frac{\Sigma X}{n}$$

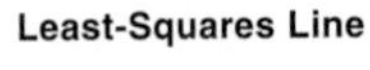

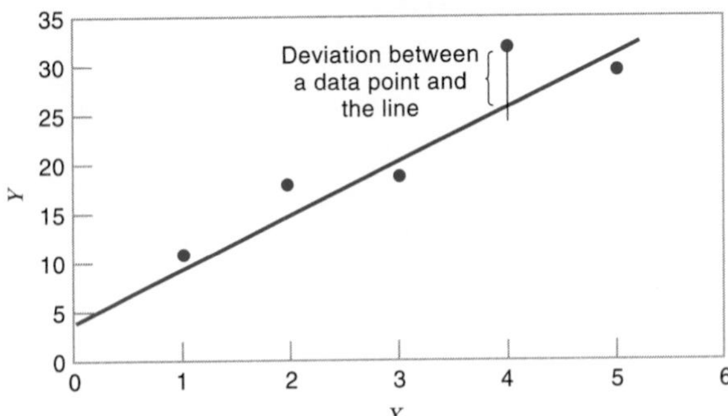

FIGURE 5.7 Deviations between the data points and the line

TABLE 5.2 Table for Calculating the Least-Squares Line

Observation number	X	Y	XY	X^2
1	x_1	y_1	$x_1 \times y_1$	$x_1 \times x_1$
2	x_2	y_2	$x_2 \times y_2$	$x_2 \times x_2$
⋮	⋮	⋮	⋮	⋮
n	x_n	y_n	$x_n \times y_n$	$x_n \times x_n$
Total	ΣX	ΣY	ΣXY	ΣX^2

Although these equations might seem too complicated to be true, if you look at them carefully you will see that really only five quantities have to be calculated. Four of the quantities are sums involving the data values x and y, and the fifth is the number of observations in the sample. As an example, look at the quantity ΣXY. This quantity is the sum of the products of the x and y values for each observation. The easiest way to calculate all of the quantities involved is to make a table with a column for each sum needed. The table will look like the one in Table 5.2.

In the table each x_i represents the value of X for the ith data point, and each y_i represents the Y value of the ith data point. The first column keeps track of the observation number, the next two columns are the values of X and Y for the observation, the next column is the product of the X and Y value for each observation, and the last column is the square of the X value of the observation.

EXAMPLE 5.10 Training and Performance

Finding the Least-Squares Line

The company looking at the relationship between training and performance decides to use the least-squares method to find the equation of the line that describes the relationship. The first thing the managers of the company do is to create the table shown here:

When you are substituting the value for b into the equation for a, do NOT round it. Round all of the values AFTER the calculations are done.

Observation number	Training days (X)	Score (Y)	XY	X^2
1	1.0	41	41.0	1.00
2	1.5	60	90.0	2.25
3	2.0	72	144.0	4.00
4	2.5	91	227.5	6.25
5	3.0	99	297.0	9.00
Total	10.0	363	799.5	22.50

Analyze the Data

Substituting the values in the last row of the table into the formulas, they obtain

$$b = \frac{(5)(799.5) - (10)(363)}{(5)(22.5) - (10^2)} = \frac{367.5}{12.5} = 29.4$$

$$a = \frac{363}{5} - (29.4)\frac{10}{5} = 13.8$$

Using these values, they find the least-squares line to be

$$\hat{y} = 13.8 + 29.4x$$

The equation tells them that the base score on the test is 13.8 points and that every day of training increases the score by 29.4 points. ■

TRY IT NOW!

Starting Salaries and Math Courses *Finding the Least-Squares Line*

The Career Planning Office at the university wants to use least squares to find the equation that relates the number of math courses taken and starting salary. The data are

Number of math courses	Starting salary ($)
1	26,284
1	25,470
2	26,777
3	27,269
4	28,553
6	30,054

Many calculators that do statistical calculations also find the least-squares line. If you have such a calculator it is probably worthwhile to learn how to do this.

(a) Find the equation for the least-squares line for the data. (*Hint:* Create a table like the one in Example 5.10 or use a computer software package.)

(b) Explain what the least-squares line tells the Career Planning Office about math courses and starting salary.

When you obtain the least-squares line it is often useful to plot the line on the same plot as the original data. This allows you to see how well the line fits the data values. Since two points determine a straight line, the easiest way to plot the line is to substitute two different values for X into the least-squares equation and solve for $\hat{y}$. Once you have two pairs of points you can plot them and draw the line.

EXAMPLE 5.11 Training and Performance

Plotting the Least-Squares Line

The company that is looking at performance scores and training days decides to plot the data and the line it had found on the same graph to see how well the line represents the data. To do this the company chooses two different values for X, 1 and 3 training days, and uses the equation to find the predicted scores. The following equations are obtained:

Analyze the Data

$$\hat{y} = 13.8 + 29.4(1) = 43.2 \quad \text{and} \quad \hat{y} = 13.8 + 29.4(3) = 102$$

ANS. $\hat{y} = 25{,}019 + 840.6x$; THE BASE SALARY IS \$25,019 AND EVERY MATH CLASS INCREASES IT BY \$840.60.

Thus, the least-squares line predicts that a person with 1 day of training would score 43.2 points and a person with 3 days of training would score 102 points. The company plots these points on the graph with the original data and draws the line. The resulting plot looks like this:

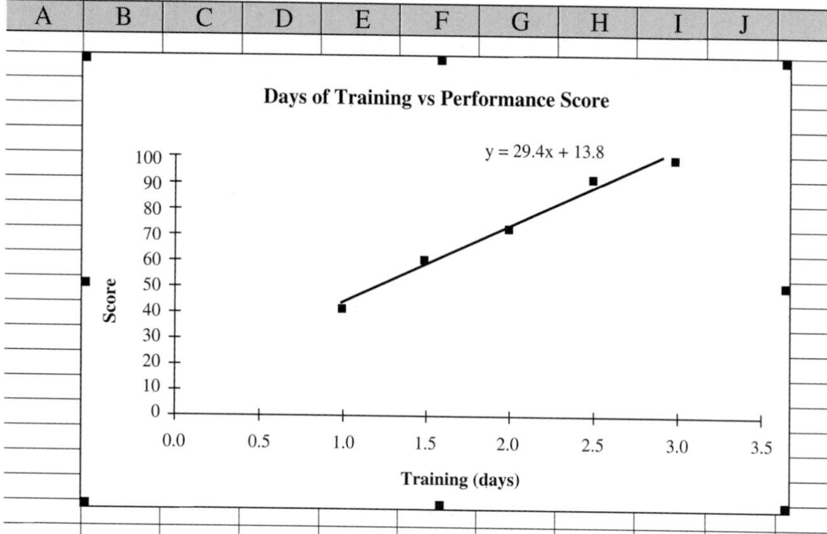

The plot shows that the line fits the data very well. ■

TRY IT NOW!

Starting Salaries and Math Courses ***Finding the Least-Squares Line***

Once the least-squares equation is obtained, the Career Planning Office wants to see whether the equation does a good job of predicting starting salary for a given number of math courses.

Plot the data and the least-squares line on the same graph.

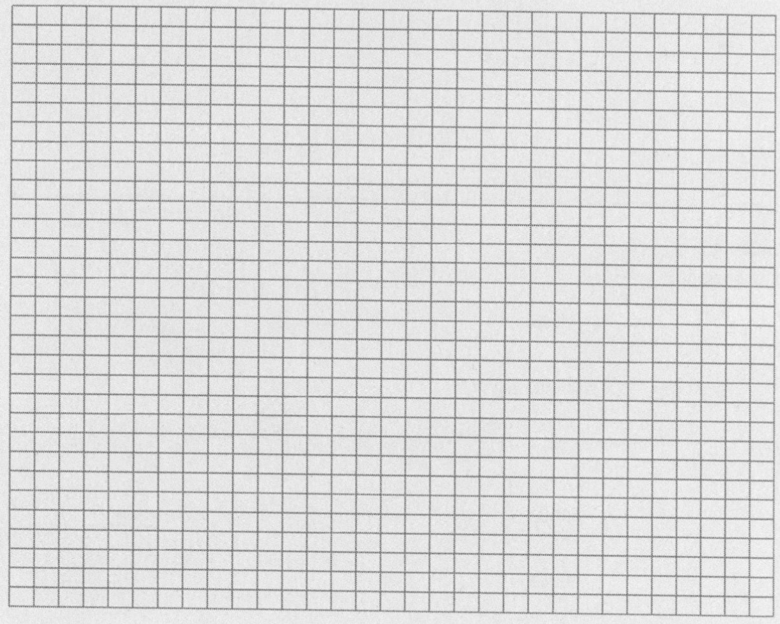

ANS. SEE PAGE 198.

Interpolation and Extrapolation

After finding the least-squares line, it might be reasonable to wonder when the equation can be used. When are the predictions useful? Are there any times when the predictions are not useful?

In the example on training days and performance score, the company used the equation of the least-squares line to predict scores for a person who was trained for 1 day and a person who was trained for 3 days. Notice that both of the values that they chose for X were *within* the range of X from the data they collected. This is called ***interpolation.*** There is another kind of prediction called ***extrapolation.***

> Predicting values for Y using values of X that are outside the data range is called ***extrapolation.*** Finding values for Y using X values that are within the data range is called ***interpolation.***

Interpolations are valid and they will produce good results if the line is a good fit. Predicting values for Y using values of X that are *outside* the data range, extrapolation, is usually quite dangerous. In reality, you have absolutely no knowledge of the relationship outside the range of the data and you have no business trying to predict it. It might be the case that the true relationship changes completely outside that range—perhaps as the number of days of training goes beyond a certain point, performance scores *decrease!* If you want to find a line to make predictions for certain values of the independent variable, it is necessary to collect data in that range.

TRY IT NOW!

Starting Salaries and Math Courses ***Finding the Least-Squares Line***

Use the equation you just found to predict the starting salary of a person who takes two mathematics courses. Do the same thing for the starting salary of a person who takes five mathematics courses.

ANS.

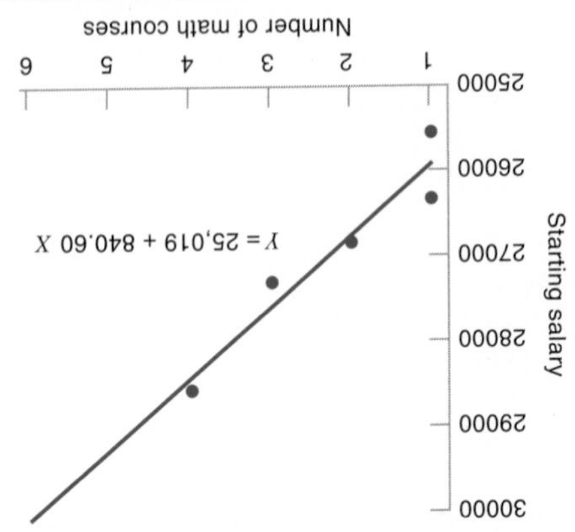

Do you think the predictions from the least-squares line are useful? Why or why not?

Is what you just did interpolation or extrapolation?

Now use the equation of the least-squares line to predict the starting salary of a person who takes no math courses. Do the same thing for a person who takes ten math courses.

Do you think these predictions are valid? Why or why not?

5.3.4 Exercises—Learning It!

5.4 In a study about postage tariffs and revenue, The European Economic Community wanted to look at the relationship between the number of postal employees in a country and the amount of domestic mail that was processed. They collected data for six different countries and found:

Country	Number of staff	Domestic traffic (billions of pieces)
Germany	342,413	18.32
France	289,156	23.87
Italy	221,534	6.62
Britain	189,000	16.75
Spain	65,355	4.06
Sweden	52,251	4.21

Source: *The Economist*, June 15, 1996.

(a) Create a scatter plot of the data and determine whether a linear relationship is appropriate.

(b) Find the equation of the least-squares line for the data.

(c) The Netherlands employs 53,560 postal workers. Use the least-squares equation to predict the domestic mail traffic for The Netherlands.

5.5 In trying to look at the effects of shopping center expansion, the Commerce Department decided to look at the relationship between the number of shopping centers and the retail sales for different states in the same region. The Department collected the data for the North Central states shown at the top of page 200.

ANS. $26,701; $29,223 INTERPOLATION $25,020, $33,426 NO. YOU ARE EXTRAPOLATING.

State	Number of Shopping Centers	Retail Sales ($ billion)	State	Number of Shopping Centers	Retail Sales ($ billion)
Illinois	2,096	41.8	Missouri	887	22.7
Indiana	905	21.4	Nebraska	264	5.7
Iowa	308	7.5	North Dakota	87	2.1
Kansas	481	11.6	Ohio	1,704	41.6
Michigan	1,018	25.3	South Dakota	58	1.3
Minnesota	471	13.9	Wisconsin	625	14.6

Source: *Statistical Abstract of the United States* 1999.

(a) Create a scatter plot of the data.

(b) Find the equation of the least-squares line relating retail sales and number of shopping centers.

(c) Plot the least-squares line and the data on the same plot. Do you think the line fits the data well? Why or why not?

(d) Use the least-squares equation to predict retail sales for each state.

5.6 As part of an international study on energy consumption, data were collected on the number of cars in a country and the total travel in kilometers. The data for 12 of the countries are shown here:

Country	Total cars (million cars)	Travel (billion km)	Country	Total cars (million cars)	Travel (billion km)
United States	142,352	3140	Netherlands	5,527	84
Finland	1,823	35	France	23,268	348
Denmark	1,664	31	Norway	1,592	24
Britain	21,316	353	Italy	26,117	368
Australia	8,534	138	Germany	43,752	609
Sweden	3,321	53	Japan	40,246	439

Source: *The Economist*, June 22, 1996.

(a) Create a scatter plot of the data. Do you think that there is a linear relationship between number of kilometers traveled and the number of cars?

(b) Find the least-squares line for the data. Interpret the value of the slope.

(c) Does the intercept make sense for these data? Why or why not?

(d) Plot the least-squares line on the same plot with the data. Does the line make you feel confident about predicting travel as a function of the number of cars?

(e) Use the least-squares equation to predict the number of kilometers traveled for Sweden and Japan. How well do the predictions agree with the original data?

5.7 In a study of why retail stores fail, data were collected on the type of retailer, the rental charges ($ per sq ft), and sales ($ per sq ft) for super regional shopping malls in the United States in 1993. The data are shown in the table:

Type of retailer	Rental charges ($/sq ft)	Sales ($/sq ft)
Department stores	2.0	131
Clothing and accessories	19.0	237
Gift/specialty	22.5	250
Shoes	22.5	259
Food service	32.0	342
Jewelry	40.0	555

Source: *The Economist*, March 1, 1997

(a) Create a scatter plot for the data. Do you think that the relationship between rental charges and sales is linear?

(b) Find the equation of the least-squares line for the data and interpret the value of the slope and the intercept.

(c) Does the intercept make sense for these data? Why or why not?

(d) Plot the least-squares line on the same plot with the data. Do you think the line does a good job of predicting sales as a function of rental charges? Why or why not?

5.4 Executive Summary

ABC COLLEGE (PART II)

Business Analysis...

TO: President, Aluacha Balaclava College
FROM: Provost, Aluacha Balaclava College
RE: Current Faculty Salaries

To increase our knowledge of faculty salaries, we decided to look at some additional variables, including Rank, Gender, School, and Tenure. These variables should provide additional insight into the makeup of the current faculty. The first phase of the analysis deals with the School for each faculty member. The other three variables will be examined in the next phase of the analysis.

When you look at faculty rank by school as shown in Figures 1 and 2, you can see that both the School of Liberal Arts and the School of Business tend to have faculty at higher ranks, whereas the School of Science and the School of Professional Studies have more faculty at the lower ranks. From Figure 2 you can see that Liberal Studies and Business have 72% and 63% of their faculty at the rank of Associate Professor or above, whereas Science and Professional Studies have 49% and 47% at these ranks.

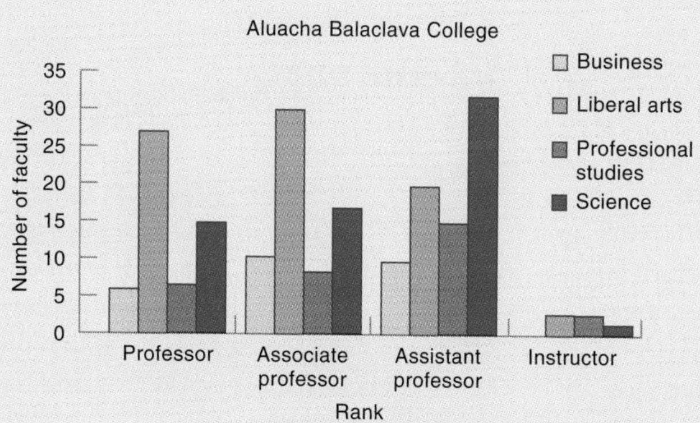

FIGURE 1

(continued)

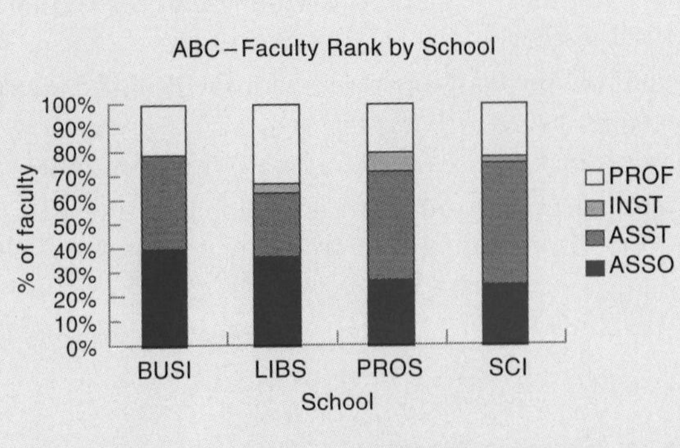

FIGURE 2

Based on the past, we expect to see a relationship between years of service and salary. Figure 3 shows that although such a relationship does appear to exist, it is not clear. When you look at a graph of salary versus years of service you can see that there is a great deal of variability in the data, as well as some anomalies that must be explained before we can understand the salary structure. For example, the faculty member with the highest salary has less than 5 years of service to the college.

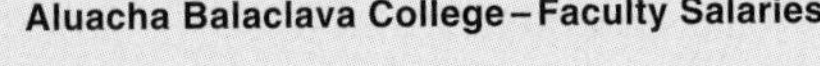

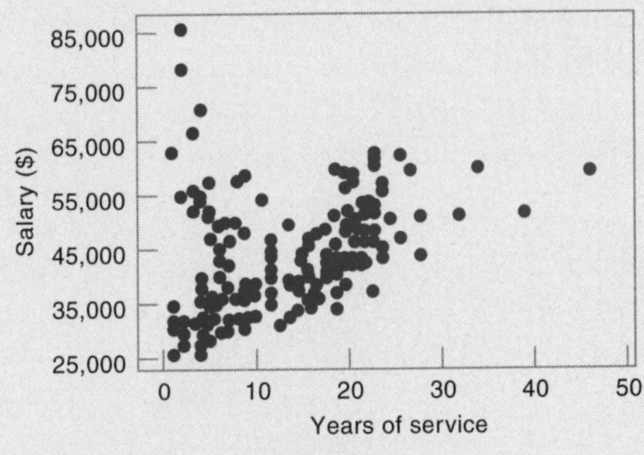

FIGURE 3

Certainly, a difference on the order of 20% in upper ranks among the various schools might influence the salary structure for each school. It is my recommendation that I continue to analyze the data by studying additional variables that might be important, particularly Rank, Gender, and Tenure, and try to identify the variable or variables that most affect salary. I will get back to you with my findings in 2 weeks.

The *Wall Street Journal* is a major source of current business news and information for the business community. If your professor has arranged for your class to have access to the Business Extra feature, you can go to it now and see the techniques of this chapter in action today. Go to the Wiley Web site at http://www.wiley.com/college/pelosi, and click on Business Extra!

5.5 BIVARIATE DATA IN EXCEL

This section covers the basics of displaying and analyzing bivariate data in Excel. Many of the steps involved are similar to those discussed in previous chapters.

5.5.1 Creating Contingency Tables in Excel

You have already learned the basics of creating tables in Excel, using the **Pivot Table** command. We will use this same tool to create contingency tables for bivariate data. Figure 5.8 shows a portion of the Aluacha Balaclava College data in an Excel worksheet. Suppose that we want to create a contingency table for the variables Rank and School. Highlight the range that contains the data you want to analyze. The steps for accomplishing this are:

Note: It is not necessary for the two columns you are interested in to be next to each other. You can highlight more than just the columns you want to analyze.

1. From the **Data** menu, select **Pivot Table and PivotChart Report.** The Pivot Table Wizard will start by asking what type of data you want to work with. Since you are using data that are already in an Excel worksheet, simply leave the default radio button checked and click on **Next>** to continue. You have the option to create only the table or a table and chart. We will create the table first and then the chart.
2. Since you have already highlighted the range that contains your data, you can just proceed by clicking **Next>.** If you have not indicated where your data are located, you can do that now by highlighting the range in the worksheet.
3. The next dialog box opens as shown here. Indicate where you want the Pivot Table to appear and click the button labeled **Layout.**

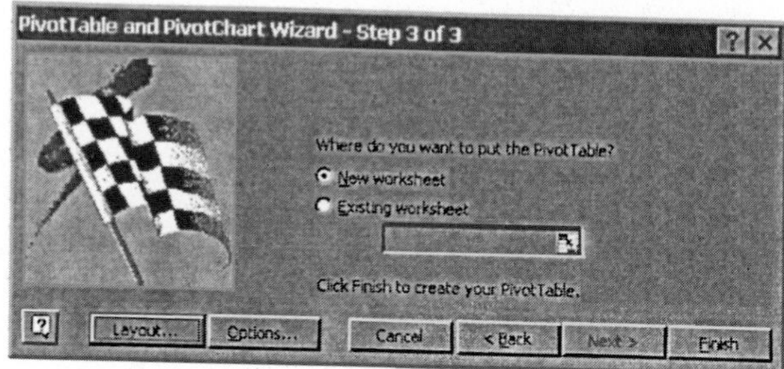

	A	B	C	D	E	F	G
1	Rank	Years at ABC	Salary 96-97	Gender	Tenure?	School	Rank
2	ASST	22	53316	F	Y	BUSI	ASST
3	PROF	11	64375	M	Y	BUSI	PROF
4	ASSO	7	63501	M	Y	BUSI	ASSO
5	ASSO	6	59426	M	N	BUSI	ASSO
6	ASSO	20	49058	M	Y	BUSI	ASSO
7	PROF	4	94969	M	N	BUSI	PROF
8	ASST	21	54762	M	Y	BUSI	ASST
9	ASSO	9	55516	M	Y	BUSI	ASSO
10	ASSO	18	45932	M	Y	BUSI	ASSO
11	ASSO	11	56871	M	Y	BUSI	ASSO

FIGURE 5.8 ABC Excel Worksheet

The last step of the process will define the table you want to create. The dialog box will show the list of variables (columns) that you highlighted. In this case, we will use the variables Rank and School to create the table, with Rank on the rows and School in the columns.

4. Drag the field box for Rank to the area marked **Row,** and the field box for School to the area marked **Column.** Now drag the field box for *either* Rank or School into the area marked **Data.** The dialog box should look like the one in Figure 5.9.

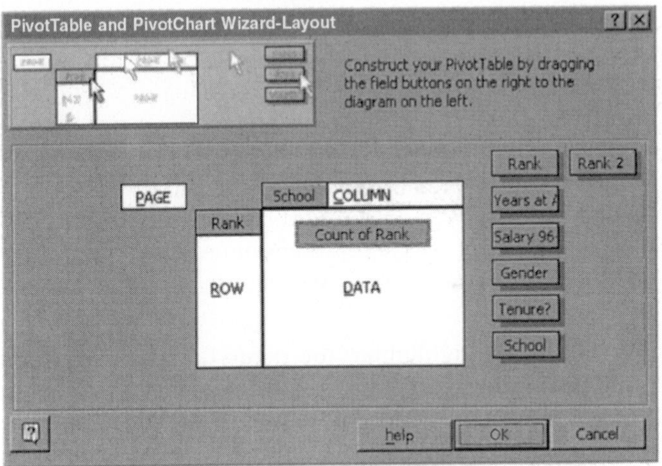

FIGURE 5.9 Creating the contingency table

5. Click on **Next** and tell Excel where you want the table to appear, either in the current worksheet or in a new worksheet.
6. Finally, click on **Finish;** the table shown in Figure 5.10 should appear.

Count of Rank	School				
Rank	BUSI	LIBS	PROS	SCI	Grand Total
ASSO	11	30	9	17	67
ASST	10	20	15	32	77
INST		3	3	2	8
PROF	6	27	7	15	55
Grand Total	27	80	34	66	207

FIGURE 5.10 Contingency table of the variables Rank and School

Note: *To change after the table is created, double click on the top left corner of the table.*

You might want to use relative frequencies instead of frequencies for the contingency table, particularly if you are going to use the table to create clustered or stacked bar charts. You can change the way the data are displayed while you are creating the contingency table.

1. After you drag the field to the **Data** section of the table, double click on it and the **Field** dialog box opens. Click on **Options>>** and the box expands, as shown in Figure 5.11.

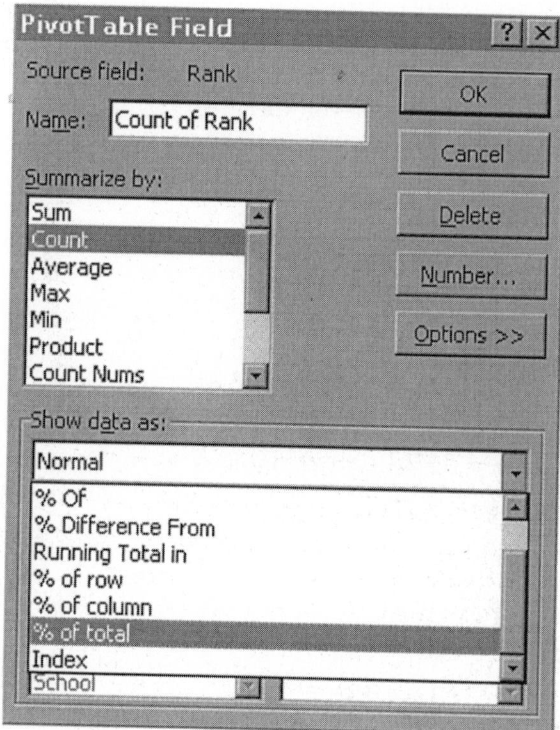

FIGURE 5.11 Changing the data display

2. Click on the drop down menu in the **Show data as** box, and select "% of total," "% of row," or "% of column." Your choice will, of course, be determined by what you want to do with the table later. Figure 5.12 shows the contingency table with the frequencies displayed as a percentage of the total number of observations.

Count of Rank	School				
Rank	BUSI	LIBS	PROS	SCI	Grand Total
ASSO	5.31%	14.49%	4.35%	8.21%	32.37%
ASST	4.83%	9.66%	7.25%	15.46%	37.20%
INST	0.00%	1.45%	1.45%	0.97%	3.86%
PROF	2.90%	13.04%	3.38%	7.25%	26.57%
Grand Total	13.04%	38.65%	16.43%	31.88%	100.00%

FIGURE 5.12 Contingency table with relative frequencies

5.5.2 Creating Clustered Bar Charts in Excel

Suppose you want to create a clustered bar chart for the faculty data, using the variable Rank as the axis variable, with a bar for each school. You can do this using either the frequency or relative frequency contingency table we just made.

The steps for creating a clustered bar chart are very similar to those for a simple bar chart. They are:

1. To highlight a portion of the pivot table, you will need to copy it to another location in the worksheet using the **Paste Special** command. To do this, click on the lower right hand corner of the table and highlight it. Select **Copy** from

Note: If the data in the copy do not appear as percents, use the ***Format cells*** *command to change the format to percentages.*

the **Edit** menu. Then, click on the location for the copy and select **Paste Special.** In the **Paste** section, click on the radio button for **Values** and in the **Operation** section, select **None,** as shown in Figure 5.13. Click **OK** and a copy of the table will appear in the location you specified.

Note: Never try to highlight the table from the top left corner—Excel will rearrange the table.

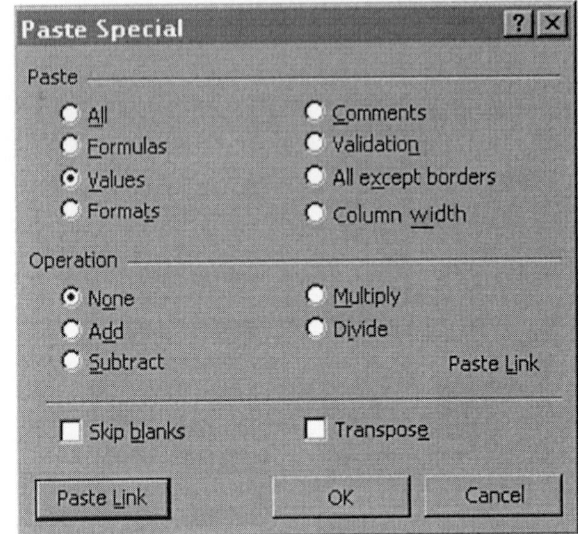

FIGIRE 5.13 Paste Special dialog box

2. Highlight the copy of the table, being careful *not* to highlight the Grand Total row or column. Then start the Chart Wizard and select **Column** as the type of chart and the clustered chart as the subtype.
3. Click **Next** twice to get to the Options step; add titles and make any desired formatting choices.
4. Click **Next** to indicate where you want the chart to be located and then click **Finish.** A chart similar to the one shown in Figure 5.14 should appear.

Note: The columns of the table will be the categories on the x axis, so plan ahead.

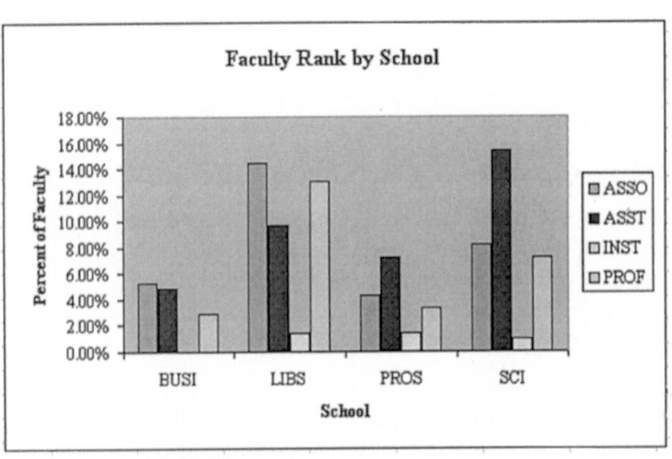

FIGURE 5.14 Clustered bar chart

5.5.3 Creating Stacked Bar Charts in Excel

To create a stacked bar chart in Excel, you will need to display the data in the contingency table differently. Suppose that you want to look at the different ranks as a percentage of the total for each school. You will need to recreate the contingency table for the data, displaying the data as a percent of the column (since School is the column variable). The new contingency table should look like Figure 5.15.

Count of Rank	School				
Rank	BUSI	LIBS	PROS	SCI	Grand Total
ASSO	40.74%	37.50%	26.47%	25.76%	32.37%
ASST	37.04%	25.00%	44.12%	48.48%	37.20%
INST	0.00%	3.75%	8.82%	3.03%	3.86%
PROF	22.22%	33.75%	20.59%	22.73%	26.57%
Grand Total	100.00%	100.00%	100.00%	100.00%	100.00%

FIGURE 5.15 Contingency table for stacked bar chart

The steps for creating a stacked bar chart are very similar to those for creating a clustered bar chart. You must make a copy of the table using the **Paste Special** command before you can highlight the data range.

1. Highlight the rows of the pivot table, being careful not to include the Grand Total row and column, and start the Chart Wizard.
2. Select Column as the chart type and 100% Stacked Column as the subtype, as shown in Figure 5.16.

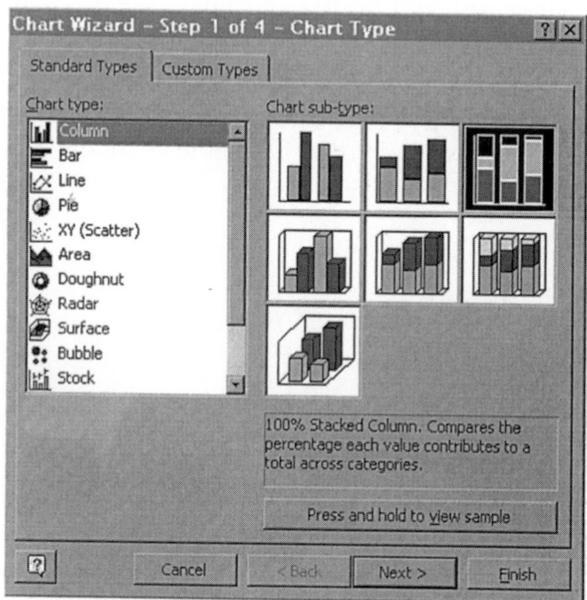

FIGURE 5.16 Selecting a stacked bar chart

3. Click **Next** twice to get to the Options step; put in titles and any other formatting changes that you want.
4. Click **Next,** enter the location for the chart, and click **Finish** to display the chart. It should look similar to the one in Figure 5.17.

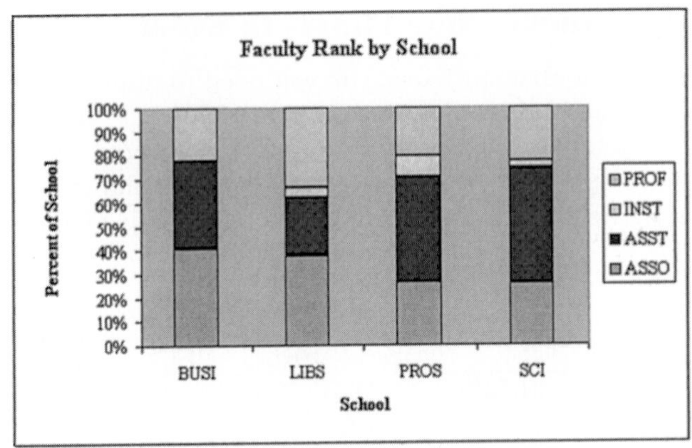

FIGURE 5.17 Stacked bar chart

5.5.4 Analyzing Quantitative Bivariate Data in Excel

When you learned how to analyze quantitative bivariate data, you learned about scatter plots and the least-squares line. Excel allows you to create a scatter plot and plot the least-squares line on the plot. Suppose that we want to plot the data for the number of training days and score on the aptitude test, and find the least-squares line. The data are shown in Figure 5.18.

When creating a scatter plot in Excel, it is important that the independent variable be in the first column, and the dependent variable in the second column. The steps for plotting the data and finding the least-squares line are as follows:

1. Highlight the range of the data and start the Chart Wizard. Select **XY** (Scatter) as the chart type and **Scatter** (no lines) for the subtype, as shown in Figure 5.19.
2. Click **Next>** twice to get to the **Chart Options** dialog box; put in titles and make any other desired formatting choices.
3. Select **Next>** to tell Excel where to locate the chart and **Finish** to display the chart. The chart should look like the one in Figure 5.20.

	A	B
1	**Training**	**Score**
2	1.0	41
3	1.5	60
4	2.0	72
5	2.5	91
6	3.0	99

FIGURE 5.18 Training data

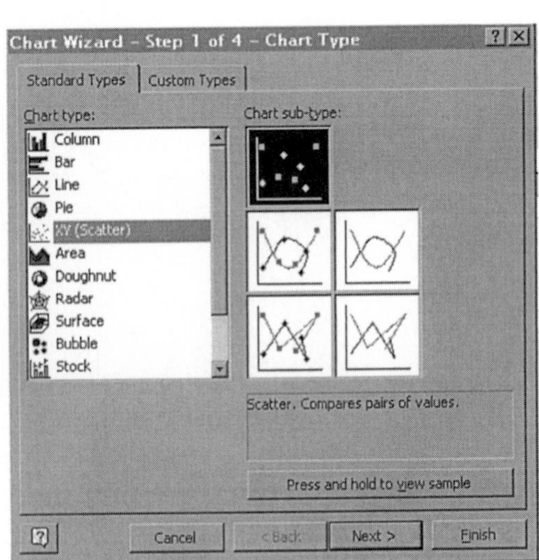

FIGURE 5.19 Selecting the scatter plot option

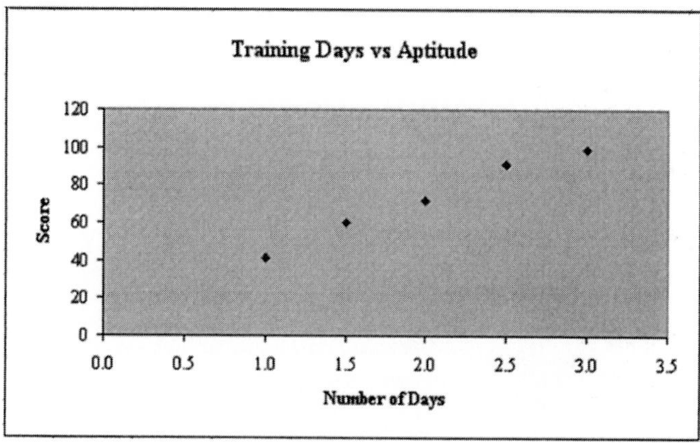

FIGURE 5.20 Finished scatter plot

Once you have the scatter plot, you can add the least-squares line as follows:

Make sure you single click here; double clicking will bring up a different dialog box.

1. Click on any one of the points in the scatter plot to highlight them all.
2. From the **Chart** menu, select **Add Trendline,** as shown in Figure 5.21. The **Add Trendline** dialog box will open.
3. In the Trend/Regression section, highlight **Linear,** as shown in Figure 5.22.

Note: If Add Trendline is not on the menu, hold the menu open for a few seconds until it expands.

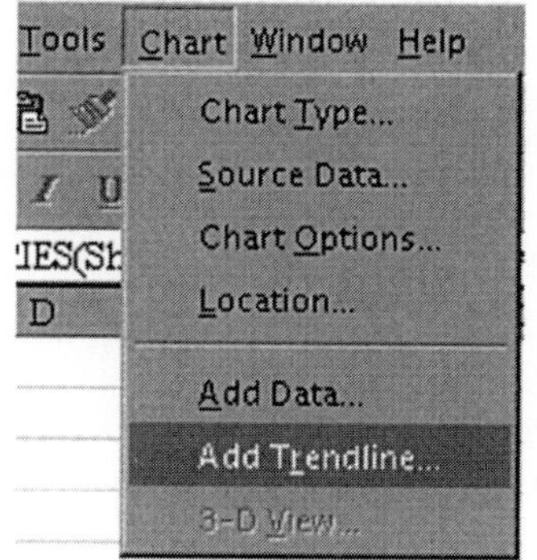

FIGURE 5.21 Chart menu

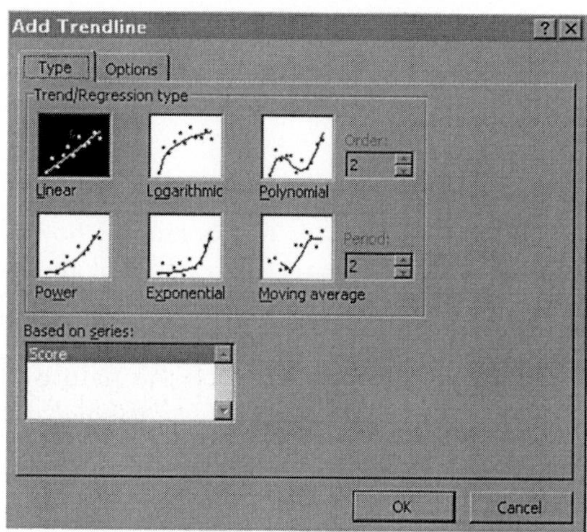

FIGURE 5.22 Selecting the type of trendline

4. Click on the **Options** tab and click the box labeled **Display equation on chart,** as shown in Figure 5.23. You can also choose to label the line with a title other than the default.
5. Click **OK;** the least-squares line and its equation will appear on the chart, as shown in Figure 5.24.

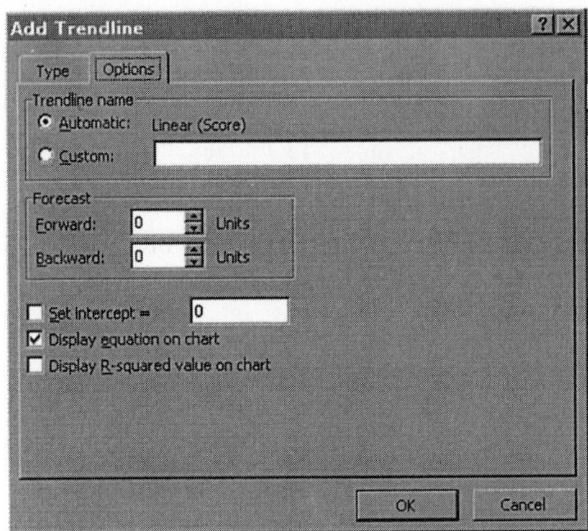

FIGURE 5.23 Trendline options

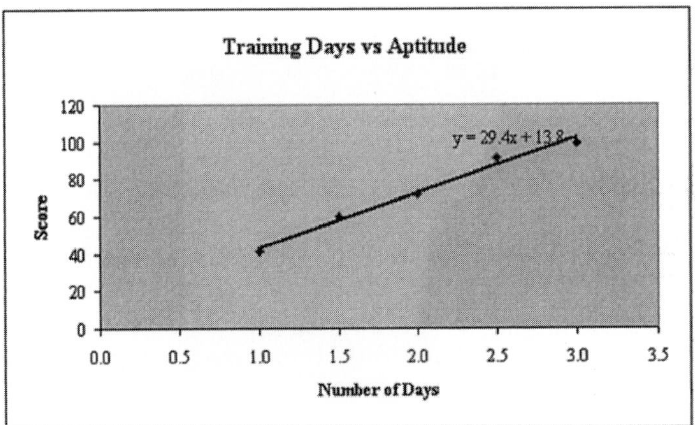

FIGURE 5.24 Scatter plot with least-squares line

Notice that Excel displays the equation with the slope term first and the intercept term last.

CHAPTER 5 SUMMARY

In this chapter you learned some methods for looking at how two variables are related. You learned that very often, we are interested not in a single variable, but rather in how variables are *related.* There are several different methods for looking at these relationships. There are graphical methods, such as *stacked bar charts, clustered bar charts,* and *scatter plots,* which allow you to see the nature of the relationships. There are also quantitative methods, such as *least-squares analysis,* which allow you to describe the relationship numerically.

By now you should be more convinced than ever that there is no standard way to analyze a set of data. Rather, various statistical tools are used together to produce the most complete *picture* of the data and the information they contain.

Key Terms

Term	Definition	Page reference
$\hat{y}$	$\hat{y}$ (**y-hat**) is the predicted value of y for a selected value of x	194
Clustered bar chart	A **clustered bar chart** is used in place of multiple bar charts to make comparisons for one of the qualitative variables. The bars are grouped according to the values of the other variable.	178
Contingency table	A **contingency table** is a table whose rows represent the possible values of one variable and whose columns represent the possible values for a second variable. The entries in the table are the number of times that each pair of values occurs.	174
Deviation (e)	The difference between the data point and the value predicted by the least-squares equation is called the **deviation, *e*.**	194
Extrapolation	Predicting values for Y using values of X that are outside the data range is called **extrapolation.**	198
Interpolation	Finding values for Y using X values that are within the data range is called **interpolation.**	198
Least squares	**Least squares** finds the equation of the line that minimizes the sum of the squared errors. between the actual data points and the line.	194
Scatter plot	A **scatter plot** is a graph used to represent bivariate quantitative data. Each of the variables and the data are plotted as points on the graph.	186
Stacked bar chart	In a **stacked bar chart** the data for the selected variable are represented as a percentage of the total for each category of the second variable. Each value of the selected variable is represented in a different way and the bars are "stacked" to total 100%.	181

Key Formulas

Term	Formula	Page reference
Least-squares equation	$\hat{y} = a + bx$	194
$\hat{y}$ (predicted value)	$\hat{y}$	194
***e* (deviation)**	$\hat{y} - y$	194
***a* (intercept estimate)**	$a = \frac{\Sigma Y}{n} - b\frac{\Sigma X}{n}$	194
***b* (slope estimate)**	$b = \frac{n\Sigma XY - \Sigma X \Sigma Y}{n\Sigma X^2 - (\Sigma X)^2}$	194

CHAPTER 5 EXERCISES

Learning It!

5.8 Consider the data on the number of students choosing different majors at Dartmouth College that you looked at in Chapter 3.

Major	1986	1991	1996
Anthropology	10	19	17
Art History	28	20	15
Asia	11	15	22

(continued)

Major	1986	1991	1996
Biology	31	44	108
Chemistry	28	15	55
Classics	2	1	8
Comparative Literature	5	6	6
Drama	13	8	5
Earth Science	8	15	7
Economics	90	66	93
English	156	143	92
French	23	15	19
Geography	23	28	28
Government	147	172	142
History	102	125	115
Mathematics	35	23	14
Music	10	3	11
Philosophy	21	28	25
Physics	13	10	16
Psychology	70	74	87
Religion	22	31	8
Sociology	17	26	15

(a) What type of bivariate chart would be appropriate for displaying these data?

(b) What variable would you choose for the *x*-axis categories?

(c) Create a clustered bar chart for the data.

5.9 In an effort to learn whether customers were correct about coupon life being shorter, the following data were collected:

	Number of coupons	
Coupon life	**1995**	**1996**
Less than 1 month	28	123
1–4 months	88	140
5–8 months	204	122
9–12 months	141	88
More than 1 year	39	27

(a) Use a clustered bar chart to display the data.

(b) Is the perception that coupon life is getting shorter justified? Why or why not?

5.10 Look again at the data on the percentage of people who reported workplace violence that were presented in Chapter 3.

Workplace violence survey	
Type of violence	**% who reported**
Harassment	19
Threat of physical harm	7
Physical attack	3

	Type of violence (%)		
Major effect on worker	**Harassment**	**Threat**	**Physical**
Psychologically	49	53	49
Disrupted work life	34	25	25
Physically injured or sick	13	9	17
No negative effect	4	13	9

Display these data on a single graph.

5.11 Large companies are always looking for expanding markets. Media companies in particular are looking at foreign markets for expansion. To obtain some information about expansion possibilities in Central Europe, a major communications company collected data on revenues from television advertising and the percentage of households with cable or satellite television for seven countries.

Country	% of households	TV advertising revenues
Hungary	55	170
Slovakia	47	28
Poland	33	369
Czech Republic	28	105
Romania	27	40
Russia	15	250
Bulgaria	9	23

Source: *The Economist*, July 6, 1996

(a) Create a scatter plot of the data. Does it appear that advertising revenues are related to the percentage of households that have cable or satellite TV?

(b) Find the equation of the least-squares line for the data.

(c) Plot the least-squares line on the same plot as the data. Do you think that the line does a good job of predicting TV advertising revenues? Why or why not?

(d) In the Ukraine, 8% of the households have cable or satellite television. Use the line to predict TV advertising revenues for the Ukraine.

5.12 For many countries, tourism contributes a large part of revenues. In trying to predict tourism revenues, one of the independent variables that is considered important is the number of foreign visitors to the country. Data for six different countries were collected:

Country	Number of visitors (million)	Tourism receipts ($ billion)
France	60	27.3
Spain	48	25.1
United States	45	58.4
Italy	30	27.1
Britain	23	17.5
Germany	15	11.9

Source: *The Economist*, July 1996

(a) Create a scatter plot of the data and find the equation of the least-squares line.

(b) Use the least-squares line to predict tourism revenues for Italy and the United States.

(c) For which country does the least-squares line do the best job of predicting tourism receipts?

5.13 As part of the anticrime bill passed in 1995, the U.S. government granted money to different cities to hire new beat-patrol officers. Nine cities in New Jersey were given grants and hired officers. In trying to assess the program, government analysts wanted to look at the relationship between the number of officers hired and the amount of the grant. The data are

Grant ($)	Number of officers
150,000	2
375,000	5
471,125	6
70,967	1
450,000	6

(continued)

Grant ($)	Number of officers
525,000	7
375,370	7
750,000	10
1,000,000	12

Source: Justice Department

(a) Create a scatter plot of the data.

(b) Find the equation of the least-squares line.

(c) Plot the least-squares line on the same plot as the data.

(d) How well do you think the line fits the data?

(e) Use the equation to predict the number of officers hired for each city.

(f) Compare the values from the least-squares line to the actual data.

5.14 As communications and the media change and become more important in the economy, the radio industry has become an area of concern. One of the major communications companies wanted to look at the relationship between the number of radio stations a company owned and the revenues generated by radio. The company collected the following data:

Company	Number of stations	Revenues ($ billion)
Westinghouse/Infinity	83	1.05
Jacor	57	0.31
Clear Channel	104	0.31
Evergreen	35	0.30
Disney/ABC	21	0.29
American Radio Systems	63	0.23
SFX	67	0.22
Chancellor	41	0.21
Cox	38	0.21
Bonneville	20	0.12

Source: *The Economist*, June 29, 1996; *Duncan's American Radio*

(a) Create a scatter plot of the data. Do you think that there is a relationship between the number of stations that a company owns and the revenues generated by radio?

(b) Find the least-squares line for the data.

Thinking About It!

5.15 The summer of 1995 is remembered as one of the hottest summers on record. The *New York Times* reported on the amount of electricity used and the temperature for ten different record breaking days:

Date	Temperature (°F)	Electrical usage (MW)
August 2, 1995	95	10,805
July 23, 1991	99	10,752
July 8, 1993	100	10,667
July 27, 1993	93	10,654
July 27, 1995	90	10,567
June 20, 1995	95	10,551
July 9, 1995	101	10,398
July 26, 1995	90	10,391
July 8, 1994	90	10,368
July 19, 1991	96	10,349

(a) Do you think it is likely that the amount of electrical usage in New York City depends on the temperature?

(b) Create a scatter plot showing the relationship between electrical usage and temperature.

(c) Do you think the data indicate a relationship between the two variables? Why or why not?

(d) Can you think of any other variables or factors that might be hiding a relationship? If so, what might that variable or factor be?

(e) Eliminate the days from years other than 1995 and replot the data. Now what do you see?

(f) Do any of the data points appear to be unusual? Can you offer any explanation for this?

(g) July 9, 1995 was a Sunday (which means that businesses in New York City were closed). Eliminate this point and replot the data. Now what do you see?

(h) Find the least-squares line for the data from the last plot.

5.16 The pharmaceutical company that is looking at the relationship between advertising expenditures and sales of over the counter drugs collects some additional data:

Drug	Advertising ($ millions)	Factory sales ($ millions)
Tylenol	143.8	855
Advil	91.7	360
Vicks	26.6	350
One Touch	2.0	220
Robitussin	37.7	205
Bayer Aspirin	43.8	170
Alka-Seltzer	52.2	160
Centrum	16.5	150
Mylanta	32.8	135
Tums	27.6	135
Excedrin	26.7	130
Benadryl	30.9	130
Halls	17.4	130
Metamucil	12.1	125
Sudafed	28.6	115

(a) Make a scatter plot of the data.

(b) What explanation can you offer for the fact that there does not appear to be a relationship between advertising expenditures and sales? What additional information do you think would help put the data in perspective?

(c) Separate the drugs listed into four categories: pain relievers, digestive, cold/allergy, and other.

(d) Create four different scatter plots. Does this change anything? If so, how?

(e) For each of the categories that show a relationship between sales and advertising, find the equation of the least-squares line.

(f) Do the equations have any similarities? If so, what are they?

5.17 Consider the data on revenue and number of radio stations owned by various companies. *Requires Exercise 5.14*

(a) Use the least-squares line to predict the radio revenues for Chancellor and Westinghouse/Infinity. Which prediction is better?

(b) Leave out the data point for Westinghouse/Infinity and recalculate the least-squares line. Do you think that this line will do a better job of predicting radio revenues? Why or why not?

5.18 The Commerce Department also has data available on number of shopping centers and retail sales for the South Central States. The data are given at the top of page 216. *Requires Exercise 5.5*

State	Number of Shopping Centers	Retail Sales ($ billion)
Alabama	630	15.5
Arkansas	370	7.5
Kentucky	616	13.9
Louisiana	700	18.7
Mississippi	430	8.2
Oklahoma	568	13.2
Tennessee	1,200	23.0
Texas	2,976	87.3

Source: *Statistical Abstract of the United States 1999*

(a) Create a scatter plot of the data. Do you think that the variables are linearly related?

(b) Find the equation of the least-squares line for the data.

(c) How does the equation for the South Central States compare to the one you found for the North Central States?

(d) Would you have expected the least-squares lines for the South Central and North Central States to be exactly the same? Why or why not?

(e) What similarities would you expect them to have? What differences?

Requires Exercises 5.5, 5.18

5.19 Combine the data on retail sales and number of shopping centers for the North Central and South Central states. Data for the North Central states are repeated here for convenience.

State	Number of Shopping Centers	Retail Sales ($ billion)
Illinois	2,096	41.8
Indiana	905	21.4
Iowa	308	7.5
Kansas	481	11.6
Michigan	1,018	25.3
Minnesota	471	13.9
Missouri	887	22.7
Nebraska	264	5.7
North Dakota	87	2.1
Ohio	1,704	41.6
South Dakota	58	1.3
Wisconsin	625	14.6

(a) Create a scatter plot of the data and find the equation of the least-squares line.

(b) Plot the least-squares line on the scatter plot.

(c) Your boss says that the model for the combined data will be better than the model for the two areas separately because there are more data for the combined equation. Write a memo to your boss explaining your results and which method you think is better. Be sure to back up your opinions with the analyses.

Doing It!

Datafile: FACULTY.XXX

5.20 The Provost at Aluacha Balaclava College wants to look at the faculty salary data in some other ways. She has collected data on salary, years of service, rank, school, gender, and tenure. A sample of the data is shown here:

Salary ($)	Years of service	Rank	Schools	Gender (M/F)	Tenure (Y/N)
53,316	22	ASST	BUSINESS	F	Y
64,375	11	PROF	BUSINESS	M	Y
63,501	7	ASSO	BUSINESS	M	Y

(continued)

Salary ($)	Years of service	Rank	Schools	Gender (M/F)	Tenure (Y/N)
59,426	6	ASSO	BUSINESS	M	N
49,058	20	ASSO	BUSINESS	M	Y
94,969	4	PROF	BUSINESS	M	N
54,762	21	ASST	BUSINESS	M	Y
55,516	9	ASSO	BUSINESS	M	Y

(a) Create graphical displays that analyze the relationship between gender and rank and gender and school. Is there anything that the Provost might find interesting? Why or why not?

(b) Create graphical displays that look at tenure by school and by rank. What can you say about these data?

(c) Look at salary versus years of service for each rank separately. Do you think that the relationship between the two variables is still valid? Is it easier to see the relationship when the data are separated like this? Why or why not?

(d) Find least-squares equations that will enable the Provost to predict salary based on years of service for each rank. Do you think the equations do a good job of predicting salary? Why or why not?

(e) Are each of the equations you found in the previous part the same? Would you have expected them to be? How do they compare?

(f) Redo the analysis of salary and years of service considering some of the other qualitative variables. Do any of them make the least-squares equations better?

(g) Which qualitative variable, if any, would you suggest that the Provost at ABC use to separate the data? Why?

(h) Write a memo to the President of the college summarizing your results. Include suggestions for the next phase of the analysis.

5.21 The following data were collected from ten big fund managers about the ways in which their holdings were distributed:

Bond Holdings by Currency (%)

Currency	Neutral weights	A	B	C	D	E	F	G	H	I	J
Dollar	33	31	54	45	38	32	32	46	27	42	31
Yen	19	19	6	15	15	15	18	0	12	11	18
Sterling	5	6	2	6	4	3	4	7	5	6	7
DM	10	8	12	18	15	13	10	18	32	14	16
FFr	7	5	12	8	2	10	8	5	5	4	8
Others	26	31	14	8	26	27	28	24	19	23	20
Sum	100	100	100	100	100	100	100	100	100	100	100

Holdings by Instrument (%)

Instrument	A	B	C	D	E	F	G	H	I	J
Equities	40	78	70	65	50	50	50	36	60	31
Bonds	50	14	20	30	42	45	45	54	40	48
Cash	10	8	10	5	8	5	5	10	0	21
Sum	100	100	100	100	100	100	100	100	100	100

Equity Holdings by Area (%)

Area	Neutral weights	A	B	C	D	E	F	G	H	I	J
Americas											
United States	42	39	46	35	24	26	41	28	28	34	29
Others	2	4	4	1	5	2	3	2	0	2	2

(continued)

Equity Holdings by Area (%)

Area	Neutral weights	A	B	C	D	E	F	G	H	I	J
Europe											
Britain	9	8	4	7	7	6	6	7	12	6	8
Germany	4	4	2	8	7	8	4	9	6	8	4
France	4	3	2	3	4	10	4	7	14	1	6
Others	11	9	8	1	15	17	8	7	13	15	13
Asia											
Japan	22	21	23	35	30	25	24	30	17	25	30
Others	6	12	11	10	8	6	10	10	10	9	8
Sum	100	100	100	100	100	100	100	100	100	100	100

Key:
FUND

A Merrill Lynch
B Lehman Brothers
C Nikko Securities
D Daiwa Europe
E Credit Agricole
F Robeco Group Asset Management
G Bank Julius Baer (Zurich)
H UBS International Investment
I Commerz International Capital Management
J Credit Suisse Asset Management

(a) Create an appropriate graphical display to show how holdings are distributed among the three instruments (equities, bonds, cash) for each of the funds.

(b) Create a graphical display of equity holdings both for continent and countries. Compare these to each other and to the neutral weights.

(c) Create a graphical summary for bond holdings by currency for each of the funds. Compare them to each other and to the neutral weights.

(d) Create any other graphs and displays that you think help to summarize the data.

(e) Prepare a report on distribution of holdings for the ten funds surveyed.

CHAPTER 6

PROBABILITY

CREDIT PROBLEMS

One of the problems facing a small business is that of borrowing money. As a result of problems with loan defaults, banks and other lending institutions have imposed more stringent conditions for obtaining loans. Thus, many small businesses find themselves forced to close because they cannot meet the stiffer requirements.

Business Dilemma...

The problems of small businesses affect the cities and towns in which the businesses are located. The towns would like to know what is going on and how they can help. A medium-size New England city has been trying to understand the problems facing the small businesses in their town by administering a questionnaire every 6 months. The questionnaire collects information on the size of the business in terms of annual sales and employees, the type of business, and whether the business is experiencing recession-related problems. A sample of the data is shown here:

Number	Size	Employee	Nature	Problem	Understand	Concerned	Call	Loan	Collateral	Access
1	2	2	1	1	2	1	2	2	0	2
2	1	2	3	1	2	2	0	2	2	1
3	4	3	1	2	1	2	2	2	2	0
4	1	1	1	2	1	2	2	2	2	2
5	1	2	1	2	0	0	0	0	0	0
6	3	1	5	2	0	2	2	2	2	1

(Credit Problems continued)

The variables and coded values are fully explained in Exercise 6.38 at the end of the chapter.

The data are categorical and are coded. For example, for the variable Size, the value 2 refers to a company that has six to ten employees.

The town has employed an analyst to help interpret the results of the study and to determine how the small businesses in the city are being affected by credit problems.

6.1 CHAPTER OBJECTIVES

In Chapters 3–5 you learned different ways to summarize and describe data that were collected. The data were usually random samples from different populations, but the techniques used really described only the sample data.

In this chapter we look at how *probability theory* can be used to measure and predict what is *likely* to happen when data are collected from different populations. This chapter covers the following topics:

- Basic Probability Rules
- Random Variables and Probability Distributions
- The Binomial Probability Distribution
- The Normal Probability Distribution

6.2 BASIC RULES OF PROBABILITY

Probability is a concept that you are most likely familiar with, although perhaps not in a formal sense. Whenever you talk about whether some event is likely to occur, such as whether it will rain tomorrow, you are using the concepts of **probability.**

> ***Probability*** is a measure of how likely it is that something will occur.

To talk about probability using the language of probability it is necessary to define some terms. In probability and statistics we often speak of **experiments.** These are not experiments in the laboratory sense, but rather are the actions we perform to collect data. As an experiment we might count the number of students who miss statistics class each day or record the color of the car parked next to us in the parking lot.

An *experiment* is any action whose outcomes are recordable data.

When we perform an experiment, or collect data, we must think about what outcomes might occur so that we know what form our data will take. This is called the **sample space** of the experiment. You remember from the previous chapters that data can be qualitative or quantitative and that we use different techniques when we analyze them.

The *sample space, S,* is the set of all possible outcomes of an experiment.

As a very simple experiment, consider rolling a single, six-sided die and recording the number of spots on the top facing side. You know that there are six possible outcomes of the experiment, so the sample space is

The brackets { } are used to indicate a sample space.

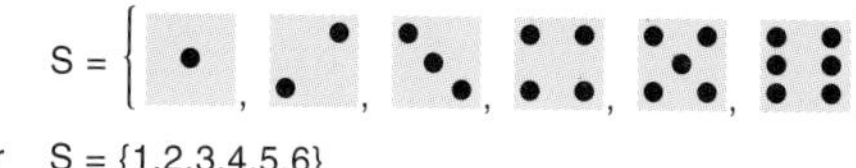

or S = {1,2,3,4,5,6}

Another example is the sample space for the experiment of tossing a coin. In this case the sample space is

or S = {H, T}, where H represents a head and T represents a tail

Depending on the experiment and the type of data collected, a sample space might have a *finite* number of elements such as the ones we just described. The word *finite* means that you can count the number of elements. This will most often happen when the experiment results in qualitative data or in quantitative data that are integer.

When the data from the experiment are quantitative and continuous, then the sample space contains an *infinite* number of possible values and must be described mathematically or in words. For example, suppose that as our experiment we decide to take college students at random and measure their heights. This is an example of *continuous* qualitative data. The number of possible values that we get will be *bounded* (there are probably not any college students shorter than one foot or taller than eight feet) but *infinite* (since height is a measurement and there are an infinite number of measurements between 1 foot and 8 feet). To describe this sample space we might write

S = {all numbers greater than or equal to 1 and less than or equal to 8}

or using mathematical notation

$$S = \{x: 1 \leq x \leq 8\}$$

Figuring out the sample space for an experiment is important in data collection, too. It helps the experimenter think about all of the possible results they might obtain and to plan for them.

EXAMPLE 6.1 Flipping Two Coins

Writing Out a Sample Space

An experiment consists of flipping two standard coins and writing down what is on the side facing up for each of the coins. If we let H represent a head and T represent a tail, then the sample space for this experiment is

$$S = \{HH, HT, TH, TT\}$$

HT and TH are different even if the coins are both quarters, but this is another way to try and think about it.

If you are thinking that HT and TH are the same outcome, then try to think of tossing the coins one after another or think of the problem as if the coins are different, such as a penny and a quarter. In writing out sample spaces it is best not to combine outcomes, but to write each one separately. ■

TRY IT NOW!

The Spinner Problem ***Writing out the Sample Space***

An experiment consists of spinning the two different spinners pictured here:

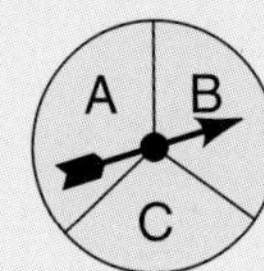

Write down the sample space for this experiment.

You may be wondering what rolling dice and spinning spinners have to do with collecting data and you are right to wonder. In fact, they have little to do with the types of problems you will encounter in statistics, but they do form an easy basis for discussing and understanding the general rules of probability.

6.2.1 Probability of an Event

Several of the sample spaces that you looked at have something in common that make calculating probabilities easy. This feature is that each of the outcomes in the sample space is equally likely to occur on any given trial of the experiment. For example, when you roll a single die, each of the six possible outcomes in **S** is equally likely to occur. The same is true about flipping coins, both one coin and two coins.

Often we are interested in knowing how likely it is that a certain outcome or outcomes of the experiment will occur. We call these outcomes the **events** of interest.

An ***event, A,*** is an outcome or a set of outcomes that are of interest to the experimenter.

ANS. {1A, 1B, 1C, 2A, 2B, 2C, 3A, 3B, 3C}

The **probability** that an event A will occur is written as P(A) and is read "the probability of A."

> The ***probability of an event A,* P(A),** is a measure of the likelihood that an event A will occur.

When each of the outcomes in a sample space *is equally likely,* then the probability of A can be calculated using the following formula:

Formula for P(A)

$$P(A) = \frac{\text{Number of ways that A can occur}}{\text{Total number of possible outcomes}}$$

or

$$P(A) = \frac{n_A}{N}$$

where n_A is the number of outcomes that correspond to the event, A, and N is the total number of outcomes in the sample space, S.

Although you have been taught to reduce fractions and use decimals, when we are calculating probabilities here we will not do this so that you can see the actual number of outcomes of interest.

If you look at the simple experiment of flipping a coin described earlier, you can see that if S = {H, T} and we look at the event A = coin turns up heads, then $P(A) = \frac{1}{2}$, since there is only one way that the event A can occur and there are two possible outcomes of the experiment. This should not be surprising, since it is one of the ways you know probability intuitively.

Similarly if we look at the experiment of rolling a die where S = {1, 2, 3, 4, 5, 6} and we let A be the event that the number that comes up is even, then

$$P(A) = \tfrac{3}{6} = \tfrac{1}{2}$$

since there are 3 even numbers possible out of the 6 possible outcomes of the experiment. Again, this is not surprising since it is somewhat intuitive.

There are some facts about probabilities that must be true:

These facts may seem trivial, but try to keep them in mind when you calculate probabilities. If you get an answer that is not a number between 0 and 1 then ***it cannot be correct!***

1. $0 \leq P(A) \leq 1$. This says that the probability of an event must be a number between 0 and 1 inclusive. Since you know that probabilities are formed by taking the ratio of the number of ways that A can happen to the total number of outcomes, the numerator is a subset of (smaller than or equal to) the denominator.
2. P(S) = 1. This says that the sum of the probabilities for the entire sample space must be equal to 1, or that essentially, when you perform an experiment, something must happen!
3. If an event A *must* happen, then P(A) = 1, and if the event cannot happen, then P(A) = 0.

EXAMPLE 6.2 Flipping Two Coins

Finding Probabilities

Joe and Tom decide to flip coins to determine who will pay for dinner. They agree that if the coins match Joe will pay and if they do not match Tom will pay. What is the probability that Tom pays for dinner?

Remember from the previous example that the sample space for this experiment is given by S = {HH, HT, TH, TT}. If we let A be the event that Tom pays, then we can write

A = the two coins do not match

It was important to list HT and TH as different outcomes so that the outcomes in S are all equally likely.

Looking at S, we see that the outcomes in the sample space are equally likely to occur and that two outcomes correspond to the event A: HT and TH. Thus, the probability that Tom pays for dinner is

$$P(A) = \tfrac{2}{4}$$

Using the same approach, if we let B be the event that Joe pays for dinner, or

$$B = \text{the two coins match}$$

then there are two outcomes in S that correspond to B, HH and TT, so

$$P(B) = \tfrac{2}{4}$$

From this we see that the arrangement is fair to both people. ■

Finding probabilities when the events are equally likely is not hard if you can write down the sample space, S, without much difficulty. These types of problems are knows as "classical" probability problems. Although the situations where the ideas of classical probability apply are limited, they do make it easy to illustrate the rules of probability.

The Spinner Problem *Classical Definition of Probability*

In the previous exercise you found the sample space for the spinner example to be

$$S = \{1A, 1B, 1C, 2A, 2B, 2C, 3A, 3B, 3C\}$$

Let A be the event that the first spinner lands on an odd number. Find P(A).

Let B be the event that the second spinner is a vowel. Find P(B).

The complement of an event A is often referred to as the event, "not A."

When the number of possible outcomes of an experiment is large, calculating probabilities can be tedious. At times it is easier to solve the opposite or **complement** of the problem you are interested in! You may wonder how this can be possible. It is possible because it makes use of one of the three rules of probabilities, the one that says that the probabilities must sum to one.

> The ***complement*** of an event A, denoted **A′**, is the set of all outcomes in the sample space, S, that do not correspond to the event A.

ANS. $P(A) = \frac{6}{9}$, $P(B) = \frac{3}{9}$

Since the event A is a set of outcomes in S and the complement of the event, A′, is the set of all outcomes in S that do NOT correspond to A, we can see that

Formula for the probability of the complement of A

$$P(A) + P(A') = 1$$

and that we can find P(A) by calculating P(A′) and subtracting it from 1. That is,

$$P(A) = 1 - P(A')$$

For the experiment of rolling a single die, the sample space was

$$S = \{1, 2, 3, 4, 5, 6\}$$

If we define the event A to be that the number that comes up is greater than 2 we can calculate $P(A) = \frac{4}{6}$ directly, since there are 4 outcomes that are larger than 2 out of the 6 possible outcomes.

We notice that the complement of A, A′, is defined as all of the numbers that are NOT larger than 2. Since two outcomes correspond to A′ we know that $P(A') = \frac{2}{6}$ and we can find $P(A) = 1 - P(A') = 1 - \frac{2}{6} = \frac{4}{6}$.

Although this seems to complicate something that was not very complicated, there are times when using the complement of an event to find a probability is much easier. Usually this is when the number of possible outcomes that correspond to the event of interest is a large part of the sample space, S.

Despite what it may look like, the idea of equally likely outcomes is not limited to dice, coins, and spinners! In fact, the ideas of classical probability apply to random sampling as well. Whenever an experiment consists of selecting an item at random from a group of items, the sample space will consist of all of the possible items. If the sample is truly random, then each item in the group is just as likely to be selected as any other item.

EXAMPLE 6.3 Credit Problems

Probabilities and Random Sampling

Understand the Problem

The Chamber of Commerce in the city looking at credit problems of small businesses administered the questionnaire to 166 random businesses out of 1536 existing small businesses. The Chamber of Commerce was worried that if the surveys were administered by mail the sample might be biased toward companies that were having problems. These companies might be more likely to respond to the survey because it would give them an opportunity to report their problems to a group who might be able to help them. To ensure that the sample was truly representative, the surveys were administered by phone. One of the questions asked was about the size of the company in annual sales. The questionnaire allowed the following responses:

Collect the Data

1 Under \$1 million
2 \$1–5 million
3 \$6–10 million
4 \$11–20 million
5 Over \$20 million

If the business did not respond to the question then the response was coded as a zero (0). The results of the questionnaire are

Size	Number of responses
No response	1
Under \$1 million	60
\$1–5 million	21
\$6–10 million	42
\$11–20 million	21
Over \$20 million	21
Total	166

The Chamber of Commerce decided to select a business at random and interview it along with the bank with which it does business. What is the probability that the company selected will have over $20 million in sales?

This is an experiment in which the sample space is the set of 166 companies that respond. That is, S = {C1, C2, C3, . . . , C166} and each element of S is equally likely to be chosen. Since we are interested in the event that the company has over $20 million in sales (call that event A) we see that 21 elements (companies) in the sample space correspond to A out of the total of 166, so

$$P(A) = \frac{21}{166}$$ ■

EXAMPLE 6.4 **Product Preference**

Random Sampling

A market research firm has conducted a product preference survey at a large manufacturing company. A group of 250 production workers were asked to use three different pairs of safety glasses and to select the one that they preferred. The results of the survey showed that 120 preferred product A, 85 preferred product B, and 45 preferred product C. The marketing research firm decides to select a worker at random and interview him more thoroughly about his choice. What is the probability that the worker interviewed prefers product B?

If you think about the problem you will see that the experiment consists of selecting a worker at random. Thus, the sample space of the experiment will consist of the 250 workers,

$$S = \{W1, W2, W3, \ldots, W248, W249, W250\}$$

Let B be the event that the worker chosen preferred product B. Then $P(B) = \frac{85}{250}$, since 85 outcomes (workers) in S corresponded to the event B, and there were 250 possible outcomes. ■

6.2.2 Combinations of Events: OR and AND

Calculating the probability of a single event is not difficult. Much of the time, however, we are interested in looking at more than one event. For example, if an experiment consisted of selecting employees at random from a company, we might be interested in the event A = the employee is an hourly worker, or the event B = the employee participates in the company's stock purchase program. From what we have learned, if we had the data on the number of employees in the company and the number that fell into each category, we could calculate P(A) and P(B) without much trouble. But suppose that the company is interested in how these two events behave *together*? We must look at the events **A OR B** and **A AND B.**

The event **A OR B** describes the event when either A happens or B happens or they both happen.

The event **A AND B** is the event that A and B both occur.

Let's look at the problem in terms of one of the smaller problems we studied earlier. When you roll a single die, the sample space is S = {1, 2, 3, 4, 5, 6}. If you let the event A = the number that comes up is even, and the event B = the number that comes up is a 3, then you can easily see that $P(A) = \frac{3}{6}$ and $P(B) = \frac{1}{6}$. What if you were interested in the event that the number that comes up is even OR a 3? The same rules that we used to calculate simple probabilities will apply here.

If we look at the sample space S we can count how many of the possible outcomes correspond to the event A OR B. We see that 2, 4, and 6 correspond to A and that 3 corresponds to B. Thus, using the rules for probability when events are equally likely, we find that P(A OR B) = $\frac{4}{6}$, since 4 outcomes out of the 6 possible outcomes correspond to what we are interested in.

You may have noticed two things about this problem. First, the answer, $\frac{4}{6}$, is simply the sum of the two individual probabilities, $\frac{3}{6}$ and $\frac{1}{6}$. This is not a coincidence. Second, the events A and B have no outcomes in common. In probability we refer to these kinds of events as **mutually exclusive.**

> Two events, A and B, are said to be ***mutually exclusive*** if they have no outcomes in common.

When two events are mutually exclusive, then the probability that A occurs or B occurs, **P(A OR B),** is the sum of the individual probabilities. This is known as the **simple addition rule** and is found by

Formula for simple addition rule: P(A OR B)

$$\mathbf{P(A\ OR\ B) = P(A) + P(B)}$$

The simple addition rule easily extends to any number of mutually exclusive events. For example, if A, B, C, and D are four mutually exclusive events, then

$$P(A\ OR\ B\ OR\ C\ OR\ D) = P(A) + P(B) + P(C) + P(D)$$

EXAMPLE 6.5 Flipping Two Coins

***Finding* P(A OR B)**

Remember that Joe and Tom were matching coin flips to see who would pay for dinner. The sample space for the experiment was S = {HH, HT, TH, TT}.

If A is the event that the two coins both come up tails, and B is the event that the two coins do not match, find P(A OR B).

You can see that one outcome, TT, corresponds to the event A and that two outcomes, HT and TH, correspond to the event B, so that

$$P(A\ OR\ B) = \tfrac{3}{4}$$

You can also see that A and B have no outcomes in common. That is, A and B are mutually exclusive, so that you should be able to find P(A OR B) by adding P(A) and P(B). Since P(A) = $\frac{1}{4}$ and P(B) = $\frac{2}{4}$ (these should be easy for you by now),

$$P(A\ OR\ B) = \tfrac{1}{4} + \tfrac{2}{4} = \tfrac{3}{4}$$ ■

In probability, as in any kind of mathematics, we must be very precise in our use of words. The word OR in probability is *inclusive.* That means when we talk about the event A OR B occurring we mean that A occurs or B occurs or BOTH occur. This was not a problem when we were talking about rolling a die, since there is no way that a number can be both even and a 3!

EXAMPLE 6.6 Credit Problems

Simple Addition Rule

In the example with the Chamber of Commerce and the small businesses, the Chamber of Commerce wants to know the probability that the company selected to be interviewed in depth is one of the largest (sales over $20 million) or one of the smallest (sales under $1 million).

In the last example we defined A to be the event that the company has sales of over $20 million and we found that P(A) was $\frac{21}{166}$. We can define event B to be the event that the company chosen has sales under \$1 million. What we are trying to determine here is P(A OR B).

It is easy to see that the events A and B are mutually exclusive, that is, that they cannot have any company in common. This is the same as saying that there is no company that has sales under \$1 million and over \$20 million. We can use the simple addition rule here since the sample space is much too large to work with comfortably:

$$P(\text{A OR B}) = P(\text{A}) + P(\text{B})$$

We need to find P(B) first. The results of the survey showed that 60 companies had sales under \$1 million, so $P(B) = \frac{60}{166}$. Thus,

$$P(\text{A OR B}) = \frac{21}{166} + \frac{60}{166} = \frac{81}{166}$$ ■

EXAMPLE 6.7 **Product Preference**

***Finding the Probability of* A OR B**

In the product preference example, a random sample of 250 production workers were asked to use three different pairs of safety glasses and to select the one that they preferred. The results of the survey found that 120 preferred product A, 85 preferred product B, and 45 preferred product C.

We defined an experiment where a worker was selected at random for further interviewing. We let the event B = the worker preferred product B and we found that $P(B) = \frac{85}{250}$. Let the event C = the worker preferred product C.

Find the probability that the worker selected for further interviewing preferred product B or C.

Since the sample space for this experiment does not help us, we must use the simple addition rule. First we need to find P(C). Since 45 outcomes (workers) in the sample space preferred product C, we know that

$$P(C) = \frac{45}{250}$$

To find P(B OR C) we use the simple addition rule and find that

$$P(\text{B OR C}) = \frac{85}{250} + \frac{45}{250} = \frac{130}{250}$$ ■

Up to this point we have been expressing probabilities as fractions without reducing them. This is only to illustrate what numbers we use to calculate the probabilities. In fact, probabilities are often expressed as decimals or percentages. In the previous example you could also say that the probability that the worker selected preferred product B or C is 0.52 or 52%. Looking at the probability as a percentage is really quite illuminating in this case. We see that although product A had the largest number of people preferring it, a majority of the workers prefer something else.

The Spinner Problem ***Calculating the Probability of* A OR B**

The sample space for the experiment of spinning the two spinners is

$$S = \{1A, 1B, 1C, 2A, 2B, 2C, 3A, 3B, 3C\}$$

Let A be the event that the first spinner comes up a 1 and let B be the event that it comes up a 3. Find the probability that A OR B occurs using the sample space.

Now find the same probability using the simple addition rule.

Why are the two answers the same?

The simple addition rule for probability that you just learned applies only when the events of interest have nothing in common, that is, they are mutually exclusive. Sometimes that will always be the case, as in the product preference example. It is not physically possible for a single worker to prefer more than one of the products, just as it is not possible for a single roll of a die to result in a 2 and a 3 at the same time. What happens when this is *not* the case, when it is possible that both of the events, A and B, can occur?

Look at the example of rolling a single die. The sample space for the experiment is

$$S = \{1, 2, 3, 4, 5, 6\}$$

When we let A be the event that the number that came up was even and B be the event that the number that came up was a 3, these events had nothing in common. It is impossible for them to both occur on a *single trial* of the experiment. The law of probability worked just fine and P(A OR B) $= \frac{3}{6} + \frac{1}{6} = \frac{4}{6}$.

Suppose that we define a new event, C, where

C = the number that comes up is exactly divisible by 3

and we want to know the probability that the number on the die is even *and* is exactly divisible by 3. Remember that our definition of the word AND is that *both* of the events occur. This means that we are looking at any outcomes in S that are both even AND exactly divisible by 3. Looking at the sample space, you can see that there is only one outcome that fits this description, 6. Thus, the probability that both events occur is P(A AND C) $= \frac{1}{6}$. The probability that both events will occur is often referred to as the probability of the intersection of the events.

This is the same as asking for the probability that A OR C *will occur.*

ANS. P(A OR B) $= \frac{6}{9} (= \frac{2}{3})$; P(A OR B) $= \frac{1}{3} + \frac{1}{3} = \frac{2}{3}$; MUTUALLY EXCLUSIVE EVENTS

EXAMPLE 6.8 Credit Problems

***Probability of* A AND B**

The size of a company does not refer to sales alone. It also reflects the number of employees that a company has. In the survey, the Chamber of Commerce also asked a question about the number of employees in a company. The data were coded into six different categories(0–5, 6–10, 11–50, 51–150, 151–250, and Over 250). The following contingency table is based on the questions about sales and number of employees:

Employees	No response	Under $1 m	$1–5 m	$6–10 m	$11–20 m	Over $20 m	Grand Total
0–5	0	44	7	7	0	0	58
6–10	0	12	9	3	3	0	27
11–50	1	4	4	14	3	3	29
51–150	0	0	1	8	5	7	21
151–250	0	0	0	6	5	6	17
Over 250	0	0	0	4	5	5	14
Grand Total	1	60	21	42	21	21	166

The Chamber of Commerce was interested in knowing how likely it was that they would be interviewing very large companies. They defined a large company as one that had sales over $20 million (A) and more than 250 employees (B). What they wanted to find was P(A AND B).

Remember that the event A AND B occurs when both of the events occur and that we often refer to this as the intersection of the two events. From the table, if we find both of the events and see where they intersect, we see that five businesses are included in both events. Therefore,

$$P(\text{A AND B}) = \frac{5}{166}$$

The Chamber of Commerce also wanted to find out how likely it was that they would interview a small company, which they defined as one with sales under $1 million (C) and 0–5 employees (D). Again, since they want to find the probability that both of these events occur, we look for the intersection and find that

$$P(\text{C AND D}) = \frac{44}{166}$$

They are more likely to interview a very small company than a very large company. In fact, the probability of getting a small company is about nine times as much as that of getting a very large company. ■

Does the fact that the events A and C have something in common change the way we look at the event A OR C? Well, remember that our definition of the word OR is that one or the other or *both* of the events can occur. This means that we are looking at any outcomes in S that are even, or exactly divisible by 3, or both even AND exactly divisible by 3. Looking at the sample space, you can see that there are four outcomes that fit this description, 2, 3, 4, and 6. Thus, using the formula for probability, P(A OR C) $= \frac{4}{6}$. What happens if we try to use the simple addition rule?

From the sample space you can see that P(A) $= \frac{3}{6}$ (there are three outcomes that are even) and P(C) $= \frac{2}{6}$ (there are two outcomes that are exactly divisible by 3). If we add these two probabilities we get: $\frac{3}{6} + \frac{2}{6} = \frac{5}{6}$. Wait! This is *not* the answer we got using the definition. What went wrong?

What went wrong is what usually goes wrong when mathematics leads to an incorrect answer—we violated the rules, in this case, the rules for using the simple addition rule. The simple addition rule is valid only if the events of interest are *mutually exclusive.* In this case, events A and C are *not* mutually exclusive; they have an outcome in common, the outcome of a 6.

When we calculated P(A), the outcome that the die turned up a 6 was included in that probability. Then, when we calculated P(C), the outcome of a 6 was included again. When we added the two probabilities together, the outcome was included twice, once for each event. Thus, the answer we obtained was too large by $\frac{1}{6}$, which is the probability that the die turns up a 6.

How can we adjust the simple addition rule of probability to work in situations when the events are NOT mutually exclusive? You can see from the example that the problem occurs when an outcome is included in *both* events, that is, in A AND C. The answer obtained by adding the individual probabilities was too large because the probability that both A AND C occur, P(A AND C), is included in both individual probabilities. If we consider this we can come up with a **general addition rule** for probability that considers the probability of A OR B when the events are not mutually exclusive:

$$P(\text{A OR B}) = P(\text{A}) + P(\text{B}) - P(\text{A AND B})$$

Formula for general addition rule: P(A OR B)

EXAMPLE 6.9 Flipping Two Coins

Calculating P(A OR B)

In the example where Joe and Tom are matching coins, the sample space is

$$S = \{HH, HT, TH, TT\}$$

We let A be the event that both coins come up tails and we know that $P(A) = \frac{1}{4}$.

Suppose we define the event B = the coins match. What is the probability that the coins match or they both come up tails?

From the sample space we can see that two outcomes (HH and TT) correspond to the event A OR B. Thus, $P(\text{A OR B}) = \frac{2}{4}$. To use the addition rule we need to look at events A and B and decide whether they have any elements in common. We see that they do, since the outcome TT satisfies both the definition of A and the definition of B. We will have to use the general rule and remember to subtract P(A AND B). Thus, we find

$$P(\text{A OR B}) = P(\text{A}) + P(\text{B}) - P(\text{A AND B})$$

or

$$P(\text{A OR B}) = \frac{1}{4} + \frac{2}{4} - \frac{1}{4} = \frac{2}{4}$$

which we know is the correct answer. ■

In Chapter 5 you learned about collecting data that involve two qualitative variables. You learned how to organize that data into a contingency table and to use the data to describe the sample. Data of this type are also important in probability problems.

EXAMPLE 6.10 Credit Problems

The General Addition Rule

Suppose that the Chamber of Commerce is interested in knowing the probability that the company chosen for further interviewing had sales over \$20 million (A) or more than 250 employees (C). How can we find this probability, P(A OR C)?

Employees	No response	Under \$1 m	\$1–5 m	\$6–10 m	\$11–20 m	Over \$20 m	Grand Total
0–5	0	44	7	7	0	0	58
6–10	0	12	9	3	3	0	27
11–50	1	4	4	14	3	3	29
51–150	0	0	1	8	5	7	21
151–250	0	0	0	6	5	6	17
Over 250	0	0	0	4	5	5	14
Grand Total	1	60	21	42	21	21	166

If we look at the two events we see that $P(A) = \frac{21}{166}$ and $P(C) = \frac{14}{166}$. Now, because we are going to *add* the probabilities, we have to determine whether the two events have any outcomes in common. We need to know whether there are any businesses that have both sales over $20 million and more than 250 employees. We found P(A AND C) $= \frac{5}{166}$ previously. We have to use the general addition rule:

$$P(\text{A OR C}) = P(\text{A}) + P(\text{C}) - P(\text{A AND C})$$

or

$$P(\text{A OR C}) = \frac{21}{166} + \frac{14}{166} - \frac{5}{166} = \frac{30}{166}$$

■

When you are looking for the probability of the event A OR B in a contingency table problem, it is not difficult to recognize when you need to use the general addition rule or when the simple addition rule will work. You can think about the outcomes that the events might have in common as the *intersection* of the two simple events in the table. If one event is represented by a row and the other by a column, then there will be a place where they intersect or overlap and you will need to use the general addition rule. If both of the simple events A and B are rows or both columns, then they cannot intersect, and the simple addition rule applies.

EXAMPLE 6.11 Student Status

Using the General Addition Rule

Remember the School of Business that is concerned about the number of upper level students who are enrolled in the Introductory Statistics course? The school collected data on 28 students and asked the students their year and whether they had transferred to the University. The data are shown in the contingency table here:

	Status		
Year	**Nontransfer**	**Transfer**	**Total**
Fr	3	1	4
So	10	2	12
Jr	2	0	2
Sr	1	9	10
Total	16	12	28

Suppose that the committee decides to select a student at random and look at that student's records more closely. The sample space of the experiment is the 28 students. Since every student is just as likely to be selected, the outcomes in S are equally likely. What is the probability that the student whose records are examined is a sophomore or a transfer student?

In general, it is helpful to use letters to represent events that are coded to the actual data rather than just A *or* B.

Let S represent the event that the student selected is a sophomore and T be the event that the student selected is a transfer student. We are looking for P(S OR T).

To start, we will find P(S) and P(T). From the table we can find that $P(S) = \frac{12}{28}$ and $P(T) = \frac{12}{28}$.

Next, we need to think about whether these events have any outcomes in common. That is, are there any students who are both sophomores AND transfer students? Again, looking at the table, we see that there are two students who are classified as sophomores and transfer students. These two students are included in both P(S) and P(T), so we will have to use the general addition rule. Thus,

$$P(\text{S OR T}) = \frac{12}{28} + \frac{12}{28} - \frac{2}{28} = \frac{22}{28}$$

If we look at the table and use the cells that correspond to S OR T instead of the totals we get

$$P(\text{S OR T}) = \frac{10 + 2 + 1 + 0 + 9}{28} = \frac{22}{28}$$

which is the same answer. ■

TRY IT NOW!

Quality Problems *Using the General Addition Rule*

The company that manufactures cardboard boxes collected data on the defect type and production shift. The data are summarized in the contingency table:

	Shift			
Defect	**1**	**2**	**3**	**Total**
Color	8	4	3	15
Printing	6	5	2	13
Skewness	0	2	0	2
Total	14	11	5	30

If a box has more than one defect, then it is classified by the more serious of the defects only.

Suppose that a box from the sample is selected at random and examined more closely. What is the probability that the box has a color defect?

What is the probability that the box was produced during the second shift?

Is it possible for the selected box to have a color defect and to have been produced on the second shift? If so, what is the probability?

What is the probability that the selected box will have a color defect or will have been produced on the second shift?

ANS. $P(C) = \frac{15}{30}$, $P(2) = \frac{11}{30}$, YES, $\frac{4}{30}$, $\frac{22}{30}$.

6.2.3 Probabilities as Relative Frequencies

At this point you may wonder why we need to study probability at all. It is a reasonable question if you think of probability only in terms of coins, dice, and spinners, or as random samples taken from known populations. These contexts are good for explaining how probabilities are calculated. The situations serve as models for examining probabilities for other situations.

In the previous chapters of this book you looked at methods for describing sample data taken from some population. We talked about the fact that the descriptions are exact for the sample, but are only estimates when applied to the whole population. How good those estimates are depends on many factors, such as the size of the sample and how well the sample represents the population of interest.

The same is true of probability models. When you collect sample data and calculate relative frequencies you can find, exactly, the probability that an item taken from the sample will have some characteristic(s) of interest. If the data are a good representation of the population, then we can also use the relative frequencies as estimates of the true probabilities for the population. Probabilities calculated in this way are often called **empirical** probabilities. The same rules of probability that you have already learned apply to these problems as well.

An ***empirical probability*** is one that is calculated from sample data and is an estimate for the true probability.

EXAMPLE 6.12 Restaurant Survey

Probabilities as Relative Frequencies

A local marketing firm took a random sample of people in a large city to learn what kind of restaurants they think the city needs. The firm asked the customers to choose the type from the following list:

- Fast food
- Family restaurant
- Adult economical
- Adult moderate
- Adult upscale

As a result of their research they obtained the following data:

Type of restaurant	Number of people	Relative frequency (%)
Fast food	127	20
Family restaurant	234	36
Adult economical	158	24
Adult moderate	72	11
Adult upscale	56	9
Total	647	100.00

If we assume that the sample was a good representation of the adult residents of the city, what is the probability that a person selected at random in the city would favor some type of adult restaurant?

This question is really asking for the probability that a person would favor either an adult economical (AE), an adult moderate (AM), or an adult upscale (AU) restaurant. Since the events are mutually exclusive, we can use the simple addition rule to find the answer. What has changed is that our sample space is no longer the

647 original respondents to the survey. Instead, the sample space of the experiment becomes the possible responses that a person can give, or

$$S = \{\text{fast food, family, adult economical, adult moderate, adult upscale}\}$$

and the outcomes are no longer equally likely. We can, however, use the relative frequencies as estimates of the probabilities for each outcome:

$$P(\text{AE OR AM OR AU}) = 24\% + 11\% + 9\% = 44\%$$ ■

6.2.4 Exercises—Learning It!

6.1 In 1997, the competition for local phone service increased significantly as a result of changes in federal law. A survey of over 10,000 people in a large metropolitan area asked whether they rated their current local phone service provider as Excellent, Very Good–Good, Satisfactory, or Poor–Very Poor. The results were tabulated and are shown in the table:

Rating	Excellent	Very Good–Good	Satisfactory	Poor–Very Poor
% Responding	12	21	25	42

(a) What is the probability that a person selected at random from the area will rate his current phone service as Excellent or Very Good–Good?

(b) What is the probability that a person selected at random from the area will not rate his service as Poor–Very Poor?

6.2 A company was interested in looking at the way in which employees used the two floating holidays that were part of their benefits packages. They surveyed 300 employees and asked them what type of job they had and how they used the holidays. The answers were tabulated into a contingency table:

	How Days Were Used		
Type of Job	**Took Actual Holiday**	**Added to Vacation**	**Took Random Days**
Professional	5	17	51
Clerical	13	46	32
Hourly	53	78	5

(a) What is the probability that an employee surveyed took the floating holidays on the actual holiday?

(b) What is the probability that an employee surveyed was professional?

(c) What is the probability that an employee surveyed was clerical and added the floating holidays to his vacation?

(d) What is the probability that an employee surveyed took the floating holidays as random days off or was an hourly worker?

6.3 A computer magazine surveyed its readers to determine how likely it was that people who planned to purchase new computers in the near future would buy a portable/notebook or desktop model. The results are tabulated in the table:

	When Purchase Will Be Made		
Type of Computer	**0–3 Months**	**3–6 Months**	**6–12 Months**
Notebook/Portable	34	156	258
Desktop	56	346	128

(a) What is the probability that a person surveyed planned to buy a desktop model in the next 3–6 months?

(b) What is the probability that a person surveyed planned to buy a computer in the next 0–3 months or that the person was planning to buy a desktop model?

(c) What is the probability that a person was planning to buy a notebook computer and that the person planned to make the purchase in the next 0–3 or 3–6 months?

(d) What is the probability that a person did not plan to make a purchase in the next 6 months?

6.4 A marketing firm in the Northeast was looking at the type of medication that people with allergies took during the autumn allergy season. In particular, the firm wanted to know whether the person took medication daily and whether that medication was prescribed by a physician or purchased over the counter. The results of the survey are in the table:

Frequency of Taking Medicine	Type of Medication	
	Prescription	**Over the Counter**
Daily	86	43
As needed (sporadic)	23	156

(a) What is the probability that an allergy sufferer took prescription medication daily?

(b) What is the probability that an allergy sufferer took over-the-counter medication or that he took the medication daily?

(c) What is the probability that an allergy sufferer took medication daily and that he used over-the-counter medication?

6.5 A report by the Department of Justice on rape victims reports on interviews with 3721 victims. The attacks were classified by age of the victim and the relationship of the victim to the rapist. The results of the study are given here:

Age of Victim	Relationship of Rapist		
	Family	**Acquaintance or Friend**	**Stranger**
Under 12	153	167	13
12 to 17	230	746	172
Over 17	269	1232	739

(a) What is the probability that a victim was under 12 years of age?

(b) What is the probability that a victim was between 12 and 17 and that the rapist was a member of the family?

(c) What is the probability that a victim was under 12 or that the rapist was an acquaintance or friend?

(d) What is the probability that the victim was not under 12 years of age?

(e) What is the probability that the rapist was not a family member, acquaintance, or friend?

6.3 CONDITIONAL PROBABILITY AND INDEPENDENCE

In the previous chapter we talked about whether two variables were related. Now we will talk about that same topic with respect to probabilities.

Suppose we are interested in marketing a particular product. If we define the event A to be the event that a person chosen at random buys the product, then, using the relative frequency approach, P(A) is simply the percentage of people in our sample space who buy the product. Suppose, however, we decide to look at a second event, B, which is the event that a person in the sample space has seen an advertisement for the product. Now, as marketers, we might be interested in whether the fact that a person sees the ad affects the probability that the person buys the product. That is, we might be interested in these questions: *If* a person has seen the advertisement, what is the probability that they will buy the product?

If a person has not seen the advertisement, what is the probability that they will buy the product? As marketers, we certainly hope that the first probability is higher than the second!

6.3.1 Conditional Probability

Up to now we have been considering problems in which we sample from the entire sample space. Now, our knowledge of the outcome of event B reduces the number of sample space elements from which we choose. This type of probability is called a **conditional probability.** Conditional probabilities are written as **P(A|B)** and are read "the probability that A will occur *given that* B has occurred" or "the probability of A given B."

Conditional probability is usually defined in terms of a formula that makes it seem more complicated than it really is. Keep in mind that, effectively, a conditional probability is simply one that is calculated from a reduced sample space.

The ***conditional probability*** of an event A given an event B is

$$P(A|B) = \frac{P(A \text{ AND } B)}{P(B)}$$

EXAMPLE 6.13 Product Marketing

Conditional Probability

A marketing research firm is interested in measuring the effectiveness of an advertisement for a new product. They take a random sample of 500 people and ask them whether they have bought the new product and whether they saw an advertisement for the product before the purchase. The results are given in the table:

	Saw advertisement	Did not see advertisement	Total
Purchased product	175	45	220
Did not purchase	100	180	280
Total	275	225	500

The marketing research firm is interested in finding out whether seeing the advertisement (B) affects the probability that a person will buy the product (A). They decide to find P(A)and P(A|B).

We already know how to do the first calculation and so, from the table, we can calculate that

$$P(A) = \frac{220}{500} = 44\%$$

Now, what does the second probability mean? Well, they want to know the probability that a person purchased the product *given that* they saw the advertisement. If we know that the person saw the advertisement, then our sample space no longer has 500 possible outcomes in it. In fact, it has been reduced to only the outcomes in the first column of the table, 275 possibilities. From our new sample space we see that 175 of those people purchased the product. Thus,

$$P(A|B) = \frac{175}{275} = 63.6\%$$

It appears that the two events might be related. ■

In Example 6.13, the two probabilities, P(A) and P(A|B), are not the same. However, this does not mean that the two events, A and B, are *definitely* related. Because our probabilities are calculated using the relative frequency method, we know that another sample might produce different results. To be able to say with some certainty that A and B are related you will need to use the methods of inferential statistics that are covered in Chapter 15. Right now, however, we see that the conditional probability leads us to believe that this might be true.

EXAMPLE 6.14 Credit Problems

Conditional Probability

Consider again the Chamber of Commerce survey. The contingency table is given here:

Several phrases mean the same thing as "given that." Some of these are "of the," "if," and "when."

Employees	No response	Under $1 m	$1–5 m	$6–10 m	$11–20 m	Over $20 m	Grand Total
0–5	0	44	7	7	0	0	58
6–10	0	12	9	3	3	0	27
11–50	1	4	4	14	3	3	29
51–150	0	0	1	8	5	7	21
151–250	0	0	0	6	5	6	17
Over 250	0	0	0	4	5	5	14
Grand Total	1	60	21	42	21	21	166

The Chamber of Commerce is wondering about the relationship between size of a company and sales. It makes sense that the size of a company would affect the amount of sales they have. The Chamber of Commerce wants to know, in particular, what percentage of the companies with over 250 employees (A) have sales over $20 million (B). That is, they want to know the probability that a company has sales over $20 million ***given that*** they have over 250 employees, or P(B|A).

Note: The strategy in solving these problems is to identify the "given" information first. This becomes the denominator of the probability.

To solve this problem, we must first determine how the given information reduces the sample space. Since we know that the company has over 250 employees, our sample space is limited to the row of the table labeled "Over 250." This reduces the sample space to 14 possibilities. Now, of those companies we see that 5 have sales over $20 million. Thus

$$P(B|A) = \tfrac{5}{14} \text{ or } 35.7\%$$

■

6.3.2 Independent Events

> Two events are ***independent*** if the probability that one event occurs on any given trial of an experiment is not affected or changed by the occurrence of the other event.

When you looked at bivariate relationships in Chapter 5 you were trying to decide whether the value of one quantitative variable depended on another or whether they were independent. We can also use the word **independent** in terms of events and probability. That is, if two events are independent, P(A|B) = P(A). In probability, two events, A and B, are independent *exactly when*

Formula for independent events

$$P(A \text{ AND } B) = P(A) \times P(B)$$

The phrase *exactly when* means that the statement can be used in both directions. That is, if we know two events are independent, then to find the probability that both will occur we can multiply the individual probabilities together. It also means that if we know that the probability that both occur is equal to the product of the individual probabilities, we can conclude that the events are independent.

EXAMPLE 6.15 Product Marketing

Independence and Probability

In Example 6.13 we can check to see whether purchasing the product (A) and seeing the advertisement (B) are independent by comparing the quantity P(A AND B) to the quantity P(A) × P(B). The data are repeated here:

	Saw advertisement	Did not see advertisement	Total
Purchased product	175	45	220
Did not purchase	100	180	280
Total	275	225	500

From the table we see that

$$P(A) = \frac{222}{500} \qquad P(B) = \frac{275}{500} \qquad P(A\text{ AND }B) = \frac{175}{500}$$

If we calculate P(A) P(B), we get $\frac{220}{500} \times \frac{275}{500} = 0.242$ and $P(A\text{ AND }B) = \frac{175}{500} = 0.35$.

Thus the events A and B are not independent *in this sample*. We know that when we use sample data the probabilities are *exactly correct* only when applied to the sample. Does it mean that the two events A and B are not independent in the population? Not really. We will need the tools of inferential statistics to answer that question. ■

In reality, knowing absolutely that two events are independent is very difficult. Most of the time, we are really trying to determine exactly that from our sample data.

Most of the examples that allow us to use the formula P(A AND B) = P(A)P(B) for independent events are limited to those classical probability examples using coins and dice that we discussed in the very beginning of this chapter. In other situations, to calculate P(A AND B) we use the definition of conditional probability with the terms rearranged:

$$P(A\text{ AND }B) = P(A|B)P(B)$$

That is, the probability that both events A and B happen is the probability that A happens *given that* B has happened, weighted by the percentage of time that B happens. You can see that if A and B are independent, the term P(A|B) reduces to P(A) and we have the formula for independent events.

6.3.3 Exercises—Learning It!

6.6 Consider the company that was interested in how employees used the two floating holidays that were part of their benefits packages. The data are shown here in a contingency table.

	How Days Were Used		
Type of Job	**Took Actual Holiday**	**Added to Vacation**	**Took Random Days**
Professional	5	17	51
Clerical	13	46	32
Hourly	53	78	5

(a) What is the probability that an employee took the floating holidays on the actual holiday given that they were professional?

(b) What is the probability that, if an employee were professional, they added the day to their vacation?

(c) Of the clerical employees, what is the probability that they took the actual holiday?

(d) Are the events that the person was an hourly worker and that they took random days off independent in this sample? Why or why not?

6.7 Consider the data on computer purchases given in the following table:

	When Purchase Will Be Made		
Type of Computer	**0–3 months**	**3–6 Months**	**6–12 Months**
Notebook/Portable	34	156	258
Desktop	56	346	128

(a) What is the probability that a person who planned to buy a computer in the next 3–6 months plans to buy a desktop?

(b) If a person plans to buy a notebook/portable computer, what is the probability that they will purchase it in the next 0–3 months?

(c) Of the people who are planning to buy a computer in 6–12 months, what percentage will buy desktops?

(d) Are the events that the person will buy a notebook computer and that they will purchase in 3–6 months independent in this sample? Why or why not?

6.8 A marketing firm in the Northeast was looking at the type of medication that people with allergies took during the autumn allergy season. The data are given here:

	Type of Medication	
Frequency of Taking Medicine	**Prescription**	**Over-the-counter**
Daily	86	43
As Needed (sporadic)	23	156

(a) What is the probability that allergy sufferers took medication daily given that they took over-the-counter medicine?

(b) Of the allergy sufferers who took prescription medicine, what is the probability that they took the medication daily?

(c) If allergy sufferers take over-the-counter medicine, what is the probability that they take it only as needed?

(d) Are the events that a person takes over-the-counter medicine and that they take it sporadically independent in this sample? Why or why not?

6.9 A report by the Department of Justice on rape victims reports on interviews with 3721 victims. The attacks were classified by age of the victim and the relationship of the victim to the rapist. The results of the study are given here:

	Relationship of Rapist		
Age of Victim	**Family**	**Acquaintance or Friend**	**Stranger**
Under 12	153	167	13
12 to 17	230	746	172
Over 17	269	1232	739

(a) What is the probability that a victim was under 12 years of age given that the rapist was a family member?

(b) If the victim was under 12, what is the probability that the rapist was a stranger?

(c) Of the victims who were raped by a family member, what is the probability that a victim was between 12 and 17?

(d) Given that the victim was not under 12 years of age, what is the probability that they were raped by a stranger?

6.4 RANDOM VARIABLES

When you learned the different techniques for summarizing and analyzing data, you learned that although qualitative data are important for understanding and interpreting the information obtained from a set of data, there is not much you can do with the data itself. Most statistical analyses use numerical or quantitative data as their basis. In much the same way, we also prefer to discuss probabilities for experiments whose outcomes are numerical.

You know from algebra that a variable is a quantity whose value can change or vary. In algebra the exact value that the variable takes on depends on the equation that includes it. We have also referred to the different kinds of data that can be collected from a population as variables. The exact value that a statistical variable will take on depends on the laws of chance or probability. When the variables in question are quantitative, they are known as **random variables.**

> A ***random variable, X,*** is a quantitative variable whose value varies according to the rules of probability.

When the outcome of an experiment is a random variable, then the elements of the sample space are all of the possible values that the variable can have. Random variables, like data, can be discrete (integers) or continuous (real numbers). In our initial discussion of random variables we will consider only the discrete case.

In the experiment of rolling a single die and recording the number of spots that are on the top face, the sample space for the experiment can be written as

$$S = \{1, 2, 3, 4, 5, 6\}$$

The outcomes are numerical and the exact value that will turn up varies. We know from the rules of probability that each of the values is equally likely, or has an equal probability of happening. Thus, $X =$ the number of spots on the top face of a die is a random variable.

EXAMPLE 6.16 Tossing Two Coins

Defining a Random Variable

In the previous section we looked at an experiment in which two coins were tossed. The sample space of that experiment was

$$S = \{HH, HT, TH, TT\}$$

This experiment does not involve a random variable, since the possible outcomes are not numerical. It is possible, however, to describe the outcomes of the experiment numerically by defining a random variable for the experiment. Let $X =$ the number of heads that appear on the two coins. The possible values of X are $x = 0$, 1, and 2. Every time you perform the experiment you do not know what will happen, but the laws of probability give you some insight into what is likely to occur. ■

We always use capital letters, like X, to represent the random variable, and lowercase letters, such as x, to represent the values of the random variable.

6.4.1 Probability Distribution of a Discrete Random Variable

The rules of probability that describe the way a random variable behaves are known as the **probability distribution** of the random variable. The probability distribution of a discrete random variable assigns a probability to each of the possible values that can happen.

We read p(x) *as "p of x."*

The ***probability distribution*** of a random variable, X, written as **p(x)**, gives the probability that the random variable will take on each of its possible values.

The notation that we use for the probability distribution of a random variable is similar to the notation for the probability of an event. For a random variable,

$$p(x) = P(X = x) \qquad \text{for all possible values of } X$$

Most often the probability distribution is written in the form of a table.

EXAMPLE 6.17 **Tossing Two Coins**

Writing the Probability Distribution

In the experiment of tossing two coins we saw that $X =$ the number of heads is a random variable that can take on three values: 0, 1, and 2. Using the rules of probability that we learned, we can find the probability distribution of X, the number of heads in two tosses of a coin:

$p(0) = P(X = 0)$ corresponds to only one outcome, TT, so $p(0) = \frac{1}{4}$
$p(1) = P(X = 1)$ corresponds to two outcomes, HT and TH, so $p(1) = \frac{2}{4}$
$p(2) = P(X = 2)$ corresponds to one outcome, HH, so $p(2) = \frac{1}{4}$

In table form we would write this as

x	0	1	2
p(x)	$\frac{1}{4}$	$\frac{2}{4}$	$\frac{1}{4}$

■

The rules for probability distributions are the same as the rules for probabilities. For each value of the random variable, X,

1. $0 \le p(x) \le 1$ (probabilities are numbers between 0 and 1 inclusive)
2. $\Sigma p(x) = 1$ for all values of x (the probabilities must sum to 1)

Notice that the outcomes of a random variable are *mutually exclusive.* This means that whenever we are interested in finding the probability that the random variable will take on one of its values OR another of its values we can use the simple addition rule.

EXAMPLE 6.18 **Newspaper Sales**

Finding Probabilities from a Probability Distribution

The number of copies of the *Wall Street Journal* (*WSJ*) that are sold daily by a convenience store is a random variable X, which is described by the probability distribution

x	0	1	2	3	4	5
p(x)	0.10	0.12	0.25	0.30	0.20	0.03

What is the probability that on any given day the convenience store sells exactly two copies of the *WSJ*?

We can obtain this answer directly from the table:

$$p(2) = 0.25$$

What is the probability that two or three copies are sold on any given day?

It is first important to recognize that we are trying to find $P(X = 2 \text{ OR } X = 3)$. Since the values of a random variable are mutually exclusive, we can simply add the probabilities to obtain the answer:

$$P(X = 2 \text{ OR } X = 3) = p(2) + p(3) = 0.25 + 0.30 = 0.55$$

■

Notation and Probabilities

Very often we are interested in the probability that a random variable takes on any one of a set of its possible values. In particular, we might be interested in finding the probability that the random variable takes on a value that is **"at least *x*," "more than *x*," "at most *x*," "less than *x*," "between x_1 and x_2,"** or **"between x_1 and x_2 inclusive."** There is nothing new that you need to know to find the probabilities. It just takes a little practice to be able to recognize each of the different problems and to write down what you are looking for. Since the words can get cumbersome, a standard notation is used.

As an example, we will use a random variable X that can take on values of $x = 0, 1, 2, 3, \ldots, n$. Table 6.1 provides a summary of each problem, what it means, and the correct notation.

TABLE 6.1 Probability Notation Summary

Find the probability that X takes on a value that is . . .	What it means	Notation
at least x	All of the values of the random variable that are the value x or larger (up to n)	$P(X \geq x)$
more than x	All of the values of the random variable that are larger than the value x (up to n)	$P(X > x)$
at most x	All of the values of the random variable that are the value x or less	$P(X \leq x)$
less than x	All of the values of the random variable that are smaller than the value x	$P(X < x)$
between x_1 and x_2 inclusive	All of the values of the random variable that start with the value x_1 and go up to and include the value x_2	$P(x_1 \leq X \leq x_2)$
between x_1 and x_2	All of the values of the random variable that are larger than the value x_1 and smaller than the value x_2	$P(x_1 < X < x_2)$

EXAMPLE 6.19 Newspaper Sales

Finding Interval Probabilities

The convenience store that sells the *WSJ* wants to know a bit more about the probability that it will sell the newspaper. The probability distribution of X, the number of copies of the *WSJ* sold per day, is given by

x	0	1	2	3	4	5
p(x)	0.10	0.12	0.25	0.30	0.20	0.03

In particular, the store needs to sell at least 3 copies per day to make a profit from the sales. What is the probability that the store will make a profit on any given day?

We are looking for the probability that the store sells at least 3 copies, or $P(X \geq 3)$. This means $P(X = 3 \text{ OR } X = 4 \text{ OR } X = 5)$, which is calculated as

$$p(3) + p(4) + p(5) = 0.30 + 0.20 + 0.03 = 0.53$$

What is the probability that the store will not make a profit?

We can answer this question directly by determining that the store will not make a profit if it sells less than 3 copies of the newspaper and finding $P(X < 3)$. We can also do this problem by making use of the complement of an event. The events "make a profit" or "$X \geq 3$" and "do not make a profit" or "$X < 3$" are complements of each other. This means that their probabilities must sum to 1. Since we already know that $P(X \geq 3) = 0.53$, we can find $P(X < 3)$ by taking

$$1 - P(X \geq 3) = 1 - 0.53 = 0.47$$

■

TRY IT NOW!

Defective Diskettes ***Finding Interval Probabilities***

A company that sells computer diskettes in bulk packages for a warehouse club outlet knows that the number of defective diskettes in a package is a random variable with the probability distribution given here:

x	0	1	2	3	4	5	6
$p(x)$	0.30	0.21	0.12	0.10	0.10	0.09	0.08

Find the probability that a package of the diskettes will contain at least 3 defective disks.

Find the probability that the package will contain between 2 and 5 defective diskettes.

Find the probability that the number of defective diskettes will be at most 2.

6.4.2 Probability Histograms

Random variables and their probability distributions are the models for the populations from which our sample data are taken. You learned in Chapter 3 that you can display quantitative data using a relative frequency table or a relative frequency histogram. In much the same way, a random variable can be displayed with a probability distribution table or a probability distribution histogram.

ANS. 0.37, 0.20, 0.63

EXAMPLE 6.20 Newspaper Sales

Creating a Probability Histogram

The convenience store that sells the *WSJ* would like to see what the distribution of newspaper sales looks like. The store creates a probability histogram for the random variable:

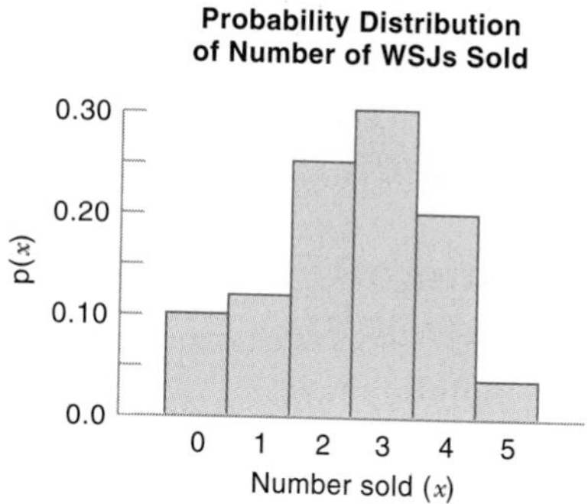

The histogram shows that the probability distribution of sales is not very variable, approximately symmetric, and centered at about 3 newspapers per day. ■

In a probability histogram the area of each rectangle is equal to the probability that the random variable will take on the given value. This may not seem important right now, but we use this fact later in the chapter when we move from discrete to continuous random variables.

TRY IT NOW!

Defective Diskettes ***Creating a Probability Histogram***

The company that sells computer diskettes in bulk packages for a warehouse club would like to have a picture of how the number of defective diskettes in a package behaves. The probability distribution is given here:

x	0	1	2	3	4	5	6
$p(x)$	0.30	0.21	0.12	0.10	0.10	0.09	0.08

Create a probability histogram for the number of defective diskettes.

(continued)

Use the probability histogram to describe the distribution of the number of defective diskettes in a package.

6.4.3 Exercises—Learning It!

6.10 The number of employees who call in sick on any given day in a small business is a random variable with probability distribution:

x	0	1	2	3	4	5	6
p(x)	0.10	0.23	0.18	0.16	0.13	0.10	0.10

(a) What is the probability that on any given day at most 4 employees call in sick?

(b) What is the probability that between 2 and 4 employees call in sick?

(c) What is the probability that more than 4 employees call in sick?

6.11 The number of members who cannot get a tee time at a local country club is a random variable with probability distribution given by

x	0	1	2	3	4	5	6	7	8
p(x)	0.11	0.12	0.13	0.19	0.12	0.09	0.09	0.08	0.07

(a) What is the probability that between 2 and 5 members inclusive cannot get tee times?

(b) What is the probability that less than 3 cannot get tee times?

(c) What is the probability that at least 6 cannot get tee times?

(d) What is the probability that at most 4 cannot get tee times?

6.12 The number of times that a person gets a busy signal when calling the local cable television office is a random variable with the following probability distribution:

x	0	1	2	3	4
p(x)	0.23	0.34	0.17	0.15	?

(a) What is p(4)?

(b) What is the probability that a person will not get a busy signal?

ANS:

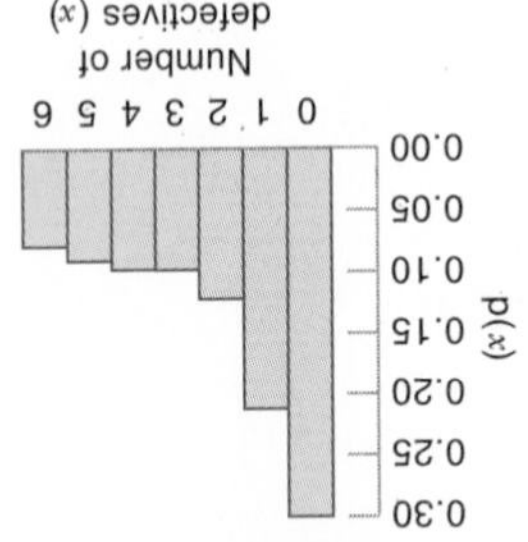

SKEWED RIGHT, MUCH MORE LIKELY TO FIND SMALL NUMBER OF DEFECTIVES

(c) What is the probability that a person gets at least 1 busy signal?

(d) What is the probability that a person gets more than 2 busy signals?

6.13 A company that packages small items for resale is looking at the problems of incorrect packaging. The company finds that in a box that is supposed to contain two dozen items, the number of missing items is a random variable with probability distribution:

x	0	1	2	3	4	5	6
p(x)	0.13	0.17	0.26	0.30	0.07	0.05	0.02

(a) What is the probability that in a box of 2 dozen, exactly 3 are missing?

(b) What is the probability that the number of missing items is less than 4?

(c) What is the probability that there are exactly 20 items in the box?

(d) What is the probability that there are more than 20 items in the box?

6.14 A large airline keeps track of the number of no-shows for one of its most important commuter flights. Over time the airline has found that the number of ticketed passengers who do not show up is a random variable with the following probability distribution:

x	0	1	2	3	4	5	6	7	8
p(x)	0.05	0.08	0.13	0.23	0.18	0.13	0.08	0.06	0.06

(a) What is the probability that at least 3 ticketed passengers do not show up for the flight?

(b) What is the probability that between 2 and 5 passengers do not show up for the flight?

(c) What is the probability that not more than 6 passengers do not show up for the flight?

(d) The aircraft used for the flight has 35 seats. If the airline routinely overbooks the flight by 4 passengers, what is the probability that on any given day every ticketed passenger who shows up will get a seat?

6.5 THE BINOMIAL PROBABILITY DISTRIBUTION

In the previous section you learned the definition of a random variable and a probability distribution. Each of the random variables that you looked at was described by a probability distribution that was given in a table. The random variables represented many different types of data that might be collected in a statistical study. In fact, most of the random variables that we see in the real world fall into specific categories and can be described by a set of special models or probability distributions. We now look at one of these models, the binomial probability distribution, in detail.

6.5.1 The Binomial Model

One of the most common types of data that people collect is data on the number of times that some phenomenon occurs in a sample of given size. For example, you may be interested in the number of people in a sample who are in favor of certain legislation or in the number of people who like a new flavor of ice cream. The sample does not have to consist of people; it could be the number of defective diskettes in a box of ten, or the number of times a coin turns up heads in a certain number of tosses. The random variable in each case is the *number of times the phenomenon occurs* in the sample. All of these types of data are examples of a **binomial random variable.**

> A ***binomial random variable*** is the number of successes in n trials or in a sample of size n.

Certain characteristics define binomial random variables:

- There are a fixed number of identical trials of an experiment. *This is the same as taking a sample of size n. Just think of each trial as selecting the next item for the sample.*
- The outcome for each trial of the experiment can be classified in one of two ways: a *success,* S (when the phenomenon of interest happens) or a *failure,* F (when the phenomenon of interest does not happen).
- The probability that a success occurs in any sample element or on any trial of the experiment, π, is the same for each element or trial. This also means that the probability of a failure, which is $1 - \pi$, is also constant. *This means that nothing happens over the course of the experiment to change the probability of a success, such as a change in population.*
- The trials of the experiment are independent. *This means that the outcome from one trial does not affect the outcomes of subsequent trials.*
- The random variable is the number of successes that occur in the n trials of the experiment.

In finding real-world situations that exactly fit the characteristics of a binomial random variable when we are sampling from a population it is difficult to ensure that the trials are independent of each other and that π, the probability of a success on any trial or the proportion of successes in the population, remains constant. Keep in mind that the reason we want the trials to be independent is that if they are not, then the probability of a success will change from trial to trial. This is a violation of the third characteristic. In fact, the only way to ensure independence when sampling, is to sample from a finite population with replacement or from an infinite population. Sampling with replacement means that when you sample an item from the population, you return it to the population, allowing for the possibility that you might sample the exact same item again.

The first problem, the idea of sampling with replacement, is not very appealing from a practical point of view. Since the purpose of statistics is to obtain information, sampling the same item or person repeatedly will not add to the information contained in the sample. The second problem, the idea of an infinite population, is more philosophical. Although there are no truly infinite populations, many populations are infinite for all practical purposes, such as the number of people in the world (or even in a large country for that matter) or all of the production, past and present, of a machine or factory.

What happens when the population from which we sample is finite and we do not sample with replacement?

EXAMPLE 6.21 CD Jewel Cases

Sampling Without Replacement

Suppose that you are inspecting a shipment of CD jewel cases for cracks in the cover. The box from which you are sampling contains 30 cases, of which 5 have cracked covers. The first time that you select an item from the population, the probability of getting a case with a cracked cover (the proportion of successes in the population) is $\frac{5}{30} = 0.167$. Now, you certainly are not going to sample with replacement in this situation. What would you gain by throwing a case you have already inspected back in the box, particularly if it is defective?

The next time you sample an item from the box, what is the probability of a success? If you are thinking, "It depends on what happened the first time," then you are absolutely correct! Look at the diagram shown here. You see that as you continue to sample from the box, the probability of obtaining a case with a cracked cover on *that trial* is different from the previous trial; that is, π changes from trial to trial. The trials are not independent because the outcome of one trial directly affects the outcome of the next!

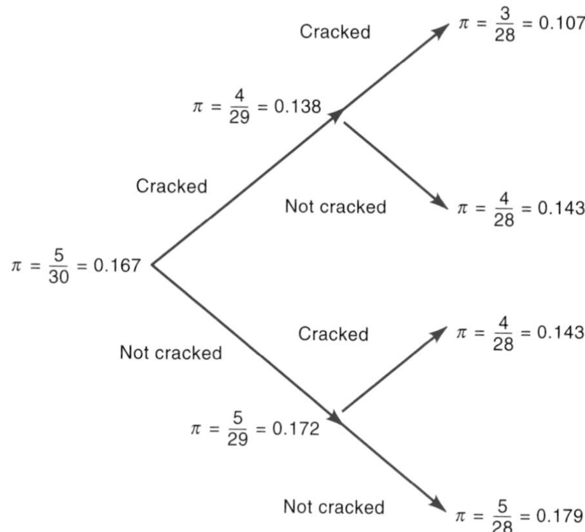

What could we do to fix the problem? The real issue is that when the denominator in the proportion is small and changing, the value of the fraction changes considerably. What happens if the denominator is much larger? Will the change still be noticeable?

Let's look at the same problem, but with everything increased proportionally. Suppose that the box contains 3000 jewel cases, of which 500 have cracked covers. In this case π, the probability or proportion of cracked cases, is still 0.167 when we begin sampling. Now what happens to π as items are sampled and not replaced in the population? The next figure illustrates the results:

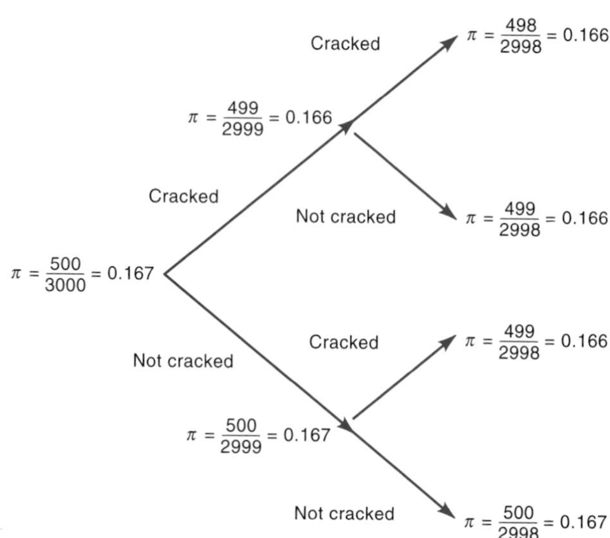

You see that although π changes, the changes are much less noticeable. In fact, if you were writing π to the nearest percent you would not see the change at all. ■

Usually the population must be at least 1000 to ensure that the changes do not occur before the third decimal place and the sample size should be no more than 10% of the population.

Clearly, as the population gets larger the problem gets smaller. The magnitude of the change in π depends on two things: the size of the population and the size of the sample that is drawn from the population. In general, if the population size is large and the sample size is small relative to the population size, then the random variable represented by the number of successes in the sample can be assumed to be binomial.

EXAMPLE 6.22 Credit Problems

Identifying a Binomial Random Variable

In addition to identifying variables, the Chamber of Commerce that is interested in the credit problems of small businesses asked these businesses a series of questions about the problems they might be experiencing. One of these questions, to which the businesses responded Yes or No, was, Are you experiencing credit problems? In previous applications of this questionnaire, the Chamber of Commerce found that approximately 10% of the businesses have reported having such problems.

Is the number of businesses who reported having credit problems in the sample of 166 a binomial random variable?

To answer this question we need to consider the five characteristics of the binomial random variable.

1. Yes. There are a fixed number of trials, in this case 166, and the selection was random.
2. Yes. Each trial can result in only one of two outcomes: a success (the company is having credit problems) or a failure (the company is not having credit problems).
3. Yes. If we assume that the time to return the survey was short enough, there would be no economic situations that would change the proportion from 10%.
4. Yes. Here we have to be careful. The sample of 166 is taken from a population of 1536 small businesses in the city. If 10% of the businesses do have credit problems, then that would correspond to 154 successes in the population. In the worst case, the probability of a success could change to 0 (if all 154 successes in the population wound up in the sample of 166), but that is nearly impossible. (If it did happen, then either the sample was not random or else the estimate of 10% is not at all realistic.) Most likely it would change from 154/1536 (10.03%) at the beginning of the sampling to about 137/1370 (10%) when the entire sample of 166 was completed.
5. Yes. The data collected are the number of businesses in the sample that are experiencing credit-related problems. ■

In general, if the sample size is about 10% of the population then the assumption that the probability of a success does not change is a reasonable one.

EXAMPLE 6.23 Wearing Seat Belts

Identifying a Binomial Random Variable

The state of Connecticut has seat-belt laws for drivers and passengers. It is known that 70% of the drivers in Connecticut wear their seat belts when they drive. A police trap selects a random sample of five drivers and counts the number that are wearing seat belts. Is the number of drivers wearing seat belts in the sample of five a binomial random variable?

To answer this question we need to consider the five characteristics of a binomial random variable.

1. Yes. There are a fixed number of identical trials if we assume that each driver is selected randomly.
2. Yes. Each trial can result in only one of two outcomes: a success (the driver is wearing a seat belt) or a failure (the driver is not wearing a seat belt).
3. Yes. If we assume that the sample is taken over a short enough period of time that driving habits will not have changed drastically, then the 70% will remain constant.
4. Yes. If we assume that there is no way that the driver of a car that is stopped can influence the outcome for the next driver then the trials are independent. The population of the drivers in Connecticut is very large and the sample size is definitely small relative to the population so the trials will be independent and the proportion of successes in the population will remain essentially constant.
5. Yes. The data that are collected are the number of people wearing seat belts in the sample of five selected at random. ■

It is important that you learn to recognize problems to which the binomial distribution applies. It is easy enough to do in a textbook (after some practice) but when you are actually practicing statistics you will need to know what to look for. Keep in mind the five characteristics of a binomial random variable when you are looking at both problems in this book and at data that have been collected in real statistical studies.

TRY IT NOW!

Loan Defaults ***Recognizing a Binomial Random Variable***

Although the Chamber of Commerce is concerned about the problems of small businesses, it must also be sensitive to the problems that the lending institutions have when issuing credit. One of the problems that banks have with small businesses is default on loan payments. It is estimated that approximately 20% of all small businesses with less than 50 employees are at least 6 months behind in loan payments. The Chamber of Commerce that surveyed the small businesses of a city wants to look at this problem in more detail. It finds that of the 1536 small businesses in the city, 965 have less than 50 employees. It randomly selects 25 of these small businesses, checks their credit histories, and counts the number of companies in the sample of 25 that are at least 6 months behind in loan payments.

Does this qualify as a binomial probability distribution?

6.5.2 The Binomial Probability Distribution

Now that we understand binomial random variables, we need to know how to find their probability distribution. The probability distribution for the binomial random variable will depend on two quantities or parameters: n, the number of trials or the sample size, and p, the proportion of successes in the population. The random variable X is the number of successes in n trials of the experiment.

Remember, we use parameters for populations, and a probability distribution is a model for a population.

ANS. YES ON ALL FIVE CRITERIA.

The probability distribution of X is determined by this formula:

Binomial probability distribution

$$p(x) = \frac{n!}{(x!)(n-x)!}\pi^x(1-\pi)^{n-x} \qquad \text{for } x = 0, 1, 2, \ldots, n$$

The formula considers the sample size, n, the probability of a success, π, and the value of X that you are interested in, x. The number of trials of the experiment defines the possible values that the random variable can have. If there are n trials of the experiment, then the smallest number of successes that can occur is 0 and the largest number of successes is n. Thus, a binomial random variable, X, can have values $x = 0, 1, 2, \ldots, n$. The probability of a success on any trial, π, will determine how the probabilities are distributed over the values of X. When π is large, then you will expect to see a lot of successes in the sample, so the higher values of X will have the larger probabilities. When π is small, the lower values of X will have the larger probabilities.

The terms that contain the ! are known as factorials. $n!$ is equal to $n \times (n-1) \times \cdots \times 1$. The other factorial terms are calculated in a similar manner.

You do not really need to know how to use the formula to find the probability distribution of a binomial random variable. There are tables for this purpose for many different combinations of n and π. These tables are identical in use to the probability distribution tables that you used in the previous section. A good set of these tables is found in Appendix A at the end of this book.

Binomial Probability Tables

Most statistical software packages, such as Minitab and SPSS, and many spreadsheets, such as Excel, find binomial probabilities.

The probability distribution tables for the binomial distribution are classified according to the value of n, the number of trials of the experiment. There are tables for values of n from 5 to 30. Each table covers a range of values for π from 0.05 to 0.95. A sample of some of the table for $n = 5$ is shown in Figure 6.1.

The two columns that are shaded make up the probability distribution table for $n = 5$ and $\pi = 0.70$ (or 70%). If you just take those columns and transpose as shown in Figure 6.2, then the result will look like every probability distribution table you have seen before!

Do not forget that decimals and percentages are equivalent!

Except for learning to recognize binomial random variables and using the tables, there is nothing new to learn about answering questions involving binomial random variables.

$n = 5$							π					
x	0.05	0.10	0.20	0.25	...	0.50	0.60	0.70	0.75	...	0.90	0.95
0	0.774	0.590	0.328	0.237	...	0.031	0.010	0.002	0.001	...	0.000	0.000
1	0.204	0.328	0.410	0.396	...	0.156	0.077	0.028	0.015	...	0.000	0.000
2	0.021	0.073	0.205	0.264	...	0.313	0.230	0.132	0.088	...	0.008	0.001
3	0.001	0.008	0.051	0.088	...	0.313	0.346	0.309	0.264	...	0.073	0.021
4	0.000	0.000	0.006	0.015	...	0.156	0.259	0.360	0.396	...	0.328	0.204
5	0.000	0.000	0.000	0.001	...	0.031	0.078	0.168	0.237	...	0.590	0.774

FIGURE 6.1 Portion of binomial table for $n = 5$

x	0	1	2	3	4	5
p(x)	0.002	0.028	0.132	0.309	0.360	0.168

FIGURE 6.2 Binomial probability distribution for $n = 5$ and $\pi = 0.70$

EXAMPLE 6.24 Wearing Seat Belts

Using the Binomial Probability Tables

The example about the Connecticut drivers identified the random variable for the problem as a binomial random variable with $n = 5$ and $\pi = 0.70$. What is the probability that, in the sample of 5 drivers, exactly 3 are wearing seat belts?

Looking at the table in Figure 6.1 or 6.2, we see that $p(3) = 0.309$.

What is the probability that in a sample of 5 drivers taken at most 2 are wearing seat belts? Again, from the table in Figure 6.1 or 6.2,

$$P(X \leq 2) = p(0) + p(1) + p(2) = 0.002 + 0.028 + 0.132 = 0.162$$

■

You can see that there is really nothing new involved in actually solving problems that involve the binomial distribution. The parts that require some thinking and work are recognizing the problem as binomial, identifying the parameters n and π for the particular problem, and finding the correct table.

It is important to recognize that the definition of a success is critical to problem solving with the binomial distribution. A success is not necessarily always something good, nor does it have to stay the same in a given problem. To determine what the success is, you must look at the question to be answered, define a success, and use the appropriate value of π.

EXAMPLE 6.25 Parking Tickets

Calculating Binomial Probabilities

A local watchdog agency has been looking at parking problems outside the city court building. It estimates that 40% of all of the cars parked in the metered lot receive parking tickets for meter violations. The agency decides to take a random sample of 10 cars from the lot and check to see whether they have a parking ticket on the windshield.

(a) Find the probability that, of the 10 cars sampled, exactly 6 have parking tickets.

For this problem a success is having a parking ticket and so we use the table with $n = 10$ and $\pi = 0.40$ and find that $P(X = 6) = 0.111$.

(b) Find the probability that between 4 and 7 inclusive do not have parking tickets.

For this problem a success is *not* having a parking ticket. Since 40% of the cars have parking tickets, we can use the definition of the complement to find that 100% − 40% = 60% do not have parking tickets.

Caution! No matter what you may think, it is NOT easier to keep using $\pi = 0.40$ and try to change the question to be in terms of cars having parking tickets!

Use $n = 10$ and $\pi = 0.60$ to get $P(4 \leq X \leq 7) = 0.111 + 0.201 + 0.251 + 0.215 = 0.778$.

If the watchdog group found in its sample of 10 cars that none of the cars had parking tickets, would you think that the estimate of 40% was reasonable?

With $n = 10$ and $\pi = 0.40$ the probability that no cars have tickets, $P(X = 0)$, is 0.006, which is very small. Thus, it is highly unlikely that, if 40% of the cars get tickets, the sample of 10 would find no cars with tickets. The estimate seems to be high. ■

The previous example is a preview of the next topic in statistics that you will study. In the first part of this book you learned how to describe data that are collected and how to calculate different sample statistics. Now you are learning about probability models and how they can be used to determine how likely it is that different events will occur when we assume some parameters for our population data. In the previous example we looked at how well what we observed (the data) fit the probability model (binomial with $\pi = 40\%$ and $n = 10$). We used the probability that such an event would happen to come to the conclusion that the model did not seem appropriate. In the remainder of this book you will learn the more formal methods of hypothesis testing to accomplish this same thing.

TRY IT NOW!

Loan Defaults ***Solving Binomial Probability Problems***

The Chamber of Commerce that is checking credit problems of small businesses estimated that 20% of all small businesses were at least 6 months behind in loan payments. The Chamber of Commerce took a random sample of 25 small businesses and counted the number of the businesses that were at least 6 months behind in loan payments.

Define a success for this problem.

Describe the random variable, X, in words.

Find the parameters of the binomial distribution for this problem.

Find the probability that in the sample of 25 businesses less than 6 were at least 6 months behind in loan payments.

Find the probability that between 4 and 9 inclusive were at least 6 months behind in loan payments.

ANS. BEHIND IN PAYMENTS; X = THE NUMBER OF COMPANIES BEHIND IN LOAN PAYMENTS; $n = 25$, $\pi = 0.20$; 0.618, 0.748

6.5.3 The Mean and Standard Deviation of the Binomial Distribution

Since probability distributions are models of populations, and random variables are numerical, it makes sense that just like quantitative sample data, they have means and standard deviations. There are some general formulas for calculating the mean and standard deviation of a random variable, but we will concentrate on the probability distributions that we study.

Since probability distributions are population models, their means and standard deviations are parameters represented by the Greek letters μ and σ. In particular, for a binomial random variable, X, the **mean, μ,** and the **standard deviation, σ,** are found using the following formulas:

Binomial mean and standard deviation

$$\mu = n\pi \quad \text{and} \quad \sigma = \sqrt{n\pi(1 - \pi)}$$

You see that the mean and standard deviation depend on the parameters of the probability distribution, n and π. The formula for the mean is actually quite intuitive if you think about it. If you knew, for example, that 40% of a certain population wore eyeglasses, and you took a sample of 10 people from that population, how many of the 10 would you *expect* to wear glasses? Instinctively you would take 40% of the 10, to get 4 people who wear glasses. From the formula for μ we would get

$$\mu = n\pi = (10)(0.40) = 4 \text{ people}$$

The formula for the standard deviation is really not at all intuitive and deriving it is beyond the scope of this text. To see how it is used, we can calculate the standard deviation of our example and find that

$$\sigma = \sqrt{n\pi(1 - \pi)} = \sqrt{(10)(0.40)(0.60)} = 1.55 \text{ people}$$

Thus, we know that if $n = 10$ and $\pi = 0.40$, then the number of people who wear glasses is a random variable with a mean of 4 and a standard deviation of 1.55.

EXAMPLE 6.26 **Credit Problems**

Calculating the Mean and Standard Deviation of a Binomial Random Variable

With a sample of $n = 166$ we could not use the tables to determine probabilities for the number of small businesses that reported having credit problems. Most statistical software packages will calculate probability distributions for binomial random variables for any values of n and π, but we can find the mean and standard deviation of this random variable without any problems.

The mean represents the expected number of businesses that are experiencing credit problems in the sample of 166. That is, with $n = 166$ and $\pi = 0.10$ the mean is

$$\mu = n\pi = (166)(0.10) = 16.6 \text{ businesses}$$

The standard deviation of the number of small businesses in 166 that report credit problems is

$$\sigma = \sqrt{n\pi(1 - \pi)} = \sqrt{(166)(0.10)(0.90)} = 3.87 \text{ businesses}$$

■

EXAMPLE 6.27 Wearing Seat Belts

Finding the Mean and Standard Deviation of a Binomial Random Variable

The Department of Transportation in Connecticut would like to know how many drivers the state troopers should expect to find wearing their seat belts at the checkpoint. It decides to calculate the mean of the binomial random variable.

In this case, $n = 5$ and $\pi = 0.70$, so it calculates that

$$\mu = n\pi = (5)(0.70) = 3.5 \text{ people}$$

The Department would also like to know the standard deviation of the number that would be wearing seat belts. In this case

$$\sigma = \sqrt{n\pi(1 - \pi)} = \sqrt{(5)(0.70)(1 - 0.70)} = \sqrt{(5)(0.70)(0.30)} = \sqrt{1.05} = 1.02 \text{ people} \quad \blacksquare$$

Remember that the mean and standard deviation tell us something about how random variables behave. In particular, they tell us where the center of the probability distribution is located and how much the random variable will vary around that center.

TRY IT NOW!

Loan Defaults ***Calculating the Mean and Standard Deviation of a Binomial Random Variable***

The Chamber of Commerce that was looking at the loan defaults for small businesses wants to know the mean and standard deviation for the binomial random variable with $n = 25$ and $\pi = 0.20$.

Find the mean and standard deviation of the number of small businesses in 25 that will default on their loans.

How can we use our knowledge of the mean and standard deviation? One thing we can do is to compare our knowledge of what *should* happen, to the reality of what *did* happen, to get some idea of how well the reality fits the theory. This is the basis for the work you will do in the remainder of this book, *inferential statistics*. Right now, we will look at this work in an informal way.

EXAMPLE 6.28 Credit Problems

Using the Mean and the Standard Deviation

The Chamber of Commerce wonders whether the current random sample of 166 businesses supports its belief that 10% of the small businesses in the city are experiencing credit problems. It already has the mean and standard deviation for its model, so it decides to compare the model to the actual data.

ANS. $\mu = 5$, $\sigma = 2$

The mean of the binomial random variable with $n = 166$ and $\pi = 0.10$ is 16.6 and the standard deviation is 3.87. From the data, the Chamber of Commerce analysts find that the number of businesses that answered yes to the question of credit problems was 25. Clearly, 25 is not equal to 16.6, but how different is it?

If they consider the standard deviation they can calculate the number of standard deviations that their data value is from the mean:

$$z = \frac{25 - 16.6}{3.87} = 2.17$$

They know that the empirical rule holds only for symmetric distributions and they have no idea whether that applies here, but they do know that 2.17 standard deviations away from the mean is at least possibly unusual.

As a second check the analysts use their data to estimate the probability that a small business will report having credit problems. They found 25 such businesses in their sample of 166, so they estimate the probability that a business will report having credit problems to be $25/166 = 0.1506$ or approximately 15%. This is different from the 10% they were expecting, but the difference may just be a result of sampling.

As a third check they use a statistical software package to calculate the probability of having 25 successes in a sample of 166 when $\pi = 0.10$. They find that the probability is 0.0108, which is only slightly more than 1%. It would seem that perhaps this sample does not fit their earlier beliefs. ■

EXAMPLE 6.29 Parking Tickets

Using the Mean and Standard Deviation

The watchdog agency that is looking at the problem of parking tickets would like to know what it should expect to see in the data it collects. The analysts in the agency decide to calculate the mean and standard deviation of the binomial random variable.

The mean is

$$\mu = (10)(0.40) = 4 \text{ cars}$$

and the standard deviation is

$$\sigma = \sqrt{n\pi(1 - \pi)} = \sqrt{(10)(0.40)(0.60)} = \sqrt{2.4} = 1.55 \text{ cars}$$

This tells the analysts that they should expect to find 4 cars with parking tickets. Wondering how much the number of cars might vary, they decide to find the probability that the number of tickets will be within 2 standard deviations of the mean. To do this they calculate $\mu \pm 2\sigma = 4 \pm (2)(1.55) = 4 \pm 3.1 = (0.9, 7.1)$. They want to find the probability that the random variable is between these two values, or $P(0.90 < X < 7.1)$.

How will they do this? The binomial tables certainly do not include numbers like 0.90 and 7.1! The analysts realize that they will have to convert the problem to the nearest integer values that satisfy the probability expression. That means they need to find $P(1 \leq X \leq 7)$. From the tables for $n = 10$ and $\pi = 0.40$ they find that the answer is 0.981. They interpret this to mean that 98.1% of the time the number of tickets they find will be between 1 and 7 inclusive. This gives them a good idea of what to expect in their data. ■

The idea of comparing what should happen to what does happen is a critical idea in statistics. In the next few chapters we develop a formal method for doing this called *hypothesis testing.*

5. Display the binomial distribution in a bar chart.

6. Compare the bar chart from step 3 to the binomial distribution displayed in step 5. How do they compare? Why are they different?

7. The following graph has a line at the theoretical value of π, 0.70. Graph your estimates of π for each sample on the same graph. What happens to your estimate as the sample size increases?

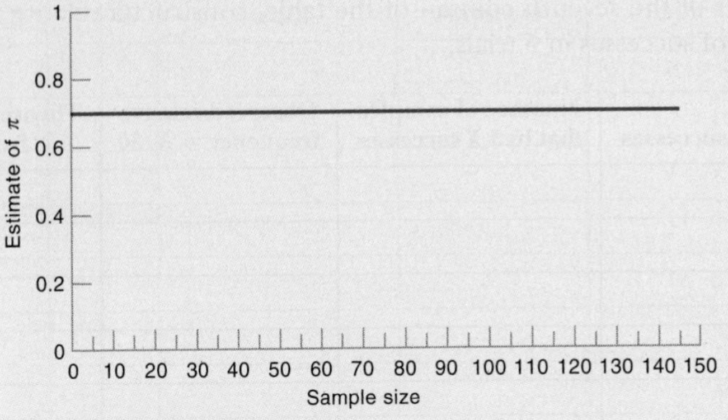

6.5.4 Exploring the Binomial Distribution

You have started to become familiar with using the binomial probability tables and solving binomial probability problems, but you still may not understand what role the parameters n and π play in determining what the probability distribution of a binomial random variable looks like.

In Figure 6.3 you see the effects of changing the value of the parameter π for a fixed value of n. What you see agrees with our earlier thoughts that when π is small it is more likely that the number of successes will be small and the distribution skews to the right. When π is large it is more likely that the number of successes will be large and the distribution is skewed to the left. You can also see that when π is equal to 0.50 the distribution is symmetric.

If you look at the binomial table for $n = 10$ you will notice, not surprisingly, that the probability distributions for $\pi = 0.20$ and $\pi = 0.80$ are mirror images of each other.

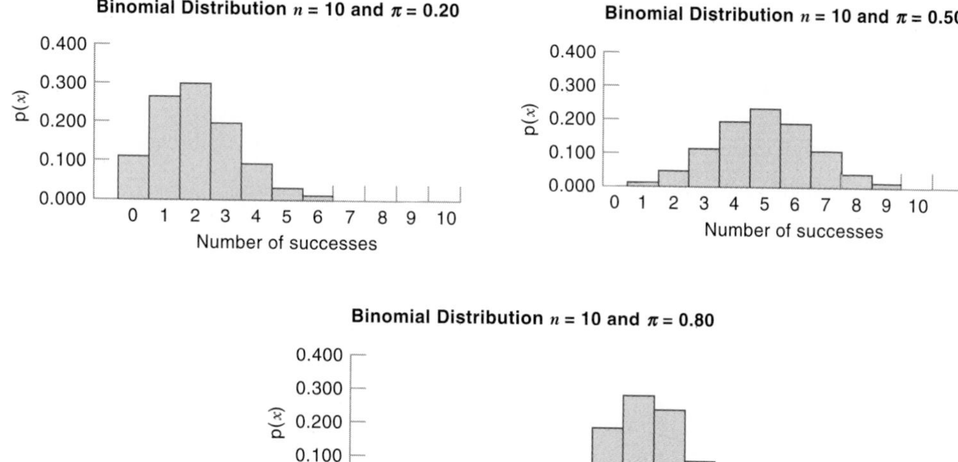

FIGURE 6.3 Effects of changing π when n is fixed

Where does the mean fit into the picture? If you remember, the mean is the value that you expect to occur, that is, it is the most likely outcome. If you look at Figure 6.3, you see that in the first probability histogram the highest bar is for $X = 2$ and the mean of a binomial random variable with $n = 10$ and $\pi = 0.20$ is $\mu = (10)(0.20) = 2$.

Figure 6.4 shows the effects of changing the value of the parameter n for a fixed value of π. The y scale for each histogram is approximately the same. From the picture you can see that, for the most part, the shape of the distribution remains the same as n varies, but the number of possible values and the probability of each value of X (bars in the histogram) changes. In fact, as n gets larger, the individual probabilities get smaller. This makes sense, since we know that the probabilities must sum to 1 and if there are more values of X, then each value will get a smaller share of the total.

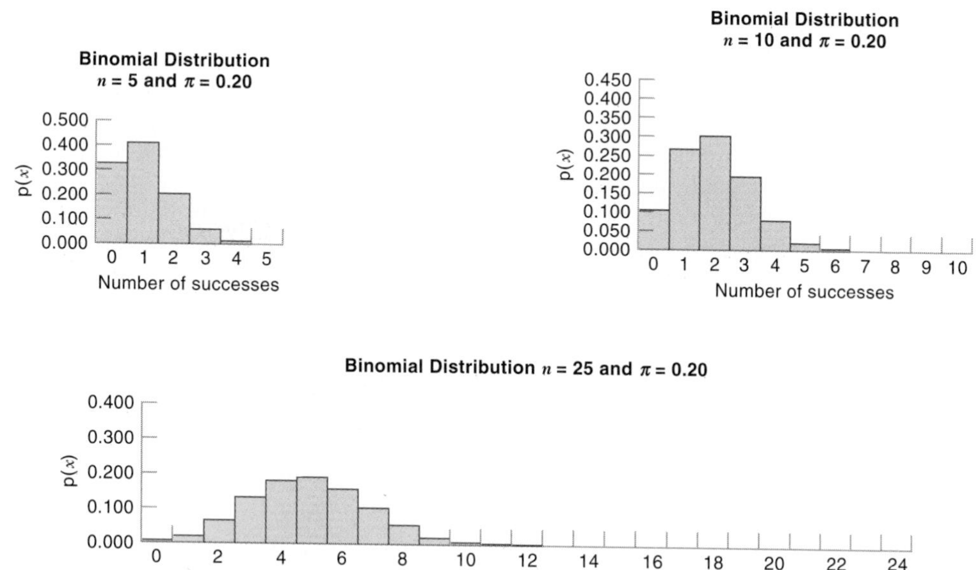

FIGURE 6.4 Effects of changing n for a fixed value of π

6.5.5 Exercises—Learning It!

6.14 The Board of Realtors of a small city reports that 80% of the homes that are sold have been on the market for more than 6 months. The Board takes a random sample of 15 homes that have recently been sold and counts the number that were on the market for more than 6 months. What is the probability that of the 15 houses in the sample

(a) less than 12 have been on the market for more than 6 months?

(b) between 8 and 13 have been on the market for more than 6 months?

(c) at least 10 have been on the market for more than 6 months?

(d) at most 4 have been on the market for less than 6 months?

6.15 The Department of Transportation for a city has found that 25% of all parking tickets that have been issued have not been paid within 1 month of issue. The Department takes a random sample of 20 parking tickets that were issued 1 month ago and counts the number that have not been paid. What is the probability that

(a) at most 5 have not been paid?

(b) between 4 and 8 inclusive have not been paid?

(c) more than 7 have not been paid?

(d) at least 6 have been paid?

6.16 A large construction firm estimates that 10% of the jobs that it manages are finished within the contracted time period. It looks at a random sample of 5 jobs that it has managed.

(a) What is the probability that 4 of the 5 jobs were not completed within the contracted time period?

(b) What is the mean number of jobs that are completed within the contracted time period?

(c) What is the standard deviation of the number of jobs in 5 that are completed within the contracted time period?

6.17 A large bank that issues many loans for General Motors estimates that 70% of the loans are approved within 24 hours of application. A consumer group takes a random sample of 25 recent GM loan applications.

(a) What is the probability that at most 5 were not approved within 24 hours?

(b) What is the probability that between 10 and 17 are approved within 24 hours?

(c) What is the mean number of loans in 25 that will be approved within 24 hours?

(d) What is the standard deviation of the number of loans in 25 that will be approved within 24 hours?

(e) What is the probability that the number of loans in 25 that are approved within 24 hours is within 3 standard deviations of the mean?

6.18 Companies have been having problems with employees playing computer games at work. As the size and complexity of such games increases, computer system administrators find that network resources are being drained and that the games are using more and more hard disk space. A recent survey across various industries revealed that 30% of workers said that the last computer game they played had been played at work. A random sample of 15 employees is taken.

(a) What is the probability that less than 6 said they played their last computer game at work?

(b) What is the probability that at least 4 said they played their last computer game at work?

(c) What is the probability that at most 10 said they did not play their last computer game at work?

(d) What is the expected number of employees in a sample of size 15 who played their last computer game at work? What is the standard deviation of the number of employees in 15 who played their last computer game at work?

(e) What is the probability that the number of employees in 15 who played their last computer game at work is within 2 standard deviations of the mean?

6.6 CONTINUOUS RANDOM VARIABLES

In Chapter 2 you learned about the different types of data. In particular, you learned that there are two types of quantitative data: discrete and continuous. Discrete data are integer and are often a count of the number of times that something happens. The binomial distribution that you just studied is one good probability model for discrete data.

Continuous data occur when the variable of interest can take on any one of an infinite number of values over some *interval* on the real number line. Much of the time, continuous data result from taking data on a *measurement*. Examples of this would be height of students or grade point averages (GPA). The actual number of values that you can obtain is limited by the measuring instrument (we choose to measure height to the nearest inch or report GPA to two decimal places) but any value in the interval is valid.

When you learned about discrete random variables you learned that to find probabilities associated with the random variable, you simply added the relevant individual probabilities. With continuous random variables you will have to shift your thinking a little bit to see how probabilities are calculated.

When we looked at the effects of changing the value of n in the binomial distribution, we saw that as n increased, the number of possible values of X increased and the individual probabilities got smaller. When $n = 10$ it is not that tedious to calculate $P(X \geq 4)$, but when $n = 20$ or $n = 25$ it is considerably more tedious to do it directly. You are adding many more terms and they are all very small numbers. If we let n get very large, say, $n = 100$, it would be tiring indeed! Figure 6.5 looks at the binomial distribution for $\pi = 0.50$ and $n = 10, 25, 50$, and 100.

You can see from the graphs that if we connect the tops of all of the histogram bars, as n gets larger, the curve becomes smooth. For continuous random variables, which can take on many more than 100 possible values, the probability distribution is called a **probability density function, $f(x)$,** and is represented by a smooth curve such as the one in Figure 6.6 at the top of page 264.

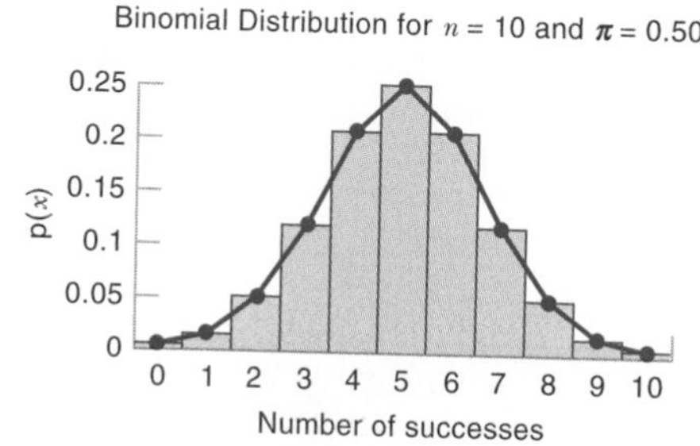

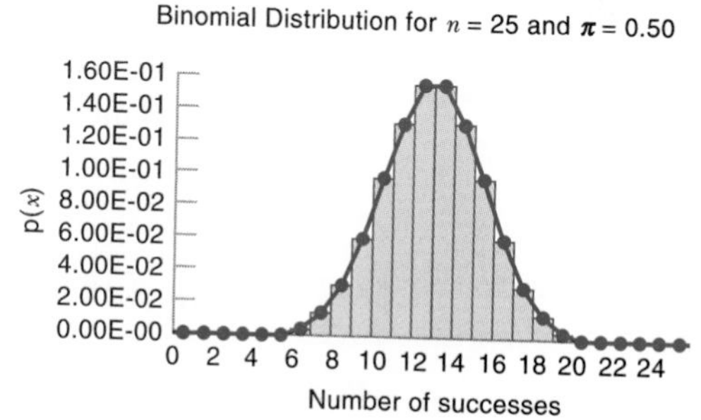

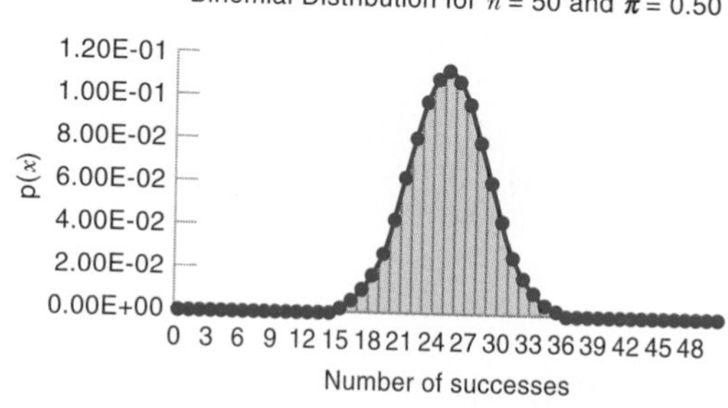

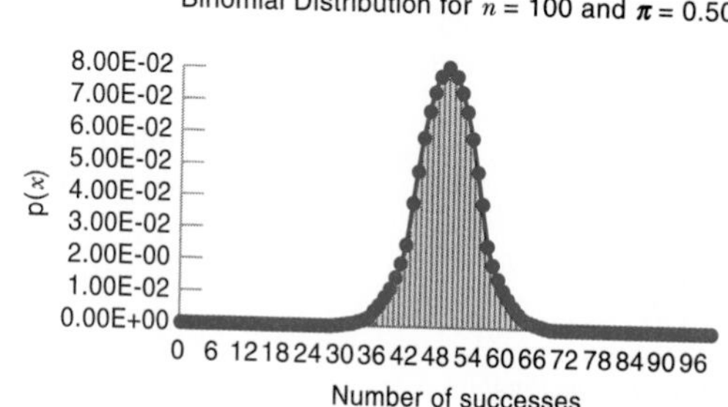

FIGURE 6.5 Binomial distribution for large values of n

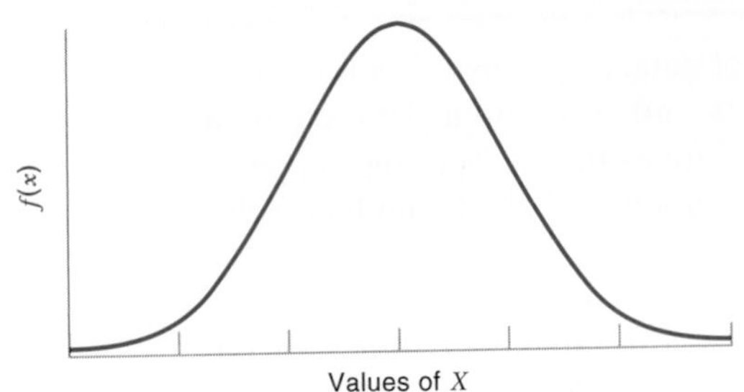

FIGURE 6.6 Probability distribution for a continuous random variable

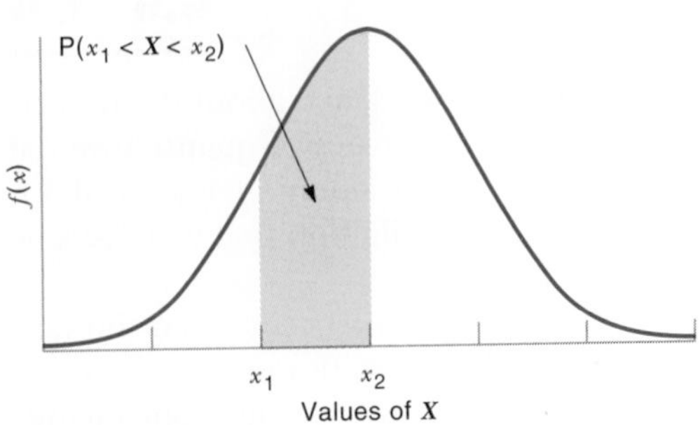

FIGURE 6.7 Probability represented by an area under the curve

A ***probability density function, f(x),*** is a smooth curve that represents the probability distribution of a continuous random variable.

You might be wondering how this curve relates to probabilities, since there is no corresponding probability table with numbers involved. How do you find the probabilities that you are interested in? These are good questions.

When we increased the value of n for the binomial distribution, you saw that the individual probabilities got much smaller. In fact, if you look at the scales on the y axes for Figure 6.5 you will see that for $n = 100$ the *largest* number on the graph is 0.08! Again, this makes sense because the total probability is always equal to 1 and when you have to divide it up over more and more possible values, each individual probability gets closer and closer to 0.

For continuous random variables $P(x_1 < X < x_2)$ is exactly the same as $P(x_1 \leq X \leq x_2)$, since $P(X = x) = 0$.

In fact, for continuous random variables we can no longer talk about the probability that the random variable will assume one particular value, $P(X = x)$, because this is equal to 0. Instead, we can talk about the probability that the random variable will take on any one of the values over an *interval* of interest; that is, we can find $P(x_1 < X < x_2)$. This probability is represented by the area under the probability density curve as shown in Figure 6.7. Finding probabilities for a particular probability density curve as shown in Figure 6.7 involves the mathematics of calculus, but for certain distributions the probabilities have already been calculated and tabulated.

In the next section we look at one particular continuous probability distribution that serves as a model for many natural phenomena. This is known as the *normal distribution.*

6.7 THE NORMAL DISTRIBUTION

6.7.1 The Normal Curve

The normal probability distribution is the symmetric, bell-shaped curve shown in Figure 6.8. It is usually referred to as the *normal curve.* This is the same curve we saw when we learned about the empirical rule.

In reality, most measurement data are modeled very well by this distribution. The actual formula for the probability density is

Normal probability density

$$f(x) = \frac{1}{\sigma\sqrt{2\pi}} e^{-(x-\mu)^2/2\sigma^2} \quad \text{for } -\infty < x < \infty$$

Here, π is the familiar constant, 3.141 . . . , not related to the binomial distribution.

where $e = 2.71828 \ldots$ and $\pi = 3.14159 \ldots$. If you look at the equation you can see that the probability density for a value, x, relies on two **parameters,** μ and σ. The normal distribution is the ultimate symmetric, bell-shaped distribution.

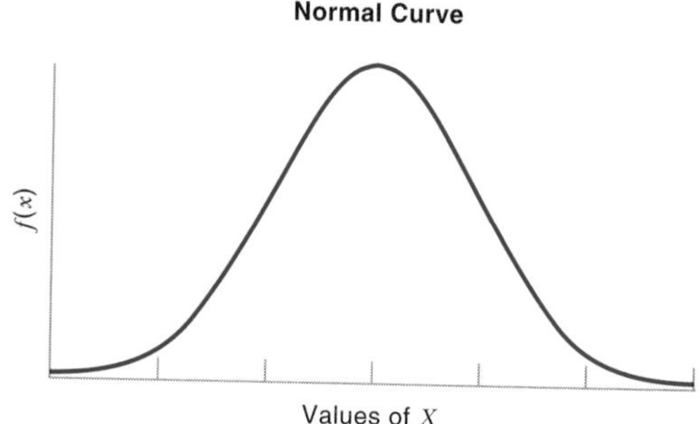

FIGURE 6.8 Normal probability curve

For a normal random variable, the parameter μ is the **mean** of the normal random variable, X, and σ is the **standard deviation.**

When we refer to a normally distributed random variable we often use a special notation

$$X \sim N(\mu, \sigma)$$

This shorthand is equivalent to saying that the random variable X is normally distributed with a mean of μ and a standard deviation of σ.

When we studied the binomial probability distribution we learned that the parameters, in that case n and π, defined how the probability was distributed over the set of possible values of X. That is, they defined the shape of the probability histogram. In a similar way, μ and σ define the way the normal distribution looks.

You have come across the mean in two other situations. When you learned about descriptive statistics, you learned that the mean was a measure of central tendency, or an estimate of the most typical data value. Then, when you studied the binomial distribution, we said that the mean is the most likely value, or the one that you expect to happen most often. For a normally distributed random variable, the mean is the center of the distribution. It is the value that determines the location of the probability density curve on the number line.

You also learned about the standard deviation. You know that the standard deviation measures how far the data are spread out around the mean. For a normally distributed random variable, σ determines how spread out the probability density is around its center. You may remember that in Chapter 4 we used the mean and the standard deviation to obtain a mental image of the distribution of the data. The empirical rule told us that for a symmetric distribution, virtually all of the data fall within 3 standard deviations of the mean. Since the normal distribution is the fundamental symmetric curve, we can use this same idea to get a picture of a normal probability distribution.

In Figure 6.9 you can see the effect that changes in μ and σ have on the way the normal curve looks.

As the standard deviation increases, the distribution gets more spread out around its center. For the curve with a mean of 30 and a standard deviation of 5 you see that the ends of the curve are around 15 and 45, 3 standard deviations away from the mean! As the mean increases, the distribution moves to the right (in the direction of increasing values of X) and when the mean decreases the distribution moves to the left. Notice that although the appearance of the normal curve does change when μ and σ are varied, the basic shape does not change. The curve is always bell-shaped and symmetric. This is an important feature of the normal probability distribution.

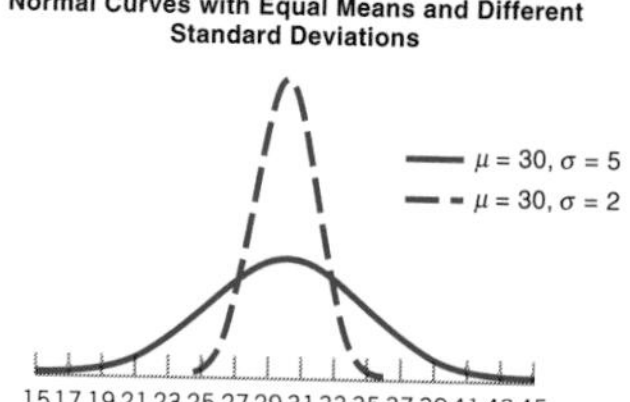

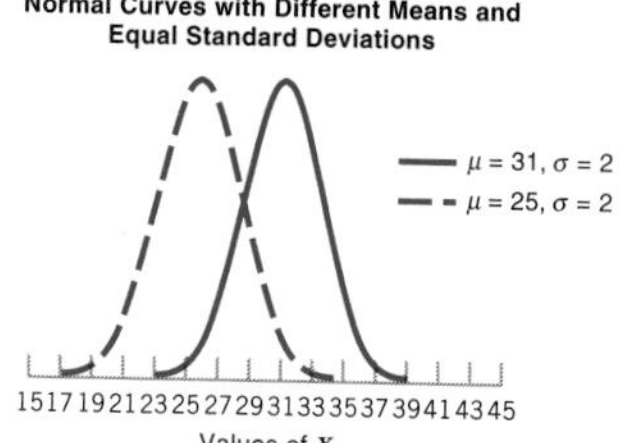

FIGURE 6.9 Effects of changing μ and σ on the normal curve

TRY IT NOW!

Food Expenditures ***Looking at the Normal Curve***

The amount of money that a person working in a large city spends each week for lunch is a normally distributed random variable. For professional and management personnel the random variable has a mean of \$35 and a standard deviation of \$5. For hourly employees the mean is \$30 with a standard deviation of \$2.

Sketch the normal curves for each of the two random variables on the same graph.

6.7.2 The Standard Normal Curve

When we learned about continuous random variables we said that the probability that the random variable takes on any value in an interval is equal to the area under the probability density curve. We also said that finding these probabilities requires the use of integral calculus, which is beyond the scope of this book. How will we find the probabilities we are interested in?

Remember that when we studied the binomial probability distribution, the formula to find probabilities was also complicated, and we solved the problem by using tables for different sets of values for n and π. Since π is constrained to be between 0 and 1, it was not hard to get tables for many different values of n.

The idea of using probability tables for the normal probability distribution seems like a good one, but there is a practical limitation. Unlike n and π, the values of μ and σ are not at all constrained. Depending on the variable of interest, there are an infinite number of different pairs of μ and σ that we might be interested in. It is not feasible to have a table for every different problem we can think of.

The problem is solved by finding a way to transform every normally distributed random variable to a single, standard normal random variable. This standard normal random variable is known as **Z** and has a mean of 0 and a standard deviation of 1. We can use the shorthand notation to write that as **Z ~ *N*(0, 1).** Once we transform the problem we can use a single normal probability table, a **standard normal table,** to solve it.

ANS.

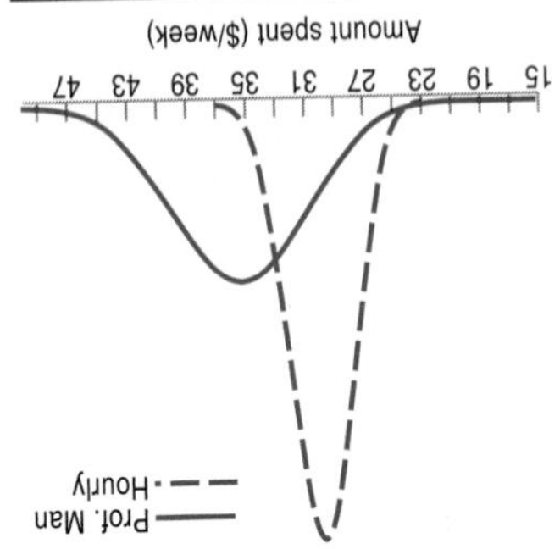

A ***Z random variable*** is normally distributed with a mean of 0 and a standard deviation 1, $Z \sim N(0, 1)$.

A ***standard normal table*** is a table of probabilities for a Z random variable.

This is not mysterious, if you think about it for a minute. If the class average on an exam were a 70 and you wanted to make it a 75, you would *add* 5 points to everyone's grade. Similarly, to move the mean from μ to 0, you subtract μ from the values.

How does the transform work? Remember that the mean of a normally distributed random variable locates the normal curve on the number line. What we want to do is move any arbitrary normal random variable that is centered at μ down the number line to center at 0. It is not hard to see that this can be accomplished by subtracting the value of μ from the random variable, X.

The change from a standard deviation of σ to a standard deviation of 1 is not difficult either. Essentially you need to scale the probability distribution so that the total area under the curve stays equal to 1 (one of the rules of probability). A value of X that is 2 standard deviations away from μ for the original random variable must stay 2 standard deviations away from 0 when it is transformed to Z. To accomplish this we describe the distance that X is from μ, $X - \mu$, in terms of the number of standard deviations it is away from μ. The transform from X to Z is then given by

Formula for Z-score

$$Z = \frac{X - \mu}{\sigma}$$

where $X \sim N(\mu, \sigma)$ and $Z \sim N(0, 1)$. At this point, an example will help you see what is happening.

This is the population version of the z-scores you calculated in Chapter 4.

EXAMPLE 6.31 Aptitude Scores

Transforming from X to Z

Scores on an aptitude test given by the training department of a large company are normally distributed with a mean of 75 points and a standard deviation of 5 points. The managers of the company are interested in knowing what proportion of the people that take the test score between 65 and 85 points.

The first thing we need to do is *draw a picture* representing the problem we are trying to solve.

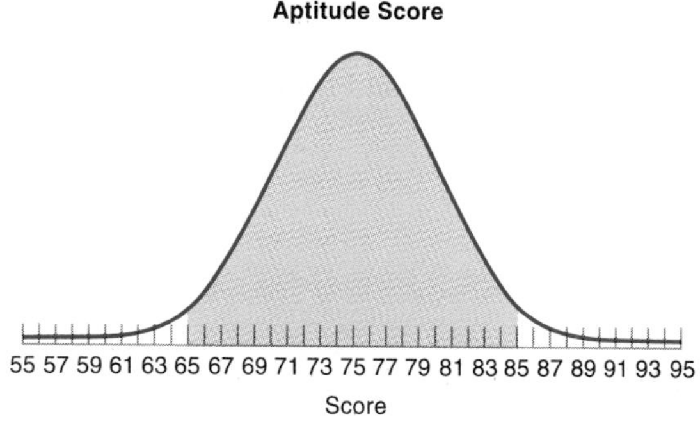

Note: It may seem to be a waste of time to you to draw the pictures. A little time spent here will avoid a LOT of time wasted later on.

The picture shows the distribution of the scores and the area under the curve that corresponds to the problem that management wants to solve. We know that to solve the problem we must transform it to a standard normal problem. To do this we must

	Second decimal place									
z	0.00	0.01	0.02	0.03	0.04	0.05	0.06	0.07	0.08	0.09
0.0	0.5000	0.5040	0.5080	0.5120	0.5160	0.5199	0.5239	0.5279	0.5319	0.5359
0.1	0.5398	0.5438	0.5478	0.5517	0.5557	0.5596	0.5636	0.5675	0.5714	0.5753
0.2	0.5793	0.5832	0.5871	0.5910	0.5948	0.5987	0.6026	0.6064	0.6103	0.6141
0.3	0.6179	0.6217	0.6255	0.6293	0.6331	0.6368	0.6406	0.6443	0.6480	0.6517
0.4	0.6554	0.6591	0.6628	0.6664	0.6700	0.6736	0.6772	0.6808	0.6844	0.6879
0.5	0.6915	0.6950	0.6985	0.7019	0.7054	0.7088	0.7123	0.7157	0.7190	0.7224
0.6	0.7257	0.7291	0.7324	0.7357	0.7389	0.7422	0.7454	0.7486	0.7517	0.7549
0.7	0.7580	0.7611	0.7642	0.7673	0.7704	0.7734	0.7764	0.7794	0.7823	0.7852
0.8	0.7881	0.7910	0.7939	0.7967	0.7995	0.8023	0.8051	0.8078	0.8106	0.8133
0.9	0.8159	0.8186	0.8212	0.8238	0.8264	0.8289	0.8315	0.8340	0.8365	0.8389
1.0	0.8413	0.8438	0.8461	0.8485	0.8508	0.8531	0.8554	0.8577	0.8599	0.8621
1.1	0.8643	0.8665	0.8686	0.8708	0.8729	0.8749	0.8770	0.8790	0.8810	0.8830
1.2	0.8849	0.8869	0.8888	0.8907	0.8925	0.8944	0.8962	0.8980	0.8997	0.9015

FIGURE 6.11 The standard normal table

For continuous random variables, probability is often referred to as the area under the curve.

must always equal 1, we can obtain $P(Z > z)$ by using the definition of the complement of an event. That is,

$$P(Z > z) = 1 - P(Z < z)$$

So, to find the area under the curve above a given value of Z you look up the Z value, find the probability below Z, and subtract it from 1. Thus, using our earlier example,

$$P(Z > 1.14) = 1 - 0.8729 = 0.1271$$

Once you are comfortable using the normal probability table you can find upper area probabilities easily by relying on the symmetry of the normal distribution. Since the normal probability distribution is symmetric about the mean, it must be true that the area to the right of a Z value must be equal to the area to the left of the negative of that Z value, or

$$P(Z > z) = P(Z < -z)$$

This is illustrated in Figure 6.12.

Using the tables to find $P(z_1 < Z < z_2)$ is not difficult either. Figure 6.13 illustrates the process.

When you look up the larger Z value, in this case $Z = +2$, the table gives the entire area under the curve to the left of 2, which is 0.9772. Looking at the picture, you

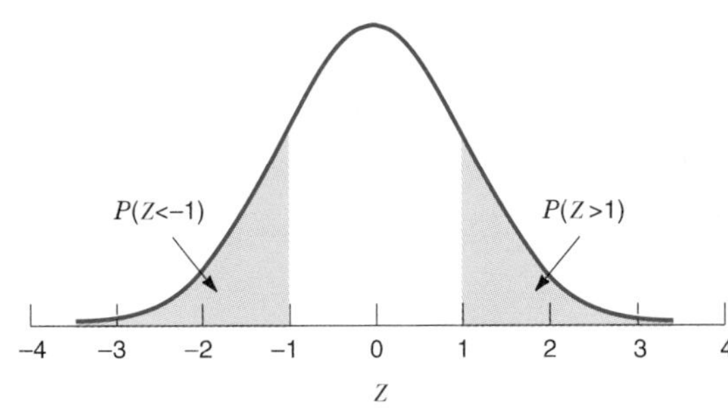

FIGURE 6.12 Comparison of upper and lower probabilities

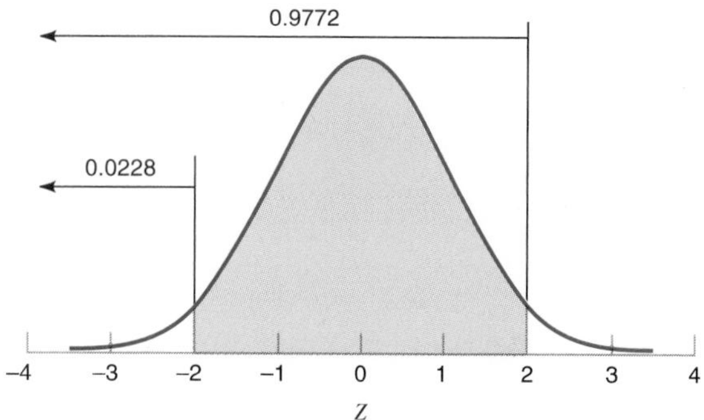

FIGURE 6.13 Finding the area between two Z values

see that this includes the piece of the curve to the left of the lower value, in this case $Z = -2$, which is 0.0228. Since we do not want to include this lower portion we must subtract it from the first value. Thus, in general,

$$P(z_1 < Z < z_2) = P(Z < z_2) - P(Z < z_1)$$

and for this example,

$$P(-2 < Z < +2) = P(Z < +2) - P(Z < -2) = 0.9772 - 0.0228 = 0.9544$$

If you think about it, you already knew this! Remember that the Z random variable is $N(0, 1)$, so finding $P(-2 < Z < +2)$ is the same as finding the probability that the random variable will be within 2 standard deviations of the mean. The answer, not surprisingly, is 0.9544 or 95.44%. Remember the empirical rule? It told us that for a symmetric distribution, approximately 95% of the data will fall within 2 standard deviations of the mean. This is where the empirical rule comes from.

Remember that Z can also be thought of as the number of standard deviations that a value is from its mean.

Table 6.2 summarizes the rules for using the standard normal probability tables.

TABLE 6.2 Rules for solving normal probability problems

To Find . . .	Area Under the Curve . . .	Look Up . . .
$P(Z < z)$	below a value of Z	the Z value and use the table directly
$P(Z > z)$	above a value of Z	1. the Z value and subtract the value in the table from 1 OR 2. the negative of the Z value and use the table directly
$P(z_1 < Z < z_2)$	between two values of Z	both Z values and subtract the lower value from the higher value

TRY IT NOW!

The Standard Normal Table *Using the Table to Find Probabilities*

For each of the following questions, *draw a picture* of what you are trying to find BEFORE you use the table to find it.

(continued)

Find the probability that a Z random variable takes on a value that is less than 2.74.

Find the probability that a Z random variable is greater than 0.85.

Drawing a picture will help you use the table correctly.

Find the probability that Z is between -1.36 and 1.87.

6.7.4 Solving Normal Probability Problems

Just as you found with the binomial distribution, once you understand how the random variable and the probability distribution work, solving problems is really not hard. The hardest part is understanding what the problem really means.

The following steps are used to solve problems that involve normally distributed random variables with mean μ and standard deviation σ:

Step 1: Write down the information about the random variable, i.e., $X \sim N(\mu, \sigma)$.

Step 2: Draw a picture that represents the problem and write down the probability statement, e.g., $P(X > 30)$.

Step 3: Transform the values of X that are involved in the problem into Z values.

Step 4: Look up the Z values on the standard normal table.

Step 5: Perform any additional calculations that need to be done, as described in Table 6.2.

EXAMPLE 6.32 Aptitude Scores

Solving Normal Probability Problems

The company that administered the aptitude test to its employees wants to know what proportion of the people who take the test score between 65 and 85 points.

ANS. 0.9969, 0.1977, 0.8824

We have essentially answered this question in the course of this section, but we can put it all together here.

We know that $X \sim N(75, 5)$ and that we are looking for $P(65 < X < 85)$ or

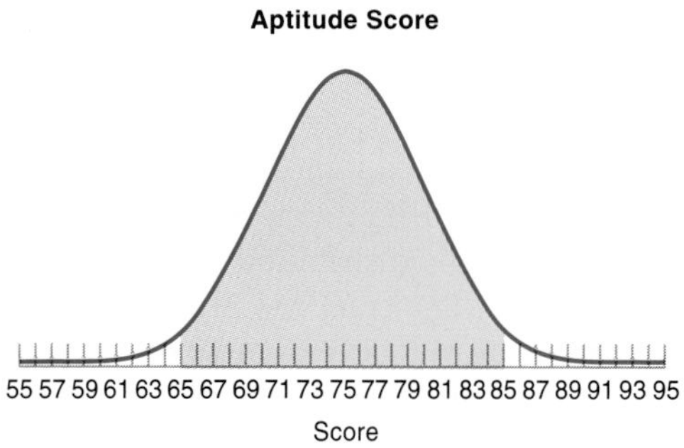

We found the Z values of interest to be -2 and $+2$. Looking these values up in the normal tables, we find that the probability for $Z = -2$ is 0.0228 and for $+2$ it is 0.9772. From the picture we see that we are trying to find the area *between* these two values and so we subtract the probability values to find

$$0.9772 - 0.0228 = 0.9544$$

The company is also interested in knowing what proportion of the people who take the test score in what is considered to be the superior range, above 87 points.

We know that $X \sim N(75, 5)$. To answer their question we need to find $P(X > 87)$. This is represented by the graph:

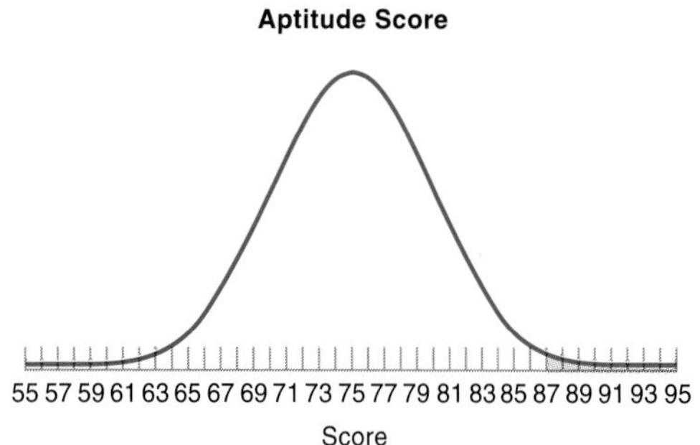

Transforming the X value of 87 to Z, we get

$$Z = \frac{87 - 75}{5} = \frac{12}{5} = 2.40$$

Notice that this answer makes sense, since it is positive and the X value of interest is to the right of the mean.

Looking the Z value of 2.40 up in the table, we get a probability of 0.9918.

Now we must decide whether there is anything left to do. The answer is most certainly YES! Common sense also tells you that 0.9918 cannot possibly be the answer. Look at how much of the area in the picture is shaded—it is very small, hardly over 99%! We are looking for the area *above* a value and the table gives the opposite area. We must subtract the value in the table from 1 to obtain

$$1 - 0.9918 = 0.0082 \text{ or } 0.82\%$$

Thus, the company sees that less than 1% of the people who take the test score in the superior range. ■

When doing problems, keep in mind that probabilities, proportions, and percentages are all ways of expressing the same quantity. Do not be misled by the way a question is asked. It is best to answer the question using the quantity type specified, but you are not wrong in using either decimals or percentages.

EXAMPLE 6.33 On-Time Flights

Calculating Normal Probabilities

The number of minutes late that a flight arrives at Chicago's O'Hare Airport from Dallas/Ft. Worth Airport is normally distributed with a mean of 5.4 minutes and a standard deviation of 1.8 minutes. The company is interested in finding out what percentage of the flights on this route are more than 10 minutes late.

The first step in solving the problem is to understand what we need to find. We know that $X \sim N(5.4, 1.8)$ and we are trying to find $P(X > 10)$. The following illustration represents the problem. Since we are looking for the probability that the flight is more than 10 minutes late, we shade the area to the right of the value 10.

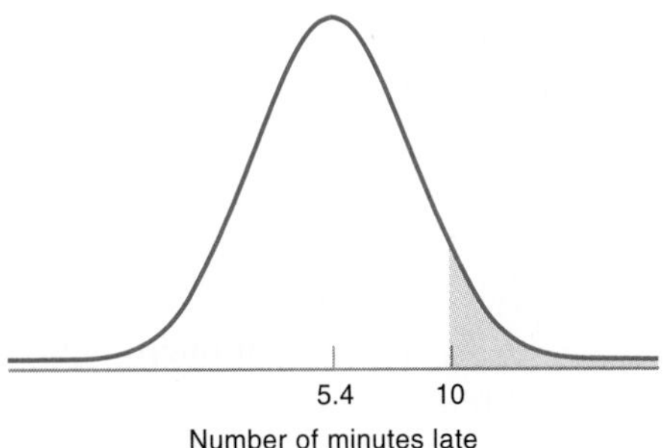

The second step is to transform the problem into a standard normal problem and use the table to look up the probability. That is, we need to find the Z-score for the value of 10.

$$Z = \frac{10 - 5.4}{1.8} = 2.56$$

Looking up the Z value in the table, we find that the probability associated with this Z-score is 0.9948.

The last step is to reconcile the number in the table to the problem. Since the table always gives the area to the left of Z and we are looking for the area to the right of Z, we need to subtract the table value from 1. Thus, the answer to the problem is

$$1 - 0.9948 = 0.0052$$

That is, 0.52% of the flights are more than 10 minutes late.

Suppose the airline also wants to know the probability that flights on this route are not late. We are looking for $P(X \leq 0)$. This is shown here in the figure:

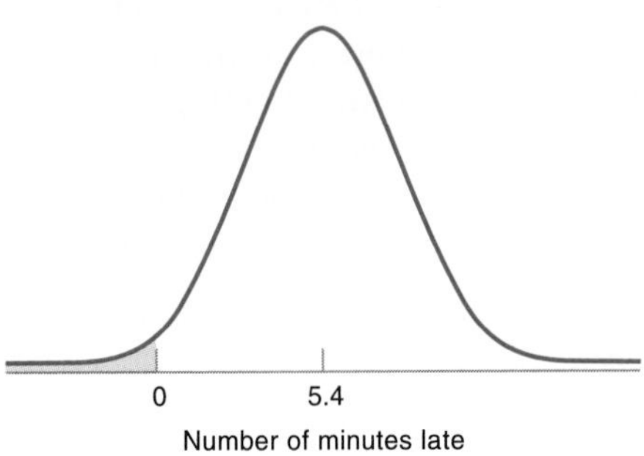

Transforming the problem into a standard normal problem, we calculate:

$$Z = \frac{0 - 5.4}{1.8} = -3.00$$

Looking the Z value up in the table, we find that the probability is 0.0013. Since the table and the problem we are trying to solve agree, this is the answer to the question.

So, the airline has learned that although a very small percentage (0.52%) of their flights on this route are more than 10 minutes late, an even smaller percentage (0.13%) are on time. ■

Speed Reading ***Solving Normal Probability Problems***

The instructor who is interested in how many pages of the statistics text that students can read in an hour knows that the random variable is $N(7, 1.5)$.

Find the probability that a student could read more than 11.5 pages in an hour.

The instructor was worried about the percentage of students who read less than a 5-page section in the given hour. What percentage of the students is this?

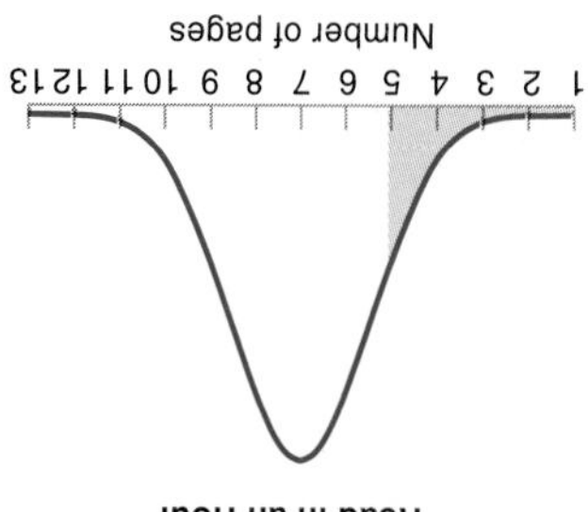

ANS. 0.0013; 0.0918

6.7.5 Finding Values That Correspond to Known Probabilities

In the previous section you learned how to use the standard normal probability tables to solve problems involving any normally distributed random variable. In these problems you were interested in finding the probability or the area under the curve that relates to a specific value of the random variable, *X*.

Another interesting type of problem that we can solve uses the normal distribution and the standard normal tables. Many people use the probabilities of the normal distribution to make decisions about what values of a variable define certain outcomes.

Suppose that a company wants to reward with an incentive bonus those salespeople whose sales are in the top 10%, or suppose that a city decides that only those people who score in the top 5% on a civil service exam will get job interviews. In many cases it does not make sense to simply take the top 5% of each group that takes the exam or the top 10% of each month's sales. If a particularly ill-suited group of people take the exam, the city could wind up interviewing people who are in no way qualified for the positions available. Similarly, the company could reward people in one month and deny people in the next who have the same sales figures.

Instead, these decision makers rely on the normal probability model to define the cutoff points for the variables of interest. How do they find the numbers that they are looking for?

You know how to use the normal probability tables to find the probability that corresponds to a given value of *X* or *Z*. The problem we just described is really the exact opposite of that problem. The decision makers know the percentage or area under the curve that they want to define. They do not know the value of *Z* (and subsequently *X*) that it corresponds to. This is illustrated in Figure 6.14.

Solving this type of problem involves using the normal probability tables "inside out." Previously, you have located the *Z* value on the *outside* of the table and determined the answer to the question by looking on the *inside* of the table. For this type of problem you will start by looking on the *inside* of the table for the known probability and move to the *outside* to find the answer. It sounds more complicated than it really is. Again, you simply need to be systematic in your approach.

To get started, we will concentrate on the technique. Suppose you want to find the value of *Z* that has 10% of the area below it. This is illustrated in Figure 6.15.

Since we know that the normal tables give the area below the value of *Z*, and that is what we are looking for, we can look the probability up directly. At first glance it may seem like you are looking for a needle in a haystack, but with a little bit of common sense and insight you will see that it is really not difficult.

If you look at the picture we drew (and this is why we draw them), you can see immediately that the value of *Z* that we want must be negative. We have already halved our search! Also, if you look at the tables, you will see that the numbers in the table are in numerical order. Once you find a suitable starting place for your search, you

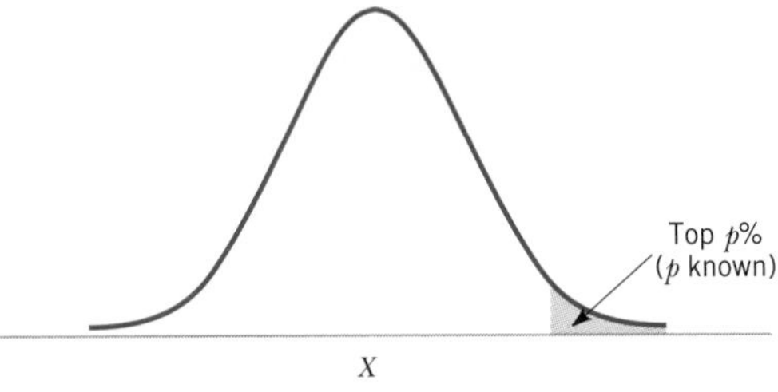

FIGURE 6.14 The "inverse" normal probability problem

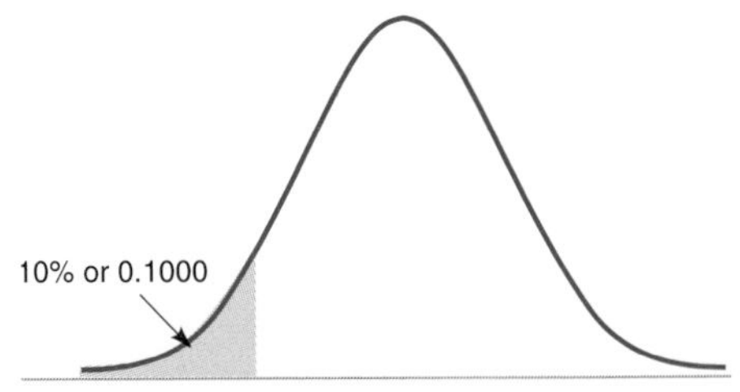

FIGURE 6.15 Bottom 10% of the normal distribution

z	0.00	0.01	0.02	0.03	0.04	0.05	0.06	0.07	0.08	0.09
−1.9	0.0287	0.0281	0.0274	0.0268	0.0262	0.0256	0.0250	0.0244	0.0239	0.0233
−1.8	0.0359	0.0351	0.0344	0.0336	0.0329	0.0322	0.0314	0.0307	0.0301	0.0294
−1.7	0.0446	0.0436	0.0427	0.0418	0.0409	0.0401	0.0392	0.0384	0.0375	0.0367
−1.6	0.0548	0.0537	0.0526	0.0516	0.0505	0.0495	0.0485	0.0475	0.0465	0.0455
−1.5	0.0668	0.0655	0.0643	0.0630	0.0618	0.0606	0.0594	0.0582	0.0571	0.0559
−1.4	0.0808	0.0793	0.0778	0.0764	0.0749	0.0735	0.0721	0.0708	0.0694	0.0681
−1.3	0.0968	0.0951	0.0934	0.0918	0.0901	0.0885	0.0869	0.0853	0.0838	0.0823
−1.2	0.1151	0.1131	0.1112	0.1093	0.1075	0.1056	0.1038	0.1020	0.1003	0.0985
−1.1	0.1357	0.1335	0.1314	0.1292	0.1271	0.1251	0.1230	0.1210	0.1190	0.1170
−1.0	0.1587	0.1562	0.1539	0.1515	0.1492	0.1469	0.1446	0.1423	0.1401	0.1379
−0.9	0.1841	0.1814	0.1788	0.1762	0.1736	0.1711	0.1685	0.1660	0.1635	0.1611
−0.8	0.2119	0.2090	0.2061	0.2033	0.2005	0.1977	0.1949	0.1922	0.1894	0.1867

FIGURE 6.16 Normal probability table containing the probability 0.1000

simply have to search systematically for the number you are looking for. The section of the normal table that contains the value we are looking for is shown in Figure 6.16.

This is probably a good place to point out that since the tables give probabilities to four decimal places, we are not likely to find the value we are looking for exactly. However, if the value you want is not there, you will always be able to locate two adjacent values, one smaller and one larger than the value you are looking for. Examining the table you see that the numbers from top to bottom are increasing and that at the row for $z = -1.3$ they are too small and at the $z = -1.2$ row they are too large. The value you want must be in there somewhere! A more careful search will lead you to the two cells that are highlighted in the table, 0.0985 and 0.1003.

As we guessed, one of these is a bit too small and the other is too large. The value of 0.0985 corresponds to a value of Z of -1.29, whereas 0.1003 corresponds to $z = -1.28$. Thus, the value of Z that we are looking for must be in between these two.

At this point we need to discuss how we will determine the Z values that we will use. Some people would suggest performing a linear interpolation between the two values to get an estimate of the correct value of Z. Even though the normal curve is certainly not linear, for small increments in Z this is not a bad approximation. The only problem is, it is not worth the trouble.

For our purposes we will use the value of the probability that is closest to the value we are looking for unless there is something in the problem that tells us to use the one that is smaller or larger. The something would be some directional description of the percentage we are looking for, like "at least 10%," in which case we would choose 0.1003, or "at most 10%," which would lead us to 0.0985. When we look at an actual application of this technique you will see how little difference the exact answer makes.

Now on to solving real problems. We start with a simple example that uses what we have already figured out.

EXAMPLE 6.34 Aptitude Scores

Solving the Inverse Problem

As hard as it may be to take, downsizing and cost cutting are a reality of business life. The company that gives employees the aptitude test has decided that people who score in the bottom 10% of the test scores will not receive any additional job training. If there are to be layoffs, these people will be among the first to be cut. The question is, what cutoff score on the test should the company use?

We already know that the bottom 10% corresponds to a Z-score of -1.28. But clearly this cannot be the answer to the question. How do we translate the Z-score back into the realm of the variable of interest, the test scores?

You know that the Z value represents the number of standard deviations away from the mean that a value is. The negative sign on the Z value tells you to move down from the mean (subtract the number of standard deviations). Thus, we know that the cutoff score must be 1.28 standard deviations *below* the mean. That is,

$$X = 75 - (1.28)(5) = 68.6 \text{ points}$$

The company will have to decide whether to use 68 points (and affect less than 10% of the people) or 69 points (and affect more than 10%). ■

From this example you see why it is not necessary to interpolate to get the exact value of Z. If the answer is to be used to make a decision, the extra precision gained by getting the exact Z value does not usually translate into any practical information. The test is not scored to the nearest tenth of a point. Even if it were, the change in the Z value affects the hundredths place of the score.

We used our understanding of the Z value to determine the cutoff score, but the formula we used really comes from algebraically solving the definition of the Z value for X:

$$Z = \frac{X - \mu}{\sigma} \longrightarrow X = \mu + Z\sigma$$

When Z is positive you will add to μ and when Z is negative you will subtract from μ.

When solving problems that define the probability and when looking for the value of the random variable, it is important to know when you are specifying an area above the value of interest or an area below the value. When the area is below the value you are looking for, you can look up the specified probability directly. When the area is above the value you are looking for you will either have to subtract the specified probability from 1 and look that up, or look up the given probability and rely on the symmetry of the table.

EXAMPLE 6.35 Aptitude Scores

Specifying Upper Area Probabilities

Although cost cutting and downsizing are negative aspects of the business world, the company with the aptitude test is also planning to give extra training to employees who score in the top 2% of those taking the test. The company would like to identify the score to use as the cutoff point.

If we draw a picture that represents the problem we see that the Z value we are looking for will most certainly be positive.

If you want to look up the value directly you will have to look up the bottom area or 0.9800. It is just as easy to use common sense and rely on the symmetry of the normal distribution. If you look up 0.0200 in the table you will find that it is not there, but that you can choose from 0.0197 and 0.0202. Since 0.0202 is closer to 2% (and slightly more generous to the employees) we will use the corresponding Z value of -2.05.

But we just said that the answer has to be positive. This is where common sense, symmetry, and the picture come together. We know the answer should be positive from the picture and common sense, but we used the symmetry feature to make the lookup easier. We will use $+2.05$ to find the correct answer.

The cutoff score for the top 2% is then

$$75 + (2.05)(5) = 85.25 \text{ points}$$

The company can use 85 (and train more than 2%) or 86 (and train less than 2%). ■

TRY IT NOW!

Speed Reading ***Solving the Inverse Problem***

The instructor who is interested in how fast students can read the statistics textbook would like to identify the bottom 25% of the class, in terms of the number of pages that they can read in an hour.

Find the number of pages per hour that defines the bottom 25% of the students.

Inverse normal probability problems are an important application of the normal distribution. These types of problems are encountered many times in real life when standards or cutoff points must be determined.

6.7.6 Exercises—Learning It!

6.19 The amount of money spent by students for textbooks in a semester is a normally distributed random variable with a mean of \$235 and a standard deviation of \$15.

(a) Sketch the normal distribution that describes the amount of money spent on textbooks in a semester.

(b) What is the probability that a student spends between \$220 and \$250 in any semester?

(c) What percentage of students spend more than \$270 on textbooks in any semester?

(d) What percentage of students spend less than \$225 in a semester?

6.20 On any given day, the number of leasable square feet of office space available in a small city is a normally distributed random variable with a mean of 850,000 square feet and a standard deviation of 25,000 square feet. The number of leasable square feet available in another small city is normally distributed with a mean of 900,000 square feet and a standard deviation of 25,000 square feet.

(a) Sketch the distribution of leasable office space for both cities on the same graph.

ANS. $Z = -0.67$, 5.995 OR 6 PAGES

(b) What is the probability that the number of leasable square feet in the first city is less than 925,000 square feet?

(c) What is the probability that the amount available in the second city is less than 925,000?

6.21 The actual amount of a certain brand of orange juice in a container marked half gallon is a normally distributed random variable with a mean of 65 oz and a standard deviation of 0.35 oz.

(a) What percentage of the containers contain more than 64.5 oz?

(b) What percentage of the containers contain between 64 and 66 oz?

(c) If federal law says that 98% of all containers must be at or above the labeled weight, does this brand of orange juice meet the requirement?

6.22 The amount of money per month earned by an auditor with 10 years experience is a normally distributed random variable with mean \$3500 and standard deviation \$240.

(a) What percentage of auditors with 10 years experience earn more than \$4000 per month?

(b) What percentage of auditors with 10 years experience earn less than \$3200 per month?

(c) What is the probability that a randomly selected auditor earns between \$3250 and \$3800 per month?

(d) What monthly income defines the top 10% of all auditors with 10 years experience?

6.8 Executive Summary

CHAMBER OF COMMERCE

Business Analysis...

TO: Chamber of Commerce
FROM: Data Analysts
RE: Random Sampling of Survey Respondents

We have done a preliminary analysis of the responses to the survey of area businesses. Based on our data, shown in the accompanying table, we have determined that if you select a single response to follow up you will most likely select a business with sales under \$1 million.

Size	Number of Responses	Probability of a Response
No response	1	1/166 = 0.6%
Under \$1 million	60	60/166 = 36.1%
\$1–5 million	21	21/166 = 12.7%
\$6–10 million	42	42/166 = 25.3%
\$11–20 million	21	21/166 = 12.7%
Over \$20 million	21	21/166 = 12.7%
Total	166	166/166 = 100%

If you intend to randomly sample more than one company that responded to the survey, your sample will still be predominantly from the same group, followed by those with sales in the \$6–10 million group.

We also looked at workforce size for these companies. Our analysis indicates that sales and workforce size might be related, as shown in the table.

Employees	No Response	Under $1 m	$1–5 m	$6–10 m	$11–20 m	Over $20 m	Grand Total
0–5	0.0	26.5	4.2	4.2	0.0	0.0	34.9
6–10	0.0	7.2	5.4	1.8	1.8	0.0	16.3
11–50	0.6	2.4	2.4	8.4	1.8	1.8	17.5
51–150	0.0	0.0	0.6	4.8	3.0	4.2	12.7
151–250	0.0	0.0	0.0	3.6	3.0	3.6	10.2
Over 250	0.0	0.0	0.0	2.4	3.0	3.0	8.4
Grand Total	0.6	36.1	12.7	25.3	12.7	12.7	100.0

If you find it acceptable that you are likely to be interviewing smaller companies, then random sampling is a good technique. If, however, you want to interview the entire spectrum of businesses, another sampling technique, such as stratified sampling where you sample from each group, might be better. We would be happy to set up such a sampling plan for you at your request.

The *Wall Street Journal* is a major source of current business news and information for the business community. If your professor has arranged for your class to have access to the Business Extra feature, you can go to it now and see the techniques of this chapter in action today. Go to the Wiley Web site at http://www.wiley.com/college/pelosi, and click on Business Extra!

6.9 USING EXCEL TO GENERATE PROBABILITY DISTRIBUTIONS

Excel has built-in functions that allow you to calculate probabilities and generate random data from many different probability distributions. In this section, we will look at using Excel with the binomial and normal probability distributions.

6.9.1 Calculating Binomial Probabilities in Excel

So far, you have relied on tables to find probabilities for the binomial probability distribution. What would you do if you needed to solve a problem for values of n and π that were not in the tables? Excel has built-in functions that calculate binomial probabilities for any values of n and π.

Suppose that you want to calculate the probability that a random sample of $n = 50$ with $\pi = 0.45$ will have exactly 25 successes. You can use the Excel function **BINOMDIST** to calculate this probability. We will look at this function using the Function Wizard so that you understand how Excel functions work and how you can find out about Excel functions you have never used. We will also look at a macro included on the disk that accomplishes the same thing. Follow these steps:

1. To use a function, position the cursor in an empty cell in the worksheet.
2. From the main toolbar, click on the **Function Wizard** icon. The **Paste Function** dialog box opens. This box lists all of the different categories of functions available in Excel. Highlight **Statistical** for the function category and **BINOMDIST** for the function, as shown in Figure 6.17 on page 282.

   At the bottom you see the format for the function you are choosing and a description of what it does. Click **OK** and the dialog box for the **BINOMDIST** function opens.

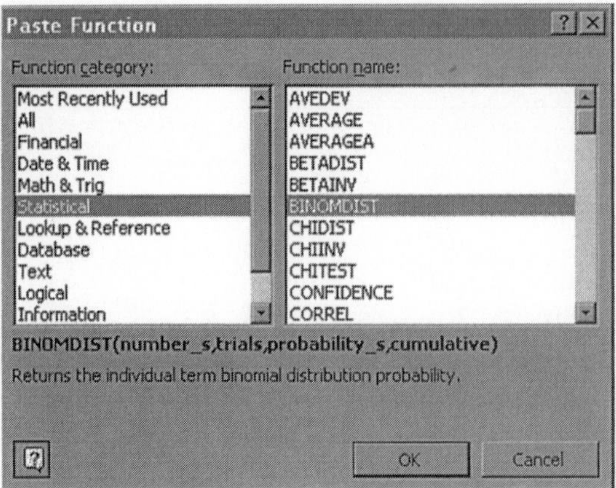

FIGURE 6.17 Choosing an Excel function

As you place the cursor in each text box, a description of the input for that box is described at the bottom of the dialog box. It is important that you read these descriptions so that you know what you are supposed to input.

3. Place the cursor in the text box labeled **Number_s.** At the bottom you can see that this is where you enter the number of successes you are interested in. Type in the number "25."
4. Now, place the cursor in the text box labeled **Trials** and enter "50," which is the number of trials that you have.
5. Place the cursor in the text box labeled **Probability_s.** Notice that the bottom of the dialog box tells you that Excel is looking for the probability of a success on any trial, π. Type in "0.45."
6. The last text box lets you indicate what kind of probability you want. Excel will calculate either $P(X = x)$ or $P(X \leq x)$, the cumulative probability. In this case we want $P(X = 25)$ so we will set this value to False. The completed dialog box should look like the one in Figure 6.18.

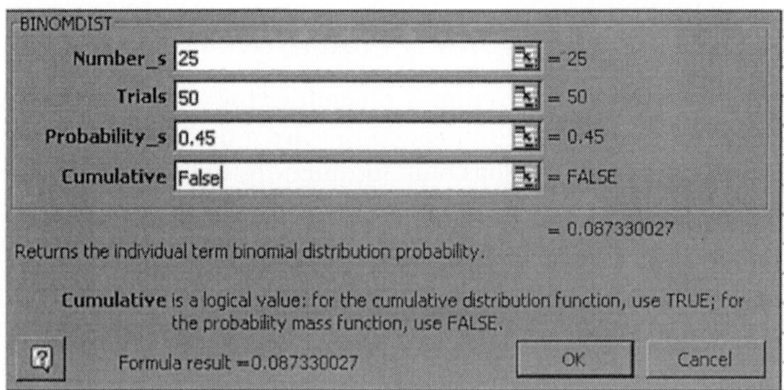

FIGURE 6.18 Completed BINOMDIST dialog box

7. Click on **OK** and the probability—in this case, 0.087330027—will appear in the cell in which you started.

You might have noticed that while you were filling in the dialog box, the status line in Excel was recording exactly what gets entered in the cell where you place the function, as shown in Figure 6.19. When you become familiar with particular functions, you can type the command in directly and bypass the Function Wizard. We will do that for the other functions in this chapter.

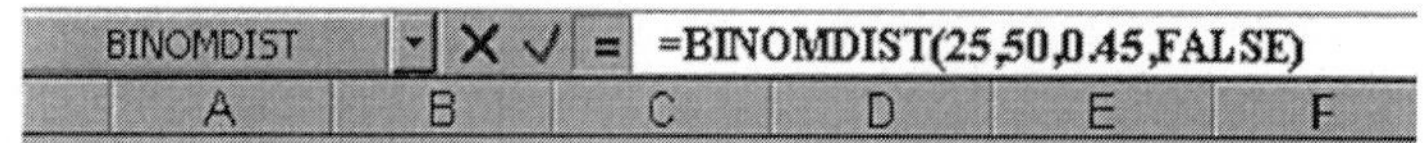

FIGURE 6.19 The BINOMDIST command

From the Kadd menu select **Probability.** You will see the choices shown in Figure 6.20. Select **Binomial** and the dialog box shown in Figure 6.21 will open. Three items must be entered to calculate the probability: the probability of a success, π, the number of trials, n, and the value of interest. You have the option of calculating several different probabilities for a specific value of interest (when you use Left and Right, you will enter two values). Table 6.3 lists the options and what they calculate.

You can also use KADD-STAT to calculate binomial probabilities.

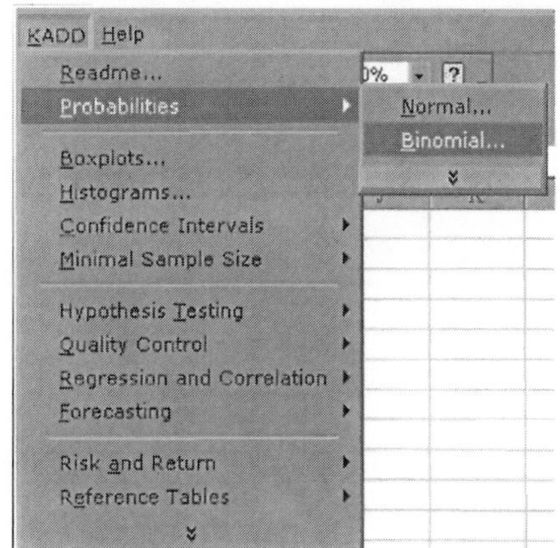

FIGURE 6.20 KADD menu

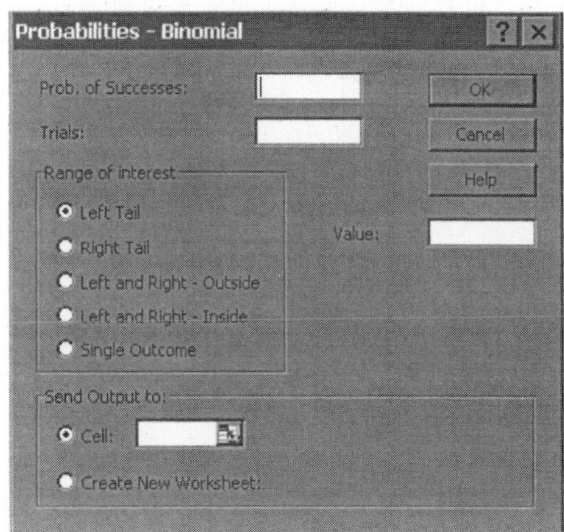

FIGURE 6.21 KADD Binomial dialog box

TABLE 6.3 Options for Probabilities

Range of Interest	What Is Calculated
Left Tail	P($X \leq$ value)
Right Tail	P($X \geq$ value)
Left and Right, Outside	P($X \leq$ lower value) + P($X \geq$ upper value)
Left and Right, Inside	P(lower value $\leq X \leq$ upper value)
Single Outcome	P($X =$ value)

To calculate the same probability we did with the **BINDIST** function, P(X = 25), the complete dialog box should look like the one in Figure 6.22. After you indicate where you want the output to appear and click **OK,** the output shown in Figure 6.23 should appear.

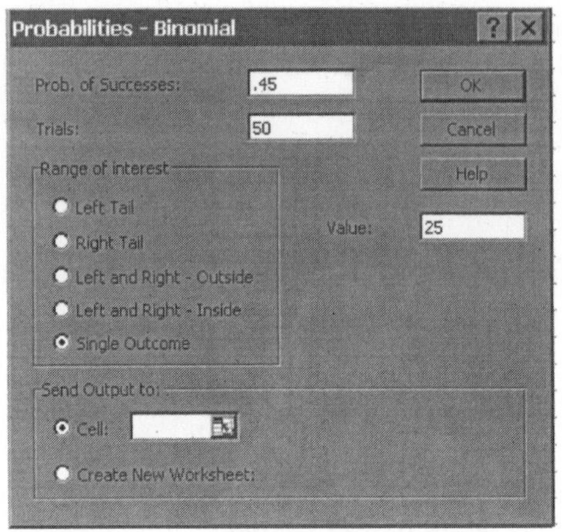

FIGURE 6.22 Binomial probability for a single value of X

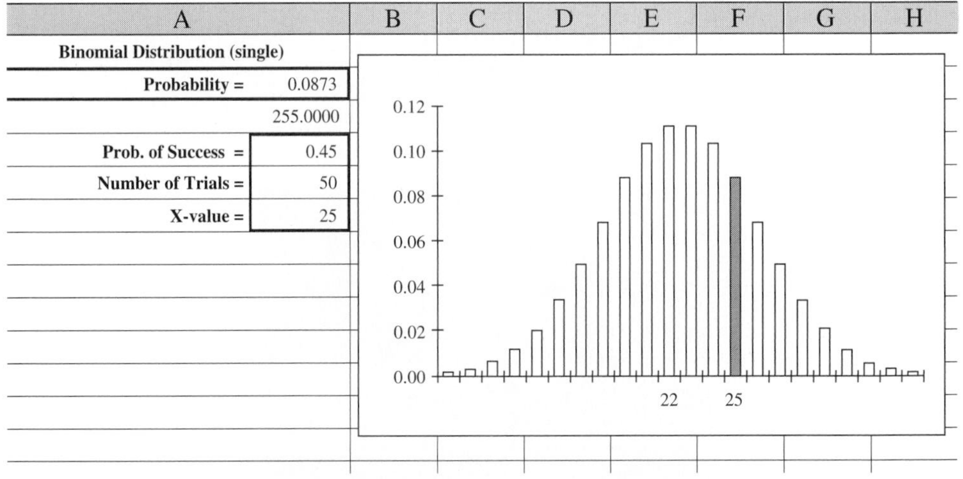

FIGURE 6.23 Binomial output from KADD

6.9.2 Calculating Normal Probabilities in Excel

Excel has functions for calculating probabilities either from a normal distribution with a given mean and standard deviation or from a standard normal. There are also functions for solving inverse normal probability problems—that is, finding the value of Z that corresponds to a given probability. Table 6.4 lists all of the functions, describes what they do, and explains what values are expected as input.

You can also find normal probabilities using KADDSTAT. From the KADD menu choose **Probability > Normal.** The dialog box shown in Figure 6.24 opens. As you can see you have several options for calculating probabilities: below and above a specific value and between or outside two specific values.

To calculate the probability for a normally distributed random variable with mean 10 and standard deviation 3, follow these steps:

TABLE 6.4

Function format	What it does	Input
NORMDIST(x, mean, standard_deviation, cumulative)	Returns $P(X \leq x)$ for a normally distributed random variable	x = value of interest; mean = mean of the random variable; standard_deviation = standard deviation of the random variable; cumulative = true for $P(X \leq x)$
NORMINV(probability, mean, standard_deviation)	Returns the value of x that has the specified probability below it	probability = the area under the curve below the X value of interest; mean = mean of the random variable; standard_deviation = standard deviation of the random variable
NORMSDIST(x)	Returns $P(z \leq x)$ for a standard normal random variable	x = value of interest for Z
NORMSINV(probability)	Returns the value of Z that has the specified probability below it	probability = area under the standard normal curve below the Z value of interest

1. Fill in the mean, μ, and the standard deviation, σ, of the random variable in the appropriate text boxes.
2. From the section labeled **Range of Interest,** select the type of probability you want. For left- and right-tail probabilities, you will enter one value of X in the text box labeled **Value.** If you select **Left and Right,** either inside or outside, the box will change and you will enter two values of X.
3. If you want to solve the inverse probability problem, select **Inverse Value** and type in the *left-tail* area in the box labeled **Cumulative Probability.**
4. Fill in where you want the output to go and click **OK** to obtain the results.

For example, if you wanted to find $P(X \leq 4)$ for the random variable that is $N(10, 3)$, fill in the dialog box as shown in Figure 6.24. The output shown in Figure 6.25 on page 286 will appear in the location you specified.

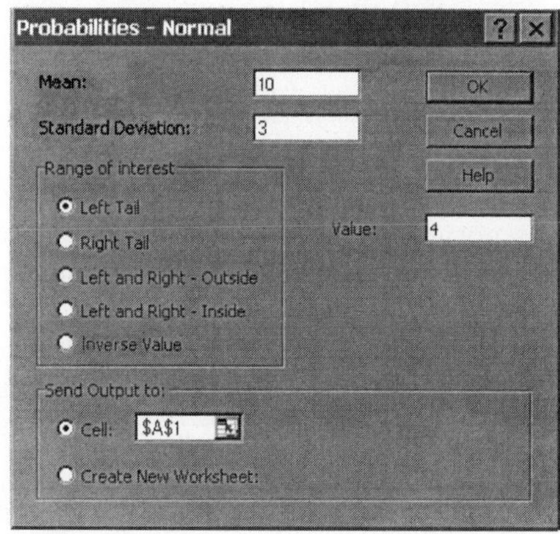

FIGURE 6.24 KADD Normal dialog box

6.9.3 Generating Random Data in Excel

In addition to calculating probabilities in Excel, you can also generate random data that come from populations with specific probability distributions. Such data are useful in simulations and other exercises. To generate data from different probability distributions, you use the **Data Analysis** tools. From the **Data Analysis** tools list, select **Random Number Generation.** The dialog box shown in Figure 6.26 opens.

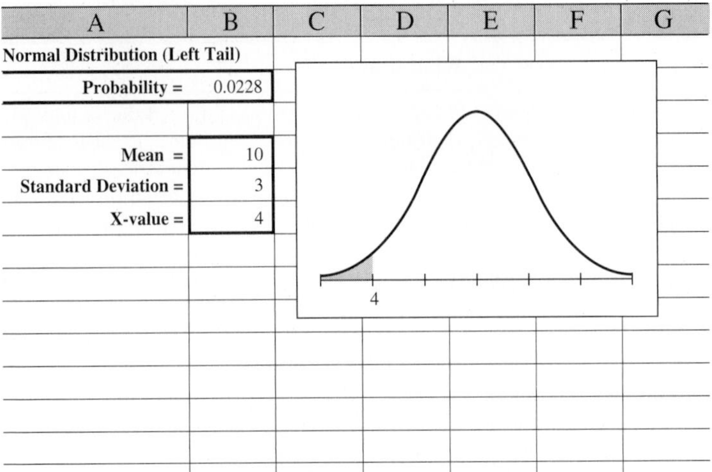

FIGURE 6.25 KADD Normal output

Random Number Generation
Number of Variables:
Number of Random Numbers:
Distribution: Discrete
Parameters
Value and Probability Input Range:
Random Seed:
Output options
Output Range:
New Worksheet Ply:
New Workbook
OK
Cancel
Help

FIGURE 6.26 Random Number Generation dialog box

Excel will generate random data from several probability distributions, including the binomial and the normal. To see the list of available distributions, click on the drop down arrow in the text box labeled **Distribution:** and the list appears as shown in Figure 6.27.

Random Number Generation
Number of Variables:
Number of Random Numbers:
Distribution: Discrete
Parameters
Value and Probability Inpu
Uniform
Normal
Bernoulli
Binomial
Poisson
Patterned
Discrete
OK
Cancel
Help

FIGURE 6.27 List of probability distributions

The top portion of the dialog box is the same for every probability distribution. In the text box labeled **Number of Variables:** you enter the number of different random variables you want to generate. In most cases, this is 1. In the second text box, labeled **Number of Random Numbers:** you input the number of observations from the probability distribution that you want to generate—usually either the sample size or the population size, depending on what you are generating.

We will generate 50 observations from a binomial distribution with $n = 20$ and $\pi = 0.70$. To do this, follow these steps.

1. Select **Binomial** from the list of distributions and the dialog box will change to allow input of the appropriate parameters.
2. In the text box for **Number of Variables:** type "1" and in the text box for **Number of Random Numbers:** type "50."
3. In the text box labeled **p Value** enter the value for μ, 0.70. Finally, in the text box for **Number of Trials:** enter 20.
4. Specify where you want the output to appear and click **OK.** The completed dialog box should look like the one in Figure 6.28.

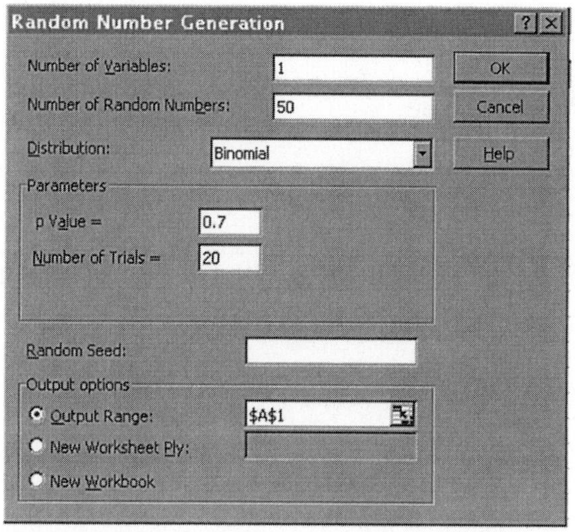

Random Number Generation

Number of Variables: 1
Number of Random Numbers: 50
Distribution: Binomial
Parameters
p Value = 0.7
Number of Trials = 20
Random Seed:
Output options
Output Range: $A$1
New Worksheet Ply:
New Workbook
OK
Cancel
Help

FIGURE 6.28 The Binomial Random Variable dialog box

The data will be output to the location you specify. Figure 6.29 shows a portion of the output. Notice that the values are all less than 20 (which you would expect) and that most of the values are higher than 10, since π is larger than 0.50.

	A
1	16
2	10
3	15
4	12
5	14
6	11
7	10
8	12
9	14
10	16
11	14
12	14
13	13
14	11
15	14

FIGURE 6.29 Random data from binomial distribution

The steps for generating data from a normal distribution are identical to those for the binomial distribution. The only difference is that the parameters you enter for the normal distribution are the mean and standard deviation, μ and σ.

CHAPTER 6 SUMMARY

Probability is an important and interesting subject in its own right, but the study of random variables and probability distributions is important in the study and development of statistics.

Probability is the bridge between what we studied in the first five chapters of this book, *descriptive statistics,* and what is to follow in subsequent chapters, *inferential statistics.* In descriptive statistics we use different techniques to describe sample data. In inferential statistics we will test hypotheses about the populations from which these samples came. Probability is the tool that allows us to reconcile what happened (descriptive) with what we think is true by determining how likely the outcomes of the experiment we perform are.

Key Terms

Term	Definition	Page reference
A AND B	The event **A AND B** is the event that A and B both occur.	226
A OR B	The event **A OR B** describes the event when either A happens or B happens or they both happen.	226
Binomial random variable	A **binomial random variable** is the number of successes in n trials or in a sample of size n.	247
Complement	The **complement** of an event **A,** denoted **A′,** is the set of all outcomes in the sample space, **S,** that do not correspond to the event **A.**	224
Empirical probability	An **empirical probability** is one that is calculated from sample data and is an estimate for the true probability.	234
Event	An **event, A,** is an outcome or a set of outcomes that are of interest to the experimenter.	222
Experiment	An **experiment** is any action whose outcomes are recordable data.	221
Independent events	Two events are **independent** if the probability that one event occurs on any given trial of an experiment is not affected or changed by the occurrence of the other event.	238
Interval probability	An **interval probability** gives the probability that a random variable will take on a value *between* two given values $P(x_1 \leq X \leq x_2)$.	269
Mutually exclusive	Two events, A and B, are said to be **mutually exclusive** if they have no outcomes in common.	227
Probability	**Probability** is a measure of how likely it is that something will occur.	220
Probability density function, $f(x)$	A **probability density function, $f(x)$,** is a smooth curve that represents the probability distribution of a continuous random variable.	264
Probability distribution, p(x)	The **probability distribution** of a random variable X, written as **p(x),** gives the probability that the random variable will take on each of its possible values.	242
Probability of an event, P(A)	The **probability of an event A, P(A),** is a measure of the likelihood that an event A will occur.	223
Random variable	A **random variable, X,** is a quantitative variable whose value varies according to the rules of probability.	241

Key Terms

Term	Definition	Page reference
Sample space, S	The **sample space, S,** is the set of all possible outcomes of an experiment.	221
Standard normal random variable, Z	A **standard normal random variable** is normally distributed with a mean of 0 and a standard deviation of 1, **$Z \sim N(0, 1)$.**	267
Standard normal table	A **standard normal table** is a table of probabilities for a Z random variable.	267

Key Formulas

Term	Formula	Page reference
Binomial mean and standard deviation	$\mu = n\pi$ and $\sigma = \sqrt{n\pi(1 - \pi)}$	255
Binomial probability formula	$p(x) = \frac{n!}{(x!)(n-x)!}\pi^x(1-\pi)^{n-x}$ for $x = 0, 1, \ldots, n$	252
Conditional probability of an event A given an event B	$P(A\|B) = \frac{P(A \text{ AND } B)}{P(B)}$	237
General addition rule	P(A OR B) = P(A) + P(B) − P(A AND B)	231
Independent events	P(A AND B) = P(A) × P(B)	238
P(A)	$P(A) = \frac{\text{Number of ways that A can occur}}{\text{Total number of possible outcomes}}$	223
	$P(A) = \frac{n_A}{N}$	
Probability of the complement, P(A′)	P(A) + P(A′) = 1	225
Simple addition rule	P(A OR B) = P(A) + P(B)	227
Z-score	$Z = \frac{X - \mu}{\sigma}$	267

CHAPTER 6 EXERCISES

Learning It!

6.22 In the survey about satisfaction with local phone service, those respondents who rated their current service as excellent and those who rated it Poor–Very Poor were asked what type of company their current local service provider was. The results are given in the table:

Current Service Source	Excellent	Poor–Very Poor
Long distance company	264	1394
Local phone company	444	1318
Power company	131	485
Cable TV company	215	431
Cellular phone company	198	572

(a) What is the probability that a person selected from this group will rate his service as excellent and will have a long distance company as his current provider?

(b) What is the probability that a person selected from this group will use a power company or a cable TV company as his current provider?

(c) What is the probability that a person selected from this group will rate his current service as Poor–Very Poor or use a local phone company?

(d) What is the probability that a person selected from this group will rate his service as Poor–Very Poor and will use a cellular phone company?

6.23 In a study on college students and binge drinking, researchers were interested in looking at binge drinking and gender. Questions were asked about the number of times that a student had five or more drinks in the last 2 weeks and gender. The results are shown in the table:

	Number of Times Had Five or More Drinks in a Row in Last 2 Weeks					
Gender	**0**	**1**	**2**	**3**	**4**	**5**
Male	55	20	18	19	8	4
Female	75	14	12	24	2	0

(a) What is the probability that a student is a male and had five or more drinks in a row 2 times in the last 2 weeks?

(b) What is the probability that a student is female or had five or more drinks in a row 3 times in the last 2 weeks?

(c) What is the probability that a student had five or more drinks in a row in the last 2 weeks 3 or 4 times?

(d) What is the probability that a student did not have five or more drinks in a row in the last 2 weeks?

6.24 In the same study of binge drinking and college students, the researchers were also interested in the number of times that student experienced hangovers in the semester. The data they collected are given here:

	Hangover Since Beginning of Semester		
Gender	**Not at All**	**Once**	**Twice or More**
Male	61	23	40
Female	66	25	36

(a) What is the probability that a student is female and had a hangover twice or more during the semester?

(b) What is the probability that a student is male and has not had a hangover during the semester?

(c) What is the probability that a student had a hangover once or more during the semester?

6.25 Surveys indicate that 40% of all small businesses do not provide any kind of health insurance options for their employees. The Chamber of Commerce in a large city takes a random sample of 20 small businesses. What is the probability that in the sample of 20 small businesses

(a) at least 12 do not provide health insurance options for employees?

(b) at most 4 do not provide health insurance options for employees?

(c) between 8 and 13 do not provide health insurance options for employees?

(d) at least 5 provide health insurance options for employees?

6.26 Recent studies have shown that 30% of employees in the insurance industry telecommute 4 days a week. If a random sample of 15 insurance industry employees is taken, what is the probability that

(a) between 4 and 7 inclusive telecommute 4 days a week?

(b) less than 6 telecommute 4 days a week?

(c) at least 9 telecommute 4 days a week?

(d) between 5 and 10 do not telecommute 4 days a week?

6.27 A survey done at a state university in New England found that 40% of all seniors have encountered academic problems related to binge drinking. If a random sample of 25 seniors at the university is taken, what is the probability that of the 25

(a) at most 6 have encountered academic problems related to binge drinking?

(b) between 4 and 9 have encountered academic problems related to binge drinking?

(c) more than 15 have encountered academic problems related to binge drinking?

(d) Find the mean and standard deviation of the number of seniors in a sample of 25 who have encountered problems related to binge drinking.

6.28 The amount of office space allocated to production planners in consumer products companies is a normally distributed random variable with a mean of 120 square feet (sq ft) and a standard deviation of 6 sq ft.

(a) What percentage of production planners' offices have more than 135 sq ft?

(b) What percentage of production planners' offices have between 110 and 125 sq ft?

(c) What percentage of production planners' offices have less than 130 sq ft?

6.29 The size of a gift/specialty store in a regional super mall is a normally distributed random variable with a mean of 8500 sq ft and a standard deviation of 260 sq ft. What is the probability that a randomly selected gift/specialty store in a regional super mall is

(a) more than 8000 sq ft?

(b) between 8300 and 9000 sq ft?

(c) less than 9500 sq ft?

6.30 A recent study done at a university in New England found that 60% of all students have missed class in the semester because of drinking. A random sample of 20 students is taken. What is the probability that

(a) at least 15 have missed class because of drinking?

(b) between 12 and 17 inclusive have missed class because of drinking?

(c) less than 5 have not missed class because of drinking?

(d) at most 13 have not missed class because of drinking?

Thinking About It!

6.31 The company that is looking at the way employees took floating holidays collected data from 300 employees. The data are shown again here: *Requires Exercise 6.2*

	How Days Were Used		
Type of Job	**Took Actual Holiday**	**Added to Vacation**	**Took Random Days**
Professional	5	17	51
Clerical	13	46	32
Hourly	53	78	5

(a) What is the probability that an employee selected at random is a clerical worker?

(b) Suppose you know that the person selected used the floating holidays as random days off. Now what is the probability that the person is a clerical worker?

(c) How do the probabilities in parts (a) and (b) compare?

(d) What is the probability that the person took the floating holidays on the actual holiday given that you know the person is a professional employee?

(e) If you know that the person selected is either a clerical worker or an hourly worker, what is the probability that the person took the days as added vacation days?

Requires Exercise 6.3

6.32 Consider the computer magazine survey about consumers' plans to buy computers. The data are given here:

	When Purchase Will Be Made		
Type of Computer	**0–3 Months**	**3–6 Months**	**6–12 Months**
Notebook/Portable	34	156	258
Desktop	56	346	128

(a) What is the probability that a person selected at random is planning to make a purchase in 0–3 months, given that the person plans to buy a notebook computer?

(b) What is the probability that a person selected is planning to buy a desktop computer, given that the person plans to make the purchase in the next 6 months?

(c) If you know that the person selected is planning to buy a desktop computer, what is the probability that the person will make the purchase in the next 3–6 months?

(d) What is the probability that a person will buy a notebook computer, given that the person is not planning to buy it within the next 0–3 months?

6.33 Consider the study of binge drinking and college students. The data are:

	Hangover Since Beginning of Semester		
Gender	**Not at All**	**Once**	**Twice or More**
Male	61	23	40
Female	66	25	36

(a) Given that the student is female, what is the probability that she had a hangover twice or more during the semester?

(b) What is the probability that a student is male given that the student had a hangover once or less during the semester?

(c) What is the probability that a student has had two or more hangovers in a semester given that the student is male?

(d) Compare your answers to parts (a) and (c) and interpret the results for the researchers.

Requires Exercise 6.25

6.34 The Chamber of Commerce that is interested in whether small businesses provide health care options for employees wants a few more questions answered. The surveys indicated that 40% of employers did not provide health insurance options for employees.

(a) In the sample of 20, how many should the Chamber of Commerce expect to provide health insurance options for employees?

(b) What is the standard deviation of the number of small businesses in the 20 that provide health insurance options?

(c) Find the probability that the number of small businesses in a sample of 20 will be within 2 standard deviations of the mean.

(d) How does this probability compare to the percentage predicted by the empirical rule? If it does not agree, why not?

Requires Exercises 6.25, 6.34

6.35 The Chamber of Commerce looking at health insurance options provided by small businesses finds four that provide health insurance options for employees and thinks this is unusual.

(a) Do you agree that the findings are unusual? Why or why not?

(b) What would you tell the Chamber of Commerce this might mean?

6.36 The manager of a regional super mall wants to compare the gift/specialty stores in her mall to the size of the smallest 20% of the gift/specialty shops in similar malls. She knows that the size of such stores is normally distributed with a mean of 8500 sq ft and a standard deviation of 260 sq ft.

(a) What square footage defines the smallest 20% of such stores?

(b) Harriet's Gift Boutique has complained that it is much smaller than any similar stores in other malls. If the size of this store is 7800 sq ft, is the complaint reasonable?

6.37 The Dean of Students at another university in New England read the report on binge drinking and decided to conduct a small survey on her own campus. She took a random sample of 20 students and found that 15 of them had missed class because of drinking. She decides that this indicates that her university is within the norm for this problem. Do you agree with her conclusion? Why or why not? *Requires Exercise 6.30*

Doing It!

6.38 The Chamber of Commerce that is studying the credit problems of small businesses asked them three questions to classify their business and seven questions related to the issue of credit problems. A portion of the datafile and an explanation of each variable are given here: ***Datafile :*** *CHAMBER.XXX*

Size	Employees	Nature	Problem	Understands	Concerned	Call	Loan	Collateral	Access
2	2	1	1	2	1	2	2	0	2
1	2	3	1	2	2	0	2	2	1
4	3	1	2	1	2	2	2	2	0
1	1	1	2	1	2	2	2	2	2
1	2	1	2	0	0	0	0	0	0
3	1	5	2	0	2	2	2	2	1
3	3	2	2	1	1	2	2	2	1
2	2	3	2	1	2	2	2	2	2
3	5	2	2	1	2	2	2	1	2

- The variable *Size* refers to the annual sales of the company and is coded as follows:

  1 under $1 million
  2 $1–5 million
  3 $6–10 million
  4 $11–20 million
  5 over $20 million

- The variable *Employees* refers to the number of employees that the company currently employs. This variable was coded as

  1 0–5 employees
  2 6–10 employees
  3 11–50 employees
  4 51–150 employees
  5 151–250 employees
  6 Over 250 employees

- The variable *Nature* refers to the type of business and is coded as

  1 Manufacturing
  2 Retail
  3 Service
  4 Real Estate
  5 Other

- The next seven variables contain the response to the questions or statements indicated and are coded as follows:

1	Yes
2	No

- *Problem* "Are you experiencing credit related problems?"
- *Understd* "The bank understands my problems."
- *Concern* "I am concerned that my note might be recalled."
- *Call* "The bank is planning to recall my loan."
- *Loan* "The bank has called my loan."
- *Collateral* "The bank has demanded more collateral."
- *Access* "Access to credit is affecting my business."

(a) Look at the variable *Problem* that was discussed in Example 6.28. Separate the respondents according to the type of company that they have. For each type of industry, generate a binomial probability distribution for $\pi = 0.10$ and $n =$ the number of that type of company. For each type of company find the probability that the number of people reporting credit problems is the actual number found in the sample.

(b) For each type of company estimate the value of π. Compare these to each other, to the overall estimated value of π and to the assumed value of 0.10. Report your conclusions.

(c) Repeat parts (a) and (b) for the different sizes of companies (both annual sales and number of employees).

(d) Now look at the variables related to loan recall, *Concern, Call,* and *Loan.* Use the data to estimate the percentage of small businesses that responded Yes to each of these questions. How does the number of nonresponses to the question affect your estimate of the percentage? Do you think that it is better to estimate the percentage of Yes respondents using the total of 166 companies or just the ones who responded to the question? Why?

(e) Investigate the variables *Concern, Call,* and *Loan* the same way you investigated *Problem.*

(f) Investigate the variable *Understd* the same way you investigated *Problem.*

(g) Investigate the variable *Access.*

(h) Prepare a report for the Chamber of Commerce about the credit problems and concerns of small businesses.

Datafile: TISSUES.XXX

6.39 In Chapter 3 you learned about some of the customer complaints that a company that manufactures tissues can get. One of the categories of complaints that made up a large percentage of the total was Dispensing. In that category, Sheets Tear on Removal was a significant factor.

The managers of the tissue company have decided to address this problem. They know that tensile strength is the factor that determines when a tissue will tear, and have decided that to solve the problem they will have to investigate the tensile strength of the tissues.

As part of the Quality Control program at the company, facial tissue has certain product specifications, that is, criteria that must be met, for the product to be acceptable to consumers. One of the characteristics that is specified is tensile strength.

The managers have decided to look at the current levels of tissue strength. They know the target values for the process and the parameters that should be met, and have decided to check to see whether the process is meeting the current specifications. If it is not, then changes will need to be made to see that it does. If it is, then perhaps the process specifications will need to be changed. The managers will collect data on two variables:

- **Machine Direction (MD) Strength:** This is the strength in the direction that the machine pulls on the tissue during manufacture. It has to be high enough that the tissues do not break, causing machine down time.
- **Cross-Direction (CD) Strength:** This is the strength in the direction that the tissue is pulled out of the box. It is the variable that determines whether the sheets tear when you remove them from the box.

Samples were taken from tissue produced on a single tissue machine. The samples were taken over three different days and the results were recorded.

A portion of the datafile and an explanation of the variables are shown here:

Day	MDStrength	CDStrength
1	1006	422
1	994	448
1	1032	423
1	875	435
1	1043	445
1	962	464
1	973	472

- ***Day*** keeps track of the day on which the sample was taken and goes from 1 to 3.
- ***MDStrength*** measures machine-directional strength and is measured in lb/ream.
- ***CDStrength*** measures cross-directional strength and is measured in lb/ream.

According to the specifications, *MDStrength* is supposed to be normally distributed with a mean of 1000 and a standard deviation of 50 lb/ream. *CDStrength* should be normally distributed with a mean of 400 and a standard deviation of 25 lb/ream.

(a) Use a computer software package to create normal probability tables for the specified distributions of *MDStrength.* Use increments of 50 and go from 800 to 1200.

(b) Use the table to determine the probability that a tissue manufactured according to specifications will have an *MDStrength* of less than 850 lb/ream.

(c) Create a relative frequency histogram for the variable *MDStrength* that goes from 800 to 1200 in class intervals of 50 units.

(d) Do the data in the histogram appear to have the shape of a normal distribution? What is the center?

(e) Look at the relative frequencies on the histogram you just created, and calculate what percentage of the data are within 1 standard deviation of the mean value of 1000. According to the empirical rule what percentage should be within 1 standard deviation? How do the actual data compare with the empirical rule prediction?

(f) Use the procedure above to determine the percentage of *MDStrength* data that are within 2 and 3 standard deviations of the mean.

(g) The critical specifications for *MDStrength* are 850 on the low side and 1075 on the high side. Use the frequency distribution to determine the percentage of the tissues that actually do not meet these specifications.

(h) How does this compare to the percent defective expected by the product specifications?

(i) Do you think that the company should be concerned about the difference? Why or why not?

(j) Create a set of normal probabilities for the theoretical distribution of *CDStrength.*

(k) The critical values for *CDStrength* are 480 on the high side and 390 on the low side. *CDStrength* that is too high creates a stiff tissue. Since the cross direction is the one in which tissues are pulled from the box, a value of *CDStrength* that is too low can cause sheets to tear on removal from the carton. According to the specifications, what percentage of the tissues should have CD strengths that are too high? too low?

(l) Create a graph of the theoretical distribution of *CDStrength.*

(m) Generate a set of descriptive statistics for the variable *CDStrength.* Compare the mean and the median. Do you think that the distribution of *CDStrength* is symmetric?

(n) Create a relative frequency histogram for the variable *CDStrength.* Does it support the assumption of normality?

(o) Compare the percentage of CD strength measurements that are within 1, 2, and 3 standard deviations of the mean to the predictions of the empirical rule. Is the assumption of normality still reasonable?

(p) Prepare a report to management that indicates whether the process appears to be running to the product specifications. In this report include any changes that need to be made (in terms of mean and standard deviation) to bring the process back to target values.

CHAPTER 7

SAMPLING DISTRIBUTIONS AND CONFIDENCE INTERVALS

THE DIAPER COMPANY

Business Dilemma...

Most large manufacturing companies use some form of Statistical Quality Control (SQC) in the manufacture of their products. One form of SQC that is often used is a control chart. A control chart looks at variation in data from samples of products taken over time.

A large company that manufactures disposable diapers collects data from its machines at random times during the workday. One of the variables that is measured is diaper weight. Diaper weight is an important factor in the manufacturing process for two reasons. First, the material that contributes most to diaper weight is the most expensive component of the diaper. Thus, it is reasonable to want to provide enough of this material, but not an excessive amount. The second reason is that the weight of a diaper relates to the consumer's perception of how well that diaper will absorb liquid. The target values, previously identified by consumer research, for diaper weight are a mean of 55 g and a standard deviation of 0.55 g.

When diapers are collected they are grouped in samples of size 5. The sample number and the individual diaper weights and bulks (in grams) are recorded. The sample averages are then calculated and plotted on charts. Machine operators use these charts to tell them whether the machine is behaving as expected or whether the machine needs adjustment. The first few lines of the data set are shown here.

Sample	Diaper	Weight	Bulk
1	1	55.87	0.419
1	2	55.35	0.380
1	3	54.50	0.365
1	4	53.97	0.406
1	5	54.29	0.360
2	1	54.85	0.397
2	2	54.79	0.405
2	3	54.65	0.393

7.1 CHAPTER OBJECTIVES

To properly use control charts and to make inferences about the population mean, you must understand the behavior of the sample mean, $\overline{X}$. Gaining an understanding of $\overline{X}$ is the focus of this chapter. We will look at control charts in more detail in Chapter 16. In Chapter 6, we saw that the behavior of a quantitative variable can be described by its probability distribution, and this distribution in turn can be described by parameters such as the mean and the variance. In this chapter we make the link from the probability concepts you learned in Chapter 6 to the inferential statistics techniques covered in the remaining chapters in this book.

Figure 7.1 is a drawing you first saw in Chapter 2. The larger circle on the left represents the population you are studying. The smaller circle on the right represents the sample you have taken from this population. This figure is being used to help you see the relationship between probability and inferential statistics. In reality, the sample circle should sit inside the population circle since it is a piece of it.

Chapters 3, 4, and 5 taught you the techniques of descriptive statistics, which help you describe the sample. These techniques work on the smaller circle and are

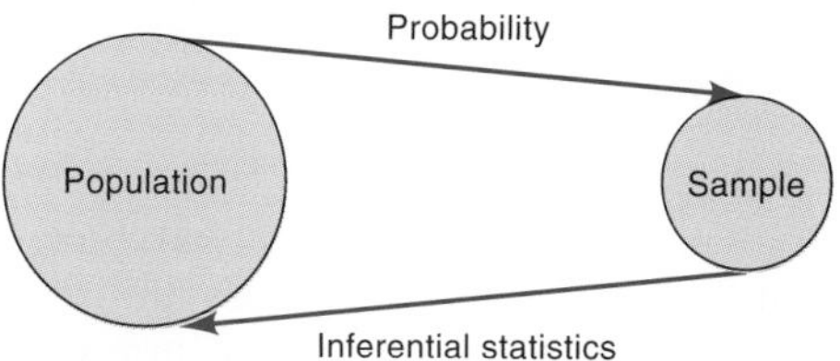

FIGURE 7.1 Relationship between probability and inferential statistics

very helpful in gaining an understanding of the sample data, but they do not let you use the information in the sample to draw conclusions or inferences about the population. In other words, you do not yet have the ability to link that smaller circle to the larger one. In the last chapter you learned some tools of probability. In particular, you learned how to calculate the likelihood of a particular sample being selected from a population. You were thus making the trip across the top arc in Figure 7.1, from the population to the sample.

The key to inferential statistics is found in this chapter.

But this is not really our desired goal. We wish ultimately to make the trip from the sample to the population along the bottom arc in Figure 7.1. We wish to use the information in the sample to make probabilistic statements about the behavior of the population. This is the goal of inferential statistics. The key that unlocks this trip is found in this chapter. The rest of the chapters in this book can be opened only with the key.

More specifically, this chapter covers:

- Motivation for Point Estimators
- Common Point Estimators
- Desirable Properties of Point Estimators
- Distribution of the Sample Mean, $\overline{X}$: The Central Limit Theorem
- The Central Limit Theorem—A More Detailed Look
- Drawing Inferences by Using the Central Limit Theorem
- Large-Sample Confidence Intervals for the Mean
- Distribution of the Sample Mean: Small Sample and Unknown σ
- Small-Sample Confidence Intervals for the Mean
- Confidence Intervals for Qualitative Data
- Sample Size Calculations

7.2 MOTIVATION FOR POINT ESTIMATORS

***Remember:** A parameter is a numerical descriptor of the population. Parameter values are typically unknown.*

Since we most likely will not know the value of the parameters that describe the population, we must resort to using the information contained in the sample. It seems logical that if we can identify a numerical descriptor for the sample, then this statistic, called a point estimate, might be used to estimate the corresponding measure for the population. This is the right idea, which leads us to the definition of a **point estimate** and a **point estimator.**

> A ***point estimate*** is a single number calculated from sample data. It is used to estimate a parameter of the population. A ***point estimator*** is the formula or rule that is used to calculate the point estimate for a particular set of data.

Sample statistics become point estimates.

Actually you have been working with point estimates without really knowing it. Up to this point, values calculated from the sample have been called sample statistics. Now we establish the link between sample statistics and the corresponding population parameters. In doing so we will have created point estimates out of these sample statistics. Let's take a look at the diaper company introduced at the beginning of the chapter.

EXAMPLE 7.1 The Diaper Company

Some Possible Point Estimates

Collect and Analyze the Data

Suppose a sample of 30 diapers was taken and the diaper weight was recorded in grams for each diaper. You decide to use the tools of descriptive statistics to describe this sample. The results of your analysis in Excel are shown here. Each of these values fits the definition of a point estimate. Each one is a single number calculated from the sample and it could be used to estimate an unknown population parameter. In the case of the sample mean, median, and mode, any of these values could be used as estimates of the true unknown mean weight of the population of all diapers manufactured.

Weight	
Mean	54.9833333
Median	54.86
Mode	#N/A
Standard deviation	0.63690162
Range	2.47
Minimum	53.97
Maximum	56.44
Count	30

Note: Excel uses #N/A to indicate that the mode was unavailable. In most cases this means that there were no values that occurred more than once.

■

Before we go any further we must consider what parameters of the population we wish to estimate.

7.3 COMMON POINT ESTIMATORS

In Chapter 2 you learned that there are two major categories that can be used to classify variables: *qualitative* and *quantitative.* You also learned that the type of tools that can be used to analyze data depends on the type of data. Statisticians must know what kind of data they are analyzing before the analysis tools are selected and the inferences made.

***Remember** that a quantitative variable is numerical and a qualitative variable is descriptive.*

7.3.1 Point Estimators for Quantitative Variables

If you are studying a *single quantitative variable,* then you typically wish to know the value of the *population mean* and the value of the *population standard deviation.* That is, you wish to know the center and the variability in the population. Remember that what you would like to know are the values of those parameters that describe the behavior of the population.

EXAMPLE 7.2 The Diaper Company

Parameters of Interest

Understand the Problem

For the diaper company, the population consists of all diapers made by this company. The characteristic that is being studied is the weight of the diapers. This is a quantitative variable and so we are interested in knowing the mean weight of all diapers made by this company and the standard deviation of the weights of all diapers made by this

7.3 Jiffy Burger does not want its customers to wait more than 3 minutes on the average for their food. A sample of the wait time in minutes for 20 customers is collected and shown here:

3.4	3.3	3.3	3.3	3.3	3.4	3.4	3.3	3.2	3.4
3.3	3.3	3.3	3.3	3.4	3.2	3.5	3.2	3.4	3.1

(a) What is your estimate of the average customer wait at Jiffy Burger?

(b) How much difference is there between your estimate and the target of 3 minutes?

7.4 A company is comparing the proportion of defective items produced by the second shift with the proportion of defective items produced by the third shift. In a sample of 100 items made by the second shift, 2 were found to be defective. In a sample of 100 items made by the third shift, 4 were found to be defective.

(a) What is your estimate of the proportion of defective items produced by the second shift?

(b) What is your estimate of the proportion of defective items produced by the third shift?

(c) What is the difference in the two estimates that you found in parts (a) and (b)?

7.5 A company that buys blank VHS tapes for video recording is concerned about the amount of time that the tapes are able to record. The tapes are rated at 120 minutes, but the company knows there is variation in the actual recording time. Data are collected on 25 randomly selected tapes and the actual recording times are listed here:

116	118	119	119	120
117	118	119	119	121
117	118	119	120	121
117	119	119	120	121
117	119	119	120	121

(a) What is your estimate of the average time available on the tape?

(b) Is your estimate different from 120 minutes? If so, by how much?

7.4 DESIRABLE PROPERTIES OF POINT ESTIMATORS

In this section, we develop the properties of point estimators. We do this by focusing on estimators for the population mean, μ. However, the resulting properties apply to any point estimator.

In Chapter 4 you learned how to calculate measures of the middle of the sample data. In particular, you learned about the sample mean, $\overline{X}$, the sample median, and the sample mode. The trimmed mean was also examined as a measure of the middle of the sample data. Based on what we have seen so far, it makes sense to consider using one or more of these statistics as our point estimator of the unknown value μ. Let's see how these might work for our diaper company.

Collect and Analyze the Data

EXAMPLE 7.4 The Diaper Company

Possible Point Estimates of μ

Suppose you took a sample of 5 diapers and recorded the diaper weight (in grams) of each of the 5 diapers. The data are shown here:

55.87   55.35   54.50   53.97   54.29

The sample mean is 54.80 and the sample median (the middle score) is 54.50. There is no mode for this data set since none of the values occur more than once. We could use the value of either 54.80 or 54.50 as our point estimate for the unknown true mean weight of the diapers being made. ■

It appears that the mean, the median, and the mode all fit the definition of a point estimator. In fact, we could dream up many other formulas that would fit the definition of a point estimator. For example, we could decide to average the minimum and maximum value in the sample and call this a point estimator. This is a legitimate point estimator, since the calculation is based only on sample data and yields a single number. Clearly, we need some criteria to judge which of these point estimators is the best one to use to estimate μ.

Let's think about the criteria that we could use to make this judgment. If the point estimate is to be used as our best guess of the value of the unknown population parameter, in this case μ, then we would like the point estimate to be close to μ. Ideally, we would like our point estimate to hit μ on the nose. But we know that the chance of that happening is pretty slim. In fact, we know from Chapter 2 that the sample is only a piece of the population and if we were to take a different sample, we would get a different sample mean, a different sample median, and a different sample mode.

Let's follow the diaper company an hour after our first sample of 5 diapers.

EXAMPLE 7.5 **The Diaper Company**

Collect and Analyze the Data

Second Sample Yields Slightly Different Values for Point Estimates

A second sample of 5 diapers is taken an hour after the first sample. The diaper weights, in grams, are as follows:

54.85 54.79 54.65 55.56 55.82

Some quick calculations yield

Sample mean = 55.13 Sample median = 54.85 Sample mode = N/A ■

The particular point estimates are different now. We used the same point estimators (formulas to calculate the sample mean and sample median) but we got different numbers because the data in this second sample were different from those of the first sample. This tells us that our point estimate depends on the particular sample we happen to choose and it changes from sample to sample. Combining this fact with the criterion of getting close to the unknown μ, we can see that we want to use the point estimator that comes closest to μ for most samples. That is, we would like a point estimator that does not yield radically different numbers from sample to sample.

Suppose for a minute that you dreamed up a formula for a point estimator for μ and you used it with two different samples from the same population. For the first sample your point estimate was calculated to be 24 and for the second sample it was calculated to be 245. How much faith would you have in your estimate? "Not much" should be your answer. Why? The feature of this point estimator that is troubling is that it yields wildly different estimates from sample to sample. The estimator has too much variability; that is, it jumps around too much from sample to sample.

In summary, what we really want is a point estimator with the following three properties:

Properties of point estimators

1. The point estimator should fairly estimate the unknown population parameter.
2. The point estimator should yield a number close to the unknown population parameter as the sample size increases.
3. The point estimator should not have a great deal of variability.

Even though we have been considering point estimators for the unknown population mean, μ, these properties are desirable for any point estimator.

TABLE 7.4 Ten 90% Confidence Intervals

$\overline{X}$	55.21	54.94	54.99	55.05	55.06	54.97	55.11	54.92	55.03	55.10
Error	0.17	0.17	0.17	0.17	0.17	0.17	0.17	0.17	0.17	0.17
Lower	55.04	54.78	54.82	54.89	54.89	54.81	54.95	54.76	54.87	54.93
Upper	55.37	55.11	55.16	55.22	55.23	55.14	55.28	55.09	55.20	55.27
Covers μ?	No	Yes	Yes	Yes	Yes	Yes	Yes	Yes	Yes	Yes

After all, μ is a number even if it is unknown to us. Therefore, there is no probability associated with it being between two other numbers; it is either in the interval or it is not.

So, then, what is the proper interpretation of those words? The correct interpretation of the 95% confidence level has to do with the chance that you have an interval that does in fact contain the population parameter. Remember that if you take 100 different samples from the same population, you will get 100 different sample means and therefore 100 different confidence intervals. If each of them is a 95% confidence interval then theoretically 95 out of the 100 intervals will contain μ and 5 of them will not.

Suppose that 10 samples of size $n = 30$ were selected from the population of diapers. For each sample, an average diaper weight was calculated and a 90% confidence interval was calculated based on this value of $\overline{X}$. These 10 confidence intervals are shown in Table 7.4. Let's assume that the manufacturing process was running properly so the population mean is 55 g. Remember that the population standard deviation is 0.55 g. According to the theory, 9 out of 10 of these intervals should include the value of $\mu = 55$ g.

The last row of Table 7.4 indicates whether the interval includes the value of 55 g. You can see in Figure 7.9 that there is only 1 interval that does not include the value of 55 g and 9 that do. This is just what we expected, since 90% of 10 intervals is 9 intervals that cover μ. The problem, of course, is that we don't know the actual value of μ and therefore we don't know whether we have an interval that actually contains μ or not. The confidence level gives us the probability of our having an interval that does in fact contain the population parameter.

To increase the probability that we have a "good" interval, we could widen the intervals. This is precisely what happens when you increase the confidence level. When you increase the confidence level from 90% to 95%, you are increasing the chance that you have a good interval, but you are losing precision by widening the interval. It is a tradeoff.

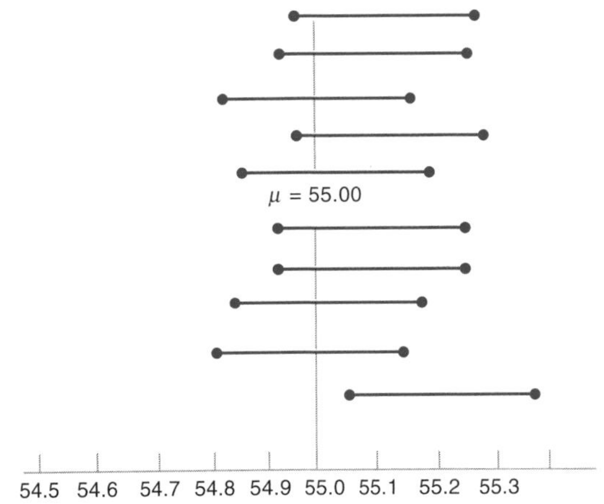

FIGURE 7.9 Comparison of confidence intervals and μ

7.8.5 Exercises—Learning It!

7.11 A university wants to estimate the average amount of money that students spend on textbooks in a semester. It takes a random sample of 45 students and finds that the average amount of money spent was \$282 with a standard deviation of \$21. Find a 98% confidence interval estimate for the true mean amount of money spent on textbooks in a semester.

7.12 The weights of jars of peanut butter are normally distributed with a standard deviation of 0.03 oz. A random sample of 12 jars has an average weight of 14.9 oz.

(a) Find a 95% confidence interval for the true mean weight of the jars.

(b) If the jars are labeled 15 oz, do you think that there is a problem?

7.13 Quality Foods' regional manager wants to determine the average fat content per pound of steak sold in Portland, Maine. She's considering quitting her job and starting a cattle ranch after reading the article "Queen of the Range" in the January 1989 issue of *Successful Farming.* Her ranch would produce low-fat beef for sale to upscale consumers. She purchased one steak from each of the 18 stores in the area and determined the fat content per pound. The data (in ounces) are shown here:

1.2	1.3
1.6	1.3
1.3	1.6
0.7	1.1
1.3	1.2
1.7	1.3
0.9	0.9
1.8	1.4
1.3	1.4

The standard deviation of fat content is known to be 0.30 oz.

(a) Assuming that the fat content is normally distributed, calculate a 95% confidence interval for the average fat content per pound in steaks sold in the Portland, Maine, area.

(b) Her research shows that the steaks from her ranch will average 1.0 oz of fat per pound. Are her steaks significantly lower in fat content than the ones available in the Portland area? Explain why or why not.

7.14 Is it a lottery jackpot or a bonus? A salary or a life's savings? No, it's the annual compensation paid out to top executives of public stock corporations. The following table shows the 1996 salary and bonus for the first few of the 43 executives, the firm they work for, and the type of firm (manufacturing or nonmanufacturing). *Datafile:* SALARY.XXX

Name	Firm	Type	1996 Salary and Bonus
Eugene Freedman	Enesco Giftware Group/Stanhome Inc.	M	\$4,505,500
Thomas Wheeler	Massachusetts Mutual	NM	3,569,998
Terrence Murray	Fleet Financial Group	NM	3,909,200
Robert Shapiro	Monsanto	M	2,920,000
David E. Sams, Jr.	Massachusetts Mutual	NM	2,760,183
Charles Gifford	BankBoston	NM	2,600,000
George David	United Technologies	M	2,375,000

SOURCE: *Springfield Sunday Republican* (July 20, 1997)

Assuming that these 43 executives represent a random sample of executives, find a 90% confidence interval for the mean salary of executives.

7.15 The United States Department of Labor publishes a great deal of data on a monthly basis. The following data on the average price of peanut butter were extracted from the World Wide Web:

[Bureau of Labor Statistics Data]
Average Price Data
Series Catalog:
Series ID: APU0000716141
Area: U.S. city average
Item: Peanut butter, creamy, all sizes, per lb (453.6 g)

Year	Jan	Feb	Mar	Apr	May	Jun	Jul	Aug	Sep	Oct	Nov	Dec
1997	1.810	1.819	1.778	1.808	1.817	1.817	1.810	1.749	1.797	1.764	1.703	1.730
1998	1.801	1.808	1.821	1.808	1.772	1.787	1.808	1.802	1.795	1.813	1.820	1.791
1999	1.769	1.788	1.818	1.822	1.809	1.817	1.831	1.819	1.823	1.830	1.835	1.861

Treating these 3 years of data as a sample, find a 90% confidence interval for the average monthly price of peanut butter. Assume that the standard deviation is $0.035.

7.16 A national grocery chain is considering opening a store at a particular location. To be sure that enough traffic goes by that location, the grocery chain took a sample of vehicles crossing the intersection on 40 days. The results are shown in the table:

Number of Cars Crossing Location/Day			
1431	1540	1293	1340
1302	1700	1533	1402
1255	1840	1272	1467
1377	1642	1572	1220
1450	1139	1520	1477
1483	1227	1227	1515
1529	1684	1257	1242
1588	1782	1238	1350
1535	1491	1276	1367
1533	1513	1420	1375

(a) Find a 95% confidence interval for the average number of cars that pass this location on a daily basis. The standard deviation is assumed to be 165 cars.

(b) The company has decided to open a store at this location only if there is a daily average of at least 1400 cars passing this location. Based on your confidence interval, would you advise the company to open a store at this location? Explain why or why not.

7.17 The amount of time that it takes a student to complete an assignment in a statistics class has a standard deviation of 5 minutes. A group of 35 students is observed and it is found that the average time to complete the assignment was 55 minutes.

(a) Find a 99% confidence interval for the true mean time to complete the assignment.
(b) If the instructor believes that the students should be spending an average of 50 minutes on the assignment, what can you say about his belief?

7.18 Most companies have increased their dependence on computers and software. As a result, more employee time is spent on the telephone with technical support for the software. A sample of 22 times spent on hold for technical support is shown here:

Time on Hold (minutes)	
8.6	12.9
12.7	11.4
8.7	10.3
12.2	7.9
11.7	9.2
7.3	10.5
9.8	11.8
14.5	10.9
13.0	11.5
12.9	10.6
11.4	11.7

Assume that the standard deviation is 2 minutes.

(a) Since the sample size is less than 30 and you are not told that the population of time on hold is normally distributed, display the data in a histogram, and comment on the shape of the data. Is it reasonable to assume that the data come from a population that has a normal distribution? Why or why not?

(b) Find a 99% confidence interval for the average amount of time spent on hold per call.

(c) Find a 95% confidence interval for the average amount of time spent on hold per call.

(d) If you are the manager of these employees and you are trying to argue for additional staff, which of the two confidence intervals would you use and why?

7.19 The symphony in a medium-size New England city is surveying the community to determine the average number of times during a year that a person would attend a concert at a particular price. The responses from 50 adults are shown here:

Number of Times Symphony Would Be Attended in One Year				
1	3	2	2	2
4	4	4	4	4
3	2	4	4	4
2	1	4	4	4
2	3	3	3	3
2	3	3	3	3
3	5	5	5	5
2	4	4	4	4
4	3	2	2	2
3	3	2	2	2

(a) Find a 90% confidence interval for the average number of times a year a person would attend a concert at the price studied.

(b) How might this confidence interval be useful to the management of the symphony?

Discovery Exercise 7.2
EXPLORING CONFIDENCE INTERVALS FOR μ

From a population of college students across the United States, a sample was selected to find out how many hours per week a typical student spends playing sports.

Part I: A random sample of 2500 students was selected. The sample mean, $\overline{X}$, was found to be 12.5 hours. The population standard deviation, σ, is known to be 1.05 hours. Given this information, find

(a) a 90% confidence interval for μ

(b) a 92% confidence interval for μ

(continued)

(c) a 94% confidence interval for μ

(d) a 96% confidence interval for μ

(e) a 98% confidence interval for μ

(f) Discuss what happens to the size of the interval as the level of confidence increases.

Part II: A random sample of 2500 students was selected. The sample mean, $\overline{X}$, was found to be 10.5 hours. The population standard deviation, σ, is known to be 1.05 hours. Given this information, find

(a) a 90% confidence interval for μ

(b) a 92% confidence interval for μ

(c) a 94% confidence interval for μ

(d) a 96% confidence interval for μ

(e) a 98% confidence interval for μ

(f) Compare the intervals found in Part I with those found in Part II. Discuss what happened to the confidence interval due to the change in the value of the sample mean, $\overline{X}$.

Part III: A random sample of 2500 students was selected. The sample mean, $\overline{X}$, was found to be 12.5 hours. Suppose you learn that the population standard deviation, σ, is actually 2.05 hours. Given this information, find

(a) a 90% confidence interval for μ

(b) a 92% confidence interval for μ

(c) a 94% confidence interval for μ

(d) a 96% confidence interval for μ

(continued)

(e) a 98% confidence interval for μ

(f) Compare the intervals found in Part I with those found in Part III. Discuss what happened to the confidence intervals due to the change in the value of the population standard deviation, σ.

Part IV: A random sample of 2000 students was selected. The sample mean, $\overline{X}$, was found to be 12.5 hours. The population standard deviation, σ, is known to be 1.05 hours. Given this information, find

(a) a 90% confidence interval for μ

(b) a 92% confidence interval for μ

(c) a 94% confidence interval for μ

(d) a 96% confidence interval for μ

(e) a 98% confidence interval for μ

(f) Compare the intervals found in Part I with those found in Part IV. Discuss what happened to the confidence intervals due to the change in the value of the sample size, n.

7.9 DISTRIBUTION OF THE SAMPLE MEAN: SMALL SAMPLE AND UNKNOWN σ

In the previous section we noted that if the standard deviation of a normally distributed population is unknown and the sample size is small ($n \leq 30$), then the sampling distribution of $\overline{X}$ does not follow a normal distribution. As we did with the large sample size situation, logic tells us to try using s in the formula for the z-score instead of σ. When we do this a t-score is created instead of a z-score. That is, the sampling distribution of $\overline{X}$ for small samples, when σ is unknown and the population is normally distributed, follows what is called *Student's t distribution.* The t-score is calculated as follows:

$$t = \frac{\overline{X} - \mu}{s/\sqrt{n}}$$

t-score

Notice that the calculation for t is just the same as for z, with σ replaced with s.

The t distribution was first developed by a man named William Gosset who was working for Guinness Brewery in Ireland. The company did not allow research results to be published so he published his results under a pen name; Student was his pen name!

This distribution is not named for you, the student!

The graph of the t distribution looks very much like the standard normal distribution. It is symmetric, it has a bell shape, and it is centered at zero just like the z distribution. The major difference between the z and the t distributions has to do with the spread or variability of the distributions. The standard deviation of the t distribution is not 1 like it is for the z distribution. Instead, the variability of the t distribution is related to a number that is called the degrees of freedom. Thus, there are many different t distributions, but they all have generally the same shape. A t distribution with 5 degrees of freedom is shown in Figure 7.10 on page 338.

Let's examine the z and t calculations. The two calculations are shown side by side:

Each sample yields a different sample mean, $\overline{X}$, and a different sample standard deviation, s.

$$z = \frac{\overline{X} - \mu}{\sigma/\sqrt{n}} \qquad t = \frac{\overline{X} - \mu}{s/\sqrt{n}}$$

Think about what causes the variability in the z statistic. For a given sample size, say $n = 26$, the only thing that causes the z values to change from sample to sample is $\overline{X}$. The other elements of the calculation stay the same from sample to sample. Now look at the t distribution. Both $\overline{X}$ and s are changing from sample to sample. This causes t to have more variability than z. Based on this discussion we would correctly

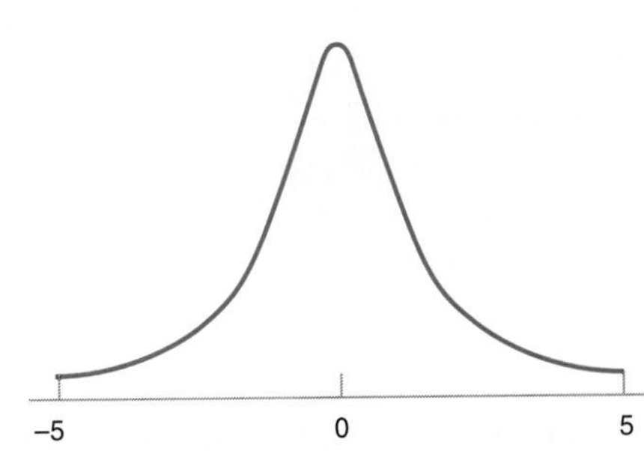

FIGURE 7.10 *t* distribution with 5 degrees of freedom

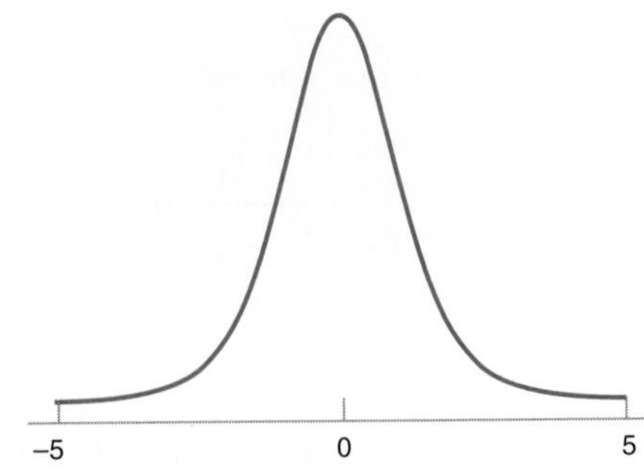

FIGURE 7.11 *t* distribution with 25 degrees of freedom

conclude that *t* will have "fatter" tails than *z* and indeed it does. The *t* distribution for a sample size of $n = 26$ is shown in Figure 7.11.

You should ask, Why do I need to know the value of *n* to draw the graph? You might remember that as we take larger and larger samples (*n* gets larger) our estimate of the unknown population standard deviation gets better and better. Why is this so? Well, just think about the whole population as a big pie. When you take a small sample it is like taking a small piece of the pie and tasting it and trying to decide how the whole pie tastes based on that piece. As the piece you taste gets bigger you have a much better idea of how the whole pie tastes. Eventually, if you take a big enough sample you will eat the whole pie and you will know exactly how the whole pie tastes! This is the same as sampling the whole population. If the whole population were sampled you wouldn't need to estimate σ because you would know it.

Better estimates of σ make t less variable.

So as you take a larger and larger sample you get a better and better estimate of σ, which, in turn, causes *t* to be less and less variable. All of this means that the graph of *t* depends on the size of your sample. In particular, the degrees of freedom associated with the *t* distribution is related to the sample size. The value for the degrees of freedom is $n - 1$, one less than the sample size. If you have taken a sample of size 26, then the *t* distribution will have 25 degrees of freedom. This is the graph shown in Figure 7.11. Examine the *t* distributions for various different degrees of freedom shown in Figure 7.12.

What do you notice about the graph of *t* as the number of degrees of freedom gets larger (i.e., as the sample size gets larger)? You should see that the *t* distribution gets tighter, meaning the variability of the distribution gets smaller. This is precisely what you should have expected to happen based on our discussion of what happens to our estimate *s* as we sample bigger pieces of the pie. In fact, eventually, if we use a large enough value for *n*, the graph of *t* will be indistinguishable from the standard normal distribution, *z*. Typically, the value of *n* that is considered large enough is $n > 30$.

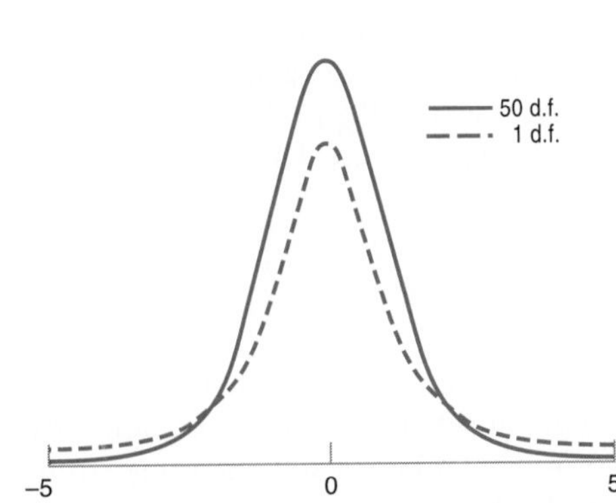

FIGURE 7.12 *t* distributions with 1 and 50 degrees of freedom

7.10 SMALL-SAMPLE CONFIDENCE INTERVALS FOR THE MEAN

Now that we have an understanding of the *t* distribution, the only thing that remains is to see how the confidence interval for μ changes for small samples. Replacing the *z* table value with a *t* value in the formulas for the upper and lower limits of the confidence interval for μ gives us the following:

Confidence Interval for μ, Small Sample and σ Unknown

Error:	$e = \dfrac{t_{\alpha/2,n-1}s}{\sqrt{n}}$
Width of the interval:	$w = 2e$
Lower bound:	$L = \overline{X} - e$
Upper bound:	$U = \overline{X} + e$

In addition, we must now assume that the underlying population of the variable we are estimating is normally distributed.

7.10.1 Using the *t* Table

The procedure for figuring out the correct *t* value for any confidence level is similar to that used to find the correct *z* value. We need to find the *t* value so that there is a total probability of α in the tails of the distribution. Since the *t* distribution is symmetric, this means there will be $\alpha/2$ in each of the tail areas. Unlike with the *z* table, there is no need to work the table backward. Typically, the *t* table is used to find the *t* value that corresponds to a certain probability in one of the tails of the distribution rather than to find probabilities under the *t* distribution. A portion of the *t* table is shown in Figure 7.13.

The complete *t* table is found in Table 4 in Appendix A. Notice that the table has several columns and several rows. The columns correspond to the tail area probability and the rows correspond to the number of degrees of freedom, which is one less than the sample size. The procedure for using the table is as follows:

Steps for Finding the Value of t for a Confidence Interval

Step 1: Take the value of α and divide it by 2.

Step 2: Use that column of the *t* table.

Step 3: Find the number of degrees of freedom by calculating $n - 1$. Use that row of the *t* table.

Step 4: Read off the corresponding *t* value at the intersection of the row and column you have identified. Label this value $t_{\alpha/2,n-1}$ to indicate that the tail area probability is $\alpha/2$ and there are $n - 1$ degrees of freedom.

Let's look at an example to see how to use the *t* table.

	Upper-Tail Areas					
Degrees of Freedom	**0.25**	**0.1**	**0.05**	**0.025**	**0.01**	**0.005**
20	0.687	1.325	1.725	2.086	2.528	2.845
21	0.686	1.323	1.721	2.080	2.518	2.831
22	0.686	1.321	1.717	2.074	2.508	2.819
23	0.685	1.320	1.714	2.069	2.500	2.807
24	0.685	1.318	1.711	2.064	2.492	2.797
25	0.684	1.316	1.708	2.060	2.485	2.787
26	0.684	1.315	1.706	2.056	2.479	2.779

FIGURE 7.13 A portion of the *t* table

Collect and Analyze the Data

EXAMPLE 7.13

Using the t Table

Find the t value for a 95% confidence interval for a sample size of 25:

1. Since a 95% confidence interval is required, α is 0.05 and so $\alpha/2$ is 0.025.
2. Use the 0.025 column of the t table.
3. Since the sample size is $n = 25$, use the row corresponding to $n - 1 = 25 - 1 = 24$ degrees of freedom.
4. The t value is 2.064 in the table shown in Figure 7.13. Label it $t_{0.025,24}$. ■

Now let's use this t value to find a confidence interval for μ in the following example.

Collect and Analyze the Data

EXAMPLE 7.14 Assembly Time

Small-Sample Confidence Interval for μ

In pricing a new product, the manufacturer must determine the average number of minutes it takes to manufacture one item. A sample of 25 items is tracked and the number of minutes to make each unit is recorded here. The assembly time of a unit is known to have a normal distribution.

Time to Assemble Item

5.2	4.4	5.0	5.2	4.7	4.6	4.8	4.8	4.0	4.5
5.7	4.8	5.2	4.4	4.3	4.5	4.0	4.6	4.9	5.8
5.2	6.0	5.6	5.7	4.5					

To find the confidence interval for μ, we need to calculate $\overline{X}$ and s and find the appropriate t value from the table shown in Figure 7.13.

$$\overline{X} = 4.90 \text{ min}$$
$$s = 0.55 \text{ min}$$

The t value with 24 degrees of freedom and a tail area of 0.025 is $t_{0.025,24} = 2.064$.

The upper and lower 95% confidence limits for μ are calculated using the following formulas:

Error:	$e = \frac{t_{\alpha/2,n-1}s}{\sqrt{n}} = \frac{(2.064)(0.55)}{\sqrt{25}} = 0.23$
Width of the interval:	$w = 2e = (2)(0.23) = 0.46$
Lower bound:	$L = \overline{X} - e = 4.90 - 0.23 = 4.67$ min
Upper bound:	$U = \overline{X} + e = 4.90 + 0.23 = 5.13$ min

Notice that the t value for the 95% confidence interval with 24 degrees of freedom is 2.064. If we had known the value of σ, then we would have used a z value of 1.96 instead of the t value. This would have made the value of e smaller, making the interval narrower. Confidence intervals constructed using t values are always wider than the corresponding interval would be if you could have used z. This is a direct result of the increased variability due to having to estimate σ. ■

The t distribution is the correct sampling distribution to use whenever σ is unknown. However, when the sample size is large, $n > 30$, it is common practice to use the z distribution instead of the t distribution because the graphs are virtually identical. The original reason for using z instead of t for large samples has all but vanished but the practice continues. Before the use of statistical software, analysts had to rely on printed t tables. Since the t distribution depends on the sample size, very large t tables were needed to allow for many different sample sizes. Thus, it was generally agreed that z could be used for sample sizes greater than 30, eliminating the need for t tables beyond 30 degrees of freedom. Software packages have eliminated the need for printed tables. Nevertheless, the convention of using z instead of t for large samples has become entrenched, and in this book, when the sample size is larger than 30 we will use the z distribution. Note that you would certainly be correct to use t whenever the standard deviation is unknown and that may be the approach taken by some software packages.

7.10.2 Exercises—Learning It!

7.20 The police department is concerned about the ability of officers to identify drunk drivers on the road. Before instituting a new training program they take a sample of 28 arrests and record the level of alcohol in the blood at the time of the arrest. Assume that the level of alcohol in the blood is normally distributed. The data are shown here:

Alcohol Level	
92	204
93	182
108	173
173	105
194	153
133	150
207	180
127	209
256	141
184	151
253	133
159	147
101	209
133	252

(a) Find a 90% confidence interval for the average alcohol level in the blood at the time of arrest.

(b) Find a 95% confidence interval for the average alcohol level in the blood at the time of arrest.

7.21 A large amusement park has recently added five new rides, including a large roller coaster called the Mind Eraser. Management is concerned about the waiting times on the new roller coaster. A random sample of 10 people is selected and the time (in minutes) that each person waits to ride the Mind Eraser is recorded and shown here:

Mind	Eraser
43	66
80	54
48	72
61	58
74	68

(a) Find a 95% confidence interval for the average waiting time for the Mind Eraser, assuming that the waiting time is normally distributed.

(b) The park management thinks that if customers have to wait more than 60 minutes for a ride, then the park should increase the staff to reduce the waiting time. Based on your confidence interval, does the park need to increase the staff? Explain why or why not.

7.22 Hospital administrators are paying increasing attention to length of stay of patients. Data from sample of 14 patient stays (in days) are shown here:

Patient Length of Stay	
7	6
2	5
6	4
7	4
8	2
8	3
3	7

(a) Find a 95% confidence interval for the length of patient stay, assuming that the length of stay is normally distributed.
(b) Find a 90% confidence interval for the length of patient stay, assuming that the length of stay is normally distributed.
(c) Which of these intervals should the administrator use in negotiating with insurance companies and why?

7.23 The number of workers per vehicle at the top 10 car assembly plants is shown here:

Nissan Smyrna	2.22
Toyota Cambridge	2.35
Honda East Liberty	2.38
Toyota Georgetown #1	2.50
Chrysler Bramalea	2.54
Honda Marysville	2.57
Ford Atlanta	2.63
Ford Chicago	2.66
Chrysler Belvidere	2.68
GM Oshawa #1	2.68

SOURCE: *Manufacturing Engineering*, August 1997

Assuming that the number of workers per vehicle has a normal distribution, find a 95% confidence interval for the average number of workers per vehicle.

7.24 The percentage of foster children adopted into families varies widely from state to state according to an August 8, 1997 article in the *Springfield Union News*. Congress is preparing bills to encourage the process in some states. The number of children adopted in 1996, as a percentage of all children available for adoption that year, is shown for a sample of 14 states:

Alabama	18.46
Alaska	31.31
California	34.78
Kansas	29.67
Kentucky	30.60
Massachusetts	46.27
Minnesota	20.66
New Hampshire	51.61
North Dakota	96.73
Ohio	25.08
Rhode Island	44.83
Texas	28.93
Utah	53.45
Wyoming	50.00

Find a 95% confidence interval for the average adoption rate, assuming that the adoption rates are normally distributed.

7.11 CONFIDENCE INTERVALS FOR QUALITATIVE DATA

Often we are interested in estimating what proportion of the population has a particular characteristic or has a particular opinion. In fact, most of the data printed in newspapers and magazines are the result of surveys and often proportions or percentages are reported. This is particularly true at election times. For example, the candidate for mayor wishes to know what proportion or percentage of voters in the city favor him.

The increasing focus on quality and meeting the needs of the customer has led to increased data collection, much of which is qualitative data. A manufacturing company is clearly interested in the proportion of products manufactured that are defective. All businesses, both manufacturing and service industries, are interested in knowing whether their products/services are meeting the needs of the customer. As a result you are often asked to fill out a questionnaire about how you liked the product and/or service you received. The data from questionnaires such as these are often qualitative data.

Remember: *Qualitative data describe a particular characteristic of a sample item. They are most often nonnumerical in nature.*

If the data we are analyzing are qualitative data, then we are most likely interested in estimating the proportion, π, of population members that have a certain characteristic (one of the categories of the nominal variable). Confidence intervals for the population proportion, π, have the same basic structure as those for μ. Remember that the sample proportion, p, is the best point estimate for π and so we should center the confidence interval at the value of p.

7.11.1 Finding the Confidence Interval for π

To develop the corresponding formulas for the lower and upper bounds of a $100(1 - \alpha)\%$ confidence interval for π, we need to know that the sampling distribution of p is a normal distribution. Again drawing on the properties of the normal distribution, we must extend the interval a certain number of standard errors to get the coverage we desire. The standard error of the point estimator, p, is $\sqrt{\pi(1 - \pi)/n}$. Notice that to calculate the standard error of p you must know the value of π. But you are trying to estimate π, so, clearly, you do not know π. It makes the most sense to use p as an estimate of π in the formula for the standard error.

The point estimate, p, should be at the center of any confidence intervals of π.

Combining these pieces of information with the knowledge that we wish to place p at the center of the confidence interval, we arrive at the following formulas for the lower and upper bounds:

Formula for Confidence Interval for π

Error: $e = z_{\alpha/2}\sqrt{\dfrac{\pi(1 - \pi)}{n}} \cong z_{\alpha/2}\sqrt{\dfrac{p(1 - p)}{n}}$

Width of the interval: $w = 2e$

Lower bound: $L = p - e$

Upper bound: $U = p + e$

where $z_{\alpha/2}$ is the z value that cuts off $\alpha/2$ in the upper tail of the standard normal distribution and $\alpha/2$ in the lower tail of the standard normal distribution.

Let's look at an example.

EXAMPLE 7.15 Beverly Hills, 90210

Collect and Analyze the Data

Confidence Interval for π

Hard times have hit the *Beverly Hills, 90210* crowd. Nearly a third of teens polled by Teenage Research Limited said they have been personally affected by the recession. Where do teens get their money? A survey of 2000 teens showed that 47% of them get some money from their parents. Find a 95% confidence interval for the proportion of teens who get some money from their parents.

Given information: $p = 0.47$
$n = 2000$

Calculations:

Standard error $= \sqrt{\dfrac{p(1-p)}{n}} = \sqrt{\dfrac{0.47(1-0.47)}{2000}} = 0.011$

Error $= e = z_{\alpha/2}\sqrt{\dfrac{p(1-p)}{n}} = (1.96)\ (0.011) = 0.022$

Lower bound $= p - e = 0.47 - 0.02 = 0.45$

Upper bound $= p + e = 0.47 + 0.02 = 0.49$

So we can state that we are 95% confident that the percentage of all teens who get money from their parents is between 45 and 49%. ■

TRY IT NOW!

Retirement Years ***Confidence Interval for π***

A survey shows that a growing number of Americans are willing to make sacrifices to become home owners despite increasing job and financial worries,. The Federal National Mortgage Association surveyed 1857 Americans and found that 67% would put off retirement for 10 years to own a home.

Find a 90% confidence interval for the proportion of all Americans who would put off retirement for 10 years to own a home.

7.11.2 Exercises—Learning It!

7.25 I asked 100 imaginary friends (only to avoid the time and cost of data collection) the following question: Do you regularly watch *The Simpsons*? Of the 100 friends, 35 of them answered yes.

(a) Calculate a 95% confidence interval for the "viewership" of this show.

(b) The network is considering canceling the show if less than one-third of the population regularly watches the show. Based on this information, what will the network do?

7.26 Many companies have been experiencing downsizing. There is some feeling that when rumors of a downsize begin to float through an organization, employees begin to use their sick days at a faster rate than normal for fear of losing them. Fifty employees were surveyed and asked whether they would use their sick days freely in the face of a potential downsizing. Of the 50 employees in the sample, 11 said they would.

ANS. $L = 0.652$, $U = 0.688$

(a) Find a 95% confidence interval for the proportion of employees who would begin to use their sick days freely when faced with a potential downsizing.

(b) Based on your confidence interval, what are some recommendations you might suggest to managers?

7.27 A poll of 450 registered Massachusetts voters found 46% of the Bay State voters opposed to allowing casino gambling in the state.

(a) Find a 95% confidence interval for the proportion of all Bay State voters opposed to allowing casino gambling in the state.

(b) Is 50% in the confidence interval? If so, what does this tell you? If not, what does this tell you?

(c) What would you recommend to the governor of Massachusetts, who is pushing for expanded gambling?

7.28 Thousands of years ago people hung the yellow blossoms of Saint-John's-wort over their doorways, hoping to ward off evil spirits. Today, German physicians write nearly 3 million prescriptions a year for pills made from extracts of the plant, meant to relieve depression. But doctors on the other side of the Atlantic haven't followed suit. Scientists in the United States say that there is no reliable evidence that the herb can help.

To find out more, researchers at the University of Munich and the University of Texas in San Antonio studied 1500 people with mild to moderate depression. One-third were treated with Saint-John's-wort, one-third were treated with antidepressant drugs, and one-third were treated with a placebo. The researchers found that after 6 weeks of treatment 64% of the people taking Saint-John's-wort pills felt markedly better, compared to 59% of those receiving synthetic antidepressant drugs.

(a) Construct a 95% confidence interval for the proportion of people who would feel markedly better using Saint-John's-wort pills.

(b) Construct a 95% confidence interval for the proportion of people who would feel markedly better using synthetic antidepressant drugs.

(c) Compare the two confidence intervals. Do they overlap at all? What is your recommendation to doctors?

7.29 In designing a new dormitory, a progressive university wishes to determine where students prefer to study in order to provide appropriate space. A survey of 100 randomly selected undergraduate students shows that 33% prefer to study in their room.

(a) Construct a 95% confidence interval for the proportion of students who prefer to study in their room.

(b) If the university has the option of making various-size rooms, what proportion of the rooms should be made larger to accommodate those who wish to study in their room?

7.30 A medium-size city hospital is concerned about the number of ventilator-acquired respiratory infections in each of the past 3 years. The random sample of infections were studied and the number of infections that were vent-related infections is shown in the table:

Year	Number of Infections	Number of Vent-Related Infections
1996	19	13
1997	14	11
1998	13	10

(a) Find the sample proportion of vent-related infections for each of the 3 years.

(b) Construct a confidence interval for the proportion of vent-related infections for each of the 3 years.

(c) Should the hospital be concerned that the proportion of vent-related infections is increasing? Justify your answer using the confidence intervals found in part (b).

7.12 SAMPLE SIZE CALCULATIONS

Confidence intervals are easy to calculate and are commonly used to provide interval estimates for either the population mean or the population proportion. In fact, often a newspaper article will report the sample mean or sample proportion and a number called the sampling error or margin of error.

Collect and Analyze the Data

EXAMPLE 7.16 Political Polls

Illustration of Sampling Error

According to an article written by the Associated Press and published in the *Springfield Union News* on October 23, 1996, a CNN–USA Today–Gallup tracking poll put the national polling gap at 23 points, with Clinton favored by 55%, Dole by 32%, and Perot by 8%. The survey of 754 likely voters had a 4-point margin of error. ■

This sampling error or margin of error is what we have labeled error. Thus, if you wanted to construct the confidence interval from such a report you simply need to add and subtract the sampling error to the point estimate.

Collect and Analyze the Data

EXAMPLE 7.17 Political Polls

Constructing the Confidence Interval

Continuing with the results of the CNN–USA Today–Gallup tracking poll, the proportion of voters who favor Clinton was 55% with a 4% margin of error. Thus, the percentage is between 51% and 59%. The article in the newspaper did not report the confidence level, but typically 95% confidence intervals are calculated. ■

7.12.1 Understanding the Error

Sampling error is due to the fact that only a piece of the population has been studied.

We have not really examined why this distance between the center of the confidence interval and either endpoint is called an *error*. As we have seen many times before, the term *sampling error* does not imply that you made an error. It does indicate that you have imperfect information about the population, since you studied only a sample of that population. There is another reason why this value is called an error. Consider the confidence interval calculated in Example 7.12 for the diaper manufacturer. In that example we found a 95% confidence interval for the mean diaper weight in grams, as shown here:

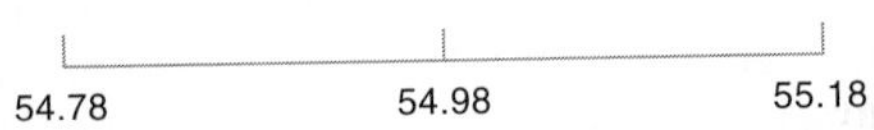

Remember that the value of 54.98 is the sample mean, $\overline{X}$. Suppose for the moment that we have found an interval that does contain μ but you don't know where in the interval μ is located. If you used $\overline{X}$ to estimate μ, what is the largest amount by which you could miss the value of μ? This *worst-case scenario* happens if μ is at either endpoint of the interval. If μ is at either of the endpoints, then our point estimate $\overline{X}$ is in error by the amount of $e = 0.20$ g. If μ is anywhere else in the interval, then our point estimate $\overline{X}$ is off by some amount less than 0.20 g. So we are 95% confident that the error is at most 0.20 g. Remember that a 95% confidence level tells you that 19 out of 20 intervals of this width contain the true population parameter. This is why we have labeled the distance from the middle of the interval to either endpoint as e, to stand for error. It is precisely this value that is often quoted in newspaper or research articles, although the newspaper rarely tells you what the corresponding level of confidence is. Typically, a 95% level of confidence has been used.

You might wonder if it is possible to specify the size of this error to achieve a certain level of accuracy. This is indeed often desirable. By specifying the amount of error that you can tolerate in a particular situation you are determining the sample size needed. Often you cannot achieve a particular level of accuracy because to do so would require a sample size that you cannot afford. This is the subject of the next subsection.

7.12.2 Determining the Sample Size

In Chapter 2, we identified the following factors that are important in determining the size of the sample needed:

- The amount of variation in the population
- The amount of error that can be tolerated
- The extent of resources available
- The size of the population

We now know enough statistics to develop a formula for the sample size that incorporates the first two of these factors. You should remember that these factors were identified as most important to the sample size determination.

Recall that the expression for e is one of the following, depending on whether you are estimating the mean, μ, or the proportion, π.

$$\text{Estimating } \mu: \qquad e = \frac{z_{\alpha/2}\sigma}{\sqrt{n}}$$

$$\text{Estimating } \pi: \qquad e = z_{\alpha/2}\sqrt{\frac{p(1-p)}{n}}$$

Each of these equations can be rewritten and solved for n, the sample size, by using some basic algebra. When this is done you get two equations for n that are algebraically equivalent to the two equations shown previously:

$$\text{Estimating } \mu: \qquad n = \frac{z_{\alpha/2}^2\sigma^2}{e^2} = \left(\frac{z_{\alpha/2}\sigma}{e}\right)^2$$

$$\text{Estimating } \pi: \qquad n = \frac{z_{\alpha/2}^2\, p(1-p)}{e^2}$$

Let's examine the equation for n if we are trying to estimate the population mean, μ. If we specify a certain level of confidence and a value for the maximum difference between $\overline{X}$ and μ, then we can calculate how large a sample we must select. Let's see how this formula could be used by the diaper manufacturer.

EXAMPLE 7.18 The Diaper Company

Sample Size Determination

Collect and Analyze the Data

The diaper manufacturer wants to be 95% confident that the estimate $\overline{X}$ is not in error by more than 0.10 g. That is, the diaper manufacturer wants to be sure that 19 out of 20 possible confidence intervals of width 0.20 g contain the true mean, μ. Recall that the manufacturing process has a standard deviation of 0.55 g. Thus, we have

$$e = 0.10 \text{ g}$$
$$z_{\alpha/2} = 1.96$$
$$\sigma = 0.55 \text{ g}$$

Using this information to calculate n yields

$$n = \frac{z_{\alpha/2}^2 \sigma^2}{e^2} = \frac{(1.96^2)(0.55^2)}{0.10^2} = 116.2$$

Since we can't sample a fractional diaper, we must round this value up to 117 diapers. ■

Always round up in sample size calculations.

For sample size calculations you should always round up to guarantee the level of confidence and error you have specified.

TRY IT NOW!

Bottle Filling ***Finding the sample size***

How many bottles does the bottle manufacturer need to sample to be 98% confident that the error is at most 0.05 oz? Remember that the population standard deviation is 0.1 oz.

Ways to handle situations in which the standard deviation is unknown

Notice that we needed a value for the population standard deviation to calculate n. If this is unknown then we must estimate it. Unfortunately, often we need to take a sample to estimate σ but we need σ to figure out how large our sample needs to be. This is a classic "catch 22" situation. There appears to be no way out.

Fortunately, there are a couple of ways to handle this dilemma. First of all, we could take a small sample to get a rough estimate of the standard deviation and use this in the formula for n. Suppose that we took a sample of size 10 and we used this sample to calculate the sample standard deviation, s. This value of s can then be used as an estimate for σ and plugged into the formula for n. Suppose when we do this the formula tells us that we need a sample of size $n = 55$. Well, we already have data on 10 observations so we need an additional 45 to complete the sample. Another way is to use information about the variability of a similar product or process. This may not be perfect but it will give a rough idea of the value of σ that can, in turn, be used in the sample size calculation.

For you to be more confident, the sample size must be larger.

Very often the sample size determined from the formula cannot be collected because of limited resources (i.e., cost). If this happens then you must be willing to accept a lower level of confidence or tolerate a higher value of e or both. Let's examine the impact on n of varying the level of confidence. Before we do the calculations, let's see what we might anticipate. We know that as the level of confidence increases, the z value also increases. Since z is in the numerator of the formula for n, we would expect the sample size needed to increase as the level of confidence increases. This should make intuitive sense as well. For us to be more confident, the sample size must be larger.

ANS: $n = 22$

EXAMPLE 7.19 The Diaper Company

Collect and Analyze the Data

Sample Sizes for Various Increasing Levels of Confidence Require Increasing Sample Sizes

Suppose the diaper manufacturer considers several different levels of confidence. The sample sizes needed to achieve an error of at most 0.10 g for various levels of confidence are calculated here:

$$\text{90\% confidence level:} \quad n = \frac{z_{\alpha/2}\sigma^2}{e^2} = \frac{(1.645^2)(0.55^2)}{0.10^2} = 81.9 \text{ rounded up to } 82$$

$$\text{95\% confidence level:} \quad n = \frac{z^2_{\alpha/2}\sigma^2}{e^2} = \frac{(1.96^2)(0.55^2)}{0.10^2} = 116.2 \text{ rounded up to } 117$$

$$\text{98\% confidence level:} \quad n = \frac{z^2_{\alpha/2}\sigma^2}{e^2} = \frac{(2.33^2)(0.55^2)}{0.10^2} = 164.2 \text{ rounded up to } 165$$

$$\text{99\% confidence level:} \quad n = \frac{z^2_{\alpha/2}\sigma^2}{e^2} = \frac{(2.58^2)(0.55^2)}{0.10^2} = 201.4 \text{ rounded up to } 202$$

■

If the sample size you calculate is too expensive, the other way you can cut costs is to increase the size of the error you can tolerate. Let's see what happens to the sample size as the maximum error is increased. Again, a quick look at the formula for n shows us that the value for e is in the denominator. So by increasing e we will be dividing by a larger number and hence the sample size needed will be smaller. Intuitively, this, too, makes sense. If you can tolerate a larger error, then you can take a smaller sample. Let's look at the diaper manufacturer from this perspective.

As the maximum error increases, the sample size decreases.

EXAMPLE 7.20 The Diaper Company

Collect and Analyze the Data

Impact of Larger Errors

Consider the following values for the maximum error that the diaper company is willing to tolerate in its estimate of μ. In all cases they wish to be 95% confident that the error is at most the specified value.

$$\text{Error} = 0.10 \text{ g} \quad n = \frac{z^2_{\alpha/2}\sigma^2}{e^2} = \frac{(1.96^2)(0.55^2)}{0.10^2} = 116.2 \text{ rounded up to } 117$$

$$\text{Error} = 0.15 \text{ g} \quad n = \frac{z^2_{\alpha/2}\sigma^2}{e^2} = \frac{(1.96^2)(0.55^2)}{0.15^2} = 51.6 \text{ rounded up to } 52$$

$$\text{Error} = 0.20 \text{ g} \quad n = \frac{z^2_{\alpha/2}\sigma^2}{e^2} = \frac{(1.96^2)(0.55^2)}{0.20^2} = 29.05 \text{ rounded up to } 30$$

$$\text{Error} = 0.25 \text{ g} \quad n = \frac{z^2_{\alpha/2}\sigma^2}{e^2} = \frac{(1.96^2)(0.55^2)}{0.25^2} = 18.6 \text{ rounded up to } 19$$

■

Calculations of the sample size for situations when you wish to estimate the population proportion, π, are done in a similar manner. The only difference is the particular formula to be used. Consider the teens who are receiving money from their parents. We looked at this situation in Example 7.15.

EXAMPLE 7.21 *Beverly Hills, 90210*

Collect and Analyze the Data

Calculation of Sample Size for Proportions

How many teens must be sampled to be 95% confident that our estimate of π is off by at most 5%? Remember that the point estimate is p, the sample proportion or percentage. If we want the sample proportion to be in error by at most 5%, then $e = 0.05$.

The formula for n is

$$n = \frac{z_{\alpha/2}^2 p(1 - p)}{e^2}$$

Plugging in the values we know gives us

$$n = \frac{(1.96^2)p(1 - p)}{0.05^2}$$

At this point we realize that we can't continue without a value for p but we need a sample to get a sample proportion. ■

This is again a circular problem. We need p to find n but we need n to get p! There are two approaches you can take here. First of all, if you have any information about the value of p from previous samples or experience, then you should use that information as an estimate of p. If you have no information at all, then you should use a value of $p = 0.50$ in the formula for the sample size calculation. When you do this the sample size that is calculated is as large as it can be for the specified confidence level and error. It is the most conservative approach you can take and will often lead to a sample size larger than you really need. Let's finish Example 7.21 by using a value of $p = 0.50$.

Collect and Analyze the Data

EXAMPLE 7.22 ***Beverly Hills, 90210*** **(cont'd)**

Sample Size Calculation for Proportion

Using a value of $p = 0.50$ in the formula for n gives us

$$n = \frac{(1.96^2)p(1 - p)}{0.05^2} = \frac{(1.96^2)(0.5)(1 - 0.5)}{0.05^2} = 384.16$$

which is rounded up to 385 teenagers. ■

TRY IT NOW!

Retirement Years ***Sample Size Calculation for π***

How many Americans must be sampled to determine the percentage who would put off retirement for 10 years to own a home? The estimate should not differ from the actual population proportion by more than 3% with a confidence of 90%.

ANS: 752 AMERICANS

The conclusions that we reached about what happens to the required sample size as the confidence level and the error vary are the same for proportions as for means. As the confidence level increases, the sample size needed to estimate the population proportion also increases. As the error that can be tolerated increases, the sample size needed decreases.

7.12.3 Exercises—Learning It!

7.31 How many stores must be sampled for the woman who wants to buy a ranch to be 95% confident that the error in estimating the average fat content per pound in steaks sold in the Portland, Maine, area is at most 0.05 oz? The standard deviation of fat content is known to be 0.30 oz.

7.32 How many months must be sampled for analysts to be 99% confident that the error in estimating the average monthly price of peanut butter is at most $0.02? Assume the standard deviation is $0.035.

7.33 How many days must be observed for the grocery store chain to be 90% confident that the error in estimating the average number of vehicles passing a certain location is at most 10 vehicles? *Requires Exercise 7.16*

7.34 How many viewers must be surveyed to be 98% confident that the estimate of the viewership is in error by at most 3%? *Requires Exercise 7.25*

7.35 How many employees must be sampled to be 95% confident that the error in estimating the proportion of employees who would begin to use sick days at a faster rate when rumors of downsizing are circulating is at most 0.02? *Requires Exercise 7.26*

7.13 Executive Summary

THE DIAPER COMPANY

Business Analysis...

TO: Quality Manager
FROM: Erica Q. Analyst
RE: Monitoring diaper weights

This company is committed to providing quality disposable diapers to our customers. We know that one of the important characteristics to the customer is the weight of the diaper because it is related to how well the diaper will absorb liquid. Target values for diaper weights are $\mu = 55$ g with a standard deviation of $\sigma = 0.55$ g. My team and I have been investigating which statistic to use to estimate the average of all the diaper weights being produced to be sure the process is running correctly.

A sample of 5 diapers was taken every hour and each diaper was weighed. The average weight and the median weight for each sample were calculated. The average weight is the sum of the 5 diaper weights divided by 5 and the median weight is the third highest weight in the sample of 5. The results of the first 10 hours of production for today are shown here:

Hour	Average Weight (g)	Median Weight (g)
1	54.80	54.50
2	55.13	54.85
3	54.81	54.42
4	54.58	54.56
5	55.18	55.50
6	55.28	55.23

(continued)

Hour	Average Weight (g)	Median Weight (g)
7	55.03	54.91
8	55.23	55.37
9	54.72	54.11
10	55.05	55.21
Average	55.06	54.97
Standard Deviation	0.22	0.51

As you can see, the median weight fluctuates much more than the sample mean. This is clear when you look at the numbers themselves but also when you compare the standard deviation of the 10 means to that of the 10 medians. It is known that the sample mean is a better estimator of the population mean and my study confirms this. I recommend that only the sample mean be calculated for each sample.

As you look at the sample means you will see that they fluctuate around 55.06 g. To help the operators on the floor, we must tell them how high and how low the sample mean can go before they should suspect a problem. If the process is running correctly, than 99.7% of the sample means should be between 54.25 g and 55.75 g. This represents a spread of 3 standard deviations around the target mean of 55 g. If a sample mean is below 54.25 g or above 55.75 g, then someone should investigate what might be wrong. For the first 10 hours of production, there were no sample means beyond these boundaries. The data and these limits are shown in the following graph.

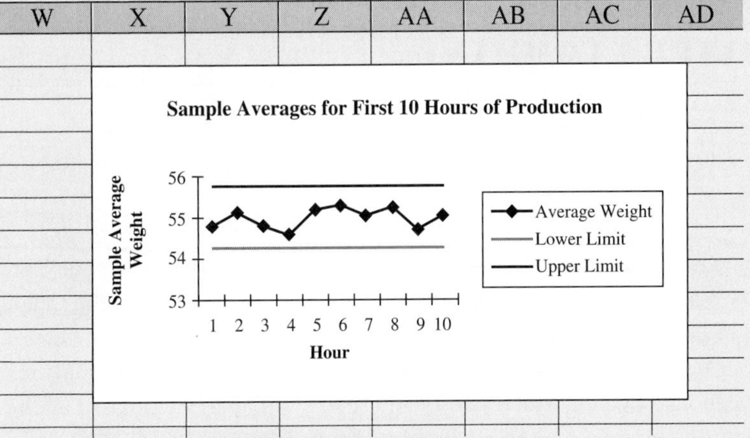

Remember that these cutoff values are based on a sample size of $n = 5$. Although this is a small sample, I know from previous studies that the individual diaper weights have a bell-shaped distribution and therefore I can use the theory to establish the cutoff values despite the small sample size. If the sample size changes, the cutoff values will need to be recalculated.

I recommend taking a sample of 5 diapers, weighing each of them, and calculating the average weight each hour. If the average goes lower than 54.25 g or higher than 55.75 g, then the quality manager should be contacted.

The *Wall Street Journal* is a major source of current business news and information for the business community. If your professor has arranged for your class to have access to the Business Extra feature, you can go to it now and see the techniques of this chapter in action today. Go to the Wiley Web site at http://www.wiley.com/college/pelosi, and click on Business Extra!

7.14 USING EXCEL TO FIND CONFIDENCE INTERVALS

Excel does not have a tool that automatically calculates confidence intervals. To do this, you will have to use some of the functions you already learned about in a formula. In this section, we will explain how to do so for a large-sample confidence interval for the mean. We will also explain how to use the Excel functions for the t distribution.

7.14.1 Large-Sample Confidence Intervals for the Mean

To find a confidence interval for a population parameter, you need a point estimate and a formula for the error of the estimate. For the population mean, when σ is known or when n is large $(n > 30)$, the formula for the confidence interval is

$$\overline{X} \pm z_{\alpha/2}\frac{\sigma}{\sqrt{n}}$$

To find a confidence interval for the mean using Excel, you must have a point estimate, $\overline{X}$. You can obtain this from the Descriptive Statistics in the Data Analysis Tools or by using the **AVERAGE** function. You will also need a value for σ, or else a sample estimate, s, based on a large sample. The last thing that you need is the z value, which you will obtain using the **NORMSINV** function discussed in Chapter 6.

Figure 7.14 shows a portion of an Excel worksheet that contains a sample of 50 diaper weights, and a set of summary statistics for the data.

To calculate a 95% confidence interval for the true weight of a diaper, follow these steps:

1. Position the cursor in the cell that you want to contain the upper limit of the confidence interval. In this case, we will use E1, which is just to the right of the summary data.
2. Since you want to let Excel know that you are entering a formula, start the formula by typing an equal sign "=". All formulas in Excel must start with an equal sign.

	A	B	C	D
1	**Weight**		*Weight*	
2	55.87			
3	55.35		Mean	54.993
4	54.50		Standard Error	0.096962964
5	53.97		Median	54.915
6	54.29		Mode	54.4
7	54.85		Standard Deviation	0.685631691
8	54.79		Sample Variance	0.470090816
9	54.65		Kurtosis	-0.848226678
10	55.56		Skewness	0.078374807
11	55.82		Range	2.84
12	54.40		Minimum	53.6
13	56.44		Maximum	56.44
14	54.11		Sum	2749.65
15	54.67		Count	50
16	54.56			
17	54.60			

FIGURE 7.14 Diaper data and summary statistics

What you want to calculate is $\overline{X} + z_{0.025}\frac{s}{\sqrt{n}}$. We will use the sample standard deviation because our sample size is large enough.

3. After you type the equal sign, position the cursor on the cell that contains the value of $\overline{X}$, in this case D3. If you look at the status line or the cell itself, you see that the cell D3 is entered in the formula. Since in our confidence interval we want to use that *specific* cell all the time for the sample mean, you need to change the cell reference to an absolute reference.
4. With the cursor still in the cell, press F4. The cell reference D3 will change to $D$3. The $ tells Excel to look *always* in column D, *always* in row 3 for this value. This is important to know when you copy formulas.
5. Now, we want to add to $\overline{X}$ the quantity $z_{0.025}\frac{s}{\sqrt{n}}$. Type in + and then type **NORMSINV(0.975)**.

Remember: The NORMSINV function returns the z value for the lower tail probability.

   Remember that the quantity $\frac{s}{\sqrt{n}}$ is referred to as the standard error of the mean. When you look at the summary statistics that Excel calculates, you see that the second value is indeed the standard error of the mean. This was not meaningful to us when we first looked at numerical descriptors, so we did not talk about it then. Now we will use it to finish our confidence interval.

6. Type in a multiplication sign, "*", and position the cursor in the cell that contains the standard error, in this case, D4. Again, press F4 to make the cell an absolute reference.
7. The finished formula is shown in Figure 7.15.
8. Hit Enter and the result, 55.18304, will be displayed.

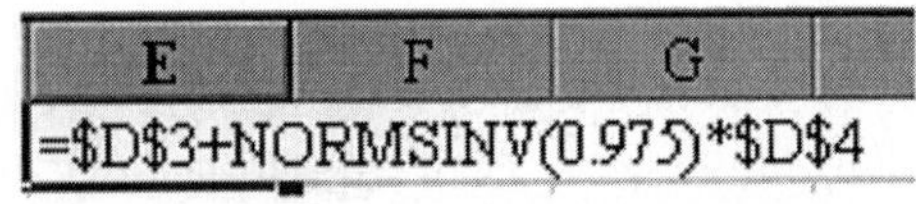

FIGURE 7.15 Formula for upper limit of confidence interval

You can calculate the lower confidence limit by typing the same equation in the cell next to the upper limit. Be sure to change the z value to a negative by using **NORMSINV(0.025).** To avoid retyping the whole equation, you can simply copy the one you just did and paste it into a new cell. Then, move to the display of the equation in the status bar and edit the **NORMSINV** parameter.

When you calculated the summary statistics, you might have noticed that there was an option available for Confidence Level for the Mean. Checking that box will add a new line to the end of the summary statistics output, which is supposed to be $z_{0.025}\frac{s}{\sqrt{n}}$. We have not used this option because the calculation is wrong (not drastically, but it is definitely not correct).

7.14.2 The *t* Distribution in Excel

The difference between large- and small-sample confidence intervals for the mean is in the sampling distribution of $\overline{X}$. You know that when σ is unknown and the sample size is not greater than 30, the Student's t distribution applies. The formula for the confidence interval is

$$\overline{X} \pm t_{\alpha/2,n-1} \frac{s}{\sqrt{n}}$$

To calculate small-sample confidence intervals for the population mean with Excel, you will use the **TINV** function to get the appropriate *t* values.

Just like other functions in Excel, the **TINV** function needs some input parameters. The format of the **TINV** function is **TINV(probability, deg_freedom).** The value that you input for **probability** is the value of α, the total tail area probability. The value for **deg_freedom** is $n - 1$, the degrees of freedom. As an example, for a 95% confidence interval for μ, based on a sample of size 25, the function would look like **TINV(0.05,24)** and would return the value 2.063898. There is no lower *t* value in Excel. To obtain the lower confidence limit, you simply subtract the quantity $t_{\alpha/2,\,n-1} \frac{s}{\sqrt{n}}$ from $\overline{X}$.

7.14.3 Confidence Intervals with KADDSTAT

KADDSTAT provides statistical functions that allow you to find confidence intervals for both means and proportions. The basic steps are the same for each, but the input supplied by the user changes. We will give detailed directions for the small-sample confidence interval for the mean.

From the KADD menu, select **Confidence intervals > One sample > Population Mean using t.** The dialog box shown in Figure 7.16 opens.

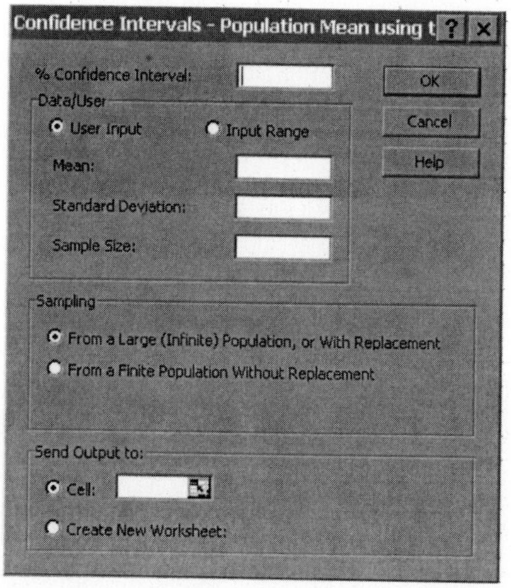

FIGURE 7.16 Dialog box for Confidence Intervals (User Input)

1. First, indicate the level of confidence, as a percentage, that you want to use.
2. You have the option of calculating a confidence interval either from raw data or from summary statistics (like a problem from a textbook). Select **User Input** if you already have the summary statistics or **Input Range** if you have raw data. As you can see from Figure 7.16, for **User Input,** you must supply Excel with the mean, the standard deviation, and the sample size. If you select **Input Range,** the dialog box will change as shown in Figure 7.17 (page 356), and you will input the location of the data. For **Input Range** you must also indicate whether the data have a header row.

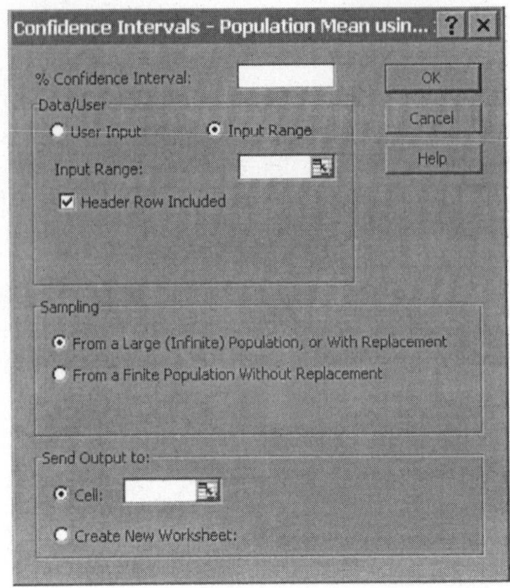

FIGURE 7.17 Dialog box for Confidence Intervals (Input Range)

3. Next you must indicate how the sampling was done, from a large (infinite) population or from a finite population without replacement.
4. Indicate where you want the output to appear and click **OK.**

Figures 7.18 and 7.19 show the dialog box and output for the first 10 diaper weights shown in Figure 7.14.

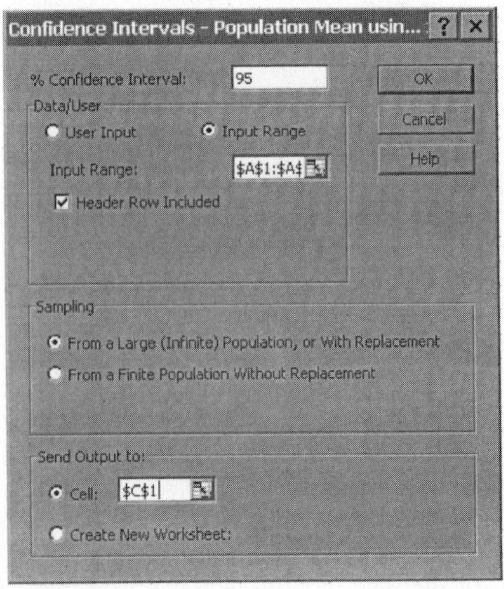

FIGURE 7.18 Completed dialog box for 10 diaper weights

C	D	E
Confidence Interval for Mean		
using t from Infinite Population		
or with Replacement		
Lower limit =	54.4967	
Upper limit =	55.4333	
Margin for Error (Half Width) =	0.4683	
Mean =	54.9650	
Standard Deviation =	0 .6547	
% Confidence Interval =	95%	
Sample Size =	10	

FIGURE 7.19 Output for Confidence Interval for Small Sample using *t*

CHAPTER 7 SUMMARY

This chapter has covered the basics of estimating population parameters. In particular, you learned how to estimate the average of a numeric characteristic of a population, μ, and the proportion of a population that has a certain characteristic, π. The estimates are calculated from a sample selected from the population. Each sample would therefore yield a slightly different estimate of the population parameter. Thus, the estimators are themselves random variables. Just like the random variables you studied in Chapter 6, the estimators have a distribution. When the random variable is an estimator, the distribution is called a sampling distribution. The sampling distribution has a mean and a standard deviation, which is called the standard error.

You have learned how to use the sampling distribution of $\overline{X}$ to calculate probabilities and make inferences about μ. You have also learned how to create confidence intervals for μ and for π. Finally, you have learned how to calculate the required sample size to achieve a certain level of precision with a specified confidence.

Key Terms

Key Term	Definition	Page Reference
Central Limit Theorem	The **Central Limit Theorem** states that in random sampling from a population with mean μ and standard deviation σ, when n is large enough, the distribution of $\overline{X}$ is approximately normal with a mean, $\mu_{\overline{X}}$, equal to μ and a standard deviation, $\sigma_{\overline{X}}$, equal to $\sigma/\sqrt{n}$.	311
Confidence interval	A **confidence interval** or an **interval estimate** is a range of values with an associated probability or confidence level, $1 - \alpha$. The probability quantifies the chance that the interval contains the true population parameter.	325
Point estimate	A **point estimate** is a single number calculated from sample data. It is used to estimate a parameter of the population.	298
Point estimator	A **point estimator** is the formula or rule that is used to calculate the point estimate for a particular set of data.	298

(continued)

Key Terms (*Continued*)

Term	Definition	Page reference
Sampling distribution	The distribution of a point estimator or a sample statistic is called a **sampling distribution.**	310
Standard error	The **standard error** is the standard deviation of the sampling distribution of a point estimator. It measures how much the point estimator or sample statistic varies from sample to sample.	310
Unbiased estimator	An **unbiased estimator** yields an estimate that is fair. It neither systematically overestimates the parameter nor systematically underestimates the parameter.	306

Key Formulas

Description	Formula	Page Reference
z score for $\overline{X}$	$z = \dfrac{\overline{X} - \mu_{\overline{X}}}{\sigma_{\overline{X}}}$	309
Mean of $\overline{X}$	$\mu_{\overline{X}} = \mu$	311
Standard error of $\overline{X}$	$\sigma_{\overline{X}} = \sigma/\sqrt{n}$	311
Confidence interval for μ when σ is known	Error: $e = \dfrac{z_{\alpha/2}\,\sigma}{\sqrt{n}}$ Width of the interval: $w = 2e$ Lower bound: $L = \overline{X} - e$ Upper bound: $U = \overline{X} + e$	327
Large-sample confidence interval for μ when σ is unknown	Error: $e = \dfrac{z_{\alpha/2}s}{\sqrt{n}}$ Width of the interval: $w = 2e$ Lower bound: $L = \overline{X} - e$ Upper bound: $U = \overline{X} + e$	329
Small-sample confidence interval for μ when σ is unknown, normal population	Error: $e = \dfrac{t_{\alpha/2,n-1}s}{\sqrt{n}}$ Width of the interval: $w = 2e$ Lower bound: $L = \overline{X} - e$ Upper bound: $U = \overline{X} + e$	339
Confidence interval for π	Error: $e = z_{\alpha/2}\sqrt{\dfrac{\pi(1-\pi)}{n}} \cong z_{\alpha/2}\sqrt{\dfrac{p(1-p)}{n}}$ Width of the interval: $w = 2e$ Lower bound: $L = p - e$ Upper bound: $U = p + e$	343
Sample size for estimating μ	$n = \dfrac{z_{\alpha/2}^2\,\sigma^2}{e^2}$	347
Sample size for estimating π	$n = \dfrac{z_{\alpha/2}^2\,p(1-p)}{e^2}$	347

CHAPTER 7 EXERCISES

Learning It!

7.36 The manufacturer of 15-oz breakfast cereal boxes samples and weighs 5 boxes every hour. The observations for 7 hours are shown here: *Requires Example 7.11*

14.91	15.23	15.34	15.40	15.48	15.59	15.62
14.96	15.24	15.34	15.42	15.49	15.60	15.62
15.11	15.28	15.36	15.45	15.50	15.60	15.63
15.21	15.30	15.38	15.46	15.52	15.61	15.64
15.22	15.30	15.39	15.48	15.58	15.61	15.67

(a) Find the upper and lower confidence limits for the average weight of the breakfast cereals. Use $\alpha = 0.05$. Is the value of 15.00 oz contained in the interval?

(b) What does that tell you about the filling process?

7.37 A company that buys blank VHS tapes for video recording is concerned about the actual amount of time that the tapes are able to record. The tapes are rated at 120 minutes, but the company knows there is variation in the actual time that the tapes can be used. The company collects data on 25 randomly selected tapes and finds the recording times listed here: *Requires Exercise 7.5*

116	118	119	119	120
117	118	119	119	121
117	118	119	120	121
117	119	119	120	121
117	119	119	120	121

(a) Find the average and the standard deviation of these data.

(b) Find a 95% confidence interval for the average recording time, assuming that the recording times are normally distributed.

(c) What do you conclude about the claim that the tapes have an average of 120 minutes of usable recording time? Use the confidence interval to support your conclusion.

7.38 A cross-country runner is evaluating his times against a team average of 18.5 minutes. The standard deviation of his times was 0.25 minute. This season the runner's average is 17.0 minutes for 10 races.

(a) Assuming that race times are normally distributed, calculate the *z*-score for the runner's average time.

(b) Using the *z*-score you found in part (a), decide whether this runner is unusally fast compared to the team.

7.39 An insurance company is concerned about the amount of time it takes for operators who are responding to calls to the 800 number to access the database. It calls this time the response time. The Management Information Systems (MIS) department claims that the average response time is 10 seconds. A sample is taken and 40 response times are recorded. The results of generating descriptive statistics in Excel are shown here:

Summary Statistics for Response Time

Mean	9.95656397
Standard Error	0.02942547
Median	9.9616274
Mode	#N/A
Standard Deviation	0.18610301
Sample Variance	0.03463433
Kurtosis	−0.29568133
Skewness	−0.31707278
Range	0.79489018
Minimum	9.49771882

(*continued*)

Summary Statistics for Response Time	
Maximum	10.292609
Sum	398.262559
Count	40

(a) What are the average and standard deviation of the response times?

(b) Calculate the standard error of $\overline{X}$ using the standard deviation and n.

(c) Do you see the number calculated in part (b) anywhere in the output?

(d) Calculate the z-score for the average response time.

(e) Based on the z-score, do you think the MIS department's claim is correct?

7.40 A company concerned about the health of its employees has offered the employees free membership in a local health club. One year after this benefit was adopted, a survey of 50 employees was done to determine the average number of hours per week they exercise. The 50 employees surveyed exercised an average of 3.5 hours a week with a standard deviation of 0.5 hour. The national average number of hours of exercise per week is 3 hours a week.

(a) Find the z-score for the average of 3.5 hours.

(b) Display the sampling distribution of $\overline{X}$.

(c) Based on the z-score, do you think the employees of this company exercise more than the national average?

7.41 The Bureau of Labor Statistics publishes a great deal of data on a monthly basis. The following data on the average price of bread were extracted from the World Wide Web.

Average Price Data
Series Catalog:
Series ID: APU0000702111
Area: U.S. city average
Item: Bread, white, pan, per lb (453.6 g)

Year	Jan	Feb	Mar	Apr	May	Jun	Jul	Aug	Sep	Oct	Nov	Dec
1997	0.862	0.858	0.855	0.855	0.854	0.874	0.872	0.872	0.885	0.899	0.897	0.884
1998	0.855	0.860	0.853	0.863	0.866	0.859	0.867	0.869	0.860	0.849	0.855	0.866
1999	0.872	0.880	0.883	0.897	0.886	0.885	0.893	0.884	0.878	0.889	0.899	0.899

Treating these 3 years of data as a sample, find a 90% confidence interval for the average price of bread. Assume that the standard deviation is $0.02 per pound.

7.42 In an effort to improve the quality of the CD players that your company makes, you have started to sample the component parts that you purchase from an outside supplier. You will accept the shipment of parts only if there is less than 1% defectives in the shipment. Recognizing that you cannot test the entire shipment (or population), you select a sample of 25 components to test. You find 3 defectives in the sample of 25.

(a) Find a 90% confidence interval for the proportion of components in the population that are defective.

(b) Based on your confidence interval, should you accept the shipment? Why or why not?

7.43 A nationwide survey of practicing physicians will be taken to estimate μ, the true mean number of prescriptions written per day. The desired margin of sampling error is 0.75. A pilot study revealed that a reasonable planning value for the population standard deviation is 5.

(a) If the desired level of confidence was 99%, how many physicians should be contacted in the survey to estimate μ?

(b) If the desired confidence level were lowered to 95%, what would be the sample size?

(c) Discuss the results of parts (a) and (b).

7.44 A hotel is studying the proportions of rooms that are not ready when customers check in to the hotel.

(a) How many rooms must be in the sample for the hotel to be 95% confident that the margin of error is at most 1%?

(b) How many rooms must be in the sample for the hotel to be 95% confident that the margin of error is at most 3%?

Thinking About It!

7.45 Suppose you are studying the length of stay at a hospital and the population had a mean of 8 days with a standard deviation of 2.5 days. The length of hospital stay has a normal distribution.

(a) Display the population distribution of hospital stay.

(b) If you observed the hospital stay of 20 patients, find the standard error of $\overline{X}$. Display the sampling distribution of $\overline{X}$ on the same graph as part (a) using a different color pen or pencil.

(c) If you observed the hospital stay of 30 patients, find the standard error of $\overline{X}$. Display the sampling distribution of $\overline{X}$ on the same graph as (a) and (b) using a different color.

(d) If you observed the hospital stay of 80 patients, find the standard error of $\overline{X}$. Display the sampling distribution of $\overline{X}$ on the same graph as (a) and (b) using a different color.

(e) What happens to the sampling distribution of $\overline{X}$ as the sample size increases? What does this tell you about the accuracy of $\overline{X}$ as an estimator for μ?

7.46 Suppose you are studying the salaries of 3 different populations that all have the same average salary: μ = \$25,000. The 3 populations have different standard deviations: accounting major, $\sigma = 1000$; computer information systems major, $\sigma = 2000$; and marketing major, $\sigma = 3000$. You select a sample of 30 from each population.

(a) Find the standard error of $\overline{X}$ for each of the three groups.

(b) What happens to the standard error as the population variability increases?

(c) What does this tell you about the accuracy of $\overline{X}$ as an estimator for μ ?

7.47 The 43 executives listed in Exercise 7.14 all work for firms that are headquartered or have significant operations in western Massachusetts. *Requires Exercise 7.14*

(a) How does this affect the usefulness of the confidence interval for μ?

(b) These firms can be divided into two groups: manufacturing (M) and nonmanufacturing (NM). Compute a 90% confidence interval for the mean executive salary for each of the two groups assuming the salaries are normally distributed.

(c) Do these confidence intervals overlap? If so, what do you think that indicates? If not, what does that tell you?

7.48 Are women more fully represented in politics in Europe today? The data shown here give the percentage of women in government as of June 1997 for some of the countries that belong to the Council of Europe.

Country	No. of Government Posts	No. of Men	No. of Women	% of Women
Sweden	22	11	11	50.00
Norway	19	11	8	42.11
Finland	18	12	6	33.33
France	27	19	8	29.63
Netherlands	14	10	4	28.57
Spain	15	11	4	26.67
Denmark	19	14	5	26.32
Austria	16	12	4	25.00
Luxembourg	12	9	3	25.00
United Kingdom	22	17	5	22.73
Slovak Republic	18	14	4	22.22
Italy	56	44	12	21.43
Liechtenstein	5	4	1	20.00

(*continued*)

CHAPTER 8

HYPOTHESIS TESTING: AN INTRODUCTION

THE TISSUE STRENGTH PROBLEM

Business Dilemma...

A manufacturer of tissues has received numerous complaints about its products. One of the frequent complaints is about the strength of the tissue. As we have noted many times before in this book, all companies are paying increasingly more attention to the customer in an attempt to "totally delight the customer." Clearly, in this case, the customers are not totally delighted with the tissues made by this company. Management has asked the statisticians to investigate the source of this problem by taking a sample.

There are two possible explanations. One possibility is that manufacturing is producing tissues that are not so strong as the specifications. In this case, an adjustment may be needed to the manufacturing process. The second possibility is that despite the fact that manufacturing is making the tissues according to specifications, the customers prefer stronger tissues. In this case, an adjustment to the specifications may be in order.

Your boss has asked you to find out whether the tissues are in fact as strong as they are designed to be. There are two measures of tissue strength: machine-directional strength *(MDStrength)* measured in lb/ream and cross-directional strength *(CDStrength)* also measured in lb/ream. You decide to collect data on 3 different days. A portion of the data file is shown in the margin.

Day	MD Strength	CD Strength
1	1006	422
1	994	448
1	1032	423
1	875	435
1	1043	445
1	962	464
1	973	472
1	1036	489
1	1084	440

The product specifications for *MDStrength* state that the mean should be 1000 lb/ream with standard deviation of 50 lb/ream. *CDStrength* is supposed to have a mean of 450 lb/ream with a standard deviation of 25 lb/ream.

8.1 CHAPTER OBJECTIVES

From Chapter 7 we learned that the sample mean is a good point estimate of the population mean. Suppose we took a sample of tissues and measured the strength of each tissue. We can use the data to calculate a sample mean strength. If that sample mean doesn't agree with the target mean strength, then we should tell the boss that the process must be adjusted. Simple, right? Well, not quite.

Remember: A point estimate is a single number, calculated from sample data, which is used to estimate a population parameter.

After a bit more thought, you remember that although the sample mean, $\overline{X}$, is a single number for any particular sample, if you pick a different sample you will probably get a different sample mean. In fact, there are many different possible values you could get for the sample mean, and virtually none of them will actually equal the true population mean, μ.

EXAMPLE 8.1 **Tissue Strength Problem**

Understand the Problem

Impact of Sampling Error

Suppose that you take a sample of tissues and find the sample average *MDStrength* to be 1010 lb. Clearly, the sample average, $\overline{X} = 1010$, does not exactly equal the specification of 1000. Does this mean that the process is not running correctly? Probably not, but we will need a more precise way of deciding. An hour later you might take another sample and get a sample *MDStrength* of 995 lb. Again, you need to decide whether the process is running correctly on the basis of that sample average, $\overline{X} =$ 995 lb. Clearly, the sample average will be different each time you take a sample and will almost never be equal to 1000 even if the process is running correctly!

Remember that you are examining only a sample of the population of tissues, and each tissue manufactured has a slightly different MD strength. The variability in the tissue strengths combined with the fact that you have data on only a piece of the population leads to variability in the sample averages, the $\overline{X}$'s. Recall that the variability of $\overline{X}$ is called the standard error and it is based on the amount of variability in the population, σ, and the sample size, n. ■

This example shows you that you should not simply compare the $\overline{X}$ value you get from the sample to the target mean strength, because even if the tissues were being made properly, the $\overline{X}$ that you observe will almost never be equal to that number. So, a simple point estimate will not do the job.

This chapter introduces the major concepts and philosophy of a technique called **hypothesis testing,** which will do the job. You might remember that when we talked about the need for inferential statistics we said that most of the techniques of inferential statistics could be classified as either estimation tools or hypothesis testing tools. This chapter lays the groundwork for hypothesis testing. The remaining chapters of the text rely heavily on the ideas developed in this chapter.

Specifically, in this chapter we will look at:

- What Is a Hypothesis Test?
- Overview of Hypotheses to Be Tested
- The Pieces of a Hypothesis Test
- Two-Tail Tests of the Mean: Large Sample
- What Error Could You Be Making?
- Which Theory Should Go Into the Null Hypothesis?
- One-Tail Tests of the Mean: Large Sample

8.2 WHAT IS A HYPOTHESIS TEST?

The word **hypothesis** has the same meaning in statistics as it does in everyday use. What does this word mean to you? Some possibilities are

- an idea
- an assumption
- a guess
- a theory

You actually work with many hypotheses on a daily basis without even realizing it. For example, you might think that exercising on a regular basis improves your overall ability to study. Your hypothesis, in this case, is that there is a relationship between exercising and effective studying. To decide whether your hypothesis is correct you might use your recollection of past experiences.

Often the hypothesis is about the value of a parameter such as the population mean.

In statistics, a ***hypothesis*** is an idea, an assumption, or a theory about the behavior of one or more variables in one or more populations.

The sample data are your evidence and on the basis of these data you must make a decision.

Once a hypothesis is formed, you must **test** it. You must decide whether to believe the hypothesis. The only information you have to help you decide is contained in your sample. Thus, to do a **hypothesis test,** you use the information in your sample data to help you decide whether you should believe the hypothesis. Basically, you are trying to decide whether the sample is consistent with the hypothesis (in which case you believe the hypothesis) or whether the sample is inconsistent with the hypothesis (in which case you choose not to believe it or to reject it).

A ***hypothesis test*** is a statistical procedure that involves formulating a hypothesis and using sample data to decide on the validity of the hypothesis.

The framework for all hypothesis tests is the same.

There are many different types of hypotheses that you could test and these are the subject of the next section. However, regardless of the specific hypothesis that you are testing, the basic procedure is the same. The purpose of this chapter is to explain the framework of the hypothesis testing procedure. The details of the test depend on the particular hypothesis that you are testing, but the purpose and general approach are the same for all tests. In fact, virtually all of the remaining chapters in this book are devoted to spelling out the details for the various tests you are likely to need for analyzing sample data and making informed business decisions. It is important that you not view these as separate and isolated chapters. They add flesh to the skeleton we will develop in this chapter. Think of each chapter as a variation on the same theme.

8.3 DESIGNING HYPOTHESES TO BE TESTED—AN OVERVIEW

Different types of data require different analysis tools

Let's start by thinking about what type of variables we might be examining. In Chapter 2 you learned that two major categories can be used to classify variables, *qualitative* and *quantitative*. The distinction was made because different techniques are used depending on the type of data you have. You have seen (Chapters 3–5 and 7) that different *descriptive* tools and point estimators are used, depending on what kind of data you wish to evaluate. Now we will see that there are different *inferential* tools for different kinds of data.

8.3.1 Hypotheses About Quantitative Variables

Sample data that are inherently numerical in form are called quantitative data. Recall from Chapter 6 that if we are analyzing a quantitative variable then we know that it can be described by its distribution. The distribution in turn can be described by parameters. Thus, if we are constructing a theory or hypothesis about a quantitative variable it might be a statement about

Hypotheses about a quantitative variable

- The shape of the distribution of the variable in one population
- The mean value, μ, of the variable in one population.
- How the mean value of the variable in one population, μ_1, compares to the mean value of the variable in a second population, μ_2
- The equality of the mean values of the variable in more than two populations
- The amount of variability, σ^2, of the variable in one population
- How the amount of variability of the variable in one population, σ_1^2, compares to the amount of variability of the variable in a second population, σ_2^2

All but the first bulleted item are generally referred to as tests on means and tests on variances. The first item requires a "goodness of fit" test. Goodness of fit tests are the subject of Chapter 15.

EXAMPLE 8.2 Tissue Strength Problem

Understand the Problem

Possible Hypotheses

For the problem that you are investigating for your boss, tissue strength is a quantitative variable. An example of each of the hypotheses just discussed is shown for this variable:

Type of Hypothesis	Specific Hypothesis
• The shape of the distribution of the variable in one population	The variable *MDStrength* has a normal distribution.
• The mean value, μ, of the variable in one population	The population mean *MDStrength* is equal to 1000 lb/ream.

(continued)

Type of Hypothesis	Specific Hypothesis
• How the mean value of the variable in one population compares to the mean value of the variable in a second population	The mean *MDStrength* of tissues made by machine 1 is greater than the mean *MDStrength* of tissues made by machine 2.
• The equality of the mean values of the variable in more than two populations	The mean *MDStrength* of tissues made by machines 1, 2, and 3 are equal.
• The amount of variability, σ^2, of the variable in one population	The variability of *MDStrength* of tissues is less than 625 $(\text{lb/ream})^2$. (Recall that the variance is the standard deviation squared.)
• How the amount of variability of the variable in one population compares to the amount of variability of the variable in a second population	The tissues made by machine 1 have more variability in the *MDStrength* variable than those tissues made by machine 2. ■

Remember: *Qualitative data describe a particular characteristic of a sample item.*

Notice that a qualitative variable, in this case the number of the machine that made the tissue, was used to divide the data into two or more populations. This is often the major use of a qualitative variable, particularly nominal data. Recall that nominal data are one type of qualitative data. They are data that are created by assigning numbers to different categories when the numbers have no real meaning.

TRY IT NOW!

7-11 Stores *Possible Hypotheses*

7-11 stores are convenience stores located all over the Northeast. Management is studying sales data. Develop a specific hypothesis for each of the different types of hypotheses that we have discussed. We've listed one specific hypothesis to get you started:

Type of Hypothesis	Specific Hypothesis
• The shape of the distribution of the variable in one population	Daily sales at store 23 are normally distributed.
• The mean value, μ, of the variable in one population	
• How the mean value of the variable in one population compares to the mean value of the variable in a second population	
• The equality of the mean values of the variable in more than two populations	

(continued)

- The amount of variability, σ^2, of the variable in one population
- How the amount of variability of the variable in one population compares to the amount of variability of the variable in a second population

8.3.2 Hypotheses About Nominal Variables

In addition to using nominal variables as a way to divide the data into two groups, we are often interested in what percentage or proportion of a population has a particular characteristic. For example, we might be interested in what proportion of the product we are manufacturing is defective. In this case, the nominal variable is the quality status of the product, nondefective or defective, and we are interested in the percentage or proportion of the population that has the quality status "defective." If the data we are analyzing are *nominal* data, the hypothesis might be a statement about

- The value of the proportion, π, of population members that have a certain characteristic (one of the categories of the nominal variable)
- How the proportion who have a certain characteristic in one population, π_1, compares with the corresponding proportion in a second population, π_2

EXAMPLE 8.3 Cereal Manufacturer

Possible Hypotheses

Understand the Problem

A cereal company is considering a new package design. The company would like to know what percentage or proportion of the consumers like this new design. An example of each of the hypotheses just discussed is shown for this variable:

Type of Hypothesis	Specific Hypothesis
• The value of the proportion, π, of the population members that have a certain characteristic	At least 50% of the customers like this new design.
• How the proportion who have a certain characteristic in one population compares with the corresponding proportion in a second population	A greater proportion of women than men like this new design.

■

Notice that, in this example, we are interested in the proportion of the population that prefers the new design. In this case, the nominal variable is whether a consumer prefers the new design. We have used a second nominal variable (gender) to divide the consumers into two populations and have then constructed a hypothesis about the proportion of women who prefer the new design compared to the proportion of men who prefer the new design.

ANS. (ANSWERS MAY VARY) THE AVERAGE DAILY SALES IS $2500. THE AVERAGE SALES IN THE MA STORES IS GREATER THAN IN THE CT STORES. THE AVERAGE DAILY SALES FOR ALL COUNTIES IN MA ARE THE SAME. THE VARIABILITY OF STORES IN NY IS 100 DOLLARS². THE VARIABILITY OF DAILY SALES IN NY IS GREATER THAN IN THE CT STORES.

Step 3: Select one of the qualitative variables and set up null and alternative hypotheses for a parameter of this variable.

Step 4: As a class, agree on several quantitative and qualitative variables that you feel are important. Record the data for all of the teams on each of these variables.

Step 5: Use the tools of descriptive statistics to display these data.

Step 6: Enjoy the M&M's!

8.4.2 Collect the Data and Define the Test Procedure

The second step of any hypothesis test is to **define the test procedure.** This includes selecting the appropriate test statistic, selecting the value of α, and finding the rejection region.

As you will see, much of the rest of this textbook is devoted to various types of hypothesis tests. So, you must decide what is the right test for your problem or situation. Table 8.1 gets you started on this task. You must decide whether you have quantitative data or nominal data. You must also decide whether you are studying one population, two populations, or more than two populations. For the moment, we will look at situations that involve hypothesis tests for the mean (μ) of a quantitative variable for one population. This is just so we can get through basics of hypothesis testing. Later, we will return to this issue and do a better job of determining which test to use.

To perform the test, you will need to choose between the null and the alternative hypotheses. To be more specific, you must decide to reject or not to reject the null hypothesis. Your decision is always phrased with regard to the null hypothesis. If you choose not to reject the null hypothesis, this means that the sample data are consistent with the null hypothesis, giving you no reason to reject it. If you choose to reject the null hypothesis, this means the sample data are sufficiently inconsistent with the null hypothesis, giving you reason to reject it.

So it seems that the information in your sample is the evidence that you will use to decide between H_0 and H_A. However, the sample consists of n observations. Somehow you must capture the information in the sample into a single number. This number is called the **test statistic.** The formula for calculating the test statistic depends on the particular test you have chosen, but its function is always the same.

A ***test statistic*** is calculated from the sample data and is used to decide between the null and alternative hypothesis.

Remember that in general a statistic is a number calculated from sample data.

What values of the test statistic lead you to reject the null hypothesis? This is precisely the question that must be answered next. To do this you must specify the **level of significance of the test** called **alpha, α.** For now, think of α as the greatest probability (or chance) of rejecting a true null hypothesis that you are willing to tolerate. In other words, α is the greatest chance of this type of error that you are willing to live with. This will become clearer in Section 8.6. Remember from Chapter 6 that probabilities correspond to areas. Alpha is the area of the **rejection region.**

Remember from Chapter 6 that areas correspond to probabilities. Alpha is the area of the rejection region.

The ***rejection region*** is the range of values of the test statistic that will lead you to reject the null hypothesis. ***Alpha, α,*** is the area of the rejection region.

For example, if z is our test statistic, the rejection region might be all values of z larger than 1.96 or smaller than -1.96. If the value of z that we calculate is less than -1.96 or greater than 1.96, then the test statistic would be in the rejection region and we would reject the null hypothesis. The value that marks the beginning of the rejection region for positive values is often called the **critical value.** In this case, 1.96 is often called the **z critical value** because the test statistic is z.

z is a common test statistic. It is the same z we discussed in Chapter 7.

The rejection region is shaded in Figure 8.1. As you can see, it has two tails and is the rejection region for a two-tail test, hence the name! The area of this rejection region is $\alpha = 0.05$.

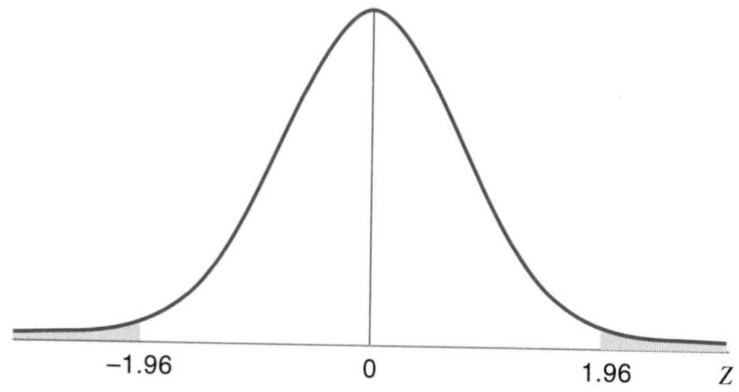

FIGURE 8.1 Possible rejection region

EXAMPLE 8.7 The Tissue Strength Problem

Define the test procedure: Select the right test statistic, pick value of α, and find the rejection region

The tissue strength manufacturer is concerned about the average strength of the tissues measured by the variable *MDStrength.* The null and alternative hypotheses have been set up in Example 8.4. The appropriate test is a one population test of the mean. The test statistic is z (you would not know this yet). The manufacturer decides that they can tolerate a certain kind of error 5% of the time, so $\alpha = 0.05$. The rejection region is therefore the one shown in Figure 8.1. ■

The specific values that define the rejection region depend on the test you are using and on the size of α. However, regardless of the particulars you must always choose a value of α at this step. If you don't, then you run the risk of waiting to see the results before deciding on the maximum chance of error you can tolerate. This is not ethical. This is somewhat like waiting to see whether you got an 85 on an exam and then declaring that you were shooting for an 85!

8.4.3 Collect the Data and Calculate the Test Statistic

The third step of any hypothesis test requires you to use the data you have collected and the test statistic you have decided is appropriate and calculate the value of the test statistic for your sample data. You will use the value of the test statistic from this step to do the next step.

8.4.4 Decide Whether to Reject the Null Hypothesis

There are two main approaches to deciding whether to reject the null hypothesis. The first is to use the rejection region you found in step 2 of the hypothesis testing procedure. If the test statistic you calculated in step 3 falls in the rejection region, then you reject the null hypothesis. If it does not fall in the rejection region, then you do not reject the null hypothesis. You say that you fail to reject the null hypothesis. It is technically incorrect to say that you accept the null hypothesis. This is because when you use the word *accept,* it implies that you have, in a sense, proven this hypothesis. But the only thing that you have done is shown that the data are not inconsistent with the null hypothesis. This point is discussed further in Section 8.7.2.

The second approach to deciding whether to reject the null hypothesis involves ***p* values.** Using *p* values frees you of having to actually find the rejection region. Hypothesis testing output from any statistical software package includes *p* values. These are the subject of Section 8.5.2.

8.4.5 Interpret the Statistical Decision in Terms of the Stated Problem

The final step in any hypothesis test is to interpret the statistical decision from step 4 in terms of the stated problem. In other words, translate the decision you made to either reject the null hypothesis or fail to reject the null hypothesis into a business decision. What are your recommendations and conclusions based on this test? This is clearly very important and goes along with the third step in our problem-solving steps called "draw conclusions and make recommendations."

Now you know enough of the basics of hypothesis testing to look at a specific situation. The first test we will look at is a two-tail test of the mean when you know the value of the population standard deviation, σ, or you have a large ($n > 30$) sample size.

8.5 TWO-TAIL TESTS OF THE MEAN: LARGE SAMPLE

There are two different cases to consider when testing the population mean: tests of the mean when you know something about the *population* standard deviation, σ, and tests of the mean when all you have is the *sample* standard deviation, *s*. The first case is covered in this chapter. This case also includes the situation where you do not know the population standard deviation, σ, but you have a sufficiently large sample size, $n > 30$. When this happens you use the sample standard deviation, *s*, as an estimate of σ. For this reason, the tests in this chapter are referred to as **large-sample tests** but they are used whenever you know the population standard deviation regardless of the sample size.

Large-sample tests are used whenever you know σ or when $n > 30$.

8.5.1 Two-Tail Test of the Mean: A Detailed Example

The first step is to take your idea or hypothesis about the mean and construct the null and the alternative hypotheses.

EXAMPLE 8.8 The Tissue Company

Understand the Problem

Step 1: Setting Up the Null and Alternative Hypotheses

Returning to the tissue strength example, suppose the manufacturer is interested in whether the *MDStrength* is different from the target value of 1000 lb/ream. This means a two-tail test must be used. Remember that if a two-tail test is used, the "=" theory must be in the null hypothesis. The first step of the procedure is then completed when we write the null and the alternative hypotheses:

$$H_0: \ \mu = 1000 \text{ lb/ream}$$
$$H_A: \ \mu \neq 1000 \text{ lb/ream}$$

■

Since we are talking about a hypothesis test of μ, it makes sense to use the value of $\overline{X}$ as our evidence from the sample. Remember that the Central Limit Theorem (Chapter 7) tells you that the sample mean, $\overline{X}$, tends to have a normal distribution with a mean equal to the true population mean, μ. It also tells you that the distribution of the sample mean, $\overline{X}$, has a standard deviation or standard error equal to $\sigma/\sqrt{n}$. We can therefore convert $\overline{X}$ to a standard normal, z, by the following formula:

Remember that $\overline{X}$ is the best point estimate for μ.

$$z = \frac{\overline{X} - \mu}{\sigma/\sqrt{n}}$$

z Test statistic

So the *test statistic* for a hypothesis test of μ should be a z test statistic.

Let's think about what z really tells us and what values of the z test statistic would lead us to reject H_0. We are interested in detecting whether the true mean, μ, has shifted from 1000. Values of $\overline{X}$ that are far from 1000 would be the ones that lead us to be suspicious of and reject H_0: $\mu = 1000$.

If the $\overline{X}$ value is considerably smaller than 1000, what will happen to the numerator of the z test statistic? The numerator is $(\overline{X} - \mu)$. If $\overline{X}$ is a lot smaller than μ, then the difference will be a negative number of large magnitude. For instance, if $\overline{X} = 950$, then the difference is -50. As a result of the "large" negative value in the numerator, z will be a "large" negative number. Keep in mind that the difference of -50 must be deemed "large" relative to the size of the standard error. Similarly, if $\overline{X}$ is a number much larger than μ (say, 1050) then the difference $(\overline{X} - \mu)$ will be a large positive number and z will be a large positive number. It seems then that "large" negative values of z (resulting from $\overline{X}$ values a lot lower than 1000) and large positive values of z (resulting from $\overline{X}$ values a lot higher than 1000) are the ones that will lead us to reject the null hypothesis, H_0. We need a cutoff or **critical value** of z to help us decide what constitutes a "large" z value.

***Note:** The expression "large" negative values means negative values of large magnitude. The term "large" negative value is not technically correct but using it might make the explanations easier to follow.*

The specification of these cutoff or critical values for z is completely determined by the size of the rejection region, α. You want the total area of the rejection region to be α and since the rejection region consists of two tails of the z distribution (large positive z values and "large" negative z values), the area in each tail must be $\alpha/2$. Combining all these ideas leads us to the rejection region shaded in Figure 8.2 on page 378. The rejection region is defined to be those values of the test statistic (in this case, z) that lead you to reject the null hypothesis. In this case, the rejection region is all z values that are greater than $z_{\alpha/2}$ or less than $-z_{\alpha/2}$. These cutoff values are so labeled because they are z values (from the Z table) and they cut off a tail area of $\alpha/2$. They are sometimes referred to as **critical values.**

We determined the rejection region by logically thinking about what z values should lead us to reject the null hypothesis.

You may recall that in Chapters 6 and 7 you learned how to find z values for given tail area probabilities. This is the procedure you need to use to get $z_{\alpha/2}$. The steps from Chapter 7 are repeated here:

Step 1: Take the value of α and divide it by 2.

Step 2: Look up that value in the body of the z table (find the one closest to it).

Steps for finding $z_{\alpha/2}$ and $-z_{\alpha/2}$

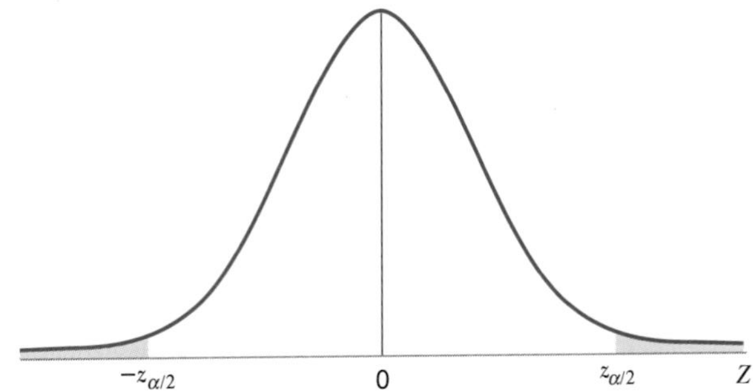

FIGURE 8.2 Rejection region for two-tail test of μ

Step 3: Read off the corresponding z value. This gives you the value of $-z_{\alpha/2}$.

Step 4: Drop the negative sign to get the value of $z_{\alpha/2}$.

Let's do the second step of the hypothesis testing procedure now.

Understand the Problem

EXAMPLE 8.9 The Tissue Company

Step 2: Define the test procedure

We have just seen that the correct test statistic is z. The tissue company decides that it does not want to reject a true null hypothesis more than 5% of the time. Thus, it sets α to be 0.05. The values of $z_{\alpha/2}$ and $-z_{\alpha/2}$ are found using the steps listed previously:

Step 1: Divide α by 2 to get $0.05/2 = 0.025$.

Step 2: Look this up in the body of the z table, a portion of which is shown here:

z	0.00	0.01	0.02	0.03	0.04	0.05	0.06	0.07	0.08	0.09
−2.1	0.0179	0.0174	0.0170	0.0166	0.0162	0.0158	0.0154	0.0150	0.0146	0.0143
−2.0	0.0228	0.0222	0.0217	0.0212	0.0207	0.0202	0.0197	0.0192	0.0188	0.0183
−1.9	0.0287	0.0281	0.0274	0.0268	0.0262	0.0256	0.0250	0.0244	0.0239	0.0233
−1.8	0.0359	0.0351	0.0344	0.0336	0.0329	0.0322	0.0314	0.0307	0.0301	0.0294
−1.7	0.0446	0.0436	0.0427	0.0418	0.0409	0.0401	0.0392	0.0384	0.0375	0.0367

Step 3: Reading off the corresponding z value, we find $z_{\alpha/2} = -1.96$.

Step 4: Dropping the negative sign gives us $z_{\alpha/2} = 1.96$.

So the rejection region for this hypothesis test is $z < -1.96$ or $z > 1.96$. This completes step 2 of the hypothesis testing procedure. ■

You should have been able to guess that the critical value of z would be close to 2. Why? Remember the empirical rule from Chapter 4 told you that about 95% of the values fall within 2 standard deviations of the mean. Well for z the mean is 0 and the standard deviation is 1, so about 95% of the z values should fall between $0 - 2(1) = -2$ and $0 + 2(1) = 2$. We just found a critical z value of 1.96, which is indeed very close to 2!

Use the bottom of the t table to quickly find the z critical value.

There is a shorter way to find the values of $z_{\alpha/2}$ and $-z_{\alpha/2}$. If you look at the bottom of Table 4 in Appendix A, you will see the z critical values for different values of α for both one-tail and two-tail tests. The value of 1.96 is found in the column that corresponds to a level of significance for a two-tail test of 0.05. You might be wondering why these z values are on the bottom of the t table. You might recall from Chapter 7 that the t distribution approaches the z distribution as the sample size (and hence the number of degrees of freedom) gets larger. To demonstrate this, the t value for 120 degrees of freedom is shown and then just below it is the corresponding z value. So you can use the row labeled z critical value to quickly find the values of $z_{\alpha/2}$ and $-z_{\alpha/2}$.

TRY IT NOW!

The Tissue Company ***Finding the Rejection Region***

Suppose the tissue company decided to set α at 0.10. Find the rejection region.

Remember that $\overline{X}$ is the best point estimator for μ.

The third step is to capture the information in the sample into a single number called the test statistic. It is the sample mean, $\overline{X}$, that is particularly relevant, since you are testing an idea about the true population mean, μ. Suppose the sample mean *MDStrength* of 36 tissue samples is found to be 980 lb/ream. On the surface it looks like the process should be adjusted. After all, 980 is 20 units less than the target value of 1000. You must remember that this $\overline{X}$ value of 980 is based on a sample. If you took another 36 tissue samples you might get a sample mean of 1020. You cannot decide whether a difference of 20 is really big until you compare it to the standard error! This is precisely what the z-score calculation does.

We can calculate z using the following formula for standardizing $\overline{X}$:

$$z = \frac{\overline{X} - \mu}{\sigma/\sqrt{n}}$$

Use the value of μ specified in the null hypothesis.

It seems like we have a problem since we need to know μ to calculate the z statistic but we don't know μ. This is easily resolved at this point because μ is the ***target*** specification value. In general, the value of μ that you use is the number that you are testing your sample evidence against, the value in your null hypothesis.

Let's see how this test statistic would be calculated for the tissue strength problem that we have been following.

Collect and Analyze the Data

EXAMPLE 8.10 The Tissue Company

Step 3: Collect the Data and Calculate the Test Statistic

The data have been collected and a portion is shown on page 364. Recall that the population standard deviation, σ, for the tissue manufacturer is 50. The z statistic is then

$$z = \frac{\overline{X} - \mu}{\sigma/\sqrt{n}}$$

$$z = \frac{980 - 1000}{50/\sqrt{36}} = \frac{-20}{8.333} = -2.40$$

Notice that you use the target value of 1000 as the value for μ in this calculation. ■

ANS. REJECT H_0 IF $z < -1.64$ OR $z > 1.64$

Which error should be avoided?

Clearly, α and β must be numbers between 0 and 1 since they are probabilities. As the investigator, you will get to decide the value of α. This means that you can specify the chances of making a Type I error to be anything you wish. Once you set α, the value of β is completely determined. Your first thought might be to set α to be as small as possible so there is hardly any chance of making a Type I error. Well, there is a price to pay for making α really small. As α gets smaller, the size of β gets larger. So, just like most things in life, there is a trade-off. You can force the chance of making a Type I error to be really small but then you have to live with a greater chance of making a Type II error.

Figure 8.3 shows the rejection region for a two-tail test of μ for α equal to 0.05. Remember that the rejection region corresponds to those values of the z test statistic that lead you to reject the null hypothesis. Also recall that the z test statistic is calculated using the value of μ from the null hypothesis. So the rejection region is drawn based on the assumption that the null hypothesis is *true.* The shaded region then corresponds to the chance of getting a "large" negative z test statistic or a large positive z test statistic when the null hypothesis is true. If we make this region smaller by making α smaller, then we reduce the likelihood of rejecting a true null hypothesis, which means we are failing to reject the null hypothesis more often. For some of those times that we fail to reject the null hypothesis, we should have rejected the null hypothesis. This is a Type II error. Thus by decreasing the chance of a Type I error, α, we increase the chance of making a Type II error, β.

Let's examine this trade-off in terms of the tissue strength problem.

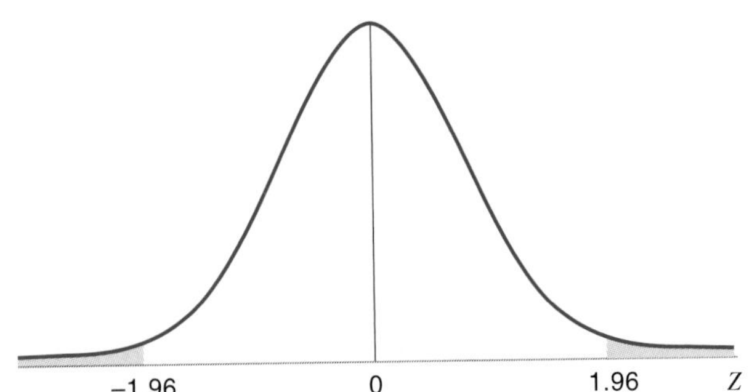

FIGURE 8.3 Rejection region for a two-tail test of μ with $\alpha = 0.05$

Understand the Problem

EXAMPLE 8.20 The Tissue Strength Problem

Possible Value for α

In terms of the tissue strengths, suppose you decide to set the chance of making a Type I error, α, really small, say, 0.01. This means that only 1% of the time will you incorrectly decide that the product specs are not being met, when really they are OK. This is the good news.

The trade-off is that the chance of making a Type II error increases. In this case, it means that the likelihood of deciding that the product specs are OK when they are not gets larger. How large the likelihood gets will depend on the real value of μ. ■

The standard value of α used to test hypotheses is 0.05. However, if making a Type I error is much more costly than making a Type II error, then you should consider testing at a value of α equal to 0.01. This will, of course, cause the value of β to increase. If, on the other hand, you feel that making a Type II error is particularly costly, then you should consider testing at a value of $\alpha = 0.10$. If both errors are equally costly then you should probably use the standard value of $\alpha = 0.05$.

Consider another example.

EXAMPLE 8.21 The Airplane Bolts Problem

Considering the Costs of the Errors

Understand the Problem

Suppose you are inspecting bolts that are used to fasten engines to airplanes. The mean strength of these bolts must be at least 100 pounds per square inch (psi). You need to decide whether a shipment of these bolts is OK—that is, whether they are strong enough. You realize that you cannot test them all because once you test a bolt it cannot be used in the airplane. This is what we call destructive sampling. If you test them all you will have none to use. You decide to take a sample of bolts, and on the basis of the mean strength of the sample you will decide whether the shipment is OK.

One possible way to set up the hypothesis test is as follows:

Remember: *A Type I error is that you reject the null hypothesis when, in fact, the null hypothesis is true.*

$$H_0: \mu \geq 100 \text{ psi} \quad \text{(The shipment is OK)}$$
$$H_A: \mu < 100 \text{ psi} \quad \text{(The shipment is not OK)}$$

For this hypothesis test, what is a Type I error? In this case, you would believe that the shipment is not OK when in fact it is OK. So, you would send the bolts back for rework when they did not need to be reworked.

Now let's look at a Type II error for this problem. In this case, you would keep the bolts even though they are not strong enough.

Recall: *A Type II error is that you fail to reject the null hypothesis when, in fact, the alternative hypothesis is true.*

Which of these errors is more costly?

- Send bolts back for rework when they did not need to be reworked.
- Keep bolts that are not strong enough.

We would probably all agree that keeping bolts that are not strong enough is the more costly error (in terms of human life). This is a Type II error. Thus, we should try to minimize the value of β by testing at α equal to 0.10. ■

TRY IT NOW!

New Package Design: ***Setting the Value of α***

We have seen that a one-sided test is often used to investigate whether a new method of advertising or producing something is better than the existing method. Consider a company that is trying a new package design for its product. The average sales for this product are currently \$1500/month. The null and alternative hypotheses would be

$$H_0: \mu \leq \$1500$$
$$H_A: \mu > \$1500$$

In terms of the company's decision to adopt or not adopt this new design, what are the Type I and Type II errors?

What value of α would you suggest be used to conduct the test?

ANS. TYPE I ERROR IS TO CONCLUDE THE NEW DESIGN IS BETTER WHEN IT IS NOT. TYPE II ERROR IS TO CONCLUDE THE NEW DESIGN IS NOT BETTER WHEN IT IS. THESE ARE EQUALLY COSTLY ERRORS SO USE $\alpha = 0.05$.

8.6.3 Exercises—Learning It!

8.7 Administrators at a small college are concerned that part-time evening students may not be familiar with all the services of the College. They wish to offer an orientation program to these students but recognize that most of the part-time students work during the day and are generally very busy. The administrators do not want to prepare an elaborate presentation if only a handful of part-time students will attend. Hence, they will conduct the orientation if more than 25% of the part-time students are interested in attending.

(a) State the consequences of a Type I error.

(b) State the consequence of a Type II error.

(c) Suggest a value for α, and justify your choice.

8.8 A company is thinking about setting up an on-site day-care program for its employees. The CEO has stated that she will do so only if more than 80% of the employees favor such a decision.

(a) State the consequences of a Type I error.

(b) State the consequence of a Type II error.

(c) Suggest a value for α, and justify your choice.

8.9 In an attempt to improve quality, many manufacturers are developing partnerships with their suppliers. A local fast-food burger outfit has partnered with its supplier of potatoes. The burger outfit buys potatoes in bags that weigh 20 lb. It does not wish to accept underweight bags of potatoes.

(a) State the consequences of a Type I error.

(b) State the consequence of a Type II error.

(c) Suggest a value for α, and justify your choice.

8.10 You are a connoisseur of chocolate chip cookies and you do not think that Nabisco's claim that every bag of Chips Ahoy cookies has 1000 chocolate morsels is correct.

(a) State the consequences of a Type I error.

(b) State the consequence of a Type II error.

(c) Suggest a value for α, and justify your choice.

8.11 Antilock brake systems (ABS) have been hailed as a revolutionary safety feature. A study by the National Highway Traffic Safety Administration looked at fatal accidents. The claim is that cars with ABS are in fewer fatal crashes than those without.

(a) State the consequences of a Type I error.

(b) State the consequence of a Type II error.

(c) Suggest a value for α, and justify your choice.

8.12 A College Placement Office wonders whether there is a difference between the average salary of engineering graduates and business school graduates.

(a) State the consequences of a Type I error.

(b) State the consequence of a Type II error.

(c) Suggest a value for α, and justify your choice.

8.13 Your new television has a 1-year warranty. You are given the option to buy a 3-year warranty and wonder if it is worth it. You wish to test the hypothesis that the average time before a problem occurs is more than 3 years.

(a) State the consequences of a Type I error.

(b) State the consequence of a Type II error.

(c) Suggest a value for α, and justify your choice.

8.14 M&M/Mars claims that at least 20% of the M&M's in each package are the new blue color.

(a) State the consequences of a Type I error.

(b) State the consequence of a Type II error.

(c) Suggest a value for α, and justify your choice.

8.15 A computer center is arguing for more computers in the lab for students at a midsize college. The computer center at a university claims that the average amount of time that students spend on-line has increased from last year's average of 1 hour per day.

(a) State the consequences of a Type I error.

(b) State the consequence of a Type II error.

(c) Suggest a value for α, and justify your choice.

8.7 WHICH THEORY SHOULD GO INTO THE NULL HYPOTHESIS?

In Section 8.4.1 we said that the first step is to construct two opposing views. We called one of them the null hypothesis and one of them the alternative hypothesis. Because of the way the hypothesis testing procedure works, it is important to carefully consider which of the views you are going to call the null hypothesis and which one you will call the alternative hypothesis.

Several different approaches may be taken to determine how the null and alternative hypotheses should be set up. These different approaches are the subject of the next two subsections. The first subsection further develops the concept of two-tail and one-tail tests, and the second subsection illustrates the conservative nature of the hypothesis testing procedure. Depending on the specifics of the problem you are trying to solve, one of these approaches will shed some light on resolving the question, Which theory should go into the null hypothesis?

8.7.1 Two-Tail Tests and One-Tail Tests

Much of our discussion so far has been about null and alternative hypotheses, which are called **two-tail tests.** The format is familiar to you by now and is shown in the following **definition.**

A **two-tail test** of the population mean has the following null and alternative hypotheses:

$$H_0: \quad \mu = \text{[a specific number]}$$

$$H_A: \quad \mu \neq \text{[a specific number]}$$

The null hypothesis of a two-tail test claims that the mean (or whatever parameter you are testing) is actually *equal* to the particular number stated. The opposing view is clearly that the mean is *not equal* to that particular value, and this is the alternative hypothesis.

Remember: You could be testing a variance or a proportion instead.

When you use a two-tail test you are interested in seeing whether the true mean is *different* from the number specified. You wish to know if the true mean is *higher than* the number or *lower than* the number. In other words, you want to test for deviations from the number in either direction—on the high side or the low side.

If you are doing a two-tail test, there is no decision to be made about how the null and the alternative hypotheses should be set up. The hypothesis testing procedure requires that the view with the equal sign be in the null hypothesis.

EXAMPLE 8.22 The Tissue Strength Problem

Understand the Problem

Set Up as a Two-Tail Test of the Mean

For the tissue strength example, we could set up the following two-tail test:

$$H_0: \quad \mu = 1000 \text{ lb/ream}$$
$$H_A: \quad \mu \neq 1000 \text{ lb/ream}$$

Here the specific number is 1000. ■

Both the soda bottle-filling problem and the potato chip packaging problem discussed in the previous section are also two-tail tests. In each of these cases the view that the true mean, μ, was equal to 32 oz (for the soda) or 10 oz (for the chips) was the null hypothesis.

TRY IT NOW!

The Chapperel Steel Company ***Setting Up the Null and Alternative Hypotheses for a Two-Tail Test of the Mean***

Another recent management approach is to have employees become actual partners of the business. Chapperel Steel Company has done exactly this, and the company feels that one of the benefits of this concept is that the average number of sick days will decrease. Before implementing this program, Chapperel had an average of 7.2 sick days per employee.

Set up the null and alternative hypotheses to test whether the average number of sick days per employee is different from 7.2.

Sometimes you really wish to see only whether the population mean (or whatever parameter you are testing) is lower than the stated value. In this case, you are interested only in testing whether the true mean, proportion, or variance is *less than* some number. Then you should use what is called a **lower-tail test.** A lower-tail test is one of two types of one-tail tests.

> A ***lower-tail test*** of a population mean has the following null and alternative hypotheses:
>
> $$H_0: \quad \mu \geq \text{[a specific number]}$$
> $$H_A: \quad \mu < \text{[a specific number]}$$

As with the two-tail test you could just as easily be testing a proportion, a variance, or the difference between two means or proportions.

Understand the Problem

EXAMPLE 8.23 The Tissue Strength Problem

Set Up as a Lower-Tail Test

Suppose the manufacturer of the tissues is worried only about the tissue strength being less than the 1000-lb/ream specified value. Then the test would be set up as follows:

$$H_0: \quad \mu \geq 1000 \text{ lb/ream}$$
$$H_A: \quad \mu < 1000 \text{ lb/ream}$$

■

Notice that the viewpoint that the manufacturer is interested in testing became the alternative hypothesis. You should also notice that the inequality sign with the equal sign attached to it (in this case $\geq$) became part of the null hypothesis.

ANS H_0: $\mu = 7.2$ DAYS; H_A: $\mu \neq 7.2$ DAYS

EXAMPLE 8.24 **The Chapperel Steel Company**

Understand the Problem

Illustrating a Lower-Tail Hypothesis Test

Reconsider the Chapperel Steel Company example. The company is particularly interested in whether their partner idea has in fact reduced the average number of sick days from 7.2 per year. It would make more sense to set this test up as a lower-tail test:

$$H_0: \quad \mu \geq 7.2 \text{ days}$$
$$H_A: \quad \mu < 7.2 \text{ days}$$

■

You can see that we have placed the theory that management wishes to test into the alternative hypothesis and again the inequality with the equal sign (in this case ≥) is placed into the null hypothesis.

TRY IT NOW!

The Bank Example ***Lower-Tail Test***

Suppose a bank knows that its customers are waiting in line an average of 10.2 minutes during the lunch hour. The branch manager has decided to add an additional teller during the 12–2 P.M. period and wishes to test the hypothesis that the average wait has decreased due to the additional teller. Set up the null and alternative hypotheses for the bank manager.

You may also wish to see whether the true mean is greater than the stated value. In this case, you are interested only in testing whether the true mean is *greater than* some number. This is also called an **upper-tail test.** An upper-tail test is the other kind of one-tail test. In general, such a test would look like this:

> An ***upper-tail test*** of a population mean has the following null and alternative hypotheses:
>
> $$H_0: \quad \mu \leq \text{[a specific number]}$$
> $$H_A: \quad \mu > \text{[a specific number]}$$

EXAMPLE 8.25 **The Tissue Strength Problem**

Understand the Problem

Set Up as an Upper-Tail Test

For example, suppose the manufacturer of the tissues is worried only about the tissue strength being greater than the 1000-lb/ream specified value. Then, the test would be set up as follows:

$$H_0: \quad \mu \leq 1000 \text{ lb/ream}$$
$$H_A: \quad \mu > 1000 \text{ lb/ream}$$

■

Here again, notice that the manufacturer's contention becomes the alternative hypothesis. The inequality with the equal sign (in this case ≤) is again placed into the null hypothesis.

ANS. H_0: $\mu \geq 10.2$ MIN; H_A: $\mu < 10.2$ MIN.

TRY IT NOW!

New Advertising Program ***Setting Up an Upper-Tail Test***

Suppose a company has implemented a new advertising program in the hopes of increasing sales from last year's annual average of \$4.3 million. Set up the null and alternative hypotheses to test the theory that sales have increased.

Summary

Two-Tail Test

- Is used to test whether the parameter has shifted away from a certain number in either direction, increased or decreased.
- Must always be set up so the "=" theory is the null hypothesis.
- Is used when the problem statement has the key words *changed* or *different* in the problem statement.

One-Tail Tests

Lower-Tail Test

- Is used to test whether the parameter has shifted to a number less than a certain number.
- Must always be set up with the "=" as part of the null hypothesis.
- Is used when the problem statement has the key words *decreased, reduced,* or *less than.*
- The theory that you wish to "prove" is placed into the alternative hypothesis.

Upper-Tail Test

- Is used to test whether the parameter has shifted to a number more than a certain number.
- Must always be set up with the "=" as part of the null hypothesis.
- Is used when the problem statement has the key words *increased* or *greater than.*
- The theory that you wish to "prove" is placed into the alternative hypothesis.

8.7.2 What View Requires No Action?

The next approach is particularly useful if you have decided to use a one-tail test. This is because, as we saw in the preceding section, there is really no choice about how to set up the null and alternative hypotheses once you decide to use a two-tail test.

This approach considers the question, What view requires that I take no action? Typically, this is the view that the population is behaving as it should be or as some-

ANS. H_0: $\mu \le \$4.3$ MILLION; H_A: $\mu > \$4.3$ MILLION

one claims it should be. This view becomes the null hypothesis. Sometimes people call this the status quo.

EXAMPLE 8.26 The Tissue Strength Problem

Understand the Problem

Manufacturing Specification Becomes the Null Hypothesis

For the tissue strength problem that we have been examining, the view that requires no action (or adjustments) is to believe that the manufacturing specification is being met. In this case, the specification is that the mean *MDStrength* is greater than or equal to 1000 lb/ream. This becomes our null hypothesis. Thus, H_0: $\mu \geq 1000$ lb/ream. Once we have the null hypothesis, it is easy to construct the alternative hypothesis since it has to cover all the other cases. So we have H_A: $\mu < 1000$ lb/ream. This hypothesis test is shown here:

$$H_0: \quad \mu \geq 1000 \text{ lb/ream}$$

$$H_A: \quad \mu < 1000 \text{ lb/ream}$$

■

Now you should ask, Why do it this way? The reason has to do with the fact that the hypothesis testing procedure is a conservative procedure. As such it behaves like a conservative person. A conservative person will take action only when he/she is very sure that action needs to be taken.

One way to help you understand what this means is to think about the belief in Santa Claus. Many young children believe in Santa Claus until they are about 7 or 8 years old. In this case, the null hypothesis would be H_0: Santa Claus exists and the alternative hypothesis would be H_A: Santa Claus does not exist. Children start off believing in Santa Claus (it is never proven to them) and they continue to believe that Santa Claus exists until there is overwhelming evidence to the contrary.

In a similar manner, the hypothesis testing procedure will tell us to believe the null hypothesis unless the evidence in the sample data overwhelmingly contradicts the null hypothesis. In other words, the status quo, or the view that implies that no action be taken, should be placed in the null hypothesis. It will be assumed to be correct until the data in the sample are *really* incompatible with it.

This approach is just like our judicial system. A person is assumed innocent until the evidence is so strong that it is impossible to continue to believe that the person is innocent. Remember that the instructions to the jurors are always to prove "beyond a reasonable doubt" that the person is guilty. This means that, even if most of the evidence indicates that the person is guilty, if there is still some reasonable doubt, the jurors must find the person not guilty.

Judicial System ***Setting Up the Null and Alternative Hypotheses***

If you think about the judicial system in terms of a hypothesis test, how would you set up the null and the alternative hypotheses?

ANS. H_0: PERSON IS INNOCENT; H_A: PERSON IS GUILTY

Consider another example.

Understand the Problem

EXAMPLE 8.27 The Soda Machine Problem

Demonstrating the Approach for a Two-Tail Test, Which View Requires That No Action Be Taken?

A soda machine should dispense, on average, 8 oz of liquid into cups. Having purchased soda from this machine in the past, you recall that sometimes you get a small amount of soda and sometimes the cup overflows. Using the approach described in this section, you would ask, What view requires that no action be taken?

Since the view that requires us to take no action is that the true mean fill is 8 oz, you should put this statement in the null hypothesis. Thus, you would get

$$H_0\text{:}\quad \mu = 8 \text{ oz}$$
$$H_A\text{:}\quad \mu \neq 8 \text{ oz}$$

■

TRY IT NOW!

VCR Manufacturer *Setting Up the Hypotheses so the Status Quo Is in the Null Hypothesis*

Suppose a manufacturer of VCRs claims that the average life of his VCRs is at least 3 years. You have a VCR made by this company and have had problems with it, and so you question this claim. Set up the hypothesis test to investigate the manufacturer's claim.

8.7.3 Exercises—Learning It!

8.16 Administrators at a small college are concerned that part-time evening students may not be familiar with all the services of the College. They wish to offer an orientation program to these students, but recognize that most of the part-time students work during the day and are generally very busy. They do not want to prepare an elaborate presentation if only a handful of part-time students will attend. They will conduct the orientation if more than 25% of the part-time students are interested in attending. Set up the null and alternative hypotheses to be used to decide whether the administrators should offer the session.

8.17 A company is thinking about setting up an on-site day-care program for its employees. The CEO has stated that she will do so only if more than 80% of the employees favor such a decision. Set up the null and alternative hypotheses to be tested.

8.18 A human resource manager feels that men use e-mail less than women. Set up the null and alternative hypotheses that should be tested to determine whether the human resource manager is correct.

8.19 In an attempt to improve quality many manufacturers are developing partnerships with their suppliers. A local fast-food burger outfit has partnered with its supplier of potatoes. The burger outfit buys potatoes in bags that weigh 20 lb. It wishes to set up the null and alternative hypotheses to test whether the bags do weigh on the average 20 lb.

8.20 You are a connoisseur of chocolate chip cookies and you do not think that Nabisco's claim that every bag of Chips Ahoy cookies has 1000 chocolate morsels is correct. Set up the null and alternative hypotheses to test this claim.

ANS. H_0: $\mu \geq 3$; H_A: $\mu < 3$

8.21 Antilock brake systems (ABS) have been hailed as a revolutionary safety feature. A study by the National Highway Traffic Safety Administration looked at fatal accidents. The claim is that cars with ABS are in fewer fatal crashes than those without. Set up the null and alternative hypotheses to test this claim.

8.22 A college placement office wonders whether the average entry level salary this year is different from last year's value of $25,000. Set up the null and alternative hypotheses to test this question.

8.23 The college placement office in Exercise 8.22 also wonders if there is a difference between the average salary of engineering graduates and business school graduates. Set up the null and alternative hypotheses to see if these averages are different.

8.24 Your new television has a 1-year warranty. You are given the option to buy a 3-year warranty and wonder if it is worth it. You wish to test the hypothesis that the average time before a problem occurs is more than 3 years. Set up the null and alternative hypotheses to test this belief.

8.25 It seems like you spend more money on groceries during the summer months when you eat more ice cream and drink more fluids. You know that you spend an average of $25/week on groceries during the winter months. Set up the null and alternative hypotheses to decide whether on the average, you spend more than this amount per week during the summer.

8.26 M&M/Mars claims that at least 20% of the M&M's in each package are the new blue color. Set up the null and alternative hypotheses to test this claim.

8.27 The computer center at a university claims that the average amount of time that students spend on-line has increased from last year's average of 1 hour per day. Set up the null and alternative hypotheses to test this claim.

8.8 ONE-TAIL TESTS OF THE MEAN: LARGE SAMPLE

In Section 8.5 you learned how to do a two-tail hypothesis test of the mean. In this section, we adapt that procedure to do a one-tail hypothesis test of the mean, μ. The procedure applies when you know the standard deviation of the population or if you have a sufficiently large sample. In the latter case, the only change in the procedure is to use the sample standard deviation, s, instead of σ. Therefore, we again use the label of "large sample" to describe these tests.

8.8.1 Lower-Tail Tests of the Mean

In Section 8.7.1 we saw that often we are interested in whether the mean has shifted in *one* direction. Reconsider the tissue strength problem. Most likely the company is interested in checking to see whether the true average *MDStrength* has decreased from the specification of 1000 lb/ream. Thus, a lower-tail test would make more sense in this case. Let's use this example to illustrate the procedure for a one-tail hypothesis test of μ when the population standard deviation is known.

Fortunately, the steps for completing a one-tail test of the mean when the population standard deviation is known are quite similar to those we used in the previous section. In fact, the only thing that will change is the procedure for finding the rejection region in step 2. Recall that we have been using the following five-step hypothesis testing procedure:

Steps for any hypothesis test

Step 1: Set up the null and alternative hypotheses.
Step 2: Define the test procedure.
Step 3: Collect the data and calculate the test statistic.
Step 4: Decide whether to reject the null hypothesis.
Step 5: Interpret the statistical decision in terms of the stated problem.

Reconsider the problem that the tissue company faces as a one-tail test. The first step is to set up the null and alternative hypotheses.

Understand the Problem

EXAMPLE 8.28 The Tissue Company

Step 1: Setting Up Null and Alternative Hypotheses

Since the tissue manufacturer is checking to see whether the true mean is *less than* 1000 lb/ream, this must go into the alternative hypothesis. So, we have the following setup.

$$H_0: \quad \mu \geq 1000 \text{ lb/ream}$$
$$H_A: \quad \mu < 1000 \text{ lb/ream}$$

■

We called this type of test a *lower-tail test.* The fact that the $<$ sign is in the alternative hypothesis makes it a lower-tail test. Next, you will see why it is called a lower-tail test as we find the rejection region.

Again, when we talk about "a lot lower" we must consider the difference in terms of the size of the standard error.

The second step includes selecting a value for α and finding the rejection region. Again, let's think about what size z values should lead us to reject the null hypothesis. We are interested in detecting whether the true mean has decreased below 1000 lb/ream. So, values of $\overline{X}$ that are much lower than 1000 would lead us to be suspicious of the null hypothesis. Following the same logic that we used in the previous section, we can see that if $\overline{X}$ is "a lot lower" than 1000 then $(\overline{X} - \mu)$ will be negative and z will be a negative number. Clearly, "large" negative z values will then lead us to reject the null hypothesis.

How about large positive z values? To get a positive z value, $\overline{X}$ would have to be bigger than 1000. If this is the case, would we ever want to reject the null hypothesis? No! An $\overline{X}$ value of, say, 1150, would certainly give us a large positive z value but a sample mean of 1150 is consistent with the null hypothesis. Remember that we reject the null hypothesis only when the sample evidence is inconsistent with the null hypothesis. Thus, any $\overline{X}$ value larger than 1000 would lead us to continue to believe the null hypothesis. In fact, we wouldn't even have to do the hypothesis test in such cases!

So we have decided that only "large" negative z values will lead us to reject the null hypothesis. We need only decide how large in the negative direction z has to be before we reject H_0. Keep in mind that we arrived at this rejection region by simple logic! The particular value of the cutoff point for z is again completely determined by the value of α and is labeled z_α.

Combining the idea that we will reject H_0 when the z value is too large in the negative direction with the requirement that we incorrectly reject H_0 only a certain percentage (α) of the time, we arrive at the following picture:

Rejection region for lower-tail test of μ—large sample

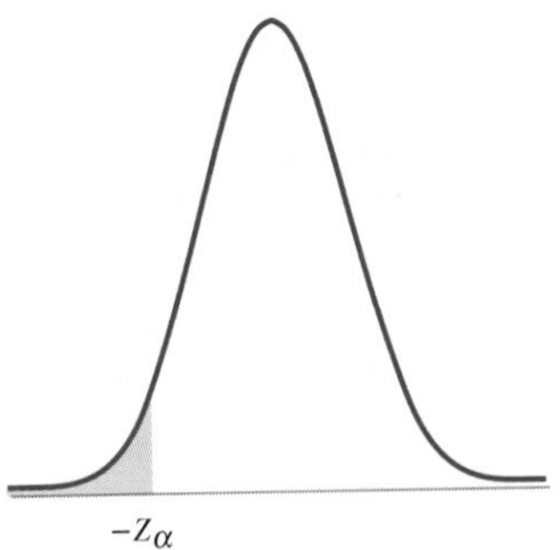

The shaded region is the rejection region. The rejection region is the *lower tail* of the normal distribution and hence the name *lower-tail test.* Remember that the rejection region consists of those values of z, the test statistic, that lead you to reject the null hypothesis. Thus, a z value smaller than $-z_\alpha$ (or a "large" negative z value) will lead you to reject the null hypothesis.

By using the standard normal table we can find this critical z value so that the probability that we are in the rejection region is α. The rejection region for the tissue company can be found using this procedure.

EXAMPLE 8.29 The Tissue Company

Understand the Problem

Step 2: Define the Test Procedure

Suppose α is set at 0.05. In this case, the shaded area must be 0.05. Since we are specifying the probability of 0.05, we look for 0.05 in the body of the standard z table and see that the closest values are 0.0495 and 0.0505 corresponding to z values of -1.65 and -1.64, respectively. It is OK to use either of these values or the average of these two numbers, which would be -1.645. Thus, we will reject H_0 if z is smaller than -1.645. ■

You may remember that for the two-tail test when we set $\alpha = 0.05$, we found the rejection region to be $z < -1.96$ or $z > 1.96$. Can you explain why the negative critical z value is different for the two-tail test? Remember that for the two-tail test, we split the value of $\alpha = 0.05$ in half before looking it up in the table. Thus, the critical value of -1.96 has an area of only 0.025 compared to the full value of 0.05 we used to get the critical value of -1.645.

Finding the Rejection Region

Try to predict what will happen to the $-z_\alpha$ value for the one-tail test if $\alpha = 0.025$. Now find it to confirm your guess.

In general, the procedure for finding the rejection region for a lower-tail test is as follows:

Steps for finding the rejection region for a lower-tail test

Step 1: Look up the value of α in the body of the z table (find the one closest to it).

Step 2: Read off the corresponding value; call it $-z_\alpha$.

Step 3: The rejection region consists of all values of z that are less than $-z_\alpha$.

The third step is to capture the information in the sample into a single number called the test statistic. It is the same calculation done in the previous section and is repeated here.

EXAMPLE 8.30 The Tissue Company

Collect and Analyze the Data

Step 3: Collect the Data and Calculate the Test Statistic

The data have been collected as described in the chapter opener. Recall that the population standard deviation, σ, for the tissue manufacturer is 50 lb/ream and that the sample mean, $\overline{X}$, was observed to be 980 lb/ream. The z statistic is then

---

ANS. -1.96

$$z = \frac{\overline{X} - \mu}{\sigma/\sqrt{n}}$$

$$z = \frac{980 - 1000}{50/\sqrt{36}} = \frac{-20}{8.333} = -2.4$$ ■

Now we can finish the tissue strength problem. At step 4 the value of the test statistic is examined to see whether it falls in the rejection region. Finally, step 5 requires that you interpret the statistical decision in terms of the problem statement.

Draw Conclusions and Make Recommendations

EXAMPLE 8.31 The Tissue Company

Step 4: Deciding Whether the Null Hypothesis Should Be Rejected

Step 5: Interpreting the Statistical Decision in Terms of the Stated Problem

The rejection region for this one-tail, lower-tail alternative hypothesis test is $z < -1.645$.

Clearly the calculated z value of -2.40 falls in the rejection region. Thus, we reject H_0 and conclude that the true mean has decreased below 1000 lb/ream.

Remember that there is less than a 5% chance of observing a sample mean as low as 980 lb/ream if in fact the true mean really has not decreased below 1000! The precise calculation can be found based on the p value.

Let's look at another example. ■

	A	B
1	One Sample Test for μ	
2	p-value =	0.0109
3		
4	Null Hypothesis: μ =	1000
5	Alternative Hypothesis:	Less Than
6	Sample Size: n =	36
7	Sample Mean: $\overline{X}$ =	980.0000
8	Population Std. Dev.: σ =	50.0000
9	Standard Error: $\sigma_{\overline{X}}$ =	8.3333
10		
11		

Understand the Problem

Collect and Analyze the Data

Draw Conclusions and Make Recommendations

EXAMPLE 8.32 The Chapperel Steel Company

Lower-Tail Hypothesis Test

In Example 8.24 we set up the hypothesis test for the company that had adopted the partnering approach with its employees. Remember that the company was interested in seeing whether this approach did in fact reduce the average number of sick days per year from 7.2. Suppose a sample of 20 employees of this company used an average of 7.0 sick days the first year after the partner approach was implemented. National personnel data indicate that the standard deviation is 1.25 days.

Is there enough evidence to conclude that the partnering approach did decrease the average number of sick days? Use $\alpha = 0.05$.

Step 1: Set up the null and alternative hypotheses.

Since the company is trying to show that the average number of sick days has decreased, that must be the alternative hypothesis. So, we have the following null and alternative hypotheses:

$$H_0: \quad \mu \geq 7.2$$
$$H_A: \quad \mu < 7.2$$

Step 2: Define the test procedure.

	A	B
1	One Sample Test for μ	
2	p-value =	0.2415
3		
4	Null Hypothesis: μ =	7.2
5	Alternative Hypothesis:	Less Than
6	Sample Size: n =	20
7	Sample Mean: $\overline{X}$ =	7.0000
8	Population Std. Dev.: σ =	1.2500
9	Standard Error: $\sigma_{\overline{X}}$ =	0.2795
10		

Lacking any specific direction from the company, set $\alpha = 0.05$. Since it is a lower-tail test, you look up 0.05 in the body of the standard normal table and find z_α to be -1.645.

Step 3: Collect the data and calculate the test statistic:

$$z = \frac{\overline{X} - \mu}{\sigma/\sqrt{n}} = \frac{7.0 - 7.2}{1.25/\sqrt{20}} = -0.72$$

Step 4: Decide whether to reject the null hypothesis. Clearly, $z = -0.72$ is not in the rejection region and we fail to reject H_0.

Step 5: Interpret the statistical decision in terms of the stated problem. In this case, the data indicate that the average number of sick days used has not been reduced. ■

TRY IT NOW!

Frozen Foods ***Lower-Tail Test of the Mean***

Jake Bramhall can identify the make, model, and number of cylinders of any passing car but he can't tell the difference between stewed tomatoes and tomato paste. Although more men are pushing shopping carts these days, many like Mr. Bramhall show little aptitude in the supermarket and display markedly different purchasing behavior than women. A study done by Consumer Network Inc. shows that the average amount of money spent by 100 single men on facial tissues was \$7.38. On the basis of these data can you conclude that men spend less money on facial tissues than the average \$8.19 spent by women on facial tissues? Use a population standard deviation of \$3.50 and an α value of 0.05.

Step 1: Set up the null and alternative hypotheses.

Step 2: Define the test procedure.

Step 3: Collect the data and calculate the test statistic.

Step 4: Decide whether to reject the null hyothesis.

Step 5: Interpret the statistical decision in terms of the stated problem.

Are the results different if you use $\alpha = 0.01$?

ANS. H_0: $\mu \geq 8.19$; H_A: $\mu < 8.19$; $z_\alpha = -1.645$; $z = -2.31$; REJECT H_0; MEN DO SPEND LESS, ON THE AVERAGE, THAN WOMEN. YES.

8.8.2 Upper-Tail Test of μ

So far all of the one-tail tests that we have performed have been lower-tail tests. That is, the $<$ symbol was used in the alternative hypothesis. We must now consider what will be different in our procedure if we need to do an upper-tail test, that is, one with the $>$ symbol in the alternative hypothesis. Let's look at an example.

Understand the Problem

EXAMPLE 8.33 Frozen Foods

Step 1: Setting Up the Null and Alternative Hypotheses

In the same study of supermarket behavior that you just looked at in the Try It Now! exercise, the average amount of money spent on frozen dinner/entrees by men was found to be \$41.48. There were 100 men in the study, and the population standard deviation can be assumed to be \$10. Is there any evidence to indicate that the men spend more than the national average for women of \$40.71?

The major steps of the hypothesis testing procedure are the same. Here again, the only difference is in the rules for finding the rejection region used in step 2. Since we are interested in showing that the men spend *more* on frozen dinner/entrees, we know it is a one-tail test with the $>$ symbol in the alternative hypothesis. That gives us the following null and alternative hypotheses:

$$H_0: \quad \mu \leq \$40.71$$
$$H_A: \quad \mu > \$40.71$$

That completes step 1. ■

Step 2 asks us to select a value for α and find the rejection region. If you look back at the logic that led us to the rejection region for the lower-tail test, you will see that in this case it is values of $\overline{X}$ that are much larger than 40.71 that will lead us to reject H_0. These values of $\overline{X}$ will yield large positive z statistics. This observation coupled with what we have learned about the behavior of the normal distribution gives the following picture:

Rejection region for upper-tail test of μ — large sample

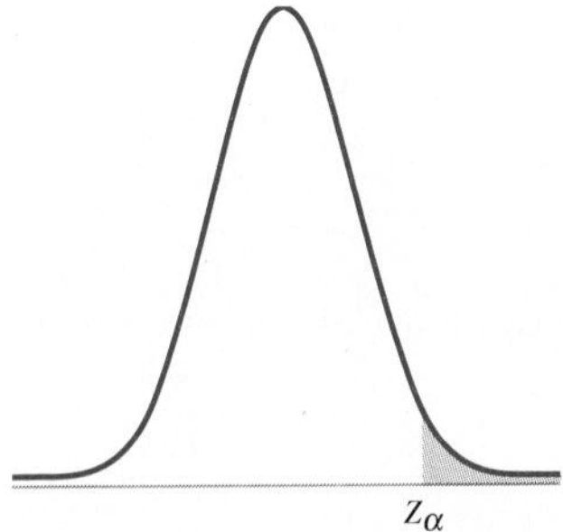

Here again the shaded region has an area of α and we will reject H_0 only when z is bigger than z_α, thus falling into the rejection region.

Understand the Problem

EXAMPLE 8.34 Frozen Foods

Step 2: Define the Test Procedure

Suppose we set $\alpha = 0.05$. In this case the area of the rejection region must equal 0.05. Remember that the normal distribution table gives us only lower-tail areas as the probabilities. But, since we know that the distribution is symmetric we can look up 0.05 and simply drop the negative sign to get z_α. The value for z_α is arrived at by dropping the negative sign in front of either -1.64 or -1.65. Hence, use either 1.64 or 1.65 or the midpoint, 1.645.

The rejection region $z > 1.645$. ■

This example has shown us the steps for the rejection region for an upper-tail test:

Steps for finding the rejection region for an upper-tail test

Step 1: Look up the value of α in the body of the z table (find the one closest to it).

Step 2: Read off the corresponding value and drop the negative sign. Call it z_α.

Step 3: The rejection region consists of all values of z that are greater than z_α.

We are now ready to complete this example.

EXAMPLE 8.35 Frozen Foods

Steps 3, 4, and 5

Collect and Analyze the Data

The data have been collected: $n = 100$, $\overline{X} = \$41.48$, and $\sigma = \$10$. For step 3 we calculate the z test statistic as follows:

$$z = \frac{\overline{X} - \mu}{\sigma/\sqrt{n}} = \frac{41.48 - 40.71}{10/\sqrt{100}} = 0.77$$

Draw Conclusions and Make Recommendations

	A	B
1	**One Sample Test for μ**	
2	p-value =	0.2216
3		
4	Null Hypothesis: μ=	40.71
5	Alternative Hypothesis:	Greater Than
6	Sample Size: n =	100
7	Sample Mean: $\overline{X}$ =	41.4800
8	Population Std. Dev.: σ =	10.0000
9	Standard Error: $\sigma_{\overline{X}}$ =	1.0000
10		
11		

Finishing this example, we do steps 4 and 5. Clearly, our z value of 0.77 does not fall in the rejection region. Therefore, we should fail to reject the null hypothesis and conclude that men do not spend more than \$40.71 on average for frozen dinners/entrees! ■

TRY IT NOW!

Supermarket Survey ***Upper-Tail Test of the Mean***

From the same supermarket survey it is found that the 100 men spent, on the average, \$19.98 on low-calorie soft drinks. Is there enough evidence to conclude that men spend more than women, who, on the average, spend \$18.86? Assume that the population standard deviation is \$10 and use $\alpha = 0.05$.

8.8.3 Adjustments to *p* Value Calculation for One-Tail Tests

In Section 8.5.2 we calculated the p value for a two-tail hypothesis test of μ when σ was known. The procedure for one-tail tests is the same except that you do not double the tail area probability. Most of the time you will get p value from the computer output.

ANS. $z = 1.12$; NO

Collect and Analyze the Data

EXAMPLE 8.36 Frozen Foods

Calculating the p Value

Consider the frozen foods example (Example 8.35). This problem used an *upper-tail test of* μ with σ known. A sample of 100 men spent $41.48 on the average on frozen foods. The z statistic was calculated to be 0.77.

The p value is calculated as follows:

$$p \text{ value} = P(z > 0.77) = 1 - 0.2206 = 0.7794$$

■

8.8.4 Exercises—Learning It!

8.28 A major manufacturer of glue products thinks it has found a way to make the glue adhere longer than the current average of 90 days. The manufacturer wishes to see whether the glue products made this way have an average time to failure greater than 90 days. A sample of 30 tubes of the new glue yields an average of 93 days before failing. The failure time is normally distributed with a standard deviation of 3 days.

(a) Set up the null and the alternative hypotheses to test whether average time to failure is greater than 90 days.

(b) Complete the remaining hypothesis testing steps using $\alpha = 0.05$.

(c) Find the p value.

(d) Based on the p value, what can you conclude about the average time to failure for the new product?

8.29 Recent medical research indicates that skin cancer patients who receive a new medication for skin cancer live longer than those who do not. The average length of life prior to the development of this medication was 18 months. The medical community wishes to test the claim made by the developers of this drug. A sample of 35 patients who received the medication lived an average of 21 months. The standard deviation is 5 months.

(a) Set up the null and the alternative hypotheses to test whether average length of life has increased from 18 months.

(b) Complete the remaining hypothesis testing steps using $\alpha = 0.10$.

(c) Find the p value.

(d) Based on the p value, what can you conclude about the average length of life for patients who receive the medication?

8.30 An automobile company thinks that with new designs, its cars will last longer before having a problem. For this reason, the company wishes to extend the warranty that comes with the vehicle in hopes of attracting more customers. Before making this change, the idea is tested. Prior to the design changes, the cars lasted on the average 43 months before having a major problem. A sample consisting of 50 cars was tested. The cars lasted an average of 44 months before having a major problem. The standard deviation is 2 months.

(a) Set up the null and the alternative hypotheses to test whether average time before having a major problem is longer than 43 months.

(b) Complete the remaining hypothesis testing steps using $\alpha = 0.05$.

(c) Find the p value.

(d) Based on the p value, what can you conclude about the average time before having a major problem?

8.31 A manufacturer of top-of-the-line tennis rackets claims that its Smack Em tennis racket will change a player's game. A tennis pro currently serves the ball at an average speed of 115 mph with a standard deviation of 2.5 mph. The speeds are normally distributed. The tennis pro decides to test the company's claim and records the speed of his serve for 15 balls using the Smack Em racket. The data are shown in the following table:

Speed (mph)	
117.3	115.9
115.1	115.2
116.0	115.0

(continued)

Speed (mph)	
116.2	113.0
112.9	120.8
115.4	116.9
113.8	114.4
114.2	

(a) Set up the null and the alternative hypotheses to test whether the average service speed has increased using the new racket.

(b) Complete the remaining hypothesis steps using $\alpha = 0.01$.

(c) Find the p value.

(d) Based on the p value, should the tennis pro invest in the new racket?

8.32 In an attempt to improve quality, many manufacturers are developing partnerships with their suppliers. A local fast-food burger outfit has partnered with its supplier of potatoes. The burger outfit buys potatoes in bags that weigh 20 lb. It does not wish to accept underweight bags of potatoes. A sample of 40 bags shows an average weight of 19.95 lb with a standard deviation of 0.1 lb.

(a) Set up the null and the alternative hypotheses to test whether the average bag weighs at least 20 lb.

(b) Complete the remaining hypothesis steps using $\alpha = 0.05$.

(c) Find the p value.

(d) Based on the p value, should the burger outfit accept the shipment of potatoes?

8.9 *Executive Summary:*
THE TISSUE COMPANY

Business Analysis...

TO: Operations Manager
FROM: Erica Q. Analyst
RE: Monitoring tissue strength

As you know, our company has been receiving complaints about the strength of our tissues. My PST (problem solving team) was assigned this problem to investigate and we have begun this task. This memo is an interim report on the investigation.

There are two measures of tissue strength: machine-directional strength (*MDStrength*) and cross-directional strength (*CDStrength*). We measured these two variables on three different days. On each day we took 75 observations of each variable. The product specifications are summarized in the table.

Variable	Mean (lb/ream)	Standard Deviation (lb/ream)
MDStrength	1000	50
CDStrength	450	25

My team and I have decided that the tool of hypothesis testing should be used to determine whether the process is producing tissues that meet the specifications. If so, then the problem is not with the process but perhaps the specifications are not consistent with what the customer needs. If the problem is with the process, then it must be examined.

We have decided to use a series of hypothesis tests to investigate this problem. For each variable, we will use the sample data to test the population mean, μ, against the specification value. We know that we can also use the sample data to test the population variance, σ^2 (recall that the variance is the standard deviation

(continued)

squared), against the specification value for each variable. We know that the procedure for testing the variances will be the same as that for testing the means, but we must read a little bit more about the details of how to do this.

For the tests of the population mean, we are proposing to use lower-tail tests to see whether the actual population mean has shifted to a number less than the desired specification value. This could be causing the customers to complain. It doesn't seem likely that the customers are complaining that the tissues are too strong, but we must check this out. If indeed some customers are complaining that the tissues are not strong enough and some are complaining that the tissues are too strong, then we would recommend using a two-tail test of the mean to detect a change from the target mean value in either direction.

We will conduct these tests and report the p value of each of the tests to you. This will give you complete information about the tests and allow you to decide what level of significance, α, is appropriate. Keep in mind that by using a very small value for α you protect the company against the mistake of fixing a process that is really running well, but you increase the chances that you fail to detect a problem with the process. The costs of each of these errors should be evaluated before deciding on a value for α. You should contact the accounting department to get estimates of the costs of these two types of errors.

My team will be completing the hypothesis tests of the mean of each of the variables within the next few days. Please contact me if you have any questions about how we are proceeding.

The *Wall Street Journal* is a major source of current business news and information for the business community. If your professor has arranged for your class to have access to the Business Extra feature, you can go to it now and see the techniques of this chapter in action today. Go to the Wiley Web site at http://www.wiley.com/college/pelosi, and click on Business Extra!

8.10 HYPOTHESIS TESTING IN EXCEL

Since this chapter covers the basics of hypothesis testing, all of the Excel instructions for hypothesis testing are found at the end of Chapter 9.

CHAPTER 8 SUMMARY

In this chapter you have learned the key steps involved in doing any hypothesis test. You first formulate two opposing viewpoints called the null and alternative hypotheses. These hypotheses are typically theories or ideas about the value of one or more population parameters. The technique of hypothesis testing helps you decide between these opposing hypotheses using the sample data as the evidence upon which to base your decision. In doing any hypothesis test there are two possible errors you can make. These are called Type I and Type II errors. The probabilities of making these errors are labeled α and β, respectively. It is desirable to make both of these probabilities small, but there is a tradeoff.

In this chapter you have also learned the procedure for doing large-sample tests of the mean. This procedure applies whenever you know the population standard deviation or you have a sufficiently large sample size, $n > 30$. Thus, the tests are called large-sample tests.

Key Terms

Term	Definition	Page Reference
Alpha (a)	The probability of making a Type I error is called $\boldsymbol{\alpha}$.	389
Alternative hypothesis	The **alternative hypothesis** is a statement about the population(s) that is opposite to the null hypothesis. It is referred to as H_A.	372
Beta (β)	The probability of making a Type II error is called $\boldsymbol{\beta}$.	389
Hypothesis	A **hypothesis** is an idea, an assumption, or a theory about the behavior of one or more variables in one or more populations.	366
Hypothesis test	A **hypothesis test** is a statistical procedure that involves formulating a hypothesis and using sample data to decide on the validity of the hypothesis.	366
Lower-tail hypothesis test	A **lower-tail hypothesis test** of the population mean has the following null and alternative hypotheses: H_0: $\mu \geq$ [a specific number] H_A: $\mu <$ [a specific number]	394
Null hypothesis	The **null hypothesis** is a statement about the population(s). It is referred to as H_0.	372
***p* value**	The ***p* value** is defined to be the smallest value of α for which you can reject H_0. This is also called the level of significance of the test.	383
Rejection region	The **rejection region** is the range of values of the test statistic that will lead you to reject the null hypothesis.	375
Test statistic	A **test statistic** is a number that captures the information in the sample. It will be used to choose between the null and alternative hypotheses.	375
Two-tail hypothesis test	A **two-tail test** of the population mean has the following null and alternative hypotheses: H_0: $\mu =$ [a specific number] H_A: $\mu \neq$ [a specific number]	393
Type I error	A **Type I error** is made when you reject the null hypothesis and the null hypothesis is actually true. In other words, you incorrectly reject a true null hypothesis.	388
Type II error	A **Type II error** is made when you fail to reject a false null hypothesis. In other words, you fail to reject H_0 when you should have rejected it.	388
Upper-tail hypothesis test	An **upper-tail hypothesis test** of the population mean has the following null and alternative hypotheses: H_0: $\mu \leq$ [a specific number] H_A: $\mu >$ [a specific number]	395

Key Formulas

Term	Formula	Page Reference
z test statistic	$z = \dfrac{\overline{X} - \mu}{\sigma/\sqrt{n}}$	377

CHAPTER 8 EXERCISES

Learning It!

8.33 The manufacturer of an over-the-counter pain reliever claims that its product brings pain relief to headache sufferers in an average of 3.5 minutes. To be able to make this claim in its television advertisements, the manufacturer was required by a particular television network to present statistical evidence in support of the claim.

(a) Is this a one-tail test or a two-tail test?

(b) Set up the null and the alternative hypotheses.

(c) What is a Type I error?

(d) What is a Type II error?

(e) A sample of 40 headache sufferers is used. They report that it took an average of 3.3 minutes to get some relief. If the standard deviation is 0.5 minute, perform the hypothesis test using $\alpha = 0.02$.

8.34 Pharmaceutical companies spend millions of dollars annually on research and development of new drugs. After a new drug is formulated, the pharmaceutical company must subject it to lengthy and involved testing before receiving the necessary permission from the Food and Drug Administration (FDA) to market the drug. The pharmaceutical company must provide substantial evidence that a new drug is safe before receiving FDA approval, so that the FDA can confidently certify the safety of the drug.

(a) Set up the null and alternative hypotheses.

(b) What is a Type I error?

(c) What is a Type II error?

8.35 Suppose a quality manager for a catsup company is interested in testing whether the mean number of ounces of catsup per family-size bottle differs from the labeled amount of 20 oz.

(a) Is this a one-tail or a two-tail test?

(b) Set up the null and the alternative hypotheses.

(c) What is a Type I error?

(d) What is a Type II error?

(e) A sample of 30 catsup bottles is checked. The average number of ounces in the sampled bottles is 19.97 oz. If the standard deviation is 0.1 oz, perform the hypothesis test using $\alpha = 0.05$.

(f) Find the p value. What conclusion can you draw about the mean number of ounces in catsup bottles?

8.36 The LEGO Group, an international company, makes the LEGO blocks that many of us have played with at some time. Many of its products require that the production process perform according to specifications. One of the products is Little People and the diameter of the neck of each of the Little People must be 0.5 inch so that it can be attached to the head properly. LEGO is interested in testing to see whether this process is performing according to specifications.

(a) Is this a one-tail test or a two-tail test?

(b) Set up the null and the alternative hypotheses.

(c) What is a Type I error?

(d) What is a Type II error?

(e) A sample of 30 blocks is tested. The average diameter of the sampled necks was 0.48 inch. If the standard deviation is 0.05 inch, perform the hypothesis test using $\alpha = 0.02$.

(f) Find the p value and make a recommendation to LEGO.

8.37 Another concept from the TQM (total quality management) movement is the idea of building better relationships with your vendor. In doing so the quality of the incoming raw material is improved. If you buy raw materials from me you may wish to sample some of the material I sell you to test the quality claims that I have made. Suppose I claim that the weight of the material I sold you was on the average 10 lb. You wish to test this claim.

(a) Is this a one-tail test or a two-tail test?

(b) Set up the null and alternative hypotheses.

(c) What is a Type I error?

(d) What is a Type II error?

(e) A sample of 30 yields an average weight of 10.03 lb. If the standard deviation is 0.03 lb, perform the hypothesis test using $\alpha = 0.05$.

(f) Find the p value and decide whether you would like to continue to purchase material from one supplier.

8.38 An up-and-coming restaurant chain is trying to decide whether to locate in the town of Longmortgage. It will locate there only if the average number of days of the week that people eat out is three or more. The company wishes to investigate the town of Longmortgage as a potential location.

(a) Is this a one-tail test or a two-tail test?

(b) Set up the null and the alternative hypotheses.

(c) What is a Type I error?

(d) What is a Type II error?

Thinking About It!

8.39 Would it be possible to switch the null and the alternative hypotheses for the ETS problem? Explain why or why not. *Requires Exercise 8.2*

8.40 For the glue manufacturer, which of the possible errors is the more costly error? Consider the consequences of making a Type I error and the consequences of making a Type II error. *Requires Exercise 8.28*

8.41 Consider the case of the medical research described in Exercise 8.29. *Requires Exercise 8.29*

(a) What position would you be taking if you had made the null hypothesis H_0: $\mu \geq 18$?

(b) What factors other than the medication might influence the length of time a cancer patient lives?

8.42 What are the implications of the car company setting the warranty too long? *Requires Exercise 8.30*

8.43 Consider the cereal manufacturer. *Requires Exercise 8.6*

(a) From the cereal manufacturer's perspective, what is the more costly error?

(b) From the consumer's perspective, what is the more costly error?

8.44 For the television network, what are the implications and consequences of a Type I error? A Type II error? *Requires Exercise 8.33*

8.45 Rewrite the hypothesis test for the FDA problem by switching the null and alternative hypotheses. *Requires Exercise 8.34*

(a) What is a Type I error for this new setup?

(b) What is a Type II error for this new setup?

(c) Compare your answers with those you found in Exercise 8.34. What has happened to the errors?

(d) Which setup do you feel is better and why?

8.46 If you took a sample of catsup bottles and observed a sample mean, $\overline{X}$ = 19.7 oz, does this automatically mean that the bottle-filling machine is not working properly? Explain why or why not. *Requires Exercise 8.35*

8.47 What are the implications for LEGO if the process that manufactures the necks for the Little People is not producing necks with the specified diameter? *Requires Exercise 8.36*

8.48 As the receiver of raw material, explain why you would not want to test every component of raw material (i.e., why not test the population instead of just examining a sample). *Requires Exercise 8.37*

8.49 From the perspective of the restaurant chain, what are the consequences of a Type I error? A Type II error? Which error is more costly? *Requires Exercise 8.38*

Doing It!

8.50 Let us return to the tissue manufacturer presented at the beginning of this chapter. Recall that the manufacturer was concerned about customer complaints involving sheets tearing on removal. The company decided to look at the manufacturing process to see how it compared to the product specification and to see whether any changes needed to be made. Making changes to the manufacturing process is a big job and before proceed- ***Datafile:*** *TISSUES.XXX* ing the manufacturer would like to be a little more certain that the changes need to be made. A sample of 225 was taken from a single tissue machine. The samples were taken over three different days and the results are stored in the data file TISSUES.XXX. A portion of the data file is shown here:

Day	MDStrength	CDStrength
1	1006	422
1	994	440
1	1032	423
1	875	435
1	1043	445

The variable *Day* keeps track of the day on which the tissue was produced and ranges from 1 to 3.

The variable *MDStrength* measures the machine-directional strength and is measured in lb/ream. The product specifications for *MDStrength* state that the measurement is normally distributed with $\mu = 1000$ lb/ream and $\sigma = 50$ lb/ream.

The variable *CDStrength* measures the cross-directional strength and is measured in lb/ream. The product specifications for *CDStrength* state that the measurement is normally distributed with a mean of 450 lb/ream and a standard deviation of 25 lb/ream.

After giving the matter some thought the engineers looking at the tissue manufacturing process wondered whether the fact that the measurements were taken on three different days might bias the analysis. Since operating conditions are not always the same on any given day, they wondered whether the process was off target on all three days or whether it was off target on one or two days. They decided to check each day individually.

(a) Perform a hypothesis test at the 0.05 level of significance to determine whether *MDStrength* was 1000 on each of the three days separately. Use the target standard deviation of 50 and write your results in the table:

Day	z Statistic	Decision (reject H_0/fail to reject H_0)
1		
2		
3		
All 3 days together		

(b) Using these results, do you think the company can assume that *MDStrength* is running on target? Why or why not?

(c) Using a 0.05 level of significance, do the sample data indicate that the variable *CDStrength* was running according to target specifications on each of the three days? Do you conclude the same for the three-day period as a whole?

Day	z Statistic	Decision (reject H_0/fail to reject H_0)
1		
2		
3		
All 3 days together		

(d) Using these results, do you think the company can assume that *CDStrength* is running on target? Why or why not?

(e) Since the consumer problem that prompted the study was sheets tearing on removal, the company decides that it is really interested in knowing only whether the average *CD-Strength* is less than the target of 450. If it is not, the company will not make any adjustments. Redo the tests in part (c) as a one-tail test to reflect this change. What is the result?

(f) One of the other variables that must be considered is some measure of total strength, which is related to both the dispensing defects and another important tissue variable, softness. Often strength and softness are tradeoffs. Using both *MDStrength* and *CD-Strength*, the company can calculate the Geometric Mean Tensile (GMT) strength, which is equal to the square root of the product of the two variables. This variable is also subject to process specifications.

Unfortunately, the group is divided on the subject of GMT. The operation's specialists think that since the company has critical specifications for the measurement, they need to check whether those specifications are being met. The machine operators say that since GMT is calculated from two other variables that have been tested, they do not need to perform a hypothesis test concerning these data.

What do you think? Is it possible for both *MDStrength* and *CDStrength* to be running according to specs but yet have GMT out of specs? Experiment with the data and see.

(g) Using the results of your analysis prepare a report to management about the current tissue manufacturing process. Make a recommendation on whether the process needs to be adjusted or whether it is running on target. Remember, if it is not running on target, the management will be considering making changes to the specifications to reduce customer complaints about dispensing. Address this point in your report.

8.51 A manufacturer of electronic telecommunications equipment was receiving complaints from the field about low volume on long-distance connections. Aunt Sue in California couldn't hear Cousin Fred in Florida.

Datafile: AMPLIF.XXX

A string of amplifiers manufactured by the company was being used to boost the signal at various points along the way. The boosting ability of the amplifiers (the "gain") was naturally the prime suspect in the case.

The design of the amplifiers calls for a gain of 10 decibels (dB). This means that the output from the amplifier should be about 10 times stronger than the input signal. This amplification makes up for the natural fading of the signal over long-distance connections. Because it is difficult to make every amplifier with a gain of exactly 10 dB, the design allows amplifiers to be considered acceptable if the gain falls between 7.75 and 12.2 dB. These permissible minimum and maximum values are sometimes called the specification (or spec) limits. The average value is to be 10 dB. Because there are literally hundreds of amplifiers boosting the signal on a long connection, low-gain amplifiers should be balanced by high-gain amplifiers to give an acceptable volume level.

The quality improvement team investigating the "couldn't hear" condition arranged to test the gain of 120 amplifiers. The results of the tests are listed below and are found on the disk file named AMPLIF.XXX.

Gain of 120 Tested Amplifiers

8.1	10.4	8.8	9.7	7.8	9.9	11.7	8.0	9.3	9.0
8.2	8.9	10.1	9.4	9.2	7.9	9.5	10.9	7.8	8.3
9.1	8.4	9.6	11.1	7.9	8.5	8.7	7.8	10.5	8.5
11.5	8.0	7.9	8.3	10.0	9.4	9.2	10.7	9.0	8.7
9.3	9.7	8.7	8.9	8.6	9.5	9.4	8.8	8.3	8.2
8.4	9.1	10.1	7.8	8.1	8.8	9.2	8.4	7.8	8.0
7.9	8.5	9.2	8.7	10.2	7.9	9.8	8.3	9.0	9.6
9.9	10.6	8.6	9.4	8.8	8.2	10.5	9.7	9.1	8.0
8.7	9.8	8.5	8.9	9.1	8.4	8.1	9.5	8.7	9.3
8.1	10.1	9.6	8.3	8.0	9.8	9.0	8.9	8.1	9.7
8.6	9.2	8.5	9.6	9.0	10.7	8.6	10.0	8.8	8.6
8.5	8.2	9.0	10.2	9.5	8.3	8.9	9.1	10.3	8.4

(a) How many of the amplifiers fell within the specification limits?

(b) Does this mean that the data were of little value?

(c) Generate a histogram of the data to get a better "picture" of the data. What shape does it have and what does that tell you about the problem?

(d) Calculate the standard summary statistics for these data: mean, median, trimmed mean, standard deviation, variance, and range.

(e) Although the amplifiers were designed to have 10-dB gain, very few of them actually had a measured gain of 10 dB. Furthermore, very few amplifiers had exactly the same gain. Speculate about what could be causing that variation.

(f) Test the hypothesis that the true average gain is 10 dB.

(g) Find a 95% confidence interval for the true average gain, μ.

(h) Based on your analysis in parts (a)–(f), what are your recommendations to the manufacturer of the amplifiers?

CHAPTER 9

INFERENCES: MORE ONE-POPULATION TESTS

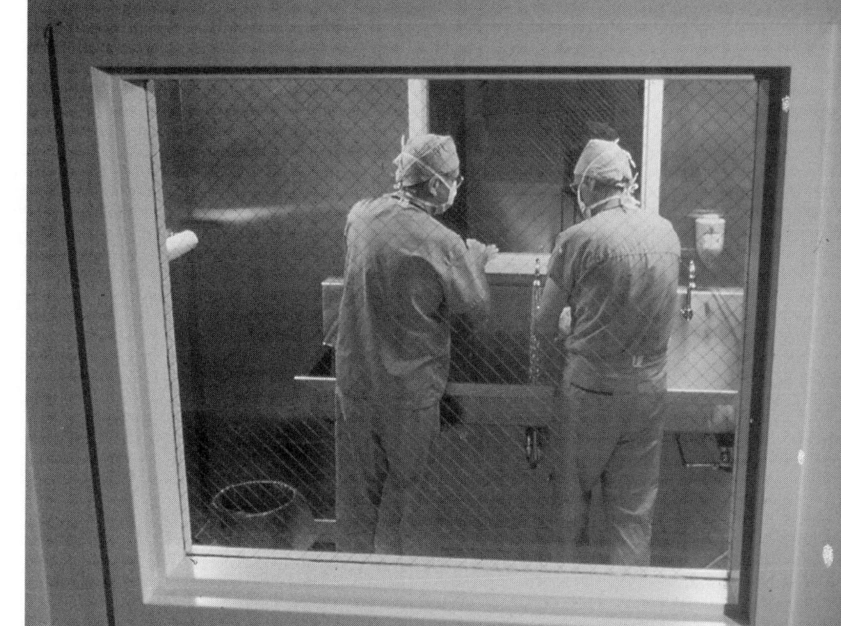

THE HOSPITAL

The health-care industry is as concerned with quality as manufacturing companies. With the rising costs of health care, many hospitals are looking for ways to contain costs without sacrificing quality of care. Studies have shown that a simple way to cut down on the spread of bacteria is to be sure that all employees wash their hands adequately. The literature indicates that a minimum of 5 seconds is needed.

Business Dilemma...

To be sure that the medical staff was washing their hands long enough, a large hospital observed a sample of employees washing their hands. The employees did not know they were being observed. In total, 28 employees were observed. The average hand-washing time was found to be 2.556 seconds with a sample standard deviation of 3.755 seconds. On the basis of these data, the hospital must decide whether the employees should participate in a training session to learn about the consequences of inadequate hand washing.

A portion of the data set is shown here:

Observation	Unit	Time 1
1	CCU	3
2	CCU	2
3	CCU	0
4	CCU	5
5	CCU	2
6	CCU	0

9.1 CHAPTER OBJECTIVES

The hospital described previously does not know the standard deviation of hand-washing times and the sample size is small ($n \leq 30$). Therefore, the hypothesis testing procedure introduced in Chapter 8 cannot be used. Now it is time to examine what to do if the population standard deviation is unknown and the sample size is small. In addition to handling small-sample tests of the mean, we will also see how to perform a hypothesis test for other population parameters.

If we are analyzing a *quantitative variable,* such as time an employee washes his/her hands, then we know that it can be described by its distribution. The distribution, in turn, can be described by parameters. Thus, if we are constructing a theory or hypothesis about a *quantitative variable* it might be a statement about

- The mean value, μ, of the variable in one population
- The amount of variability, σ^2, of the variable in one population

If the data we are analyzing are *nominal data,* such as whether an employee is satisfied with the job, the hypothesis might be a statement about

- The value of the proportion, π, of population members that have a certain characteristic (one of the categories of the nominal variable)

In this chapter we look at the numerical details of the test statistics and rejection regions for hypothesis tests about a single population parameter. We will be studying only one population. For example, we will look at the average sales of a particular product or the proportion of people who favor legalizing marijuana. In Chapter 10 we extend these results to compare the behavior of two populations. This might entail comparing the average sales of two products or comparing the views of men and women on the issue of legalizing marijuana.

This chapter covers the following material:

Remember: *Both μ and π describe the behavior of the population not the sample. They are typically unknown.*

- Hypothesis Test of the Population Mean, μ: Small Sample
- Hypothesis Test of the Population Variance, σ^2
- Hypothesis Test of the Population Proportion, π
- Summary of One-population Tests
- The Relationship Between Hypothesis Testing and Confidence Intervals

9.2 HYPOTHESIS TEST OF THE MEAN: SMALL SAMPLE

In the previous chapter you learned to perform a large-sample hypothesis test of the mean. In our examples, we have seen that sometimes there is information about the population standard deviation from either the product specs or from some previous study. However, more often than not, the population standard deviation is not known. In this case the sample standard deviation, s, must be used to calculate an estimate of the unknown population standard deviation, σ. If the sample is sufficiently large, $n > 30$, then you can use the Z test statistic from Chapter 8 to do a hypothesis test on the mean. However, very often you have a small sample.

Remember: To find the sample variance you use: $s^2 = \dfrac{n \sum x^2 - (\sum x)^2}{n(n-1)}$

Now let us think about the implications of having a small sample on our hypothesis test. The steps of any hypothesis test are repeated here. Notice that step 3 has been modified to include the calculation of the p value. As we saw in Chapter 8, this gives you an alternative way to make the decision at step 4 and it provides the manager with more information. However, for small-sample tests of μ and tests of σ^2, you cannot calculate the p values by hand with the tables you have in Appendix A. You would need probability tables similar to the normal distribution table to calculate the p value. We will follow standard procedure and get our p value from software output.

Use p value from the output of Excel or Minitab.

Step 1: *Set up the null and alternative hypotheses.*
Step 2: *Define the test procedure.*
Step 3: *Collect the data and calculate the test statistic and the p value.*
Step 4: *Decide whether to reject the null hypothesis.*
Step 5: *Interpret the statistical decision in terms of the stated problem.*

Steps for any hypothesis test

Only the details of steps 2 and 3 change.

Step 1 will not be affected since we are just setting up the null and the alternative hypotheses. If you guessed that steps 2 and 3 are affected then you were right. In Chapter 8, we calculated a Z statistic as our test statistic in step 3. But the formula for Z uses σ, which is now unknown, and our estimate is based on a small sample. Logic tells us simply to use s in the formula instead of σ. However, when we do this the test statistic no longer follows a normal distribution. Instead, it has a *t distribution.*

The Central Limit Theorem does not apply because $n \leq 30$.

You used the t distribution in Chapter 7 when you learned how to find a confidence interval for the mean of a normally distributed population when σ was unknown and the sample size was small. We will use our knowledge of the t distribution to do a hypothesis test of μ for precisely this situation.

The test statistic is calculated as follows:

Remember that a test statistic is a single number, based on the sample, that allows you to decide between the null and the alternative hypotheses.

$$t = \frac{\overline{X} - \mu}{s/\sqrt{n}}$$

t test statistic

Notice that the calculation for the t statistic is just the same as Z with σ replaced with s.

Remember: The population must have a normal distribution to use the t statistic.

9.2.1 Two-Tail Test of the Mean: Small Sample

Let's first look at two-tail tests of the mean when σ is unknown.

EXAMPLE 9.1 The Hospital

Two-Tail Test of μ: Small Sample

Understand the Problem

The hospital wishes to test whether the population average washing time is different from 5 seconds.

Step 5: Interpret the statistical decision in terms of the stated problem.

9.2.2 One-Tail Test of the Mean: Small Sample

In the previous subsection we learned that the two-tail hypothesis testing procedure for μ is affected in two major ways by the lack of knowledge about σ. The test statistic becomes a t test statistic instead of a Z test statistic, and the rejection region cutoff values must be found from the t table rather than the Z table. The same can be said about one-tail tests of the mean when σ is unknown.

The only step in the procedure that we need to update is finding the rejection region using the t table for one-tail tests. The form of the rejection region is the same as when σ is known. The only difference is in finding the critical values. Remember that we constructed the rejection regions by following a series of logical arguments as to what values of $\overline{X}$ would lead us to reject the null hypothesis. These arguments still apply.

For a one-tail test we want to reject H_0 if the calculated t statistic is too small. Thus, we have the rejection region shaded in Figure 9.1.

For an upper-tail test we want to reject H_0 if the calculated t statistic is too large. The rejection region for this type of test is shaded in Figure 9.2.

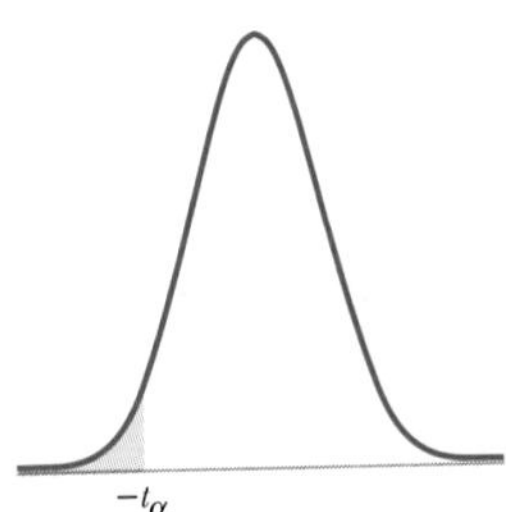

FIGURE 9.1 Rejection region for a lower-tail test of μ

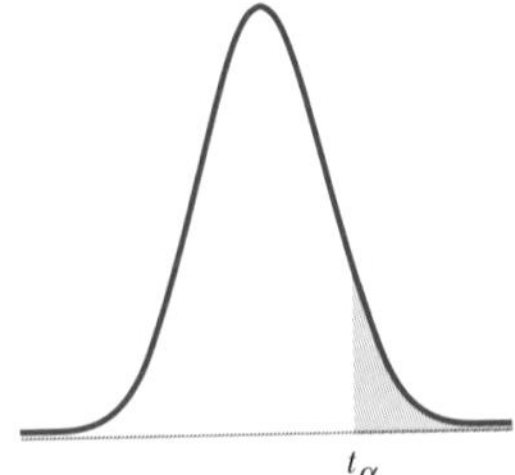

FIGURE 9.2 Rejection region for an upper-tail test of μ

The cutoff values are found in a manner similar to that used for the two-tail test except that there is no reason to split the value of α in half. These steps are summarized here:

Steps for finding the rejection region for one-tail tests of μ: small sample

Step 1: *Use the column of the t table that corresponds to the value of α you have selected.*

Step 2: *Find the number of degrees of freedom by calculating $n - 1$ and use that row of the t table.*

Step 3: *For upper-tail tests the desired t_α value is found at the intersection of that row and column. For lower-tail tests, place a negative sign in front of the value to get the value of $-t_\alpha$.*

Step 4: *For upper-tail tests the rejection region is $t > t_\alpha$. For lower-tail tests the rejection region is $t < -t_\alpha$.*

Let's look at some examples.

ANS. H_0: $\mu = 32$, H_a: $\mu \neq 32$, $t = 2.045$, $t = 2.23$, $p = 0.03$, REJECT H_0.

EXAMPLE 9.3 The Hospital

One-Tail Test of μ: Small Sample

The hospital is most likely interested in testing whether the mean hand-washing time is less than 5 seconds. This is a one-tail test of μ.

Understand the Problem

Step 1: *Set up the null and alternative hypotheses.* Since the hospital is interested in seeing whether average hand-washing times are *less than 5 seconds,* this is a lower-tail test. The null and alternative hypotheses are shown here:

$$H_0: \quad \mu \geq 5 \text{ s}$$
$$H_A: \quad \mu < 5 \text{ s}$$

Step 2: *Define the test procedure.* The data were collected and are shown in Example 9.1. The value of α has been set at 0.05. The specific value of t_α is found by looking in the t table. Use the column labeled 0.05 and the row corresponding to 27 degrees of freedom $(28 - 1 = 27)$. The table value at the intersection of this column and row is -1.703. This is the value of t_α.

Analyze the Data

Step 3: *Collect the data and calculate the test statistic and the p value.* The data were collected and are shown in Example 9.1. Since the value of σ is not known we must calculate both $\overline{X}$ and s from the sample data. These values and the t test statistic were calculated in Example 9.1. They are $\overline{x} = 2.536$ s and $s = 3.687$ s and

$$t = \frac{\overline{X} - \mu}{s/\sqrt{n}} = \frac{2.536 - 5}{3.687/\sqrt{28}} = -3.54$$

The p value is found by calculating the chance of observing $t = -3.54$ or smaller. Notice that since this is a one-tail test, you do not double the p value:

$$p \text{ value} = P(t < -3.54) = 0.0007$$

The output from Excel using the KADDSTAT add-in is shown here. The "one-sample test for mu" option was selected from the KADD main menu and the alternative hypothesis was specified as "less than."

One Sample Test for μ	
p-value =	0.0007
Null Hypothesis: μ =	5
Alternative Hypothesis:	Less Than
Sample Size: n =	28
Sample Mean: X̄ =	2.5357
Sample Std. Dev.: S =	3.6866
Standard Error: $S_{\overline{X}}$ =	0.6967

Alternatively, the output from Minitab is shown here:

```
T-TEST OF THE MEAN

Test of mu = 5.000 vs mu < 5.000

Variable    N    Mean    StDev    SE Mean      T        P
Hand was   28   2.536    3.687     0.697    -3.54   0.0007
```

Draw Conclusions

Step 4: *Decide whether to reject the null hypothesis.* Since the calculated test statistic of $t = -3.54$ is in the rejection region and the p value is less than 0.05, we reject H_0.

Step 5: *State the statistical decision in terms of the problem.* Based on these data, we can conclude that the average hand-washing time is less than 5 seconds. ■

Let's look at one more example.

EXAMPLE 9.4 New Marketing Plan

Upper-Tail Test of μ When σ Is Unknown

A company is trying out a new marketing plan and wishes to evaluate its success. Prior to the new advertising scheme the average store sales per week was $4000. The new method is tried on a random sample of 15 stores.

Can the company conclude that the new marketing plan worked? The weekly sales are assumed to be normally distributed. Use $\alpha = 0.05$.

Understand the Problem

Step 1: *Set up the null and alternative hypotheses.* Since the company is interested in seeing whether average sales have *increased,* this is an upper-tail test. The null and alternative hypotheses are shown here:

$$H_0:\quad \mu \leq \$4000$$
$$H_A:\quad \mu > \$4000$$

Step 2: *Define the test procedure.* The value of α has been set at 0.05. The specific value of t_α is found by looking in the t table. Use the column labeled 0.05 and the row corresponding to 14 degrees of freedom (15 − 1 = 14). The table value at the intersection of this column and row is 1.761. This is the value of t. The rejection region is $t > 1.761$.

Step 3: *Collect the data and calculate the test statistic and the p value.* The following sales data were collected:

Collect and Analyze the Data

$4128	$4132	$4163
$4148	$4157	$4039
$4028	$4146	$4174
$4190	$4054	$4181
$4088	$4069	$4099

Since the value of σ is not known we must calculate both $\overline{X}$ and s from the sample data:

$$\overline{X} = \$4119.7 \qquad s = \$53.4 \qquad t = \frac{4119.7 - 4000}{53.4/\sqrt{15}} = 8.69$$

The output from Excel using the KADDSTAT add-in is shown here. The "one-sample test for mu" option was selected from the KADD main menu and the alternative hypothesis was specified as "less than."

One Sample Test for μ	
p-value =	0.0000
Null Hypothesis: μ =	4000
Alternative Hypothesis:	Greater Than
Sample Size: n =	15
Sample Mean: $\overline{X}$ =	4119.7333
Sample Std. Dev.: S =	53.3646
Standard Error: $S_{\overline{X}}$ =	13.7787

Alternatively, Minitab can be used, providing the following output:

```
T-TEST OF THE MEAN

Test of mu = 4000.0 vs. mu > 4000.0

Variable    n      Mean     StDev    SE Mean      T          P
sales      15     4119.7     53.4      13.8      8.69     0.0000
```

Draw Conclusions

Step 4: *Decide whether to reject the null hypothesis.* Since the calculated test statistic of $t = 8.69$ is in the rejection region, we reject H_0. The p value of 0.0000 also tells us to reject H_0.

Step 5: *State the statistical decision in terms of the problem.* Based on these data, we can conclude that the advertising scheme has indeed increased sales. ■

Diameter of Washers *Lower-Tail Test of μ: Small Sample*

Your company purchases washers. It is important that the diameter of the hole not be more than 0.5 inch. If the hole in the center of the washer is too large then your company will not be able to use the washer. The diameters are assumed to be normally distributed. You have just received a shipment of 10,000 of these washers. You decide to sample 20 to check to be sure that the diameters are not more than 0.5 inch, on the average. Should you accept the shipment? Use $\alpha = 0.05$.

Step 1: *Set up the null and the alternative hypotheses.*

Step 2: *Define the test procedure.*

Step 3: *Collect the data and calculate the test statistic and the p value.* Your measurements (in inches) are

0.5053	0.5098	0.4606	0.4606
0.4711	0.4627	0.4800	0.4800
0.4672	0.5642	0.5495	0.5495
0.4672	0.5346	0.5745	0.5745
0.5340	0.3767	0.3933	0.3933

Step 4: *Decide whether to reject the null hypothesis.*

(continued)

Step 5: *Interpret the statistical decision in terms of the stated problem.*

9.2.3 Summary of Tests of the Mean: Small Sample

In the last two sections we have seen several more examples of the five-step hypothesis testing procedure. In each case, regardless of whether it was a two-tail or one-tail test, the same five steps were utilized. There were two major differences from the tests of μ when σ is known: (1) a t test statistic was used instead of Z and (2) the cutoff values for the rejection region were found by using the t table instead of the Z table.

The rejection regions are summarized here:

Type of Test	Rejection Region
Two-tail test of μ	Reject H_0 if $t < -t_{\alpha/2}$ or if $t > t_{\alpha/2}$
H_0: $\mu =$ [a specific number]	
H_A: $\mu \neq$ [a specific number]	
Lower-tail test of μ	Reject H_0 if $t < -t_\alpha$
H_0: $\mu \geq$ [a specific number]	
H_A: $\mu <$ [a specific number]	
Upper-tail test of μ	Reject H_0 if $t > t_\alpha$
H_0: $\mu \leq$ [a specific number]	
H_A: $\mu >$ [a specific number]	

9.2.4 Exercises—Learning It!

9.1 The cost of common goods and services in five cities is shown in the table *(USA Today)*:

City	Aspirin (100)	Fast food (hamburger, fries, soft drink)	Woman's haircut/blow dry	Toothpaste (6.4 oz)
Los Angeles	$7.69	$4.15	$20.11	$2.42
Tokyo	$35.93	$7.62	$76.24	$4.24
London	$9.69	$5.80	$44.35	$3.63
Sydney	$7.43	$4.53	$29.93	$2.08
Mexico City	$1.16	$3.63	$17.94	$1.08

(a) You have just returned from a business trip and you lost your receipt for the aspirin you purchased but would like to be reimbursed by your company (since you had to take the aspirin after a stressful business meeting!). You guesstimate a cost of $10.00. Your boss claims that the average cost of aspirin is less than $10.00. Using these data, can you "prove" your boss wrong? Conduct the necessary hypothesis test. Assume that all costs are normally distributed.

(b) Based on these data, is there enough evidence to support your submitting a cost of $10.00 for the fast-food meal on your trip?

ANS. $t = -0.72$, FAIL TO REJECT THE NULL HYPOTHESIS. ACCEPT THE SHIPMENT.

(c) If you remove Tokyo from the data set do your answers to parts (a) and (b) change? What does this tell you about the effect of outliers on the hypothesis test of μ when you have a small sample?

9.2 The marketing material for a New England ski resort advertises that they can make snow whenever the temperature is 32°F or below. To demonstrate how often this happens their material includes the following line graph of the weekly average temperatures.

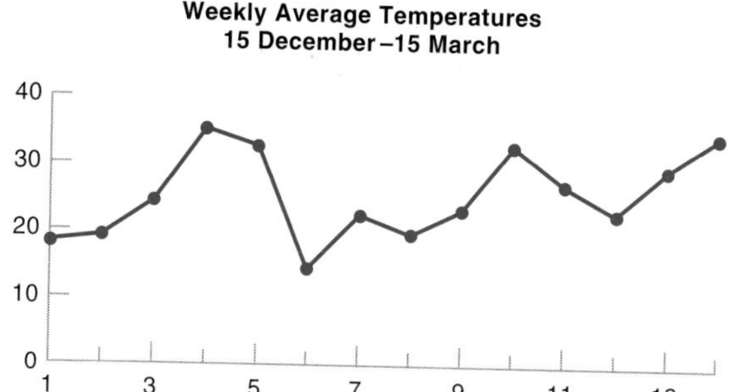

The data that generated this graph are shown here:

Week	1	2	3	4	5	6	7	8	9	10	11	12	13	14
Temperature	18	19	24	35	33	14	22	20	23	33	27	23	30	35

Is there enough evidence for the ski resort to claim that the average weekly temperature is less than 32°F? Assume that the average weekly temperature is normally distributed.

9.3 Although job prospects for nurses were once good, many nurses now face an uncertain future as hospitals cut staff and train unlicensed workers to do some of their jobs. The change is reflected in enrollment at several area nursing schools. The following table shows the enrollment at nursing schools in Western Massachusetts:

School	1995	1996
Holyoke Community College	60	45
Berkshire Community College	96	96
Greenfield Community College	90	79
Springfield Technical Community College	146	135
American International College	189	180
Elms College	298	300
UMass–Amherst	411	429
Baystate Medical Center	150	130

Using the 1996 data, test the hypothesis that the average enrollment in nursing programs has decreased from the average of 180 in 1995. Assume that enrollment in nursing programs is normally distributed.

9.4 If you like shopping for the best deal on long-distance phone service, then you'll enjoy sorting through offers from 10 different marketers vying to be your energy supplier. Residents of 16 communities will be the first in Massachusetts to wade into the coming nationwide experiment in deregulation of the natural gas industry. The average customer uses 1232 therms of natural gas, for which the average cost has been \$520.24. The table shows the proposed costs to deliver 1232 therms of natural gas from 10 competitors:

Company	Cost ($)
All Energy Marketing Co.	478.66
Broad Street/Energy One	450.24
Global Energy Services	468.16

(continued)

Company	Cost ($)
Green Mountain Energy Partners	471.24
KBC Energy Services	435.53
Louis Dreyfus Energy Services	472.24
National Fuel Resources	468.22
NorAm Energy	442.20
WEPCO Gas	443.52
Western Gas Resources	457.81

Is there enough evidence to conclude that the average cost to the customer from the competitors is less than $520.24? Assume that the costs are normally distributed.

9.5 Computer centers at universities and colleges are certainly aware of the increased number of Web surfers. To begin to understand the demands that will be made on the computer center resources, one school studied 25 children in grades 7 to 12. The number of hours that these children spent on the Internet in 1 week is shown here:

5.0	4.4	5.7	5.6	5.5
5.2	5.0	4.8	3.6	4.1
4.6	4.9	4.0	6.7	5.5
5.4	6.7	5.8	5.4	4.8
5.9	5.1	3.8	4.1	6.7

Is there enough evidence to indicate that children spend more than an average of 5 hours per week Web surfing? Assume that the time spent Web surfing is normally distributed.

9.3 χ^2 TEST OF A SINGLE VARIANCE

Remember: The variance is the standard deviation squared.

Hypothesis tests of the population variance, σ^2, follow the same basic steps that were used to do a hypothesis test of the population mean.

There are two types of situations for which you might be interested in doing a hypothesis test of the population variance. First, you may wish to see whether a manufacturing process is running to the specified standard deviation. You cannot test the standard deviation but must instead test the population variance. This was the case in Chapter 7 for the tissue manufacturer. Second, to perform some other statistical analysis of the data, you may need to know the population variance. In this case you would use sample data to test to see whether the population variance is, in fact, a particular value.

Just like with tests of the mean, you can do a two-tail or a one-tail test of the variance. To decide which type of test you need, you must determine what you are trying to learn from your study. The key words and guidelines are found in Chapter 8.

9.3.1 Two-Tail Hypothesis Test of the Variance

To learn how to do a two-tail test of the variance we will complete the five steps of the hypothesis testing procedure for the tissue manufacturer introduced in Chapter 8.

Understand the Problem

EXAMPLE 9.5 The Tissue Manufacturer

Test of Population Variance

Step 1: *Set Up the Null and Alternative Hypotheses for a Test of the Population Variance.* The variable *MDStrength* should have a standard deviation of 50 lb/ream. So, the population variance should be $50^2 = 2500$ (lb/ream)^2. This gives us the following null and alternative hypotheses:

$$H_0: \quad \sigma^2 = 2500 \text{ (lb/ream)}^2$$
$$H_A: \quad \sigma^2 \neq 2500 \text{ (lb/ream)}^2$$

■

The next step in the hypothesis testing procedure is to collect data and define the test procedure. To do this we must decide what test statistic to use. This is the main difference between a hypothesis test of the population mean, μ, and a hypothesis test of the population variance, σ^2. In testing means, we used the sample mean as the basis for our decision to reject or fail to reject the null hypothesis. Because the Central Limit Theorem told us that $\overline{X}$ has an approximately normal distribution for sufficiently large sample sizes, the appropriate test statistic for a large-sample test of the mean is a Z statistic and thus the rejection region is determined by Z values. As we have seen, in the small-sample case, $\overline{X}$ follows a t distribution for normally distributed populations.

If we are testing the population variance then the sample variance, s^2, will be used as the basis for deciding between H_0 and H_A. Relying once again on the mathematical statisticians to do the theoretical work, we learn that the sampling distribution associated with the sample variance, s^2, is called the chi-square (χ^2) distribution. The rejection region will be determined by critical values from the chi-square distribution. An example of a chi-square distribution is shown in Figure 9.3.

Use s^2 as the basis for deciding between H_0 and H_A.

The chi-square distribution, just like any distribution, describes how the random variable behaves. Recall from Chapter 6 that a distribution tells you the most likely values of the random variable (where there is the most area under the curve) and the least likely values of the random variable (where there is little to no area under the curve). You will see the chi-square distribution again in Chapter 15.

If the variable being studied is assumed to be normally distributed, then the statistic to test whether the population variance is equal to a particular value is calculated as follows:

$$\chi^2 = \frac{(n-1)\, s^2}{\sigma^2}$$

Chi-square test statistic for testing σ^2

where

n = sample size
s^2 = the sample variance
σ^2 = the hypothesized value of the population variance under the null hypothesis

Notice that this test statistic is basically comparing the variability contained in the sample and reflected in the sample variance to the value of the population variance that is being tested. In this case, the comparison takes the form of a ratio. In testing means, the comparison of the sample evidence, reflected in $\overline{X}$, to the value of the population mean being tested is accomplished by a subtraction. In both cases the idea is the same: Is the sample evidence consistent with the null hypothesis?

The chi-square test assumes that the underlying population distribution is normal.

This test statistic has been labeled with the Greek letter χ (chi) and a squared symbol, hence the name chi-square test statistic. Like the t distribution, the shape

The χ^2 distribution is not symmetric.

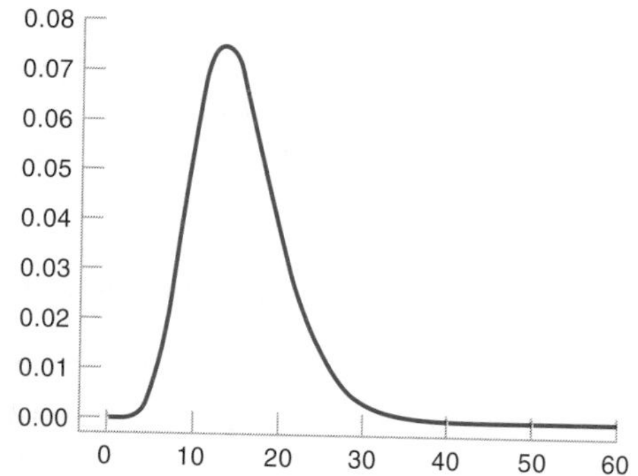

FIGURE 9.3 A chi-square distribution

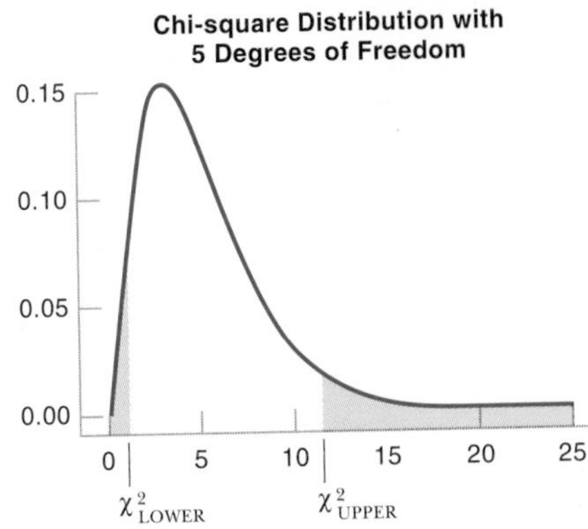

FIGURE 9.4 Rejection region for a two-sided test of the variance

of the chi-square distribution is determined by the number of degrees of freedom. This test statistic has $n - 1$ degrees of freedom. Unlike the Z and t distributions, the χ^2 distribution is not symmetric. In particular, you can never get a negative χ^2 value since $(n - 1)$, s^2, and σ^2 are all always positive.

Recall that the rejection region is the set of those values of the test statistic that would lead you to reject the null hypothesis. Let's think a minute about what values of the chi-square test statistic would lead us to reject the null hypothesis. Clearly, if the sample variance exactly equals the population variance, then the ratio of s^2 to σ^2 will be 1 and the test statistic will be equal to $n - 1$. In the case of the tissue manufacturer, this would be $36 - 1 = 35$. In this situation the sample evidence is clearly consistent with the null hypothesis and we would fail to reject H_0.

If the sample variance is quite different from the population variance being tested then it will be either larger or smaller than σ^2. If the sample variance is a great deal lower than the population variance being tested, then the ratio of s^2 to σ^2 will be a fraction and the test statistic will be some value less than $n - 1$. A similar analysis tells us that if the sample variance is a great deal larger than the population variance being tested, then the ratio of s^2 to σ^2 will be greater than 1 and the test statistic will be larger than $n - 1$. These are the situations that would lead us to reject H_0. This gives us the basic structure for the rejection region. We will reject H_0 if the value of the test statistic is much less than $n - 1$ or much greater than $n - 1$. Since this is a two-sided rejection region, the area in each tail must be $\alpha/2$. A typical rejection region is shown as the shaded region in Figure 9.4. It is defined by values greater than χ^2_{upper} or smaller than χ^2_{lower}.

Remember: *The total area of the rejection region is α.*

The specific values for χ^2_{lower} and χ^2_{upper} must be found from the chi-square table. A portion of this table is shown in Table 9.1. The complete table is found in Table 5 in Appendix A.

Note: *We cannot use +/− the same critical value since the distribution is not symmetric.*

Let's use this table to complete step 2 of the hypothesis testing procedure for the tissue company.

TABLE 9.1 A Portion of the Chi-square Table

	Upper-Tail Areas											
Degrees of Freedom	**0.995**	**0.99**	**0.975**	**0.95**	**0.9**	**0.75**	**0.25**	**0.1**	**0.05**	**0.025**	**0.01**	**0.005**
32	15.134	16.362	18.291	20.072	22.271	26.304	36.973	42.585	46.194	49.480	53.486	56.328
33	15.815	17.073	19.047	20.867	23.110	27.219	38.058	43.745	47.400	50.725	54.775	57.648
34	16.501	17.789	19.806	21.664	23.952	28.136	39.141	44.903	48.602	51.966	56.061	58.964
35	17.192	18.509	20.569	22.465	24.797	29.054	40.223	46.059	49.802	53.203	57.342	60.275

EXAMPLE 9.6 The Tissue Company

Rejection Region for Variance Test

Collect and Analyze the Data

Step 2: *Define the test procedure.*

The 36 sample data values were collected in Chapter 8. The company has been using $\alpha = 0.05$. Since the sample size was $n = 36$, we must use the row with $n - 1 =$ 35 degrees of freedom. To get the value for χ^2_{upper}, use the column labeled 0.025 in the upper tail.

The table value at the intersection of the correct row and column is 53.203. You may have noticed that the column values correspond to upper-tail areas. There is no need to have another table for lower-tail areas. To have the area of the lower tail be 0.025, the upper tail must be 0.975.

To get the value for χ^2_{lower} use the column labeled 0.975 in the upper tail. The table value at the intersection of the row with 35 degrees of freedom and 0.975 in the upper tail is 20.569. ■

To get a sense of how different the sample variance must be from the population variance in order to reject H_0, let's examine this rejection region for a moment. The upper cutoff value is 53.203. If we divide this by 35, the number of degrees of freedom, we get 1.52. Thus, even if the sample variance is 1.5 times larger than the population variance you are testing it against, you would not yet be in the rejection region. Likewise if we take the lower cutoff value of 20.569 and divide it by 35 we get 0.588. So, if the sample variance is, for example, 60% (0.60) of the population variance you are testing it against, you would not reject the null hypothesis. This tells us that the sample evidence must be "pretty different" from the population variance you are testing it against in order to reject the null hypothesis. The chi-square table quantifies "pretty different" for us.

Now we can complete step 3 of the hypothesis testing procedure. Remember that at this step the test statistic is calculated.

EXAMPLE 9.7 The Tissue Company

Calculating the Chi-square Test Statistic

Step 3: *Collect the data and calculate the test statistic and the p value.*

A sample of 36 tissues had a sample standard deviation of 60.1 lb/ream. The test statistic is

$$\chi^2 = \frac{(n-1)s^2}{\sigma^2}$$

$$= \frac{(36-1)(60.1)^2}{2500} = 50.57$$

The p value must be obtained from the output of software. ■

The fourth step of the hypothesis testing procedure is to decide whether to reject the null hypothesis on the basis of the test statistic. The fifth step is to interpret this decision in terms of the original problem statement. Let's complete the test of the variance for the tissue manufacturer.

EXAMPLE 9.8 The Tissue Company

Draw Conclusions

Steps 4 and 5 of the Hypothesis Testing Procedure

Since the value of 50.57 does not fall in the rejection region, we fail to reject the null hypothesis. This tells us that the manufacturing process is running according to specifications for the variability of the variable *MDStrength*. ■

TRY IT NOW!

The Cereal Company ***Testing the Variance***

A cereal manufacturer wishes to test whether the population variance of the weight of the boxes is equal to 0.0500 oz^2.

Step 1: *Set up the null and alternative hypotheses.*

Step 2: *Define the test procedure.* A random sample of 20 boxes has a standard deviation of s = 0.25oz. Use $\alpha = 0.05$.

Step 3: *Collect the data and calculate the test statistic and the p value.*

Step 4: *Decide whether to reject the null hypothesis.*

Step 5: *Interpret the statistical decision in terms of the stated problem.*

9.3.2 One-Sided Tests of the Variance

If you are testing the population variance, most of the time you are interested in doing a two-sided test. However, it is possible to do a one-sided test of the variance. The only change in the procedure needed to complete a one-sided test of the variance is in step 2. A one-sided rejection region is used in this case. The rejection regions for the two possibilities are shown in Figure 9.5.

H_0: $\sigma^2 \geq$ [a specific number]	H_0: $\sigma^2 \leq$ [a specific number]
H_A: $\sigma^2 <$ [a specific number]	H_A: $\sigma^2 >$ [a specific number]

ANS. H_0: $\sigma^2 = 0.0500$, H_A: $\sigma^2 \neq 0.0500$; $\chi^2_{\text{upper}} = 32.852$, $\chi^2_{\text{lower}} = 8.907$; TEST STATISTIC = 23.75; DO NOT REJECT H_0.

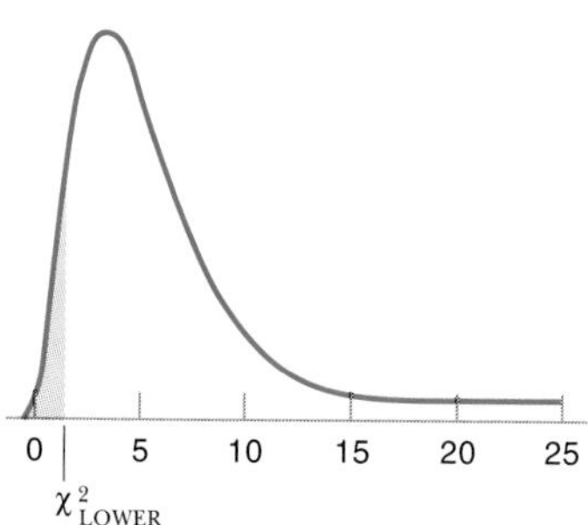

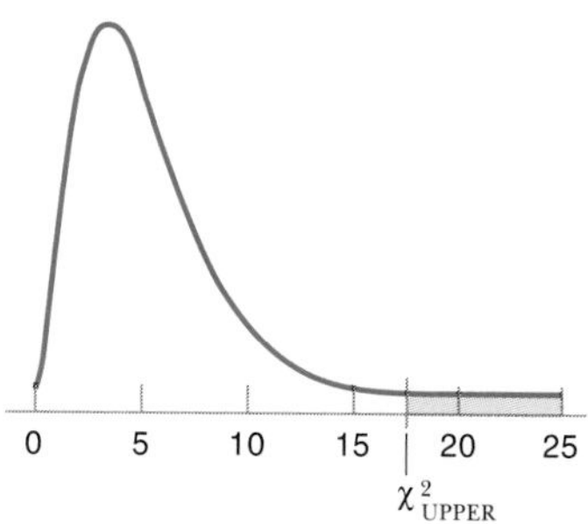

FIGURE 9.5 Rejection regions for one-sided tests of the variance

EXAMPLE 9.9 The Tissue Company

One-Sided Test of the Variance

Let's reconsider the variability for *MDStrength* for the tissue manufacturer. Suppose that the company wishes to be sure that the variance is at most 2500 lb/ream. The key words "at most" tell us this is an upper-tail test of the variance.

Understand the Problem

Step 1: Set up the null and alternative hypotheses.

$$H_0: \ \sigma^2 \leq 2500 \text{ lb/ream}$$

$$H_A: \ \sigma^2 > 2500 \text{ lb/ream}$$

Step 2: Define the test procedure. Set $\alpha = 0.05$. Use the chi-square table with 35 degrees of freedom to find the rejection region. The table value at the intersection of the row for 35 degrees of freedom and the column with 0.05 in the upper-tail area is 49.802. Note that we did not divide α in half because this is a one-sided test with a one-sided rejection region.

Analyze the Data

Step 3: Collect the data and calculate the test statistic and p value. The data were collected in Chapter 8, Exercise 8.50. There were 2500 observations. The test statistic is calculated here:

$$\chi^2 = \frac{(n-1)s^2}{\sigma^2}$$

$$= \frac{(36-1)(60.1)^2}{2500} = 50.57$$

Step 4: Decide whether to reject the null hypothesis. This test statistic falls in the rejection region, so we reject the null hypothesis.

Step 5: Interpret the statistical decision in terms of the stated problem. We conclude that the population variance is greater than 2500 lb/ream and the process should be adjusted. ■

Draw Conclusions

You should notice that we got two different results based on the same sample of data. When we used a two-sided test of the variance we failed to reject the null hypothesis and concluded that the process was running properly. But when we used an upper-tail test of the variance we concluded that the population variance was greater than 2500 lb/ream and that the process was not running properly. You must decide what you are interested in detecting before you do the test. This is an example of how to "lie with statistics." You might say that the data do not lie. You are right about that in one sense. However, by manipulating the type of test that is done and the value of α that is used, you can change the conclusions of the analysis. If you are using the results of someone else's data analysis you must ask the right questions to be sure that the data have not been unfairly manipulated to support a particular position.

9.3.3 Summary of Tests on the Variance

In this section all of the tests used the same test statistic in steps 2 and 3. The purpose of the test statistic is always the same: It gives you a single number that summarizes the sample information and helps you to decide between the null and alternative hypotheses. The test statistic for tests on variances is

$$\chi^2 = \frac{(n-1)s^2}{\sigma^2}$$

At step 2 we did see that the rejection region is different depending on what type of test we are doing. These differences are summarized in the next table.

Type of Test	Rejection Region
Two-tail test of σ^2	Reject H_0 if $\chi^2 < \chi^2_{\text{lower}}$ or if $\chi^2 > \chi^2_{\text{upper}}$
H_0: $\sigma^2 =$ [a specific number]	
H_A: $\sigma^2 \neq$ [a specific number]	
Lower-tail test of σ^2	Reject H_0 if $\chi^2 < \chi^2_{\text{lower}}$
H_0: $\sigma^2 \geq$ [a specific number]	
H_A: $\sigma^2 <$ [a specific number]	
Upper-tail test of σ^2	Reject H_0 if $\chi^2 > \chi^2_{\text{upper}}$
H_0: $\sigma^2 \leq$ [a specific number]	
H_A: $\sigma^2 >$ [a specific number]	

9.3.4 Exercises—Learning It!

9.6 A company that sells mail-order computer systems has been planning inventory and staffing based on an assumption that the variance of their weekly sales is 180 ($\$1000^2$). The weekly sales are normally distributed. The company selects 15 weeks at random from the past year and obtains the data (in thousands of dollars) shown here:

Weekly sales	191	222	222	223	223	225	227	228	229	232	234	234	236	244	253

(a) What is the sample variance for these data?

(b) Set up the hypotheses to test whether the population variance is different from 180.

(c) At the 0.05 level of significance, what can you conclude about the company's assumption?

9.7 In manufacturing, the amount of material that is wasted or lost during a process is very important. In preparing financial estimates, a company assumes that the percent material lost for its new process has a variance of $10\%^2$. After the new process has been running for a month and appears to be stable, the cost analyst looks at the percent material lost and finds the following data:

Daily Loss	10	12	12	13	14	14	18	19	19	20

(a) What is the sample variance for these data?

(b) Set up the hypotheses to test whether the actual variance is greater than the value the company has been assuming. Assume that the daily loss is normally distributed.

(c) At the 0.05 level of significance, what can you conclude?

9.8 Lead time for an order is a critical factor in inventory planning. A company has noticed that inventory for assembling its new product line has been consistently short in the past few months. It has been assumed that lead time is normally distributed with a standard deviation of 2 days. The company decides to look at the last 20 orders placed, and finds that the lead times (in days) are

1	4	6	7
4	5	6	8
4	5	7	8
4	6	7	10
4	6	7	11

(a) What is the sample variance for these data?

(b) Set up the hypotheses to test whether the actual variance is greater than the value the company has been assuming. Be sure you use the variance here.

(c) At the 0.05 level of significance, what can you conclude?

9.9 In an effort to understand the cost overruns by a particular department in a company, data were collected on the amount of the overrun ($) for 24 different days:

87.3	93.7	96.8	98.4	100.9	107.8
89.9	94.9	97.0	99.6	101.3	109.7
91.5	96.5	97.1	100.3	105.7	111.5
93.6	96.7	97.3	100.4	107.7	114.2

(a) Calculate the sample variance for the daily cost overrun.

(b) At the 0.05 level of significance, do the data agree with the assumption that the variance of the daily overrun is 50 (dollars)^2. Assume that the cost overruns are normally distributed.

9.4 TEST OF A SINGLE PROPORTION

All of the tests that we have done thus far in the chapter have been tests on quantitative data. However, very often it is not the average or variance that we are interested in but rather some proportion of the population that behaves in a certain manner. If the data we are analyzing are *nominal data*, the hypothesis might be a statement about

- The value of the proportion, π, of population members that have a certain characteristic (one of the categories of the nominal variable)

For example, the hypothesis might be a statement about the proportion of

- Residents of Swingfield who are in favor of a casino
- Students who are interested in graduate school
- Vaccinated patients who remain cancer free
- CEOs who use computers as a major tool
- People who are unemployed

In these cases, the parameter of interest is a proportion. In Chapter 7 you learned that an estimator for the true unknown proportion, π, is the corresponding sample proportion, p. For example, if 100 people are surveyed and 58 are in favor of a casino, then the sample proportion, p, is 58/100 or 0.58.

__Remember:__ We are using π to represent the population proportion. The Greek letter tells you it's a parameter.

Like $\overline{X}$, the sample proportion, p, rarely if ever actually equals the true population proportion, π. Remember that this is not because you did something wrong but rather because you are looking at only a piece of the population and not the entire population. This is what we have called sampling error. It is a fact of life in statistics. You cannot eliminate sampling error unless you examine the entire population.

Since the sample proportion is not likely to equal the population proportion, we again see that the estimate alone is inadequate for making decisions. Suppose, for example, that more than 60% of the voters must be in favor of a casino and the sample proportion comes out to be 0.58. Does this automatically mean that the casino should be killed? Is it possible that more than 60% of the population favors the casino but only 58% of those sampled favor the casino? Possibly. How possible again depends on the standard error. So we need to develop the hypothesis testing procedure for tests on proportions. We start by looking at two-tail tests of proportions.

9.4.1 Two-Tail Tests of Proportions

Fortunately much of what we have already learned about hypothesis testing can be easily adapted to tests of proportions. In fact, we will use precisely the same five steps that we have been following for any hypothesis test.

Let's use an example to see how these steps work for a two-tail test of proportions.

Understand the Problem

EXAMPLE 9.10 Beverly Hills, 90210

Two-Tail Test of Proportions

Hard times have hit the *Beverly Hills, 90210* crowd. Nearly a third of teens polled by Teenage Research Limited said they have been personally affected by the recession. Where do teens get their money? Suppose you wish to do a hypothesis test to see whether half or 50% of all teens get some money from their parents.

Step 1: *Set up the null and alternative hypotheses.* The same general guidelines from Chapter 8 apply to setting up the null and the alternative hypotheses for a test of proportions. Since we are interested in seeing if the true proportion *differs* from 50% in either direction, we use a two-tail test. For this example, the null and alternative hypotheses are

$$H_0: \quad \pi = 0.50$$
$$H_A: \quad \pi \neq 0.50$$

Step 2: *Define the test procedure.* A survey of 1000 teens showed that 47% of them get some money from their parents. In Chapter 7 you learned that the sampling distribution for p is the normal distribution. Therefore, the test statistic for proportions is a Z statistic. Thus, the form of the rejection region is exactly the same as the rejection region for a two-tail test on the mean when the standard deviation is known. If we set $\alpha = 0.05$, then the rejection region is as follows: reject H_0 if $Z > 1.96$ or $Z < -1.96$.

Collect and Analyze the Data

Step 3: *Collect the data and calculate the test statistic and the p value.* Now we must consider what information in the sample will help us make a decision between the null and the alternative hypotheses. Clearly, we must use the sample proportion, p. But we know that we cannot simply use the value of p alone. We must take into account the fact that p will vary from sample to sample. As we have repeatedly seen, this is taken into account by dividing by the standard error of the estimator. The appropriate test statistic is

Z test statistic for proportions

$$Z = \frac{p - \pi}{\sqrt{\pi(1 - \pi)/n}}$$

where π is the hypothesized value of the population proportion.

This test statistic has the same basic form as the Z statistic we used in testing μ. In that case we used

$$Z = \frac{\overline{X} - \mu}{\sigma/\sqrt{n}}$$

In the numerator we are calculating the difference between the value of the population proportion, π, and the sample proportion, p. This is equivalent to the calculation that we did in the numerator of the Z calculation for μ. In the denominator of both Z statistics we use the standard error of the estimator. In the case of proportions, this is $\sqrt{\pi(1-\pi)/n}$.

For this example the Z statistic is

$$Z = \frac{0.47 - 0.50}{\sqrt{0.50(1 - 0.50)/1000}} = -1.90$$

Remember that the p value is the smallest value of α for which you can reject H_0. To complete the hypothesis test you should calculate the p value. The p value for a test of proportions is calculated the same way as it was for the test of means. Since this is a two-tail test we must double the tail area probability. The Z statistic for this example was found to be -2.68. So, the p value is found as follows:

$$p \text{ value} = 2P(Z > 2.68) = (2)(0.0287) = 0.0574$$

If you select an α of 0.05 as we have done in this example, then you will fail to reject H_0. The output from Excel using the KADDSTAT add-in is shown here. The "one-sample test for pi" option was selected from the Kadd main menu and the alternative hypothesis was specified as "not equal."

One Sample Test for π	
p-value =	0.0574
Null Hypothesis: π =	0.5
Alternative Hypothesis:	Not Equal
Number of Trials: n =	1000
Number of Successes:	470
pi-hat =	0.4700

Step 4: *Decide whether to reject H_0.* Since the value of $Z = -1.90$ is not in the rejection region, we do not reject H_0.

Draw Conclusions

Step 5: *Interpret the statistical decision in terms of the stated problem.* We conclude that the true proportion of teenagers who receive spending money from their parents is not different from 0.50. ■

TRY IT NOW!

Poll of Americans *Test of Proportion*

She did it again. For the zillionth time, your mother casually asked you when you are going to get married and you've been seething ever since. How do you get it off your chest? These days, you might e-mail her. The Pew Internet and American Life Project, based on a telephone survey of 3533 randomly selected adults, recently (July 2000) calculated that 64 million of us e-mail our family members. Thirty-one percent of those who send family e-mail find it an easier way to say frank or unpleasant things to their relatives. Is there evidence that more than 30% of those who send family e-mail use it to communicate unpleasant things? Use $\alpha = 0.05$.

Step 1: *Set up the null and alternative hypotheses.*

(continued)

Step 2: *Define the test procedure.*

Step 3: *Collect the data and calculate the test statistic and the p value.*

Step 4: *Decide whether to reject the null hypothesis.*

Step 5: *Interpret the statistical decision in terms of the stated problem.*

9.4.2 One-Tail Test of Proportions

Finally, we move to one-tail tests of proportions. Here again the five-step hypothesis testing procedure is identical to the one we have been using. The test statistic is the same as that used for a two-tail test of proportions and the rejection regions are the same as those used for one-tail tests of the mean.

Step 1: *Set up the null and alternative hypotheses.* There are two possible ways to set up a one-tail test of proportions. We have already looked at the issues that should be addressed in deciding how to set up the hypothesis test. Here we will simply present the two forms again using the terms upper-tail and lower-tail test.

Remember *that the specific number must be a number from 0 to 1.*

Upper-Tail Test	Lower-Tail Test
H_0: $\pi \leq$ [a specific number]	H_0: $\pi \geq$ [a specific number]
H_A: $\pi >$ [a specific number]	H_A: $\pi <$ [a specific number]

Step 2: *Define the test procedure.* Since the test statistic is a Z test, the rejection regions for the one-tail tests are precisely the same as the ones we used in testing means.

Step 3: *Collect the data and calculate the test statistic and the p value.* We have seen in the previous section that the appropriate test statistic is

$$z = \frac{p - \pi}{\sqrt{\pi(1 - \pi)/n}}$$

For an upper-tail test, the p value is the probability of observing a z value greater than this test statistic value. For a lower-tail test, the p value is the

ANS. H_0: $\pi \leq 0.30$, H_A: $\pi > 0.30$; CRITICAL VALUE $= \pm 1.96$; $Z = -1.30$; FAIL TO REJECT H_0; p VALUE $= 0.0968$

probability of observing a z value less than this test statistic value. Note that the p value is not doubled for a one-tail test as it is for a two-tail test.

Steps 4 and **5** remain the same. ■

Consider an example.

EXAMPLE 9.11 Testing Raw Materials

An Upper-Tail Test of Proportions

Your company has been building a long-term relationship with one of its suppliers in the spirit of TQM. The supplier claims that at most 5% of its products are defective. Should you believe the supplier's claim? Test using $\alpha = 0.05$.

Understand the Problem

Step 1: *Set up the null and alternative hypotheses.* Since you are interested in seeing whether there is at most 5% defectives, this is an upper-tail test. You will believe the supplier's claim unless the data indicate otherwise. This is an upper-tail test with the following setup:

H_0: $\pi \leq 0.05$ (Supplier's claim is correct.)

H_A: $\pi > 0.05$ (Supplier's claim is incorrect.)

Step 2: *Define the test procedure.* You take a sample of 100 items and find six defectives. Since $\alpha = 0.05$, the rejection region is $z > 1.645$.

Step 3: *Collect the data and calculate the test statistic and the p value.* The sample proportion was found to be $p = 6/100 = 0.06$ and the sample size was $n = 100$. Using this information we can calculate the test statistic:

Collect and Analyze the Data

$$Z = \frac{p - \pi}{\sqrt{\pi(1 - \pi)/n}} = \frac{0.06 - 0.05}{\sqrt{0.05(1 - 0.05)/100}} = 0.46$$

Notice that 0.05 is used as the value for π since that is the hypothesized value of the population proportion under H_0.

This is an upper-tail test so we do not double the tail area probability. The p value is found as follows:

$$p \text{ value} = P(Z > 0.46) = 0.3228$$

The output from Excel using the KADDSTAT add-in is shown here. The "one-sample test for pi" option was selected from the KADD main menu and the alternative hypothesis was specified as "greater than."

One Sample Test for π	
p-value =	0.3228
Null Hypothesis: π =	0.05
Alternative Hypothesis:	Greater Than
Number of Trials: n =	100
Number of Successes:	6
pi-hat =	0.0600

Step 4: *Decide whether to reject H_0.* Since $Z = 0.46$ does not fall in the rejection region, we fail to reject H_0. The p value is 0.3228, which is greater than $\alpha = 0.05$ so we fail to reject H_0.

Draw Conclusions

Step 5: *Interpret the statistical decision in terms of the problem.* You cannot conclude with confidence that the vendor has more than 5% defectives in the entire shipment. There is not enough evidence that the supplier's claim is incorrect. ■

Try It Now!

The Soft Drink Company *One-Tail Test of Proportion*

The Coca-Cola Company is interested in entering the fruit drink market. Before bringing its new product, Fruitopia, to the market the company wishes to be sure that it will capture more than 20% of the fruit drink market. Is there enough evidence to allow Coca-Cola to proceed with the new product? Use $\alpha = 0.05$.

Step 1: *Set up the null and alternative hypotheses.*

Step 2: *Define the test procedure.* A survey of 1000 people shows that 225 respondents prefer Fruitopia to other fruit drinks.

Step 3: *Collect the data and calculate the test statistic and the p value.*

Step 4: *Decide whether to reject the null hypothesis.*

Step 5: *Interpret the statistical decision in terms of the stated problem.*

9.4.3 Summary of Tests on Proportions

In this section all of the tests use the same test statistic in steps 2 and 3. The purpose of the test statistic is always the same: It gives you a single number that summarizes the sample information and helps you to decide between the null and alternative hypotheses. The test statistic for tests on proportions is

$$z = \frac{p - \pi}{\sqrt{\pi(1 - \pi)/n}}$$

ANS. H_0: $\pi \leq 0.20$, H_A: $\pi > 0.20$; CRITICAL VALUE = 1.645; $Z = 1.98$; p VALUE = 0.0240; FAIL TO REJECT H_0; THEY SHOULD PROCEED WITH FRUITOPIA.

At step 2 we did see that the rejection region is different depending on what type of test we are performing. This is summarized here:

Type of Test	Rejection Region
Two-tail test of π	Reject H_0 if $z < -z_{\alpha/2}$ or if $z > z_{\alpha/2}$
H_0: $\pi =$ [a specific number between 0 and 1]	
H_A: $\pi \neq$ [a specific number between 0 and 1]	
Lower-tail test of π	Reject H_0 if $z < -z_\alpha$
H_0: $\pi \geq$ [a specific number between 0 and 1]	
H_A: $\pi <$ [a specific number between 0 and 1]	
Upper-tail test of π	Reject H_0 if $z > z_\alpha$
H_0: $\pi \leq$ [a specific number between 0 and 1]	
H_A: $\pi >$ [a specific number between 0 and 1]	

9.4.4 Exercises—Learning It!

9.10 Companies are increasingly concerned about employees playing video games at work. In addition to reducing productivity, this habit slows down networks and uses valuable storage space. A recent article stated that 80% of all employees play video games at work at least once a week. A large company that employs many engineers wonders whether its employees are as bad as the article claims. If they are, the company will install software that detects and removes video games from the network. The company surveys (anonymously) 100 employees and finds that 85 of the employees surveyed had played video games at work in the past week.

(a) Set up the null and alternative hypotheses to test whether the proportion of the company's employees that play video games is greater than the proportion stated in the article.

(b) At the 0.05 level of significance, test the hypotheses.

(c) What do you recommend that the company do?

9.11 An alumni office is interested in serving their alumni better to encourage more donations to the college. A survey of 200 alumni was conducted to determine whether half-day training sessions offered on the campus were of interest. If more than 75% of the alumni were interested, the college would start a program. The survey showed that 160 of the alumni surveyed were interested in such a program.

(a) Set up the null and alternative hypotheses to test whether the college should implement the program.

(b) At the 0.05 level of significance, test the hypotheses.

(c) What do you recommend that the college do?

9.12 A company that makes computer keyboards has specifications that allow it to produce a product that has a maximum of 3% defective. The company has been receiving more customer complaints than usual. A sample of 50 keyboards has 2 defectives.

(a) Set up the null and alternative hypotheses to test whether the proportion defective keyboards has exceeded the amount allowed by the specifications.

(b) At the 0.05 level of significance, test the hypotheses.

(c) What do you recommend that the company do?

9.13 A university in the Northeast claims in its brochures that it has an acceptance rate of 60%. A sample of 300 high school seniors who applied to this university shows that 148 of them were accepted.

(a) Set up the null and alternative hypotheses to test whether the acceptance rate is what the university claims.

(b) At the 0.05 level of significance, test the hypotheses.

(c) Is there a need for the university to change its literature?

9.14 "Computer Jobs Increase by 6%" is the headline on an article in a national newspaper. A study of the classified job ads in that same newspaper indicates that out of 2202 advertisements in a typical Sunday edition, 502 were for computer related jobs. Statistics released by the Bureau of Labor Statistics for the last 12 months show that 15% of available jobs were computer related.

(a) Set up the null and alternative hypotheses to test whether the headline is correct.

(b) At the 0.05 level of significance, test the hypotheses.

(c) What conclusion can you reach?

9.5 SUMMARY OF ONE-POPULATION TESTS

We have now finished with the tests of parameters of one population variables. In the next chapter you will learn how to extend these tests to compare the parameters from two populations. Before leaving this chapter, it might be helpful to summarize all the one-population tests from this chapter and from Chapter 8.

We have said repeatedly that the steps for *any* hypothesis test are the same and the only thing that changes is the test statistic, which impacts the determination of the rejection region and the p value calculation. However, it is easy to get lost in the details of the particulars for each test. To help you, the flow chart below suggests a number of questions that you could ask yourself to help you decide which test to use. The diamond shape symbols indicate a decision point for you.

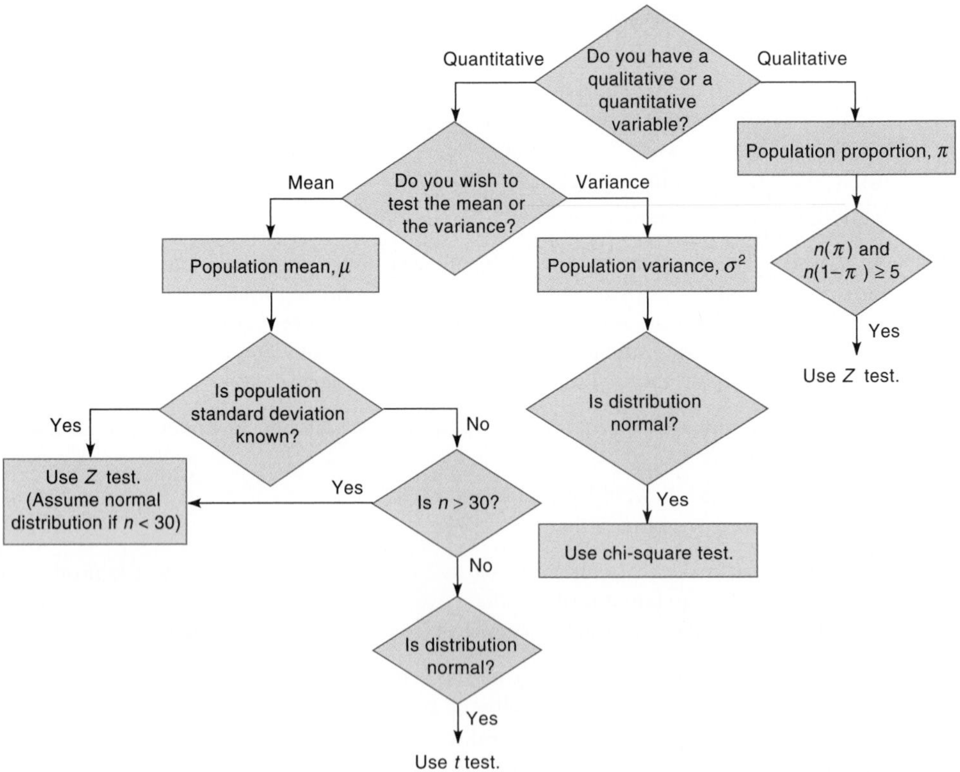

Notice that many of the tests require that the underlying population distribution be normal. Most of the time you will not know this for sure. There is a hypothesis test for testing whether the underlying distribution is normal. It is another chi-square test, which is covered in Chapter 15. For now, you should get used to displaying the data as a histogram or a boxplot when you have a quantitative variable. Visually check to see whether the histogram is "reasonably" bell shaped.

Also notice that there is an assumption to be checked when you are testing a population proportion. Technically, you should use a binomial distribution to test a hypothesis about π. However, when $n(\pi)$ and $n(1 - \pi)$ are greater than or equal to 5, then the binomial distribution can be approximated by the normal or the Z distribution. Be sure to check this condition before using the Z test to test proportions.

Discovery Exercise 9.1

EXPLORING THE CONNECTION BETWEEN CONFIDENCE INTERVALS AND HYPOTHESIS TESTING

Part I

A recent survey is offering the first evidence that PCs are replacing TVs as the primary source of home recreation, information, and entertainment. The survey was conducted among 1200 homes nationwide. The average computer user spends 9.5 hours per week in front of the PC but only 8 hours per week watching prime-time TV. Assume that the standard deviation of hours spent in front of a PC is 3 hours/week.

(a) Test the hypothesis that the average number of hours per week a computer user spends in front of a PC is different from 8 hours. Use $\alpha = 0.05$.

(b) Using the same data, construct a 95% confidence interval for μ, the population average time spent in front of a PC.

(c) Is the value of 8 in the confidence interval you constructed in part (b)?

(d) Did you reject the null hypothesis in part (a)?

Part II

The Casual Businesswear Employee Survey was conducted to assess the attitudes and behavior of white-collar employees whose companies allow casual dress on some basis. The study was national in scope and the sample size was 752 people. Of those in the sample, 609 agree that allowing casual dress improves morale.

(a) Test the hypothesis that the proportion of white-collar employees who agree that allowing casual dress improves morale is different from 80%. Use $\alpha = 0.05$.

(b) Construct a 95% confidence interval for π.

(continued)

(c) Is the value of 0.80 in the confidence interval?

(d) Did you fail to reject the null hypothesis?

Part III

Summarize.

Based on these two situations, speculate how you would complete the following statements:

If the value of the parameter being tested (the one in the null hypothesis) is not in the confidence interval then I will ________ the null hypothesis.

If the value of the parameter being tested (the one in the null hypothesis) is in the confidence interval then I will ________ the null hypothesis.

9.6 CONNECTION BETWEEN HYPOTHESIS TESTING AND CONFIDENCE INTERVALS

Now you have learned about both confidence intervals and hypothesis testing. These two techniques are actually closely related even though they are used for different purposes. You can see the relationship between these techniques easily if we reconsider one of the hypothesis testing examples from this chapter and calculate the corresponding confidence interval. Let's look at the tissue company.

EXAMPLE 9.12 The Tissue Company

Understand the Problem

Relationship of Confidence Interval to Hypothesis Test

Analyze the Data

A sample of 36 tissues was taken and the average *MDStrength* was 980 lb/ream. The standard deviation of the process is 50 lb/ream. In Example 8.11, we tested the hypothesis that the population mean *MDStrength* was 1000 lb/ream. The following hypothesis test was done:

$$H_0: \quad \mu = 1000 \text{ lb/ream}$$
$$H_A: \quad \mu \neq 1000 \text{ lb/ream}$$

Draw Conclusions

The value of the test statistic was $Z = -2.4$. Based on this Z value and an α value of 0.05, the null hypothesis was rejected, leading us to conclude that the population mean, μ, was not 1000 lb/ream.

Now construct a 95% confidence interval for μ using these data:

$$\text{Upper} = \overline{X} + Z(\sigma/\sqrt{n}) = 980 + (1.96)(50/\sqrt{36}) = 980 + 16.33 = 996.33 \text{ lb/ream}$$

$$\text{Lower} = \overline{X} - Z(\sigma/\sqrt{n}) = 980 - (1.96)(50/\sqrt{36}) = 980 - 16.33 = 963.67 \text{ lb/ream}$$ ■

Notice that the value of μ of 1000 lb/ream is not in the confidence interval. This means that 1000 is not a likely value of μ. Using the same data we rejected the null hypothesis, concluding that μ was not 1000 lb/ream. You can see that the results from the confidence interval are consistent with the conclusions drawn from the hypothesis test.

This result can be stated in general for any hypothesis test, whether it be a test of μ, σ^2, or π. If the value of the parameter being tested (the one in the null hypothesis) is in the confidence interval, then you will fail to reject the null hypothesis of a two-tail test. If the value of the parameter being tested is not in the confidence interval, then you will reject the null hypothesis. Of course, the same value of α must be used for both the confidence interval construction and the hypothesis test, and the hypothesis test must be a two-tail test.

9.7 Executive Summary:

THE HOSPITAL

Business Analysis...

TO: Human Resource Manager
FROM: Erica Q. Analyst
RE: Training

You asked my department to make a recommendation on whether hospital employees should participate in a training session to learn about the consequences of inadequate hand washing. To make this decision we needed to find out how long, on the average, employees are washing their hands. The literature indicates that at least 5 seconds of hand washing is necessary to cut down on the spread of bacteria.

A sample of 28 employees were observed. This was a particularly challenging data collection because if people knew they were being observed, they would most likely wash their hands for longer than usual. So, employees did not know they were being observed. **The average hand washing time is statistically less than 5 seconds.** The results are summarized in the table:

Sample Size	28
Sample Mean	2.536 sec
Sample Standard Deviation	3.687 sec
t statistic	−3.54
p value	0.0007

A histogram of the data is shown here:

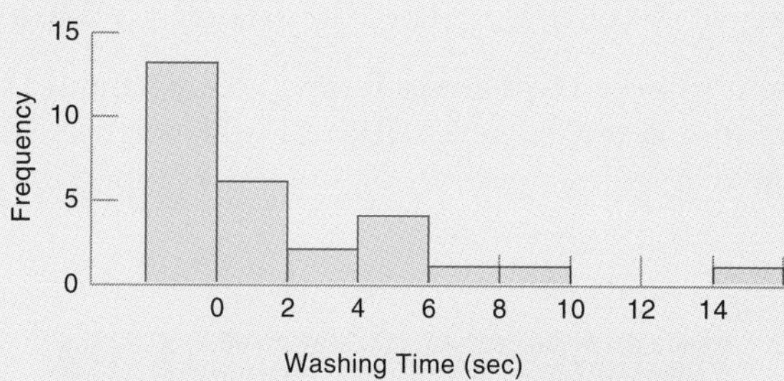

No one washed their hands a negative amount of time; the first column of the graph corresponds to those employees who did not wash their hands (time = 0 sec). Since our sample size was less than 30, the *t* test was used in the analysis. This test requires the underlying assumption that the variable of interest is normally distributed. As you can see from the graph, the washing times do not appear to be normally distributed and therefore we must be concerned about the size of the sample. To avoid this problem, a sample size greater than 30 should be taken. We understand that this is particularly difficult given the nature of the data collection.

Even though we have probably violated the assumption of normality for the *t* test, the large number of people who are not washing their hands suggests that some training in this area is necessary. We suggest that you proceed with the plans for training. In addition, the washing times should be analyzed by department.

(continued)

Clearly, it is more critical in some areas of the hospital than in others. We also suggest that data on hand washing time be collected after the training to see whether the training was effective.

The *Wall Street Journal* is a major source of current business news and information for the business community. If your professor has arranged for your class to have access to the Business Extra feature, you can go to it now and see the techniques of this chapter in action today. Go to the Wiley Web site at http://www.wiley.com/college/pelosi, and click on Business Extra!

9.8 HYPOTHESIS TESTING IN EXCEL

One of the things you learned in this chapter is that all hypothesis tests have the same basic form. What changes from test to test is how to calculate the test statistic and which sampling distribution applies. It is most important to understand when each test is appropriate.

This is also true about using Excel to perform hypothesis tests. All that changes for the different tests is the input.

KADDSTAT provides statistical functions that allow you to perform hypothesis tests for both means and proportions. The basic steps are the same for each. The only differences are the input that the user must supply. We will give detailed directions for the small-sample hypothesis test for the mean. Once you understand this procedure, the others are very similar.

9.8.1 Small-Sample Tests for the Population Mean

From the KADD menu choose **Hypothesis Testing > One Sample.** You will see a list of the one-sample hypothesis tests that KADDSTAT will perform. Choose **Population Mean using t** and the dialog box shown in Figure 9.6 will open.

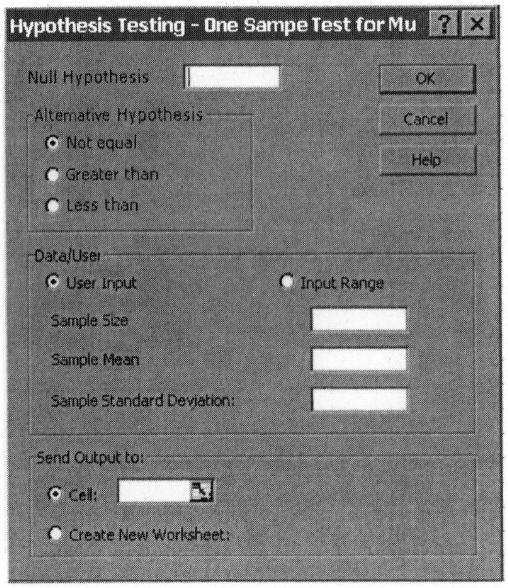

FIGURE 9.6 Dialog box for small-sample test of μ

The dialog boxes for hypothesis testing have three main parts: Null Hypothesis, Alternative Hypothesis, and Data/User.

Suppose that we are looking at the hand washing data and we want to perform a test to see whether the mean time spent washing hands is different from 5 seconds. Since this is a small sample, 28 employees, and we do not have the population standard deviation, the t test is appropriate. We will use a level of significance of 0.05.

1. In the box labeled Null Hypothesis, input the value of the hypothesized mean, 5 seconds.
2. Next we must identify the form of the alternative hypothesis. Since we want to know whether the mean has *changed*, this is a two-sided test. Click on the radio button next to **Not Equal.**
3. Now we must indicate whether we are doing the test from raw data or from a set of summary statistics. If you have summary statistics only, you would input the sample size, the sample mean, and the sample standard deviation. In this case we have the data so click on the button labeled **Input Range.** The dialog box will change to allow you to input the range in the Excel worksheet that contains the data. Position the cursor in the box labeled **Input Range** and highlight the data in the Excel worksheet. Click on **Header Row Included** if your data range is labeled with a variable name.
4. Last, indicate where you want the results of the test to be located.

The completed dialog box should look like the one in Figure 9.7. Click **OK** and the output shown in Figure 9.8 will appear in the location you specified.

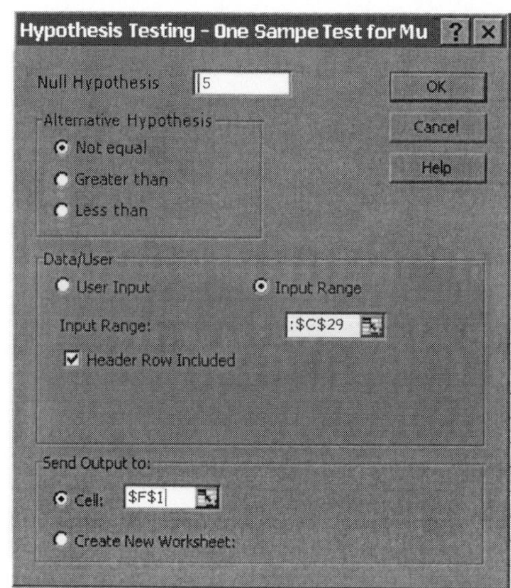

FIGURE 9.7 Completed dialog box for hand washing data

F	G
One Sample Test for μ	
p-value =	0.0015
Null Hypothesis: μ=	5
Alternative Hypothesis:	Not Equal
Sample Size: n =	28
Sample Mean: $\bar{X}$ =	2.5357
Sample Std. Dev.: S =	3.6866
Standard Error: $S_{\bar{X}}$ =	0.6967

FIGURE 9.8 Output from the t test for the hand washing data

From the output section, we see that the p value of the test is 0.0015. This means that unless our chosen level of significance is less than 0.0015, we will reject H_0 and conclude that the hand washing time has changed.

9.8.2 χ^2 Tests for the Variance in Excel

There is no built-in tool or macro for the χ^2 test for the variance, but the test can be performed by using some built-in Excel functions. Most of these functions should be familiar to you.

We will look at the problem of the tissue manufacturer. When we did the test on the mean tissue strength in Chapter 8, we used the target value for the standard deviation, 50 lb/ream. Now we will test to see whether it was reasonable to assume that the population variance is 2500 $(\text{lb/ream})^2$, using a χ^2 test. The data are the same data that we used in Chapter 8.

Since we want to know whether the true population variance is different from the target value of 2500 $(\text{lb/ream})^2$, we will do a two-tailed test. To do the test, we will need to calculate the value of the test statistic and the critical value for the test. We will also calculate the p value for the test.

The test statistic for a χ^2 test for the variance is

$$\chi^2 = \frac{(n-1)s^2}{\sigma^2}$$

To calculate this using Excel, the following steps are used:

E	F
s^2	
σ^2	
n	
Test Statistic	
Critical Value	
p value	

FIGURE 9.9 Setup for χ^2 test

1. To organize the output, put labels in worksheet cells to identify all of the output values. Then when you are done, you will know which value is which. In this case, label cells for s^2, σ^2, the sample size, the test statistic, the critical value of the test, and the p value of the test. An example of this is shown in Figure 9.9.
2. In the cell adjacent to the one labeled s^2, use the **STDEV** function to calculate the sample standard deviation, and then square it. The formula will look like the one shown in Figure 9.10.

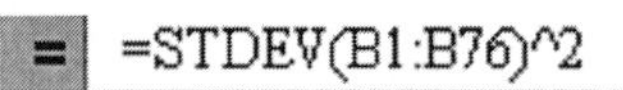

FIGURE 9.10 Formula for variance

As an alternative to this, you can use the **VAR** function, which calculates the sample variance. The input for this function is the data range, just as in the **STDEV** function.

3. In the cell adjacent to the one labeled σ^2, type in **2500**, and type **75** in the one adjacent to n.
4. To calculate the test statistic, we will need the three values just input. In the cell adjacent to Test Statistic, type in the following formula:

Note: You need parentheses for $n - 1$.

```
=(F3-1)*F1/F2
```

These are the cell locations from the worksheet we are using as an example. Be sure to use the cell locations from *your* worksheet if they are different. You could enter the numbers directly in the formula, but it really is easier to use the cell locations.

5. We will use the **CHIINV** function to find the two critical values for the test. The **CHIINV** function works the same way as the **TINV** function. The input values are the upper-tail probability and the degrees of freedom. Since α for this test is 0.05 and it is a two-tail test, the probability for the lower critical value will be 0.975, and 0.025 for the upper value. The degrees of freedom are $75 - 1 = 74$. The upper-tail formula is shown here:

```
=CHIINV(0.025,74)
```

The output value is 99.67838. Place the formulas for the upper and lower critical values in the two cells adjacent to the one labeled Critical Value.

6. Remember that the p value of the test is associated with the test statistic. To find the p value of the test, we will use the **CHIDIST** function. This function accepts as input the value of the χ^2 variable and the degrees of freedom, and outputs the tail area probability. In the cell adjacent to the one labeled p value, type

```
= =CHIDIST(F4,74)*2
```

The cell F4 is the reference of the cell that contains the test statistic value. We multiply the p value by 2 because this is a two-tail test.

The complete output is shown in Figure 9.11.

E	F	G
s^2	3334.307	3334.307
σ^2	2500	
n	75	
Test Statistic	98.6955	
Critical Value	99.67838	52.10282
p value	0.058305	

FIGURE 9.11 Output for χ^2 test

Comparing the test statistic to the critical value, we find that we cannot reject H_0. That is, it is reasonable to assume that the population variance is 2500 $(\text{lb/ream})^2$. The decision is a rather close one, as you can see from the p value.

Remember that the χ^2 test, just like the t test, assumes that the population is normally distributed. Before you report any results, you should check this assumption with some type of graphical display.

Any hypothesis test can be done in Excel using the same type of procedure outlined here, although it is easier if there are built-in tools or macros available.

CHAPTER 9 SUMMARY

In this chapter you have learned how to do a hypothesis test of the population mean, population variance, and population proportion. The five-step hypothesis testing procedure is the same for any hypothesis test. The differences in the tests are in the rejection regions and the calculation of the test statistic and the p value. For a test of the population mean, you use a Z test if the population standard deviation is known or if $n > 30$; otherwise you use a t test. For a hypothesis test of the population variance use a chi-square test, and for a test of proportions use a Z test.

You have seen that in any hypothesis test the rejection region and thus the final decision depend on the value of α. You can alter the outcome of the test by adjusting the value of α. To handle the potential unethical use of hypothesis testing and to provide management with more information than simply whether the null hypothesis was rejected, you learned about p values. You have seen that the p value frees you from specifying a value of α for the test. By reporting the p value for the test, you put the decision to reject or fail to reject the null hypothesis in the hands of management. The decision maker must weigh the costs of Type I and Type II errors and make a decision using these costs and the p value. The final section of this chapter ties the results of a hypothesis test to the corresponding confidence interval calculation.

Key Formulas

Term	Formula	Page Reference
t test statistic	$t = \dfrac{\overline{X} - \mu}{s/\sqrt{n}}$	417
Chi-square statistic	$\chi^2 = \dfrac{(n-1)s^2}{\sigma^2}$	429
Z test statistic for proportions	$Z = \dfrac{p - \pi}{\sqrt{\pi(1-\pi)/n}}$	436

CHAPTER 9 EXERCISES

Learning It!

9.15 Most traffic lights are set so that there is enough time for pedestrians to cross the road safely. A recent study indicates that a large number of elderly cannot get across the road in the usual 15 seconds allowed. To determine the average amount of time it takes senior citizens to cross the street, a study was taken of 25 seniors. On the average, it took them 19.5 seconds to cross the street, with a sample standard deviation of five seconds. Assume the time to cross the road has a normal distribution.

(a) Set up the null and alternative hypotheses to see whether the data show that it does indeed take seniors longer than 15 seconds to cross the street.

(b) In terms of traffic flow, what are the implications of a Type I error?

(c) What are the implications of a Type II error?

(d) Find the value of the test statistic.

(e) If $\alpha = 0.05$, what is the rejection region?

(f) What is your recommendation to the city?

9.16 Kids think Moms are doing a great job! According to a recent poll conducted by Massachusetts Mutual Insurance Company, 90% of children feel their mothers spend enough time with them. A similar survey was conducted in New York to see whether children there felt the same way. Of 1000 children surveyed in New York 880 felt that their mothers spend enough time. Do these data indicate that less than 90% of the New York children feel their mothers spend enough time with them?

(a) Set up the null and alternative hypotheses.

(b) What is the value of the test statistic?

(e) If $\alpha = 0.10$, what is the rejection region?

(d) What do you conclude about the children of New York?

(e) What might be causing this difference?

9.17 In a new advertising campaign, Coca-Cola pokes fun at the decision to revive its famous contoured bottle. Atlanta-based Coke faced significant technical hurdles in bringing out the well-known bottle in a new material: plastic. Coke also conducted extensive marketing tests to make sure that one of the world's best-known packages, seldom seen since the 1970s, would be a hit in the 1990s.

Coca-Cola wishes to be sure that at least 60% of the consumers prefer the contoured bottle. Of 3,000 consumers nationwide, 1900 prefer the new bottle. Is this sufficient evidence to give the new bottle the go-ahead?

(a) Set up the null and alternative hypotheses for Coca-Cola.

(b) In terms of Coke's decision to introduce the new bottle or not, what is a Type I error?

(c) In terms of Coke's decision to introduce the new bottle or not, what is a Type II error?

(d) What is the value of the test statistic?

(e) If $\alpha = 0.05$, what is the rejection region? What is your decision?

9.18 You purchased your home in 1987 for \$165,000, which was the average price at that time. Now you are thinking of selling your home. You take a sample of homes sold in your neighborhood during the past 2 months and find the following sale prices in \$:

130,000	135,500	136,000	140,000	160,000
167,000	168,000	174,500	177,400	180,000

(a) Based on these data, conduct the hypothesis test to see whether the average selling price has increased from \$165,000. Assume that the selling price of homes in this town is normally distributed.

(b) What advice would you give this homeowner regarding selling his home at this time? Explain your answer in terms of the results of the hypothesis test.

9.19 The Charlotte Sting is a team in the Women's NBA. The manager is concerned about attendance during the 2000 season and has collected the following data through July 15, 2000:

Opponent	# Home Games	Total Home Attendance	# Away Games	Total Away Attendance
Cleveland	2	9364	1	6039
Detroit	1	3801	1	5135
Houston	1	5402	1	12196
Los Angeles	0	0	1	4847
Miami	2	10544	0	0
New York	0	0	1	14073
Orlando	1	5003	2	13693
Phoenix	1	8425	0	0
Portland	0	0	1	6569
Sacramento	1	3946	0	0
Seattle	1	3946	0	0
Utah	0	0	1	4582
Washington	1	5509	1	18713

(a) Calculate the average and standard deviation of attendance at home games.

(b) Calculate the average and standard deviation of attendance at away games.

(c) Suppose that last year the average home attendance was 5000. Test this year's home attendance against 5000 to see whether the average attendance is different from last year. Assume the attendance figures are normally distributed.

(d) Suppose that last year the average away attendance was 8000. Test this year's away attendance against 8000 to see whether the average attendance is different fiom last year. Assume the attendance figures are normally distributed.

(e) What additional data do you think the manager should be tracking with regard to attendance? Explain your answer.

9.20 In the wake of a large number of repeat crime offenders, many states are considering the death penalty. A sample of 100 citizens of a New England state was taken and 56 of the 100 people favored the death penalty.

(a) Legislatures in favor of the death penalty are using the results of this survey to say that the majority of the people in the state are in favor of the death penalty. Conduct the appropriate hypothesis test to determitme whether these legislatures are justified in their remark.

(b) What conclusion can be reached from this survey about the preference for citizens of this state toward the death penalty?

Thinking About it!

Requires Exercise 9.17

9.21 Coca-Cola has asked you your recommendation about their new bottle. Basically, the company wants to know whether you are secure in your decision before it makes any drastic changes. You decide to test how much the procedure you chose affected your decision.

(a) Suppose you had used $\alpha = 0.10$. What is your decision?

(b) Now use $\alpha = 0.01$. What is your decision?

(c) Find the p value for this problem.

(d) Based on this new information, what would you tell the Coca-Cola company to do?

Requires Exercise 9.15

9.22 Look again at your recommendation to the city about the length of its walk light signal. In writing your report, you start to think about whether the study you did was adequate.

(a) What other factors might be useful in determining the length of time to allow people to cross the street safely?

(b) What are the drawbacks of making decisions such as this based on the mean?

(c) What might be a better statistic to use in this case?

9.23 Many states are considering allowing casino gambling in an attempt to revitalize urban areas. Opponents say gambling would be a magnet for crime and would shift spending away from entertainment and other industries. A recent poll conducted by the Boston *Sunday Herald* found that 46% of the Bay State voters are opposed to gambling, whereas 36% support the proposal. Eighteen percent of those surveyed had no opinion or were neutral. The poll of 450 registered voters across the state was conducted between a Tuesday and a Friday. Legislatures will endorse the casinos if less than 50% of the voters oppose it. Do the data indicate that this is the case?

(a) Set up the null and the alternative hypotheses.

(b) What should you do with the 18% who had no opinion or were neutral?

(c) Find the value of the test statistic.

(d) If the members of the legislature wish to be conservative, how should they set α?

(e) If the members of the legislature wish to be more aggressive on this issue, how should they set α?

(f) Using the value of α set in part (d), find the rejection region.

(g) What is your recommendation to your local representative?

(h) Using the value of α set in part (e), find the rejection region.

(i) What is your recommendation now to your local representative?

Requires Exercise 9.1

9.24 Remember the problem where you were trying to convince your boss that your expense report for the aspirin purchase was justified? Your boss just asked you for the data you used to justify the expense. He points out that the price of aspirin in Tokyo seems a bit high and asks you to reduce your estimate. The data are repeated here:

City	Aspirin (100)	Fast food (hamburger, fries, soft drink)	Woman's haircut/blow dry	Toothpaste (6.4 oz)
Los Angeles	\$7.69	\$4.15	\$20.11	\$2.42
Tokyo	\$35.93	\$7.62	\$76.24	\$4.24
London	\$9.69	\$5.80	\$44.35	\$3.63
Sydney	\$7.43	\$4.53	\$29.93	\$2.08
Mexico City	\$1.16	\$3.63	\$17.94	\$1.08

(a) If you remove Tokyo from the data set should you change your expense report?

(b) What does this tell you about the effect of outliers on the hypothesis test of μ when you have a small sample?

Doing It!

9.25 A portion of the data file for the hospital that collected the data on hand washing is shown here:

Datafile: HOSPITAL.XXX

Observation	Unit	Time 1	Time 2
1	CCU	3	16
2	CCU	2	7
3	CCU	0	5
4	CCU	5	8
5	CCU	2	15
6	CCU	0	15
7	CCU	2	20
8	CCU	3	16
9	CCU	0	18
10	IMCU	1	16
11	IMCU	2	8

You can see that information was also collected on the unit of the employee and a second time, labeled Time 2, was also recorded. Assume that the hand washing times are normally distributed and are recorded in seconds.

(a) Find the sample means and sample standard deviations for the first hand washing time, Time 1, for each unit.

(b) Test to see if any of the units had an average hand-washing time, Time 1, less than 5 seconds.

(c) The second hand washing time, Time 2, was recorded after the employees received some training on the effects of not washing their hands long enough. Find the sample means and sample standard deviations for the second hand washing time, Time 2, for each unit.

(d) Test to see whether any of the units had an average hand washing time after training, Time 2, of less than 5 seconds.

(e) Display all the initial hand-washing times, Time 1, in a histogram. Is the assumption of normality reasonable?

(f) Display all the second hand-washing times, Time 2, in a histogram. Is the assumption of normality reasonable?

(g) Test the hypothesis that the variance of the initial hand washing time is 14 seconds.

(h) Test the hypothesis that the variance of the hand washing times after training is greater than 14 seconds.

(i) Find the sample proportion of employees who increased their hand-washing time after training. Test the hypothesis that the proportion of employees who increased their time after training is greater than 0.80.

(j) Based on your analysis, write a report to the manager of the hospital.

- Test for the Variance of One Population
- Test of the Difference in Two Population Means—Paired Data
- Hypothesis Test of the Difference in Two Population Proportions
- Hypothesis Test of the Difference in Two Population Variances

10.2 COLLECTING DATA FROM TWO POPULATIONS

When you are comparing characteristics of two different populations, you must have a sample from each of the populations. These samples are usually selected independently of each other. In other words, the selection of one sample should not have any effect on the selection of the second sample. We will label all of the parameters of one population with a subscript 1 and all the parameters of the second population with a subscript 2. It does not matter which population you label 1 or 2. The populations and samples are shown in Figure 10.1.

Consider the question posed about whether men or women spend more money on frozen foods. We could label the population of males as population 1 and the population of females as population 2. If we do this then the parameters and statistics corresponding to the male population will be identified with a subscript 1 and those describing the female population will carry a subscript 2. These are shown in the following lists.

	Population 1: Males	Population 2: Females
Size of population	N_1	N_2
Population mean	μ_1	μ_2
Population standard deviation	σ_1	σ_2
Sample size	n_1	n_2
Sample mean	$\overline{X}_1$	$\overline{X}_2$
Sample standard deviation	s_1	s_2

For this example, we would select a sample of men shoppers and a separate sample of women shoppers. We would ask all members of the sample how much money they spent on frozen foods in the past week. It is not necessary that the sample sizes be equal, but if possible it is desirable to have both sample sizes (n_1, n_2) greater than or equal to 30. The reason for this stems from the fact that the Central Limit Theorem generally applies when the sample size is 30 or greater. Remember that we developed the z test statistic based on the knowledge that the sample mean, $\overline{X}$, has a normal distribution.

Qualitative variables are often used to identify two populations for comparison.

However, often a single sample is selected and a qualitative variable is used to identify two populations for comparison. For the food shoppers example, we might select one sample of shoppers and then record the gender of the respondent as part of the data. This means that the data can then be divided into the two comparison

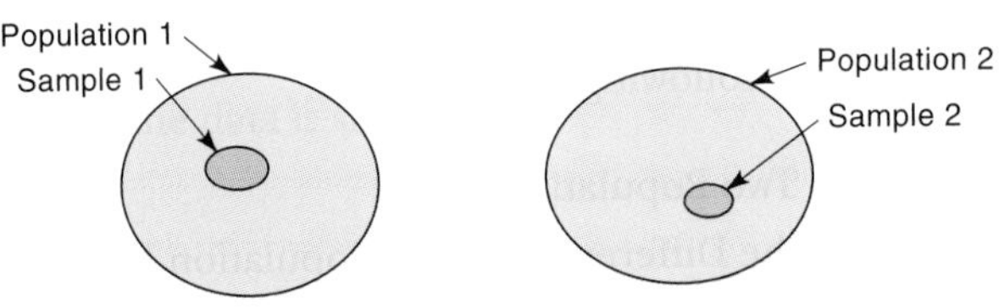

FIGURE 10.1 Two populations and two samples

populations after the data have been collected. If at the same time you collect data on the age of the person as "under 40" or "40 and over" then you can also compare the average frozen food expenditure for younger buyers to that of older buyers. Clearly, spending differences that are identified by gender or age could be of great assistance in developing a marketing strategy.

10.3 HYPOTHESIS TEST OF THE DIFFERENCE IN TWO POPULATION MEANS—OVERVIEW

There are several different cases to consider if you are testing a hypothesis of the difference in two population means. To determine into which case your data fit, you must first see if you have information on the population standard deviation of both populations. As you saw in Chapter 9, sometimes you know the value of the population standard deviation but most of the time you do not. If you know the value of the standard deviation for each of the two populations that you are comparing, then you will use a z test statistic. In this case, it does not matter how large the samples are. The underlying populations must be normally distributed. This is covered in Section 10.4.

Population standard deviations are known or the sample sizes are large.

If you do not know the value of the standard deviation for each of the two populations, then you must check the size of the sample. If each of the samples has 30 or more observations then you will be in what is commonly referred to as the "large-sample" case. This case is very similar to the situation when you know the standard deviations.

Remember that when $n \geq 30$ the Central Limit Theorem generally applies.

If you do not know the population standard deviations and one or both of your samples has less than 30 observations, then you will be in the "small-sample" case. You must then decide whether the variances in each of the two populations are the same, even though they are unknown, or different. Section 10.5 covers the case when you do not know the value of the standard deviations but you do know that the populations are normally distributed.

Population standard deviations are unknown and sample sizes are small.

Finally, sometimes the data are collected in such a way that the samples are not independent. This happens quite often when you are comparing two different medical procedures or treatments. You wish to be sure that the differences that you observe are not simply due to the fact that you have different patients with different medical histories. In this case you might use the same patients in both samples. If your samples are dependent then you must use what is known as a paired t test to compare the population means. This is the subject of Section 10.7.

Paired data must be analyed differently.

In summary, three sections will be devoted to hypothesis testing of the difference in means. Section 10.4 will cover tests when the standard deviation is known, Section 10.5 will cover the cases when the standard deviation is not known, and Section 10.7 will cover the test for paired data. Regardless of the particular case, each hypothesis test will follow the five-step procedure outlined in Chapters 8 and 9. It is repeated here for you:

Steps for any hypothesis test

Step 1: Set up the null and alternative hypotheses.

Step 2: Set the significance level and define the test procedure.

Step 3: Collect the data and calculate the test statistic and the p value.

Step 4: Make a statistical conclusion (reject or fail to reject the null hypothesis).

Step 5: Make a managerial decision.

Since you are already familiar with hypothesis testing, in this chapter we often combine the first two steps, which define the test procedure, into a single step.

10.4 LARGE-SAMPLE TESTS OF THE DIFFERENCE IN TWO POPULATION MEANS

10.4.1 Large-Sample Tests of Two Means With Known Standard Deviations

The basic test concerning two population means occurs when we want to know whether the two samples come from populations with equal means and we *assume that the population standard deviations are known.* Although this may not seem reasonable, there are cases where a historical or specified standard deviation is appropriate.

EXAMPLE 10.1 The Tissue Manufacturer

Identifying the Two Populations

Understand the Problem

The company that is looking at tissue strength wants to look at the problem again. Since tissue strength seems to vary quite a bit, your boss has asked you to find out whether there is any difference in the strength of the tissues made on one day compared to another day. The company uses two measures of tissue strength: machine-directional strength *(MDStrength)* measured in lb/ream and cross-directional strength *(CDStrength)* also measured in lb/ream. Right now he wants you to look at the *MDStrength.*

The product specifications for *MDStrength* state that the mean should be 1000 lb/ream with standard deviation of 50 lb/ream. You have collected data on 75 sheets for each of three different days. For each sheet you recorded the *MDStrength* and the *CDStrength.*

Collect the Data

The first thing to do is to identify the two populations to be compared. The tissue manufacturer wants to compare the strength of tissues made on day 1 to the strength of tissues made on day 2. Population 1 is all tissue sheets made on day 1 and we have a sample of size $n_1 = 75$ from this population. All tissue sheets made on day 2 comprise population 2 and we have a sample of $n_2 = 75$ from this population. ■

Use the techniques of Chapter 9 to test the variance for each of the populations.

In this case, we will use the specified values of the population variance to perform the test. Of course, this is not something you want to do blindly. Just because you have specifications does not mean that you have compliance. Still, for our example we already established that the specified values for the population standard deviation are valid.

Once you can establish that the values of the population standard deviations for both populations are known, you know what case we are dealing with and we are ready to proceed with the hypothesis test.

- *The first step of the procedure is to construct the null and alternative hypotheses.*

As with tests of a single mean, there are three different ways to set up the hypothesis test. The guidelines for determining which of these tests you should use are the same as presented in Chapter 9. The three possible setups are shown here:

Remember the key words different, less than, *and* greater than *tell you which test to use.*

Two-Sided Test

H_0: $\mu_1 = \mu_2$ or H_0: $\mu_1 - \mu_2 = 0$
H_A: $\mu_1 \neq \mu_2$ $\quad$ H_A: $\mu_1 - \mu_2 \neq 0$

Use this test if you wish to test whether the mean of population 1 is *different* from the mean of population 2.

Lower-Tail Test

H_0: $\mu_1 \geq \mu_2$ or H_0: $\mu_1 - \mu_2 \geq 0$
H_A: $\mu_1 < \mu_2$ $\quad$ H_A: $\mu_1 - \mu_2 < 0$

Use this test if you wish to test whether the mean of population 1 is *less than* the mean of population 2.

Upper-Tail Test

H_0: $\mu_1 \le \mu_2$ or H_0: $\mu_1 - \mu_2 \le 0$
H_A: $\mu_1 > \mu_2$ H_A: $\mu_1 - \mu_2 > 0$

Use this test if you wish to test whether the mean of population 1 is *greater than* the mean of population 2.

Note: You should never have $\bar{X}$'s in the statement of the hypotheses. There is no need to formulate a hypothesis about the sample means because you know the values. You do not know the population means.

Notice that the equals sign is always part of the null hypothesis. Also notice that the hypotheses are statements about the *relationship* between the size of the mean of population 1 and the mean of population 2. The tests do not give you information about the value of the means, only about how the value of μ_1 compares to the value of μ_2.

You can see that there are two ways to state each of the hypotheses. For each setup shown here, the first way of writing the test makes a statement about the relative value of μ_1 to μ_2. The second way of writing the same test makes a statement about the value of the difference, $\mu_1 - \mu_2$. They are equivalent to each other. Look at the two-sided test. Clearly, if $\mu_1 = \mu_2$ then the difference between them must be zero. It is also possible to test for differences of values other than zero. For example, you could test that the difference between the two means is 10 or any other value you like. The procedure is basically the same with only a slight difference in the test statistic formula.

EXAMPLE 10.2 The Tissue Manufacturer

Setting Up the Test

The tissue manufacturer wishes to see whether the mean tissue strengths are the same for day 1 and day 2 tissues. The variable to be examined is *MDStrength.* The null and alternative hypotheses are

Understand the Problem

$$H_0: \mu_1 = \mu_2$$
$$H_A: \mu_1 \neq \mu_2$$

In addition to setting up the hypotheses, the test is defined by choosing a level of significance, α.

The rejection regions are found using the procedures from Chapter 8.

Suppose for this test we choose $\alpha = 0.05$. The test statistic to be calculated in step 3 is a z statistic so we know how to find the rejection region for the two-sided test. Since we know that the total area of the rejection region must be equal to α and $\alpha =$ 0.05, we split it in half and require the area of each tail of the normal distribution to be 0.025. From the standard normal tables we find the critical values for the test to be ±1.96. ■

Once the test has been defined, the data are collected and processed. This allows us to proceed with the third step of the procedure, calculating the value of the test statistic.

Remember that the test statistic is calculated from sample data and is used to decide between the null and the alternative hypotheses. If we are trying to decide whether $\mu_1 = \mu_2$, then it makes sense to look at the size of the difference between $\bar{X}_1$ and $\bar{X}_2$. We know that even if the two population means are exactly the same, we will almost never get two equal sample means. So we don't expect the difference $\bar{X}_1 - \bar{X}_2$ to be zero even if the null hypothesis is true. However, if the null hypothesis is true, then the difference $\bar{X}_1 - \bar{X}_2$ should be small relative to the size of the standard error. Clearly, large differences in the sample means would lead us to be suspicious of the null hypothesis. The appropriate test statistic is a z statistic and is calculated as follows:

$$z = \frac{(\bar{X}_1 - \bar{X}_2) - 0}{\sqrt{\sigma_1^2/n_1 + \sigma_2^2/n_2}}$$

Formula for test statistic for difference between two population means

Remember: A point estimator is calculated from sample information only and is used to estimate an unknown population parameter.

The numerator of the test statistic is simply comparing the evidence, $\overline{X}_1 - \overline{X}_2$, to the difference in the population means if H_0 is true. For the hypotheses we are using, if H_0 is true then the true difference is zero, so you see that the comparison is between $\overline{X}_1 - \overline{X}_2$ and zero. As we saw in Chapter 9, the size of the difference is always measured in terms of the standard error. Thus, the denominator is the standard error of the point estimator. In this case we are trying to estimate $\mu_1 - \mu_2$ and the natural point estimator is $\overline{X}_1 - \overline{X}_2$. The standard error of $\overline{X}_1 - \overline{X}_2$ is a natural extension of the standard error $\overline{X}$, $\sqrt{\sigma^2/n}$, which we often wrote as $\sigma/\sqrt{n}$.

When we are testing for a difference of zero, the last part of the numerator is often left out entirely. This makes sense, but it is important that you know what you are really testing. When you need to test for a difference equal to some value other than zero, then you need to put that value in the formula for the test statistic in place of the zero. For example, if you wished to test to see whether the difference in the populations means was equal to 10, then you would change the null and alternative hypotheses to the following:

$$H_0: \ \mu_1 - \mu_2 = 10$$
$$H_A: \ \mu_1 - \mu_2 \neq 10$$

You would then use the value of 10 in the formula for the test statistic instead of zero. This is called the hypothesized difference and is labeled *d*.

EXAMPLE 10.3 The Tissue Manufacturer

Calculation of Test Statistic

Now we are ready to calculate the test statistic for the tissue manufacturer. The relevant data are shown here:

Analyze the Data

Population 1: Day 1 Tissues	Population 2: Day 2 Tissues
$n_1 = 75$	$n_2 = 75$
$\overline{X}_1 = 990.8$	$\overline{X}_2 = 977.0$
$\sigma_1 = 50$ lb/ream	$\sigma_2 = 50$ lb/ream

We can calculate the value of the test statistic z as follows:

$$z = \frac{(990.8 - 977.0) - 0}{\sqrt{50^2/75 + 50^2/75}} = 1.69$$

Using the standard normal table, we can find the p value of the test by looking up the test statistic of 1.69. We find that the area to the right of $z = 1.69$ is 0.0455. Since this is a two-sided test, we double that and find that the p value is 0.09. ■

Although much of the work is done at this point, the test procedure is not. The fourth step of the hypothesis testing procedure requires you to reject or fail to reject the null hypothesis on the basis of the test statistic. At the fifth step of the procedure you interpret this decision in terms of the problem. Let's finish the tissue manufacturer problem now.

EXAMPLE 10.4 Tissue Manufacturer

Finishing the Test

The test statistic for the comparison of tissue strengths was 1.69. The rejection region for the test had critical values of ± 1.96. Since 1.69 is not outside the critical values, that is, it is not in the rejection region of the test, we fail to reject the null hypothesis.

Draw Conclusions

Our conclusion is that there is no evidence that the mean *MDStrength* of tissues made on day 1 is different than that of those made on day 2.

From previous experience in hypothesis testing, you know that you should also examine the p value for these data. The p value is less than 0.10. This means that if you set α larger than the p value, say, at 0.10, then you would reject the null hypothesis of equal means. The decision, in this case, depends very much on the choice of α. We might say that the decision is "on the fence" with regard to these two hypotheses. Perhaps we should compare day 2 to day 3 to get a better understanding of what is happening. ■

TRY IT NOW!

The tissue manufacturer also recorded values of *MDStrength* for 75 tissues made on day 3. The sample mean *MDStrength* for that day was found to be 1000.32 lb/ream. Is there any evidence that the average *MDStrength* is different on day 2 than day 3? Use $\alpha = 0.05$.

Identify

Population 1 :

Population 2 :

Step 1:

Step 2:

Step 3:

Step 4:

Step 5:

ANS. $z = -2.86$ AND P VALUE $= 0.0042$. REJECT H_0 AND CONCLUDE THAT THE AVERAGE *MDSTRENGTH* IS DIFFERENT ON DAY 2 AND DAY 3.

Once the conclusion of the test is reached, the real work in terms of decision making begins. The statistical analysis simply confirms or fails to confirm a hypothesis. It does not help you make decisions about the problem you are trying to solve.

EXAMPLE 10.5 Tissue Strength

Interpreting and Using the Results of a Test

Draw Conclusions

As a result of our tests, we have concluded that the average *MDStrength* of the tissues made on day 1 and day 2 are equal but the average *MDStrength* of the tissues made on day 2 and day 3 are different. Clearly, something is not quite right with this process. How can we interpret this? What should we do next?

What we know as a result of this test is that the tissue strength is not behaving entirely as it is supposed to. It is not clear *how* the mean strength differs, or whether it is *always* different or just *sometimes different.* It is also not clear on which, if any, of the three days the *MDStrength* is correct.

This would be a good time to graph the data and see what is happening. This would help us look for any patterns in the data. ■

To answer the question we started with, we would like to compare all 3 days. That is, we would like to do a hypothesis test that looks like this:

H_0: $\mu_1 = \mu_2 = \mu_3$

H_A: At least one of them is different.

This is a test of more than two means and you cannot do such a test using the techniques of this chapter. You need to use a technique called analysis of variance, which is covered in Chapter 12.

10.4.2 Large-Sample Tests of Two Means With Unknown Standard Deviations

The large-sample test for the difference between two population means requires that *both* of the sample sizes be greater than 30. Remember that the only differences in the various hypothesis tests are in the calculation of the test statistic.

Large-sample test of the difference between two means

The test statistic for this case is very similar to the case when you know the standard deviations. Since the sample sizes are large, each individual sample standard deviation is a good estimate of the corresponding unknown population standard deviation. So, we simply use each of the sample standard deviations in the formula instead of the corresponding values of σ.

The test statistic becomes

$$z = \frac{(\overline{X}_1 - \overline{X}_2) - 0}{\sqrt{s_1^2/n_1 + s_2^2/n_2}}$$

Finding the rejection region is the same as it is for any hypothesis test involving the z distribution—it depends on α and whether the test is one-sided or two-sided.

EXAMPLE 10.6 Training Issues

Setting Up the Hypotheses

Recall the corporation that was interested in whether there was a difference in the results of in-house versus outside training programs. The employees involved in the training completed a sample copy of the CMI certification examination at the end of each of the respective training programs. The company wants to know whether the outside trainers achieve better results. In this case the two populations are:

Population 1: Employees trained by an outside consultant
Population 2: Employees trained in-house

Understand the Problem

Since the company is interested in whether one group is *better* than the other, it will use a one-sided test and the hypotheses are

$$H_0\text{: } \mu_1 \leq \mu_2$$
$$H_A\text{: } \mu_1 > \mu_2$$

■

Once the hypotheses are set up and you know the population parameters you are testing, you need to make a decision about which specific type test you will use. To do this you need to assemble the data you have and look at standard deviation and sample size. With tests about the mean, the first question is whether the population standard deviation is known. If it is, then you would perform the z test defined in the previous section. If it is not, then you need to look at the sample sizes to make the next decision. When both sample sizes n_1 and n_2 are large (≥ 30), then the test is also a z test with the test statistic just described.

EXAMPLE 10.7 Training Issues

Setting Up the Test

The company looking at training issues assembled and processed its data as shown here:

Collect the Data

	Population 1 (Outside Consultant)	Population 2 (In-house Training)
Sample size	$n_1 = 50$	$n_2 = 47$
Sample mean	$\overline{X}_1 = 75.46$	$\overline{X}_2 = 63.55$
Sample standard deviation	$s_1 = 4.12$	$s_2 = 7.69$

You see that the company had 50 employees in the group receiving outside training and 47 people in the group being trained in-house. Since the study was a new one, the company had only sample measures of variation. It will be able to use a z test, because of the large sample sizes.

Once the company knows it will use a z test, it can find the rejection region. In this case there is no real reason to choose a level of significance other than $\alpha = 0.05$, so that is what is used.

The one-sided rejection region is found using the techniques of Chapter 9. The value of z is found to be 1.645. That is, the rejection region is to the right of the value 1.645.

■

Steps 1 and 2 of the hypothesis test define the test procedure to be used. The only other computational portion of the test is to calculate the test statistic. This is completely determined by the test procedure and so it is a matter of using the correct formula.

EXAMPLE 10.8 Training Issues

Performing the Test

The corporation looking at training issues knows that it is using a z test for its data. The test statistic is calculated as follows:

$$z = \frac{(75.46 - 63.55) - 0}{\sqrt{4.12^2/50 + 7.69^2/47}}$$

$$z = \frac{11.91}{1.2640} = 9.42$$

Analyze the Data

To find the p value of the test, we look up the z score of 9.42 on the standard normal table and find that the p value is 0.0000.

■

The remainder of the hypothesis testing procedure is the same for this test as it has been for any of the tests we have done. So let's complete the test by doing steps 4 and 5.

EXAMPLE 10.9 Training Issues

Conclusions and Interpretation

Step 4: *Make a statistical conclusion.* Since $z = 9.42$ is most definitely in the rejection region, we reject the null hypothesis.

Step 5: *Make a managerial decision.* Since we reject the null hypothesis, we conclude that the mean post-test score for the group trained by an outside consultant is higher than that for the group trained in-house. ■

Draw Conclusions

Remember that the standard error is the standard deviation of the point estimator. It is the yardstick by which we judge all differences.

You are probably not surprised at this conclusion since the average for the outside group was higher than the one for the inside group. However, this is not sufficient reason to conclude that they are different. You cannot simply look at the two $\overline{X}$ values and conclude that employees trained by an outside consultant did better on the post-test than those trained by an in-house person. Yes, $\overline{X}_1$ is higher than $\overline{X}_2$ if you look only at the observed difference. It is possible that such a difference might occur due to the random nature of the sampling and testing procedure. The only way you can tell if there is a "significant" difference is to compare the observed difference in the sample means to the size of the standard error. This is precisely what the test statistic does for you.

Try It Now!

The management of the corporation looking at training issues are not convinced that they should switch to outside consultants for all of their training programs. They want to look at how the two groups compared on the pretest.

The relevant data are given here:

	Population 1 (Outside Consultant)	Population 2 (In-house Trainer)
Sample size	$n_1 = 50$	$n_2 = 47$
Mean score on pretest	$\overline{X}_1 = 43.52$	$\overline{X}_2 = 47.66$
Standard deviation of pretest score	$s_1 = 14.80$	$s_2 = 12.80$

Test to see whether there is a difference in the mean pretest scores. Use $\alpha = 0.05$.

Step 1:

Step 2:

(continued)

Step 3:

Step 4:

Step 5:

10.4.3 Exercises—Learning It!

10.1 Many studies have been done comparing consumer behavior of men and women. One such on-going study concerns take-out food. In particular, the study focuses on whether there is a difference in the mean number of times per month that men and women buy take-out food for dinner. The most recent results of the study are shown here:

	Population	
	Men	Women
Sample size	$n_1 = 34$	$n_2 = 28$
Sample mean	$\overline{X}_1 = 25.6$	$\overline{X}_2 = 21.2$
Population standard deviation	$\sigma_1 = 4.2$	$\sigma_2 = 3.8$

Because the study has so much historical data, information is known about the population standard deviations.

(a) Set up the hypotheses to test whether there is a difference in the mean number of times per month that a person buys take-out food for dinner for men and women.

(b) Use the z test with known population variances to set up and perform the test. Use a level of significance of 0.05.

(c) Find the p value for the test.

(d) Do the data provide evidence that the mean number of times per month for men differs from that for women?

(e) Does the choice of α in this case affect the decision?

10.2 Professional employees who work for large corporations often contend that the mean salary paid by a company differs by location in the United States. To test that claim, data were collected on financial analysts working for a large corporation at locations in New England and in the upper Midwest. Because there is an extensive history of salary data, the population standard deviations are available. The study found the following results:

ANS. H_0: $\mu_1 = \mu_2$, H_A: $\mu_1 \neq \mu_2$; CRITICAL VALUE = ± 1.96; $z = -1.48$; FAIL TO REJECT; THERE IS NO DIFFERENCE.

	Population	
	New England	Upper Midwest
Sample size	$n_1 = 25$	$n_2 = 18$
Sample mean	$\overline{X}_1 = \$38,348$	$\overline{X}_2 = \$36,782$
Population standard deviation	$\sigma_1 = \$2336$	$\sigma_2 = \$2258$

(a) Set up the appropriate hypotheses to test whether the company's analysts in New England were paid more, on the average, than those working in the upper Midwest.

(b) Use the z test with known population variances to set up and perform the test. Use a level of significance of 0.05.

(c) Find the p value for the test.

(d) Do the data support the contention that the mean pay for analysts in New England is higher than that of analysts in the upper Midwest?

10.3 A study at a university in New England focuses on binge drinking by students. The people who administered the study wanted to determine whether students who lived on campus had more episodes of binge drinking per semester on the average than those who lived at home. They surveyed all students who were enrolled in a required health course and obtained the following data:

	Population	
	On Campus	At Home
Sample size	$n_1 = 220$	$n_2 = 196$
Sample mean	$\overline{X}_1 = 37.3$	$\overline{X}_2 = 35.6$
Population standard deviation	$\sigma_1 = 8.6$	$\sigma_2 = 10.1$

The study used the same survey instrument used in many other similar studies and so they used the population standard deviation.

(a) Set up the appropriate hypotheses to test whether students who live at home have fewer episodes of binge drinking per semester, on the average, than those who live on campus.

(b) Use the z test with known population variances to set up and perform the test. Use a level of significance of 0.05.

(c) Find the p value for the test.

(d) Do the data indicate that students who live at home binge less on the average?

10.4 A company uses two suppliers to provide paper for the copy machines. The company has experienced an excessive number of paper jams and wonders whether there is a difference in the paper provided by each supplier. The company collects data on the number of jams per ream of paper (500 sheets) over a period of 2 months. The summary data are

	Population	
	Supplier 1	Supplier 2
Sample size	$n_1 = 45$	$n_2 = 52$
Sample mean	$\overline{X}_1 = 8.1$	$\overline{X}_2 = 9.3$
Population standard deviation	$\sigma_1 = 1.1$	$\sigma_2 = 1.2$

(a) Set up the appropriate hypotheses to test whether paper from the two suppliers results in the same average number of jams per ream.

(b) Use the z test with known population variances to set up and perform the test. Use a level of significance of 0.05.

(c) Find the p value for the test.

(d) Do the data indicate that there is a difference between suppliers on average?

10.5 You are considering selling your house and need to choose between two real estate agencies. You collect data on the number of weeks that a house is on the market for both agencies. The summary statistics are shown here:

	Population	
	Agency A	Agency B
Sample size	$n_1 = 25$	$n_2 = 20$
Sample mean	$\overline{X}_1 = 22.3$	$\overline{X}_2 = 18.5$
Population standard deviation	$\sigma_1 = 1.5$	$\sigma_2 = 2.2$

(a) At the 0.05 level of significance, test to see whether houses listed with agency A are on the market on the average longer than those listed with agency B.

(b) Find the p value for the test.

(c) Which agency would you use and why?

10.5 SMALL-SAMPLE TESTS OF THE DIFFERENCE IN TWO POPULATION MEANS

When the population standard deviation is unknown and the sample size is large, the z test can be used. If the sample size is not large, then it is necessary to use a t test, just as we did in the one-population tests.

10.5.1 Small-Sample Tests of Two Means With Unknown But Equal Standard Deviations

Unfortunately, we do not always have the luxury of large samples. Remember that data collection is expensive, so often the sample size for one or both of the samples is less than 30. This is called the "small-sample" case.

The reason that 30 is used as the cutoff point has to do with the fact that the Central Limit Theorem applies for sample sizes of 30 or more.

Just as in the one-population case, the small-sample tests for two population means will involve the t distribution. The t test carries with it the same assumption that the populations involved in the test are normally distributed. In addition, though, the two-population case requires that you know whether the two population variances can be considered equal. In this section, we look at both cases.

EXAMPLE 10.10 Training and Gender

Setting Up the Hypotheses

Understand the Problem

In addition to looking at the results of training in-house versus using an outside consultant, the company decided to look at gender issues in training. It took the group of people that had been trained in-house and differentiated them according to gender. The company wanted to know whether there was any difference in the post-test scores for males versus females.

We can call the females population 1 and the males population 2. Since the company is interested only in whether the groups are different, it can use a two-sided test. The hypotheses are

$$H_0: \mu_1 = \mu_2$$
$$H_A: \mu_1 \neq \mu_2$$

■

The first approach is to assume that even though you don't know the variability in the two populations, you know enough to believe that there is the same amount of variability in each population. At first this may seem a bit odd to you but actually it is not such a ridiculous assumption. Remember that you are comparing the means of two populations. Since you are measuring the same variable in both populations, it is quite possible that the two populations have a normal distribution with the same shape but with different means. Figure 10.2 on page 468 illustrates such a situation.

There is, of course, a way to tell by doing a hypothesis test to compare two variances. This is the subject of Section 10.9.

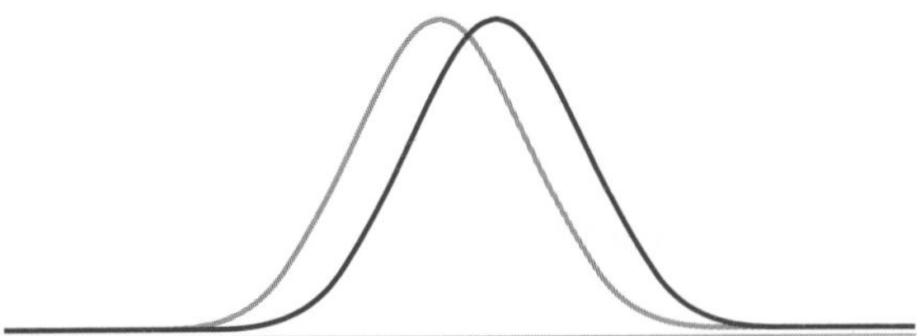

FIGURE 10.2 Two normally distributed populations with the same variance but different means

For now, we will assume that equal variance has been confirmed through a statistical procedure. We have two estimates of this variance, one from each sample. We have s_1^2 and s_2^2, which are two different estimates of the same number. Instead of using two different estimates of the unknown but common population variance, it makes more sense to combine the data and find one better estimate of the variance. That is, instead of using s_1^2 and s_2^2 in the formula for the test statistic, we will "pool" the data from the samples and get one estimate of the common variance. This is called the **pooled variance.**

One way to estimate the pooled variance is simply to put all the data together from both samples and calculate the sample variance of this "big" sample. There are two reasons for not doing that. One reason is that if, indeed, the two population means are different, then the consolidated data will have a mean that is not from *either* population. This will result in a distorted measure of variance. In addition, at this point most people have already calculated the sample variances for each sample individually. Thus, we will find the pooled variance by building from the individual sample variances. Your first thought might be to average the two sample variances. This is the right idea, but instead we will use a weighted average. If, for example, one of the samples sizes is 10 and the other one is 25, then the sample variance from the sample based on 25 observations is more accurate and should carry a greater weight in calculating the pooled variance. The formula for the pooled variance, s_p^2, is shown here:

Formula for the pooled variance

$$s_p^2 = \frac{(n_1 - 1)s_1^2 + (n_2 - 1)s_2^2}{n_1 + n_2 - 2}$$

This formula weights the sample variances by one less than the sample size. If the sample sizes are the same, this formula is the same as a simple average of the two sample variances.

EXAMPLE 10.11 **Training and Gender**

Calculating the Pooled Variance

The data for the post-tests on the in-house group are given here:

Analyze the Data

	Population 1 Females Trained In-House	Population 2 Males Trained In-House
Sample size	$n_1 = 20$	$n_2 = 27$
Sample average	$\overline{X}_1 = 63.95$	$\overline{X}_2 = 63.26$
Sample standard deviation	$s_1 = 8.86$	$s_2 = 6.87$

As a double check, be sure the number you end up with for the pooled standard deviation is in between the two sample standard deviations. If it is not, recheck your work, as you have made a mistake.

The calculation of the pooled variance of the in-house post test scores is then

$$s_p^2 = \frac{(20 - 1)(8.86^2) + (27 - 1)(6.87^2)}{20 + 27 - 2}$$

$$s_p^2 = \frac{1491.4924 + 1227.1194}{45} = \frac{2718.6118}{45} = 60.4136$$

$$s_p = \sqrt{60.4136} = 7.77$$

■

Now we are ready to consider the test statistic for the small-sample case when the population variances are equal. The test statistic in this case has a t distribution with $(n_1 + n_2 - 2)$ degrees of freedom. Remember that for simpler notation we can write the t value as $t_{\alpha,n-1}$. The test statistic is calculated as follows:

Test statistic using pooled variance

$$t = \frac{\overline{X}_1 - \overline{X}_2}{\sqrt{s_p^2/n_1 + s_p^2/n_2}}$$

or equivalently

$$t = \frac{\overline{X}_1 - \overline{X}_2}{s_p\sqrt{1/n_1 + 1/n_2}}$$

Knowing the degrees of freedom and the formula for the test statistic, we can complete the hypothesis test.

EXAMPLE 10.12 Gender and Training

Conducting the Hypothesis Test

Now the company looking at training issues can find the rejection region for the test and calculate the test statistic. Since it is doing a two-tail test, the cutoff values will be the t statistic with 0.025 in the tail area and 45 degrees of freedom, $t_{0.025,\,45}$. From the t table the critical values are found to be ±2.014. The test statistic is calculated as

$$t = \frac{63.95 - 63.26}{7.77\sqrt{\frac{1}{20} + \frac{1}{27}}}$$

$$t = \frac{0.69}{7.77\sqrt{0.08704}} = \frac{0.69}{(7.77)(0.2950)} = 0.3010$$

Analyze the Data

The company uses a statistical software package to look up the t statistic and finds that the area outside the test statistic is 0.3823. Since this is a two-sided test, it doubles that to find that p value = 0.7646. The results of the test follow:

P	Q	R
t-Test: Two-Sample Assuming Equal Variances		
	Males	*Females*
Mean	63.25925926	63.95
Variance	47.1994302	78.47105263
Observations	27	20
Pooled Variance	60.40300412	
Hypothesized Mean Difference	0	
df	45	
t Stat	-0.301254646	
P(T<=t) one-tail	0.38230401	
t Critical one-tail	1.679427442	
P(T<=t) two-tail	0.764608019	
t Critical two-tail	2.014103302	

The results of the test show that since 0.3010 is not in the rejection region of the test, the company cannot reject H_0. There is not enough evidence to say that the mean test score for the male in-house group is different than the mean post-test score for the female in-house group. ■

TRY IT NOW!

The company also wants to look at gender differences in the test scores for the group of employees trained by the outside consultant. It assembles the relevant data and finds the following:

	Population 1 Females Trained by Outside Consultant	Population 2 Males Trained by Outside Consultant
Sample size	$n_1 = 21$	$n_2 = 29$
Sample mean	$\overline{X}_1 = 75.9$	$\overline{X}_2 = 75.2$
Sample standard deviation	$s_1 = 3.9$	$s_2 = 4.4$

Find the pooled variance for the data.

Test to see whether there is evidence that the mean post-test score for the females trained by the outside consultant is different than the mean post-test score for the males trained by the outside consultant. Use a level of significance of 0.05.

Step 1:

Step 2:

Step 3:

Step 4:

Step 5:

ANS. $s_p = 4.15$; H_0: $\mu_1 = \mu_2$; H_A: $\mu_1 \neq \mu_2$; CRITICAL VALUE $= \pm 2.009$; $t = 0.58$; FAIL TO REJECT; THERE IS NO DIFFERENCE.

10.5.2 Small-Sample Tests of Two Means With Unknown and Unequal Standard Deviations

If you test for equality of variances and find that the population variances are not equal, then you cannot pool the data. This is known as the Behrens–Fisher problem. Figure 10.3 depicts this situation. In this case both of the populations have a normal distribution with different variances.

Second way to handle small samples

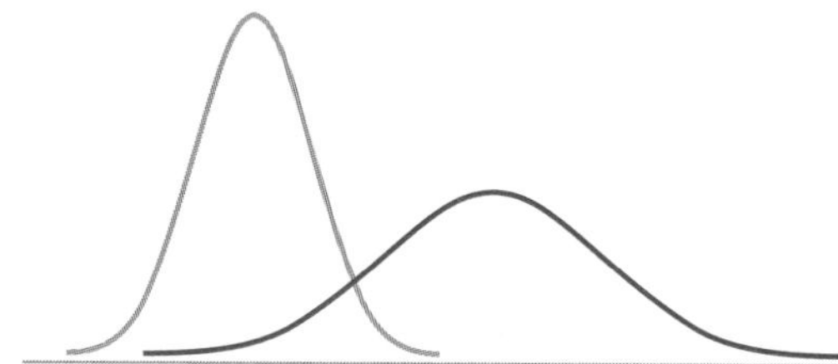

FIGURE 10.3 Two normally distributed populations with unequal variances

The test statistic is called a separate-variance t test. As the name indicates, you must use the individual sample variances in the test statistic. In fact, the formula for calculating the test statistic looks exactly like the z statistic for the large-sample case when the variances are unknown. It is calculated as follows:

Small-sample test with unknown standard deviations

$$t = \frac{(\overline{X}_1 - \overline{X}_2) - d}{\sqrt{s_1^2/n_1 + s_2^2/n_2}}$$

It does not follow a z distribution because the estimates of the unknown variances are based on small samples. We know from our work in Chapter 9 that the appropriate distribution for small-sample situations is the t distribution. This is the case here as well, but the number of degrees of freedom is found according to a rather more complicated formula than you have seen thus far. This test statistic can be approximated by a t distribution with ν (Greek letter pronounced "new") degrees of freedom. The formula for ν is given as follows:

Formula for degrees of freedom for small samples and unequal variances

$$\nu = \frac{\left(\dfrac{s_1^2}{n_1} + \dfrac{s_2^2}{n_2}\right)^2}{\dfrac{(s_1^2/n_1)^2}{n_1 + 1} + \dfrac{(s_2^2/n_2)^2}{n_2 + 1}} - 2$$

When you calculate ν you will most likely get a fractional result. But we know that degrees of freedom are integer values. Simply drop the fractional portion of the result to get just an integer value for the degrees of freedom. You may wonder why we do this. The reason is that the number that results for the degrees of freedom in this case will be smaller than the one used in the pooled variance case. The number of degrees of freedom in the test defines the test's ability to detect significant differences in the population means. That is, when you assume that the population variances are *not* equal, your hypothesis test becomes less *powerful* and the chances that you will make a Type II error for a given value of α increase. By not pooling variances you are more likely to miss true differences in the population means.

Note: *There are several equivalent formulas for calculating the degrees of freedom in this case.*

EXAMPLE 10.13 Training and Gender

Small-Sample Test with Unequal Variances

Suppose we repeat the test on gender in the in-house group, this time assuming that the population variances are not equal. How does this change the analysis? The relevant data are again given at the top of page 472.

Analyze the Data

	Population 1 Females Trained In-House	Population 2 Males Trained In-House
Sample size	$n_1 = 20$	$n_2 = 27$
Sample average	$\bar{X}_1 = 63.95$	$\bar{X}_2 = 63.26$
Sample standard deviation	$s_1 = 8.86$	$s_2 = 6.87$

Section 10.9 will cover the procedure for testing for equal variances.

Step 1: Construct the null and the alternative hypotheses.

$$H_0: \quad \mu_1 = \mu_2$$
$$H_A: \quad \mu_1 \neq \mu_2$$

Step 2: Select α and find the rejection region.

To do this we need to find the degrees of freedom to use. Substituting in the formula we get

$$\nu = \frac{\left(\frac{8.86^2}{20} + \frac{6.87^2}{27}\right)^2}{\frac{(8.86^2/20)^2}{20+1} + \frac{(6.87^2/27)^2}{27+1}} - 2$$
$$= \frac{32.18308\ldots}{0.84272\ \ldots} - 2$$
$$= 38.18939 - 2 = 36.189$$

Taking the integer portion gives us 36 degrees of freedom. The value $t_{0.025,36}$ is found using a computer software package to be ± 2.0281. ■

Many statistical packages offer you the option of doing the t test assuming equal variances or assuming unequal variances. To make an informed choice about whether you should pool the data, you must do a test for the equality of the variances. This is the subject of Section 10.9.

10.5.3 Exercises—Learning It!

10.6 The Board of Realtors for Greater Bridgeport, CT, wants to know whether the average price of a single family home in the area has increased in the past. They take a random sample of homes sold in 1995 and 1996 and calculate the following statistics:

	Population 1995	Population 1996
Sample size	$n_1 = 25$	$n_2 = 25$
Sample mean	$\bar{X}_1 = \$151,166$	$\bar{X}_2 = \$160,669$
Sample standard deviation	$s_1 = \$5332$	$s_2 = \$6468$

(a) Set up the appropriate hypotheses to test whether there has been an increase in the mean selling price of a home in Greater Bridgeport.

(b) Calculate the pooled variance for the data.

(c) Assuming that the data are normally distributed, use the small-sample test with equal variances to test the hypotheses. Use a level of significance of 0.10.

(d) Do the data provide evidence that the average price of a home in 1996 is higher than it was in 1995?

10.7 The cost of shipping is of great concern to mail-order businesses. Traditionally, mail-order companies have used United Parcel Services (UPS) for their shipping. The U.S. Postal Service has been promoting its parcel post service as a competitor for this service. To determine whether parcel post is better than UPS ground, a mail-order company sent 20 packages via UPS ground and 20 packages via parcel post and tracked the number of working days for the packages to reach their intended destinations. A summary of the data is given here:

	Population	
	UPS Ground	U.S. Postal Service
Sample size	$n_1 = 20$	$n_2 = 20$
Sample mean	$\bar{X}_1 = 7.3$	$\bar{X}_2 = 7.1$
Sample standard deviation	$s_1 = 0.9$	$s_2 = 2.3$

(a) Set up the appropriate hypotheses to test whether the U.S. Postal Service is better than UPS Ground.

(b) Assuming that the data are normally distributed, use the small-sample test with unequal variances to test the hypotheses. Use a level of significance of 0.05.

(c) Do the data provide evidence that the average delivery time for parcel post is less than for UPS Ground?

10.8 After months of working overtime, you have saved some money for a set of new golf clubs and you want to make sure that you are buying the best. You can get a really good deal on brand X clubs, but would make the sacrifice to buy brand Z if they really improve your game. The salesperson allows you to take the number 3 wood from each brand and use them to hit balls on a driving range. The data for your efforts are summarized here:

	Population	
	Brand X	Brand Z
Sample size	$n_X = 15$	$n_Z = 15$
Sample mean	$\bar{X}_X = 255$	$\bar{X}_Z = 271$
Sample standard deviation	$s_X = 8.7$	$s_Z = 9.1$

(a) Set up the appropriate hypotheses to test whether brand Z clubs are better than brand X.

(b) Calculate the pooled variance for the data.

(c) Assuming that the data are normally distributed, use the small-sample test with equal variances to test the hypotheses. Use a level of significance of 0.05.

(d) Should you spend the extra cash or save it for golf balls?

10.9 Few things are more frustrating than needing information and having to wait for it. The time spent on hold waiting for technical support to resolve software problems is one of the largest drains on productivity experienced by small businesses. Before a company will consider switching from its current word processing software (Microsoft Word) to a competitor (WordPerfect) the company will have to be convinced that it will spend less time on hold. The company decides to perform a test by placing 10 calls to each technical support line and recording the amount of time (in minutes) that the caller is on hold. The summary data follow:

	Population	
	MS Word	WordPerfect
Sample size	$n_1 = 10$	$n_2 = 10$
Sample mean	$\bar{X}_1 = 11.2$	$\bar{X}_2 = 9.7$
Sample standard deviation	$s_1 = 3.4$	$s_2 = 1.6$

(a) Assuming that the data are normally distributed, use the small-sample test with unequal variances to test the hypotheses that the company will spend less time per call, on the average, with WordPerfect technical support.

(b) Should the company switch software?

10.10 Are all discount mail-order companies the same? In an attempt to answer this question, data were collected on the price of software for the top ten business software packages reported by *PC Magazine*, August 1997. Two well-known mail-order companies were asked for prices on each piece of software. The data are shown at the top of page 474.

population 2. For example, in studying the effect on sales of a new product display, you would want to compare stores that are either similar in size or in similar locations. Otherwise, the apparent increase in sales that is observed might simply be due to the fact that a larger, busier store was randomly chosen to try out the new display. In this case, it is possible that the sales did not really increase due to the new display.

Dependent samples are related to each other. The members of one sample are identical to or matched or paired with the members in the other sample according to some characteristic.

Discovery Exercise 10.1
INTRODUCTION TO EXPERIMENTAL DESIGN

Did you ever wonder why the restrooms in restaurants have a sign instructing all employees to wash their hands before returning to work? The owner of a large restaurant chain wanted to increase the amount of time that employees washed their hands after reading about the health implications of washing for only a few seconds. A random sample of 10 employees was selected. The amount of time each employee washed was recorded. The data were collected in such a way that the employees did not know they were being observed.

These employees were then educated on the benefits of hand washing. They watched a health video that detailed the benefits of increasing the amount of time they washed. One week after the training, employee hand washing was timed again. The times (in seconds) are shown in the next table:

Employee	Before Training	After Training
1	3	3
2	3	3
3	2	4
4	4	4
5	3	5
6	3	4
7	4	4
8	3	4
9	5	6
10	2	3

(a) Use a two-population paired t test to test the hypothesis that no learning has occurred. Use a pooled variance.

$$H_0: \mu_1 = \mu_2$$
$$H_A: \mu_1 \neq \mu_2$$

(b) What is your conclusion?

(c) Why is this surprising? (*Hint:* Of the 10 employees, how many of them washed at least as long after the training?)

(d) Explain how these data are different from most of the two-sample data sets you have looked at up to this point in the chapter. Why might this be important?

(e) Suppose 10 different employees were used for the second timing. Would this make a difference? Explain why or why not.

In the situation described previously, one of the characteristics that could be used to pair or match the sample members is the size of the store. A second is the location of the store. This is the first departure we have seen from random sampling. In fact, you are *trying* to match the items that are sampled in an attempt to control other variables that influence the data. Clearly, the size of the store will influence sales. In a sense, you match sample elements to keep the comparison "fair." Similarly, it would not be fair to compare the average miles per gallon of two cars driven by two people with very different driving styles. You would want either the same person testing both cars or people matched on the basis of their driving styles. There may be more than one characteristic that you wish to use to match the members of the two samples. This discussion is really the beginning of a topic known as experimental design. In designing the statistical experiment, you are trying to get the most information for your money. Paired data are the simplest case of a designed experiment. It fits naturally here because often paired data are collected to compare two population means and yet the data are incorrectly analyzed using the methods discussed in the last section.

You should *not* analyze these paired or matched data using the small-sample t test that was described in the previous section. If you do, you might miss differences that exist but are masked by improper analysis. In this section we see how to analyze dependent or paired data.

10.7.2 The Paired Sample Test

The problem with using the tests for independent populations is that if there is a large amount of variation among the sample elements, then the standard errors of the estimates will be high. Since we divide by the standard error to obtain our test statistic, this value is often smaller than it should be. Real differences in the populations are *hidden* by the amount of variation among the sample elements.

How can we fix this problem? Well, if you think about it, the real question we are asking is whether the difference between the pretest and post-test measurements is significantly different from zero. In that case, we can look at the differences as our measurements and perform a test about them. The hypotheses for this test are then

$$H_0\colon\ \mu_d = 0 \qquad H_0\colon\ \mu_d \le 0 \qquad H_0\colon\ \mu_d \ge 0$$
$$H_A\colon\ \mu_d \ne 0 \qquad H_A\colon\ \mu_d > 0 \qquad H_A\colon\ \mu_d < 0$$

Table 10.2 shows how the data for such a test are set up. Each observation in the sample is a row in the table. The second and third columns are the values of the pretest (population 1) and post-test (population 2). For example, in the second column, the entry x_{13} is the pretest value for the third sample element. The fourth column, labeled Difference, is calculated by subtracting the pretest score from the post-test score. These differences are labeled $d_1, d_2, \ldots, d_n$. Finally, the average of these difference is found and labeled $\bar{d}$. That is,

Average difference

$$\bar{d} = \frac{\sum_{i=1}^{n} d_i}{n}$$

TABLE 10.2 Data Set Up for Paired Difference Test

	Variable		
Observation	**Pretest** X_1	**Post-test** X_2	**Difference** $d = (X_2 - X_1)$
1	x_{11}	x_{21}	d_1
2	x_{12}	x_{22}	d_2
3	x_{13}	x_{23}	d_3
⋮	⋮	⋮	⋮
n	x_{1n}	x_{2n}	d_n
Average			$\bar{d}$

Understand the Problem

EXAMPLE 10.15 Training Issues

Setting Up the Hypotheses for a Paired Difference Test

The company that was looking at the results of two different types of training programs wonders whether there is really an improvement realized from any type of training program. It decides to analyze the in-house training program it has and look at the difference in the pretest and post-test scores for the people who have gone through the training. The company wants to know whether the training increases the scores. The company knows it must use a paired difference test because the two populations are dependent. Since it wants to know if the program *increases* scores, it will use a one-sided test. The question is, In what direction do each of the hypotheses go?

If the training program does increase scores, then the differences (post-test − pretest) will be positive. In this case, the test should be an upper-tail test and the appropriate hypotheses are

$$H_0\colon\ \mu_d \le 0$$
$$H_A\colon\ \mu_d > 0$$

■

You see that the direction of the test depends on what the experimenter thinks the effect of the experiment will be and the order in which you subtract the pretest and post-test values. Most paired difference tests are one-sided.

EXAMPLE 10.16 Sleep Apnea

Setting up Hypotheses

Because of skyrocketing health-care costs, many hospital administrators are working to contain costs. Studies are being done to see whether diagnosis and treatment of some conditions can be done at home at a significantly reduced cost. One such area of study is in the diagnosis and treatment of obstructive sleep apnea syndrome (OSAS), which affects 2% to 5% of the adult male population and is characterized by extremely heavy snoring. As a result of OSAS, breathing is suspended either partially or entirely, which can lead to suffocation.

Understand the Problem

Once OSAS is diagnosed, the traditional treatment calls for hospitalization to begin nasal continuous positive airway pressure (NCPAP). In an effort to reduce costs, a study was done where NCPAP was initiated at home.

One of the variables observed for each patient before and after treatment was the number of obstructions. If the treatment worked, then the average number of obstructions post-treatment should be less than the pretreatment average. The hospital running the study wants to know whether home treatment of OSAS was effective.

Since the number of obstructions should decrease after NCPAP if treatment is effective, the analyst knows that the test should be one-tailed, and the differences (post-test − pretest) should be negative. This means that the test should be a lower-tail test and the appropriate hypotheses are

$$H_0: \quad \mu_d \geq 0$$
$$H_A: \quad \mu_d < 0$$

■

The hypothesis test is now essentially a test of a single mean. We know how to do this test from Chapter 9. The paired difference test is considered to be a small-sample test, so the test statistic will be a t statistic. The only difference is that the mean we are testing is the mean difference between two populations rather than the mean of a single population. Otherwise, the procedure is the same.

We need to define the test statistic for the test. For a paired difference test, the test statistic has a t distribution with $n - 1$ degrees of freedom. Remember that in this test n is the *number of pairs* and not the number of data points:

$$t = \frac{\bar{d}}{s_d/\sqrt{n}}$$

Paired difference test

where s_d is the standard deviation of the differences and is found in the usual way. Since the test is a t test, we must, as always, have normally distributed populations.

Figure 10.4 Shows typical data for a paired sample test. Since the data are plotted by observation, you can clearly see that the values after treatment are higher than

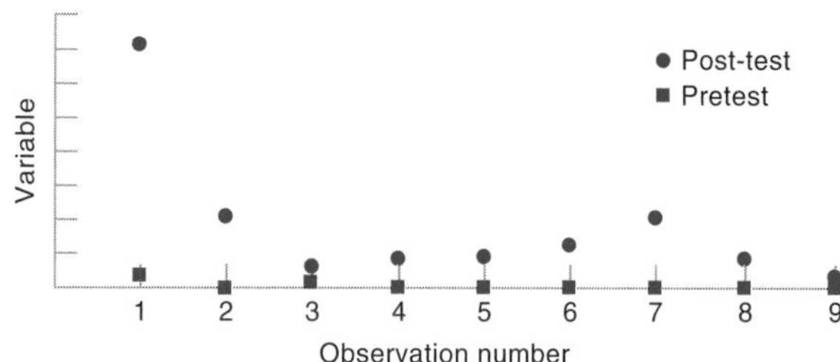

FIGURE 10.4 Pretest and post-test data for similar obersations

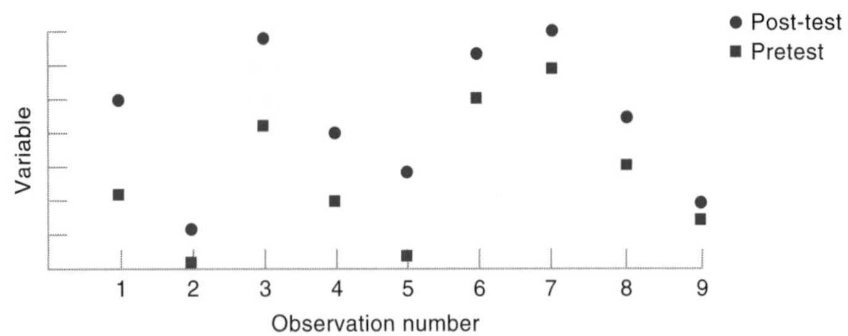

FIGURE 10.5 Pretest and post-test data for highly variable observations

the values before treatment for every observation in the sample. The statistical test will see whether the differences are statistically significant.

If we used the small, independent sample t test we would average all of the values in the first sample and all of the values in the second sample. In doing so we would lose some of the information contained in the sample. To see this effect, let's look at some different data to make a point. When you look at Figure 10.5, it is not obvious that the post-test data have a higher average if you do not view the data in pairs. The variation from sample element to sample element hides the differences between the pretest and post-test data. This is what happens when you simply average all of the pretreatment values and all of the post-treatment values and compare the sample means using a t test.

EXAMPLE 10.17 Training Issues

Performing the Paired Sample Test

The company that wants to know the value of training programs has 47 people who participated in the in-house training program. It analyzes the data and finds the following summary statistics:

$$n = 47$$
$$\bar{d} = 15.89$$
$$s_d = 8.45$$

Analyze the Data

The company decides to test with $\alpha = 0.05$. Since there are 47 pairs of data, the t test will have $n - 1 = 46$ degrees of freedom and the critical values will be $t_{0.05,46} = 1.679$, obtained from statistical software.

The test statistic is calculated to be

$$t = \frac{15.89}{8.45/\sqrt{47}} = 12.89$$

Clearly, this has a p value of 0.0000. ■

EXAMPLE 10.18 OSAS Data

Doing the Paired Sample Test

Let's complete the OSAS example using a level of significance of 0.05. If the treatment was effective, then the average difference should be significantly less than zero. If the treatment was not effective, then the pretest and post-test values would be close and the differences small, resulting in an average difference close to zero. The actual data for the $n = 9$ patients are shown in the table:

Patient	Number of Obstructions Pretreatment	Post-Treatment	Difference
1	365	22	−343
2	107	1	−106
3	28	12	−16
4	40	8	−32
5	48	3	−45
6	64	8	−56
7	109	0	−109
8	55	4	−51
9	20	0	−20
$\bar{d}$			−86.44
s_d			101.83

Analyze the Data

The test statistic follows a t distribution with $n - 1$ degrees of freedom. The value of n is equal to the number of pairs or the number of differences. In this case, $n = 9$ so there are 8 degrees of freedom. We need to find $t_{0.05,8}$. From the t table, the critical value is −1.860.

The test statistic looks just like the t statistic for a single population mean. It is calculated as

$$t = \frac{-86.44}{101.83/\sqrt{9}}$$
$$= -2.546$$

The p value of the test is found by looking up the test statistic in the t distribution with 8 degrees of freedom. We find that the p value is 0.0172. ■

Once the testing procedure is done we require a decision and then an interpretation.

EXAMPLE 10.19 Does Training Work?

Deciding What the Test Results Mean

The company looking at whether training programs are effective looks at the results of the test. Management sees that the test statistic is in the rejection region, so they will reject H_0.

Draw Conclusions

The company concludes that the average difference in score before and after the training program is greater than zero. This means that the training program is effective. ■

EXAMPLE 10.20 OSAS Data

Conclusions

In the study looking at the effectiveness of home treatment of sleep apnea, we see that the test statistic of −2.546 is in the rejection region, so we reject H_0.

Draw Conclusions

The hospital administration can conclude that the average difference between the number of obstructions after and before home treatment is less than zero—that is, it has gone down. Therefore, the home treatment is effective. ■

Print Sales	Radio Sales
28.3	22.1
24.6	19.1
23.1	20.3
21.0	24.4
25.7	22.4
22.5	19.2
32.0	22.8
23.5	20.3
24.3	25.5
25.2	22.6
23.3	24.9
25.3	29.7
22.2	22.2
23.4	28.5
23.9	28.2
25.7	21.6

10.13 Although it cannot be denied that advertising impacts sales, it is also true that advertising is expensive and companies want to advertise in ways that have the greatest benefit for the amount of money spent. A company that sells snack food designs two different advertising strategies, one focusing on print media and the other on radio. It ran the campaigns in a total of 16 different cities, paired on population size, and measured the sales ($1000) in the week directly following the beginning of the campaign. The data are given in the margin.

(a) Calculate the differences in sales for each pair of cities.

(b) Based on these differences, do you think there is a difference in mean sales for the two types of advertising campaigns? Why or why not?

(c) Calculate the average difference and the standard deviation of the differences.

(d) Set up the hypotheses to test whether there is a difference in mean sales due to type of advertising.

(e) Assuming that the data are normally distributed, at the 0.01 level of significance, what can you conclude?

10.14 How does time spent using the computer impact the speed with which you work? A software company ran a study that looked at the effectiveness with which a person uses a mouse. It selected 10 people, matched on computer skills, and measured the speed with which they moved a mouse at the beginning of a long session of computer use and after 2 hours of use. The data (in hundredths of a second) are shown here:

67	57
64	53
69	71
88	61
72	73
80	50
85	53
116	80
77	63
78	41

(a) Calculate the differences between the times for each person. Just looking at the differences, do you think that there was a change in the average speed after 2 hours? Why or why not?

(b) Calculate the average difference and the standard deviation of the differences.

(c) Set up the hypotheses to test whether there was a change in the mean speed with which the people moved the mouse.

(d) Assuming that the data are normally distributed, at the 0.05 level of significance, what can you conclude?

10.15 Does gender impact the use of electronic mail (e-mail)? An insurance company studied the use of e-mail in its organization by counting the number of business-related e-mails generated by 10 men and 10 women matched on job position in a day. The data are given here:

Men	Women
82	48
77	61
78	56
83	59
82	58
78	56
81	60
74	64
86	59
76	63

(a) Calculate the differences in the number of business-related e-mails for each male/female pair. Just looking at the differences, do you think that men use e-mail more? Why or why not?

(b) Calculate the average difference and the standard deviation of the differences.

(c) Set up the hypotheses to test whether the average number of business-related e-mails generated by men is greater than that generated by women.

(d) Assuming that the data are normally distributed, at the 0.05 level of significance, what can you conclude?

10.8 HYPOTHESIS TEST FOR THE DIFFERENCE IN TWO POPULATION PROPORTIONS

10.8.1 Two-Population Tests With Qualitative Data

One of the things you should realize by now is that different types of data require different statistical techniques. So far, all of the two-population tests that we have looked at involve quantitative data. In this section, we look at the two-population tests for a kind of qualitative data—population proportions or percentages.

A lot of data are available in the form of proportions or percentages. You see this type of data all the time in the newspaper. Here are some examples taken from the newspaper.

- A study of Americans in the 1980s found that 71% said the government should take care of people who can't take care of themselves. In the 1990s the percentage was 57%. Is there evidence that Americans have become more cynical and less compassionate?
- A recent nationwide poll of 1225 adults showed that blacks and whites differ in their opinions of the causes and solutions of society's problems. But do they really? Seventy percent of blacks feel progress has been made in easing racial tension in the past decade compared to 65% of whites. Based on these data, do blacks and whites really feel differently about this issue?
- Researchers in San Francisco using the diseased cells of melanoma patients have developed a vaccine that they say dramatically reduces the recurrence of the deadliest form of skin cancer. After three years, 70% of those vaccinated remained cancer-free, compared to 20% of patients treated with surgery alone.
- A study of 1049 men and women aged 18 to 65 shows that a greater percentage of women (86%) find it difficult to have sex without emotional involvement compared to men (71%).
- A study conducted by an on-line service found that 30% of respondents under age 45 drove sports cars compared to 17% of the 45 or over population.

Each of the studies cited has a structure similar to those we have already looked at in this chapter. In each case two populations are being compared and we have taken a sample from each population. What has changed is that the parameter being analyzed is no longer the mean, but the population proportion. For each sample, the percentage of the sample that has a certain characteristic is found. These percentages then need to be compared.

10.8.2 The Test for Two Population Proportions

We know that even if the percentage of two populations that have a certain characteristic were exactly the same, we would almost never get exactly the same percentage in two samples from the populations. This is due to sampling error. The question then

$$H_0: \pi_M = \pi_W \quad \text{or} \quad H_0: \pi_M - \pi_W = 0$$
$$H_A: \pi_M \neq \pi_W \quad \text{or} \quad H_A: \pi_M - \pi_W \neq 0$$

■

Recall that the test statistic of a single-population proportion was a z statistic. The extension to comparing two-population proportions is also a z test statistic. Therefore, we already know how to find the rejection region.

The test statistic for this test is constructed using logic similar to what we have used before. The two sample proportions are compared by subtracting one from the other. To determine whether this difference is "large," it is compared to the standard error of the estimate. In this case, the estimate of the true difference in the population proportions, $\pi_1 - \pi_2$, is the difference in the sample proportions, $p_1 - p_2$. The standard error of this estimate is similar to the standard error for a single-sample proportion. The test statistic is then given by the formula

Test statistic for comparing two population proportions

$$z = \frac{p_1 - p_2}{\sqrt{\bar{p}(1-\bar{p})\left(\frac{1}{n_1} + \frac{1}{n_2}\right)}}$$

Remember that the test statistic is calculated under the assumption that the null hypothesis is true.

Notice that $\bar{p}$ is used in the calculation of the standard error. The value of $\bar{p}$ is similar to the pooled variance in the sense that it combines all of the sample data. If the null hypothesis is true and the population proportions are equal, then the best estimate of the common but unknown population proportion is obtained by pooling the data. The formula for $\bar{p}$ is then

Common population proportion

$$\bar{p} = \frac{x_1 + x_2}{n_1 + n_2}$$

EXAMPLE 10.23 Is Training Really Better?

Performing the Test

After thinking about the problem, the company testing to see whether the proportion of passes from the in-house training group is lower than that of the outside training group decides that a Type I error will be more costly. The managers reason that if they reject H_0 in error and conclude that the in-house group has a significantly lower percentage of passes, they will wind up making changes and implementing expensive programs in error. They decide to test at the 0.01 level of significance.

Analyze the Data

The critical value for the test is $z = -2.33$.

They calculate the value of $\bar{p}$ to be

$$\frac{13 + 20}{47 + 50} = 0.340 \text{ or } 34\%$$

The value of the test statistic is then

$$z = \frac{0.277 - 0.400}{\sqrt{(0.340)\,(0.660)\left(\frac{1}{47} + \frac{1}{50}\right)}}$$
$$= -1.28$$

■

EXAMPLE 10.24 E-Mail Usage

Doing the Test

For the study of e-mail usage, there is no reason to test at any level other than 0.05. The rejection region for a two-tail z test is defined by the critical values ± 1.96.

Analyze the Data

The value of $\bar{p}$ is calculated as follows:

$$\bar{p} = \frac{13 + 27}{35 + 35} = 0.571$$

and the test statistic is found to be

$$z = \frac{0.371 - 0.771}{\sqrt{(0.571)\,(0.429)\left(\frac{1}{35} + \frac{1}{35}\right)}} = -3.39$$

■

As in any hypothesis test, we are not finished until we make a decision about H_0 and interpret that decision in terms of the problem we are trying to solve.

EXAMPLE 10.25 Is Training Really Better?

Draw Conclusions

Conclusions

The group of managers who are looking at training programs found that the test statistic for their data was -1.28. Since this is not in the rejection region, they fail to reject H_0. Thus, they conclude that there is not enough evidence to say that the group trained in-house has a lower percentage of passes on the certification exam than the group trained by the outside consultant.

Does this end the issue? Not by a long shot. The managers who are promoting the idea of using outside consultants are still not convinced that it is not a better route. They argue that even if the percentage of passes *is* the same in both groups there are other factors to consider. They want to look at employee perceptions about the training programs. They also argue that the higher test scores on the post-test must mean something. Perhaps the true difference will be evident in subsequent job performance.

What you see here is that statistics *cannot* solve the problem. Both groups have legitimate arguments. What the group doing the study has to decide on is *what* measurable outcome they really want to see. If it is the percentage of their employees who pass the certification exam, then in-house training is probably sufficient. If they are interested in employee attitudes and job performance issues, then they have a lot more work to do before they can make a good decision. ■

EXAMPLE 10.26 E-Mail Usage

Draw Conclusions

Conclusions

For the question about using e-mail we see that the test statistic is in the rejection region, so we reject the null hypothesis. We conclude that a different proportion of men and women use e-mail to communicate decisions. Although this tells the company something, the results of the test do not indicate whether men or women use e-mail more. If this is what the company wanted to know, then it should have done a one-sided test. ■

As you can see, testing the difference in two population proportions is not very different from testing the difference in two population means. This test has been developed parallel to the procedure for testing the difference in two population means. It has also been developed as a natural extension of the test of a single-population proportion.

TRY IT NOW!

E-mail Usage *Tests of Two Proportions*

The company looking at use of e-mail is also interested in the use of e-mail for personal messages. After seeing the results of the last test, the company decides that it really wants to know whether a higher proportion of women than men use e-mail to send personal messages. The data are shown here:

	Population 1 Men	Population 2 Women
Sample size	35	35
Population proportion	π_1	π_2
Number that use e-mail	15	18
Sample proportion		

Finish the table and then complete the hypothesis test.

Step 1:

Step 2:

Step 3:

Step 4:

Step 5:

ANS. $\hat{p}_1 = 0.43$; $\hat{p}_2 = 0.51$; H_0: $\pi_2 \le \pi_1$; H_A: $\pi_2 > \pi_1$; C.V. = 1.645; $\bar{p} = 0.47$; $z = 0.67$; FAIL TO REJECT H_0; MEN

10.8.3 Exercises—Learning It!

10.16 Does television match reality? A recent study looked at the percentage of television characters who survived cardiopulmonary resuscitation (CPR) compared to those who survive in real life. The study looked at 34 instances where CPR was applied to a television character and found that 25 survived, whereas data provided by Emergency Medical Technicians found that in 40 similar cases, only 16 survived.

(a) Calculate the sample proportion of people who survive CPR for television and for reality.

(b) Set up the hypotheses to test whether there is a difference in the proportion of people who survive CPR in the two groups.

(c) At the 0.05 level of significance, does television reflect reality?

10.17 Women who smoke suffer an increased risk of dying of breast cancer, according to a recently published study. In the study, out of 319,000 women who never smoked there were 468 deaths from breast cancer, whereas out of 120,000 smokers, there were 187 deaths.

(a) Calculate the sample proportion of women who died of breast cancer for smokers and nonsmokers.

(b) Set up the hypotheses to test whether the proportion of women who die of breast cancer is higher for smokers than for nonsmokers.

(c) At the 0.05 level of significance, can you conclude that smoking causes breast cancer? If not, what can you conclude?

10.18 Selling personal computers is big business and consumers are becoming increasingly aware of vendor reputation. A recent study of two vendors of desktop personal computers reports on the units that need repair for Dell Computer and Gateway 2000. Of 1584 computers manufactured by Dell Computer, 427 needed repair, whereas for Gateway 2000, 825 of 2662 computers needed repair.

(a) Calculate the sample proportion of computers needing repair for each company.

(b) Set up the hypotheses to test whether the proportion of computers needing repairs is different for the two companies.

(c) At the 0.05 level of significance, what can you conclude?

10.19 How punctual are Amtrak trains? One of the reasons that passenger trains are late is that almost all of the tracks are owned and maintained by freight companies who control the schedules for use. Amtrak's definition of on time is based on trip length. After customer complaints about late trains, Amtrak has tried to improve and claims that it has. Of 100 runs of the Metroliner between New York City and Washington, D.C., in March 1993, 87 were on time, whereas in the same period in 1994, 90 were on time.

(a) Calculate the sample proportion of on-time trips for each time period.

(b) Can Amtrak really claim it has improved ($\alpha = 0.05$)? Why or why not?

10.9 HYPOTHESIS TEST OF THE DIFFERENCE IN TWO POPULATION VARIANCES

10.9.1 The *F* Test for Comparing Population Variances

Remember the test to compare population means when the samples are small and the standard deviations are unknown? In working with small samples, we had to decide whether the populations had a common but unknown variance. If they did then we pooled the data and calculated a pooled estimate of the variance, s_p^2. We did not, however, discuss how to decide whether the populations had a common variance. Now it is time to learn how to determine this. A hypothesis test of variances follows the same five steps that we have repeatedly used. Once again, the only difference is the test statistic.

To decide whether we should pool the data we need to test to see if two population variances are *equal*. Thus, we should use a two-sided test. The null and alternative hypotheses are shown here:

Remember: The key words different, less than, *and* greater than *tell you which test to use.*

Two-sided Test

H_0: $\sigma_1^2 = \sigma_2^2$ or H_0: $\sigma_1^2/\sigma_2^2 = 1$
H_A: $\sigma_1^2 \neq \sigma_2^2$ or H_A: $\sigma_1^2/\sigma_2^2 \neq 1$

Use this test if you wish to test whether the variance of population 1 is *different* from the variance of population 2.

As with the tests to compare two population means or proportions, it is also possible to do one-sided tests. These are shown here:

Lower-Tail Test

H_0: $\sigma_1^2 \geq \sigma_2^2$ or H_0: $\sigma_1^2/\sigma_2^2 \geq 1$
H_A: $\sigma_1^2 < \sigma_2^2$ or H_A: $\sigma_1^2/\sigma_2^2 < 1$

Use this test if you wish to test whether the variance of population 1 is *less than* the variance of population 2.

Because of the difficulty in finding the rejection region for a lower-tail test, most one-sided tests are conveniently done as upper-tail tests.

Upper-Tail Test

H_0: $\sigma_1^2 \leq \sigma_2^2$ or H_0: $\sigma_1^2/\sigma_2^2 \leq 1$
H_A: $\sigma_1^2 > \sigma_2^2$ or H_A: $\sigma_1^2/\sigma_2^2 > 1$

Use this test if you wish to test whether the variance of population 1 is *greater than* the variance of population 2.

Since we are trying to decide how two population variances compare, it makes sense to compare the sample variances. We have seen two ways of comparing numbers. One way is to subtract one number from the other and see how close the difference is to zero. If the two numbers are estimates of the same unknown population parameter, then their difference will be close to zero. The other way to compare two numbers is to divide one number by the other and see how close the ratio is to one. If the two numbers are estimates of the same unknown population parameter, then their ratio will be close to one. Notice that the second way of writing each of the variance tests shown previously uses a ratio and a comparison to 1.0. When comparing variances, you should always use a ratio to compare them and not a difference.

The test statistic for comparing variances is an F statistic.

We know from our work in Chapter 7 that the best estimator of the population variance is the sample variance. Extending this idea to two populations, the point estimate for the ratio of the population variances is the ratio of the sample variances. This is also the test statistic, shown here:

Formula for test statistic for comparing two variances

$$F = \frac{s_1^2}{s_2^2}$$

The F distribution is determined by two sets of degrees of freedom.

Notice that this ratio is labeled F. This means that the test statistic follows an F distribution, if the two original populations are normally distributed. The F distribution was briefly introduced to you in Chapter 7. It is named after the famous statistician R. A. Fisher. Like the χ^2 distribution, which we used to test a single-population variance, the specific shape of the F distribution is determined by its degrees of freedom. But the F distribution has not one, but two values that determine its shape. One of these is called the degrees of freedom in the numerator and it is equal to one less than the sample size on which s_1^2 is based, $n_1 - 1$. The other one is called the degrees of freedom in the denominator and is equal to one less than the sample size on which s_2^2 is based, $n_2 - 1$.

The procedure for finding the rejection regions is similar to that which we have used for other tests. If you are a doing a two-sided test, then the rejection region is two-sided; if you are doing a one-sided test, then the rejection region is one-sided. These are shown in Figure 10.6.

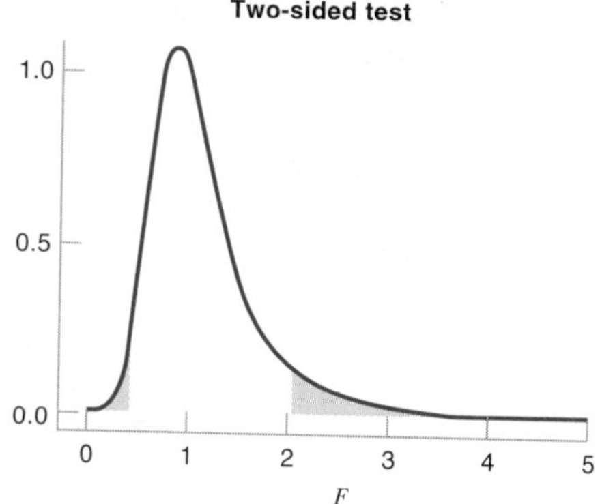

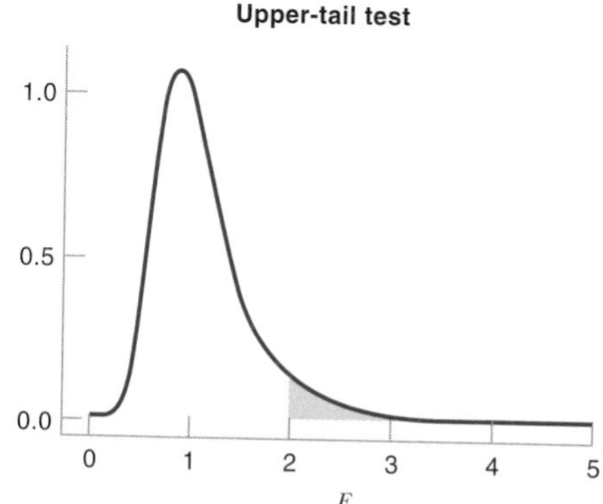

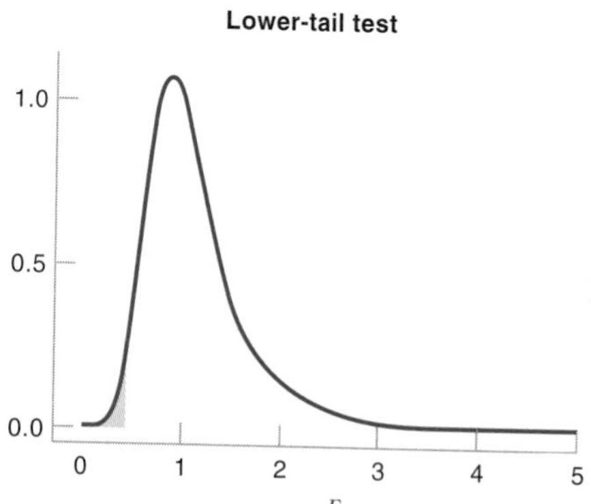

FIGURE 10.6 Rejection regions for test of variances

The critical values that define the rejection region are labeled $F_{\text{upper,df1,df2}}$ and $F_{\text{lower,df1,df2}}$ rather than F_{cutoff} and $-F_{\text{cutoff}}$, the notation you might have expected. To find the values for $F_{\text{upper,df1,df2}}$, and $F_{\text{lower,df1,df2}}$ we need to notice that the shape of the F distribution is not symmetric and the distribution is not centered at zero. Therefore, the absolute values of F_{upper} and F_{lower} are not the same and they will always be greater than zero. This is why they are not labeled F_{cutoff} and $-F_{\text{cutoff}}$. It happens that there is a relationship between the upper and lower F values. In particular, $F_{\text{lower,df1,df2}}$ can be found from an upper-tail value as follows:

The symbols df_1 and df_2 stand for the number of degrees of freedom in the numerator and the denominator, respectively.

$$F_{\text{lower,df1,df2}} = \frac{1}{F_{\text{upper,df2,df1}}}$$

Formula for findng the lower critical value for an F test

That is, the lower critical value is found by taking the reciprocal of the upper critical value *with the degrees of freedom reversed.* Therefore, we need table values only for F_{upper}.

Since the F distribution is determined by two sets of degrees of freedom, labeled df_1 and df_2, we will need an entire table to specify the values for F_{upper} that cut off a certain amount of probability in the upper tail of the distribution. Unlike the other tables that we have encountered so far, each upper-tail area probability requires a separate table. For instance, Table 6a in Appendix A shows the values for F_{upper} that cut off an area of 0.01 in the upper tail. The row and column we need to use depends on the number of degrees of freedom in the numerator and the denominator. However, if we need 0.05 in the upper-tail area, then we must use Table 6b in Appendix A. This is the first time we have encountered a different table for each value of α. When we used the t or the χ^2 distribution, each column corresponded to a different value of α.

EXAMPLE 10.27 Training and Gender

Setting Up the Test

When the company looking at training programs wanted to know whether there was a difference in the post-test scores for males versus females, we made an assumption about whether the population variances were equal. The relevant data from the problem follow:

	Population 1 Females Trained In-House	Population 2 Males Trained In-House
Sample size	$n_1 = 20$	$n_2 = 27$
Sample average	$\bar{X}_1 = 63.95$	$\bar{X}_2 = 63.26$
Sample standard deviation	$s_1 = 8.86$	$s_2 = 6.87$

To really determine whether this assumption is reasonable we need to test the hypotheses:

Analyze the Data

$$H_0: \sigma_1^2 = \sigma_2^2$$
$$H_A: \sigma_1^2 \neq \sigma_2^2$$

With these hypotheses, if we reject H_0, then we will conclude that the variances *are* different and we will know that we cannot pool the variances. For the moment we will assume that the populations are normally distributed and we will do the test at the 0.10 level of significance, which means that we need to use the F table with the upper-tail area of 0.05, Table 6b. A portion of that table is shown here:

		Numerator Degrees of Freedom (df_1)									
		18	19	20	21	22	23	24	25	26	27
Denominator degrees of freedom (df_2)	18	2.217	2.203	2.191	2.179	2.168	2.159	2.150	2.141	2.134	2.126
	19	2.182	2.168	2.155	2.144	2.133	2.123	2.114	2.106	2.098	2.090
	20	2.151	2.137	2.124	2.112	2.102	2.092	2.082	2.074	2.066	2.059
	21	2.123	2.109	2.096	2.084	2.073	2.063	2.054	2.045	2.037	2.030
	22	2.098	2.084	2.071	2.059	2.048	2.038	2.028	2.020	2.012	2.004
	23	2.075	2.061	2.048	2.036	2.025	2.014	2.005	1.996	1.988	1.981
	24	2.054	2.040	2.027	2.015	2.003	1.993	1.984	1.975	1.967	1.959
	25	2.035	2.021	2.007	1.995	1.984	1.974	1.964	1.955	1.947	1.939
	26	2.018	2.003	1.990	1.978	1.966	1.956	1.946	1.938	1.929	1.921
	27	2.002	1.987	1.974	1.961	1.950	1.940	1.930	1.921	1.913	1.905

To find $F_{\text{lower},df1,df2}$ you must reverse the degrees of freedom and find the corresponding F_{upper} value and then take the reciprocal.

To find the upper critical value we will use the numerator degrees of freedom as $20 - 1 = 19$ and the denominator degrees of freedom as $27 - 1 = 26$. The value of $F_{\text{upper},19,26}$ is 2.003. Now, the lower critical value that we want is $F_{\text{lower},19,26}$, so using the relationship that

$$F_{\text{lower},19,26} = \frac{1}{F_{\text{upper},26,19}}$$

we find that

$$F_{\text{lower},19,26} = \frac{1}{2.098} = 0.3356$$

■

This example has illustrated the procedure for finding the rejection region for a two-sided test. Let's summarize the steps for finding a two-sided rejection region and note the differences for a one-sided rejection region.

Two-sided rejection region:

Step 1: Divide the value of α in half.

Step 2: Find the F table that corresponds to those values that cut off $\alpha/2$ in the upper tail of the distribution.

Step 3: Find $F_{\text{upper df1,df2}}$ at the intersection of the column corresponding to $\text{df}_1 = n_1 - 1$ and the row corresponding to $\text{df}_2 = n_2 - 1$.

Step 4: Find F_{lower} by first finding $F_{\text{upper df2,df1}}$ with $n_2 - 1$ degrees of freedom in the numerator and $n_1 - 1$ degrees of freedom in the denominator. Then take the reciprocal of this number.

Step 5: Reject H_0 if the F statistic is larger than F_{upper} or less than F_{lower}.

If we are using a one-sided test of the variances, the main difference in finding the rejection region is that you do not split α in half. In addition, you need to find only one of the critical values: either F_{upper} or F_{lower}.

Upper-tail rejection region:

Steps for finding the rejection regions for the F distribution

Step 1: Find the F table that corresponds to those values that cut off α in the upper tail of the distribution.

Step 2: Find $F_{\text{upper,df1,df2}}$ at the intersection of the column corresponding to a $\text{df}_1 = n_1 - 1$ and the row corresponding to $\text{df}_2 = n_2 - 1$.

Step 3: Reject H_0 if the F statistic is larger than F_{upper}.

Lower-tail rejection region:

Step 1: Find the F table that corresponds to those values that cut off α in the upper tail of the distribution.

Step 2: Find F_{lower} by first finding $F_{\text{upper,df2,df1}}$ with $n_2 - 1$ degrees of freedom in the numerator and $n_1 - 1$ degrees of freedom in the denominator. Then take the reciprocal of this number.

Step 3: Reject H_0 if the F statistic is less than F_{lower}.

To avoid the tedious problem of finding the lower-tail rejection region for a one-tail test, it is easier to just set the test up as an upper-tail test by defining population 1 as the one with the larger of the two sample variances.

The remainder of the hypothesis testing procedure involves calculating the test statistic and making a decision both in terms of the null and alternative hypotheses and the original problem. We can now finish the example.

EXAMPLE 10.28 Training and Gender

Concluding the Test

For the training data we can calculate the test statistic as

$$F = \frac{8.86^2}{6.87^2} = 1.663$$

Analyze the Data

Since the critical values for the test were 0.3356 and 2.003, we see that we cannot reject H_0. This means that there is not enough evidence to say that the variances are different, and so the assumption that they are equal is reasonable. ■

TRY IT NOW!

Training and Gender *Test for Equality of Variances*

When you looked at gender differences for the group of employees trained by the outside consultant, you did the test using the pooled variance. That is, you assumed the population variances were equal. The relevant data are shown in the following table:

	Population 1 Females Trained by Outside Consultant	Population 2 Males Trained by Outside Consultant
Sample size	$n_1 = 21$	$n_2 = 29$
Sample mean	$\overline{X}_1 = 75.9$	$\overline{X}_2 = 75.2$
Sample standard deviation	$s_1 = 3.9$	$s_2 = 4.4$

Assume that the data are normally distributed and perform a test to see whether the assumption of equal variances was reasonable. Use a level of significance of 0.10.

Step 1:

Step 2:

Step 3:

Step 4:

Step 5:

ANS. H_0: $\sigma_1^2 = \sigma_2^2$, H_A: $\sigma_1^2 \neq \sigma_2^2$; $F_{\text{lower},20,28} = 0.487$, $F_{\text{upper},20,28} = 1.959$; $F = 0.786$; DO NOT REJECT H_0; THE ASSUMPTION OF EQUAL VARIANCES IS REASONABLE.

10.9.2 Exercises—Learning It!

10.20 Consider the problem in which The Board of Realtors for Greater Bridgeport, CT, was looking at the average selling prices of homes. The data are given again:

	Population	
	1995	**1996**
Sample size	$n_1 = 25$	$n_2 = 25$
Sample mean	$\overline{X}_1 = \$151{,}166$	$\overline{X}_2 = \$160{,}669$
Sample standard deviation	$s_M = \$5332$	$s_W = \$6468$

(a) Assuming that the populations are normally distributed, set up the hypotheses to test whether the population variances are equal at the 0.10 level of significance.

(b) Was the decision to test using the pooled variance justified?

10.21 In your quest for the perfect golf clubs you made an assumption about the population variances when you tested your hypotheses. The data you collected are given here:

	Population	
	Brand X	**Brand Z**
Sample size	$n_X = 15$	$n_Z = 15$
Sample mean	$\overline{X}_X = 255$	$\overline{X}_Z = 271$
Sample standard deviation	$s_X = 8.7$	$s_Z = 9.1$

(a) Set up the appropriate hypotheses to test whether the variance of brand Z clubs is the same as the variance for brand X.

(b) Assuming that the populations are normally distributed, at the 0.10 level of significance was your decision to pool the variances a good one?

(c) In general, would a difference in variation between the clubs be a factor in your purchase decision?

10.22 The members of the Chamber of Commerce of a small city in Fairfield County, CT, are looking at the amount of vacant office space in their city compared to a similar city. The data are given here:

	Population	
	Our City	**Their City**
Sample size	$n_1 = 12$	$n_2 = 12$
Sample mean	$\overline{X}_1 = 210{,}700$	$\overline{X}_2 = 167{,}607$
Sample standard deviation	$s_1 = 2200$	$s_2 = 2100$

Assuming that the populations are normally distributed, at the 0.02 level of significance, should they have pooled the variances?

10.23 A company has two different production lines that make the plastic cards used for credit cards and ATM cards. Both lines use $\overline{X}$ control charts to make sure that they run to the target specification, and both have been in control for the past six weeks. Recently, however, the quality manager has noticed that one of the machines (machine A) has many more items being rejected for the measurement on the width of the card. Since both machines are running to target, he decides the problem must be with the variability and decides to run a test. He samples 40 items from each production line and calculates the following summary statistics:

	Population	
	Machine A	**Machine B**
Sample size	$n_A = 40$	$n_B = 40$
Sample standard deviation	$s_A = 1.1$ mm	$s_B = 0.62$ mm

(a) Set up the hypotheses to test whether the variance of machine A is greater than the variance of machine B.

(b) Assuming that the populations are normally distributed, perform the test at the 0.10 level of significance.

(c) Is the quality manager correct in his perception that machine A is more variable?

10.24 A large utility company is considering two sites for locating a large-scale wind energy conversion system (windmill). In selecting a site both the average speed and the variation in speed are important: the more consistent the wind speeds, the more efficient the energy conversion. The variability for the two sites is measured using a sample of 30 wind speed observations at each site. The summary data are given here:

	Population	
	Site 1	**Site 2**
Sample size	$n_1 = 30$	$n_2 = 30$
Sample standard deviation	$s_1 = 1.8$ mph	$s_2 = 2.62$ mph

(a) Set up the hypotheses to test whether the variability in wind speed at the two sites is the same.

(b) Assuming that the populations are normally distributed, perform the test at the 0.10 level of significance.

(c) What can you tell the utility company about the variability at the two sites?

10.10 Executive Summary:
TRAINING PROGRAMS

Business Analysis...

TO: CEO
FROM: Human Resources
RE: Training Programs

A study was conducted to determine whether training by an outside consultant is more effective than our in-house training programs. The study was done in the Quality Department with people training as Certified Mechanical Inspectors for the American Society for Quality (ASQ). One hundred people were randomly assigned to one of the two groups. A total of 97 people completed the training and took the certification exam: 50 from the group that received outside training and 47 from the in-house group.

The final result is that, although the group that received outside training scored, on average, higher than the group that trained in-house ($p < 0.05$), there is no statistically significant difference in the percentage who passed the certification exam between the two groups. The table summarizes some of the results.

	Outside Consultant	In-house Training
Post-Test Score Mean	75.5	63.5
Standard Deviation	4.12	7.69
Percent Passing Certification	27.7%(13/47)	40.0%(20/50)
Sample Size	50	47

The group that had outside training scored, on average, ten points higher on the post-test exam. There was also more variability in the scores of the in-house group. To be certain that differences in the post-test scores were real and not a result of inherent differences in the two groups, we also used a *t* test to see whether there was a difference in the pretest scores of the two groups. The results of the test found no significant difference, so the two groups were evenly matched.

Although the conclusion seems to be that the two methods of training produce the same percentage of passes, it is important to note several things. First, the percentages are not different "statistically," but this could be due to very small sample sizes. Second, although the percentage passing the exam is the same, the scores on the post-test are not—they differ by more than 10 points. This difference might show up later in job performance.

Other issues to consider are cost and employee morale. There were no dropouts from the outside training group, whereas three people did not finish the in-house training session. We conducted a satisfaction survey at the end of each training program, and we intend to analyze the data to see whether there are any significant results.

Although we cannot say that outside training is absolutely better, the results do show that training in either form is good. There is a significant difference in test scores before and after training $(p < 0.05)$.

At this time we must decide what we think the most important outcomes of training are and then make decisions based on these outcomes. We suggest tracking the job performance of both of these employee groups to see whether there are any real differences in issues such as job evaluations, raises, and promotions.

The *Wall Street Journal* is a major source of current business news and information for the business community. If your professor has arranged for your class to have access to the Business Extra feature, you can go to it now and see the techniques of this chapter in action today. Go to the Wiley Web site at http://www.wiley.com/college/pelosi, and click on Business Extra!

10.11 TWO-POPULATION HYPOTHESIS TESTS IN EXCEL

Excel has built-in data analysis tools for two-population hypothesis tests. Once you know which test to use, the procedure is not very different from test to test.

10.11.1 Large-Sample Tests of Two Means

For a large-sample test of two population means, either the population standard deviations must be known or else the sample size from each population must be large—that is, greater than 30. Suppose that we want to consider the data from the company that was looking at in-house versus outside consultant training. They want to know whether the results obtained by the outside consultant are better than those of the in-house trainers. This is a one-tail test, and the hypotheses are

$$H_0: \quad \mu_1 \leq \mu_2$$
$$H_A: \quad \mu_1 > \mu_2$$

To use Excel to perform the hypothesis test, the data must be in a spreadsheet. If you do not know the population standard deviations and are using the sample standard deviations, you must first calculate these using either the Descriptive Statistics tool or the **STDEV** or **VAR** functions. The value you will actually need is the variance, so if you calculate the standard deviation, you will have to square it to find the variance.

In our example, the population standard deviations are not known, but the sample sizes are $n_1 = 50$ and $n_2 = 47$, respectively. To perform the test, open the **Tools > Data Analysis** menu and from the list choose **z Test: Two Sample for Means.** This will open the dialog box for the test as shown in Figure 10.7.

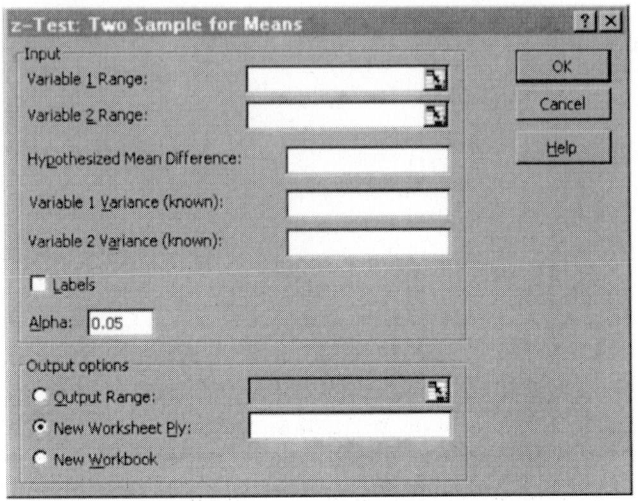

FIGURE 10.7 Dialog box for z test for two means

Use the following procedure to perform the test:

1. Position the cursor in the text box next to **Variable 1 Range:** and highlight the range that contains the post-test data for the first population—in this case, the group trained by the outside trainer.
2. With the cursor in the text box for **Variable 2 Range:** highlight the location of the data for the second population, the in-house group.
3. Position the cursor in the text box for **Hypothesized Mean Difference** and enter **0.** Since we want to know whether $\mu_1 > \mu_2$, this is the same as $\mu_1 - \mu_2 > 0$.
4. Now, put the cursor in the text box for **Variable 1 Variance (known)** and enter the *value* of the variance for population 1. For the training example, the variance in post-test scores for the outside group is $(4.12)^2 = 16.97$.

***Note:** You must enter the value of the variance itself. You cannot enter a formula or highlight a data range here.*

5. Repeat this for **Variable 2 Variance (known).**
6. If there were labels in any of the data ranges you highlighted, check **Labels** check box.
7. Enter the level of significance for the test. In this case, we will use the default value of $\alpha = 0.05$.
8. Finally, indicate where you want the output from the test to appear.

When you have entered all the data, the dialog box should look like the one in Figure 10.8.

9. Hit Enter to perform the test. The resulting output is shown in Figure 10.9.

From the output, we see that the value of the test statistic, labeled z in the output, is 9.419937922 (which is the same as the 9.42 we obtained by hand). Since the critical value for a one-tailed test is 1.644853, we can reject H_0 and conclude that the mean for the outside group is higher than the mean for the in-house group.

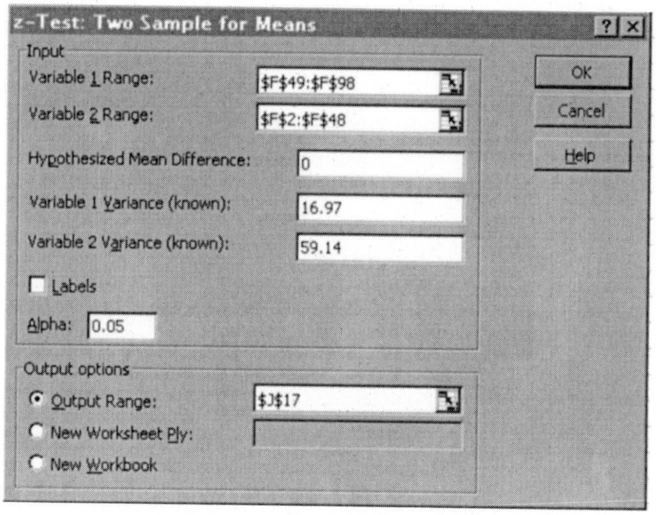

z-Test: Two Sample for Means

Input

Variable 1 Range: $F$49:$F$98

Variable 2 Range: $F$2:$F$48

Hypothesized Mean Difference: 0

Variable 1 Variance (known): 16.97

Variable 2 Variance (known): 59.14

Labels

Alpha: 0.05

Output options

Output Range: $J$17

New Worksheet Ply:

New Workbook

OK

Cancel

Help

FIGURE 10.8 z test dialog box

z-Test: Two Sample for Means		
	Variable 1	*Variable 2*
Mean	75.46	63.55319
Known Variance	16.97	59.14
Observations	50	47
Hypothesized Mean Difference	0	
z	9.419937922	
P(Z<=z) one-tail	0	
z Critical one-tail	1.644853	
P(Z<=z) two-tail	0	
z Critical two-tail	1.959961082	

FIGURE 10.9 Output from z test for two sample means

The procedure gives the p value for the test, but does not label it as such. The value labeled $P(Z <= z)$ one-tail is the p value for the one-tailed test, and $P(Z <= z)$ two-tail is the p value for the two-tailed test.

10.11.2 Small-Sample Tests for Two Population Means

When you do not know the population standard deviations and the sample sizes are not large, the appropriate test is the t test. To choose the correst t test, you must decide whether the two population variances are the same or whether they differ from each other. Excel provides t test procedures for both cases.

Let's look at the training data for the outside consultant. Suppose that now we want to know whether there is a difference in post-test scores for males and females. Since there were only 50 people in the original sample, it is not possible that both sample sizes are larger than 30. Therefore, we must use a t test. We will use the t test that assumes the two population variances are equal.

From the **Data Analysis Tools** menu, select **t-Test: Two Sample Assuming Equal Variances.** The dialog box that opens should look very similar to the one for the z test. The only difference is that you are not required to put in the population variances. The t test assumes that they are unknown and the procedure will calculate them from the data. Fill in the dialog box, just as you did for the Z test. An example of the completed box is shown in Figure 10.10.

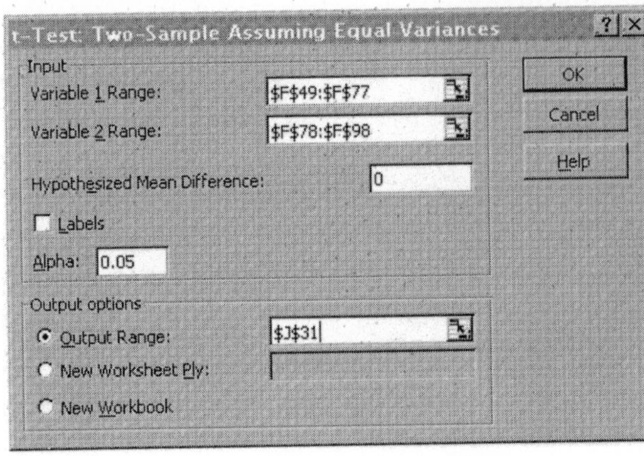

t-Test: Two-Sample Assuming Equal Variances

Input
Variable 1 Range: $F$49:$F$77
Variable 2 Range: $F$78:$F$98
Hypothesized Mean Difference: 0
Labels
Alpha: 0.05
Output options
Output Range: $J$31
New Worksheet Ply:
New Workbook
OK
Cancel
Help

FIGURE 10.10 *t* test for two means, variances assumed equal

Click **OK;** the output is placed in the location you specified. The output for this test is shown in Figure 10.11.

t-Test: Two-Sample Assuming Equal Variances		
	Variable 1	*Variable 2*
Mean	75.17241379	75.85714
Variance	18.93349754	14.82857
Observations	29	21
Pooled Variance	17.22311166	
Hypothesized Mean Difference	0	
df	48	
t Stat	-0.575819805	
P(T<=t) one-tail	0.283713515	
t Critical one-tail	1.677224191	
P(T<=t) two-tail	0.567427031	
t Critical two-tail	2.01063358	

FIGURE 10.11 Output for *t* test assuming equal variances

From the output, we see that the value of the t statistic is -0.575819805. Since we wanted to determine whether there was a difference between males and females, it is a two-sided test and the critical values are ± 2.01063358. Comparing the test statistic and the critical value, we fail to reject H_0 and conclude that there is no difference in the scores for males and females in the outside group. The output from the t test does include the p value of the test, although it is not labeled as such. The value labeled P(T <= t) two-tail is the p value for the two-tail test. Notice that it is twice the value for the one-tail test.

What if we cannot assume that the variances are equal? In this case, the two variances are 18.93 and 14.83, which do not appear to be that different. However, we can do the same test, assuming that the variances are not equal, and see what changes. From the list of **Data Analysis** tools, select **t Test: Two Sample Assuming Unequal Variances.** There are no differences in the dialog box. This makes sense, because there are no differences in the test inputs, just the outputs. Entering the same data as in the previous test produces the output shown in Figure 10.12.

t-Test: Two-Sample Assuming Unequal Variances		
	Variable 1	*Variable 2*
Mean	75.17241379	75.85714
Variance	18.93349754	14.82857
Observations	29	21
Hypothesized Mean Difference	0	
df	46	
t Stat	-0.58736595	
P(T<=t) one-tail	0.2799151	
t Critical one-tail	1.678658919	
P(T<=t) two-tail	0.559830201	
t Critical two-tail	2.012893674	

FIGURE 10.12 Output from t test assuming unequal variances

From the output, you see that the only real difference is in the value for degrees of freedom. The test assuming unequal variances is a more conservative test. Since the degrees of freedom have changed, the critical values will also change. The conclusion of the test in this example is the same.

Do not forget that all of the t tests *assume the populations are normally distributed.* You need to check this assumption before reporting any results.

10.11.3 Paired Difference Test in Excel

When the two populations in a hypothesis test are related, we must use a paired difference test. There is an Excel data analysis tool for the paired difference test.

Suppose that we want to look at the training scores to determine whether training really changes test scores. In this case, the two populations are related; they are the same people, so we must use a paired difference test. We will look at the in-house group, using the same data as for the previous examples. The hypothesis test is a one-sided test, because we want to know whether training increases test scores. We will define the difference in scores to be post-test − pretest.

From the list of data analysis tools, select **t Test: Paired Two Sample for Means.** The dialog box is the same as the dialog boxes for the other t tests that we have looked at. In this case, the first variable is the post-test scores for the in-house group, and the second variable is the pretest scores for the same group. The output from the test is shown in Figure 10.13. By now, the output should look familiar.

t-Test: Paired Two Sample for Means		
	Variable 1	*Variable 2*
Mean	63.55319149	47.65957
Variance	59.20906568	163.7946
Observations	47	47
Pearson Correlation	-0.040209148	
Hypothesized Mean Difference	0	
df	46	
t Stat	7.170308992	
P(T<=t) one-tail	2.53155E-09	
t Critical one-tail	1.678658919	
P(T<=t) two-tail	5.0631E-09	
t Critical two-tail	2.012893674	

FIGURE 10.13 Output from paired difference test

From the output, you can see that the value of the test statistic is 7.17031. Comparing this to the one-tail critical value of 1.678658919, we reject H_0 and conclude that the test scores have increased. The p value of the test is 0.0000.

10.11.4 Two Population Tests of Proportions

Excel does not have a built-in test for comparing two population proportions, but we have supplied a macro that will perform the test. The macro assumes that you have the proportion of frequency of successes calculated for each population. You can use pivot tables to do this.

The company looking at training scores wants to determine whether the proportion of people who pass the test from the outside training group is greater than the proportion for the in-house group. An example of the pivot table is shown in Figure 10.14. The counts for each cell are displayed as percentage of row.

Count of Certificaton Exam	Certificaton Exam		
Training	F	P	Grand Total
I	0.723	0.277	1.000
O	0.600	0.400	1.000
Grand Total	0.660	0.340	1.000

FIGURE 10.14 Pivot table for training data

From the list of MacDoIt macros, choose **TwoPropTest** and click **Run.** A table will open in a new worksheet, just as in the macros for the one-population tests. We will let the outside group be population 1 and the in-house group be population 2. In the top portion of the table, type in the sample proportions and sample sizes for each group. The table will update automatically. The results of the test are shown in Figure 10.15.

	A	B	C	D	E
2					
3		Proportion		Sample Size	
4	Sample 1	p1	0.4000	n1	50
5	Sample 2	p2	0.2770	n2	47
6	Pooled	pp	0.3404		
7					
8	Test Statistic	Z	1.2777		
9	Significance Level	α	0.05		
10	*Critical Values*				
11	Lower Tail	Z1	-1.6449	p-value1	0.100684
12	Upper Tail	Z2	1.6449	p-value2	0.100684
13	Two Tail	Z3	-1.9600	p-value3	0.201367

FIGURE 10.15 Table for two proportion test

The test statistic is 1.2777. The test is an upper-tail test so the critical value is 1.6449 with a p value of 0.1007. From the results, we conclude that we cannot reject H_0. There is not enough evidence to say that the proportion that passes from the outside group is higher.

10.11.5 *F* Test for Comparing Two Variances

When we looked at the small-sample tests for comparing population means, we had to make a decision about whether the population variances were equal. Excel has an analysis tool to test hypotheses about population variances.

We can use this test to determine which t test was correct. From the list of Data Analysis tools, select **F Test Two Sample for Variances.** The dialog box is the same one we have seen for the other two population tests.

The only difference is not obvious from the dialog box—the test is done as an upper-tail test. So, to test whether the variances are not equal, you must enter *half* the value of α that you want to use and you must enter the larger variance as population 1. Finish filling out the dialog box and click **OK.** The output is shown in Figure 10.16.

F-Test Two-Sample for Variances		
	Variable 1	*Variable 2*
Mean	75.17241379	75.85714286
Variance	18.93349754	14.82857143
Observations	29	21
df	28	20
F	1.27682546	
P(F<=f) one-tail	0.289003794	
F Critical one-tail	2.365666774	

FIGURE 10.16 Output from two-sample variance test

From the output, the test statistic is labeled F and is 1.27682546. Comparing this to the critical value of 2.365666774, we conclude that we cannot reject H_0 and that it is reasonable to assume that the variances are equal. The p value of 0.289003794 given is the one-tailed p value.

CHAPTER 10 SUMMARY

Key Terms

Term	Definition	Page Reference
Dependent samples	**Dependent samples** are related to each other. The members of one sample are identical to or matched or paired with the members in the other sample according to some characteristic.	476
Pretest and post-test	**Pretest** and **post-test** conditions exist when data are collected on the same sample elements before and after some experiment is performed.	475

Key Formulas

Term	Formula	Page Reference
Formula for average difference, $\bar{d}$	$\bar{d} = \dfrac{\sum_{i=1}^{n} d_i}{n}$	478
Formula for common population proportion, $\bar{p}$	$\bar{p} = \dfrac{x_1 + x_2}{n_1 + n_2}$	488
Formula for degrees of freedom for small-sample, unequal variances test	$\nu = \dfrac{\left(\dfrac{s_1^2}{n_1} + \dfrac{s_2^2}{n_2}\right)^2}{\dfrac{(s_1^2/n_1)^2}{n_1 + 1} + \dfrac{(s_2^2/n_2)^2}{n_2 + 1}} - 2$	471

Key Formulas *(continued)*

Term	Formula	Page Reference
Variances test formula for F_{lower}	$F_{\text{lower,df1,df2}} = \dfrac{1}{F_{\text{upper,df2,df1}}}$	493
Formula for pooled variance, s_p^2	$s_p^2 = \dfrac{(n_1 - 1)s_1^2 + (n_2 - 1)s_2^2}{n_1 + n_2 - 2}$	468
Test for paired difference	$t = \dfrac{\bar{d}}{s_d/\sqrt{n}}$	479
Test for two population means:		
• Variances known	$z = \dfrac{(\bar{X}_1 - \bar{X}_2) - 0}{\sqrt{\sigma_1^2/n_1 + \sigma_2^2/n_2}}$	459
• Variances unknown, $n_1, n_2 \geq 30$	$z = \dfrac{(\bar{X}_1 - \bar{X}_2) - 0}{\sqrt{s_1^2/n_1 + s_2^2/n_2}}$	462
• Variances unknown and not equal, n_1, $n_2 < 30$; degrees of freedom adjusted	$t = \dfrac{(\bar{X}_1 - \bar{X}_2) - d}{\sqrt{s_1^2/n_1 + s_2^2/n_2}}$	471
• Variances unknown but equal, $n_1, n_2 < 30$	$t = \dfrac{(\bar{X}_1 - \bar{X}_2)}{s_p\sqrt{1/n_1 + 1/n_2}}$	469
Test for two population proportions	$z = \dfrac{p_1 - p_2}{\sqrt{\bar{p}(1 - \bar{p})\left(\dfrac{1}{n_1} + \dfrac{1}{n_2}\right)}}$	488
Test for two population variances	$F = \dfrac{s_1^2}{s_2^2}$	492

CHAPTER 10 EXERCISES

Learning It!

10.25 The members of the Chamber of Commerce of a small city in Fairfield County, CT, are wondering whether they need to worry about the amount of vacant office space in the city. They would consider lobbying for tax incentives for businesses if they find that there is more vacant office space in their city than in a comparable area. They take weekly data on the number of square feet of vacant office space, for the second quarter of 1996 for each city and find the following:

	Population	
	Our City	**Their City**
Sample size	$n_1 = 12$	$n_2 = 12$
Sample mean	$\bar{X}_1 = 210{,}700$	$\bar{X}_2 = 167{,}607$
Sample standard deviation	$s_1 = 2200$	$s_2 = 2100$

(a) Calculate the pooled variance for the data.

(b) Assuming that the data are normally distributed, at the 0.01 level of significance, should they lobby for tax incentives?

10.26 A recent study of consumer behavior focused on the amount of money spent monthly on frozen foods. The study wanted to determine whether there was a difference in the average amount of money spent for men and women. Data were collected on samples of 50 men and 50 women and the following information was found:

	Population	
	Men	Women
Sample size	$n_M = 50$	$n_W = 50$
Sample mean	$\overline{X}_M = \$72.24$	$\overline{X}_W = \$67.44$
Sample standard deviation	$s_M = \$8.23$	$s_W = \$8.12$

(a) Set up the appropriate hypotheses to test whether men spend more per month, on the average, for frozen foods than women.

(b) Use the large-sample test with unknown variances to test the hypotheses. Use a level of significance of 0.10.

(c) Do the data provide evidence that the average amount spent per month on frozen food by men is greater than by women?

(d) What is the p value of the test?

10.27 The nurses who were part of the hand washing experiment are still not convinced that the length of time spent washing hands makes that much difference. They design their own study and decide to have each nurse in the CCU wash his or her hands twice, once for 2.5 seconds and once for 15 seconds. After each washing they do a bacteria culture and measure the number of bacteria that remain on the person's hands. The data are shown in the next table.

Observation	Culture 1 2.5 s	Culture 2 15 s
1	66	78
2	132	115
3	120	93
4	187	48
5	190	77
6	17	3
7	33	12
8	92	12
9	1000	146

(a) Calculate the differences between the number of bacteria for each nurse. Just looking at the differences, do you think that washing longer decreased the amount of bacteria? Why or why not?

(b) Calculate the average difference and the standard deviation of the differences.

(c) Set up the hypotheses to test whether there was a decrease in the average amount of bacteria after washing longer.

(d) Assuming that the data are normally distributed, at the 0.05 level of significance, what can you conclude?

(e) Suppose that you were told that the second episode of hand washing was done right after the first. Would that change the way you interpret the results of the study?

Thinking About It!

10.28 It has been a widely held belief that the switch to participative management would increase employees' buy-in to the company. One of the benefits that should be realized is a reduction in the number of sick days that employees use. A company that has made the switch in some departments wonders whether this has been true. It decides to sample 25 employees from each of two manufacturing departments. The first has been using a participative management style for almost 2 years and the second is still using a traditional management style. The data on the number of sick days used by each employee in the past 12 months follow:

Participative					Traditional				
1	3	5	5	6	0	5	6	7	9
1	4	5	6	7	3	5	7	7	9
2	4	5	6	8	4	6	7	7	10
2	4	5	6	8	4	6	7	8	11
3	4	5	6	8	5	6	7	8	11

At the 0.05 level of significance, do the data provide enough evidence to say that employees who use participative management styles use, on the average, fewer sick days than those who use a traditional management style? Be sure to justify any assumptions you make in selecting the test procedure you use.

10.29 The software company that is looking at the time to failure of the diskettes (hours) it uses decides to look at an alternative supplier of the product. The data for the current supplier and for the new supplier are shown here:

Current Supplier				Alternative Supplier			
486	494	502	508	489	492	495	498
490	496	504	510	489	492	496	499
491	498	505	514	491	493	497	502
491	498	506	515	492	493	497	503
494	498	507	527	492	494	497	505

The company has decided that if the mean time to failure for the new supplier is longer than it is for the current supplier, it will switch suppliers.

(a) What level of significance would you suggest the company use? Justify your choice.

(b) Assuming that the data are normally distributed, should the company switch suppliers? Use the level of significance you chose in part (a).

(c) What impact did your choice of α have on the decision?

Requires Exercise 10.11

10.30 You are still wondering about the results of the test on the difference in software prices. You wonder why the two tests came to different conclusions and figure that it must be the amount of variability in the software prices for the packages chosen.

Top Ten Business Software	Computability Price ($)	PC Connection Price ($)
Norton Anti-Virus 2000 v 6.0	29	32
Microsoft W98 Second Edition Upgrade	95	90
Norton System Works 2000 v 3.0	59	60
VirusScan 5.0	29	24
QuickBooks 2000 Pro	200	200
Norton Internet Security 2000	58	48
QuickBooks 2000	120	120
Microsoft W98 Second Edition	180	179
Microsoft Office 2000 Upgrade	220	230
VirusScan 5.0 Deluxe	38	33

(a) Look at the data again. Do any of the software have prices that seem to be *very* different from the others? If so, which ones?

(b) Drop the data for the most unusual observations and perform the hypothesis test again using the test for independent samples.

(c) Does anything change from the last time you did the test? If so, what?

(d) Does dropping the observations change the decision?

(e) Do you think this was the right test to use? Why or why not?

10.31 A study was recently completed by an insurance company concerning a particular surgical procedure. The study looked at the hospital records of 40 patients at two different hospitals and compared the length of patient stay. The data were analyzed using Minitab. Output showing the descriptive statistics for the data is given here:

```
DESCRIPTIVE STATISTICS

Length of Stay    N      Mean     Median    Trim Mean    St.Dev.    SE Mean

Hospital 1        40     7.725     7.500       7.667      2.562      0.405
Hospital 2        40    10.350    10.000      10.222      3.340      0.528

Length of Stay     Min       Max        Q1         Q3

Hospital 1        2.000    14.000     6.000       9.000
Hospital 2        5.000    18.000     8.000      13.500
```

(a) Set up the hypotheses necessary to test whether the patients at hospital 1 had, on the average, a shorter stay than those at hospital 2.

(b) What type of test would you use to make this decision? Why?

(c) Perform the appropriate hypothesis test. Use a level of significance of 0.05.

(d) Do the data provide evidence that the mean stay at hospital 1 is shorter than at hospital 2?

10.32 After looking at the results of the data analysis, the Director of Human Resources at the company looking at sick days and type of management writes a memo to the Vice President of Human Resources suggesting that the company change all units over to participative management. He cites the results of the test and states that the data "provide evidence that participative management causes people to take fewer sick days." Since you did the analysis, he gives you the memo to read before he sends it. *Requires Exercise 10.28*

(a) Do you agree with the Director of Human Resources? Why or why not?

(b) Write a memo to the Director of Human Resources explaining your reaction. Include plans for further study if you think it is warranted.

10.33 Reconsider the study of the amount of money spent monthly on frozen foods. Data were collected on samples of 50 men and 50 women: *Requires Exercise 10.26*

	Population	
	Men	**Women**
Sample size	$n_M = 50$	$n_W = 50$
Sample mean	$\bar{X}_M = \$72.24$	$\bar{X}_W = \$67.44$
Sample standard deviation	$s_M = \$8.23$	$s_W = \$8.12$

(a) Do you think your decision was sensitive to the value chosen for α? Why or why not?

(b) Suppose that you were interested only in whether the average spent by men was different than the average spent by women. How would this have changed the setup of the test? Would it have changed the conclusion?

10.34 After looking at the software price data again, and based on the results of the paired test, you are considering buying your software from Computability. You decide to check the ads for each company one more time to see whether there are any hidden catches and you notice that shipping charges for PC Connection are \$5 whereas for Computability they are \$16.95. At the 0.05 level of significance, who will you buy your software from? *Requires Exercises 10.11, 10.30*

10.35 Since the data were available, the Nursing Supervisor was interested in knowing whether there was a difference in the average amount of time that nurses from two different departments spent washing their hands. She was not sure whether to pool the variances, and Minitab does not do an F test on variances, so she decided to run the t test both ways. The Minitab output is shown at the top of page 510.

```
Two Sample T-Test and Confidence Interval

Two sample T for C9
C8        N      Mean      StDev      SE Mean
IMCU     10      1.00      1.89       0.60
N4        8      4.87      5.79        2.0
95% CI for mu (IMCU) - mu (N4 ): (-8.79, 1.0)
T-Test mu (IMCU) = mu (N4 ) (vs not =): T = -1.82 P = 0.11 DF = 8

Two Sample T-Test and Confidence Interval

Two sample T for C9
C8        N      Mean      StDev      SE Mean
IMCU     10      1.00      1.89       0.60
N4        8      4.87      5.79        2.0
95% CI for mu (IMCU) - mu (N4 ): (-7.98, 0.2)
T-Test mu (IMCU) = mu (N4 ) (vs not =): T = -2.00 P = 0.063 DF = 16
```

(a) Interpret the results of the output for the first test, without pooling the variances. How many degrees of freedom are there for this test? If you use a level of significance of 0.10 what would you conclude about the two departments?

(b) Interpret the results of the output for the second test, pooling the variances. How many degrees of freedom are there for this test? If you use a level of significance of 0.10, what would you conclude about the two departments?

(c) How does this example confirm what you learned about the effects of pooling the variances?

Doing It!

Datafile: BOSSSAL.XXX

10.36 Every year the *Wall Street Journal* has a feature on compensation of CEOs of different companies. The data include type of company, amount of salary, amount of bonus, % change from the previous year, and several other compensation forms. A sample of the data is shown here:

Company	1996 Salary (000)	1996 Bonus (000)	% Change from 1995	Options Gains	Other	Total Direct Compensation (000)	Present Value of Options Grants (000)
Basic materials							
Air Products	$738.10	$473.00	−8.70	$ 560.60	$390.50	$2162.10	$ 887.00
Alcoa	750	810	−22	6113.60	0	7673.60	13,905.60
Alumax	800	797.1	27.3	0	670	2267.10	8,491.10
Armco	559.2	0	−42.2	0	0	559.2	422.7
Asarco	811.7	485	−20.5	0	539.8	1836.40	571.6

(a) Look at the 1996 salary data for cyclical and noncyclical companies. Create a plot of salaries for each group. Based on the graphs do you think the data are normally distributed? Why or why not?

(b) Perform the appropriate hypothesis test to determine whether the variances in salary for the two types of companies are equal. Based on this test, can you assume equal variances?

(c) Based on the results of your answers to parts (a) and (b) select the appropriate test procedure to test whether the mean salary for cyclical and noncyclical companies is the same.

(d) Perform the test at the 0.05 level of significance. What is your conclusion?

(e) Repeat the procedure you used to answer parts (a)–(d) to determine whether the mean bonus for the two types of companies is different.

(f) Look at the entire set of data. One variable that is reported is the change in compensation level from the previous year (%). Calculate the proportion of companies whose CEOs received increases in compensation. Do the same thing for the proportion who received decreases in compensation.

(g) At the 0.05 level of significance, is the proportion of those receiving positive increases greater than the proportion of those receiving decreases?

(h) Do the necessary analysis to compare the mean salaries of the technology companies to those of the industrial companies.

(i) Write a memo summarizing your analysis. Include the answers to parts (a) – (h) as appendix items in your report.

CHAPTER **11**

REGRESSION ANALYSIS

IS TQM WORKING?

Business Dilemma...

A company that manufactures computer storage media has had a Total Quality Management (TQM) program in place for the past 2 years. The program incorporates Quality Circles, Statistical Quality Control, and Team-Based Decision Making in the production of removable storage media, i.e., floppy diskettes. Before the company decides to expand the program to other departments it would like to assess whether the program has been effective. According to the literature, when TQM programs are used they should result in increased productivity and quality, and decreased waste and delay.

The company asked the production team to assemble some data so that it can decide whether the program is successful. The team decided to collect data on five different variables, machine speed, waste, delay, rate of operation, and average outgoing quality for the 2-year period that the program has been in place. A sample of the data is shown here:

Month	Speed	Waste (%)	RateOper	Delay (h)	Quality
1	375	8.9	14.5	6.2642	95
2	334	9.9	12.8	6.4854	93
3	356	8.7	12.7	6.8372	94
4	378	9.5	13.9	5.7134	93
5	373	9.8	13.7	6.3136	94
6	381	8.8	14.7	6.2034	92

In particular, the company managers would like to know how production rate, waste, and delay are related to the speed at which a machine runs. They know that they have been able to run the production process at a faster speed in the past 2 years, but they are not sure that the increase in speed translates to an increase in productivity or a decrease in waste and delay.

11.1 CHAPTER OBJECTIVES

In Chapter 5 you learned a little bit about relationships between quantitative variables. In particular, you learned that there are different types of relationships between two variables and that when the relationship is linear you can use least squares to find the equation to describe the relationship.

For example, a company might want to predict sales of a particular product. The company knows that there are many different variables that might affect sales, but it does not know which variable(s) are most important or exactly how they relate to sales. The company needs to find a model that will enable it to predict sales as a function of the other variables. In *regression analysis,* this model is an *equation.*

In the first part of the chapter we look at *simple linear regression,* which predicts the value of Y as a linear function of a single independent variable, X. Once we have established the basics of regression analysis in the simple linear case we will look at *multiple regression models,* which predict the value of Y as a function of a set of independent variables.

In this chapter you will learn how to

- Find the linear regression equation for a dependent variable Y as a function of a single independent variable X
- Determine whether a relationship between X and Y exists
- Analyze the results of a regression analysis to determine whether the simple linear model is appropriate

11.2 THE SIMPLE LINEAR REGRESSION MODEL

11.2.1 Deterministic and Statistical Relationships

In some cases where two variables, x and y, are related, the relationship is *deterministic,* or *functional.* This means that when a value of x is selected, the value of y is uniquely determined. For example, if we were interested in the relationship between the total

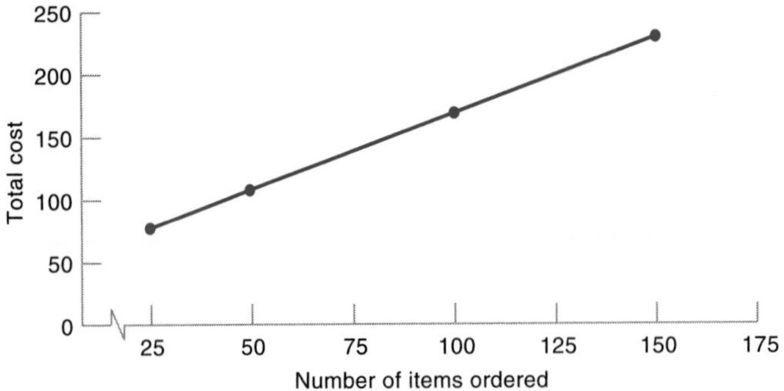

FIGURE 11.1 Deterministic relationship between total order cost and number of items ordered

cost of an order, y, and the number of items ordered, x, we can describe this relationship by an equation such as

$$y = \$50 + \$1.20x$$

where the value of \$50 might represent an ordering cost and the \$1.20 is the cost per item ordered. Figure 11.1 illustrates this type of relationship.

If a person were to order $x = 100$ items, then the corresponding cost would be $y = \$50 + (\$1.20)(100) = \$170$. Every person who orders 100 items will incur the cost of \$170. That is, the value of y is *unique,* for a given value of x.

Although many real problems are described by this type of relationship, we are interested in a different situation when we study *linear regression.* When we look at the relationship between two variables, X and Y, we are interested in situations where the value of Y varies for a given value of X. That is, we are interested in the *statistical relationship* between two variables.

Suppose that we are looking at the relationship between dollars spent in advertising and the revenues from sales. Clearly, we expect the two variables to be related, but we do not expect that every time a company spends \$$x$ in advertising it will always have \$$y$ in revenues. We know that there are other *factors,* or *variables,* such as the type of product, location, and various economic factors that will affect the value of Y for a given value of X.

When we collect our data we are collecting *pairs* of observations on the two variables, X and Y. Thus, we will have a set of n data pairs:

$$(x_1, y_1), (x_2, y_2), \ldots, (x_n, y_n)$$

A plot of the data might look like the one in Figure 11.2. You can see that the two variables are related, but that a particular value of advertising expenditures can

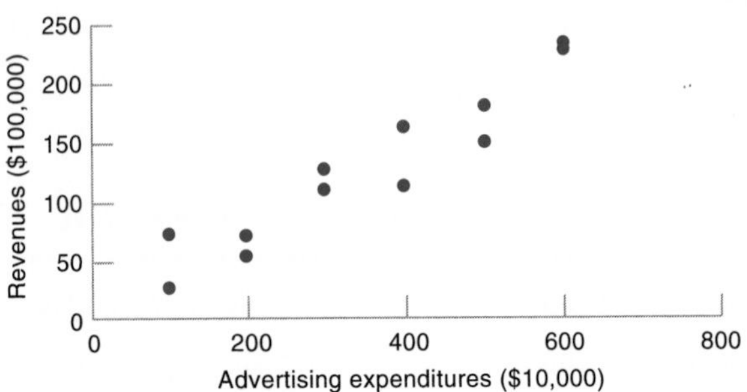

FIGURE 11.2 Statistical relationship between revenue and advertising expenditures

result in more than one value for revenue. This type of plot, a scatter plot, is of primary importance in exploring relationships between variables and should be done *before* any type of statistical analysis is performed.

EXAMPLE 11.1 Is TQM Working?

Plotting the Data to Look for a Linear Relationship

The company that is looking at its TQM program has decided that if the program is effective then the observed increase in machine speed should be accompanied by an increase in productivity and a decrease in waste and delay.

Understand the Problem

The company decides to look at productivity and machine speed to see whether there is any relationship between them that can be investigated further. The machine speed is measured in items per minute that the machine is set to produce. The measure chosen for productivity is rate of operation, which is a measure of the usable throughput of the machine per hour (in thousands of units).

Collect and Analyze the Data

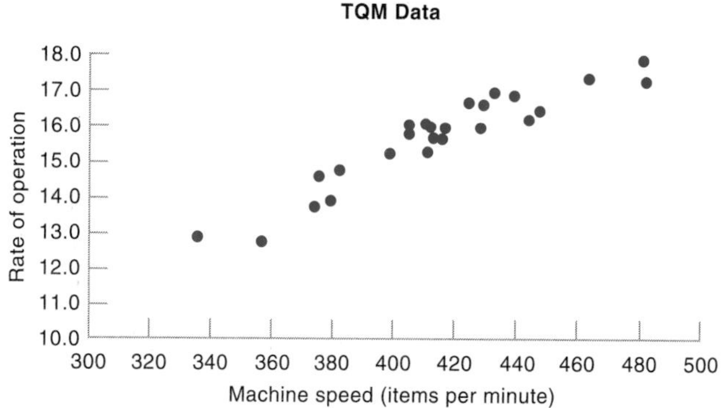

After looking at the plot it seems that a linear relationship is a reasonable model, and so the company decides to proceed with a simple linear regression analysis. ■

In the case of simple linear regression we would like to find an equation, or model, that will allow us to predict a value for a variable, Y. Ideally, since the value of Y depends on many different factors, we would like to find some variable X that does a good job of predicting Y with a linear equation. By a "good" job of predicting, we mean that the prediction we obtain is *useful* for purposes of planning or problem solving. In regression analysis, the X variable is assumed to be controlled or at least controllable. This means that its values can be fixed by the person collecting the data.

EXAMPLE 11.2 HMO Health

Looking at the Relationship Between Variables

Understand the Problem

As approaches to health-care coverage change, Health Maintenance Organizations (HMOs) are growing in popularity. Some business analysts wondered how the increase in popularity affected the financial health of the HMOs. They collected data on revenue and number of members for ten different HMOs:

Collect the Data

HMO	Members (million)	Revenue ($ billion)
United HealthCare	4.24	5.49
Humana	3.19	4.63
FHP International	1.83	3.86
PacifiCare Health Systems	1.62	3.60
U.S. Healthcare	2.07	3.43
WellPoint Health Network	2.30	2.91
Health Systems International	1.83	2.74
Foundation Health	2.15	2.40
Oxford Health Plans	0.97	1.71
Physician Corp. of America	0.89	1.20

SOURCE: *The Economist,* April 6, 1996

In this case the dependent variable is revenue, measured in billions of dollars and the independent variable is number of members, in millions. The analysts looked at a scatter plot of the data to see whether a relationship existed:

Analyze the Data

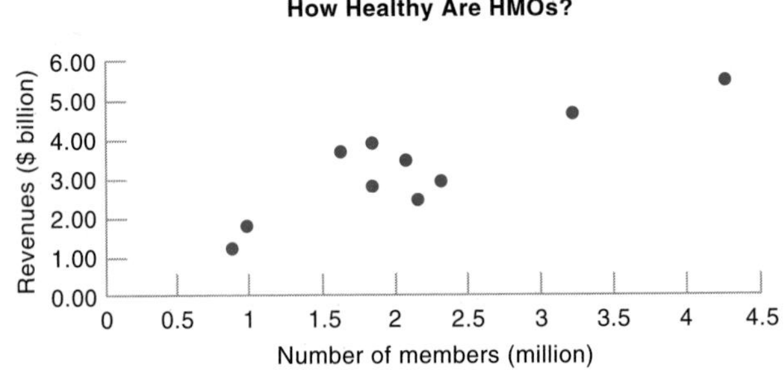

Draw Conclusions

From the plot it appeared that a linear relationship existed between revenue and number of members. This meant that a straight line should provide a good model for predicting revenue for an HMO as a function of the number of members of the HMO. ■

As you learn additional and more sophisticated statistical tools, you should not lose sight of the descriptive tools you learned first. Plotting data is essential to any statistical analysis and should be one of the first things you do so that you can determine what analysis, if any, is appropriate.

Increasing Capacity *Plotting Data to Look at the Relationship*

An oil company is trying to determine how the number of refining sites available for refining crude oil relates to the overall refining capacity. It would use this information to determine whether expansion will provide the increase in capacity that it wants or whether other steps to increase capacity will be necessary. The company collects data on other competitive companies and finds the following:

Oil Company	Number of Sites	Refining Capacity (million tons per year)
Royal Dutch/Shell	13	81.82
Exxon	10	81.82
Agip	13	58.18
BP	8	43.64

(continued)

Oil Company	Number of Sites	Refining Capacity (million tons per year)
Repsol	5	40.00
Total	7	36.36
Turkish Petroleum	4	34.55
Elf	8	32.73
Mobil	7	29.09
Petrofina	3	25.45

SOURCE: *The Economist,* July 15, 1995

Use the accompanying grid to create a scatter plot of the data.

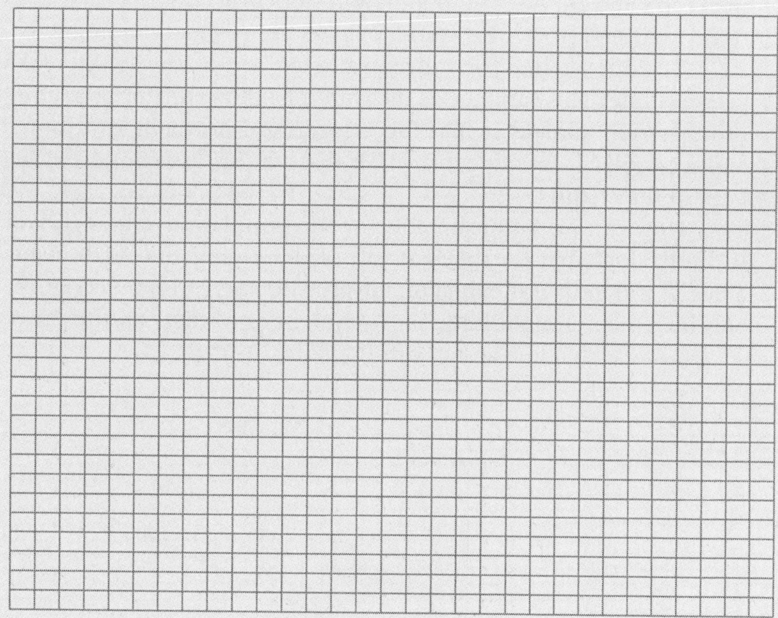

Do you think that a linear model is a good one?

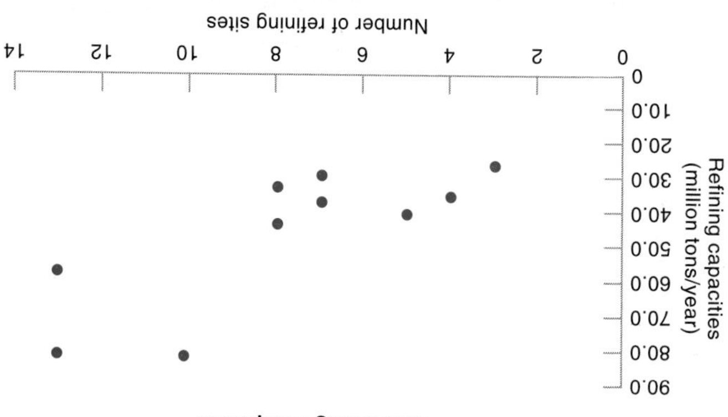

ANS. YES

11.2.2 The Simple Linear Regression Model

The objective of simple linear regression is to find a linear equation that describes the existing relationship between two variables, X and Y. The equation we find will be based on data taken from some population. Just as in any problems involving sampling from a population, we are trying to find an *estimate* for the true **regression model** between the two variables.

> The true relationship between the variables X and Y, the ***simple linear regression model,*** can be described by the equation
> $$y = \beta_0 + \beta_1 x + \varepsilon$$

*At this point we are assuming that a plot of the data has determined that a **linear model** is appropriate.*

This equation says that for a given value of the variable $X = x$, the actual value of Y will be determined by the expression $\beta_0 + \beta_1 x$, plus some random variation, ε, due to other, unmeasured, factors. Thus, if we knew the values of β_0, the true population intercept, and β_1, the true population slope, we could predict the value of Y to within some random error, ε. Figure 11.3 shows the population model for a linear regression.

You can see that for a given value of $X = x_1$, the values of Y vary around the regression line. This variation is measured by the error term, ε. One of the assumptions of regression analysis is that the ε terms are normally distributed with a mean of 0 and a standard deviation of σ. We discuss this assumption along with some others later in the chapter.

How can we find estimates for the population values β_0 and β_1? We would like to find values that do the best job of describing the relationship between the variables. If you look at the data on advertising and revenue in Figure 11.2, you can probably imagine a straight line that you might draw that captures the relationship. Figure 11.4 shows such a line along with the data.

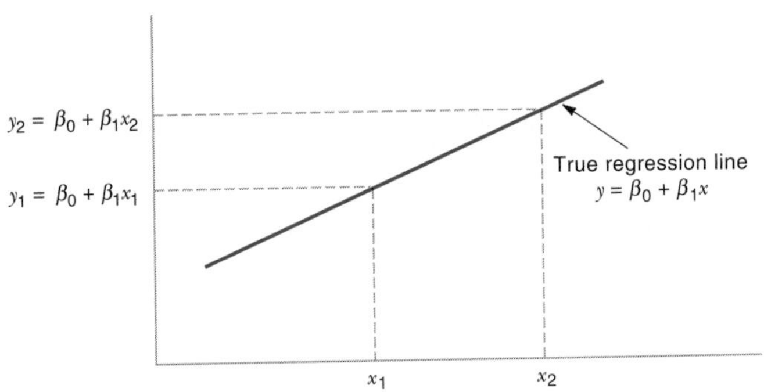

FIGURE 11.3 The true regression model showing how Y varies for a given value of X

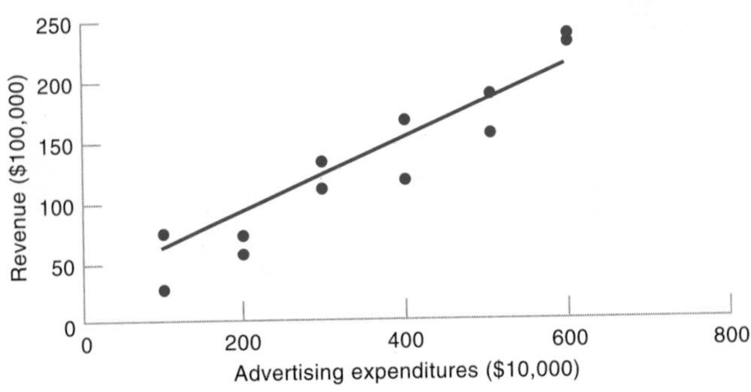

FIGURE 11.4 Straight line approximating the relationship between advertising and revenue

The equation of the line that we draw will be:

$$\hat{y} = b_0 + b_1 x$$

where $\hat{y}$ is the predicted value of Y for a particular value of $X = x$. The quantities b_0 and b_1 are the *estimates* of the population values β_0 and β_1. This line is called the *regression line of y on x* or the estimate of the *simple regression model.*

The problem is that there are many different lines that we might draw depending on what our criterion for "best" is. A list of possible criteria might be

- Hit as many points as possible.
- Have an equal number of points above and below the line.
- Pick two representative points and connect them.
- Connect the first and the last points.

The trouble with these criteria is that they do not produce a unique line. That is, there are many lines that hit 3 or 4 or 5 points and many lines that have an equal number of points above and below the line. (The last criterion actually produces a unique line, but it is not a very good criterion.) Figure 11.5 illustrates the problem. In Figure 11.5a both of the lines drawn have six points above and six points below. Figure 11.5b has several different lines, all of which go through exactly three of the data points.

You may wonder why it is important that we find a unique line to fit the data. Remember that we want to use the model (the equation) to predict values for Y, the dependent variable, for different possible values of X, the independent variable. One of the important features of a good model is that it be consistent. If the technique we use to find the line can produce many different models, then how will the user know which model or prediction to use? If everyone is allowed to choose the model he or she likes best, then the technique is, for all practical purposes, useless. You might as well just pick a number out of a hat.

11.2.3 The Least-Squares Line

At this point, we are sure about two things. We want the method we use for finding the equation of the line to produce one that is unique, and we want it to be a *good* representation of reality. Although there are certainly many ideas about what is good, we

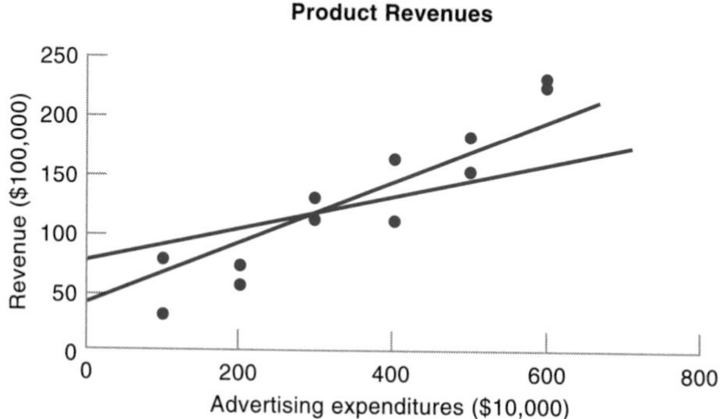

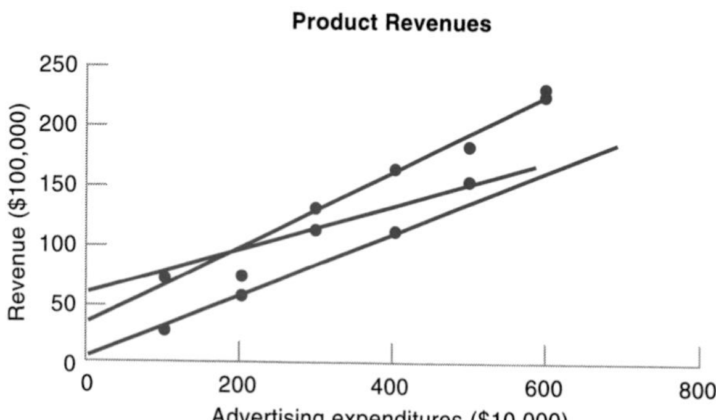

FIGURE 11.5 A single criterion can produce many different lines.

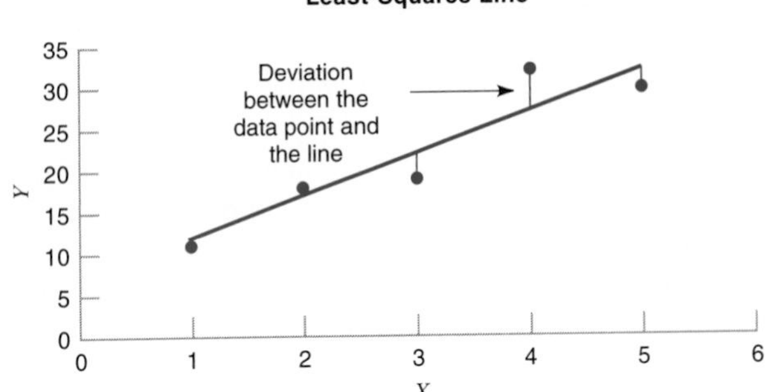

FIGURE 11.6 Deviations between the data points and the line

can agree that the line should be close to as many of the data points as is possible. Figure 11.6 shows a set of data and a line drawn to represent the relationship between the variables. Although the line does not actually go through any of the data points, it is very close to most of them. The distance from each data point to the line is shown. These distances are called the **deviations** or **errors** of the line. We would like to find a line that somehow minimizes the overall deviation of the data points from the line.

> The distance between the predicted value of Y, $\hat{y}$, and the actual value of Y, y, is called the ***deviation*** or ***error.***

When you learned about the variance in Chapter 4, you learned that when deviations are both positive and negative (in this case because the data points fall both above and below the line) you cannot simply look at the *sum* or *total* deviation, because it will be 0. For the variance, you solved the problem by squaring the deviations and then adding them together. We will use a similar approach to solving this problem.

The technique that we will use to find the line that best fits the data will be the **least-squares method.**

> The technique that finds the equation of the line that minimizes the total or sum of the squared deviations between the actual data points and the line is called the ***least-squares method.***

You may wonder why we always square negative quantities to make them positive instead of just taking the absolute value. One reason is that mathematically the square is a nicer quantity to work with than the absolute value. The other reason, in the case of fitting a line to a set of data, is that using the square of the error makes the line try to fit *all* of the points. This is because the penalty for avoiding certain points is much larger. Suppose that the actual distance from a data point to the line is -10 units. If we simply wanted to minimize the *absolute* deviation, then the penalty attached to missing that point is $|-10| = 10$. When we minimize the square of the distance, the penalty for missing that point becomes $(-10)^2 = 100$ and so the line tries to get closer to that point.

Note: *Sometimes, when a data point is a true outlier, this leads to problems with the model.*

The least-squares method finds the equation of the line

$$\hat{y} = b_0 + b_1 x$$

that minimizes

$$\sum_{i=1}^{n} (y_i - \hat{y}_i)^2$$

the total of squared deviations from the data points to the line. The values for $\boldsymbol{b_0}$ (the intercept of the line) and $\boldsymbol{b_1}$ (the slope of the line) are found by using the following equations:

$$b_1 = \frac{n\sum_{i=1}^{n} x_i y_i - \sum_{i=1}^{n} x_i \sum_{i=1}^{n} y_i}{n\sum_{i=1}^{n} x_i^2 - \left(\sum_{i=1}^{n} x_i\right)^2} \quad \text{or} \quad \frac{n\sum xy - \sum x \sum y}{n\sum x^2 - \left(\sum x\right)^2}$$

and

Formulas for the slope and intercept of a least-squares line

$$b_0 = \frac{\sum_{i=1}^{n} y_i}{n} - b_1\frac{\sum_{i=1}^{n} x_i}{n} \quad \text{or} \quad b_0 = \bar{y} - b_1\bar{x}$$

Although these equations may seem a bit complex, if you look at them carefully you will see that only five quantities have to be calculated. Four of the quantities involve the data values for X and Y, and the fifth is simply the number of observations in the sample, n. For example, look at the quantity Σxy. This is simply the sum of the products of the x and y values for each data point. The easiest way to look at what is involved in the calculations is to make a table with a column for each sum needed. The table will look like the one in Table 11.1.

TABLE 11.1 Table for Calculating the Least-Squares Line

Observation Number	x	y	xy	x^2
1	x_1	y_1	$x_1 y_1$	$x_1 x_1$
2	x_2	y_2	$x_2 y_2$	$x_2 x_2$
.	.	.	.	.
.	.	.	.	.
.	.	.	.	.
n	x_n	y_n	$x_n y_n$	$x_n x_n$
Totals	Σx	Σy	Σxy	Σx^2

EXAMPLE 11.3 Is TQM Working?

Finding the Least-Squares Line

Do not round until you have done the calculations.

The manufacturing company that is trying to assess the effectiveness of its TQM program is looking at the relationship between productivity as measured by rate of operation (Y) and machine speed (X). It has plotted the data and thinks that the plot indicates that the linear model is a good one. To find the equation of the least-squares line, the managers of the company have assembled the following information:

Analyze the Data

$$\Sigma x = 10{,}340 \qquad \Sigma y = 391.4 \qquad \Sigma xy = 162{,}951.9 \qquad \Sigma x^2 = 4{,}306{,}918 \qquad n = 25$$

They first calculate b_1, the estimate of the slope:

Although we would never use the estimate of b_1 to this many decimal places in the final equation, again, you should not round until after you use the value in the equation for b_0. In the final equation, the values for b_0 and b_1 should be rounded to reflect the precision of the original data.

$$b_1 = \frac{(25)(162{,}951.9) - (10{,}340)(391.4)}{(25)(4{,}306{,}918) - (10{,}340)^2} = \frac{26{,}721.5}{757{,}350} = 0.035282894$$

and then use that estimate to find b_0, the estimate of the y intercept of the line:

$$b_0 = \frac{391.4}{25} - (0.035282894)\left(\frac{10{,}340}{25}\right) = 1.062995$$

The equation of the regression line relating rate of operation to machine speed is

$$\hat{y} = 1.06 + 0.035x$$

Draw Conclusions

This means that there is a positive relationship between machine speed and productivity; that is, as machine speed increases, so does productivity. In fact, the equation tells the managers that for every unit increase in machine speed, the productivity goes up by 0.035. This is the definition of the slope of a line.

Although the positive relationship is encouraging, the people looking at the equation wonder whether it really means anything. That is, they wonder whether the increase in productivity realized by increasing speed is *significant.* The equation of the line alone cannot tell them that. They need to do further analysis. ■

The equation of the least-squares regression line does give some information about the relationship between the independent variable Y and the dependent variable, X. The *sign* of the slope estimate tells whether the relationship is positive or negative. The *value* of the slope gives the change that will occur in Y when X is changed by one unit.

It is more difficult to explain the interpretation of the intercept. By definition, the intercept of a line is the value of Y when $X = 0$. In some situations, this number can be thought of as the value of the dependent variable that is related to *other factors* that are not considered in this model. For example, when we look at the relationship between sales and advertising, it is possible that for \$0 spent on advertising, there will still be sales of a product.

In many cases, however, it does not make sense for the value of Y to be nonzero when $X = 0$. In the TQM example, if the machine speed is 0 there *is no productivity,* that is, Y must be 0. We discuss this problem in more detail as we proceed.

EXAMPLE 11.4 HMO Health

Calculating the Least-Squares Line

After they plotted the data and looked at the graph, the analysts who were interested in the relationship between HMO revenues (Y), and number of members (X), decided to use least squares to find the equation of the regression line relating the two variables. They assembled the data shown in the next table.

Although finding the equation of the regression line by hand is not difficult, it is tedious, even for small data sets. Many calculators have the capability to find the equation of the least-squares line. If you have such a calculator you might want to learn how to use it now.

Analyze the Data

Observation Number	Members, X (million)	Revenue, Y (\$ billion)	XY	X^2
1	4.24	5.49	23.2776	17.9776
2	3.19	4.63	14.7697	10.1761
3	1.83	3.86	7.0638	3.3489
4	1.62	3.60	5.8320	2.6244
5	2.07	3.43	7.1001	4.2849
6	2.3	2.91	6.6930	5.29
7	1.83	2.74	5.0142	3.3489
8	2.15	2.40	5.1600	4.6225
9	0.97	1.71	1.6587	0.9409
10	0.89	1.20	1.0680	0.7921
Total	21.09	31.97	77.6371	53.4063

Substituting into the equations they found

$$b_1 = \frac{(10)(77.6371) - (21.09)(31.97)}{(10)(53.4063) - (21.09)^2} = \frac{102.1237}{89.2749} = 1.143924$$

$$b_0 = \frac{31.97}{10} - (1.143924)\left(\frac{21.09}{10}\right) = 0.7844643$$

Thus, the regression equation of HMO revenues on number of members is

$$\hat{y} = 0.78 + 1.14x$$

Draw Conclusions

They realize that the equation means that for an increase in members of 1 million, the revenues will increase by \$1.14 billion. The intercept of the line is 0.78, which would mean that when an HMO has no members, it will still generate \$0.78 billion in revenues. This is a case where interpretation of the intercept does not make sense. ■

Because least-squares analysis is mechanical, the equation alone cannot tell us whether the relationship is real or whether, in fact, the two variables are unrelated. You can find a least-squares line relating any two variables, but that certainly does not mean that the two variables are really related. To make that decision, further statistical tools are needed.

Most spreadsheet programs and all statistical software also perform regression analysis. It is not necessary to use the computer just to find the equation of the regression line, but further analysis can really only be done using a computer package. Although it is not necessary now, the remainder of this chapter assumes that you have access to some statistical software package. At the end of this section we look at regression output from different software packages. As the chapter progresses we will use the output extensively to make decisions about the problems we are trying to solve.

Try It Now!

Increasing Capacity *Finding the Equation of the Least-Squares Regression Line*

The oil company that is looking at increasing refining capacity has decided that a linear relationship is appropriate.

Fill in the table or use some other means to find the equation of the least-squares line:

Observation Number	Number of Sites, X	Capacity, Y	XY	X^2
1	13	81.82		
2	10	81.82		
3	13	58.18		
4	8	43.64		
5	5	40.00		
6	7	36.36		
7	4	34.55		
8	8	32.73		
9	7	29.09		
10	3	25.45		
Total				

Interpret the meaning of the estimate of the slope of the line. Does the y intercept make sense for these data?

ANS. $\hat{y} = 9.03 + 4.79x$ CAPACITY WILL INCREASE BY 4.79 M TONS FOR EVERY NEW SITE ADDED. NO.

When using a regression model we must remember that the model is constructed only from sample data. It is really relevant only *over the range of observed values.* The equation tells you about the relationship between the dependent and independent variables, only in this range. There are two kinds of predictions that you can make, **interpolation** and **extrapolation.**

> Using the equation to predict values of Y within the range of the X data is called ***interpolation.*** Predicting values of Y for values of X outside the observed range is called ***extrapolation.***

Extrapolation is risky and really should almost never be done. Without data you have no idea what the relationship beyond your "boundaries" is like. Over a larger range of the dependent variable, the relationship might change shape and be nonlinear. It might even change direction, making your predictions totally inappropriate.

Increasing Capacity ***Using the Regression Equation to Predict the Value of Y***

Use the equation of the regression line you found previously to predict the refining capacity for each of the observed values of X, the number of sites. Put the calculated values into the table below.

Observation Number	Number of Sites, X	Capacity, Y	$\hat{y} = 9.03 + 4.79x$
1	13	81.82	
2	10	81.82	
3	13	58.18	
4	8	43.64	
5	5	40.00	
6	7	36.36	
7	4	34.55	
8	8	32.73	
9	7	29.09	
10	3	25.45	

11.2.6 Calculating Residuals

We used least squares to find the line for regression analysis, because we wanted the line we obtained to be close to the actual data points. How can we assess how well the regression line accomplishes this?

If we plot the regression line on the same plot with the data we can get a *visual* or *graphical* idea of the connection between the model and the data. The proximity of the data points to the line will give an overall picture of how well the regression line describes the relationship between the variables.

EXAMPLE 11.7 **Is TQM Working?**

Plotting the Regression Line and Calculating Residuals

The company assessing its TQM decided to plot its data and the regression equation together to try to get a visual idea of what the least-squares line did.

ANS. 71.3, 56.9, 71.3, 47.4, 33.0, 42.6, 28.2, 47.4, 42.6, 23.4

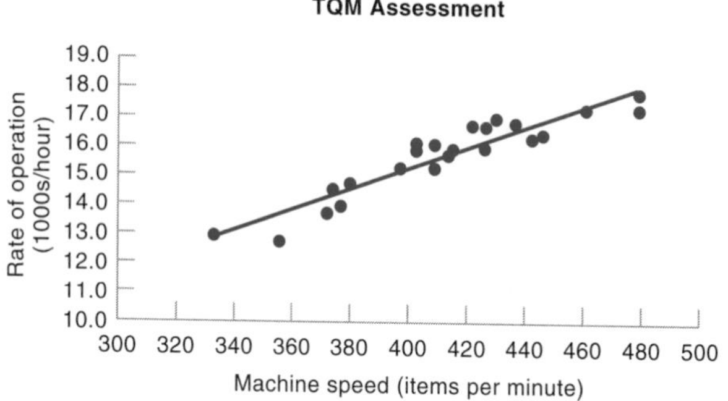

Draw Conclusions

The graph shows that most of the data points are very close to the line. The company felt that the line it obtained did a pretty good job of describing the relationship between machine speed and productivity. ■

EXAMPLE 11.8 HMO Health

Plotting the Regression Line

The analysts who are looking at the relationship between revenues and number of members of HMOs created a plot of the data and the regression equation that they calculated.

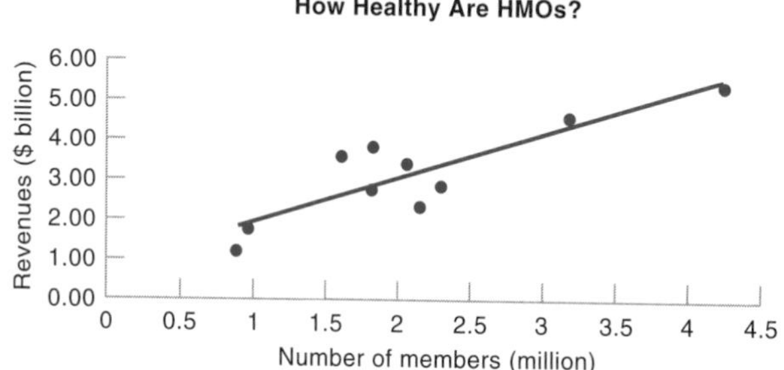

Draw Conclusions

They see that some of the points are very close to the line, but others are farther away. Still, it looks like the line does a pretty good job of describing the relationship between revenues and number of members. The analysts wonder whether they can get a numerical measure of the differences between the predicted values and the actual data. ■

A *numerical* measure of the agreement between the line and the data is obtained by looking at the differences between the observed and expected values of Y for each value of X. In regression analysis, these differences are known as the **residuals.**

> The difference between the observed value of Y (y_i), and the predicted value of Y from the regression equation ($\hat{y}_i$), for a value of $X = x_i$ is called the ith ***residual,*** e_i.

The *sign* of the residual, positive or negative, tells whether the prediction was lower or higher than the actual data value. The *size* of the residual gives an idea of how much the actual data vary around the line.

EXAMPLE 11.9 Is TQM Working?

Calculating Residuals

Analyze the Data

To obtain a better idea of how well the regression line agreed with their data, the workers decided to calculate the residuals for two predicted values close to the ones that they were interested in. They looked at their data and found that they had data for machine speeds of 373 and 447 items per minute, which were close to the 375 and 450 speeds. They used the regression equation to find the predicted values for $X = 373$:

$$\hat{y} = 1.06 + 0.035(373) = 14.1$$

and for $X = 447$:

$$\hat{y} = 1.06 + 0.035(447) = 16.7$$

and calculated the residuals, $y - \hat{y}$, for $X = 373$:

$$y - \hat{y} = 13.7 - 14.1 = -0.4$$

and for $X = 447$:

$$y - \hat{y} = 16.4 - 16.7 = -0.3$$

In each case, the difference between the observed data and the line was negative. The magnitude of the deviation was about 0.3 or 0.4, which is about 300 or 400 items per hour. ■

The residuals play a very important role in regression analysis. As you just saw, they give a numerical value to the differences between the model and the actual data for each of the data points in the sample. We have already discussed that, for a statistical relationship, the actual values of Y will vary for a fixed value of X. The residuals also provide a means to measure the overall variation in Y for any value of X. In addition, as we will see later on in this chapter, the residuals are used to determine the appropriateness of a linear model.

EXAMPLE 11.10 HMO Health

Calculating Residuals

For the HMO problem, the analysts wanted to use the model to predict revenues for different size HMOs. They were interested in predicting Y for $X = 1.0$ (1 million members) and 2.0 (2 million members). To have a way to compare the predicted values to the actual data, they chose the data points with $X = 0.97$ and 2.07, since these points were closest to the values of interest. The analysts calculated the predicted values using the equation $\hat{y} = 0.78 + 1.14x$ for each value and then calculated the residuals. The results were

Analyze the Data

Observation Number	x_i	y_i	$\hat{y}_i = 0.78 + 1.14x_i$	$e_i = y_i - \hat{y}_i$
9	0.97	1.71	$\hat{y}_9 = 0.78 + 1.14(0.97) = 1.89$	$e_9 = 1.71 - 1.89 = -0.18$
5	2.07	3.43	$\hat{y}_5 = 0.78 + 1.14(2.07) = 3.14$	$e_5 = 3.43 - 3.14 = 0.29$

The differences between the predicted revenues and the actual revenues were $180 million and $290 million or about 10%. ■

Although residuals are important, they cannot tell you everything about how good the model will be for predicting values of Y. Just because the residual for a certain data point is large, it does not mean that the regression equation does a poor job of predicting Y for values of X near that point. It may be that the data point used for the residual is unusually far from the regression line and that the prediction is actually more representative of the population. For this reason it helps to look at the residuals in context. Graphing the regression line with the data points provides additional insight about individual residuals.

EXAMPLE 11.11 HMO Health

Looking at the Residuals Graphically

When the HMO analysts looked at the plot of the data and the regression line, they saw that the data points that they used to calculate the residuals were actually very close to the regression line.

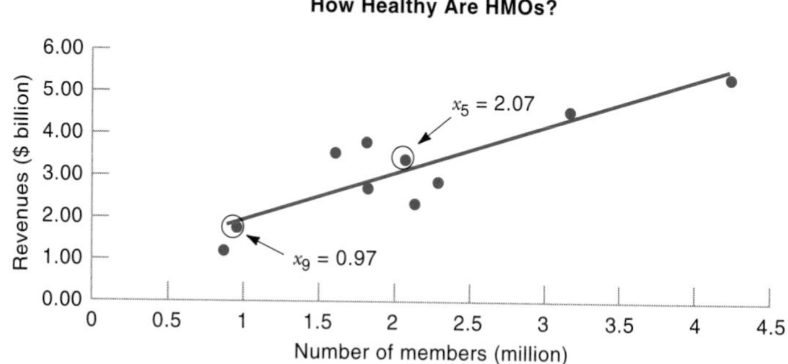

They felt that the errors for the number of members that they were interested in were not unusually large. ■

TRY IT NOW!

Increasing Capacity ***Calculating the Residuals***

The oil company that is looking at the relationship between refining capacity and the number of refining sites wants to get a better idea of how the regression line relates to the actual data. It decides to calculate the residuals for each observed value of *X*, the number of sites. Find the residuals and fill in the table:

Observation Number	Number of Sites, *X*	Refining Capacity *Y*	$\hat{y} = 9.03 + 4.79x$	$e_i = y_i - \hat{y}_i$
1	13	81.82	71.3	
2	10	81.82	56.9	
3	13	58.18	71.3	
4	8	43.64	47.4	
5	5	40.00	33.0	
6	7	36.36	42.6	
7	4	34.55	28.2	
8	8	32.73	47.4	
9	7	29.09	42.6	
10	3	25.45	23.4	

SOURCE: *The Economist*, July 15, 1995

To get a picture of how the residuals and the regression line fit together, the company also decides to graph the regression line on a plot of the data. Graph the regression line on the data plot. How well do you think the line represents the data?

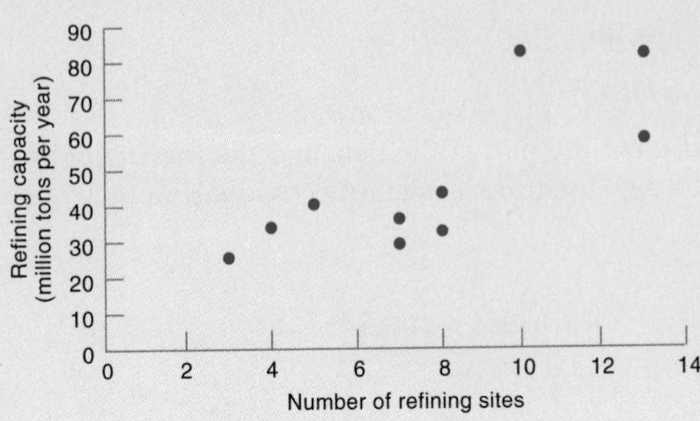

11.2.7 The Standard Error of the Estimate

Since each residual corresponds to a single data point we know that we cannot use any single residual to determine how much the data differ from the model. Still, we would like some way to measure how much the data points vary around the regression line. This measure is known as the **standard error of the estimate, $s_{y|x}$**.

> ***The standard error of the estimate,*** $s_{y|x}$ is a measure of how much the data vary around the regression line.

The quantity that we are trying to measure is the *overall* or *average* variation of the data around the line. Remember that the residuals measure the *individual* variation of each data point from the line. We can obtain an overall measure of this variability by using something similar to the formula we used to measure the variability of the data from its mean in Chapter 4. In fact,

$$s_{y|x} = \sqrt{\frac{\Sigma(y - \hat{y})^2}{n - 2}} = \sqrt{\frac{\Sigma e^2}{n - 2}}$$

There are several different computational formulas for finding the standard error of the estimates. The one we have shown makes it easiest to understand what the

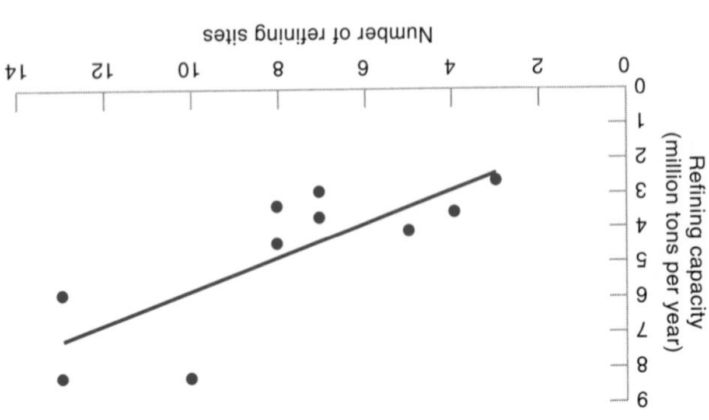

ANS. THE LINE DOES A PRETTY GOOD JOB EXCEPT FOR A FEW POINTS.

quantity really measures. It is most convenient if you have already calculated the residuals. We will not look at any other formulas, because, as we already said, beyond finding the least-squares equation, regression analysis should be done using a computer.

EXAMPLE 11.12 HMO Health

Calculating the Standard Error of the Estimate

Since they knew that any single residual might be unusually large or small, the analysts decided to calculate the standard error of the estimate for the regression line. They calculated the residuals and squared residuals for each data point as

Analyze the Data

Observation Number	Members, X	Revenue, Y	$\hat{y}$	$e = y - \hat{y}$	e^2
1	4.24	5.49	5.61	−0.12	0.01
2	3.19	4.63	4.42	0.21	0.04
3	1.83	3.86	2.87	0.99	0.98
4	1.62	3.60	2.63	0.97	0.94
5	2.07	3.43	3.14	0.29	0.08
6	2.30	2.91	3.40	−0.49	0.24
7	1.83	2.74	2.87	−0.13	0.02
8	2.15	2.40	3.23	−0.83	0.69
9	0.97	1.71	1.89	−0.18	0.03
10	0.89	1.20	1.79	−0.59	0.35
Total					**3.38**

Then, the standard error of the estimate is

$$s_{y|x} = \sqrt{\frac{3.38}{8}} = \sqrt{0.423} = 0.65$$

This means that the typical deviation or distance of each data point from the line is 0.65 or \$650 million. ■

The standard error of the estimate is analogous to the standard deviation of data from the mean and to the standard error of the mean, which we have studied before. From our knowledge of what these quantities measure, and the empirical rule, we can get an intuitive sense of what the quantity $s_{y|x}$ means. We can get a *mental image* of how the data are spread out around the line. Later on in the chapter we develop some more formal ways to use the standard error of the estimate to look at predictions.

In Section 11.2.4 we looked at the computer output for the HMO problem for several different software packages. Figure 11.8 shows the portion of the output from

SUMMARY OUTPUT

Regression Statistics	
Multiple R	0.879773847
R Square	0.774002022
Adjusted R Square	0.745752275
Standard Error	0.65297731
Observations	10

Excel

```
The regression equation is
Rev $bn = 0.784 + 1.14 Members (m)

Predictor      Coef    StDev      T       P
Constant     0.7845   0.5050   1.55   0.159
Members      1.1439   0.2185   5.23   0.000

S = 0.6530    R-Sq = 77.4%    R-Sq(adj) = 74.6%
```

Minitab

FIGURE 11.8 Computer output showing the standard error of the estimate

(a) Create a scatter plot of the data. Does it appear that advertising revenues are related to the percentage of households that have cable or satellite TV?

(b) Find the equation of the regression line for the data.

(c) Plot the regression line on the same plot as the data. Do you think that the line does a good job of predicting TV advertising revenues? Why or why not?

(d) From the plot, which country do you think will have the largest residual? Which will have the smallest?

(e) In the Ukraine, 8% of the households have cable or satellite television. Use the line to predict TV advertising revenues for the Ukraine.

(f) Find the residuals for each country. Do the values support your answer to part (d)?

(g) Calculate the standard error of the estimate for the regression line.

11.5 As part of the anticrime bill passed in 1995, the U.S. government granted money to different cities to hire new beat-patrol officers. Nine cities in New Jersey were given grants and hired officers. In trying to assess the program, government analysts wanted to look at the relationship between the number of officers hired and the amount of the grant. The data are

Grant ($)	Number of Officers
150,000	2
375,000	5
471,125	6
70,967	1
450,000	6
525,000	7
375,370	7
750,000	10
1,000,000	12

SOURCE: *Justice Department*

(a) Create a scatter plot of the data.

(b) Find the equation of the linear regression line.

(c) Plot the regression line on the same plot as the data.

(d) How well do you think the line fits the data?

(e) Use the regression equation to predict the number of officers hired for each city.

(f) Calculate the residuals and the standard error of the estimate.

11.6 For many countries, tourism is an important part of revenues. In trying to predict tourism revenues, one of the independent variables that is considered important is the number of foreign visitors to the country. Data for six different countries were collected:

Country	Number of Visitors (million)	Tourism Receipts ($ billion)
France	60	27.3
Spain	48	25.1
United States	45	58.4
Italy	30	27.1
Britain	23	17.5
Germany	15	11.9

SOURCE: *The Economist*, July 1996

(a) Create a scatter plot of the data and find the equation of the linear regression line.

(b) Use the regression line to predict tourism revenues for Italy and the United States.

(c) For which country does the regression line do a better job of predicting tourism receipts?

(d) Calculate the residuals and the standard error of the estimate.

11.7 As communications and the media change and become more important in the economy, the radio industry has become an area of concern. One of the major communications companies wanted to look at the relationship between the number of radio stations a company owned and the revenues generated by radio. It collected the following data:

Company	Number of Stations	Revenues ($ billion)
Westinghouse/Infinity	83	1.05
Jacor	57	0.31
Clear Channel	104	0.31
Evergreen	35	0.30
Disney/ABC	21	0.29
American Radio Systems	63	0.23
SFX	67	0.22
Chancellor	41	0.21
Cox	38	0.21
Bonneville	20	0.12

SOURCE: *The Economist*, June 29, 1996, *Duncan's American Radio*

(a) Create a scatter plot of the data. Do you think that there is a relationship between the number of stations that a company owns and the revenues generated by radio?

(b) Find the linear regression line for the data.

(c) Use the regression line to predict the radio revenues for Chancellor and Westinghouse/Infinity. Which prediction is better?

(d) Leave out the data point for Westinghouse/Infinity and recalculate the regression line. Do you think that this line will do a better job of predicting radio revenues? Why or why not?

11.3 INFERENCES ABOUT THE LINEAR REGRESSION MODEL

The tools you have learned for finding the simple linear regression equation are descriptive. The method of least squares allows you to find the equation of the line that best describes the sample data. Looking at the residuals allows you to get some idea about how well the line fits the data. Residuals are useful to some degree but, as in most cases, we would really like to be able to make *inferences* about the population based on our sample data.

In particular, we would like to know

- whether the relationship described by the regression equation is *meaningful.*
- how well the equation enables us to predict values of the dependent variable.
- how useful the predictions are for decision making.

To accomplish these tasks we need to learn some inferential methods related to regression analysis.

11.3.1 Hypothesis Testing About the Slope, β_1

Saying that there is a linear relationship between X and Y means that as X changes, Y changes in some predictable, corresponding way. The parameter that describes the magnitude of the relationship is the slope of the line. Remember that the definition of slope is the change in Y for a unit change in X. Thus, if the variables X and Y are related, the slope of the line will be some number. If there is no relationship between X and Y, then the slope of the line is zero. That is, we say that as X changes, Y *does not*

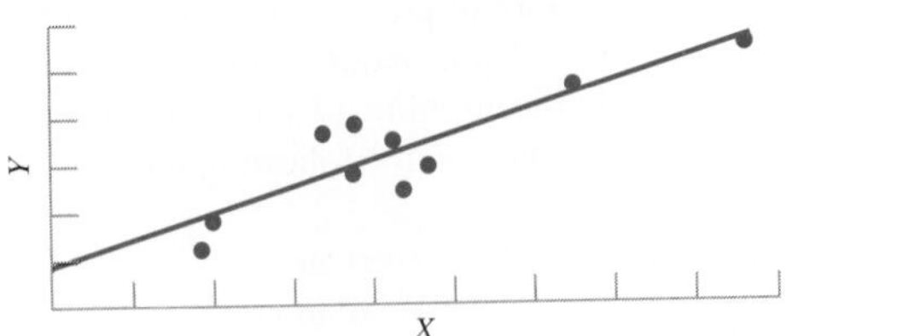

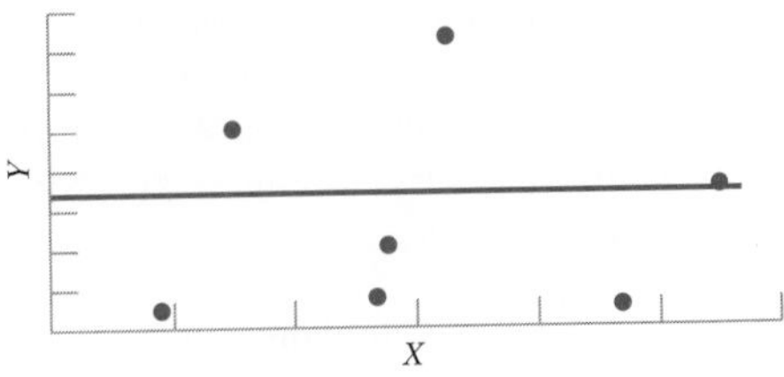

FIGURE 11.9 (a) Line with nonzero slope; (b) line with zero slope

change in a related way (Figure 11.9). Thus, one of the ways that we can determine whether the relationship between the two variables is real is to decide whether the slope of the regression line is equal to zero.

Although looking at data gives you an idea about what might be true in the population, you know quite well by now that you cannot simply look at the numbers to make these decisions. If the data consist of small numbers, the slope and intercept values, b_1 and b_0, will naturally be small. In the same way, if the data are large numbers, the corresponding slope and intercepts might or might not be large. You must consider the *standard error* of the statistic in question to make decisions involving the values. We will use hypothesis testing to decide whether the slope of the regression line is *significantly different from zero.*

You know that if you took a different sample your calculated regression line would not have exactly the same slope and intercept values. Thus, these estimates are sample statistics and have sampling distributions.

The first step in testing a hypothesis is to set up the appropriate hypotheses. In this case we want to test

$$H_0:\ \beta_1 = 0$$
$$H_A:\ \beta_1 \neq 0$$

If the test results in rejecting the null hypothesis, then we will conclude that the slope of the regression line is not equal to zero, and that the relationship between the X and Y variables is real.

Our estimate of β_1 is b_1, and to proceed with the steps of the hypothesis test we need to know about the sampling distribution of b_1. It turns out that the sampling distribution associated with the least-squares estimate of the slope is the Student t distribution. The test statistic for our hypothesis test is therefore

Formula for t statistic

$$t = \frac{b_1 - \beta_1}{s_{b_1}}$$

which has a t distribution with $n - 2$ degrees of freedom. In the formula, s_{b_1} is the **standard error of the slope** b_1 and is calculated by

Formula for standard error of b_1

$$s_{b_1} = \frac{s_{y|x}}{\sqrt{\Sigma x^2 - (\Sigma x)^2/n}}$$

This does not mean that the values cannot be calculated by hand. Once you find the regression coefficients and the standard error you have all of the pieces you need to find the test statistic.

Although the equation may look complicated we have said that for any purposes other than finding the regression line, we will be using statistical software to find the values we need. Since the test is a two-sided test, once the significance level of the test, α, is chosen, the critical values of the test are $\pm t_{\alpha/2,n-2}$. We now have the test set up. All that remains is to perform the test and make a decision.

EXAMPLE 11.13 Is TQM Working?

Hypothesis Test About the Slope Coefficient

The company looking at its TQM program has determined that the equation of the regression line relating productivity to machine speed is

$$\hat{y} = 1.06 + 0.035x$$

When the regression line and the data are graphed, it appears that the regression line does a good job of representing the data. Still, the company looks at the value of the slope, 0.035, and wonders if it really means anything. The company decides to perform a hypothesis test at the 0.05 level of significance, to see whether the relationship is real.

Analyze the Data

The hypotheses are

$$H_0: \beta_1 = 0$$
$$H_A: \beta_1 \neq 0$$

Since the value of α is 0.05 and there are 25 data points, the critical values of the test are $\pm t_{0.025,23}$ or ± 2.069.

From previous analyses the company knows that $\Sigma x = 10{,}340$, $\Sigma x^2 = 4{,}306{,}918$, and $s_{y|x} = 0.4544$. The value of the test statistic is

$$t = \frac{0.035 - 0}{\dfrac{(0.4544)}{\sqrt{4{,}306{,}918 - (10{,}340)^2/25}}} = \frac{0.035}{0.00261} = 13.51$$

Remember that the hypothesized value for β_1 is zero.

Comparing the value of the test statistic to the critical values, the company sees that 13.51 is definitely beyond the critical values and so it will reject H_0 and conclude that the slope of the regression line is not equal to zero. That is, there is a significant linear relationship between productivity and machine speed. ■

When we first talked about computer output, we said that there are usually three sections in the output. We are interested in the section with information about the regression coefficients. Figure 11.10 shows the relevant sections of the computer output for two different statistical packages.

In the output you are given all of the information needed to perform the hypothesis test about the slope coefficient. You can either look up the critical value for the level of significance that you have chosen and compare it to the t statistic, or use the p value of the test, which is also included in the output. In all cases, the p value of the test is 0.000. Since this is less than our chosen α, we reject H_0.

Predictor	Coef	StDev	T	P
Constant	1.063	1.084	0.98	0.337
Speed	0.035283	0.002611	13.51	0.000

Minitab

	Coefficients	Standard Error	t Stat	P-value
Intercept	1.062994916	1.083622206	0.980964501	0.336817039
Speed	0.035282894	0.002610746	13.51448824	1.9909E-12

Excel

FIGURE 11.10 t-test portion of computer output

EXAMPLE 11.14 HMO Health

Hypothesis Test About the Slope of the Regression Line

The analysts who were looking at the relationship between HMO revenues and number of members used statistical software to perform the regression analysis and to determine whether the relationship is significant. They want to test, at the 0.05 level of significance, the hypotheses

$$H_0: \beta_1 = 0$$
$$H_A: \beta_1 \neq 0$$

Analyze the Data

At the 0.05 level of significance with 10 − 2 = 8 degrees of freedom, the critical values for the test are ±2.306.

They obtained the following output:

```
Regression Analysis

The regression equation is
Rev $bn = 0.784 + 1.14 Members (m)

Predictor        Coef      St Dev        T        P
Constant       0.7845      0.5050     1.55    0.159
Members        1.1439      0.2185     5.23    0.000
```

From the output line that corresponds to the slope estimate, they see that the coefficient is 1.1439 and the standard error of the slope is 0.2185. The corresponding t statistic is 5.23. Since the critical value for the test is 2.306, they reject H_0 and conclude that the slope of the regression line is not zero. That is, there is a significant linear relationship between revenues and number of members.

They can also use the p value of the test to make the decision. From the output, the p value of the test is 0.000. Since that is less than the specified α of 0.05, they know that they should reject H_0. ■

You might have noticed that in the computer output there is corresponding information about b_0, the intercept of the regression line. It is tempting to want to test hypotheses about β_0, the intercept, in particular whether it is equal to zero. *Do not do this.* Remember that the regression line is valid only in the range of X that has been observed in the data. If you do not have X data for $X = 0$, then you cannot make a determination about whether the intercept should remain in the equation. Removing the intercept from the equation when the slope is not equal to zero means that the regression line will move downward, parallel to itself, and will no longer be the line of best fit for the data.

Increasing Capacity *Testing for Significance of the Regression Model*

The oil company that is looking at increasing capacity wants to determine whether the relationship between refining capacity and number of refining sites that it calculated is significant.

Write down the hypotheses that the company must test.

The company decides to use a 0.01 level of significance for the test. Find the critical values for the test.

Remember that you need to find the degrees of freedom, in this case n − 2.

It used a computer software package to run the analysis and obtained the following output:

	Coefficients	*Standard Error*	*tStat*	*P-value*	*Lower 95%*	*Upper 95%*
Intercept	9.028295455	11.04587353	0.817345539	0.437393793	−16.44355105	34.50014196
Number of sites	4.786628788	1.307226853	3.661666509	0.006385827	1.77215631	7.801101266

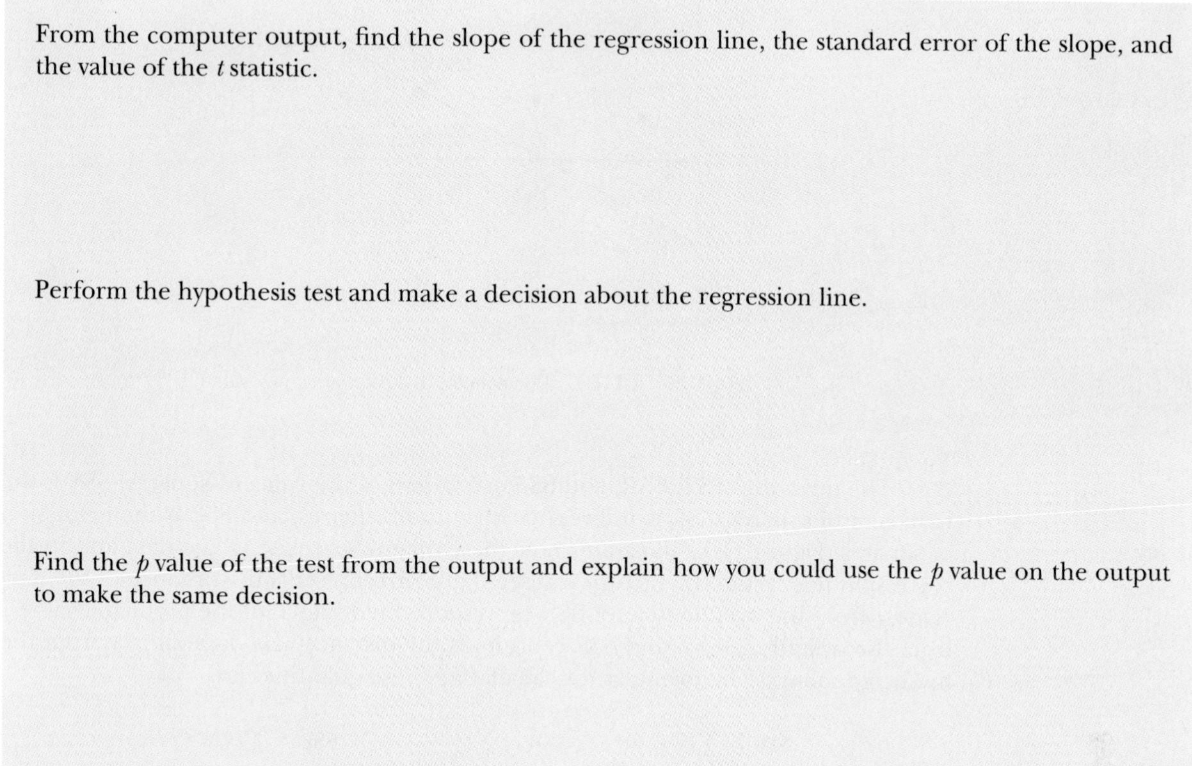

From the computer output, find the slope of the regression line, the standard error of the slope, and the value of the t statistic.

Perform the hypothesis test and make a decision about the regression line.

Find the p value of the test from the output and explain how you could use the p value on the output to make the same decision.

Once we have determined that the relationship between X and Y is significant, we can perform some additional analyses to see whether the predictions we obtain are useful for the purposes of decision making and to determine the strength of the relationship.

11.3.2 Partitioning the Variance in Linear Regression

In statistics, we are always interested in looking at the *variation* in data. In Chapter 4 you learned about the standard deviation and how that can be used to measure the variation of data around its mean value. When we are looking at the relationship between two variables, Y (the dependent variable) and X (the independent variable), we are interested in how Y *varies*, considering the values of the variable, X.

When two variables, X and Y, are linearly related, the variation of the y values from the overall mean of Y can be attributed to two different factors: its relationship with X and pure chance. In fact, the variation in the y values from the overall mean of Y can be partitioned, or divided, into parts called **sums of squares:**

SST: the total variation in the y values around the mean $\bar{y}$
SSR: the variation in Y that is caused by Y's relationship with X
SSE: the variation in Y that remains unexplained

ANS. H_0: $\beta_1 = 0$, H_A: $\beta_1 \neq 0$; ± 3.355; 4.79, 1.81, 3.66; REJECT H_0. THE REGRESSION IS SIGNIFICANT. SINCE $0.01 > 0.0064$, WE CAN REJECT H_0.

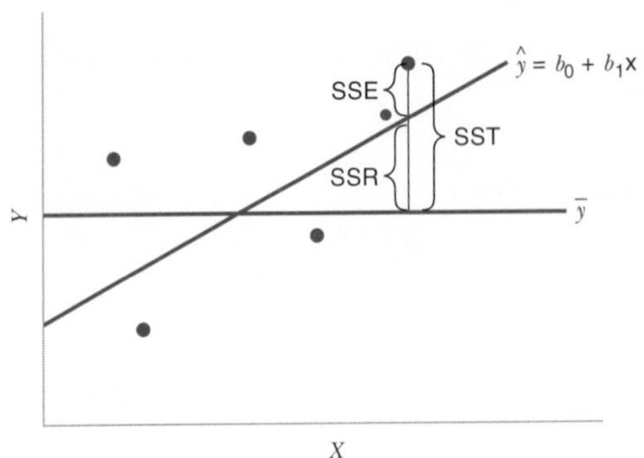

FIGURE 11.11 Components of the variation in y value

Notice that SSE is related to the residuals that you learned about previously.

The quantities **SST, SSR,** and **SSE** are known as the **sums of squares:** SST is the total sum of squares, SSR is the regression sum of squares, and SSE is the error sum of squares. Figure 11.11 illustrates how these quantities relate to the data and to the regression line. From the picture you see that SST represents the distance of the data value y_i from the overall mean $\bar{y}$. SSR represents the distance of the predicted value $\hat{y}$ from the overall mean $\bar{y}$, and SSE represents the distance of a data value y_i from the predicted value $\hat{y}$. The formulas for calculating these quantities are

$$\text{SST} = \sum(y - \bar{y})^2 \qquad \text{SSR} = \sum(\hat{y} - \bar{y})^2 \qquad \text{SSE} = \sum(y - \hat{y})^2$$

In addition you see that

$$\text{SST} = \text{SSR} + \text{SSE}$$

When X and Y are related, SSR is a large part of the total variation. This implies that a major reason that Y varies so much is *because* it is related to X. When this is true, the SSE component of the variation is small and is the variation in Y that happens "naturally" or entirely due to chance.

When X and Y are not related, the regression line is horizontal ($\beta_1 = 0$) and the SSR component of the variation disappears. The SSE part of the variation becomes dominant and we say that we cannot really explain the variation in Y using the linear model with X.

We can use these ideas to create a formal test for the significance of the linear regression model. The test is referred to as an *analysis of variance (ANOVA)* test, because it is based on looking at the *variation* in the Y variable.

The hypotheses that we test are

H_0: The linear regression model is significant.
H_A: The linear regression model is not significant.

The test statistic for this test uses the **mean squares,** which are obtained by dividing the sums of squares, SSR and SSE, by their respective degrees of freedom:

$$\text{MSR} = \frac{\text{SSR}}{1} \quad \text{and} \quad \text{MSE} = \frac{\text{SSE}}{n - 2}$$

You saw the F distribution when you looked at the test for comparing the variances of two normal populations in Chapter 10.

The test looks at the ratio of the regression mean square (MSR) to the error mean square (MSE). As we just saw, when the regression model is really significant (that is, when X and Y are really linearly related), SSR (and therefore MSR) will be much larger than SSE (and therefore MSE). The ratio of the two mean squares has an F distribution with 1 and $n - 2$ degrees of freedom. If the ratio is larger than the critical F value, then the model is significant. Thus, the ANOVA test is a one-sided or one-tail test.

ANOVA

	df	*SS*	*MS*	*F*	*Significance F*
Regression	1	37.7124744	37.7124744	182.6413924	1.9909E-12
Residual	23	4.749125596	0.206483722		
Total	24	42.4616			

Excel

```
Analysis of Variance

Source        DF       SS       MS       F       P
Regression     1   37.712   37.712  182.64   0.000
Error         23    4.749    0.206
Total         24   42.462
```

Minitab

FIGURE 11.12 Computer ANOVA output for regression analysis

Calculation of SST, SSR, and SSE is not difficult, but for even small data sets it can be computationally exhausting. If you have any two of the components, you can obtain the third by subtraction. You can see from the formulas that SSE is really the sum of the squared residuals that you used to find $s_{y|x}$, and that SST is really the numerator portion of the variance of Y.

If you have been doing the analyses by hand or using a calculator, you probably have already calculated most of the quantities you need. However, if you are doing this much analysis you really should be using a statistical software package to do the job. You remember that we learned that output from a statistical analysis program includes a section known as the ANOVA section. Figure 11.12 shows the ANOVA output for Excel and Minitab.

You might wonder why you need another method for testing significance of a linear regression model. In reality you need only one method, since both tests (the t test and the F test) yield the same decision. The difference is, to some degree, a matter of preference. Other statistical analyses use the ANOVA approach and some people prefer that type of test. In addition, the ANOVA approach is used in multiple regression and model building, as you will see in the next chapter.

The quantities SST, SSR, and SSE generated during the ANOVA approach also yield additional information about how good the linear regression model is. One of the reasons that we would like to know whether two variables are related is so that we can use the information to predict one given the other. Another reason is so that we can control or reduce the variation in one quantity by controlling the variation in the other. The regression sum of squares (SSR) measures the amount of the variation in the Y variable that can be accounted for or *explained by* Y's relationship with X. If you look at SSR as a portion of SST, then you can determine the amount of the variability in Y that can be explained, or accounted for. This value is called the **coefficient of determination, R^2:**

$$R^2 = \frac{\text{SSR}}{\text{SST}}\,100\%$$

Formula for coefficient of determination

R^2 is usually part of the general information in the output from statistical packages.

The coefficient of determination gives you a measure of how much the variation in Y could be reduced if X were controlled to a single value. This is a way of measuring how useful a model is for planning purposes. Even if a linear regression model is significant, it may not explain enough of the variation in the Y variable to be useful for planning. When this is the case, you may want to use a regression model with more than one independent or *explanatory* variables. These models are called multiple regression models and are discussed in Chapter 12.

11.3.3 Exercises—Learning It!

11.8 The data on the number of postal employees and the amount of mail processed were analyzed using Minitab. A portion of the output is given here:

```
Predictor         Coef          StDev        T       P
Constant         0.955          4.608     0.21   0.846
  Staff     0.00005872     0.00002087     2.81   0.048

S = 5.461    R-Sq = 66.4%        R-Sq(adj) = 58.1%
```

(a) Set up the hypotheses to test whether the slope coefficient is equal to 0.

(b) There were six observations in the sample. At the 0.05 level of significance what are the critical values of the test?

(c) From the output, find the value of the coefficient, the standard error of the slope, and the value of the *t* statistic.

(d) Compare the *t* statistic to the critical value and determine whether the relationship between the number of postal employees and the amount of mail processed is significant.

11.9 Consider the data from Exercise 11.4 which looked at the relationship between the percentage of households with cable TV in Central Europe and TV advertising revenues. The regression model is

$$\hat{y} = 127.2 + 0.442x \qquad s_{y|x} = 143.2 \qquad \Sigma x = 214 \qquad \Sigma x^2 = 8142$$

(a) Find the standard error of the slope.

(b) Set up the appropriate hypotheses and find the value of the test statistic.

(c) At the 0.10 level of significance, test to see whether the slope coefficient is significantly different from 0.

11.10 In Exercise 11.6 you looked at the relationship between the number of visitors to a country, *X*, and the receipts from tourism, *Y*. The regression equation is

$$\hat{y} = 9.95 + 0.487x \qquad s_{y|x} = 15.50 \qquad \Sigma x = 221 \qquad \Sigma x^2 = 9583$$

(a) Calculate the standard error of the slope.

(b) Set up the hypotheses to determine whether the regression equation is significant at the 0.05 level.

(c) Find the critical values of the test and calculate the test statistic.

(d) Is the relationship between number of visitors and tourism receipts significant?

11.11 Consider the data from Exercise 11.3 on the number of kilometers of travel, *Y*, and the number of cars, *X*, for different countries. The results of a regression analysis using Microsoft Excel are given here:

	Coefficients	*Standard Error*	*t Stat*	*P-value*
Intercept	−106.212984	55.14747208	−1.92598102	0.082984278
Total Cars	2.15816E-05	1.194E-06	18.07496921	5.75839E-09

(a) From the output, find the slope coefficient, the standard error of the slope, the *t* statistic, and the *p* value of the test.

(b) At the 0.01 level of significance use the *p* value to determine whether the relationship between number of kilometers traveled and the number of cars is significant. (The *p* value in Excel is a one-sided *p* value.)

(c) There were 12 observations in the data set. Find the critical values for the test and verify your answer to part (b).

11.12 In Exercise 11.5 you looked at the relationship between the amount of money, *X*, that a city was granted and the number of new police officers hired, *Y*, for nine different cities in New Jersey. The Minitab output from the regression analysis is shown here:

```
Predictor         Coef         StDev        T
Constant        0.7077        0.5360     1.32
Grant ($)   0.00001191    0.00000100    11.88
```

(a) Use the output to find the regression equation relating *X* and *Y*.

(b) Use the output to test whether the relationship between the amount of the grant and the number of new officers is significant.

11.13 Data on the number of radio stations owned by 10 different companies, *X*, and the revenues generated by radio, *Y*, were examined in Exercise 11.7. The data were analyzed using Microsoft Excel and the output is given here:

	Coefficients	*Standard Error*	*t Stat*	*P-value*
Intercept	0.085444208	0.176860232	0.483117131	0.641956743
# of Stations	0.004546468	0.003006584	1.512170824	0.16894211

Use the output to determine whether there is a significant relationship between the number of radio stations owned and the revenues generated by radio for a company.

11.14 Consider the data from Exercise 11.2 on the number of shopping centers and retail sales for the 12 North Central states. The data were analyzed with Minitab and the output is shown here:

```
Predictor        Coef       StDev        T        P
Constant        1.331       1.006     1.32    0.215
No. Shop     0.019021    0.001129    16.84    0.000
```

At the 0.01 level of significance, is the relationship between the number of shopping centers and retail sales significant?

11.4 PREDICTION AND CONFIDENCE INTERVALS

We have discussed the fact that in a *statistical* relationship the values of the dependent variable will vary for any single value of the independent variable. No matter how strong the relationship between *X* and *Y* is, there is some amount of inherent variation that will exist in *Y* for any given value of *X*. This natural variation is identified in the population regression model $y = \beta_0 + \beta_1 x + \varepsilon$ as the quantity ε.

When the relationship between *X* and *Y* is strong, the variation in *Y* for a given value of *X* is small and can be thought of simply as *natural* variation. If you look at a plot of the data and the regression line, the points will be very close to the line. That is, the variation that exists is entirely due to chance and we should not waste time trying to figure out why it happens. In this case, the predictions we obtain from our estimate of the regression line will be fairly precise and can be used for the purposes of making decisions.

When the relationship between *X* and *Y* is not so strong, the variation in *Y* for a given value of *X* will be variation present because our linear model is *not adequate*. In this case, the data points will not be close to the regression line, the relationship might not be linear, or there may be other factors that cause *Y* to vary. In this case, even if *X* and *Y* have a statistically significant relationship, the predictions obtained from the regression model might not be precise enough for purposes of decision making.

In Section 11.2 you learned that the standard error of the estimate, $s_{y|x}$, is a measure of the overall variation in Y for any value of X. In this section we put that value in context and see how it can be used to evaluate the usefulness of a regression model.

11.4.1 Confidence Intervals for Regression Analysis

The value of $\hat{y}$ obtained from the regression model is an estimate of the *mean value of Y for a given value of X*. That is, the value $\hat{y}$ is an *estimate* of the true mean, $\mu_{y|x}$. If the variable X represented advertising expenditures, then the regression model relating X to sales of a product, Y, would predict the *average* sales for a given level of advertising. Because our estimate is based on sample data, we know that there is some error in that estimate.

In Chapter 9 you learned how to find confidence intervals for the mean of a population μ, based on a sample estimate, $\overline{X}$. We can use the same ideas to create a confidence interval for $\mu_{y|x}$ based on our sample estimate, $\hat{y}$.

To find a confidence interval for a population parameter we need to know the sampling distribution of the estimate and the standard error of the sample statistic. The estimate $\hat{y}$ has a Student t distribution with $n - 2$ degrees of freedom. The standard error is related to the standard error of the estimate, $s_{y|x}$. The formula for a $(1 - \alpha)100\%$ **confidence interval** for the mean value of Y for a given value of $X = x_i$, $\mu_{y|x_i}$, is

$$\hat{y}_i - t_{\alpha/2,\, n-2} s_{y|x} \sqrt{\frac{1}{n} + \frac{(x_i - \bar{x})^2}{\Sigma x^2 - (\Sigma x)^2/n}} \le \mu_{y|x_i} \le \hat{y}_i + t_{\alpha/2,\, n-2} s_{y|x} \sqrt{\frac{1}{n} + \frac{(x_i - \bar{x})^2}{\Sigma x^2 - (\Sigma x)^2/n}}$$

A ***confidence interval*** provides an estimate for the mean value of Y ($\mu_{y|x}$) at a particular value of X.

Again, the expression looks formidable, but it does not contain anything we have not already dealt with!

Previously, when you found confidence intervals, you found that the width of the interval was related to the level of confidence that you wanted. This is also true for the confidence interval for $\mu_{y|x_i}$, but the width of the interval also depends on how far the selected value of X is from the average value of X. The farther the value of interest is from the average X value, the wider (and less precise) the confidence interval becomes! Figure 11.13 illustrates how the confidence interval is related to the values of the X variable.

If you look at the formula for the confidence interval again, you will see that when $X = \overline{X}$, the part of the formula in the square root reduces to $1/\sqrt{n}$ and the formula looks exactly like the confidence interval for the mean that you learned previously.

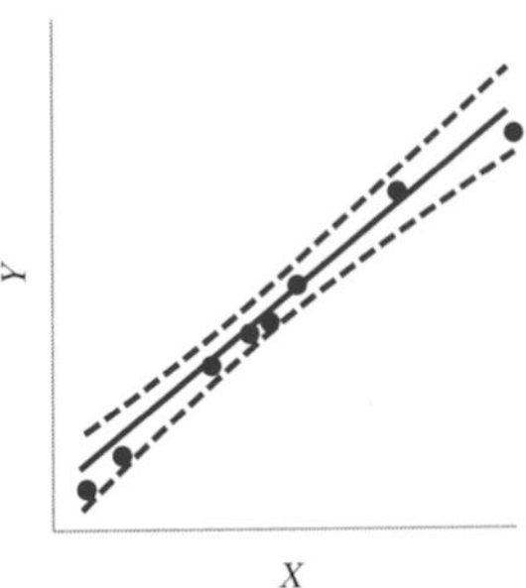

FIGURE 11.13 Confidence interval for the mean estimate

EXAMPLE 11.15 Is TQM Working?

Calculating a Confidence Interval for the Mean Response

The manufacturing group that is looking at the effectiveness of TQM wants to know something about the accuracy of the predictions from the regression model. To accomplish this, it decides to find 95% confidence intervals for two machine speeds that it runs frequently, 400 and 450 items per minute. The regression model is

$$\hat{y} = 1.06 + 0.035x$$

The first step is to find the predicted value for the 400 speed:

$$\hat{y} = 1.06 + 0.035(400) = 15.06$$

Analyze the Data

From previous work the manufacturers know the predicted value for 450 is 16.81 and $s_{y|x} = 0.4544$, $\Sigma x = 10{,}340$, and $\Sigma x^2 = 4{,}306{,}918$. They calculate that $\overline{X} = 413.6$.

For a 95% confidence interval the t values are $\pm t_{0.025,23} = \pm 2.069$, so they calculate

To actually calculate the interval it is probably easiest to calculate the ± part and then add and subtract that value from the prediction, ŷ.

$$(2.069)(0.4544)\sqrt{\frac{1}{25} + \frac{(400 - 413.6)^2}{4{,}306{,}918 - (10{,}340)^2/25}}$$

$$= (2.069)(0.4544)\sqrt{0.0461054\ldots} = 0.202$$

So, the confidence limits are

$$15.06 \pm 0.20 = (14.86, 15.26)$$

or

$$(14.86 \le \mu_{y|400} \le 15.26)$$

The manufacturers see that the estimate of the mean productivity is somewhere between 14.86 (or 14,860 units) per hour and 15.26 (or 15,260 units) per hour. The width of the interval is

$$15.06 - 14.86 = 0.40 \text{ or } 400 \text{ units/hour}$$

which is fairly precise for their purposes.

They do a similar calculation for a speed of 450 items per minute and obtain:

$$(2.069)(0.4544)\sqrt{\frac{1}{25} + \frac{(450 - 413.6)^2}{4{,}306{,}918 - (10{,}340)^2/25}}$$

$$= (2.069)(0.4544)\sqrt{0.0837367\ldots} = 0.272$$

Notice that the only change in the calculation is substituting 450 for 400 in the square root part of the formula.

So the 95% confidence interval for a speed of 450 items per minute is

$$16.81 \pm 0.27 = (16.54, 17.08)$$

or

$$(16.54 \le \mu_{y|450} \le 17.08)$$

Analyze the Data

That means that at a speed of 450 items per minute, average hourly production will be between 16,540 and 17,080 items. ■

It is not really difficult to calculate confidence intervals for one or two estimates, but if you want intervals for more estimates, using a computer is much easier.

EXAMPLE 11.16 HMO Health

Finding Confidence Intervals for the Mean Estimate

The analysts who are looking at the relationship between HMO revenues and number of members would like to know how accurate the estimates from the regression model are. They use Minitab to find 95% confidence intervals for the mean for each value of X in the data set. The output (edited) from the analysis is shown here:

Analyze the Data

X Value	Fit	95.0% CI
0.89	1.803	(1.025, 2.580)
0.97	1.894	(1.148, 2.640)
1.62	2.638	(2.101, 3.174)
1.83	2.878	(2.381, 3.374)
1.83	2.878	(2.381, 3.374)
2.07	3.152	(2.676, 3.629)
2.15	3.244	(2.767, 3.721)
2.30	3.415	(2.930, 3.901)
3.19	4.434	(3.710, 5.157)
4.24	5.635	(4.460, 6.809)

Draw Conclusions

They see that the uncertainty in the estimated revenue (the width of the interval) goes from a low of \$0.953 billion to a high of \$2.349 billion. For the middle X values (close to the mean) the width of the interval is about \$1 billion. They feel that the confidence intervals are very wide, especially considering the size of the actual estimates. It might not be practical to use this model to predict mean revenues. ■

Most statistical software packages will calculate the confidence intervals for either a single X value or for an entire set of X values. If you are using a spreadsheet program, entering the formula is not a difficult task.

TRY IT NOW!

Increasing Capacity *Finding Confidence Intervals for the Mean Predicted Value*

After calculating the regression model and deciding that the model is significant, the analysts at the oil company would like to know about the accuracy of the estimates from the model. They decide to calculate 95% confidence intervals for $X = 8$ and 13 sites. They know from previous work that for the set of 10 observations in the model, $s_{y|x} = 13.43$, $\Sigma x = 78$, and $\Sigma x^2 = 714$.

Find 95% confidence intervals for the mean estimates.

Do you think that these estimates would be useful for planning purposes? Why or why not?

ANS. FOR $X = 8$ (37.51, 57.14) AND FOR $X = 13$ (52.77, 89.74).

11.4.2 Prediction Intervals for Regression Analysis

A confidence interval for the mean estimate from the regression model gives the decision maker an idea of just how accurate the estimate is *over a long period of time.* That is, it is an interval estimate for the mean. This is certainly of importance for decisions that involve long-time horizons, but what about models that are important for predictions in a single instance?

If a company is looking at the relationship between sales and advertising, a confidence interval will tell it that, for a specific level of advertising, the *average* sales will vary between these two amounts. This is certainly useful information, but some additional information might also be helpful. The company might be interested in the accuracy of a *single observation.* For example, it might like to have an interval estimate for next month's sales for some specific advertising outlay. In a problem related to cash flow, this information would be more important than an overall mean. Intervals for individual estimates are called **prediction intervals** in regression analysis.

A ***prediction interval*** gives an estimate for an individual value of Y at a particular value of X.

The formula used to calculate a $(1 - \alpha)100\%$ prediction interval for a regression model is almost identical to the one for the confidence interval:

$$\hat{y}_i - t_{\alpha/2,n-2}s_{y|x}\sqrt{1 + \frac{1}{n} + \frac{(x_i - \bar{x})^2}{\Sigma x^2 - (\Sigma x)^2/n}} \le y \le \hat{y}_i + t_{\alpha/2,n-2}s_{y|x}\sqrt{1 + \frac{1}{n} + \frac{(x_i - \bar{x})^2}{\Sigma x^2 - (\Sigma x)^2/n}}$$

You see that the only difference is the "1" in the square root part of the formula. The impact of this change is that the prediction intervals for a specific value of X will be *wider* than the corresponding confidence interval. If you think about it, a wider interval for prediction makes sense. You know from the ideas of sampling and the Central Limit Theorem that the distribution of individual observations is always more variable than the distribution of the sample means.

EXAMPLE 11.17 Is TQM Working?

Finding a Prediction Interval for a Regression Model

The company that is looking at the TQM program thinks that the estimates for the mean production are useful, but the analysts would like to know how much variability there is in the estimate for the hourly productivity. They decide to find 95% prediction intervals for the estimates for speeds of 400 and 450 units per min. The relevant values for the 25 observations are $\hat{y}_{400} = 15.06$, $\hat{y}_{450} = 16.81$, $s_{y|x} = 0.4544$, $\Sigma x = 10{,}340$, and $\Sigma x^2 = 4{,}306{,}918$. The t value has not changed from the confidence interval calculations and so the analysts calculate the interval as follows:

$$(2.069)(0.4544)\sqrt{1 + \frac{1}{25} + \frac{(400 - 413.6)^2}{4{,}306{,}918 - (10{,}340)^2/25}}$$

$$= (2.069)(0.4544)\sqrt{1.0461055\ldots} = 0.962$$

Analyze the Data

The 95% prediction interval is then

$$15.06 \pm 0.96$$

or

$$(14.10 \le y \le 16.02)$$

So, in a given hour, at 400 units per minute, production might vary from 14,100 to 16,020 units. Similarly for the 450 speed they find

$$(2.069)(0.4544)\sqrt{1+\frac{1}{25}+\frac{(450-413.6)^2}{4{,}306{,}918-(10{,}340)^2/25}}$$

$$=(2.069)(0.4544)\sqrt{1.0837367\ldots}=0.979$$

The prediction interval is

$$16.81 \pm 0.98$$

or

$$(15.83 \leq y \leq 17.79)$$

At 450 units per minute, hourly production will vary from 15,830 to 17,790 units.

Draw Conclusions

They see that the variability for an individual month's productivity is greater than the variability for average production. The width of the intervals is about 0.97 or 970 items, which is still useful for planning purposes. ■

Prediction intervals are important when the individual values for the Y variable are critical to the decision process. If, for example, the company looking at TQM is interested in planning warehouse capacity based on the amount of usable product it has, then a long-term estimate might not make sense.

Increasing Capacity ***Calculating Prediction Intervals for Regression Estimates***

The oil company analysts decide to calculate 95% prediction intervals for the two X values that they are interested in. The relevant values from the set of 10 observations are $s_{y|x} = 13.43$, $\Sigma x = 78$, and $\Sigma x^2 = 714$.

Find 95% prediction intervals for $X = 8$ and $X = 13$ refining sites.

Do you think that confidence intervals or prediction intervals would be more appropriate for the oil company's purposes?

11.4.3 Exercises—Learning It!

Requires Exercise 11.5

11.15 For the data on federal grant money and police officers hired the relevant data are

$$\Sigma x = 4{,}167{,}462 \qquad \Sigma x^2 = 2{,}571{,}647{,}717{,}614 \qquad s_{y|x} = 0.8033 \qquad n = 9$$

(a) Find a 95% confidence interval for the mean number of officers hired when the amount of the grant is \$350,000.

(b) Find a 95% prediction interval for the number of officers hired when the amount of the grant is \$350,000.

Requires Exercise 11.1

11.16 For the data on the number of postal workers in a country and the amount of mail processed, the relevant data are:

ANS. (14.83, 79.82) AND (35.18, 107.33), PROBABLY CONFIDENCE INTERVALS

$\Sigma x = 1{,}159{,}709 \qquad \Sigma x^2 = 292{,}657{,}611{,}087 \qquad s_{y|x} = 5.4614 \qquad n = 6$

(a) Find 95% confidence intervals for the mean amount of mail processed when the number of postal workers is 50,000 and 250,000.

(b) Find 95% prediction intervals for the same two values of *X*.

11.17 For the data on the number of shopping centers and retail sales for the North Central States, the relevant data are: *Requires Exercise 11.2*

$$\Sigma x = 8308 \qquad \Sigma x^2 = 9{,}517{,}766 \qquad s_{y|x} = 2.1918 \qquad n = 12$$

(a) Find 98% confidence intervals for the mean retail sales when the number of shopping centers is 1000 and 1500.

(b) Which interval is wider? Why?

(c) Find 98% prediction intervals for the same values of *X*.

(d) Do you think that prediction or confidence intervals are more appropriate for these data?

11.18 For the data on the number of automobiles in a country and the total number of kilometers traveled, the relevant data are *Requires Exercise 11.3*

$$\Sigma x = 319.51 \qquad \Sigma x^2 = 25{,}598.8975 \qquad s_{y|x} = 156.0981 \qquad n = 12$$

(a) Find 99% confidence intervals for the number of kilometers traveled for $X = 1.5$ and 10 (million) cars.

(b) Find 99% prediction intervals for the two values of *X* from part (a).

11.5 CORRELATION ANALYSIS

In many instances, when people talk about regression analysis they also talk about *correlation analysis.* The two topics are related, but not interchangeable. Both regression and correlation analyses deal with bivariate quantitative data and the relationship between the two variables. The main purpose of regression analysis is to find an equation or model that allows the decision maker to predict the value of the dependent variable. On the other hand, *correlation analysis* simply *measures the strength* of the linear relationship between two quantitative variables. The output of the analysis is a single number. In correlation analysis, there is no need to identify which variable is dependent and which is independent, since prediction is not the end result.

11.5.1 The Correlation Coefficient

We have talked about the types of linear relationships that can exist between two variables. In Figure 11.14 you see three types of relationships: perfect negative, none, and perfect positive.

If we simply want to measure the strength of a relationship between two variables, we use the **correlation coefficient.**

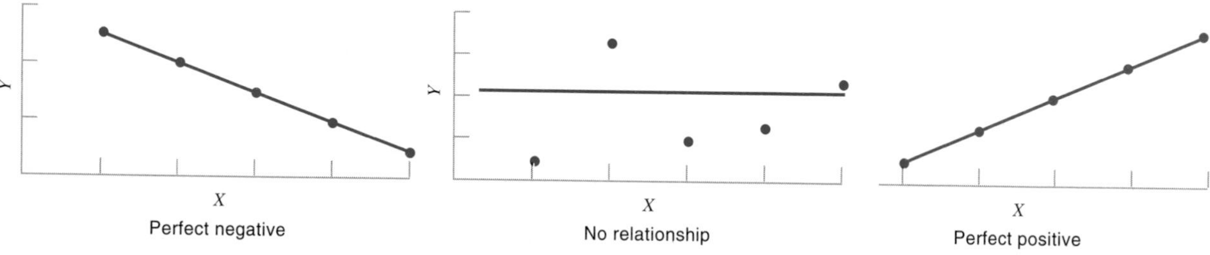

FIGURE 11.14 Three types of relationships: perfect negative, no relationship, and perfect positive

> The *correlation coefficient* is used as a measure of the strength of a linear relationship. A correlation of −1 corresponds to a perfect negative relationship, a correlation of 0 corresponds to no relationship, and a correlation of +1 corresponds to a perfect positive relationship.

The **correlation coefficient,** r, is calculated using the formula

$$r = \frac{\Sigma xy - (\Sigma x)(\Sigma y)/n}{\sqrt{\Sigma x^2 - (\Sigma x)^2/n}\sqrt{\Sigma y^2 - (\Sigma y)^2/n}}$$

Again, we have a complicated formula, but it uses all of the familiar elements. Any scientific calculator that does regression will output the correlation coefficient. Software that performs regression analysis usually does not output the correlation coefficient directly because correlation and regression are not interchangeable. In the next section you will learn a statistic that is part of regression that can be used to obtain the correlation coefficient.

In many cases, the correlation coefficient is used along with regression analysis as another measure of how good the regression model is. It is important to recognize that the correlation coefficient can be used as a statistic in its own right when prediction of one variable as a function of the other is not appropriate or not necessary.

For example, suppose that a company is interested in knowing whether there is a relationship between the score on an aptitude test and the number of months that a person remains in an entry level position. The company does not necessarily want to *predict* the number of months in the entry level position; it simply wants to know if the test score is related to that variable. In this case the company could calculate the correlation between score on the test and number of months in the entry level job.

EXAMPLE 11.18 Is TQM Working?

Calculating the Correlation Coefficient

The company looking at its TQM program wonders what the correlation coefficient is for the relationship between machine speed and productivity. It decides to calculate the correlation. The relevant numbers are

Analyze the Data

$$\Sigma x = 10{,}340 \qquad \Sigma y = 391.4 \qquad \Sigma xy = 162{,}951.9 \qquad \Sigma x^2 = 4{,}306{,}918$$
$$\Sigma y^2 = 6170.22 \qquad n = 25$$

The calculation is

$$r = \frac{162{,}951.9 - (10{,}340)(391.4)/25}{\sqrt{4{,}306{,}918 - (10{,}340)^2/25}\sqrt{6170.22 - (391.4)^2/25}}$$
$$= \frac{1068.86}{(174.051\ldots)(6.516\ldots)} = 0.9424$$

The correlation coefficient is very close to +1, which indicates a strong, positive relationship between machine speed and productivity. ■

You may know what values indicate good correlation and what values indicate that there is not really a relationship between two variables. The answer is, It depends. When data are collected under uncontrolled circumstances, there is usually a lot of variation in the data from other, uncontrolled, unmeasured variables. When this happens, the correlation between two variables might not appear to be strong because of the additional factors. This will also be reflected in the widths of the confidence and prediction intervals. Sometimes a correlation in the range of 0.6 to 0.7 (or −0.6 to −0.7), which might not provide *useful* information, is an indication that further investigation is appropriate.

EXAMPLE 11.19 HMO Health

Calculating the Correlation Coefficient

The analysts looking at the relationship between revenues and number of members for various HMOs are pretty certain that the relationship between the two variables will be a strong, positive one, so they decide to calculate the correlation coefficient to check their assumption. The numbers that they need to perform the calculation are

Analyze the Data

$$n = 10 \qquad \Sigma x = 21.09 \qquad \Sigma y = 31.97 \qquad \Sigma xy = 77.6371$$
$$\Sigma x^2 = 53.4063 \qquad \Sigma y^2 = 117.3013$$

The calculation is

$$\frac{77.6371 - (21.09)(31.97)/10}{\sqrt{53.4063 - (21.09)^2/10}\sqrt{117.3013 - (31.97)^2/10}} = \frac{10.2124}{11.60795\ldots} = 0.8798$$

Looking at the value, the analysts feel that the number does indicate the strong positive correlation that they expected to find. ■

TRY IT NOW!

Increasing Capacity ***Calculating the Correlation Coefficient***

The relevant data to calculate the correlation coefficient for the oil company problem are

$$n = 10 \qquad \Sigma x = 78 \qquad \Sigma y = 463.64 \qquad \Sigma xy = 4121.86 \qquad \Sigma x^2 = 714$$
$$\Sigma y^2 = 25{,}359.3224$$

Find the correlation coefficient for the data.

The correlation coefficient is also related to one of the quantities that we looked at in regression analysis, the coefficient of determination, R^2. The value of r is equal to the square root of R^2. The sign of r is the same as the sign of the slope coefficient.

$$r = \pm\sqrt{R^2}$$

11.6 REGRESSION ASSUMPTIONS AND RESIDUAL ANALYSIS

Although regression is certainly one of the most powerful and frequently used tools in statistical analysis, it is also one that is often misused. This sometimes happens because the model is built on certain *assumptions* and people are often unaware of the assumptions or choose to ignore them. As you have learned before in this book, when you ignore the *assumptions* behind a statistical tool, the results of the analysis

ANS. 0.791

might be totally incorrect. In this section we will look at the assumptions of the simple linear regression model and the ramifications of violating those assumptions. We will also look at some simple techniques for determining whether the assumptions of the model are appropriate for a particular set of data.

Another reason that the simple linear model is misused is that people do not realize that the model is inappropriate for the data being analyzed. This can be true even when the results of the analysis indicate that the simple linear model is appropriate. We will also look at ways to determine when the simple linear model is not appropriate.

11.6.1 Assumptions and Problems in the Regression Model

Remember that the simple linear model is given by

$$y = \beta_0 + \beta_1 x + \varepsilon$$

and that ε represents the random error in the model. Most of the assumptions that are built into the simple linear regression model involve this error term.

The basic assumptions about the error ε follow:

1. It has a mean value of zero $(\mu_\varepsilon = 0)$.
2. For every value of X, the standard deviation, σ, of ε is the same.
3. The distribution of ε is normal.
4. The error terms for the different observations are not correlated with each other.

What happens if these assumptions are not valid? Obviously, the simple linear model is not correct, but what does that really mean? It may mean several different things. One possible result of violating the assumptions is that you may decide that a model is significant when it is not, or vice versa. Another result is that although you may be correct in your decision about the significance of the model, the equation you obtain is completely wrong. That is, although the model may give reasonable predictions for Y, the coefficients in the model, b_0 and b_1, cannot be interpreted correctly. When this is the case, using the model for planning or control purposes is very risky.

In addition to violating the assumptions of the regression model, there are other factors that make the linear model inappropriate. Some of these factors are

- Fitting a linear model when the true relationship is nonlinear
- Influence of outliers on the regression equation

Sometimes data that appear to have a linear relationship in a scatter plot may actually have a nonlinear relationship. It is very often hard to see curves or nonlinear patterns when looking at scatter plots. The results of the analysis might indicate that the linear model is appropriate when in fact a nonlinear model would be better. Also, sometimes certain observations in the data set have a large influence on the regression equation. This often happens when the X value for an observation is far away from the other values. When these data points are removed, the entire analysis may change.

How can we tell if we are violating the assumptions or using the linear model incorrectly? One tool that answers many of these questions is called *residual analysis*. You have already learned how to calculate residuals. Now we will look at them as a diagnostic tool.

According to the assumptions of linear regression, for all values of the independent variable, the residuals of the model should be normally distributed random variables with a mean of zero and a standard deviation of σ. That is, the ε are $N(0, \sigma)$.

If we plot the residuals from the regression model, the e_i's, as a function of X, we should expect to see that they are randomly distributed around a value of 0. Furthermore, the amount of variation around 0 should be the same for all values of X. When the plot exhibits departures from this, it indicates that certain of the model assumptions are not valid or that a linear model was not appropriate.

In Figure 11.15 we see several different plots of the residuals versus the values of the independent variable, X. The first plot shows what the residual plot should look like when the assumptions of the linear regression model are met and when the simple linear model is appropriate. You can see that the residuals are randomly distributed around the mean value of 0 and that there is no apparent pattern in the plot. The others plots show different patterns that can result when the assumptions are violated or when the model is not appropriate. Figure 11.15b shows a typical plot that results when the linear model is used on data that have a nonlinear relationship. The residuals have a systematic pattern to them. Figures 11.15c and d show plots that can result when the assumption of equal variances is violated.

Certain statistical packages plot the residuals against the fitted values ($\hat{y}$) instead of X. When the regression model is significant, X and Y are related and so the plots will not be different in shape. Also, some packages use "standardized residuals" (the residuals divided by the standard error of the residuals) instead of the residuals. Again, this does not produce a difference in the plots.

In addition to checking that the residuals have a mean of zero and that they are randomly dispersed around this value, we must check the shape of the distribution to see if it is normal. You remember that this is also an assumption for some of the hypothesis tests that you learned in Chapters 9 and 10. How can we check to see whether data come from a normal distribution? There are several ways to

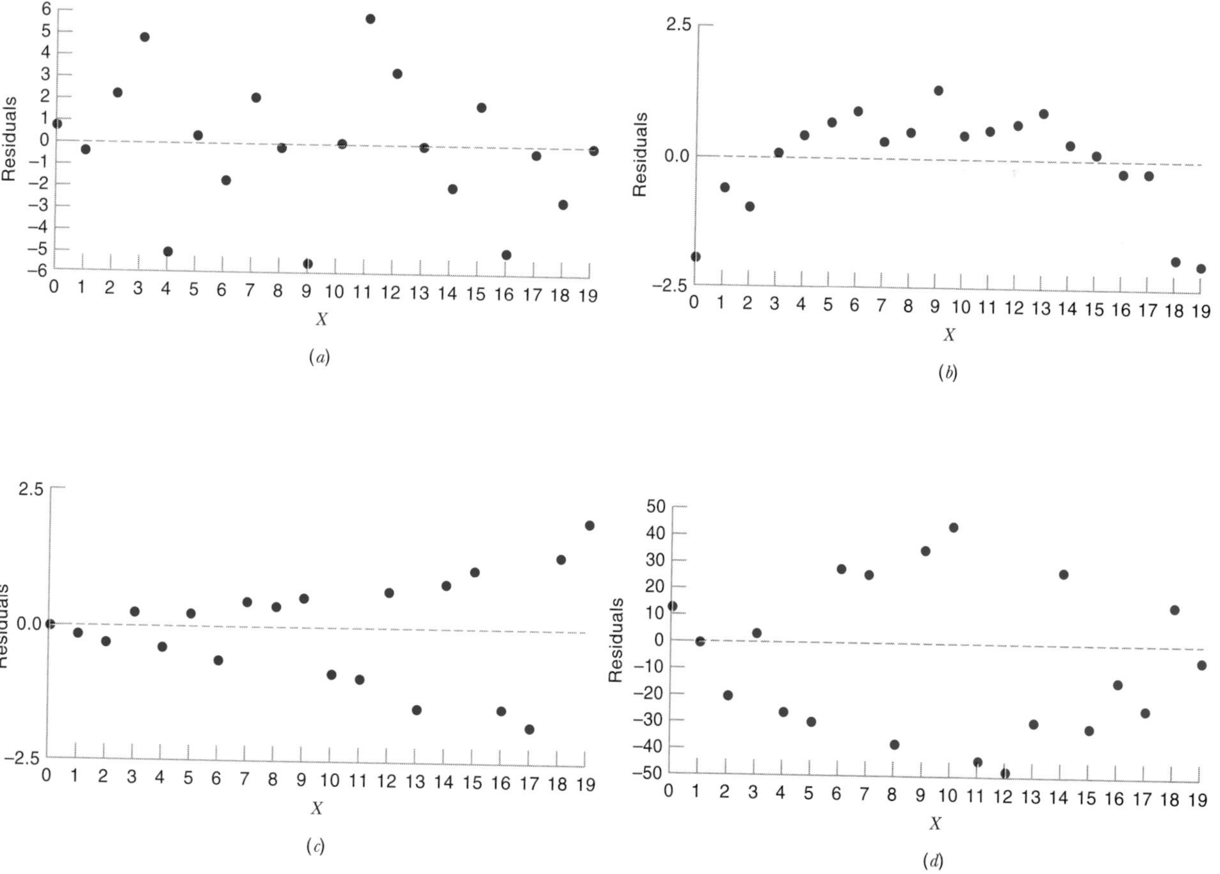

FIGURE 11.15 Examples of residual plots

accomplish this. We will look at one *informal* method, making a histogram, and one *formal* method, a normal probability plot, that is available in many statistical software packages.

Note: For small data sets histograms may be misleading. You might want to use dotplots or normal plots.

If you look at a data distribution to see whether it might be normally distributed, you will look to see that it is approximately bell-shaped, that is, unimodal and symmetric. Figure 11.16 shows histograms of the residuals from the same plots that you looked at in Figure 11.15. In each case, a normal curve with a mean of 0 is overlaid on the histogram.

You may notice that even in the case where the residuals looked randomly distributed, it does not look like the residuals come from a normal distribution. It may be that the residuals are not normally distributed, or it may be that there is just not enough data to make a really good histogram. This is one of the problems with such an informal method.

Another, more formal method for determining whether data are normally distributed is a plot called a **normal probability plot.**

A ***normal probability plot*** is a plot of the ordered data against their expected values under a normal distribution. When data are normally distributed, the plot will be a straight line.

The methods for creating a normal plot are well beyond the scope of this book, but they are easily created with statistical software packages. In fact, most statistical

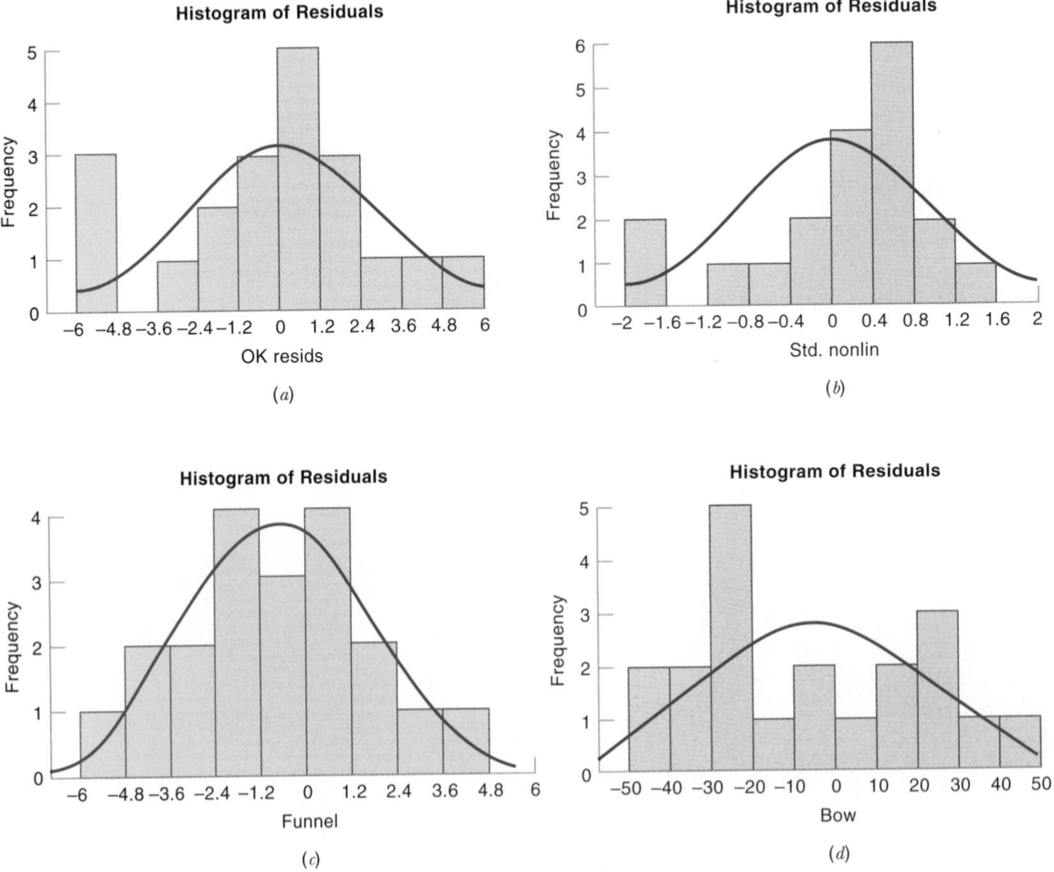

FIGURE 11.16 Histograms of residuals

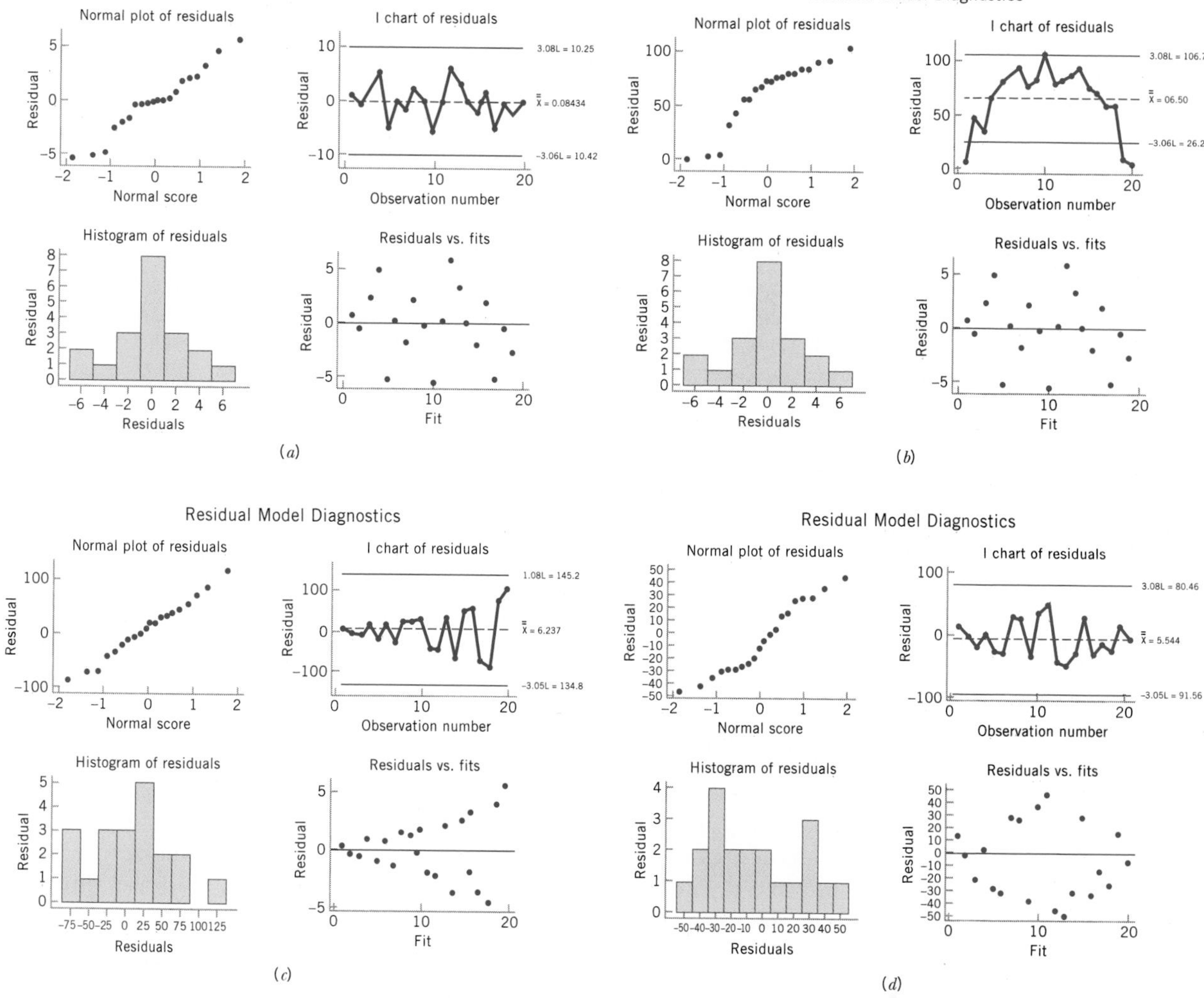

FIGURE 11.17 Regression diagnostic plots (Minitab)

software make normal plots as part of their output from regression analysis. Figure 11.17 shows a set of residual plots, including a normal plot from Minitab, for each of the sets of residuals we have been looking at.

Another factor that can cause problems in using the linear regression model is the effects of observations that have excessive influence on the equation of the line. This can happen as a result of two things: data pairs that are outliers, and data points whose X values are very far removed from the rest of the data. Both of these factors can cause the regression model to shift toward the suspect data point and skew the resulting regression line.

There are a few ways to determine whether a data set has such an observation. One visual method, as seen in the Minitab output in Figure 11.17, is to create a control chart for the residuals and see whether any of the values indicate an "out of control" situation. Another visual method is to make a boxplot of the residuals or the X data values and see whether any are determined to be outliers.

It is also possible to determine whether a data point has a large influence on the model by using some statistical techniques. Many statistical software packages use these techniques and report the problem as part of the output. Figure 11.18 on page 556 shows this part of the output for Minitab.

Obs	Members	HMORev $	Fit	StDev Fit	Residual	St Resid
1	4.24	5.486	5.631	0.509	−0.146	−0.36 X
2	3.19	4.629	4.432	0.313	0.197	0.34
3	1.83	3.857	2.878	0.215	0.979	1.59
4	1.62	3.600	2.639	0.232	0.961	1.58
5	2.07	3.429	3.153	0.206	0.276	0.45
6	2.30	2.914	3.415	0.210	−0.501	−0.81
7	1.83	2.743	2.878	0.215	−0.136	−0.22
8	2.15	2.400	3.244	0.206	−0.844	−1.37
9	0.97	1.714	1.896	0.323	−0.182	−0.32
10	0.89	1.200	1.805	0.336	−0.605	−1.08

X denotes an observation whose X value gives it large influence.

Obs	of Sta	RadioRev	Fit	StDev Fit	Residual	St Resid
1	83	1.0500	0.4628	0.1191	0.5872	2.75P
2	57	0.3143	0.3446	0.0783	−0.0303	−0.13
3	104	0.3143	0.5583	0.1720	−0.2440	−1.40
4	35	0.3048	0.2446	0.0942	0.0602	0.27
5	21	0.2857	0.1809	0.1232	0.1048	0.50
6	63	0.2286	0.3719	0.0831	−0.1433	−0.62
7	67	0.2190	0.3901	0.0882	−0.1710	−0.75
8	41	0.2095	0.2718	0.0852	−0.0623	−0.27
9	38	0.2095	0.2582	0.0894	−0.0487	−0.21
10	20	0.1238	0.1764	0.1256	−0.0526	−0.25

FIGURE 11.18 Warning output from Minitab

EXAMPLE 11.20 Is TQM Working?

Checking Regression Assumptions Using Residuals

The company that is using linear regression to determine whether its TQM program is working decides to make sure that what it has done so far is correct. Since the linear regression model is significant, the analysts want to make sure that it is valid and that they can use it for decision-making purposes. They use Minitab to analyze the data and look at the output of residual plots. The output is shown here:

Analyze the Data

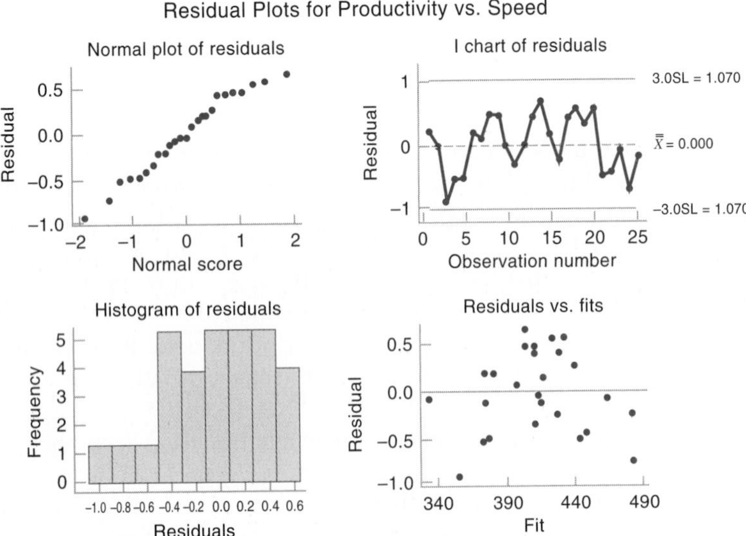

Draw Conclusions

From the histogram and normal probability plots it appears that there might be a problem with the assumption of normality. The plot of the residuals versus the $\hat{y}$'s appears to be random, although there is an impression that the data actually might

have a nonlinear relationship. The control chart indicates that there are no problems with extreme values.

Before the analysts decide to use this model, they will look more carefully at the data and see whether another, perhaps nonlinear model, would be better. ■

11.6.2 Exercises—Learning It!

11.19 Look at the regression model you developed for the data on federal grant money and police officers hired.

Requires Exercises 11.5, 11.15

(a) Make a plot of the residuals versus the values of the independent variable.

(b) Look at the plot you obtained. Does it appear that a linear model is really appropriate for these data? Why or why not?

(c) Looking at the same residual plot, does the assumption of equal variances appear reasonable? Why or why not?

(d) Use an appropriate graphical technique to display the distribution of the residuals. Be sure to consider how many residuals you have in selecting the technique. Does the assumption of normality appear to be reasonable?

(e) Create a normal probability plot of the residuals. What does this make you think about the normality assumption?

(f) Considering your answers to parts (a)–(e), do you think that the linear regression model was a good one for these data? Be sure to cite specifics in your answer.

11.20 Consider the regression model you found for the data on the number of postal workers in a country and the amount of mail processed.

Requires Exercises 11.1, 11.16

(a) Make a plot of the residuals versus the values of the independent variables.

(b) What does this lead you to believe about the appropriateness of the linear model?

(c) Now plot the residuals versus the predicted values of y.

(d) How do the two graphs compare? Why do you think this happened?

(e) Make a normal probability plot of the data. Do you think the assumption of normality is reasonable?

(f) Considering your answers to parts (a)–(e), do you think that the linear regression model is appropriate for these data. Why or why not?

11.21 Look at the model you found for the data on the number of shopping centers and retail sales for the North Central states.

Requires Exercises 11.2, 11.17

(a) Make a plot of the residuals versus the independent variable.

(b) From the plot, does it appear that a linear model is appropriate?

(c) Looking at the residual plot, do you think that the assumption of equality of variances is violated?

(d) Make a graph that shows the distribution of the residuals.

(e) Does it appear that the residuals are normally distributed?

(f) Considering your answers to parts (a)–(e), do you think that the linear regression model is appropriate for these data? Why or why not?

11.22 Look at the model you found for the data on the number of automobiles in a country and the total number of kilometers traveled.

Requires Exercises 11.3, 11.18

(a) Make a residual plot of the data versus the independent variables.

(b) What does the residual plot tell you about the assumption of a linear relationship? The assumption of equal variances?

(c) Using the residual plot, the computer output, or a plot of the values of the independent variable, do you think that any observation had a lot of influence on the model? If so, which point(s) are they?

(d) Do you think that the assumption of normality is reasonable?

(e) Considering your answers to parts (a)–(d), do you think that the linear model is appropriate for these data? Why or why not?

4. In the bottom part of the dialog box indicate which plots you want included in the output.
5. Indicate where you want the output to appear and click **OK.**

The output is rather extensive. The main portion of the output shown in Figure 11.27 contains the same information that is in the linear regression output from the Data Analysis Tools. The remainder of the output consists of the graphs requested and the residuals and standardized residuals, as shown in Figure 11.28.

Regression and Correlation

Observations	10
R Square	0.7740
Standard Error	0.6530
Adjusted R Square	0.7458
Multiple R	0.8798

ANOVA

	df	SS	MS	F	p value
Regression	1	11.6822	11.6822	27.3985	0.0008
Residual	8	3.4110	0.4264		
Total	9	15.09321022			

	Coefficients	Standard Error	t value	p value
Intercept	0.7845	0.5050	1.5533	0.1590
Members (m)	1.1439	0.2185	5.2344	0.0008

Forecast?

Caution: If any independent variable can be perfectly predicted using one or more of the other independent variables, then the regression analysis may give an error message, or it may yield results which are not reasonable.

FIGURE 11.27 Main output from regression analysis

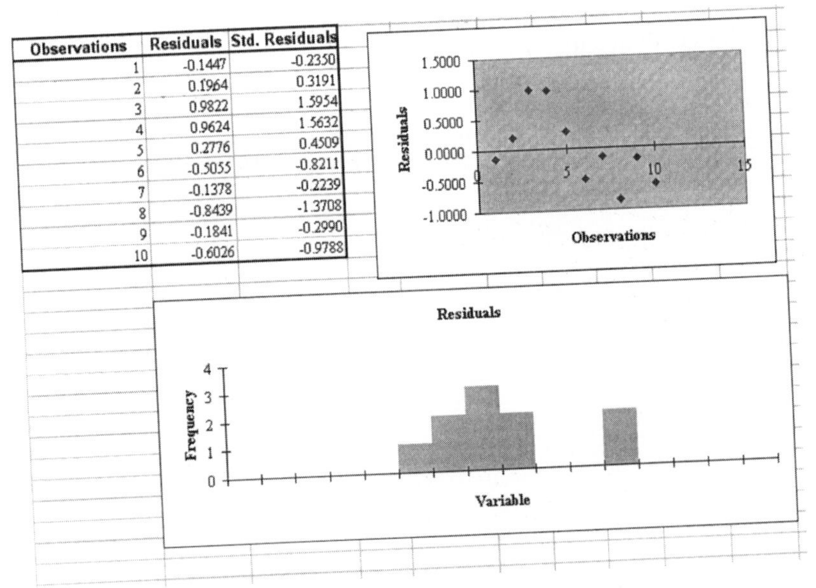

Observations	Residuals	Std. Residuals
1	-0.1447	-0.2350
2	0.1964	0.3191
3	0.9822	1.5954
4	0.9624	1.5632
5	0.2776	0.4509
6	-0.5055	-0.8211
7	-0.1378	-0.2239
8	-0.8439	-1.3708
9	-0.1841	-0.2990
10	-0.6026	-0.9788

FIGURE 11.28 Additional regression output

Rather than inputting the equation of the regression line as a formula, KADD will calculate the predicted values for the data points or for any other x values that you want to use. In the main portion of the output, click on the box labeled **Forecast** and the dialog box shown in Figure 11.29 opens. Place the cursor in the **Forecast Data Range:** box and highlight the location of the values of the independent variable for which you want predictions. Then indicate where you want the output located and click **OK.** The output shown in Figure 11.30 appears.

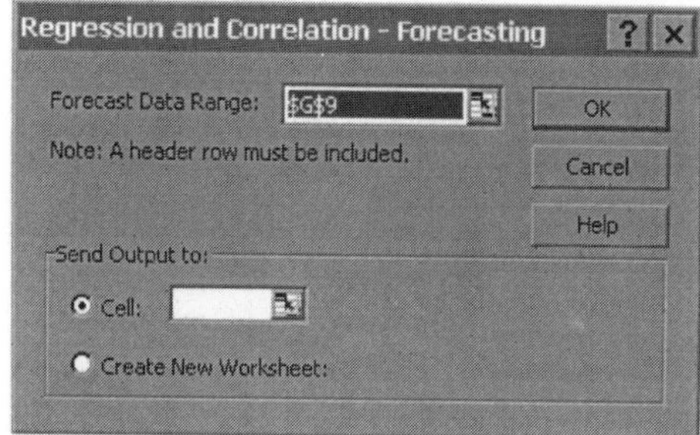

FIGURE 11.29 Forecasting dialog box

T	U	V	W
Regression and Correlation - Forecasting			
	Intercept	Members (m)	
Coefficient	0.7845	1.1439	
	Observations		Forecasted Value
	1	4.24	5.6347
	2	3.19	4.4336
	3	1.83	2.8778
	4	1.62	2.6376
	5	2.07	3.1524
	6	2.3	3.4155
	7	1.83	2.8778
	8	2.15	3.2439
	9	0.97	1.8941
	10	0.89	1.8026

FIGURE 11.30 Predictions for the values of the independent variable

CHAPTER 11 SUMMARY

Linear regression analysis is a powerful tool for determining how two variables are related. The regression equation can be used for *description, control,* and *prediction.* Description is important when the user is simply trying to understand the way that two variables are related. Control describes when the model is used to set standards or reduce variability. Prediction is when the model is used to determine what the resulting Y value should be when X takes on certain values. Although finding the simple linear model itself is not numerically difficult, performing a complete regression analysis requires the use of computer software to completely understand the model.

We have also seen that even though the simple linear model may be significant, it might not be correct. It is necessary to test the *assumptions* of the linear model to see whether the model you obtain is appropriate.

Key Terms

Term	Definition	Page Reference
Confidence interval	A **confidence interval** provides an estimate for the mean value of Y ($\mu_{y\|x}$) at a particular value of X.	544
Correlation coefficient	The **correlation coefficient** is used as a measure of the strength of a linear relationship. A correlation of −1 corresponds to a perfect negative relationship, a correlation of 0 corresponds to no relationship, and a correlation of +1 corresponds to a perfect positive relationship.	550
Deviation	The distance between the predicted value of Y, $\hat{y}$, and the actual value of Y, y, is called the **deviation** or error.	520

Key Terms (continued)

Term	Definition	Page Reference
Interpolation and extrapolation	Using the equation to predict values of Y within the range of the X data is called **interpolation.** Predicting values of Y for values of X outside the observed range is called **extrapolation.**	526
Least-squares method	The technique that finds the equation of the line that minimizes the total or sum of the squared deviations between the actual data points and the line is called the **least-squares method.**	520
Normal probability plot	A **normal probability plot** is a plot of the ordered against their expected values under a normal distribution. When data are normally distributed, the plot will be a straight line.	554
Prediction interval	A **prediction interval** gives an estimate for an individual value of Y at a particular value of X.	547
Residual (e_i)	The difference between the observed value of Y (y_i), and the predicted value of Y from the regression equation, ($\hat{y}_i$), for a value of $X = x_i$ is called the ith **residual,** e_i.	527
Simple linear regression model	The true relationship between the variables X and Y, the **simple linear regression model,** can be described by $y = \beta_0 + \beta_1 x + \varepsilon$	518
Standard error of the estimate ($s_{y\mid x}$)	The **standard error of the estimate,** $s_{y\mid x}$, is a measure of how much the data vary around the regression line.	530
Sums of squares	**SST:** the total variation in the y values around the mean $\bar{y}$. **SSR:** the variation in Y that is caused by Y's relationship with X. **SSE:** the variation in Y that remains unexplained.	539
$\hat{y}$ **(y hat)**	The value of y that we find is really a prediction of the mean value of Y for a given value of X.	525

Key Formulas

Term	Formula	Page Reference
b_1	$b_1 = \dfrac{n\sum_{i=1}^{n} x_i y_i - \sum_{i=1}^{n} x_i \sum_{i=1}^{n} y_i}{n\sum_{i=1}^{n} x_i^2 - \left(\sum_{i=1}^{n} x_i\right)^2}$ or $\dfrac{n\sum xy - \sum x \sum y}{n\sum x^2 - \left(\sum x\right)^2}$	521
b_0	$b_0 = \dfrac{\sum_{i=1}^{n} y_i}{n} - b_1 \dfrac{\sum_{i=1}^{n} x_i}{n}$ or $b_0 = \bar{y} - b_1\bar{x}$	521
Standard error of the estimate $s_{y\mid x}$	$s_{y\mid x} = \sqrt{\dfrac{\Sigma (y - \hat{y})^2}{n - 2}} = \sqrt{\dfrac{\Sigma e^2}{n - 2}}$	530
Standard error of the slope	$s_{b_1} = \dfrac{s_{y\mid x}}{\sqrt{\Sigma x^2 - (\Sigma x)^2/n}}$	536
Test statistic for slope	$t = \dfrac{b_1 - \beta_1}{s_{b_1}}$	536
Sums of squares	$\text{SST} = \Sigma(y - \bar{y})^2$ $\text{SSR} = \Sigma(\hat{y} - \bar{y})^2$ $\text{SSE} = \Sigma(y - \hat{y})^2$	540
Mean squares	$\text{MSR} = \dfrac{\text{SSR}}{1}$ and $\text{MSE} = \dfrac{\text{SSE}}{n - 2}$	540

Key Formulas (*continued*)

Term	Formula	Page Reference
Coefficient of determination, R^2	$R^2 = \frac{\text{SSR}}{\text{SST}} 100\%$	541
Confidence interval	$\hat{y}_i - t_{\alpha/2,n-2}\, s_{y\mid x}\sqrt{\frac{1}{n} + \frac{(x_i - \bar{x})^2}{\Sigma x^2 - (\Sigma x)^2/n}} \leq \mu_{y\mid x_i} \leq \hat{y}_i + t_{\alpha/2,n-2}\, s_{y\mid x}\sqrt{\frac{1}{n} + \frac{(x_i - \bar{x})^2}{\Sigma x^2 - (\Sigma x)^2/n}}$	544
Prediction interval	$\hat{y}_i - t_{\alpha/2,n-2}\, s_{y\mid x}\sqrt{1 + \frac{1}{n} + \frac{(x_i - \bar{x})^2}{\Sigma x^2 - (\Sigma x)^2/n}} \leq \mu_{y\mid x_i} \leq \hat{y}_i + t_{\alpha/2,n-2}\, s_{y\mid x}\sqrt{1 + \frac{1}{n} + \frac{(x_i - \bar{x})^2}{\Sigma x^2 - (\Sigma x)^2/n}}$	547
Correlation coefficient, r	$r = \frac{\Sigma xy - (\Sigma x)(\Sigma y)/n}{\sqrt{\Sigma x^2 - (\Sigma x)^2/n}\,\sqrt{\Sigma y^2 - (\Sigma y)^2/n}}$	550

CHAPTER 11 EXERCISES

Learning It!

11.23 How much does advertising impact market penetration? To assess the impact of advertising in the tobacco industry, a study looked at the amount of money spent on advertising a particular brand of cigarettes and brand preference among adolescents and adults. The data are shown here:

Brand	Advertising ($ million)	Brand Preference: Adolescent (%)	Brand Preference: Adult (%)
Marlboro	75	60	23.5
Camel	43	13.3	6.7
Newport	35	12.7	4.8
Kool	21	1.2	3.9
Winston	17	1.2	3.9
Benson & Hedges	4	1.0	3.0
Salem	3	0.3	2.5

SOURCE: *Centers for Disease Control Web site*

(a) Look at the data for brand preference for adolescents and amount spent on advertising. Which variable is the dependent variable? Which is the independent variable?

(b) Create a scatter plot of advertising and adolescent brand preference. Do you think that there is a linear relationship between the two variables? Why or why not?

(c) Now create another scatter plot using adult brand preference instead. How does this plot compare to the one for adolescent brand preference? From the plots, do you think that adolescent or adult brand preference is more strongly related to advertising expenditures? Why?

(d) Find the least-squares line for adolescent brand and advertising expenditures.

(e) Interpret the meaning of the slope and intercept for the model. Do they make sense?

(f) Use the model to predict adolescent brand preference for each brand studied. How well do the predicted values agree with the actual data?

(g) Using $\alpha = 0.05$, is the model significant?

11.24 Retention of students is one of the largest problems facing colleges and universities today. Loss of students impacts revenues not only from tuition but from state and federal funding programs. If a university can understand what factors impact student retention it can form strategic plans aimed at keeping students enrolled. Academic performance is often cited as one reason that students leave. Data were collected from 20 colleges in the Midwest on the freshman retention rate (% of freshmen who stay for a second year) and the 25th percentile score on the American College Testing (ACT) examination. (The ACT test is a college entrance examination similar to the Scholastic Assessment Test, SAT.) The data are given here:

Freshman Retention Rate	ACT 25th Percentile
0.84	22
0.82	22
0.86	22
0.88	23
0.83	23
0.87	21
0.87	22
0.85	25
0.84	22
0.85	23
0.84	21
0.81	22
0.81	22
0.83	21
0.75	20
0.86	20
0.79	20
0.82	20
0.81	18
0.77	21
0.80	22
0.78	21
0.73	18
0.75	18
0.73	20
0.78	18
0.77	24
0.73	21
0.78	19
0.72	21
0.77	21
0.74	19
0.72	21

(a) Which variable is the independent variable? Which is the dependent variable?

(b) Create a scatter plot of the data. Does it appear that freshman retention rate is related to the 25th percentile on the ACT exam?

(c) Find the equation of the regression line for the data.

(d) Plot the regression line on the same plot as the data. Do you think that the line does a good job of predicting freshman retention at a college or university? Why or why not?

(e) Calculate the standard error of the estimate, $s_{y|x}$, for the regression line.

(f) At the $\alpha = 0.05$ level, is the model significant?

11.25 The British Bankers' Association wanted to look at the relationship between the amount of deposits made (in billions of £) and the number of customers that a bank had. Analysts collected data on six different large banks and found the following information:

Bank Name	Deposits (£ billion)	Customers (million)
Abbey National	101.7	13.6
Barclays	108.2	10.0
Lloyds	96.9	15.0
National Westminster	113.8	7.5
Woolrich	27.5	4.0
Halifax	77.1	7.6

(a) Which variable is the independent variable? Which is the dependent variable?

(b) Create a scatter plot of the data. Does it appear that the amount of deposits is related to the number of customers?

(c) Find the equation of the regression line for the data.

(d) Plot the regression line on the same plot as the data. Do you think that the line does a good job of predicting the amount of deposits? Why or why not?

(e) Calculate the standard error of the estimate, $s_{y|x}$, for the regression line.

(f) At the 0.05 level, is the model significant?

11.26 An education task force looking at poverty levels in the United States has collected data for each state and the District of Columbia on the total number of people below the poverty level and the number of adults over the age of 25 who did not graduate from high school for the year 1993. The data are shown in the table:

Datafile: *POVERTY.XXX*

State	Number Not HS Graduates	Number (1000) Below Poverty Level
Alabama	922,624	609
Alaska	57,717	60
Arizona	845,022	812
Arkansas	588,886	377
California	6,500,643	5,118
Colorado	412,981	363
Connecticut	533,673	310
Delaware	110,053	80
District of Columbia	84,746	114
Florida	2,699,792	1,923
Georgia	1,528,441	1,034
Hawaii	183,722	131
Idaho	212,562	165
Illinois	1,903,162	1,234
Indiana	973,367	547
Iowa	352,081	257
Kansas	283,939	250
Kentucky	869,966	521
Louisiana	934,959	821
Maine	165,485	131
Maryland	785,626	359
Massachusetts	885,187	528
Michigan	1,433,317	1,099
Minnesota	500,894	498
Mississippi	624,725	486
Missouri	929,994	531
Montana	95,969	153
Nebraska	204,514	211
Nevada	190,412	195
New Hampshire	189,608	119
New Jersey	1,095,526	693
New Mexico	354,334	371
New York	3,362,431	3,068
North Carolina	1,403,648	1,039

(continued)

State	Number Not HS Graduates	Number (1000) Below Poverty Level
North Dakota	100,204	97
Ohio	1,546,910	1,253
Oklahoma	515,394	458
Oregon	475,886	503
Pennsylvania	1,908,231	1,338
Rhode Island	190,777	112
South Carolina	820,896	527
South Dakota	101,129	77
Tennessee	1,254,473	749
Texas	4,287,836	2,994
Utah	224,674	190
Vermont	78,587	58
Virginia	1,181,694	589
Washington	455,141	512
West Virginia	427,433	312
Wisconsin	626,820	449
Wyoming	48,091	51

(a) The task force would like to find a model that will predict the number of people living below the poverty level from the number of adults who are not high school graduates. Which is the dependent variable, and which is the independent variable?

(b) Create a scatter plot of the data. Do you think that a linear relationship exists between the two variables?

(c) Find the linear regression model for the data.

(d) Interpret the meaning of the slope and the y intercept of the model. Do you think that the y intercept makes sense for these data?

(e) Use the model to predict the number of people who are below the poverty level for the states of Wyoming, Connecticut, and North Carolina. What are the residuals for these three observations?

(f) At the 0.05 level of significance, is the model significant?

Thinking About It!

Requires Exercises 11.2, 11.17

11.27 The Commerce Department also has data available on number of shopping centers and retail sales for the South Central states. The data are given here:

State	Number of Shopping Centers	Retail Sales ($ billion)
Kentucky	616	13.9
Alabama	630	15.5
Tennessee	1,200	23.0
Arkansas	370	7.5
Mississippi	430	8.2
Louisiana	700	18.7
Oklahoma	568	13.2
Texas	2,976	87.3

SOURCE: *Statistical Abstract of the United States 1999*

(a) Find the linear regression model for the South Central states.

(b) How does the equation for the South Central states compare to the one you found for the North Central states?

(c) Would you have expected them to be exactly the same? Why or why not?

(d) What similarities would you expect them to have? What differences?

(e) Combine the data from the North Central and South Central states and find the linear regression model for the combined data.

(f) Do you think that the individual models are better or worse than the combined model? On what criteria do you base your conclusion?

11.28 Look at the data on advertising and brand preference for cigarettes again. *Requires Exercise 11.23*

(a) Find the simple linear regression model that relates adult brand preference to advertising expenditures.

(b) At the 0.05 level, is the model significant?

(c) What is R^2 for this model? What does it mean? What is the correlation coefficient?

(d) Compare the model for adult brand preference to the one you found for adolescent brand preference. Which variable do you think is more strongly related to advertising expenditures? Why?

(e) Do you think that these data help to support the claims against the tobacco industry that its advertising targeted teenagers? Why or why not?

11.29 Consider the model you developed relating poverty levels and education. *Requires Exercise 11.26*

(a) Find 95% confidence intervals for the mean number of people who live below the poverty level when the number of adults who are not high school graduates is (i) 500,000, (ii) 1,000,000, and (iii) 2,000,000.

(b) Find 95% prediction intervals for the number of people who live below the poverty level when the number of adults who are not high school graduates is (i) 500,000, (ii) 1,000,000, and (iii) 2,000,000.

(c) Do you think that the model is useful for predicting the number of people below the poverty level? Why or why not?

(d) The task force contends that if it can institute programs to reduce the number of adults who have not finished high school by 10% in each state, it will have a significant impact on the number of people who are living below the poverty level. Do you agree or disagree with this statement? Why?

11.30 Consider the data on the British banks. *Requires Exercise 11.25*

(a) What is R^2 for this model? What does it mean? What is the correlation coefficient?

(b) Find 95% confidence intervals for the mean amount of deposits when the number of customers is (i) 12 million, (ii) 15 million, and (iii) 7 million.

(c) Find 95% prediction intervals for the amount of deposits when the number of customers is (i) 12 million, (ii) 15 million, and (iii) 7 million.

(d) Do you think that the model is useful for predicting the amount of deposits? Why or why not?

11.31 The British Bankers' Association decided to look at another variable to predict deposits. It chose the number of branches for each bank. The data are given here: *Requires Exercises 11.25, 11.30*

Bank Name	Deposits (£ billion)	Branches 1996
Abbey National	101.7	867
Barclays	108.2	1997
Lloyds	96.9	2797
National Westminster	113.8	1920
Woolrich	27.5	430
Halifax	77.1	938

(a) Find the simple linear regression model that relates deposits to number of branches.

(b) At the 0.05 level, is the model significant?

(c) What is R^2 for this model? What does it mean? What is the correlation coefficient?

(d) Compare the model for predicting deposits using the number of branches to the one you found for number of customers. Which variable do you think is more strongly related to deposits? Why?

Requires Exercises 11.23, 11.28

11.32 Look at the model that you developed for adolescent brand preference for cigarettes and the amount of money spent on advertising.

(a) Make a plot of the residuals versus the values of the independent variables.

(b) What does this lead you to believe about the appropriateness of the linear model?

(c) Now plot the residuals versus the predicted values of y.

(d) How do the two graphs compare? Why do you think this happened?

(e) Make a normal probability plot of the data. Do you think the assumption of normality is reasonable?

(f) Considering your answers to parts (a)–(e), do you think that the linear regression model is appropriate for these data? Why or why not?

Requires Exercises 11.17, 11.27

11.33 Look at the model you developed for shopping centers and retail sales for the South Central states.

(a) Make a plot of the residuals versus the values of the independent variables.

(b) What does this lead you to believe about the appropriateness of the linear model?

(c) Now plot the residuals versus the predicted values of y.

(d) How do the two graphs compare? Why do you think this happened?

(e) Make a normal probability plot of the data. Do you think the assumption of normality is reasonable?

(f) Considering your answers to parts (a)–(e), do you think that the linear regression model is appropriate for these data? Why or why not?

Requires Exercises 11.26, 11.29

11.34 Consider the model that you developed for poverty levels and education.

(a) Make a plot of the residuals versus the values of the independent variables.

(b) What does this lead you to believe about the appropriateness of the linear model?

(c) Now plot the residuals versus the predicted values of y.

(d) How do the two graphs compare? Why do you think this happened?

(e) Make a normal probability plot of the data. Do you think the assumption of normality is reasonable?

(f) Considering your answers to parts (a)–(e), do you think that the linear regression model is appropriate for these data? Why or why not?

Doing It!

Datafile: *FACULTY.XXX*

11.35 The Provost at Aluacha Balaclava College wants to look at the faculty salary data in some other ways. She has collected data on salary, years of service, rank, school, gender, and tenure. A sample of the data is shown here:

Salary ($)	Years of Service	Rank	Schools	Gender M/F	Tenure Y/N
53,316	22	ASST	BUSINESS	F	Y
64,375	11	PROF	BUSINESS	M	Y
63,501	7	ASSO	BUSINESS	M	Y
59,426	6	ASSO	BUSINESS	M	N
49,058	20	ASSO	BUSINESS	M	Y
94,969	4	PROF	BUSINESS	M	N
54,762	21	ASST	BUSINESS	M	Y
55,516	9	ASSO	BUSINESS	M	Y

(a) Make scatter plots of salary versus years of service for the entire faculty. Do you think that there is a linear relationship between the two variables? Why or why not?

(b) Find the simple linear regression model with salary as the dependent variable and years of service as the independent variable.

(c) At the 0.05 level, is there a significant linear relationship between salary and years of service?

(d) What is the value of R^2 for this model? What does it mean?

(e) Separate the data by rank and create scatter plots of salary versus years of service for each rank. How do these plots compare to the one for all of the faculty?

(f) Find a simple linear regression model for salary versus years of service for each rank. How do the regression coefficients for each rank compare to each other? How do they compare to the overall model for all of the faculty?

(g) At the 0.05 level of significance, are any of the models significant?

(h) What are the R^2 values for each of the models?

(i) Calculate the residuals for all significant models. Create a plot of residuals versus predicted values for each model. Is the simple linear model appropriate for these data? Why or why not?

(j) For each significant model, investigate the assumption of normality. Do you think the assumption is valid for these data? Why or why not?

(k) Are there any data values that might be exerting a strong influence on the model? If so, which ones? Drop any unusual values from the data and rerun the models. How does this change the results?

(l) Perform any additional analyses that you feel would be helpful to determine whether the simple linear model is an appropriate one for these data.

(m) Write a report with your conclusions.

CHAPTER 12

MULTIPLE REGRESSION MODELS

WHERE SHOULD WE LIVE?

One of the problems that face city planners and real estate developers is the price of homes in an area. What factors influence the prices of homes? On a microlevel, real estate developers can look at factors directly related to the individual dwelling, such as square footage, number of bedrooms, and number of bathrooms. For large-scale planning purposes, a micromodel is not appropriate. Many other global factors affect the price of a home, such as location, school systems, and access to public transportation.

The cities of Dallas and Fort Worth, Texas, wanted to look at the various "commuter" suburbs of the city that have grown up over the years and find a model that would enable them to understand what factors play a role in the prices of homes in these areas. They decided to look at 41 different communities regarded as "commuter" suburbs of Dallas/Fort Worth, and collected data on five different variables that they thought would impact the average selling price of a home. The variables that they looked at were average household income, total instructional expenditures, mean SAT scores, population diversity, and the violent crime rate. A portion of the data is shown here:

Suburb	1994 Avg.Value of Home Sold	Avg. Household Income	Total Instructional Expenditures per Pupil	Mean SAT Score	Population Diversity (% nonwhite)	1993/94 Violent Crime (per 1000)
Addison	$204,800	$49,803	$2,600	980	32.40%	4.5
Allen	$99,000	$60,031	$2,185	955	9.30%	1.9
Arlington	$97,613	$50,188	$2,154	929	14.70%	8.3
Balch Springs	$48,300	$37,111	$1,947	935	24.00%	14.6
Bedford	$173,073	$58,982	$2,473	951	10.10%	2.3
Carrollton	$108,700	$58,551	$2,600	980	22.10%	2.5
Cedar Hill	$84,500	$55,768	$2,174	901	24.10%	1.1
Cockrell Hill	$58,200	$30,434	$2,714	775	70.10%	8.3
Colleyville	$235,427	$121,962	$2,471	952	4.90%	0.4
Coppell	$149,500	$78,917	$2,472	925	13.80%	0.5
Desoto	$109,300	$62,575	$2,306	885	27.20%	3.1

They wanted to find a model that would explain the average value of homes in a location based on these variables. They felt that this model would help them make decisions about current as well as future communities.

12.1 Chapter Objectives

The purposes of regression models are to *predict,* to *explain,* and to *control.* Many real-world phenomena are too complex for the simple linear model that we looked at in Chapter 11. Some variables that we are interested in depend on *more than one* independent variable. When this is the case, we use *multiple regression models* to describe the relationship between the independent variable, Y, and the set of dependent variables, $X_1, X_2, \ldots, X_k$.

In this chapter you will learn how to

- find the regression equation for a dependent variable Y as a function of a set of independent variables, $X_1, X_2, \ldots, X_k$.
- determine whether the relationship is significant
- determine which variables contribute to the model and which do not
- analyze the results of a regression analysis to determine whether the model is appropriate

12.2 THE MULTIPLE REGRESSION MODEL

12.2.1 A Description of the Multiple Regression Model

When two quantitative variables are related in a linear manner, we can use a simple linear regression model to describe the relationship. We saw that, in many cases, the simple linear model does a good job of predicting or describing the way one variable behaves relative to another. In some cases, though, the simple linear model was not appropriate because the relationship between the variables was not linear, or because one or more of the assumptions of the simple linear model was violated. In other cases, the simple linear model may have been appropriate and even statistically significant, but the results might not have been *useful* for the purposes of making decisions.

One of the quantities that we looked at in simple linear regression was the value of R^2, the coefficient of determination. You remember that R^2 is a measure of the amount of variation in the dependent variable, Y, that can be explained by the linear model involving the independent variable X. Sometimes even when a linear model is significant, the independent variable, X, does not do a good enough job of explaining how Y behaves. One possible solution to this problem is to find another, better, independent variable to work with, but there may not be a single variable that will do the job. Another solution, the one we will look at in this chapter, is to find a *set* of independent variables, known as **input variables,** that together provide a good model for predicting the dependent variable known as the **output variable.**

> The dependent variable, Y, is often referred to as the ***output variable,*** whereas the independent variables $X_1, X_2, \ldots, X_k$ are referred to as the ***input variables.***

Models that describe this type of relationship are known as **multiple regression models.**

> The true relationship between the independent variable Y and the set of independent variables, $X_1, X_2, \ldots, X_k$, the ***multiple regression model,*** can be described by the equation
>
> $$y = \beta_0 + \beta_1 x_1 + \beta_2 x_2 + \cdots + \beta_k x_k + \varepsilon$$

This equation says that the actual value of the variable Y will be determined by the equation $\beta_0 + \beta_1 x_1 + \beta_2 x_2 + \cdots + \beta_k x_k$, plus some random variation, ε, due to other, unmeasured, factors.

The coefficients $\beta_1, \beta_2, \ldots, \beta_k$ are similar to the slope coefficient β_1 in the simple linear model, $y = \beta_0 + \beta_1 x_1 + \varepsilon$, with just a small difference. In the simple linear model, β_1 represents the slope of the line, or the change in the dependent variable, Y, for a unit change in the independent variable, X. In the multiple regression model, the parameters $\beta_1, \beta_2, \ldots, \beta_k$ are really not the slope, because we are not talking about a line, but they have a similar interpretation. Each of the β_i coefficients represents the change that will occur in the independent variable, Y, if the variable associated with the coefficient of interest, X_i, is changed by one unit *and all other variables in the model are held constant.* In the case of only two independent variables, the multiple regression equation has a physical interpretation: The equation is the *plane* that describes the relationship, similar to the line in the one-variable model.

12.2.2 The Least-Squares Multiple Regression Model

Our objective in the multiple regression model is to find the estimates for the population values $\beta_1, \beta_2, \ldots, \beta_k$ that do the "best" job of describing the real relationship between Y and the set of X variables that we have chosen.

You remember that, in the simple linear model, we used the method of least squares to find the equation of the line that minimized the sum of the squared differences between the actual values of Y and the values predicted by the model. In the simple linear model you were given equations to find the values of b_0 and b_1, although you found out that, except for finding the equation of the model, most of the analysis in simple linear regression is best done using an appropriate computer software package, such as Minitab or Excel.

Least squares can also be extended to models with more than one independent variable. That is, we want to find the equation

$$\hat{y} = b_0 + b_1x_1 + b_2x_2 + \cdots + b_kx_k$$

that minimizes the total squared deviation between the actual data and the values obtained from the regression model. Remember that $\hat{y}$ is the value of the dependent variable as predicted by the model *for a specific set of values of the independent variables*, $X_1 = x_1$, $X_2 = x_2, \ldots, X_k = x_k$. Finding the values of $b_0, b_1, b_2, \ldots, b_k$ involves solving a system of k simultaneous equations and is entirely too tedious to do by hand. For such an analysis, an appropriate software package is essential for finding the regression model.

EXAMPLE 12.1 Texas Real Estate

Understand the Problem

Finding the Multiple Regression Model

The city planners that are looking at the prices of homes in the suburbs of Dallas/Fort Worth, Texas, are trying to find the relationship between the average price of a home (Y) and a set of five independent variables, *average household income* (X_1), *total instructional expenditures* (X_2), *mean SAT scores* (X_3), *population diversity* (*% nonwhite*) (X_4), and the *violent crime rate* (per 1000) (X_5). Their equation will be

$$\hat{y} = b_0 + b_1x_1 + b_2x_2 + b_3x_3 + b_4x_4 + b_5x_5$$

The analysts use Minitab to find the equation of the multiple regression model that best fits the data. The results follow.

Analyze the Data

```
Regression Analysis

The regression equation is
1994 Avg. Value _of Home Sold = - 140352 + 1.64 Avg. Household Income
     + 39.2 Total Instructional Expenditure + 90 Mean SAT Score
     - 47820 Diversity - 1132 1993/94 Avg. Violent Crime
```

The computer output gives the values of the coefficients as $b_0 = -140{,}352$, $b_1 = 1.64$, $b_2 = 39.2$, $b_3 = 90$, $b_4 = -47{,}820$, and $b_5 = -1132$.

The analysts interpret the coefficients as the change in the average selling price of a home in dollars for a unit change in each of the variables. That is, if the average household income in a location increases by one dollar, the average selling price of a home in that location will increase by \$1.64, *as long as all other variables remain constant.* Similarly, if the mean SAT score increases by one point, the average price of a home will increase by \$90. Again, this assumes that nothing else in the model has changed.

Draw Conclusions

From the coefficients the analysts see that for the most part the model makes sense. That is, as income, total educational expenditures, and SAT scores go up, so do the selling prices of homes. Similarly, as the violent crime rate increases, the price of the homes goes down. The analysts are not pleased about the coefficient of X_4, but they know that it reflects a reality. ■

The output from statistical software for multiple regression models is almost identical to the output for the simple linear model. Figure 12.1 on the facing page shows the output from Excel and Minitab. The section of the output that contains the coefficients of the multiple regression model is highlighted.

You see that the basic sections of the output are the same, general information about the model, information about the coefficients, and the ANOVA information. We will look at the output in more detail as the chapter progresses.

EXAMPLE 12.2 Phillips Petroleum

Finding the Regression Model

Understand the Problem

Financial analysts would like to understand the relationship among common stockholders' equity ($/share), total revenue (billions of dollars), and total assets (billions of dollars). Data on these variables for Phillips Petroleum from 1986 to 1996 are shown in the table:

Collect the Data

Year	Equity, Y	Revenue, X_1	Assets, X_2
1986	7.55	10.018	9.186
1987	7.08	10.917	8.772
1988	8.69	11.490	8.417
1989	8.74	12.492	7.832
1990	10.51	13.975	8.301
1991	10.61	13.259	8.298
1992	10.37	12.140	8.489
1993	10.28	12.545	7.961
1994	11.29	12.367	8.042
1995	12.16	13.521	8.493
1996	16.15	15.807	9.120

The analysts decide to use a multiple regression model to find a model with equity as the dependent variable and revenue and assets as the independent variables. A portion of the computer output for their analysis follows.

Analyze the Data

SUMMARY OUTPUT

Regression Statistics	
Multiple R	0.923228385
R Square	0.852350651
Adjusted R Square	0.815438314
Standard Error	1.067662859
Observation	11

ANOVA

	df	*SS*	*MS*	*F*	*Significance F*
Regression	2	52.64353179	26.32176589	23.09121324	0.000475254
Residual	8	9.119231848	1.139903981		
Total	10	61.76276364			

	Coefficients	*Standard Error*	*tStat*	*P-value*	*Lower 95%*
Intercept	−16.71847039	7.179010344	−2.328798761	0.048252087	−33.27330864
Revenue	1.452643014	0.216118353	6.721516208	0.00014936	0.954272876
Assets	1.034291795	0.769247372	1.344550312	0.215646057	−0.739596974

Excel output for Example 12.2

SUMMARY OUTPUT

Regression Statistics	
Multiple R	0.866778185
R Square	0.751304423
Adjusted R Square	0.715776483
Standard Error	37957.7302
Observation	41

ANOVA

	df	*SS*	*MS*	*F*	*Significance F*
Regression	5	1.52341E+11	30468171569	21.14686162	1.08463E-09
Residual	35	50427624859	1440789282		
Total	40	2.02768E+11			

	Coefficients	*StandardError*	*tStat*	*P-value*	*Lower 95%*	*Upper 95%*	*Lower 95.0%*
Intercept	−140351.6689	112957.8302	−1.242513853	0.222307657	−369668.5358	88965.198	−369668.5358
Avg. Household Income	1.637671454	0.312118144	5.246960128	7.59702E-06	1.004037162	2.271305746	1.004037162
Total Instructional Expenditures per pupil	39.15871129	21.78140875	1.797804345	0.080839566	−5.059953319	83.3773759	−5.059953319
Mean SAT	89.63285763	113.8778516	0.787096493	0.436523067	−141.5517541	320.8174694	−141.5517541
Population Diversity (% non-white)	−47820.09741	62143.05497	−0.769516359	0.446749366	−173977.3601	78337.1653	−173977.3601
1993/94 Avg. Violent Crime (per 100)	−1132.378569	2146.787097	−0.527475952	0.601191161	−5490.5934	3225.836262	−5490.5934

Excel

Note: The software packages do not highlight these areas.

```
Regression Analysis

The regression equation is
1994 Avg. Value _of Home Sold = - 140352 + 1.64 Avg. Household_ Income
          + 39.2 Total Instructional_ Expenditur + 90 Mean SAT_ Score
          - 47820 Population Diversity_ (% non-white
          - 1132 1993/94 Avg. Violent _Crime (per 1000)

Predictor       Coef        StDev          T        P
Constant     -140352       112958      -1.24    0.222
Avg. Hou      1.6377       0.3121       5.25    0.000
Total In       39.16        21.78       1.80    0.081
Mean SAT        89.6        113.9       0.79    0.437
Populati      -47820        62143      -0.77    0.447
1993/94        -1132         2147      -0.53    0.601

S = 37958       R-Sq = 75.1%       R-Sq(adj) = 71.6%

Analysis of Variance

Source        DF           SS           MS          F        P
Regression     5  1.52341E+11  30468171569      21.15    0.000
Error         35  50427624859   1440789282
Total         40  2.02768E+11

Source        DF       Seq SS
Avg. Hou       1  1.46103E+11
Total In       1   3261836377
Mean SAT       1   1202680560
Populati       1   1372121063
1993/94        1    400872070

Unusual Observations
Obs  Avg. Hou   1994 Avg       Fit  StDev Fit   Residual   St Resid
  1     49803     204800    110273      13150      94527      2.65R
  8     30434      58200     42311      28127      15889      0.62 X
 21    196697     361100    397689      30411     -36589     -1.61 X
 38     84007     269926    178710       9319      91216      2.48R
 39     87854     269926    178242      13518      91684      2.58R
```

Minitab

FIGURE 12.1 Computer output from Excel and Minitab

The model is $\hat{y} = -16.72 + 1.45x_1 + 1.03x_2$.

Draw Conclusions

From this model, they see that an increase in revenue of 1 billion dollars will increase equity by $1.45/share for a fixed value of assets, whereas an increase in assets of 1 billion dollars will increase equity by $1.03/share for a fixed revenue. The constant for the model is −16.72, which indicates that with revenue and assets equal to zero, shareholder equity is −16.72 billion dollars. This does not make much sense, but it would be extrapolating anyway. ■

TRY IT NOW!

Order Filling *Finding the Multiple Regression Model*

A mail-order catalog company is looking at the time it takes to prepare an order for shipping. In particular, the company is looking for the amount of time that is spent collecting the items ordered and packing them. In this operation, an employee (a checker) is given an order to fill. Items are located in bins in one of six different sections of the warehouse. The checkers move around the warehouse retrieving the items and packing them into the shipping cartons. The company has looked at the operation in some detail and believes that three major variables are involved in the process: the number of items ordered, the number of different locations (sections of the warehouse) in which the items are located, and the experience level (in months) of the checker. Data are collected on 45 orders. A portion of the data is shown here:

Time (min)	Items	Locations	Experience (months)
9.3	1	6	8
4.4	1	3	13
4.4	5	2	3
5.6	3	3	5
4.9	11	1	4
8.8	14	3	5

The company wants to know how the time it takes to fill an order is related to the other three variables, so it decides to use a multiple regression model. The output from the computer software is given here.

SUMMARY OUTPUT

Regression Statistics	
Multiple R	0.915838993
R Square	0.838761061
Adjusted R Square	0.82696309
Standard Error	1.021396967
Observations	45

ANOVA

	df	*SS*	*MS*	*F*	*Significance F*
Regression	3	222.5057888	74.16859627	71.09366969	2.71039E-16
Residual	41	42.7733223	1.043251763		
Total	44	265.2791111			

	Coefficients	*Standard Error*	*tStat*	*P-value*	*Lower 95%*
Intercept	0.215224599	0.55856837	0.385314691	0.701996141	−0.912827729
Number of Items	0.281391801	0.029191616	9.639473395	4.26275E-12	0.222438105
Locations	1.259340956	0.103175681	12.20579253	3.10059E-15	1.050973327
Experience	0.019087782	0.047667374	0.400437032	0.690913642	−0.0077178487

Write down the equation of the regression model.

Interpret the value of each of the coefficients of the model.

12.2.3 Using the Multiple Regression Model for Prediction

Just as in the case with the simple linear model, the multiple regression equation can be used to predict the value of the dependent variable for a specific set of values of the independent variables. We must ask the same question: How useful are these predictions?

You remember from the simple linear model that one way to determine the usefulness of a model is to look at the *residuals*, the differences between the actual values of the dependent variable and the values predicted by the model for a specific set of input variables. The value of the residual for the ith observation is

$$e_i = y_i - \hat{y}_i$$

The size of the residual gives a measure of how good a particular model is at predicting the value of the dependent variable.

EXAMPLE 12.3 Texas Real Estate

Using the Model to Make Predictions

The group looking at average selling prices of homes in Dallas/Fort Worth suburbs decides to use the model to predict the selling price for two of the communities in the data set to see how well the values predicted by the model agree with the data. To decide which locations to pick, the analysts make a boxplot of the data, as shown at the top of page 582.

ANS. $\hat{y} = 0.21 + 0.28x_1 + 1.26x_2 + 0.02x_3$; ASSUMING THAT ALL OTHER FACTORS REMAIN CONSTANT, IF YOU INCREASE THE NUMBER OF ITEMS BY 1 THEN THE TIME INCREASES BY 0.28 MINUTE; IF YOU INCREASE THE NUMBER OF LOCATIONS, THEN THE TIME INCREASES BY 1.26 MINUTES; AND IF YOU INCREASE EXPERIENCE BY 1 MONTH, THEN THE TIME INCREASES BY 0.02 MINUTE.

Analyze the Data

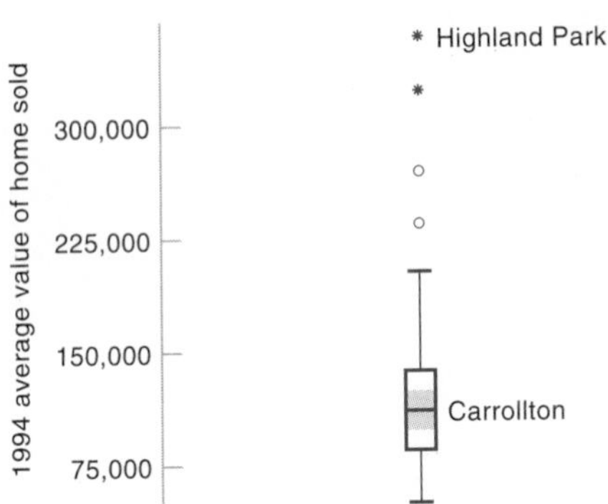

After looking at the boxplot, they decide to look at Highland Park because it appears to be an outlier and Carrollton because it is at the center of the data. Using the regression model

$$\begin{aligned}\text{1994 avg. value of home sold} = & -140{,}352 + 1.64 \text{ avg. household income} \\ & + 39.2 \text{ total instructional expenditure} \\ & + 90 \text{ mean SAT score} \\ & - 47{,}820 \text{ population diversity} \\ & - 1132 \text{ 1993/94 avg. violent crime}\end{aligned}$$

for Carrollton they calculate

$$\begin{aligned}\hat{y} &= -140{,}352 + 1.64(58{,}551) + 39.2(2600) + 90(980) - 47{,}820(0.221) - 1132(2.5) \\ &= \$132{,}393\end{aligned}$$

and for Highland Park

$$\begin{aligned}\hat{y} &= -140{,}352 + 1.64(196{,}697) + 39.2(3159) + 90(1070) - 47{,}820(0.037) - 1132(1.7) \\ &= \$398{,}670\end{aligned}$$

They compare this to the actual data of \$361,100 for Highland Park and \$108,700 for Carrollton and find the actual deviations to be

Carrollton:	\$108,700 − \$132,393 = − \$23,693	% error = (\$23,693/\$108,700)(100) = 21.8%
Highland Park:	\$361,100 − \$398,670 = − \$37,570	% error = (\$37,570/\$361,100)(100) = 10.4%

They observe that whereas the actual deviation is larger for Highland Park, the percent error is larger for Carrollton. ■

As you saw in the previous example, it is not difficult to use the multiple regression model to predict the values of the independent variable. However, as models become more complex, it can get tedious. In fact, if you want to compare the predicted and actual values for every observation in the sample, it will certainly be time-consuming. For this reason, almost all software used for regression analysis allows you to find predicted values of Y, either for all of the actual sets of X data or for some specific data of interest as well as the residuals.

EXAMPLE 12.4 Phillips Petroleum

Using the Model for Prediction

The people looking at a model to predict equity using revenue and assets wonder how well the multiple regression model does the job. They analyze the data, and as part of the output, they have the software calculate, for each set of input data, the predicted equity and the residual. A portion of the output is shown here:

Residual Output

Observation	Predicted Equity	Residuals
1	7.335111748	0.214888252
2	8.212841015	−1.132841015
3	8.678031875	0.011968125
4	9.528519475	0.788519475
5	12.16787192	−1.657871917
6	11.12467664	−0.514676643
7	9.696718843	0.673281157
8	9.738933196	0.541066804
9	9.564140375	1.725859625
10	11.70695601	0.453043987
11	15.6761989	0.473801102

Analyze the Data

They see that the largest deviation is about \$1.73/share, whereas the smallest is \$0.01/share. ■

Another way to look at how good a job the model does at predicting the values of the independent variable is to create a scatter plot of the predicted values. If the model is a perfect fit then you would expect the predicted values to be equal to the actual data, that is, $\hat{y} = y$. If you plot the predicted values versus the actual values, the results should form a straight line that intercepts the origin if the fit is good.

EXAMPLE 12.5 Phillips Petroleum

Plotting the Predicted versus the Actual Values

The analysts in the group looking at predicting equity want to look at how well the model predicts equity graphically. They decide to plot the predicted values ($\hat{y}$'s) versus the actual values (y's). They also plot the line $\hat{y} = y$ on the plot for reference. They see that the points fall very close to the line. It appears that the model provides a good fit.

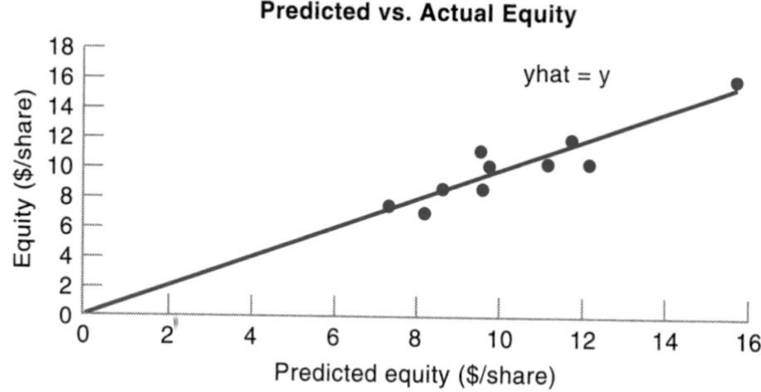

■

Order Filling *Finding Predicted Values*

The mail-order catalog company that is looking at the time it takes to prepare an order for shipping wants to see how well the model it has found predicts the time to fill an order. The data for six of the observations are here:

Time (min)	Items	Locations	Experience (months)
9.3	6	1	8
4.4	3	1	13
4.4	5	2	3

(continued)

Time (min)	Items	Locations	Experience (months)
5.6	3	3	5
4.9	11	1	4
8.8	14	3	5

Use the model to find the predicted time to fill an order for each of the six sets of input data you have.

Compare the predicted results to the actual data. Do you think that this model does a good job of predicting the time to fill an order? Why or why not?

12.2.4 Exercises—Learning It!

Datafile: TRAFFAT.XXX

12.1 A group of legislators wanted to look at factors that affect the number of traffic fatalities. They collected some data for 1994 from the National Transportation Safety Board on the number of fatalities for 50 states and the District of Columbia (DC), the number of licensed drivers, the number of registered vehicles, and the number of vehicle miles traveled. A portion of the data is shown here:

State	Fatalities	Population	Licensed Drivers, X_1 (thousands)	Registered Vehicles X_2 (thousands)	Vehicle Miles X_3 (millions)
AL	1083	4,219	3,043	3,422	48,956
AK	85	606	443	508	4,150
AZ	903	4,075	2,654	2,980	38,774
AR	610	2,453	1,770	1,560	24,948
CA	4226	31,431	20,359	23,518	271,943
CO	585	3,656	2,620	3,144	33,705

SOURCE: *Statistical Abstract of the United States 1996*

As you can see from the data table, they also had information on population for each state, but they did not think that it would prove useful. They decided to find a multiple regression model that predicts the number of fatalities using the other variables as the set of independent variables. The output from the computer software is shown here:

ANS. 8.2, 4.5, 4.2, 4.9, 4.6, 8.0

SINCE THE LARGEST RESIDUAL IS JUST ABOUT ONE MINUTE, THE MODEL APPEARS TO DO A GOOD JOB.

SUMMARY OUTPUT

Regression Statistics	
Multiple R	0.982548538
R Square	0.96540163
Adjusted R Square	0.963193224
Standard Error	154.5407481
Observations	51

ANOVA

	df	*SS*	*MS*	*F*	*Significance F*
Regression	3	31321046.9	10440348.97	437.1485021	2.54274E-34
Residual	47	1122493.613	23882.84282		
Total	50	32443540.51			

	Coefficients	*Standard Error*	*tStat*	*P-value*	*Lower 95%*
Intercept	51.7481659	30.43306219	1.700392999	0.095666076	−9.475200509
X Variable 1	0.06294764	0.048829545	1.289130172	0.20366155	−0.035284642
X Variable 2	−0.211896991	0.055989427	−3.784589385	0.000435566	−0.324533083
X Variable 3	0.029349954	0.003525079	8.326041167	8.34285E-11	0.022258416

(a) How many independent variables are there in the model proposed? What are they?

(b) Use the computer output to write down the regression model.

(c) Interpret the coefficients of the model.

(d) Use the model to predict the number of traffic fatalities for the states shown in the data table.

(e) Compare the predicted values from the model to the actual values. Based on the plot, does the model do a good job of predicting the number of traffic fatalities?

12.2 In a study on mandatory seat-belt laws, a group of lobbyists wanted to determine whether there was a relationship among the percentage of motorists who comply with the law, the size of the fine for violation of the law, and the amount of time that the law has been in effect. They decided to look at data on 48 locations with mandatory seat-belt laws. A portion of the data that they had available is shown here:

Datafile: SEATBELT.XXX

State	Percent Compliance	Fine	Years in Effect
AL	55	25	5.0
AK	69	15	6.8
AZ	60	10	6.5
AR	51	30	6.0
CA	83	20	11.5
CO	54	15	10.0

Note. ME and NH do not have mandatory seat-belt laws. Data not available for Wyoming.
SOURCE: Bureau of Transportation

(a) Which variable do you think is the dependent variable and which are the independent variables? Why?

(b) The output from a multiple regression model is shown here. Does this model agree with your answer to part (a)?

```
Regression Analysis

The regression equation
Percent Compliance = 0.416 + 0.00187 Fine + 0.0194 Years In Effect

47 cases used 4 cases contain missing values

Predictor       Coef        StDev       T       P
Constant     0.41558      0.05153    8.06   0.000
Fine        0.001874     0.001050    1.78   0.081
Years In    0.019397     0.004672    4.15   0.000
```

(continued)

```
S = 0.09682        R-Sq = 30.8%        R-Sq(adj) = 27.7%

Analysis of Variance

Source        DF          SS          MS        F        P
Regression     2    0.183552    0.091776     9.79    0.000
Error         44    0.412431    0.009373
Total         46    0.595983

Source        DF      Seq SS
Fine           1    0.021952
Years In       1    0.161600
```

(c) Interpret the values of the coefficients in the model.

(d) Use the model to predict the percent compliance with the law for the six states shown in the data table.

(e) Make a plot of the values of $\hat{y}$ versus y for these states.

(f) From the plot, do you think that the model does a good job of predicting compliance with seat-belt laws? Why or why not?

Datafile:
CRIME.XXX

12.3 A committee studying the issue of crime in large cities wanted to know whether it was possible to find a relationship between the number of serious crimes in the city and several other crime/sociological variables. The committee members decided to focus their study on the number of police officers in the city, the percentage of arrested males who tested positive for drugs, the number of families in the city below the poverty level, the number of people between 16 and 19 who were not enrolled in school and were not high school graduates, and the number of single female parent households. They were focusing on 23 large cities, but all of the data were not available for all of the cities in the study. A portion of the latest data is shown here:

City	Police Officers	Nonenrolled/ Not Grad	Familes Below Poverty Level	Serious Crimes	Single Female Parent Households	Male Arrests Drugs (%)
Atlanta, GA	1,533	3,247	21,686	76,398	36,577	69
Birmingham, AL	724	1,891	14,075	33,895	22,391	64
Chicago, IL	12,132	27,838	116,645	NA	197,631	69
Cleveland, OH	1,682	5,262	31,340	45,610	45,455	64
Dallas, TX	2,857	10,702	35,085	154,929	54,434	59
Denver, CO	1,361	3,312	14,417	36,558	24,215	60
Detroit, MI	3,954	13,455	71,673	127,080	113,553	58
Fort Lauderdale, FL	463	1,212	4,545	24,334	7,346	64

SOURCE: *County and City Data Book 1994*

(a) Which variable is the dependent variable? Which are the independent variables?

(b) Look at the set of input variables. Do you think that it is reasonable that there is a relationship between the number of serious crimes in a city and these variables? Why or why not? Can you think of other variables that the committee should consider?

(c) Use a computer software package to find the multiple regression model for the data. Interpret the coefficients in the model.

(d) Use the software package to find the predicted value of the number of serious crimes for each of the cities in the study and calculate the residuals. Which city has the best fit? Which has the worst?

(e) Use the model to predict the number of serious crimes for the three cities that were missing those data. How do these predictions fit into the overall data set?

(f) Make a plot of the predicted versus actual data. Overall, how well do you think the model predicts the number of serious crimes in a city?

Datafile:
INTERNET.XXX

12.4 A survey done by a local Internet provider in a medium-size city focused on the amount of time per week that the computer was used for Internet access. Analysts surveyed 35 households and collected data on the number of hours of Internet use per week, the number of computers in the household, the number of children in the household, household income, and the education level of the head of the household (in years of education).

(a) Decide which variable in this study is the dependent variable and which are the independent variables.

(b) Which two independent variables do you think are most likely related to the number of hours of Internet use per week?

(c) Use a computer software package to find the model that predicts hours of use using the two variables that you identified in part (b). Interpret the coefficients of the model.

(d) Use the computer software to find predicted values and residuals for each of the 35 households in the survey. Make a plot of the predicted values versus the actual data.

(e) Based on the plot do you think that the model you found does a good job of predicting the number of hours of Internet use per week? Why or why not?

12.3 ASSESSING THE MULTIPLE REGRESSION MODEL

In the previous section you learned about the multiple regression model and what it means. In addition to finding the multiple regression model you did some investigation of the *quality* of the model. This investigation, looking at the size of the residuals, was subjective in that there was no formal statistical test attached to it. In this section we look at formal, *statistical* methods for assessing the multiple regression model we obtain.

12.3.1 Testing the Significance of the Model

Once we have the regression equation, we would like to know whether that relationship is *statistically significant.* That is, we want to know whether the model, defined by the set of input or independent variables, does a good job of explaining or accounting for the variation in the output or dependent variable.

In the simple linear model, you learned two ways to test the significance of the model. The t test tested whether the slope coefficient, β_1, was nonzero. If β_1 is not zero, then there is a significant relationship between the dependent and independent variables. The F test, the ANOVA test, tested whether the amount of variation in the dependent variable that was explained by the linear model was larger than the amount left unexplained. In multiple regression analysis we test the significance of the *model as a whole.* The hypotheses are

$$H_0:\ \beta_1 = \beta_2 = \cdots = \beta_k = 0$$
$$H_A:\ \text{At least one of the } \beta_i\text{'s} \neq 0$$

To do this, we use the F test. Remember that the variation in the y values from the overall mean of Y can be partitioned, or divided, into parts called sums of squares:

SST: the total variation in the y values around the mean $\bar{y}$

SSR: the variation in Y that is caused by Y's relationship with X

SSE: the variation in Y that remains unexplained

You remember from the simple linear model that SST = SSR + SSE and that SST is known as the total sum of squares and represents the distance of the data value y_i from the overall mean $\bar{y}$. SSR is the regression sum of squares and represents the distance of the predicted value $\hat{y}$ from the overall mean $\bar{y}$. SSE is the error sum of squares and represents the distance of a particular data value y_i from the predicted value $\hat{y}$. The formulas for calculating these quantities are

$$\text{SST} = \Sigma(y - \bar{y})^2 \qquad \text{SSR} = \Sigma(\hat{y} - \bar{y})^2 \qquad \text{SSE} = \Sigma(y - \hat{y})^2$$

When the dependent variable, Y, is related to the set of independent variables included in the model, then SSR is large and SSE is small. When Y is not related to the set of X variables, then SSE will dominate. The test statistic, F, uses the mean squares, MSR and MSE, which are calculated by dividing the sums of squares by their respective degrees of freedom.

Formula for F statistic

$$F = \frac{\text{MSR}}{\text{MSE}}$$

How many degrees of freedom does each sum of squares have? The entire model with n observations has $n - 1$ degrees of freedom, so SST has $n - 1$ degrees of freedom. Since the model has k independent variables, SSR has k degrees of freedom, and by subtraction SSE has $(n - 1) - k$ or $n - k - 1$ degrees of freedom. Figure 12.2 shows a general ANOVA table for a multiple-regression model:

Source of Variation	Degrees of Freedom	Sum of Squares	Mean Square	F Value
Regression	k	SSR	$\text{MSR} = \frac{\text{SSR}}{k}$	$\frac{\text{MSR}}{\text{MSE}}$
Error	$n - k - 1$	SSE	$\text{MSE} = \frac{\text{SSE}}{n - k - 1}$	
Total	$n - 1$	SST		

FIGURE 12.2 ANOVA table for multiple regression model

EXAMPLE 12.6 Texas Real Estate

The ANOVA Table

The planners who are interested in predicting the average selling price of a home in the Dallas/Fort Worth area used Minitab to perform the regression analysis and to get the multiple regression model. They looked at the residuals to see how well the model was able to predict the selling price, but now they need to see whether the model is significant.

They want to test the hypotheses

$$H_0\text{: } \beta_1 = \beta_2 = \beta_3 = \beta_4 = \beta_5 = 0$$
$$H_A\text{: At least one of the coefficients is not equal to 0.}$$

To do this they look at the output from the Minitab analysis again:

```
Regression Analysis

The regression equation is
1994 Avg. Value of Home Sold = - 140352 + 1.64 Avg. Household Income
     + 39.2 Total Instructional Expenditure + 90 Mean SAT Score
     - 47820 Population Diversity - 1132 1993/94 Avg. Violent Crime

Predictor        Coef      StDev        T        P
Constant      -140352     112958    -1.24    0.222
Avg. Hou       1.6377     0.3121     5.25    0.000
Total In        39.16      21.78     1.80    0.081
Mean SAT         89.6      113.9     0.79    0.437
Populati       -47820      62143    -0.77    0.447
1993/94         -1132       2147    -0.53    0.601

S = 37958         R-Sq = 75.1%     R-Sq(adj) = 71.6%
```

Analyze the Data

(continued)

```
Analysis of Variance

Source        DF           SS            MS          F        P
Regression     5   1.52341E + 11   30468171569    21.15    0.000
Error         35    50427624859     1440789282
Total         40    2.02768E+11
```

They look at the section of the output labeled Analysis of Variance. From the table they see that the value of the test statistic, F, is

$$\frac{\text{MSR}}{\text{MSE}} = \frac{30{,}468{,}171{,}569}{1{,}440{,}789{,}282} = 21.15$$

Now they must determine what this means. ■

In an ANOVA test we are looking at the ratio of the explained variation to the unexplained variation. If it is high enough (if the explained variation is significantly larger than the unexplained part), then we can conclude that the model is significant. The F test is then a one-sided, right-tail test.

You remember that an F statistic has two parameters, the numerator degrees of freedom and the denominator degrees of freedom. In this case the numerator, MSR, has k (the number of variables in the model) degrees of freedom and the denominator, MSE, has $n - k - 1$ degrees of freedom. For a test at the α level of significance, the F critical value is

$$F_{\alpha,k,n-k-1}$$

Symbol for F critical value

EXAMPLE 12.7 Texas Real Estate

Testing the Significance of the Multiple Regression Model

The planners looking at the average selling price of houses want to perform the test at the 0.05 level of significance. Since they are looking at 41 different locations and their model has 5 different independent variables, they know that they need an F critical value with 5 degrees of freedom in the numerator and $41 - 5 - 1 = 35$ degrees of freedom in the denominator. From the tables of the F distribution, they find that the critical value is $F_{0.05,5,35} = 2.4852$.

Analyze the Data

The test statistic is 21.15, which is definitely outside the critical value. They reject H_0 and conclude that the model is significant. ■

In the previous example, we showed the calculation for the test statistic and found the critical value using the F distribution tables. When you are using the computer to perform the analysis this is not always necessary. Most statistical software packages print out the value of the test statistic. Unless the software asks for the level of significance of the test it will not print out the critical value, but many packages do print out the p value of the test. Remember that you can use the p value to determine whether to reject H_0 by comparing it to the level of significance you choose. If the p value is less than the chosen level of significance, then you reject H_0; if not, then you fail to reject.

EXAMPLE 12.8 Phillips Petroleum

Testing Significance of the Multiple Regression

The analysts who are looking at predicting shareholders' equity using total revenues and assets need to know whether their model is significant. They want to test the hypotheses

H_0: $\beta_1 = \beta_2 = 0$

H_A: At least one coefficient is not equal to 0.

at the 0.05 level of significance.

They look again at the output from the Excel computer analysis:

Analyze the Data

SUMMARY OUTPUT

Regression Statistics	
Multiple R	0.923228385
R Square	0.852350651
Adjusted R Square	0.815438314
Standard Error	1.067662859
Observations	11

ANOVA

	df	*SS*	*MS*	*F*	*Significance F*
Regression	2	52.64353179	26.32176589	23.09121324	0.000475254
Residual	8	9.119231848	1.139903981		
Total	10	61.76276364			

	Coefficients	*Standard Error*	*tStat*	*P-value*	*Lower 95%*
Intercept	−16.71847039	7.179010344	−2.328798761	0.048252087	−33.27330864
Revenue	1.452643014	0.216118353	6.721516208	0.00014936	0.954272876
Assets	1.034291795	0.769247372	1.344550312	0.215646057	−0.739596974

From the output they see that the F statistic is 23.09 and that the p value is 0.0005. Since 0.0005 is less than their specified level of significance, 0.05, they reject H_0 and conclude that the model is significant. ■

Order Filling *Testing the Significance of the Model*

The mail-order company looking at factors related to the time to fill an order wants to know whether its model is significant.

Write down the hypotheses that it must test.

The Excel output from the company's analysis is shown here:

SUMMARY OUTPUT

Regression Statistics	
Multiple R	0.915838993
R Square	0.838761061
Adjusted R Square	0.82696309
Standard Error	1.021396967
Observations	45

ANOVA

	df	*SS*	*MS*	*F*	*Significance F*
Regression	3	222.5057888	74.16859627	71.09366969	2.71039E-16
Residual	41	42.7733223	1.043251763		
Total	44	265.2791111			

	Coefficients	*Standard Error*	*tStat*	*P-value*	*Lower 95%*
Intercept	0.215224599	0.55856837	0.385314691	0.701996141	−0.912827729
Number of Items	0.281391801	0.029191616	9.639473395	4.26275E-12	0.222438105
Locations	1.259340956	0.103175681	12.20579253	3.10059E-15	1.050973327
Assets	0.019087782	0.047667374	0.400437032	0.690913642	−0.077178487

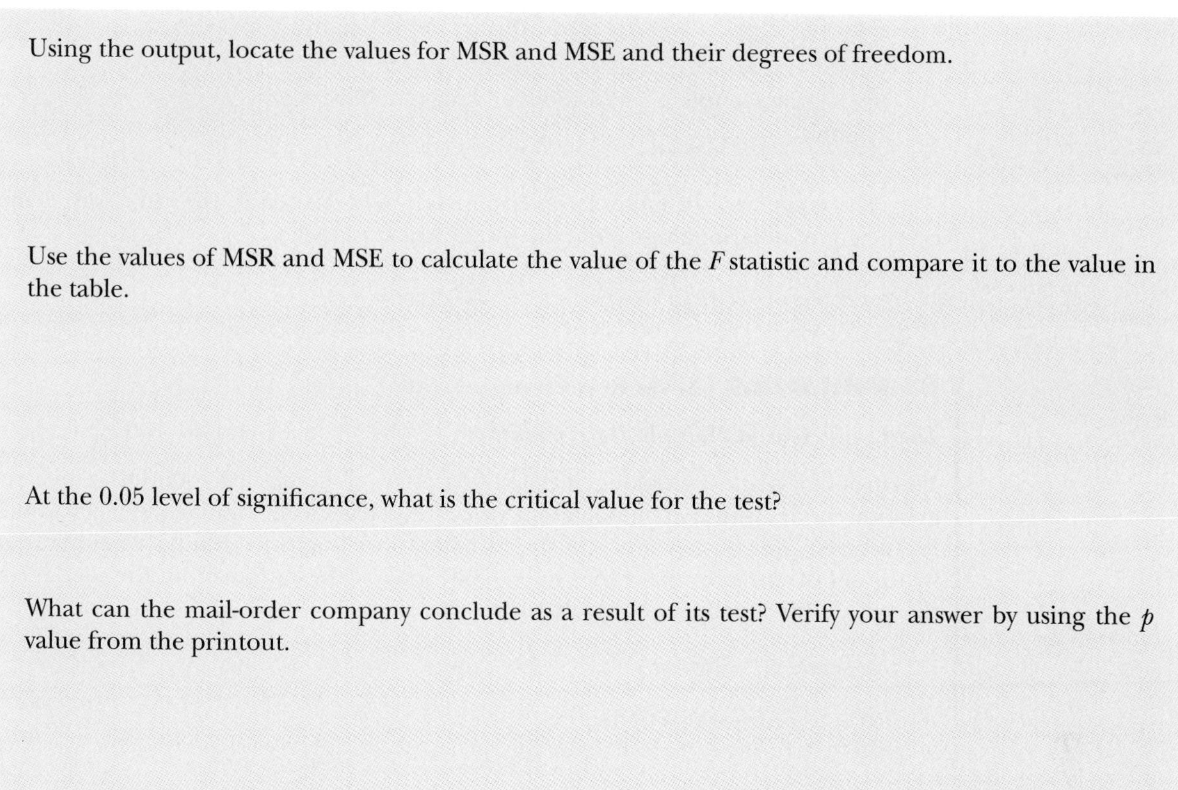

Using the output, locate the values for MSR and MSE and their degrees of freedom.

Use the values of MSR and MSE to calculate the value of the F statistic and compare it to the value in the table.

At the 0.05 level of significance, what is the critical value for the test?

What can the mail-order company conclude as a result of its test? Verify your answer by using the p value from the printout.

At this point you should realize that just because the result of a statistical analysis is *statistically significant* does not mean that it will be useful or meaningful for purposes of decision making. If you have a lot of data, it might result in significant but essentially useless results.

The results of the significance test for a multiple regression model tell us that the *model* as a whole is significant, specifically that at least one of the coefficients is not zero. The F test tells us that the amount of variation in the dependent variable that is explained by the model is significantly larger than the amount left unexplained. These results lead to some questions; in particular, which coefficients are nonzero and how much of the variation in the dependent variable has been accounted for by the model? These questions can be answered by looking at some additional results of the analysis.

12.3.2 The Coefficient of Multiple Determination

In the simple linear regression model you learned that it is sometimes useful to look at the amount of the variation in Y that can be explained by its association with X (SSR) as a percentage of the total variation in Y (SST). This measure is called the coefficient of determination, R^2, which can be interpreted as the amount by which the variation in Y *could be reduced* if the value of X is held constant. This type of interpretation is particularly useful in manufacturing control applications where the objective is to reduce the variation in the output (product) by controlling the variation in the input (raw materials, machine settings).

In multiple regression models there is an analogous measure, called the **coefficient of multiple determination, R^2.**

ANS. MSR = 74.17, DF = 3, MSE = 1.04, DF = 41, F = 74.17/1.04. CRITICAL VALUE IS 2.8327. SINCE 71.09 > 2.8327 THE COMPANY KNOWS THAT THE MODEL IS SIGNIFICANT, AT LEAST ONE OF THE COEFFICIENTS IN THE MODEL IS NOT = 0. SINCE p IS LESS THAN 0.05, THE COMPANY REJECTS H_0.

The ***coefficient of multiple determination, R^2,*** is a measure of the percentage of the variation in the dependent variable, Y, that can be accounted for by the complete set of independent variables, $X_1, X_2, \ldots, X_k$, in the model.

The coefficient of multiple determination is calculated in the same way as the coefficient of determination from the simple linear model:

Formula for coefficient of multiple determination

$$R^2 = \frac{\text{SSR}}{\text{SST}} 100\%$$

EXAMPLE 12.9 Texas Real Estate

The Coefficient of Multiple Determination

The group of planners looking at the selling prices of homes has found that their regression model with five independent variables is statistically significant. They would like a better idea of how much of the variation in selling price can be accounted for by the set of variables that they chose. They look at the output from the model for the value of the coefficient of multiple determination:

```
Regression Analysis

The regression equation is
1994 Avg. Value of Home Sold = - 140352 + 1.64 Avg. Household Income
      + 39.2 Total Instructional Expenditure + 90 Mean SAT Score
      - 47820 Population Diversity - 1132 1993/94 Avg. Violent Crime

Predictor        Coef      StDev         T        P
Constant      -140352     112958     -1.24    0.222
Avg. Hou       1.6377     0.3121      5.25    0.000
Total In        39.16      21.78      1.80    0.081
Mean SAT         89.6      113.9      0.79    0.437
Populati       -47820      62143     -0.77    0.447
1993/94         -1132       2147     -0.53    0.601

S = 37958        R-Sq = 75.1%        R-Sq(adj) = 71.6%
```

From the output they see that the value of R^2 is 75.1%, which means that the set of five variables that they chose accounts for 75.1% in the variation of the average selling price of a house. The value makes them feel good about the set of variables that they chose, but at the same time they wonder if there is a better set of variables that they could use. ■

At this point you may be thinking that "more is better" applies to the multiple regression model. Certainly, the more variables we add to the model the larger SSR will get, and therefore R^2 will increase. This is true in an absolute sense—numerically adding variables will never decrease SSE, so that as you add variables, R^2 will increase—but that does not mean that the model is better.

One of the objectives of modeling in general, and in the multiple regression model in particular, is to create a model that does a good job of predicting the value of the dependent variable, *with as small a set of input variables as possible.* There are several reasons for this. As the number of variables in a model increases, so does the complexity of the model. Complex models are harder to maintain and harder to explain to the people who want to use them. Also, as you increase the number of independent variables in a model, you increase the number of ways in which these variables may interact *with each other.* This results in unstable models—models that are very sensitive to small changes in the inputs. For these reasons, more is not necessarily better.

Another measure that is used in looking at multiple regression models is called the **adjusted R^2.**

The ***adjusted R^2*** is the value of the coefficient of multiple determination adjusted to reflect the number of variables in the model.

Although it is true that as you increase the number of variables SSR will always increase, you know that increasing the number of variables also *decreases* the number of degrees of freedom in the model. It is possible that adding a variable will increase SSR, and thereby decrease SSE, in such a way that the MSE actually increases! This happens because although the value you are dividing into (SSE) decreases, the value you are dividing by (degrees of freedom) decreases even more. The adjusted R^2 may actually decrease as variables are added to the model! We will talk about the adjusted R^2 further when we discuss model building.

EXAMPLE 12.10 Phillips Petroleum

The Coefficient of Multiple Determination

The financial analysts who created a model for shareholders' equity want to see how the variables they selected account for the variation in shareholders' equity. They look at the output from their computer analysis and find

Analyze the Data

SUMMARY OUTPUT

Regression Statistics	
Multiple R	0.923228385
R Square	0.852350651
Adjusted R Square	0.815438314
Standard Error	1.067662859
Observations	11

From this output they see that the two variables in the model account for about 85% of the variation in shareholders' equity. They notice that the value of the adjusted R^2 is about 82%, but they are not sure how this number should be interpreted. ■

TRY IT NOW!

Order Filling ***The Coefficient of Multiple Determination***

The mail-order company looking at factors related to the time to fill an order wants to know whether the set of independent variables that it selected does a good job of accounting for the variation in the time to fill an order. The relevant output from the model is shown here:

SUMMARY OUTPUT

Regression Statistics	
Multiple R	0.915838993
R Square	0.838761061
Adjusted R Square	0.82696309
Standard Error	1.021396967
Observations	45

(continued)

Using the output, find the value of the coefficient of multiple determination.

If you were the manager of the company would you be satisfied with this model? Why or why not?

Look at the value of adjusted R^2. What do you think this value might be telling the company?

12.3.3 Testing the Individual Coefficients

In the simple linear regression model you learned that one way to test whether a model is significant is to perform a t test on the slope coefficient. This tests the hypotheses

$$H_0: \beta_1 = 0$$
$$H_A: \beta_1 \neq 0$$

In the simple linear model, the t test for β_1 and the ANOVA test are equivalent. In the multiple regression model the ANOVA tests all of the coefficients simultaneously. The result of rejecting the null hypothesis in this test of significance is that we know that at least one of the coefficients is nonzero. Although this tells us, to some extent, whether we are on the right track, it does not tell us whether all of the variables in the model are useful or necessary in predicting the value of the dependent variable. It is certainly possible that in a model with three independent variables, only one of the coefficients is nonzero and that the other two variables are not adding any information to the model. If this were the case, it would be nice to be able to identify which variables contribute to the model and which variables do not.

This process is actually the beginning of a complex process called "model building," which we will discuss later in the chapter. At this point we will simply look at how to do a simple assessment of the value of each of the individual variables in the model.

We can test whether individual coefficients in a multiple regression model are equal to zero using a t test like the one used in the simple linear model. The major difference in this test is that we are testing whether the coefficient of the particular variable is equal to zero *assuming that all other variables remain in the model.* This assumption is critical because it does not allow you to simply toss out all of the variables that do not prove to be significant. To test whether the coefficient of some variable X_i in the model is different from zero we test the hypotheses

$$H_0: \beta_i = 0$$
$$H_A: \beta_i \neq 0$$

using a t test. The test statistic is given by

ANS. 83.9%; YES, THE R^2 IS HIGH; 82.7%; THIS IS CONSIDERABLY LOWER THAN R^2—SOME VARIABLES MIGHT NOT BE IMPORTANT.

$$t = \frac{b_i}{s_{b_i}}$$

Formula for test statistic for individual coefficients

Most computer packages give the information necessary to perform this test as part of their standard output. It is important that you understand exactly what it tells you so that you do not make errors in formulating your model.

EXAMPLE 12.11 Texas Real Estate

t Tests for Individual Coefficients

The planners who are looking at the average selling price of homes in the Dallas/Fort Worth area are pleased with the results of their model, but they wonder whether all of the variables in the model are really contributing to the final result. They decide to look at the computer output again and see whether they can obtain any additional information about the model. The relevant portion of the output is shown here:

Analyze the Data

```
Regression Analysis

The regression equation is
1994 Avg. Value of Home Sold = - 140352 + 1.64 Avg. Household Income
      + 39.2 Total Instructional Expenditure + 90 Mean SAT Score
      - 47820 Population Diversity - 1132 1993/94 Avg. Violent Crime

Predictor        Coef      StDev        T        P
Constant      -140352     112958    -1.24    0.222
Avg. Hou       1.6377     0.3121     5.25    0.000
Total In        39.16      21.78     1.80    0.081
Mean SAT         89.6      113.9     0.79    0.437
Populati       -47820      62143    -0.77    0.447
1993/94         -1132       2147    -0.53    0.601

S = 37958          R-Sq = 75.1%       R-Sq(adj) = 71.6%
```

The planners figure that what they want to do is perform five individual t tests to see whether the individual coefficients are equal to zero. They decide to do this at the 0.05 level of significance and look at the p values from the output. They see that only one variable, *average household income,* has a p value less than 0.05. They reason that this means that the coefficient of X_1 is not zero. Using the same approach, they see that the result of the other four tests is that the coefficients of those variables, β_2 through β_5, are not nonzero.

What does this mean? Can the planners simply drop the other four variables from the model? What would happen if they did? ■

EXAMPLE 12.12 Phillips Petroleum

Looking at Individual Coefficients

Although the model for predicting shareholders' equity had only two variables in it, the analysts still wondered whether both variables were necessary. They decide to look at the relevant output again:

Analyze the Data

SUMMARY OUTPUT

Regression Statistics	
Multiple R	0.923228385
R Square	0.852350651
Adjusted R Square	0.815438314
Standard Error	1.067662859
Observations	11

(continued)

ANOVA

	df	*SS*	*MS*	*F*	*Significance F*
Regression	2	52.64353179	26.32176589	23.09121324	0.000475254
Residual	8	9.119231848	1.139903981		
Total	10	61.76276364			

	Coefficients	*Standard Error*	*tStat*	*P-Value*	*Lower 95%*
Intercept	−16.71847039	7.179010344	−2.328798761	0.048252087	−33.27330864
Revenue	1.452643014	0.216118353	6.721516208	0.00014936	0.954272876
Assets	1.034291795	0.769247372	1.344550312	0.215646057	−0.739596974

They see that the t statistic for *revenue* is 6.72 and p value is essentially zero, indicating that the coefficient of that variable is nonzero. They also see that the t statistic for *assets* is 1.34 and that the p value for that test is 0.22. This would lead to the conclusion that the coefficient of the *assets* variable is zero.

Should the analysts drop the variable? At this point they are unsure about what to do. ■

What do we learn from testing the individual coefficients in a model? We do learn something about the utility of the variables. Clearly, some of the variables are important and should stay in the model, but what about the others? It would appear that we cannot throw them all out because of the assumption, but what happens if we do? If we don't throw them all out, which ones should we discard?

EXAMPLE 12.13 Texas Real Estate

Adjusting the Model

The planners looking at the real estate model decide to drop all of the variables with low t statistics out of the model. They are pretty sure this is not the right thing to do, but they want to see what happens if they take the most drastic approach.

Analyze the Data

```
Regression Analysis

The regression equation is
1994 Avg. Value of Home Sold = − 1167 + 2.09 Avg. Household Income

Predictor        Coef      StDev         T         P
Constant        −1167      14281     −0.08     0.935
Avg. Hou       2.0894     0.2084     10.03     0.000

S = 38118          R-Sq = 72.1%       R-Sq(adj) = 71.3%

Analysis of Variance

Source          DF            SS              MS          F         P
Regression       1    1.46103E+11     1.46103E+11    100.56     0.000
Error           39    56665134929      1452952178
```

The first thing they notice is that the model itself has changed. The intercept value has decreased from −\$140,352 to −\$1167. This is quite a change. In addition, the coefficient of the variable *average household income* has increased from 1.64 to 2.09.

Interestingly, the value of R^2 has not changed much, from 75.1% to 72.1%. It certainly appears that the variables that were dropped were not of any use, but the planners are still not convinced they should drop them all. ■

The answer to the question of dropping variables is not a simple yes or no. The t statistics and/or p values for the individual coefficients give a hierarchy for the variables in the model. With all variables in the model, we can consider the variable with the smallest t value (or largest p value) to be contributing the least to the model and we can eliminate that variable. But the simple approach stops there. If we drop a variable then the *entire model changes.* It is necessary to rerun the analysis and get a new model and look at those results in the same way we did the original model.

EXAMPLE 12.14 Phillips Petroleum

Looking at Individual Coefficients

The financial analysts from Phillips Petroleum decide to see what the effect of dropping assets from the model is, so they rerun the model as a simple linear model. The results of that analysis are shown here:

SUMMARY OUTPUT

Regression Statistics	
Multiple R	0.904978067
R Square	0.818985302
Adjusted R Square	0.798872558
Standard Error	1.114548637
Observations	11

ANOVA

Analyze the Data

	df	*SS*	*MS*	*F*	*Significance F*
Regression	1	50.58279565	50.58279565	40.71971956	0.000128074
Residual	9	11.17996798	1.242218665		
Total	10	61.76276364			

	Coefficients	*Standard Error*	*tStat*	*P-value*	*Lower 95%*
Intercept	−7.795059065	2.857364461	−2.728059081	0.023298434	−14.25887147
Revenue	1.437769522	0.225313329	6.381200479	0.000128074	0.928074973

The first thing they look at is the model itself. Without including assets as a variable, the new model is

$$\hat{y} = -7.80 + 1.44x$$

The intercept term has changed considerably, but the coefficient for the revenue variable is essentially the same.

The analysts also notice that the R^2 value has changed. Without assets in the model, the model accounts for only 81.9% of the variation in shareholders' equity, whereas the two-variable model had an R^2 of 85.2%. The analysts also notice that the new R^2 is close to the value of the adjusted R^2 for the two-variable model. They wonder how to interpret this.

At this point they cannot decide what to do. They like the model with the larger R^2 value, but it seems pointless to leave the variable in if it is not contributing significantly to the model. They decide to try to find a model that has a higher R^2 by looking for other independent variables that might prove to be significant. ■

You can see that there are no easy answers here. In the two examples we looked at, dropping the variables with low t values had different impacts. In one case the model changed but the value of R^2 did not, whereas in the other case the R^2 value dropped but the model coefficients remained essentially the same. In other cases both the model and the R^2 values can change.

TRY IT NOW!

Order Filling *Testing Individual Regression Coefficients*

The mail-order company looking at factors related to the time to fill an order wants to know how the individual variables contribute to the model. It decides to look at the computer analysis again:

SUMMARY OUTPUT

Regression Statistics	
Multiple R	0.915838993
R Square	0.838761061
Adjusted R Square	0.82696309
Standard Error	1.021396967
Observations	45

ANOVA

	df	*SS*	*MS*	*F*	*Significance F*
Regression	3	222.5057888	74.16859627	71.09366969	2.71039E-16
Residual	41	42.7733223	1.043251763		
Total	44	265.2791111			

	Coefficients	*Standard Error*	*tStat*	*P-value*	*Lower 95%*
Intercept	0.215224599	0.55856837	0.385314691	0.701996141	−0.912827729
Number of Items	0.281391801	0.029191616	9.639473395	4.26275E-12	0.222438105
Locations	1.259340956	0.103175681	12.20579253	3.10059E-15	1.050973327
Experience	0.019087782	0.047667374	0.400437032	0.690913642	−0.077178487

Look at the coefficients of each of the three variables in the model and perform the appropriate hypothesis tests.

Which variables have nonzero coefficients? Which variables have coefficients that are equal to zero?

As a result of these tests, what recommendation would you make?

ANS. FOR NUMBER OF ITEMS, REJECT H_0; FOR LOCATIONS, REJECT H_0; FOR EXPERIENCE, FAIL TO REJECT H_0. THE COEFFICIENTS OF NUMBER OF ITEMS AND LOCATIONS ARE NOT 0; THE COEFFICIENT OF EXPERIENCE IS 0. TRY RUNNING THE MODEL WITHOUT EXPERIENCE.

The questions faced as a result of looking at the individual model coefficients are not ones that have simple answers. They give rise to a group of techniques called model-building techniques, which try to find the "best" model from a set of input variables. By "best" we generally mean the model with the smallest number of variables that explains the largest portion of the variation in the dependent variable.

12.3.4 Exercises—Learning It!

12.5 Consider the model on traffic fatalities for the different states. The variable X_1 represents the number of licensed drivers, X_2 is the number of registered vehicles, and X_3 is the number of vehicle miles driven annually. The output from the computer analysis is shown here: *Requires Exercise 12.1*

SUMMARY OUTPUT

Regression Statistics	
Multiple R	0.982548538
R Square	0.96540163
Adjusted R Square	0.963193224
Standard Error	154.5407481
Observations	51

ANOVA

	df	*SS*	*MS*	*F*	*Significance F*
Regression	3	31321046.9	10440348.97	437.1485021	2.54274E-34
Residual	47	1122493.613	23882.84282		
Total	50	32443540.51			

	Coefficients	*Standard Error*	*tStat*	*P-value*	*Lower 95%*
Intercept	51.7481659	30.43306219	1.700392999	0.095666076	−9.475200509
X Variable 1	0.06294764	0.048829545	1.289130172	0.20366155	−0.035284642
X Variable 2	−0.211896991	0.055989427	−3.784589385	0.000435566	−0.324533083
X Variable 3	0.029349954	0.003525079	8.326041167	8.34285E-11	0.022258416

(a) Set up the hypotheses to test whether the model as a whole is significant.

(b) Use the output to test the hypotheses at the 0.05 level of significance.

(c) What is the coefficient of multiple determination for this model?

(d) Do you think that the model does a good job of explaining the variation in the number of traffic fatalities in a state? Why or why not?

(e) Set up the hypotheses to test each regression coefficient individually.

(f) Perform the tests at the 0.05 level of significance.

(g) What can you conclude about the coefficient of variable X_2?

(h) What are your conclusions about X_1? About X_3?

(i) Would you recommend dropping any of these variables from the model? Why or why not?

12.6 The analysts looking at the model on compliance with mandatory seat-belt laws is wondering whether their model is statistically significant. They look at the output from the model: *Requires Exercise 12.2*

```
Regression Analysis

The regression equation
Percent Compliance = 0.416 + 0.00187 Fine + 0.0194 Years In Effect

47 cases used 4 cases contain missing values
```

(continued)

```
Predictor        Coef        StDev        T        P
Constant      0.41558      0.05153     8.06    0.000
Fine         0.001874     0.001050     1.78    0.081
Years In     0.019397     0.004672     4.15    0.000

S = 0.09682        R-Sq = 30.8%        R-Sq(adj) = 27.7%

Analysis of Variance

Source        DF          SS          MS          F        P
Regression     2    0.183552    0.091776       9.79    0.000
Error         44    0.412431    0.009373
Total         46    0.595983

Source       DF      Seq SS
Fine          1    0.021952
Years In      1    0.161600
```

(a) Set up the hypotheses to test whether the model is significant.

(b) At the 0.01 level of significance, is the model they tested significant? What does this mean?

(c) What is the value of R^2 for this model? Do you think that the model does a good job of explaining the variation in compliance with the seat-belt laws? Why or why not?

(d) Set up the hypotheses to test for each of the regression coefficients individually and perform the test at the 0.05 level of significance.

(e) What are your conclusions from the tests on individual coefficients? What recommendations would you make about including the variables currently under consideration?

Requires Exercise 12.3

12.7 Consider the problem of the committee that is looking at the issue of serious crimes in some large cities.

Data file: *CRIME.XXX*

(a) Set up the hypotheses to test whether the multiple regression model is significant.

(b) Use the output from your analysis to perform the test at the 0.05 level of significance. What is your conclusion?

(c) What percentage of the variation in the number of serious crimes in a city is accounted for by the set of variables in the model? Based on this number, do you think that the set of variables chosen by the committee does a good job of explaining the number of serious crimes in a large city?

(d) Set up the hypotheses to test the individual regression coefficients.

(e) At the 0.01 level of significance, what are your conclusions? What recommendations would you make about the set of variables currently in the model?

Requires Exercise 12.4

12.8 Look at the data on Internet usage again and consider the two-variable model that you developed.

Datafile: *INTERNET.XXX*

(a) At the 0.05 level of significance, what can you conclude about the significance of your model?

(b) What percentage of the variation in hours of Internet usage is explained by the set of variables in your model? Based on this percentage, do you think your model is a good one? Why or why not?

(c) Set up the hypotheses and test the individual regression coefficients in your model at the 0.05 level of significance. What are your conclusions?

(d) Based on the results of the tests on individual coefficients, what would you do next? Why?

12.9 In the problem about number of traffic fatalities the model was rerun, dropping the data on number of licensed drivers that had the lowest t statistic. The output is shown here:

Requires Exercises 12.1, 12.5

SUMMARY OUTPUT

Regression Statistics	
Multiple R	0.981925801
R Square	0.964178279
Adjusted R Square	0.962685707
Standard Error	155.6025568
Observations	51

ANOVA

	df	*SS*	*MS*	*F*	*Significance F*
Regression	2	31281357.04	15640678.52	645.9845512	1.99303E-35
Residual	48	1162183.473	24212.15568		
Total	50	32443540.51			

	Coefficients	*Standard Error*	*tStat*	*P-Value*	*Lower 95%*
Intercept	46.03605608	30.31563375	1.518558262	0.135433408	−14.91757512
X Variable 2	−0.162799336	0.041321977	−3.939776022	0.000263617	−0.245882691
X Variable 3	0.029996183	0.003513227	8.538070709	3.42795E-11	0.02293237

(a) Write down the equation of the new two-variable model.

(b) Compare the new model to the model with three variables. How much does the model change when number of licensed drivers is dropped?

(c) Compare the value of R^2 for both models. What does this make you think about the decision to drop number of licensed drivers from the model?

(d) Would you consider the two-variable model a good model? Why or why not?

(e) Based on the value of R^2 would you be satisfied with this model or would you want to consider other variables?

12.10 The lobbyists looking at compliance with seat-belt laws decided to drop the variable associated with the amount of the fine for noncompliance from the model. The output from the modified model is shown here:

Requires Exercises 12.2, 12.6

```
Regression Analysis

The regression equation is
Percent Compliance = 0.462 + 0.0188 Years In

48 cases used 3 cases contain missing values

Predictor        Coef      StDev       T       P
Constant      0.46203    0.04443   10.40   0.000
Years In     0.018846   0.004673    4.03   0.000

S = 0.09806       R-Sq = 26.1%       R-Sq(adj) = 24.5%

Analysis of Variance

Source        DF        SS        MS        F       P
Regression     1   0.15642   0.15642    16.27   0.000
Error         46   0.44231   0.00962
Total         47   0.59873
```

(a) Write down the equation for the new model and compare it to the model with two independent variables. Do you think that the coefficients have changed significantly? Why or why not?

(b) Test the significance of the new model at the 0.05 level of significance.

(c) Compare the value of R^2 from the new model to R^2 from the old model. What does this make you think about the decision to drop the variable associated with the fine from the model?

(d) If you were among the group of lobbyists would you be satisfied with this model? Why or why not? Can you suggest any other variables that might be considered?

Discovery Exercise 12.1
FINDING THE BEST MODEL

The Office of Institutional Planning at a university in the Far West is interested in understanding what factors influence the graduation rate, that is, the percentage of entering freshmen who actually graduate from the university. The university planners have collected data on 46 universities with traits similar to theirs and have selected three variables that they think are related to the graduation rate: 25th percentile combined SATs of accepted students, the acceptance rate (percentage of students who apply that are accepted by the university), and educational expenditure per student ($) by the university. A sample of the data is shown here:

Rank/School Name	1995 Actual Graduation Rate (%)	SAT/ACT 25th	Acceptance Rate (%)	Education Expenditures per Student
Indiana University—Bloomington	59	NA	80	9,713
SUNY—Binghamton	74	NA	40	9,080
Allegheny University	52	786	61	33,270
Univ. of California—Riverside	56	910	78	13,403
Oregon State University	53	949	89	10,182
University of Hawaii—Manoa	55	960	65	13,360
New Jersey Inst. of Technology	63	970	67	14,030

The entire data set is found in the datafile GRADRATE.XXX.

(a) Which variable do you think will have the greatest effect on graduation rate? Explain why you chose this variable.

(b) Find a simple linear model that predicts graduation rate using the variable that you think is most important. What is the value of R^2 for your model? Is the model significant?

(c) Do this again using the other two independent variables, and fill in the table:

Independent Variable	R^2	p Value

(d) Which one-variable model do you think is the best? Why?

(e) How many different models with two independent variables could you find? List them all.

(f) Find the multiple regression models for all of the two-variable models. Fill in the table:

Independent Variables	R^2	p Value

(g) Which two-variable model do you think is best? Why? Does the two-variable model you think is best contain the variable from the best one-variable model? Would you expect it to?

(h) Find the multiple regression model that predicts graduation rate using all three independent variables. What is R^2 for this model? Is it significant?

(i) Now, fill in the table for each of the "best" models that you have found.

Number of Independent Variables	Independent Variables	R^2	p Value
1			
2			
3			

(j) If you were going to use a model to predict graduation rate, which of these three models would you choose? Why?

12.4 BUILDING A MULTIPLE REGRESSION MODEL

At the end of the last section we saw that the problem of deciding which variables to include in the multiple regression model is not an easy one. The objective is to find the "best" model, but that is not really well defined. Two somewhat conflicting criteria are involved in the definition: The model should do an acceptable job of predicting or explaining the dependent variable, and the model should use the smallest possible set of independent variables.

The task of deciding which variables should be included/excluded from the model must be done in a systematic way. If variables are dropped from a model, then the entire analysis must be redone. To keep the analysis from being chaotic and unproductive, several methods known as **model-building techniques** have been developed.

> ***Model-building techniques*** are methods used for identifying the best multiple regression model from a set of independent variables. These methods include forward selection, backward elimination, stepwise regression, and all possible regressions.

This section focuses on the issues of choosing the set of independent variables to be considered in a model as well as some of the model-building techniques available in most statistical software packages. We will not go into the technical details of most of the techniques since they can be quite complex, but rather we discuss the ideas behind the techniques and how to interpret the results.

12.4.1 Choosing a Set of Independent Variables

After reading the examples in this chapter and doing some of the exercises presented so far, you may be wondering how and why the people doing the analyses chose the variables they did. In many cases, you might have chosen an entirely different set of variables! The choice of the dependent variable is usually quite straightforward. There is a problem to be solved or a decision to be made that involves the variable in question. The choice for the set of independent variables is not quite as easy. Many factors are involved in the decision procedure.

One thing that can heavily impact the decision process is the experience and intuition of the "experts" involved. It is difficult, if not impossible, to solve a problem or make a decision if you know nothing about the subject. Often the group involved in the problem will brainstorm to find a list of variables that might be related to the dependent variable. Once this list is established and prioritized, other factors influence the final choice.

A factor that must be considered in the decision process is whether the data for the study will come from existing data or whether they will be collected especially for this analysis. When the data are to come from existing sources, availability and cost are two important considerations. Sometimes variables that the group considers important might be too expensive to obtain or might not even be available. In this case, similar variables that are less desirable might have to be included. Occasionally, the set of available data is overwhelming and decisions have to be made about which variables to include.

EXAMPLE 12.15 Texas Real Estate

Choosing the Set of Input Variables

The planners looking at the selling price of homes in different locations in the Dallas/Fort Worth area had 56 different variables on their list of possible variables. They were able to obtain data for all of the locations of interest for 20 of the 56 variables.

They felt that 20 variables were too many to work with, so after some discussion they decided to try to find a set of 5 that they felt were most important. The question was how should they choose the 5 variables?

Understand the Problem

Of course, everyone in the group had opinions about which variables to include, and there was some overlap, but in the end the planners decided on a more objective approach. They knew that the correlation coefficient measured the strength of the relationship between two variables, and so they decided to calculate the correlation coefficient for each of the 20 variables with the average selling price of a home. They would try to pick the five variables with the highest correlation. The correlations are shown in the table here:

Avg. household income	0.84885	Square miles	−0.25142
Percent passing AA	0.63989	Population density	0.20480
Percent taking SAT	0.51699	Property tax rate	−0.20097
Mean SAT	0.50495	1994 pop	−0.19425
Total instructional exp.	0.48006	Distance to Dallas/Fort Worth	−0.12979
Population diversity	−0.44283	Annual insurance	−0.10825
1993/94 violent crime	−0.42840	Percent owner occupied	0.09989
Hazardous waste sites	−0.28200	Median age	−0.09370
Appreciation of sale price	0.27094	Park land	−0.05087
1993/94 nonviolent crime	−0.26457	Annual growth rate	0.01887

They looked at the five variables that were most highly correlated with the average selling price of a home and decided not to use all five of them. The reason for this was that four out of the five variables were related to education, and they wanted some diversity in the variable set. They decided to take two of the education-related variables, and agreed on mean SAT scores and total instructional expenditures. ■

When data come from existing sources it is often tempting to include every bit of data that is available. This approach can be counterproductive and can lead to overly complex and unstable models. We will talk more about these and other problems with models in the next section of the chapter. If a model from a subset of available data is not acceptable, it is always possible to add more variables to the set under consideration.

When data are going to be collected as part of an analysis it is wise to include as many possible variables as you can afford. If you collect data by means of a survey or an experiment, then usually the only way to add variables to the study is to repeat the entire data collection procedure. This can be time-consuming and expensive, if not impossible.

GPA ***Choosing the Independent Variables***

Many studies have been done on what factors are related to a college student's grade point average (GPA). These studies often focus on precollege factors, such as high school performance, SAT or ACT scores, and general socioeconomic factors such as family income and race. Students know that once they are in college, many other factors influence their GPA.

(continued)

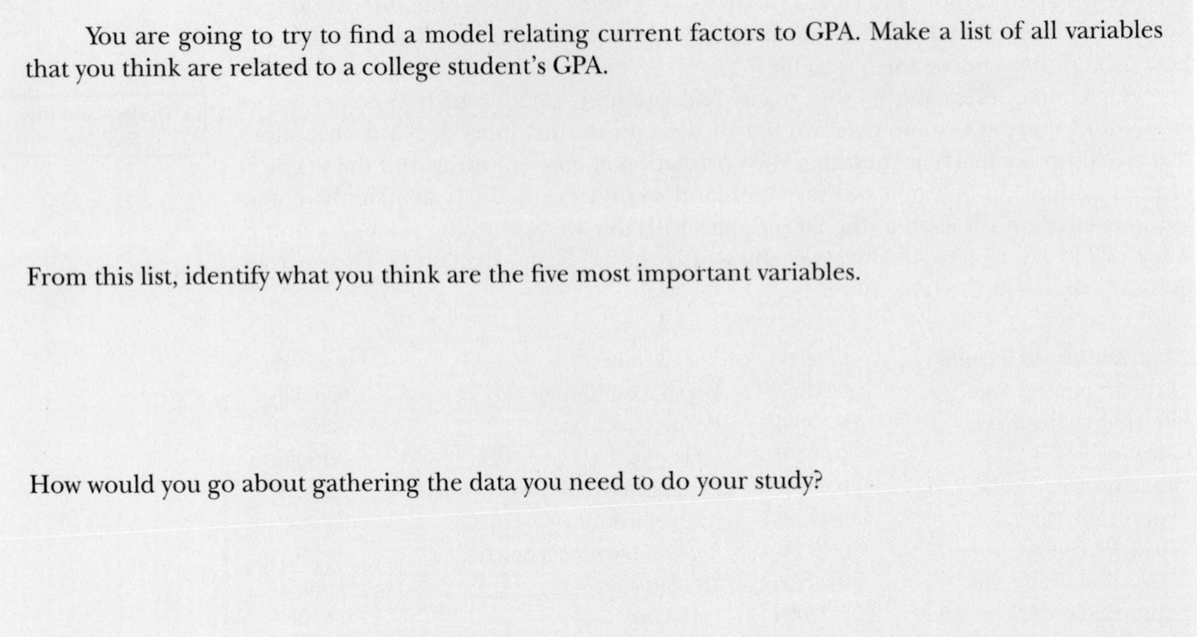

You are going to try to find a model relating current factors to GPA. Make a list of all variables that you think are related to a college student's GPA.

From this list, identify what you think are the five most important variables.

How would you go about gathering the data you need to do your study?

Once the set of variables is chosen and the analysis begins, statistical software is used to actually find the "best" model from the set of variables under consideration.

12.4.2 Forward Selection and Backward Elimination

The simplest of the model-building techniques are forward selection and backward elimination. The techniques are very well described by their names. In forward selection, a model is built by adding variables one at a time, until adding variables does not cause the model to improve. In the backward elimination model, all variables are included at first and then dropped one by one until the model begins to degrade. There are several different ways to define improvement and degradation of a model. We will focus on the most commonly used methods.

Forward selection starts by running all possible one-variable models and selecting the "best" one. There are several equivalent measures of "best": largest R^2, smallest MSE, largest F statistic, and largest t statistic. After the one-variable model is found, each of the remaining unchosen variables is combined with the current model. Again, the "best" of these is chosen. Most computer packages define "best" in terms of something called the partial F statistic, which is equivalent to the increase in the MSR, the decrease in MSE, or the highest t statistic. The technique continues adding variables until the change in the model is not significant at some specified level.

Backward elimination works the same way as forward selection, except that it starts with the full model and drops the "worst" (using the same criteria) until dropping a variable causes the model to become significantly worse.

EXAMPLE 12.16 Texas Real Estate

Forward Selection

The planners looking at the real estate problem decided to use forward selection to try to find the "best" model for their set of five variables. The computer output from the procedure is enlarged here:

```
* * * *  M U L T I P L E   R E G R E S S I O N  * * * *

Listwise Deletion of Missing Data

Equation Number 1    Dependent Variable..   1994 Avg.   Value of Home

Block Number 1.  Method:  Forward  Criterion  PIN .0500  AVG. HOU TOTAL IN MEAN SAT 1993 94 POPULATION

Variable(s) Entered on Step Number 1.     AVG. HOU.Avg. Household Income

Multiple R              .84885   Analysis of Variance
R Square                .72054                       DF      Sum of Squares           Mean Square
Adjusted R Square       .71338   Regression           1  146103347775.79370    146103347775.794
Standard Error     38117.60981   Residual            39   56665134929.23070     1452952177.67258

                                 F =    100.55620          Signif F =    .0000
```

Analyze the Data

```
-------------------Varaiables not in the Equation------------
Variable                B           SE B       Beta        T    Sig T

AVG. HOU         2.089442        .208365   .848848    10.28    .0000
(Constant)  -1166.758282     14280.72621              -.082    .9353
```

```
--------------Variables not in the Equation------------
Variable    Beta In     Partial     Min Toler       T    Sig T

TOTAL IN    .140535     .239924      .814503    1.523    .1359
MEAN SAT    .072320     .115670      .714894     .718    .4772
1993 94    -.066667    -.113157      .805119    -.702    .4869
POPULATI   -.049250    -.081890      .772608    -.507    .6154
```

```
----------------Variables not in the Equation----------------
Variable                B           SE B       Beta         T    Sig T

AVG. HOU         2.089442        .208365   .848848    10.028    .0000
(Constant)  -1166.758282     14280.72621               0.082    .9353

-----------------Variables not in the Equation---------------
Variable      Beta In      Partial      Min Toler        T      Sig T

TOTAL IN      .140535      .239924       .814503    1.523      .1359
MEAN_SAT      .072320      .115670       .714894     .718      .4772
1993_94_     -.066667     -.113157       .805119    -.702      .4869
POPULATI     -.049250     -.081890       .772608    -.507      .6154
```

From the output they saw that only one variable was included in the final model. They notice that the next variable for consideration is total instructional expenditure, which had the second highest t statistic from the original model.

The model is $\hat{y} = -1167 + 2.09$ average household income. ■

TRY IT NOW!

Order Filling *Forward Selection*

The mail-order company wants to use a standard method to find the best model from its set of three variables. It decides on forward selection because this method is the easiest to understand. The relevant portions of the computer output are shown here:

```
Method:  Forward    Criterion  PIN  .0500   NUMBER_O LOCATION EXPERIEN

Variable(s) Entered on Step Number 1..    LOCATION  Locations
```

(continued)

```
Multiple R              .68766        Analysis of Variance
R Square                .47287                        DF    Sum of Squares     Mean Square
Adjusted R Square       .46061        Regression       1         125.44303       125.44303
Standard Error         1.80333        Residual        43         139.83608         3.25200

                                      F =       38.57409        Signif F =      .0000

------------------Variables in the Equation------------------

Variable              B          SE B        Beta          T      Sig T

LOCATION        1.116792      .179814     .687657      6.211      .0000
(Constant)      2.650287      .704624                  3.761      .0005

          Variable(s) Entered on Step Number 2..     NUMBER_O Number of Items

Multiple R              .91549        Analysis of Variance
R Square                .83813                        DF    Sum of Squares     Mean Square
Adjusted R Square       .83042        Regression       2         222.33850       111.16925
Standard Error         1.01114        Residual        42          42.94061         1.02240

                                      F =      108.73411        Signif F =   .0000

------------------Variables in the Equation------------------

Variable              B          SE B        Beta          T      Sig T

Number_O         .281325      .028898     .610427      9.735      .0000
Location        1.256149      .101834     .773465     12.335      .0000
(Constant)       .338773      .460945                   .735      .4665

END PIN =  .050 Limits reached.
```

What variable is added on the first step of the procedure? What is its coefficient? What is the value of R^2 for the first model considered?

What variable is added on the second step? What is its coefficient? What does R^2 change to after this step?

Does the coefficient of the first variable change when the second variable is added? If so, what is the new value?

Write down the final model.

ANS. LOCATIONS, 1.12, 47.3%; NUMBER OF ITEMS, 0.28, 83.8%; YES, 1.26; $\hat{y} = 0.34 + 1.26\text{LOCATION} + 0.28\text{NUMBER OF ITEMS}$

Forward selection and backward elimination are straightforward techniques, but there is no guarantee that they will find the "best" model. In fact, as you can see, many combinations of variables are not even considered as part of the process. For this reason, a technique called stepwise regression, which is a variation on these methods, is often used.

12.4.3 Stepwise Regression

Stepwise regression is actually a combination of the forward selection and backward elimination methods. It starts the same way as forward selection, by running all of the one-variable models and selecting the variable with the largest F or t statistic. It then adds variables one at a time to the current model using the same type of criteria as forward selection. The difference occurs when three variables have been included in the model. Stepwise regression includes a routine that considers dropping previously added variables from the model using criteria similar to the ones used by backward elimination. In this way the method considers combinations of variables that were never considered in either of the other methods.

For example, suppose that five variables are being considered for addition in the model and that the first variable chosen is X_2, the second is X_1, and the third is X_5. Up to this point the stepwise procedure is the same as forward selection. However, at this point the stepwise regression procedure considers dropping either X_1 or X_2 from the model, looking at the possible combinations of X_1 and X_5 or X_2 and X_5. Although the second of these combinations, X_2 and X_5, was considered in the second iteration, the combination X_1 and X_5 was not. In this way, stepwise regression considers many more combinations of variables than the other two methods.

If it sounds complicated, it is. Many people make errors in using the stepwise regression technique because they do not understand it well enough. The method is very sensitive to the choice of significance levels chosen for adding and dropping variables. Small changes in these values can lead to completely different models being picked as the "best" model. If people are not familiar with the technique or with the software package they are using, they can get easily confused. Minitab requires that the user specify the criteria for adding and dropping variables from the model in terms of an F statistic and defaults to the same value, 4.00 for each. Other packages may allow the user to choose between significance levels or F statistics.

Clearly, the defaults and options are different among the packages and in many cases will produce different results. A powerful mainframe statistical package called SAS defaults to 0.15 for both significance levels. Without knowing what they are doing, users can get very different results!

EXAMPLE 12.17 Texas Real Estate

Stepwise Regression

Knowing that forward selection does not consider many different combinations of variables, the group studying the real estate problem decided to use stepwise regression to see whether it resulted in a different model. The output from the Minitab procedure is given below. The parts in ***bold italic*** indicate responses made by the user to questions from the procedure.

Analyze the Data

```
Stepwise Regression

 F-to-Enter:      4.00     F-to-Remove:      4.00

 Response is 1994 Avg on 5 predictors, with N = 41
```

(continued)

```
 Step              1
 Constant      -1167
 Avg. Hou       2.09
 T-Value       10.03

 S             38118
 R-sq          72.05

 More? (Yes, No, Subcommand, or Help)
SUBC>y

  No variables entered or removed

  More? (Yes, No, Subcommand, or Help)
SUBC>no
```

The output is not very helpful, but after looking at it, the planners found that one variable, average household income, was added to the model and that its coefficient was 2.09. The R^2 from the model was 72.05.

In this case, the model from stepwise regression is the same as that from forward selection. ■

The output from the stepwise regression procedure varies among software packages. The output from Minitab is interactive, requiring the user to make decisions at several points, and very lengthy, since it gives the results of each iteration. The output from KADDSTAT is slightly less involved, with only the end results output. The major portion of the output contains information on the variables included in the model and those considered but not included. If you want the additional information available with standard regression output, such as predicted values and residuals, you need to rerun the model with the common regression routine.

Order Filling ***Testing Individual Regression Coefficients***

The mail-order company looking at the model for order filling decides to use stepwise regression to see whether it finds a model that is different from the one found using forward selection. The Minitab results (with the interactive parts edited out) are given here.

```
Stepwise Regression

F-to-Enter:      4.00      F-to-Remove:      4.00

Response is     Time     on 3 predictors, with N =     45

Step               1
Constant       2.650

Location        1.12
T-Value         6.21

S               1.80
R-Sq           47.29

Step               2
Constant      0.3388

Location        1.26
T-Value        12.34
```

(continued)

```
Number o      0.281
T-Value        9.74

S              1.01
R-Sq          83.81

No variables entered or removed
```

From the output, how many iterations did the procedure take?

Which variable was added to the model first? What is its coefficient?

Which variable was added second? What is its coefficient?

Did the coefficient for the first variable change? If so, what is its coefficient after the second variable is added?

What is the final model from the stepwise procedure?

12.4.4 All Possible Regressions

One method of finding the "best" regression model that has been largely overlooked in the past is the method known as all possible regressions or all subsets. Practitioners have hesitated to use this technique because of the number of calculations that must be done. In the past, the technique has proved to be too computer-intensive for most situations. With the advent of powerful personal computers, this is no longer an issue and the technique is becoming widely used.

The method does exactly what its name states. Given a set of candidate variables, it runs regression models for all of the possible combinations of variables and then identifies the "best" model for each different size. For example, if there were five variables under consideration for a model, the all subsets method would run all models with one variable, all possible combinations of two variables, all three-variable combinations, etc. It then chooses, according to one or several criteria, the best one-variable model, the best two-variable model, and so on. The user is then free to choose among the models presented based on other decision criteria, such as cost, ease of access to the data, and personal preferences.

ANS. TWO; LOCATION, 1.12; NUMBER OF ITEMS, 0.281; YES, FROM 1.12 TO 1.26; $\hat{y} = 0.3888 + 1.26$LOCATION $+ 0.281$NUMBER OF ITEMS

TABLE 12.1 Number of subsets

Number of Variables	Number of Subsets	Result
1	$2^1 - 1$	1
2	$2^2 - 1$	3
3	$2^3 - 1$	7
4	$2^4 - 1$	15
5	$2^5 - 1$	31
⋮	⋮	⋮
10	$2^{10} - 1$	1,023
⋮	⋮	⋮
20	$2^{20} - 1$	1,048,575

The reason that the technique is so computer-intensive is the way the number of possible combinations grows with respect to the number of variables. If there are k variables under consideration, then there are $2^k - 1$ combinations to consider. Table 12.1 gives you an idea of how large this number gets.

The number of possible models for 5 variables is not unreasonable; even for 10 it is manageable, but doubling the number of variables from 10 to 20 multiplies the result by a factor of 1000!

The method of all possible regressions usually uses several criteria to define "best" for each level of model. Two of the criteria are ones you are already familiar with, R^2 and adjusted R^2. The third criterion is called the $\boldsymbol{C_p}$ **statistic,** which is a measure of the total squared error. The quantity p is the number of *terms* in the model being evaluated, including the intercept:

$$C_p = \frac{\text{SSE}_p}{\text{MSE}_{\text{ALL}}}(n - 2p)$$

The C_p statistic uses the SSE from the model being evaluated and the MSE from the "full" model, the model that contains all of the potential variables. Using C_p, the "best model" with p terms will result in $C_p = p$. For this model the estimates of the coefficients are unbiased.

EXAMPLE 12.18 Texas Real Estate

All Subsets

Although the results of forward selection and stepwise regression procedures both came up with the same "best" model, the planners were not sure they wanted a one-variable model. They decided to use the all possible regressions method. The Minitab output from the procedure is shown on the facing page. In this case, the output was the best two models for each size considered.

The planners found the results of this model to be quite helpful. They saw that the best one-variable model was the same one found by the forward and stepwise procedures. By looking at the value of adjusted R^2, they saw that by going from a three-variable model to a four-variable model the value actually decreased from 72.5 to 72.1, indicating that adding the variable mean SAT scores provided no additional information. They also saw that there was a two-variable model that was the best on all criteria and that according to the C_p index was better than the one-variable model. This model had both average household income and total instructional expenditure included.

```
Best Subsets Regression

Response is 1994 Avg

                                          A P   M T
                                          v o l e o
                                          g p 9 a t
                                          . u 9 n a
                                            1 3   1
                                          H a / S
                   R-Sq                   o t 9 A I
Vars   R-Sq   (adj)    C-p       S        u i 4 T n

   1   72.1    71.3    2.3   38118        X
   1   25.5    23.6   67.9   62238              X
   2   73.7    72.3    2.1   37488        X       X
   2   72.4    71.0    3.8   38357        X     X
   3   74.5    72.5    2.8   37351        X X     X
   3   74.3    72.2    3.2   37561        X     X X
   4   74.9    72.1    4.3   37575        X X   X X
   4   74.7    71.9    4.6   37742        X   X X X
   5   75.1    71.6    6.0   37958        X X X X X
```

Analyze the Data

■

One of the benefits of the all possible regressions procedure is that, for reasonably sized sets of input variables, it can be done with any software package that does regression analysis. The evaluation criteria R^2 and adjusted R^2 are included with normal regression output; the exception is C_p, which is often omitted but easy to calculate from the information available. The user simply needs to carefully list and run all of the combinations of independent variables.

TRY IT NOW!

Order Filling *All Possible Regressions*

The mail-order company is pretty sure that it has identified the best model, but it decides to use the all possible regressions method to make sure that it is not missing something. The output from the analysis follows.

```
Best Subsets Regression

Response is Time
                                                      N L E
                                                      u o x
                                                      m c p
                                                      b a e
                                                      e t r
                                                      r i i
                    R-Sq                                o e
Vars     R-Sq      (adj)        C-p          S        o n n

   1     47.3       46.1       93.0     1.8033          X
   1     25.2       23.4      149.3     2.1486        X
   2     83.8       83.0        2.2     1.0111        X X
   2     47.3       44.8       94.9     1.8239          X X
   3     83.9       82.7        4.0     1.0214        X X X
```

(continued)

Is there a one-variable model that is best on all criteria? If so, what is it?

What is the best two-variable model?

Is there any benefit from moving to a three-variable model? Why or why not?

What model do you recommend the company use? Why?

The relative ease with which all possible regressions can be done has made the use of the forward, backward, and stepwise procedures less popular. These latter techniques are still used to reduce an extremely large set of input variables down to a smaller set so that all subsets can be used.

12.5 CHECKING MODEL ADEQUACY

Just as in the simple linear model, some assumptions in the model must be checked to ensure that the model is appropriate. A model may appear to give good predictions and have a large value of R^2 and still not be a good multiple regression model. In this section, we discuss some of the problems that can occur in a multiple regression model.

12.5.1 Residual Analysis

In the linear model some of the assumptions involved the error term in the model. Remember that the multiple regression model is given by

$$y = \beta_0 + \beta_1 x_1 + \beta_2 x_2 + \cdots + \beta_k x_k + \varepsilon$$

and that ε is the error term. The basic assumptions about the error term ε follow:

1. It has a mean value of zero ($\mu_\varepsilon = 0$).
2. For every value of X, the standard deviation, σ, of ε is the same.
3. The distribution of ε is normal.
4. The error terms for the different observations are not correlated with each other.

ANS. YES, THE ONE WITH LOCATION, THE ONE WITH LOCATION AND NUMBER OF ITEMS; NO, ADJ. R^2 DECREASES; TWO VARIABLE, BEST USING ALL METHODS.

These assumptions also hold for the multiple regression model. In the simple linear model we used residual plots to tell us whether the assumptions were violated. These same plots help in the multiple regression model.

A plot of the residuals versus the predicted values gives information about whether the relationship is linear and whether the error terms have equal variances. If the plot of the residuals versus the $\hat{y}$ values shows a pattern, then the relationship between Y and the set of predictor variables might be nonlinear. Similarly, if the amount of scatter in the residuals varies as the level of Y varies, then the assumption of equal variances may be violated.

In addition to these plots, in multiple regression models it is also useful to plot the residuals against each of the independent variables to obtain additional information. If there are any problems indicated by the plot of the residuals versus the predicted values, you have information about a problem with the model as a whole. Plots against the individual variables can pinpoint whether the problem exists with all or just specific variables. If the problem exists with just one or two variables, the analyst can look at alternative models that do not contain these variables. Although the residual plots can be done in any package that creates scatter plots, Excel and Minitab include the plots as part of the output options in their regression routines.

To decide whether the assumption that the residuals are normally distributed is valid, you can use a normal probability plot or a histogram, just as you did in the simple linear model.

EXAMPLE 12.19 Texas Real Estate

Residual Plots

The real estate planners have decided to use the two-variable model identified by all possible regressions. They decide to plot the residuals from the model against each of the independent variables. The plots are shown here:

Analyze the Data

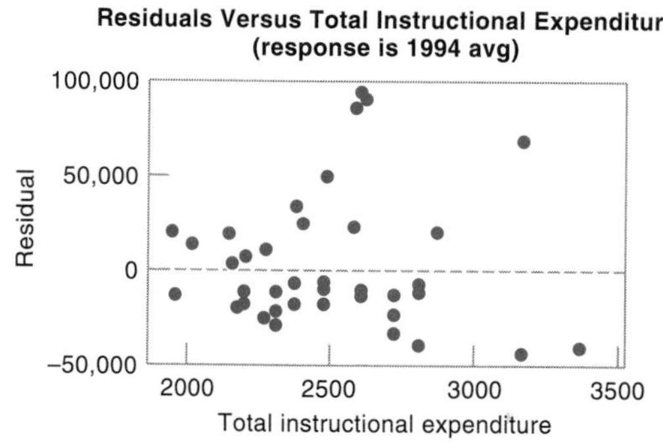

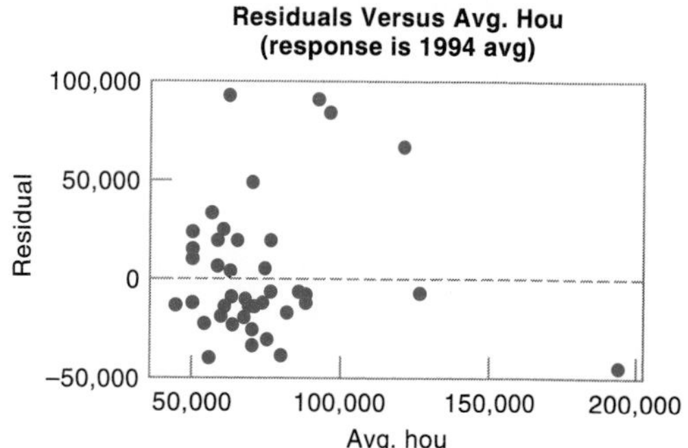

Both plots exhibit more variation on the high side than on the low side. In the plot against the total instructional expenditures it appears that the variance of the residuals increases as the variable increases. In the second plot, against average household income, the problem is not as severe, although it is more difficult to evaluate because there are some isolated values at the high end of the variable range.

A normal plot of the residuals was also done, as shown at the top of page 616.

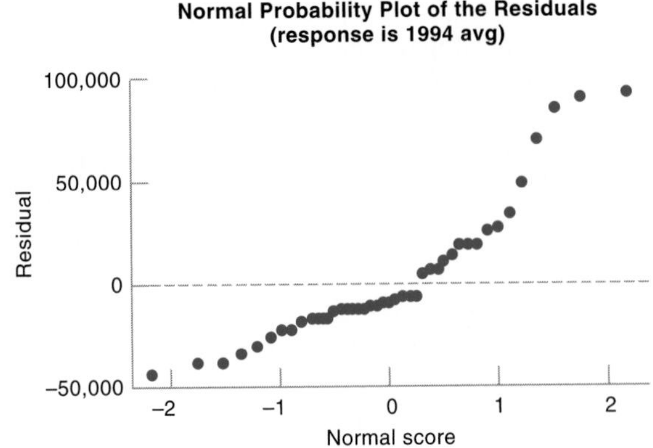

Draw Conclusions

From the plot it appears that the normality assumption is not valid because the points do not fall in a straight line.

From the diagnostic plots, it appears that the "best" model they have found violates some of the regression model assumptions. ■

At this point you might be thinking that you would be really upset if, after doing all that work and finding the "best" model, there is a problem with it. You might wonder why you didn't check these things before all that work. In fact, modeling is not a sequential procedure. It is an iterative procedure from which a solution gradually evolves. Checking earlier would involve a lot more checks than might be necessary with the final, candidate model.

Order Filling *All Possible Regressions*

Now that it has a model it likes, the mail-order company would like to make sure that the model does not violate any assumptions of the multiple regression model. The company creates a set of residual plots, which are shown here:

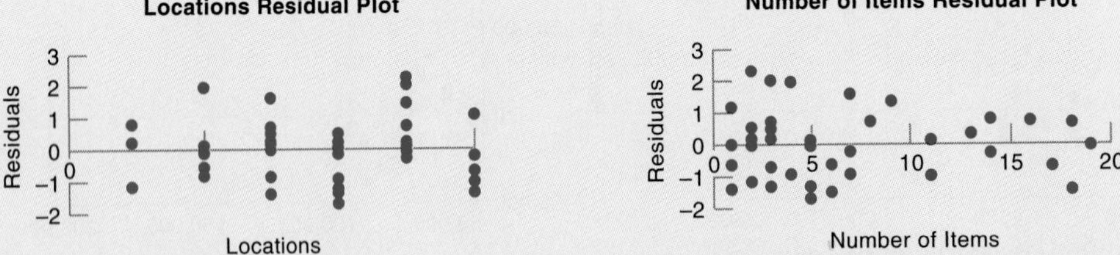

Look at the plot of residuals versus the locations. Does it appear that there is a problem with the assumption of equal variances?

Look at the plot of residuals versus the number of items. Does it appear that there is a problem with the assumption of equal variances?

The company also created a normal probability plot of the residuals:

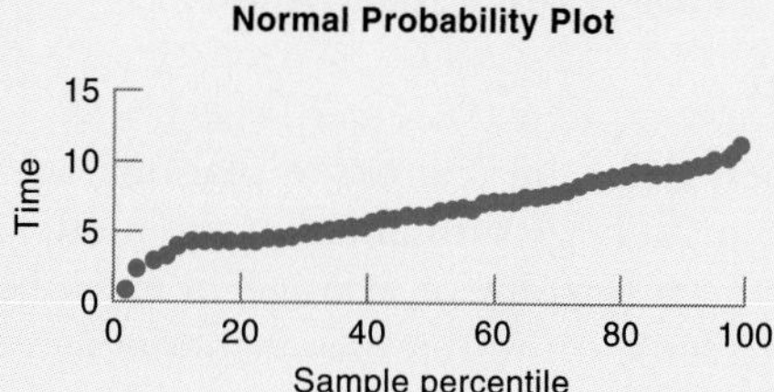

From this plot, what can you say about the assumption of normality?

12.5.2 Values With Large Influence

Another problem that we encountered in the simple linear model was the problem of data points that exerted a large influence on the model. This could happen when the value of the dependent variable did not agree with the model or when an observation had an X value that was distant from the other data points. Since there was only one independent variable, we could use plots such as scatter plots and boxplots to help identify these observations.

The problem of observations exerting a large influence can also happen in the multiple regression model, but it is more difficult to detect. This is because the influence might come from a combination of values of the independent variables and we lose the element of visualization that we had in the one-variable model. In multiple regression it is necessary to rely on other measures to identify observations with a large influence. As we saw with the linear model, as part of the output Minitab generates a warning about observations that exert a large influence on the model either because of a large residual or because of X values that are significantly larger.

One method that has emerged as a way to detect influential values uses a statistic called the **Cook's distance, *D*.**

The ***Cook's distance*** method compares the values of the regression coefficents with all observations to the values when the *i*th observation is removed from the model.

ANS. NO; YES, THE VARIANCES APPEAR TO DECREASE; RESIDUALS APPEAR NORMAL.

If the ith observation is influencing the model, then the difference in coefficients between the two models will be large and the corresponding value of Cook's distance is also large. A suggested definition of large is to compare D to $F_{0.5,k+1,n-k-1}$, an F statistic of a tail area of 0.50 and with $k + 1$ degrees of freedom in the numerator and $n - k - 1$ in the denominator. A rougher rule of thumb is to compare Cook's distance to 1. If, in either case, D exceeds the critical value, then the observation in question should be removed from the model. Outputting Cook's distance is an option of the regression routine in many statistical packages.

EXAMPLE 12.20 Texas Real Estate

Residual Plots

Looking at their data, the real estate planners wonder whether one of the locations might be exerting a large influence on the model. In particular, they remember that when they made a boxplot of average home values, Highland Park was an outlier. They decide to look at the regression model again and to calculate Cook's distance for their model and see whether they should eliminate those data. They specify for Minitab to calculate Cook's distances and also to output warnings about the data. The warning output is shown here:

Analyze the Data

```
Unusual Observations
Obs    Avg. Hou   1994 Avg      Fit   Stdev Fit   Residual   St Resid
  1       49803     204800   108753        7458      96047      2.61R
 21      196697     361100   410877       28165     -49777    -2.01RX
 25       42483      71800   117684       20993     -45884     -1.48X
 38       84007     269926   175521        7392      94405      2.57R
 39       87854     269926   181703        7868      88223      2.41R
 40      115368     324990   253062       15077      71928      2.10R
R denotes an observation with a large standardized residual
X denotes an observation whose X value gives it large influence
```

The planners notice that observation 21 has both a large residual and a large X value influence. They check and find that it is indeed Highland Park. Minitab outputs Cook's distance for Highland Park to be 1.749 and compares it to $F_{0.5,3,38} = 0.803$. Since Cook's distance is so much larger than the F value, the planners will have to think about redoing the analysis without that bit of data. None of the other Cook's distances exceed the critical value. ■

12.5.3 Multicollinearity

One problem that occurs in the multiple regression model that is not a factor in the simple linear model is known as **multicollinearity.**

A multiple regression model has ***multicollinearity*** when variables in the set of independent variables are correlated with each other.

It is not at all unusual to find that some of the variables in the set of independent variables are related to each other. This is especially likely to happen when the data used for a model come from existing sources. When data come from experimentation, it is possible to control elements that might cause multicollinearity. When data come from existing sources, this is not easy.

Suppose you were trying to find a model to predict the amount of money that a family spends on food, and that in your set of independent variables you had family income, house value, number of children, family size, and level of education of the head of the household. It would seem almost certain that some of these variables would be related to each other. It is also possible that variables in the set are related to other variables that are not included in the model. When this happens, the results of a multiple regression analysis may be affected.

The main effect of multicollinearity on the model is instability of the regression coefficients. When two variables in the set of independent variables are highly correlated, then the coefficients of the model are not stable. This means that when you remove one of the variables and rerun the model the coefficients will change—sometimes even changing sign from negative to positive! If this is the case, then interpretation of the coefficients is not meaningful. We know that the coefficient in the model represents the change in the dependent variable when the variable of interest is changed *and all other variables are held constant.* If two variables are highly correlated, then it may not be possible to vary one variable without also having the other variables change too.

Another problem that occurs when multicollinearity is present in a model is that the individual coefficients have large standard errors and therefore small t statistics. It is possible that a model might test significant as a whole, but that no individual coefficient will be significantly different from zero. This is certainly a contradiction and an indication that something is wrong!

There are several complex statistical procedures to find out whether a model has multicollinearity, but some simple procedures work well too. One method for detecting multicollinearity is to calculate the correlations between every pair of independent variables and look for large values near 1 or -1. If it appears that some variables are highly correlated, then the analyst may wish to concentrate on models that do not include both variables. Some statistical packages, such as Minitab, will warn the user when variables are highly correlated and in cases where the problem is severe, will refuse to include a variable in the model.

EXAMPLE 12.21 Texas Real Estate

Checking for Multicollinearity

The planners doing the real estate model know that their data came from existing sources and so might exhibit multicollinearity. They decide to run correlations for the set of five variables that they are considering.

Analyze the Data

Correlations (Pearson)

	Avg. Hou	Populati	1993/94	Mean SAT
Populati	−0.477			
1993/94	−0.441	0.436		
Mean SAT	0.534	−0.400	−0.208	
Total In	0.431	0.073	−0.163	0.138

From the correlation matrix the planners see that the highest correlation is 0.534, which is not high at all. The correlation between the two variables used in the model is 0.434. Hence, they know that they do not have to worry about multicollinearity. ■

A way to examine the effects of the multicollinearity in a model is to run the model with and without one of the variables. If the coefficients change to an unacceptable degree, for example, a complete change in sign from positive to negative, then another analysis method should be used. One method that produces coefficients that are not affected by multicollinearity is called ridge regression.

Order Filling ***Checking for Multicollinearity***

The mail-order company wants to check to see whether the model it is thinking about using has any problems with multicollinearity. It calculates the correlation between the two variables that are in the final model and finds that the correlation is −0.141.

Based on this information do you think that multicollinearity is a problem in their model? Why or why not?

Although multicollinearity causes big problems with the regression coefficients, the overall ability of the model to predict values of the dependent variable is not affected. If the users of the model are not looking at the actual equation but only at the predictors, the model may still be useful.

12.5.4 Using the Model

We have discussed some of the problems that can occur in a multiple regression model. Although none of the problems make the model unusable, we must understand the impact on the decision-making process. The biggest problem in terms of the usefulness of the model is instability of the regression coefficients. When the coefficients are unstable, then they really do not represent the change in the dependent variable that results from a corresponding change in one of the independent variables. If you try to use the model to bring about such a change, you may find that the result does not even resemble what you expect.

Problems with coefficient instability or error result from multicollinearity, overspecified models, and influential observations. Unless the multicollinearity is severe (variables correlated with a correlation coefficient of 0.9999 and above), instability is not much of a problem.

Overspecification of a model occurs when the "more is better" approach is taken to modeling. If you add enough variables to a model you can get an almost perfect fit to the set of input data you are using. The problem is that the perfect fit is just for that particular set of data. If you vary the data set at all you will find that the model varies wildly, which makes it almost useless for "what if" analysis and scenario management. Overspecification can be avoided by using one of the techniques designed to find the "best" regression model.

Observations that exert a large influence on the model also cause the coefficients of the model to be inaccurate. Often dropping the observations that are erroneous will solve the problem.

It is useful to check the stability of the model you find. One simple way to do this is to run the regression with the selected independent variables on subsets of the original data. If you have a large enough data set then you could divide it into two randomly chosen subsets and run the model on both subsets. If the resulting models are not similar, then the model may have problems with stability. If you do not have a large enough data set to run two separate analyses then you can choose two or more random samples of a fixed size from the set of data and run the regression on each subset. Again, if the models do not agree, then there is a problem that you must be aware of before using the model to make decisions.

ANS. NO, CORRELATION IS VERY LOW.

12.6 Executive Summary: Housing Prices

Business Analysis...

TO: City Councils, Cities of Dallas and Fort Worth
FROM: City Planners
RE: Housing Price Study

We recently conducted a study to try to determine what factors, if any, can be used to predict the selling prices of houses in the commuter suburbs of Dallas/Fort Worth. In this study we considered a macromodel, concentrating on characteristics of the towns rather than characteristics of the houses themselves.

After some deliberation we decided to use five different variables in our model: average household income, total instructional expenditures per pupil, mean SAT score, population diversity (% nonwhite), and number of violent crimes (per 1000 population). There are many other variables that might be considered, but we wanted to keep the analysis reasonable.

Using multiple regression models, we found two models that might be considered "best." Each was statistically significant and no one model was clearly better than the other. The result of the first model is

$$\text{Average selling price} = -1167 + 2.09(\text{average household income})$$

This says that, for every thousand dollar increase in household income, the selling price will increase by $2090. The intercept term is essentially zero, which makes sense. This model was considered best using two different methods of analysis.

We also looked at a model that considered an additional variable, total instructional expenditure per pupil. The result of this model is

$$\begin{aligned}\text{Average selling price} = {} & -67346 + 1.94(\text{average household income}) \\ & + 30.6(\text{total instructional expenditure per pupil})\end{aligned}$$

From a statistical perspective the two models are not very different. The coefficients in the one-variable model make more sense, but that model does not tell us anything about what characteristics of the town are related to selling prices. In the two variable model, the intercept is very large and might be misleading. It is our conclusion that neither model is satisfactory.

We would like to continue the analysis by considering a different set of variables. In particular we would like to replace average household income with town characteristics to see whether we can find a model that will help us in our planning. We will keep you informed of our progress.

The *Wall Street Journal* is a major source of current business news and information for the business community. If your professor has arranged for your class to have access to the Business Extra feature, you can go to it now and see the techniques of this chapter in action today. Go to the Wiley Web site at http://www.wiley.com/college/pelosi, and click on Business Extra!

12.7 MULTIPLE REGRESSION MODELS IN EXCEL

The tools used in Excel for multiple regression models are the same ones that are used for the simple linear model. The only difference is that the data range for the X variables will cover more than one column. It is *very* important, however, that the X variable columns be adjacent to each other. If they are not, you will have to rearrange the worksheet before you do the analysis.

The output section includes information about each of the regression coefficients. If you choose the residual plots option, you will get a plot of residuals versus each independent variable. This is also true for the line fit plots. These plots allow you to look at the assumptions of the multiple regression model and decide whether the model is appropriate.

Excel does not have any tools for finding the "best" regression model. These are sophisticated statistical tools, and Excel is not really a statistics software package. If you want to find the best model using Excel, you will have to use the all possible regressions approach.

KADDSTAT makes it easier to do multiple regression using Excel because it does not require that the data be in adjacent columns, unlike the Data Analysis Tools routine. Using KADDSTAT for multiple regression is almost identical to using it for simple linear regression. The only difference is that you will select more than one variable from the list of independent variables. To accomplish this, press the control (Ctrl) key while you click on each variable that you want to include in the analysis. If you want to include the entire list, you can just click on the **Select All** button.

12.7.1 Stepwise Regression with KADDSTAT

KADDSTAT has a routine that will allow you to perform stepwise regression, both forward and backward, in Excel. From the **KADD** menu select **Regression and Correlation > Forward Stepwise** and the dialog box shown in Figure 12.3 opens. The dialog box is identical to the one for Single/Multiple regression with two additional inputs.

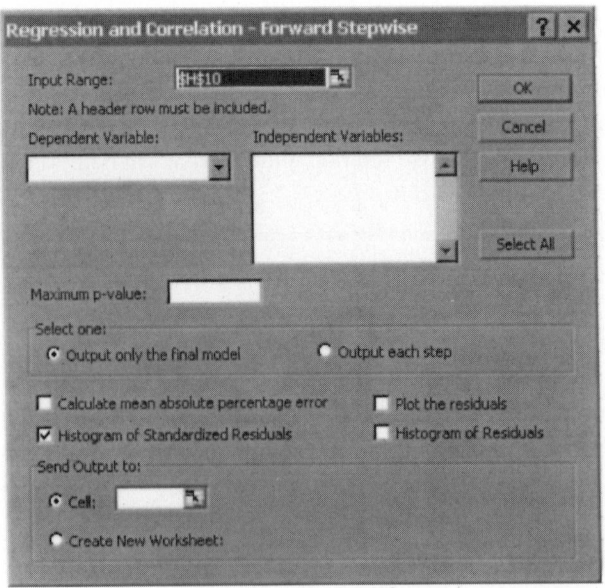

FIGURE 12.3 Dialog box for forward stepwise regression

Just above the area where you indicate which graphical output you want is a section labeled **Select one:**. This allows you to indicate whether you want to have only the final model output or whether you want each step output. In addition, you need to specify the p value to be used for adding and dropping variables from the model. KADDSTAT uses the same p value for both.

CHAPTER 12 SUMMARY

Finding a multiple regression model is easy. Finding a multiple regression model that is useful for the purposes of decision making is really an art. Modeling is an iterative process for which there is no single correct answer. The answer you choose depends on what you know and understand about the problem to be solved and how you intend to use the model.

There are several steps to the modeling process: Identifying potential independent variables, collecting data, and finding a potential model are the beginning steps. Once a potential model is found, the process of *model building* takes place to find a "best" model. The objective of this process is to find a model that does an acceptable job of explaining or predicting the dependent variable with as few independent variables as possible. Some of the model-building techniques used are *forward selection, backward elimination, stepwise regression,* and *all possible regressions.* Finally, once the "best" model is identified, it must be checked for problems such as *violation of assumptions, influential observations,* and *multicollinearity* before it can be used for decision-making purposes.

Key Terms

Term	Definition	Page Reference
Adjusted R^2	The **adjusted R^2** is the value of the coefficient of multiple determination adjusted to reflect the number of variables in the model.	593
Coefficient of multiple determination, R^2	The **coefficient of multiple determination, R^2,** is a measure of the percentage of the variation in the dependent variable, Y, that can be accounted for by the complete set of independent variables, $X_1, X_2, \ldots, X_k$, in the model.	592
Cook's distance	The **Cook's distance** method compares the values of the regression coefficients with all observations to the values when the ith observation is removed from the model.	617
Input variable	The set of independent variables, $X_1, X_2, \ldots, X_k$, are referred to as the **input variables.**	576
Model-building techniques	**Model-building techniques** are methods used for identifying the best multiple regression model from a set of independent variables. These methods include forward selection, backward elimination, stepwise regression, and all possible regressions.	604
Multicollinearity	A multiple regression model has **multicollinearity** when variables in the set of independent variables are correlated with each other.	618
Multiple regression model	The true relationship between the independent variable Y and the set of independent variables, $X_1, X_2, \ldots, X_k$, the **multiple regression model,** can be described by the equation $y = \beta_0 + \beta_1 x_1 + \beta_2 x_2 + \cdots + \beta_k x_k + \varepsilon$	576
Output variable	The dependent variable, Y, is often referred to as the **output variable.**	576

Key Formulas

Term	Formula	Page Reference
F test statistic	$F = \dfrac{\text{MSR}}{\text{MSE}}$	588
F critical value	$F_{\alpha,k,n-k-1}$	589
R^2	$R^2 = \dfrac{\text{SSR}}{\text{SST}}100\%$	592
t test statistic	$t = \dfrac{b_i}{s_{b_i}}$	595

CHAPTER 12 EXERCISES

Learning It!

12.11 The analysts looking at the model for equity ($/share) at Phillips Petroleum decided that the model they had was not adequate for their needs. They decide to try the model with a different set of independent variables: debt ($ billions) and number of employees (thousands). The data and output of the regression analysis are given here:

Year	Equity	Debt	Employees	Year	Equity	Debt	Employees
1986	7.55	6.2	21.8	1992	10.37	3.8	21.4
1987	7.08	5.8	22.5	1993	10.28	3.2	19.4
1988	8.69	4.9	21.0	1994	11.29	3.1	18.4
1989	8.74	4.0	21.8	1995	12.16	3.1	17.4
1990	10.51	3.9	22.4	1996	16.15	3.0	17.2
1991	10.61	4.0	22.7				

SUMMARY OUTPUT

Regression Statistics	
Multiple R	0.848198989
R Square	0.719441525
Adjusted R Square	0.649301907
Standard Error	1.471736507
Observations	11

ANOVA

	df	*SS*	*MS*	*F*	*Significance F*
Regression	2	44.43469688	22.21734844	10.2572774	0.006195745
Residual	8	17.32806676	2.166008345		
Total	10	61.76276364			

	Coefficients	*Standard Error*	*tStat*	*P-value*	*Lower 95%*
Intercept	25.01669053	4.991469246	5.011889145	0.001037315	13.50633437
Debt	−1.187745989	0.571806762	−2.077180733	0.07142751	−2.506335599
Employees	−0.47922578	0.303483518	−1.579083382	0.152970523	−1.179060481

(a) Write down the equation of the regression model and interpret the coefficients.

(b) Use the regression equation to predict shareholders' equity for each year from 1986 through 1996.

(c) Calculate the residuals and compare the actual data to the predicted values. Which year has the largest residual? Which has the smallest?

(d) Do you think that the model does a good job of predicting shareholders' equity? Why or why not?

(e) Set up the hypotheses to test the significance of the overall model.

(f) At the 0.05 level of significance, what is your conclusion about the model?

(g) What is the value of R^2 for this model? What does it mean?

(h) Compare this model to the model using revenue and assets developed in the chapter. Which model do you think is better? Why?

12.12 Analysts at a company that produces small appliances are looking at sales of 24 food preparation products in a medium-size city in the Midwest. They have noticed that sales in this city have not been meeting forecast values for several months and want to look at the problem in more detail. They have collected data on monthly sales ($), advertising expenditure ($), number of competing products available, number of discount opportunities (sales, coupons, etc.) offered during the month, and the warranty period of the item. A portion of the data is shown here:

Datafile: *SALES.XXX*

Sales ($)	Advertising ($)	Number of Competitors	Discounts	Warranty (years)
4565	459	1	1	2.00
4896	545	0	0	0.25
4480	472	2	2	1.00
4300	482	3	3	2.00
3502	435	3	3	0.25
4413	499	3	3	1.00
5868	604	0	0	1.00
4527	501	1	1	1.00
3849	370	3	3	1.00

(a) Consider the problem that must be solved. What do you think is the dependent variable in this problem? Which are the independent variables?

(b) As advertising expenditures increase, what do you think the effect on sales will be? Will they increase or decrease? How do you think that each of the other independent variables will affect monthly sales?

(c) Use a computer package to find the multiple regression model you identified in part (a).

(d) Write down the regression equation and interpret the coefficients in the model. How did the actual coefficients agree with your expectation of their effect?

(e) Use the software package to calculate the predicted sales for each of the products in the data set and compare them to the actual sales.

(f) Make a plot of predicted versus actual sales.

(g) How well do you think the model predicts monthly sales?

(h) Set up the hypotheses and test the significance of the model using $\alpha = 0.05$.

(i) What is the value of R^2 for this model and what does it mean?

12.13 The Department of the Interior is looking at state parks in the United States. It is wondering what variables might affect revenues and has assembled data for each state consisting of the number of acres, number of day visitors, number of overnight visitors, and operating expenses for 1992. A portion of the data is shown here:

Datafile: *NATLPARK.XXX*

State	Acreage (1000)	Day Visitors (1000)	Overnight Visitors (1000)	Total Revenue ($1000)	Operating Expenses (1000)
Alabama	50	4,740	1,175	25,724	28,279
Alaska	3,250	3,567	703	1,957	5,294
Arizona	46	1,721	580	4,114	11,392
Arkansas	51	6,931	683	12,805	23,364
California	1,345	64,765	6,187	63,689	175,189
Colorado	347	11,973	727	10,708	15,771
Connecticut	176	7,672	357	3,571	8,875
Delaware	17	2,795	207	5,013	8,829

SOURCE: *Statistical Abstract of the United States 1999*

(a) Find a multiple regression model that predicts revenue as a function of the number of acres of parkland, the number of day visitors, the number of overnight visitors, and operating expenses.

(b) Interpret the coefficients of the model.

(c) Use the model to predict the revenues for each state.

(d) Calculate the residuals and compare them to the actual data.

(e) Which state has the largest residual? Which state has the smallest?

(f) What is the value of R^2 for this model? Do you think that the model does a good job of predicting revenues for state parks? Why or why not?

Datafile: MALL.XXX

12.14 A national chain of women's clothing stores with locations in large shopping malls thinks that it can do a better job of planning store renovations and expansions if it understands what variables impact sales. It plans a small pilot study on stores in 24 different mall locations. The data it collects consist of monthly sales, store size (sq ft), number of linear feet of window display, number of competitors located in mall, size of the mall (sq ft), and distance to nearest competitor (ft). A sample of the data is shown here:

Store	Sales	Size	Windows	Competitors	Mall Size	Nearest Competitor
1	4453	3860	39	12	943,700	227
2	4770	4150	41	15	532,500	142
3	4821	3880	39	15	390,500	263
4	4912	4000	39	13	545,500	219
5	4774	4140	40	10	329,600	232
6	4638	4370	48	14	802,600	257

(a) What is the dependent variable in this model? Which variables are the independent variables?

(b) How do you think that the size of a store will impact sales? How do you think the other independent variables will impact sales?

(c) Use a computer software package to find a multiple regression model for the data.

(d) Interpret the values of the coefficients in the model. Do they agree with how you expected them to behave?

(e) Set up the hypotheses to test whether the model as a whole is significant. At the 0.05 level of significance, what is your conclusion?

(f) Use the model to predict monthly sales for each of the stores in the study. Calculate the residuals.

(g) Which store had the largest residual? Which had the smallest?

(h) Plot the residuals versus the actual values. Do you think that the model does a good job of predicting monthly sales? Why or why not?

Thinking About It!

Requires Example 12.2, Exercise 12.11

Datafile: MOBIL.XXX

12.15 The financial analysts looking at a model for shareholders' equity at Phillips Petroleum have obtained similar data from Mobil Oil. They would like to construct models for Mobil similar to the two that they have already constructed for Phillips. The data are not available for all of the years of interest. The data for Mobil are shown here:

Year	Assets ($ million)	Revenue ($ million)	Shareholder Equity ($/share)	Total Debt ($ million)	Employees (1000)
1986	NA	44,936	32.86	NA	70.9
1987	NA	51,678	36.46	NA	68.1
1988	NA	54,740	38.19	NA	69.4
1989	NA	56,388	39.84	NA	67.9
1990	NA	64,774	42.44	NA	67.3
1991	25,464	63,311	43.74	8229	67.5

(continued)

Year	Assets ($ million)	Revenue ($ million)	Shareholder Equity ($/share)	Total Debt ($ million)	Employees (1000)
1992	25,075	64,456	41.06	8520	63.7
1993	25,037	63,975	42.74	8027	61.9
1994	25,503	67,383	42.61	7727	58.5
1995	24,850	75,370	44.71	6756	50.4
1996	27,479	81,503	47.62	6581	43.0

SOURCE: *Mobil Oil Annual Report*, World Wide Web site: www.mobiloil.com

(a) Using the data that are available, create a model for Mobil that relates shareholder equity to assets and revenue.

(b) In what ways might you expect the model for Mobil to be similar to the one for Phillips? In what ways might they be different?

(c) Compare the model for Mobil to the one found in Example 12.2 for Phillips Petroleum. Do the models agree with your answer to part (b)?

(d) Find a model for Mobil that relates shareholder equity to total debt and number of employees.

(e) Compare the model for Mobil to the one for Phillips from Exercise 12.11. How are they similar? How are they different?

(f) Which of the two models for Mobil do you think does a better job of predicting shareholder equity?

12.16 Automobile salespeople want to understand the amount of driving done by a household so that they can plan advertising campaigns. They propose to use data from a survey sponsored by the Department of Transportation to help them understand what factors affect the annual number of miles driven by a household.

Datafile: MILES.XXX

(a) What variables do you think might influence the number of miles driven annually by a household? Why did you choose these variables?

As part of the study, data were extracted from a data base containing the survey information. The data used consisted of 85 households with two or more people for a small city in the Northeast. The variables in the study were total miles driven in the previous 12 months, number of drivers in the household, number of vehicles in the household, number of children ages 5 to 19 in the household, total number of trips taken in the 24-hour period prior to the survey, and total number of miles driven in the same 24-hour period.

(b) Do you see any problems with these data? If so, what are they? Suggest any additional variables that you think would help to eliminate or clarify the problems.

(c) A portion of the data available from the Department of Transportation is shown here:

HHVMILES	DRVRCNT	VEHCOUNT	NUM_KIDS	DTVCNT_H	DTVMILH
0	2	0	2	3	3
20,975	2	2	1	6	35
23,000	3	2	0	7	99
36,000	1	1	0	2	70
6,327	2	2	2	2	10
27,423	2	2	0	5	58
7,058	1	2	0	0	0
24,365	1	3	1	4	10
101,313	1	2	1	4	13
2,519	2	2	0	2	6

The six variables are defined as follows:

HHVMILES	*total annual miles for all vehicles in household*
DRVRCNT	*number of drivers in household*
VEHCOUNT	*number of vehicles in household*
NUM_KIDS	*number of children in household age 5 through 21*
DTVCNT_H	*number of travel day vehicle trips for the household*
DTVMILH	*travel day vehicle miles for household*

The travel day is the 24-hour period prior to the survey.

(d) Use a computer software package to find the multiple regression model that predicts total annual vehicle miles using the other five variables as the set of independent variables.

(e) Write down the model and interpret the coefficients. Do they make sense?

(f) At the 0.05 level of significance what can you say about the model?

(g) What is the value of R^2 for this model? Do you think that the model will be useful for predicting total annual vehicle miles for a household? Why or why not?

Requires Exercise 12.14

12.17 The planners looking at store characteristics and sales want to know more about the model that they have found.

(a) Find and interpret the value of R^2 for this model.

(b) Do you think that this model will be useful in helping the planners? Why or why not?

(c) Set up the hypotheses to test the individual regression coefficients. At the 0.05 level of significance, what are your conclusions?

(d) If you were going to drop just one variable from the model, which one would you choose? Why?

Requires Exercise 12.11

Datafile:
PHILLIPS.XXX

12.18 The analysts looking at financial data from Phillips Petroleum are not satisfied with either of the two models that they have developed. They want to combine the two models and determine if there is a better model available.

(a) Based on the results of the previous models, which two variables do you think will be most helpful in predicting shareholder equity? Why?

(b) Use the all possible regressions method to find the best one-, two-, three-, and four-variable models.

(c) From the list of best models for each size, pick the model that you think should be used to predict shareholder equity.

(d) Write a memo to the Chief Financial Officer of the company explaining your model and justifying your choice.

Requires Exercise 12.12

12.19 Look at the output from the analysis of the monthly sales data for the small appliances manufacturer. There were four variables in the original analysis, but the company wants to know whether they were all important in the model.

(a) Set up the hypotheses to test whether the individual coefficients are different from zero and perform the tests at the 0.05 level of significance.

(b) What are your conclusions from this test?

(c) Consider the variables that have coefficients that are zero. Which of these would you recommend dropping from the model? Why?

(d) Rerun the analysis, dropping the variable you identified in part (c). How does this change the model as a whole?

(e) Does dropping this variable change the contribution of the other variables? If so, how?

(f) Would you consider dropping another variable? If so, which one?

(g) If you answered yes to part (f), then rerun the analysis dropping that variable.

(h) Based on all of your analyses, what model do you think the company should use?

(i) Does this approach to finding a model resemble any of the model building techniques you learned about? If so, which one?

Requires Exercises 12.14, 12.17

12.20 The store planners for the women's clothing chain want to find the best model that they can for understanding what store characteristics impact monthly sales.

(a) Use stepwise regression or all possible regressions to find the best model for the data.

(b) Analyze the model you have identified to determine whether it has any problems.

(c) Write a memo reporting your findings to your boss. Identify the strengths and weaknesses of the model you have chosen.

12.21 Look again at the data on monthly sales of small appliances.

Requires Exercises 12.12, 12.19

(a) Use stepwise regression or all possible regressions to find the best model from the set of four variables.

(b) Compare the results of the formal procedure to the model you chose in Exercise 12.19. Are the two models the same? Would you expect them to be?

(c) Consider the two "best" models you have. If they are different, which one would you choose as your model? Why?

12.22 Look at the results of the analysis on the state park data collected by the Department of the Interior.

Requires Exercise 12.13

(a) Set up the hypotheses for testing individual regression coefficients. At the 0.01 level of significance, what are your conclusions?

(b) Drop any of the variables whose coefficients tested to be zero from the model and rerun the analysis.

(c) How does the model change?

(d) Are you satisfied with this model or do you think that additional analysis must be done to find the best model?

(e) Perform any additional analyses you think are necessary to find the best model for predicting revenues.

12.23 Look again at the model for predicting the total annual miles driven by a household.

Requires Exercise 12.16

(a) At the 0.05 level of significance, what can you say about the individual regression coefficients?

(b) Which variables would you consider dropping from the model? Why?

(c) Consider what the model is trying to predict. Do you think that households with no vehicles should be included in these data? Why or why not?

(d) Identify the observations that have no vehicles and drop them from the data. Rerun the analysis. Does this change anything?

(e) Again, think about what the model is trying to predict. What other data values do not represent the population of interest? Why?

(f) Drop any observations that correspond to your answer to part (e) and rerun the model. How do the results compare with the other two models? Do you feel more confident with this model? Why or why not?

12.24 Look at the model that you decided on for the monthly small appliance sales.

Requires Exercises 12.12, 12.19, 12.21

(a) Prepare a set of residual plots for the model. Does the model appear to violate any of the assumptions of the multiple regression model? If so, what are the problems?

(b) Calculate the correlations between each pair of independent variables. Does there appear to be multicollinearity in the model? If so, what would you recommend doing?

(c) Divide the data set in half using some random selection process and run the model on each subset. Compare the models. Do the coefficients of the model appear stable? Why or why not?

(d) Use either Cook's distance or some other measure available in your software to determine whether any of the observations are exerting a strong influence on the model.

(e) Drop these observations from the data and rerun the analysis. How does this change the model?

(f) Prepare a memo describing your findings and suggesting a model to use for predicting revenue. Be sure to include any limitations of the model you suggest.

12.25 Consider the model that you feel is currently best for predicting total annual miles for a household.

Requires Exercises 12.16, 12.23

(a) Prepare a set of residual plots for the model. Does the model appear to violate any of the assumptions of the multiple regression model? If so, what are the problems?

(b) Calculate the correlations between each pair of independent variables. Does there appear to be multicollinearity in the model? If so, what would you recommend doing?

(c) Use either Cook's distance or some other measure available in your software to determine whether any of the observations are exerting a strong influence on the model.

(d) Drop these observations from the data and rerun the analysis. How does this change the model?

(e) Prepare a memo describing your findings and suggesting a model to use for predicting revenue. Be sure to include any limitations of the model you suggest.

Doing It!

12.26 As we saw in the example about Texas Real Estate, there are many factors that might affect home prices. A group looking at the city of Boston collected data on a number of variables believed to be predictors of home prices. The variables are

CRIM	per capita crime rate by town
ZN	proportion of residential land zoned for lots over 25,000 sq ft
INDUS	proportion of nonretail business acres per town
CHAS	Charles River dummy variable (=1 if tract bounds river, 0 otherwise)
NOX	nitric oxides concentrations (parts per 10 million)
RM	average number of rooms per dwelling
AGE	proportion of owner-occupied units built prior to 1940
DIS	weighted distances to five Boston employment centers
RAD	index of accessibility to radial highways
TAX	full-value property-tax rate per $10,000
PTRATIO	pupil–teacher ratio by town
LSTAT	% lower status of population
MEDV	median value of owner-occupied homes in $1000s

CRIM	ZN	INDUS	CHAS	NOX	RM	AGE	DIS	RAD	TAX	PTRATIO	LSTAT	MEDV
0.00632	18.0	2.31	0	0.538	6.575	65.2	4.0900	1	296	15.3	4.98	24.0
0.02731	0.0	7.07	0	0.469	6.421	78.9	4.9671	2	242	17.8	9.14	21.6
0.02729	0.0	7.07	0	0.469	7.185	61.1	4.9671	2	242	17.8	4.03	34.7
0.03237	0.0	2.18	0	0.458	6.998	45.8	6.0622	3	222	18.7	2.94	33.4
0.06905	0.0	2.18	0	0.458	7.147	54.2	6.0622	3	222	18.7	5.33	36.2
0.02985	0.0	2.18	0	0.458	6.430	58.7	6.0622	3	222	18.7	5.21	28.7
0.08829	12.5	7.87	0	0.524	6.012	66.6	5.5605	5	311	15.2	12.43	22.9

(a) Calculate the correlation coefficients of each variable with the median value of owner-occupied homes (MEDV).

(b) Select a set of no more than five variables to use as the set of independent variables.

(c) Using the variables you selected, find the best model for predicting the median value of homes.

(d) Test to see whether your model is appropriate.

(e) Summarize your findings in a memo to the group.

CHAPTER **13**

TIME SERIES AND FORECASTING

TAKE ME OUT TO THE BALL GAME

American Pastime, Inc. is a company that provides high-quality entertainment to communities. With a clear focus on families, American Pastime plans to offer people of all ages an affordable opportunity to view exciting Double A baseball in a clean and safe environment.

Business Analysis...

To plan for this facility, American Pastime must forecast ticket sales. This information will help the company determine the number of ticket windows and the ordering/inventory plan for the food and souvenir items to be sold in such a way that costs are minimized.

The facility will consist of a state-of-the-art 200,000-square-foot stadium. Seating for approximately 6000 fixed seats for baseball attendees will be available: 4200 chair reserved seats and 1800 bench with back general admission seats. There will be 61 home games.

The population figures for the past 10 years for the area are available to you. The data are divided into two groups: the number of people in families with children (FWC) and the number of people in the age group from 20 to 40 with no children (NC). These two groups are your target population. Once you have the forecast for the two population groups, you must predict the number of people who will attend each game. Past experience shows that the attendance rate is 1.91 per 1000 for the FWC group and 1.75 per 1000 for the NC group.

13.1 Chapter Objectives

The problem of forecasting ticket sales described in the chapter opener is similar to many business problems that require the prediction of some variable. For example, you may wish to predict sales of a new or existing product, the closing price of a stock, the yield of an agricultural crop, the attendance at a meeting, or the donations to a nonprofit organization.

The problem of forecasting is the problem of prediction. It is an important problem in many arenas. Imagine your financial success if you could develop a really accurate forecasting model to predict stock prices in the future! The techniques presented in this chapter will get you off the ground with forecasting tools. Forecasting is a field in which there are great job opportunities.

Two major approaches to forecasting

There are two major approaches to developing a forecasting model. One approach is a **qualitative** approach. This approach relies on experience and expert opinion. Such an approach is used when little or no historical data are available. For instance, if you are introducing a brand-new product, you will not have any past sales data, or if you are penetrating a new market, you will not have any historical data. The other major approach is to use a **quantitative model.** These models are used when historical data are available. Since this is a course in quantitative methods, we will focus our attention in this chapter on quantitative models.

> A ***qualitative model*** for forecasting relies on experience and expert opinion. It is used when there are little or no historical data available. A ***quantitative model*** uses past data to predict future values.

Let's consider the daily sales of loaves of bread at your local convenience store. The manufacturer would like to know precisely how many loaves of bread will be sold each day. Then the manufacturer could supply exactly that number and know that it will not lose any customers due to a stock out and it will not be left with loaves of bread at the end of the day that cannot be sold. But the number of loaves of bread sold per day probably depends on a number of factors, such as the number of loaves sold the previous day, the weather, the traffic, and other things. We could try to build a regression model treating the number of loaves of bread sold as the dependent variable and the others as independent variables. However, in many instances such as this one there are few data available on the independent variables. Hence, it is often impossible to build a *causal* model.

In these cases, the only alternative is to use a time series forecasting model. The main idea behind any time series forecasting model is that we can predict future values by studying the behavior of the past values. There is not a sense of cause and effect in these models but simply an attempt to *see patterns, repetitive or systematic behavior, and/or trends in the data.*

So you can see that there are two major types of quantitative models: **causal** and **time series models.** Causal models exploit the *relationship* between the variable you wish to predict and *other variables.* You have already studied some causal models in the last chapter on multiple regression. There are also other techniques that can be used to develop a causal model, but they are beyond the scope of this text. The field of econometrics is the study of this topic.

Causal models exploit the relationship between the dependent variable and other related variables in predicting future values for the dependent variable.

Time series models use only data on the variable of interest. They exploit the patterns and trends in the data. The remainder of this chapter will focus on time series models.

Time series models use only data on the variable of interest. They exploit patterns, repetitive or systematic behavior, and/or trends in the data to predict future values for the dependent variable.

The following simple example may help you understand what this means.

Suppose you observe the time that Mr. Russell goes to work every morning for 10 mornings. The data are shown here:

Monday	8:02 AM	Monday	7:59 AM
Tuesday	9:15 AM	Tuesday	9:20 AM
Wednesday	7:55 AM	Wednesday	8:10 AM
Thursday	9:08 AM	Thursday	9:09 AM
Friday	8:06 AM	Friday	8:05 AM

A quick look at these times would tell you that on Mondays, Wednesdays, and Fridays, Mr. Russell leaves somewhere around 8 AM, whereas on Tuesdays and Thursdays he leaves shortly after 9 AM. We could use this pattern to predict his departure times for the next few days. We are banking on the fact that Mr. Russell, like most of us, is a creature of habit and therefore the future looks much like the past in terms of general patterns. We do not know what is causing this pattern and we cannot know the cause by simply examining these data. In a time series method, we do not need to know what is causing the difference in his departure times on MWF versus TuTh.

Remember: *The independent variable is displayed on the x axis and the dependent variable on the y axis.*

Typically, when you are looking at time series data, you have several observations of the variable of interest (the dependent variable) observed over time. So, in effect, time becomes the independent variable. The graph shown in Figure 13.1 on page 634 displays the number of loaves of bread sold at a typical convenience store for the last 25 days.

This scatter plot depicts the number of loaves sold along the y axis and the number of the day along the x axis. It is the same scatter plot technique that you learned in Chapter 5 except now the data points are connected. The days are arbitrarily numbered beginning with day 1. To predict the number of loaves of bread to be sold on day 26 we should exploit the information in the scatter plot. This means we should try to identify any patterns that exist in the sales over time.

This small example illustrates the nature of **time series** data.

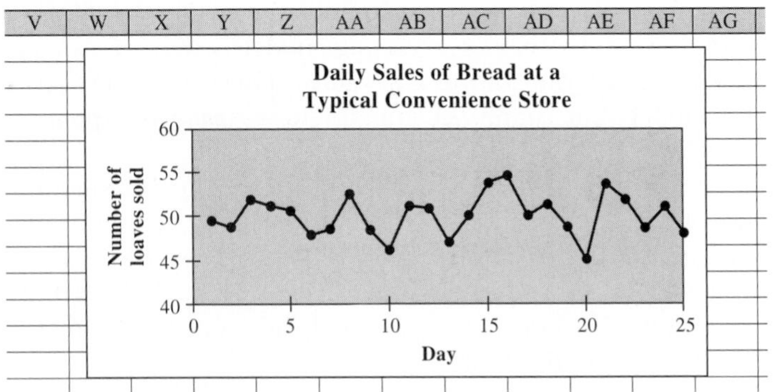

FIGURE 13.1 Sample scatter plot of loaves sold by time

A *time series* is a set of observations of a variable at regular time intervals, such as yearly, monthly, weekly, daily, etc.

Time series models are used to ***extrapolate*** *past behavior to predict future behavior.*

There are many different ways of extracting the information in a time series to predict the value of the variable in the next time period or beyond. In this chapter you will learn how to analyze time series data using four different methods: simple moving average, weighted moving average, exponential smoothing, and regression. These are the most commonly used techniques. The moving average and exponential smoothing techniques are appropriate for **stationary time series.** This simply means there is no significant upward or downward long-term trend in the data. The technique of regression is appropriate for **nonstationary time series,** where there is some upward or downward trend over time. This is the same basic technique you learned in Chapter 11 only with the variable time as the independent variable now.

A *stationary time series* is one with no significant upward or downward trend. A *nonstationary time series* has some type of trend.

This chapter covers the following material:

- Getting Started with Time Series Data
- Components of the Multiplicative Time Series Model
- Simple Moving Average Models
- Weighted Moving Average Models
- Exponential Smoothing Models
- Regression Models
- Seasonal Indexes
- Other Forecasting Techniques

13.2 GETTING STARTED WITH TIME SERIES DATA

13.2.1 Time Series Notation

To study time series data we must introduce some general notation. Consistent with the notation from regression, we will label the variable that we are trying to predict with the letter Y. Since each observation is taken at a particular *time*, we will subscript Y with the letter t. Thus, the data in a time series are labeled

Time series notation

$$y_1, y_2, \ldots, y_t$$

where

y_1 is the observation of the variable at time period 1

y_2 is the observation of the variable at time period 2

y_t is the observation of the variable at time period t

The observation that is the oldest in terms of the time that it was observed compared to the present is labeled y_1. For the bread example, the daily sales 25 days ago is the oldest observation and is therefore labeled y_1. The second oldest observation is labeled y_2 and so forth. With t observations of the variable of interest, the current time is labeled time period t. We are typically trying to predict the value for the next time period, $t + 1$. This prediction will be labeled $\hat{y}_{t+1}$. Remember that we used the notation $\hat{y}$ as the predicted value of y from the regression model. In a similar manner, the caret in $\hat{y}_{t+1}$ tells you it is an estimate and the subscript $t + 1$ tells you that it is an estimate for the next time period, $t + 1$. Sometimes you may wish to predict beyond this point. In this case you may wish to predict the value of y for time periods $t + 2$, $t + 3$, etc. These would be labeled $\hat{y}_{t+2}$, $\hat{y}_{t+3}$, etc.

Consider how the data would be labeled for the baseball problem.

EXAMPLE 13.1 Baseball Attendance

Population Data for the Past 10 Years

Understand the Problem

Collect the Data

The population data for the community surrounding the location of the new baseball stadium are shown below. Remember that FWC is the number of people in families with children and NC is the number of people in the age group from 20 to 40 with no children.

	A	B	C
1	Year	FWC	NC
2	1991	1,098,909	564,790
3	1992	1,197,185	556,734
4	1993	1,169,860	653,134
5	1994	1,350,675	632,459
6	1995	1,335,213	642,387
7	1996	1,207,658	654,890
8	1997	1,379,723	657,238
9	1998	1,321,457	657,238
10	1999	1,387,692	717,903
11	2000	1,546,920	692,340

There are really two time series here: the time series consisting of observations of the number of people in families with children and those for the families with no children. For the moment, just consider the time series labeled FWC. The value from the year 1991 is the oldest so it is labeled y_1. The most recent observation is 2000 and so it is labeled y_{10}. Thus, the current time is $t = 10$ and we wish to predict the value for $t = 11$ or the year 2001. ■

The time period should be selected to fit the needs of the problem.

Note that the time period could be every minute, every hour, every day, every week, every month, every year, or any other period that makes sense for the particular application you are working with. For the loaves of bread example in the previous section, the time period is every day since we observed daily sales. For the baseball ticket sales example, the population must be predicted for the next year based on the last 10 years of data. So the time period is every year. If you are predicting the closing price of a stock, the time period would be every day.

13.2.2 Displaying the Time Series

Always display the data before deciding on a method of analysis.

Once you have identified the data and labeled them properly, you should display them using a line graph. This is like a scatter plot but it connects the points. The x axis should be time and the y axis should be the variable of interest. Let's continue working with the FWC time series.

Analyze the Data

EXAMPLE 13.2 Baseball Attendance

Line Graph for FWC Time Series

The line graph for the FWC time series follows.

Use a Line graph from the Chart Wizard in Excel. Note the dates don't line up perfectly with the "dots." This is due to limitations in Excel.

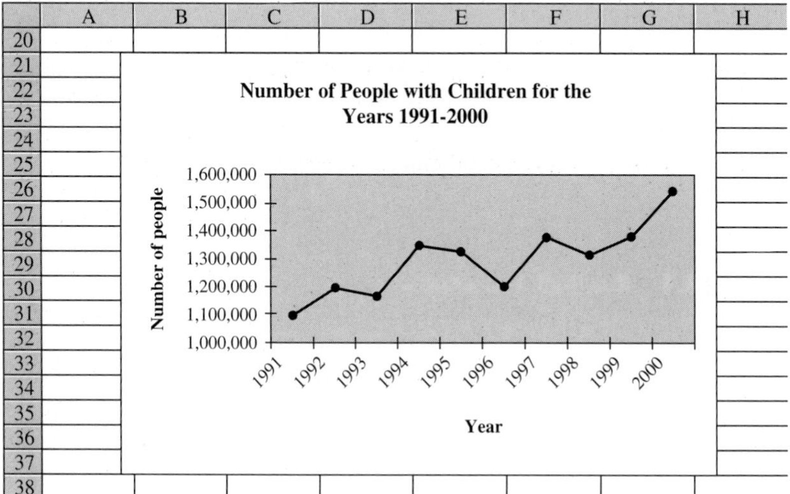

Note that alternatively the x axis could have been labeled year 1 to year 10. In this case, it is probably preferable to use the actual years for the x axis, whereas for the bread data example, it was easiest to label the days from 1 to 25. ■

After you plot the data, you should examine the plot to see whether there are any obvious patterns or trends. In this case, the time series seems to have a slight upward trend but there are no regular patterns. Now you plot the scatter plot for the NC time series and examine it for patterns or trends.

Baseball Attendance ***Line Graph of NC Time Series***

Display the NC time series as a line graph.

Do you see any patterns or trends? If so, what are they?

The next section gives names to the various patterns and trends you have been noticing.

13.2.3 Exercises—Learning It!

13.1 By participating in the AP program, high school students may acquire college credit for their knowledge of college-level subjects. The following data are the number of students who took AP examinations (per 1000 12th graders) by gender from 1984 to 1997.

Year	Male	Female
1984	50	50
1985	61	58
1986	65	63
1987	68	65
1988	76	85
1989	86	90
1990	101	98
1991	96	111
1992	102	117
1993	108	127
1994	101	129
1995	111	140
1996	117	144
1997	117	145

Source: The College Board, Advanced Placement Program, *National Summary Reports*

(a) Display both time series on the same graph.

(b) Do you see any patterns or trends? Is the time series for males stationary or nonstationary? Is the time series for females stationary or nonstationary?

(c) What other information might be useful in evaluating these time series?

13.2 The graph at the top of page 638 shows the daily closing price of John Wiley and Sons stock from April 17, 2000, to July 17, 2000. Do you see any patterns in the time series?

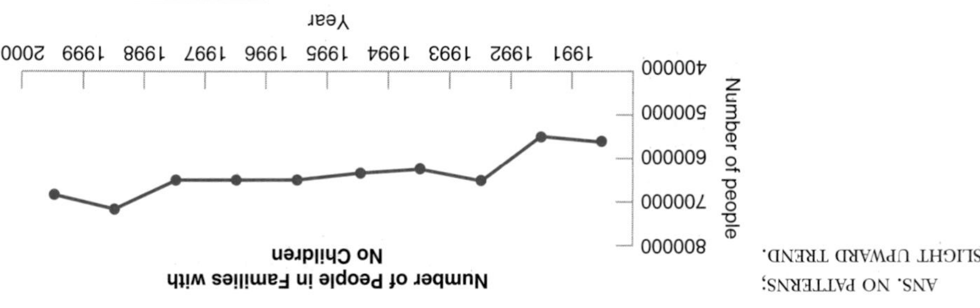

ANS. NO PATTERNS;
SLIGHT UPWARD TREND.

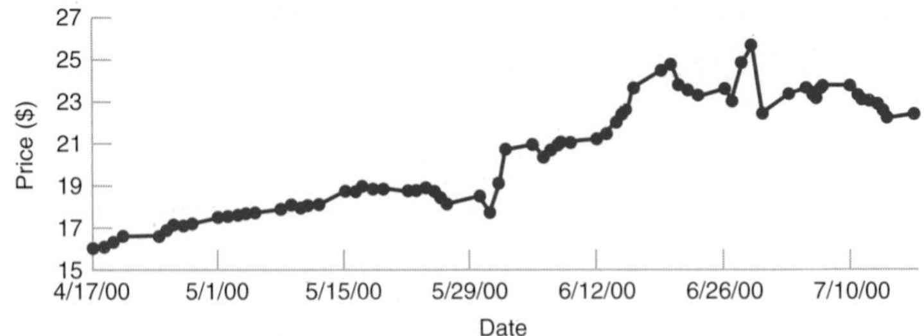

Datafile: *SCHOOLS.XXX*

13.3 In planning for schools, the Department of Education keeps data on public elementary and secondary school enrollment in grades 1–12 (in thousands) by region. The data in the Schools.XXX file show these figures from 1965 to 1997 for the Northeast, Midwest, South, and West regions of the United States. The data are also shown here. Notice that the data are available every 5 years until 1990 and after that annually.

Year	Northeast	Midwest	South	West
1965	8155	10907	13701	7045
1970	9136	11950	14416	7829
1975	8994	11360	13872	7622
1980	7711	9929	13259	7289
1985	6772	9019	12994	7445
1990	6662	9061	13478	8406
1991	6774	9176	13724	8687
1992	6881	9301	13940	8884
1993	6993	9374	14126	9049
1994	7086	9461	14312	9206
1995	7210	9560	14529	9369
1996	7332	9675	14762	9640
1997	7421	9738	14947	9822

(a) Display the four time series on one graph.

(b) Which of the time series are stationary and which are nonstationary? Explain.

(c) Which area of the country seems to be growing in population?

(d) Which area of the country seems to be decreasing in population?

Datafile: *APPLES.XXX*

13.4 The U.S. Department of Agriculture maintains a database of crop yield for various crops. The data in the file called Apples.XXX show the holdings of apples in cold storage for the state of New York from 1989 to 1998 by month. The data are also shown here:

Month	1989	1990	1991	1992	1993	1994	1995	1996	1997	1998
					1,000 bushels					
January	4,838	5,550	5,435	7,140	5,365	5,959	5,789	5,641	7,302	6,160
February	3,753	4,021	4,051	5,737	4,214	4,773	4,338	4,759	6,056	4,653
March	2,724	2,737	2,689	3,859	2,938	3,108	3,176	3,449	4,752	3,344
April	1,757	1,450	1,480	2,662	2,010	1,887	1,915	1,941	3,182	1,932
May	798	625	605	1,468	1,116	840	1,037	1,016	2,150	1,000
June	303	240	161	535	421	286	415	440	1,286	523
July	158	106	61	252	NA	68	243	201	751	
August	52	117	66	NA	NA	NA	NA	NA	433	
September	2,954	3,569	4,962	2,677	2,286	3,163	3,731	3,319	3,715	4,425
October	6,397	8,572	8,722	9,115	8,321	8,380	8,139	7,891	8,874	8,427
November	6,740	7,874	7,921	9,199	7,420	8,347	7,861	8,135	9,279	7,620
December	5,976	6,539	6,910	8,170	6,463	7,321	7,019	7,021	8,429	6,696

(a) Display the apples holdings for New York as a line graph.

(b) What can you learn about the amount of apples available over any given year?

(c) As you look at the data across the years, do you see any trend in the apple holdings in New York?

13.5 The U.S. Bureau of Census records the population of other countries in its international data base. The following data show the total mid-year population of the United Kingdom from 1950 to 2000. *Datafile: UKPOP. XXX*

Year	Population	Year	Population	Year	Population	Year	Population	Year	Population
1950	50,127,000	1960	52,372,000	1970	55,632,000	1980	56,314,000	1990	57,620,937
1951	50,290,000	1961	52,807,000	1971	55,907,000	1981	56,382,597	1991	57,807,900
1952	50,430,000	1962	53,292,000	1972	56,079,000	1982	56,353,589	1992	58,015,103
1953	50,593,000	1963	53,625,000	1973	56,210,000	1983	56,410,413	1993	58,207,959
1954	50,765,000	1964	53,991,000	1974	56,224,000	1984	56,503,978	1994	58,408,622
1955	50,946,000	1965	54,350,000	1975	56,215,000	1985	56,676,069	1995	58,613,976
1956	51,184,000	1966	54,643,000	1976	56,206,000	1986	56,866,272	1996	58,814,763
1957	51,430,000	1967	54,959,000	1977	56,179,000	1987	57,065,918	1997	59,006,721
1958	51,652,000	1968	55,214,000	1978	56,167,000	1988	57,258,270	1998	59,187,127
1959	51,956,000	1969	55,461,000	1979	56,228,000	1989	57,437,574	1999	59,355,419
								2000	59,508,382

(a) Display the population data as a line graph.

(b) Do you see any patterns or trends?

(c) What do you notice about the data after 1980? Why do you think this happened?

Discovery Exercise 13.1 LOOKING FOR PATTERNS AND TRENDS

Examine the time series displayed in the accompanying graphs and identify any patterns and trends that you see. Use what you know about the particular data being collected to help you identify why the data look the way they do.

(a) This chart shows the average monthly price (cents per kilowatt·hour) of electricity across the United States from January 1988 to January 2000.

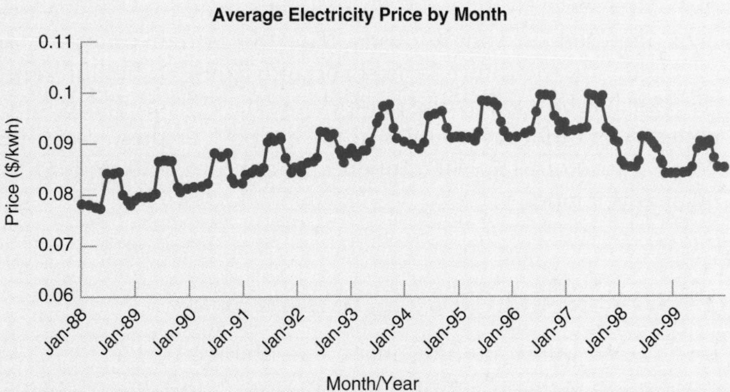

(b) The Bureau of Labor Statistics (BLS) reports data on commodity prices on a monthly basis. These data are reported on a regional and national basis. The graph at the top of page 640 displays the monthly average price (cents per pound) of white bread (pan) in the United States for the years 1980–2000.

(continued)

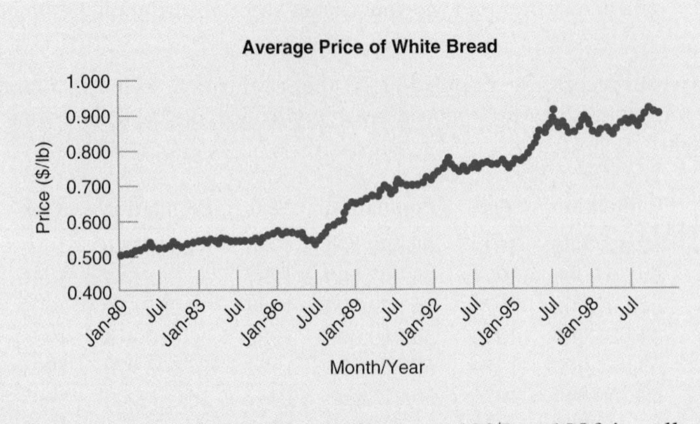

(c) The number of electric ranges shipped annually from 1987 to 1996 is collected by the appliance industry.

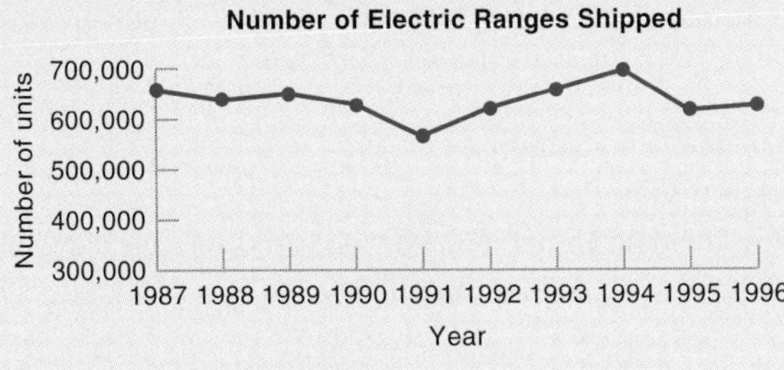

13.3 COMPONENTS OF THE MULTIPLICATIVE MODEL

Time series models assume that the future mirrors the past.

Remember that the main idea in time series analysis is to detect patterns, systematic behavior, and/or trends in the data and use this information to predict future values. Implicit in this approach is the idea that the future "looks like" the past. If it does not, then analyzing the past will not help us much in predicting the future. As you consider any time series be sure that the forces that influenced the variable in the past have not changed. Suppose, for example, that a new regulatory law has been imposed on your industry. The forces that influence sales have most likely changed, and the future is most certainly going to be different from the past in this case. Or maybe two leading competitors have merged; the future is almost definitely going to be different for sales in this market. In these cases, historical data may not be indicative of what will happen in the future, and perhaps you should consider a qualitative model.

13.3.1 Classical Multiplicative Model

In the case where nothing major has changed (that we know about), we wish to decompose or break down the time series into component parts. This approach is called the **multiplicative model.** The idea is that each observation is the product of four components:

- Trend component, T
- Seasonal component, S
- Cyclical component, C
- Random component, R

Some time series have all of these components and some just have one or more of these components. However, every time series has a random component. The multiplicative model is spelled out in the following definition.

In a ***multiplicative model*** any observation in the time series can be written as the product of four components:

$$y_t = \text{T} \times \text{S} \times \text{C} \times \text{R}$$

13.3.2 Components of a Multiplicative Time Series Model

Let's consider each of these components one at a time. If there is a **trend component,** then there is a systematic, long-term tendency of the values of the variable to increase or decrease. There is a trend in the number of families with children as seen in Example 13.1, but there is no trend in the number of loaves of bread sold over time shown in Figure 13.1. Notice that there are what look like short-term trends in the bread data, but over the 25 days there is no significant change in the number of loaves sold.

The ***trend component*** describes a systematic, long-term tendency of the data to increase or decrease over time.

There are many reasons why a trend might be present in the time series. Clearly, if we are observing the closing price of a stock we own, then we hope to see an upward trend! There may be more sales due to increased marketing or an increase in the target population. There may be more people using the Internet due to increased availability. We will use the technique of regression to model the trend in a time series in Section 13.7.

If there is a **seasonal component,** then the values in the time series follow a predictable pattern over the course of a year. For example, if you are selling swimwear, you probably will see a seasonal component because the months of May, June, and July have higher sales than the other months and this happens each year. If you are selling flowers or candy, you might expect December, February, and April to be higher each year due to Christmas, Valentines Day, and Easter! If you are observing weekly box office sales, you might find that the first week of every month has higher sales because many people get paid at the end of the month and thus have more disposable income in the beginning of the month. These would be examples of a seasonal component.

The ***seasonal component*** describes a systematic pattern that repeats itself year after year.

We will use seasonal indexes to model the seasonal component. This is covered in Section 13.8.

If there is a **cyclical component,** then there is a systematic pattern in the data that mirrors what is happening with the economy. The cyclical component is similar to the seasonal component except that instead of happening every year it might happen, say, every 5 or 10 years. For instance, the time series might reflect the effects of an economy moving from a recession to a depression to recovery and growth every 10 years.

The ***cyclical component*** models systematic ups and downs in the time series; these ups and downs repeat every 2 to 10 years and are typically tied to the business economy.

We will not learn any techniques to model the cyclical component explicitly.

Finally, we have already noted that every time series has a **random component.** If there were no random component, then once we modeled the other components we would have a perfect prediction of the future values! This seems unlikely. There are always random fluctuations that are not predictable, are not systematic, and cannot be modeled.

> The ***random component*** describes the irregular, unsystematic "bumps" in the values of the time series.

If the time series has only the random component present, then you can use a smoothing method to forecast this variable. We will look at three smoothing techniques: moving averages, weighted moving averages, and exponential smoothing. These are covered in the next three sections. When you use the smoothing methods to model the random component, you might "see" other components in the time series that were masked or hidden by the random bumps in the data.

Before moving on to the smoothing techniques, let's look at some time series to determine whether we can identify the components that are present.

Understand the Problem

EXAMPLE 13.3 Hospital Staffing

Identifying Components in a Time Series

Collect the Data

A hospital is concerned about providing quality care for patients. To predict their staffing needs, they observe the number of patients in the hospital for a month. The time series is displayed in the Excel line graph shown here:

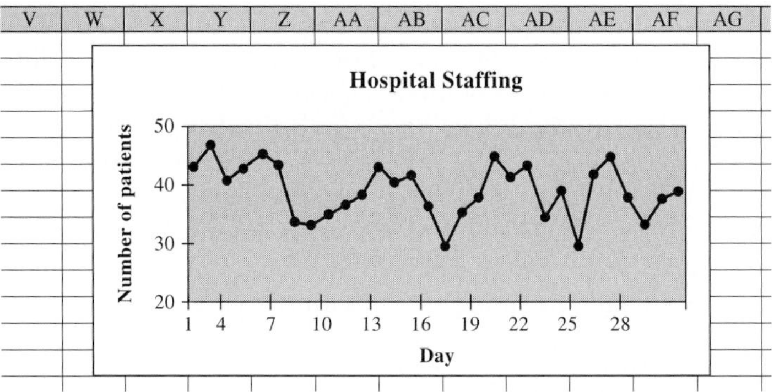

There does not appear to be a trend component in this time series since there is no systematic increase or decrease in the number of hospital patients over the month. There are not enough data to observe either a seasonal or a cyclical component. The only component present, therefore, is a random component, which accounts for the nonsystematic "bumps" in the data values. ■

Here's another time series to consider.

Understand the Problem

EXAMPLE 13.4 Mail Orders Received

Identifying Components of a Time Series

Collect the Data

A mail-order company has recorded the number of *Harry Potter* books it has sold over the past 15 weeks. A line graph of the data follows:

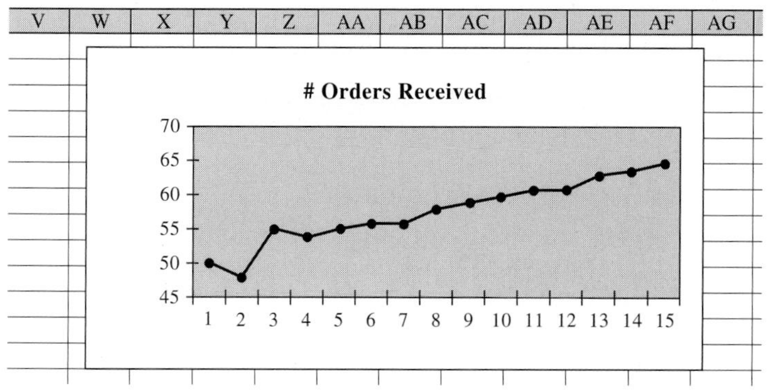

Clearly, a trend component as well as a random component are present. ■

Now you try one.

TRY IT NOW!

Components of a Time Series *Electricity Prices*

Reconsider the time series (Discovery Exercise 13.1(a)) showing the average monthly price of electricity across the United States from January 1988 to January 2000. A line graph of the data is displayed here:

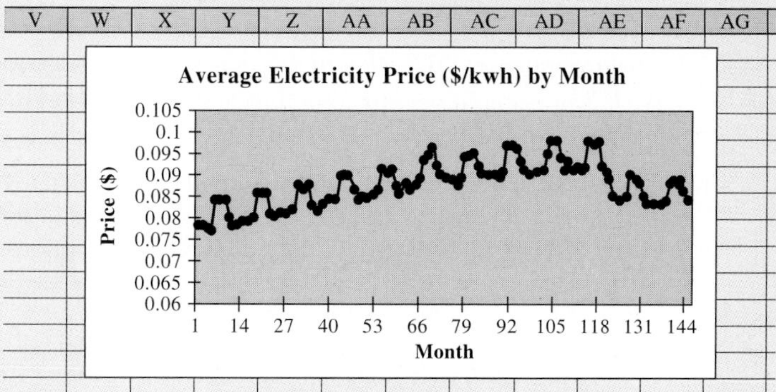

Which of the four components are present in this time series?[1]

13.3.3 Exercises—Learning It!

13.6 The number of employees working in any industry is tracked by the Bureau of Labor Statistics. The graph shows the number of employees working full time in the child day-care industry.

Datafile: CHILDCARE.XXX

---

[1] ANS. TREND, SEASONAL, AND RANDOM.

(a) What components does this time series have?

(b) Suggest a possible explanation for each of the components you have found.

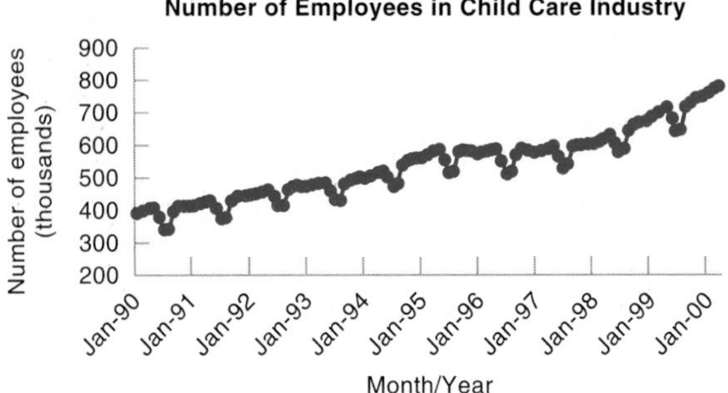

Datafile: GAS.XXX

13.7 The average monthly price of a gallon of unleaded, midgrade gasoline is shown in the graph. The data from January 1994 to May 2000 are given in the GAS.XXX datafile.

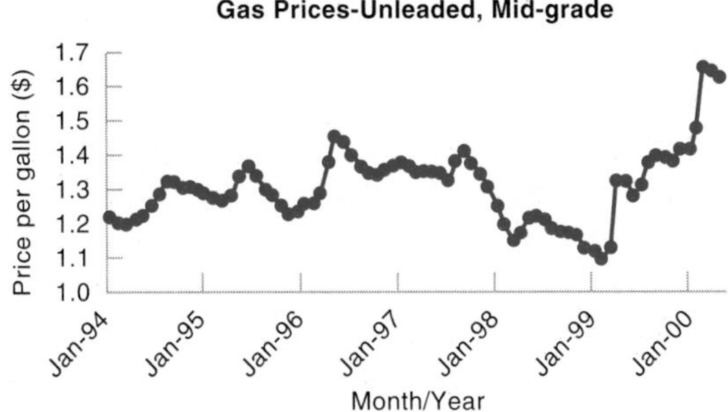

(a) What components do you see in this time series? Give a reason for each.

(b) What factors might be used to predict gas price if you were to use a causal model instead of a time series model?

13.8 Business is being conducted more frequently via the Internet. The following table shows the total on-line advertising revenue from 1995 to 2000 and the Internet-generated revenue from 1996 to 2000. Although the number of observations is small, you can still get a sense of the components of these time series.

Year	Internet-generated Revenue ($ billions)	Total On-line Advertising Revenue ($ billions)
1995	0.10	0.008
1996	0.39	0.436
1997	0.94	2.9
1998	1.9	21.8
1999	3.0	73.9
2000	4.4	180

(a) What components do you see in each of these time series?

(b) Do you think the trend component is linear?

Datafile: CIG.XXX

13.9 Recently, the cigarette industry has been under heavy criticism. Examine the total domestic cigarette sales (billions of cigarettes) for the years 1963 to 1994.

Year	Sales	Year	Sales	Year	Sales	Year	Sales
1963	516.5	1967	525.8	1971	547.2	1975	603.2
1964	505	1968	540.3	1972	561.7	1976	609.9
1965	521.1	1969	527.9	1973	584.7	1977	612.6
1966	529.9	1970	534.2	1974	594.5	1978	615.3

(continued)

Year	Sales	Year	Sales	Year	Sales	Year	Sales
1979	621.8	1983	603.6	1987	575.4	1991	510.9
1980	628.2	1984	608.4	1988	560.7	1992	506.4
1981	636.5	1985	599.3	1989	525.6	1993	461.4
1982	632.5	1986	586.4	1990	523.7	1994	490.2

(a) Display this time series as a line graph.

(b) What components do you see in this time series?

(c) Describe what has happened to the sale of cigarettes in the United States over these 30 years.

13.10 The daily opening, closing, high, and low prices (in $) of Microsoft stock are found in the datafile MSFT.XXX. The volume of shares traded is also in the datafile. A portion of the file is shown here. The data in the file are from May 1, 2000, to August 1, 2000.

Datafile: MSFT.XXX

Date	Open	High	Low	Close	Volume
1-May-00	72.875	74	71.6875	73.4375	53905500
2-May-00	72.8125	73.5	69.5	69.875	48858100
3-May-00	70.375	70.8125	68.8125	70.5625	27677400
4-May-00	70.3125	71.25	69.3125	70.4375	21658600
5-May-00	70.25	71.8125	69.875	71.125	18201100
8-May-00	70.9375	71.375	69.6875	69.8125	18093800
9-May-00	70.1875	70.4375	67.5	67.8125	30389200
10-May-00	67.75	67.875	65.75	66.1875	33870000
11-May-00	66.625	68.125	65.75	67.875	29195400
12-May-00	68.4375	69.75	68.25	68.8125	18943000

(a) On one graph, display the opening, high, low, and closing prices of the stock.

(b) For each time series, identify the components that are present.

(c) Display the volume as a line graph.

(d) Does the volume of stocks traded have the same components as the closing price of the stock?

13.4 SIMPLE MOVING AVERAGE MODELS

Let's look again at the problem on baseball attendance. If you had to forecast the number of people in families with children for 2001 right now, how would you use the data? If it helps, think about forecasting the number of loaves of bread to be sold on day 26. Remember you have data on only the past behavior of the variable of interest. Nothing else.

If you suggested finding the average of all of the data and using that as your forecast for time period $t + 1$, then you would be thinking along the right lines. Figure 13.2 on page 646 redisplays the FWC time series with an additional line drawn at the average, $\bar{y}$.

The average FWC population over the past 10 years is 1,299,529. This, then, would become our forecast for 2001 if we decided to use the overall average as our forecast. By doing so we would be saying that we believe that the time series is stationary and that all of the data, even the 10-year-old data, are equally valuable in constructing our forecast.

We are trying to find a model that comes close to as many data points as possible.

How good is this model? The graph of the straight line at the average value tells us that our forecast of the overall average is not terribly close to the data points that we have already observed. For instance, if we used the forecast of 1,299,529 to forecast for the year 2001 we would have been off by 1,546,920 − 1,299,529 = 247,391 people. Although there is not a strong trend in the data, it should be clear that the

Datafile:
COTTON.XXX

13.19 The number of acres (1,000) planted with cotton crops is collected by the U.S. Department of Agriculture. The data are shown here for the years 1960 through 1998:

1960	16,080	1980	14,534
1961	16,588	1981	14,330
1962	16,293	1982	11,345
1963	14,843	1983	7,926
1964	14,836	1984	11,145
1965	14,152	1985	10,685
1966	10,349	1986	10,045
1967	9,450	1987	10,397
1968	10,913	1988	12,515
1969	11,883	1989	10,587
1970	11,945	1990	12,348
1971	12,355	1991	14,052
1972	14,001	1992	13,240
1973	12,480	1993	13,438
1974	13,679	1994	13,720
1975	9,478	1995	16,931
1976	11,636	1996	14,653
1977	13,680	1997	13,898
1978	13,375	1998	13,393
1979	13,978		

(a) Display this time series as a line graph.

(b) Use a 6-period simple moving average to predict the number of acres of cotton for 1999.

(c) Find the MSE for this model.

(d) Use a 6-period weighted moving average to predict the number of acres of cotton for 1999. Use $w_t = 0.50$, $w_{t-1} = 0.30$, $w_{t-2} = 0.10$, $w_{t-3} = 0.05$, $w_{t-4} = 0.03$, and $w_{t-5} = 0.02$.

(e) Find the MSE for the model in part (d).

(f) Which model do you recommend and why?

(g) How might this model be useful to the government?

13.20 The Bureau of Labor Statistics annually conducts a survey called the Consumer Expenditure Survey. Data on the amount of money consumers spend on various categories of products are collected and published. The data for the average amount of money ($) spent on alcohol from 1984 to 1998 is shown here:

Year	Money Spent on Alcohol
1984	275
1985	306
1986	271
1987	289
1988	269
1989	284
1990	293
1991	297
1992	301
1993	268
1994	278
1995	277
1996	309
1997	309
1998	309

(a) Display this data as a line graph.

(b) What are the components of this time series?

(c) Use a 3-period weighted moving average to predict the alcohol expenditure for 1999. Use $w_t = 0.60$, $w_{t-1} = 0.30$, and $w_{t-2} = 0.10$.

13.6 EXPONENTIAL SMOOTHING MODELS

In the last section we saw that it is often difficult to determine the "best" values for the weights to be used in the weighted moving average model. The **exponential smoothing model** to be discussed in this section is another averaging technique that allows you to use unequal weights. This technique specifies a formula for the assignment of these weights.

An ***exponential smoothing model*** is an averaging technique that uses unequal weights. The weights applied to past observations decline in an exponential manner.

13.6.1 Forecasting Using an Exponential Smoothing Model

The exponential smoothing model is different from the weighted moving average model because *all* of the historical data in the time series are used to generate the forecast for the next period. It is similar to a weighted MA model because the forecast is a weighted average. The weights are assigned in such a way that the most recent observation, y_t, carries the largest weight. The second most recent observation, y_{t-1}, carries the second largest weight and the weights assigned to the other data points decrease *systematically*.

Weighted MA models use only k periods of historical data in the calculation of the forecast for the next period.

Remember that the weights must be positive fractions and sum to one.

What does the word *systematically* mean? Generally, it means that there is some order or pattern. Let's see how we could assign the weights systematically. Use the FWC time series for the baseball attendance problem again. Suppose we decided to assign a weight of 0.70 to the most recent observation in the time series. Call this weight α. So $w_{10} = \alpha = 0.70$. We know from the previous discussion that the weight for the observation at time period 9 should be less than 0.70. If we calculate the weight for this second most recent time period as $\alpha(1 - \alpha)$, then we know it would always be less than α. In this case, $w_9 = 0.70(1 - 0.70) = 0.21$. The weight for the third most recent observation should be less than 0.21. It is calculated as $\alpha(1 - \alpha)^2 = (0.70)(1 - 0.70)^2 = 0.063$. If we continue with this pattern the weights to be used in forecasting for period 11 are shown in the table and in the associated graph of Figure 13.4. The table and the graph show that the weights decrease rather quickly as the age of the data increases. In fact, the graph looks like the graph of an exponential curve. Hence, the name given to this technique is exponential smoothing.

The definition of α is not the same as that used in hypothesis testing. We could use a different Greek letter to avoid any confusion with the earlier definition of α, but most forecasting books use α so we will do so as well. In this case, α is called the **smoothing constant.**

Time Period	Weight
10	0.7000000
9	0.2100000
8	0.0630000
7	0.0189000
6	0.0056700
5	0.0017010
4	0.0005103
3	0.0001531
2	0.0000459
1	0.0000138

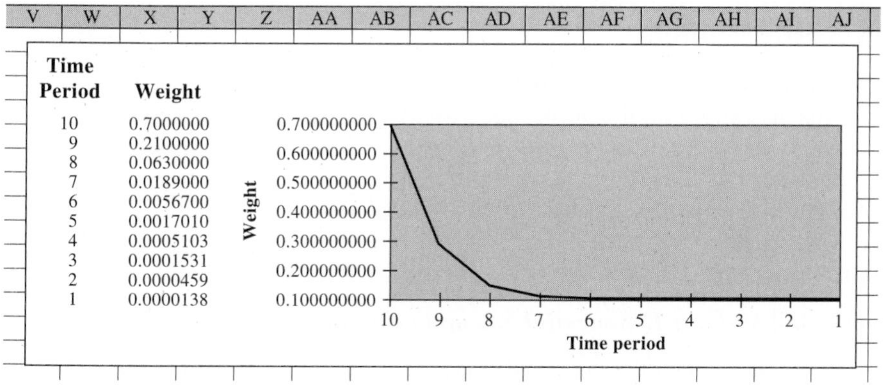

FIGURE 13.4 Weights for exponential smoothing model with $\alpha = 0.70$

The ***smoothing constant, α,*** is the weight assigned to the most recent observation in an exponential smoothing model.

Let's see how to calculate the forecast for the FWC time series using a smoothing constant of $\alpha = 0.7$.

EXAMPLE 13.8 **Baseball Attendance**

Exponential Smoothing Model

Analyze the Data

The forecast for period 11 (FWC population for the year 2001) is calculated as a weighted average of all of the historical data using the weights shown in Figure 13.4:

$$\begin{aligned}\hat{y}_{11} &= (0.7)(1{,}546{,}920) + (0.21)(1{,}387{,}692) + (0.063)(1{,}321{,}457) \\ &\quad + \cdots + (0.0000138)(1{,}098{,}909) \\ &= 1{,}493{,}651\end{aligned}$$

■

The general formula for the forecast for the next period, $t + 1$, is

Formula for exponentially smoothed forecast for the next period

$$\begin{aligned}\hat{y}_{i+1} &= \sum_{i=1}^{t} w_i y_i \\ &= \alpha y_t + \alpha(1-\alpha)y_{t-1} + \alpha(1-\alpha)^2 y_{t-2} + \cdots + \alpha(1-\alpha)^n y_{t-n} + \cdots\end{aligned}$$

Notice that the sum starts with the most recent observation weighted by α and includes data all the way back to the beginning of the time series. By examining the weights used when $\alpha = 0.7$, you can see that any data older than 3 time periods contributes virtually nothing. Why then should we bother to include these observations in the weighted average? The answer to that rather appropriate question has to do with a practical consideration. It can be shown that the exponentially smoothed forecast calculated using the previous formula is algebraically equivalent to the following equation:

Alternative formula for computing the exponentially smoothed forecast for period t + 1

$$\hat{y}_{t+1} = \hat{y}_t + \alpha(y_t - \hat{y}_t)$$

It is not immediately obvious when you look at the formula that all of the data in the time series are actually being used. All of the data are rolled into the forecast made for time period t, $\hat{y}_t$. The new forecast $\hat{y}_{t+1}$ is equal to the previous forecast plus some adjustment. The adjustment is based on how much error there was in the previous forecast, that is, the difference between the forecast for period t and the observation for period t, $(y_t - \hat{y}_t)$. If your previous forecast was "too high," then you need to adjust the forecast in the downward direction and the adjustment will be negative since $\hat{y}_t$ was larger than y_t. If, on the other hand, your previous forecast was "too low," then you need to make the forecast a bit larger and the adjustment will be positive since y_t was bigger than $\hat{y}_t$.

13.6.2 Evaluating the Exponential Smoothing Model

The last equation shown previously is the best one to use to actually calculate the forecast using exponential smoothing. This is true because you need only the most recent forecast, $\hat{y}_t$, the most recent observation, y_t, and α to complete the computation. Let's see how to use this equation and find the MSE of the exponential smoothing model for the FWC time series.

EXAMPLE 13.9 **Baseball Attendance**

Forecast and MSE for Exponential Smoothing Model

Analyze the Data

The first five columns of the table display the year, the population for families with children, the forecast for each year, the error, and the adjustment to be made for the next forecast. The last column is used to find the mean square error.

Year	FWC y_t	Forecast $\hat{y}_t$	Error, $y_t - \hat{y}_t$	Alpha × Error $a(y_t - \hat{y}_t)$	Error Squared $(y_t - \hat{y}_t)^2$
1991	1,098,909	1,098,909	0	0	0
1992	1,197,185	1,098,909	98,276	68,793.20	9,658,172,176
1993	1,169,860	1,167,702	2,158	1,510.46	4,656,101
1994	1,350,675	1,169,213	181,462	127,023.64	32,928,580,838
1995	1,335,213	1,296,236	38,977	27,283.69	1,519,183,299
1996	1,207,658	1,323,520	−115,862	−81,103.39	13,424,000,588
1997	1,379,723	1,242,417	137,306	96,114.48	18,853,048,354
1998	1,321,457	1,338,531	−17,074	−11,951.86	291,524,175
1999	1,387,692	1,326,579	61,113	42,778.94	3,734,771,425
2000	1,546,920	1,369,358	177,562	124,293.28	31,528,204,498
	Forecast	1,493,651		MSE	11,194,214,145

■

Notice that to create the table shown in Example 13.9, we needed a forecast for period 1. Generally, you simply set the forecast for the first time period equal to the observation for the first time period. The effect of doing this is quickly washed out. As a result, the error for period 1 is always zero, making the second forecast precisely the same as the first forecast. Notice also that you cannot really forecast beyond period $t + 1$ because you do not know what the error will be for future forecasts. Since you have assumed a stationary time series (or you wouldn't be using simple exponential smoothing), your forecast for any period beyond $t + 1$ is the same as your forecast for period $t + 1$.

The observation for the first period becomes the forecast for the first period to get the technique started.

To compare the usefulness of the exponential smoothing model to the moving average and weighted moving average models that we have considered, we again use the mean square error (MSE). The MSE is computed in precisely the same manner as we have done before. It turns out that to calculate the forecast for $\hat{y}_{t+1}$ you need to calculate the error and so it is a simple matter of squaring these errors and averaging them to get the MSE.

EXAMPLE 13.10 Baseball Attendance

Make a Recommendation

Evaluating the Exponential Smoothing Model

In this case the MSE for the exponential smoothing model with a smoothing constant of 0.7 is smaller than for any other model we have tried for this time series. The graph shown here clearly depicts this as the time series and the forecasts are very close to each other for most periods.

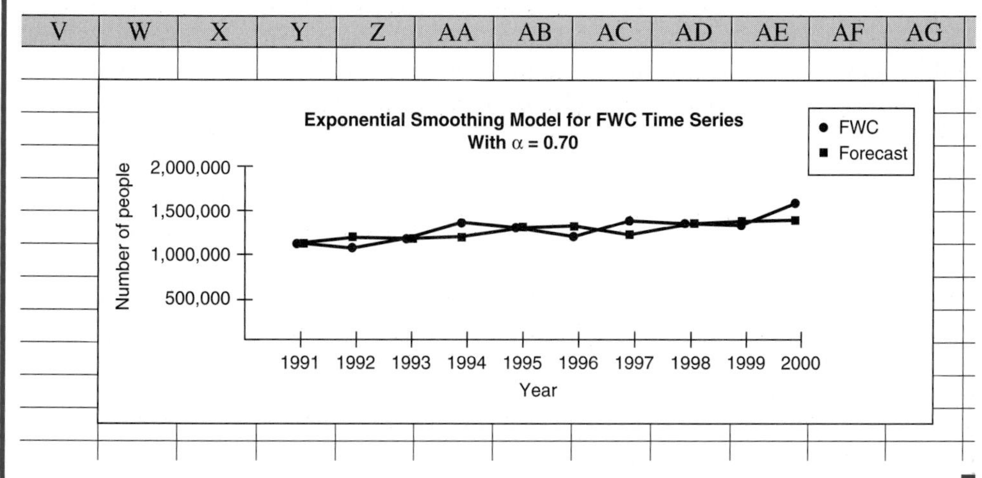

■

Perhaps the MSE could be made even smaller with a different smoothing constant. Try it and see for yourself!

Try It Now!

Baseball Attendance ***Exponential Smoothing Model***

Find the forecast for the number of people in families with children for 2001 using an exponential smoothing model with a smoothing constant of 0.6.

Complete the table to find the MSE for the exponential smoothing model ($\alpha = 0.6$) for the FWC time series.

Year	*FWC*	*Forecast*	*Error*	*Alpha × Error*	*Error Squared*
1991	1,098,909				
1992	1,197,185				
1993	1,169,860				
1994	1,350,675				
1995	1,335,213				
1996	1,207,658				
1997	1,379,723				
1998	1,321,457				
1999	1,387,692				
2000	1,546,920				
	Forecast			MSE	

Is this a better model than the model with a 0.7 smoothing constant?

Some software packages allow you to optimize the value of α. For example, in Excel you can use the Solver feature of the Tools menu to find the value of α that gives you the smallest MSE.

As you can see, the selection of the smoothing constant affects both the forecast and the MSE for the model. Since α can vary anywhere from 0 to 1, it is impossible to try all values of α to find the model with the least MSE. Just as we did with the weighted moving average models, we can vary α and observe what happens to the MSE and attempt to zero in on a good value for α.

13.6.3 Exercises—Learning It!

Requires Exercises 13.11, 13.16

13.21 Use the baseball attendance for the population with no children (NC) time series.

(a) Forecast the attendance for 2001 using an exponential smoothing model with a value of $\alpha = 0.90$.

(b) Find the MSE for this model.

ANS. $\hat{y}_{11}$ = 1,473,021; MSE = 11,378,876,397; No

(c) How does this model compare with the weighted moving average models and the simple moving average models you tried in Exercises 13.11 and 13.16?

(d) Which model do you recommend and why?

13.22 Use an exponential smoothing model with $\alpha = 0.65$ to forecast the domestic cigarette sales. *Requires Exercise 13.9*

(a) Forecast the domestic cigarette sales for 1995.

(b) Find the MSE for this model.

(c) Based on the components present in this time series, is exponential smoothing an appropriate choice? Explain.

13.23 Use an exponential smoothing model with $\alpha = 0.55$ to forecast the sales for the next month for the pizza restaurant. *Requires Exercise 13.18*

(a) Find the MSE for this model.

(b) How does this model compare with the weighted moving average model developed in Exercise 13.18?

(c) Which model do you recommend and why?

13.24 Use an exponential smoothing model to forecast the number of patients seen in the emergency room for the next day. The data are shown in Exercise 13.15. Use $\alpha = 0.85$. *Requires Exercise 13.15*

13.25 Use an exponential smoothing model to forecast the amount of money spent on alcohol. *Requires Exercise 13.20*

(a) Use an exponential smoothing model with $\alpha = 0.75$ to predict the amount of money spent on alcohol in 1999.

(b) Find the MSE for this model.

(c) Based on the components present in this time series, is exponential smoothing an appropriate model? Explain.

13.7 REGRESSION MODELS

All of the models that have been considered thus far in the chapter are models that could be used if you have a time series that has no trends. But what if there is a long-term trend in the data, either upward or downward? In this case you should use a technique that explicitly models the trend. You are already familiar with one such technique, regression. There are other techniques that can be used to model trends in the data. Two of these are second-order moving averages and double exponential smoothing. These are extensions of the techniques covered in the previous sections. However, the most commonly used technique when a trend is present is the technique of regression. This is the only one that will be covered in this chapter.

Remember: A stationary time series is one that exhibits no long-term trend.

13.7.1 Finding the Linear Regression Model

The first step to analyzing time series data is to display the data using a scatter plot. After you construct a scatter plot and visually examine the time series data, you may observe a clear upward or downward linear trend. In this case you should try a regression model. However, it is not always crystal clear that there is a trend in the data. This is the case with the FWC time series we have been working with. There appears to be a slight upward trend, but is that enough to warrant the use of regression? You may decide, as we have done, to use a stationary technique for such data. Upon examination of the errors (or residuals as they are called in regression) you may see a pattern. If there is a pattern, there probably is some more information in the time series data that you have not explicitly modeled. In this case you may also try a regression model.

In Chapter 11, you learned all about the technique of simple linear regression. The same technique is used to model time series data. Recall that the general model for a simple linear regression model is

$$y = \beta_0 + \beta_1 x + \varepsilon$$

where

y is the dependent variable

x is the independent variable

β_0 is the theoretical, unknown y intercept of the line

β_1 is the theoretical, unknown slope of the line

ε are independent with a normal distribution with a mean of zero and a constant standard deviation

Using observations of x and y, estimates of β_0 and β_1 can be computed. The prediction equation is given as

$$\hat{y} = b_0 + b_1 x$$

where

b_0 is the estimate of the y intercept

b_1 is the estimate of the slope

It makes more sense to label the independent variable as t when using regression to model a time series.

When using regression to model time series data, the independent variable is time and the dependent variable is the variable you are interested in forecasting. The prediction model thus becomes

$$\hat{y} = b_0 + b_1 t$$

Typically, you number the first time period as $t = 1$, the second time period as $t = 2$, and so forth. This is what we have done with the FWC time series. It would not be wrong to use the actual years for the independent variable in this case and you would get the same results for the slope (b_1) but different intercepts (b_0). You will get the same forecast as long as you use the correct number for time in the prediction equation.

Let's check to see that this is the case.

Analyze the Data

EXAMPLE 13.11 Baseball Attendance

Regression Model for FWC Time Series

The output from running regression in Excel follows. The column of numbers containing the population for families with children (FWC) was identified as the dependent (or y) values and the column of numbers ranging from 1 to 10 was identified as the range for the independent variable (or x values).

	A	B	C	D	E	F
62	SUMMARY OUTPUT					
63						
64	*Regression Statistics*					
65	Multiple R	0.848512409				
66	R Square	0.719973308				
67	Adjusted R Square	0.684969971				
68	Standard Error	73836.86001				
69	Observations	10				
70						
71	ANOVA					
72		*df*	*SS*	*MS*	*F*	*Significance F*
73	Regression	1	1.12138E+11	1.12138E+11	20.5687051	0.001911048
74	Residual	8	43615055164	5451881895		
75	Total	9	1.55753E+11			
76						
77		*Coefficients*	*Standard Error*	*t Stat*	*P-value*	
78	Intercept	1096755.133	50440.17795	21.74368089	2.1102E-08	
79	Time	36868.01212	8129.17074	4.535273437	0.00191105	
80						

Extracting the values for b_0 and b_1 from this output, we can write the regression model as

$$\begin{aligned}\hat{y}_t &= b_0 + b_1 t \\ &= 1{,}096{,}755.1 + 36{,}868.012t\end{aligned}$$

The forecast for time period 11 (year 2001) is calculated by using the regression model and substituting the value of 11 for $t =$ time. This calculation is

$$\begin{aligned}\hat{y}_{11} &= 1{,}096{,}755.1 + (36{,}868.012)(11) \\ &= 1{,}502{,}303\end{aligned}$$

If we used the actual years as the independent variable values instead, we would get the following results:

	A	B	C	D	E	F
42	SUMMARY OUTPUT					
43						
44	*Regression Statistics*					
45	Multiple R	0.848512409				
46	R Square	0.719973308				
47	Adjusted R Square	0.684969971				
48	Standard Error	73836.86001				
49	Observations	10				
50						
51	ANOVA					
52		*df*	*SS*	*MS*	*F*	*Significance F*
53	Regression	1	1.12138E+11	1.12138E+11	20.5687051	0.001911048
54	Residual	8	43615055164	5451881895		
55	Total	9	1.55753E+11			
56						
57		*Coefficients*	*Standard Error*	*t Stat*	*P-value*	
58	Intercept	-72270588.99	16221777.02	-4.455158576	0.00212468	
59	Year	36868.01212	8129.17074	4.535273437	0.00191105	
60						

The model is

$$\hat{y}_t = -72{,}270{,}589 + 36{,}868.012t$$

Notice that the estimate of the slope, b_1, is the same but the intercept term, b_0, is different. The same forecast is obtained as long as we use the year 2001 as the value for time to be predicted:

$$\begin{aligned}\hat{y}_{2001} &= -72{,}270{,}589 + (36{,}868.012)(2001) \\ &= 1{,}502{,}303\end{aligned}$$

■

It is clearly possible to forecast more than one period into the future. If we wished to estimate the population for the year 2002 we would simply use the year 2002 (or time $t = 12$) as the value for time in the regression model. Thus,

$$\begin{aligned}\hat{y}_{2002} &= -72{,}270{,}589 + (36{,}868.012)(2002) \\ &= 1{,}539{,}171.279\end{aligned}$$

The farther out in time that you try to forecast, the less reliable your forecast will be since you have no additional actual data.

A word on extrapolation

It should be noted that, by using a regression model to forecast for the next period or beyond, you are extrapolating. You were warned not to do this in the chapter on regression. However, in analyzing time series data the objective is to make a prediction for the next time period or beyond that will always be outside the range of the data. You are always extrapolating the past into the future when you work with time series data. The assumption for any time series model is that the future "looks" like the past. Without this assumption you cannot do anything with the historical data. So it is not that you were unduly cautioned in the chapter on regression but that the objective is now slightly different.

Remember to label time starting with $t = 1$.

Now that you have seen that there is no difference in the forecast resulting from different ways of coding the time values, we will always number the values of time starting with the value $t = 1$. This is often the easiest thing to do because sometimes your time variable is a calendar date, an hour of the day, or a day of the week.

Baseball Attendance ***Regression Model***

Find the regression model and forecast for the number of people with no children (NC) for 2001 (time $t = 11$).

The data are shown here:

Time	*Year*	*NC*
1	1991	564,790
2	1992	556,734
3	1993	653,134
4	1994	632,459
5	1995	642,387
6	1996	654,890
7	1997	657,238
8	1998	657,238
9	1999	717,903
10	2000	692,340

13.7.2 Evaluating the Regression Model

We have been using the mean square error to evaluate the moving average and exponential smoothing models. This is easily done for the regression model because any software package that you use to run the regression model will calculate the predicted values and the residuals for each value of y_t. These residuals can then be squared and averaged to get the MSE. These values are shown in the next example.

ANS. $b_0 = 563,461.53$
$b_1 = 14,445.412$
$\hat{y}_{11} = 722,361$

EXAMPLE 13.12 Baseball Attendance

Finding the MSE for the Regression Model

Analyze the Data

The first three columns of the accompanying table were generated by Excel as part of the output of regression. The last column is simply the residuals (or errors) squared and then this column is averaged to get the MSE.

	A	B	C	D
83	RESIDUAL OUTPUT			
84				
85	*Observation*	*Predicted FWC*	*Residuals*	*Residuals Squared*
86	1	1133623.145	-34714.14545	1205071895
87	2	1170491.158	26693.84242	712561223.4
88	3	1207359.17	-37499.1697	1406187728
89	4	1244227.182	106447.8182	11331137996
90	5	1281095.194	54117.80606	2928736933
91	6	1317963.206	-110305.2061	12167238484
92	7	1354831.218	24891.78182	619600802.1
93	8	1391699.23	-70242.2303	4933970918
94	9	1428567.242	-40875.24242	1670785443
95	10	1465435.255	81484.74545	6639763742
96				
97			MSE	4,361,505,516

■

Notice that the MSE of 4,361,505,516 is a little different from the value listed in the Excel output under MS for residual. That value is found in the output shown in Example 13.11 as 5,451,881,895. The reason for the difference is that the MS for regression is found by dividing the sum of squares (SS), which corresponds to the sum of the residuals squared, by the degrees of freedom for that term in regression, which is 8 in this case. We divided the sum of the residuals squared by the number of observations, which in this case is 10. The calculation of the MSE for regression will always yield a higher number than the calculation of the MSE for forecasting purposes because of this difference in the denominator. It is not that Excel is wrong, it is simply that we are using the MSE as a measure of the model's goodness rather than in the calculation of the F statistic (Significance F in Excel).

A comparison of the MSE for the regression model to the MSE values for all of the other models of this time series that we have tried shows that the regression model is the best. This makes sense since we did see a slight upward trend in the data when we examined the line graph and we saw a pattern in the errors when we used a moving average model (all but one were positive).

In addition to using the MSE as a way to evaluate the regression model, we can also use the methods learned in Chapter 11. Specifically, the value of R^2 should be examined and a hypothesis test for the significance of the slope term should be done. The next example serves as a reminder of these methods using the FWC time series.

EXAMPLE 13.13 Baseball Attendance

Analyze the Data

R^2 and Test for Significance for the Regression Model

The information needed to evaluate the regression model is shown in the output in Example 13.11. The coefficient of determination for the regression model is $R^2 =$ 72%. Thus, 72% of the variability in the y values is explained by the independent variable of time.

The hypothesis test for the slope is

$$H_0: \beta_1 = 0$$
$$H_A: \beta_1 \neq 0$$

Draw Conclusions

The t test statistic is shown in the coefficient table as 4.535273 with a p value of 0.0019. The low p value (less than 0.01) tells us to reject the null hypothesis and conclude that the slope is nonzero. This tells us that the model is useful. ■

Baseball Attendance ***Evaluating the Regression Model for the NC Time Series***

Evaluate the regression model for the number of people in families with no children (NC). Find the MSE, the value of R^2 and test for the significance of the slope term.

13.7.3 Exercises—Learning It!

13.26 The Bureau of Labor Statistics (BLS) reports data on commodity prices on a monthly basis. These data are reported on a regional and national basis. The following graph displays the monthly average price (cents per pound) of white bread in the United States for January 1980 to June 2000.

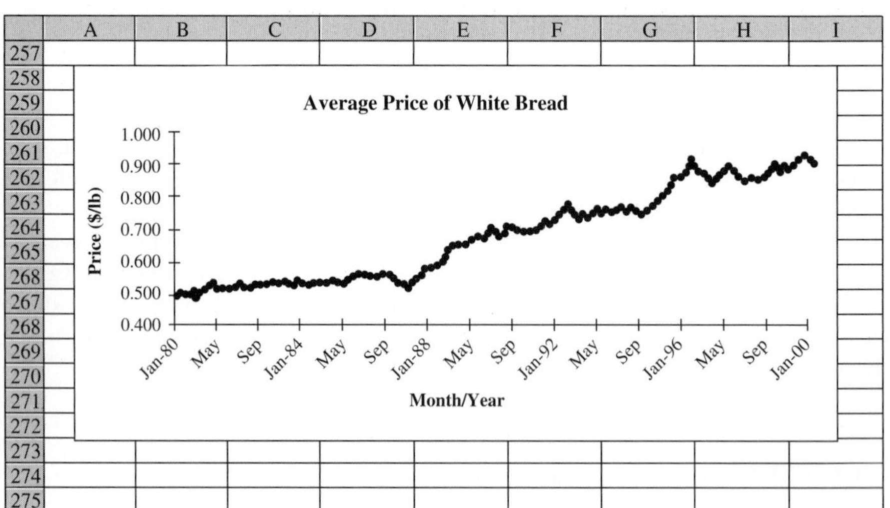

ANS. MSE = 514,917,365; R^2 = 76.98%; t = 5.17
REJECT H_0 AND CONCLUDE THE SLOPE IS NONZERO.

The output from running regression in Excel is shown here:

	K	L	M	N	O	P	Q
1	SUMMARY OUTPUT						
2							
3	*Regression Statistics*						
4	Multiple R	0.974976					
5	R Square	0.950577					
6	Adjusted R Square	0.950375					
7	Standard Error	0.030276					
8	Observations	246					
9							
10	ANOVA						
11		*df*	*SS*	*MS*	*F*	*Significance F*	
12	Regression	1	4.301705885	4.301706	4693.019	2.3855E-161	
13	Residual	244	0.223654819	0.000917			
14	Total	245	4.525360703				
15							
16		*Coefficients*	*Standard Error*	*t Stat*	*P-value*	*Lower 95%*	*Upper 95%*
17	Intercept	0.45325	0.003872417	117.0456	2.3E-216		
18	Time	0.001862	2.71823E-05	68.50561	2.4E-161	0.001808596	0.00191568
19							

(a) Predict the average price of bread for the next 3 months (time = 247, 248, 249).

(b) Test the significance of the slope for this model.

(c) Is the graph consistent with the results of your hypothesis test? Explain why or why not.

13.27 Some people thought that the movie rental business would decrease the number of people who go to the movie theaters. Let's look at the evidence. The data in the MOVIE.XXX datafile show the number of employees (in thousands) in the movie industry from January 1990 to April 2000. The data are shown here: ***Datafile:*** *MOVIE.XXX*

Data Type: ALL EMPLOYEES (in thousands)

Jan-90	386.8	Jan-91	413.4	Jan-92	398.9	Jan-93	411.6	Jan-94	423.2
Feb-90	387.3	Feb-91	411.7	Feb-92	395.8	Feb-93	407.1	Feb-94	430.9
Mar-90	395.7	Mar-91	411	Mar-92	400.8	Mar-93	403.6	Mar-94	438.3
Apr-90	399.3	Apr-91	410.1	Apr-92	396.7	Apr-93	404.6	Apr-94	438.5
May-90	406.3	May-91	409.8	May-92	397.7	May-93	404.2	May-94	434.5
Jun-90	414.3	Jun-91	416.7	Jun-92	403.8	Jun-93	411.9	Jun-94	440.2
Jul-90	420.4	Jul-91	417.7	Jul-92	405.5	Jul-93	415	Jul-94	442.7
Aug-90	429.3	Aug-91	425.5	Aug-92	405	Aug-93	422.3	Aug-94	452.9
Sep-90	407.3	Sep-91	402.4	Sep-92	387.9	Sep-93	407.6	Sep-94	433.3
Oct-90	408.7	Oct-91	399	Oct-92	396.4	Oct-93	409.5	Oct-94	440.4
Nov-90	415.8	Nov-91	405.8	Nov-92	406.2	Nov-93	417	Nov-94	456.1
Dec-90	421.3	Dec-91	407.3	Dec-92	416	Dec-93	430	Dec-94	463.4
Jan-95	460.5	Jan-96	505	Jan-97	534.5	Jan-98	567.5	Jan-99	577.0
Feb-95	477.4	Feb-96	508.9	Feb-97	536.3	Feb-98	575.5	Feb-99	592.0
Mar-95	480.1	Mar-96	521.1	Mar-97	540.4	Mar-98	574.5	Mar-99	590.3
Apr-95	483.9	Apr-96	519.2	Apr-97	537.2	Apr-98	569.5	Apr-99	593.4
May-95	484.8	May-96	524.9	May-97	542.4	May-98	574.6	May-99	612.9
Jun-95	484.9	Jun-96	530.1	Jun-97	551.7	Jun-98	568.6	Jun-99	622.1
Jul-95	497	Jul-96	537.7	Jul-97	558.2	Jul-98	585.4	Jul-99	628.2
Aug-95	499.1	Aug-96	538.6	Aug-97	570.2	Aug-98	590	Aug-99	630.9
Sep-95	488.8	Sep-96	524.3	Sep-97	551.3	Sep-98	573.3	Sep-99	611.4
Oct-95	489.6	Oct-96	522.1	Oct-97	550.5	Oct-98	571.3	Oct-99	613.3
Nov-95	500.1	Nov-96	528.7	Nov-97	558.3	Nov-98	574.5	Nov-99	618.7
Dec-95	505.5	Dec-96	536.1	Dec-97	573.7	Dec-98	587.2	Dec-99	626.8

(continued)

Data Type: ALL EMPLOYEES (in thousands) ***(continued)***

Jan-00	619.4
Feb-00	623.4
Mar-00	627.9
Apr-00	627.6

(a) Display the data as a line graph.

(b) What are the components of this time series?

(c) Find the slope and intercept for the regression model to predict the number of employees in the movie industry.

(d) Interpret the slope in terms of the problem.

(e) Comment on the thought that the movie industry is on the decline as a result of video rentals.

Datafile: *GAS.XXX*

13.28 The price of a gallon of gas has been steadily increasing. Use the data in the GAS.XXX datafile to predict future gas prices using a regression model. Prices are given from January 1994 to May 2000.

(a) Find the slope and intercept for the regression model.

(b) Predict the gas price for June 2000 and July 2000.

(c) Interpret the slope in terms of this problem.

(d) Test the significance of the slope using $\alpha = 0.05$.

(e) Who might be interested in using this model?

Requires Exercises 13.18, 13.23

13.29 Reconsider the sales of pizzas shown in Exercise 13.18.

(a) Find the slope and intercept of the regression model for these time series data.

(b) Compare the MSE for the regression model to the MSE for the weighted moving average model and the exponential smoothing model.

13.8 SEASONAL INDEXES

So far we have looked at ways to model the random component using one of several smoothing methods and the trend component using regression. In this section we look at how to model the seasonal component. There are many ways to model the seasonal component in a time series. We will look at a method called seasonal indexes. To do this we will rely on our knowledge of moving averages and regression.

13.8.1 Setting Up the Time Frame for Seasonal Indexes

The name **seasonal** comes from the fact that some products were traditionally tied to the weather of the season. For example, you would typically think of boats and skis as seasonal products. In the case of skis, you would expect sales to be higher in the winter months. If the time series has a seasonal component, then that means that there are some observations that are consistently higher or lower than the other observations. It could be that first-quarter production is always a bit lower than the rest of the year or perhaps the number of defects or errors is greater than usual on Fridays. If you ever tried to reach the doctor's office on a Monday morning, you would know that the number of calls to his/her office is a seasonal variable!

Always display the data as a line graph.

To model the seasonal component you need to identify a **time frame.** In particular, you need to know how often the data are collected and over what period of

Variable	Data Collected Every	Pattern Repeats Every
Sale of skis	Month	Year
Sale of boats	Month	Year
Number of defects	Day	Week
Number of employees working in the music industry	Quarter	Year
Number of calls	Day	Week
Number of customers at a fast-food chain	Hour	Day

FIGURE 13.5 Examples of seasonal time frames

time the pattern of highs and lows repeats itself. This might be months in a year or quarters in a year or days in a week or hours in a day. Your knowledge about the data being collected will help you identify the likely time frame. However, as with any time series data analysis, the *first step is to display the time series as a line graph.* This will give you a way to verify the presence of a seasonal component and to see how often the pattern repeats itself. You should also identify any other components in the time series.

Figure 13.5 gives some examples.

Once you have the time frame you can begin to model the seasonal component.

13.8.2 Steps for Finding Seasonal Indexes

Use the following steps to model the seasonal component:

STEPS FOR FINDING SEASONAL INDEXES

Step 1. Display the time series as a line graph. Identify the time frame for the seasonal component and identify any other components.

Step 2. Estimate the value for each observation if there were no seasonal component present.

Step 3. Calculate the raw seasonality for each observation by dividing the observation by the estimate from step 2.

Step 4. Average all the individual indexes for the same "season."

Step 5. Deseasonalize the data by dividing each observation by the seasonal index.

Step 6. Model the trend component (if there is one) using regression on the deseasonalized data.

Step 7. Find the deseasonalized predicted values using the regression equation.

Step 8. Calculate final predictions by putting the seasonal component back. Multiply the values at step 7 by the appropriate seasonal index.

To develop this approach we will work through an example.

EXAMPLE 13.14 **Sales of Four-wheel-drive Vehicles**

Collect the Data

Step 1: Identify time frame

The data are the dollar sales of four-wheel-drive utility vehicles (in $1000) of a local car dealer during the past 5 years. The data are displayed as a line graph.

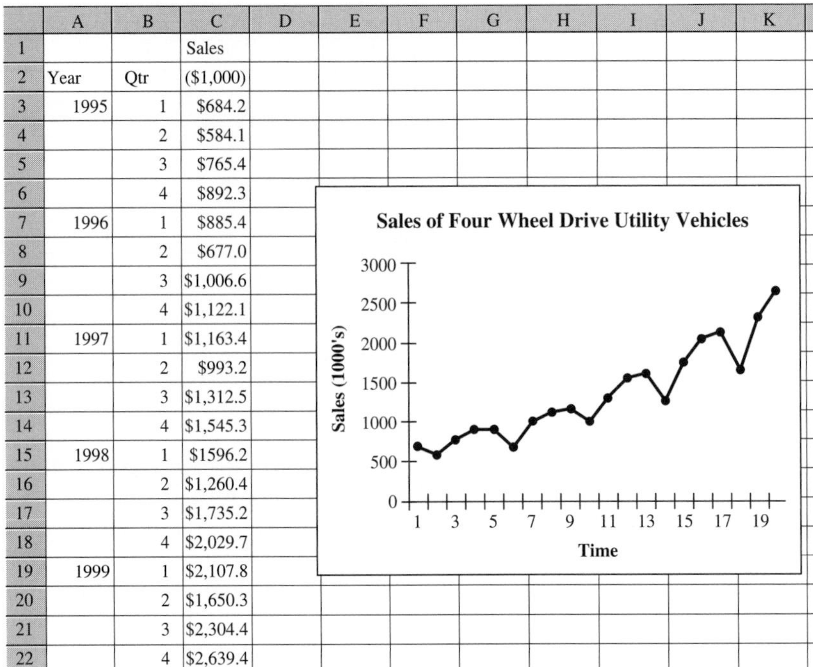

	A	B	C
1			Sales
2	Year	Qtr	($1,000)
3	1995	1	$684.2
4		2	$584.1
5		3	$765.4
6		4	$892.3
7	1996	1	$885.4
8		2	$677.0
9		3	$1,006.6
10		4	$1,122.1
11	1997	1	$1,163.4
12		2	$993.2
13		3	$1,312.5
14		4	$1,545.3
15	1998	1	$1596.2
16		2	$1,260.4
17		3	$1,735.2
18		4	$2,029.7
19	1999	1	$2,107.8
20		2	$1,650.3
21		3	$2,304.4
22		4	$2,639.4

Analyze the Data

The data are collected every *quarter*, and a pattern of highs and lows repeats every *year*. So the season is a quarter. The second quarter is always lower than the rest of the year, and the fourth quarter is always higher than the rest of the year. There is also a trend and a random component present in the time series. ■

Step 3 is to estimate the values for each time period if no seasonal component were present. This is where we need our moving averages. You should average the values for the time period that corresponds to how often the pattern repeats. If there were no seasonal component, this would be your estimate. In our example this will be a 1-year estimate.

Analyze the Data

EXAMPLE 13.15 Sales of Four-wheel-drive Vehicles

Step 2: Estimate values as if no seasonal component present

Since the pattern repeats every year we will calculate a yearly average. So we average the sales for four quarters of 1995. We get $731.5 (thousands).

If there were no seasonal component, then we would expect the "middle" quarter to have $731.5 (1,000) for sales. So this is our estimate for quarter $2\frac{1}{2}$! But of course there is no quarter $2\frac{1}{2}$. For the moment, place this number in the column labeled "4Qtr MA" in the row for quarter 3. Now we must average the sales for the next 1-year period of time, which runs from quarter 2 of 1995 through and including quarter 1 of 1996. This gives us $781.8 (thousands).

This average should correspond to quarter $3\frac{1}{2}$! Place the value $781.8 in the column labeled 4 Qtr MA in the row for quarter 4 of 1995. So to get the "right" average for quarter 3 we average the two four-quarter moving averages we just found (one for quarter $2\frac{1}{2}$ and one for quarter $3\frac{1}{2}$). We get $756.7 (thousands).

This is called a **centered moving average.** It is only necessary when you have no "middle" value for the period of time over which the pattern repeats. Place this value in the column labeled "Centered 4 Qtr MA" for quarter 3 of 1995. So if there were no seasonal component, you would expect sales for quarter 3 in 1995 to be $756.7

	A	B	C	D	E
1			Sales		Centered
2	Year	Qtr	($1,000)	4 QTR MA	4 QTR MA
3	1995	1	$684.2		
4		2	$584.1		
5		3	$765.4	$731.5	$756.7
6		4	$892.3	$781.8	$793.4
7	1996	1	$885.4	$805.0	$835.2
8		2	$677.0	$865.3	$894.1
9		3	$1,006.6	$922.8	$957.6
10		4	$1,122.1	$992.3	$1,031.8
11	1997	1	$1,163.4	$1,071.3	$1,109.6
12		2	$993.2	$1,147.8	$1,200.7
13		3	$1,312.5	$1,253.6	$1,307.7
14		4	$1,545.3	$1,361.8	$1,395.2
15	1998	1	$1596.2	$1,428.6	$1,481.5
16		2	$1,260.4	$1,534.3	$1,594.9
17		3	$1,735.2	$1,655.4	$1,719.4
18		4	$2,029.7	$1,783.3	$1,832.1
19	1999	1	$2,107.8	$1,880.8	$1,952.0
20		2	$1,650.3	$2,023.1	$2,099.3

(1,000). The rest of the values are found in a similar manner. Notice that the last value you can find an estimate for is quarter 2 of 1999. ■

This is not the usual way we have calculated moving averages because we are using future values to estimate past values. Usually we use past values to estimate future values. But our purpose here is different. We wish simply to see what the annual estimate would have been if there were no seasonal component. You only need to go though the extra step of getting a centered MA if you have an even number of seasonal periods such as 4 quarters in a year, 12 months in a year, or 24 hours in a day. If you had a daily seasonality, then you would have 7 days in a week and you would have a middle value.

You would need a centered MA for monthly seasons too but not for daily.

Sales of Four-wheel-drive Vehicles ***Finding Centered Moving Averages***

Verify the centered MAs for the year 1996.

Now let's look at step 3.

ANS. ALL ANSWERS ARE ROUNDED TO ONE DECIMAL PLACE: Q1: (805.0 + 865.3)/2 = 835.2; Q2: (865.3 + 922.8)/2 = 894.1; Q3: (922.8 + 992.3)/2 = 957.5; Q4: (992.3 + 1071.3)/2 = 1031.8

Analyze the Data

EXAMPLE 13.16 Sales of Four-wheel-drive Vehicles

Step 3: Calculate raw seasonality

For each observation, find a raw seasonality by dividing the actual value, y_t, by the estimate found in step 2. The calculation for quarter 3 of 1995 is

$$\text{Raw seasonality} = \frac{765.4}{756.7} = 1.01$$

Time	*Year*	*Qtr*	*Sales ($1,000)*	*4 Qtr MA*	*Centered Raw 4 Qtr MA*	*Seasonality*
1	1995	1	$684.2			
2		2	$584.1			
3		3	$765.4	$731.5	$756.7	1.01
4		4	$892.3	$781.8	$793.4	1.12
5	1996	1	$885.4	$805.0	$835.2	1.06
6		2	$677.0	$865.3	$894.1	0.76
7		3	$1,006.6	$922.8	$957.5	1.05
8		4	$1,122.1	$992.3	$1,031.8	1.09
9	1997	1	$1,163.4	$1,071.3	$1,109.6	1.05
10		2	$993.2	$1,147.8	$1,200.7	0.83
11		3	$1,312.5	$1,253.6	$1,307.7	1.00
12		4	$1,545.3	$1,361.8	$1,395.2	1.11
13	1998	1	$1,596.2	$1,428.6	$1,481.4	1.08
14		2	$1,260.4	$1,534.3	$1,594.8	0.79
15		3	$1,735.2	$1,655.4	$1,719.3	1.01
16		4	$2,029.7	$1,783.3	$1,832.0	1.11
17	1999	1	$2,107.8	$1,880.8	$1,951.9	1.08
18		2	$1,650.3	$2,023.1	$2,099.3	0.79
19		3	$2,304.4	$2,175.5		
20		4	$2,639.4			

■

Notice that all the raw seasonal values are around 1. This should not be surprising. If there were no seasonality present, then when you compare your estimate to the actual value you would get a ratio of 1. Think about what the raw seasonality tells you. For quarter 2 of 1995, it was 1.01. This tells you that quarter 2 of 1995 was a pretty "average" quarter, whereas quarter 4 of 1997 had a raw seasonality of 1.11 and thus it was about 111% of an "average" quarter. Raw seasonal values greater than 1.00 tell you that the season was higher than average, and raw seasonal values less than 1.00 mean that the season was lower than average. If all your seasonal values are really close to 1.00, then there really is not a seasonal component!

TRY IT NOW!

Sales of Four-wheel-drive Vehicles ***Finding Raw Seasonalities***

Verify the raw seasonality for Q1 in the year 1996.

ANS: 885.4/835.2 = 1.06

Analyze the Data

EXAMPLE 13.17 Sales of Four-wheel-drive Vehicles

Step 4: Calculate average seasonality

Average all the quarter 1 raw seasonal values to get a seasonal index for quarter 1. Notice that there are 4 raw quarter 1 seasonal values. This is *not* because there are 4 quarters but rather because of the amount of data we have. Do this for each quarter.

The calculation for the first two are shown here:

Seasonal index Q1 = (1.06 + 1.05 + 1.08 + 1.08)/4 = 1.07
Seasonal index Q2 = (0.76 + 0.83 + 0.79 + 0.79)/4 = 0.79

Time	Year	Qtr	*Sales ($1,000)*	*4 Qtr MA*	*Centered Raw 4 Qtr MA*	*Seasonality*	*Average Seasonality*
1	1995	1	$684.2				1.07
2		2	$584.1				0.79
3		3	$765.4	$731.5	$756.7	1.01	1.02
4		4	$892.3	$781.8	$793.4	1.12	1.11
5	1996	1	$885.4	$805.0	$835.2	1.06	1.07
6		2	$677.0	$865.3	$894.1	0.76	0.79
7		3	$1,006.6	$922.8	$957.5	1.05	1.02
8		4	$1,122.1	$992.3	$1,031.8	1.09	1.11
9	1997	1	$1,163.4	$1,071.3	$1,109.6	1.05	1.07
10		2	$993.2	$1,147.8	$1,200.7	0.83	0.79
11		3	$1,312.5	$1,253.6	$1,307.7	1.00	1.02
12		4	$1,545.3	$1,361.8	$1,395.2	1.11	1.11
13	1998	1	$1,596.2	$1,428.6	$1,481.4	1.08	1.07
14		2	$1,260.4	$1,534.3	$1,594.8	0.79	0.79
15		3	$1,735.2	$1,655.4	$1,719.3	1.01	1.02
16		4	$2,029.7	$1,783.3	$1,832.0	1.11	1.11
17	1999	1	$2,107.8	$1,880.8	$1,951.9	1.08	1.07
18		2	$1,650.3	$2,023.1	$2,099.3	0.79	0.79
19		3	$2,304.4	$2,175.5			1.02
20		4	$2,639.4				1.11
21	2000	1					1.07
22		2					0.79
23		3					1.02
24		4					1.11

■

TRY IT NOW!

Sales of Four-wheel-drive Vehicles ***Finding Seasonal Indexes***

Verify the seasonal indexes for Q3 and Q4.

Notice that the column labeled "Average Seasonality" has the four values repeated down the column. This is because we will use the same Q1 seasonal index to get our predictions for all historical quarter 1 values to get an MSE or MAD. Once we get a new quarter 1 value, everything must be updated.

ANS: ALL ANSWERS ARE ROUNDED TO ONE DECIMAL PLACE: Q3: (1.01 + 1.05 + 1.01 + 1.0)/4 = 1.02; Q4: (1.12 + 1.09 + 1.11 + 1.11)/4 = 1.11

Analyze the Data

EXAMPLE 13.18 Sales of Four-wheel-drive Vehicles

Step 5: Deseasonalize the data

Remember that we are using a multiplicative model so to remove the seasonal component we must divide.

Remove the seasonal component from the time series by dividing each observation by the appropriate seasonal index. The first one is done for you.

$$\text{Quarter 1 year 1995:} \quad \text{Deseasonalized data} = \frac{684.2}{1.07} = 639.44$$

Time	*Year*	*Qtr*	*Sales (\$1,000)*	*4 Qtr MA*	*Centered Raw 4 Qtr MA*	*Seasonality*	*Average Seasonality*	*Deseasonal data*
1	1995	1	$684.2				1.07	$639.44
2		2	$584.1				0.79	$739.37
3		3	$765.4	$731.5	$756.7	1.01	1.02	$750.39
4		4	$892.3	$781.8	$793.4	1.12	1.11	$803.87
5	1996	1	$885.4	$805.0	$835.2	1.06	1.07	$827.48
6		2	$677.0	$865.3	$894.1	0.76	0.79	$856.96
7		3	$1,006.6	$922.8	$957.6	1.05	1.02	$986.86
8		4	$1,122.1	$992.3	$1,031.8	1.09	1.11	$1,010.90
9	1997	1	$1,163.4	$1,071.3	$1,109.6	1.05	1.07	$1,087.29
10		2	$993.2	$1,147.8	$1,200.7	0.83	0.79	$1,257.22
11		3	$1,312.5	$1,253.6	$1,307.7	1.00	1.02	$1,286.76
12		4	$1,545.3	$1,361.8	$1,395.2	1.11	1.11	$1,392.16
13	1998	1	$1,596.2	$1,428.6	$1,481.5	1.08	1.07	$1,491.78
14		2	$1,260.4	$1,534.3	$1,594.9	0.79	0.79	$1,595.44
15		3	$1,735.2	$1,655.4	$1,719.4	1.01	1.02	$1,701.18
16		4	$2,029.7	$1,783.3	$1,832.1	1.11	1.11	$1,828.56
17	1999	1	$2,107.8	$1,880.8	$1,952.0	1.08	1.07	$1,969.91
18		2	$1,650.3	$2,023.1	$2,099.3	0.79	0.79	$2,088.99
19		3	$2,304.4	$2,175.5			1.02	$2,259.22
20		4	$2,639.4				1.11	$2,377.84
21	2000	1					1.07	
22		2					0.79	
23		3					1.02	
24		4					1.11	

■

TRY IT NOW!

Sales of Four-wheel-drive Vehicles ***Deseasonalize the Data***

Verify the deseasonalized value for quarter 1 of 1999.

Notice that you can deseasonalize every observation. This time series can now be analyzed for trend, cycle, and random components.

The deasonalized time series for the sales of four-wheel-drive vehicles is shown in Figure 13.6. Clearly, the seasonal component is gone and there is a linear trend present. We will run regression on the deseasonalized data using time as the independent variable and the deseasonalized values as the dependent variable to model the linear trend. This is step 6.

Analyze the Data

EXAMPLE 13.19 Sales of Four-wheel-drive Vehicles

Step 6: Model the trend using regression

We wish to find the values of the y intercept, b_0, and the slope, b_1, that give us the line through the deseasonalized data with the least error. The output from a regression

ANS: 2107.8/1.07 = 1969.91

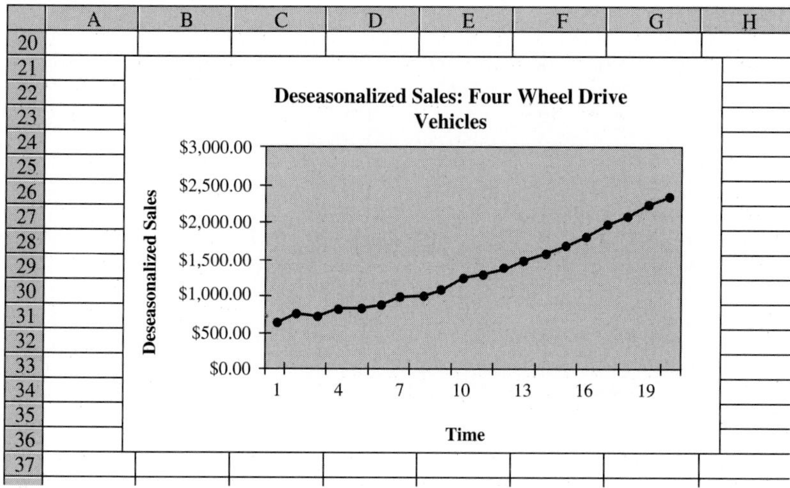

FIGURE 13.6 Deseasonalized sales

using Excel with time as the independent variable (X) and the deseasonalized data as the dependent (Y) values follows.

SUMMARY OUTPUT

Regression Statistics	
Multiple R	0.983399
R Square	0.967073
Adjusted R	0.965244
Standard E	101.4645
Observations	20

ANOVA

	df	*SS*	*MS*	*F*	*Significance F*
Regression	1	5442697	5442697	528.671234	8.565E-15
Residual	18	185310.9	10295.05		
Total	19	5628007			

	Coefficients	*Standard Errors*	*t Stat*	*P-value*	*Lower 95%*	*Upper 95%*	*Lower 95.0%*	*Upper 95.0%*
Intercept	397.6637	47.13346	8.436971	1.1398E-07	298.63984	496.6874591	298.6398441	496.6874591
Time	90.46826	3.934625	22.99285	8.565E-15	82.201912	98.73460774	82.20191226	98.73460774

The predicted deseasonalized time series can be found using

$$y_t = 397.66 + 90.47t$$

So, for quarter 1 of 1995 the predicted deseasonalized value would be

$$y_1 = 397.66 + 90.47(1) = 488.13$$

The other values are shown in the column labeled Predicted Sales Deseasonalized.

Time	Year	Qtr	Sales ($1,000)	Deseasonal data	Predicted production Deseasonalized
1	1995	1	$684.2	$639.44	488.13
2		2	$584.1	$739.37	578.60
3		3	$765.4	$750.39	669.07
4		4	$892.3	$803.87	759.54
5	1996	1	$885.4	$827.48	850.01
6		2	$677.0	$856.96	940.48
7		3	$1,006.6	$986.86	1030.95
8		4	$1,122.1	$1,010.90	1121.42

(continued)

Time	Year	Qtr	Sales ($1,000)	Deseasonal data	Predicted production Deseasonalized
9	1997	1	$1,163.4	$1,087.29	1211.89
10		2	$993.2	$1,257.22	1302.36
11		3	$1,312.5	$1,286.76	1392.83
12		4	$1,545.3	$1,392.16	1483.30
13	1998	1	$1,596.2	$1,491.78	1573.77
14		2	$1,260.4	$1,595.44	1664.24
15		3	$1,735.2	$1,701.18	1754.71
16		4	$2,029.7	$1,828.56	1845.18
17	1999	1	$2,107.8	$1,969.91	1935.65
18		2	$1,650.3	$2,088.99	2026.12
19		3	$2,304.4	$2,259.22	2116.59
20		4	$2,639.4	$2,377.84	2207.06
21	2000	1			2297.53
22		2			2388.00
23		3			2478.47
24		4			2568.94

■

TRY IT NOW!

Sales of Four-wheel-drive Vehicles ***Predict the Deseasonalized Values***

Verify the deseasonalized predicted value for quarter 1 of 2000.

Notice that we can predict deseasonalized values by using future values of time. Now we need to arrive at final predictions by putting the seasonal component back in. This is step 7.

EXAMPLE 13.20 **Sales of Four-wheel-drive Vehicles**

Step 7: Calculate final predictions by putting the seasonal component back

Multiply the predicted deseasonalized values by the appropriate seasonal index to make the final predictions for the historical data and the future values. Remember that the four quarterly seasonal indexes were found in step 4 to be 1.07, 0.79, 1.02, and 1.11.

The prediction for quarter 1 of 2000: $y_2 = 2297.53(1.07) = \$2458.36$

The prediction for quarter 4 of 2000: $y_{24} = 2568.94(1.11) = \$2851.52$

The remaining values are shown in the last column of the spreadsheet.

Time	*Year*	*Qtr*	*Sales ($1,000)*	*Deseasonal data*	*Predicted production Deseasonalized*	*Re-seasonalized Predictions*	*Abs Error*	*Error Squared*
1	1995	1	$684.2	$639.44	488.13	522.30	161.90	26211.61
2		2	$584.1	$739.37	578.60	457.09	127.01	16131.54
3		3	$765.4	$750.39	669.07	682.45	82.95	6880.70
4		4	$892.3	$803.87	759.54	843.09	49.21	2421.62

ANS. $\hat{y}_{21} = 397.66 + 90.47(21) = 2297.53$

Time	Year	Qtr	Sales ($1,000)	Deseasonal data	Predicted production Deseasonalized	Re-seasonalized Predictions	Abs Error	Error Squared
5	1996	1	$885.4	$827.48	850.01	909.51	24.11	581.29
6		2	$677.0	$856.96	940.48	742.98	65.98	4353.36
7		3	$1,006.6	$986.86	1030.95	1051.57	44.97	2022.30
8		4	$1,122.1	$1,010.90	1121.42	1244.78	122.68	15050.38
9	1997	1	$1,163.4	$1,087.29	1211.89	1296.72	133.32	17774.22
10		2	$993.2	$1,257.22	1302.36	1028.86	35.66	1271.64
11		3	$1,312.5	$1,286.76	1392.83	1420.69	108.19	11705.08
12		4	$1,545.3	$1,392.16	1483.30	1646.46	101.16	10233.35
13	1998	1	$1,596.2	$1,491.78	1573.77	1683.93	87.73	7696.55
14		2	$1,260.4	$1,595.44	1664.24	1314.75	54.35	2953.92
15		3	$1,735.2	$1,701.18	1754.71	1789.80	54.60	2981.16
16		4	$2,029.7	$1,828.56	1845.18	2048.15	18.45	340.40
17	1999	1	$2,107.8	$1,969.91	1935.65	2071.15	36.65	1343.22
18		2	$1,650.3	$2,088.99	2026.12	1600.63	49.67	2467.11
19		3	$2,304.4	$2,259.22	2116.59	2158.92	145.48	21164.43
20		4	$2,639.4	$2,377.84	2207.06	2449.84	189.56	35932.99
21	2000	1			2297.53	2458.36	Predictions	
22		2			2388.00	1886.52		
23		3			2478.47	2528.04		
24		4			2568.94	2851.52		
							84.68	9475.84
							MAD	MSE

■

The effect of reintroducing the seasonal component for quarter 2 values is to decrease the predicted values. This is of course because we know from historical data that quarter 2 sales are lower than average. Perhaps, people don't buy new vehicles in the dead of winter!

TRY IT NOW!

Sales of Four-wheel-drive Vehicles ***Predict the Values***

Verify the prediction for quarter 2 of 2000.

13.8.3 Exercises—Learning It!

13.30 Consider the following products and fill in the table below:

Variable	What time frame for a seasonality component would you expect?	What reasons might there be for this seasonality?
Sale of flowers		
Sale of candy		
Sale of movie tickets		
Number of employees working in camps		
Number of people calling in to a radio show		
Number of people on-line		

ANS. $\hat{y}_{22} = 2388.00(0.79) = \$1886.52$

Datafile:
ELECT.XXX

13.31 The average price of electricity in a U.S. city is given in the file called ELECT.XXX. The data are from January 1988 to December 1999.

(a) Display this time series as a line graph.

(b) What components do you find in this line graph?

(c) Find a seasonal index for each month of the year.

(d) Deseasonalize the data and find the slope and intercept for the trend that is present.

(e) Using both the regression model and the seasonal indexes, predict the average monthly price of electricity for 2000.

Datafile:
CHILD.XXX

13.32 The number of employees in the child-care industry is given from January 1990 to April 2000.

(a) Display these data as a line graph.

(b) Find a seasonal index for each month of the year.

(c) Which months have unusually high employment?

(d) Is there a trend component in this time series? If so, model it using regression on the deseasonalized data.

(e) Forecast the number of employees in the child-care industry for the rest of the months of the year 2000.

(f) Find the MSE for this model.

Datafile:
HOUSINGSALES.XXX

13.33 Consider the number of months it takes to sell a house. These data are in the datafile HOUSINGSALES.XXX.

(a) Display this time series as a line graph.

(b) Is there a seasonal component?

(c) Is there a trend component?

(d) Model the seasonal component for the number of months it takes to sell a house using the method of seasonal indexes. Use regression if there is also a trend component.

(e) Use your model to predict the number of months it will take to sell a house for each of the months from July through December 2000.

(f) Find the MSE for your model.

Datafile:
APPLEPRICES.XXX

13.34 The price of fruit is often a function of time of year and weather conditions. Consider the average price of a pound of red delicious apples in an average U.S. city.

(a) Display this time series as a line graph.

(b) Use a seasonal index and a regression model if needed to develop a forecasting model for these data.

(c) Forecast the average monthly price of apples for the year 2000.

(d) Find the MSE for this model.

13.35 The local liquor store has a bottle redemption center attached to it. The management is trying to determine staffing needs for the redemption center. The number of bottles brought into the redemption center varies from day to day. The data from the last 8 weeks are shown here:

	Week 1	Week 2	Week 3	Week 4	Week 5	Week 6	Week 7	Week 8
Mon	148,454	154,737	133,633	144,836	112,442	118,233	152,319	146,798
Tue	180,000	183,968	180,202	128,024	145,972	133,185	143,714	141,173
Wed	147,053	137,972	151,757	154,201	168,834	136,696	144,376	183,922
Thu	152,197	132,140	136,850	171,955	131,309	113,572	143,632	164,890
Fri	150,583	135,596	156,593	170,612	138,128	140,232	173,093	190,861
Sat	172,366	183,452	170,539	219,810	150,925	173,050	178,533	188,736

(a) What do you notice about the values for Saturdays?

(b) Use a 7-period MA and create a daily index for each of the days of the week.

(c) Is there a trend component as well?

(d) What recommendations can you make to management about staffing and why?

13.9 OTHER FORECASTING METHODS

In this chapter we have introduced the vocabulary for forecasting methods and some of the basic techniques of forecasting. There are many other models that can be used, depending on the nature of the data. For example, the exponential smoothing technique is a special case of **autoregressive integrated moving average models (ARIMA)** developed by Box and Jenkins. We have looked at moving average models, but we have not considered **autoregressive modeling.**

Sometimes we find that the values in our time series are related to earlier values in the time series. This is similar to the approach we took in the last section when we said that the January observation was most similar to the previous January observation as opposed to the previous observation, which would have been a December value. You might find that every third observation is related but not really have any reason for this relationship. When the data are correlated to themselves, this is called **autocorrelation.** You would want to exploit this pattern in building your model. In this case, you should consider using an ARIMA model.

Also, when we looked at techniques to model the trend component, we only considered linear models. Clearly, you might have a nonlinear trend. In this case, you would need to consider other **nonlinear regression models.**

Despite the fact that we have not covered a full semester's worth of forecasting models, you have learned enough to analyze time series data and to model the data in many cases. Always remember to visually analyze the data first and examine the components of the time series before deciding on a model. Once you have developed a model, be sure to find the MSE and the MAD as measures of error and to examine the residuals to be sure there is no pattern remaining. If there is a pattern remaining in the residuals, then there is something else in the data that you can model.

13.10 Executive Summary:
The Baseball Stadium

Business Analysis...

TO: General Manager
FROM: Erica Q. Analyst
RE: Forecast for attendance

To assist American Pastime, Inc. in planning for the new stadium, I have analyzed the 10 years of population data that you provided to me. I have developed a forecasting model for the population of families with children (FWC) and the number of people in the age group from 20 to 40 with no children (NC).

First, I visually examined the historical data for the two time series. The graphs are shown here:

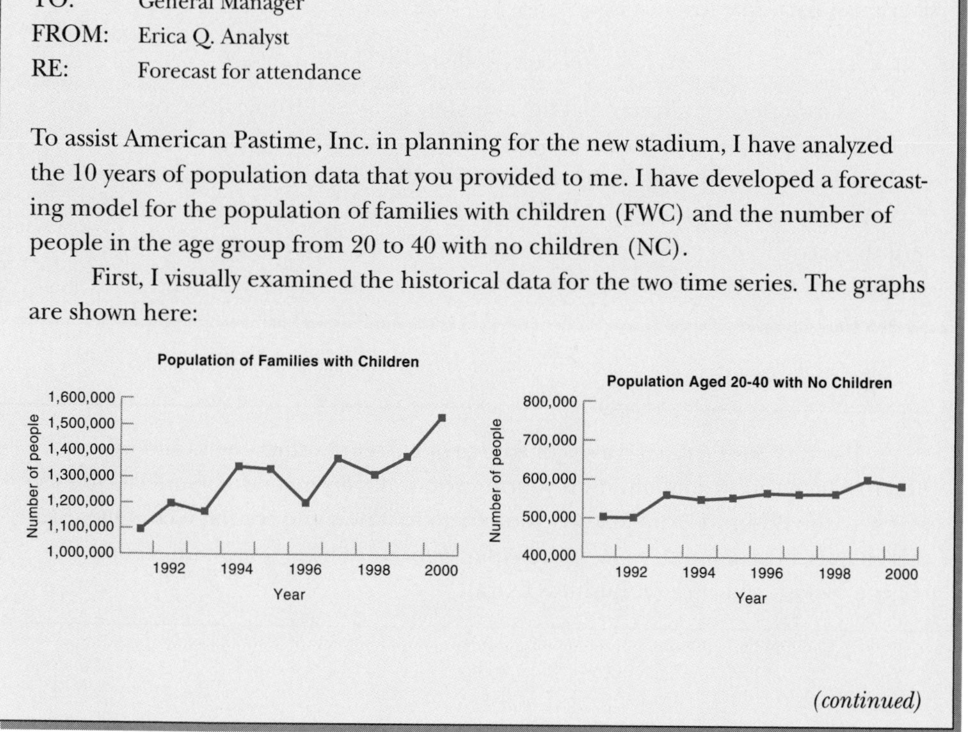

(continued)

You can see that the FWC time series is nonstationary because it has an upward trend in addition to a random component. The NC time series seems to have only a random component. Neither time series has a seasonality or a cyclical component.

I developed a variety of models for the FWC time series. For each model, I found the mean squared error (MSE) to compare the models. The results are summarized in the table:

Model	Parameters	MSE
3-period moving average	none	14,473,870,385
2-period moving average	none	12,900,675,743
3-period weighted moving average	$w_t = 0.50$, $w_{t-1} = 0.25$, $w_{t-2} = 0.25$	14,065,205,328
3-period weighted moving average	$w_t = 0.60$, $w_{t-1} = 0.30$, $w_{t-2} = 0.10$	14,123,783,596
2-period weighted moving average	$w_t = 0.75$, $w_{t-1} = 0.25$	12,735,801,453
Exponential smoothing model	$\alpha = 0.70$	11,194,214,145
Exponential smoothing model	$\alpha = 0.60$	11,378,876,397
Regression model	$b_0 = 1{,}096{,}755.133$ $b_1 = 36{,}868.01212$ (time as Y)	4,361,505,516

Clearly, the regression model gives the smallest MSE. This is consistent with the fact that we noticed a trend component in the FWC time series. The moving average, weighted moving average, and exponential smoothing models all lag the time series because they are really meant to be used when there is only a random component present. You can see this clearly when you examine the residuals for each of these models.

American Pastime, Inc. should use the regression model shown here to forecast the population of families with children for the year 2001:

$$y_t = 1{,}096{,}755.133 + 36{,}868.01(\text{time})$$

Time $t = 11$ corresponds to the year 2001 since the model was developed with 10 years of data. The forecast is

$$y_{11} = 1{,}096{,}755.1 + 36{,}868.012(11) = 1{,}502{,}303$$

Past experience indicates that the attendance rate is 1.91 per 1000 people for the FWC group. Applying this ratio to the estimate for the year 2001, I forecast the attendance to be $(1{,}502{,}303/1000)1.91 = 2869.39$ or 2870 baseball attendees.

A similar analysis must be done for the population without children. I will forward those results to you when they are finished. Please feel free to contact me if you have any questions about this analysis.

The *Wall Street Journal* is a major source of current business news and information for the business community. If your professor has arranged for your class to have access to the Business Extra feature, you can go to it now and see the techniques of this chapter in action today. Go to the Wiley Web site at http://www. wiley.com/college/pelosi, and click on Business Extra!

13.11 TIME SERIES ANALYSIS IN EXCEL

You learned how to do one of the forecasting methods described in this chapter when you learned about the linear regression model. Excel also has analysis tools for moving average and exponential smoothing models. In this section, we will look at two methods for the moving average model. For the exponential smoothing model, we will use the Excel data analysis tool.

Look at the problem of predicting the number of families with children that will attend Double A baseball games in a new stadium that is being built. The data collected are population data from the area from 1991 to 2000. The population figures are for two groups, families with children (FWC) and people 20–40 years old with no children (NC), both groups the stadium would like to attract. The data, in an Excel worksheet, are shown in Figure 13.7.

	A	B	C
1	Year	FWC	NC
2	1991	1,098,909	564,790
3	1992	1,197,185	556,734
4	1993	1,169,860	653,134
5	1994	1,350,675	632,459
6	1995	1,335,213	642,387
7	1996	1,207,658	654,890
8	1997	1,379,723	657,238
9	1998	1,321,457	657,238
10	1999	1,387,692	717,903
11	2000	1,546,920	692,340

FIGURE 13.7 Population data for baseball stadium

13.11.1 Moving Average Models in Excel

It is possible to analyze a moving average forecasting model in Excel using the **Add Trendline** option with a graph. To do this, you must first create a graph of the time series you want to analyze. The type of graph you want to create in Excel is a scatter plot, which you learned about in Chapter 5. Select the range that contains your data and make a scatter plot of the data. It should look similar to the one in Figure 13.8.

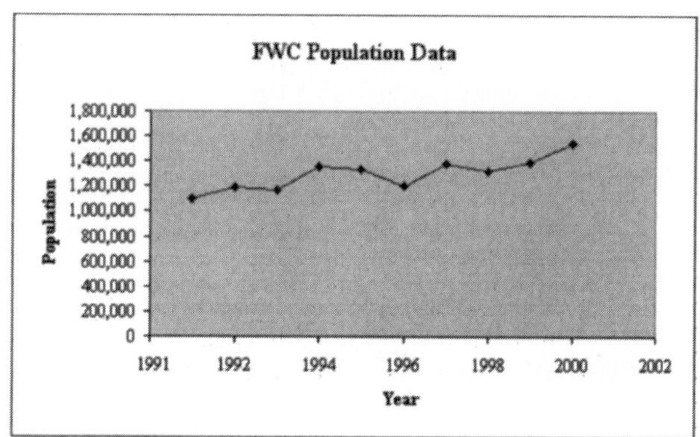

FIGURE 13.8 Scatter plot of FWC population data

Once the chart is created, follow these steps:

1. Click on the chart to select it, and click on any point on the line to select the data series. When you click on the chart to select it, a new option, **Chart,** is added to the menu bar.
2. From the **Chart** menu, select **Add Trendline**. The dialog box shown in Figure 13.9 (page 684) opens.
3. Click on the **Trend/Regression** text box for **Moving average.** You can specify the number of periods you want to use in the model by entering the value in the text box labeled **Period:.** Type in 3, since we want a 3-period moving average for this example. Click **OK;** a new line for the moving average model is inserted into the chart, as shown in Figure 13.10.

Although this tool is simple to use, it is limited. The trendline appears on the chart, but you do not get the actual predicted values from the model anywhere in the worksheet; thus, you will be unable to calculate the error. Also, there is a trendline model only for the moving average model, and not for exponential smoothing. For

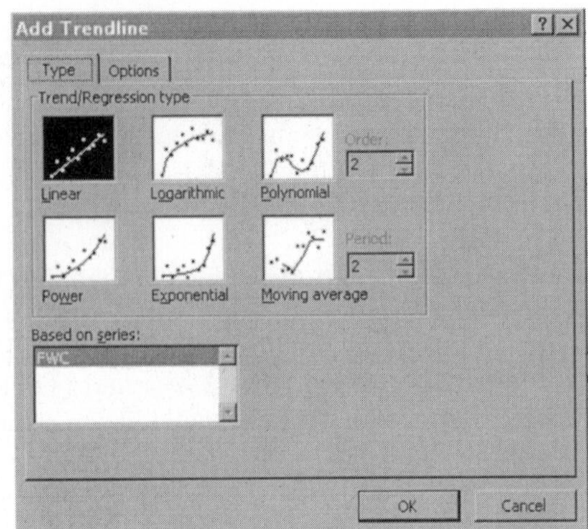

FIGURE 13.9 The Add Trendline dialog box

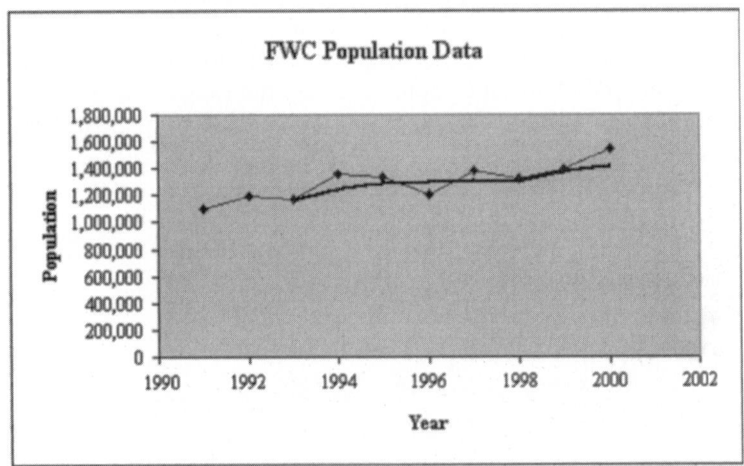

FIGURE 13.10 Chart with moving average trendline

these reasons, you might want to use the data analysis tools for time series. You can do this as follows:

1. From the list of Analysis Tools, select **Moving Average** and the dialog box shown in Figure 13.11 opens.
2. Position the cursor in the text box labeled **Input Range:** and highlight the range that contains the data. Highlight only the actual data, not the column with the time periods. Put a check in the **Labels in First Row** box if the range contains a label.
3. Position the cursor in the text box for **Interval:** and type in the number of periods you want to use for the moving average.
4. Now, position the cursor in the box labeled **Output Range:** and enter the location in the worksheet where you want the predicted values from the model to be located. Excel automatically skips the first value and enters NA for any values that cannot be predicted. For example, in a 3-period moving average, the first value that can be predicted is y_4. To line up the predicted values with the actual data, position the cursor in the cell adjacent to the *second* data value. You cannot have the output from this tool placed in a new worksheet or new workbook.

We do not use the standard errors for the predicted values, so there is no reason to include them.

5. Finally, put a check in the box for **Chart Output** and click **OK.** The worksheet will update to show the predicted values from the moving average model and a

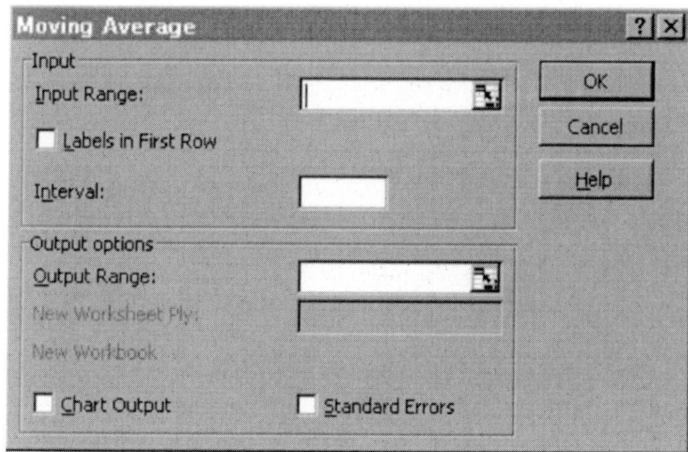

FIGURE 13.11 Moving Average dialog box

	A	B	C
1	Year	FWC	
2	1991	1,098,909	
3	1992	1,197,185	#N/A
4	1993	1,169,860	#N/A
5	1994	1,350,675	1,155,318
6	1995	1,335,213	1,239,240
7	1996	1,207,658	1,285,249
8	1997	1,379,723	1,297,849
9	1998	1,321,457	1,307,531
10	1999	1,387,692	1,302,946
11	2000	1,546,920	1,362,957
12			
13			

Moving Average
Value
2,000,000
1,000,000
0
1 3 5 7 9
Data Point
Actual
Forecast

FIGURE 13.12 Output from moving average tool

graph of the actual data and the predictions from the model, as shown in Figure 13.12.

If you are going to look at several models and try to choose the best model, then you will need to calculate the MSE for the model. To do this, we will use formulas in the worksheet:

1. First, you must calculate the error for each prediction. Just as we saw in regression analysis, the errors provide valuable information about how well the predicted values match the actual data. Position the cursor in the cell adjacent to the first predicted value and type in a formula to find the difference between the data value and the predicted value.

Be sure to remember the equal sign to tell Excel you are entering a formula.

2. Next, you need to square the deviations. Position the cursor in the cell adjacent to the first error, and type in the formula =**E5^2.**

***Note:** Your cell references should be the ones for your own data locations.*

3. Copy these formulas to the appropriate cells for the other data values and predicted values.
4. In the cell directly below the squared errors, you will need to type in the rest of the formula for the MSE. That is, you must add up all of the squared deviations and divide by the number of values, $t - k$, in this case, 7. We can use the **SUM** and **COUNT** functions to do this, as shown in Figure 13.13.

The MSE will now appear in the cell just below the squared deviations. Figure 13.14 shows the worksheet with all of the calculated values.

= =SUM(E5:E11)/COUNT(E5:E11)

FIGURE 13.13 Summing the squared deviations

	A	B	C	D	E
1	Year	FWC		Error	Squared Error
2	1991	1,098,909			
3	1992	1,197,185	#N/A		
4	1993	1,169,860	#N/A		
5	1994	1,350,675	1,155,318	195,357	38,164,357,449
6	1995	1,335,213	1,239,240	95,973	9,210,816,729
7	1996	1,207,658	1,285,249	-77,591	6,020,415,008
8	1997	1,379,723	1,297,849	81,874	6,703,406,459
9	1998	1,321,457	1,307,531	13,926	193,924,192
10	1999	1,387,692	1,302,946	84,746	7,181,884,516
11	2000	1,546,920	1,362,957	183,963	33,842,262,727
12				MSE	14473866726
13					

FIGURE 13.14 Table with errors and MSE

13.11.2 Exponential Smoothing Models in Excel

The simplest way to analyze a time series using an exponential smoothing model in Excel is to use the data analysis tool. This tool works almost exactly like the one for moving average, except that you will need to input the value of $1 - \alpha$ instead of the number of periods, k. The dialog box for the exponential smoothing analysis tool is shown in Figure 13.15.

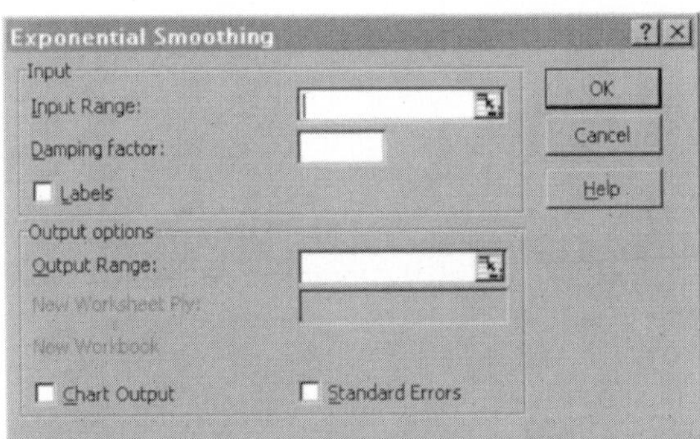

FIGURE 13.15 The Exponential Smoothing dialog box

Once you have entered the data range and the damping factor, $1 - \alpha$, and indicated what output you want and a location, the analysis is the same as the one for the moving average model.

CHAPTER 13 SUMMARY

A lot of time series data are collected on virtually every aspect of life. The government, businesses, and even individuals keep track of many variables over periods of time. This type of data contains information on patterns and trends that can be used to forecast the behavior of the variable for the future. According to Peter Bernstein in his book entitled *Against the Gods: The Remarkable Story of Risk,* the idea that defines the boundary between modern times and the past is the mastery of risk. This means that the future is more than a whim of the gods and that men and women are not passive. Bernstein says that the ability to define what may happen in the future and to choose among alternatives lies at the heart of contemporary societies.

This chapter has provided you with a brief introduction to the topic of forecasting. You have learned some of the basic terminology and techniques in this interesting discipline. You learned how to use moving averages and weighted moving averages to predict future values of a numeric variable. You also saw an additional application of the technique of regression. Finally, in this chapter you learned how to evaluate the model to choose the "best" model.

Key Terms

Term	Definition	Page Reference
Causal model	A **causal model** exploits the relationship between the dependent variable and other related variables in predicting future values for the dependent variable.	633
Cyclical component	The **cyclical component** models systematic ups and downs (in the time series) that repeat every 2 to 10 years and are typically tied to the business economy.	641
Exponential smoothing model	An **exponential smoothing model** is an averaging technique that uses unequal weights. The weights applied to past observations decline in an exponential manner.	659
***k*-period moving average**	A ***k*-period moving average** is the average of the most recent *k* observations.	646
Multiplicative model	The **multiplicative model** says that any observation in the time series can be written as the product of four components: $y_t = \mathrm{T} \times \mathrm{S} \times \mathrm{C} \times \mathrm{R}$	641
Qualitative model	A **qualitative model** for forecasting relies on experience and expert opinion. It is used when there are little or no historical data available.	632
Quantitative model	A **quantitative model** uses past data to predict future values.	632
Random component	The **random component** describes the irregular, unsystematic "bumps" in the values of the time series.	642
Seasonal component	The **seasonal component** describes a systematic pattern that repeats itself year after year.	641
Simple moving average model	A **simple moving average model** uses the simple average of the most recent *k* observations to predict for the next time period.	650
Smoothing constant	The **smoothing constant, α,** is the weight assigned to the most recent observation in an exponential smoothing model.	660
Stationary time series	A **stationary time series** is one with no significant upward or downward trend. A **nonstationary time series** has some type of trend.	634
Time series	A **time series** is a set of observations of a variable at regular time intervals, such as yearly, monthly, weekly, or daily.	634
Time series model	A **time series model** uses only data on the variable of interest. It exploits patterns, repetitive or systematic behavior, and/or trends in the data.	633
Trend component	The **trend component** describes a systematic long-term tendency of the data to increase or decrease over time.	641
Weighted moving average model	A **weighted moving average model** is a moving average model with unequal weights.	654

Key Formulas

Term	Formula	Page Reference
Simple moving average forecast	$\hat{y}_{t+1}$ = average of the most recent k observations $= \frac{y_t + y_{t-1} + \cdots + y_{t-k+1}}{k}$	646
Mean square error (MSE)	$\text{MSE} = \frac{\sum_{i=k+1}^{t} (y_i - \hat{y}_i)^2}{t - k}$	648
Mean absolute deviation (MAD)	$\text{MAD} = \frac{\sum_{i=k+1}^{t} \lvert y_i - \hat{y}_i \rvert}{t - k}$	650
Weighted moving average forecast	$\hat{y}_{t+1}$ = weighted average of the most recent k observations $= w_t y_t + w_{t-1} y_{t-1} + \cdots + w_{t-k+1} y_{t-k+1}$	656
Exponential smoothing forecast	$\hat{y}_{t+1} = \alpha y_t + \alpha(1-\alpha)y_{t-1} + \alpha(1-\alpha)^2 y_{t-2} + \cdots + \alpha(1-\alpha)^n y_{t-n} + \cdots$	660

CHAPTER 13 EXERCISES

Learning It!

Datafile: OZONE.XXX

13.36 A number of cities in the United States have had severe ozone problems caused by the burning of fossil fuels. The problem has been severe in cities such as Denver and Los Angeles (LA). The average monthly ozone rate in LA from 1979 to 1996 is given in the datafile. The first few lines of this datafile are shown here:

Jan 1979	2.7
Feb	2
Mar	3.6
Apr	5
May	6.5
Jun	6.1

(a) Find the MSE for a 12-month simple moving average model of these data.

(b) Find the MSE for an exponential smoothing model of these data with $\alpha = 0.90$.

(c) Find the MSE for the regression model of these data.

(d) Select the model with the lowest MSE and forecast the average monthly ozone rate for January 1997.

Datafile: HOSPITAL.XXX

13.37 Most hospitals monitor length of stay of patients. These data help administrators to effectively use resources and staff. The average length of stay (in days) by month for a medium-size New England city hospital are shown here:

Month/year	Length of Stay	Month/year	Length of Stay	Month/year	Length of Stay
Jan-97	4.69	Jan-98	4.6	Jan-99	6.43
Feb-97	2.7	Feb-98	5.42	Feb-99	6.66
Mar-97	5.28	Mar-98	4.01	Mar-99	4.43
Apr-97	3.53	Apr-98	6.62	Apr-99	4.43
May-97	3.16	May-98	5.7	May-99	6.09
Jun-97	4.56	Jun-98	2.79	Jun-99	4.7
Jul-97	7.72	Jul-98	5.3	Jul-99	6.52
Aug-97	4.03	Aug-98	6.44	Aug-99	5.68
Sep-97	2.29	Sep-98	6.21	Sep-99	5.29
Oct-97	7.41	Oct-98	3.22	Oct-99	2.45
Nov-97	4.47	Nov-98	8.46	Nov-99	5.29
Dec-97	5.27	Dec-98	6.91	Dec-99	4.32

(a) Display these data as a line graph.

(b) Find the MSE for a 3-month simple moving average model of these data.

(c) Find the MSE for a 3-month weighted moving average model using $w_t = 0.70$, $w_{t-1} = 0.20$, and $w_{t-2} = 0.10$.

(d) Find the MSE for an exponential smoothing model of these data with $\alpha = 0.80$.

(e) Select the model with the lowest MSE and forecast the average length of stay for January 2000.

13.38 Technology is affecting every aspect of our lives. An increasing amount of research is being done via on-line databases. The data in the LIBRARY.XXX file shows the monthly usage of ABI/Inform at Lancaster University in England for 1997 and 1998. The data are shown here.

Datafile: LIBRARY.XXX

Date	ABI/Inform	Date	ABI/Inform
Jan-97	928	Jan-98	1617
Feb-97	991	Feb-98	1387
Mar-97	890	Mar-98	1031
Apr-97	647	Apr-98	525
May-97	775	May-98	832
Jun-97	855	Jun-98	412
Jul-97	395	Jul-98	320
Aug-97	736	Aug-98	458
Sep-97	650	Sep-98	167
Oct-97	1184	Oct-98	365
Nov-97	2201	Nov-98	377
Dec-97	710	Dec-98	277

(a) Display these data as a line graph.

(b) Which of the forecasting techniques would you recommend and why?

(c) Develop a model to predict the usage of ABI/Inform for January 1999 using the technique you proposed in part (b).

13.39 Virtually all medical research involves the collection and analysis of data. There are many job opportunities in the field of biostatistics. The American Statistical Association (ASA) did a salary survey of faculty teaching in Biostatistics Departments. The data shown here are the median starting salaries (in $) for assistant professors, associate professors, and full professors.

Year	Assistant	Associate	Full
1993	52,735	62,300	92,000
1994	50,866	62,000	92,308
1995	56,000	64,500	97,516
1996	57,000	68,234	98,296
1997	62,804	73,840	106,438
1998	63,860	76,200	117,695
1999	72,580	78,749	136,217

(a) Display the three time series on the same graph.

(b) Do they have the same components?

(c) Recommend a forecasting model for the assistant professors.

(d) Using the model, predict the salary in 2000 for assistant professors of biostatistics with more than 3 years of experience.

(e) What factors other than time do you think might be important in predicting salaries?

13.40 The data presented in the file RIVER.XXX show the average monthly flow of the Elbe River in Canada from 1982 to 1996. The Department of Natural Resources monitors the water flow to detect any shifts in the ecology of the region. The first few lines of the data file are shown at the top of page 690.

Datafile: RIVER.XXX

Jan 1982	170
Feb	376
Mar	658
Apr	311
May	205
Jun	385

(a) Find the MSE for a 12-month moving average model.

(b) Find the MSE for a 12-month weighted moving average model with the following weights: 0.34, 0.10, 0.11, 0, 0, 0, 0, 0, 0.02, 0.14, 0.25, 0.04. These weights are the optimal weights for a 12-month moving average model.

(c) Find the MSE for an exponential smoothing model with $\alpha = 0.55$. This is the optimal value of α for an exponential smoothing model.

(d) Find the MSE for a regression model.

(e) Using the model with the smallest MSE, predict the average monthly river flow for January 1997.

Datafile: *FIRES.XXX*

13.41 Each year during the "dry" season, a number of western states experience forest fires. Some of these fires are ignited by natural elements such as lightning, whereas others are started by arson. The FIRES.XXX file shows the number of acres lost in forest fires by year from 1941 to 1996. The first few lines of this datafile are

1941	1,009,000
1942	1,475,000
1943	856,000
1944	3,027,000
1945	4,271,000
1946	3,126,000
1947	1,115,000

(a) Find the MSE for a 3-year, 6-year, and 9-year moving average model.

(b) Using the model with the smallest MSE, forecast the number of acres to be lost in 1997.

Thinking About It!

Requires Exercises 13.4 and 13.34

13.42 Examine the prices of apples in Exercise 13.34 and the holdings of apples in Exercise 13.4.

(a) Do these time series have the same components?

(b) Do they seem to be related?

(c) Try using the data in the holdings file as the independent variable to predict the price of apples in the price file. How does the error for this model compare to the one developed in Exercise 13.34?

Requires Exercise 13.12

13.43 Many critics have suggested that students are less prepared for college these days.

(a) Use regression with time as the independent variable to predict the average verbal and math SAT scores for the data in Exercise 13.12.

(b) Find the MSE for these models and compare them to the MSE for the moving average models you developed in Exercise 13.12.

(c) Which model gives you the least error for each time series?

(d) Does your analysis support the critics? Explain why or why not.

(e) In 1996 the SAT scores were recentered. How will this affect your model when you include data from 1996 forward?

Datafile: *HOUSINGSALES.XXX*

Requires Exercises 13.14 and 13.33

13.44 Look over your analysis of the HOUSINGSALES.XXX data. When is the best time of year to sell your house? Explain.

13.45 On the Internet, find the population data for the United States that corresponds to the same period of time as Exercise 13.5. Do you see the same components in this time series as the population data for the United Kingdom? *Requires Exercise 13.5*

13.46 Very often data are available as both seasonally adjusted and not seasonally adjusted. Consider the housing data. The table shows both the seasonally adjusted values and the non–seasonally adjusted values. Examine the seasonally adjusted data and compare to the nonadjusted data. What do you think they have done to seasonally adjust these data?

New One-Family Houses Sold and For Sale-Monthly

	Seasonally adjusted				Not seasonally adjusted					
	Houses sold during month		Houses for sale at end of month		Houses sold during month				Houses for sale at end of month	
Period	Total (000's)	Median month start to sale	Total (000's)	Median month start to EOM	Total (000's)	Median sales price	Median months start to sale	Average sales price	Total (000's)	Median months start to EOM
Jan-95	626	4.1	341	5.0	47	$127,900	4.7	$147,400	340	5.3
Feb-95	559	4.0	346	5.1	47	$135,000	4.4	$160,200	341	5.6
Mar-95	616	4.4	346	5.2	60	$130,000	4.5	$153,300	343	5.8
Apr-95	621	4.7	348	5.5	58	$134,000	4.7	$157,800	344	5.9
May-95	674	5.0	349	5.7	63	$133,900	4.9	$158,000	346	5.8
Jun-95	725	4.8	348	5.9	64	$133,700	4.3	$160,200	349	5.6
Jul-95	765	4.8	344	5.7	64	$131,000	4.6	$154,200	343	5.3
Aug-95	701	4.4	350	5.4	63	$134,900	3.9	$162,000	350	5.0
Sep-95	678	4.2	353	5.4	54	$130,000	4.0	$155,600	354	5.1
Oct-95	696	4.2	359	5.3	54	$135,200	3.8	$156,200	361	5.0
Nov-95	664	4.2	366	5.2	46	$137,000	4.3	$160,700	371	5.0
Dec-95	709	3.8	370	5.2	45	$138,600	4.2	$165,600	374	5.3
Jan-96	714	4.1	369	5.1	54	$131,900	4.7	$155,300	370	5.5
Feb-96	769	3.9	355	5.0	68	$139,400	4.5	$163,700	362	5.7
Mar-96	721	4.4	368	5.2	70	$137,000	4.4	$162,100	362	5.8
Apr-96	736	4.0	368	5.3	70	$140,000	4.2	$170,000	366	5.6
May-96	746	4.5	361	5.4	69	$136,400	4.4	$163,300	360	5.4
Jun-96	721	4.9	355	5.2	65	$140,000	4.3	$166,500	355	4.9
Jul-96	770	4.3	350	4.9	66	$144,200	4.2	$168,400	351	4.5
Aug-96	826	3.7	342	4.8	73	$137,000	3.4	$159,700	342	4.4
Sep-96	770	4.5	330	4.8	62	$139,000	4.1	$167,400	332	4.5
Oct-96	720	4.4	328	4.8	56	$143,800	4.0	$168,400	332	4.5
Nov-96	771	4.0	330	4.6	54	$143,500	4.3	$172,000	330	4.5
Dec-96	805	4.1	322	4.7	51	$144,900	4.4	$171,800	326	4.8
Jan-97	830	4.2	308	4.8	61	$145,000	4.8	$171,900	309	5.1
Feb-97	801	4.0	301	4.8	69	$143,000	4.5	$171,100	296	5.3
Mar-97	831	3.9	288	4.9	81	$148,000	3.9	$172,700	284	5.4
Apr-97	744	4.0	290	4.8	70	$150,000	4.1	$179,500	289	5.2
May-97	760	4.0	287	4.7	71	$141,000	3.8	$170,700	286	4.7
Jun-97	793	3.0	288	4.7	71	$145,000	2.7	$179,400	288	4.4
Jul-97	805	3.6	289	4.7	69	$145,900	3.4	$175,500	289	4.3
Aug-97	815	3.4	287	4.8	72	$144,000	3.1	$170,700	284	4.4
Sep-97	840	3.5	284	4.7	67	$146,300	3.2	$177,500	285	4.4
Oct-97	800	3.6	284	4.7	62	$141,500	3.4	$172,900	287	4.4
Nov-97	864	3.7	281	4.8	61	$145,000	3.8	$175,400	281	4.6
Dec-97	793	3.5	281	4.8	51	$145,900	3.8	$175,800	287	4.9

(continued)

Notice that if you concluded that there was no treatment effect (by failing to reject H_0), then each response would be equal to the overall mean plus some random variation called error.

We must use the data to estimate the grand mean and the treatment effect. As you will see in Section 14.4 on the assumptions of ANOVA, the error term is assumed to have an average of zero. The grand mean can be estimated by $\bar{\bar{x}}$ and the treatment effect is the adjustment that must be made to the grand mean to predict a response. The treatment effect can be estimated by taking the difference between the treatment mean and the overall mean, $\bar{x}_j - \bar{\bar{x}}$. Thus, the estimate of the response is

$$\text{Response} = \bar{\bar{x}} + (\bar{x}_j - \bar{\bar{x}}) + \text{Error} = \bar{x}_j + \text{Error}$$

or just the treatment mean + error.

Analyze the Data

EXAMPLE 14.12 Airspace Data

A Prediction Model

For the airspace data consider $x_{11} = 23$ mm. Writing this in terms of its components gives us

$$\text{Response} = \text{Grand mean} + \text{Treatment effect} + \text{Error}$$
$$23 = 17.32 + (21.01 - 17.32) + \text{error}$$
$$23 = 17.32 + 3.69 + 1.99$$

Our model would predict an average of 21.01 mm of airspace in process. In this case we would be in error by 1.99 mm. ■

TRY IT NOW!

Tissue Strength Data ***Prediction Model***

For the tissue strength data, write x_{11} in terms of its components.

What is your error for this particular observation?

14.3.8 The Next Step: Multiple Comparisons

Remember that your goal is to understand how the airspace changes as the tissue box sits on the shelf.

If you have rejected the null hypothesis of equal population means, as we have in the case of the airspace data, you can say that there is sufficient evidence in the data to state that not all the population means are the same. Clearly, this is only the first step. To decide what type of experiment to run next to further investigate the effect this factor has on the variable of interest, we should try to learn a little bit more from this data set.

ANS. 1006 = 988.4 + (900 − 988.4) + 16
ERROR = 16 LB/REAM

```
Analysis of Variance

Source    DF        SS       MS        F        P
Time       3   2554.75   851.58   239.13    0.000
Error    476   1695.12     3.56
Total    479   4249.87

                                    Individual 95% CIs For Mean
                                    Based on Pooled StDev
Level      N      Mean    StDev     -------+---------+---------+---------
  1      120    21.008    1.526                                (-*-)
  2      120    17.458    1.483                      (*-)
  3      120    15.783    2.083           (-*-)
  4      120    15.017    2.319     (-*-)
                                    -------+---------+---------+---------
Pooled StDev =   1.887                   16.0      18.0      20.0
```

FIGURE 14.4 Confidence intervals for airspace data from Minitab

Let's see what tools we have already learned that might help us with our detective work. We started off by simply looking at the sample mean for each of the levels of the factor. But we know from our work in Chapter 7 that the sample mean is a point estimate and is never likely to actually "hit" the population mean right on the money. To get an idea of how far off our point estimate was likely to be, we constructed confidence intervals for the population mean. It seems that this might be a useful tool at this point. In fact, most statistical software packages calculate the individual sample means and the corresponding confidence intervals when you run ANOVA. This portion of the Minitab output for the airspace data is shown in Figure 14.4. Excel ANOVA output does not include confidence intervals.

Visual analysis for pairwise comparison gets you started

By this point in the text, you have seen that you can learn a great deal by examining graphs and noticing patterns. As you examine these confidence intervals you can see that some of them overlap and some do not. For example, the confidence interval for the mean airspace in process (population or level 1) seems particularly different from the confidence interval for the mean airspace after 4 weeks (level 4). However, the confidence intervals for the mean airspace for levels 3 (2 weeks) and 4 (4 weeks) overlap a bit. Although this is not a formal statistical test, you can certainly intelligently speculate about whether there is one population mean that is causing the F value in ANOVA to be large (leading to a rejection of the null hypothesis) or whether all of the means are different from each other. In the case of the airspace data it seems that there is a great difference between the in-process data and the 24-hour data. Perhaps it would be a good idea to look at the differences in the sample means. Table 14.1 shows the amount of growback (in mm) in the tissues from the time of manufacturing until 4 weeks after manufacturing. These values are easily found by subtracting pairs of sample means. For example, the difference between $\bar{x}_1$ and $\bar{x}_2$ is (12.01 − 17.46 mm) = 3.55 mm.

This table tells us that the airspace decreases 3.55 mm between the time of manufacturing (level 1) and 24 hours later (level 2), it decreases an additional 1.68 mm between the 24-hour mark and 2 weeks later, and it decreases only an additional 0.76 mm between 2 weeks and 4 weeks. In total, the tissues "grow back" about 6 mm from the time of manufacturing until the customer opens the box 4 weeks later. Clearly, our idea that most of the growback occurs during the first 24 hours after manufacturing seems to be correct. In fact, the tissues are greatly compressed at the time of manufacturing to get them into the box, so perhaps focusing on the first 24 hours is a good approach for your next experiment.

Table 14.1 Difference in Sample Means of Airspace Data

Level	1	2	3
1			
2	3.55		
3	5.23	1.68	
4	5.99	2.44	0.76

This analysis also points out how much easier it is to do data analysis when you are actually involved in the manufacturing process or the situation that generated the data. If you understand the situation you are much more likely to be able to make sense of the data and make relevant recommendations.

The intuitive, visual approach we have taken here works well at pointing you in the right direction and will not differ much from the conclusions you could draw from formal techniques if the sample sizes are equal, as they were in the airspace data. In fact, the most common formal statistical test done at this point uses the difference between two of the sample means as the center of a confidence interval, which estimates the difference in the corresponding population means. Several techniques could be used to do this. Alternatively, a hypothesis test of the difference in the two population means can be done. It might seem that a t test or a paired t test from Chapter 10 would work here. It is natural to think so since we now wish to compare two population means. Although the setup of the null and alternative hypotheses is the same here, unfortunately we cannot use either a t test or a paired t test to do the test. The reason for this has to do with the fact that you are making multiple pairwise comparisons from a single data set and in addition to that you are doing the comparison after the data have been analyzed.

Techniques for doing pairwise comparisons sometimes give conflicting conclusions.

There are several techniques that could be used and most statistical software packages will have several options for doing the pairwise comparisons. For example, if you are using Minitab, then you can use any one of four techniques to do the pairwise comparisons. Sometimes these techniques lead to conflicting conclusions. Many issues need to be addressed to properly explain these techniques and they will not be addressed here. However, by examining the confidence intervals for the mean of each level of the factor, looking at how they overlap and how much the sample means change as you change levels of the factor, you will detect a good deal about how the factor influences the variable you are studying. This will help guide the design of your next experiment.

14.3.9 Exercises—Learning It!

14.1 A diaper company is considering 3 different filler materials for their disposable diapers. Eight diapers were tested with each of the 3 filler materials, and 24 toddlers were randomly given a diaper to wear. As the child played, fluid was injected into the diaper every 10 minutes until the product failed (leaked). The amount of fluid (in grams) at the time of failure was recorded for each diaper. The data are shown here:

Material 1	Material 2	Material 3
791	809	828
789	818	814
796	803	855
802	781	844
810	813	847
790	808	848
800	805	836
790	811	873

(a) What is the response variable and what is the factor?

(b) How many levels of the factor are being studied?

(c) Is there any difference in the average amount of fluid the diaper can hold using the 3 different filler materials? If so, which ones are different?

(d) What is your recommendation to the company and why?

Datafile: *DISKFAIL.XXX*

14.2 In Chapter 4 you looked at a large company that sells software. The company had received complaints that the disks provided by the company failed to work properly after extended use. The company has decided to investigate the complaint. Data are collected on the time to failure for disks from their current supplier and two alternative suppliers. The data are shown here:

Current Supplier	Alternative 1 Supplier	Alternative 2 Supplier
486	489	508
490	489	510
491	491	517

(continued)

Current Supplier	Alternative 1 Supplier	Alternative 2 Supplier
491	492	506
494	492	515
494	492	520
496	492	503
498	493	524
498	493	515
502	494	503
504	495	507
505	496	515
506	497	509
507	497	518
508	497	495
510	498	499
514	499	510
515	502	503
527	503	533
498	505	517

(a) What is the response variable and what is the factor?

(b) How many levels of the factor are being studied?

(c) Is there any difference in the average time to failure of the disks from the 3 different suppliers? If so, which ones are different?

(d) What is your recommendation to the company and why?

14.3 Grading homework is a real problem. It takes an enormous amount of time and many students do not do a very good job or copy answers from other students or the back of the book. A teacher of elementary statistics decided to conduct a study to determine what effect grading homework had on her students' exam scores. She taught 3 sections of Elementary Statistics and randomly assigned each class one of three conditions: (1) no homework given, (2) homework given but not collected, and (3) homework given, collected, and graded. After the first exam, she collected the data (exam scores). They are shown below:

Datafile: HOMEWORK.XXX

No Homework	Homework, Not Collected	Homework, Collected
69	73	83
69	63	97
92	68	72
84	79	79
79	57	84
84	68	76
76	72	91
63	74	76
76	49	83
82	84	88
89	79	91
72	71	96
72	80	68
65	74	99
73	71	89
47	63	80
92	88	79
71	83	91
83	89	83
81	82	83
92	69	76
80	92	90
64	79	79
72	81	67

(continued)

No Homework	Homework, Not Collected	Homework, Collected
84	76	86
79	81	86
74	81	82
81	75	84

(a) What is the response variable and what is the factor?

(b) How many levels of the factor are being studied?

(c) Is there any difference in the average exam scores using the 3 different approaches to homework? If so, which ones are different?

(d) What is your recommendation to the teacher and why?

14.4 Two tissue strength measurements were studied: machine-directional strength (*MD-Strength*) and the cross-directional strength (*CDStrength*). They are both measured in lb/ream. We will look at only the *CDStrength* in this exercise. The data were collected over 3 days and the company would like to know whether the average *CDStrength* is the same for all 3 days.

In the complete data set there are 75 observations per day. In this example we will look at only five observations per day. At the end of the chapter you will have the opportunity to do a complete analysis of this data set.

The five CD strengths for each of the 3 days are shown here:

Day	*CDStrength*	Day	*CDStrength*	Day	*CDStrength*
1	422	2	436	3	473
1	448	2	468	3	440
1	423	2	419	3	441
1	435	2	458	3	443
1	445	2	459	3	400

(a) Display the data as a dotplot.

(b) Find the grand mean and the treatment means.

(c) Mark the grand mean and the treatment means on the dotplot.

(d) Examine the first observation for day 1: 422 lb/ream. Find the difference between the first treatment mean and the grand mean. This is the treatment effect for the first treatment. On the dotplot mark off this difference.

(e) Continue to examine the first observation for day 1: 422 lb/ream. Find the difference between this observation and the first treatment mean and the grand mean. This is the error for this observation. On the dotplot mark off this difference.

(f) Analyze these data using one-way ANOVA. Is there a significant treatment effect?

Datafile: BALLDESN.XXX

14.5 The sports industry is a large and competitive market. A manufacturer of golf balls is considering 4 new ball designs. A sample of 36 balls from each of the 4 models is tested and the distance the balls carry (in yards) is recorded. The balls are hit by a machine. The data follow.

M1 Model	M2 Model	M3 Model	M4 Model
257	256	244	250
255	255	243	255
256	258	241	251
255	257	243	249
255	257	240	250
256	257	249	251
255	258	244	251
258	258	249	248
252	256	248	247
256	258	243	253
253	258	242	250
254	256	245	255
260	259	253	250

(continued)

M1 Model	M2 Model	M3 Model	M4 Model
258	255	250	256
258	259	251	260
257	257	249	259
259	256	249	252
257	255	249	253
255	255	255	257
256	257	249	255
259	260	251	251
261	255	250	255
260	261	248	253
257	262	250	256
260	258	258	262
262	260	258	258
258	260	257	263
260	256	258	259
258	255	254	256
258	256	256	261
258	257	255	258
256	251	254	258
260	253	255	256
260	254	260	263
261	254	254	264
257	255	253	257

(a) What is the response variable and what is the factor?

(b) How many levels of the factor are being studied?

(c) Is there any difference in the average distance the ball carries?

(d) What is your recommendation to the golf manufacturer and why?

14.4 ASSUMPTIONS OF ANOVA

We have already mentioned that ANOVA is a very commonly used technique. Unfortunately, many times ANOVA is used when it is not the appropriate technique. This may be partly due to the fact that it is relatively easy to run ANOVA using a statistical package and most software tools simply do the calculations but do not check that it is the appropriate technique. This is your job as the data analyst. As with many of the tools presented in this book, the tool of ANOVA gives you valid conclusions if your data meet certain assumptions. If your data do not meet these assumptions and you use ANOVA, you could easily draw the wrong conclusions. Thus, you should always check that the three major assumptions of ANOVA are met *before* you use this technique.

The three major assumptions of ANOVA are as follows:

1. The errors are random and independent of each other.
2. Each population has a normal distribution.
3. All of the populations have the same variance.

14.4.1 Assumption About the Errors

The first assumption talks about the behavior of the errors. What are these errors? The term error refers to the difference between any observed value and the sample mean of its group. We looked at these differences when we developed the formula for SSE in Section 14.3.3. Remember that SSE is found by adding up the squared differences of the form $x_{ij} - \overline{x}_{j}$. Each term in the sum for SSE is considered an "error." Thus, the first assumption says that these differences should be random and the error for one observation should not influence the error for another observation. If you have randomly selected a sample from each of the populations then typically this assumption is met.

Time series data may violate this assumption.

The most common situation in which this assumption is violated is when you have time series data. In this case, the observation at time period t may influence the observation at time period $t + 1$ (in fact, it is precisely this dependency that you exploit when you build a time series model). If the observations are dependent, then the errors will be dependent. A violation of this assumption could seriously affect the conclusions reached using ANOVA. If you are suspicious of a bias in the sampling process or if you have time-dependent data, then you should consult a more advanced textbook.

14.4.2 Assumptions About the Underlying Populations

The second and third assumptions of ANOVA refer to the behavior of the variable being collected. The second assumption says that the variable should have a normal distribution in each of the populations (each level of the factor). You can check this assumption formally using a chi-square goodness of fit test, which is the subject of the next chapter. At this point you should visually check the shape of the data in each sample by displaying a histogram of the data.

Analyze the Data

EXAMPLE 14.13 Airspace Data

Looking at Histograms for Normality

Histograms for all 4 levels of the factor *time* for the airspace data are shown here:

Note: If you use Excel's Histogram command, change the gap width to zero.

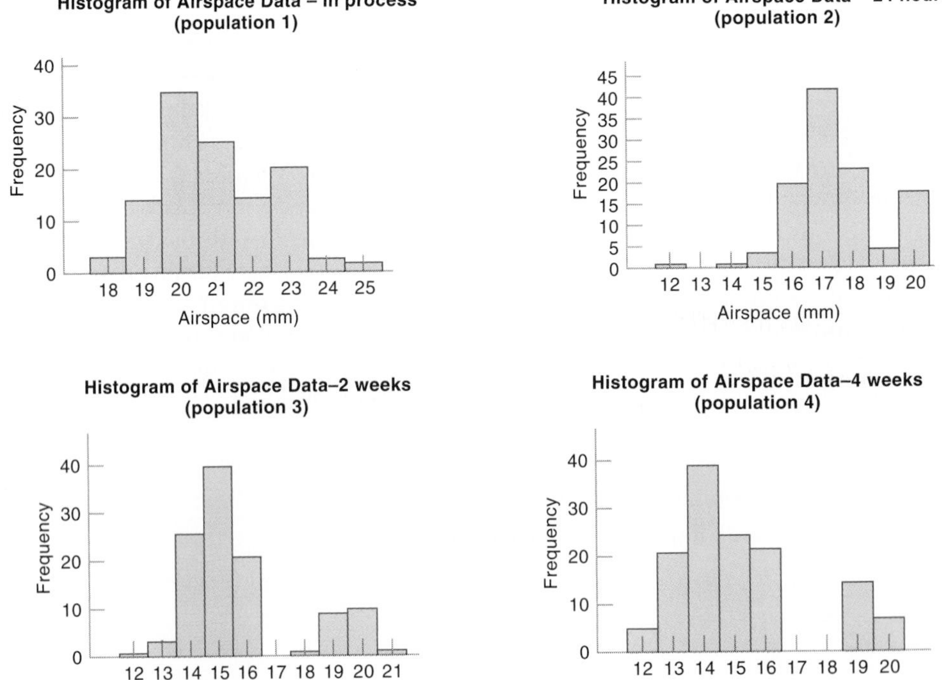

A look at these graphs tells us that we may be in violation of the assumption of normality for at least one of the populations. ■

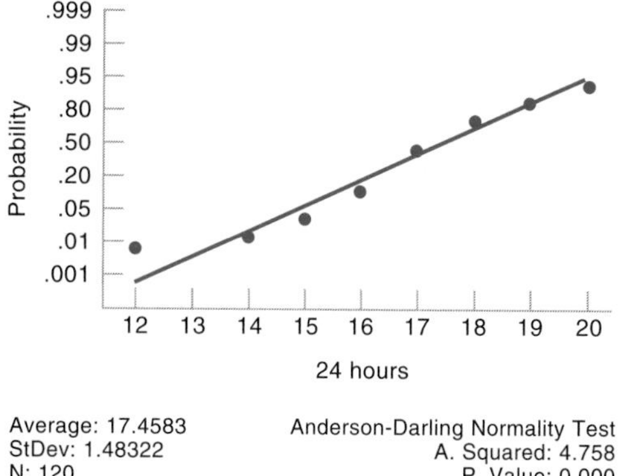

FIGURE 14.5 Normal probability plot of 24-hour airspace data

The normal probability plot in Excel should not be used as it is not correct.

Another way to test for the assumption of normality is to use a normal probability plot. You were introduced to this concept in the discussion of the assumptions of simple linear regression in Section 11.6.1. A normal probability plot for the in-process data is shown in Figure 14.5. It was generated by Minitab.

__Remember:__ When the data are normally distributed, the plot will be a straight line.

Fortunately, the technique of ANOVA is not particularly sensitive to violations of the normality assumption. This means that if your data follow a distribution that is not extremely different from a normal distribution, then your conclusions from ANOVA are probably fine, especially for a large sample size.

The third assumption of ANOVA also has to do with the behavior of the distribution of the variable in each of the populations. Once you have checked to see that the second assumption has been met, or at least is not severely violated, then you must check to see that the amount of variability in each of the populations is the same. That is, the variance within each population should be equal. This is necessary to combine the data from the various samples to get an estimate of the inherent variability measured by SSE.

__Remember:__ You are using ANOVA to test equality of means.

At a minimum, you should compare the size of the sample variances and do a visual check of the data by looking at a boxplot of the data to see whether the spread in each sample looks about the same. Neither of these approaches constitutes a test for equal variances and, of course, there are such tests, but they will certainly identify glaring violations of this assumption.

EXAMPLE 14.14 Airspace Data

Analyze the Data

Checking for Equal Variances Using a Boxplot

The sample variances for the airspace data are shown in the table:

Time	Sample Standard Deviation	Sample Variance
1	1.53	2.34
2	1.48	2.19
3	2.08	4.33
4	2.32	5.38

The boxplots of airspace by time follow.

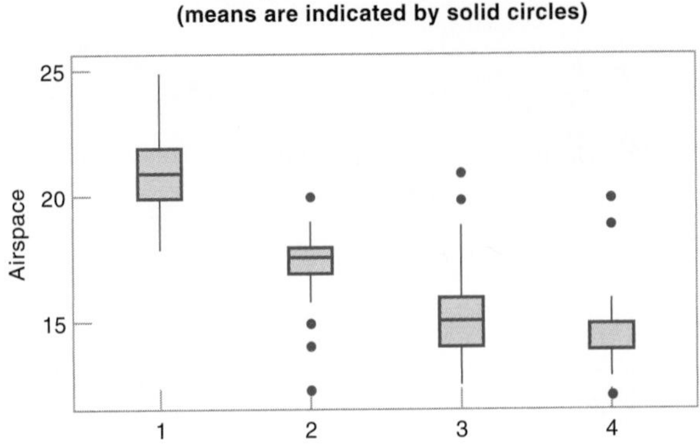

The largest sample variance (5.38) is almost 2.5 times larger than the smallest sample variance (2.19). This represents a large difference in the variances given the size of this sample. These data may be in violation of the third assumption of ANOVA. ■

Transformations can be used to stabilize the variance.

There are formal statistical procedures to test the assumption of equal variances. The statistical software you are using will most likely have more than one way to test this assumption. If the data are in violation of the third assumption, you will need to use an appropriate data transformation to normalize the data and stabilize the variance. Alternatively, you could use a nonparametric technique.

14.4.3 Exercises—Learning It!

Refers to Exercise 14.1

14.6 Check the ANOVA assumptions for the disposable diaper company interested in testing different materials.

(a) Is there any reason to believe that the errors are not independent?

(b) Construct histograms of the amount of fluid in the diapers at the time of failure for each of the 3 different materials. Do they look normally distributed?

(c) Calculate and compare the size of the sample variances and do a visual check of the data by looking at boxplots of the data to see whether the spread in each sample looks about the same.

(d) Comment on the validity of the assumptions of ANOVA for these data.

Refers to Exercise 14.2

14.7 Check the ANOVA assumptions for the software company.

(a) Is there any reason to believe that the errors are not independent?

(b) Construct histograms of the time to failure for each of the 3 different suppliers. Do they look normally distributed?

(c) Calculate and compare the size of the sample variances and do a visual check of the data by looking at boxplots of the data to see whether the spread in each sample looks about the same.

(d) Comment on the validity of the assumptions of ANOVA for these data.

Refers to Exercise 14.3

14.8 Check the ANOVA assumptions for the statistics teacher investigating the effect of homework on exam scores.

(a) Is there any reason to believe that the errors are not independent?

(b) Construct histograms of the exam scores for each of the 3 different methods. Do they look normally distributed?

(c) Calculate and compare the size of the sample variances and do a visual check of the data by looking at boxplots of the data to see whether the spread in each sample looks about the same.

(d) Comment on the validity of the assumptions of ANOVA for these data.

14.9 Check the ANOVA assumptions for the golf ball manufacturer.

Refers to Exercise 14.5

(a) Is there any reason to believe that the errors are not independent?

(b) Construct histograms of the distance the balls carried for the 4 different ball designs. Do they look normally distributed?

(c) Calculate and compare the size of the sample variances and do a visual check of the data by looking at boxplots of the data to see whether the spread in each sample looks about the same.

(d) Comment on the validity of the assumptions of ANOVA for these data.

14.5 ANALYSIS OF DATA FROM BLOCKED DESIGNS

14.5.1 Motivation for Block Designs

In this chapter we have looked at two issues for the tissue company: the effect of time on the airspace in the box and the strength of the tissues being manufactured as measured by the variable *MDStrength*. In both of these situations there was one factor of interest and the company was able to collect a sample of *comparable* observations from each population.

Use block design when it is difficult to get comparable samples.

Often there is one factor of interest but the observations in the sample may not be comparable due to some other factor. Consider the effect on sales of product display. One factor is being studied here: the product display. Suppose we are considering 3 different product displays; then there are 3 levels for this factor. To use a one-way ANOVA we would need to collect sales data from a sample of stores using display method 1, a sample of stores using display method 2, and a sample of stores using display method 3. This is not a problem, but the question that arises is, Are the sales from these stores different due to some reason other than the display method being used? It is likely that the answer to this question is yes. The stores are probably different in size and geographic location. These factors of size and location would not matter if they did not affect the variable we were studying: sales. If they did not affect sales, then we could happily use a one-way ANOVA, randomly assigning stores to use one of the three product display methods. But they most likely do affect sales. We are not going to find a sample of like size stores in the same location! So we cannot get a sample of *comparable* stores to sample.

In this example, it seems as though we actually have 3 factors: product display method, size, and location of the store. But really we are interested only in the effect of the product display method on sales. The other 2 factors are in a sense "nuisance factors." They need to be taken into account, but we are not directly interested in their effect on sales at this point. The factors size and location need to be blocked out so that we may see the effect of the product display on sales. Otherwise, there is no way to tell whether the differences we see in sales are a result of the differing product displays or the differing size and/or location of the store.

There are two possible ways to handle the data collection for this example. We could find 3 stores that are similar in size and location (large city, small city, rural, etc.) and randomly assign a product display method to each store. Then we would need to find another 3 stores that are similar in size and location and do the same thing. Each set of 3 stores becomes what is called a **block.** We would use as many blocks as feasible given the amount of time, the amount of money, and the availability of stores.

Alternatively, we could observe a set of 20 stores for 3 weeks. During the first week, each store would randomly be assigned to use one of the 3 product display methods, during the second week, the store would use a second product display method, and during the third week, the store would use the remaining product display method. In this case each store is a **block.**

A ***block*** is a group of objects or people that have been matched. An object or person can be matched with itself, meaning that repeated observations are taken on that object or person and these observations form a block.

If the realities of data collection lead you to use blocks, then you must take this into account in your analysis. Your experimental design is called a **randomized block design.** Instead of using a one-way ANOVA you must use a block ANOVA.

An experiment has a ***randomized block design*** if several different levels of one factor are being studied and the objects or people being observed/measured have been matched. Each object or person is randomly assigned to one of the c levels of the factor.

14.5.2 Partitioning the Total Variation in a Block Design

Analysis approach is conceptually the same as a one-way ANOVA.

The analysis of data from a block design is conceptually the same as that of a one-way design. You essentially still have just one factor of interest. You are still interested in deciding whether there is a treatment effect. That is, you are interested in seeing if the population means are all equal or if at least one is different. The null and alternative hypotheses remain as follows:

$$H_0: \ \mu_1 = \mu_2 = \mu_3 = \cdots = \mu_c$$

H_A: At least one of the means is different.

Like the approach we took with data from a one-way design, the idea is to take the total variability as measured by SST and break it down into its components. With a block design there is one additional component: the variability between the blocks. It is called the **sum of squares blocks** and is labeled **SSBL.**

The ***sum of squares blocks*** measures the variability between the blocks. It is labeled ***SSBL.***

Block factor is probably significant but you must test it.

The difference between each observation and the mean of its block is squared and these squared differences are accumulated into the sum of squares blocks. This component measures the portion of the variation that is attributable to the fact that the data were collected in blocks. Since we used blocks because we thought that there were some "interfering factors," we would expect this component to be of significant size. If it is not, then we probably worried about factors that do not, in fact, affect the variable of interest.

For a block design, the variation we see in the data is due to one of three things: the level of the factor, the block, or the error. Thus, the total variation is divided into three components:

Formula for SST in terms of other components in a block design

$$\text{SST} = \text{SSA} + \text{SSBL} + \text{SSE}$$

The terms SSA and SSE have the same formulas and definition as for a one-way ANOVA. The effect of partitioning the total variation into another component is to reduce the error term, SSE. Recall that SSE is used to find MSE, which becomes the denominator of the F test statistic. If you can reduce SSE by the use of blocks, then the MSE term will be smaller, making the F test statistic larger. Since "big" F values lead you to reject the null hypothesis of equal means, the use of blocks allows you to see differences in the treatment means that you might not have seen otherwise.

SSA and SSE have the same formulas as a one-way ANOVA.

14.5.3 Using the ANOVA Table in a Block Design

Consider a randomized block design with r blocks and c groups. There are a total of $n = rc$ observations. The ANOVA table for such a block design looks just like the ANOVA table for a one-way design with an additional row. It is shown below:

Source of Variation	SS	df	MS	F	p Value
Between groups	SSA	$c - 1$	$\text{MSA} = \frac{\text{SSA}}{c-1}$	$F = \frac{\text{MSA}}{\text{MSE}}$	
Between blocks	SSBL	$r - 1$	$\text{MSBL} = \frac{\text{SSBL}}{r-1}$		
Within groups	SSE	$(r-1)(c-1)$	$\text{MSE} = \frac{\text{SSE}}{(r-1)(c-1)}$		
Total	**SST**	$rc - 1$			

The last 2 columns of the ANOVA table are used to do the hypothesis test of the equality of the population means. The hypothesis test is easily done by determining if the F value is in the rejection region. If the F test statistic is "too large," that is, larger than the critical F value from the table, then you conclude that MSA and MSE are not, in fact, estimates of the same number and there is a treatment effect. If the software you are using does not provide you with the critical F value, you can look it up in the F table in Appendix A. The F statistic has $(c - 1)$ degrees of freedom in the numerator (from the MSA term) and $(r - 1)(c - 1)$ degrees of freedom in the denominator (from the MSE term).

Use the F test statistic and p value to test the hypothesis of equal means.

Let's see how this works by following the sales and product display example.

EXAMPLE 14.15 **Product Display Location**

Collect and Analyze the Data

A Block Design

A national chain of stores is investigating the effect of the product display on sales of the product. The analysts are interested in 3 product display locations: on the shelf (group 1), at the end of the aisle (group 2), and at the entrance to the store (group 3). They have matched stores with respect to size and location and have created 10 blocks of stores. The stores in the blocks were randomly assigned a product display location and the monthly sales were recorded. The data are shown here:

	A	B	C	D
1	Block	Shelf	End of Aisle	Front of Store
2	1	4457	4500	5800
3	2	4400	4370	5290
4	3	4310	4300	5000
5	4	4600	4400	5600
6	5	5000	5000	6000
7	6	4500	4500	5300
8	7	4700	5100	5900
9	8	4590	4280	5460
10	9	8510	8670	10600
11	10	6470	6500	8410
12				
13	Average	**5153.7**	**5162**	**6336**

What do you notice about the "front of store" sales?

The data are displayed by location in the graph.

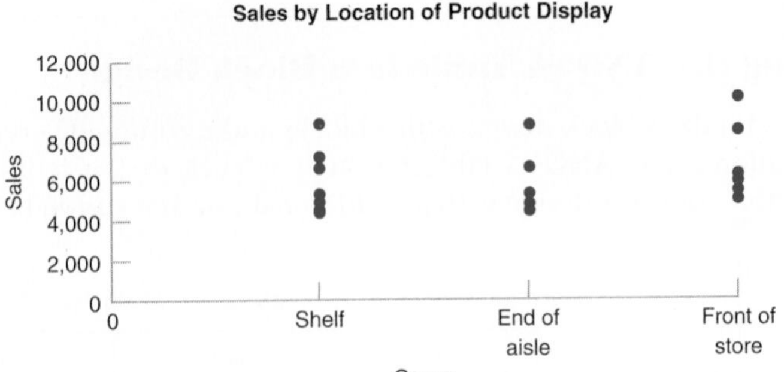

The ANOVA table and the group sample means and confidence intervals generated by Minitab are shown here:

```
Analysis of Variance of Sales

Source      DF        SS         MS        F        P
Location     2   9253927    4626964    60.70    0.000
Block        9  60738440    6748716    88.54    0.000
Error       18   1371972      76221
Total       29  71364339

                               Individual 95% CI
Location             Mean    ------+---------+---------+---------+-----
End of Aisle         5162    (----*----)
Front of Store       6336                                (---*---)
Shelf                5154    (----*---)
                             ------+---------+---------+---------+-----
                                 5200      5600      6000      6400
```

Looking at the sample means and the confidence intervals for the individual population means, we can see that locating the product at the front of the store generates considerably more sales.

To complete the hypothesis test we need to find the F value and then use the F table to find the rejection region. Minitab does not calculate the F or p values for a block design.

The null and alternative hypotheses are

H_0: $\mu_1 = \mu_2 = \mu_3$

H_A: At least one population mean is different.

The F statistic is MSA/MSE = 4,626,964/76,221 = 60.7. The critical value for the rejection region is found from the F table with 2 $(c - 1)$ and 18 $(r - 1)(c - 1)$ degrees of freedom. If $\alpha = 0.05$, then the critical F value is 3.55. Clearly, $F = 60.7$ is larger than the critical F value and we reject H_0.

Draw Conclusions

The null hypothesis is rejected and we conclude that the location of the product display affects the average sales. Our confidence interval plot tells us that it is probably group 3 (front of store) that has the different mean, since the other two sample means are quite similar and the confidence intervals overlap substantially. ■

Be sure to check your assumptions!

All of the assumptions of one-way ANOVA pertain to the block design. Thus, you should be sure to check these assumptions for your data set.

TRY IT NOW!

Participative Management *Block Design*

In Chapter 10 you looked at the number of sick days used by employees in the past 12 months by employees who were traditionally managed and those who were involved in a participative management style. Management is now considering a third approach that is a mixture of the old structure with the team-based approach. The study involves 75 employees matched by age, type of work, and gender.

Use the Minitab output shown here to determine whether there are any differences in the mean number of sick days used by the different populations.

```
Analysis of Variance for Sick Day

Source    DF        SS        MS
Style      2    57.680    28.840
Block     24   336.213    14.009
Error     48    24.987     0.521
Total     74   418.880

                        Individual 95% CI
Style    Mean    -------+---------+---------+---------+----
Part.    4.72      (----*----)
Hybrid   6.56                                (----*----)
Trad     6.60                                 (----*----)
                 -------+---------+---------+---------+----
                      4.80      5.40      6.00      6.60
```

14.5.4 Benefits of Blocking

The purpose of blocking is to allow you to see a treatment effect with a smaller sample size. However, it is often difficult to set up the blocks and so it is interesting to examine whether the effort to set up the blocks is worth it. The following formula gives you a measure of the relative efficiency of the block design compared to a one-way design:

Was it worth it to use a block design?

$$\text{Relative efficiency} = \frac{(r-1)\text{MSBL} + r(c-1)\text{MSA}}{(n-1)\text{MSE}}$$

Formula for relative efficiency of block design

The terms in this formula are all found in the ANOVA table from a block design. The value of n is the total sample size. The relative efficiency value tells you by what factor the sample size would have to be increased to see the treatment effect without using a block design. Clearly, if the relative efficiency is a low number such as 1.5, then perhaps it is not worth the effort to set up the blocks. Let's see how this formula works for the product display location.

ANS. $F = 55.35$; $F_{\text{crit}} = 3.23$ USING 2 AND 40 DEGREES OF FREEDOM AND $\alpha = 0.05$; REJECT H_0. AT LEAST ONE GROUP IS DIFFERENT. FROM THE CONFIDENCE INTERVALS, IT APPEARS THAT PARTICIPATIVE GROUP IS DIFFERENT FROM THE OTHER TWO.

Analyze the Data

Draw Conclusions

EXAMPLE 14.16 **Product Display Location**

Efficiency of Block Design

The ANOVA table for the product display location exercise is shown here:

Source	DF	SS	MS
Display	2	9,253,927	4,626,964
Block	9	60,738,440	6,748,716
Error	18	1,371,972	76,221
Total	**29**	**71,364,339**	

The relative efficiency of this design is calculated as follows:

$$\text{Relative efficiency} = \frac{(10 - 1)6{,}748{,}716 + 10(3 - 1)4{,}626{,}964}{(30 - 1)76{,}221} = 69.3$$

This number tells us that we would have needed 69 times as many observations to see the treatment effect if we did not use a block design. Clearly, the blocking was worth it in this case. ■

Participative Management ***Efficiency of Block Design***

Calculate the relative efficiency of the block design for the data on sick days. Comment on the usefulness of the blocking.

14.5.5 Exercises—Learning It!

Datafile: *AMPS1.XXX*

14.10 A manufacturer of electronic components was concerned about the reliability of one of its products. The company wished to see whether the input current that the component would draw from a power source such as a battery changed over time. Twenty components were pretested at the time of manufacture, 9 days later, and 58 days later. The data (in milliamps) are shown here:

Number	Pretest	9 Days	58 Days
1	26.1	27.0	27.5
2	26.2	27.4	27.8
3	26.3	27.8	28.5
4	27.4	28.1	28.3
5	27.8	29.5	29.8
6	26.8	27.9	27.8
7	28.2	28.9	29.3
8	28.2	29.3	29.3

(continued)

ANS. RELATIVE EFFICIENCY = 46.1; CLEARLY WORTH IT.

Number	Pretest	9 Days	58 Days
9	27.1	28.1	28.9
10	26.9	27.9	28.0
11	27.8	28.9	29.0
12	27.4	28.8	28.8
13	27.1	28.0	27.7
14	27.4	29.0	29.5
15	26.5	27.7	27.8
16	27.0	27.6	27.7
17	28.3	29.1	29.6
18	28.2	29.1	29.1
19	27.0	27.5	28.0
20	28.1	29.7	30.4

(a) What is the factor and how many levels are there in this design?

(b) What is the blocking factor?

(c) Is there a significant difference in the power drawn over time?

(d) Calculate the relative efficiency of the blocking. Is the blocking effective?

14.11 Many techniques for finding the "best" or optimal solution to a problem require that you provide the computer software with a starting solution. There are often different ways to get this starting solution. Four algorithms for generating starting solutions are run on 30 different problems. The number of iterations required to move from the starting solution to the optimal solution was recorded. A portion of the data is shown here:

Datafile: *ALGORTH.XXX*

Problem	Method	Iteration
1	1	5
2	1	4
3	1	4
4	1	4
5	1	2
6	1	2

(a) Is there any difference in the number of iterations required to find the optimal solution that is due to the difference in the method used to generate the starting solution?

(b) Which method would you recommend and why?

14.12 No. 1 Foods contracts with colleges and universities to provide the food services for the school. It has 3 different cafeteria layouts, which it is evaluating in terms of the time (in minutes) it takes for a "typical" student to get his/her food. To do a fair comparison No. 1 Foods has blocked on the size of the school. Is there a difference in the average time spent getting food for the 3 different layouts? If so, which layout is best? The data are shown here:

	Layout 1	Layout 2	Layout 3
1	6.5	2.9	6.9
2	5.8	4.5	6.1
3	5.8	4.1	7.0
4	6.7	4.2	7.4
5	6.4	5.1	6.9
6	5.8	4.7	7.7
7	6.2	5.2	7.8
8	5.7	4.9	8.1
9	6.9	4.8	7.8
10	5.0	4.3	8.2
11	5.8	4.2	7.1
12	4.8	4.1	7.4
13	6.7	4.7	7.2
14	6.6	4.3	7.6
15	4.7	4.4	7.5

14.13 Should you listen to classical music, watch TV, or just have silence when you study? To answer this question a group of 10 undergraduate students were randomly selected from a large university. For one semester they listened to classical music while they studied, for the next semester they watched TV while they studied, and for the third semester they studied in the library. Their GPA for each semester was recorded. The data are shown below:

Student	Music	TV	Library
1	3.62	3.35	3.23
2	3.38	3.23	3.07
3	3.09	2.24	2.70
4	2.69	1.88	2.41
5	3.29	2.31	3.01
6	2.97	2.75	2.82
7	2.60	1.98	2.14
8	3.56	3.26	3.07
9	3.50	2.74	3.23
10	3.74	3.19	3.55

(a) What is the response variable?

(b) What is the factor? How many levels are there?

(c) What is the blocking factor?

(d) Use block ANOVA to determine where there are any differences in the average GPA scores for the three treatment groups.

(e) What other factors would you suggest be included in a subsequent study?

Datafile: GRADSAL.XXX

14.14 What can I expect as a starting salary if I major in Business? Engineering? Education? This is a commonly asked question. The career office at a university decided to see if there were any differences in the starting salaries of these 3 majors. Analysts selected 50 students from last year's graduating class and recorded the starting salary for each student. To do a fair comparison, the students were matched on the basis of the overall grade point average. The data are shown here:

Business	Engineering	Education
27,220	35,685	24,476
26,204	33,500	24,246
28,065	32,955	24,612
28,778	32,878	25,057
28,498	32,802	24,821
29,150	33,389	25,588
25,389	33,875	24,562
27,310	32,435	24,390
28,501	33,131	23,689
26,433	33,556	24,832
26,557	32,996	24,698
25,707	33,545	25,214
25,297	33,705	24,222
26,636	35,324	24,632
26,624	31,834	24,661
25,447	33,309	23,711
26,943	34,988	24,688
27,064	33,941	24,732
27,666	33,628	24,092
27,150	32,888	24,916
27,230	32,950	24,800
27,042	33,735	24,617
28,949	34,607	24,218
27,240	33,921	24,191
27,512	34,573	24,726
27,031	32,849	24,417

(continued)

Business	Engineering	Education
29,402	33,686	24,226
28,487	33,839	24,424
29,841	33,770	24,411
26,408	33,017	23,915
29,049	34,669	24,333
26,191	35,282	24,638
28,137	33,676	25,528
28,347	34,547	25,034
29,584	33,065	25,062
27,569	33,938	24,434
26,976	33,686	24,853
27,960	33,094	24,459
26,835	33,494	24,609
28,228	33,414	23,643
25,731	32,811	25,267
26,554	34,200	23,586
25,770	32,487	24,578
27,307	34,261	24,880
27,498	33,211	24,783
27,235	33,320	24,144
27,227	33,385	25,203
29,677	33,736	24,538
25,758	34,803	24,359
27,073	33,694	24,166

(a) What is the response variable?

(b) What is the factor? How many levels are there?

(c) What is the blocking factor?

(d) Use block ANOVA to determine whether there are any differences in the average starting salary for the three groups.

(e) What other factors would you suggest be included in a subsequent study?

14.15 Surely you have heard of the "freshman ten," referring to the average weight gain of 10 lb by students during the freshman year. Does the same phenomenon occur to graduate students? A sample of 15 students was taken and their weight (in lb) was recorded in September, February of the following year, July of the following year, and then July 2 years later. The data are shown here:

Datafile: *WEIGHT.XXX*

Person	Sept	Feb	July	July, 1 Year Later
1	110	115	115	111
2	140	144	146	141
3	165	169	171	165
4	123	128	131	124
5	158	167	169	159
6	180	187	187	181
7	173	179	179	173
8	178	185	190	180
9	195	203	207	196
10	145	154	158	145
11	136	137	137	137
12	170	179	180	170
13	166	168	171	168
14	180	184	185	181
15	130	136	138	130

A new student of statistics decided to use a one-way ANOVA for these data. The results from Minitab follow.

```
Analysis of Variance for Weight

Source    DF       SS      MS        F         P
Month      3      634     211     0.36     0.784
Error     56    33108     591
Total     59    33742
```

(a) Using this ANOVA table, what would you conclude about the average weights at the 4 times the data were collected?

(b) Explain why this analysis is incorrect and why it must be analyzed as a block design.

(c) What are the blocks?

(d) The Minitab output for the block ANOVA is shown here. What can you conclude about the average weights for the 4 time periods?

```
Analysis of Variance for Weight

Source      DF          SS         MS
Person      14    32990.73    2356.48
Month        3      633.87     211.29
Error       42      117.13       2.79
Total       59    33741.73
```

Discovery Exercise 14.1
THE BENEFITS OF BLOCKING

In manufacturing electronic products such as loudspeakers, it is important that connections are strong and hold so that they do not disconnect. The same is true for commercial heaters. One of the customers of a manufacturer of heaters complained that the pull poundage was too low. Thus, the customer did not have confidence in the terminal connection. New wires with the terminals attached were made and a pull test was done on a sample of 25. The terminals were connected and pulled apart. The pull poundage at which the terminals would disconnect from each other was recorded. Then the same terminals were reconnected and the test was repeated a total of 6 times. The object was to determine if the pull poundage changed over time. The minimum pull poundage required by the customer was 5 lb. The data (datafile HEATERS.XXX) are shown here:

Trial 1	Trial 2	Trial 3	Trial 4	Trial 5	Trial 6
11.0	12.3	9.8	12.3	10.8	8.5
8.5	10.8	7.5	11.0	8.0	8.0
9.5	10.0	9.0	9.0	9.0	7.8
10.0	7.5	8.0	9.8	10.5	8.5
10.5	7.5	10.3	9.0	9.0	9.8
11.8	11.8	10.0	9.0	9.5	10.3
11.5	10.0	14.0	11.3	14.0	13.0
10.0	9.5	10.0	8.0	8.3	8.0
11.3	12.0	11.0	11.3	10.5	10.3
10.3	10.5	9.8	9.8	11.8	10.5
11.0	15.0	13.5	11.5	9.8	10.0
11.3	10.8	9.8	10.3	10.0	9.5
10.5	10.0	10.5	10.5	10.0	9.5
11.8	10.8	10.0	11.8	9.8	9.5
10.0	10.0	9.5	11.8	9.0	9.3
11.5	11.0	11.0	9.8	9.0	9.8
10.5	9.0	12.5	11.3	11.0	11.8
11.3	11.0	9.5	9.0	10.0	8.0

(continued)

Trial 1	Trial 2	Trial 3	Trial 4	Trial 5	Trial 6
11.0	11.3	11.3	10.0	11.3	9.5
11.0	8.0	10.5	7.0	7.0	12.0
11.8	10.3	12.3	11.8	12.5	11.0
12.0	12.3	11.5	12.0	12.3	11.0
11.5	12.0	11.0	10.0	11.5	11.5
12.0	9.5	12.5	9.5	9.0	9.3
10.0	7.5	10.5	10.3	9.5	9.0

Part I: One-Way ANOVA

Use a one-way ANOVA to analyze these data.

(a) What is the response variable and what is the factor?
(b) How many levels of the factor are being studied?
(c) Is there any difference in the average pull poundage among the trials? If so, which ones are different?
(d) What is your recommendation to the company and why?

Part II: Block Design

Since the same terminals were connected and pulled apart 6 times, each row is actually a block. Reanalyze these data using a block design.

(a) Is there any difference in the average pull poundage among the trials? If so, which ones are different?
(b) Explain why you got a different answer when you analyzed the data as a one-way design.
(c) Calculate the sample size needed to see the treatment effect using a randomized one-way design.
(d) Now, what is your recommendation to the company?

14.6 ANALYSIS OF DATA FROM TWO-WAY DESIGNS

After learning about block designs and thinking a bit more about the results of the airspace analysis, you wonder whether there might be some other factor that influences the airspace in the box (something other than the length of time that the box sits on the shelf). You return to talk to the people who work in manufacturing to ask them about how the tissue boxes are made.

14.6.1 Motivation for a Factorial Design Model

In Figure 14.6 you see a picture of a hardroll, which is a large roll of raw paper stock. Each box of 250 tissues is made from 25 hardrolls, each of which has 10 different slit positions. Four such slit positions are shown in the diagram. One tissue is taken from each slit and they are pressed into a tissue box and sealed. A hardroll lasts for 4 hours in production.

The manufacturing personnel feel that the mean airspace might differ by position in the hardroll from which the tissues were made. This hypothesis was proposed because of two facts:

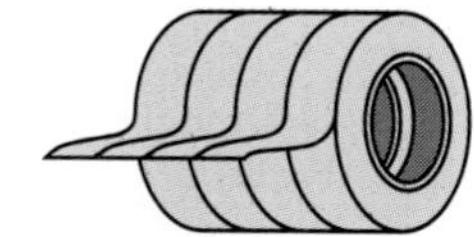

FIGURE 14.6
Schematic of a hardroll

1. As the hardroll sits in the warehouse, the outside collects moisture. Thus boxes made from tissues taken from the outside of the roll might have less growback.

2. The core (very center) of the roll is very compressed (a hardroll weighs 1000 pounds). Thus, boxes of tissues made from the core have the "life stretched out of them."

As a result of this discussion you have identified another potential factor, the position in the hardroll from which the box was produced. This is not a blocking factor because you are interested in knowing whether this factor affects the airspace in the box. Hence, it is not a nuisance factor. You return to look at your data and realize that a total of 4 cases of tissue boxes were sampled, one case every hour for 4 hours. One case was used to obtain in-process measurements. The other 3 cases were saved for observations taken after 24 hours, 2 weeks, and 4 weeks. Each case contained 24 cartons of tissue boxes or 120 tissue boxes. This means that the tissues that were allowed to sit on the shelf for 24 hours were made from a different part of the hardroll than the ones that sat on the shelf for 2 weeks or 4 weeks. You cannot tell from this data set if the position in the hardroll is indeed a significant factor because you did not account for this factor in your experimental design.

Based on this new information you suggest the following sampling plan:

Revised sampling plan for the tissue company

1. Sample 5 times through the hardroll. Since a hardroll lasts for 4 hours the 5 observations were taken at the beginning and once an hour thereafter. This results in observations at the top, the core, and 3 in the middle of the hardroll.
2. Each sample consists of a case of tissues (24 cartons or 120 tissue boxes).
3. A total of 4 cases is sampled every hour. One was used to obtain in-process measurements. The other 3 cases are saved for observations taken after 24 hours, 2 weeks, and 4 weeks.

Each airspace measurement is taken on a tissue box made from a certain position in the hardroll and allowed to sit on the shelf a certain amount of time before measurement. Thus, we have two factors: position and time. The position indicates from what part of the hardroll the sample was taken. The values for position are 1, 2, 3, 4, and 5. Position 1 indicates that it was taken from the outside of the roll and position 5 indicates it was taken from the core. The factor time indicates when the measurement was taken: 1 = in process, 2 = after 24 hours, 3 = after 2 weeks, and 4 = after 4 weeks.

This experimental design is an example of a **factorial design with two factors.** The two factors do not need to have the same number of levels but we will assume that the sample size is the same for each combination of the levels. For the airspace data this means that the number of tissue boxes sampled from position 1 and tested in process is the same as the number of tissue boxes sampled from position 3 and allowed to sit 2 weeks on the shelf, and this is the same as the number of tissue boxes sampled from each of the 5 positions and allowed to sit for each of 4 different time possibilities. In this design, a sample of 1 case (24 cartons or 120 boxes) is selected from each of the $5 \times 4 = 20$ populations. This is referred to as **equal replication.** Each observation within a population is referred to as a **replicate.** If you have unequal sample sizes, you must refer to a more advanced text.

> An experimental design is called a ***factorial design with two factors*** if there are several different levels of two factors being studied. The first factor is called ***factor A*** and there are r levels of factor A. The second factor is called ***factor B*** and there are c levels of factor B.

Understand the Problem

EXAMPLE 14.17 Airspace Data

Two-Factor Design

For the airspace data, we can label the position factor as factor A and the time factor as factor B. There are $r = 5$ levels of factor A: positions 1, 2, 3, 4, and 5. Position 1 refers to tissues made from the very outside of the hardroll and position 5 refers to tissues made from the core of the hardroll. There are $c = 4$ levels of the factor B, as we had before. ■

The design is said to have ***equal replication*** if the same number of objects or people being observed/measured are randomly selected from each population. The population is described by a specific level for each of the two factors. Each observation is called a ***replicate.*** There are n' observations or replicates observed from each population. There are $n = n'rc$ observations in total.

EXAMPLE 14.18 Airspace Data

Collect the data

Number of Replicates

For the airspace data, one case or 120 tissue boxes is selected for each combination of position and time. There are 20 combinations of position and time ($rc = (5)(4) = 20$). Thus, n' is 120 and there are $(2)(120) = 2400$ observations in total. ■

The tissue company wishes to know whether there is a difference in airspace due to position in the hardroll and whether there is a difference in airspace by time tested. To answer these questions we must extend our analysis technique to handle this second factor.

14.6.2 Partitioning the Variation

The underlying concept in analyzing data from a two-factor design is the same as the approach we took in analyzing data from a one-way design. Remember that we looked at the relative sizes of the components of variation. For a two-factor design the variation we see in the data is due to one of four things: factor A, factor B, the interaction between factors A and B, and error. The idea is to take the total variability as measured by SST and break it down into four component sum of squares.

Break down SST into four components.

The names and labels for these are **sum of squares due to factor A (SSA), sum of squares due to factor B (SSB), sum of squares due to the interacting effect of A and B (SSAB),** and **sum of squares error (SSE).** Although the names are a bit different from those we used in a one-way ANOVA, they are an extension of the same concept.

The ***sum of squares due to factor A*** is labeled ***SSA.*** It measures the squared differences between the mean of each level of factor A and the grand mean.

The ***sum of squares due to factor B*** is labeled ***SSB.*** It measures the squared differences between the mean of each level of factor B and the grand mean.

The ***sum of squares due to the interacting effect of A and B*** is labeled ***SSAB.*** It measures the effect of combining factor A and factor B.

The ***sum of squares error*** is labeled ***SSE.*** It measures the variability in the measurements within the groups.

Thus, the total variation is divided into four components:

Formula for SST in terms of other components in a two-way design

$$SST = SSA + SSB + SSAB + SSE$$

The terms SSA and SSE have the same formulas and definitions as for a one-way ANOVA. The SSB and SSAB terms are calculated in a similar fashion. If you are using a two-way experimental design, you will need to use software to do the calculations. The formulas for the sum of squares terms are long and tedious and any statistical software will generate the ANOVA table for a two-way design.

14.6.3 Using the ANOVA Table in a Two-Way Design

Consider a factorial design with r levels of factor A and c levels of factor B with n' replicates in each combination of factors A and B. There are a total of $n = n'rc$ observations. The ANOVA table for such a design looks just like the ANOVA table for a one-way design with two additional rows. It is shown below:

Source of Variation	SS	df	MS	F	p Value
Factor A	SSA	$r - 1$	$\text{MSA} = \dfrac{\text{SSA}}{r-1}$	$F = \dfrac{\text{MSA}}{\text{MSE}}$	
Factor B	SSB	$c - 1$	$\text{MSBL} = \dfrac{\text{SSB}}{c-1}$	$F = \dfrac{\text{MSB}}{\text{MSE}}$	
Interaction of A and B	SSAB	$(r - 1)(c - 1)$	$\text{MSAB} = \dfrac{\text{SSAB}}{(r-1)(c-1)}$	$F = \dfrac{\text{MSAB}}{\text{MSE}}$	
Error	SSE	$rc(n' - 1)$	$\text{MSE} = \dfrac{\text{SSE}}{rc(n'-1)}$		
Total	**SST**	$rcn' - 1$			

The last 2 columns of the ANOVA table are used to do the hypothesis tests. In a two-way ANOVA, three hypothesis tests should be done. (1) To test the hypothesis of no difference due to factor A we would have the following null and alternative hypotheses:

Hypothesis test for factor A

H_0: There is no difference in the population means due to factor A.

H_A: There is a difference in the population means due to factor A.

This hypothesis test is easily done by determining whether the F value in the row of the ANOVA table corresponding to factor A is in the rejection region. If the F test statistic is "too large," that is, larger than the critical F value from the table, then you conclude that factor A is significant. If the software you are using does not provide you with the critical F value, you can look it up in the table of F distribution values. The F statistic has $(r - 1)$ degrees of freedom in the numerator (from the MSA term) and $rc(n' - 1)$ degrees of freedom in the denominator (from the MSE term).

(2) To test the hypothesis of no difference due to factor B we would have the following null and alternative hypotheses:

Hypothesis test for factor B

H_0: There is no difference in the population means due to factor B.

H_A: There is a difference in the population means due to factor B.

This hypothesis test is easily done by determining whether the F value in the row of the ANOVA table corresponding to factor B is in the rejection region. If the F test statistic is "too large," that is, larger than the critical F value from the table, then you conclude that factor B is significant. If the software you are using does not provide you with the critical F value, you can look it up in the F distribution table. The F statistic has $c - 1$ degrees of freedom in the numerator (from the MSB term) and $rc(n' - 1)$ degrees of freedom in the denominator (from the MSE term).

(3) To test the hypothesis of no difference due to the interaction of factors A and B, we would have the following null and alternative hypotheses:

H_0: There is no difference in the population means due to the interaction of factors A and B.
H_A: There is a difference in the population means due to the interaction of factors A and B.

Hypothesis test for interaction of factors A and B

This hypothesis test is easily done by determining whether the F value in the row of the ANOVA table corresponding to the interaction of factors A and B is in the rejection region. If the F test statistic is "too large," that is, larger than the critical F value from the table, then you conclude that the interaction is significant. If the software you are using does not provide you with the critical F value, you can look it up in the F distribution table. The F statistic has $(r-1)(c-1)$ degrees of freedom in the numerator (from the MSAB term) and $rc(n'-1)$ degrees of freedom in the denominator (from the MSE term). The interaction effect is discussed further in the next section. But first let's look at the airspace data.

EXAMPLE 14.19 Airspace Data

Analyze the Data

Two-Way ANOVA

The output from Minitab for the airspace data is shown here. Factor A is position and factor B is time.

```
Two-way Analysis of Variance

Analysis of Variance for Airspace

Source            DF          SS         MS
Position           4     5942.98    1485.74
Time               3    12773.75    4257.92
Interaction       12      865.52      72.13
Error           2380     1667.08       0.70
Total           2399    21249.33
```

To test the hypothesis of no difference due to factor A, we would have the following null and alternative hypotheses:

H_0: There is no difference in the population means due to position.
H_A: There is a difference in the population means due to position.

The F value is MSA/MSE $= 1485.74/0.70 = 2122.5$. With such a large F value we really don't need an F critical to tell us that our F value is bigger than F critical. However, for completeness the table F value is found for $\alpha = 0.05$ with 4 degrees of freedom in the numerator and 2380 degrees of freedom in the denominator. F critical $= 2.37$, so, clearly, position is a significant factor.

To test the hypothesis of no difference due to factor B, we would have the following null and alternative hypotheses:

H_0: There is no difference in the population means due to time.
H_A: There is a difference in the population means due to time.

The F value is MSB/MSE $= 4257.92/0.70 = 6082.7$. With such a large F value we really don't need an F critical to tell us that our F value is bigger than F critical. However, for completeness the table F value is found for $\alpha = 0.05$ with 3 degrees of freedom in the numerator and 2380 degrees of freedom in the denominator. F critical $= 2.60$ so, clearly, time is a significant factor.

To test the hypothesis of no difference due to the interaction of factors A and B we would have the following null and alternative hypotheses:

H_0: There is no difference in the population means due to the interaction of position and time.
H_A: There is a difference in the population means due to the interaction of position and time.

The F value is MSAB/MSE = 72.13/0.70 = 103.0. With such a large F value we really don't need an F critical to tell us that our F value is bigger than F critical. However, for completeness the table F value is found for $\alpha = 0.05$ with 12 degrees of freedom in the numerator and 2380 degrees of freedom in the denominator. F critical = 1.75, so, clearly, the interaction is significant.

Draw Conclusions

At this point we know from the analysis that both position in the hardroll from which the tissue box is made and the length of time the box sits on the shelf affect the average airspace in the box. We also know that these two factors interact. ■

Participative Management ***Two-Way Design***

In a previous Try It Now! exercise you looked at the number of sick days used in the past 12 months by employees who were traditionally managed, employees who were involved in a participative management style, and employees who were involved in a management style that was a mixture of the old structure with the team-based approach. Management is wondering whether the employee's department is a factor as well.

Use the accompanying Minitab output to determine if there are any differences in the mean number of sick days by management style and by department and if there is any interaction effect.

Analysis of Variance for Sick Day

Source	DF	SS	MS
Department	4	298.187	74.547
Mgt Style	2	51.440	25.720
Interaction	8	4.293	0.537
Error	60	42.000	0.700
Total	74	395.920	

14.6.4 Understanding the Interaction Effect

In the previous section we performed a hypothesis test to determine whether the two factors had a significant interaction effect. The easiest way to understand this effect is to look at a graph of the sample averages for each of the possible combinations of the two factors. The line graph shown in Figure 14.7 displays the 20 sample means for airspace.

From this graph you can see that the mean airspace decreases the longer the box sits on the shelf, regardless of from what position in the hardroll the box was made. However, the line connecting the sample means for those made from position 2 crosses the line connecting the sample means for those made from position 5. This indicates that the amount of growback in the tissue box between the 24-hour mark and the 2-week mark depends on where in the hardroll the tissue came from. Thus, the airspace behavior is affected by the interaction of the time on the shelf and the position in the hardroll from which it was made. This is what we expected based on our hypothesis test.

ANS. AT $\alpha = 0.05$, DEPARTMENT $F = 106.50$, $F_{crit} = 2.53$; MANAGEMENT STYLE $F = 36.74$, $F_{crit} = 3.15$; INTERACTION $F = 0.767$, $F_{crit} = 2.10$. THERE IS A DIFFERENCE DUE TO DEPARTMENT AND MANAGEMENT STYLE, BUT THE INTERACTION IS NOT SIGNIFICANT.

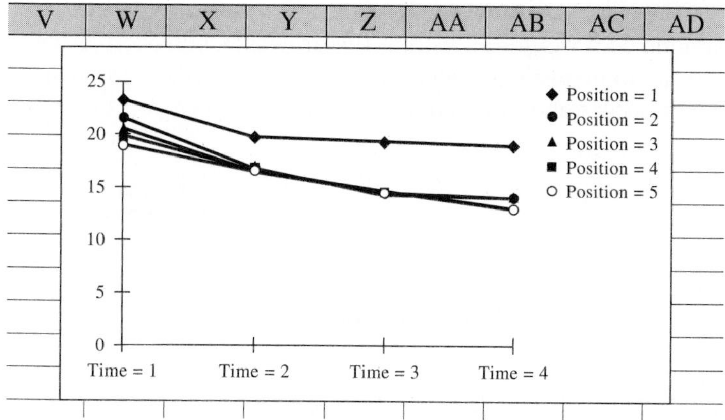

FIGURE 14.7 Average airspace based on time on shelf for different positions

The information needed to look at the interaction effect graphically is the average of the observed variable for each group. Such information can be generated by using a statistical software package. Sometimes it is part of the output of ANOVA and sometimes it is a separate command.

EXAMPLE 14.20 Airspace Data

Analyze the Data

Sample Means for All Combinations for Position and Time Tested

In Minitab the analysis of means command generates output as shown here for the airspace data.

```
Rows: Position  Columns: Time

         1         2         3         4        All
1     120       120       120       120       480
       23.00     19.75     19.58     19.33     20.42
        0.648     0.523     0.705     0.473     1.613

2     120       120       120       120       480
       20.83     16.88     15.08     14.13     16.73
        0.803     1.171     0.762     0.668     2.713

3     120       120       120       120       480
       20.25     17.08     14.54     14.08     16.49
        0.664     1.120     0.916     0.705     2.605

4     120       120       120       120       480
       19.29     16.67     15.04     13.29     16.07
        0.679     0.853     0.938     0.938     2.371

5     120       120       120       120       480
       21.67     16.92     14.67     14.25     16.88
        1.286     0.816     0.690     0.882     3.096

All   600       600       600       600      2400
       21.01     17.46     15.78     15.02     17.32
        1.521     1.478     2.076     2.311     2.976

Cell Contents-

    Airspace:N

          Mean

         StDev
```

■

If there were no interaction effect, the lines connecting the sample means would be parallel. This would tell us that the growback behavior of the tissues in the box was the same no matter from what position in the hardroll the tissues were made. The graph might look something like the one shown in Figure 14.8.

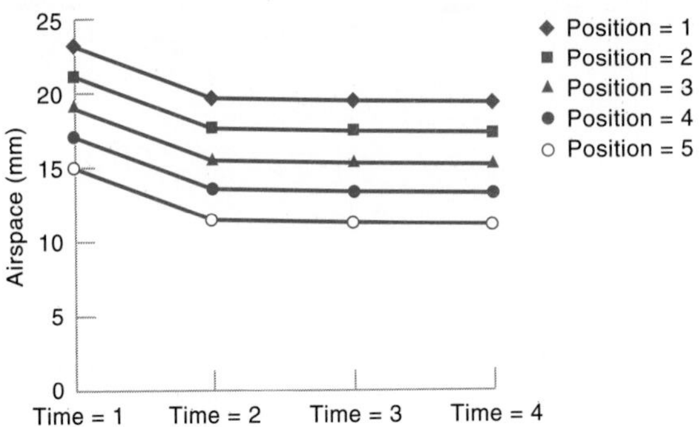

FIGURE 14.8 Hypothetical average airspace if there were no interaction effect

14.6.5 Exercises—Learning It!

14.16 The manufacturer of batteries is designing a battery to be used in a device that will be subjected to extremes in temperature. The company has a choice of 3 materials to use in the manufacturing process. An experiment is designed to study the life of the battery when it is made from materials A, B, and C and is exposed to temperatures of 15, 70, and 125°F. For each combination of material and temperature, 4 batteries are tested. The lifetimes in hours of the batteries are shown here:

	Temperature		
	15°F	**70°F**	**125°F**
Material A	130,155,74,180	34,40,80,75	20,70,82,58
Material B	150,188,159,126	126,122,106,115	25,70,58,45
Material C	138,110,168,160	174,120,150,139	96,104,82,60

(a) Calculate the average life for each of the 3 materials.

(b) Calculate the average life for each of the 3 temperatures.

(c) Calculate the average life for each of the 9 treatment groups.

(d) Plot the 9 treatment means on a graph with temperature factor on the x axis, and the life of the battery in hours on the y axis. Use a different color for each of the 3 materials and connect the averages for those of the same material. What do you speculate about the interaction effect based on the graph?

(e) Confirm your suspicions by doing a two-way ANOVA and testing to see if there is a significant interaction effect.

(f) What material do you recommend to this manufacturer and why?

Refers to Exercise 14.5

14.17 The golf ball data that you analyzed as a one-way ANOVA in Exercise 14.5 were actually collected at three different times of day. To see if the time of day is a factor, reanalyze the data using a two-way ANOVA. The first 12 observations of each model were taken early in the morning, the second 12 observations were taken mid-day, and the last 12 observations were taken late in the afternoon.

(a) Is there any difference in the average distance the ball carries by design?

(b) Is there any difference in the average distance the ball carries by time of day?

(c) Is there any interaction effect? If so, interpret this in terms of the application.

(d) Check the assumptions of ANOVA for these data.

Refers to Exercise 14.10
***Datafile:** AMPS2.XXX*

14.18 The company that tested the power supplies in Exercise 14.10 wished to see whether the input current that the component would draw from a power source, such as a battery, changed over time. Twenty components were pretested at the time of manufacture, 9 days later, and 58 days later. The company was also concerned about the possible differences in the product performance from lot to lot. The entire experiment was repeated for a sample taken from another lot. The data (in milliamps) are shown here:

Number	Pretest	9 Days	58 Days
1	25.6	27.3	28.5
2	27.9	30.0	30.5
3	25.7	27.1	27.8
4	25.9	27.6	29.1
5	25.2	26.6	27.5
6	26.1	27.9	29.4
7	26.5	28.8	29.4
8	29.9	32.1	33.2
9	27.9	29.1	30.3
10	27.3	29.8	32.0
11	25.1	27.2	28.5
12	25.7	27.2	27.9
13	27.0	28.3	29.2
14	25.6	26.2	26.8
15	26.2	27.1	27.6
16	26.5	28.3	28.9
17	24.7	25.8	26.8
18	29.5	33.1	34.7
19	25.3	27.2	28.2
20	24.9	26.2	27.4

(a) With the additional lot this can now be considered a two-factor design. What is factor A? Factor B? How many replicates are there?

(b) Analyze both lots as a two-factor ANOVA.

(c) Is there any difference in the amount of power drawn from the battery over time?

(d) Is there any difference in the amount of power drawn from the battery by lot?

(e) Is there any interaction effect? If so, interpret this in terms of the application.

14.19 With the increased use of computers at all levels of the organization, many managers are finding themselves faced with new and different problems. One manager wished to study the effect of the employees' efficiency measured by how long it took to complete a particular task (in seconds). Twenty employees were timed at the beginning of the day and at 2, 4, and 6 hours after the employee had been doing intensive work. In each case the employee used his/her right hand to complete the task 20 times and the left hand 20 times. The data are shown here:

Datafile: *MOUSE1.XXX*

Beginning of Day		After 2 hr Intensive Work		After 4 hr Intensive Work		After 6 hr Intensive Work	
Right	Left	Right	Left	Right	Left	Right	Left
67	162	84	63	52	89	57	114
64	86	78	71	53	53	53	61
69	88	74	86	56	122	71	61
88	99	91	111	66	88	61	61
72	83	70	99	59	93	73	53
80	88	73	88	77	116	50	43
85	113	86	121	64	104	53	56
116	69	71	66	62	53	80	111
77	88	76	56	54	58	63	38
78	101	76	56	65	119	41	40
68	73	61	48	71	96	63	58
51	61	62	51	92	104	41	41
54	76	94	123	71	146	53	84
75	53	63	56	50	81	63	58

(continued)

Beginning of Day		After 2 hr Intensive Work		After 4 hr Intensive Work		After 6 hr Intensive Work	
Right	Left	Right	Left	Right	Left	Right	Left
71	71	70	83	71	53	61	136
64	61	63	63	58	58	46	93
86	63	66	86	77	73	68	71
98	101	71	63	53	56	64	68
103	86	53	61	81	136	49	73
91	71	81	171	70	83	70	74

(a) Is there any difference in the average time to complete the task after differing amounts of computer intensive work?

(b) Is there any difference in the average amount of time to complete the task for the right hand versus the left hand?

(c) Is there a significant interaction effect?

(d) Display the treatment means to get some additional insight into the interaction effect. What does the graph tell you that the hypothesis test does not tell you?

(e) What is your recommendation to this manager?

14.20 A manufacturer of adhesive products designed an experiment to compare a new adhesive product to a competitor's product. The adhesive product, or glue, is used by automobile manufacturers. The response variable was the strength of the glue measured by tensile strength in pounds per square inch (psi). The ability to adhere to oil-contaminated surfaces under different humidity conditions was studied. There were 2 levels for factor A: no oil or oil. Oil contamination was applied by hand dipping the samples in an oil solution and allowing them to air dry at room temperature for 2 hours. There were 2 levels for factor B: 50% humidity and 90% humidity. Three samples were tested for each of the combinations of factor A and factor B. The tensile values (psi) for the new product are shown here:

Humidity	No Oil	Oil
50%	175,100,175	43,42,44
90%	95,115,85	95,105,116

(a) Does the product behave significantly differently if the surface is oil contaminated?

(b) Does the product behave significantly differently at different humidity levels?

(c) Is there any significant interaction effect present?

14.7 OTHER TYPES OF EXPERIMENTAL DESIGNS

Two-way ANOVA extends to factorial design.

Often you wish to investigate more than 2 factors. The analysis technique of ANOVA extends directly to what is known as a factorial design with more than 2 factors. The interaction terms become a bit more complicated and the required sample size increases as you consider additional factors. However, the basic approach that we have taken works and the concepts you have learned extend directly to handle more than 2 factors.

We can see from our work in the previous section that the number of observations that you need increases very quickly as you increase the number of factors. For the airspace data we ended up with 20 groups from 2 factors. This means your total sample size increases. Suppose, for example, that the tissue company wished to consider a third factor that had 3 levels. We would have (20)(3) or 60 groups to study. If we selected a sample of 5 from each of these populations we would need a total sample size of 300. You often do not have the resources to collect this many data.

With the addition of a third factor you could perform more hypothesis tests. You would have 3 hypothesis tests for the effect of the individual factors; 3 hypothesis tests to test for interactions between 2 of the variables (factor A and factor B; factor B and factor C; factor A and factor C), and 1 hypothesis test to check for interaction between all 3 variables. Although there are more tests to be performed, each one is done using an F test just as we have seen in this chapter.

Higher order interactions are often difficult to interpret.

The two-way interaction terms are often relatively easy to interpret, as we have seen in the previous section. However, the higher order interactions are typically difficult to interpret and often do not tell you much. Thus, instead of using a full factorial design as we have done with two factors, we use a technique that helps keep the sample size down while still giving information about the main effect of the factors on the variable we are studying. These are called fractional factorial designs. In the case of the tissue company faced with 60 groups to study, the fractional design may call for a sample to be selected from only 30 groups. Thus, half the number of groups is studied, hence the term fractional design. You want to select the 30 groups to be studied judiciously so that you get information on the 3 factors and some of the important interaction effects. You lose information on some of the higher order interactions, but at least you have information on the major factors individually and some of the two-way interactions. This is better than not doing the experiment at all because of cost reasons. If you are in a situation where you wish to study more than 2 factors you should consult an advanced text on experimental design.

Fractional designs help reduce the cost.

14.8 *Executive Summary:*
THE AIRSPACE PROBLEM

Business Analysis...

TO: Tissue Manufacturing Manager
FROM: Erica Q. Analyst
RE: Analysis of tissue airspace

This report addresses the customer complaints that have been received regarding tissues tearing when a new box of tissues is opened. As you know this is caused because there is not enough airspace at the top of the box. Although there is sufficient airspace in the tissue box at the time of manufacturing, as the tissues sit on the shelf they "grow back," leaving less airspace in the box.

To understand this "growback" phenomenon, we designed an experiment, collected the data, and analyzed the data. This memo will summarize the experiment and the results.

The airspace in 120 tissue boxes (24 cartons) was measured at four different time periods: in process, 24 hours after manufacturing, 2 weeks after manufacturing, and 4 weeks after manufacturing. Clearly, this was destructive sampling because we could not sell the tissue boxes after they had been opened and the airspace measured! Also, we were looking at four populations, so we could not use a t test to compare the means. In this case the correct technique to use is ANOVA. Because we were interested only in one factor, time, a one-way ANOVA analysis was done. The output from Excel is shown here.

(continued)

	J	K	L	M	N	O	P
3	Anova: Single Factor						
4							
5	SUMMARY						
6	*Groups*	*Count*	*Sum*	*Average*	*Variance*		
7	In Process	120	2521	21.00833	2.327661		
8	24 hours	120	2095	17.45833	2.19993		
9	2 weeks	120	1894	15.78333	4.339216		
10	4 weeks	120	1802	15.01667	5.377871		
11							
12							
13	ANOVA						
14	*Source of Variation*	*SS*	*df*	*MS*	*F*	*P-value*	*F crit*
15	Between Groups	2554.75	3	851.5833	239.1302	1.34E-94	2.623636
16	Within Groups	1695.117	476	3.561169			
17							
18	Total	4249.867	479				
19							

From the summary section of this output you can see that the average amount of airspace decreases from 21 mm to just over 15 mm as the boxes sit on the shelf. The F value for the between groups variation ($F = 239.1302$) is larger than the F critical value (labeled F crit) ($F\text{ crit} = 2.62$). The F value and the tiny p value (1.34×10^{-94}) indicate that the mean airspace is different for at least one of the time periods. The one most likely to be different is the in-process time period. Within 4 weeks of the time of manufacture the airspace decreases on the average about 6 mm.

A word of caution should be added at this point regarding the assumptions of ANOVA. The major assumptions of this statistical technique were checked, and it is possible that the assumption of equal variance for the four time periods may not hold. Further testing of this assumption should be done and if necessary a transformation should be used to stabilize the variance.

After doing this analysis we talked to your employees and learned that the mean airspace might be different by position in the hardroll from which the tissues were made. A new experiment was designed and data were collected to investigate this possibility. Two factors were used in this experiment: time (with the same 4 levels as the first experiment) and position in the hardroll (5 levels ranging from the outside of the roll to the core of the roll). A two-way ANOVA was done on these data. We conclude that the mean airspace differs with time and with position in the hardroll and that these two factors interact with each other.

Ideally, we would like to specify a target amount of airspace to be left at the time of manufacturing so that by the time the customer opens the box 4 weeks later there will be sufficient airspace left in the box to keep the tissues from tearing. The original estimate of a 6-mm change in airspace due to the time factor must now be adjusted to reflect the position in the hardroll from which the tissues are made. It is possible that different target values should be specified for different parts of the hardroll. We will continue to investigate this problem.

The *Wall Street Journal* is a major source of current business news and information for the business community. If your professor has arranged for your class to have access to the Business Extra feature, you can go to it now and see the techniques of this chapter in action today. Go to the Wiley Web site at http://www.wiley.com/college/pelosi, and click on Business Extra!

14.9 ANOVA IN EXCEL

Although Excel is not really a statistical software package, it does have some built-in tools for performing the basics of analysis of variance. We will look at how to use these tools for one- and two-way designs.

14.9.1 One-Way Analysis of Variance in Excel

To perform a one-factor ANOVA using Excel, the data must be in a worksheet with the data for each factor level in separate, adjacent columns. A portion of the airspace data is shown in Figure 14.9.

	A	B	C	D
1	Time 1	Time 2	Time 3	Time 4
2	23	20	19	19
3	25	19	19	19
4	23	20	20	19
5	23	20	20	19
6	23	20	19	19
7	23	19	20	19
8	23	20	20	19
9	23	20	19	19
10	22	20	19	19
11	22	20	20	20
12	23	20	19	20
13	23	19	19	19
14	22	20	19	19
15	22	20	21	19
16	24	20	20	19
17	23	20	18	20
18	23	20	19	20

FIGURE 14.9 Airspace data in Excel

To perform the analysis to see whether there is a difference in mean airspace for the different times, we will use the **ANOVA: Single Factor** tool from the **Tools > Data Analysis** menu. The dialog box shown in Figure 14.10 opens.

Anova: Single Factor

Input
Input Range:
Grouped By: Columns / Rows
Labels in First Row
Alpha: 0.05

Output options
Output Range:
New Worksheet Ply:
New Workbook

OK
Cancel
Help

FIGURE 14.10 ANOVA: Single Factor dialog box

The input is similar to most Excel data analysis tools.

1. Enter the range that contains the data in the **Input Range:** text box. If your data range contains labels, click on the text box for **Labels in First Row.**
2. Since each factor is in a different column, click the radio button for **Grouped By: Columns.** This is the default value.

3. In the text box for **Alpha,** enter the level of significance that you want to use for the test.
4. Finally, indicate where you want Excel to put the output from the analysis.
5. Click **OK;** the output will appear in the location specified. The output for the airspace data is shown in Figure 14.11. As with the output from the regression analysis, you might want to select **Format > Column > AutoFit Selection** while the output is still highlighted.

F	G	H	I	J	K	L
Anova: Single Factor						
SUMMARY						
Groups	*Count*	*Sum*	*Average*	*Variance*		
Time 1	120	2521	21.00833333	2.327661064		
Time 2	120	2095	17.45833333	2.199929972		
Time 3	120	1894	15.78333333	4.339215686		
Time 4	120	1802	15.01666667	5.377871148		
ANOVA						
Source of Variation	*SS*	*df*	*MS*	*F*	*P-value*	*F crit*
Between Groups	2554.75	3	851.5833333	239.1302467	1.34182E-94	2.623636419
Within Groups	1695.116667	476	3.561169468			
Total	4249.866667	479				

FIGURE 14.11 Output from ANOVA on airspace data

Excel provides some summary statistics for each factor and the ANOVA table as output. From the ANOVA table, you see that the F value for Between Groups is 239.13, compared to the critical value of 2.6236. The p value of the test is zero for all practical purposes. Thus, the conclusion is that there is a difference in the mean airspace values for the different time periods.

Excel does not provide any tools for doing multiple comparisons to determine which levels are different, nor does it provide any diagnostic plots for checking assumptions. Since the fitted values are not provided, there is no way to find the residuals and perform the analysis yourself.

14.9.2 Two-Way ANOVA Designs in Excel

The data analysis tools in Excel allow you to analyze two-way designs for situations where there are no replications, and for situations where there are replications. The

	A	B	C	D
1	Store	Shelf	End of Aisle	Front of Store
2	1	4457	4500	5800
3	2	4400	4370	5290
4	3	4310	4300	5000
5	4	4600	4400	5600
6	5	5000	5000	6000
7	6	4500	4500	5300
8	7	4700	5100	5900
9	8	4590	4280	5460
10	9	8510	8670	10600
11	10	6470	6500	8410

FIGURE 14.12 Display/sales data

no-replication tool is similar to the method you would use to analyze a blocked design, whereas the replications tool allows you to analyze a full two-way design.

To analyze a blocked design, we will look at the data on the effects of display type on sales. The data should be in a spreadsheet with the factors (display type) in columns and the blocks (stores) in rows, as shown in Figure 14.12.

1. From the analysis tools list, select **ANOVA: Two-Factor Without Replication** and the dialog box shown in Figure 14.13 opens.

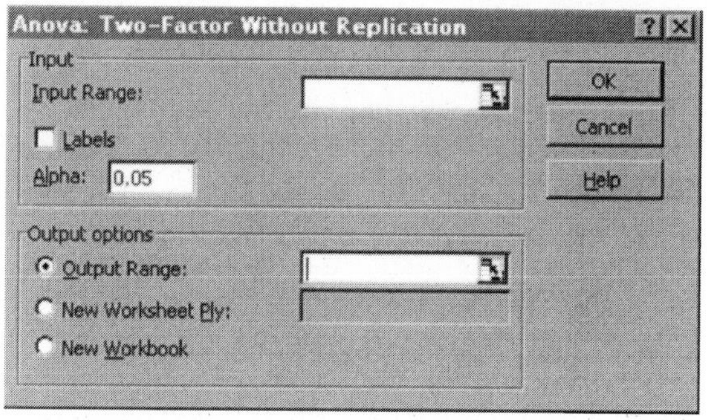

Anova: Two-Factor Without Replication

Input
Input Range:
Labels
Alpha: 0.05

Output options
Output Range:
New Worksheet Ply:
New Workbook

OK
Cancel
Help

FIGURE 14.13 Two-way without replication dialog box

2. Enter the worksheet range for the data and fill in the other text boxes with the appropriate information.
3. Click **OK;** the output will be placed in the location specified. The output for the store display data is shown in Figure 14.14.

F	G	H	I	J	K	L
Anova: Two-Factor Without Replication						
SUMMARY	Count	Sum	Average	Variance		
1	3	14757	4919	582583		
2	3	14060	4686.667	273233.3		
3	3	13610	4536.667	161033.3		
4	3	14600	4866.667	413333.3		
5	3	16000	5333.333	333333.3		
6	3	14300	4766.667	213333.3		
7	3	15700	5233.333	373333.3		
8	3	14330	4776.667	374233.3		
9	3	27780	9260	1353100		
10	3	21380	7126.667	1235433		
Shelf	10	51537	5153.7	1782646		
End of Aisle	10	51620	5162	1970196		
Front of Store	10	63360	6336	3148316		
ANOVA						
Source of Variation	SS	df	MS	F	P-value	F crit
Rows	60738440.03	9	6748716	88.5418	4.73E-13	2.456282
Columns	9253927.267	2	4626964	60.70484	9.97E-09	3.554561
Error	1371972.067	18	76220.67			
Total	71364339.37	29				

FIGURE 14.14 Output for blocked design

The output includes summary information for each factor level and block in addition to the ANOVA table. We see from the p values that both the blocks (located in the rows) and the display types (located in the columns) were significant.

The method for analyzing a full two-way design with replications is very similar to the method for the one-way and two-way without replications. The only difference is in the way Excel expects the data to be stored in the worksheet.

Excel expects to find the data in table format, with the levels of one factor in columns and the levels of the other factors in rows. Each replicate (observation) for a pair of levels is placed in a cell under the previous one. An explanation of this data setup from the Excel documentation is shown in Figure 14.15.

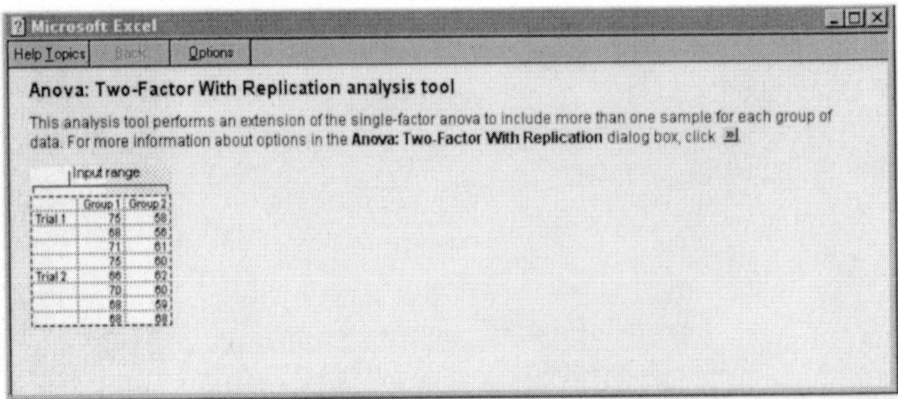

FIGURE 14.15 Data setup for two-way with replications

A subset of the airspace data is shown in Figure 14.16. In this example there are 24 boxes taken from each of five positions. The airspace is measured at four different times.

	A	B	C	D	E	F
1			Time1	Time2	Time 3	Time 4
2		Position 1	23	20	19	19
3			25	19	19	19
4			23	20	20	19
5			23	20	20	19
6			23	20	19	19
7			23	19	20	19
8			23	20	20	19
9			23	20	19	19
10			22	20	19	19
11			22	20	20	20
12			23	20	19	20
13			23	19	19	19
14			22	20	19	19
15			22	20	21	19
16			24	20	20	19
17			23	20	18	20
18			23	20	19	20
19			23	20	20	19
20			23	18	20	20
21			23	20	20	19
22			23	20	20	19
23			23	20	21	20
24			24	20	20	20
25			23	19	19	20
26		Position 2	20	18	14	14
27			20	17	15	14
28			21	17	15	14
29			20	16	16	14
30			21	17	14	15
31			21	18	15	14
32			20	17	15	14

FIGURE 14.16 Airspace data for two-way analysis

The completed dialog box for the two-way with replications analysis tool is shown in Figure 14.17.

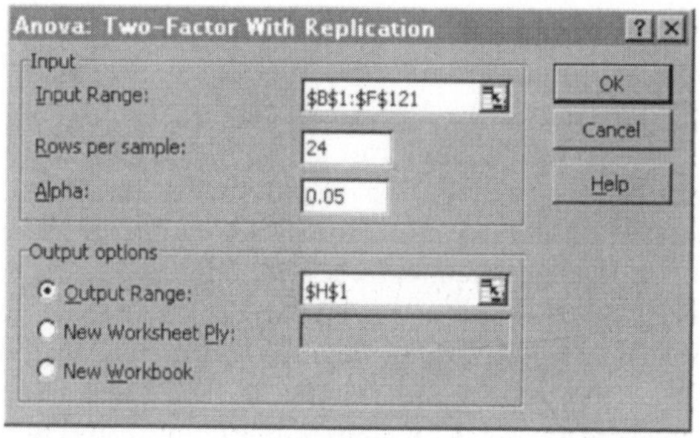

Anova: Two-Factor With Replication

Input
Input Range: $B$1:$F$121
Rows per sample: 24
Alpha: 0.05

Output options
Output Range: $H$1
New Worksheet Ply:
New Workbook

OK
Cancel
Help

FIGURE 14.17 Two-way with replications dialog box

The only difference in the input is that you need to tell Excel how many replications there are by filling in the text box labeled **Rows per sample:**. In this case there were 24. You *must* highlight the row with the first factor labels and the column with the second factor labels. Excel does not give you a choice here. The output is shown in Figure 14.18. It is very similar to the output from the other ANOVA tools.

H	I	J	K	L	M	N
Anova: Two-Factor With Replication						
SUMMARY	Time1	Time2	Time 3	Time 4	Total	
Position 1						
Count	24	24	24	24	96	
Sum	552	474	470	464	1960	
Average	23	19.75	19.5833333	19.3333333	20.4166667	
Variance	0.43478261	0.2826087	0.51449275	0.23188406	2.6245614	
Position 2						
Count	24	24	24	24	96	
Sum	500	405	362	339	1606	
Average	20.8333333	16.875	15.0833333	14.125	16.7291667	
Variance	0.66666667	1.41847826	0.60144928	0.46195652	7.42061404	
Position 3						
Count	24	24	24	24	96	
Sum	486	410	349	338	1583	
Average	20.25	17.0833333	14.5416667	14.0833333	16.4895833	
Variance	0.45652174	1.29710145	0.86775362	0.51449275	6.84199561	
Position 4						
Count	24	24	24	24	96	
Sum	463	400	361	319	1543	
Average	19.2916667	16.6666667	15.0416667	13.2916667	16.0729167	
Variance	0.47644928	0.75362319	0.91123188	0.91123188	5.6683114	
Position 5						
Count	24	24	24	24	96	
Sum	520	406	352	342	1620	
Average	21.6666667	16.9166667	14.6666667	14.25	16.875	
Variance	1.71014493	0.6884058	0.49275362	0.80434783	9.66842105	
Total						
Count	120	120	120	120		
Sum	2521	2095	1894	1802		
Average	21.0083333	17.4583333	15.7833333	15.0166667		
Variance	2.32766106	2.19992997	4.33921569	5.37787115		
ANOVA						
Source of Variation	*SS*	*df*	*MS*	*F*	*P-value*	*F crit*
Sample	1188.59583	4	297.148958	409.963072	3.869E-150	2.39132447
Columns	2554.75	3	851.583333	1174.89128	3.56E-215	2.62429012
Interaction	173.104167	12	14.4253472	19.9020037	4.7221E-35	1.77324111
Within	333.416667	460	0.72481884			
Total	4249.86667	479				

FIGURE 14.18 Output from airspace two-way design

CHAPTER 14 SUMMARY

In this chapter you have learned the tool of analysis of variance (ANOVA), which is used to draw inferences about more than two population means. It directly extends the two-population tests to compare means which you learned in Chapter 10. You typically find yourself comparing more than two populations when you are trying to determine what factors influence the variable you are studying.

Regardless of the specific number of factors you are investigating, the technique of ANOVA partitions the variation in the data into components and compares the relative sizes of these components. So it is through an analysis of the variation in the data that we learn something about the means. It is a clever approach and one that draws on many of the basic concepts and tools that you have learned in earlier chapters.

The results of the hypothesis tests that you can perform will guide you in your design of subsequent experiments as you try to understand the factors that cause your variable of interest to vary. Ultimately you are interested in building a model to predict or control this variation. Remember that unexpected variation is the enemy according to Deming, and customers are demanding higher quality in products and services. It is only by understanding variation that we can produce quality products.

Key Terms

Term	Definition	Page Reference
ANOVA	**Analysis of variance (ANOVA)** is the technique used to analyze the variation in the data to determine if more than two population means are equal.	700
Block	**A block** is a group of objects or people that have been matched. An object or person can be matched with itself, meaning that repeated observations are taken on that object or person and these observations form a block.	724
Factor	**A factor** is a variable that can be used to differentiate one group or population from another.	698
Factorial design with two factors	An experimental design is called a **factorial design with two factors** if there are several different levels of two factors being studied. The first factor is called **factor A** and there are r levels of factor A. The second factor is called **factor B** and there are c levels of factor **B**.	734
Grand mean	The **grand mean** or the **overall mean** is the sample average of all the observations in the experiment. It is labeled $\bar{\bar{x}}$.	702
Level	A **level** is one of several possible values or settings that the factor can assume.	698
Mean squares	The **mean square among** is labeled **MSA.** The **mean square error** is labeled **MSE** and the **mean square total** is labeled **MST.**	710
One-way or completely randomized design	An experiment has a **one-way** or completely **randomized design** if several different levels of one factor are being studied and the objects or people being observed/measured are randomly assigned to one of the c levels of the factor.	699
Randomized block design	An experiment has a **randomized block design** if there are several different levels of one factor being studied and the objects or people being observed/measured have been matched. Each object or person is randomly assigned to one of the c levels of the factor.	724

Key Terms (*continued*)

Term	Definition	Page Reference
Replicate	The design is said to have **equal replication** if the same number of objects or people being observed/measured are randomly selected from each population. The population is described by a specific level for each of the two factors. Each observation is called a **replicate.** There are n' observations or replicates observed from each population. There are $n = n'rc$ observations in total.	735
Response variable	The **response variable** is a quantitative variable that you are measuring or observing.	698
Sum of squares among (SSA)	**Between groups variation** measures how different the individual treatment means are from the overall grand mean. It is often called the **sum of squares between** or the **sum of squares among (SSA).**	704
Sum of squares blocks (SSBL)	The **sum of squares blocks** measures the variability between the blocks. It is labeled **SSBL.**	724
Sum of squares error (SSE)	Within groups variation measures the variability in the measurements within the groups. It is often called **sum of squares within** or **sum of squares error (SSE).**	705
Sum of squares due to factor A (SSA)	The **sum of squares due to factor A** is labeled **SSA.** It measures the squared differences between the mean of each level of factor A and the grand mean.	735
Sum of squares due to factor B (SSB)	The **sum of squares due to factor B** is labeled **SSB.** It measures the squared differences between the mean of each level of factor B and the grand mean.	735
Sum of squares due to the interacting effect of A and B (SSAB)	The **sum of squares due to the interacting effect of A and B** is labeled **SSAB.** It measures the effect of combining factor A and factor B.	735
Sum of squares total (SST)	The **total variation** or **sum of squares total (SST)** is a measure of the variability in the entire data set considered as a whole.	702
Treatment	A **treatment** is a particular setting or combination of settings of the factor(s) being studied.	700
Treatment mean	**A treatment mean** is the average of the response variable for a particular treatment.	704

Key Formulas

Term	Formula	Page Reference
SST, one-way design	$\sum_{j=1}^{c}\sum_{i=1}^{n_j}(x_{ij} - \bar{\bar{x}})^2$	702
SSA, one-way design	$\text{SSA} = \sum n_j(\bar{x}_j - \bar{\bar{x}})^2$	704
SSE, one-way design	$\sum_{j=1}^{c}\sum_{i=1}^{n_j}(x_{ij} - \bar{x}_j)^2$	705
MSA, one-way design	$\dfrac{\text{SSA}}{c - 1}$	710

(continued)

Key Formulas (*continued*)

Term	Formula	Page Reference
MSE, one-way design	$\frac{\text{SSE}}{n - c}$	710
MST, one-way design	$\frac{\text{SST}}{n - 1}$	710
***F* statistic, one-way design**	$\frac{\text{MSA}}{\text{MSE}}$	711
SST, block design	SST = SSA + SSBL + SSE	724
Relative efficiency of block design	$\frac{(r - 1)\text{ MSBL} + r(c - 1)\text{ MSA}}{(n - 1)\text{ MSE}}$	727
SST, two-way design	SST = SSA + SSB + SSAB + SSE	735

CHAPTER 14 EXERCISES

Learning It!

14.21 A manufacturer of watches is concerned about the defective rate. There have been numerous customer complaints. The watches are made on 3 shifts and the company wishes to see if there is any difference in the average percent defective on the 3 shifts. The defective rate for each shift for 10 days is recorded and shown here:

	Shift 1	Shift 2	Shift 3
Day 1	0.020	0.037	0.036
Day 2	0.016	0.032	0.032
Day 3	0.018	0.028	0.037
Day 4	0.021	0.029	0.033
Day 5	0.020	0.031	0.038
Day 6	0.022	0.034	0.035
Day 7	0.019	0.028	0.034
Day 8	0.019	0.032	0.027
Day 9	0.019	0.031	0.036
Day 10	0.021	0.030	0.034

(a) What type of design is this?

(b) Is there any difference in the percent defective by shift? If so, which one(s)?

(c) Check the assumptions of ANOVA for these data.

Datafile: DISHWASH.XXX

14.22 A manufacturer of dishwashers was concerned about the consistency of measuring the resistance of the heater in the dishwasher product from one meter to another. A sample of 30 heaters was selected. The resistance of each heater was measured by 4 meters. The data (in ohms) follow.

Sample	Meter 1	Meter 2	Meter 3	Meter 4
1	14.5	14.4	14.3	14.63
2	14.8	14.8	14.7	14.98
3	14.8	14.8	14.7	14.93
4	14.6	14.6	14.5	14.80
5	15.8	15.7	15.6	15.95

(*continued*)

Sample	Meter 1	Meter 2	Meter 3	Meter 4
6	14.6	14.6	14.5	14.80
7	14.8	14.8	14.7	14.99
8	14.4	14.4	14.3	14.62
9	14.6	14.5	14.4	14.71
10	14.3	14.2	14.2	14.43
11	14.3	14.3	14.2	14.49
12	14.6	14.6	14.5	14.75
13	14.3	14.2	14.2	14.44
14	15.0	14.9	14.8	15.11
15	14.5	14.5	14.4	14.68
16	14.7	14.7	14.5	14.86
17	14.6	14.6	14.5	14.76
18	14.7	14.6	14.5	14.81
19	14.7	14.7	14.6	14.85
20	14.6	14.5	14.4	14.71
21	14.5	14.4	14.3	14.58
22	14.4	14.3	14.3	14.50
23	15.3	15.3	15.2	15.44
24	14.4	14.4	14.3	14.54
25	14.5	14.4	14.3	14.58
26	14.8	14.7	14.6	14.86
27	14.6	14.5	14.4	14.72
28	14.5	14.4	14.3	14.57
29	14.4	14.3	14.2	14.50
30	14.6	14.6	14.5	14.75

(a) What type of design is this?

(b) Is there any difference in the measurements taken by the different operators? If so, which one(s)?

(c) Check the assumptions of ANOVA for these data.

14.23 The dishwasher company wondered whether it mattered if the meters had time to warm up before being used. In addition to the 4 meters used in Exercise 14.22, another meter of the same type as meter 4 was allowed a 2-hour warm-up period before being used. The readings on this meter for the same 30 sample products are shown here:

Requires Exercise 14.22

Samples 1–5	14.62	15.00	14.95	14.78	15.93
Samples 6–10	14.79	15.01	14.61	14.70	14.45
Samples 11–15	14.48	14.76	14.45	15.09	14.67
Samples 16–20	14.86	14.77	14.79	14.84	14.71
Samples 21–25	14.58	14.50	15.45	14.55	14.59
Samples 26–30	14.85	14.72	14.58	14.51	14.76

(a) Rerun the ANOVA including these data as a fifth treatment.

(b) Do any of your conclusions change?

14.24 Many on-line service companies have a technical support telephone service to assist users who are having difficulty getting connected or using the service. Recently there has been a concern about the amount of time that a customer has to wait "on hold" before hearing a human voice. In an effort to decide which on-line service to purchase, a study was conducted. Thirty calls were made to 4 on-line services during 3 times of day: early morning (6–8 AM), midday (noon to 2 PM), and late afternoon (4–6 PM). The amount of time spent on hold in minutes was recorded. A portion of the data is shown in the next table.

Datafile: *ONHOLD.XXX*

	Company 1	Company 2	Company 3	Company 4
Early AM	11	11	7	3
	8	11	9	8
	7	11	7	6
	8	9	9	9

(continued)

Company 1	Company 2	Company 3	Company 4
8	9	8	11
7	6	8	9
8	9	5	9

(a) Is there any difference in the average time on hold among the four companies?

(b) Is there any difference in the average amount of time on hold by time of day?

(c) Is there any interaction between the time of day and the four companies?

(d) If you could use more than one of the companies, which company would you use during each of the three time periods? Explain your reasoning.

(e) If you cannot use more than one company, which company would you select? Explain your reasoning.

(f) What other factors might influence the time on hold?

14.25 One of the benefits of implementing a Total Quality Management program is the decreased time it takes to go from product design to market sales. This is often referred to as the cycle time. An automobile company recently implemented a TQM program companywide. The cycle times (in months) for 3 new cars before TQM and 1 year after TQM are shown here:

Before TQM	After TQM
26, 29, 22	17, 9, 13

(a) Based on these data, what can you conclude about the average cycle time before and after the implementation of TQM?

(b) What else would you like to know about these products to be certain that the reduction in cycle time is a result of the TQM program and not something else?

Datafile: *SCORES.XXX*

14.26 There has been increasing concern about the declining reading and math levels of American students. A study was conducted to determine the effect of income on four response variables: behavior problems index, reading score, math score, and vocabulary score. All three of the scores were from 0 to 100. The behavior index ranges from 0 to 100 with low scores indicating fewer behavior problems. One hundred children age 5 to 7 were tested from families with varying income levels. Three income levels were used: an annual income of $15,000 or less, an annual income of $25,000, and an annual income of $40,000. The results are found in the datafile named SCORES.XXX.

(a) For each of the response variables, test to see whether there is a difference in the average score for the 3 levels of the income factor.

(b) Have any of the assumptions of ANOVA been violated?

(c) What recommendations can you make based on your analysis?

Refers to Exercise 14.19
Datafile: *MOUSE2.XXX*

14.27 The manager from Exercise 14.19 is also concerned about the accuracy of her employees after many hours of intensive computer work. At the same time as the data on time to complete the task was taken, a measure of accuracy (% correct) was also recorded. These data are shown here:

Beginning of Day		After 2 hr Intensive Work		After 4 hr Intensive Work		After 6 hr Intensive Work	
Right	Left	Right	Left	Right	Left	Right	Left
95.88	89.70	93.60	90.78	87.96	82.54	79.88	92.38
91.94	90.00	98.00	94.17	96.39	87.96	84.70	86.58
92.79	85.68	90.10	94.17	98.59	95.76	93.68	94.17
95.76	95.53	97.00	89.70	96.00	91.00	93.92	95.00
91.46	81.97	87.96	96.84	84.35	83.24	97.76	96.84
92.72	90.15	95.53	90.78	96.39	95.00	74.68	84.48
93.60	92.72	96.84	92.72	94.90	94.61	86.40	89.23
94.61	83.45	80.76	91.00	94.61	87.96	99.00	90.00
99.00	98.00	95.53	92.19	79.38	79.60	94.61	86.11
97.76	88.30	92.00	88.82	89.70	85.00	76.65	82.91

(continued)

Beginning of Day		After 2 hr Intensive Work		After 4 hr Intensive Work		After 6 hr Intensive Work	
Right	Left	Right	Left	Right	Left	Right	Left
100.00	93.60	96.39	97.17	93.68	96.84	98.59	94.17
89.18	89.23	80.90	85.58	98.59	90.00	81.13	90.00
87.47	97.00	85.68	94.61	92.93	91.75	86.96	95.88
94.17	96.39	93.29	91.94	85.68	94.90	92.72	83.00
91.40	91.94	96.00	84.97	93.60	87.27	91.94	94.90
95.53	84.19	94.90	90.15	90.57	89.70	80.69	94.61
93.68	96.39	94.34	89.00	96.39	84.70	91.75	87.79
94.90	84.44	92.19	87.79	87.96	95.53	95.00	95.00
97.76	94.17	95.00	91.40	94.90	93.92	85.58	82.97
97.00	93.29	98.59	91.40	95.53	90.57	96.84	88.69

(a) Is there any difference in the averagse accuracy level after differing amounts of computer intensive work?

(b) Is there any difference in the average accuracy level to complete the task for the right hand versus the left hand?

(c) Is there a significant interaction effect?

(d) What is your recommendation to this manager?

14.28 In an effort to reduce crime, several cities have implemented a plan that encourages members of the police force to live in the city they patrol. These police officers have been given the opportunity to purchase homes at half-price, the other half of the cost being funded by the city budget. To see whether this program has had the desired effect, data were recorded on the yearly number of murders in 5 cities the year before the program was initiated, 1 year after the program started, and 2 years after the program was initiated. The data are shown here:

City	Year Before Program Started	1 Year After Program Started	2 Years After Program Started
Los Angeles	44	43	43
Chicago	35	34	33
Detroit	41	39	38
Springfield	21	20	19
Philadelphia	29	28	27

(a) What type of experimental design was used in this situation?

(b) Has the program been effective? Why or why not?

(c) Have any of the assumptions of ANOVA been violated?

(d) A government publication states that the average number of murders has dropped from 34 to 31.8 for the cities that have adopted this program. The publication uses this statement to propose expanding this program to other cities. Do you agree with this analysis? Why or why not? Should this program be adopted by other cities or should it be scrapped?

14.29 The adhesive company in Exercise 14.20 was interested in comparing its new product with that of its competitor. The same experimental conditions were used to test the competitor's product. The tensile values (psi) for the competitor's product are shown here: *Requires Exercise 14.20*

Humidity	No Oil	Oil
50%	437, 437, 450	9, 10, 6
90%	115, 115, 50	105, 87, 105

(a) Does the competitor's product behave significantly differently if the surface is oil contaminated?

(b) Does the competitor's product behave significantly differently at different humidity levels?

(c) Is there a significant interaction effect for the competitor's product?

(d) Summarize your findings about the new product and the competitor's product in terms of the response to oil-contaminated surfaces and varying levels of humidity. Should this company continue to develop the new product?

Thinking About It!

Refers to Exercises 14.22, 14.23

14.30 Upon further thought about the dishwasher company, you have decided to compare just 2 of the columns of data: meter 4 and meter 4 after a warm-up period.

(a) Use a paired t test to make this comparison. Is there any difference in the readings if you let the meter warm up?

(b) Run the appropriate ANOVA using just meter 4 and meter 4 after warm-up as the data set. Does the ANOVA indicate any difference in the treatment means?

(c) Should you have expected the same answer using the paired t test and the ANOVA? Explain why or why not.

(d) Take the value of the t statistic from the paired test and square it. Compare it to the F statistic from the ANOVA. What do you notice? Do you think this will always happen or is this just a coincidence for this data set?

Refers to Exercise 14.3

14.31 Reconsider the teacher of statistics who was wondering whether to assign and grade homework. The teacher used 3 different classes to investigate the 3 different possible ways of dealing with homework. The teacher used a one-way design thinking that students randomly select sections of a course to take and so they should be comparable. Is there any reason to think that a block design should have been used in this situation instead of the one-way design that was used? Explain why or why not.

Refers to Exercise 14.1

14.32 When the diaper company tested absorbency the product was actually placed on a child and the child was allowed to play during the testing. As the child played, fluid was injected into the diaper every 10 minutes until the product failed (leaked). The amount of fluid (in grams) at the time of failure was recorded for each diaper. This experiment was set up as a one-way design. Can you think of any reason why a block design might be better?

14.33 In any ANOVA you test the null hypothesis of equal means using an F statistic. If you fail to reject the null hypothesis and you construct a confidence interval for the difference in two of the treatment means, what number should you expect to find in the confidence interval? Explain why.

Refers to Exercise 14.18

14.34 In Exercise 14.18 you analyzed a data set with two factors: time and lot. Since then, two more months have gone by and data have been collected on two more lots. Unfortunately, for the third lot the experiment was run only for the pretest and 9 days later. For the fourth lot, data were collected during the pretest and 9 days and 16 days later (instead of 58 days). The data are shown here:

Number	Pretest	9 Days
1	26.1	31.5
2	26.8	29.8
3	25.3	28.7
4	28.1	32.2
5	25.3	30.3
6	27.3	31.7
7	26.5	30.4
8	24.8	28.0
9	26.1	28.6
10	26.2	29.1
11	25.3	27.4
12	28.0	31.6
13	25.5	29.1
14	24.8	28.2
15	27.2	31.0

(continued)

Number	Pretest	9 Days	16 Days
1	30.8	34.6	35.0
2	27.5	30.9	31.4
3	26.8	31.3	31.8
4	29.4	32.8	33.5
5	28.7	32.6	32.0
6	24.0	26.5	26.9
7	26.4	30.9	31.2
8	28.3	31.0	31.2
9	30.0	32.4	32.8
10	25.0	27.3	27.4
11	26.8	30.3	30.8
12	26.7	30.9	31.2
13	26.1	27.9	28.2
14	27.6	31.5	31.7
15	27.4	29.7	30.0

(continued)

Number	Pretest	9 Days
16	25.1	27.1
17	26.2	28.2
18	26.8	29.5
19	27.3	29.4
20	27.1	28.8

Number	Pretest	9 Days	16 Days
16	26.3	29.0	29.5
17	28.0	31.5	32.0
18	25.3	27.1	27.5
19	26.4	28.3	28.4
20	27.2	30.0	30.7

(a) Explain why you cannot simply add two more levels to the lot factor and reanalyze the entire data set using ANOVA.

(b) What analysis do you suggest be done to use these additional data?

14.35 You have decided to use your newly acquired data analysis skills in your coaching of a 6th-grade girls' basketball team. You want to see whether there is any difference in the average number of points your team scores when you use different defense strategies. You suggest the following design: use "man-to-man" defense strategy for the first third of the season and record the number of points scored for each game. Switch to full-court press strategy for the second third of the season and record the number of points scored for each game. During the last third of the season use a mixture of defense strategies.

(a) Will you be able to tell which strategy is best from the data collected from this experiment?

(b) Suggest an alternative experimental design.

14.36 In Exercise 14.15 you concluded that the average weights for the students were different at the four different times the data were collected. Suppose you now learned that these students were enrolled in a 1-year weekend MBA program starting in September of 1 year and ending a year later and that they were all working at full-time jobs during this time. *Refers to Exercise 14.15*

(a) What might be causing the weight differences that you observed?

(b) Support your theory by taking another look at this data set and analyzing it differently.

14.37 In Exercises 14.19 and 14.27 you analyzed the amount of time to complete a task and the accuracy level after varying amounts of time of intensive computer work. What other factors would you suggest be studied in a subsequent experiment on this subject? *Refers to Exercises 14.19, 14.27*

Doing It!

14.38 A manufacturing company that makes paper products is having trouble with its paper towel line. When a roll of paper towels is manufactured, the last step before the roll is put in a case is to wrap it with the poly wrapper in which the consumer sees it on the store shelf. A large amount of product is scrapped because it is not being wrapped properly.

The problem appears to be that the diameters of the towel rolls are too large and the wrapper does not go all the way around and seal properly. There are many factors in the manufacturing process that would appear to affect roll diameter, but the engineers involved were not sure exactly how the different machine settings really impacted roll diameter. In fact, they were not convinced that all of the factors made a difference! The towel machine team designed a study to determine the effect that different machine settings actually had on roll diameter. The specifications for the diameter of the roll of towels is 5.35 inches. Several different people on the team expressed a concern that some settings that would result in a good roll diameter might have an adverse impact on another towel roll characteristic, roll firmness.

If a towel is not firm its wrapping will also be affected, and if it is too firm consumers will still react negatively. Fixing the roll diameter problem at the expense of firmness was not an option.

The team decided to look at two machine factors:

1. Embosser roll gap: the mechanism that puts the pattern in the towel
2. Speed: the speed at which the machine winds the rolls of towels

The machine was run at two different settings for speed and two different sizes of the embosser roll gap. The response variables were diameter of the roll of paper towels in inches and firmness measured on a specialized scale. Lower numbers indicate softer rolls, whereas larger numbers indicate firmer rolls. A portion of the data set is shown here:

Speed	Embosser	Diameter	Firmness
0	0	5.43307	0.271667
0	0	5.39370	0.336667
0	0	5.47244	0.260333
0	0	5.39370	0.261333
0	0	5.43307	0.297000
1	0	5.39370	0.312000
1	0	5.47244	0.294667
1	0	5.43307	0.342333
1	0	5.47244	0.306000
1	0	5.43307	0.365667

Datafile: TOWEL.XXX

The variable *Speed* is a 0–1 variable that indicates the machine speed. A 0 indicates that the slower machine speed was used and a 1 indicates that the faster machine speed was used. The variable *Embosser* is a 0–1 variable that indicates the size of the embosser roll gap. A 0 indicates that the smaller gap measurement was used, whereas a 1 indicates that the larger gap measurement was used.

(a) Is there a difference in the diameter of the paper towel roll due to the speed at which the machine is run?

(b) Is there a difference in the diameter of the paper towel roll due to the size of the embosser roll gap?

(c) Is there any interaction of the two factors with respect to the diameter of the paper towel roll?

(d) Is there a difference in the firmness of the paper towel roll due to the speed at which the machine is run?

(e) Is there a difference in the firmness of the paper towel roll due to the size of the embosser roll gap?

(f) Is there any interaction of the two factors with respect to the firmness of the paper towel roll?

(g) Check the ANOVA assumptions for both response variables.

(h) Prepare a report for management explaining the effects that each of the machine settings have on *Diameter* and *Firmness*. Indicate which settings result in acceptable values for roll diameter. Make a recommendation on machine settings, if you can.

14.39 In several of the worked examples in this chapter we looked at a portion of a data set measuring tissue strength. The management of the tissue company was concerned about complaints involving sheets tearing on removal. One possibility was the lack of airspace in the box. We have studied that data set extensively in this chapter. Another possible explanation is that the tissues are not strong enough. Two tissue strength measurements were studied: machine-directional strength (*MDStrength*) and the cross-directional strength (*CDStrength*). They are both measured in lb/ream. The data were collected over 3 days and the company would like to know if the average *MDStrength* and the average *CDStrength* are the same for all 3 days. There are 75 observations per day. A portion of the data set is shown here:

Datafile: TISSUE.XXX

Day	*MDStrength*	*CDStrength*	Day	*MDStrength*	*CDStrength*
1	1006	422	1	962	464
1	994	448	1	973	472
1	1032	423	1	1036	489
1	875	435	1	1084	440
1	1043	445			

The specifications indicate that *MDStrength* should have a mean of 1000 lb/ream and a standard deviation of 50 lb/ream. The specifications indicate that *CDStrength* should be normally distributed with a mean of 450 and a standard deviation of 25 lb/ream.

(a) Is there any difference in the average *MDStrength* for the 3 days? If so, which day(s) are different?

(b) Is the *MDStrength* running to specification?

(c) Is there any difference in the average *CDStrength* for the 3 days? If so, which day(s) are different?

(d) Is the *CDStrength* running to specification?

(e) Check the assumptions of ANOVA for both response variables.

(f) Using the results of your analysis, prepare a report to management telling them about the current tissue manufacturing process. Make recommendations to them on whether the process must be adjusted or whether it is running to target. Remember, if it is running to target they will consider making changes to the specifications to reduce customer complaints about dispensing.

CHAPTER 15

THE ANALYSIS OF QUALITATIVE DATA

COLLEGE DRINKING

Business Dilemma...

For many students, consumption of alcohol is part of the "college experience." Some colleges and universities attract students based on their reputation as "party schools." Students do not often think about the ramifications of their drinking until they experience problems related to it, such as failing classes or flunking out entirely, unwanted pregnancies, or encounters with law enforcement. University administrations are often unaware of or in denial of the problems and do not have programs in place to help students address the problems of drinking and alcohol-related health behaviors.

The problem of excessive alcohol consumption in college is one that has been documented many times, in many different ways. A random national survey involving 140 colleges and universities, conducted by Harvard University, looked at the problems connected with *binge drinking*, which is defined as the consumption of five or more drinks during one episode of drinking for men and consumption of four or more drinks during one episode of drinking for women. The study found that as the number of binge drinking episodes for an individual increased, the number of alcohol-related problems experienced increased as well. The types of problems that the two studies examined included having a hangover, missing class, having unplanned sex, and driving while intoxicated.

A senior Public Health major at a university in the Northeast conducted a survey similar to the Harvard survey to examine the problem of binge drinking on the officially "alcohol-free" campus. The survey was administered to students registered in a Public Health course entitled "Wellness." Although the sample is not really a random sample of the student population, the course was one that is required of all students at the University. The study was limited to students 25 years of age or under and participation was voluntary.

The study resulted in 221 usable responses. Data were collected in four different areas: information about drinking habits (4 questions), problems experienced related to the students' drinking (15 questions), problems experienced because of other students' drinking (8 questions), and some demographic information (9 questions).

A sample of some of the data is shown here:

Five	Four	Three	Last	Binger	Hangover	Miss	Behind
0	0	0	2	1	1	1	1
0	0	0	4	1	1	1	1
0	1	1	3	2	1	1	1
0	0	0	3	1	1	1	1
0	0	0	3	1	1	1	1
0	0	0	4	1	1	1	1

(The variable names are abbreviated and are explained in the text as needed.)

15.1 Chapter Objectives

You have learned that although *qualitative data* are important in understanding the results of statistical analyses, there are not many statistical tools that deal specifically with these types of data. You learned some graphical techniques for displaying qualitative data in Chapters 3 and 5 and you learned how to calculate probabilities for these variables in Chapter 6. In Chapters 9 and 10 you learned some techniques for testing hypotheses about population proportions, which arise from *qualitative data.*

This chapter deals primarily with the analysis of qualitative data. Almost all of the techniques that are used to analyze qualitative data are known as *chi-square tests.* In this chapter you will learn to use chi-square tests for

- testing whether a particular probability model fits a set of data (goodness of fit test)
- testing equality of proportions for more than two populations
- testing whether two qualitative variables are dependent or independent

15.2 TEST FOR GOODNESS OF FIT

In Chapters 9 and 10 you learned several different hypothesis tests that *assumed* that the data came from a population that was normally distributed. At the time you may have wondered how you could know if the assumption was valid for a particular set of data. In Chapter 11 you saw a normal probability plot, which you used informally to determine whether the residuals were normally distributed.

There are some other, *informal*, ways to check to see whether the assumption of normality is valid, such as creating a histogram, dotplot, or boxplot of the data and seeing whether the shape resembles that of the normal distribution. This is not a bad idea, but whenever we can substantiate an *eyeball* test with a formal statistical technique, we are more secure in the decisions we make.

One method of testing to see if data come from a population with a certain distribution is to perform a test called a **chi-square goodness of fit test.**

A ***chi-square goodness of fit test*** checks to see how well a set of data fit the model for a particular probability distribution.

15.2.1 The Chi-Square Test

You know by now that every hypothesis test has

- a set of hypotheses, H_0 and H_A
- a test procedure that defines how the data are collected and processed
- a test statistic that has a certain sampling distribution
- one or more critical values
- a decision or conclusion that can be made as a result of the test

For a chi-square goodness of fit test, the hypotheses are

The chi-square goodness of fit test is always a one-tail or one-sided test.

H_0: The data come from a population with a specific probability distribution (normal, binomial, etc.).

H_A: The data do not come from a population with the specified distribution.

The test procedure is to collect a set of sample data and to create a frequency histogram for the data. The test then compares the **observed** frequency distribution of the data to the frequency distribution that would be **expected** if the null hypothesis were true.

The ***observed frequencies*** are the actual number of observations that fall into each class in a frequency distribution or histogram.

The ***expected frequencies*** are the number of observation that should fall into each class in a frequency distribution under the hypothesized probability distribution.

EXAMPLE 15.1 College Drinking

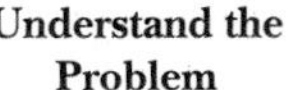

Choosing the Hypothesized Distribution

Because the data collected for the survey on binge drinking were not a random sample, the researcher was interested in knowing how well the sample represented the actual student population. The researcher thought that the distribution of students among the four classes—freshman, sophomore, junior, and senior—was approximately uniform. That is, the probability distribution for the students he expected was

Class	Freshman	Sophomore	Junior	Senior
Probability	25%	25%	25%	25%

This type of distribution is known as a **uniform distribution.** ■

A ***uniform distribution*** is one in which each outcome or class of outcomes is equally likely to occur.

EXAMPLE 15.2 College Drinking

Understand the Problem

Setting Up the Goodness of Fit Test

In this situation, the hypotheses we wish to test are

H_0: The distribution of students is uniform over the classes.

H_A: The distribution of students is not uniform.

Because of a mixup in the early administration of the survey, the question about class was left off some of the surveys. As a result there were only 171 responses to this question. The data are shown here:

Class	Observed Frequency
Freshman	86
Sophomore	36
Junior	30
Senior	19
Total (n)	**171**

From simply looking at the data it might be reasonable to wonder whether the distribution is uniform, since the number of freshmen is larger than that of the other classes combined. ■

Remember that we often test hypotheses when observed data seem unusual or inconsistent with what we expect.

EXAMPLE 15.3 Quality Problems

The Chi-Square Goodness of Fit Test

Understand the Problem

A company that manufactures CD jewel cases contracts with various computer software manufacturers to provide a product that is 10% defective. One of the software manufacturers is wondering about the quality of the product it receives and decides to check on the quality of the cases.

Since the company has just received a shipment of product it decides to sample 1000 boxes of the jewel cases and take 5 jewel cases from each. The reason for checking 5 jewel cases is that this is consistent with the company's current acceptance sampling procedures. The company will inspect and count the number of defective cases. If the vendor is conforming to the contract, then the data collected on the number of defective cases should have a binomial distribution with $\pi = 0.10$ (or 10%).

Collect the Data

The hypotheses the company wishes to test are

H_0: The distribution of defective cases is binomial with $n = 5$ and $\pi = 0.10$.

H_A: The distribution of defective cases is NOT binomial with $n = 5$ and $\pi = 0.10$.

The company decides to perform the test at the 0.05 level of significance. ■

You might be wondering why we would want to do this, since you already know how to do hypothesis tests about proportions. This is a good question. The reason is tied to the *information* we are trying to obtain. If the software manufacturer tests the hypothesis $\pi = 0.10$ (against $\pi \neq 0.10$ or $\pi > 0.10$), then the conclusion will only be about the percent defective over the 5000 jewel cases in the sample. Depending on the length of time over which the product was manufactured, an average percent defective may not be a good indication of what is happening.

The chi-square goodness of fit test will give information about the distribution of the number of defective cases in a sample of size 5, which may enable the software manufacturer to obtain additional information about when or how the population changed. Remember that when you learned about the binomial probability distribution, one of the assumptions we made was that π, the proportion of successes in the population, remains constant over time. In a manufacturing process this is not always a safe assumption, since the process may shift over time. If the process changes but *averages* 0.10 over time, the hypothesis test about proportions might not be able to identify the problem. If we test the distribution as well as the value of π, we may be able to identify a problem. You will see what we mean as the example progresses.

TRY IT NOW!

Seat-Belt Usage ***Setting Up the Hypotheses for the Goodness of Fit Test***

Analysts for insurance companies assume that the number of drivers who wear seat belts is a binomial random variable with $\pi = 0.70$. To test this assumption they decide to set up checkpoints and sample 10 drivers every 2 hours. Set up the hypotheses to perform an appropriate chi-square goodness of fit test.

In a chi-square goodness of fit test, we are always trying to decide whether the data we observed fit a particular probability distribution model. We can use this model to determine how many data points we would *expect* to fall in each class of the frequency distribution since we know the theoretical probabilities of observing any of the possible values.

ANS. H_0: THE NUMBER OF DRIVERS WEARING SEAT BELTS IS BINOMIAL WITH $n = 10$ AND $\pi = 0.70$; H_A: THE NUMBER OF DRIVERS WEARING SEAT BELTS IS NOT BINOMIAL WITH $n = 10$ AND $\pi = 0.70$.

EXAMPLE 15.4 College Drinking

Finding the Expected Frequencies

If the distribution of students over the classes is really uniform, then we would expect there to be the same number of students in each class; that is,

$$(25\%)(171) = 42.75 \text{ students in each year}$$

If we add a column to the frequency table we see that indeed the observed frequency does differ from what we expected to happen.

Analyze the Data

Class	Observed Frequency	Expected Frequency
Freshman	86	42.75
Sophomore	36	42.75
Junior	30	42.75
Senior	19	42.75
Total (n)	**171**	**171**

We can see the deviation from what is expected visually by looking at the frequency histograms for both the observed and expected distributions.

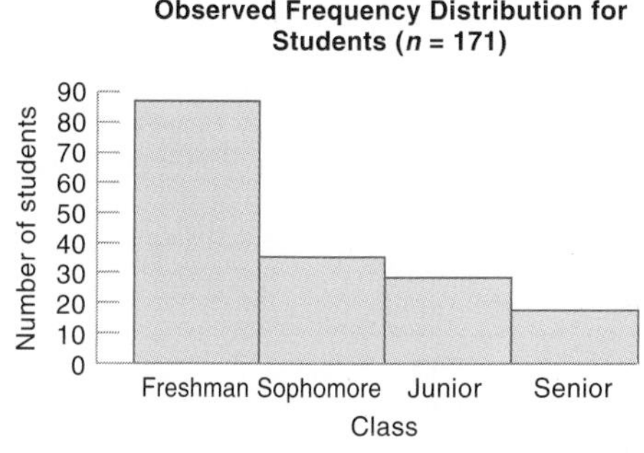

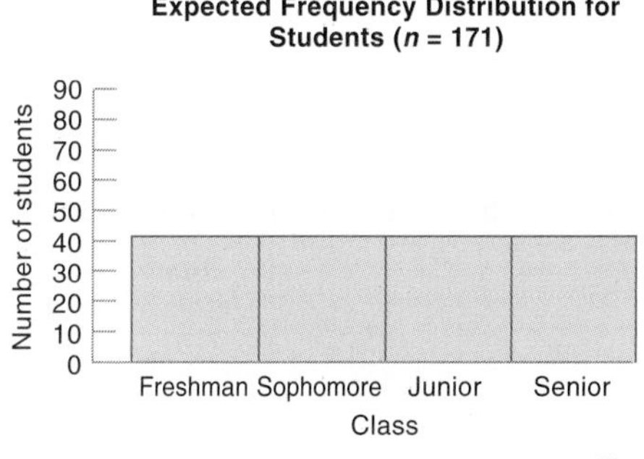

■

In the case of the uniform distribution, there is not much calculation involved in finding the expected frequencies of the probability distribution. For other probability distributions, you will need to do some additional calculations to find the expected frequencies.

EXAMPLE 15.5 Quality Problems

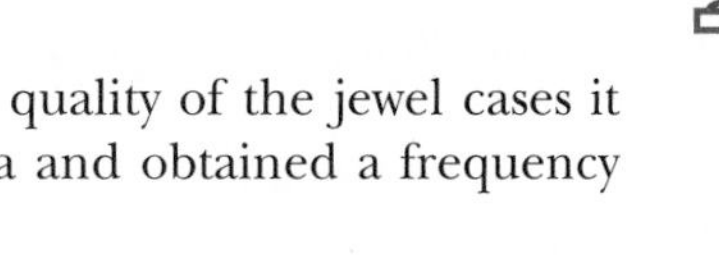

Calculating the Expected Frequencies

The software manufacturer who is wondering about the quality of the jewel cases it purchases from an outside vendor has collected the data and obtained a frequency distribution and histogram:

Number of Defective Cases	Frequency
0	485
1	340
2	127
3	48
4	0
5	0
Total	**1000**

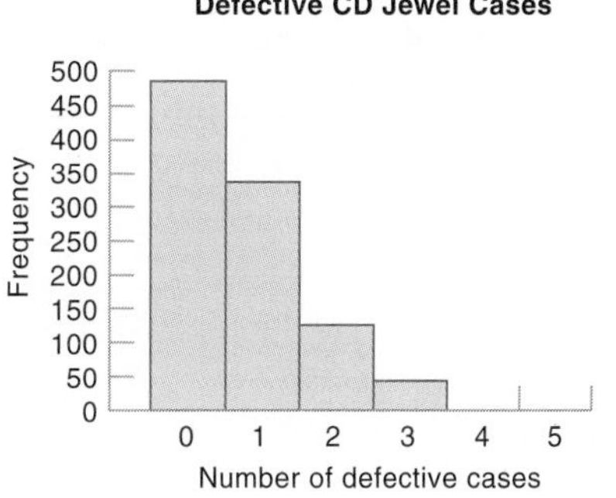

Analyze the Data

The data have the right shape for a binomial distribution with a small value of π but there seem to be too many crates that have a high number of defective cases.

The next step is to determine the expected frequencies for the binomial distribution with $n = 5$ and $\pi = 0.10$. Looking in the binomial tables, the manufacturer finds that the probability distribution is

x	0	1	2	3	4	5
$p(x)$	0.590	0.328	0.073	0.008	0.000	0.000

The *expected* frequency for each class of the frequency distribution, e_i, is calculated by multiplying the probability for that class by the sample size:

$$e_i = np_i$$

where n is the sample size of the data, and p_i is the probability that the value in the ith class will occur. For this problem, $n = 1000$, so we have

x	np_i
0	$(1000)(0.590) = 590$
1	$(1000)(0.328) = 328$
2	$(1000)(0.073) = 73$
3	$(1000)(0.008) = 8$
4	$(1000)(0.000) = 0$
5	$(1000)(0.000) = 0$

Putting it all together in one table, we see that there is definitely a difference between the observed and expected frequencies.

The reason for the discrepancy in the totals is rounding. If the binomial tables had 4 decimal places you could find the expected frequencies to 1 decimal place and avoid the problem.

Number of Defective Cases	Observed Frequency	Expected Frequency
0	485	590
1	340	328
2	127	73
3	48	8
4	0	0
5	0	0
Total	**1000**	**999**

■

TRY IT NOW!

Seat-Belt Usage *Calculating the Expected Frequencies*

The insurance analysts collect data for 1000 samples of 10 drivers and obtain the frequency distribution shown in the table. Find the expected frequency distribution for the data if the distribution is really binomial with $n = 10$ and $\pi = 0.70$.

Number Wearing Seat Belts (x)	Observed Frequency	$p(x)$	Expected Frequency
0	0		
1	0		
2	1		
3	6		
4	33		
5	116		
6	213		

For the moment, don't worry about rounding if the expected frequency column does not add to 1.

(continued)

Number Wearing Seat Belts (x)	Observed Frequency	$p(x)$	Expected Frequency
7	275		
8	216		
9	119		
10	21		
Total	**1000**		

Create frequency histograms for both the observed and the expected frequency distributions. At this point, does it appear that the observed data conform to the binomial distribution with $n = 10$ and $\pi = 0.70$? Why or why not?

Once we have collected the data, formed a hypothesis, and found the expected frequencies for the hypothesized distribution, we need to find a way to quantify the results of the test. The next section describes how to do this.

15.2.2 The Chi-Square Statistic

You know from previous work that often it is departure from what we expect to happen that leads us to perform a hypothesis test. The question is, How can we quantify the "deviation" from what is expected, and how will we know when what we observe deviates by more than it should or more than is likely by pure chance? To answer

---

ANS.

$p(x)$	EXPECTED F
0.000	0
0.000	0
0.001	1
0.009	9
0.037	37
0.103	103
0.200	200
0.267	267
0.233	233
0.121	121
0.028	28

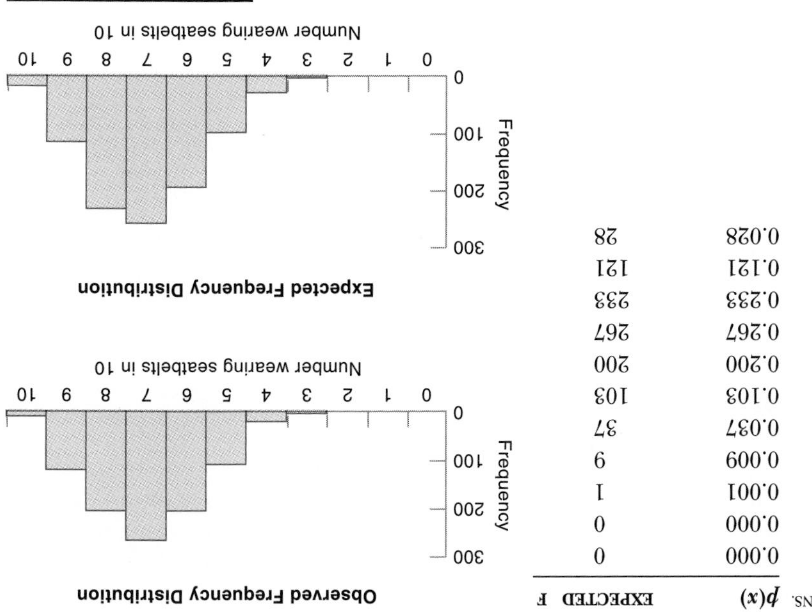

these questions we need to define a test statistic that measures the deviation of interest and has a sampling distribution whose behavior we understand. This test statistic is known as the **chi-square statistic** and is calculated as

Chi-square statistic

$$\chi^2 = \frac{\sum_{i=1}^{k} (o_i - e_i)^2}{e_i}$$

where

o_i = observed frequency in the ith class of the frequency distribution
e_i = expected frequency in the ith class of the frequency distribution
k = the number of classes in the frequency distribution

Don't worry too much abut the value of p right now. It will explained in detail later on when we need it.

This test statistic has a chi-square distribution with $k - p - 1$ degrees of freedom, where p = the number of parameters of the theoretical distribution that were estimated from the data.

This statistic is a little different from any that you have encountered before. We are trying to measure the amount by which the observed frequency distribution deviates from the expected frequency distribution. Clearly, looking at the difference between the two quantities, $o_i - e_i$, is a good start. Just as clearly, though, if you simply add the deviations they will cancel each other out, since some will be positive and some will be negative. So, just as we did when we learned about the variance and the standard deviation, we square the quantities so that they are all positive. Adding the squared deviations together is a measure of *total* deviation. Dividing by e_i is similar to calculating the *percent error* instead of the *absolute error*.

EXAMPLE 15.6 College Drinking

Calculating the Chi-Square Statistic

For the example about the distribution of students, we can calculate the chi-square statistic by extending the frequency table that we have developed:

Analyze the Data

Class	Observed Frequency (o_i)	Expected Frequency (e_i)	$o_i - e_i$	$\frac{(o_i - e_i)^2}{e_i}$
Freshman	86	42.75	43.25	43.76
Sophomore	36	42.75	−6.75	1.07
Junior	30	42.75	−12.75	3.80
Senior	19	42.75	−23.75	13.19
Total (n)	**171**	**171**		**61.82**

You see that the value of the test statistic is 61.82. This is a measure of the **total** deviation of the observed frequencies from the expected frequencies. The question now is, What does this tell us about the distribution of students? ■

EXAMPLE 15.7 Quality Problems

Calculating the Chi-Square Statistic

From the data that were collected it appears that there are definitely differences between the observed data and what would be expected if indeed the population is binomial with $\pi = 0.10$ and $n = 5$. To quantify the total difference we need to calculate the chi-square test statistic:

Number of Defective Cases	Observed Frequency	Expected Frequency	$o_i - e_i$	$\frac{(o_i - e_i)^2}{e_i}$
0	485	590.5	−105.5	18.85
1	340	328.1	11.9	0.43
2	127	73.0	54	39.95
3	48	8.1	39.9	196.54
4	0	0.5	−0.5	0.5
5	0	0.0	0.0	0.0
Total	**1000**	**1000.2**	**−0.2**	**256.27**

To avoid large errors from rounding, the probabilities were calculated with a computer package and the expected frequencies were calculated to 1 decimal place.

Analyze the Data

From the calculation of the chi-square statistic we see that the measure of total deviation between the expected and observed frequencies is 256.77. We also see that the classes in the frequency distribution for values of 2 and 3 contribute the most to the total. ■

TRY IT NOW!

Seat-Belt Usage ***Calculating the Chi-Square Statistic***

Fill in the table to calculate the value of the chi-square statistic for the data obtained by the insurance analysts.

Number Wearing Seat Belts	Observed Frequency	$p(x)$	Expected Frequency	$o - e$	$\frac{(o - e)^2}{e}$
0	0	0.000	0		
1	0	0.000	0		
2	1	0.001	1		
3	6	0.009	9		
4	33	0.037	37		
5	116	0.103	103		
6	213	0.200	200		
7	275	0.267	267		
8	216	0.233	233		
9	119	0.121	121		
10	21	0.028	28		
Total	**1000**	**0.999**	**999**		

ANS.

$o - e$	$(o - e)^2/e$
0	—
0	—
0	0.00
−3	1.00
−4	0.43
13	1.64
13	0.85
8	0.24
−17	1.24
−2	0.03
−7	1.75
	7.18

Once we have quantified the difference between the observed and expected frequency distributions, we are ready to determine whether the difference is significant.

15.2.3 The Critical Value and the Decision Rule

We now have a way to measure the deviation of the observed data from what is expected, the chi-square statistic, and we know that this test statistic has a χ^2 distribution with $k - 1 - p$ degrees of freedom. All that remains of the test is finding the critical value and making a decision about our hypothesis.

To find the appropriate critical value we will need a level of significance for the test, α. Chi-square goodness of fit tests are always one-sided and upper-tail tests. This is because we are looking at the *total deviation* and trying to see if that *exceeds* some reasonable level. To find the critical value we look up $\chi^2_{\alpha,k-p-1}$ for the appropriate values of α and $k - p - 1$, as shown in Figure 15.1.

To make a decision about our hypothesis we compare the value of the test statistic to the critical value. Since it is an upper-tail test, if the chi-square test statistic is greater than the χ^2 value from the table we will reject H_0 and conclude that the data did not come from the hypothesized distribution. If the chi-square statistic is less than the critical value, we fail to reject H_0 and conclude that there is no evidence that the hypothesized distribution is not appropriate.

There are two things we must know to find the critical value for the test: the level of significance of the test, α, and the degrees of freedom, $k - p - 1$.

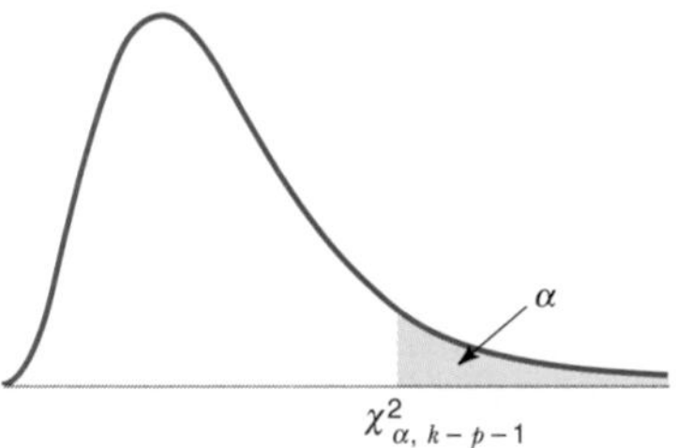

FIGURE 15.1 The upper tail of a chi-square distribution

EXAMPLE 15.8 College Drinking

Performing the Chi-Square Test

For the problem with the student distribution, suppose we would like to perform the test at the 0.05 level of significance. This would mean that there is a 5% chance that the test will conclude that the data collected did not come from the uniform distribution when in fact it did.

Analyze the Data

To determine the number of degrees of freedom, we first look at the number of classes in the frequency distribution, k. In this case, $k = 4$. The value p represents the number of population parameters we estimated from the data. In this case we did not use the data to estimate any parameters. Thus, the number of degrees of freedom for the test is $4 - 0 - 1 = 3$. From the chi-square table, we look up $\chi^2_{0.05,3}$ and find that the critical value is 7.82.

To make a decision, we compare the chi-square test statistic, 61.82, to the critical value of 7.82. Since 61.82 is larger than 7.82 (the test statistic falls beyond or outside the critical value) we reject H_0. That is, the conclusion of the test is that the data do not come from a population that has a uniform distribution. This indicates that the survey was not evenly spread out over the 4 years. ■

Draw Conclusions

EXAMPLE 15.9 Quality Problems

Performing the Chi-Square Test

The software company found the value of the chi-square statistic for the data on the defective jewel cases to be 256.27. To decide what this means, it needs to find the critical value for the test, compare the test statistic to the critical value, and make a decision.

Analyze the Data

To find the critical value the company analysts must know α and the degrees of freedom for the test. They have already decided to test at the 0.05 level of significance. The number of degrees of freedom for the test is calculated to be

$$\text{Degrees of freedom} = k - p - 1 = 6 - 0 - 1 = 5$$

Remember that p is the number of parameters of the hypothesized distribution that were estimated from the data. The binomial distribution has 2 parameters, n and π, both of which were given or assumed, not estimated.

Draw Conclusions

This critical value, $\chi^2_{0.05,5}$, is 11.07. Since 256.27 is clearly beyond the critical value, the software company can reject H_0 and conclude that the number of defective jewel cases in a sample of 5 does not have a binomial distribution with $\pi = 0.10$. That is, the data do not fit the assumed probability model. ■

TRY IT NOW!

Seat-Belt Usage ***Finding the Critical Value and Performing the Test***

The insurance analysts decide that they want to test the goodness of fit hypotheses at the 0.01 level of significance.

How many degrees of freedom will the critical value for the test have?

Find the critical value for the test.

Based on the chi-square test statistic and the critical value, what can you conclude about the distribution of the number of people in a sample of size 10 that wear seat belts?

One of the things that happens as we learn more and more statistical techniques is that we lose sight of the fact that we are doing the analyses to help us identify problems, that is, to understand why things happen and to make informed decisions. After the chi-square goodness of fit test, what do we know and how can we use the information?

ANS. DEGREES OF FREEDOM = 10. CRITICAL VALUE IS 23.21. WE CANNOT REJECT H_0. THERE IS NO REASON TO BELIEVE THAT THE HYPOTHESIZED DISTRIBUTION IS INCORRECT.

Understand the Problem

EXAMPLE 15.10 College Drinking

After the Test Is Over . . .

As a result of the chi-square test, the researcher who administered the survey on binge drinking knows that the distribution of students in his sample is not uniformly distributed over the four classes. This *means* that his sample *may not be representative of the population he is trying to study* and that he will have to be careful about any conclusions or generalizations he makes.

In this case, the researcher began to think a little more about his null hypothesis. Does it really make sense that students are uniformly distributed over the four classes? After some thought he realized that if you consider the problems of student retention (loss of students from transfer or dropout) and the transfer in of students from other universities and community colleges, it is more likely that the true percentage of students in each class decreases as the class level increases. He contacted the university administrator who keeps track of such things and found out that the historical distribution of students is the one in the table:

Collect the Data

Class	Expected Distribution (%)	Expected Frequency
Freshman	45.2	77.3
Sophomore	18.6	31.8
Junior	18.0	30.8
Senior	18.2	31.1
Total (n)	**100**	**171**

The researcher then decided to compare the actual frequency distribution to the new distribution obtained from the university and redo the chi-square test. The comparison is shown here in the table:

Analyze the Data

Class	Observed Frequency (o_i)	Expected Frequency (e_i)	$o - e$	$\frac{(o-e)^2}{e}$
Freshman	86	77.3	8.7	0.98
Sophomore	36	31.8	4.2	0.55
Junior	30	30.8	−0.8	0.02
Senior	19	31.1	−12.1	4.71
Total (n)	**171**	**171.0**		**6.26**

Draw Conclusions

Since nothing else changed, the critical value of the test is still $\chi^2_{0.05,3} = 7.82$. The value of the test statistic, 6.26, is not outside the critical value so there is not sufficient evidence to reject H_0. This means that there is no reason to say that the sample did not come from a population with the hypothesized distribution and so it is reasonable to assume that the sample is representative of the student population of the university *as defined by the university administration.* ■

One of the benefits of the chi-square test is that it lets us proceed with confidence in our analysis. Knowing that the sample does indeed represent the population of interest gives much more credibility to any conclusions drawn from the analysis.

EXAMPLE 15.11 Quality Problems

After the Test Is Over . . .

The company that used the outside vendor as a source of CD jewel cases knows as a result of the test that the number of defective cases in a sample of size 5 does not have a binomial distribution with $\pi = 0.10$. The company does *not* know whether the distribution is binomial with a different value of π or whether some other factor makes the binomial distribution inappropriate. This is the time to use some common sense, knowledge of how the data were collected, and descriptive and graphical statistics to see if the company can identify the problem.

There are many things that the company analysts could do, depending on how they collected the data and what variables they recorded, but in this case they decided to plot the data in the order in which the cases were produced. Each sample that they took came from a different box and they recorded the lot number and production data along with the data on the number of defective cases. A time plot of the data indicated that there was an increase in the number of defectives in the sample starting at about the 750th sample. Since the first plot was very dense the analysts decided to also plot every fifth sample so that they could see the shift more clearly.

Draw Conclusions

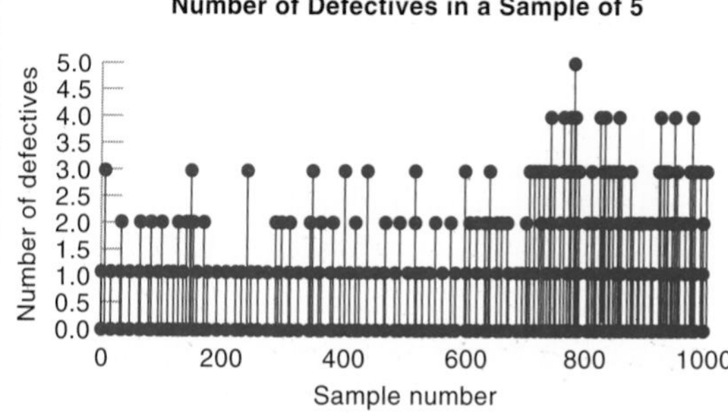

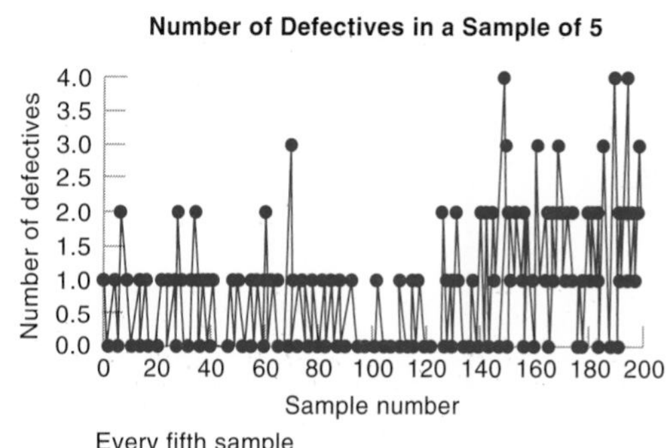

As a result of the chi-square test and the plot of the data they learned that the percent defective had apparently changed during production. This is why the binomial distribution was not correct. ■

15.2.4 Testing for Normality and Other Considerations

The results of the chi-square goodness of fit test are similar to the test you learned for testing whether the variances of two populations are equal. The test does not result in a definitive answer that the hypothesized distribution is correct, just as the hypothesis test to see if two variances are equal does not tell you that the variances are equal. Rather, if you reject H_0, it will tell you when the hypothesized distribution is *not* correct. When you are using a chi-square test to test the assumption of normality, you will either decide that the assumption of normality is not appropriate, or that since there is no evidence to the contrary, the assumption is a reasonable one.

EXAMPLE 15.12 Jar Weights

Testing for Normality

The quality specifications for a 15.0-ounce jar of peanut butter state that the weights of the jars should be normally distributed with a mean of 15.1 oz. The Quality Focus Group for the product line selects a random sample of 500 jars to determine whether the specifications are being met. It decides to test at the 0.05 level of significance.

Understand the Problem

Collect the Data

The hypotheses for the test are

H_0: The jar weights are normally distributed with $\mu = 15.1$ oz.

H_A: The jar weights are not normally distributed with $\mu = 15.1$ oz.

The group collects the data and uses a computer package to create a frequency distribution and histogram.

Weights (<)	Observed Frequency
14.75	3
14.80	5
14.85	34
14.90	43
14.95	79
15.00	83
15.05	92
15.10	77
15.15	56
15.20	20
15.25	5
15.30	1
15.35	1
15.40	1
Total	**500**

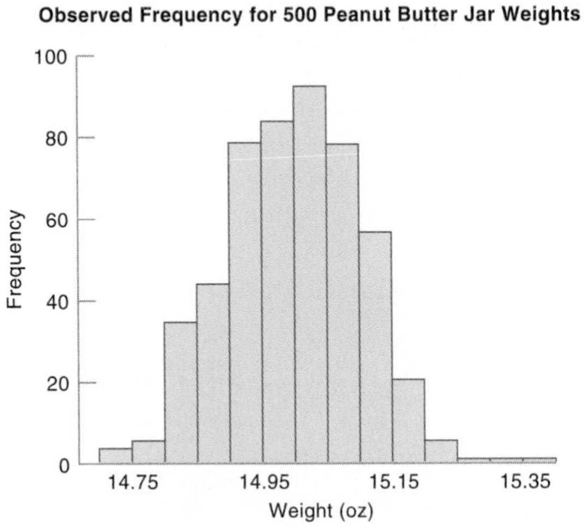

The software package creates classes the same way you have learned. For example, 14.80 is the same as $14.75 < x \leq 14.80$.

The data are symmetric, although this does not mean that they are definitely normally distributed.

To calculate the expected frequency for each class the analysts need to calculate the probability that a randomly selected jar will fall into the weight range defined by each class. For the first class they need to find $P(14.70 < X \leq 14.75)$.

Remember from Chapter 6 that you need to turn the two values into standard normals (Z's) and look them up. But to do that you need μ and σ! The specifications for the jars give only a value for μ, so the analysts will have to use the data to estimate σ.

Analyze the Data

Using the same software package, they find that the sample standard deviation, s, is 0.102 oz. So, to find the probability of interest they use

$$\text{For } 14.70: \quad z = \frac{14.70 - 15.10}{0.102} = -3.92$$

$$\text{For } 14.75: \quad z = \frac{14.75 - 15.10}{0.102} = -3.43$$

Looking up the Z values in the table and subtracting the results, they find that $P(14.70 < X \leq 14.75) = 0.0003 - 0.0000 = 0.0003$. When they were doing the calculations, they noticed that there was a discrepancy between the total for the expected frequency and the total of 500 observations. Looking at the table, they realized that this was probably because there were a few additional classes on the high side that had nonzero probabilities. They expanded the table to include these classes.

To find the expected number of jars out of the 500 that would weigh between 14.70 and 14.75 oz the analysts multiplied the probability by 500 and obtained (0.0003) (500) = 0.15. They found the probabilities and expected frequencies for all of the classes:

Weight (<)	Frequency	Observed $P(a < X < b)$	Expected Frequency	$\frac{(o_i - e_i)^2}{e_i}$
14.75	3	0.0003	0.1	84.10
14.80	5	0.0013	0.7	28.13
14.85	34	0.0055	2.7	355.99
14.90	43	0.0179	8.9	130.33
14.95	79	0.0458	22.9	137.71
15.00	83	0.0927	46.4	28.93
15.05	92	0.1486	74.3	4.23
15.10	77	0.1879	94.0	3.07
15.15	56	0.1879	94.0	15.36
15.20	20	0.1486	74.3	39.66
15.25	5	0.0927	46.4	36.91
15.30	1	0.0458	22.9	20.92
15.35	1	0.0179	8.9	7.03
15.40	1	0.0055	2.7	1.11
15.45	0	0.0013	0.7	0.67
15.50	0	0.0003	0.1	0.13
Total	**500**	**1.0000**	**500**	**894.28**

Looking at the chi-square statistic, there would appear to be some kind of problem. The data may not be *exactly* normally distributed, but they are not that far off. Why is the value of the test statistic so large? ■

Before we proceed any further with the example we need to discuss some of the problems with the chi-square goodness of fit test. The problems are related to the number of observations that are used to create the frequency distribution.

You may remember from Chapter 3 that a fairly large sample size is required to obtain a good frequency distribution. If your frequency histogram is highly variable due to lack of data, the frequencies in some classes will have greater differences from the expected frequencies.

Another related problem is that when the total sample size is small, the expected frequencies for each class will also be small. Since the chi-square statistic divides by the expected frequency, this can inflate the value of the statistic artificially and lead to rejection of H_0 when, in fact, it is true. For this reason, it is recommended that the chi-square test not be used if the expected frequency in any cell is less than 5. If this is not the case, it is possible to combine adjacent cells to get the expected frequencies above 5, but this results in a loss of degrees of freedom.

Remember, dividing by numbers close to 0 causes the result to be large.

EXAMPLE 15.13 Jar Weights

Analyze the Data

Collapsing Classes When the Expected Frequencies Are <5

Looking at the table of the observed and expected frequencies, the Quality Focus Group for the product called in a statistician to help them. The statistician explained that there are too many classes with very small expected frequencies that are causing the chi-square statistic to be inflated. The group decides to collapse cells on both ends of the distribution to get the expected frequencies above 5. The table was adjusted and the chi-square statistic recalculated:

Weight (<)	Observed Frequency		P(a<X<b)	Expected Frequency		$\frac{(o_i - e_i)^2}{e_i}$
14.75	3	85	0.0003	0.1	12.4	423.89
14.80	5		0.0013	0.7		
14.85	34		0.0055	2.7		
14.90	43		0.0179	8.9		
14.95	79		0.0458	22.9		137.71
15.00	83		0.0927	46.4		28.93
15.05	92		0.1486	74.3		4.23
15.10	77		0.1880	94.0		3.07
15.15	56		0.1880	94.0		15.36
15.20	20		0.1486	74.3		39.66
15.25	5		0.0927	46.4		36.91
15.30	1		0.0458	22.9		20.92
15.35	1	2	0.0179	8.9	12.4	8.78
15.40	1		0.0055	2.7		
15.45	0		0.0013	0.7		
15.50	0		0.0003	0.1		
Total	**500**		**1.0000**	**500**		**719.46**

After collapsing classes there were only 10 classes left. Also, the normal distribution has two parameters, μ and σ, and the data were used to estimate one of them, σ.

Clearly, the chi-square statistic is still large, but it has been considerably reduced.

To complete the test, the Quality Focus Group found the critical value for the test. It calculated the degrees of freedom to be

$$\text{Degrees of freedom } = k - p - 1 = 10 - 1 - 1 = 8$$

Since it wanted to test at $\alpha = 0.05$, it used $\chi^2_{0.05,8} = 15.51$.

Since the value of the test statistic, 719.46, is beyond the critical value of 15.51, the group rejects H_0 and concludes that the jar weights are not normally distributed with a mean of 15.1 oz and a standard deviation of 0.102 oz. ■

Again, we need to look at the conclusion of the chi-square goodness of fit test and realize that, in fact, the conclusion comes as a package deal. In the previous example the conclusion is that the data do not come from a normal distribution with a mean of 15.1 oz. It is not necessarily true that the data are not normally distributed—they might be normally distributed with a *different mean* than the one hypothesized. It is also not necessarily true that the mean is not 15.1 oz; the mean could be 15.1 oz, but the distribution *might not be normal.* To really know what is going on here, the Quality Focus Group might want to perform a hypothesis test about the value of the mean to see whether that is the problem, or rerun the chi-square test using the data to estimate μ.

15.2.5 Exercises—Learning It!

15.1 The administration of a university has been using the following distribution to classify the ages of their students:

Age Group	Estimated % of Student Population
Less than 18	2.7
18–19	29.9
20–24	53.4
Older than 24	14

A recent student survey provided the following data on age of students:

Age Group	Frequency
Less than 18	6
18–19	118
21–24	102
Older than 24	26

(a) Set up a table that compares the expected and observed frequencies for each group.

(b) Based on the table, do you think that the data represent the estimated distribution?

(c) Set up the hypotheses for the chi-square goodness of fit test.

(d) Perform the goodness of fit test at the 0.05 level of significance.

(e) Based on the chi-square test, is the estimated age distribution that the university is using correct?

15.2 As part of a survey on the use of Office Suites Software, the company doing the polling wanted to know whether its population was uniformly distributed over the following age distribution: under 25, 25 to 44, 45 and up. The company looked at the data it had collected so far and found the following distribution:

Age Group	Number of Respondents
Under 25	73
25 to 44	61
45 and up	66
Total	**200**

(a) Based on the data, do you think that the respondents are uniformly distributed over the age categories?

(b) Set up the hypotheses to test whether the data are uniformly distributed over the age categories.

(c) Find the expected frequency distribution and perform the chi-square goodness of fit test.

(d) At the 0.05 level of significance, would you say that the respondents were uniformly distributed over the age groups?

15.3 The Transit Authority in a large city estimates that 80% of business commuters get a seat for their entire commute. It decided to take a random sample of its subway system over the course of a 12-week period to see whether its estimate is correct. It set up an exit poll at the most common destination station and asked 15 randomly selected commuters whether they got a seat for the entire commute. The data the Transit Authority obtained are as follows:

Number of Commuters in 15 Who Got Seats	Count
0	0
1	0
2	0
3	0
4	0
5	0
6	0
7	0
8	1
9	3
10	10
11	21
12	31
13	20
14	9
15	5
Total	**100**

(a) Why is the number of commuters in 15 who got seats a binomial random variable?

(b) Set up the hypotheses to test whether the sample data come from a binomial distribution with $n = 15$ and $\pi = 0.80$.

(c) Find the expected frequencies for the hypothesized distribution.

(d) Perform the chi-square goodness of fit test at the 0.01 level of significance.

(e) Is it reasonable to assume that the data come from a binomial distribution with $n = 15$ and $\pi = 0.80$?

15.4 One of the assumptions of the small sample (t) hypothesis test about a mean is that the underlying population is normally distributed. The accompanying data represent the diameter of the holes in washers that were purchased by a company. The specification on the washers is that the mean diameter of the hole be 0.5000 in.

0.5053	0.5098	0.4606	0.4606
0.4711	0.4627	0.4800	0.4800
0.4672	0.5642	0.5495	0.5495
0.4672	0.5346	0.5745	0.5745
0.5340	0.3767	0.3933	0.3933

(a) Make a frequency distribution and a histogram for the data. Do not use more than 5 classes.

(b) From the histogram, would you be willing to believe that the data are normally distributed?

(c) Set up the hypotheses to test that the data come from a normal distribution with a mean of 0.5000 and a standard deviation of 0.0600 in.

(d) Find the expected frequency distribution of the data.

(e) At the 0.05 level of significance, does it appear reasonable to assume that the data are normally distributed?

15.5 A large banking corporation believes that 80% of the loan applications it receives are approved within 24 hours. It decides to take a random sample of 10 loan applications every day for 3 months and record the number of the applications that are approved within 24 hours. The following data are obtained:

Number of Loan Applications in 10 Approved in 24 Hours	Frequency
4	1
5	5
6	11
7	19
8	27
9	18
10	7
Total	**88**

(a) Set up the necessary hypotheses to test whether the data come from a binomial distribution with $n = 10$ and $p = 0.80$.

(b) Find the expected frequency distribution for the data.

(c) At the 0.05 level of significance, is it reasonable to assume that the number of loan applications that are approved in 24 hours has a binomial distribution with $\pi = 0.80$?

15.3 TESTING PROPORTIONS FROM MORE THAN TWO POPULATIONS

In Chapter 10 you learned how to compare parameters from two different populations. In particular, you learned that you can use a Z test to determine whether the population proportions for two populations are equal. What if you are interested in comparing the population proportions for *more than two populations?*

Using a chi-square test, it is possible to compare proportions for more than two populations. Although it would be possible to compare a set of c populations by using the Z test you learned in Chapter 10 to test all of the possible pairs of populations, this is not a good thing to do. The reason for doing the single test is that each hypothesis test you do has a type I error probability associated with it. When you do multiple tests there is an increased chance that you will decide that two population proportions are different when in fact they are not. The single test controls the probability of making this mistake.

15.3.1 Testing Proportions for More Than Two Populations

In general, some characteristic of importance (a success) is defined for several different populations. We want to determine whether the proportion of successes in each population is the same. That is, the general set of hypotheses we wish to test is

$$H_0: \ \pi_1 = \pi_2 = \cdots = \pi_c$$

$$H_A: \ \text{At least one } \pi_i \text{ is different.}$$

To test these hypotheses for two populations you take a sample from each population and count the number of times that the characteristic of interest occurs. The data collection for more than two populations is the same.

In Chapter 5 you learned how to summarize data that involved two qualitative variables—the contingency table. For this test the two variables are the population that the sample item comes from ($i = 1, 2, \ldots, c$) and whether the item is a success (the characteristic is present) or a failure (the characteristic is not present). An example of the contingency table is shown in Table 15.1.

The proportion of successes for each population can be calculated as

$$p_i = \frac{s_i}{n_i}$$

TABLE 15.1 Data Table for Testing Equality of Proportions

	Population				
Number of	**1**	**2**	**. . .**	**c**	**Totals**
Successes	s_1	s_2	. . .	s_c	s
Failures	f_1	f_2	. . .	f_c	f
Total	n_1	n_2	. . .	n_c	n

EXAMPLE 15.14 College Drinking

Understand the Problem

Setting Up a Chi-Square Test of Proportions

For the purposes of the study on binge drinking, students were classified as nonbinge drinkers, infrequent binge drinkers, and frequent binge drinkers. One question of interest to the researcher was whether there was a difference in academic responsibility among the three different categories of drinkers. He decided to look at the question of whether the proportion of people who missed class because of drinking is the same for each of the three groups. He created the contingency table shown here:

	Type of Drinker			
Miss Class	**Nonbinge**	**Infrequent**	**Frequent**	**Total**
Never	77	39	31	**147**
Once or More	7	19	39	**65**
Total	**84**	**58**	**70**	**212**

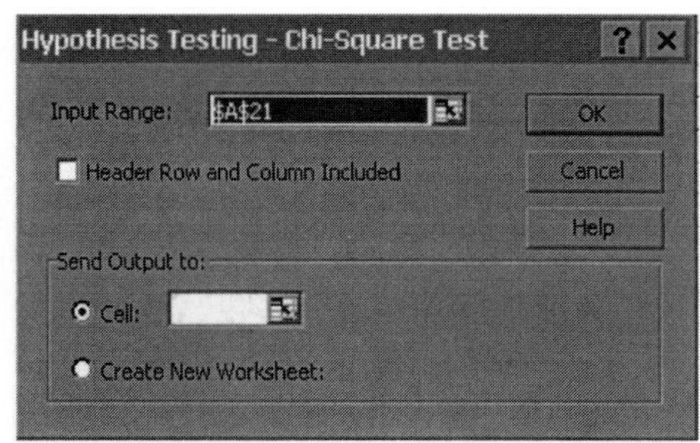

FIGURE 15.7 Dialog box for Chi-Square Test

Indicate where you want the output located and then click **OK.** The output for the binge drinking data is shown in Figure 15.8.

Chi-square test statistic	= 15.3884	Number of:	
p-value	= 0.0174	rows =	4
		columns =	3

Actual frequencies

		Variable B			
		Non-binge	Infrequent	Frequent	Totals
Variable A	Residence Hall or Dormitory	35	25	46	106
	Fraternity or Sorority	0	1	0	1
	Other University Housing	0	2	1	3
	Off Campus House or Apartment	49	30	24	103
	Totals	84	58	71	213

Chi-square calculations

		Variable B		
		Non-binge	Infrequent	Frequent
Variable A	Residence Hall or Dormitory	1.1071	0.5172	3.2201
	Fraternity or Sorority	0.3944	1.9447	0.3333
	Other University Housing	1.1831	1.7135	0.0000
	Off Campus House or Apartment	1.7289	0.1360	3.1100

Expected frequencies

		Variable B			
		Non-binge	Infrequent	Frequent	Totals
Variable A	Residence Hall or Dormitory	41.8028	28.8638	35.3333	106
	Fraternity or Sorority	0.3944	0.2723	0.3333	1
	Other University Housing	1.1831	0.8169	1.0000	3
	Off Campus House or Apartment	40.6197	28.0469	34.3333	103
	Totals	84	58	71	213

NOTE: Expected frequencies should not be less than 5.0

FIGURE 15.8 KADDSTAT output from Chi-Square Test

CHAPTER 15 SUMMARY

The chi-square test involves comparing observed and expected frequencies for different classes of data. The test is quite versatile and can be used to test *goodness of fit, equality of proportions for more than two populations,* and *independence of qualitative variables.*

As is true with *any* statistical tool, the results of a chi-square test do not *solve* a problem or make a decision for the user. They simply point out when further action is indicated and when it is not. Solving the real problem requires knowledge of the situation and sometimes further data collection and analysis.

Key Terms

Term	Definition	Page Reference
Chi-square goodness of fit test	The **chi-square goodness of fit test** checks to see how well a set of data fits the model for a particular probability distribution.	762
Expected frequencies, e_i	The **expected frequencies** are the number of observations that should fall into each class in a frequency distribution under the hypothesized probability distribution.	762
Independent events	Two events are independent if the probability that one event occurs is not affected or changed by the occurrence of the other event.	238
Observed frequencies, o_i	The **observed frequencies** are the actual number of observations that fall into each class in a frequency distribution or histogram.	762
Uniform distribution	A **uniform distribution** is one in which each outcome or class of outcomes is equally likely to occur.	763

Key Formulas

Term	Formula	Page Reference
Chi-square critical value	$\chi^2_{\alpha, k-p-1}$	770
Chi-square statistic	$\chi^2 = \dfrac{\sum_{i=1}^{k} (o_i - e_i)^2}{e_i}$	768
Degrees of freedom for goodness of fit test	$k - p - 1$	768
Degrees of freedom for test for independence	$(r - 1)(c - 1)$	795
Expected frequency for test for independence	$e_{ij} = \left(\dfrac{r_i}{n}\dfrac{c_j}{n}\right)n = \dfrac{r_i c_j}{n}$	792
Expected frequency for test for proportions	$e_i = \dfrac{s}{n} n_i = \dfrac{sn_i}{n} = pn_i$	781
Overall proportion of success	$p = \dfrac{s_1 + s_2 + \cdots + s_c}{n_1 + n_2 + \cdots + n_c} = \dfrac{s}{n}$	781
Probability for independent events	P(A AND B) = P(A) × P(B)	238

CHAPTER 15 EXERCISES

Learning It!

15.14 A random sample of 69 Porsche drivers were asked how many miles they had driven their vehicle in the past calendar year. A frequency table for the data is given here:

Number of Miles	Observed Frequency
$0 < x \leq 4000$	20
$4000 < x \leq 8000$	22
$8000 < x \leq 12{,}000$	14
$12{,}000 < x \leq 16{,}000$	6

(continued)

Number of Miles	Observed Frequency
$16{,}000 < x \leq 20{,}000$	1
$20{,}000 < x \leq 24{,}000$	4
$24{,}000 < x \leq 28{,}000$	0
$28{,}000 < x \leq 32{,}000$	2

(a) Set up the hypotheses to test whether the number of miles driven by Porsche drivers is normally distributed with a mean of 7500 miles with a standard deviation of 6500 miles.

(b) Find the expected frequencies for each cell.

(c) Calculate the chi-square test statistic. If necessary, collapse cells so that the expected frequency for each category is at least 5.

(d) At the 0.05 level of significance, what can you conclude about the number of miles driven annually by Porsche drivers?

15.15 To begin a study comparing the monthly salaries of the auditors for a particular company to accountants' salaries in the industry in general, a random sample of 30 auditors was taken and their monthly salaries recorded. The data are shown here:

3069	3276	3333	3484	3570
3072	3310	3383	3498	3593
3137	3313	3412	3515	3603
3144	3323	3446	3532	3649
3269	3330	3456	3551	3659

(a) Create a frequency distribution for the data using six classes and display the data graphically.

(b) Do you think that the assumption that the data are normally distributed is at least reasonable? Why or why not?

(c) Set up the hypotheses to test whether the data come from a normal population that has a mean of \$3150 and a standard deviation of \$165.

(d) Perform the chi-square goodness of fit test with a level of significance of 0.05.

(e) What does the test tell you about the data?

15.16 The problem of workplace violence is growing. A survey of 600 full-time American workers on workplace violence concentrated on those respondents who were victims of harassment, threat of physical violence, and actual physical violence. In follow-up interviews the victims were asked to identify the major effect that the violence had on them. The data are shown here:

Major Effect on Worker	Type of Violence		
	Harassment	Threat	Physical
Psychological	56	28	15
Disrupted work life	39	13	12
Physical injury or sickness	15	5	10
No negative effect	5	7	6

(a) Suppose that the group that conducted the study was interested in whether the type of violence that a person experienced is related to the effect of the violence on their life. Set up the hypotheses for this test.

(b) Find the expected frequencies for each cell.

(c) Without collapsing any categories, how many degrees of freedom will the test have?

(d) At the 0.05 level of significance, are type of violence and effect on a worker independent?

15.17 Through the 1990s the number of people taking the drug Prozac increased dramatically. As part of the General Social Survey done in 1998, information was collected on whether the respondents had ever taken Prozac and the region of the country in which they lived. The data follow.

Taken Prozac	Region of Interview: New England	Middle Atlantic	East North Central	West North Central	South Atlantic	East South Atlantic	West South Central	Mountain	Pacific
Yes	8	11	17	10	25	8	6	7	5
No	52	148	188	84	202	67	108	81	148

(a) Set up the hypotheses to test whether the proportion of people who take Prozac is the same for all regions of the United States.

(b) Calculate the overall proportion of people who take Prozac.

(c) Find the expected frequencies for each cell.

(d) Calculate the chi-square statistic.

(e) At the 0.05 level of significance, do the data indicate that the proportion of people who take Prozac is the same for all regions?

15.18 In the survey about using Office Suite software the researchers were interested in finding whether the proportion of people who installed the software themselves was different for different age groups. They created the contingency table shown here:

Install Software	Age Group: Under 25	25 to 44	45 and Up
Yes	8	45	94
No	9	14	31

(a) Set up the hypotheses to test whether the proportion of people who install their own Office Suite software is the same for all three age groups.

(b) Use the data to calculate the overall proportion of people who install their own Office Suite software.

(c) Find the expected frequencies for each cell and calculate the chi-square statistic.

(d) At the 0.05 level of significance, what can you conclude about the proportion of people who install their own Office Suite software?

15.19 A software company that was looking at the time to failure of the diskettes it uses decides to look at its two suppliers of the product. The specifications for the product state that the life of the diskette should be normally distributed with a mean of 500 hours and a standard deviation of 5 hours. The data for each of the suppliers are shown here:

Supplier A					Supplier B				
474	492	498	504	511	487	492	495	497	499
486	492	500	505	511	488	492	495	497	499
489	494	501	506	512	489	492	495	497	499
490	494	501	507	513	489	492	495	497	501
490	494	501	508	514	489	493	495	498	502
490	495	502	508	515	491	493	496	498	503
491	496	502	509	517	491	494	496	498	503
491	498	504	509	519	491	494	496	498	505
491	498	504	510	528	492	494	496	499	506

(a) Create a frequency distribution and a histogram for each supplier.

(b) From the histogram, does it appear that the data for each supplier are normally distributed?

(c) Perform a chi-square goodness of fit test for each supplier to see if it is reasonable to say that the diskettes meet the specifications. Use a level of significance of 0.05.

15.20 As part of an annual survey by the Department of Transportation, randomly selected households are asked, among other questions, about the number of vehicles in the household and the availability of public transportation. The results for people who lived in urban areas are tabulated as follows:

Public Transportation?	Number of Vehicles 0	1	2	3	4	5+
Yes	974	2592	2427	687	194	59
No	98	378	540	199	58	23

(a) Set up the hypotheses to determine whether the number of vehicles in a household and the availability of public transportation are independent.

(b) How many degrees of freedom will the critical value for the test have?

(c) Calculate the expected frequencies and compute the test statistic.

(d) At the 0.05 level of significance, what can you conclude about the number of vehicles in a household and the availability of public transportation for households in urban areas?

15.21 In the same poll sponsored by NBC News and the *Wall Street Journal* in December 1999, people were asked how much of their holiday shopping they intended to do over the Internet. The results, by gender of the respondent, were

	Holiday Shopping over the Internet				
Gender	**All of it**	**Most of it**	**Some of it**	**None of it**	**Not sure**
Male	4	17	94	346	3
Female	2	14	85	431	7

(a) Set up the hypotheses to test whether gender and the amount of holiday shopping done on the Internet are independent.

(b) Find the expected frequencies for each cell.

(c) Perform the chi-square test for independence.

(d) At the 0.05 level of significance, is the amount of holiday shopping done over the Internet independent of gender?

15.22 In a poll sponsored by NBC News and the *Wall Street Journal* in December 1999, 1003 people were asked whether or not they intended to do any of their holiday shopping over the Internet. They were also asked their annual household income. The results are found in the table below.

	Household Income							
Internet?	**Less than \$10,000**	**Between \$10,000 and \$20,000**	**Between \$20,000 and \$30,000**	**Between \$30,000 and \$40,000**	**Between \$40,000 and \$50,000**	**Between \$50,000 and \$75,000**	**Between \$75,000 and \$100,000**	**More than \$100,000**
No	31	57	101	113	90	12	54	61
Yes	2	5	9	20	19	3	49	44

Note: Not all 1003 respondents chose to answer both questions.

(a) Set up the hypotheses to test whether the proportion of people who intend to do some holiday shopping over the Internet is the same for each income level.

(b) Calculate the overall proportion of people who intend to do some holiday shopping over the Internet.

(c) Calculate the expected frequency for each cell.

(d) At the 0.10 level of significance, what can you say about the proportion of people who intend to do some holiday shopping over the Internet for the different income levels?

Thinking About It!

15.23 One of the big controversies during the Vietnam War era was whether the draft lottery was truly random. Many people thought that the lottery was biased against people who were born in certain months of the year. The accompanying data show the number of birth dates in each month that were chosen in the first half of the draft lottery (there are 366 possible birth dates, so these are the first 183 birth dates that were chosen).

Month	Number of Birth Dates in the First Half of the Draft	Month	Number of Birth Dates in the First Half of the Draft
January	13	July	14
February	12	August	18
March	9	September	19
April	11	October	13
May	14	November	21
June	14	December	25

(a) Just by looking at the data, do you think that the claim was worth investigating? Why or why not?

(b) At the 0.05 level of significance do the data indicate that the distribution of the first 183 draft dates was something other than random? (*Hint:* Think about what random would mean in this situation.)

15.24 Consider the company that is looking at the relationship between type of advertising media and age of customer. The data are shown again here: *Requires Exercise 15.12*

Type of Advertisement	Age of Customer				
	21–30	31–40	41–50	Over 50	Total
Store display	21	28	8	6	**63**
Catalog	8	5	1	1	**15**
Magazine	1	23	8	1	**33**
Newspaper	18	14	2	4	**38**
Total	**48**	**70**	**19**	**12**	**149**

(a) Create a revised contingency table that collapses categories and fixes the problem of cells with expected frequencies less than 5.

(b) Perform the chi-square test for independence again.

(c) Compare the results of this test with the results of the test where categories were not collapsed.

15.25 Consider the data from the problem about the diskette suppliers. *Requires Exercise 15.19*

(a) Why is doing a chi-square goodness of fit test for each supplier to see if they meet specifications different than doing a test to see whether the mean for each supplier is 500 hours and a test to see if the variance for each supplier is 25 hours^2?

(b) Just because you reject the hypothesis that the data are normally distributed with a mean of 500 hours and a standard deviation of 5 hours, does that mean that the data are *not* normally distributed?

(c) Calculate the sample mean and standard deviation for each supplier from the data provided.

(d) Do a chi-square test for each supplier to see if the data are normally distributed using the sample means and standard deviations.

(e) How does this change the test procedure itself?

(f) How do the results of these tests compare to the results of the previous tests?

15.26 Look at the results of the chi-square test on proportions for the data on Prozac use. *Requires Exercise 15.17*

(a) Prepare a plot of the proportion of people who take Prozac by region.

(b) When you reject H_0 you decide that at least one population (in this case region) is different. Use your plot to come to a more informative conclusion.

15.27 Look at the data on the number of miles driven by the sample of Porsche drivers. ***Datafile:*** *PORSCHE.XXX*

(a) Make a boxplot of the data.

(b) Do the data look normally distributed?

(c) Delete the outliers and replot the data. Did this change your opinion about the normality of the data? Why or why not?

(d) Calculate the mean and standard deviation of the data without the outliers.

(e) Perform a chi-square goodness of fit test to determine whether the data come from a normally distributed population with the calculated mean and standard deviation.

(f) What are your conclusions?

Doing It!

15.28 The Public Health student who was looking at the issue of college drinking administered a survey that asked questions on four different areas: drinking habits, problems related to drinking, problems related to other people's drinking, and living habits. A portion of the data from the survey and an explanation of the variables are given here:

Five	Four	Three	Last	Binger	Hangover	Miss	Behind	Regret	Forget
0	0	0	2	1	1	1	1	1	1
0	0	0	4	1	1	1	1	1	1
0	1	1	3	2	1	1	1	1	1
0	0	0	3	1	1	1	1	1	1
0	0	0	3	1	1	1	1	1	1
0	0	0	4	1	1	1	1	1	1

Argue	Engage	Protect	Damage	Police	Injured	Medical	Drive	DWI	Ride
1	1	1	1	1	1	1	1	1	1
1	1	1	1	1	1	1	1	1	1
1	1	1	1	1	1	1	1	1	1
1	1	1	1	1	1	1	1	1	1
1	1	1	1	1	1	1	3	1	3
1	1	1	1	1	1	1	1	1	1

Age	Gender	Fulltime	Greek	Live	Roommate	Race	Class
18	1	Y	N	4	P	2	1
62	2	Y	N	4	S	1	
18	2	Y	N	1	R	1	1
31	1	Y	N	4	R	1	
19	2	Y	N	4	P	1	2
20	2	Y	N	1	R	1	2

For the purposes of this survey a "drink" means any of the following:

12-ounce can or bottle of beer
4-ounce glass of wine
12-ounce bottle or can of wine cooler
1 oz (shot) of liquor straight or in a mixed drink

Binge drinking is defined as

The consumption of five or more drinks in one episode of drinking for males.
The consumption of four or more drinks in one episode of drinking for females.

The variables *Five, Four,* and *Three* refer to the 2-week period just before the survey was administered and answer the questions indicated. They are coded as follows:

0	None
1	Once
2	Twice
3	Three to five times
4	Six to nine times
5	Ten or more times

- *Five* "How many times have you had five or more drinks in a row?"
  Four "How many times have you had four drinks in a row (but no more than that)?"
  Three "How many times have you had three drinks in a row (but no more than that)?"

- The variable *Last* answers the question, When did you have your last drink? The answers are coded as follows:

  0 I never had a drink
  1 Not in the past year
  2 More than 30 days ago, but less than a year ago
  3 More than one week ago, but less than 30 days ago
  4 Within the last week

- The variable *Binger* is defined as the type of drinker that a student is based on his or her answer to the first four questions.

  0 Nondrinker
  1 Nonbinge drinker
  2 Infrequent binge drinker
  3 Frequent binge drinker

The next 15 variables answer questions that start with the statement "Since the beginning of the school year, how often has your drinking caused you to. . . " The answers are coded as follows:

0 Not at all
1 Once
2 Twice or more

- *Hangover* ". . . have a hangover?"
- *Miss* ". . . miss a class?"
- *Behind* ". . . get behind in school work?"
- *Regret* ". . . do something you later regret?"
- *Forget* ". . . forget where you were or what you did?"
- *Argue* ". . . argue with friends?"
- *Engage* ". . . engage in unplanned sexual activity?"
- *Protect* ". . . not use protection when you had sex?"
- *Damage* ". . . damage property?"
- *Police* ". . . get into trouble with campus or local police?"
- *Injured* ". . . get hurt or injured?"
- *Medical* ". . . require medical treatment for an alcohol overdose?"
- *Drive* ". . . drive after drinking alcohol?"
- *DWI* ". . . drive after having five or more drinks?"
- *Ride* ". . . ride with a driver who was high or drunk?"
- The variable *Age* is the age of the student.
- The variable *Gender* is the gender of the student and is coded as

  1 Male
  2 Female

- The variable *Fulltime* is Y if the student is full-time and N if the student is part-time.
- The variable *Greek* is Y if the student is a member of a fraternity or sorority and N if not.
- The variable *Live* records where the student lives and is coded as follows:

  1 Residence hall or dormitory
  2 Fraternity or sorority house
  3 Other university housing
  4 Off-campus house or apartment

- The variable *Roommate* describes with whom the student lives and is coded as follows:

  A Alone
  R Roommate(s) or housemate(s)
  S Spouse
  P Parent(s) or other relative(s)
  O Significant other
  C Children

- The variable *Race* describes the race or ethnic category of the student and is coded as

Blank	Hispanic (separate question)
1	White
2	Black/African American
3	Asian/Pacific Islander
4	Native American/Native Alaskan
5	Other

- The variable *Class* describes the student's year at the university and is coded as

1	Freshman
2	Sophomore
3	Junior
4	Senior

(a) Look at the variable *Drive,* which refers to whether a student drove after drinking. Create a contingency table for this variable and the variable *Binger.*

(b) At the 0.05 level of significance, is whether a student drove after drinking independent of the type of drinker he or she is?

(c) If you exclude nondrinkers and look at only those students who drink, does the answer change?

(d) From the variables *Live* and *Roommate* derive a way to classify students as residents/commuters and to separate commuters living at home from commuters living with nonrelatives.

(e) Create contingency tables that will allow you to look at the relationship between how often a student missed class *(Miss)* and resident/commuter students. Would you expect these two variables to be related? Why or why not?

(f) Do a chi-square test to determine whether these two variables are related.

(g) Look at the variables *Miss* and *Gender* and do the same analysis.

(h) Look at the variables *Binger* and *Age.* Is there a relationship between them?

(i) From the variable *Age* create a new variable that classifies students as above and below the legal drinking age (assume that it is age 21 in the state of interest). How is this new variable related to the type of drinker that a student is? To *Drive*? To *Miss*?

(j) Is there a relationship between *Race* and *Binger*?

(k) Consider all of the other variables relating to behavior after drinking. Determine whether these variables are related to the type of drinker that a student is.

(l) Consider any other variables and relationships that you think are important and investigate them. Prepare a report for the university administration that describes the drinking behaviors of the students at the university.

15.29 The Chamber of Commerce that is studying the credit problems of small businesses asked the businesses three questions to classify their business and seven questions related to the issue of credit problems. A portion of the datafile and an explanation of each variable follow:

Size	Employees	Nature	Problem	Understd	Concern	Call	Loan	Collateral	Access
2	2	1	1	2	1	2	2	0	2
1	2	3	1	2	2	0	2	2	1
4	3	1	2	1	2	2	2	2	0
1	1	1	2	1	2	2	2	2	2
1	2	1	2	0	0	0	0	0	0
3	1	5	2	0	2	2	2	2	1
3	3	2	2	1	1	2	2	2	1
2	2	3	2	1	2	2	2	2	2
3	5	2	2	1	2	2	2	1	2

- The variable *Size* refers to the annual sales of the company and is coded as follows:

1	Under $1 million	4	$11–20 million
2	$1–5 million	5	Over $20 million
3	$6–10 million		

- The variable *Employees* refers to the number of employees that the company currently employs. This variable was coded as

1 0–5 employees
2 6–10 employees
3 11–50 employees
4 51–150 employees
5 151–250 employees
6 Over 250 employees

- The variable *Nature* refers to the type of business and is coded as

1 Manufacturing
2 Retail
3 Service
4 Real Estate
5 Other

The next seven variables contain the response to the questions or statements indicated and are coded as follows:

1 Yes
2 No

- *Problem* "Are you experiencing credit-related problems?"
- *Understd* "The bank understands my problems."
- *Concern* "I am concerned that my note might be recalled."
- *Call* "The bank is planning to recall my loan."
- *Loan* "The bank has called my loan."
- *Collateral* "The bank has demanded more collateral."
- *Access* "Access to credit is affecting my business."

(a) Look at the variable *Nature,* which refers to the type of business. Is the sample of businesses that were surveyed by the Chamber of Commerce uniformly distributed over the different types of companies?

(b) Answer the question posed in part (a) for *Size* and *Employees.*

(c) Create a contingency table for the variables *Problem* and *Nature.* Is the proportion of companies that are having credit-related problems different for the different types of companies?

(d) Answer the same question for the variable *Nature* and each of the variables *Understd* and *Access.*

(e) Investigate the relationship between the variables *Size* and *Access* and between the variables *Size* and *Problem.*

(f) Investigate the relationship between the variables *Employees* and *Access* and the variables *Employees* and *Problem.*

(g) Is there a relationship between the size of the company and the type of business that the company does?

(h) Is there a relationship between the size of the company and the number of employees in the company?

(i) Look at the variables related to loan recall, *Concern, Call,* and *Loan.* Investigate whether these variables are related to *Size, Employees,* and *Nature.*

(j) Look at any other relationships that you think might be useful to the Chamber of Commerce.

(k) Prepare a report for the Chamber of Commerce about your findings.

CHAPTER 16

IMPROVING AND MANAGING QUALITY

THE PLASTICS COMPANY

Business Dilemma...

One of the quality characteristics of plastic is the melt flow (min) at 200°F. This measures the viscosity of the liquid. The plastic is poured into molds to make razors, pens, disposable lighters, and many other familiar products. The melt flow indicates how the plastic will fill the molds. The plastics company monitors the process that manufactures the plastic by regularly measuring the melt flow and plotting the data on a control chart. By analyzing the data, the company determines whether the plastic is ready for sale. If the plastic does not have the correct melt flow, then air bubbles may form when the plastic is poured into a mold, causing underfilling or overfilling of the mold.

The plastics company sells its product to other manufacturers to be used in making such consumer products as automobile bumpers and pens. The company that purchases the plastic is also concerned about the melt flow of the material it is purchasing and so it checks a sample of the raw material. The melt flow results for five tests done by the manufacturer and the customer are shown in the portion of the data set displayed here:

Manufacturer	Customer
10.2	8.7
9.4	9.2
9.5	9.2
9.4	8.8
9.9	9.1

Clearly, the manufacturer and the customer are not getting the same results and something must be done to resolve these differences.

16.1 CHAPTER OBJECTIVES

The story of the plastics company detailed in the chapter opener is an example of the increased attention being paid to quality by manufacturers and customers. This book has repeatedly emphasized the importance of data analysis as a tool for improving quality both in the manufacturing environment and more recently in service industries, such as health care, and the entertainment industry. In the face of increased competition, companies must continuously monitor and improve the products and services they are marketing. To do this data must be collected, analyzed, and used to improve the products or services being sold. This idea is known as continuous improvement.

There are many definitions of the word quality, but in this chapter we will focus on the idea that a quality product or service should have the same characteristics regardless of when it was made, what shift it was made on, who was working, or which day it is. That is, the product or service should have predictable characteristics. Control charts are one of a group of tools known as the "7 Tools of Quality," which are used to deliver products or services that are consistent.

In particular, this chapter will cover:

- Supplier/Customer Relations—A New Paradigm
- The Language of Control Charts
- Types of Control Charts
- Individual or *x*-charts
- Xbar- and *R*-charts
- The *p*-chart

16.2 SUPPLIER/CUSTOMER RELATIONS—A NEW PARADIGM

As a result of the quality movement, the relationship between supplier and customer has changed dramatically. Formerly, the job of the purchasing agent was to purchase raw materials as inexpensively as possible without being much concerned with quality. The performance of the purchasing agent was judged on how inexpensively he/she was able to purchase raw material. But we all know the old adage "garbage in, garbage out." The quality movement has helped companies see the importance of changing this paradigm and treating the steps involved in bringing the product to market as a **process.**

> A ***process*** is a series of actions that changes inputs to outputs.

You are familiar with many processes. The process of getting ready for class involves all the steps you take to change yourself into a student prepared for a day of school. This might involve showering, packing the needed books and notebooks into your backpack, completing the homework due that day, and grabbing your keys and ID so you can eat and get back into your room!

Manufacturers use processes to turn raw materials into products. Sometimes those products are products that we buy directly, such as a car or a computer. Sometimes they are products that are sold to another company to be used to manufacture another item that we may buy directly or might in turn be sold to another manufacturer. The plastic made by the company described in the opening scenario, for example, is manufactured and then sold to another company to be made into car bumpers that are then sold to car manufacturers.

You may be familiar with more processes than you think. Services such as getting admitted to a hospital are processes, too; the way you sign up for courses for the upcoming semester is a process; and the way your paycheck is created is a process.

Certainly, if the inputs to the process are not of high quality then the outputs will not be either. This realization has changed the way companies work with suppliers. In particular, the job of purchasing is now to build partnerships with suppliers. This idea of a partnership means that the company will show some loyalty to the supplier and not change suppliers month to month based solely on price and the supplier will in turn work with the company to improve the quality of the inputs. In many cases, purchasing managers visit companies to see the quality initiatives that the supplier has in place. Both sides can benefit from the team approach. The supplier has a more committed customer and the customer can trust the quality of the inputs.

16.3 THE LANGUAGE OF CONTROL CHARTS

Two important points must be made about processes. First, no two items produced by a process are the same. And second, variability is to be expected in the output of all processes. What does this mean? It means that no matter how hard we try, we cannot completely eliminate variation. So, no two sheets of plastic will be exactly the same, no two golf balls will be exactly the same, no two tissue boxes will be exactly the same, and no two experiences at a hospital check-in will be exactly the same. However, we can identify the sources of variation.

If you think about where the variation in a product or service comes from you might identify the following sources: people, machines, materials, methods, measurement, and the environment. These are considered to be the six major sources of variation. A **control chart** is a graphical tool used to monitor process variation. Walter Shewhart of Bell Laboratories originally developed control charts during the 1920s.

A ***control chart*** is a graph that allows us to study variation in a product or service.

EXAMPLE 16.1 **The Soup Company**

Sources of Variation

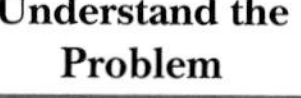

Suppose you are filling cans of soup and there should be 10.5 oz of soup in each can. Consider each of the six sources of variation for the process of filling the cans with soup.

People: Different operators of the machines might do the filling.

Machines: Different machines might be used for the process.

Materials: Different ingredients might be used to make the soup.

Methods: The way in which the cans are filled might differ.

Measurement: More than one instrument might be used to check the ounces.

Environment: The temperature of the plant might vary from day to day. ■

Coffee and a Bagel ***Identifying Possible Sources of Variation***

Suppose you go to a donut shop for coffee and a bagel. Consider the service and quality of your food. Using the six categories of sources of variation, identify where variation might come from.

16.3.1 Changes in the Distribution of a Variable

To get a better handle on describing variation and determining the causes of the variation we need to rely on some of the concepts developed in Chapters 6 and 7. Consider the process of filling the cans of soup again. The variable of interest is the number of ounces in the can. The values that this variable can assume and their corresponding likelihood can be described by a probability distribution. We studied the normal distribution in Chapter 6 and learned that many quantitative variables can be described by this bell-shaped distribution. Any single observation of the variable, such as the ounces of soup in one can, is governed by the underlying distribution. The distribution can change.

Figure 16.1 on page 816 shows the number of ounces in cans of soup. The measurements are taken every hour. There are four different scenarios depicted in this figure: (a) the underlying distribution is not changing over time; (b) the mean of the distribution is increasing over time; (c) the variance of the distribution is increasing; and (d) there was a shift in the mean of the distribution at one point in time.

Control charts help us detect situations (b) – (d). You can see by looking at the graphs that it is not easy to do. If the normal distributions were not displayed it would be difficult to see the changes that have occurred. This is because you cannot eliminate variation. Therefore, it is difficult to tell if the variation you are seeing in the variable is what is reasonable to expect or if something has happened to the process that needs attention.

ANS. ANSWERS VARY. PEOPLE: SERVER; MACHINES: OVEN USED FOR BAKING; MATERIALS: FLOUR, SUGAR; METHODS: TIME TO BAKE BAGEL OR BREW COFFEE; MEASUREMENT: AMOUNT OF COFFEE USED; ENVIRONMENT: TEMPERATURE OF SHOP.

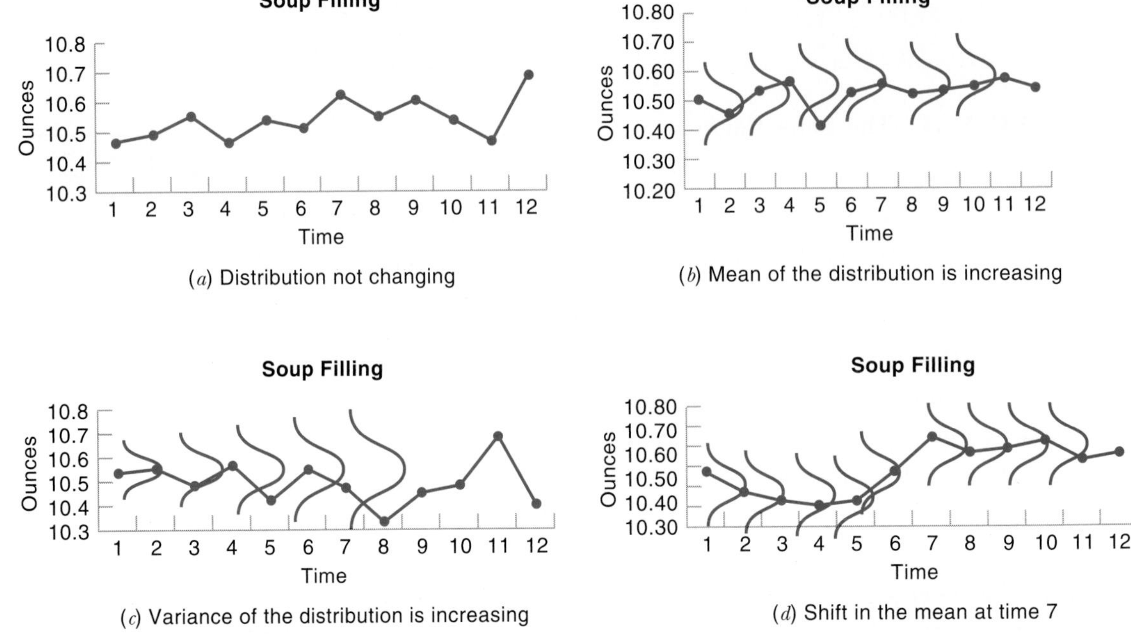

FIGURE 16.1 Different possibilities for changes in the distribution of the variable

> A process whose distribution does not change over time is said to be in a state of ***statistical control*** or ***in control.*** If it does change over time, it is said to be ***out of statistical control*** or ***out of control.***

Figure 16.1*b* shows what the observations could look like if the mean of the process, in this case the average amount of soup going into the cans, was gradually increasing. This could happen as a machine part wears out. Figure 16.1*c* shows what the observations could look like if the variance in the process increases, causing the soup amount dispensed into the can to vary more. This could happen if the person running the machine or providing the service gets tired or fatigued. Figure 16.1*d* shows what the observations might look like if there were a change in the raw materials at some point in time. In this case there is not a gradual shifting of the mean but a jump in the mean, perhaps due to a different batch of raw materials or a new operator.

16.3.2 Types of Variation

As you can see from Figure 16.1*a*, the output of a process that is in control still exhibits variation but there is no pattern to the data. The data exhibit random behavior. Such variation is said to be due to **common causes of variation.**

> ***Common causes of variation*** are the methods, machines, people, and environment that are an inherent part of a process. They are part of the design of the process.

To reduce variability in a stable process, you must eliminate some common cause of variation by changing the process in some way. This is the job of management.

Out of control processes exhibit variation that is the result of both common causes and **special causes of variation.**

> ***Special causes of variation*** are events or actions that are not part of the process design.

Control charts are one of the tools used to detect the presence of special causes of variation.

EXAMPLE 16.2 The Plastics Company

Understand the Problem

Common and Special Causes of Variation

Consider the plastics company. Possible common causes of variation in the melt flow of the plastic might be poor lighting in the plant or inconsistent raw materials. Possible special causes of variation might be the accidental setting of the controls of a machine incorrectly or a negligent supplier. ■

16.3.3 Exercises—Learning It!

16.1 A fast-food chain monitors the amount of time it takes between the customer placing the order and the customer receiving the order. Identify some potential sources of variation in this time variable.

16.2 The percentage of free throw shots that a player makes varies from game to game. Identify some causes of variation.

16.3 The diameter of a golf ball varies from ball to ball. Identify some causes of variation.

16.4 The strength of a tissue varies from tissue to tissue. Identify some causes of variation.

16.5 The average grade in an introductory statistics course varies from semester to semester. Identify some causes of variation.

16.4 TYPES OF CONTROL CHARTS

In the opening problem statement at the beginning of the chapter, you read that the machine operators plot data on control charts. There are several different types of control charts. As we have emphasized in this book on many occasions, the type of data you have dictates the tools that you can use. The same is true for control charts. The type of control chart you use depends on whether you have quantitative or qualitative data and also on the sample size you use each time you collect data.

The following decision tree appeared in the February 1998 issue of *Quality Digest.* The article was entitled "When in Doubt, Get the *x*-chart Out" by Thomas Pyzdek. The decision tree gives us a nice way to look at the types of control charts and how to decide which type to use.

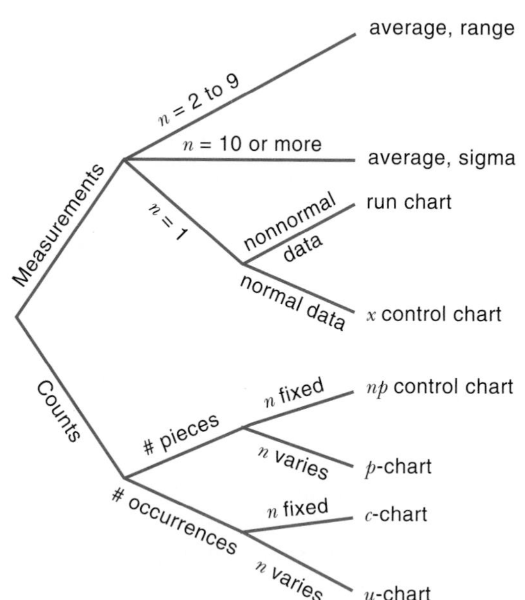

The first decision you need to make is whether you have quantitative (measurement) data or qualitative (counts) data. Following the quantitative data branch at the top of the tree, your next decision is with regard to the sample size that is used each time data are collected. If you are observing single observations each time you collect data, then you must decide if you have normal or non-normal data. The next two sections cover *x*-charts, Xbar-charts, and *R*-charts (referred to as "average, range" in the tree diagram).

Following the bottom branch of the decision tree when you have qualitative data, you must next decide whether you are counting the number of units that have a defect or the number of defects per unit. In the first case a unit is either defective or not. For instance, there is either an error in the bill or not. The latter situation occurs when you are counting, for instance, the number of errors in each bill. Once you have established which situation you have, then you must decide if your sample size is fixed or if it varies from time to time. Section 16.7 covers *np* and *p* control charts. This book does not cover the other types of control charts, but they are based on the same concepts.

16.5 INDIVIDUAL OR *x*-CHARTS

In this section we learn about individual or *x*-charts. They are called individual charts because individual values ($n = 1$) of the variable are plotted. The theory of the individual control chart is based on the normal distribution.

16.5.1 Constructing an *x*-Chart

An ***x*-chart** is a graph that plots the sample values in chronological order along the *x* axis. There are three lines on a control chart that tell the operator whether the process is in control.

> An ***x-chart*** is a control chart used to monitor individual observations of a variable over time. Time is plotted on the *x* axis and the quality characteristic being monitored is plotted on the *y* axis. The graph also has three lines drawn parallel to the *x* axis. These are called the center line, the upper control limit, and the lower control limit.

These lines are constructed using the following steps:

Steps for constructing an x-chart

Step 1: The center line (CL) of the chart is drawn at the theoretical or desired value for the mean of the distribution, μ.

Step 2: The upper control limit (UCL) of the chart is a horizontal line drawn at a value that is three standard deviations above the center line (called the 3 sigma limit), $\mu + 3\sigma$.

Step 3: The lower control limit (LCL) of the chart is a horizontal line drawn at a value that is 3 standard deviations below the center line (called the 3 sigma limit), $\mu - 3\sigma$.

Analyze the Data

EXAMPLE 16.3 The Plastics Company

Finding CL, UCL, and LCL

Suppose the desired value for the mean melt flow is $\mu = 9.5$ and the standard deviation is 0.60. The center line (CL) is drawn parallel to the *x* axis at the value $y = 9.5$. The upper control limit (UCL) of the chart is drawn parallel to the *x* axis at the value $y = 9.5 + 3(0.6) = 11.3$. The lower control limit (LCL) of the chart is drawn parallel to the x axis at the value of $y = 9.5 - 3(0.6) = 7.7$. These lines are shown in the graph.

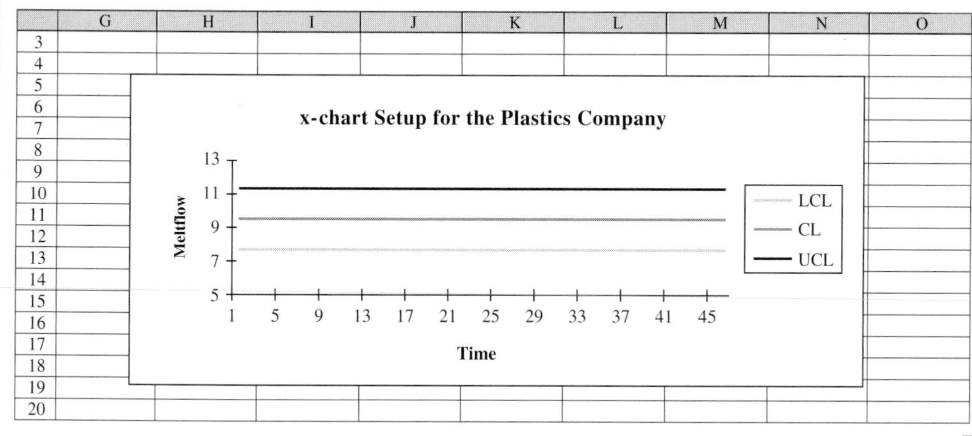

Once the upper and lower control limits have been established, the observations of the quality characteristic, such as the melt flow, are plotted on the graph. If the process is working properly, that is, if the only variation is due to natural variation, then the observations should fall between the upper and lower control limits with no discernable pattern.

The completed x-chart for the melt flow is shown in the next example.

EXAMPLE 16.4 The Plastics Company

Analyze the Data

***x*-Chart for Melt Flow**

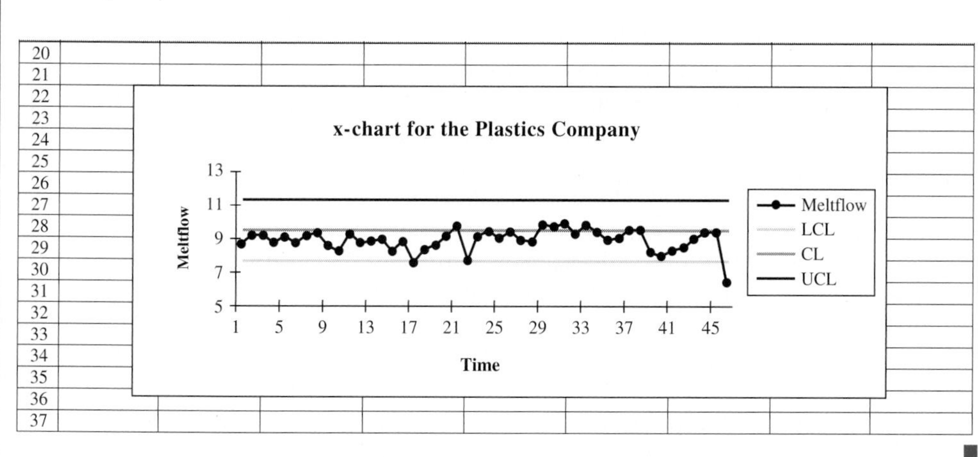

TRY IT NOW!

The Plastics Company ***x*-Chart for the Customer Data**

Use the same upper and lower control chart limits but plot the first 10 melt flows that the customer observed. They are as follows:

(continued)

8.7	9.2	9.2	8.8	9.1	8.8	9.2	9.4	8.6	8.3

In the Try It Now! that you just completed, you should see that all the melt flows fall between the upper and lower limits, and that they all fall below the center line. This is a pattern that cannot be ignored. To resolve the differing results the customer and the manufacturer will have to engage in conversation and utilize another of the "7 Tools of Quality" known as a ***fishbone diagram.*** The fishbone diagram is a tool to examine the major and secondary causes of a problem. It gets its name from the fact that it looks like the skeleton of a fish. Since the intent of this chapter is to introduce the basic idea of control charts, we will leave fishbone diagrams to be covered in a course on quality management.

16.5.2 False Alarms

You might wonder why the control limits are set 3 standard deviations above and below the mean. Would it be better to set the limits at 2 standard deviations? The answer to this question lies in our understanding of the normal distribution.

We know from our study of the normal distribution (see Figure 7.6) that 99.73% of all values should fall within 3 standard deviations of the target or population mean. Thus, the probability that a value will fall outside the control limits is 0.0027 or 27 in 10,000 if the process is working properly. If we observe a value outside the limits, then the process should be examined, because it is highly unlikely that we would see values outside these limits if the process is working properly. It may seem to you that we would be better off setting the limits at only 2 standard deviations above and below the target mean. Then we would detect problems sooner. That part of your thinking is correct but there is a trade-off.

The flip side of this issue is that no matter how small, there is some nonzero chance (in this case 0.0027) of observing values outside the limits when the process really is working properly. Using our control chart, we would flag these observations as unusual and conclude that there was some special cause of the variation. It is possible, however, that there is nothing unusual happening and that it was just chance (albeit a small chance) that the values would be outside the control chart limits. This is known as a false alarm. If we were to drop the limits to 2 standard deviations above and below the mean, we would increase the chance of a false alarm to 0.0456 or 4.56%. This is the probability of observing values above or below 2 standard deviation limits if the mean has not shifted. It is generally felt that 4.56% is too great a chance

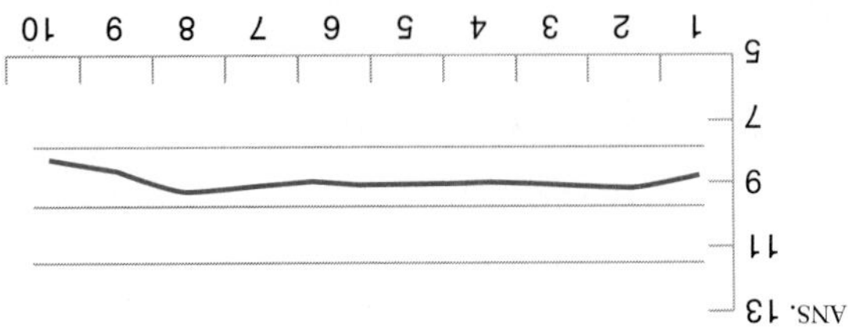

of a false alarm, although clearly the cost of making a false alarm versus the cost of missing a problem should be factored into the decision.

16.5.3 Exercises—Learning It!

16.6 A manufacturer of golf balls monitors the weight of its golf balls. Suppose the target weight is 45 g and the target standard deviation is 0.15 g.

(a) Construct the x-chart and plot the following observations on the chart:

45.3	45.2	45.2	45.3	45.5	45.3	45.2	45.1	45.3	45.2	45.3

(b) Are any of the points out of control?

16.7 A soda machine is supposed to dispense an average of 8 oz of soda with a standard deviation of 0.03 ounce into cups. A representative from the company checks the machines in use every 2 weeks. The following data show the actual soda dispensed over the last 25 weeks.

8.09	8.01	7.98	7.97	7.94
8.07	8.01	7.98	7.97	7.92
8.06	8.00	7.98	7.96	7.91
8.06	7.99	7.98	7.95	7.89
8.05	7.99	7.98	7.95	7.89

(a) Construct the x-chart for the soda machine company.

(b) Plot the observations on the chart.

(c) Are any points out of control?

16.8 You are interested in monitoring the number of minutes you can work out before you get fatigued. You think you are increasing your stamina but are not sure if what you see in the data is just natural variation. You have recorded the following number of minutes for your workout over the past 30 days. The first column of data shows the first 10 days, the second column the next 10 days, and the third column the last 10 days.

61.54	51.13	66.37
66.02	65.29	78.42
62.08	58.77	73.83
55.20	59.46	66.32
49.93	66.15	78.80
55.76	64.89	68.86
58.32	69.12	77.45
60.55	72.04	76.73
53.83	69.11	68.48
55.53	69.95	64.13

(a) If your average has been 60 minutes with a standard deviation of 5 minutes, construct the x-chart for these data.

(b) Does it appear that your process is in control?

(c) If not, does that mean you are increasing your stamina?

16.9 A company that manufactures tissues is concerned about the cross-directional strength of its tissues. The target mean is 450 lb/ream with a standard deviation of 25 lb/ream. The following data were taken over 15 hours:

422	464	437
448	472	396
423	489	432
435	440	475
445	441	439

(a) Construct the x-chart for the tissue company.

(b) Plot the observations on the chart.

(c) Are any points out of control?

16.10 A mail-order company monitors the amount of time that customers are on hold before being serviced. The company randomly monitors one call every hour. The target on-hold time is 1 minute with a standard deviation of 0.5 minute. The following on-hold times (in minutes) were recorded for one day:

0.82	0.57
0.60	0.78
1.22	0.03
1.31	0.81
0.84	0.99
0.77	0.45

(a) Construct the x-chart for the mail-order company.

(b) Plot the observations on the chart.

(c) Are any points out of control?

16.6 XBAR- AND *R*-CHARTS

Although the individual x-charts developed in the previous section are useful, it is more common to monitor the average of a sample of observations. These are called Xbar-charts and they are used to detect the presence of special causes of variation. The Xbar-chart is almost always used with the R-chart and so they are presented together in this section.

16.6.1 Xbar-charts

The **Xbar-chart** is constructed the same way that an x-chart is constructed: There is a center line and an upper and lower control limit. Instead of plotting individual observations$(n = 1)$ on the y axis, the average of n observations is plotted over time. So the variable being monitored is $\overline{X}$.

> The ***Xbar-chart*** is a control chart used to monitor the mean of a variable over time. Time is plotted on the x axis and the sample means are plotted on the y axis. The graph also has three lines drawn parallel to the x axis. These are called the center line, the upper control limit, and the lower control limit.

From our study of the central limit theorem (Chapter 7) we know that the standard deviation of $\overline{X}$ is called the standard error and is labeled $\sigma_{\overline{X}}$. The standard error is $\sigma/\sqrt{n}$. We also know that the mean of $\overline{X}$ is labeled $\mu_{\overline{X}}$ and is the same as the population or target mean, μ. Using this information, we arrive at the following steps for constructing an Xbar-chart:

Steps for constructing an Xbar-chart

Step 1: The center line (CL) of the chart is drawn at the theoretical or desired value for the mean of the distribution, μ.

Step 2: The upper control limit (UCL) of the chart is a horizontal line drawn at a value that is 3 standard deviations above the center line (called the 3 sigma limit), $\mu + 3\,\sigma/\sqrt{n}$.

Step 3: The lower control limit (LCL) of the chart is a horizontal line drawn at a value that is 3 standard deviations below the center line (called the 3 sigma limit), $\mu - 3\,\sigma/\sqrt{n}$.

The values for μ and σ come from the specifications of the manufacturing process or they may be estimated by $\overline{X}$ and s from sample data. You might remember the diaper company that we looked at in Chapter 7. The company sampled 5 diapers every hour and measured the diaper weight in grams. Let's see how to set up the Xbar-chart for the diaper company.

EXAMPLE 16.5 The Diaper Company

Analyze the Data

Calculation of Upper and Lower Control Limits for Xbar-Chart

For the diaper weight the target mean is 55 g with a target standard deviation of 0.55 g. Using these values in the formulas for UCL and LCL, you get

$$\begin{aligned} \text{UCL} &= 55 + (3)(0.55)/\sqrt{5} \\ &= 55 + 0.738 = 55.738 \text{ g} \end{aligned}$$

and

$$\begin{aligned} \text{LCL} &= 55 - (3)(0.55)/\sqrt{5} \\ &= 55 - 0.738 = 54.262 \text{ g} \end{aligned}$$

The chart setup looks like this:

V W X Y Z AA AB AC AD AE

Setup for Xbar–The Diaper Company

Weight (g)

56, 55.5, 55, 54.5, 54

UCL

CL

LCL

■

EXAMPLE 16.6 The Diaper Company

Analyze the Data

Control Chart for Average Diaper Weight

Plotting the sample averages for the weight for 52 hours gives you the following chart:

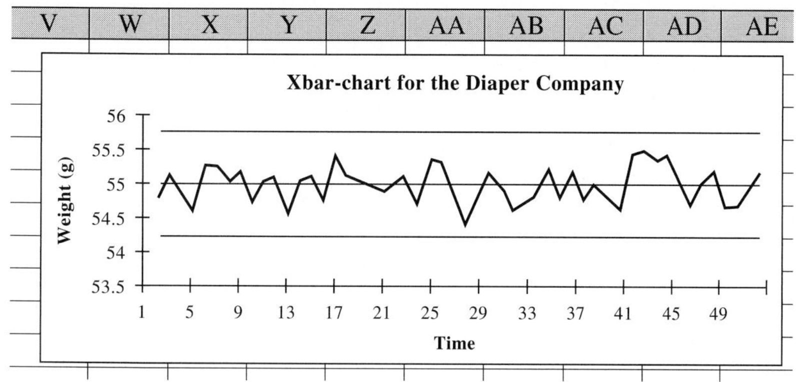

Clearly none of the sample means are outside the control limits in this case. ■

Sometimes we do not have the values of μ and σ from the specifications or we wish to develop the control chart independently of these values. In this case we use the overall mean, $\overline{\overline{X}}$, for the center line. The upper and lower control limits are calculated as follows:

Steps for constructing Xbar-chart when μ and σ are unavailable

$$\text{UCL} = \overline{\overline{X}} + A_2\overline{R}$$
$$\text{Center line} = \overline{\overline{X}}$$
$$\text{LCL} = \overline{\overline{X}} - A_2\overline{R}$$

Remember that the sample range is the Max − Min.

where $\overline{R}$ is the average of the sample ranges, and A_2 is a constant that depends on the sample size, n.

The value of $A_2\overline{R}$ is an estimate of $(3\sigma/\sqrt{n})$. You can see this when you know that

A table of A_2 values is in the Appendix.

$$\hat{\sigma}_{\overline{X}} = \frac{\overline{R}}{d_2\sqrt{n}} \quad \text{and} \quad A_2 = \frac{3}{d_2\sqrt{n}}$$

so

$$A_2\overline{R} = \frac{3}{d_2\sqrt{n}}\overline{R} = 3\left(\frac{\overline{R}}{d_2\sqrt{n}}\right) = 3\hat{\sigma}_{\overline{X}} = 3 \text{ sigma}$$

TABLE 16.1
Values of A_2

n	A_2
2	1.88
3	1.023
4	0.729
5	0.577
6	0.483
7	0.419
8	0.373
9	0.337

Table 16.1 shows the value of A_2 for a variety of different sample sizes, n. A complete table of A_2 values is in Table 7 of the Appendix.

The use of $A_2\overline{R}$ as an estimate of $(3\sigma/\sqrt{n})$ was developed to simplify the calculations. It is easier to find the range of a sample than the standard deviation. Despite the fact that the need for ease of calculation is considerably less important with the technology that we have today, these formulas continue to be favored by industry. The following example gives the observations for the first 3 samples of diaper weights. Remember that each sample is of $n = 5$ observations. The sample average and range are shown for each of these samples and the values of $\overline{\overline{X}}$ and $\overline{R}$ are shown if we were to construct the control chart based on only these 3 samples.

Analyze the data

EXAMPLE 16.7 **The Diaper Company**

Limits for Xbar-chart from the Data

In this example the upper and lower control chart limits will be constructed from these 3 samples only so you can see where the values come from. The value of A_2 is 0.577 since $n = 5$.

Sample	Diaper	Weight	Sample	Diaper	Weight	Sample	Diaper	Weight
1	1	55.87	2	1	54.85	3	1	54.40
1	2	55.35	2	2	54.79	3	2	56.44
1	3	54.50	2	3	54.65	3	3	54.11
1	4	53.97	2	4	55.56	3	4	54.67
1	5	54.29	2	5	55.82	3	5	54.56
Average		54.80			55.13			54.84
Range		1.90			1.17			2.33
Grand average		54.92						
Average range		1.80						

$$\text{UCL} = \overline{\overline{X}} + A_2\overline{R} = 54.92 + (0.577)1.80 = 55.96$$
$$\text{Center line} = \overline{\overline{X}} = 54.92$$
$$\text{LCL} = \overline{\overline{X}} - A_2\overline{R} = 54.92 - (0.577)1.80 = 53.88$$

■

Consider a different example. The sleeve shown in Figure 16.2 contains three inside diameter key characteristics. They are all machined on the same lathe but with

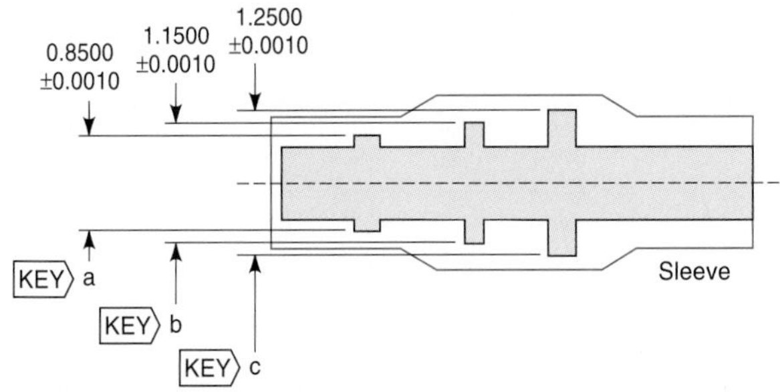

FIGURE 16.2 Three key characteristics of sleeve inside diameter

different tools. Each inside diameter is a different size. The customer requires stability of the lathe process.

The time required to manufacture a sleeve is 3 minutes. The measurements are taken every hour from three consecutive sleeves. The following table shows the data collected for 9 samples.

		Characteristic		
Sample	**Sleeve**	**a**	**b**	**c**
1	1	0.8500	1.1494	1.2494
1	2	0.8512	1.1494	1.2489
1	3	0.8501	1.1491	1.2494
2	1	0.8507	1.1498	1.2494
2	2	0.8498	1.1491	1.2488
2	3	0.8510	1.1499	1.2497
3	1	0.8509	1.1496	1.2494
3	2	0.8507	1.1498	1.2490
3	3	0.8506	1.1497	1.2496
4	1	0.8504	1.1499	1.2849
4	2	0.8502	1.1496	1.2943
4	3	0.8512	1.1497	1.2500
5	1	0.8512	1.1500	1.2490
5	2	0.8499	1.1498	1.2496
5	3	0.8508	1.1497	1.2497
6	1	0.8511	1.1498	1.2493
6	2	0.8507	1.1501	1.2497
6	3	0.8505	1.1498	1.2493
7	1	0.8512	1.1498	1.2490
7	2	0.8506	1.1494	1.2498
7	3	0.8500	1.1501	1.2496
8	1	0.8506	1.1498	1.2495
8	2	0.8506	1.1501	1.2497
8	3	0.8512	1.1500	1.2492
9	1	0.8510	1.1501	1.2495
9	2	0.8518	1.1498	1.2498
9	3	0.8499	1.1503	1.2492

EXAMPLE 16.8 The Sleeve Company

Analyze the Data

Xbar-chart

Let's construct the Xbar-chart for sleeve characteristic a using the data shown in the table above. First we must calculate the average and range for each of the 9 samples. Then we can calculate $\overline{\overline{X}}$ and $\overline{R}$ using the sample averages and sample ranges:

	Sample Averages			Sample Ranges		
Sample	a	b	c	a	b	c
1	0.8504	1.1493	1.2492	0.0012	0.0003	0.0005
2	0.8505	1.1496	1.2493	0.0012	0.0008	0.0009
3	0.8507	1.1497	1.2493	0.0003	0.0002	0.0006
4	0.8506	1.1497	1.2764	0.0010	0.0003	0.0443
5	0.8506	1.1498	1.2494	0.0013	0.0003	0.0007
6	0.8508	1.1499	1.2494	0.0006	0.0003	0.0004
7	0.8506	1.1498	1.2495	0.0012	0.0007	0.0008
8	0.8508	1.1500	1.2495	0.0006	0.0003	0.0005
9	0.8509	1.1501	1.2495	0.0019	0.0005	0.0006
Overall average	0.8507	1.1498	1.2524	0.0010	0.0004	0.0055

$$\overline{\overline{X}} = \text{average of the 9 sample means} = 0.850663$$
$$\overline{R} = \text{average of the 9 sample ranges} = 0.001033$$
$$\text{UCL} = \overline{\overline{X}} + A_2\overline{R} = 0.850663 + 1.023(0.001033) = 0.8517$$
$$\text{Center line} = \overline{\overline{X}} = 0.850663$$
$$\text{LCL} = \overline{\overline{X}} - A_2\overline{R} = 0.850663 - 1.023(0.001033) = 0.8496$$

Finally, the graph is created by plotting the control limits and the sample averages for each of the 9 samples:

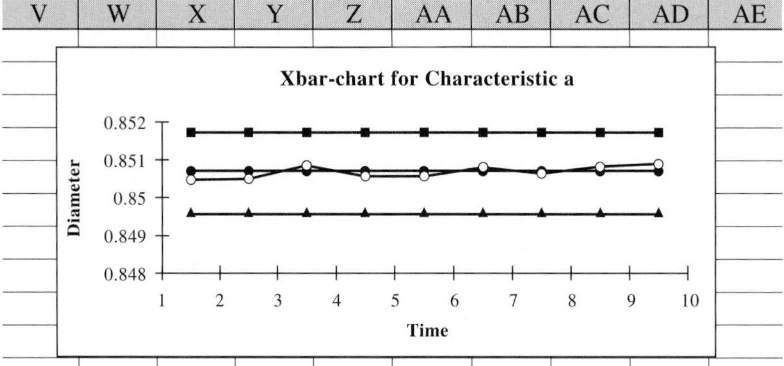

■

TRY IT NOW!

The Sleeve Company ***Xbar-chart for Characteristic b***

Using the sample averages shown in Example 16.8, create the Xbar-chart for characteristic b for the manufacturer of the sleeves.

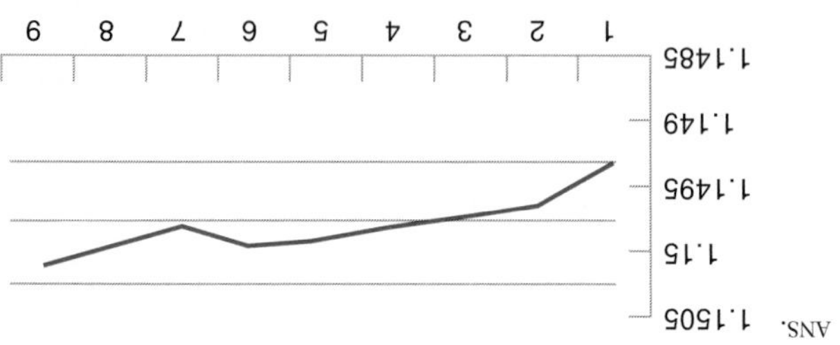

16.6.2 *R*-charts

At the beginning of the chapter we looked at 4 different scenarios for a soup can filling process. The 4 scenarios showed a stable process, two ways that the mean of the process could change, and one illustration of a change in the process variability. We learned that control charts are used to help detect changes in the mean of the distribution and changes in the variance of the distribution. The Xbar-chart developed in the previous section is used to detect changes in the mean of the distribution. In this section we look at a control chart to detect changes in the variability of the distribution. It is called the ***R*-chart.**

> The ***R*-chart** is a control chart used to monitor the variation of a process over time. Time is plotted on the x axis and the sample range, R = Max − Min, of the quality characteristic being monitored is plotted on the y axis. The graph also has three lines drawn parallel to the x axis. These are called the center line, the upper control limit, and the lower control limit.

You might wonder why we don't plot the sample standard deviations in an effort to detect changes to the process variability. This is a good question since we have repeatedly said that the standard deviation is the most commonly used measure of variability. There is, in fact, the s-chart, which is a plot of the sample standard deviations over time. However, for small sample sizes ($n = 9$ or less), the s-chart and the R-chart provide about the same information and R-charts are widely used by industry. For this reason, we will look only at R-charts.

The logic used to construct the R-chart is the same as that used to construct the x-chart and the Xbar-chart. There is a center line and upper and lower control limits that are set 3 standard deviations above and below the center line. Instead of plotting sample averages on the chart, sample ranges are plotted. To construct the upper and lower control limits we must estimate the standard deviation of R. The most commonly used estimate is $d_3(\overline{R}/d_2)$, where d_3 and d_2 are constants that depend on the size of the sample. They are found in Table 7 of the Appendix. Using this estimate for the standard deviation of R, the procedure for setting up the R-chart is as follows:

Steps for constructing an R-chart

Step 1: The center line (CL) of the chart is drawn at the average of all the sample ranges, $\overline{R}$.

Step 2: The upper control limit (UCL) of the chart is a horizontal line drawn at a value that is 3 standard deviations above the center line (called the 3 sigma limit), $\overline{R} + 3d_3(\overline{R}/d_2)$.

Step 3: The lower control limit (LCL) of the chart is a horizontal line drawn at a value that is 3 standard deviations below the center line (called the 3 sigma limit), $\overline{R} - d_3(\overline{R}/d_2)$.

By doing some algebra on the formulas for the upper and lower control limits, you can rewrite them as

Simpler steps for constructing an R-chart

$$\text{UCL} = \overline{R}\left(1 + \frac{3d_3}{d_2}\right) = \overline{R}D_4$$

$$\text{LCL} = \overline{R}\left(1 - \frac{3d_3}{d_2}\right) = \overline{R}D_3$$

In these formulas $D_4 = 1 + 3d_3/d_2$ and $D_3 = 1 - 3d_3/d_2$. They have been calculated from d_3 and d_2 and can be found in the same table in the Appendix, Table 7. Using these formulas for the upper and lower control limits makes the calculation much easier.

Constants d_2, d_3, and d_4 are found in Appendix Table 7.

Analyze the Data

EXAMPLE 16.9 The Diaper Company

R-chart

The sample ranges for 20 hours of data from the diaper company are shown here. Recall that the diaper company samples 5 diapers every hour and checks the weight in grams.

Sample	Range	Sample	Range
1	1.9	11	0.81
2	1.17	12	1.36
3	2.33	13	1.44
4	0.65	14	2.11
5	1.86	15	1.62
6	0.86	16	1.92
7	1.46	17	1.2
8	1.64	18	1.2
9	2.37	19	1.55
10	1.83	20	0.93

The center line is found by averaging the 20 sample ranges to get $\overline{R} = 1.511$ g. The upper control limit is $\overline{R}D_4 = (1.511)(2.114) = 3.193$. The lower control limit is $\overline{R}D_3 = (1.511)(0) = 0$.

Plotting these lines and the sample ranges gives you the *R*-chart shown here:

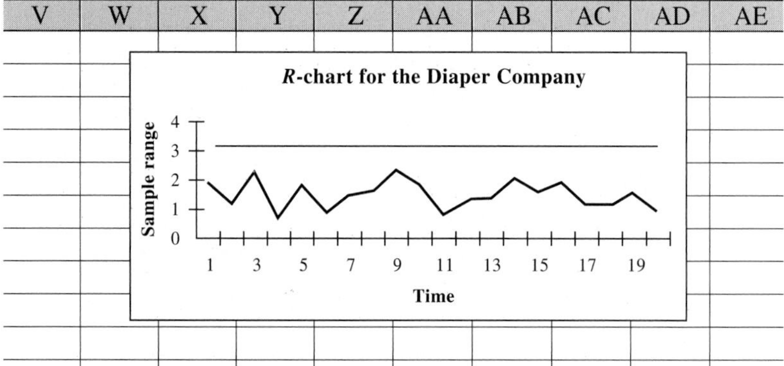

■

TRY IT NOW!

The Sleeve Company *R-chart for Characteristic b*

Using the sample ranges shown in Example 16.8, create the *R*-chart for characteristic b for the manufacturer of the sleeves.

ANS. SEE NEXT PAGE.

16.6.3 Guidelines for Sampling

The data required for both the Xbar-chart and the *R*-chart come from sampling *n* observations periodically over time. To collect such data you must decide the sample size, *n*, and the frequency with which samples are to be taken (once an hour, every 10 minutes, etc.). These samples are often referred to in the quality literature as **rational subgroups.**

There are some guidelines for selecting rational subgroups. Basically you want the sample observations in a subgroup to be similar to each other since you are finding the sample average and the sample range. Thus, you usually select consecutively produced items or consecutively served customers. Typically, sample sizes of 4 to 10 are used.

Guidelines for selecting rational subgroups

To determine the frequency of sampling you need to think about the potential sources of variation. Then you need to sample with a frequency that will allow the samples to differ from each other. For example, suppose you were manufacturing tubes of glue and the tubes were filled 8 at a time. If the timing of your sampling always got you a sample of the 8th tube, then you could be missing some variation simply because you have not looked at the other tube positions in the filling process.

16.6.4 Exercises—Learning It!

16.11 Set up the Xbar- and *R*-charts for characteristic c of the sleeve company.

16.12 An instructor wonders whether the average grade in the introductory statistics course is a stable process. The average course grade for the past 10 semesters is shown here as well as the range for each semester. The average and ranges are based on classes of size 15.

Semester	Average grade	Range
1	2.92	3.2
2	2.68	2.5
3	3.06	3.1
4	3.32	3
5	3.30	2
6	3.43	4
7	2.45	3.5
8	2.94	3.1
9	3.27	2.9
10	2.73	2.9

(a) Construct the Xbar-chart.

(b) Construct the *R*-chart.

(c) Has there been any change to the mean or variability of the grading process over the past 10 semesters? Explain why or why not.

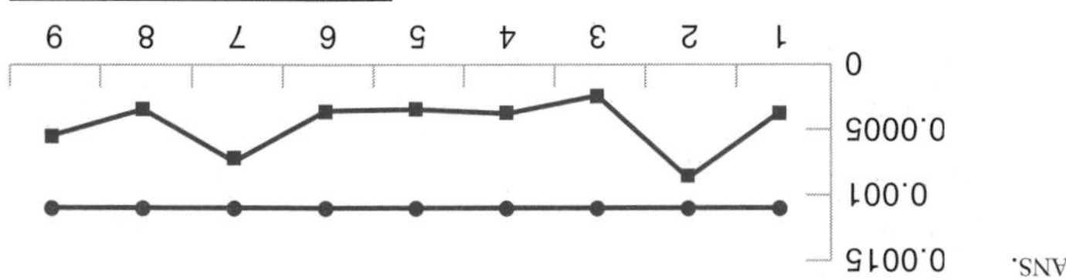

Datafile: FASTFOOD.XXX

16.13 A fast-food chain is concerned about putting the "fast" back into fast food. The variable to be monitored is the time between when the customer finishes placing his order and when he leaves the register after receiving his food. Five customers are sampled every hour during the peak hours and the following times in minutes were recorded.

Hour 1	Hour 2	Hour 3	Hour 4	Hour 5	Hour 6	Hour 7	Hour 8	Hour 9	Hour 10
4.81	3.74	4.88	4.91	5.06	5.40	3.94	4.64	4.85	4.44
4.77	4.03	5.27	3.93	4.64	3.23	4.92	4.46	5.33	4.71
4.62	4.39	4.11	3.97	4.30	4.28	4.64	4.68	4.86	4.95
4.61	4.29	5.07	4.50	4.82	4.71	4.44	4.19	3.93	4.74
3.59	3.21	4.18	5.17	4.48	4.31	5.24	4.33	5.57	4.50

(a) Construct the Xbar- and *R*-charts for this process.

(b) Has there been any change to the process mean overtime?

(c) Has there been any change to the process variability over time?

(d) If the process is in control, why might customers still be unhappy with service times?

(e) What recommendations would you make to the fast-food chain?

16.14 The golf ball company has decided to sample 4 golf balls every 2 hours to check the weight of the balls. The sample averages and sample ranges for 24 samples are shown here:

Sample	Xbar	Range
1	45.02	0.09
2	45.09	0.01
3	45.03	0.00
4	44.98	0.16
5	44.93	0.12
6	44.99	0.08
7	45.04	0.08
8	45.08	0.10
9	44.95	0.12
10	44.98	0.04
11	45.03	0.00
12	44.98	0.04
13	45.04	0.11
14	44.98	0.04
15	45.02	0.18
16	45.01	0.04
17	44.97	0.20
18	44.98	0.06
19	44.97	0.15
20	44.94	0.22
21	44.95	0.32
22	44.99	0.16
23	44.96	0.03
24	45.03	0.07

(a) Construct the Xbar- and *R*-charts for the golf ball weights. The company has a target mean of 45 g and a target standard deviation of 0.1 g.

(b) What recommendations would you make to the company?

16.15 A company that manufactures tissues has discovered that the amount of airspace left in the box at the time of production impacts the customer complaints about the first tissue tearing. The target airspace at the time of production is 20 mm with a standard deviation of 1 mm. A sample of 4 tissue boxes is checked every hour. The sample means and ranges for 20 hours follow.

Sample	Xbar	Range
1	21.96	2.10
2	18.63	1.92
3	21.63	2.21
4	20.34	2.67
5	20.46	3.20
6	21.85	2.51
7	19.18	2.46
8	20.17	1.81
9	20.07	2.27
10	19.23	1.78
11	17.94	0.90
12	17.24	2.67
13	16.85	1.15
14	16.96	2.78
15	14.45	2.06
16	17.91	2.39
17	17.66	2.23
18	17.93	1.97
19	17.29	1.61
20	18.20	1.53

(a) Construct the Xbar- and R-charts for the airspace data.

(b) What can you conclude about the packaging process from these data?

16.7 THE p-CHART

The tree diagram shown in Section 16.4 indicates that the first question you must ask to decide which control chart to use has to do with whether you have quantitative or qualitative data. The control charts we have presented so far in this chapter have dealt with quantitative data such as melt flow, weight, and diameter. However, very often we wish to monitor the number of defects, the number of errors, etc. In this case a product or service either has the attribute of interest (e.g., a defect or an error) or it does not. For such qualitative or attribute data, the most commonly used control chart is called the ***p*-chart.**

> The ***p*-chart** is a control chart used to monitor the proportion, p, of items that have a particular attribute or characteristic over time. Time is plotted on the x axis and the sample proportion, p = number in the sample with the attribute/n, is plotted on the y axis. The graph also has three lines drawn parallel to the x axis. These are called the center line, the upper control limit, and the lower control limit.

There are many situations in which you might use the p-chart, for example, the proportion of invoices processed with at least one error, the proportion of restaurant customers that have to wait more than 10 minutes for a table, the proportion of free throw shots missed, the proportion of bytes transmitted incorrectly. In each of these situations you are interested in monitoring the proportion of items or people that have these attributes.

The underlying assumption in situations like these is that the proportion of the population that has the attribute, π, remains constant over time. Thus, the population distribution is a binomial distribution, which you learned about in Chapter 6. To monitor π, samples of size n are selected over time. The number of items in the sample that have the attribute you are monitoring is observed and labeled x. This number is divided by the sample size, n, to get a sample proportion, p:

$$p = \frac{x}{n}$$

If the process is a stable process then there will, of course, be common variation in the sample proportion, p. If the process is unstable, then the sample proportion will have both common and special variation. The p-chart is used to detect this latter situation. Variation in p is displayed in the p-chart and when the sample proportion goes outside the control chart limits or exhibits a pattern, then the process needs to be examined.

16.7.1 Constructing the *p*-chart

To determine the control chart limits we need to know the mean and standard deviation of the sample proportion, p. You might recall from Chapter 7 that if the sample size is large enough the estimate p has a normal distribution with

- a mean equal to population proportion, π, and
- a standard deviation of

$$\sqrt{\frac{\pi(1-\pi)}{n}}$$

Using this information, we can construct the upper and lower control chart limits in the same basic manner as we have done for the other charts. The population proportion, π, could be known if there is a target proportion, but most of the time π must be estimated from the data. This is analogous to the situation we found ourselves in for the Xbar-chart when the population mean was unknown. In that case we used $\bar{\bar{X}}$ to estimate μ. In this case we will use $\bar{p}$ to estimate π. The estimate $\bar{p}$ is found by averaging all the sample proportions. This is equivalent to totaling the number of items with the attribute and dividing by the total number of items sampled:

Formula for $\bar{p}$

$$\bar{p} = \frac{\Sigma x}{\Sigma n}$$

The center line and the upper and lower control limits are found using the following steps:

Steps for constructing a p-chart

Step 1: The center line (CL) of the chart is drawn at the average of all the sample proportions, $\bar{p}$

Step 2: The upper control limit (UCL) of the chart is a horizontal line drawn at a value that is 3 standard deviations above the center line (called the 3 sigma limit),

$$\bar{p} + 3\sqrt{\frac{\bar{p}(1-\bar{p})}{n}}$$

Step 3: The lower control limit (LCL) of the chart is horizontal line drawn at a value that is 3 standard deviations below the center line (called the 3 sigma limit),

$$\bar{p} - 3\sqrt{\frac{\bar{p}(1-\bar{p})}{n}}$$

Once the upper and lower control chart limits have been graphed, the sample proportions are graphed over time. An example will help illustrate the construction of the p-chart.

Analyze the Data

EXAMPLE 16.10 Software Company

***p*-chart for Proportion of Defective Disks**

A manufacturer of computer disks is concerned about the proportion of defective disks. Each day a sample of 50 disks are tested and the number of defectives is reported. The proportion of defects found for the past 20 days is shown here:

Days 1–10	0.00	0.02	0.04	0.02	0.02	0.00	0.04	0.02	0.06	0.02
Days 11–20	0.02	0.02	0.00	0.00	0.04	0.02	0.00	0.02	0.02	0.04

The center line is at $\bar{p}$ = average of all the sample proportions = 0.021. The upper control limit is at

$$\bar{p} + 3\sqrt{\frac{\bar{p}(1-\bar{p})}{n}} = 0.021 + 3\sqrt{\frac{0.021\,(1-0.021)}{50}} = 0.021 + 3(0.0203) = 0.082$$

The lower control limit is at

$$0.021 - 3\sqrt{\frac{0.021\,(1-0.021)}{50}} = 0.021 - 3(0.0203) = 0$$

(since the proportion cannot be negative). The center line, the control limits, and the sample proportions are shown in the following p-chart.

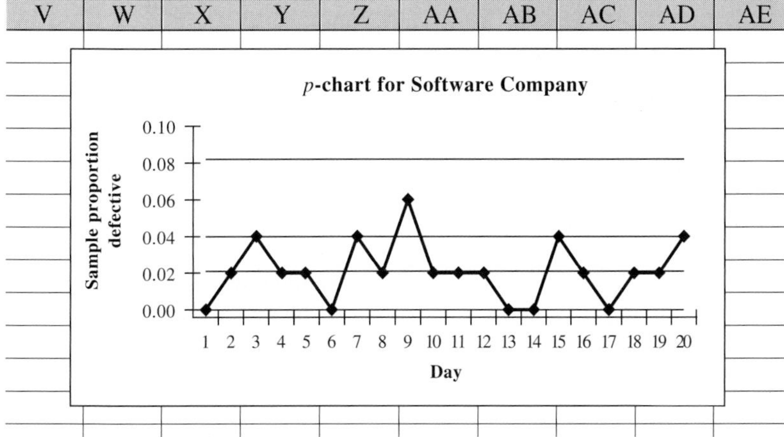

All of the sample proportions are in between the control limits, so we conclude that the process is stable. ■

Notice that the sample size remains constant from sample to sample in a p-chart. If you have a varying sample size, then you must use what is called the np-chart. This is very similar to the p-chart but accommodates the changing sample size.

The Basketball Player ***p*-chart for Proportion of Successful Free Throws**

A basketball player is monitoring his free throw percentage. He keeps track of the number of baskets made in 50 practice shots on each day. His data are shown on page 834 for the past 15 days of practice:

(continued)

Practice Session	Shots Made	Practice Session	Shots Made
1	37	9	38
2	34	10	33
3	35	11	30
4	35	12	41
5	29	13	37
6	32	14	34
7	39	15	37
8	36		

Create the p-chart to monitor the percentage of free throw shots that he makes.

Is this player consistent?

16.7.2 Exercises—Learning It!

Datafile: PATIENT.XXX

16.16 The emergency room at a major hospital is concerned about the number of patients who must wait more than 1 hour to be seen by a doctor. For the past 35 days the hospital has sampled 30 patients a day and recorded the number of patients who had to wait more than one hour to be seen. The data are shown here:

Day	Day of the week	Number of patients who waited more than 1 hour
1	Monday	19
2	Tuesday	17
3	Wednesday	19
4	Thursday	22
5	Friday	19
6	Saturday	25
7	Sunday	15
8	Monday	14
9	Tuesday	12
10	Wednesday	19
11	Thursday	15
12	Friday	15
13	Saturday	28

(continued)

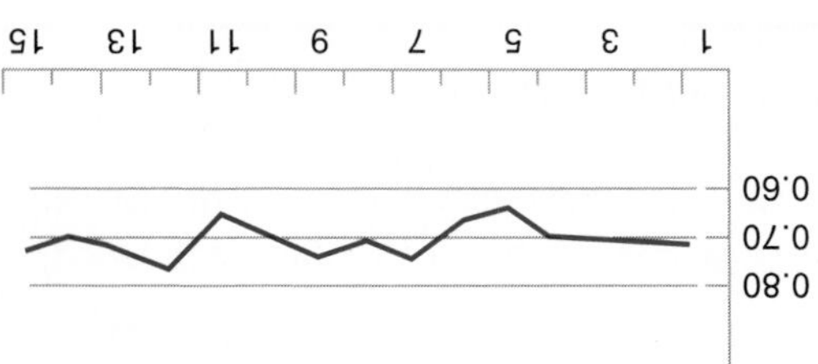

ANS. YES, NO POINTS OUT OF CONTROL.

Day	Day of the week	Number of patients who waited more than 1 hour
14	Sunday	17
15	Monday	17
16	Tuesday	18
17	Wednesday	12
18	Thursday	15
19	Friday	17
20	Saturday	22
21	Sunday	17
22	Monday	17
23	Tuesday	16
24	Wednesday	12
25	Thursday	15
26	Friday	11
27	Saturday	27
28	Sunday	20
29	Monday	20
30	Tuesday	15
31	Wednesday	20
32	Thursday	18
33	Friday	20
34	Saturday	21
35	Sunday	15

(a) Find the sample proportion who waited longer than 1 hour each day.

(b) Find the values for the center line and the upper and lower control limits.

(c) Construct the p-chart for these data.

(d) Is the process in control? If not, which points are out of control? Can you offer any explanation to the hospital?

16.17 A college registrar's office is auditing the process by which transfer credits are awarded. A sample of 50 student records is checked for each of the past 8 semesters. The number of records with errors is tabulated. The data are shown here:

Semester	Number with errors	Semester	Number with errors
1	7	5	9
2	7	6	11
3	6	7	10
4	6	8	13

(a) Find the sample proportion of records with errors for each semester.

(b) Construct a p-chart for the registrar.

(c) Is this process under control? Why or why not?

16.18 A manufacturer of T-shirts checks to be sure that the design printed on the shirt is straight. The company checks a sample of 100 shirts a day. The number of defects found for each of the past 20 days is shown here:

Day	Number defective	Day	Number defective
1	2	8	2
2	1	9	2
3	2	10	4
4	2	11	2
5	2	12	2
6	4	13	2
7	2	14	1

(continued)

Day	Number defective	Day	Number defective
15	2	18	2
16	2	19	0
17	3	20	2

(a) Find the sample proportion defective for each day.

(b) Construct the p-chart for these data.

(c) Is the process in control? Explain why or why not.

16.19 A mail-order company monitors a sample of 25 calls a day to see if a sales representative is following the company guidelines. The number of calls that have quality problems (e.g., the sales representative did not provide accurate information or did not treat the customer with respect) is recorded. The data are shown here:

Day	Number of calls with quality problems	Day	Number of calls with quality problems
1	4	11	3
2	3	12	2
3	3	13	2
4	3	14	4
5	4	15	3
6	4	16	2
7	1	17	4
8	3	18	2
9	3	19	3
10	2	20	2

(a) Find the sample proportion of calls with quality problems for each day.

(b) Construct a p-chart for these data.

(c) Is this process in control? Explain why or why not.

16.20 A manufacturer of heaters for dishwashers performs a number of different quality checks on the heaters before they are shipped. The number of heaters with defects in samples of size 25 are recorded by shift. The data are shown here:

Day	Shift 1	Shift 2	Shift 3	Day	Shift 1	Shift 2	Shift 3
1	0	2	5	9	0	3	5
2	0	3	5	10	2	3	6
3	1	3	4	11	1	3	5
4	0	3	6	12	2	3	5
5	1	3	5	13	1	3	5
6	1	4	5	14	1	2	5
7	1	3	5	15	2	4	5
8	1	3	5				

(a) Construct a p-chart for the proportion of defects produced during the day shift, shift 1.

(b) Construct a p-chart for the proportion of defects produced during the evening shift, shift 2.

(c) Construct a p-chart for the proportion of defects produced during the graveyard shift, shift 3.

(d) Which of the processes are under control?

16.8 *Executive Summary:*

THE MELT FLOW PROBLEM

Business Analysis...

TO: Quality Manager
FROM: Erica Q. Analyst
RE: Analysis of melt flow data

As you know, one of the quality characteristics of our plastic is melt flow (min) at 200°F. This measures the viscosity of the liquid. One of our customers has been checking the melt flow of the plastic we sell him and has been getting results that differ from ours.

To investigate this issue, we have looked at the sources of variation in the melt flow. Some possible common causes of variation might be poor lighting in the plant and inconsistent raw materials. I recommend that we check the lighting. We already test the quality of our raw materials, but we should check with purchasing to see whether there has been any recent change in our suppliers. Possible special causes of variation might be the accidental setting of the controls on a machine incorrectly. We should check to be sure that all of the operators have been properly trained.

In addition, we have constructed an x-chart for the last 47 melt flow observations. The chart is shown here:

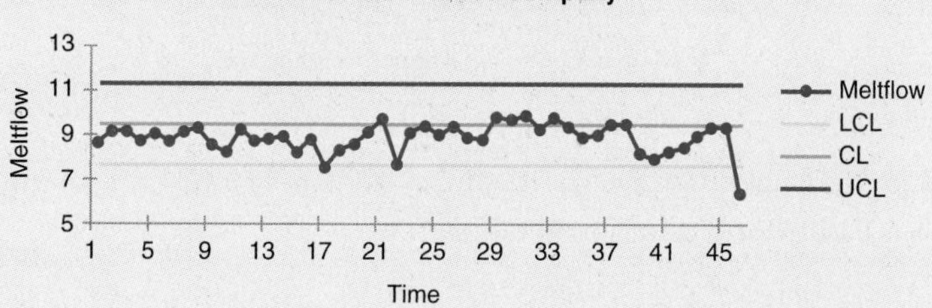

As you can see, there is only one point out of control, but there are quite a few points below the center line. We must investigate possible reasons for this.

In conclusion, we cannot yet determine whether our customer is correct but we must continue to work with the customer to resolve this difference. I recommend the continued use of control charts and the use of a fishbone diagram to identify the possible causes of this problem. I will provide you with a report next week.

The *Wall Street Journal* is a major source of current business news and information for the business community. If your professor has arranged for your class to have access to the Business Extra feature, you can go to it now and see the techniques of this chapter in action today. Go to the Wiley Web site at http://www.wiley.com/college/pelosi, and click on Business Extra!

16.9 CREATING CONTROL CHARTS IN EXCEL

Although Excel has no built-in tools for creating control charts, you can use several of the tools you already know about to create them. In this section we will detail the procedure for creating an Xbar-chart. The procedures for the other control charts are very similar.

16.9.1 Creating Subgroup Statistics in Excel

Suppose that we want to create an Xbar-chart for the diaper data. The variable measured was diaper weight for samples of size 5. The data are shown in Figure 16.3.

	A	B	C	D
1	*Sample*	*Diaper*	*Weight*	*Bulk*
2	1	1	55.87	0.419
3	1	2	55.35	0.380
4	1	3	54.50	0.365
5	1	4	53.97	0.406
6	1	5	54.29	0.360
7	2	1	54.85	0.397
8	2	2	54.79	0.405
9	2	3	54.65	0.393
10	2	4	55.56	0.413
11	2	5	55.82	0.367
12	3	1	54.40	0.397

FIGURE 16.3 Diaper weight data

To create the control chart, we need to calculate the mean and range for each sample. This is easily done using pivot tables.

1. Create a pivot table for the data by dragging the **Sample** field button to the Row area and the **Weight** field button to the Data area. Double click on **Weight** to open the Pivot Table Field box and change **Summarize by:** to **Average.** Finish making your selections and click **Finish.**
2. You cannot summarize the data in a pivot table using the range, but you can do it for the maximum and minimum values. Create pivot tables for the **Max** and **Min** of each sample and locate them adjacent to the one for average. After you have done this, the worksheet will look like the one in Figure 16.4

	A	B	C	D	E	F	G	H	I	J
1	*Sample*	*Diaper*	*Weight*	*Bulk*	Average of Weight		Max of Weight		Min of Weight	
2	1	1	55.87	0.419	Sample	Total	Sample	Total	Sample	Total
3	1	2	55.35	0.380	1	54.796	1	55.87	1	53.97
4	1	3	54.50	0.365	2	55.134	2	55.82	2	54.65
5	1	4	53.97	0.406	3	54.836	3	56.44	3	54.11
6	1	5	54.29	0.360	4	54.59	4	54.87	4	54.22
7	2	1	54.85	0.397	5	55.268	5	56.3	5	54.44
8	2	2	54.79	0.405	6	55.276	6	55.75	6	54.89
9	2	3	54.65	0.393	7	55.026	7	55.78	7	54.32
10	2	4	55.56	0.413	8	55.232	8	55.78	8	54.14
11	2	5	55.82	0.367	9	54.718	9	55.97	9	53.6
12	3	1	54.40	0.397	10	55.054	10	55.7	10	53.87
13	3	2	56.44	0.345	11	55.116	11	55.55	11	54.74
14	3	3	54.11	0.421	12	54.542	12	55.22	12	53.86
15	3	4	54.67	0.419	13	55.06	13	55.87	13	54.43

FIGURE 16.4 Data and summary pivot tables

Since we really don't need all of those columns labeled Sample, you can hide those columns to make the worksheet less crowded. To work easily with the pivot table columns, you might want to use **Copy > Paste Special > Value.**

3. Use a formula in the cell adjacent to the minimum value to calculate the range for each sample by subtracting the minimum weight value from the maximum.

16.9.2 Calculating the Control Limits in Excel

Now that you have the summary information for each sample, you need to calculate the values for the center line and upper and lower control limits. In this example, we will use the target specification of 55.00 g for the center line, but we will use the sample range data to find the upper and lower control limits. That is, we want to create a chart with a known population mean, but unknown standard deviation. Remember that the formulas for the control limits are:

$$\text{LCL} = \mu - A_2\overline{R}$$
$$\text{UCL} = \mu + A_2\overline{R}$$

The factor A_2 depends on the sample size. In this case, from Table 7 in the Appendix for $n = 5$, the value of A_2 is 0.577.

1. Use a formula to find the average of the sample ranges, $\overline{R}$. The formula should be = AVERAGE(data range), where data range is the cell reference that contains the sample ranges. For this example, the value of $\overline{R}$ is 1.44.
2. Insert three new columns next to the column that contains the sample means and label them CL, LCL, and UCL.
3. In the first cell under the label CL, type **55.00** and copy it to the cells next to each of the sample means.
4. In the first cell under the label LCL, type in the formula **= 55 − 0.577*1.44.** Copy this formula down the column for each sample.
5. In the first cell under the label UCL, type in the formula **= 55 + 0.577*1.44,** and copy this formula to the cells below.

Note: You could use cell references instead of the actual values, but be sure you use absolute cell referencing.

Your worksheet should contain columns that look like the ones shown in Figure 16.5.

L	M	N	O	P
Average of Weight				
Sample	Average	CL	LCL	UCL
1	54.796	55	54.16912	55.83088
2	55.134	55	54.16912	55.83088
3	54.836	55	54.16912	55.83088
4	54.59	55	54.16912	55.83088
5	55.268	55	54.16912	55.83088
6	55.276	55	54.16912	55.83088
7	55.026	55	54.16912	55.83088
8	55.232	55	54.16912	55.83088
9	54.718	55	54.16912	55.83088
10	55.054	55	54.16912	55.83088
11	55.116	55	54.16912	55.83088
12	54.542	55	54.16912	55.83088
13	55.06	55	54.16912	55.83088
14	55.136	55	54.16912	55.83088
15	54.73	55	54.16912	55.83088
16	55.45	55	54.16912	55.83088

FIGURE 16.5 Worksheet with CL, LCL, and UCL

16.9.3 Creating the Control Chart

In Excel you will use the Chart Wizard to create the control chart from the worksheet that you have prepared.

1. Highlight the columns in the worksheet that contain the sample means, CL, LCL, and UCL, and start the Chart Wizard.
2. From the list of **Chart types,** choose **Line** and **Lines with Markers** as the **Chart sub-type** as shown in Figure 16.6. Click **Next >** twice to continue.

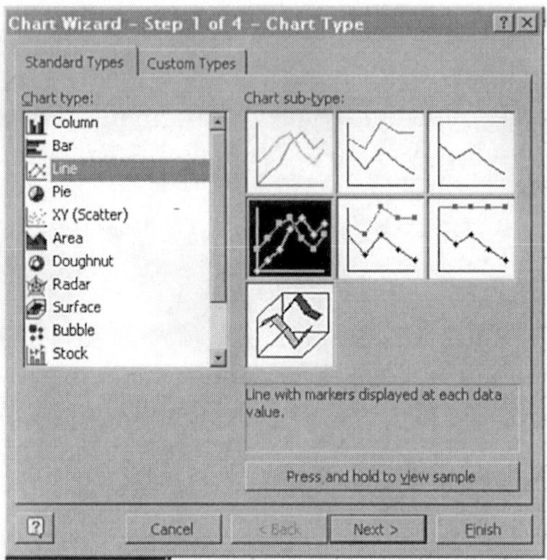

FIGURE 16.6 Choosing a line chart

3. Add titles and other formatting changes, and click **Finish.** The chart will be placed on the worksheet.

If you want the control limits to be plotted without markers, you can accomplish this quite easily.

4. Click on the chart to select it, and then click on one of the three limits. The **Format Data Series** dialog box will open. Select the **Patterns** tab, and under **Marker,** click the radio button for **None.** The dialog box is shown in Figure 16.7.

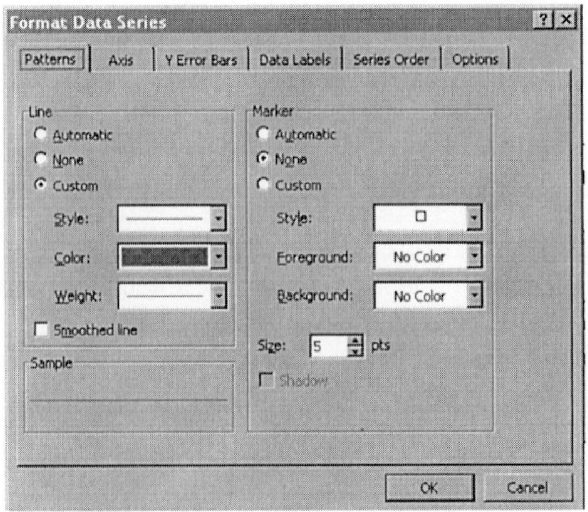

FIGURE 16.7 Removing markers from lines

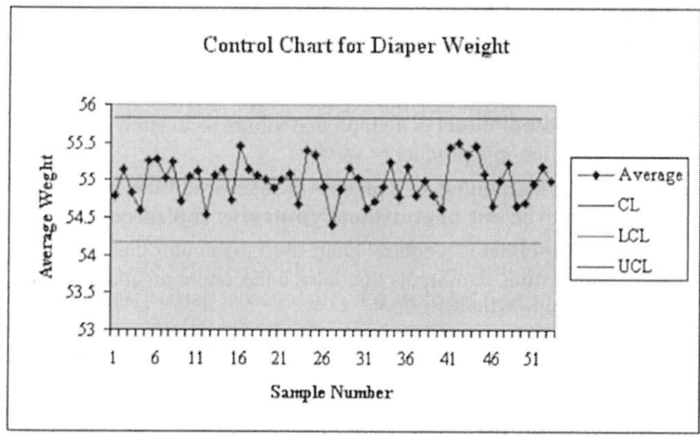

FIGURE 16.8 Control chart for diaper weight

5. Repeat this for the other two control lines. The finished graph is shown in Figure 16.8.

The steps for creating other types of control charts such as *R*- and *p*-charts are very similar to the ones for the Xbar-chart. The only changes are the calculation of the summary values for each sample and the formulas for the control limits.

CHAPTER 16 SUMMARY

Control charts are one of many quality tools being used with increasing frequency by both manufacturers and service companies. Customers are also beginning to partner with suppliers and in doing so are also monitoring the quality of their suppliers. This is a growing and dynamic area and we have just introduced the basics in this chapter.

In this chapter you learned the basics about constructing and using control charts. You have seen that there are many different kinds of charts but they all are constructed using the same logic. In all cases a sample of data is collected periodically over time to monitor some characteristic of a process. Depending on the process you are monitoring, you might observe a quantitative variable or you might observe the presence or lack of presence of some characteristic. Regardless of the situation, a control chart is used to detect the presence of special cause variation. If a process has some special cause variation, then one or more of the plotted points will go outside the upper and lower control limits.

The center line is located at the average value of the variable being plotted. The upper and lower control limits are typically set 3 standard deviations above and below the center line. This allows for detection of the presence of special variation without setting off false alarms very often. A false alarm occurs when you conclude that there is some special variation in the process when there is not any.

Key Terms

Term	Definition	Page Reference
Common causes of variation	**Common causes of variation** are the methods, machines, people, and environment that are an inherent part of a process. They are part of the design of the process.	816

(continued)

CHAPTER 17

MAKING YOUR CASE

THE GREAT DIVIDE

"The earnings gap between executives at the very top of corporate America and middle managers and workers has stretched into a vast chasm."
(Wall Street Journal, April 11, 1996)

Business Dilemma...

A *Wall Street Journal* article reports that in 1995 the heads of about 30 major companies received compensation that was 212 times higher than the pay of the average American employee. The widening gulf has ignited a political firestorm and CEOs are scurrying to explain their pay increases. Compensation of chief executives "has reached Marie Antoinette proportions," says Nell Minow, a principal at Lens Inc., an activist investment fund in Washington, D.C. "People are getting disgusted with it."

William M. Mercer Inc., New York compensation consultants, analyzed 350 proxy statements of the biggest U.S. businesses. The Securities and Exchange Commission (SEC) rules for proxy statements require disclosure of the compensation of the chief executive officer plus four or more other highly compensated executives. For each individual the following data were collected:

Company name
Type of business
Standard Industrial Classification Code (SIC)
Number of employees—1995

Company revenue—1995

CEO's name

1995 Salary—base salary earned in 1995

1995 Bonus—annual bonus earned in 1995

Percent change from 1994—change in salary/bonus from 1994 to 1995. Percent change data have been excluded for new CEOs and in cases where salary/bonus data for 1995 or 1994 are not valid.

Long-term compensation: options gain—gains from the exercise of stock options and/or stock appreciation rights during 1995

Long-term compensation: other—includes 1995 (1) value of shares of restricted stock or restricted stock units at grant, and (2) value of payouts under any other long-term incentive compensation plan.

The furor over the great pay divide is creating pressure for higher tax rates on the rich and new federal limits on executive compensation. One idea is to give tax breaks for businesses that treat their workers well—for example, by capping the highest-paid executive's pay at perhaps 50 times the lowest-paid employee's.

17.1 CHAPTER OBJECTIVES

This is the final chapter of the book. It is a good time to look back on the techniques that have been covered and use them to "make your case"! We have been building up to this point throughout the entire book.

Each of the chapters in this book has started with a business problem. That problem was used to explain the specific techniques of the chapter. Most of the worked examples in the chapter pertained to this opening business problem. Finally, each chapter ended with an Executive Summary that could be sent to management. The Executive Summary included the analysis and resulting conclusions based on the work done on that business problem in the examples in that chapter. Often the Executive Summary was more of an in-progress report, and you completed the remaining analysis as part of the Doing It! exercise at the end of the chapter. In completing the analysis you were completing a structured case. You received some guidance in the analysis by the nature of the questions that were asked, and you knew to apply the techniques that had been presented in the chapter.

Now it is time to complete the course and to solve some cases without any guidance. These are called Making Your Case exercises. This is, after all, what you will need to be able to do as you enter the workforce. You must use all that you have learned about data analysis to make some sense out of these data sets, see the information in the data, draw some conclusions, and make your case. Hopefully you have completed the paradigm shift that we started talking about in Chapter 1, and you now see the world through a "statistical thinking" lens. It is this vision that will make you an important member of any team in the workplace.

Specifically, this chapter will include:

- Summary of the Techniques Covered in This Book
- How to Analyze the "Great Divide" Data Set

17.2 SUMMARY OF THE TECHNIQUES COVERED IN THIS BOOK

As you look back over the material covered in this book, try not to see the small numerical details of each of the techniques; instead, look for the unifying themes that underlie what you have learned. Take a global look at the book and use this summary to identify the major threads that tie the book together.

This book has been divided into 17 chapters. Now, let's take the chapters and group them into six major parts.

Part	Chapters		Topic
Part I	Chapters 1 and 2		*Getting Started*
	Main idea:	Sample as a snapshot of the population	
Part II	Chapters 3, 4, and 5		*Exploratory Data Analysis*
	Main ideas:	Summarize the data in picture and numerical form	
		Look for the center, the spread, and trends	
Part III	Chapters 6 and 7		*The Keys That Unlock the Door to Inferential Statistics*
	Main ideas:	Distributions and parameters	
		Link between probability and inferential statistics	
Part IV	Chapters 8, 9, and 10		*Inferential Statistics*
	Main idea:	Use the sample to draw conclusions about the population	
Part V	Chapters 11, 12, and 13		*Model Building*
	Main idea:	Use sample data to build a model to explain the relationship between two or more variables	
Part VI	Chapters 14, 15, 16, and 17		*Additional Topics*

We have managed to reduce the book to five main ideas! Now let's see if there are some major themes that tie these ideas together.

1. Early in the text we learned that even if we did our sampling perfectly, we would still undoubtedly have incomplete information. This is not because we made any mistakes but because of what is called *sampling error*. Sampling error is the difference between what the sample predicts and what is true for the population. It is due to the fact that the sample is only a piece of the popula-

tion. No matter what you do in statistics, unless you take a census (examine the entire population), you will have some sampling error. We have learned that even if the sample data are "a bit" inconsistent with the hypothesized theory, this doesn't automatically mean the theory is wrong. It is possible and maybe even likely to find that 52% of a sample of employees feel the company has empowered them when in fact less than half of all of the employees feel this way.

2. Without a doubt, the concept of *variability* has been a common thread from the beginning of this book. One of the great quality gurus, W. Edwards Deming, said that variation is our greatest enemy. We have indeed seen this ourselves. In fact, we observed that if there were no variability in the population we could take a sample of size $n = 1$ and have perfect information. The *standard deviation*, which is the square root of the variance, is the yardstick by which we evaluate all differences when analyzing data.
3. Another theme that you may have noticed throughout the text is the focus on *relationships* between variables. Right from the beginning of descriptive statistics you compared graphs of variables and used scatter plots to look for relationships between variables. This theme was extended when you learned to do hypothesis tests to compare two or more population means or proportions. In one of the later chapters you learned how to build models that would allow you to exploit the relationship between two or more variables for prediction purposes.
4. *Decision making in any form should be based on a proper analysis of data.* To remain competitive in today's fast-changing business environment, more data than ever before are being collected. However, the data alone are useless. They must be properly analyzed to reveal the information they contain. The entire quality movement depends on the proper use of data to make informed business decisions.

So now we have reduced the entire book to four fundamental themes. Despite the many different techniques that have been covered and even some that have not been covered, there are really only a few fundamental concepts that you need to learn in statistics.

17.3 HOW TO ANALYZE THE "GREAT DIVIDE" DATA SET

Datafile: DIVIDE.XXX

The "story" presented at the beginning of this chapter is a real-life case. Your job is to analyze this data set to reveal the information they contain. The data are found in the file named DIVIDE.XXX on the CD. This section will provide you with some ideas for your analysis. Before we look at the particulars of this data set, let's see if we can identify some basic steps that should be followed anytime we begin to analyze data to solve a problem.

The material in the text has been presented in the order that you would use the techniques.

Step 1: Explore the data visually using the graphical techniques of descriptive statistics. These include bar charts, pie charts, and histograms.

Step 2: Summarize the data numerically. This includes finding the mean, median, quartiles, range, and standard deviation (at a minimum).

Step 3: Look for relationships in the data visually and numerically. Visually you would examine scatter plots. Numerically, you should use cross-tabulation tables to examine averages and standard deviations for subsets of the data.

Step 4: On the basis of the results of steps 1–3, formulate some hypotheses that might help you answer your questions and solve the problem.

Step 5: Test the hypotheses, being sure to check that the assumptions of the test are not violated. For example, if the variables must be normally distributed for the test to be valid, then first run a chi-square goodness of fit test. If the technique requires you to assume a common variance, use an F test to be sure this is a reasonable assumption.

Step 6: If there appears to be a pattern in the data over time, use a time series technique.

Step 7: If appropriate, estimate the parameters of a multiple regression model for the variable you are trying to predict. Be sure that you check the assumptions of the model. Determine whether your model is useful by testing for the significance of each of the variables and the significance of the regression model.

Step 8: Draw some conclusions from your analysis and make some recommendations.

First, examine the data visually using the graphical techniques of descriptive statistics.

Let's look at the details of implementing these eight steps for the "great divide" data set. At step 1, you should visually explore the data. You should consider using pie charts and bar charts for the qualitative variables such as type of business and SIC code. You should consider using histograms for the quantitative variables such as 1995 salary, 1995 bonus, number of employees, and annual revenue.

Next, calculate numerical descriptors for the quantitative variables.

At step 2, for each of the quantitative variables you should calculate summary statistics including the mean, median, quartiles, range, and standard deviation.

At step 3 you should start to look for patterns, trends, and relationships among the variables. You should also calculate some summary statistics for subsets of the data. For example, you might wish to calculate the average CEO salary for all "Energy" companies. For these data you might construct scatter plots to see whether

Look for relationships in the data.

- salary and/or bonus is related to type of business
- salary and/or bonus is related to annual revenue of the company
- salary and/or bonus is related to size of the company as measured by the number of employees.

Formulate hypotheses based on your analysis of the sample.

Step 4 is the point at which you summarize what you have learned from your exploratory data analysis. Remember that the tools you have used thus far in the procedure simply describe the sample. At this step you formulate some hypotheses in an attempt to use the sample to answer questions about the population related to the problem you are trying to solve.

Use hypothesis testing and ANOVA to determine if the differences in the sample are significant.

At step 5, you should consider using t tests to test for differences in the average salary. For example, you could divide the companies into two groups: companies with less than 500 employees and those with more than 500 employees. Then you could test to see if the average salary is different for the two groups. To see whether salary is related to the type of business, you would use ANOVA to see whether the average CEO salaries are equal across the various types of businesses. If they are not, determine which ones are different.

Use time series analysis if there appears to be a pattern in a variable over time.

Step 6 proposes that you examine the data over time when appropriate. For this data set, you essentially have 2 years worth of data because you have the percent change in salary and bonus from 1994 to 1995. This is not really enough data to do any time series analysis but you could look for patterns in the percent changes by type of business, SIC code, or size of the company.

Use regression to develop a prediction model.

At step 7 you should try to make some predictions. For this data set, you should consider trying to predict the salary of the CEO based on the type of business, size of the company, SIC code, and annual revenue of the company. To do this you would use a multiple regression model and determine which factors are significant.

Draw some conclusions.

At step 8, you should reach some conclusions and make some recommendations on the basis of your analysis. Perhaps the "great divide" is most pronounced in large companies or in a particular type of business. This type of conclusion might influence the type of legislation that would help solve the problem. Your data analysis must support your case but it must do it ethically.

CHAPTER 17 SUMMARY

In this chapter we have taken a global look at the techniques you learned in this book. Despite the large number of different techniques and many formulas presented in this book, we looked at the "bigger picture." We have grouped the chapters into six main parts and found four themes that tie all of our work in this book together.

With the increasing emphasis on quality and increasing international competition, there is clearly a need for business people to use data to make informed business decisions. You have learned the basic tools to allow you to see the world through a statistical paradigm. It is this lens that will help you advance in your career.

At whatever level you find yourself in an organization, you may be called upon to analyze data. You have learned how to do this, and remember that this analysis must always be done ethically and fairly. This has been a constant point throughout the discussions in this book. Lives have been lost and saved by fair data analysis. You must use your statistical paradigm responsibly.

CHAPTER 17 EXERCISES

Thinking About It!

17.1 After you received your master's degree in statistics last year, you took the only statistical job you could find near your fiancée. It is with a large pharmaceutical corporation, where you are now the only statistician. You spend most of your time supporting some randomized clinical trials initiated during the tenure of your predecessor, who left on very short notice and for reasons referred to rather vaguely in terms of "mutual agreement." The company has been losing ground to the competition, and management is now counting on new product development to "save the company."

The protocol for the largest of the ongoing trials, now coming to a close, clearly states the null hypothesis to be that cancer patients treated by a new procedure will have the same 2-year survival as those treated by the standard regimen X, but no statistical method for the comparison is specified. Your analysis produces a two-tail *p*-value of 0.08. Your boss says that switching the hypothesis to a one-tail test yields a *p*-value of 0.05 and the data clearly support the alternative hypothesis. He is prepared to recommend that the CEO approve a large budget (including your salary) to further develop this new procedure.

What do you do now? OK, what do you *really* do now?

17.2 You have been hired by an attorney to "prove" that Company ZZZ does not practice age discrimination. The specifics of the case are that Mr. Oldstone, who had worked for the company for over 20 years, lost his job a year ago. Mr. Oldstone is suing Company ZZZ for 1 million dollars claiming age discrimination. The company claims that it reorganized and that Mr. Oldstone's position was eliminated in the reorganization. Since that time Ms. Youngsville has been hired to perform tasks similar in nature to those formerly performed by Mr. Oldstone. Ms. Youngsville is a recent college graduate and is paid $30,000 less than Mr. Oldstone's salary. You have access to the company's human resource records. An initial review of the data seems to support Mr. Oldstone's claim. However, you are being paid to disprove this claim. You are a poor, starving graduate student and you and your spouse are expecting your first child in 3 months. You also know that there are several other companies with similar suits against them and they are watching the results of this trial. You know that you can probably manipulate the highly disorganized human resource data to support the company's claim that it does not practice age discrimination.

What do you do now? OK, what do you *really* do now?

Doing It!

17.3 Complete the analysis of the "great divide" data set by following the suggestions that were outlined for each of the eight steps in Section 17.3.

CASE STUDIES

Explanation of the variables in these case studies can be found in Appendix B.

MAKING YOUR CASE
Advising the President: Exploratory Data Analysis

You have taken a job at the White House on the staff of the President's Council of Economic Advisors. As the new kid on the block, you have been given the assignment of providing the President with a view of the country. The President wants you to capture the country with statistics, so that he understands how the different demographic and economic factors vary around the country.

You have data available to you from the U.S. Census Bureau by state and region of the country. The Census Bureau tracks 63 different variables covering nine main categories: population, health, education, income, crime, employment, banking, transportation, and housing. A very small portion of the data follows.

	Resident population\1			Resident population\1		
Region division, and state	**Total,\2 1994 (1,000)**	**Percent increases,\3 1990–94 (%)**	**65 years old and over, 1994 (%)**	**Householder 65 years old and over, 1994\3 (%)**	**In metro areas, 1992\4 (%)**	**Net domestic immigration, 1990–94\1**
United States	260,341	4.7	12.7	21.8	79.7	0
Northeast	51,396	1.2	14.1	23.7	89.4	(1,439,371)
New England	13,270	0.5	13.9	22.9	84.1	(364,734)
Maine	1,240	1.0	13.9	22.8	35.7	(12,109)
New Hampshire	1,137	2.5	11.9	19.5	59.4	(9,912)
Vermont	580	3.1	12.1	20.1	27.0	2,287
Massachusetts	6,041	0.4	14.1	23.3	96.2	(183,995)
Rhode Island	997	−0.7	15.6	25.6	93.6	(35,219)
Connecticut	3,275	−0.4	14.2	23.1	95.7	(125,786)

The data are found in a file named CENSUS.XXX. Looking at the data, you notice that they cover the time period from 1990 to 1994. You wonder about the data in parentheses and remember from your accounting course that this means negative numbers. You also notice that there are summary lines for geographic regions and realize that you had better remove them before you do any type of analysis by state.

Completely overwhelmed, you decide to approach your boss and ask for some direction. She tells you that the President is looking for summaries and relationships among the variables and regions of the country and that reminds you of the popularity of Ross Perot's charts and graphs. In addition, she tells you that the President wants to be prepared for attacks from Capitol Hill on health care and education, and that you should start your analysis there.

1. Prepare a set of graphical displays and statistics that summarize the availability of health care in the country. Do any of the states or regions exhibit unusual behavior? If so, which ones are they? Is any state or region consistently low or high on all aspects of health care?
2. Of particular interest is the cost of health care. Does there appear to be any relationship between the cost of hospital care and the other variables? If so, how are they related?

Now that you have gotten the idea, you understand what you need to do for each of the rest of the categories in order to have your report on the President's desk by the end of the week. Oh, by the way, the President is wondering where the best place in the country to live is.

MAKING YOUR CASE
What's on the Road? Who's Driving It?: Exploratory Data Analysis

Before you can make decisions about the future, you need to understand the current situation. The transportation industry controls the infrastructure of the country, and decisions it makes impact everyone.

One method that the industry uses to understand current trends is the Nationwide Personal Transportation Survey (NPTS). This survey is done approximately every 7 years under the sponsorship of the U.S. Department of Transportation. The NPTS compiles national data on the nature and characteristics of personal travel. NPTS data may be used to describe current travel patterns, and given projections of demographic change, can provide a valuable tool to forecast future travel demand. One aspect of transportation planning is knowing what is currently on the road. The NPTS data include motor vehicle information such as year, make, model, and other vehicle-related information.

You are asked to describe the current vehicle population of the United States. To assist in this, you have been given a portion of the NPTS data from the 1990 survey, in which data were collected on 26,172 households using computer-assisted telephone interviewing (CATI). Specifically, you have been given data from all survey interviews conducted in April 1990. A portion of the data is shown here:

CMSA	HHFAMINC	HHLOC	HHMSA	HHSIZE	HH_RACE	HOUSEID	LIF_CYC	MAKECODE
5602	05	1	5640	01	01	00038	01	014
5602	04	1	5640	06	01	00039	08	038
5602	04	1	5640	06	01	00039	08	022
5602	04	1	5640	06	01	00039	08	021
5602	98	1	5640	05	01	00041	06	021
5602	98	1	5640	05	01	00041	06	021
5602	98	1	5640	05	01	00041	06	035
5602	14	2	5190	02	01	00045	10	009
5602	14	2	5190	02	01	00045	10	006
5602	99	2	5190	03	01	00047	06	019

The data are found in a datafile called CARS.XXX. As is the case with much publicly available data, the variable names are cryptic and the qualitative variables are coded. Clearly, you will need to know what each variable and code mean. This information is detailed in Appendix B at the end of the book.

Of particular interest to automobile manufacturers is information about the age and type of vehicles on the road.

1. Use graphical and numerical summary tools to describe the distribution of vehicles by make and year.
2. Are the distributions affected by various demographics? Who drives foreign cars? Who drives old cars?
3. Is the distance driven annually impacted by where people live, gender, age, or type of vehicle?

Using these questions as a starting point, prepare a report that completely describes the vehicle population of the United States. Be sure to include any limitations of the data.

MAKING YOUR CASE
Who Spends Money? What Do They Buy?: Inferential Statistics

A large marketing research firm has an international client that has business interests in many consumer industries such as food, apparel, alcohol, and automobile fuel. As a person with some statistical experience, you have been hired by this marketing research company. Before spending any of the client's money on surveying consumers, the client has asked you to report on general trends in consumer spending. Specifically, you are asked which business areas have experienced increases, and what are the characteristics of people who are spending money in these areas. Your report will guide future survey design and eventually new product development and advertising expenditures.

Using your Internet-surfing skills, you find the Web site for the U.S. Census Bureau and find the results of the Consumer Expenditure Survey conducted periodically by the Census Bureau. The most recent survey available on-line is from 1993 and so you decide to use it. The Consumer Expenditure Survey includes information on many variables but you select for study only 49 variables that you think would be helpful. A portion of the data is shown here:

AGE2	AGE_REF	ALCBEVCQ	ALCBEVPQ	APPARCQ	APPARPQ	AS_COMP1	AS_COMP2
	46	97	30	0	33	2	1
	78	0	0	0	0	0	1
	55	0	65	0	159	0	1
73	78	0	40	0	145.83	1	1
45	45	85	170	482	845.4	1	1
52	56	54	27	175	840	2	1
36	35	40	20	375.38	120	1	1
	63	0	0	22	10	1	0

Each row in the datafile (CONSEXP.XXX) represents one person's (the Reference Person) responses to the survey questions. As is the case with much publicly available data, the variable names are cryptic and the qualitative variables are coded. Clearly, you need to know what each variable means and also what the codes mean. This information is detailed in Appendix B.

One portion of your client's business is in the food industry. The company owns restaurants and supermarkets. The first thing you decide to do is examine trends in the amount of money spent on food. You have information on the amount of money spent in the current quarter of the survey year and the amount spent in the previous quarter.

1. Did consumers spend significantly more money in the current quarter of the survey year than in the previous quarter on food? If so, is the difference meaningful?
2. Was there a change in how the money spent on food was distributed between the amount of money spent on eating out and the amount of money spent for food eaten at home?
3. Do households with teenagers spend more money on food eaten at home?
4. Do households where both adults are working spend more money on eating out?

Having done the analysis of food expenditures, you decide to take the same approach for the other business areas. In addition to looking for changes in expenditures between quarters, you wonder what other demographic factors affect spending habits. You set about doing the appropriate statistical tests to provide your client with a report by the end of the week.

MAKING YOUR CASE
Advising the President: Inferential Statistics

The President is pleased with your exploratory data analysis. Although he agrees with your impressions, he is hesitant to propose new legislation based on subjective interpretation of the data. You are smarter now, too, and you recognize the need for the formal statistical tools of hypothesis testing.

Remember the data available to you are from the U.S. Census Bureau and are found in a datafile named CENSUS.XXX. A portion of the data follow.

	Resident population\1			Resident population\1		
Region division, and state	**Total,\2 1994 (1,000)**	**Percent increase,\3 1990-94 (%)**	**65 years old and over, 1994 (%)**	**Householder 65 years old and over, 1994\3 (%)**	**In metro areas, 1992\4 (%)**	**Net domestic immigration, 1990-94\1**
United States	260,341	4.7	12.7	21.8	79.7	0
Northeast	51,396	1.2	14.1	23.7	89.4	(1,439,371)
New England	13,270	0.5	13.9	22.9	84.1	(364,734)
Maine	1,240	1.0	13.9	22.8	35.7	(12,109)
New Hampshire	1,137	2.5	11.9	19.5	59.4	(9,912)
Vermont	580	3.1	12.1	20.1	27.0	2,287
Massachusetts	6,041	0.4	14.1	23.3	96.2	(183,995)
Rhode Island	997	−0.7	15.6	25.6	93.6	(35,219)
Connecticut	3,275	−0.4	14.2	23.1	95.7	(125,786)

The attacks continue on the health-care front. Specifically, legislators from the South Central region claim that they need additional federal funding to encourage doctors and nurses to practice there. Before the President supports such legislation he wants to know the following:

1. Is the availability of medical professionals in the South Central states really lower than the availability in the rest of the country?

2. Are the South Central states the only area of the country that need this type of support? If you had to make a recommendation, what area(s) would you support?

A group of Senators from the Midwest region says that they will support the health-care initiatives for the South Central region only if they are assured that they have equity in the area of education, specifically teachers' salaries.

3. Can the President ignore their lobbying? Why or why not?

You now know that you need to be prepared to advise the President if legislators from other regions are going to try similar tactics in other categories. Do the necessary analyses and prepare your report.

MAKING YOUR CASE
Responding to the Customer: Pulling It All Together

Congratulations! You have completed your introductory statistics course and been hired by a company that is interested in applying for ISO (International Standards Organization) certification. You know that this certification requires the company to document all its processes, including the process by which it obtains and uses customer feedback to continuously improve.

The company has provided the customers with a fax number and an e-mail address to report complaints or problems. When a complaint comes in, the company must respond to the customer. Your job is to analyze the complaint data collected when customers call to complain about the product.

Your boss is most concerned about the time it takes to respond to a customer complaint. The response time is the number of minutes from receipt of the fax or e-mail until first contact with the customer. Clearly, lower response times are desirable, with all response times targeted at less than one-half day (240 minutes). The data include the number of staff personnel scheduled for that day, whether that type of problem had been encountered previously (1 = yes; 0 = no), how the issue was received (via fax or e-mail), whether the issue statement was transferred into a written resolution log, and, finally, the volume (or number) of issues electronically recorded for that day. Information is also provided on the coded volume level (Cvol = 1 if Volume ≤ 25; Cvol = 2 if $26 <$ Volume ≤ 50; Cvol = 3 for [51, 75]; Cvol = 4 for [76, 100]; Cvol = 5 for > 100). A small portion of the data set is shown here.

Run	Staff	Exper	Type	Log	Volume	Cvol	RespTime
1	5	1	E	Y	114	5	97
2	8	1	E	Y	54	3	39
3	6	1	F	Y	36	2	54
4	9	1	F	Y	66	3	55
5	10	0	E	Y	125	5	125
6	5	1	E	Y	121	5	108
7	8	0	F	Y	69	3	115
8	6	1	F	Y	40	2	60

The data are found in a file named CUSTOMER.XXX. Looking at the data, you notice that some of the variables are qualitative variables, some are quantitative variables, and some of the variables are coded responses. You know that the type of data will certainly influence what techniques you use to analyze the data.

Your boss would like you to

1. Describe the data to him. This would include graphs and numerical summaries when appropriate.
2. Look for relationships in the data. Check to see whether the response time to the customer is related to any of the other variables and, if so, how are they related.
3. Test to see what factors impact the response time.
4. Look for patterns or trends in the complaints over time.

Prepare a report for your boss addressing these issues and make recommendations based on your findings.

MAKING YOUR CASE
Too Much Scrap: Pulling It All Together

A manufacturing company that makes paper products has been having trouble with its paper towel line. When a roll of paper towels is manufactured, the last step before the roll is put in a case is to wrap it with plastic wrapper that the customer sees on the store shelf. A large amount of the product is being scrapped because it is not being wrapped properly.

Because of your data analysis skills, you have been assigned to be a member of the team formed to solve this problem. Clearly, the first thing to do is to decide why the towels are not being wrapped properly. To help you understand the problem, you decide to collect data on the towels that have been manufactured over a 3-day period. This includes information regarding the date the roll was manufactured, the shift during which the roll was manufactured, the diameter of the roll, and whether the roll was scrapped. A small portion of the data set is shown here:

Day	Shift	Diameter	Scrapped
1	A	5.35433	N
1	A	5.51181	Y
1	A	5.31496	N
1	A	5.35433	N
1	A	5.35433	N
1	A	5.27559	N

The data are found in a datafile named ROLLS.XXX. It seems to you that the roll cannot be properly wrapped if the diameter of the roll is too large. Use graphs, numerical summaries, and hypothesis testing to determine if there is any difference in the average diameter of the rolls that are scrapped and those that are not scrapped. Also investigate whether or not there is any difference in the average roll diameter over time or by shift.

After doing this analysis, you ask the engineers on the team what factors affect the roll diameter. They were not sure but they helped you understand the manufacturing process. You learn that there are several machine settings that might affect the roll diameter. They are:

1. Embosser roll gap: the mechanism that puts the pattern in the towel
2. Draw roll gap: the opening through which the towel material is pulled into the winders
3. Speed: the speed at which the machine winds the rolls of towels

The engineers also told you to be sure to pay attention to the firmness of the towel roll. They warned you that in fixing the diameter problem, you might cause a different problem. If the towel roll is not firm that will also affect wrapping, and if it is too firm consumers will perceive it as stiff and complain.

The machine was run at different settings for each factor and rolls of towels were taken from the end of the production line. The towel diameter and roll firmness were measured. A small portion of the data set is shown below:

Drawroll	Speed	Embosser	Diameter	Firmness
0	0	0	5.43307	0.271667
0	0	0	5.39370	0.336667
0	0	0	5.47244	0.260333
0	0	0	5.39370	0.261333
0	0	0	5.43307	0.297000
0	1	0	5.39370	0.312000
0	1	0	5.47244	0.294667

The data are found in a file named FACTORS.XXX.

Prepare a report for management explaining the effects that each of the machine settings has on roll diameter and firmness. Management also wishes to know whether the rolls meet the specifications for the mean roll diameter set at 5.35 inches and the maximum roll diameter of 5.50 inches. Indicate which settings result in the best values for roll diameter. Make a recommendation on machine settings if you can.

Before your report is completed, someone on the team reminds you that the roll diameter was measured to the nearest millimeter and converted to inches because the product specifications for the paper towel product are given in English measures, not metric. You remember your statistics teacher pointing out the fact that statistically different and practically different are *not* necessarily the same. Perhaps you should reconsider your conclusions.

APPENDIX A

STATISTICAL TABLES

TABLE I Random Number Table

Row #	Column # 1	2	3	4	5	6	7	8	9
1	094632795	711501513	537971597	562758635	410398128	182794408	773761503	455139927	132682754
2	033413186	653475420	289063704	485441982	460744361	328703833	289612212	569540556	620271271
3	297556368	658953044	738968017	414437050	296126017	075254187	702140315	467039889	762226273
4	472960570	785645638	574817322	817883255	976076280	843373358	118284363	445336907	327380271
5	256883707	716249997	378236162	467694224	193707682	380141891	605807481	180164558	473854769
6	179451522	878902420	602450872	987686989	686677180	242196303	517640224	691116863	275385608
7	894964682	704841116	241902107	750429362	794778197	693242123	316755091	193593484	913974355
8	738120861	744470405	873393138	758824215	394004646	496696605	006936567	163371217	727267920
9	803156944	653387115	716335974	835667154	066959782	908783760	165946696	735683921	894672507
10	187636922	953598780	481536873	055734541	493193305	566923120	435549770	007706188	839596393
11	102021077	286953643	851411058	132935798	745770831	187026467	363837178	791264282	107184709
12	734254842	133959443	113708008	443989454	786207141	772432741	682053431	048076059	617648837
13	757417865	524596578	240504889	544970942	340054233	417544234	302126745	003333205	250247568
14	227658086	233543943	487116060	577966118	524453480	934483237	367425608	431112250	536516890
15	746794759	557361146	826373105	870360802	412399571	804914923	128067420	659566961	452000520
16	235158119	336776002	728424416	086967212	040966064	335090111	985461873	832921870	461741235
17	944558037	787700710	060386364	635482046	558143223	600009181	448499754	064172342	713707601
18	658344036	271853277	275251035	744269244	877186509	130398637	367142231	846275675	485443650
19	179411521	104680475	020354893	576185422	778014690	380931445	886031872	320231466	062555147
20	865570814	699503925	628956988	683503622	276170341	744494133	081246804	523527226	198219562
21	984902072	022065717	504274676	136174524	195356906	027900159	809382340	381669407	544140648
22	139846732	496390379	582502144	768571665	177715615	830320391	105937107	329901920	618226629
23	492146502	493503513	138813631	479880385	684082619	010963692	268892703	552334849	488002392
24	739727377	916314641	263944162	861966588	286459084	491798049	760316559	837966446	371951811
25	075823838	115491339	547215506	007869049	323138362	193432798	361574944	787418390	016648846
26	915745558	104176259	349828840	546922404	266406684	490531595	336155799	242136076	641061181
27	136001350	309685268	986533618	587428568	052231831	422269870	302793461	564542482	915031158
28	691703257	926306032	988266746	716231516	519662016	986665536	993015206	066999095	731533696
29	154222042	316334873	963715901	044966315	846937935	104409586	768790545	113341348	108261519
30	983823702	641345385	203912928	219869690	208288383	861497163	149918954	160034550	759951927
31	277515731	805241329	549047139	285206828	534033122	130094940	970748730	798208639	485614463
32	566308464	543263173	711363354	339738940	051286779	714375200	698531722	072971345	762369710
33	533605194	994619567	798813607	079914804	405016946	275797011	801942743	814124918	033457635
34	374266385	237398626	014653680	107885763	848594153	093210516	751461171	121583622	388598493
35	739563239	736604709	251789737	480977217	432264262	975146204	639768152	455086460	573742841
36	539277994	536590953	293592699	279474008	525803109	281596944	199856046	646139218	124051051
37	609535944	455877404	251255783	334162937	523110770	461537085	359043224	423641232	223047648
38	254030985	962503045	747584829	988588554	631976076	901087130	961891746	149014870	557453130
39	869881662	489992047	240739861	875737562	237409010	135678267	196964820	343397286	364892121
40	935509137	382168564	659392779	628617853	533473897	569590209	333032014	937163707	460780426
41	727184789	651476235	562537081	259345598	118701307	970343244	678458590	189103174	840164700
42	076139028	276588587	329963439	184510242	904140612	761154973	175127287	520167477	242700207
43	181087637	087629199	028292894	460181436	623140518	207937371	238398056	136009368	581975565
44	514095654	401875869	095986936	976620836	391483115	713574093	679457157	184527765	553593737
45	804743163	129181317	005547120	712455031	948648814	909230622	839276576	726704039	427115217
46	492640056	038991626	749280637	430162677	414656226	603291802	983746203	756647413	333907575
47	105925664	168586200	348119547	829517480	244539107	448715108	154400559	634475954	701530403
48	688908833	510541646	706386776	935447659	798110618	127019341	889979390	455625169	283128630
49	806445894	067701203	566577304	808746117	093933115	198530698	142531634	042491555	776838859
50	249997369	047395403	102944245	987149692	239682871	971259345	193515078	797533485	459099813

TABLE 2 Binomial Probability Tables

P(X = x)

n = 5

x	0.05	0.10	0.20	0.25	0.30	0.40	0.50	0.60	0.70	0.75	0.80	0.90	0.95
0	0.774	0.590	0.328	0.237	0.168	0.078	0.031	0.010	0.002	0.001	0.000	0.000	0.000
1	0.204	0.328	0.410	0.396	0.360	0.259	0.156	0.077	0.028	0.015	0.006	0.000	0.000
2	0.021	0.073	0.205	0.264	0.309	0.346	0.313	0.230	0.132	0.088	0.051	0.008	0.001
3	0.001	0.008	0.051	0.088	0.132	0.230	0.313	0.346	0.309	0.264	0.205	0.073	0.021
4	0.000	0.000	0.006	0.015	0.028	0.077	0.156	0.259	0.360	0.396	0.410	0.328	0.204
5	0.000	0.000	0.000	0.001	0.002	0.010	0.031	0.078	0.168	0.237	0.328	0.590	0.774

n = 10

x	0.050	0.100	0.200	0.250	0.300	0.400	0.500	0.600	0.700	0.750	0.800	0.900	0.950
0	0.599	0.349	0.107	0.056	0.028	0.006	0.001	0.000	0.000	0.000	0.000	0.000	0.000
1	0.315	0.387	0.268	0.188	0.121	0.040	0.010	0.002	0.000	0.000	0.000	0.000	0.000
2	0.075	0.194	0.302	0.282	0.233	0.121	0.044	0.011	0.001	0.000	0.000	0.000	0.000
3	0.010	0.057	0.201	0.250	0.267	0.215	0.117	0.042	0.009	0.003	0.001	0.000	0.000
4	0.001	0.011	0.088	0.146	0.200	0.251	0.205	0.111	0.037	0.016	0.006	0.000	0.000
5	0.000	0.001	0.026	0.058	0.103	0.201	0.246	0.201	0.103	0.058	0.026	0.001	0.000
6	0.000	0.000	0.006	0.016	0.037	0.111	0.205	0.251	0.200	0.146	0.088	0.011	0.001
7	0.000	0.000	0.001	0.003	0.009	0.042	0.117	0.215	0.267	0.250	0.201	0.057	0.010
8	0.000	0.000	0.000	0.000	0.001	0.011	0.044	0.121	0.233	0.282	0.302	0.194	0.075
9	0.000	0.000	0.000	0.000	0.000	0.002	0.010	0.040	0.121	0.188	0.268	0.387	0.315
10	0.000	0.000	0.000	0.000	0.000	0.000	0.001	0.006	0.028	0.056	0.107	0.349	0.599

n = 15

x	0.050	0.100	0.200	0.250	0.300	0.400	0.500	0.600	0.700	0.750	0.800	0.900	0.950
0	0.463	0.206	0.035	0.013	0.005	0.000	0.000	0.000	0.000	0.000	0.000	0.000	0.000
1	0.366	0.343	0.132	0.067	0.031	0.005	0.000	0.000	0.000	0.000	0.000	0.000	0.000
2	0.135	0.267	0.231	0.156	0.092	0.022	0.003	0.000	0.000	0.000	0.000	0.000	0.000
3	0.031	0.129	0.250	0.225	0.170	0.063	0.014	0.002	0.000	0.000	0.000	0.000	0.000
4	0.005	0.043	0.188	0.225	0.219	0.127	0.042	0.007	0.001	0.000	0.000	0.000	0.000
5	0.001	0.010	0.103	0.165	0.206	0.186	0.092	0.024	0.003	0.001	0.000	0.000	0.000
6	0.000	0.002	0.043	0.092	0.147	0.207	0.153	0.061	0.012	0.003	0.001	0.000	0.000
7	0.000	0.000	0.014	0.039	0.081	0.177	0.196	0.118	0.035	0.013	0.003	0.000	0.000
8	0.000	0.000	0.003	0.013	0.035	0.118	0.196	0.177	0.081	0.039	0.014	0.000	0.000
9	0.000	0.000	0.001	0.003	0.012	0.061	0.153	0.207	0.147	0.092	0.043	0.002	0.000
10	0.000	0.000	0.000	0.001	0.003	0.024	0.092	0.186	0.206	0.165	0.103	0.010	0.001
11	0.000	0.000	0.000	0.000	0.001	0.007	0.042	0.127	0.219	0.225	0.188	0.043	0.005
12	0.000	0.000	0.000	0.000	0.000	0.002	0.014	0.063	0.170	0.225	0.250	0.129	0.031
13	0.000	0.000	0.000	0.000	0.000	0.000	0.003	0.022	0.092	0.156	0.231	0.267	0.135
14	0.000	0.000	0.000	0.000	0.000	0.000	0.000	0.005	0.031	0.067	0.132	0.343	0.366
15	0.000	0.000	0.000	0.000	0.000	0.000	0.000	0.000	0.005	0.013	0.035	0.206	0.463

$n = 20$

	π												
x	**0.050**	**0.100**	**0.200**	**0.250**	**0.300**	**0.400**	**0.500**	**0.600**	**0.700**	**0.750**	**0.800**	**0.900**	**0.950**
0	0.358	0.122	0.012	0.003	0.001	0.000	0.000	0.000	0.000	0.000	0.000	0.000	0.000
1	0.377	0.270	0.058	0.021	0.007	0.000	0.000	0.000	0.000	0.000	0.000	0.000	0.000
2	0.189	0.285	0.137	0.067	0.028	0.003	0.000	0.000	0.000	0.000	0.000	0.000	0.000
3	0.060	0.190	0.205	0.134	0.072	0.012	0.001	0.000	0.000	0.000	0.000	0.000	0.000
4	0.013	0.090	0.218	0.190	0.130	0.035	0.005	0.000	0.000	0.000	0.000	0.000	0.000
5	0.002	0.032	0.175	0.202	0.179	0.075	0.015	0.001	0.000	0.000	0.000	0.000	0.000
6	0.000	0.009	0.109	0.169	0.192	0.124	0.037	0.005	0.000	0.000	0.000	0.000	0.000
7	0.000	0.002	0.055	0.112	0.164	0.166	0.074	0.015	0.001	0.000	0.000	0.000	0.000
8	0.000	0.000	0.022	0.061	0.114	0.180	0.120	0.035	0.004	0.001	0.000	0.000	0.000
9	0.000	0.000	0.007	0.027	0.065	0.160	0.160	0.071	0.012	0.003	0.000	0.000	0.000
10	0.000	0.000	0.002	0.010	0.031	0.117	0.176	0.117	0.031	0.010	0.002	0.000	0.000
11	0.000	0.000	0.000	0.003	0.012	0.071	0.160	0.160	0.065	0.027	0.007	0.000	0.000
12	0.000	0.000	0.000	0.001	0.004	0.035	0.120	0.180	0.114	0.061	0.022	0.000	0.000
13	0.000	0.000	0.000	0.000	0.001	0.015	0.074	0.166	0.164	0.112	0.055	0.002	0.000
14	0.000	0.000	0.000	0.000	0.000	0.005	0.037	0.124	0.192	0.169	0.109	0.009	0.000
15	0.000	0.000	0.000	0.000	0.000	0.001	0.015	0.075	0.179	0.202	0.175	0.032	0.002
16	0.000	0.000	0.000	0.000	0.000	0.000	0.005	0.035	0.130	0.190	0.218	0.090	0.013
17	0.000	0.000	0.000	0.000	0.000	0.000	0.001	0.012	0.072	0.134	0.205	0.190	0.060
18	0.000	0.000	0.000	0.000	0.000	0.000	0.000	0.003	0.028	0.067	0.137	0.285	0.189
19	0.000	0.000	0.000	0.000	0.000	0.000	0.000	0.000	0.007	0.021	0.058	0.270	0.377
20	0.000	0.000	0.000	0.000	0.000	0.000	0.000	0.000	0.001	0.003	0.012	0.122	0.358

$n = 25$

	π												
x	**0.050**	**0.100**	**0.200**	**0.250**	**0.300**	**0.400**	**0.500**	**0.600**	**0.700**	**0.750**	**0.800**	**0.900**	**0.950**
0	0.277	0.072	0.004	0.001	0.000	0.000	0.000	0.000	0.000	0.000	0.000	0.000	0.000
1	0.365	0.199	0.024	0.006	0.001	0.000	0.000	0.000	0.000	0.000	0.000	0.000	0.000
2	0.231	0.266	0.071	0.025	0.007	0.000	0.000	0.000	0.000	0.000	0.000	0.000	0.000
3	0.093	0.226	0.136	0.064	0.024	0.002	0.000	0.000	0.000	0.000	0.000	0.000	0.000
4	0.027	0.138	0.187	0.118	0.057	0.007	0.000	0.000	0.000	0.000	0.000	0.000	0.000
5	0.006	0.065	0.196	0.165	0.103	0.020	0.002	0.000	0.000	0.000	0.000	0.000	0.000
6	0.001	0.024	0.163	0.183	0.147	0.044	0.005	0.000	0.000	0.000	0.000	0.000	0.000
7	0.000	0.007	0.111	0.165	0.171	0.080	0.014	0.001	0.000	0.000	0.000	0.000	0.000
8	0.000	0.002	0.062	0.124	0.165	0.120	0.032	0.003	0.000	0.000	0.000	0.000	0.000
9	0.000	0.000	0.029	0.078	0.134	0.151	0.061	0.009	0.000	0.000	0.000	0.000	0.000
10	0.000	0.000	0.012	0.042	0.092	0.161	0.097	0.021	0.001	0.000	0.000	0.000	0.000
11	0.000	0.000	0.004	0.019	0.054	0.147	0.133	0.043	0.004	0.001	0.000	0.000	0.000
12	0.000	0.000	0.001	0.007	0.027	0.114	0.155	0.076	0.011	0.002	0.000	0.000	0.000
13	0.000	0.000	0.000	0.002	0.011	0.076	0.155	0.114	0.027	0.007	0.001	0.000	0.000
14	0.000	0.000	0.000	0.001	0.004	0.043	0.133	0.147	0.054	0.019	0.004	0.000	0.000
15	0.000	0.000	0.000	0.000	0.001	0.021	0.097	0.161	0.092	0.042	0.012	0.000	0.000
16	0.000	0.000	0.000	0.000	0.000	0.009	0.061	0.151	0.134	0.078	0.029	0.000	0.000
17	0.000	0.000	0.000	0.000	0.000	0.003	0.032	0.120	0.165	0.124	0.062	0.002	0.000
18	0.000	0.000	0.000	0.000	0.000	0.001	0.014	0.080	0.171	0.165	0.111	0.007	0.000
19	0.000	0.000	0.000	0.000	0.000	0.000	0.005	0.044	0.147	0.183	0.163	0.024	0.001
20	0.000	0.000	0.000	0.000	0.000	0.000	0.002	0.020	0.103	0.165	0.196	0.065	0.006
21	0.000	0.000	0.000	0.000	0.000	0.000	0.000	0.007	0.057	0.118	0.187	0.138	0.027
22	0.000	0.000	0.000	0.000	0.000	0.000	0.000	0.002	0.024	0.064	0.136	0.226	0.093
23	0.000	0.000	0.000	0.000	0.000	0.000	0.000	0.000	0.007	0.025	0.071	0.266	0.231
24	0.000	0.000	0.000	0.000	0.000	0.000	0.000	0.000	0.001	0.006	0.024	0.199	0.365
25	0.000	0.000	0.000	0.000	0.000	0.000	0.000	0.000	0.000	0.001	0.004	0.072	0.277

TABLE 3 Standard Normal Table

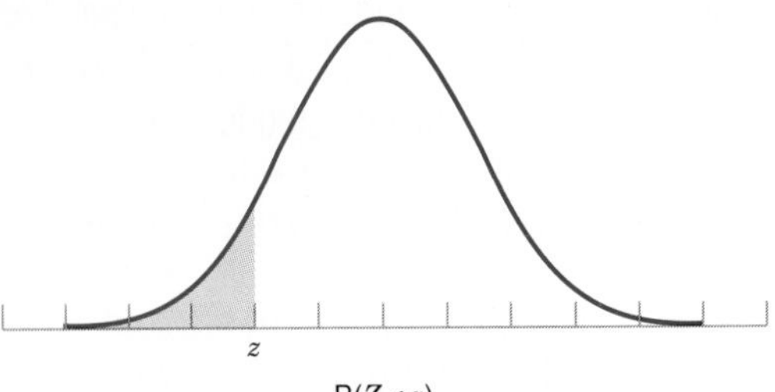

z	0.00	0.01	0.02	0.03	0.04	0.05	0.06	0.07	0.08	0.09
	Second Decimal Place									
-3.9	0.0000	0.0000	0.0000	0.0000	0.0000	0.0000	0.0000	0.0000	0.0000	0.0000
-3.8	0.0001	0.0001	0.0001	0.0001	0.0001	0.0001	0.0001	0.0001	0.0001	0.0001
-3.7	0.0001	0.0001	0.0001	0.0001	0.0001	0.0001	0.0001	0.0001	0.0001	0.0001
-3.6	0.0002	0.0002	0.0001	0.0001	0.0001	0.0001	0.0001	0.0001	0.0001	0.0001
-3.5	0.0002	0.0002	0.0002	0.0002	0.0002	0.0002	0.0002	0.0002	0.0002	0.0002
-3.4	0.0003	0.0003	0.0003	0.0003	0.0003	0.0003	0.0003	0.0003	0.0003	0.0002
-3.3	0.0005	0.0005	0.0005	0.0004	0.0004	0.0004	0.0004	0.0004	0.0004	0.0003
-3.2	0.0007	0.0007	0.0006	0.0006	0.0006	0.0006	0.0006	0.0005	0.0005	0.0005
-3.1	0.0010	0.0009	0.0009	0.0009	0.0008	0.0008	0.0008	0.0008	0.0007	0.0007
-3.0	0.0013	0.0013	0.0013	0.0012	0.0012	0.0011	0.0011	0.0011	0.0010	0.0010
-2.9	0.0019	0.0018	0.0018	0.0017	0.0016	0.0016	0.0015	0.0015	0.0014	0.0014
-2.8	0.0026	0.0025	0.0024	0.0023	0.0023	0.0022	0.0021	0.0021	0.0020	0.0019
-2.7	0.0035	0.0034	0.0033	0.0032	0.0031	0.0030	0.0029	0.0028	0.0027	0.0026
-2.6	0.0047	0.0045	0.0044	0.0043	0.0041	0.0040	0.0039	0.0038	0.0037	0.0036
-2.5	0.0062	0.0060	0.0059	0.0057	0.0055	0.0054	0.0052	0.0051	0.0049	0.0048
-2.4	0.0082	0.0080	0.0078	0.0075	0.0073	0.0071	0.0069	0.0068	0.0066	0.0064
-2.3	0.0107	0.0104	0.0102	0.0099	0.0096	0.0094	0.0091	0.0089	0.0087	0.0084
-2.2	0.0139	0.0136	0.0132	0.0129	0.0125	0.0122	0.0119	0.0116	0.0113	0.0110
-2.1	0.0179	0.0174	0.0170	0.0166	0.0162	0.0158	0.0154	0.0150	0.0146	0.0143
-2.0	0.0228	0.0222	0.0217	0.0212	0.0207	0.0202	0.0197	0.0192	0.0188	0.0183
-1.9	0.0287	0.0281	0.0274	0.0268	0.0262	0.0256	0.0250	0.0244	0.0239	0.0233
-1.8	0.0359	0.0351	0.0344	0.0336	0.0329	0.0322	0.0314	0.0307	0.0301	0.0294
-1.7	0.0446	0.0436	0.0427	0.0418	0.0409	0.0401	0.0392	0.0384	0.0375	0.0367
-1.6	0.0548	0.0537	0.0526	0.0516	0.0505	0.0495	0.0485	0.0475	0.0465	0.0455
-1.5	0.0668	0.0655	0.0643	0.0630	0.0618	0.0606	0.0594	0.0582	0.0571	0.0559
-1.4	0.0808	0.0793	0.0778	0.0764	0.0749	0.0735	0.0721	0.0708	0.0694	0.0681
-1.3	0.0968	0.0951	0.0934	0.0918	0.0901	0.0885	0.0869	0.0853	0.0838	0.0823
-1.2	0.1151	0.1131	0.1112	0.1093	0.1075	0.1056	0.1038	0.1020	0.1003	0.0985
-1.1	0.1357	0.1335	0.1314	0.1292	0.1271	0.1251	0.1230	0.1210	0.1190	0.1170
-1.0	0.1587	0.1562	0.1539	0.1515	0.1492	0.1469	0.1446	0.1423	0.1401	0.1379
-0.9	0.1841	0.1814	0.1788	0.1762	0.1736	0.1711	0.1685	0.1660	0.1635	0.1611
-0.8	0.2119	0.2090	0.2061	0.2033	0.2005	0.1977	0.1949	0.1922	0.1894	0.1867
-0.7	0.2420	0.2389	0.2358	0.2327	0.2296	0.2266	0.2236	0.2206	0.2177	0.2148
-0.6	0.2743	0.2709	0.2676	0.2643	0.2611	0.2578	0.2546	0.2514	0.2483	0.2451
-0.5	0.3085	0.3050	0.3015	0.2981	0.2946	0.2912	0.2877	0.2843	0.2810	0.2776
-0.4	0.3446	0.3409	0.3372	0.3336	0.3300	0.3264	0.3228	0.3192	0.3156	0.3121
-0.3	0.3821	0.3783	0.3745	0.3707	0.3669	0.3632	0.3594	0.3557	0.3520	0.3483
-0.2	0.4207	0.4168	0.4129	0.4090	0.4052	0.4013	0.3974	0.3936	0.3897	0.3859
-0.1	0.4602	0.4562	0.4522	0.4483	0.4443	0.4404	0.4364	0.4325	0.4286	0.4247
0.0	0.5000	0.4960	0.4920	0.4880	0.4840	0.4801	0.4761	0.4721	0.4681	0.4641

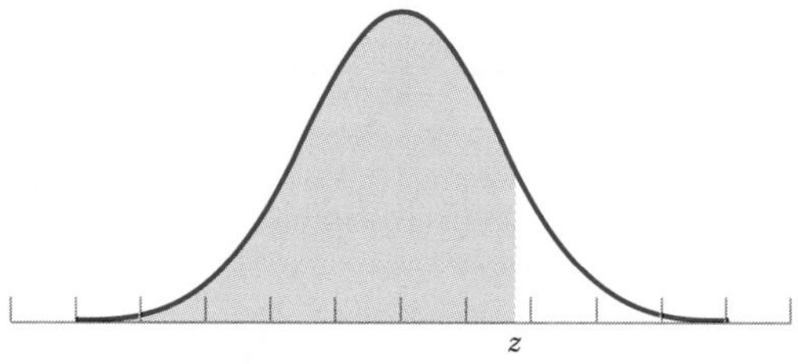

P(Z < z)

Second Decimal Place

z	0.00	0.01	0.02	0.03	0.04	0.05	0.06	0.07	0.08	0.09
0.0	0.5000	0.5040	0.5080	0.5120	0.5160	0.5199	0.5239	0.5279	0.5319	0.5359
0.1	0.5398	0.5438	0.5478	0.5517	0.5557	0.5596	0.5636	0.5675	0.5714	0.5753
0.2	0.5793	0.5832	0.5871	0.5910	0.5948	0.5987	0.6026	0.6064	0.6103	0.6141
0.3	0.6179	0.6217	0.6255	0.6293	0.6331	0.6368	0.6406	0.6443	0.6480	0.6517
0.4	0.6554	0.6591	0.6628	0.6664	0.6700	0.6736	0.6772	0.6808	0.6844	0.6879
0.5	0.6915	0.6950	0.6985	0.7019	0.7054	0.7088	0.7123	0.7157	0.7190	0.7224
0.6	0.7257	0.7291	0.7324	0.7357	0.7389	0.7422	0.7454	0.7486	0.7517	0.7549
0.7	0.7580	0.7611	0.7642	0.7673	0.7704	0.7734	0.7764	0.7794	0.7823	0.7852
0.8	0.7881	0.7910	0.7939	0.7967	0.7995	0.8023	0.8051	0.8078	0.8106	0.8133
0.9	0.8159	0.8186	0.8212	0.8238	0.8264	0.8289	0.8315	0.8340	0.8365	0.8389
1.0	0.8413	0.8438	0.8461	0.8485	0.8508	0.8531	0.8554	0.8577	0.8599	0.8621
1.1	0.8643	0.8665	0.8686	0.8708	0.8729	0.8749	0.8770	0.8790	0.8810	0.8830
1.2	0.8849	0.8869	0.8888	0.8907	0.8925	0.8944	0.8962	0.8980	0.8997	0.9015
1.3	0.9032	0.9049	0.9066	0.9082	0.9099	0.9115	0.9131	0.9147	0.9162	0.9177
1.4	0.9192	0.9207	0.9222	0.9236	0.9251	0.9265	0.9279	0.9292	0.9306	0.9319
1.5	0.9332	0.9345	0.9357	0.9370	0.9382	0.9394	0.9406	0.9418	0.9429	0.9441
1.6	0.9452	0.9463	0.9474	0.9484	0.9495	0.9505	0.9515	0.9525	0.9535	0.9545
1.7	0.9554	0.9564	0.9573	0.9582	0.9591	0.9599	0.9608	0.9616	0.9625	0.9633
1.8	0.9641	0.9649	0.9656	0.9664	0.9671	0.9678	0.9686	0.9693	0.9699	0.9706
1.9	0.9713	0.9719	0.9726	0.9732	0.9738	0.9744	0.9750	0.9756	0.9761	0.9767
2.0	0.9772	0.9778	0.9783	0.9788	0.9793	0.9798	0.9803	0.9808	0.9812	0.9817
2.1	0.9821	0.9826	0.9830	0.9834	0.9838	0.9842	0.9846	0.9850	0.9854	0.9857
2.2	0.9861	0.9864	0.9868	0.9871	0.9875	0.9878	0.9881	0.9884	0.9887	0.9890
2.3	0.9893	0.9896	0.9898	0.9901	0.9904	0.9906	0.9909	0.9911	0.9913	0.9916
2.4	0.9918	0.9920	0.9922	0.9925	0.9927	0.9929	0.9931	0.9932	0.9934	0.9936
2.5	0.9938	0.9940	0.9941	0.9943	0.9945	0.9946	0.9948	0.9949	0.9951	0.9952
2.6	0.9953	0.9955	0.9956	0.9957	0.9959	0.9960	0.9961	0.9962	0.9963	0.9964
2.7	0.9965	0.9966	0.9967	0.9968	0.9969	0.9970	0.9971	0.9972	0.9973	0.9974
2.8	0.9974	0.9975	0.9976	0.9977	0.9977	0.9978	0.9979	0.9979	0.9980	0.9981
2.9	0.9981	0.9982	0.9982	0.9983	0.9984	0.9984	0.9985	0.9985	0.9986	0.9986
3.0	0.9987	0.9987	0.9987	0.9988	0.9988	0.9989	0.9989	0.9989	0.9990	0.9990
3.1	0.9990	0.9991	0.9991	0.9991	0.9992	0.9992	0.9992	0.9992	0.9993	0.9993
3.2	0.9993	0.9993	0.9994	0.9994	0.9994	0.9994	0.9994	0.9995	0.9995	0.9995
3.3	0.9995	0.9995	0.9995	0.9996	0.9996	0.9996	0.9996	0.9996	0.9996	0.9997
3.4	0.9997	0.9997	0.9997	0.9997	0.9997	0.9997	0.9997	0.9997	0.9997	0.9998
3.5	0.9998	0.9998	0.9998	0.9998	0.9998	0.9998	0.9998	0.9998	0.9998	0.9998
3.6	0.9998	0.9998	0.9999	0.9999	0.9999	0.9999	0.9999	0.9999	0.9999	0.9999
3.7	0.9999	0.9999	0.9999	0.9999	0.9999	0.9999	0.9999	0.9999	0.9999	0.9999
3.8	0.9999	0.9999	0.9999	0.9999	0.9999	0.9999	0.9999	0.9999	0.9999	0.9999
3.9	1.0000	1.0000	1.0000	1.0000	1.0000	1.0000	1.0000	1.0000	1.0000	1.0000

TABLE 4 *t* Critical Values

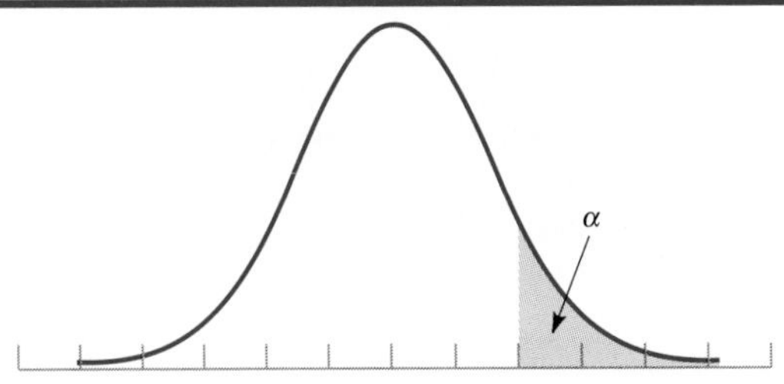

Degrees of Freedom	Upper Tail Probability (α)								
	0.15	**0.10**	**0.05**	**0.025**	**0.015**	**0.01**	**0.005**	**0.001**	**0.0005**
1	1.963	3.078	6.314	12.706	21.205	31.821	63.657	318.309	1273.155
2	1.386	1.886	2.920	4.303	5.643	6.965	9.925	22.327	44.703
3	1.250	1.638	2.353	3.182	3.896	4.541	5.841	10.215	16.326
4	1.190	1.533	2.132	2.776	3.298	3.747	4.604	7.173	10.305
5	1.156	1.476	2.015	2.571	3.003	3.365	4.032	5.893	7.976
6	1.134	1.440	1.943	2.447	2.829	3.143	3.707	5.208	6.788
7	1.119	1.415	1.895	2.365	2.715	2.998	3.499	4.785	6.082
8	1.108	1.397	1.860	2.306	2.634	2.896	3.355	4.501	5.617
9	1.100	1.383	1.833	2.262	2.574	2.821	3.250	4.297	5.291
10	1.093	1.372	1.812	2.228	2.527	2.764	3.169	4.144	5.049
11	1.088	1.363	1.796	2.201	2.491	2.718	3.106	4.025	4.863
12	1.083	1.356	1.782	2.179	2.461	2.681	3.055	3.930	4.717
13	1.079	1.350	1.771	2.160	2.436	2.650	3.012	3.852	4.597
14	1.076	1.345	1.761	2.145	2.415	2.625	2.977	3.787	4.499
15	1.074	1.341	1.753	2.131	2.397	2.602	2.947	3.733	4.417
16	1.071	1.337	1.746	2.120	2.382	2.583	2.921	3.686	4.346
17	1.069	1.333	1.740	2.110	2.368	2.567	2.898	3.646	4.286
18	1.067	1.330	1.734	2.101	2.356	2.552	2.878	3.611	4.233
19	1.066	1.328	1.729	2.093	2.346	2.539	2.861	3.579	4.187
20	1.064	1.325	1.725	2.086	2.336	2.528	2.845	3.552	4.146
21	1.063	1.323	1.721	2.080	2.328	2.518	2.831	3.527	4.109
22	1.061	1.321	1.717	2.074	2.320	2.508	2.819	3.505	4.077
23	1.060	1.319	1.714	2.069	2.313	2.500	2.807	3.485	4.047
24	1.059	1.318	1.711	2.064	2.307	2.492	2.797	3.467	4.021
25	1.058	1.316	1.708	2.060	2.301	2.485	2.787	3.450	3.997
26	1.058	1.315	1.706	2.056	2.296	2.479	2.779	3.435	3.974
27	1.057	1.314	1.703	2.052	2.291	2.473	2.771	3.421	3.954
28	1.056	1.313	1.701	2.048	2.286	2.467	2.763	3.408	3.935
29	1.055	1.311	1.699	2.045	2.282	2.462	2.756	3.396	3.918
30	1.055	1.310	1.697	2.042	2.278	2.457	2.750	3.385	3.902
40	1.050	1.303	1.684	2.021	2.250	2.423	2.704	3.307	3.788
50	1.047	1.299	1.676	2.009	2.234	2.403	2.678	3.261	3.723
60	1.045	1.296	1.671	2.000	2.223	2.390	2.660	3.232	3.681
120	1.041	1.289	1.658	1.980	2.196	2.358	2.617	3.160	3.578
***Z* critical value**	1.036	1.282	1.645	1.960	2.170	2.326	2.576	3.090	3.290
Level of Significance for a one-tailed test	**0.15**	**0.10**	**0.05**	**0.025**	**0.015**	**0.01**	**0.005**	**0.001**	**0.0005**
Level of Significance for a two-tailed test	**0.30**	**0.20**	**0.10**	**0.05**	**0.03**	**0.02**	**0.01**	**0.002**	**0.001**

TABLE 5 Chi-Square Distribution Table

The entries in this table give the critical values of χ^2 for the specified number of degrees of freedom and areas in the right tail.

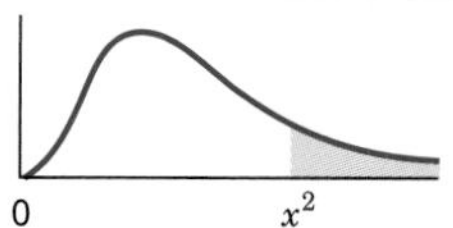

Degrees of Freedom	Upper Tail Areas											
	0.995	0.99	0.975	0.95	0.9	0.75	0.25	0.1	0.05	0.025	0.01	0.005
1	0.000	0.000	0.001	0.004	0.016	0.102	1.323	2.706	3.841	5.024	6.635	7.879
2	0.010	0.020	0.051	0.103	0.211	0.575	2.773	4.605	5.991	7.378	9.210	10.597
3	0.072	0.115	0.216	0.352	0.584	1.213	4.108	6.251	7.815	9.348	11.345	12.838
4	0.207	0.297	0.484	0.711	1.064	1.923	5.385	7.779	9.488	11.143	13.277	14.860
5	0.412	0.554	0.831	1.145	1.610	2.675	6.626	9.236	11.070	12.832	15.086	16.750
6	0.676	0.872	1.237	1.635	2.204	3.455	7.841	10.645	12.592	14.449	16.812	18.548
7	0.989	1.239	1.690	2.167	2.833	4.255	9.037	12.017	14.067	16.013	18.475	20.278
8	1.344	1.647	2.180	2.733	3.490	5.071	10.219	13.362	15.507	17.535	20.090	21.955
9	1.735	2.088	2.700	3.325	4.168	5.899	11.389	14.684	16.919	19.023	21.666	23.589
10	2.156	2.558	3.247	3.940	4.865	6.737	12.549	15.987	18.307	20.483	23.209	25.188
11	2.603	3.053	3.816	4.575	5.578	7.584	13.701	17.275	19.675	21.920	24.725	26.757
12	3.074	3.571	4.404	5.226	6.304	8.438	14.845	18.549	21.026	23.337	26.217	28.300
13	3.565	4.107	5.009	5.892	7.041	9.299	15.984	19.812	22.362	24.736	27.688	29.819
14	4.075	4.660	5.629	6.571	7.790	10.165	17.117	21.064	23.685	26.119	29.141	31.319
15	4.601	5.229	6.262	7.261	8.547	11.037	18.245	22.307	24.996	27.488	30.578	32.801
16	5.142	5.812	6.908	7.962	9.312	11.912	19.369	23.542	26.296	28.845	32.000	34.267
17	5.697	6.408	7.564	8.672	10.085	12.792	20.489	24.769	27.587	30.191	33.409	35.718
18	6.265	7.015	8.231	9.390	10.865	13.675	21.605	25.989	28.869	31.526	34.805	37.156
19	6.844	7.633	8.907	10.117	11.651	14.562	22.718	27.204	30.144	32.852	36.191	38.582
20	7.434	8.260	9.591	10.851	12.443	15.452	23.828	28.412	31.410	34.170	37.566	39.997
21	8.034	8.897	10.283	11.591	13.240	16.344	24.935	29.615	32.671	35.479	38.932	41.401
22	8.643	9.542	10.982	12.338	14.041	17.240	26.039	30.813	33.924	36.781	40.289	42.796
23	9.260	10.196	11.689	13.091	14.848	18.137	27.141	32.007	35.172	38.076	41.638	44.181
24	9.886	10.856	12.401	13.848	15.659	19.037	28.241	33.196	36.415	39.364	42.980	45.558
25	10.520	11.524	13.120	14.611	16.473	19.939	29.339	34.382	37.652	40.646	44.314	46.928
26	11.160	12.198	13.844	15.379	17.292	20.843	30.435	35.563	38.885	41.923	45.642	48.290
27	11.808	12.878	14.573	16.151	18.114	21.749	31.528	36.741	40.113	43.195	46.963	49.645
28	12.461	13.565	15.308	16.928	18.939	22.657	32.620	37.916	41.337	44.461	48.278	50.994
29	13.121	14.256	16.047	17.708	19.768	23.567	33.711	39.087	42.557	45.722	49.588	52.335
30	13.787	14.953	16.791	18.493	20.599	24.478	34.800	40.256	43.773	46.979	50.892	53.672
31	14.458	15.655	17.539	19.281	21.434	25.390	35.887	41.422	44.985	48.232	52.191	55.002
32	15.134	16.362	18.291	20.072	22.271	26.304	36.973	42.585	46.194	49.480	53.486	56.328
33	15.815	17.073	19.047	20.867	23.110	27.219	38.058	43.745	47.400	50.725	54.775	57.648
34	16.501	17.789	19.806	21.664	23.952	28.136	39.141	44.903	48.602	51.966	56.061	58.964
35	17.192	18.509	20.569	22.465	24.797	29.054	40.223	46.059	49.802	53.203	57.342	60.275
40	20.707	22.164	24.433	26.509	29.051	33.660	45.616	51.805	55.758	59.342	63.691	66.766
60	35.534	37.485	40.482	43.188	46.459	52.294	66.981	74.397	79.082	83.298	88.379	91.952
120	83.852	86.923	91.573	95.705	100.624	109.220	130.055	140.233	146.567	152.211	158.950	163.648

TABLE 6 The *F* Distribution Table

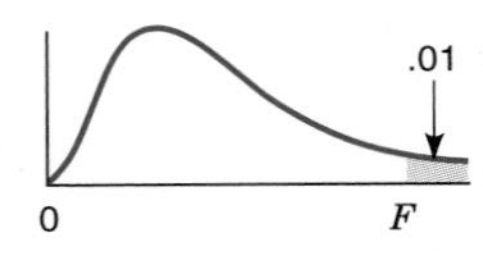

a. Area in the Right Tail under the *F* Distribution Curve = .01

Degrees of Freedom Denominator	Degrees of Freedom - Numerator 1	2	3	4	5	6	7	8	9	10	11	12	13	14	15	16	17
1	4052.185	4999.340	5403.534	5624.257	5763.955	5858.950	5928.334	5980.954	6022.397	6055.925	6083.399	6106.682	6125.774	6143.004	6156.974	6170.012	6181.188
2	98.502	99.000	99.164	99.251	99.302	99.331	99.357	99.375	99.390	99.397	99.408	99.419	99.422	99.426	99.433	99.437	99.441
3	34.116	30.816	29.457	28.710	28.237	27.911	27.671	27.489	27.345	27.228	27.132	27.052	26.983	26.924	26.872	26.826	26.786
4	21.198	18.000	16.694	15.977	15.522	15.207	14.976	14.799	14.659	14.546	14.452	14.374	14.306	14.249	14.198	14.154	14.114
5	16.258	13.274	12.060	11.392	10.967	10.672	10.456	10.289	10.158	10.051	9.963	9.888	9.825	9.770	9.722	9.680	9.643
6	13.745	10.925	9.780	9.148	8.746	8.466	8.260	8.102	7.976	7.874	7.790	7.718	7.657	7.605	7.559	7.519	7.483
7	12.246	9.547	8.451	7.847	7.460	7.191	6.993	6.840	6.719	6.620	6.538	6.469	6.410	6.359	6.314	6.275	6.240
8	11.259	8.649	7.591	7.006	6.632	6.371	6.178	6.029	5.911	5.814	5.734	5.667	5.609	5.559	5.515	5.477	5.442
9	10.562	8.022	6.992	6.422	6.057	5.802	5.613	5.467	5.351	5.257	5.178	5.111	5.055	5.005	4.962	4.924	4.890
10	10.044	7.559	6.552	5.994	5.636	5.386	5.200	5.057	4.942	4.849	4.772	4.706	4.650	4.601	4.558	4.520	4.487
11	9.646	7.206	6.217	5.668	5.316	5.069	4.886	4.744	4.632	4.539	4.462	4.397	4.342	4.293	4.251	4.213	4.180
12	9.330	6.927	5.953	5.412	5.064	4.821	4.640	4.499	4.388	4.296	4.220	4.155	4.100	4.052	4.010	3.972	3.939
13	9.074	6.701	5.739	5.205	4.862	4.620	4.441	4.302	4.191	4.100	4.025	3.960	3.905	3.857	3.815	3.778	3.745
14	8.862	6.515	5.564	5.035	4.695	4.456	4.278	4.140	4.030	3.939	3.864	3.800	3.745	3.698	3.656	3.619	3.586
15	8.683	6.359	5.417	4.893	4.556	4.318	4.142	4.004	3.895	3.805	3.730	3.666	3.612	3.564	3.522	3.485	3.452
16	8.531	6.226	5.292	4.773	4.437	4.202	4.026	3.890	3.780	3.691	3.616	3.553	3.498	3.451	3.409	3.372	3.339
17	8.400	6.112	5.185	4.669	4.336	4.101	3.927	3.791	3.682	3.593	3.518	3.455	3.401	3.353	3.312	3.275	3.242
18	8.285	6.013	5.092	4.579	4.248	4.015	3.841	3.705	3.597	3.508	3.434	3.371	3.316	3.269	3.227	3.190	3.158
19	8.185	5.926	5.010	4.500	4.171	3.939	3.765	3.631	3.523	3.434	3.360	3.297	3.242	3.195	3.153	3.116	3.084
20	8.096	5.849	4.938	4.431	4.103	3.871	3.699	3.564	3.457	3.368	3.294	3.231	3.177	3.130	3.088	3.051	3.018
21	8.017	5.780	4.874	4.369	4.042	3.812	3.640	3.506	3.398	3.310	3.236	3.173	3.119	3.072	3.030	2.993	2.960
22	7.945	5.719	4.817	4.313	3.988	3.758	3.587	3.453	3.346	3.258	3.184	3.121	3.067	3.019	2.978	2.941	2.908
23	7.881	5.664	4.765	4.264	3.939	3.710	3.539	3.406	3.299	3.211	3.137	3.074	3.020	2.973	2.931	2.894	2.861
24	7.823	5.614	4.718	4.218	3.895	3.667	3.496	3.363	3.256	3.168	3.094	3.032	2.977	2.930	2.889	2.852	2.819
25	7.770	5.568	4.675	4.177	3.855	3.627	3.457	3.324	3.217	3.129	3.056	2.993	2.939	2.892	2.850	2.813	2.780
26	7.721	5.526	4.637	4.140	3.818	3.591	3.421	3.288	3.182	3.094	3.021	2.958	2.904	2.857	2.815	2.778	2.745
27	7.677	5.488	4.601	4.106	3.785	3.558	3.388	3.256	3.149	3.062	2.988	2.926	2.872	2.824	2.783	2.746	2.713
28	7.636	5.453	4.568	4.074	3.754	3.528	3.358	3.226	3.120	3.032	2.959	2.896	2.842	2.795	2.753	2.716	2.683
29	7.598	5.420	4.538	4.045	3.725	3.499	3.330	3.198	3.092	3.005	2.931	2.868	2.814	2.767	2.726	2.689	2.656
30	7.562	5.390	4.510	4.018	3.699	3.473	3.305	3.173	3.067	2.979	2.906	2.843	2.789	2.742	2.700	2.663	2.630
40	7.314	5.178	4.313	3.828	3.514	3.291	3.124	2.993	2.888	2.801	2.727	2.665	2.611	2.563	2.522	2.484	2.451
60	7.077	4.977	4.126	3.649	3.339	3.119	2.953	2.823	2.718	2.632	2.559	2.496	2.442	2.394	2.352	2.315	2.281
120	6.851	4.787	3.949	3.480	3.174	2.956	2.792	2.663	2.559	2.472	2.399	2.336	2.282	2.234	2.191	2.154	2.119

TABLE 6 (*Continued*)

Degrees of Freedom Denominator	Degrees of Freedom - Numerator 18	19	20	21	22	23	24	25	26	27	28	29	30	40	60	120
1	6191.432	6200.746	6208.662	6216.113	6223.097	6228.685	6234.273	6239.861	6244.518	6249.174	6252.900	6257.091	6260.350	6286.427	6312.970	6339.513
2	99.444	99.448	99.448	99.451	99.455	99.455	99.455	99.459	99.462	99.462	99.462	99.462	99.466	99.477	99.484	99.491
3	26.751	26.719	26.690	26.664	26.639	26.617	26.597	26.579	26.562	26.546	26.531	26.517	26.504	26.411	26.316	26.221
4	14.079	14.048	14.019	13.994	13.970	13.949	13.929	13.911	13.894	13.878	13.864	13.850	13.838	13.745	13.652	13.558
5	9.609	9.580	9.553	9.528	9.506	9.485	9.466	9.449	9.433	9.418	9.404	9.391	9.379	9.291	9.202	9.112
6	7.451	7.422	7.396	7.372	7.351	7.331	7.313	7.296	7.281	7.266	7.253	7.240	7.229	7.143	7.057	6.969
7	6.209	6.181	6.155	6.132	6.111	6.092	6.074	6.058	6.043	6.029	6.016	6.003	5.992	5.908	5.824	5.737
8	5.412	5.384	5.359	5.336	5.316	5.297	5.279	5.263	5.248	5.234	5.221	5.209	5.198	5.116	5.032	4.946
9	4.860	4.833	4.808	4.786	4.765	4.746	4.729	4.713	4.698	4.684	4.672	4.660	4.649	4.567	4.483	4.398
10	4.457	4.430	4.405	4.383	4.363	4.344	4.327	4.311	4.296	4.283	4.270	4.258	4.247	4.165	4.082	3.996
11	4.150	4.123	4.099	4.077	4.057	4.038	4.021	4.005	3.990	3.977	3.964	3.952	3.941	3.860	3.776	3.690
12	3.910	3.883	3.858	3.836	3.816	3.798	3.780	3.765	3.750	3.736	3.724	3.712	3.701	3.619	3.535	3.449
13	3.716	3.689	3.665	3.643	3.622	3.604	3.587	3.571	3.556	3.543	3.530	3.518	3.507	3.425	3.341	3.255
14	3.556	3.529	3.505	3.483	3.463	3.444	3.427	3.412	3.397	3.383	3.371	3.359	3.348	3.266	3.181	3.094
15	3.423	3.396	3.372	3.350	3.330	3.311	3.294	3.278	3.264	3.250	3.237	3.225	3.214	3.132	3.047	2.959
16	3.310	3.283	3.259	3.237	3.216	3.198	3.181	3.165	3.150	3.137	3.124	3.112	3.101	3.018	2.933	2.845
17	3.212	3.186	3.162	3.139	3.119	3.101	3.083	3.068	3.053	3.039	3.026	3.014	3.003	2.920	2.835	2.746
18	3.128	3.101	3.077	3.055	3.035	3.016	2.999	2.983	2.968	2.955	2.942	2.930	2.919	2.835	2.749	2.660
19	3.054	3.027	3.003	2.981	2.961	2.942	2.925	2.909	2.894	2.880	2.868	2.855	2.844	2.761	2.674	2.584
20	2.989	2.962	2.938	2.916	2.895	2.877	2.859	2.843	2.829	2.815	2.802	2.790	2.778	2.695	2.608	2.517
21	2.931	2.904	2.880	2.857	2.837	2.818	2.801	2.785	2.770	2.756	2.743	2.731	2.720	2.636	2.548	2.457
22	2.879	2.852	2.827	2.805	2.785	2.766	2.749	2.733	2.718	2.704	2.691	2.679	2.667	2.583	2.495	2.403
23	2.832	2.805	2.780	2.758	2.738	2.719	2.702	2.686	2.671	2.657	2.644	2.632	2.620	2.536	2.447	2.354
24	2.789	2.762	2.738	2.716	2.695	2.676	2.659	2.643	2.628	2.614	2.601	2.589	2.577	2.492	2.403	2.310
25	2.751	2.724	2.699	2.677	2.657	2.638	2.620	2.604	2.589	2.575	2.562	2.550	2.538	2.453	2.364	2.270
26	2.715	2.688	2.664	2.642	2.621	2.602	2.585	2.569	2.554	2.540	2.526	2.514	2.503	2.417	2.327	2.233
27	2.683	2.656	2.632	2.609	2.589	2.570	2.552	2.536	2.521	2.507	2.494	2.481	2.470	2.384	2.294	2.198
28	2.653	2.626	2.602	2.579	2.559	2.540	2.522	2.506	2.491	2.477	2.464	2.451	2.440	2.354	2.263	2.167
29	2.626	2.599	2.574	2.552	2.531	2.512	2.495	2.478	2.463	2.449	2.436	2.423	2.412	2.325	2.234	2.138
30	2.600	2.573	2.549	2.526	2.506	2.487	2.469	2.453	2.437	2.423	2.410	2.398	2.386	2.299	2.208	2.111
40	2.421	2.394	2.369	2.346	2.325	2.306	2.288	2.271	2.256	2.241	2.228	2.215	2.203	2.114	2.019	1.917
60	2.251	2.223	2.198	2.175	2.153	2.134	2.115	2.098	2.083	2.068	2.054	2.041	2.028	1.936	1.836	1.726
120	2.089	2.060	2.035	2.011	1.989	1.969	1.950	1.932	1.916	1.901	1.886	1.873	1.860	1.763	1.656	1.533

TABLE 6 (Continued)

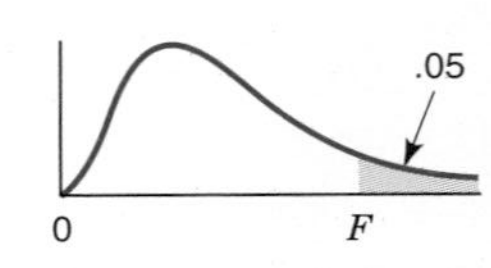

b. Area in the Right Tail under the F Distribution Curve = .05

Degrees of Freedom Denominator	Degrees of Freedom - Numerator 1	2	3	4	5	6	7	8	9	10	11	12	13	14	15	16	17
1	161.446	199.499	215.707	224.583	230.160	233.988	236.767	238.884	240.543	241.882	242.981	243.905	244.690	245.363	245.949	246.466	246.917
2	18.513	19.000	19.164	19.247	19.296	19.329	19.353	19.371	19.385	19.396	19.405	19.412	19.419	19.424	19.429	19.433	19.437
3	10.128	9.552	9.277	9.117	9.013	8.941	8.887	8.845	8.812	8.785	8.763	8.745	8.729	8.715	8.703	8.692	8.683
4	7.709	6.944	6.591	6.388	6.256	6.163	6.094	6.041	5.999	5.964	5.936	5.912	5.891	5.873	5.858	5.844	5.832
5	6.608	5.786	5.409	5.192	5.050	4.950	4.876	4.818	4.772	4.735	4.704	4.678	4.655	4.636	4.619	4.604	4.590
6	5.987	5.143	4.757	4.534	4.387	4.284	4.207	4.147	4.099	4.060	4.027	4.000	3.976	3.956	3.938	3.922	3.908
7	5.591	4.737	4.347	4.120	3.972	3.866	3.787	3.726	3.677	3.637	3.603	3.575	3.550	3.529	3.511	3.494	3.480
8	5.318	4.459	4.066	3.838	3.688	3.581	3.500	3.438	3.388	3.347	3.313	3.284	3.259	3.237	3.218	3.202	3.187
9	5.117	4.256	3.863	3.633	3.482	3.374	3.293	3.230	3.179	3.137	3.102	3.073	3.048	3.025	3.006	2.989	2.974
10	4.965	4.103	3.708	3.478	3.326	3.217	3.135	3.072	3.020	2.978	2.943	2.913	2.887	2.865	2.845	2.828	2.812
11	4.844	3.982	3.587	3.357	3.204	3.095	3.012	2.948	2.896	2.854	2.818	2.788	2.761	2.739	2.719	2.701	2.685
12	4.747	3.885	3.490	3.259	3.106	2.996	2.913	2.849	2.796	2.753	2.717	2.687	2.660	2.637	2.617	2.599	2.583
13	4.667	3.806	3.411	3.179	3.025	2.915	2.832	2.767	2.714	2.671	2.635	2.604	2.577	2.554	2.533	2.515	2.499
14	4.600	3.739	3.344	3.112	2.958	2.848	2.764	2.699	2.646	2.602	2.565	2.534	2.507	2.484	2.463	2.445	2.428
15	4.543	3.682	3.287	3.056	2.901	2.790	2.707	2.641	2.588	2.544	2.507	2.475	2.448	2.424	2.403	2.385	2.368
16	4.494	3.634	3.239	3.007	2.852	2.741	2.657	2.591	2.538	2.494	2.456	2.425	2.397	2.373	2.352	2.333	2.317
17	4.451	3.592	3.197	2.965	2.810	2.699	2.614	2.548	2.494	2.450	2.413	2.381	2.353	2.329	2.308	2.289	2.272
18	4.414	3.555	3.160	2.928	2.773	2.661	2.577	2.510	2.456	2.412	2.374	2.342	2.314	2.290	2.269	2.250	2.233
19	4.381	3.522	3.127	2.895	2.740	2.628	2.544	2.477	2.423	2.378	2.340	2.308	2.280	2.256	2.234	2.215	2.198
20	4.351	3.493	3.098	2.866	2.711	2.599	2.514	2.447	2.393	2.348	2.310	2.278	2.250	2.225	2.203	2.184	2.167
21	4.325	3.467	3.072	2.840	2.685	2.573	2.488	2.420	2.366	2.321	2.283	2.250	2.222	2.197	2.176	2.156	2.139
22	4.301	3.443	3.049	2.817	2.661	2.549	2.464	2.397	2.342	2.297	2.259	2.226	2.198	2.173	2.151	2.131	2.114
23	4.279	3.422	3.028	2.796	2.640	2.528	2.442	2.375	2.320	2.275	2.236	2.204	2.175	2.150	2.128	2.109	2.091
24	4.260	3.403	3.009	2.776	2.621	2.508	2.423	2.355	2.300	2.255	2.216	2.183	2.155	2.130	2.108	2.088	2.070
25	4.242	3.385	2.991	2.759	2.603	2.490	2.405	2.337	2.282	2.236	2.198	2.165	2.136	2.111	2.089	2.069	2.051
26	4.225	3.369	2.975	2.743	2.587	2.474	2.388	2.321	2.265	2.220	2.181	2.148	2.119	2.094	2.072	2.052	2.034
27	4.210	3.354	2.960	2.728	2.572	2.459	2.373	2.305	2.250	2.204	2.166	2.132	2.103	2.078	2.056	2.036	2.018
28	4.196	3.340	2.947	2.714	2.558	2.445	2.359	2.291	2.236	2.190	2.151	2.118	2.089	2.064	2.041	2.021	2.003
29	4.183	3.328	2.934	2.701	2.545	2.432	2.346	2.278	2.223	2.177	2.138	2.104	2.075	2.050	2.027	2.007	1.989
30	4.171	3.316	2.922	2.690	2.534	2.421	2.334	2.266	2.211	2.165	2.126	2.092	2.063	2.037	2.015	1.995	1.976
40	4.085	3.232	2.839	2.606	2.449	2.336	2.249	2.180	2.124	2.077	2.038	2.003	1.974	1.948	1.924	1.904	1.885
60	4.001	3.150	2.758	2.525	2.368	2.254	2.167	2.097	2.040	1.993	1.952	1.917	1.887	1.860	1.836	1.815	1.796
120	3.920	3.072	2.680	2.447	2.290	2.175	2.087	2.016	1.959	1.910	1.869	1.834	1.803	1.775	1.750	1.728	1.709

TABLE 6 (*Continued*)

Degrees of Freedom Denominator	Degrees of Freedom - Numerator 18	19	20	21	22	23	24	25	26	27	28	29	30	40	60	120
1	247.324	247.688	248.016	248.307	248.579	248.823	249.052	249.260	249.453	249.631	249.798	249.951	250.096	251.144	252.196	253.254
2	19.440	19.443	19.446	19.448	19.450	19.452	19.454	19.456	19.457	19.459	19.460	19.461	19.463	19.471	19.479	19.487
3	8.675	8.667	8.660	8.654	8.648	8.643	8.638	8.634	8.630	8.626	8.623	8.620	8.617	8.594	8.572	8.549
4	5.821	5.811	5.803	5.795	5.787	5.781	5.774	5.769	5.763	5.759	5.754	5.750	5.746	5.717	5.688	5.658
5	4.579	4.568	4.558	4.549	4.541	4.534	4.527	4.521	4.515	4.510	4.505	4.500	4.496	4.464	4.431	4.398
6	3.896	3.884	3.874	3.865	3.856	3.849	3.841	3.835	3.829	3.823	3.818	3.813	3.808	3.774	3.740	3.705
7	3.467	3.455	3.445	3.435	3.426	3.418	3.410	3.404	3.397	3.391	3.386	3.381	3.376	3.340	3.304	3.267
8	3.173	3.161	3.150	3.140	3.131	3.123	3.115	3.108	3.102	3.095	3.090	3.084	3.079	3.043	3.005	2.967
9	2.960	2.948	2.936	2.926	2.917	2.908	2.900	2.893	2.886	2.880	2.874	2.869	2.864	2.826	2.787	2.748
10	2.798	2.785	2.774	2.764	2.754	2.745	2.737	2.730	2.723	2.716	2.710	2.705	2.700	2.661	2.621	2.580
11	2.671	2.658	2.646	2.636	2.626	2.617	2.609	2.601	2.594	2.588	2.582	2.576	2.570	2.531	2.490	2.448
12	2.568	2.555	2.544	2.533	2.523	2.514	2.505	2.498	2.491	2.484	2.478	2.472	2.466	2.426	2.384	2.341
13	2.484	2.471	2.459	2.448	2.438	2.429	2.420	2.412	2.405	2.398	2.392	2.386	2.380	2.339	2.297	2.252
14	2.413	2.400	2.388	2.377	2.367	2.357	2.349	2.341	2.333	2.326	2.320	2.314	2.308	2.266	2.223	2.178
15	2.353	2.340	2.328	2.316	2.306	2.297	2.288	2.280	2.272	2.265	2.259	2.253	2.247	2.204	2.160	2.114
16	2.302	2.288	2.276	2.264	2.254	2.244	2.235	2.227	2.220	2.212	2.206	2.200	2.194	2.151	2.106	2.059
17	2.257	2.243	2.230	2.219	2.208	2.199	2.190	2.181	2.174	2.167	2.160	2.154	2.148	2.104	2.058	2.011
18	2.217	2.203	2.191	2.179	2.168	2.159	2.150	2.141	2.134	2.126	2.119	2.113	2.107	2.063	2.017	1.968
19	2.182	2.168	2.155	2.144	2.133	2.123	2.114	2.106	2.098	2.090	2.084	2.077	2.071	2.026	1.980	1.930
20	2.151	2.137	2.124	2.112	2.102	2.092	2.082	2.074	2.066	2.059	2.052	2.045	2.039	1.994	1.946	1.896
21	2.123	2.109	2.096	2.084	2.073	2.063	2.054	2.045	2.037	2.030	2.023	2.016	2.010	1.965	1.916	1.866
22	2.098	2.084	2.071	2.059	2.048	2.038	2.028	2.020	2.012	2.004	1.997	1.990	1.984	1.938	1.889	1.838
23	2.075	2.061	2.048	2.036	2.025	2.014	2.005	1.996	1.988	1.981	1.973	1.967	1.961	1.914	1.865	1.813
24	2.054	2.040	2.027	2.015	2.003	1.993	1.984	1.975	1.967	1.959	1.952	1.945	1.939	1.892	1.842	1.790
25	2.035	2.021	2.007	1.995	1.984	1.974	1.964	1.955	1.947	1.939	1.932	1.926	1.919	1.872	1.822	1.768
26	2.018	2.003	1.990	1.978	1.966	1.956	1.946	1.938	1.929	1.921	1.914	1.907	1.901	1.853	1.803	1.749
27	2.002	1.987	1.974	1.961	1.950	1.940	1.930	1.921	1.913	1.905	1.898	1.891	1.884	1.836	1.785	1.731
28	1.987	1.972	1.959	1.946	1.935	1.924	1.915	1.906	1.897	1.889	1.882	1.875	1.869	1.820	1.769	1.714
29	1.973	1.958	1.945	1.932	1.921	1.910	1.901	1.891	1.883	1.875	1.868	1.861	1.854	1.806	1.754	1.698
30	1.960	1.945	1.932	1.919	1.908	1.897	1.887	1.878	1.870	1.862	1.854	1.847	1.841	1.792	1.740	1.683
40	1.868	1.853	1.839	1.826	1.814	1.803	1.793	1.783	1.775	1.766	1.759	1.751	1.744	1.693	1.637	1.577
60	1.778	1.763	1.748	1.735	1.722	1.711	1.700	1.690	1.681	1.672	1.664	1.656	1.649	1.594	1.534	1.467
120	1.690	1.674	1.659	1.645	1.632	1.620	1.608	1.598	1.588	1.579	1.570	1.562	1.554	1.495	1.429	1.352

TABLE 7 Quality Control Chart Constants

Number of Observations in Subgroup, n	A_2	d_2	d_3	D_3	D_4
2	1.880	1.128	0.853	0.000	3.267
3	1.023	1.693	0.888	0.000	2.574
4	0.729	2.059	0.880	0.000	2.282
5	0.577	2.326	0.864	0.000	2.114
6	0.483	2.534	0.848	0.000	2.004
7	0.419	2.704	0.833	0.076	1.924
8	0.373	2.847	0.820	0.136	1.864
.9	0.337	2.970	0.808	0.184	1.816
10	0.308	3.078	0.797	0.223	1.777
11	0.285	3.173	0.787	0.256	1.744
12	0.266	3.258	0.778	0.283	1.717
13	0.249	3.336	0.770	0.307	1.693
14	0.235	3.407	0.762	0.328	1.672
15	0.223	3.472	0.755	0.347	1.653
16	0.212	3.532	0.749	0.363	1.637
17	0.203	3.588	0.743	0.378	1.622
18	0.194	3.640	0.738	0.391	1.608
19	0.187	3.689	0.733	0.403	1.597
20	0.180	3.735	0.729	0.415	1.585
21	0.173	3.778	0.724	0.425	1.575
22	0.167	3.819	0.720	0.434	1.566
23	0.162	3.858	0.716	0.443	1.557
24	0.157	3.895	0.712	0.451	1.548
25	0.153	3.931	0.709	0.459	1.541

APPENDIX **B**

EXPLANATION OF LARGE DATA SETS

THE INFORMATION THAT FOLLOWS WILL HELP YOU UNDERSTAND THE DATA FILE CARS.XXX.

Explanation of the Variable Names in CARS

CMSA	Household location—CMSA
HHFAMINC	Household family income category
HHLOC	MSA status
HHMSA	Household location—MSA
HHSIZE	Total number of persons in household
HH_RACE	Race of household reference person
HOUSEID	Household identification number
LIF_CYC	Family life cycle
MAKECODE	NASS Code for vehicle make
MSASIZE	Size of MSA/CMSA of household
MSTR_MON	Date of household master interview—Month
POPDNSTY	Population density of household ZIP code area
POVERTY	Household below, near, or above poverty level
REF_AGE	Age of household reference person
REF_EDUC	Education of household reference person
REF_SEX	Sex of household reference person
URBAN	Urbanized area indicator
URBNAREA	Urbanized area status
URBNSIZE	Size of urbanized area
VEH12MNT	Vehicle received in last 12 months
VEHHHOWN	Vehicle owned by household member
VEHMILES	Reported vehicle mileage previous 12 months
VEHNEW	Vehicle new or used when received
VEHTYPE	Vehicle type
VEHYEAR	Model year of vehicle

Explanation of Coded Values for Variables in CARS

CMSA Household location—CMSA

Value	Label
1122	Boston-Lawrence-Salem, MA-NH
1282	Buffalo-Niagara Falls, NY
1602	Chicago-Gary-Lake County, IL-IN-WI
1642	Cincinnati-Hamilton, OH-KY-IN
1692	Cleveland-Akron-Lorain, OH
1922	Dallas-Fort Worth, TX
2082	Denver-Boulder, CO
2162	Detroit-Ann Arbor, MI
3282	Hartford-New Britain-Middletown, CT
3362	Houston-Galveston-Brazoria, TX
4472	Los Angeles-Anaheim-Riverside, CA
4992	Miami-Fort Lauderdale, FL
5082	Milwaukee-Racine, WI
5602	New York-Northern New Jersey-Long Island, NY-NJ-CT
6162	Philadelphia-Wilmington-Trenton, PA-NJ-DE-MD
6282	Pittsburgh-Beaver Valley, PA
6442	Portland-Vancouver, OR-WA
6482	Providence-Pawtucket-Fall River, RI-MA
7362	San Francisco-Oakland-San Jose, CA
7602	Seattle-Tacoma, WA

HHFAMINC Household family income category

Value	Label
01	Less than $5,000
02	$5,000 to $9,999
03	$10,000 to $14,999
04	$15,000 to $19,999
05	$20,000 to $24,999
06	$25,000 to $29,999
07	$30,000 to $34,999
08	$35,000 to $39,999
09	$40,000 to $44,999
10	$45,000 to $49,999
11	$50,000 to $54,999
12	$55,000 to $59,999
13	$60,000 to $64,999
14	$65,000 to $69,999
15	$70,000 to $74,999
16	$75,000 to $79,999
17	$80,000 or over
98	Not Ascertained
99	Refused

HHLOC MSA status

Value	Label
1	In MSA central city
2	In MSA, not in central city
3	Not in MSA

HHSIZE Total number of persons in household

Value	Label
01	One person in household
02	Two people in household
03	Three people in household
04	Four people in household
05	Five people in household
06	Six people in household
07	Seven people in household
08	Eight people in household
09	Nine people in household
10	Ten people in household

HH_RACE Race of household reference person

Value	Label
01	White
02	Black
03	Other
98	Not Ascertained
99	Refused

HOUSEID Household identification number

(This is just an index number that is used to keep track of each interview.)

LIF_CYC Family life cycle

Value	Label
01	Single adult, no children
02	Two or more adults, no children
03	Single adult, youngest child age 0–5
04	Two or more adults, youngest child age 0–5
05	Single adult, youngest child age 6–15
06	Two or more adults, youngest child age 6–15
07	Single adult, youngest child age 16–21
08	Two or more adults, youngest child age 16–21
09	Single adult, retired, no children
10	Two or more adults, retired, no children
98	Not Ascertained

MAKECODE NASS code for vehicle make

Value	Label	Value	Label	Value	Label
001	American Motors	030	Volkswagen	048	Subaru
002	Jeep (includes Kaiser-Jeep)	031	Alfa Romeo	049	Toyota
003	AM General	032	Audi	050	Triumph
006	Chrysler	033	Austin/Austin Healey	051	Volvo
007	Dodge	034	BMW	052	Mitsubishi
008	Imperial	035	Nissan/Datsun	053	Suzuki
009	Plymouth	036	Fiat	054	Acura
010	Eagle	037	Honda	055	Hyundai
012	Ford	038	Isuzu	056	Merkur
013	Lincoln	039	Jaguar	057	Yugo
014	Mercury	040	Lancia	058	Infiniti
018	Buick	041	Mazda	059	Lexus
019	Cadillac	042	Mercedes-Benz	060	Daihatsu
020	Chevrolet	043	MG	069	Other foreign
021	Oldsmobile	044	Peugeot	084	International Harvester/Navistar
022	Pontiac	045	Porsche	089	Other medium/heavy trucks and buses
023	GMC	046	Renault	099	Unknown
024	Saturn	047	Saab	994	Legitimate skip
029	Other domestic				

MSASIZE Size of MSA/CMSA of household

Value	Label
01	Less than 250,000
02	250,000 to 499,999
03	500,000 to 999,999
04	1,000,000 to 2,999,999
05	3,000,000 or more
94	Not in MSA

MSTR_MON Date of household master interview—Month

Value	Label
01	January
02	February
03	March
04	April
05	May
06	June
07	July
08	August
09	September
10	October
11	November
12	December
98	Not ascertained

POPDNSTY Population density of household ZIP code area

Value	Label
01	0 to 99
02	100 to 249
03	250 to 499
04	500 to 749
05	750 to 999
06	1,000 to 1,999 and in MSA
07	2,000 to 2,999 and in MSA
08	3,000 to 3,999 and in MSA
09	4,000 to 4,999 and in MSA
10	5,000 to 7,499 and in MSA
11	7,500 to 9,999 and in MSA
12	10,000 to 49,999 and in MSA
13	50,000 or more and in MSA
14	1,000 or more and not in MSA

POVERTY Household below, near, or above poverty level

Value	Label
01	Below poverty level
02	Near poverty level
03	Above poverty level
98	Not Ascertained
99	Refused

REF_AGE Age of household reference person

Number except the following:

Value	Label
077	Reference person age 76 through 79
082	Reference person age 80 through 84
088	Reference person age 85 and over
998	Not Ascertained
999	Refused

REF_SEX Sex of household reference person

Value	Label
01	Male
02	Female
98	Not Ascertained
99	Refused

REF_EDUC Education of household reference person

Value	Label
01	First grade
02	Second grade
03	Third grade
04	Fourth grade
05	Fifth grade
06	Sixth grade
07	Seventh grade
08	Eighth grade
09	Ninth grade
10	Tenth grade
11	Eleventh grade
12	Twelfth grade
13	Technical school after high school
21	1st (Freshman) year of college or equivalent
22	2nd (Sophomore) year of college or equivalent
23	3rd (Junior) year of college or equivalent
24	4th (Senior) year of college or equivalent
31	One year of graduate school
32	Two or more years of graduate school
98	Not Ascertained
99	Refused

THE FOLLOWING INFORMATION WILL HELP YOU UNDERSTAND THE DATA FILE CONSEXP.XXX.

Explanation of Variable Names Used in the Consumer Expenditures Survey

Variable	Description
AGE2	Age of Spouse
AGE_REF	Age of Ref. Person
ALCBEVCQ	Alcoholic Beverages This Quarter
ALCBEVPQ	Alcoholic Beverages Last Quarter
APPARCQ	Apparel and Services This Quarter
APPARPQ	Apparel and Services Last Quarter
AS_COMP1	No. of Males Age 16 and Over in Cu
AS_COMP2	No. of Females Age 16 and Over
AS_COMP3	No. of Males Age 2 Through 15
AS_COMP4	No. of Females Age 2 Through 15
AS_COMP5	No. of Members Under Age 2 in Cu
BLS_URBN	Urban/rural
CUTENURE	Housing Tenure
EARNINCX	Cu Earned Inc. Before Taxes
EDUCA2	Education of Spouse
EDUC_REF	Education of Ref. Person
ENTERTCQ	Entertainment This Quarter
FAMTFEDX	Fed Inc. Tax Deducted From Last Pay
FAM_SIZE	No. of Members in Cu
FDAWAYCQ	Food Away From Home This Quarter
FDAWAYPQ	Food Away From Home Last Quarter
FDHOMECQ	Food At Home This Quarter
FDHOMEPQ	Food At Home Last Quarter
FINCATAX	Cu Inc. After Taxes
FINDRETX	Money Placed in Individual Retirement Account (IRA)
FOODCQ	Total Food This Quarter
FOODPQ	Total Food Last Quarter
FRRETIRX	Soc. Sec. and Railroad Income
FSALARYX	Cu Wage and Salary Inc. Before Taxes
GASMOCQ	Gasoline and Motor Oil This Quarter
GASMOPQ	Gasoline and Motor Oil Last Quarter
HEALTHCQ	Health Care This Quarter
HEALTHPQ	Health Care Last Quarter
HOUSEQCQ	House furnishings, Equip. This Quarter
HOUSEQPQ	House furnishings, Equip. Last Quarter
INC_HRS1	Wkly. Hrs. Reference Person Usually Worked
INC_HRS2	Weekly Hrs. Spouse Usually Worked
NEWID	Cu Identification Number
NUM_AUTO	No. of Automobiles
PUBTRACQ	Pub. Transportation This Quarter
PUBTRAPQ	Pub. Transportation Last Quarter
RENTEQVX	Approx. Mthly. Rental Value of Home
SAVACCTX	Savings Accts. Balances At Banks
SECESTX	Est. Market Value of Securities
TRANSCQ	Transportation This Quarter
TRANSPQ	Transportation Last Quarter
UTILCQ	Utilities, Fuels, Public Services This Quarter
UTILPQ	Utilities, Fuels, Public Services Last Quarter
VEHQ	Number of Vehicles

Explanation of Code Values for Variables in Consumers Expenditure Survey

BLS_URBN—Whether the location of the household is urban or rural

Value	Label
1	Urban
2	Rural

CUTENURE Type of ownership of house

Value	Label
1	Owned With Mortgage
2	Owned Without Mortgage
3	Owned Mort. Not Reported
4	Rented
5	Occ. Without Payment of Cash Rent
6	Stud. Housing

EDUCA2 and EDUC_REF Education level of head of household

Value	Label
1	Elementary 1–8 Yrs.
2	High School, Less Than H.S. Grad.
3	High School Graduate
4	Coll., Less Than Coll. Grad.
5	Coll. Graduate
6	Graduate School
7	Never Att. School

URBAN Urbanized area indicator

Value	Label
1	Household in urbanized area
2	Household not in urbanized area

URBNAREA Urbanized area status

Value	Label
1	Urbanized, in MSA central city
2	Urbanized, not in MSA central city
3	Not in urbanized area

URBNSIZE Size of urbanized area

Value	Label
01	50,000 to 199,999
02	200,000 to 499,999
03	500,000 to 999,999
04	1,000,000 or more without subway/rail
05	1,000,000 or more with subway/rail
94	Not in urbanized area

VEH12MNT Vehicle received in last 12 months

Value	Label
01	Yes
02	No
98	Not ascertained
99	Refused

VEHHHOWN Vehicle owned by household member

Value	Label
01	Yes
02	No
98	Not ascertained
99	Refused

VEHMILES Reported vehicle mileage previous 12 months

Value	Label
999994	Legitimate skip
999998	Not ascertained

VEHNEW Vehicle new or used when received

Value	Label
01	New
02	Used
98	Not ascertained
99	Refused

VEHTYPE Vehicle type

Value	Label
01	Automobile (includes station wagon)
02	Passenger van
03	Cargo van
04	Pickup truck (including pickup with camper)
05	Other truck
06	RV or motor home
07	Motorcycle
08	Moped
09	Other
98	Not Ascertained
99	Refused

VEHYEAR Model year of vehicle

Value	Label
055	1919–1959
063	1960–1964
065	1965
066	1966
067	1967
068	1968
069	1969
070	1970
071	1971
072	1972
073	1973
074	1974
075	1975
076	1976
077	1977
078	1978
079	1979
080	1980
081	1981
082	1982
083	1983
084	1984
085	1985
086	1986
087	1987
088	1988
089	1989
090	1990
091	1991
994	Legitimate skip
998	Not Ascertained
999	Refused

APPENDIX **C**

AN INTRODUCTION TO MICROSOFT EXCEL

This appendix will introduce you to the basics of Microsoft Excel 97, if you are not familiar with the program. If you are already familiar with Excel, you can simply refer to the sections on using Excel for statistics at the end of each chapter.

C.1 STARTING MICROSOFT EXCEL

You can start Microsoft Excel 97 in several different ways:

- from the **Start > Programs** menu
- from the Microsoft Office shortcut bar

To open Excel from the Program menu, click on **Start > Programs** and then on the icon for Excel. Excel is usually located in a folder for MS Office 97 as shown in Figure C.1. If there is not a folder for Office 97, then Excel might be a separate icon on the program menu.

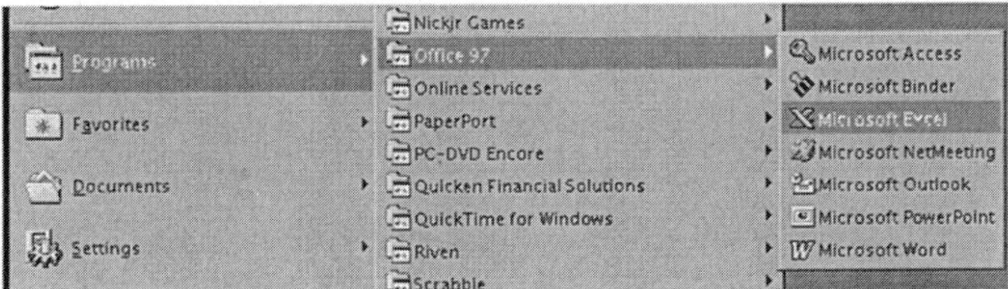

FIGURE C.1 Starting Excel from the Start button

If your computer has the Microsoft Office shortcut bar running, you will see an icon for Excel on the toolbar, as shown in Figure C.2. Clicking on the icon will launch Excel.

FIGURE C.2 The Microsoft Office toolbar

C.2 THE EXCEL WORKBOOK

Excel starts by opening a new workbook. A workbook in Excel is a collection of worksheets. Each worksheet is a grid with 256 columns and 65,536 rows. An Excel workbook, the menus, and toolbars are shown in Figure C.3. We will now look at the different parts of the workbook and talk about their functions.

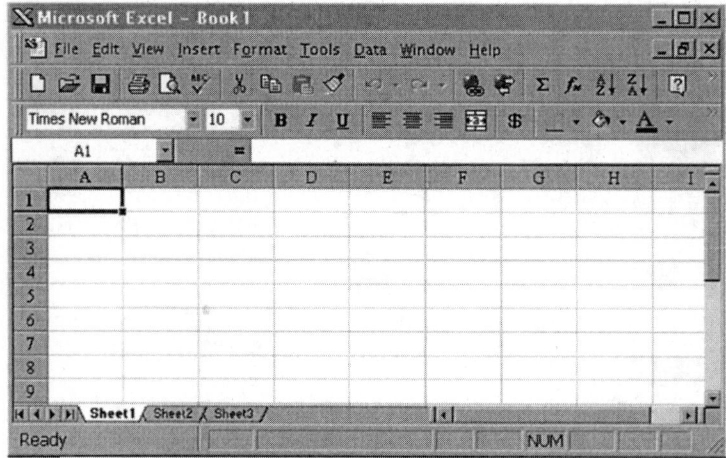

FIGURE C.3 The Excel workbook

The Worksheet

The worksheet portion of the Excel workbook is where you will store your data and do all of your calculations. A worksheet consists of 256 columns labeled with letters and 65,536 rows, labeled with numbers. An individual location in a worksheet is called a **cell.** Each cell in a worksheet is identified by its **location.** Locations are described in terms of the column letter followed by the row number. In Figure C.4, you see a typical worksheet and its formula bar. The important parts of the worksheet are labeled.

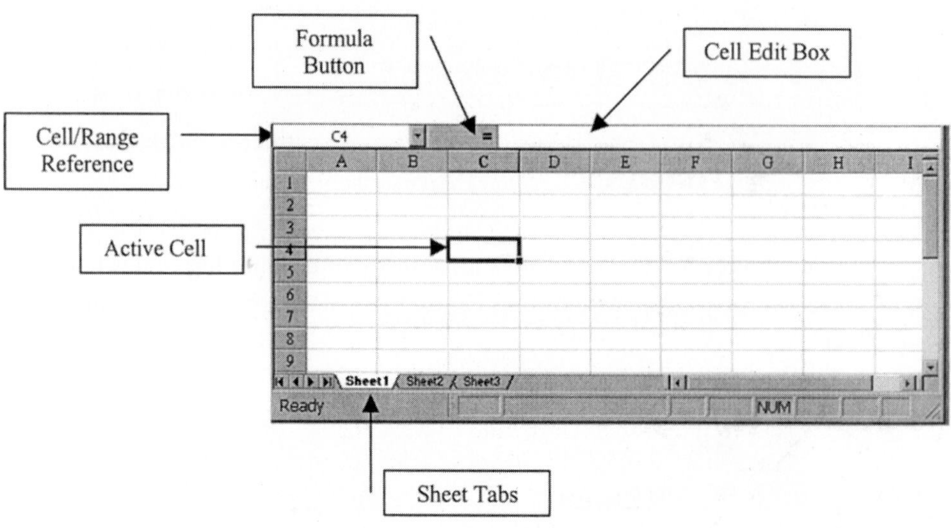

FIGURE C.4 The Excel worksheet

In this worksheet, cell C4 is the **active cell.** A cell is made active by either clicking on it or by moving to the cell using the directional keys. The active cell will have a darker border around it. The location of the active cell is shown in the Cell/Range Reference and the contents of the active cell appear in the Cell Edit box.

A workbook consists of a collection of worksheets. You can move from sheet to sheet, by clicking on the **sheet tabs** at the bottom of the workbook. It is a good idea to give different names to the worksheets to keep your worksheet organized and so that you don't waste time looking for something important. To change the name of a worksheet, double-click on the sheet tab and type in the new name.

The Excel Menu and Toolbars

The other portion of the workbook that you see when you use Excel consists of the Excel menu bar and some toolbars as shown in Figure C.5. You can specify exactly which toolbars Excel shows, but the ones shown by default are the standard and formatting toolbars.

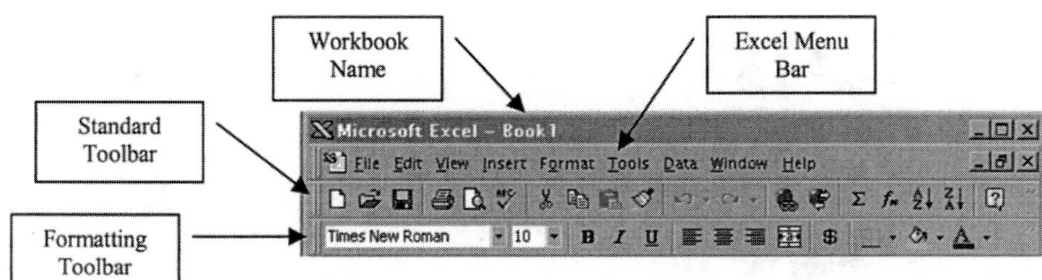

FIGURE C.5 Excel menus and toolbars

The **Standard Toolbar** contains icons for often-used tasks from the Excel menu bar. Some of these tasks are **New, Open, Print, Print Preview,** and **Save** from the File menu, **Copy, Cut,** and **Paste** from the Edit menu, and **Sort** from the Data menu. The **Formatting Toolbar** includes icons for changing the appearance of entries in the worksheet.

C.3 FILE OPERATIONS IN EXCEL

When you start Excel a new workbook automatically opens. After you have been working in Excel awhile you might want to save your work and to open your own workbooks the next time you start Excel.

Opening an Existing Workbook in Excel

There are two basic ways to open workbook files in Excel. One way is simply to double-click on the name of the file in Windows Explorer or My Computer. Excel files have the file extension **".xls"** after the name of the file. When you open the file this way, Excel will start automatically with the file as the open workbook.

If you have already started Excel, then you can open a file using the **File** menu. Click on the **File** in the menu bar and the menu shown in Figure C.6 (page C4) will appear.

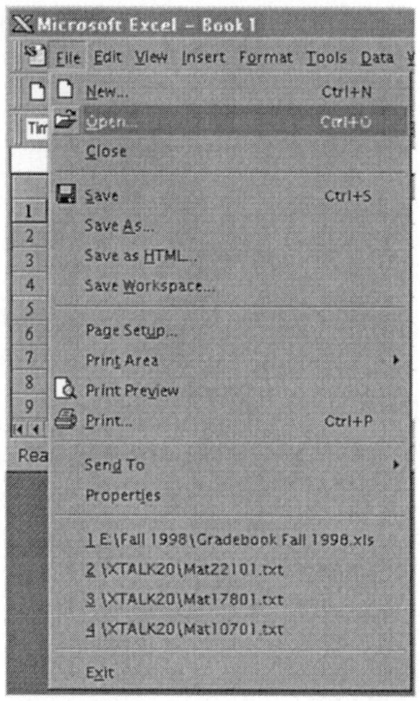

FIGURE C.6 The File menu in Excel

Choose **Open** and the dialog box shown in Figure C.7 opens.

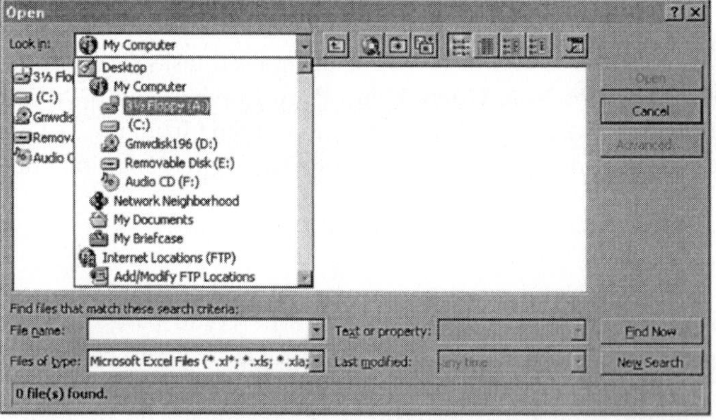

FIGURE C.7 The Open File dialog box

Clicking on the arrow next to the **Look in:** box will bring up a list of possible locations for your file. Most of the time your files will be on a floppy disk or on one of the hard drives of the computer. If the file is located on a floppy disk, choose the $3\frac{1}{2}$ Floppy option. If it is located on some other drive such as your hard drive or a network drive, you should choose the appropriate disk letter.

After you choose the drive that contains your file, a list of all Excel files on that drive will appear in the dialog box, as shown in Figure C.8. To open the file, click on the name of the file you want and choose **Open** or simply double-click on the file name.

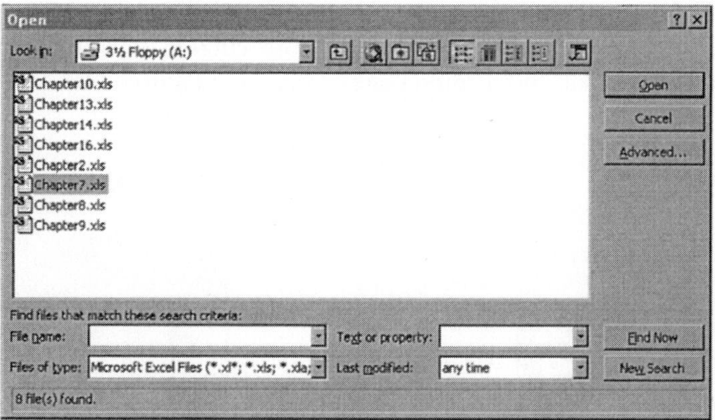

FIGURE C.8 List of Excel files on the A: drive

Saving a File in Excel

After you have done some work in Excel you will want to save your file, perhaps to work on at a later time or to hand in to your instructor. The process of saving a file in Excel is very similar to that of opening a file. Choose **File > Save** from the menu bar. If the workbook is a new one *that has not been saved before,* the **Save As** dialog box will open as shown in Figure C.9.

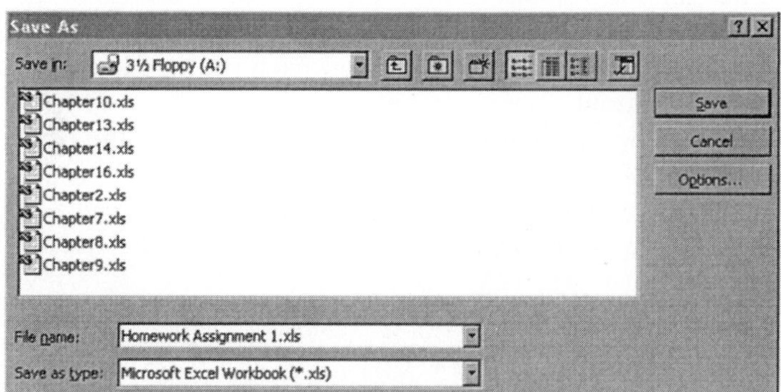

FIGURE C.9 The Save As dialog box

Use the **Save in:** list to choose the location where you want to save the file. In the **File name:** box, type in a name for the file that will help you remember what the file contains. Cute names, however funny, do not help you when you have ten files saved on the same disk! Click **Save** to save the file to the location you selected.

This is only one way to save a file. You can also click on the floppy disk icon in the Standard Toolbar, or hit Ctrl+ S.

No computer or computer network is foolproof. Even if you are not finished with your work, you will want to save your file regularly. If you do not, and the system crashes, you will lose any work you have done. Once the file has been saved for the first time, selecting **File > Save** will automatically save the file to its previous location.

C.4 PRINTING IN EXCEL

You will most likely want to print out some of your work in Excel. This can be done in several different ways.

To start printing, you can click on the printer icon in the **Standard Toolbar** or select **File > Print.** This will print your current worksheet using the current printing setup. You might not like the way your output appears if you do this. You can customize the way your printout appears by using the **Print Preview** option.

To use **Print Preview** click on the icon in the **Standard Toolbar** or choose **File > Print Preview.** When you select Print Preview your current worksheet will be shown exactly as it will appear on the printed page as shown in Figure C.10.

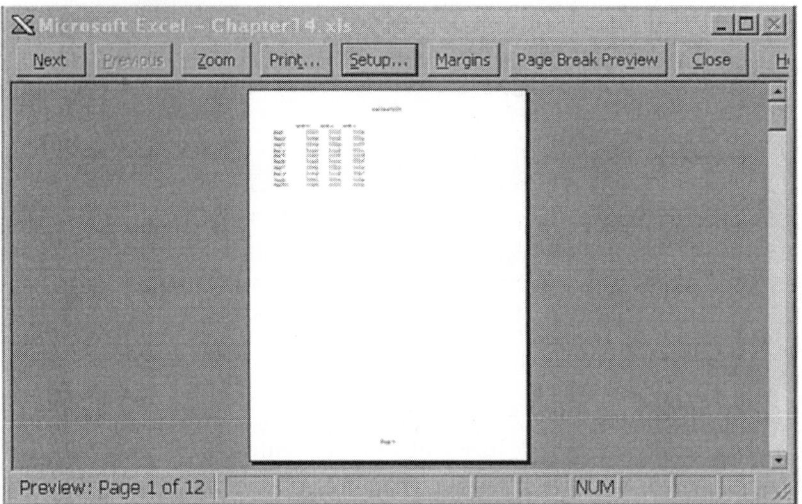

FIGURE C.10 The Print Preview dialog box

If you like the way it looks you can simply click **Print . . .** and it will be printed. If you do not like the way it looks you can change several aspects of the printout by selecting **Setup . . . .** The **Page Setup** dialog box opens. The dialog box has four tabs: **Page, Margins, Header/Footer,** and **Sheet.** Each of these lets you control a different aspect of the printout.

The **Page** tab shown in Figure C.11 allows you to choose the page orientation, portrait or landscape. Your choice will depend on how the data are located in your spreadsheet. If you use a lot of columns and not many rows, you will want Landscape. If you have many rows and not so many columns you will want Portrait.

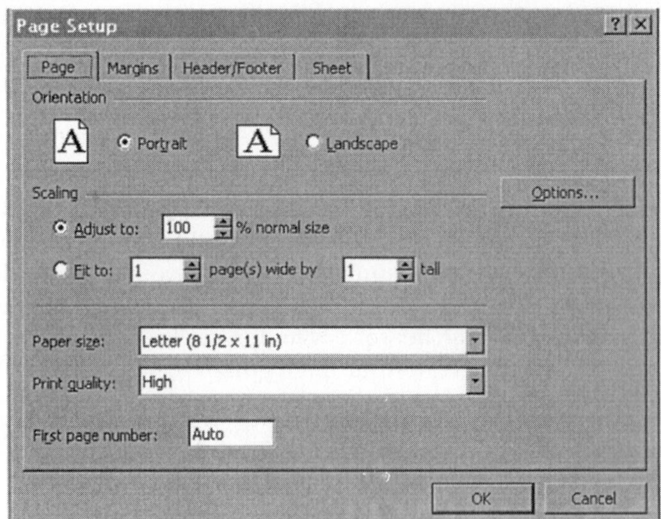

FIGURE C.11 The Page tab

The other tabs in the Page Setup dialog box let you adjust other aspects about how your selection will print. You can adjust the margins, add headers and footers (or delete the default headers and footers that Excel uses), and choose whether or not you want the gridlines on the sheet to print.

C.5 OTHER USEFUL TIPS FOR EXCEL

Selecting a Range

Many activities in Excel require you to select a range of cells in the worksheet. A range of cells might be in a single column or in several columns. There are several ways to select a range:

1. Make the first cell in the range active by moving the cursor to that cell. Press the left mouse button and drag the cursor to highlight the remaining cells in the range.
2. Click the first cell in the range, and then hold down SHIFT and click the last cell in the range. You can scroll to make the last cell visible.
3. To select non-adjacent ranges, select the first range and then hold down the CTRL button while you select the other range(s).

Copying, Cutting, and Pasting

Some of the actions that you will perform most often in Excel are copying, cutting, and pasting. These commands are found in the **Edit** menu and allow you to manage the data in your worksheets. To copy a range of cells from one location in a workbook to another, you must first select the range of cells as just described. Then, from the **Edit** menu, select **Copy,** or click on the **Copy** icon on the toolbar. Move the cursor to the first cell where you want to place the copy and then select **Paste** from the edit menu or click on the **Paste** icon on the toolbar.

If you want to move a range of cells from one location to another, after selecting the range of cells, choose **Cut** from the **Edit** menu or click on the **Cut** icon on the toolbar. Then move the cursor to the destination cells and select **Paste.**

Right Clicking

Clicking the right mouse button in Excel is a useful action. When you click the right mouse button, a pop-up context-sensitive menu appears. The commands on this menu are the ones that most likely apply to the action you are performing.

Switching Among Workbooks

In Excel it is possible to keep more than one workbook open at a time. This is useful if you need to copy information or sheets from a workbook to another workbook. To switch among open workbooks in Excel, select **Window** from the menu bar. At the bottom of the menu is a list of all open workbooks, as shown in Figure C.12.

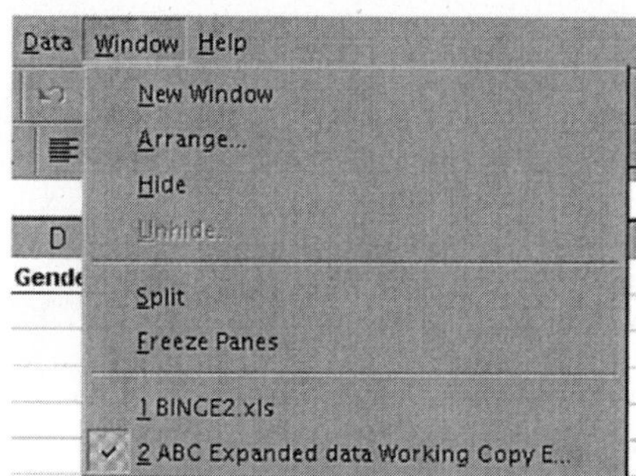

FIGURE C.12 The Window menu

To select a different workbook, click on the name of the workbook you want to use.

PHOTO CREDITS

Chapter 1: Tom & Dee Ann McCarthy/The Stock Market. ***Chapter 2:*** David Joel/Stone. ***Chapter 3:*** Jose L. Pelaez/The Stock Market. ***Chapter 4:*** Gary Holscher/Stone. ***Chapter 5:*** Yellow Dog Productions/The Image Bank. ***Chapter 6:*** Kunio Owaki/The Stock Market. ***Chapter 7:*** Stewart Cohen/Stone. ***Chapter 8:*** Don Klumpp/The Image Bank. ***Chapter 9:*** Tom Stewart/The Stock Market. ***Chapter 10:*** Henry Sims/The Image Bank. ***Chapter 11:*** © Telegraph Colour Library/FPG International. ***Chapter 12:*** David Barnes/The Stock Market. ***Chapter 13:*** Yellow Dog Productions/The Image Bank. ***Chapter 14:*** Rosanne Olson/Stone. ***Chapter 15:*** Rob Crandall/The Image Works. ***Chapter 16:*** James Rudnick/The Stock Market. ***Chapter 17:*** Doug Armand/Stone.

INDEX

TABLE 4 *t* Critical Values

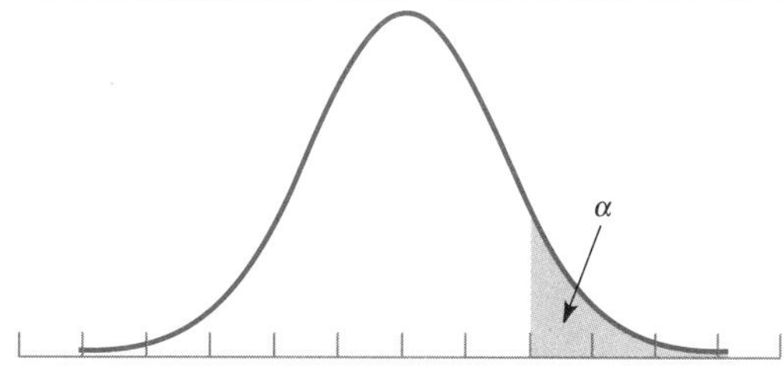

Degrees of Freedom	Upper Tail Probability (α)								
	0.15	**0.10**	**0.05**	**0.025**	**0.015**	**0.01**	**0.005**	**0.001**	**0.0005**
1	1.963	3.078	6.314	12.706	21.205	31.821	63.657	318.309	1273.155
2	1.386	1.886	2.920	4.303	5.643	6.965	9.925	22.327	44.703
3	1.250	1.638	2.353	3.182	3.896	4.541	5.841	10.215	16.326
4	1.190	1.533	2.132	2.776	3.298	3.747	4.604	7.173	10.305
5	1.156	1.476	2.015	2.571	3.003	3.365	4.032	5.893	7.976
6	1.134	1.440	1.943	2.447	2.829	3.143	3.707	5.208	6.788
7	1.119	1.415	1.895	2.365	2.715	2.998	3.499	4.785	6.082
8	1.108	1.397	1.860	2.306	2.634	2.896	3.355	4.501	5.617
9	1.100	1.383	1.833	2.262	2.574	2.821	3.250	4.297	5.291
10	1.093	1.372	1.812	2.228	2.527	2.764	3.169	4.144	5.049
11	1.088	1.363	1.796	2.201	2.491	2.718	3.106	4.025	4.863
12	1.083	1.356	1.782	2.179	2.461	2.681	3.055	3.930	4.717
13	1.079	1.350	1.771	2.160	2.436	2.650	3.012	3.852	4.597
14	1.076	1.345	1.761	2.145	2.415	2.625	2.977	3.787	4.499
15	1.074	1.341	1.753	2.131	2.397	2.602	2.947	3.733	4.417
16	1.071	1.337	1.746	2.120	2.382	2.583	2.921	3.686	4.346
17	1.069	1.333	1.740	2.110	2.368	2.567	2.898	3.646	4.286
18	1.067	1.330	1.734	2.101	2.356	2.552	2.878	3.611	4.233
19	1.066	1.328	1.729	2.093	2.346	2.539	2.861	3.579	4.187
20	1.064	1.325	1.725	2.086	2.336	2.528	2.845	3.552	4.146
21	1.063	1.323	1.721	2.080	2.328	2.518	2.831	3.527	4.109
22	1.061	1.321	1.717	2.074	2.320	2.508	2.819	3.505	4.077
23	1.060	1.319	1.714	2.069	2.313	2.500	2.807	3.485	4.047
24	1.059	1.318	1.711	2.064	2.307	2.492	2.797	3.467	4.021
25	1.058	1.316	1.708	2.060	2.301	2.485	2.787	3.450	3.997
26	1.058	1.315	1.706	2.056	2.296	2.479	2.779	3.435	3.974
27	1.057	1.314	1.703	2.052	2.291	2.473	2.771	3.421	3.954
28	1.056	1.313	1.701	2.048	2.286	2.467	2.763	3.408	3.935
29	1.055	1.311	1.699	2.045	2.282	2.462	2.756	3.396	3.918
30	1.055	1.310	1.697	2.042	2.278	2.457	2.750	3.385	3.902
40	1.050	1.303	1.684	2.021	2.250	2.423	2.704	3.307	3.788
50	1.047	1.299	1.676	2.009	2.234	2.403	2.678	3.261	3.723
60	1.045	1.296	1.671	2.000	2.223	2.390	2.660	3.232	3.681
120	1.041	1.289	1.658	1.980	2.196	2.358	2.617	3.160	3.578
Z critical value	1.036	1.282	1.645	1.960	2.170	2.326	2.576	3.090	3.290
Level of Significance for a one-tailed test	**0.15**	**0.10**	**0.05**	**0.025**	**0.015**	**0.01**	**0.005**	**0.001**	**0.0005**
Level of Significance for a two-tailed test	**0.30**	**0.20**	**0.10**	**0.05**	**0.03**	**0.02**	**0.01**	**0.002**	**0.001**

TABLE 3 Standard Normal Table

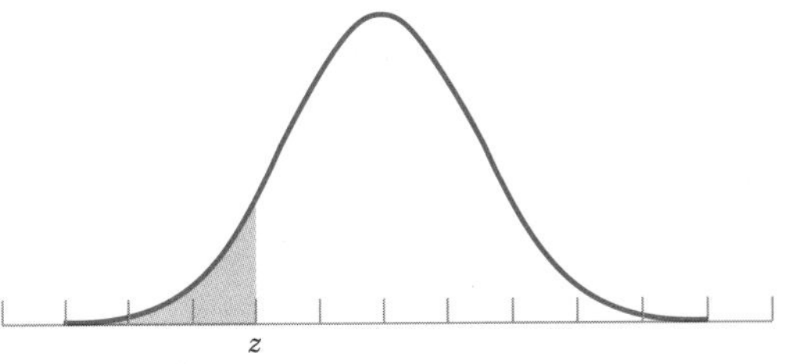

$P(Z < z)$

z	Second Decimal Place									
	0.00	**0.01**	**0.02**	**0.03**	**0.04**	**0.05**	**0.06**	**0.07**	**0.08**	**0.09**
-3.9	0.0000	0.0000	0.0000	0.0000	0.0000	0.0000	0.0000	0.0000	0.0000	0.0000
-3.8	0.0001	0.0001	0.0001	0.0001	0.0001	0.0001	0.0001	0.0001	0.0001	0.0001
-3.7	0.0001	0.0001	0.0001	0.0001	0.0001	0.0001	0.0001	0.0001	0.0001	0.0001
-3.6	0.0002	0.0002	0.0001	0.0001	0.0001	0.0001	0.0001	0.0001	0.0001	0.0001
-3.5	0.0002	0.0002	0.0002	0.0002	0.0002	0.0002	0.0002	0.0002	0.0002	0.0002
-3.4	0.0003	0.0003	0.0003	0.0003	0.0003	0.0003	0.0003	0.0003	0.0003	0.0002
-3.3	0.0005	0.0005	0.0005	0.0004	0.0004	0.0004	0.0004	0.0004	0.0004	0.0003
-3.2	0.0007	0.0007	0.0006	0.0006	0.0006	0.0006	0.0006	0.0005	0.0005	0.0005
-3.1	0.0010	0.0009	0.0009	0.0009	0.0008	0.0008	0.0008	0.0008	0.0007	0.0007
-3.0	0.0013	0.0013	0.0013	0.0012	0.0012	0.0011	0.0011	0.0011	0.0010	0.0010
-2.9	0.0019	0.0018	0.0018	0.0017	0.0016	0.0016	0.0015	0.0015	0.0014	0.0014
-2.8	0.0026	0.0025	0.0024	0.0023	0.0023	0.0022	0.0021	0.0021	0.0020	0.0019
-2.7	0.0035	0.0034	0.0033	0.0032	0.0031	0.0030	0.0029	0.0028	0.0027	0.0026
-2.6	0.0047	0.0045	0.0044	0.0043	0.0041	0.0040	0.0039	0.0038	0.0037	0.0036
-2.5	0.0062	0.0060	0.0059	0.0057	0.0055	0.0054	0.0052	0.0051	0.0049	0.0048
-2.4	0.0082	0.0080	0.0078	0.0075	0.0073	0.0071	0.0069	0.0068	0.0066	0.0064
-2.3	0.0107	0.0104	0.0102	0.0099	0.0096	0.0094	0.0091	0.0089	0.0087	0.0084
-2.2	0.0139	0.0136	0.0132	0.0129	0.0125	0.0122	0.0119	0.0116	0.0113	0.0110
-2.1	0.0179	0.0174	0.0170	0.0166	0.0162	0.0158	0.0154	0.0150	0.0146	0.0143
-2.0	0.0228	0.0222	0.0217	0.0212	0.0207	0.0202	0.0197	0.0192	0.0188	0.0183
-1.9	0.0287	0.0281	0.0274	0.0268	0.0262	0.0256	0.0250	0.0244	0.0239	0.0233
-1.8	0.0359	0.0351	0.0344	0.0336	0.0329	0.0322	0.0314	0.0307	0.0301	0.0294
-1.7	0.0446	0.0436	0.0427	0.0418	0.0409	0.0401	0.0392	0.0384	0.0375	0.0367
-1.6	0.0548	0.0537	0.0526	0.0516	0.0505	0.0495	0.0485	0.0475	0.0465	0.0455
-1.5	0.0668	0.0655	0.0643	0.0630	0.0618	0.0606	0.0594	0.0582	0.0571	0.0559
-1.4	0.0808	0.0793	0.0778	0.0764	0.0749	0.0735	0.0721	0.0708	0.0694	0.0681
-1.3	0.0968	0.0951	0.0934	0.0918	0.0901	0.0885	0.0869	0.0853	0.0838	0.0823
-1.2	0.1151	0.1131	0.1112	0.1093	0.1075	0.1056	0.1038	0.1020	0.1003	0.0985
-1.1	0.1357	0.1335	0.1314	0.1292	0.1271	0.1251	0.1230	0.1210	0.1190	0.1170
-1.0	0.1587	0.1562	0.1539	0.1515	0.1492	0.1469	0.1446	0.1423	0.1401	0.1379
-0.9	0.1841	0.1814	0.1788	0.1762	0.1736	0.1711	0.1685	0.1660	0.1635	0.1611
-0.8	0.2119	0.2090	0.2061	0.2033	0.2005	0.1977	0.1949	0.1922	0.1894	0.1867
-0.7	0.2420	0.2389	0.2358	0.2327	0.2296	0.2266	0.2236	0.2206	0.2177	0.2148
-0.6	0.2743	0.2709	0.2676	0.2643	0.2611	0.2578	0.2546	0.2514	0.2483	0.2451
-0.5	0.3085	0.3050	0.3015	0.2981	0.2946	0.2912	0.2877	0.2843	0.2810	0.2776
-0.4	0.3446	0.3409	0.3372	0.3336	0.3300	0.3264	0.3228	0.3192	0.3156	0.3121
-0.3	0.3821	0.3783	0.3745	0.3707	0.3669	0.3632	0.3594	0.3557	0.3520	0.3483
-0.2	0.4207	0.4168	0.4129	0.4090	0.4052	0.4013	0.3974	0.3936	0.3897	0.3859
-0.1	0.4602	0.4562	0.4522	0.4483	0.4443	0.4404	0.4364	0.4325	0.4286	0.4247
0.0	0.5000	0.4960	0.4920	0.4880	0.4840	0.4801	0.4761	0.4721	0.4681	0.4641